Social Psychology in Sport

SECOND EDITION

Louise Davis, PhD
Umeå University
Richard Keegan, PhD
University of Canberra
Sophia Jowett, PhD
Loughborough University

Editors

Library of Congress Cataloging-in-Publication Data

Names: Davis, Louise, 1982- editor. | Keegan, Richard (Sport psychologist), editor. | Jowett, Sophia, 1969- editor.
Title: Social psychology in sport / [edited by] Louise Davis, Richard Keegan, Sophia Jowett.
Description: Second edition. | Champaign, IL : Human Kinetics, 2024. | Includes bibliographical references and index.
Identifiers: LCCN 2023021625 (print) | LCCN 2023021626 (ebook) | ISBN 9781718201811 (paperback) | ISBN 9781718201828 (epub) | ISBN 9781718201835 (pdf)
Subjects: LCSH: Sports--Psychological aspects. | Social psychology.
Classification: LCC GV706.4 .S57 2024 (print) | LCC GV706.4 (ebook) | DDC 796.01/9--dc23/eng/20230530
LC record available at https://lccn.loc.gov/2023021625
LC ebook record available at https://lccn.loc.gov/2023021626

ISBN: 978-1-7182-0181-1

The web addresses cited in this text were current as of May 2023, unless otherwise noted.

Acquisitions Editor: Diana Vincer; **Developmental Editor:** Jacqueline Eaton Blakley; **Managing Editor:** Kevin Matz; **Copyeditor:** Patricia L. MacDonald; **Proofreader:** Leigh Keylock; **Indexer:** Dan Connolly; **Permissions Manager:** Hannah Werner; **Graphic Designer:** Julie L. Denzer; **Cover Designer:** Keri Evans; **Cover Design Specialist:** Susan Rothermel Allen; **Photograph (cover):** Brett Wilhelm/NCAA Photos via Getty Images; **Senior Art Manager:** Kelly Hendren; **Illustrations:** © Human Kinetics; **Printer:** Sheridan Books

Printed in the United States of America 10 9 8 7 6 5 4 3 2 1

The paper in this book is certified under a sustainable forestry program.

Human Kinetics
1607 N. Market Street
Champaign, IL 61820
USA

United States and International
Website: **US.HumanKinetics.com**
Email: info@hkusa.com
Phone: 1-800-747-4457

Canada
Website: **Canada.HumanKinetics.com**
Email: info@hkcanada.com

E8253

We would like to dedicate this book to the new generation of inquisitive minds, starting with our children, Ethan, Noah, and Arwyn, Charlie, and Christina and Phillippa.

Contents

PART II LEADERSHIP IN SPORT

PART III MOTIVATIONAL CONSIDERATIONS IN SPORT

Foreword

In 2007, Sophia Jowett and David Lavallee published the first edition of their landmark textbook, *Social Psychology in Sport*. Providing a thorough and comprehensive examination of the sporting literature from the social-psychological lens, it was a must-read for those of us studying how the thoughts, feelings, and behaviors of various individuals influenced other human beings. Personally, I remember how many of those chapters greatly influenced my own coaching and research on group dynamics. A lot has happened since 2007, and I am personally delighted to see that the second edition is ready to bring new research in social psychology to those of us working in this domain. Edited by researchers Louise Davis, Richard Keegan, and Sophia Jowett, the second edition of this textbook once again brings together some of the leading researchers from around the globe to facilitate a comprehensive understanding of research and practice in the social-psychological aspects of sport. The chapters in this book are divided into five parts, and all of them do a great job of discussing a broad range of relevant theories, presenting historical and current empirical research, and providing recommendations from both a theoretical perspective and an applied perspective.

The book begins with part I, Relationships in Sport. This section covers some of the newest and impactful developments in research in social psychology and sport, such as athlete maltreatment, coach–athlete conflict, and novel approaches to explaining and understanding relationships in sport, including parental involvement in youth sport.

Part II is called Leadership in Sport, and information in this section brings together the latest developments in this ever-evolving field of research. Topics such as transformational leadership, the social identity approach to leadership, and aspects of athlete peer leadership and development have become popular topics among both researchers and practitioners in the global sport environment, and each of these topics gets its own chapter in part II.

The four chapters in part III, Motivational Considerations in Sport, address the social psychology of how athlete motivation is influenced. Collectively, they help us understand ways to create more supportive sport environments. Specifically, these chapters enhance our understanding of personal and situational factors that help create a nurturing and facilitative sport environment.

Part IV, Key Social and Cognitive Processes in Sport, contains a wide variety of topics that have evolved since the first edition of the text was written. For example, the consideration of mental health in sport is an emerging area of research and is now included as its own chapter. Other chapters cover the latest developments in more established areas of research, such as the influences of social support, stress and coping, efficacy beliefs, team cohesion, and effective youth sport coaching practices that collectively contribute to the preferred outcomes for individuals, dyads, and teams in sport.

The final part of the book, The Athlete in the Wider Sport Environment, contains the largest amount of material and is the most diverse section of the book. Additionally, it brings to life thought-provoking topics that are widely debated by sport science scholars. For example, given the many forms of abuse in sport that have been reported around the world, reading about ways to create safe cultures in sport for young athletes is both timely and necessary. Related to that, ways to thrive in sport, develop talent, and transition in your career effectively are also important. Additionally, part V covers two other important topics: gender and resilience.

In sum, the second edition of *Social Psychology in Sport* is a thought-provoking and valuable addition to the literature because it covers many of the most current topics in the domain of social psychology of sport. This text should be a helpful resource to students in upper-undergraduate and graduate courses and for researchers who are conducting behavioral science research in the psychosocial aspects of sport. Kudos to editors Davis, Keegan, and Jowett for pulling together a renowned group of scholars who have brought this second edition to life.

Gordon Bloom
McGill University

Preface

When the first edition of this book was initially published in 2007, the idea was to have a single textbook that focused on topics underpinned by social-psychological frameworks. At the time, the study of social issues in sport psychology was growing quickly. The first edition provided an in-depth understanding of the theoretical, empirical, and applied advances of both established social psychological topics, and it put the spotlight on topics that remained less researched but had great potential to inform our understanding.

This second edition, written over a decade and a half later, retains many of the original topics that are pertinent to social psychology in sport while showcasing the progress that has been made since. For example, the topics of motivation climate, coach leadership, coach–athlete relationship quality and communication, social support, team cohesion, efficacy beliefs, moral behaviors, and career transitions of elite athletes (to name a few) still appear as chapters in this edition but have been updated. The expansion of topics in this volume underlines the growth of social psychology in sport. For example, the topic of relationships in sport has now grown to include chapters on attachment theory and its applicability to relationships, parental involvement, and athlete maltreatment in sport. Similarly, the topic of sport leadership has grown to include chapters on coach transformational leadership, social identity approaches, and athlete leadership. The topic of motivational environments has been expanded beyond motivational climate to include chapters on caring climates, environments supportive of interpersonal needs, and complex adaptive systems. Finally, this edition includes an eclectic mix of additional chapters that aim to capture the breadth and depth of social psychology in sport. Our expert contributors showcase important topics such as the influence of environmental and sociocultural factors on resilience in competitive sport, psychosocial aspects of mental health, psychosocial enablers of athletic thriving, stress and emotion regulation, creating safe cultures in sport, gender perspectives, and talent development and performance. In essence the second edition brings together diverse yet interconnected topics from distinct scholars who offer breadth and richness as well as creative new thinking, offering the reader a unique opportunity to learn about the state of scientific inquiry of social psychology within the context of sport. The result is an extended volume likely to be an indispensable resource to undergraduate, postgraduate, and research students as well as academics and practitioners. At the very least, we hope that the text provides an impetus for the creation of more courses around the world that focus on the psychosocial aspects in sport and that it results in the creation of interesting and interdisciplinary social psychology research in sport settings.

What Is Social Psychology?

Social psychology has been defined as the scientific investigation of how the feelings, thoughts, and behaviors of individuals are influenced by the actual, imagined, or implied presence of others. Social psychologists are interested in explaining human social behavior as well as feelings, thoughts, beliefs, attitudes, intentions, and goals. Overt behavior can be objectively measured, while unobservable processes such as thoughts and feelings can be inferred from behavior. Unobservable processes such as thoughts and feelings are crucial because they may affect or directly determine overt behavior. What makes social psychology social is that it deals with how people are influenced by other people who are physically present or who are imagined or implied to be present.

Social psychology employs scientific methods to construct and test theories in a systematic and organized way. Social psychology contains numerous and rather abstract concepts (e.g., leadership, relationships, motivation, self-concept) that explain social behavior. These concepts are described and explained by theories (sets of interrelated constructs and principles) developed by social psychologists to make better sense of social behavior. Social-psychological theories are developed through the generation of data or from previous theories. Then empirical research is conducted by collecting data to test the theory. This book sees social psychology as the scientific study of the way individuals think, feel, and behave in social situations.

Organization of This Volume

The organization of this book offers readers an opportunity to consider one or more topics in isolation should they so choose. Thus, it is not essential to read the text from beginning to end. The chapters are cross-referenced so that, with a few exceptions, chapters or parts of chapters can be read independently in almost any order. Each chapter is devoted to an important social-psychological topic and is presented with the necessary breadth and depth. Chapters in this volume share five characteristics. First, they provide clear descriptions and definitions of the topic. Second, the majority of the chapters present concise theoretical overviews that focus on the topic of interest alongside a discussion of existing programs of research. Third, the chapters introduce an array of new empirical research ideas and previously unstated or untested theoretical connections. Fourth, the chapters offer a discussion of practical applications of the research conducted thus far and applications that may be generated by future research. Fifth, all chapters conclude with a summary of what has been discussed. Educational features designed to promote pedagogy are also included. For example, each chapter includes learning objectives and discussion questions.

The chapters are organized into five distinct yet interrelated parts. Part I contains five chapters that focus on social relationships in sport and showcases the importance of interactions, relationships, and communication processes between coaches, athletes, peers, and parents. The first chapter focuses on the coach–athlete relationship phenomenon. A conceptual framework to capture this phenomenon based on evidence is discussed, and research findings that have explored the factors that affect the quality of the coach–athlete relationship are presented. The role of interpersonal communication and conflict in this unique coach–athlete relationship is subsequently addressed in the second chapter, while the third chapter provides evidence to indicate how individuals' attachment styles can affect relationships that develop in sport settings. The final two chapters of part I shed light on areas that have recently attracted increasing attention: athlete maltreatment and parental involvement.

Part II of this volume contains four chapters that highlight the development of leadership theory, research, and practice in sport. All four chapters illustrate the significant advancements in sport leadership research, especially as this pertains to research relating to coaches as well as alternative leaders in sport settings (e.g., athlete leaders, mentors, parents). The first chapter sets the foundation for sport leadership research, illustrating the role of coach leadership in promoting athletes' outcomes such as performance and satisfaction. The following three chapters shed light on how transformational leadership, social identity approaches to leadership, and athlete leadership can be extended and used within the field of sport.

In part III, the four chapters relate to motivation in sport. Motivation is a crucial contributor to athletic performance and, to date, leading researchers from around the world have illustrated how motivation can be influenced by the dynamic interplay between athletes, coaches, and the team environment. This volume presents extended insights into traditional motivational climate research and self-determination theory, with additional consideration of empowerment and coaches' interpersonal styles. Modern concepts related to caring climates are explored to better understand which practices can lead to perceptions of a caring climate as well as antecedents to and outcomes associated with a caring climate. Finally, a chapter on complex adaptive systems offers up new avenues for researching motivational climates in sport through the lens of complex systems science.

In part IV, we turn the focus toward key cognitive and social factors that describe and influence behavior. We present six diverse chapters that provide insight into how social and interpersonal phenomena can feed into concepts we often view as individualistic, such as experiences, attributes, and capabilities. The first chapter sheds light on the influence of social support on athletes, followed by contributions that focus on efficacy beliefs within relational and group contexts, stress, coping and emotions, psychosocial aspects of mental health, team cohesion, and coaching effectiveness in youth sport contexts. Together these chapters illustrate the social determination of others' experiences and perceptions, which are central to social psychology.

Part V, the final section of the book, presents seven chapters that explores topics that have generated significant interest in social psychology in sport settings. This is partly because of the intuitively appealing nature of the topics but also as a result of the potentially practical and applied significance of the research. Career transitions of elite athletes, safe sport cultures, moral behavior, resilience in competitive sport, thriving, gender perspectives, and talent development are all important factors that shape the quality of experiences, developmental processes, and performance outcomes of those involved in sport.

It is with immense pleasure that we present the second edition of *Social Psychology in Sport*, a comprehensive yet readable volume that is both empirically and practically oriented. This volume has been purposefully written for a wide range of audiences but primarily for students in upper-level undergraduate and graduate courses as well as researchers interested in the psychosocial aspects of sport. That said, our aim was for each chapter to bridge the gap between research and practice, so we have included a section on practical implications within each chapter. Therefore, we hope this book will also be applicable for sports coaches and practitioners such as sport psychology consultants working in sport. We are grateful to any among you who take the time to read *Social Psychology in Sport* and share your thoughts with us.

Acknowledgments

It is with great appreciation that we thank the following people for playing central roles in the completion of what we thought to be an ambitious project. First, we would like to thank the authors of these chapters, who produced thoughtful, relevant, and timely contributions, who not only met our rigid deadlines (even during the pandemic!), but also revised their chapters—often substantially—in light of our suggestions.

We are also grateful to Diana Vincer of Human Kinetics, who was always ready to help at each juncture, to share our excitement as new ideas came along, and to serve as a facilitator of this volume coming to fruition. In addition, acknowledgments are extended to Jackie Blakley for her meticulous work as developmental editor, Hannah Werner for her assistance with permissions, Patricia L. MacDonald for her work as copyeditor, as well as Kevin Matz and Julie Denzer.

Finally, we thank our spouses, Paul Davis, Sarah Keegan, and Peter Jowett, for supporting us consistently throughout this most rewarding project.

PART

I

Relationships in Sport

The chapters contained in part I showcase the importance of interactions, relationships, and communication between key stakeholders in sport—namely, coaches, athletes, peers, and parents. Essentially, these important people have the capacity to shape the essence of the social environment of sport. For example, coaches and athletes are at the heart of sport and are inevitably locked into a dyadic relationship. This unique dyadic coach–athlete relationship was put under the microscope fairly recently with the turn of the 21st century. Alongside this research focus, related research areas started to emerge. Examples include (1) the role of interpersonal communication and conflict, especially as they pertain to the development and maintenance of relationships; (2) coaches' and athletes' attachment styles as individual difference characteristics that can potentially affect the dyadic relationship quality, including other important outcomes; (3) parents' involvement in their child athletes' sport experience and the quality of interactions between parents, athletes, and significant others; and (4) the devastation that can occur when relationships and interactions break down to the extent that athletes are maltreated and harmed psychologically, emotionally, socially, and physically. This part contains five chapters and aims to showcase the work that has been done thus far in these areas while providing recommendations for the work that is needed to further advance knowledge and understanding.

In chapter 1, Quality Coach–Athlete Relationships, Sophia Jowett and Luke Felton explore the meaning of coaching and key terms including *relationship*, *dyad*, *group*, and *team*. Early on, they ask the reader to consider the dyadic relationship between the coach and the athlete as a team of two, where relationship, leadership, and communication aspects are considered as the golden triad of functional dyadic teams. Focusing on the dyadic relationship, a detailed description follows of the theoretical model known as the 3+1Cs of coach–athlete relationship quality. This is then followed by an exploration of the main intrapersonal factors that affect the relationship quality—namely, gender, personality, passion for sport, coach behaviors, and leadership. They explain the instrumental role of communication as a fuel of good-quality relationships and present the COMPASS model containing seven strategies. A better understanding of antecedents provides information on the circumstances in which the quality of the relationship is good, moderate, or bad, and thus more research in this area is encouraged.

In chapter 2, Conflict and Communication in Coach–Athlete Relationships, Svenja Wachsmuth and Kristen Dieffenbach consider the structural and dynamic nature of interpersonal conflict between coaches and athletes and how environmental and personal factors influence their experiences of conflict. They remind us that while conflict is inevitable in relationships, it does not need to be negative, destructive, or damaging. Providing a thorough theoretical treatise of interpersonal conflict and explaining its multidimensional nature, the discussion explores types and topics of conflict. Conflict is a process, and its onset can be described by a sequence of events that coaches and athletes can learn to identify. The discussion expands to group conflict and finishes with a section on conflict prevention and management of conflict. The recommendations for future research revolve around antecedents of interpersonal conflict: intrapersonal (e.g., personality), interpersonal (e.g., social networks), and environmental (e.g., organizational culture). The chapter ends with practical suggestions for conflict management that can be readily used.

In chapter 3, Applying Attachment Theory to the Study of Relationships in Sport, Louise Davis and Sam Carr introduce attachment theory as a framework to study coach–athlete and parent–athlete relationships in sport. The chapter outlines the fundamental concepts of attachment theory. The seminal work of Bowlby focusing on the attachment behavioral system and of Ainsworth focusing on the creation of attachment bonds leads to an explanation of the development of young people's internal working models. A discussion of the stability of attachment ensues alongside the number of attachment figures any given person can have. Subsequently, attention shifts to attachment research in sport, examining peer and parental as well as coach–athlete attachment relationships. Research in this area remains in its infancy, and thus the authors advocate for more research. Questions to explore include the following: When is the attachment system active in sporting contexts? What activates it? When it is not active, does it still play a role? To complete the chapter, the authors highlight the important implications of this research for sport parents and coaches.

In chapter 4, Athlete Maltreatment, Gretchen Kerr and Erin Willson consider the role of power in interpersonal relationships within the sporting environment. Their chapter explains the conceptualization of maltreatment as well as the definitions and classifications of maltreatment based on the existence or not of a critical relationship. It is underlined that the misuse of power (as this transpires in coach–athlete interactions and those with peers or teammates) is at the core of athlete maltreatment experiences. They further highlight that the emphasis on winning at all costs or on performance enhancement as opposed to the holistic development of the athlete contributes to less than optimal sport systems. Suggestions are put forward as to how to eradicate athlete maltreatment, such as athletes' assuming more power, use of law and arbitration, formal athlete representation, and use of athletes' voices and platforms. There is more research to be carried out around interventions that aim to shift from coach-centered to athlete-centered or coach–athlete-centered approaches to coaching as well as around the effectiveness of advocacy efforts to influence policy toward healthier relationships where power is balanced for the safety of athletes.

In chapter 5, Parental Involvement in Youth Sport, Camilla Knight, Chris Harwood, Olivier Rouquette, and Nicholas Holt offer a comprehensive review of this area. This chapter starts with characterizations of parents' involvement in their children's sport before attention is shifted to the theories and the research that has been conducted thus far. The review includes methods empirically tested to enhance parental involvement in ways that improve young people's experiences in sport. While parental involvement is an ever-evolving area of research, the authors explain that numerous avenues for further research remain. They conclude that parental involvement in youth sport is a complicated matter that affects not only the young sport participant but also the lives of the parents themselves.

1

Quality Coach–Athlete Relationships

Sophia Jowett, PhD, and Luke Felton, PhD

LEARNING OBJECTIVES

On completion of this chapter, the reader should have the following:

- Understanding of coaching as an interpersonal process and practice
- Knowledge of the key terms *dyad*, *group*, and *team*
- Comprehension of the interpersonal constructs that define the quality of a coach–athlete relationship
- Awareness of factors that affect relationship quality
- Appreciation of the role of communication in building strong relationships

There is considerable evidence, even as far back in history as the Olympic Games held in ancient Greece, of athletes being trained by coaches (trainers) who were usually former champions (see Lehmann, 2009). Accordingly, coaches not only were responsible for their athletes' physical conditioning and health but also accompanied their charges to competitions, worked with them, and encouraged them to win. The English word *coach* is believed to come from the Hungarian village Kocs, where the first large four-wheeled wooden covered carriage, known as a *kocsi*, was produced in the 15th century (O'Connor & Lages, 2009). The word first appeared in education around the 1850s at Oxford University to refer to tutors carrying students to their goal of passing their exams. In sport, coaches were known as "coachers" until the late 1880s—when the name changed to coaches.

In this chapter, we explore coaching as a relational or interpersonal process that joins the coach and the athlete in the pursuit of excellence. Such a conceptualization of coaching aligns somewhat with Jones and colleagues' view of coaching as "social orchestration," where the relationship between the coach and the athlete takes center stage (Jones et al., 2016; Jones & Wallace, 2006). Subsequently, this chapter invites the reader to consider coaching as a practice or process that resides within both the coach and the athlete because ultimately neither of them can do it alone. These two individuals depend on each other to bring about change, and this interdependence is captured in the relationship quality they develop and maintain over time.

The Coach–Athlete Team

While the term *relationship* simply connotes connection or association between two people, there are other relevant terms within the coaching context that involve the coach and the athlete—namely, *dyad*, *group*, and *team*. The term *dyad* comes from the Greek word *dyás*, meaning a pair, or a group of two people. A dyad is the smallest possible social group (Kozlowski & Ilgen, 2006). *Group* and *team* are often used interchangeably, and the coach–athlete dyad can be viewed as both a group and a team. However, these terms differ in important ways. A *group* is defined as simply a collection of individuals who coordinate their individual efforts (e.g., the coach instructs and the athletes execute instructions), whereas a team is defined as a group of people who share a common purpose and a number of challenging goals (e.g., the coach and the athletes are mutually committed to the performance goals and to each other) (Kozlowski, 2018). The shared purpose or common objective transforms, energizes, and guides the members of the team. The coach–athlete dyad becomes more than a group and forms a team when both the coach and the athlete share responsibility, when they both have opportunities to lead (e.g., the coach leads in training and the athlete leads in competition), when a coach and an athlete focus on achieving combined goals (e.g., performance is the product of efforts exerted by both), and when they discuss and solve a problem collectively. The agenda of the coach–athlete dyad is "I have your back, you have mine, and together we can achieve anything," and thus the coach and the athlete of every given dyad form a team within a team (e.g., football, basketball, hockey) or a team within a group (e.g., athletics, swimming, gymnastics).

Coaching is a process and a practice that a coach and an athlete produce together because neither the coach nor the athlete possesses all the knowledge, skills, and experiences needed to succeed.

To establish an effective performing team of two or more individuals, three key characteristics or processes need to be fulfilled (see, e.g., Edmondson & Harvey, 2017; Kozlowski & Ilgen, 2006):

- Strong relationship
- Effective communication
- Sound leadership

Teamwork has become the favored means through which coaches and athletes aim to achieve their goals within sport. This emphasis on teamwork may be one reason for the shift we are observing in coaching whereby the coach-centered coaching approach (e.g., the coach controls and commands) and the athlete-centered coaching approach (e.g., the athlete leads and initiates) have given way to the combined coach–athlete approach to coaching (see Jowett & Slade, 2021; Jowett & Wachsmuth, 2020). This combined approach to coaching acknowledges the joint contributions coaches and athletes make and emphasizes the reciprocation that exists in their exchanges (e.g., a continual give and take). According to this approach, coaching is a process and a practice that a coach and an athlete produce together because neither the coach nor the athlete possesses all the knowledge, skills, and experiences needed to succeed. Making the most of their sporting journey in terms of striving to achieve common performance goals, meeting performance potential, and reaching psychological well-being can lead to personal and interpersonal flourishing and thriving (Gosai, Jowett, & Nascimento-Júnior, 2023). Subsequently, any given coach–athlete dyad creates a unique coaching environment of mutual learning determined by the quality of the aforementioned three main factors: strong relationship, effective communication, and sound leadership. This chapter focuses on exploring the nature of the coach–athlete relationship and the role of communication in establishing relationships that work. While references will be made to leadership, readers can find more detailed information around leadership elsewhere in this book (see chapters 6-9).

Coach–Athlete Relationship Quality

A coach–athlete dyad qualifies as a relationship when there is a genuine and enduring connection, strong or weak, between its members (Reis, 2001). The nature of the relationship includes what these two people do as well as what they think and feel (Hinde et al., 1993). Accordingly, the coach–athlete relationship has been defined as a social situation within which a coach's and an athlete's interpersonal feelings, thoughts, and behaviors are mutually and causally interconnected (Jowett, 2007). Subsequently, a coach and an athlete are in a relationship with one another if (1) they have an impact on each other and (2) they are interdependent in the sense that a change in one person causes genuine change in the other.

Over the past 20 years, Jowett and her research team (e.g., Gosai, Jowett, & Nascimento-Júnior, 2023; Gosai, Jowett, & Rhind, 2021; Wachsmuth et al., 2018) have interviewed hundreds of coaches and athletes, as well as collected data via surveys from thousands of coaches and athletes, to unravel the complex and elusive nature of the coach–athlete relationship. The results of this research provided the basis for the development of the 3+1Cs model of coach–athlete relationship quality, comprising the following interpersonal dimensions: closeness, commitment, complementarity, and co-orientation. Figure 1.1 illustrates this model.

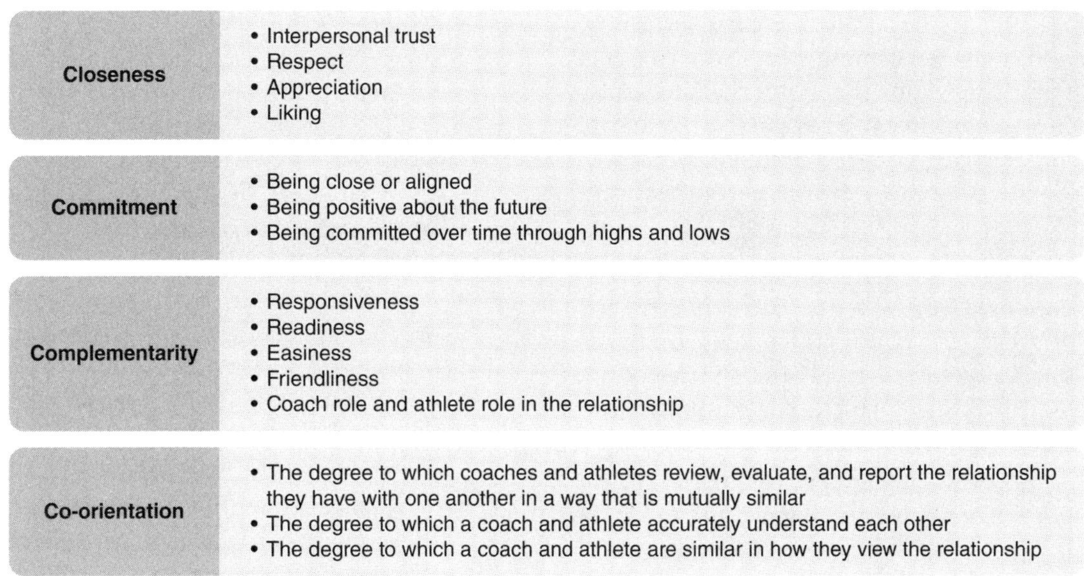

FIGURE 1.1 The 3+1Cs model.

Closeness

Closeness refers to the emotional or affective tone of the relationship and describes the interpersonal feelings experienced between a coach and an athlete. The interpersonal feelings at the core of closeness include interpersonal trust, respect, appreciation, and liking.

- *Interpersonal trust.* Affective trust encapsulates mutual interpersonal care, consideration, and concern within the social relationship expressed through support, understanding, vulnerability, validation, confidence, and belief. With belief in mind, trust can be extended to capture faith in the other's ability, including the belief that the coach, for example, has the athlete's best interests at heart. Trust is an important ingredient for building a common ground (shared knowledge), whereas distrust is a sign of incongruent and conflicting values (e.g., "I don't believe in the same things as you"). If distrust (not necessarily low levels of trust) characterizes the relationship, then establishing shared values and experiences may help the coach and the athlete (re)connect and (re)build trust (see Jowett & Cockerill, 2003).
- *Respect.* Interpersonal respect communicates fair and respectful treatment and suggests that individuals within the context of the relationship are valued, included, and accepted. Respect reflects and creates a sense of belonging, togetherness, and unity. Respect is the glue that binds coaches and athletes in every exchange or interaction.
- *Appreciation.* Appreciation encompasses feeling gratitude for a perceived benefit or recognizing and affirming the value of another's behavior or contribution to the relationship. When one expresses or shows appreciation, it cultivates a sense of positive rapport, including empathy and affiliation.
- *Liking.* Liking the other within the relationship may be thought of as the degree to which a coach and an athlete are attracted to each other (bondedness, pleasantness, and warmth toward the other). It is expressed through exchanging admiration for each other, by being curious about the other person, and also by being motivated and energized by one another. In many respects, its net effect reflects similarity and congruence (e.g., a shared outlook, shared experiences, or common interests).

Commitment

Commitment refers to the intention, willingness, or desire to maintain a close and positive relationship over time. During their sporting journey, a coach and an athlete experience highs (e.g., progress, success, media attention) and lows (e.g., burnout, injury, deselection), and their commitment to each other is the energetic connection that holds them together. This type of commitment is not passive but active. At its core lies a sense of *psychological attachment* ("we" rather than "I") that enables them to view the future confidently even when there are twists and turns and barriers along the way.

- *Being close.* Being close captures the strength of the psychological attachment or affiliation between the coach and the athlete; it is the degree to which they think they are connected.
- *Being positive.* Being positive for the future or perceiving there is promise and prospect in the relationship suggests that the other can be relied on, and thus there is an important element that keeps these individuals together—namely, predictability and consistency.
- *Being committed.* Being committed to each other highlights the degree to which dependability and thus honesty and reliability are expressed through adapting and accommodating (versus retaliating) behaviors, especially when the relationship is undergoing a challenging period.

Complementarity

Complementarity reflects a coach's and an athlete's collaboration and coordination in behavioral terms. There are two sets of complementary behaviors: corresponding and reciprocal. Corresponding behaviors encapsulate the positive actions that both the coach and the athlete are expected to manifest in their interpersonal exchanges during training and competition, whereas reciprocal behaviors are associated with the unique roles they assume as a coach and as an athlete.

At the core of corresponding complementarity are four interpersonal behaviors (responsiveness, readiness, easiness, and friendliness).

- *Responsiveness.* Responsiveness reflects a coach's and an athlete's interactions on and off the field of play that are open, sensitive, and accessible (as opposed to unforthcoming, restraining, or ignoring), aiming to meet their (inter)personal needs and fulfill their goals.
- *Readiness.* Readiness within the relationship suggests that a coach and an athlete are ready to engage, influence, energize, act, and get involved—an important interpersonal behavior underlying energy, work rate, intensity, and change, all of which are important for personal growth, progress, and performance advancement.
- *Easiness.* Easiness, or the interpersonal aspect of candidness, reflects interactions between a coach and an athlete that are free flowing, warm, compassionate, and sensitive, making them feel comfortable and at ease in each other's presence, listened to, and understood.
- *Friendliness.* Friendliness underlines the attitudes and the broader interpersonal climate within which a coach and an athlete interact—for example, friendly, approachable, pleasant, kind, and welcoming (inter)actions as opposed to unfriendly, hostile, snobbish, cold, or distant ones.

In terms of reciprocal behaviors, coaches and athletes have specific roles to play. In broad terms, coaches are expected to lead, direct, and orchestrate—they are the ones whose authority and leadership, expertise, and experience benefit athletes. Athletes are expected to follow, execute, refine, filter, practice, engage, and apply (e.g., Felton et al., 2021; Yang & Jowett, 2013). This crude description of roles needs to be understood within a fluid, malleable, and changeable operational environment. For example, in a certain training session the athlete may assume the role of a follower, yet in a competition the athlete may assume the role of a leader. The idea is that at any given time there is one leader and one follower to maintain reciprocal complementarity (cf. Kiesler, 1996) and in turn collaboration and coordination in their interactions.

It is also important to mention that a coach and an athlete may be less inclined to resort to role-prescribed behaviors the more committed they become. Indeed, as the relationship connections grow via closeness, commitment, and complementarity (3Cs), it is plausible that a coach and an athlete will be more comfortable exercising power in an equal fashion or a dialogical way (cf. Baxter & Montgomery, 1998).

Co-orientation

Co-orientation describes the degree to which coaches and athletes view, evaluate, and report the relationship they have with one another in a way that is mutually similar (Lorimer & Jowett, 2013). In short, it captures the degree to which a coach and an athlete accurately understand each other and the degree to which they are (dis)similar in the ways they evaluate their relationship. Co-orientation within the 3+1Cs model reflects a dyad's perceptual consensus, or common ground, and it may be comparable to the shared mental model as this relates to team functioning (see Van den Bossche et al., 2011). If there is high co-orientation—that is, an athlete and a coach can understand and assess their relationship accurately—then it is also likely that a coach and an athlete share mental models or have mutual understandings about other important facets, including performance goals, planning of training, and preparation for competition, enabling them to function as an effective and well-coordinated unit. This area warrants investigation because it is likely to benefit our understanding of both dyadic coach–athlete relationships (or teams of two) embedded within sport teams (e.g., football) or squads (e.g., swimming) while facilitating knowledge of group dynamics, including team cohesion and collective efficacy (e.g., Hampson & Jowett, 2012).

The 3+1Cs emerged from sustained research over the past 25 years (e.g., Davis et al., 2019; Felton & Jowett, 2013; Jowett & Carpenter, 2015; Jowett & Meek, 2000; Olympiou et al., 2008), guided by important and well-established psychosocial research and theory (see Jowett & Felton, 2014, for an overview). The aim has been to build a systematic body of knowledge about relationships in sport coaching. The 3+1Cs is a conceptual model, and its measures (Coach–Athlete Relationship Questionnaires, CART-Qs; e.g., Jowett, 2009; Jowett & Ntoumanis, 2004; Yang & Jowett, 2013) have provided a sound platform to study the quality of the coach–athlete relationship. The quality of the coach–athlete relationship as defined by the 3+1Cs interpersonal constructs is affected by

- *environmental factors* (e.g., the sport culture and the rules or norms of the sport; whether the sport is individual or team),
- *intrapersonal factors* (e.g., the individual difference characteristics such as gender, age, race or ethnicity, trait dispositions, or other orientations), and
- *interpersonal factors* (e.g., whether the dyadic relationship is atypical or typical; the relationship length) (see Jowett & Poczwardowski, 2007).

Intrapersonal factors have attracted most of the research thus far, and this research is discussed in some detail in the next section.

If there is high co-orientation—that is, an athlete and a coach can understand and assess their relationship accurately—then it is also likely that a coach and an athlete share mental models or have mutual understandings about other important facets, including performance goals, planning of training, and preparation for competition, enabling them to function as an effective and well-coordinated unit.

Intrapersonal Factors Associated With Relationship Quality

This section outlines research that has employed CART Questionnaires to investigate intrapersonal factors affecting the quality of the coach–athlete relationship—namely, gender, personality traits, and passion for sport and coaching, as well as coach leadership and behaviors. Such factors are important to consider because they provide a context from which to understand the state of any given coach–athlete relationship while discerning its future prospect more fully.

Coach and Athlete Gender

The research on gender is somewhat limited yet insightful. Employing coach–athlete dyadic research designs, Jowett and Clark-Carter (2006) found that female athletes were more likely to perceive the quality of the coach–athlete relationship in similar terms as their male coaches, while same-gender coach–athlete dyads reported better relationships than other gender dyads (Jowett & Nezlek, 2012). Thus, while female athletes attempt to align their perspectives with their coaches' perspectives, same-gender coach–athlete dyads would seem to experience higher levels of the 3Cs and to be more satisfied with interactions related to training and instruction. These results are in line with the similarity-attraction hypothesis, which states that attraction increases between those with similar characteristics (e.g., similar attitudes or judgments as well as similar gender) (see Dryer & Horowitz, 1997).

Lorimer and Jowett (2011) also found that female coaches were more understanding of their male and female athletes' feelings and thoughts than were male coaches. This is significant because coaches' perceived empathy (e.g., knowing and understanding the other), regardless of their gender, was found to be a mechanism by which the quality of the coach–athlete relationship transfers its effect onto athletes' satisfaction with training and instruction (Jowett et al., 2012). In other words, empathy, just like the coach–athlete relationship, is important to coaching. However, ample evidence suggests gendered coaching exists, meaning coaches and athletes behave according to societal expectations about gender roles. Subsequently, the expectation that females are more empathic, caring, and relationship oriented than males is well-embedded within coaching practices. For example, Gosai, Jowett, and Rhind (2021) found that male coaches coach their female athletes comparatively differently from their male counterparts (e.g., provide more reinforcement and less instruction and longer sessions to females than males) and concluded that gender perceptions determine coaches' approaches, potentially limiting female athletes' physical, social, and psychological development. Correspondingly, it can be argued that male athletes lose out too because they are less likely to be offered by coaches (often male) a more interpersonal environment in which to practice and perform.

A line of research shows that male athletes want performance-oriented behaviors and a "command and control" style of leadership from their coaches (Navarre, 2011; Singh et al., 2012), while a personal coach–athlete relationship is not important to male athletes according to Gosselin (2002). In contrast, Norman (2015) found that female athletes value the coach–athlete relationship and view coaching as a joint endeavor. In general, female athletes prefer coaching that is democratic, underlined by empathy and communication (Longshore & Sachs, 2015), the capacity to ask questions (de Haan & Norman, 2020), and support, warmth, and openness (White et al., 2017). Moreover, this line of research has brought to sharp focus that female athletes, because of the gendered coaching approaches, feel less challenged physically and stretched technically while encouraged more than needed when compared with their male counterparts (e.g., de Haan & Norman, 2020; Norman & French, 2013).

Coach and Athlete Personality

Social and personality psychologists have long been interested in understanding how personality traits influence the quality of close and personal relationships (Caspi et al., 2005). Personality has been found to predict relationship quality (e.g., Heller et al., 2004; Solomon & Jackson, 2014) as well as life satisfaction (Karney & Bradbury, 1997) and relationship satisfaction (Claxton et al., 2012). Such associations have also been documented by sport psychology researchers (Allen et al., 2013). For example, Baudin and colleagues (2011), employing a sample of athletes, showed that personality dimensions related to both life and sport satisfaction, while Jackson and colleagues (2011) determined that athletes' and coaches' personality traits were associated with their perceptions of relationship quality and concluded that dyadic dissimilarity, concerning dyad members' personality, may lead to poorly functioning coach–athlete relationships and interactions. In this section, we outline research conducted since the early 2000s, with the aim to explore the associations between personality and relationship quality.

Since most of the research conducted thus far employs the big five model to assess athletes' and coaches' personality, we provide a brief overview of the model here (and encourage readers to see McCrae & Costa [2008] for a full overview of the model). The big five model (see figure 1.2) is made up of five personality traits:

- Extraversion—includes on one hand sociability and assertiveness and on the other hand introversion and reservedness or shyness
- Agreeableness—includes compassion, respectfulness, caring, responsibility, and accountability
- Conscientiousness—includes such characteristics as organization, productiveness, and responsibility
- Neuroticism—includes tendencies toward stress, anxiety, and depression as well as psychopathological disorders (e.g., eating disorders)
- Openness to experience—includes such elements as intellectual curiosity and creative imagination as well as originality and innovation

From a relationship perspective, people high in extraversion (e.g., extraverts) perceive their relationships as positive and close. Similarly, agreeableness

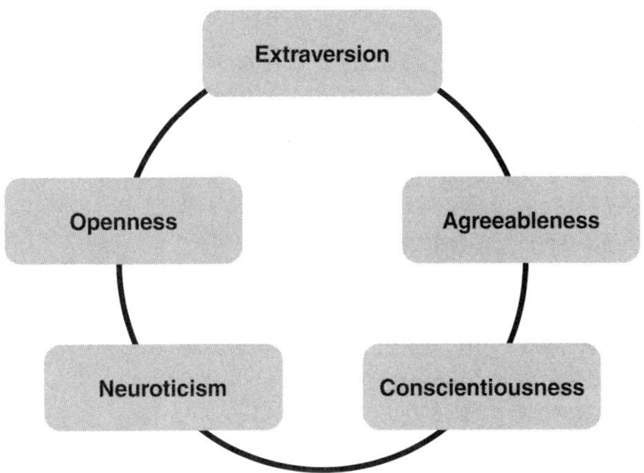

FIGURE 1.2 The big five personality model.

is associated with perceptions of relationships that are supportive, committed, and nonconflictual. High conscientiousness is related to more satisfied and committed relationships, while in contrast neuroticism is associated with viewing relationships as stressful, conflictual, and dissatisfying. Finally, openness is associated with relationships that are close, empathetic, and satisfying.

Yang and colleagues (2015) examined coach–athlete dyads and found that each relationship member's personality traits (neuroticism, extraversion, and conscientiousness) contributed independently to relationship quality. On the one hand, a coach's neuroticism negatively affected that coach's perceptions of relationship quality, and correspondingly an athlete's neuroticism negatively affected that athlete's perceptions of relationship quality (actor effects). On the other hand, a coach's conscientiousness and extraversion positively affected that coach's perceptions of relationship quality, and correspondingly an athlete's conscientiousness and extraversion positively affected that athlete's perceptions of relationship quality (actor effects). In effect, individuals with high neuroticism tended to have lower levels of closeness, commitment, and complementarity, while individuals with high extraversion and conscientiousness tended to have higher levels of closeness, commitment, and complementarity. However, only athletes' personality traits were found to affect their coaches' perceptions of relationship quality (partner effects), suggesting that coaches' perceptions of relationship quality were influenced by their athletes' personality type.

Personality is an important predictor of relationship quality and interpersonal functioning.

In another study by Jowett and colleagues (2012) that measured all five personality traits, only agreeableness was found to associate with athletes' perceptions of relationship quality and in turn empathy (i.e., perceptions of coaches' levels of understanding). It was concluded that athletes' agreeableness is a resource that enables them to nurture their relationship with their coaches, and in turn supports their coaches to develop the understanding, knowledge, and sensitivity needed to coach them effectively. The findings of this study support the importance of agreeableness in fostering better working relationships; this trait has been seen as the least understood among the big five (Caspi et al., 2005). A handful of studies have examined the associations of personality and coach–athlete relationship quality by using different constructs to assess the relationships (e.g., Aşçi et al., 2015; Jackson et al., 2011). Collectively, these findings highlight that personality shapes how athletes and coaches experience, interpret, and understand their relationships with one another, as well as provide additional evidence that personality is an important predictor of relationship quality and interpersonal functioning.

Coach and Athlete Passion for Sport

Coaches and athletes enter coaching or sport with passion and continue because of the passion they have for what they do. Passion is motivational in nature because it implies an energized and directed inclination toward the activity (coaching or sport); however, passion differs from motivation in that it targets activities that have been internalized in the person's identity (Koestner & Losier, 2002). Such passion becomes a central feature of a coach's and athlete's identity. Those who have a passion for coaching a sport like gymnastics, swimming, handball, or hockey do not merely coach a sport; they are a "gymnastics coach" or a "swimming coach," for instance. The passionate activity is part of their identity—of who they are. Vallerand and colleagues (2003) explained that representations of activities that a person likes and engages in on a regular basis are incorporated into the person's identity to the extent that they are important and highly valued, and the person invests time and energy into them, leading to a passion for these activities. Passion is an individual difference characteristic that may hinder or facilitate the development and maintenance of good-quality coach–athlete relationships. A series of studies were conducted to understand the role of passion in the development of functional relationships. Before we discuss this research, we briefly discuss two types of passion.

Vallerand and colleagues (2003) developed a dualistic approach to passion for sport activities that separates passion into *harmonious* and *obsessive*. Obsessive passion refers to a motivational force that pushes a coach or athlete toward coaching or sport. For example, a coach likes coaching but feels compelled to engage in it because of an internal force that is controlling them. Harmonious passion refers to a motivational force that leads a coach or athlete to engage in the coaching or sport willingly and produces a sense of desire and personal support about pursuing the activity. For example, an athlete doesn't feel compelled and controlled to engage in the sport; they do it because they choose to do so.

Lafrenière and colleagues (2008, 2011) and others (e.g., Kim et al., 2019) conducted several studies that explored the links between passion and relationship quality. While coaches' and athletes' harmonious passion has been found to positively link to coach–athlete relationship quality (e.g., Jowett et al., 2013; Kim et al., 2019; Lafrenière et al., 2008), coaches' and athletes' obsessive passion is either unrelated or negatively related to the relationship quality (Kim et al., 2019). Nonetheless, Lafrenière and colleagues (2008) found that athletes with obsessive passion can be highly committed to the relationship with their coach, yet they can view them as being uncooperative, hostile, or unapproachable (low complementarity). It seems paradoxical that athletes would commit to a nonoptimal relationship with their coach. However, this result is in line with the dualistic model of passion, which posits that obsessive passion leads to rigid persistence in situations (including relationships). Moreover, Lafrenière and colleagues (2011) demonstrated that the link between coaches' passion and athletes' relationship quality can be explained through the behaviors coaches deploy to coach their athletes. Their results highlighted that coaches with harmonious passion are more likely to use autonomy-supportive behaviors and in turn to have high-quality relationships, whereas coaches with obsessive passion are more likely to use controlling behaviors to coach their athletes. Controlling behaviors did not seem to significantly influence the relationship quality, though, which is an area that warrants further investigation.

Finally, the findings of Jowett and colleagues (2013) suggest that coaches may value more highly the relationships they develop with athletes who are obsessive about their sport—positive links were found between athletes' obsessive passion and coaches' perceptions of high relationship quality. In contrast, athletes may value less highly the relationships they develop with coaches who are obsessively passionate about their coaching—negative links were found between coaches' obsessive passion and athletes' perceptions of relationship quality. In addition, athletes perceived more interpersonal conflict with coaches who were obsessively passionate about coaching. Overall, research that focuses on passion and relationships would seem to suggest that harmonious passion is adaptive while obsessive passion can be maladaptive to relationship quality.

Coach Behaviors and Leadership

As Mageau and Vallerand (2003) highlighted, coaches can make a significant difference in athletes' satisfaction, motivation, and performance, and the relationship coaches and athletes develop is instrumental in achieving these outcomes. The researchers postulated that coaches' autonomy-supportive behaviors can play a crucial role in athletes' motivation. Athletes' motivation is instrumental to sporting success, and thus coaches who place value on self-initiation, as well as encourage choice, independent problem solving, and participation in decision making, are more likely to develop self-determined and by extension responsible and accountable athletes. Using Bartholomew and colleagues' (2010) psychometric tool for assessing autonomy and controlling coach behaviors, Lafrenière and colleagues (2011) found that coaches' autonomy behaviors were positively linked to good-quality coach–athlete relationships; it is thus possible that athletes who rate the coach–athlete relationship as more optimal do so because they feel respected and understood by autonomy-supportive coaches. Correspondingly, Felton and Jowett (2013) found that athletes who perceived better coach–athlete relationships were more likely to perceive their coaches as more autonomy supportive and as such providing them with choice, independence, and a framework to work within.

Jowett and colleagues (2017), employing the Coaching Behaviour Scale for Sport (Côté et al., 1999), found that athletes who perceived better relationships with their coaches reported a more positive coaching approach—athletes' closeness and commitment were consistently linked with coach behaviors that promoted planning and goal setting as well as physical development, technical skill development, and competition strategy development. It was concluded that coaches' behaviors may be influenced by the quality of the coach–athlete relationship and that it pays dividends for athletes to consciously try to develop better relationships with their coaches, because better relationships may provide the stimulus for coaches to work harder and better with them.

The potential synergies between coach leadership behaviors and the quality of the coach–athlete relationship have started to emerge (see Jowett & Arthur, 2019 for a review). Research has examined the links between leadership behaviors and relationship quality (e.g., Gosai, Jowett, and Nascimento-Júnior, 2023; Hampson & Jowett, 2012; Vella et al., 2013). Overall, this research highlights that a combination of coach transformational leadership behaviors (e.g., articulating vision, individualized support, intellectual stimulation) and coach–athlete relationship quality predicts important outcomes—for instance, developmental experiences such as personal, social, and cognitive skills, as well as goal setting and initiative (Vella et al., 2013) and collective efficacy (Hampson & Jowett, 2012).

More recently, Gosai, Jowett, and Nascimento-Júnior (2021) found that perceived coach transformational leadership behaviors predicted athletes' perceptions of both relationship quality with their respective coaches and the team's psychological safety. Zhao and Jowett (2022) found that certain coach transformational leadership behaviors, such as articulating a vision, providing an appropriate model, and providing intellectual stimulation, were linked highly to good-quality relationships, especially closeness, whereas coaches' high-performance expectations were linked highly with commitment. Interestingly, individualized support was linked negatively with commitment. This is an interesting finding and resonates with research (e.g., Brummelman et al., 2017) showing that too much encouragement, praise, or reinforcement can damage an individual's esteem—and more so female athletes' esteem because they receive more encouragement and reinforcement than their male counterparts (Gosai, Jowett, & Rhind, 2021).

Future Research Directions

This section provides some important future research directions in relation to intrapersonal factors affecting the coach–athlete relationship and the use of communication strategies, outlined in the COMPASS model, for developing and maintaining relationship quality.

In reference to the role of gender within the coach–athlete relationship, if the emphasis is on tailoring the coaching to the gender of the athlete (e.g., Longshore & Sachs, 2015; MacKinnon, 2011; Norman, 2018), then coaches miss the opportunity to genuinely connect with their athletes at a more humane and personal level—a level that goes beyond one's gender. When coaches connect with their athletes (and vice versa) and are open and curious to learn about each athlete's history, values, experiences, personality, and motivation, it not only helps develop good-quality dyadic relationships as defined by the 3+1Cs model but also more accurately informs a coaching approach (e.g., how to coach technical, mental, strategical, physical aspects; how to motivate or build confidence) devoid of gender misconceptions, prejudice, and discrimination. As LaVoi and Butcher highlighted in this book, the focus should be on the individual athlete regardless of gender because this is the most effective way to coach (see chapter 25). Therefore, future research should further our understanding of how best to develop high-quality coach–athlete relationships universally, without gender bias. Experimental and intervention-based research would be valuable in demonstrating to coaches that they do not need to provide gender-tailored coaching to achieve their desired outcomes (e.g., quality relationships, performance success, and personal well-being).

Earlier in the chapter we highlighted the associations that exist between different forms of passion and the quality of the coach–athlete relationship, specifically the favorable nature of harmonious passion in comparison with obsessive passion (e.g., Lafrenière et al., 2011). Nonetheless, more research is warranted in this area to understand the role of passion in coaches' and athletes' relationships, including (inter)actions in the pursuit of successful performances—especially in an era where the meaning of sporting success is challenged, debated, and redefined (Bishop, 2020). In addition, the research to date has been cross-sectional in nature, which limits our ability to infer causality. Future research should adopt experimental designs so the directionality of effects between passion and coach–athlete relationship quality can be assessed. Longitudinal research designs should also be encouraged so that the role of passion in predicting changes in coach–athlete relationship quality can be determined over time (e.g., do changes in the coach's level of harmonious passion across a competitive season result in changes in an athlete's perceptions of the relationship quality?).

With respect to coaching behavior and leadership research, future directions similar to those mentioned for gender and passion are recommended. There is a need for future research to move beyond the current cross-sectional designs to enable greater insight into causality and changes over time. To accomplish this goal, research should employ experimental and longitudinal designs to establish the causal inferences that exist between transformational leadership behavior and the quality of the coach–athlete relationship. In addition, the recent work of Gosai, Jowett, and Nascimento-Júnior (2023) was the first to establish associations between leadership behaviors, the coach–athlete relationship, psychological safety, and flourishing in sport. Future research should look to replicate and extend this study to enhance our understanding of how the coach–athlete relationship can influence important factors related to positive psychology (e.g., flourishing and thriving).

Finally, in relation to the COMPASS model and the communication strategies for developing and maintaining the coach–athlete relationship, future research should investigate the emotional component of communication (i.e., how the coach and athlete communicate) within the coach–athlete relationship in addition to the content of the communication (i.e., what is communicated) (Davis et al., 2019). Intervention-based studies are also recommended to gain objective assessment of how effective the COMPASS communication strategies are when used by coaches and athletes.

Practical Implications

This chapter has so far outlined what the coach–athlete relationship is and provided insight into some of the main intrapersonal factors that can influence its development. In this section, we examine the implications for practice by presenting communication as a central tool in the development of better working relationships, regardless of the effects of gender, personality, and passion, as well as coach behaviors and leadership. The starting point is that relationships are dynamic, never static. The relationship requires closeness, commitment, and complementarity to grow and develop. The 3Cs are active ingredients and need constant nourishing, otherwise they wither and die. Good communication can nurture, sustain, cultivate, and foster good-quality relationships. As regards the coach–athlete relationship, the COMPASS model was developed as an evidence-based tool for maintaining relationship quality. The COMPASS model contains seven communication strategies that were developed following a series of qualitative studies (Rhind & Jowett, 2010, 2011, 2012) aimed at uncovering the ways coaches and athletes build and maintain good-quality relationships as defined by the 3+1Cs (table 1.1).

TABLE 1.1 Overview of the COMPASS Model

COMPASS strategies	Demonstrated through
Conflict management	Efforts made by the coach and athlete to identify, discuss, monitor, and resolve possible areas of disagreement
Openness	Efforts by the coach and athlete to engage in and maintain open lines of communication
Motivation	Efforts by the coach and athlete to show effort, have enjoyable interactions, and demonstrate ability
Preventative strategies	Efforts by the coach and athlete to outline expectations, roles, and rules (and consequences for not meeting them); for example, creating a "relationship contract"
Assurance	Efforts by the coach and athlete to build confidence and show they will be there for one another when needed
Support	Efforts by the coach and athlete to help one another through difficult and challenging times, both performance related and nonsport related
Social networks	Efforts by coaches and athletes to socialize away from the track, field, or court and to develop relationships with other significant others (e.g., parents, friends, managers) that help the coach and athlete avoid working in an isolated "bubble"

Over the past decade, a handful of studies exploring the links between the COMPASS communication strategies and the 3Cs have emerged. For example, correlational research highlighted that certain COMPASS strategies are more strongly associated with certain 3Cs:

- Conflict management, motivation, and assurance are associated with commitment and complementarity.
- Openness and social networks are associated with closeness.
- Preventative strategies are associated with complementarity.
- Support is associated with closeness and commitment (see Rhind & Jowett, 2011).

Although causality cannot be readily inferred from this study, the findings suggest that coaches and athletes who employ open channels of communication and who share information without holding back are more likely to experience high closeness (mutual trust, respect, appreciation, and liking). By the same token, closeness in relationships may allow for more openness or free-flowing communication between a coach and an athlete. From an applied point of view, if a coach–athlete dyad suffers from lack of closeness, then openness, support, and social network strategies could function as an intervention to enhance closeness. In contrast, if commitment requires a dyad's attention, the strategies of choice would most probably be conflict management, motivation, assurance, and support.

Davis and colleagues (e.g., 2019, 2022) conducted a series of studies further examining the links between relationship quality and COMPASS. In their 2019 paper, they found positive associations between relationship quality and the following strategies: conflict management, support, and motivational communication. They also found that these strategies explained the association between relationship quality and athlete satisfaction with sport performance, as well as instruction and treatment received by the coach. The most predictive power in athletes' satisfaction for performance was shown by the two communication strategies of support and motivation. More recently, Davis and colleagues (2022) found that relationship quality predicts all COMPASS strategies. Athletes' perceptions of relationship quality were most strongly associated with openness, motivation, assurance, and support strategies. Their study also found that these strategies, most notably motivation (competency, autonomy, and relatedness), support (competence and autonomy), openness (competence), and assurance (autonomy) can create a positive environment within which athletes can satisfy the three basic psychological needs of competence, relatedness, and autonomy.

The COMPASS model can be embedded in the wider literature to help practitioners readily use it. Here we focus on the following three strategies to illustrate how theory and research can be translated into evidence-informed practice: conflict management and preventative strategies as well as openness. The idea of *openness*, or open channels of communication, is not new (e.g., Stafford & Canary, 1991). However, creating an environment of openness whereby athletes (and coaches) offer their thoughts and opinions in an ongoing, candid, and unrestrained manner is not easy (see Gosai, Jowett, & Nascimento-Júnior, 2023). The desirability of such a safe social environment is reflected in coaches' desire for athletes to take an active role in their own development and in turn to play an active part within the coaching process (see Jowett et al., 2022). Coaches often want their athletes to be more autonomous, volitional, self-reliant, accountable, and responsible. The display of such important characteristics requires an environment that values athletes' active (versus passive) involvement. If athletes are not given opportunities to get involved, are not encouraged to engage, or are not permitted to participate, then invaluable information and insights are withheld and in turn the value of their knowledge is inevitably lost. Without reciprocal openness, there is no trust, respect, or appreciation (closeness).

Coaches are best placed to create environments where openness is embraced, allowing all voices to be heard by empowering all athletes to become part of the coaching process.

Coaches are best placed to create environments where openness is embraced, allowing all voices to be heard by empowering all athletes to become part of the coaching process. In such environments, there is recognition that coaching is knowledge dependent and thus athletes' capacity to share and offer information is valued. Here are three simple steps to create openness:

- *Set the stage.* Coaches should keep reminding their athletes of the following: No one has a crystal ball; producing high performance is an inherently interdependent activity; speaking up is important; sharing information and being honest are key; sharing information is the responsibility of both the coach and the athlete.

- *Invite athletes in.* Coaches should invite their athletes to be open and highlight the importance of every voice; every voice needs to be heard because coaches have a limited view, and their athletes can help put the missing pieces together.
- *Respond productively.* Openness requires courage, and thus coaches should show their appreciation when ideas are shared; the athletes have fulfilled their responsibility to speak up and have shared their thoughts and opinions. If the ideas are good, then coaches can explore how they can be used; if the ideas are not applicable or relevant, then coaches should explain why the athletes' contributions may not fit in or why they may need further consideration.

Openness allows coaches and athletes to communicate freely so that everyone is engaged and feels part of the coaching process, part of the growth and development. Nonetheless, even in such a positive environment, interpersonal conflict is always lurking. Preventative strategies aim to prevent conflict by attempting to keep disagreements, misunderstandings, and incompatibility from occurring. Coaches and athletes who can talk about where they stand and clearly express their expectations are more likely to experience less interpersonal conflict. Research has suggested that relationship contracts (Jowett, 2008) and relationship rules (Jowett & Carpenter, 2015) are important because they (1) regulate behavior to minimize conflict that may disrupt the relationship and (2) provide an exchange of rewards that motivates the relationship members to stay in the relationship. Contracts and rules create a dyad's shared understanding of expectations and interests, and in doing so they enhance the dyad members' co-orientation, alignment, or common ground. While these methods may seem transactional, research outside sport settings indicates that relationship contracts, for example, are associated with psychological ownership in work settings (Aggarwal & Bhargava, 2010; see also Woodrow & Guest, 2017). Both methods may require close monitoring and updating at frequent intervals and most certainly from season to season.

Next, we outline an example of a set of relationship rules and an example of a relationship contract developed with the goal of promoting harmonious relationships that last the test of time.

A Sample of Relationship Rules

- We should respect each other (e.g., experience, knowledge, goals).
- We should trust each other (e.g., what we each say, do, and believe).
- We should be committed to each other (e.g., sacrifice personal time if necessary to talk or practice; go the extra mile).
- We should be prepared and organized (e.g., equipment, training plan).
- We should be ready (e.g., psychologically and physically).
- We should always put 100% effort into training and competition (e.g., work hard; lead by example).
- We should be appreciative of each other's efforts (e.g., acknowledge good performance, goodwill, good character).
- We should communicate important information (e.g., share information, engage, and get actively involved).
- We should show up to practice on time and leave the practice field in an organized and timely fashion.

A Sample of a Relationship Contract

- If we have an argument or disagreement, we will talk things out instead of ignoring the problem.
- We need a day in the week or month to meet and discuss one on one any issues (performance and personal) that may have arisen.
- We need to have trust in each other.
- Coaches will inform athletes before training sessions what training is being planned and the reasons for the session.
- Athletes will come mentally and physically ready to train and compete.
- We will share important information that affects performance and well-being.
- We will not share confidential information with others (third parties).
- The first week of every month, the entire team will meet for lunch or dinner.

The quality of a relationship lays the foundation for productive conflict management (Wachsmuth et al., 2018). According to Metcalfe and Mischel (1999), we process events through two cognitive systems: hot and cool. On the one hand, when the hot system (also known as the emotional "go" system) is engaged, it triggers people to respond emotionally, fervently, and quickly. For example, coaches and athletes speak or act in the heat of the moment. On the other hand, the cool system (also known as the cognitive "know" system) is deliberate and careful and slow. The cool system is the basis for self-regulation and self-control (willpower). For example, when a coach and an athlete use the cool system, they slow down and essentially gather their thoughts. Employing this approach, we propose a way to cool hot topics in often fast-paced coach–athlete interactions to manage conflict when it occurs.

Managing Oneself

- Identify your own emotions.
- Slow down so you can pay attention to what is happening; emotions let you know that you care about the discussion at hand.
- Turn your curiosity inward and ask yourself the following: Why am I feeling anxious, frustrated, angry? Am I missing part of the picture (the part that my coach or athlete sees)? Could I possibly contribute to the conflict in the same way I am convinced that the other person does?

Managing Conversations

- Conversations do not manage themselves; commit to the responsibility of managing the conversation.
- To facilitate good communication in the face of conflict, it is necessary to slow down the conversation:
    - This allows both the coach and the athlete to think and ask questions to increase understanding in a thoughtful manner.
    - The process of thinking, questioning, and deliberating allows the coach and the athlete to appreciate the basis of the conflict or disagreement and consider the reasons for the discrepancies in opinion.
    - Subsequently, the process may uncover new perspectives and supply a whole host of facts the dyad was previously unaware of or unfamiliar with.

Overall, the 3+1Cs model provides a method for understanding relationships, and the COMPASS model provides the medium to nurture better working relationships. For practitioners, both models are evidence-based tools that can be readily used to help coaches and athletes develop valuable relationship and communication skill sets, helping them reach performance success and personal well-being.

Summary

The quality of the coach–athlete relationship is at the heart of coaching, so much so that it defines it (Jowett, 2017; Jowett & Shanmugam, 2016; Jowett & Slade, 2021). The systematic study of the relationship between coach and athlete started in the early 2000s (Jowett & Meek, 2000; Wylleman, 2000) and gained momentum over the years (e.g., Antonini Philippe et al., 2011; Jowett & Wylleman, 2006). The emphasis placed on the relationship between the coach and the athlete in both academic and applied settings aligns with recent efforts to redefine performance and success as a worthwhile pursuit that is positively and personally fulfilling (and not simply or only about personal bests or gold medals) (Bishop, 2020). The research thus far suggests that coaches and athletes would do well to recognize the transformational power of their relationships as they explore alternative ways to fulfill such important goals as performance enhancement and psychological health. Such ways require coaches and athletes to connect with one another, get to know and understand one another, and work together in the pursuit of common goals.

Zooming in on the dyadic coach–athlete relationship is where coaching advantage can be found because it can provide the medium for interpersonal success and satisfaction as well as self-understanding and self-change. Although athletes do massive amounts of work, it is through strong relationships with their coaches that they find and activate their abilities and capacities. When coaches and athletes are locked into a high-quality relationship characterized by the 3+1Cs, then coaches have more capacity to influ-

Overall, the 3+1Cs model provides a method for understanding relationships, and the COMPASS model provides the medium to nurture better working relationships.

ence their athletes positively, while athletes place confidence in the contributions their coaches make by fully exploiting them.

Figure 1.3 emphasizes that having a good-quality coach–athlete relationship opens up the door for challenges (e.g., delivering hard feedback, making hard calls, setting difficult performance goals, asking questions, demanding increased intensity, pushing each other) that are received and accepted by both members of the relationship. In a strong relationship, challenge is often expected by athletes in the knowledge that coaches have their best interests at heart. In such situations, athletic and personal growth can be achieved. When relationship quality is poor and challenges or standards are high or low, then its members may feel disrespected, disliked, or disengaged. Caution may be required when relationships are great yet challenges or standards are low or modest. While there may be various reasons for this situation to occur (e.g., coaches are in favor of protecting and nurturing the happiness and comfort of their athletes), its outcome is that of trivial growth and learning.

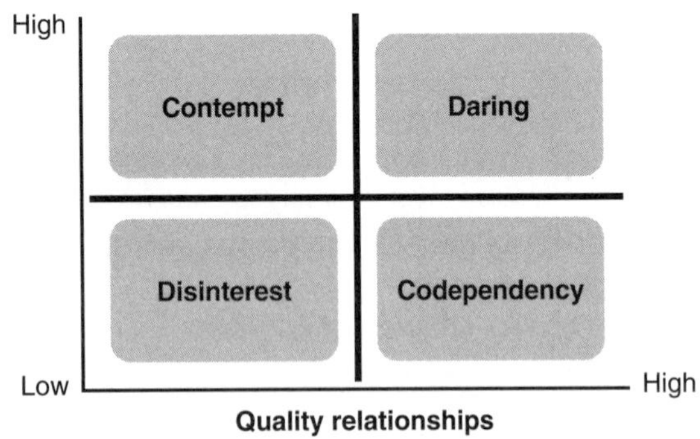

FIGURE 1.3 A 2 × 2 matrix of the coach–athlete relationship quality and challenge in competitive sport.

In this chapter, we also discussed communication strategies as building blocks to the development and maintenance of quality relationships (as defined by the 3+1Cs) despite individual difference factors affecting them positively and negatively. Effective communication is the fuel of coach–athlete relationships that work. Extending this work may require us to go beyond understanding the quality of the coach–athlete relationship and communication patterns to understanding the interplay of leadership within every given coach–athlete dyad through the lenses of the concept of effective teams (teams of two).

DISCUSSION QUESTIONS

1. Why is coaching as a process or practice better viewed through interpersonal or relational lenses?
2. Discuss the terms *dyad, group,* and *team* and describe their differences.
3. What are the psychological constructs that define the quality of the coach–athlete relationship?
4. What factors affect the quality of the coach–athlete relationship? Can you think of any other factors that are not covered in the chapter?
5. How can COMPASS communication strategies promote better relationships between coaches and athletes over time?
6. How could the research progress further to address the current gaps in knowledge and solve real practical issues in relation to the coach–athlete relationship?

2

Conflict and Communication in Coach–Athlete Relationships

Svenja Wachsmuth, PhD, and Kristen Dieffenbach, PhD, CMPC

LEARNING OBJECTIVES

On completion of this chapter, the reader should have the following:

- Understanding of the structural and dynamic nature of interpersonal and group conflict in sport
- Appreciation of environmental, intrapersonal, and interpersonal factors influencing coaches' and athletes' experiences of conflict
- Insights about how communication influences the onset and management of conflict
- Knowledge of how to implement conflict management strategies within sport relationships

> The basis of trust is repeatedly tested and sometimes even gets damaged. It is the duty of both [coach and athlete] to strengthen the relationship that has been disturbed by conflict. . . . Our communication skills are key. I often had the feeling that I talked a lot with the players. The truth is: it was always far too little.
>
> —Markus Weise, field hockey coach and three-time gold medalist at the Olympic Summer Games (Wachsmuth et al., 2021, p. 11)

Within sport relationships, as within any type of relationship, conflict is more likely to occur than not. In fact, its likelihood increases the closer a relationship is. The media have portrayed numerous high-profile coaches and athletes who found themselves and their conflicts in the headlines—for instance, Sir Alex Ferguson kicking a boot at David Beckham's head; the screaming matches between Michael Phelps and his career-long coach, Bob Bowman; and Kevin Pietersen getting dismissed from the English cricket squad because of internal quarrels. While all three situations are different in terms of reasons for and consequences of conflict, one common feature is a high degree of interdependence between the involved parties. Although these are just anecdotes that have made it to the press exemplifying incidents of conflict between a high-performance athlete and their coach or even an entire sporting association, this list could certainly be extended by numerous examples. Research suggests that conflicts are a recurrent element of relationships in sport; according to a survey of elite British sport participants conducted by Mellalieu and colleagues (2013), up to 84% of athletes, coaches, and support staff experienced incidents of interpersonal conflict during major competitions.

Yet most conflicts between athletes and coaches take place unwitnessed by the public and are often brushed off by the people around them, too. Conflicts do not look nice, nor do they feel pleasant; they may even endanger the professional and inspirational image that stakeholders in performance sport want to convey. Moreover, when conflicts become public, they are likely portrayed in a way that exaggerates the disruptive nature and damaging outcomes because confrontation makes for a better story in the media. However, placing a negative emphasis on conflict acknowledges only one side of this interaction; the side that is nasty and destructive and needs to be avoided at all costs. Viewed holistically, though, there is also a positive side of conflict as reflected by its effective management and resolution. When a conflict is resolved, the involved individuals may reframe it as a constructive experience where nothing more than a "difficult conversation" took place. The key to meeting the challenge of successfully managing conflict is open, honest, and empathic communication that enables the involved individuals to share their personal thoughts, feelings, experiences, needs, and hopes with one another. Such communication requires sound intrapersonal and interpersonal skills, especially from coaches, who are often perceived to be the more powerful partner within this relationship (Jowett & Wachsmuth, 2020; Potrac & Jones, 2009; see also chapter 4).

The key to meeting the challenge of successfully managing conflict is open, honest, and empathic communication that enables the involved individuals to share their personal thoughts, feelings, experiences, needs, and hopes with one another.

To discuss conflict and its management within a sport setting, especially the conflict within coach–athlete dyads, it is essential to reflect on the positioning of this relationship and the responsibilities that result from coaches' professional role within it. First and foremost, as the more experienced and professionally trained member, coaches carry a duty of care for the athlete, which includes building healthy and supportive relationships (Becker, 2013). Coaches should further facilitate the development of not only sport-specific but also intra- and interpersonal skills in their athletes so that both can meaningfully contribute to their relationship. This seems especially important for coaches who work with young athletes who have not yet developed such competencies (see chapter 21). Thus, coaches have the capacity and arguably the responsibility through their position to create a psychologically safe environment that empowers athletes to address concerns and together with the coach develop solutions that enable both to thrive to their full potential (Gosai et al., 2021).

In this chapter we explore conflict, considering its positive as well as its negative features. After a definition of interpersonal conflict is forwarded and discussed, conflict will be linked to communication processes as they relate to its prevention, escalation, and management. The outlined theoretical considerations are complemented with an overview of sport science research focusing on athletes' and coaches' conflict experiences within dyadic and team settings. Considering the scarcity of systematic investigations on interpersonal conflict in sport relationships, the chapter also presents potential avenues to advance research in this area. Finally, practical recommendations for working with sport participants through conflictual situations are offered. Special attention is given to equipping coaches with the skills necessary to be capable conflict managers.

Since most of the research on coach–athlete conflict has been conducted within performance environments, the content of this chapter should be viewed within this capacity and in relation to performance sport settings in which athletes and coaches work together within purposeful, goal-directed relationships. Relationships between coaches and athletes are unique from other (work) relationships—for example, in terms of their degree of interdependence and emotional closeness, as well as other dyadic characteristics (e.g., age differences, competence levels, time spent together). Thus, experiences of conflict are likely to differ from traditional work settings, and strategies for conflict management need to be adjusted to this particular context. Therefore, the theoretical underpinnings of conflict research, which traditionally originate from other academic disciplines (e.g., organizational psychology), are discussed in light of recent research developments in sport.

Theory and Research on Interpersonal and Group Conflict in Sport

Research examining the processes that govern interpersonal communication and conflict within coaching relationships and in sport more broadly has been sparse (Paradis et al., 2014a; Wachsmuth et al., 2017). Instead, the social and organizational psychology literature can provide a theoretical and empirical foundation from which experiences of conflict in sport relationships can initially be understood, and which are complemented by recent context-specific conceptualizations coming out of sport psychology.

Structural Conceptualizations of Conflict in Sport Relationships

Within social psychology, interpersonal conflict is commonly understood as a dynamic process grounded in a disagreement between interdependent parties that when unresolved leads to negative emotional responses and interfering behaviors in the attainment of an individual's goal (Barki & Hartwick, 2004). Based on this conceptualization, interpersonal conflict in sport has been defined as "a situation in which relationship partners perceive a disagreement about values, needs, opinions or objectives that is manifested through (negative) affective, cognitive and behavioral responses" (Wachsmuth et al., 2017, p. 87). This conceptualization allows researchers to investigate a range of individuals (e.g., athletes, coaches, staff) and relationships (e.g., dyads, groups), as well as contexts (e.g., professional or private, competition or practice) and topics (e.g., task and social conflict) by considering emotions, thoughts, and behaviors experienced during conflict and its management. From a theoretical perspective, this definition also highlights that disagreement represents the cognitive component of conflict. Yet not all relationship disagreements necessarily lead to interfering behaviors and negative emotions. Whether conflict arises from a disagreement depends on a range of factors (e.g., goal incompatibility, perceived influence, likelihood of change) presented later in this chapter.

The Multidimensional Nature of Conflict

Except for Partridge and Knapp (2016), who investigated conflict from a behavioral perspective, most studies within sport highlight the importance of considering all three dimensions—emotion, cognition, and behavior—to fully comprehend conflict within interpersonal and intrateam relationships (e.g., Mellalieu et al., 2013; Paradis et al., 2014a; Wachsmuth et al., 2018a). Accordingly, *cognitive* disagreements about goals, values, or personal characteristics are often perceived to be "at the heart" of conflict (Paradis et al., 2014a, p. 12). When experiencing conflict, thoughts such as blaming the other, generalizing negative behaviors and attitudes of the other, or seeking explanations that are beneficial for oneself may contribute to an escalation of the situation. In contrast, a problem-oriented cognitive response to conflict that encapsulates thoughts that help the individual understand the issue and identify possible solutions to the problem may increase the likelihood of engaging successfully in conflict management (Wachsmuth et al., 2018a).

Interpersonal conflict is experienced on an *emotional* level as well. Thus, individuals involved in conflict may recognize a range of negative emotional responses that can be directed against the other person (i.e., hard negative emotions: anger, frustration) or relate to one's own vulnerability in the relationship (i.e., soft negative emotions: disappointment, fear, sadness). Some athletes and coaches may even experience positive emotions, such as relief or hope, during encounters of conflict if an opportunity for open communication and change is perceived (Mellalieu et al., 2013; Wachsmuth et al., 2018a). Lastly, conflict also implies some form of *behavioral* reaction toward a perceived disagreement. These displayed acts of conflict may include escalating responses (e.g., shouting, throwing equipment), avoiding or withdrawing from a conflictual situation, and even problem-oriented behaviors (e.g., seeking help, individual problem solving) (Partridge & Knapp, 2016; Wachsmuth et al., 2018a).

Types and Topics of Conflict

Other structural components that determine the nature of conflict are its *type* and *topic*. Generally, researchers have differentiated between two overarching types of conflict: task and social. *Task conflict* usually revolves around what should be achieved within a particular situation (i.e., aim; e.g., team goals vs. individual goals) and how a task may be accomplished (i.e., strategies; e.g., training content, setup, or schedule). While inevitable, task conflicts are usually rational and problem oriented and thus easier to resolve. Within sport they are often associated with such matters as defining common norms, role responsibilities, or training procedures (Holt et al., 2012; Paradis et al., 2014a). *Social conflict*, on the other hand, typically emerges from perceived interpersonal incompatibilities linked to individual characteristics, opinions, or values. It is often described as emotional, personal, and persistent. Within sport, social conflicts are often expressed through confrontational or aggressive behaviors, social or sport-specific isolation, and victimization of individual team members; they may also result from deliberately manipulating interpersonal relationships (Paradis et al., 2014a; Partridge & Knapp, 2016; Wachsmuth et al., 2018a).

Following the task and social conflict categorization, Wachsmuth and colleagues (2018a) have identified four main topics of conflict within coach–athlete relationships. Typical task conflicts revolved around *sport-related* topics, such as practice content, competition strategies, or selection criteria, and *lifestyle-related* topics, such as choices on nutrition, alcohol consumption, school or work, or public demeanors. On the other hand, social conflicts usually revolved around personal *misconduct* (e.g., violation of rules and norms) or conflicting values and characteristics (e.g., dishonesty, clash of personalities). Additionally, task and social conflicts emerged from difficulties within other critical relationships (e.g., among coaches) or from the *involvement of others* (e.g., partners, parents, staff) in decision-making processes between a coach and an athlete.

Conflict originates from an individual's cognition, affect, and behavior; is perpetuated via interpersonal interactions; and in turn is manifested as a collective experience within a dyad or group.

The distinction between task and social conflict can be problematic when the individual perspectives of those involved in the conflict are considered. In other words, conflict can be perceived vastly differently by coaches and athletes with regard to its content and significance (Korsgaard et al., 2014). For instance, differing values and norms linked to time management may cause trouble if one person perceives being late as simply a bad habit while the other interprets being late as disrespectful and unappreciative. A more severe example may occur if an athlete perceives their coach to be intruding in private matters (e.g., schoolwork, friendships, recreational activities) that are viewed as being personally significant, whereas the coach may view it as their right or responsibility to know about the athlete's life and lifestyle outside of training.

In summary, an individual's perception of conflict depends on a range of external factors (e.g., cultural norms, social network), as well as their intra- and interpersonal skills (e.g., self-reflection, communication, empathy, coping with stress) and attributes (e.g., personality, relationship quality) (Mellalieu et al., 2013; Wachsmuth et al., 2017). It is also necessary to recognize that interpersonal conflict is dynamic. As such, task conflict may develop into social conflict (and vice versa), or one conflict may turn into multiple conflicts if not properly managed and defused over time.

Conflict as a Process: Emergence, Escalation, and Contagion of Conflict

A range of process models aim to explain the dynamics of conflict with regard to its underlying mechanisms and temporal nature (e.g., emergence and onset, escalation) as well as its ability to become contagious (Jehn et al., 2013; Korsgaard et al., 2014; Roberts, 2006). Thus, conflict is a process that is influenced by and takes place on multiple interconnected levels (i.e., the individual, the dyad, the group, or a dyad's broader social surrounding, and across time). These different levels become visible throughout the onset and spread of conflict. Korsgaard and colleagues (2014) theoretically described this phenomenon as a process of emergence. Thus, conflict originates from an individual's cognition, affect, and behavior; is perpetuated via interpersonal interactions; and in turn is manifested as a collective experience within a dyad or group.

The Emergence and Onset of Conflict in Sport Relationships

The onset of conflict can be described by a sequence of events leading up to a perceived destructive interpersonal situation (figure 2.1; Korsgaard et al., 2008). These events include the following:

- The existence of *conflict-prone circumstances*; for example, the interdependence of individuals who pursue incompatible goals, failed communication, or ambiguous role responsibilities (Mellalieu et al., 2013; Wachsmuth & Jowett, 2020)
- *Provoking events*, such as confrontational or aggressive interpersonal interactions, that may trigger a cognitive response aiming at evaluating the disruptive encounter
- A *sensemaking process* in which individuals may consider the relevance (quality, significance) of the relationship or problem, who is to blame (e.g., self, other, nobody) and their accountability (e.g., intent, capacity), and the likelihood of change if one would engage in conflict (e.g., efficacy expectation)

These considerations may further elicit emotional and behavioral responses that are linked to the manifestation of conflict or the de-escalation of the situation (Korsgaard et al., 2008). However, even if an individual perceives conflict, they may choose not to openly engage in it. During such covert conflict, the other person(s) may not have (yet) realized or acknowledged the dispute (Korsgaard et al.,

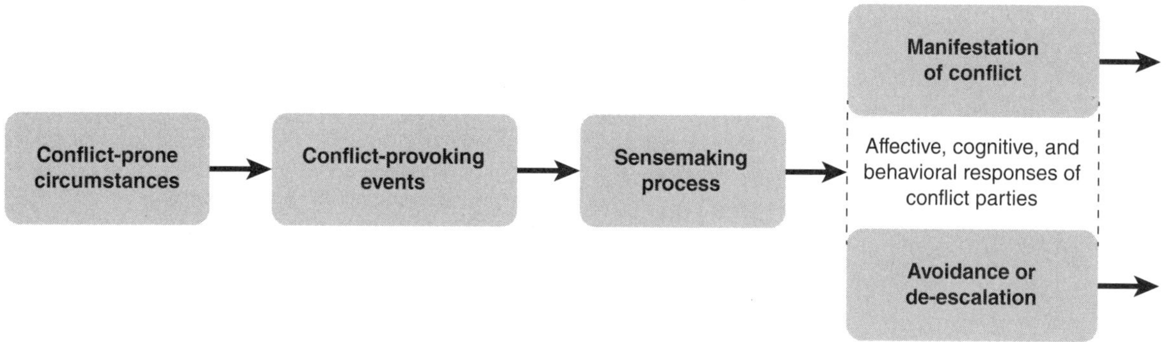

FIGURE 2.1 Events leading to the onset of interpersonal conflict.

Adapted from M.A. Korsgaard, S. Soyoung Jeong, D.M. Mahony, and A.H. Pitariu, "A Multilevel View of Intragroup Conflict," *Journal of Management* 34, no. 6 (2008): 1227.

2014). For example, an athlete may avoid bringing a conflict to their coach's attention because they may not feel safe enough within the relationship to initiate difficult conversations, or they may feel like they lack the agency and power needed for evoking change (Stirling & Kerr, 2009). Therefore, it is important that coaches be equipped with the skills necessary to demonstrate that they care for their athlete and value the relationships, as well as those skills needed to create a safe and open environment for athletes to express themselves. Coaches should also develop those skills needed to constructively respond to concerns and disagreements because poor awareness and conflict management skills can result in situations in which a small or avoidable conflict festers unnoticed until it becomes a major unresolvable problem.

The Escalation and Contagion of Conflict in Sport Relationships

Following the initial appraisal of a conflict, Wachsmuth and colleagues (2018a) identified three response patterns experienced by coaches and athletes:

- Problem-oriented response
- Uncertain response
- Escalating response

A problem-oriented response was marked by coaches' and athletes' positive emotions (e.g., relief) as well as thoughts and behaviors that were directed toward resolving the underlying issue of the dispute. Uncertain responses were linked to negative soft emotions (e.g., worry, disappointment, fear), self-doubt, a perceived lack of power, and withdrawal from or avoidance of conflict. Lastly, expressing negative hard emotions (e.g., anger, frustration), mutual blame and insults, verbal aggression, or even emotional abuse constituted an escalating response to conflict (Paradis et al., 2014a; Partridge & Knapp, 2016; Wachsmuth et al., 2018a). Such negative responses tend to form a negative cyclical process driving conflict escalation within a *self-reinforcing feedback loop* (Roberts, 2006) that may cause athletes and coaches to get caught in destructive ways of feeling, thinking, and acting. As a result, they may miss more constructive alternatives and soon view the original conflict topic as a more general and abstract issue within the relationship, which becomes difficult to manage. Moreover, individuals who lack the capacity to regulate their emotions, to self-reflect, or to listen to and understand others can perpetuate a subconscious self-centered bias (i.e., blind spot) and thus promote conflict engagement. Considering that constructive communication relies on the skills and knowledge of individuals involved in conflict, self-serving behaviors (e.g., excuses) and reciprocating aggression or defensiveness are unlikely to resolve any dispute (Canary et al., 2001; Roberts, 2006).

While conflict can certainly fester within a single relationship, negative dyadic interactions increase the likelihood of its contagion across other relationships, within and across groups (Jehn et al., 2013; Korsgaard et al., 2008, 2014). There seem to be three common ways through which conflict spreads: *direct contact* within a group through which information is shared and similarly understood (e.g., as violation of norms, respect, fairness); *indirect contact* or social contagion based on the exposure to and an adoption of observed behaviors, emotions, and opinions; and *conflict alignment*, the active formation of coalitions to achieve a common, negotiated outcome for the coalition members (Korsgaard et al., 2014). The latter can, for example, be envisaged when an entire team forms an alliance against one team member, a coach, or coaching staff. Such a situation would represent a *one versus many* intragroup conflict, which has the potential to change the power dynamics significantly within a group. More common, however, are *aggregated-dyadic* or *aggregated-multiple* types of intragroup conflict in which either two distinct or multiple coalitions actively pursue different interests. Typical aggregated-dyadic conflicts may, for example, arise if two high-status team members (e.g., coach vs. captain) continuously clash because of their differing personalities, values, or agendas. Situations in which difficult nonbinary decisions need to be made (e.g., training schedule, travel organization, room sharing) can further lead to aggregated-multiple conflicts. It should be noted that not all individuals will choose to actively respond; some may choose not to get involved within an alliance and will seek to avoid quarrels (i.e., *active-passive conflict*) (Korsgaard et al., 2014).

While the group dynamics of forming alliances and coalitions have been acknowledged within sport teams and coach–athlete dyads (Partridge & Knapp, 2016; Vealey, 2017; Wachsmuth et al., 2018b), neither the processes of contagion nor the type of intragroup conflict have been examined within the different contextual levels of sport (e.g., grassroots, professional sport, individual or team sport) and thus warrant attention. Such research may have significant implications when developing educational resources for both athletes and coaches that support skill development for effectively managing interpersonal difficulties and preempting the manifestation of a destructive culture in which open antagonism and power struggles between opposing coalitions impair nurturing learning and performance environments (Feddersen et al., 2020; Vealey, 2017).

Current Research: Determinants of Interpersonal and Group Conflict in Sport

How conflict may take place, spread, and be experienced by the involved individuals is influenced by a multitude of co-existing and interdependent variables related to the individual, the relationship, and the environment, some of which are outlined next; for a more comprehensive summary, see Wachsmuth and colleagues (2017).

Intrapersonal Factors Influencing Conflict Experiences in Sport

Within the literature, gender and personality are typical intrapersonal attributes considered to affect conflict experiences. For example, male compared with female team-sport athletes seem to engage more frequently in conflict behavior and communication in which the task rather than the social aspect of conflict is emphasized (Sullivan, 2004). Moreover, dyadic differences in personality (e.g., extraversion, conscientiousness) have been linked to dysfunctional relationships and an increase of conflict, as have been high dispositions of neuroticism and impulsivity—metaphorically described as "red temper" (Jackson et al., 2010, 2011; Yang et al., 2015). Also, an individual's attachment style (see chapter 3) appears to correlate with the frequency of conflict within relationships and seems to influence the effectiveness of conflict management strategies (Overall & McNulty, 2017). While individuals who have developed a secure attachment style over their life span experience low levels of conflict and can form lasting interpersonal bonds, individuals who developed insecure attachment styles struggle to engage in emotionally close and committed relationships (Davis & Jowett, 2014). This insecurity may have different consequences for avoidant and ambivalent attached individuals, with the former avoiding and the latter seeking conflict to meet relational expectations (Overall & McNulty, 2017).

Further to this, Jackson and colleagues suggested that if athletes and coaches possess mutually high self- and other-efficacy beliefs, they are less likely to experience conflict or part ways than if one or both perceive low-efficacy beliefs (Jackson et al., 2008, 2010). Considering the purposeful nature of interactions between athletes and coaches, perceived incompetence and lacking confidence with regard to interpersonal and sport-specific skills can pose a significant threat to the achievement of athletic goals and in turn to the relationship (Becker, 2009; Greenleaf et al., 2001; Jowett & Slade, 2021). In addition to those stable intrapersonal characteristics, situational attributes such as high levels of stress, fatigue, or performance pressure or the experience of injury or illness can increase the risk for conflict between coaches and athletes (Wachsmuth et al., 2017).

Interpersonal Factors Influencing Conflict Experiences in Sport

Individual attributes (e.g., motivation) and experiences (e.g., stress) may also expose athletes and coaches to conflict by affecting the quality of their interactions (e.g., communication, leadership, teamwork). For example, personal expectations and performance pressure within an Olympic season may strain the relationship between a coach and an athlete, leading to a breakdown of open communication that in turn causes conflict (Mellalieu et al., 2013). Generally, communication is a central element with regard to both the onset and escalation as well as the prevention and management of conflict. Effective communication enables individuals to understand one another, share critical information, and manage problems before they turn into conflict. Yet failing to communicate effectively—with regard to quantity and quality—is also the most cited reason for conflict in sport across organizational levels (i.e., athletes, coaches, staff) (Mellalieu et al., 2013). There is no such thing as "not communicating." Avoidance can occur when an individual feels uncomfortable or ill equipped to handle a situation or as a means of disengaging oneself. Avoiding a direct exchange, however, sends a message that may be interpreted as "I'm [angry, frustrated, disappointed] with you" or "I don't care about you," either of which can lead to conflict and a breakdown of the relationship if not addressed.

Depending on the study, somewhere between 66% and 93% of all communication occurs nonverbally in the form of our body language, facial expressions, and tone (Eaves & Leathers, 2018). In addition to the influence of nonverbal communication on relationship interactions, discrepancies between what is said (i.e., verbally) and what is done (i.e., behavior, facial expressions, gestures) may cause further irritation. Therefore, it is essential to be aware of the messages one is sending, both verbally and nonverbally, and to reflect on and check in on how these may be interpreted. For example, a coach may use a loud, commanding voice to convey a clear message toward an athlete, who may perceive such communication as hostile and controlling. The athlete might interpret such behavior as a show of dominance and power, and consequently feel intimidated or distressed, and therefore withdraw from a discussion or dispute. Yet another athlete may not accept such coaching behavior and reciprocally engage in equally abrasive communication, raising the risk of conflict (e.g., d'Arripe-Longueville et al., 1998; Heelis et al., 2020; Purdy et al., 2008).

Failing to communicate effectively—with regard to quantity and quality—is also the most cited reason for conflict in sport across organizational levels.

Although the abuse of power in the form of relational maltreatment is extensively covered elsewhere in the book (see chapter 4), a few words shall be spared here too. While coach–athlete conflict may be both a consequence and a determinant of abusive coaching behaviors, it is important to distinguish conflict as an interpersonal process from any form of maltreatment. The latter represents "volitional acts [within a critical relationship role] that result in or have the potential to result in physical injuries and/or psychological harm" of, for example, the athlete (Stirling, 2009, p. 1091). As such, maltreatment is a one-directional intentional behavior of the perpetrator, who holds the power over the victim. In contrast, interpersonal conflict is (at least) a dyadic process that constitutes an expression of and struggle for influence over the other. The suggestion here is that individuals in conflict have some degree of power and influence over the other, which is, for example, determined by their formal position and status as well as their skill.

Understanding power as a dyadic concept enables both individuals to possess power (i.e., exercise influence) and to give or withhold power (i.e., permit influence or not) within a conflictual situation (Jowett & Wachsmuth, 2020).

While coaches' professional role and experience place them in charge of managing relationships within the sport setting, athletes can gain power and influence by demonstrating sound interpersonal skills and showing commitment to their sport development. However, it is important to recognize the distinction between adult athletes and adolescent athletes, who, regardless of their performance level, need to be afforded specific support and guidance for the development of healthy relationship and communication skills in support of their holistic development (Wylleman et al., 2020). Thus, viewing power from a dyadic perspective, athletes and coaches are in a position in which they are both responsible for creating and maintaining effective relationships in which conflict may well occur but is readily managed by communicating openly and constructively.

Within a team setting, this dyadic view of power seems especially pertinent for the relationship between a coach and a captain or an athlete leader who is designated to act as the link between staff and team (Loughead, 2017). Consider a scenario where a captain's interpersonal difficulties with the coach can impede an entire team's performance when miscommunication and a lack of trust, respect, and commitment contribute to an insufficient flow of information, leading to conflict contagion among other athletes (Dupuis et al., 2006). Such a coach–athlete conflict can fester and escalate, fostering an ego-involving climate, jealousy, rivalry, and power struggles among team members (Holt et al., 2012; Kristiansen et al., 2012; Partridge & Knapp, 2016). However, even high-task cohesion may disturb interpersonal relationships within a competitive team environment and can contribute to conflict if team members' roles are not clear, accepted, or carried out sufficiently (Benson et al., 2013; Vealey, 2017). A conflict that has spread within an entire team is difficult to manage not only because of the differing interests of the involved individuals but also because an important social network (i.e., the team) that usually helps to negate or repair disrupted relationships between individual members breaks down (Vealey, 2017; Wachsmuth et al., 2018b).

The onset and course of conflict are never determined just by the individuals who are actively involved but also by the social and physical environments surrounding them.

Environmental Factors Influencing Conflict Experiences in Sport

Environmental constraints can predispose sport participants to conflict. Within the microsystem of a sport organization, (in)formal hierarchies, organizational culture and leadership, performance expectations, practice and competition structures, and selection procedures can have an impact on whether and how conflict is experienced (e.g., d'Arripe-Longueville et al., 1998; Feddersen et al., 2020; Henriksen et al., 2014). Poor communication between an organization's stakeholders (i.e., coaches, sport directors), conflictual interactions with significant others (e.g., parents, partners), and insufficient collaboration between club and regional or national coaches can further impede the relationships coaches have with their athletes (Feddersen et al., 2020; O'Malley et al., 2018). Additionally, a "win at all costs" culture within a performance environment can leave little room for vulnerability, empathy, and compassion, all important factors for healthy relationships, and may instead promote autocratic leadership or even abusive behaviors (Komaki & Tuakli-Wosornu, 2021; Roberts et al., 2020). Under these circumstances, open communication and constructive conflict management seem hardly achievable.

Taking an even broader view, larger cultural factors such as ethnic backgrounds, political views, and stereotypical beliefs contribute to the experiences of conflict. Explicit discrimination and prejudice as well as microaggression have repeatedly been reported within sport, both exhibited within the performance setting (e.g., coaches, team members) and imposed from the outside (e.g., media coverage, fans, opponents) (Gearity & Metzger, 2017; Jowett & Frost, 2007; Khomutova, 2015). After all, interpersonal relationships in sport do not take place in a vacuum but merge diverse sporting and nonsporting environments that directly and indirectly shape the interactions between and among coaches, athletes, staff members, and other social agents. From this perspective, the onset and course of conflict are never determined just by the individuals who are actively involved but also by the social and physical environments surrounding them. Therefore, it is important to consider these external factors when aiming to prevent, manage, and resolve conflict effectively.

Conflict Prevention and Management in Sport Relationships

While this chapter so far has focused on the immediate correlates and experiences of conflict in high-performance coach–athlete relationships, this section outlines practical insights that can be used to effectively manage interpersonal and group conflicts.

Communication Strategies for Conflict Management

Skilled communication is vital for successful conflict prevention and management—but which strategies are most effective for dealing with conflict and facilitating positive interpersonal outcomes in an adult relationship? According to Canary and colleagues (2001), two criteria seem to be relevant: the other's perceived communication competence and one's own satisfaction. A person's communication competence can be evaluated on the grounds of appropriateness (i.e., extent to which relational and contextual expectations are met) and effectiveness (i.e., interaction promotes own goal achievement). Satisfaction, in turn, represents one's own affective response to this evaluation. Competence can therefore be judged only within the context of the situation and relationship because these determine the standards that are applied (Canary and Lakey, 2006). Consequentially, different patterns of collaborative or competitive or of direct or indirect communication may be considered appropriate and effective based on the characteristics of the conflicting parties, their relationship, and the issue at hand as well as environmental constraints.

For example, Overall and McNulty (2017) reported in their review on conflict communication in close relationships that direct collaborative strategies (e.g., solution-oriented discussion) and competitive strategies (e.g., demanding change) could facilitate the resolution of severe problems and enhance relationship satisfaction in the long run, whereas indirect strategies (e.g., competitive: inducing guilt; collaborative: softening conflict) may not evoke any lasting change. However, indirect approaches may be more effective and appropriate if problems are less severe, change is not readily achievable, or the individuals lack self-confidence and security within the relationship. Thus, if there are concerns about communication or conflict management skills, coaches may consider alternative approaches to supporting athlete behavior change instead of using a direct and possibly confrontational approach, especially for minor issues.

Considering that the coach–athlete relationship is not just about having a satisfying rapport but is rather a collaboration to support the achievement of individual as well as team and often program goals, viewing conflict management from an organizational perspective provides helpful insights. Within this context, Pruitt's (1983) *dual-concern model* represents another situational (or contingency) approach to conflict management. Instead of prioritizing relationship satisfaction, it asks individuals to weigh up their concern for themselves (i.e., personal goals) versus the concern for the other individual with whom they are in conflict (Pruitt, 1983; cited from Rahim, 2002). In an extension of this model, Rahim (2002) proposes five approaches to handling interpersonal conflict, as illustrated in table 2.1.

Research in organizational settings indicates that the strategies proposed by Rahim (2002) may be used in combination to cope with different elements of conflict. A sequence of collaborative behaviors (e.g., finding mutually acceptable agreements, win-win solutions) and dominating behaviors (e.g., forcing decisions, overpowering the other) may lead to high levels of satisfaction with a conflict agreement if negotiations close with a collaborative problem-solving strategy (Van de Vliert et al., 1999). Ending with a competitive strategy, though, could decrease dyadic effectiveness or may even re-escalate a dispute because at least one conflict partner would feel dissatisfied. Thus, the order in which concerns are addressed and the strategies applied at the various stages of conflict negotiations need to be carefully thought through. This process requires a high degree of reflection and skill, so it is advisable that coaching professionals have the proper training as well as appropriate support for guiding these critical conversations. It is also important to recognize that athletes may not be in the position nor possess the skills to successfully structure such negotiations, depending on a wide range of factors such as age, personal experiences, and cultural background. As such, it may be necessary to ensure that athletes are given guidance and opportunities to learn these skills and are supported in navigating challenging conversations.

Research on Conflict Prevention and Management in Sport Relationships

In the realm of sport relationships, the COMPASS model (Rhind & Jowett, 2010; see chapter 1) presents a valuable framework for developing sound communication skills that help coaches and athletes create and maintain effective relationships. Encompassing seven different communication strategies (conflict management, openness, motivation, prevention, assurance, support, social network), conflict prevention and management are two essential parts of this model, discussed more in depth next.

Implicit and Explicit Conflict Prevention Strategies

Conflict prevention can include both explicit strategies aimed at minimizing the risk of conflict and implicit strategies to facilitate high-quality

TABLE 2.1 Conflict Management Approaches and Examples

Conflict management style	Description	Possible circumstances for effectively using this strategy
Avoidance or withdrawal	Conflict may be avoided if the issue is not perceived as important for the task or the relationship. For more complex situations or those where conflict cannot be solved for personal or circumstantial reasons, withdrawal, as an avoidance tactic, may allow an individual to avoid conflict through an opportunity to regulate emotions and reflect.	• Choosing to ignore or overlook frustrating comments made by someone you know has had a rough day • Leaving a noisy team setting prior to a major competition when stress levels are high
Dominating	A decisive approach that forces the other party to acquiesce may be deemed appropriate if speedy or unpopular decisions need to be made. However, dominating requires a high degree of influence and is therefore often (rightly or wrongly) an available strategy only to those in power. Because misuse can endanger relationships, it should be used scarcely and with sufficient communication competence. It is a strategy typically used if the problem is more important than the relationship.	• Setting strict no-discussion safety rules for the weight room • Choosing an unpopular early morning team flight due to budgetary and scheduling concerns • Setting personal boundaries that may not be popular (e.g., prioritizing self-care or academic work over team requirements)
Obliging	Giving in may be an appropriate strategy if the issue is more important to the other or if the importance of the relationship outweighs the importance of the conflict. It may also be used by an individual who perceives a lack of personal power to change a situation.	• Understanding the importance of an individual's religious faith and making a decision about required attendance when there is a scheduling conflict
Collaborating or integrating	A collaborative approach is often referred to as the gold standard; however, it requires sufficient time and resources as well as willingness to engage in an open exchange and problem-solving strategies. The aim of collaborative strategies is to find sustainable solutions that are mutually acceptable for all. Collaborative strategies should be used for complex problems that are of importance to all involved and require a long-term solution.	• Jointly defining role expectations and creating individualized development plans or training and competition schedules
Compromising	Compromise may be considered for situations where collaboration or domination do not work, such as in situations where goals are mutually exclusive or both parties hold equal power. Compromises are often only a short-term solution to a complex problem and require regular reevaluation.	• Agreeing to move the team curfew back an hour in exchange for an expanded practice session on the weekend at the start of the season

relationships and nurturing performance environments (Wachsmuth et al., 2018b). The strategies presented within the COMPASS model (Rhind & Jowett, 2010) can effectively reduce conflict by increasing mutual trust and respect and teaching coaches and athletes to show empathy, work together, and support one another to achieve shared goals. Relationships characterized by such positive relational qualities provide a secure base for constructive conflict management if problems do occur (Evans et al., 2013; Holt et al., 2012). In this regard, coaches can set standards by being approachable, establishing rapport, and providing guidance and structure through difficult situations (Becker, 2009; Wachsmuth et al., 2018b). Additionally, establishing a team culture that evolves around common values and goals can reduce individuals' ego involvement, promote collectivistic behaviors, and build trust, which enables athletes and coaches to focus on the task rather than on personal problems if (when) they occur (Vealey, 2017). Coaches can facilitate this sense of togetherness by recruiting athletes based not only on performance but also on their intra- and interpersonal skills as well as character so that they fit into the team (Wachsmuth et al., 2018b).

Explicit measures for reducing conflict can complement implicit strategies. These include agreeing on clear rules and expectations that provide a structure for working together (Heelis et al., 2020; Jowett & Carpenter, 2015) as well as anticipating and addressing concerns early on (Wachsmuth et al., 2018b). Careful consideration should be given to leadership style and communication strategies to ensure consistency between verbal and nonverbal messages and between words and actions. A coach's approach for providing growth-related feedback, for example, should be intentionally constructed so as not to create friction and promote negativity. Finding the balance between the inherent need to critique when giving feedback and providing encouragement while avoiding a feeling of criticism is crucial. Location and timing are also important considerations that coaches and athletes should carefully think about when preparing to address critical feedback or a difficult topic: Are they in the right physical place, and is there enough time to deal with the conflict? Are they in the right frame of mind, and do they have the energy to keep their emotions under control? Have they attempted to understand the problem and the other person's perspective before speaking? Being appropriately prepared to engage in a potentially problematic conversation with a clear head and sufficient time as well as demonstrating empathy and a willingness to listen, understand, and remain open minded can reduce the escalation of a stressful situation (Wachsmuth et al., 2018b).

Finding the balance between the inherent need to critique when giving feedback and providing encouragement while avoiding a feeling of criticism is crucial.

Conflict Management in Interpersonal and Group Relationships in Sport

In the case where conflict does erupt, coaches and athletes should neither be surprised by nor scared of the conflict experience itself—accepting that conflict happens in all relationships is already a constructive step toward managing it (Wachsmuth et al., 2020). Nevertheless, many individuals (including coaches and athletes) initially withdraw from conflict (Mellalieu et al., 2013) to either avoid it entirely or to first regulate emotions, self-reflect, or provide space to the other party before seeking a conversation. Sport participants may also use this time to vent frustration or seek advice from friends, family, or team members as well as to gather information about the other person or problem (Mellalieu et al., 2013; Wachsmuth et al., 2018b). Moreover, third parties (e.g., sport psychology consultants) can directly support situations of conflict between coaches and athletes as well as within teams by consulting with the involved individuals and preparing them for difficult conversations as well as by mediating between the conflicted parties (Vealey, 2017; Wachsmuth et al., 2020).

Nevertheless, within the sport performance setting, the coach as the professional is most directly responsible for solving problems and managing conflict within the team (Gould & Dieffenbach, 2021). While athletes often show reconciliatory behaviors instead of addressing a conflict directly, coaches are expected to initiate and calmly guide difficult conversations. This becomes a challenge if coaches are unaware of trouble, do not recognize signs of friction (e.g., withdrawal, body language), or do not have the time or resources to deal with a conflictual situation—barriers that likely leave a conflict to grow over time. As such, it is essential for coaches to be aware of the responsibilities and expectations that come with their professional role (Wachsmuth et al., 2018b), accept them, and have appropriate and adequate training and support for interpersonal and intrapersonal skills essential for relationship development and management (Dieffenbach, 2019).

In the long run, conflict can be managed constructively only when all parties know about its existence, are willing to find a solution, and have the skills and influence to constructively seek resolutions to problems or issues by having difficult and challenging conversations. Engaging in integrative strategies, such as compromising or collaborating, has commonly been viewed as most effective by coaches and athletes. These approaches involve sharing information, questioning, listening actively, reasoning through solutions, setting new goals, and defining behavioral strategies to achieve them (e.g., Wachsmuth et al., 2018b). However, while there was no mention of competitive or forceful conflict management strategies in Mellalieu and colleagues' (2013) study, Wachsmuth and colleagues (2018b) reported coaches' and athletes' use of dominating styles for dealing with severe conflict and misconduct, or conflict related to matters concerning one's private life. Coaches especially shut conflict down if the morale or discipline of an entire team was in danger, or if they believed their position would be fragile if they failed to deal with a problem. Further, athletes seemed to readily accept or oblige coaches' dominating, controlling, or abusive behaviors if they felt a lack of power within the relationship (Gearity & Murray, 2011; Stirling & Kerr, 2008). In the long run, though, such competitive strategies are not sustainable, may lead to strained relationships and future conflict, and can impede athletes' well-being and performance (Wachsmuth et al., 2018b).

Conflict Outcomes: Performance, Well-Being, and Relationships

Constructive conflict management is key to facilitating positive outcomes of disputes among sport participants. If conflict management fails or is perceived as inappropriate, disputes may have detrimental consequences for some or all involved parties. For example, athletes and coaches may experience higher levels of stress, negative mood, worry, or anxiety throughout or subsequent to conflict. They can feel less confident in their own or the other's interpersonal and sport-specific skills, causing a lack of motivation or a stagnation of performances. Sport development and performance may also suffer because athletes are distracted, are physically and mentally exhausted, or have stopped adhering to their coaches' training schedule. Athletes may thus consider parting from their coach or team, or leaving the sport entirely, whereas a coach may recommend that the athlete move on (Heelis et al., 2020; Wachsmuth et al., 2017, 2018b). Within a team setting, some relationships may suffer and others get stronger as alliances form; however, cohesion and collective efficacy of the team as a whole are likely to decrease (Leo et al., 2015; Paradis et al., 2014b). Moreover, conflict may not only spread among athletes and coaches but also infiltrate entire sporting organizations, creating performance environments that are marked by mistrust, antagonism, and power struggles (Feddersen et al., 2020). This may not leave any room for openness, understanding, and compassion and as such can cause a "whole world of pain" for athletes and coaches (Wachsmuth et al., 2020, p. 16).

Despite its negative connotation, conflict can also facilitate positive change if managed in a constructive fashion. Commonly cited benefits are improved problem solving and performance facilitated through collaborative conflict management processes, including open communication pathways that increase the amount and depth of shared information, promote mutual understanding, and permit open-minded thinking about creative strategies to address an issue. Sport participants, for example, reported they were able to jointly construct better training schedules, set clear expectations, and agree on long-term development goals when dealing constructively with conflict (Holt et al., 2012; Wachsmuth et al., 2018b). Last but not least, managing conflict in a collaborative manner can strengthen the relationships of the involved individuals—not just because of the gained information and insights, but especially because the individuals can trust that the relationship allows for dissent and can survive conflict without breaking apart. Such positive conflict experiences may empower athletes to openly speak with their coaches and thus further diminish the distance caused by formal hierarchies and traditional expectations and beliefs that portray coaches as unapproachable and not to be questioned.

Future Research Directions

Examining the extant scientific literature on interpersonal and group conflict within social and organizational psychology highlights the need for more research in this field. Within sport, initial studies have merely scratched the surface of understanding the complex nature of conflict as experienced by coaches and athletes across the wide range of sport performance contexts. Thus, instead of proposing explicit questions to be asked within future studies, we suggest some wider areas of inquiry to be considered.

- To better understand conflict processes, it is important to systematically investigate reciprocal emotional responses (e.g., emotional linkage and contagion), cognitive responses (e.g., attribution of blame, shared realities, empathic accuracy), and behavioral responses (e.g., body language, verbal communication, coalition seeking) of individuals engaged in conflict.

- The effectiveness of, appropriateness of, and satisfaction with conflict management strategies applied by coaches and athletes should be examined with regard to individuals' well-being and development, sport performance, and relationship quality.
- Because conflict between two (or more) individuals always takes place within a broader environment, it is vital to study factors that ease or promote its escalation.
- In a similar vein, reoccurring conflict between sport participants can instigate or be an expression of a destructive organizational culture within sport systems (Feddersen et al., 2020). Further research is warranted to examine the contagion of conflict within and across organizational levels (e.g., athletes, coaches, sport science staff, management) in order to gain in-depth knowledge of the nature, manifestation, and management of dysfunctional performance environments.
- Applied research is required to identify development opportunities for equipping sport participants with the intra- and interpersonal skills needed to form and maintain effective relationships by employing a constructive approach to conflict and by developing healthy and nurturing sporting environments. Specifically, research should examine existing strategies within coach education programs and explore ongoing development and support efforts for coaching professionals regarding intra- and interpersonal skill development. It will also be critical to consider age and developmentally appropriate expectations and best practices from an athlete perspective to create suitable resources for facilitating inter- and intrapersonal skills and thus supporting athletes on the ground.
- Finally, work is needed to explore cultural, cross-cultural, and unique sport culture factors that influence individuals' expectations, skill development, and skill application relative to relationship building, negotiating power, and conflict management.

Practical Implications: A Coach's Guide Through Conflict Management

As part of their professional responsibilities (Côté & Gilbert, 2009), coaches play a crucial role in constructing sound relationships, including managing conflict within the sport setting. In their role as conflict solvers, the coach should support healthy communication strategies for athletes and staff that minimize and manage situations that may lead to conflict, in addition to maintaining strong relationships overall. Being able to model and teach effective communication and conflict management will help coaches support the holistic development of their athletes with regard to forming the intra- and interpersonal skills necessary to build quality relationships with others. To this end, coaches need to receive sufficient education and training themselves about the establishment of appropriate teaching- and leadership-based relationships. Additionally, conflict management training can provide essential skills for handling the inherent stressors that lead to conflict in sport. The five Rs presented in figure 2.2 offer a structure to guide coaches through conflict management with or among athletes, or indeed among the coaching team or more broadly.

Coaches who speak openly about constructive conflict management provide a role model and encourage athletes to address difficulties more willingly. While managing interpersonal or intrateam conflict is never easy, such situations provide worthy teachable moments, especially for coaches working in youth or talent development settings. Figure 2.3 provides a framework for consciously working through minor conflicts. Engaging in structured conversations and collaborating to develop win-win solutions present great opportunities to teach by doing. Further, modeling consistency, managing temper, being patient, and showing empathy in challenging relationship situations will facilitate trust and help create a psychologically safe performance environment in which athletes are willing to challenge themselves without fearing negative consequences.

Recognize	• Pay attention to small changes (e.g., depth of conversations, body language, withdrawal) during interpersonal interactions and observe social dynamics in the environment (e.g., emotional climate, energy and motivation, cliques). Acknowledge negative affects and emotions by asking whether such feelings may be caused by conflict which has not been addressed. Assistant coaches and other (trustworthy) staff members may provide further information or act as sounding boards in assessing changes. Concerns should be addressed through nonconfrontational private conversations that share your observations and ask supportive questions (e.g., showing interest and care).
Reflect	• Whenever possible, take time to step away from disagreements and encourage others to do the same to help provide everyone with an opportunity to reflect. While sometimes a "quick fix" can resolve a trivial disagreement before it becomes conflict, it is still important to identify what caused the situation and what may prevent it in the future. When reflecting, prepare for a conflict conversation by considering questions such as "What is my part in this situation?," "What are my needs and objectives?," "What might the other hope for and why?," and "What time/resources can I invest?" versus "How important/urgent is the issue?." It is helpful to prepare discussion points and consider communication strategies (e.g., role play, moving chairs). If not directly involved, helping individuals reflect on their answers to these questions can help them be better prepared to handle challenging conversations.
React	• Identify strategies that help you cope with personal stress, negative emotions, and ruminating thoughts to avoid additional negative consequences (e.g., impact on immediate behavior or well-being). Try to schedule a meeting with the involved parties in a neutral location, with a set time frame and schedule. When appropriate, consider the support of a mediator (e.g., sport psychologist). While a coach may feel the need to mediate conflicts between other individuals, it is important to be mindful of the potential negative impact that their positional power can have on the individuals and situation that may impede a quality outcome. It is essential that mediators are clear on their role and have the necessary skills to be a neutral third party without giving personal opinions or recommendations.
Resolve	• Follow-up is essential for resolving conflict and maintaining or rebuilding relationship trust. Before agreeing on solutions, be sure to evaluate and reflect on whether the defined strategies will address the conflict (needs) and whether they are workable in the long run. Implement the solutions developed in the meeting by recognizing and coping with obstacles and maintaining open lines of communication. Regularly reflect about the effectiveness of the agreed solution and jointly adjust strategies if needed.
Reevaluate	• Conflicts may not be solved within one meeting, and adjustments may be necessary to address complex concerns over time. This is especially true if the individuals in conflict could only agree upon compromises or if situational circumstances change. To jointly reflect, once the crisis has passed, upon a common experience with conflict can support skill growth for future relationship development.

FIGURE 2.2 The five Rs for constructive conflict management.

1. Create safe meeting environment
Welcome individuals; set ground rules (e.g., speaking time, manners, time-outs, etc.); invite conflict parties to recall positive memories or shared goals

2. Openly share experience and expectations
Invite conflict parties to present personal experiences of the conflict (including emotions, worries, hopes, reasons for actions); reinforce ground rules; encourage questions that aim to facilitate understanding; show interest and care—allow vulnerability

3. Define conflict
Mutually identify the core issue of the conflict; prioritize multiple issues; go back to (2) if conflict parties cannot agree on a conflict definition

4. Brainstorm solutions
Motivate conflict parties to think of a wealth of *possible and impossible* solutions (the latter stimulate out-of-the-box thinking and highlight what aspects of a problem are most important); maybe new revelations require defining the conflict

5. Define and record solution
Evaluate identified solutions with regard to appropriateness, feasibility, and expected effectiveness; develop sustainable solution (including strategies and expectations); consider possible obstacles; record agreement (including objectiveness, strategies, reevaluation date, and criteria)

FIGURE 2.3 Guidelines for structuring constructive conflict conversations.

Summary

The network of relationships formed among the coach, the athletes, and the team is at the heart of sport performance. Psychologically safe, mutually respectful, and overall high-quality relationships that can withstand challenges, constructive criticism, differing opinions, and even conflict are essential for the pursuit of performance and development goals. As noted in this chapter, conflict is not in and of itself negative, and when managed properly it can help solve important concerns, foster personal growth, and improve relationships. At the same time, conflict has the potential to fester and spread within a group, promoting a destructive culture of power struggles and rivalry, and as a consequence, individuals inhibit rather than support each other's sport and personal development. As a coach, athlete, staff member, or sport psychology consultant, understanding how to recognize and manage factors that influence the perceptions of conflict, and how to build the intra- and interpersonal skills necessary to manage conflict, is therefore central to supporting the development of healthy relationships and teaching others to do so as well.

To help sport participants deal with difficult interpersonal situations and create nurturing sport environments, researchers need to invest resources into studying the determinants of functional and dysfunctional social interactions within sport settings—including attributes of the individual as well as cultural and systemic features of the sport (organization) itself. Such research can provide a foundation for evidence-based educational materials and training programs aimed at maximizing the skills of coaches, athletes, and other stakeholders to effectively engage in healthy relationships as they pursue sporting excellence.

DISCUSSION QUESTIONS

1. Define interpersonal conflict, and describe its multidimensional nature.
2. Describe the role of communication skills in conflict escalation and de-escalation.
3. What strategies can coaches and athletes employ to manage conflict, and what should they consider when choosing an approach?
4. Conflict can be characterized as a functional or a dysfunctional process. Explain.
5. How might the power dynamics within the sport environment influence the development, management, and resolution of conflict?
6. What resources and support do coaches and athletes need in order to prevent, manage, and solve conflict?
7. How can coaches educate and support athletes to prevent, manage, and solve conflict?

3

Applying Attachment Theory to the Study of Relationships in Sport

Louise Davis, PhD, and Sam Carr, PhD

LEARNING OBJECTIVES

On completion of this chapter, the reader should have the following:

- Understanding of the fundamental concepts of attachment theory
- Awareness of applications of attachment theory within the context of sport
- Deeper comprehension of both the parent–athlete and coach–athlete attachment relationship and their implications for developmental- and performance-related outcomes
- Recognition of areas for future research
- Insight into practical considerations as they pertain to education and applied interventions

Attachment theory (Bowlby, 1969/1982) is a long-established and well-developed framework for the exploration of human relationships and psychological development across the life span. Initially, attachment theory was a popular framework for understanding parent–child relationships, but the theory has also become prominent for understanding personality and individual difference characteristics across multiple close relationships (e.g., teacher–student, leader–follower, therapist–client) and contexts (e.g., organizational, clinical, academic) during adolescence and adulthood. Waters (2000) has suggested that attachment theory is one of the last surviving grand theories in psychology because it (1) is grounded in evolutionary principles, (2) helps in understanding a range of dimensions of human experience, (3) is relevant across the life span, (4) offers a developmental analysis, (5) appeals to both individual difference and normative ways of thinking, (6) incorporates both stability and change, and (7) provides guidance on what constitutes close human relationships. Nonetheless, the application of attachment theory in the context of sport has been slow to emerge, and there is a need for conceptual direction, clarity, and synthesis of ideas in this area.

The purpose of this chapter is to introduce attachment theory as an emerging perspective on the topic of close relationships within the context of sport. First, we briefly present the history of attachment theory and outline its core concepts. Within this, we explain what an attachment relationship is, how individual differences in attachment develop across the life span, and the role of early attachment experiences with primary caregivers in shaping differences in attachment styles and a person's internal working model. We discuss how these differences are sustained across time as well as how they transfer within adolescence and adulthood and across various types of relationships and contexts.

We then highlight advancements and integration of attachment theory in the context of sport.

In addition to reviewing the fundamental ideas underlying attachment theory, we highlight some research developments and illustrate the relevance of the theory for understanding the role of parent–athlete and coach–athlete attachment relationships. Here we also address emergent advancements such as context-specific attachment and the implications that such new ideas might have for sport research and practice, while also addressing methodological considerations in assessing attachment. We then provide a broader array of new empirical research ideas and offer a discussion on the practical applications of research conducted thus far. Finally, we conclude our chapter with a summary of what has been discussed, alongside some key discussion questions.

The Fundamentals of Attachment Theory

Attachment theory was pioneered by John Bowlby (1969/1982, 1973, 1977) to explain the origins of social behavior and the emotional bonds formed between infants and their primary caregivers (usually the mother, known as an attachment figure). He argued that infants are born with a repertoire of behaviors aimed at seeking and maintaining proximity to a primary caregiver. In Bowlby's view, proximity seeking is an innate affect-regulation device that protects an individual from physical and psychological harm or threat and alleviates distress. Bowlby (1988) noted that the successful achievement of these affect-regulation functions results in a sense of attachment security—that is, a sense that the world is a safe place, that one can rely on significant others, and that one can as a result confidently and autonomously explore their environment. In the development of attachment theory, Bowlby (1969/1982) drew on concepts from ethology, cybernetics, developmental psychology, and psychoanalysis, and although John Bowlby was a psychoanalyst by training, "he was really an ethologist at heart" (Van der Horst, 2009, p. 105). Accordingly, a core evolutionary assumption of attachment theory (Bowlby, 1969/1982) is the innate human tendency to seek proximity to an attachment figure in response to perceived threat. From an evolutionary perspective, proximity-seeking behaviors are part of a hypothesized goal of the *attachment behavioral system*, a critical relational mechanism through which infants, adolescents, and adults across a range of species maintain a subjective sense of safety.

A sense of attachment security is a sense that the world is a safe place, that one can rely on significant others, and that one can as a result confidently and autonomously explore their environment.

Attachment Behavioral System

Bowlby believed instinctive behaviors have evolved to bind human infants to a primary caregiver (usually the mother) and that attachment behavior is likely both instinctive and "built on the same general patterns as in other mammalian species" (Bowlby, 1979/2005, p. 37). He described a fixed set of behavioral patterns, such as crying, smiling, and clinging, that he saw primarily as evolutionary behavioral apparatus to facilitate the development of a bond between infant and caregiver. It is important to note that the internal goal of the attachment system is not proximity or contact per se but a sense of felt psychological security (Bischof, 1975; Bretherton, 1985). Bowlby (1969/1982) proposed that the attachment system is likely to be most active or activated in situations where individuals are under stress, frightened, fatigued, or ill and that the system is toned down when an attachment figure provides needed comfort and a felt sense of safety and security is restored. If the primary strategy does not work, secondary strategies such as hyperactivating or deactivating the attachment system occur (Mikulincer & Shaver, 2003).

Cassidy (1999) has outlined how maintenance of proximity and contact with a caregiver could change in accordance with the balance of the systems of attachment and exploration. For example, the sudden presence of a stranger or threat of physical harm theoretically activates the attachment system and diminishes the exploratory system. However, when a child perceives that an attachment figure is nearby and responsive, the child experiences a sense of security and safety and is more likely to explore the environment again, restoring a sense of homeostasis. Although the attachment system is most critical during the early years of life, Bowlby (1988) assumed it is active over the entire life span and is manifested in thoughts and behaviors related to support seeking.

Development of Attachment Bonds

Bowlby identified individual differences in the way children appraise the availability of an attachment figure and how they regulate their attachment behavior in response to perceived threats. Attachment behavior tends to be most obvious when the attached person feels threatened, frightened, or sick and is eased when an attachment figure provides protection, reassurance, and support. This was further evidenced when Mary Ainsworth and colleagues began to systematically study infant–parent separations and individual differences in the regulation of attachment behavior. They developed an empirical protocol: a laboratory paradigm for studying infant–parent attachments. Specifically, Ainsworth and colleagues' (1978) Strange Situation Procedure (SSP) activated an infant's attachment system and involved placing the infant in an unfamiliar environment, often with a stranger, and separating them from their primary caregiver (usually the mother) for short periods before reuniting them. This allowed for distinctly different patterns of responses to separations and reunions with a primary attachment figure to be observed. Furthermore, the protocol was designed to assess the mother's behaviors and the characteristics of their interactions with their infant. From this research, Ainsworth and her colleagues (1978) were able to categorize these differences in attachment behaviors into three primary psychological constructs, known as *attachment styles*: secure, insecure anxious-ambivalent, and insecure avoidant. The three types are described in table 3.1.

Van Ijzendoorn and colleagues (1999) outlined how the secure, insecure anxious-ambivalent, and insecure-avoidant models of attachment reflect organized patterns of attachment; that is, each pattern reflects a developed attachment strategy

TABLE 3.1 Attachment Styles and Their Characteristics and Origins

Ainsworth's attachment styles	Characteristics of children	Origins: caregiving style
Secure	• Comfortable with closeness and depending on others • No worry about being abandoned • Happy to be separated from caregiver • Happy to seek comfort during times of need or when frightened • Will perceive their caregiver as someone who is responsive and attentive to their needs • Greet caregiver with positive emotions	• Responsive to the needs of the child • Sensitive to emotional signals and signs of distress • Interact and play more with the child
Insecure anxious-ambivalent	• Will appear generally anxious and clingy • Difficulty depending on and trusting their caregiver • May experience problems regulating and controlling emotions (cry a lot) • Highly dependent on others • Strong fear of abandonment	• Inconsistency in caregiving behaviors (patterns, routines, and responses) • Unpredictable caregiving behaviors • Inconsistent in acknowledging emotional signals
Insecure avoidant	• Will not seek much contact or comfort • Will show little distress when separated from their caregiver • Will avoid contacting their caregiver, even when in distress or frightened • Will show little preference for their caregiver over strangers	• Emotionally unavailable • Consistently unresponsive when called on • Consistently rejecting and neglectful of care • Angry and rejecting of proximity-seeking efforts • Openly discouraging of outward displays of emotion

that can be considered adaptive in the sense that it is an internalized pattern of responses based on expectations of typical caregiver responses to expression of distress. That said, researchers (e.g., Main & Solomon, 1986, 1990) have identified a fourth pattern that has been labeled *disorganized attachment*. This pattern reflects the absence of a coherent and organized strategy for dealing with distress and the breakdown or absence of a consistent strategy for emotional regulation. Main and Solomon (1990) identified features such as contradictory behavior (e.g., the infant shows marked distress when separated from the caregiver but then complete indifference when they return), freezing (e.g., apparent difficulty deciding whether to seek proximity to the parent or to avoid them completely), and apprehension (e.g., displaying an apparent fear of the parent following the separation) as indicators of a disorganized pattern of attachment. This attachment strategy may be an indication that infants are experiencing anxiety, fear, and distress that they are unable to resolve in an organized fashion because the caregiver seems to simultaneously represent the source of the fear and the potential safe haven (van Ijzendoorn et al., 1999). A disorganized attachment pattern may stem from parenting that is abusive or when parents themselves are dealing with unresolved loss of an attachment figure or with issues such as depression or other mental disturbances (Hazan & Shaver, 1994; van Ijzendoorn et al., 1999). However, for the remainder of this section, Ainsworth's taxonomy of attachment will be considered.

Internal Working Models of Attachment

Ainsworth's work was important in demonstrating how the behavioral responses and interactions of primary caregivers indicate an infant's underlying knowledge structures, or *internal working models*, and contribute to the regulation of the attachment system (Bretherton & Munholland, 2008). Bowlby (1973) hypothesized that infants and children—based on their experiences of caregiver availability, responsiveness, and willingness in relation to their attachment needs—construct complex mental models about themselves and others. These internal working models are thought to provide the basis for subsequent psychological and social development. Over time, through continual transactions, Bowlby (1969/1982, 1973) suggested that children develop an internal working model that reflects a generalized mental representation of the world, of significant others, and of the self in relation to significant others.

He further hypothesized that internal working models would guide children in formulating expectations and behavior surrounding caregiver availability and responsiveness. For example, if experience leads a child to develop an internal representation of the caregiver as someone who cannot be counted on for support and comfort, the child often develops an internalized lack of trust toward the caregiver. This type of internalized model is likely to guide attachment-related behavior and expectations, perhaps resulting in a more intense and pervasive monitoring of caregiver whereabouts than would be necessary had the child developed trust in caregiver availability.

Internal working models also relate to "whether or not the self is judged to be the sort of person towards whom anyone, and the attachment figure in particular, is likely to respond in a helpful way" (Bowlby, 1973, p. 238). Hence, attachment theory also suggests that elements of self-concept and self-perception are linked to the internal working models that begin to unfold. For example, Bowlby (1973) believed that when attachment figures provide comfort and support, children develop an internal working model both of the caregiver as loving and supportive and of themselves as deserving of such love and support. In contrast, when an attachment figure is consistently rejecting, children develop a representation of the caregiver as unavailable and unloving and of themselves as unworthy of support and love. Those who have positive working models of the self and of others have a secure attachment style, while negative working models of self and others are associated with insecure attachments in the form of anxiety or avoidance. The internal working models are thought to act as a guide when entering adolescence and adulthood.

The Shift to Adolescence and Adult Attachment

When entering into adolescence and adulthood, there are numerous questions surrounding the central tenets of attachment theory. For example, are patterns of attachment stable or open to change? Can individuals develop multiple attachment relationships? Are some attachment relationships more or less important or significant than others?

Stability of Attachment

Bowlby (1973) explicitly stated that internal working models of attachment are gradually constructed out of experiences throughout infancy, childhood, and adolescence. Only then do they become relatively resistant to, but still not impervious to, change. Bowlby (1973) suggested that internal working models of attachment are not necessarily fixed throughout life and that they are likely to involve a degree of malleability and a degree of stability. While a person's initial prototypical working model can influence how they engage in various relationships across the life span, changes in familial circumstances, social contexts, and significant life events or transitions can affect the quality of attachment interactions (Davila & Sargent, 2003; Simpson et al., 2003), thereby inducing revisions and modifications within early working models. That said, modification does not imply replacement. A prototypical model of attachment could still maintain particular significance because it provides the initial parameters within which subsequent modifications take place.

Additionally, throughout childhood, adolescence, and adulthood, individuals are developmentally expected to form attachments with individuals outside and unrelated to those developed with parents (Bowlby, 1988). This is not to say that parents are relinquished as attachment figures; it is simply that normative developmental processes entail changes in the meaning and functioning of these relationships (Collins, 1996), allowing for the formation of affectional ties to significant others (e.g., close friends, romantic partners, therapists, teachers, sport coaches, leaders). Hence, it is possible for working models to undergo revision based on the experiences that individuals gain in these new relationships. Furthermore, considering that people are expected to form attachments with individuals outside of their parents, a social-cognitive model (e.g., Baldwin, 1995; Baldwin & Fehr, 1995) suggests that individuals are likely to internalize multiple models of attachment or relational schemata that could each be activated should the current context provide relevant cues.

Multiple Attachment Figures

Bretherton (1985) notes that in the most technical sense the term *attachment figure* describes the use of a relationship for the functions of a secure base (e.g., the attachment figure is seen to provide a platform for autonomous exploration), a safe haven (e.g., the attachment figure is perceived to provide comfort during distress), and proximity maintenance (e.g., the attached feels the need to be close to the attachment figure) (see figure 3.1). For Hazan and Shaver (1994), when a bond with any significant other satisfies these criteria, they are likely to form one of multiple attachment bonds that constitute an attachment hierarchy or network of individuals who are each perceived to serve attachment functions (although they likely do not all have the same relative degree of importance with regard to such functions) across the life span.

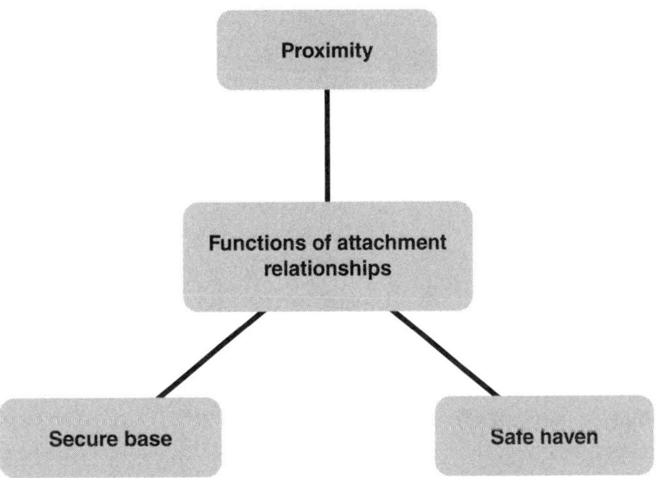

FIGURE 3.1 Three main functions of an attachment relationship.

During infancy and early childhood, parental figures may be positioned at the top of the hierarchy, but research suggests that during adolescence and adulthood, other relationship partners such as close friends and romantic partners become the preferred attachment figure as a target for proximity, safe haven, and a secure base (Hazan & Zeifman, 1994). In fact, the size and diversity of the network of attachment figures increase, and both adolescents and adults can seek proximity to and comfort from friends, teachers, mentors, managers at work, and sport coaches given they fulfill the functions identified earlier in this chapter. This does not mean that parental figures are removed from the attachment hierarchy; it is simply that their position and functions change (Bowlby, 1969/1982).

Adult Attachment

Researchers acknowledge the continuity of the attachment behavioral system during adolescence and adulthood. Bowlby (1969/1982) believed that no one of any age is completely free from reliance, and therefore the attachment system remains active over the life span. Although the same kinds of attachment system activation occur in adulthood when there are perceived threats or stressors, the threshold for activation of the attachment system is generally higher than in childhood (Mikulincer & Shaver, 2016). This happens because adults have developed an array of coping strategies as well as a strong capacity for symbolic thought, which allows a person to be comforted and soothed internally when, for example, the need for actual proximity cannot be met. Nevertheless, the attachment behavioral system is very much active during adulthood, and as in childhood, any event perceived as threatening or stressful tends to activate the attachment system.

During adolescence and adulthood, other relationship partners such as close friends and romantic parters become the preferred attachment figure.

Hazan and Shaver (1987; Shaver & Hazan, 1988; Shaver et al., 1988) were the first to employ attachment theory as a framework for understanding adult relationships. For example, in a now classic study, Hazan and Shaver (1987) translated Ainsworth's categorizations of infant attachment patterns to adult romantic love, asking participants to choose descriptors that best reflected their style of adult love relations (i.e., secure, insecure-avoidant, insecure-anxious). Secure individuals had relationships characterized by high levels of trust, happiness, and friendship, showing comfort with closeness within the relationship, whereas insecure-anxious individuals tended to experience a roller coaster of emotionality, tending to be jealous, obsessive, and unhealthily preoccupied with their partners while never feeling satisfied. Avoidant individuals tended to experience a discomfort with closeness and interdependence and showed distrust in their partner's good intentions. These styles were linked to parenting experiences in childhood, with secure individuals reporting more accepting and sensitive parenting than insecure individuals. This initial study opened up a major paradigm of research on adult close relationships that has grown immensely both in conceptualization and in measurement (see Mikulincer & Shaver, 2016, for a full overview). The research has also evolved to consider attachment in other adult relationships beyond romantic partners and across various contexts, including relationships with leaders in organizational settings (Mayseless, 2010), therapists in therapeutic settings (Parish & Eagle, 2003), and teachers in educational settings (Bergin & Bergin, 2009).

Researchers in sport have become increasingly interested in attachment theory. Sport researchers have not only applied attachment theory to enhance our understanding of well-being, relationships, and performance in sport but have also begun to use the context of sport to facilitate new developments in the direction of attachment theory itself. For example, sport researchers (e.g., Davis & Jowett, 2010) have proposed that the relationships between coaches and athletes can be viewed as forms of emotional attachment, conceptually similar to some of the central characteristics of attachment bonds and meaningful in a number of senses. Furthermore, researchers (e.g., Carr, 2009b; Carr & Fitzpatrick, 2011; Felton & Jowett, 2013a) have explored how parent–child attachment characteristics influence the nature of young people's involvement in the sporting context, shaping the quality of youth sport friendships and psychological well-being.

Recent developments in sport (e.g., Lai & Carr, 2020) have explored the possibility for within-relationship variation in parent–child attachment that is context specific. Lai and Carr (2020) raised the possibility that parents might create more or less secure experiences of attachment in relation to their children depending on the context in which they are interacting. Many children experienced their attachment to a nominated parent differently when engaging in sport as compared with other contexts (e.g., home life). Such research illustrates the potential for within-parent contextual variability in relation to attachment and is an intriguing avenue for future research. The remainder of this chapter provides an overview of advancements in the integration of attachment theory to the context of sport before outlining issues related to the measurement of attachment.

Key Advances in Attachment Research in Sport

In this section, we briefly review research in relation to the parent–athlete and coach–athlete attachment relationship and discuss how such attachment bonds provide a platform from which to understand important psychological and psychosocial outcomes related to sport development and performance.

Parental and Peer Attachment and Sport-Related Outcomes

West and colleagues (1998) have outlined that "adolescents' success in creating new supportive relationships is critically influenced by the affectively charged pattern of attachment behaviors and beliefs about attachment carried forward from the attachment history with their parents" (p. 662). Accordingly, researchers (e.g., Carr, 2009a, 2009b; Carr & Fitzpatrick, 2011; Diaconu-Gherasim & Duca, 2018) examined whether friendship quality in youth sport settings was related to the internal working models of attachment the adolescents held with a parent or primary caregiver. They also examined whether friendship quality in adolescent sport was related to the attachment characteristics of each individual within a dyadic friendship. To elaborate, Carr (2009b) hypothesized that adolescent–parent attachment characteristics reflecting more secure models of attachment would correspond to more positive friendship characteristics (e.g., companionship and pleasant play, self-esteem enhancement and support, loyalty and intimacy, things in common, and conflict resolution) in sport, while insecure attachment characteristics would be associated with more negative friendship characteristics. Employing the Adolescent Attachment Questionnaire (AAQ), West and colleagues (1998) found that attachment security with a parent or primary caregiver was the only significant predictor of positive sport friendship characteristics. This suggests that secure parent–child attachment characteristics may guide certain aspects of how peer relations in sport are experienced. This was further supported by Diaconu-Gherasim and Duca (2018), who found that adolescents with a more secure attachment also reported a higher quality of friendships, and this was particular to friendships developed within sport teams.

The effects of adolescents' attachment styles were not limited to effects experienced solely within the adolescents themselves but appeared also to be transmitted to and received by the relationship partners with whom they elected to form close friendships in the context of sport.

These findings were explored in a study by Carr and Fitzpatrick (2011), where both actor and partner effects were examined. Specifically, adolescents' perceptions of the quality of their sport friendships were examined as a function of their own (actor) and their friends' (partner) attachment characteristics. Results suggested that the effects of adolescents' attachment styles were not limited to effects experienced solely within the adolescents themselves but appeared also to be transmitted to and received by the relationship partners with whom they elected to form close friendships in the context of sport. As the authors noted,

> Perceptions of sporting friendships are complex in the sense that they are ultimately *individual* perceptions. However, they are individual perceptions of a relationship that takes place *with* another person.

In this sense, perceptions of sport friendship quality may be derived from both actor and partner attachment characteristics in a complex process of interaction.

Ullrich-French and colleagues (2011) connected parental attachment relationships to motivation-related perceptions in the physical domain with a sample of undergraduate students. Employing the Inventory of Parent and

Peer Attachment (IPPA; Armsden & Greenberg, 1987), the researchers examined the associations of mother, father, and best friend attachment with self-determined physical activity motivation and physical activity behavior with the mediating role of basic psychological need satisfaction. It has been reasoned (e.g., Carr, 2012) that internal working models of attachment may reflect individual difference factors that affect individuals' ability to orchestrate an environment in which they are able to fulfill their basic psychological needs. In support of this, Ullrich-French and colleagues (2011) showed that more secure attachment relationships with parents and best friends were associated with more adaptive physical activity motivation and behavior.

Li and colleagues (2016) tested the association between physical activity behavior during adolescence and the degree of perceived attachment security regarding mother, father, and best friend. Furthermore, they examined the mediating role of physical self-perception (a perception of self as fit, strong, and a good performer). Findings showed that attachment security to mother and best friend influenced levels of physical activity engagement through the mediation of physical self-perception, while attachment security to father directly increased activity levels in adolescence. These findings suggest that attachment-related influences are of importance for valued outcomes in the context of physical activity among adolescents. Felton and Jowett (2013a) explored the importance of attachment relationships with parents in relation to the athlete's psychological well-being (vitality, positive and negative affect) and whether this relationship can be explained by the satisfaction of the basic psychological needs of autonomy, competence, and relatedness. Their findings revealed that the association between an athlete's insecure attachment (anxious and avoidant) to parents with indexes of well-being can be explained by the satisfaction of the needs for autonomy, competence, and relatedness. The findings particularly suggest that athletes with an insecure anxious attachment style may benefit greatly from having their needs satisfied within the parent–athlete relationship.

As noted earlier in the chapter, research in the sporting context (e.g., Lai & Carr, 2018, 2020) is also raising interesting and potentially significant questions around the extent to which parental attachment might fluctuate from context to context, with some parents demonstrating significantly more or less secure or insecure attachment bonds depending on the context within which they engage with their child. Lai and Carr (2018) noted the following:

> Environmental characteristics (e.g., highly public, competitive arenas, evaluation/reward systems, interpersonal complexity) emphasized in contexts such as school or sport are likely to induce parental focus on specific goals and expectations for their children, and this has been shown to influence psychological outcomes (e.g., enjoyment, cognitive anxiety, attention, needs satisfaction). . . . In short, there are reasons to believe specific contexts have the capacity to fundamentally alter the quality of parent-child interactions to the extent that they may constitute dramatic shifts in the nature of the child-parent attachment relationship. (p. 118)

The significance of the sporting context and how parents and children interact within it and around it may have important implications for better understanding how within-person attachment relationships are experienced and fluctuate.

Coach–Athlete Attachment Relationships

Davis and Jowett (2010) first examined attachment bonds in the coach–athlete relationship. Specifically, they were initially concerned with whether the coach could satisfy the fundamental functions (secure base, safe haven, and a target for proximity maintenance) of an attachment figure forwarded by adult attachment researchers (e.g., Hazan & Shaver, 1987). Using an adapted version of the Components of Attachment Questionnaire (CAQ; Parish, 2000), Davis and Jowett (2010) examined the basic functions of an attachment bond. They found that athletes viewed the coach as an attachment figure, fulfilling the three basic functions. Subsequently, this gave them assurance to further explore how self-reported perceptions of athlete attachment style relative to their coach were associated with satisfaction within the coach–athlete relationship and with sport in general. The Experiences in Close Relationships (ECR) scale (Brennan et al., 1998) was adapted to reflect athletes' attachment toward their principal sport coach, and results indicated that athlete avoidant and anxious attachment styles were negatively linked to relationship satisfaction and sport satisfaction, including athletes' satisfaction with their training and instruction, personal treatment, and performance. Findings also revealed that satisfaction within the coach–athlete relationship mediated the association between athlete attachment styles and sport satisfaction dimensions, demonstrating relationship satisfaction as a process that links athlete attachment styles to their satisfaction with sport.

Davis and colleagues (2013b) also adopted a dyadic perspective involving actor and partner effects of athletes' and coaches' avoidant and anxious attachment styles. Specifically, they examined linear associations between attachment styles, relationship quality, and relationship satisfaction. For actor effects, results revealed a negative yet significant association with athletes' and coaches' avoidant attachment styles and their own perceptions of relationship quality (i.e., as determined by the 3Cs), which in turn associated positively with one's own perceptions of relationship satisfaction. Furthermore, the findings also revealed partner effects—athletes' avoidant attachment styles had a negative yet significant association with coaches' perceptions of relationship quality.

Scholars have branched out to examine the impact of coach–athlete attachment on broader psychological and social outcomes, including well-being (Davis & Jowett, 2014; Felton & Jowett, 2013a), basic psychological needs (Felton & Jowett, 2013b), eating psychopathology (Shanmugam et al., 2012), help-seeking behavior (Milroy et al., 2018), and athletic thriving (Davis et al., 2021). For example, Felton and Jowett (2013a) examined the associations between adolescent and adult athletes' avoidant and anxious attachment and well-being indexes (e.g., vitality, positive and negative affect) and whether this relationship could be explained by the satisfaction of the three basic psychological needs. Findings revealed that when athletes reported low levels of attachment anxiety and avoidance (i.e., a secure attachment), they reported high levels of well-being (vitality, positive and negative affect), and this relationship was most significant when all three psychological needs (e.g., autonomy, competence, and relatedness) were satisfied. Davis and Jowett's (2014) study supported these findings by illustrating a secure attachment to be associated with high well-being (positive and negative affect) in comparison with athletes high in avoidance. Such research has also begun to reveal mechanisms or mediators that link attachment and satisfaction of athletes' basic psychological needs. These include social factors such as autonomy-supportive and controlling coach behaviors as well as interpersonal communication strategies (Davis & Jowett, 2014; Davis et al., 2022; Felton & Jowett, 2013a; Felton & Jowett, 2013b). Felton and Jowett's (2013b) findings revealed that autonomy-supportive behaviors mediated the link between athletes' avoidant attachment style and basic need satisfaction, implicating autonomy-supportive behaviors as mechanisms to alleviate the negative effects of an avoidant attachment style.

In a more recent study, Davis and colleagues (2021) examined basic psychological need satisfaction as a mechanism to transfer the effects from athletes' secure, avoidant, and anxious attachment onto athletic thriving (e.g., high performance and well-being). Findings revealed a negative association between avoidant and anxious attachment and thriving via a perceived lack of need satisfaction; that is, athletes with an avoidant or anxious attachment style (relative to their coach) who also perceive their needs (i.e., autonomy, competence, and relatedness) as not being satisfied are likely to experience less thriving in their sport. In contrast, a secure coach–athlete attachment is associated with thriving via greater perceived need satisfaction.

Overall, these findings appear to suggest that athletes can thrive when their coach is engaging in coaching behaviors that create an environment in which the athlete feels their needs are being satisfied. This is of particular importance for athletes with an anxious or avoidant attachment style, because basic needs satisfaction may alleviate some levels of dysfunctionality and promote thriving in addition to well-being alone (Felton & Jowett, 2013a). Next, Felton and Jowett (2013b) attempted to understand the mechanisms by which athletes' attachment styles associated with their basic psychological needs. Results suggested that autonomy-supportive behavior and social support received from the coach positively transfer the effects of an avoidant attachment style onto athletes' perceptions of their basic psychological needs. Together, these findings point toward manipulating the athletes' social environment to alleviate any potential negative effects that may arise from having an avoidant or anxious attachment style relative to their coach. For

Athletes can thrive when their coach is engaging in coaching behaviors that create an environment in which the athlete feels their needs are being satisfied.

example, Felton and Jowett (2013b) and Davis and colleagues (2021) both suggest that increasing social support and autonomy-supportive behaviors versus controlling behaviors from the coach may create a more optimal environment where athletes are able to feel their needs are being satisfied. Controlling behaviors are likely to induce feelings of fear, nervousness, and hostility, which may interrupt the secure attachment bond required for optimal functioning in sport.

Many critical questions remain in relation to the connection between attachment styles and optimal functioning in sport. For example, Ein-Dor and colleagues (2012) raised the possibility that insecure attachment styles may be positively linked to optimal functioning in elite tennis players, arguing that self-reliance, independence, and an ability to work without proximal social support from loved ones (characteristics of avoidant individuals) may be strengths in certain contexts. Their data supported this hypothesis in a sample of elite tennis players, revealing that attachment avoidance positively predicted overall tour ranking scores, over and above the predictive contributions of training and coping resources. Such studies raise interesting possibilities about the potential value of attributes associated with insecure attachment styles in relation to optimal functioning in sport.

In a critique of Ein-Dor and colleagues' (2012) paper, Carr and Batlle (2015) argued that an association between attachment insecurity and objective performance data does not necessarily mean that such insecurity does not "come at a price" in relation to other well-being-related variables. Related to this, Güllich and colleagues' (2019) qualitative exploration of the biographies of elite and superelite athletes revealed that success at such a markedly high level in elite sport was connected to factors such as (1) sport as a compensatory activity for early, difficult, and painful loss and (2) a deep-seated need to succeed and a persistent drive to excel, together with strong obsessiveness or perfectionism; selfishness or ruthlessness; and a very high relative importance of sport in athletes' lives, above all else. The hypothesis that high-level functioning in sport is not necessarily connected to attachment in an adaptive manner warrants further investigation.

Individual differences in athletes' attachment styles relative to their coach are likely to influence how the quality of the coach–athlete relationship is viewed and how sport-related outcomes are experienced as a result.

Overall, the studies reviewed in this section indicate that individual differences in athletes' attachment styles relative to their coach are likely to influence how the quality of the coach–athlete relationship is viewed and how sport-related outcomes are experienced as a result. It appears that the research so far highlights the difficulties of an insecure attachment style (anxiety and avoidance), and while an avoidant athlete may be difficult to coach because of their unwillingness (or inability) to show enthusiasm, it is the coach's responsibility to ensure fair opportunities for all and that the welfare of the athlete is at the center of their coaching. With this in mind, the previously mentioned research findings touch on particular mechanisms that can help insecure athletes experience their relationship with their coach and their sporting outcomes more positively, despite their attachment style. Finally, the research presented here has conceptualized the coach–athlete relationship as an attachment bond in its own right. However, although the research discussed taps into attachment relative to a sport coach, a limitation is that we cannot ascertain whether the attachment characteristics of the coach–athlete relationship are a product of this relationship alone or of broader internal working models that athletes have previously developed.

Measurement of Individual Differences in Attachment Patterns

It has been noted (e.g., Bartholomew & Shaver, 1998) that the research on attachment outside of sport has diverged into two distinct traditions. On the one hand, psychodynamic and developmental psychologists tend to think on a *psychodynamic* level and prefer tests that do not rely on conscious evaluation; they are interested in clinical problems and prefer interview measures and behavioral observations over self-report questionnaires while focusing on smaller groups (Bartholomew & Shaver, 1998). On the other hand, personality and social psychologists tend to think in terms of *personality traits* and *social interactions* and prefer conscious self-report measures of attachment patterns (Bartholomew & Shaver, 1998). For the purpose of this section, we focus on how social and personality psychologists measure individual differences in attachment patterns, while also addressing commonly used and well-validated measures for assessing attachment across diverse contexts including sport.

Self-Report Measures of Adolescent and Adult Attachment

Self-report instruments most often focus on views individuals hold about themselves and others in close relationships and thus probe conscious attitudes and experiences in terms of relationships; they cannot detect when defenses distort responses. Measures of attachment either assign individuals to categories of attachment style or measure the degree to which various dimensions of attachment style are present.

Hazan and Shaver (1987) developed a self-report adult attachment questionnaire by translating Ainsworth and colleagues' (1978) three-category typology of attachment classifications (secure, insecure-avoidant, and insecure-anxious, identified in the Strange Situation Procedure) into brief categorical multisentence descriptions. This required individuals to select a statement they felt best captured the way they generally experienced and acted in their romantic relationships. In their initial studies, Hazan and Shaver (1987) found these self-selected styles to be linked to recollections of early experiences with parents during childhood as well as their beliefs about relationships (internal working models). Many personality and social psychologists have adopted Hazan and Shaver's categorical measure because of its brevity, face validity, and ease of administration. Nonetheless, categorical measures of attachment in the self-report tradition have been criticized on a theoretical level for assuming that individuals do not differ in the way they approach close relationships (Fraley et al., 2015). On an analytical level, attachment categories may misclassify some individuals on the borderlines, thereby compromising reliability and statistical power (Roisman, 2009). As a result, researchers in subsequent attachment studies have created multi-item inventories to assess adult attachment (e.g., Collins & Read, 1990; Feeney et al., 1994; Simpson, 1990) and to identify more continuous attachment scores. Researchers have also adopted approaches that deviate from Ainsworth's three-category typology in terms of how attachment is conceptualized.

The Adult Attachment Questionnaire (AAQ; Simpson, 1990; Simpson et al., 1996) and the Adult Attachment Scale (AAS; Collins & Read, 1990) were constructed from the original sentence fragments within each broad statement of the three attachment classifications described by Hazan and Shaver (1987). The AAQ comprises 17 items, representing two dimensions of attachment anxiety and attachment avoidance. The AAS comprises 18 items and represents three constructs of closeness, dependency, and anxiety. While both the AAQ and AAS demonstrate good construct and criterion validity and are widely used, the items themselves are oriented toward a romantic partner. Feeney and colleagues (1994) presented the Attachment Style Questionnaire (ASQ) to offer less of an emphasis on romantic relationships as a reference point. They went back to the attachment literature and developed new items that better captured some of the themes presented in Bowlby's and Ainsworth's writings. The ASQ consists of 40 items, with five composites:

- Self-confidence
- Discomfort with closeness
- Need for approval
- Preoccupation with relationships
- Belief that relationships are of secondary importance

In addition to yielding these five factors, the ASQ items can also be used to form scores for attachment anxiety and attachment avoidance. For example, discomfort with closeness, viewing relationships as secondary, and a lack of confidence are related conceptually to an avoidant attachment style. Preoccupation with relationships and need for approval are conceptually related to an anxious attachment style. Unlike the AAQ and AAS, the ASQ measures individual differences in attachment toward relationships and people in general rather than toward romantic partners. It has been used to measure attachment style in samples of adolescents and adults and where specific facets of anxiety and avoidance are in question.

By the mid-1990s, a complex upsurge of multi-item scales (e.g., AAQ, AAS, ASQ) had been published. In an attempt to overcome the proliferation of self-report inventories, Brennan and colleagues (1998) gathered the items from all the available self-report measures of adult attachment, as well as items from some instruments that appeared in conference presentations, and presented all 323 items to 1,086 undergraduate students. Factor analysis identified two relatively orthogonal dimensions, labeled as attachment *anxiety* and *avoidance*. The resulting 36 items that loaded highest on each of the dimensions (18 items for avoidance and 18 items for anxiety) were retained, resulting in the Experiences in Close Relationships (ECR) inventory. People who score high on either or both of these dimensions are assumed to have an insecure adult attachment style. Although it may appear that the security dimension is missing from the ECR inventory, people with low levels of attachment anxiety and avoidance can be viewed as having a secure adult attachment style. The psychometric properties have been supported in additional studies (Lopez et al., 2001; Lopez et al., 2002) and derivatives of the ECR, including the Revised Experiences in Close Relationships (ECR-R; Fraley et al., 2000) and the Experiences in Close Relationships Short Form (ECR-S; Wei et al., 2007), have also been developed. Psychometric properties of reliability and validity support the derivatives of the ECR as also being highly reliable and valid measures that have been widely used to assess variations in adult attachment relationships.

Measurement Advancements Within the Context of Sport

The domain of social relationships in sport has advanced quickly in recent years, and as a result, the field has been quick to recognize the potential of the theoretical integration of attachment theory. The first emerging body of research (discussed in this chapter) focused on the parent–athlete attachment relationship, and the second focused on the coach–athlete attachment relationship. Both bodies of literature have been heavily aligned with the self-report measurement tradition, situated within the social psychological school of thought.

For research that has focused on the parent–child attachment relationship within the context of sport (Carr, 2009; Li et al., 2016), studies have predominantly used the Inventory of Parent and Peer Attachment (IPPA; Armsden & Greenberg, 1987) or the Adolescent Attachment Questionnaire (AAQ; West et al., 1998). The IPPA assesses adolescents' perceptions of their relationships with parents and friends; it consists of 25 items that represent three broad constructs with respect to mother, father, and peers, including mutual trust, quality of communication, and the degree of anger and alienation. The three dimensions are frequently aggregated to produce composite indexes of attachment security versus attachment insecurity. The IPPA has not been designed to differentiate according to the attachment patterns described by Ainsworth and colleagues. However, the measure has been used extensively to assess attachment security as well as general insecurity. On the other hand, the AAQ (West et al., 1998) assesses only adolescents' perceptions of relationship security with a nominated attachment figure (often parents). The AAQ consists of nine items across three dimensions including availability, angry distress, and goal-corrected partnership. All nine items are averaged (angry distress items reversed) to obtain an overall rating of attachment that varies according to the degree of security.

As discussed earlier in the chapter, Lai and Carr (2020) have explored the possibility that children's perceptions of attachment security within a nominated parental relationship might change according to context; that is, perhaps attachment security would be different in a given relationship depending on the context within which interactions take place. To this end, the authors explored the validity and plausibility of context-specific attachment scales in the realms of sport (CAS-S) and academics (CAS-A). Taiwanese children responded to stems (e.g., "When I am participating in sport . . ." and "When I am involved in academic-related activities . . .") designed to focus them on attachment security and insecurity with a nominated parent in the contexts of sport and academics. While the study identified numerous complexities that require further research, there was a suggestion that (1) children may experience context-related variation in attachment security within a given parental relationship and (2) it may be possible to measure such variation using self-report tools designed to tease out context-specific attachment variation.

Additionally, Davis and Jowett (2013) developed and validated a coach–athlete-specific self-report instrument, namely the Coach–Athlete Attachment Scale (CAAS). While initial studies that assessed an athlete's attachment style relative to their coach (Davis & Jowett, 2010; Davis et al., 2013) modified the gold standard ECR scale (Brennan et al., 1998), upon psychometric evaluation, the ECR was found to display poor psychometric properties (Davis, 2012). In addition, the wording of items that reflected romantic relationships appeared most problematic, both in relation to psychometric evaluation and from a child protection consideration.

Therefore, Davis and Jowett took steps to validate the CAAS to accurately assess an athlete's attachment relative to their sport coach. Similar to Brennan and colleagues (1998), Davis and Jowett (2013) brought together existing measures of attachment and adopted De Vellis's (2003) eight-stage framework for developing and validating self-report instruments. Using confirmatory factor analysis (CFA), Davis and Jowett (2013) proposed both a two first-order factor model of the CAAS and a three first-order factor model. The two first-order factor model is in line with scales that assess adult attachment in close and romantic or marital relationship contexts, such as the ECR scale (Brennan et al., 1998). The two-dimensional CAAS contains 14 items that focus on directly assessing insecure attachment styles (anxiety and avoidance), while the secure attachment style is inferred by low scores on both the anxious and avoidant attachment dimensions. The three-dimensional CAAS contains 19 items that measure attachment anxiety, avoidance, and security. Both models have been found to have sound psychometric properties of validity and reliability (Davis & Jowett, 2013; Davis & Jowett, 2014).

Future Research Directions

Attachment research in sport is in its infancy. Research is just beginning to cement two key points. First, many of the central propositions predicted by attachment theory seem to hold true in the context of sport. Individuals hold affectively charged attachment patterns and internal working models of attachment that seem to orchestrate sport-related relationships and context-specific psychological responses. Furthermore, the language for conceptualizing and measuring attachment relationships offered by attachment theory can be employed and adapted as a meaningful lens through which relationships in sport (e.g., with peers, coaches, or parents) might be understood. There is a need, however, to further explore and elaborate upon these early efforts. Many key questions remain, such as the following:

- When is the attachment system active in sporting contexts? What activates it? When it is not active, does it still play a role or lie dormant?
- To what extent are attachment characteristics in the coach–athlete relationship a product of characteristics of the coach–athlete relationship or of internal working models carried over from previous relationships (e.g., with parents or primary caregivers)?
- How important are sport-specific attachment relationships (i.e., head coach, assistant coach, sport friendships) relative to other relationships (parents, peers) in an individual's attachment hierarchy?

Second, sport is a context that offers exciting possibilities for extending our ideas and thinking around attachment theory. Perhaps the sporting context, with its unique environmental characteristics, can offer up new questions that further extend the boundaries of attachment research. For example, as discussed in this chapter, does sport create a unique context for a relationship between parent and child that leads to children's "experiencing parents differently" in an attachment sense? Does this mean parental attachment might be context specific? If this was the case, why would this matter? How would it be explained? What would the implications be? And how might we measure this? These questions could be answered with traditional self-report data, via cross-sectional or longitudinal designs, or qualitatively through semi-structured interviews.

Further research should also consider dyadic research designs. An interesting area of research would be to study the cross-correlations between athletes' and coaches' attachment styles (e.g., anxious vs. secure) on relationship quality and subsequent performance outcomes (e.g., motivation, well-being). This would possibly inform future interventions that enhance relationship quality within the coach–athlete dyad. Dyadic research in the realm of sport friendships (e.g., Carr and Fitzpatrick, 2011), for example, has identified that individuals' experiences and well-being in the context of a given relationship are likely to be a function of the complex interplay ("an attachment dance") between the attachment characteristics of relationship partners and how these characteristics interact. Exploring similar interactive dyadic effects in coach–athlete relationships will be an important step.

As we have already noted, this research has predominantly relied on the use of self-report measures. Further studies in this field are encouraged to embrace other methodological stances. Another potential direction for research would be to extend methodological approaches to qualitatively explore the functions of a coach–athlete attachment bond, specifically what athletes mean when they report that coaches satisfy the attachment functions of proximity seeking, safe haven, and a secure base. It may be that when we unravel the idiosyncrasies of these functions and how athletes interpret such statements in regard to the coach–athlete relationship (as opposed to their relationships with a primary attachment figure), this would help us to further confirm that the coach–athlete relationship is used to satisfy attachment functions in a manner that seems emotionally similar to other established attachment bonds. Furthermore, as addressed earlier in this chapter, Davis and Jowett (2010) have conceptualized the coach–athlete relationship as an attachment bond in its own right, providing evidence that the attachment characteristics of this single relationship are likely to underpin significant contextual responses. However, because more general internal organizations in relation to attachment were not assessed outside of the context of the coach–athlete relationship, it is difficult to be certain whether the attachment characteristics of this relationship are a product of the specific relationship interactions alone or of broader internal working models that individuals had previously developed. Again, further research is needed in order to unravel these complexities.

Understanding athletes' attachment styles may help coaches adjust their approach, including communication and interaction, to ensure coaching is effective and successful.

Finally, there has also been development within experimental paradigms outside of the context of sport. For example, Mikulincer and colleagues (2002) focused on subliminal activation of the attachment system in adult subjects to examine how symbolic threats activated attachment-related thoughts that would subsequently influence performance during a series of cognitive tasks (i.e., lexical decision tasks and a Stroop color-naming task). Future sport research could consider adopting similar experimental designs to examine the activation of the attachment system and athletes' sensitivity toward various attachment figures within their network of potential attachment figures (e.g., parents, coaches, peers). This would allow us to gain deeper insight into an athlete's attachment hierarchy during potentially threatening situations. Additionally, this approach may also provide greater insight into how the arousal of the attachment system during threatening situations has the capacity to influence cognitive and physical performance in sport.

Practical Implications

On a more practical level, if attachment in sport matters, then attention might turn to education and applied intervention. For example, education that helps parents and coaches understand, consider, and work with attachment characteristics to their advantage would be advisable. From a parental perspective, educating parents on how to provide a secure base and supportive behavior within the sporting context (e.g., availability, noninterference, and encouragement; Feeney, 2010) and how to consistently communicate trust, reassurance, and acceptance may divert parents away from maladaptive parenting practices. Within achievement contexts such as sport, parents have often been observed offering either more or less affection, accessibility, and recognition, depending on how the child performs and meets their expectations. This is known as parental conditional regard (PCR; Assor et al., 2004). Parents' subjective evaluation of their children's successes and failures has the potential to serve as influential contextual cues that shape children's internal working models and thus their attachment beliefs within a given context (Lai & Carr, 2018). Therefore, parental education is an important consideration moving forward.

From a coaching perspective, research illustrates that insecure avoidant and anxious attachment styles negatively predict coaches' and athletes' perceptions of their own relationship quality as well as how the coach views the relationship with the athlete. When this view is negative and there is no connection with an athlete, it is possible that the coach reduces efforts to coach the athlete, overlooking the athlete's potential in relation to skill ability and effort. Understanding athletes' attachment styles may help coaches adjust their approach, including communication and interaction, to ensure coaching is effective and successful. Educating coaches to recognize individual difference characteristics such as attachment styles may help them overcome interpersonal difficulties that may arise from athletes' apparent lack of connection, unwillingness to invest in the relationship, overbearing need for coaches' attention, and so on. Such awareness may also help coaches to support athletes in developing secure and positive relationships over time (Côté & Gilbert, 2009; Felton & Jowett, 2015). This type of training is important to ensure coaches provide effective and fair instruction to all athletes in their care.

Additionally, educating coaches to create environments that are underpinned with greater autonomy-supportive behaviors as opposed to controlling behaviors might enhance the quality of the coach–athlete relationship as well as enhance athletes' basic psychological needs (Felton & Jowett, 2013a). Coaches displaying controlling behaviors are likely to induce athletes' experience of feeling fearful, upset, nervous, and hostile, which interrupts a secure attachment bond and may activate attachment insecurity. Second, if coaches are able to satisfy athletes' basic psychological needs through implementation of more autonomy-supportive behaviors, this could provide a buffer against neglectful parent–athlete relationships (insecure attachments) and support the athlete to thrive during adversity in the context of competition (Davis et al., 2021). Furthermore, from an applied intervention perspective, enhancing the quality of the coach–athlete relationship through autonomy-supportive behavioral styles versus controlling behavioral styles may give athletes choice and initiative, allowing more avoidant athletes to feel happier and engaged.

There are also potentially useful implications of the idea that young people's working models of attachment may be active in the context of sport. This suggests that such working models may therefore be accessible to interventions, raising the possibility that models of attachment not only could exert an influence on how sporting relationships are experienced but also could themselves be reworked (e.g., in children with maladaptive beliefs about relationships) through the medium of sport. It may be that internal working models of attachment are not only active but also open to influence from relationships developed in the context of sport and physical activity. There have been hints in the literature that involvement in sport can have a variety of individual-, family-, and community-level benefits in relation to youth development. For example, Riley and Anderson-Butcher (2012) identified a number of significant relational, emotional, and familial benefits for disadvantaged youths involved in a sport development program. The extent to which the relationships and characteristics fostered by such sport development programs translate to positive changes in working models of attachment remains to be seen, but this will be a crucial development in the sporting and youth development literature.

Summary

As we outlined at the beginning of this chapter, attachment theory is one of the final remaining grand theories in psychology; one of the benefits of such a theory is its potential to stimulate the integration of ideas and frameworks *within* and *across* fields of psychology. While sport psychology has historically been slow to integrate attachment theory within applied research, more recently the theory has received increasing interest in the field. Therefore, the purpose of this chapter was to outline attachment theory as an emerging perspective on the topic of close relationships within the context of sport. We have offered an overview of the basic concepts and fundamental ideas surrounding attachment theory and discussed how differences in attachment styles and a person's internal working models are sustained and transferred across the life span through childhood, adolescence, and adulthood, as well as across various types of relationships and contexts. Further, we have put forward a concise outline of the integration of attachment theory to the sport context and highlighted some research examining the parent–child attachment relationship, as well as coach–athlete attachment relationships, while addressing methodological considerations. We then provided a broader array of new empirical research ideas for sport-related researchers to explore, with the goal of encouraging future research. Finally, we proposed practical considerations for optimizing athletes' involvement in sport.

DISCUSSION QUESTIONS

1. Why is it important to understand individual differences in athletes' attachment styles to significant others within the context of sport?
2. Discuss the three attachment styles proposed by Ainsworth and colleagues. How do you differentiate insecure avoidance from insecure anxiety?
3. Under what circumstances might a coach be considered a potential attachment figure?
4. Consider future research directions that would generate knowledge about the role that individual differences in attachment styles play within the context of sport. What might be the practical ramifications of such research?
5. Consider how insecure attachment styles may be viewed as a strength within the context of sport. Consider the implications for an individual's well-being and performance.
6. Why is it important to consider the attachment characteristics that both members of a peer–peer or coach–athlete dyad bring to a relationship?
7. How could sport play a role in positively shaping people's internal working models of attachment? How would this work? What are the implications of this possibility?

4

Athlete Maltreatment

Gretchen Kerr, PhD, and Erin Willson, MSc

LEARNING OBJECTIVES

On completion of this chapter, the reader should have the following:

- Knowledge of the definition of maltreatment and the various forms of maltreatment
- Understanding of power and examples of the positive and negative use of power
- Understanding of athlete maltreatment within a culture of control in sport
- Knowledge of ways in which athletes have exercised power and agency

Sport provides important opportunities to build and experience social relationships. Millions of parents enroll their children in sport every year in Western countries, in part, to develop social relationships outside of the family. Researchers have provided evidence for the strongly held belief that engagement in organized sport helps young people advance their overall health and develop important life skills, such as collaboration, leadership, and cooperation, through social relationships in sport (Holt et al., 2020). For athletes, important and influential relationships experienced in sport are with their coach(es) and their teammates or training partners. Even in individual sports such as athletics, swimming, tennis, and gymnastics, athletes develop relationships with the other athletes from their clubs with whom they train, travel, and compete.

With respect to coaches, substantial evidence exists to highlight the critical role coaches have in developing young athletes through their approach to coaching, their training methods, and the relationships they build and nurture with athletes (Gould et al., 2007; Jowett & Cockerill, 2003; Kuhlin et al., 2020; Vella et al., 2013). Jowett and Shanmugam (2016) presented four essential components of a quality coach–athlete relationship, known as the 3+1C framework as discussed in chapter 1:

- Closeness—the bond between the coach and athlete, which includes trust, respect, care, support, and appreciation
- Commitment—the dedication the coach and athlete have to each other, particularly over an extended period
- Complementarity—the cooperation between the coach and athlete, which includes corresponding behaviors of the two actors and the reciprocity of their roles (e.g., the coach instructs, and the athlete completes the task)
- Co-orientation—the interdependency of the coach's and athlete's thoughts, feelings, and behaviors, such that the coach and athlete are on the same page

Numerous sport researchers have argued that a strong connection between a coach and an athlete is critical for athletes' performance success and enjoyment in sport, and that this relationship should be nurtured and prioritized along with technical coaching (Hampson & Jowett, 2012; Jowett, 2007; Jowett & Shanmugam, 2016).

At its best, the coach–athlete relationship promotes enjoyment of the sport, the actualization of athletic talent in young people, the learning of life skills, and enhancement of the athlete's well-being, self-awareness, autonomy, and agency. However, at its worst, the coach–athlete relationship can be characterized by exploitation and by psychological and physical harms to the athlete. There is no shortage of highly publicized cases around the world of sexual, psychological, and physical abuse of athletes by their coaches, from the Barry Bennell case in the United Kingdom where hundreds of young male football (soccer) players experienced sexual abuse at the hands of their coach (Taylor, 2018) to the Gymnastics New Zealand investigation that revealed ongoing patterns of physical and psychological abuse of athletes by their coaches (George, 2020). Similarly, teammates in sport can have very positive, growth-enhancing influences on each other, leading to a sense of belonging, friendship, and camaraderie (Bruner et al., 2017; Fry & Gano-Overway, 2010). On the other hand, teammates have also been cited as bullies (Evans et al., 2016; Jewett et al., 2020; Mishna et al., 2019) and perpetrators of sexual assaults, psychological humiliation, and even death as documented in the literature related to hazing and initiation practices (Waldron & Kowalski, 2009; Waldron et al., 2011).

At its best, the coach–athlete relationship promotes enjoyment of the sport, the actualization of athletic talent in young people, the learning of life skills, and enhancement of the athlete's well-being, self-awareness, autonomy, and agency.

In this chapter, we address the research on harms experienced within coach–athlete and athlete–athlete relationships, the misuse of power as a contributor to experiences of harm, and ways athletes have responded to regain power. Physical, psychological, and social harms of athletes have been conceptualized by some as maltreatment, stemming from the child abuse and neglect literature. In the following sections, definitions and descriptions of types of maltreatment and the research on maltreatment in sport will be reviewed.

Understanding Athlete Maltreatment

The World Health Organization defines child maltreatment as "the abuse and neglect that occurs to children under 18 years of age. It includes all types of physical and/or emotional ill-treatment, sexual abuse, neglect, negligence and commercial or other exploitation, which results in actual or potential harm to the child's health, survival, development or dignity in the context of a relationship of responsibility, trust or power" (WHO, n.d.). Similarly, Crooks and Wolfe (2007) define maltreatment as "*volitional acts* that result in, or have the potential to result in, physical injuries and/or psychological harm" (p. 3). There are several important aspects of this definition, including the volitional or deliberate nature of the act, which distinguishes it from an accident. Also, there is a focus on the objective behavior in question and whether this behavior has the potential to cause harm; a preventative approach is represented because there is no requirement to show evidence of harm. Finally, the intent of the actor or perpetrator of the behavior is irrelevant; in other words, no consideration is given to whether or not the perpetrator intended to cause harm through the act.

Maltreatment in sport has been classified into two categories, distinguished by the types of relationships in which the behaviors occur (Stirling, 2009). One category is *relational maltreatment*, which includes sexual, physical, and psychological abuse as well as neglect. Relational maltreatment is characterized by a *critical relationship*, which is a relationship that exists when one person depends on the other for a sense of trust, security, and need fulfillment (Crooks & Wolfe, 2007). The most intuitive example of a critical relationship is that between a child and their parent or caregiver, but critical relationships have been extended to include teacher–student and coach–athlete relationships (Stirling, 2009). A significant body of research in sport illustrates the authority and power held by the coach, which can create coach–athlete relationships in which athletes depend on their coaches for many needs (Brackenridge, 2001), including physical and psychological health and safety and the fulfillment of performance aspirations. Although the notion of critical relationships has primarily been applied to children and youths, we suggest that athletes within the emerging adulthood stage and adulthood also depend on their coaches for health and safety and the fulfillment of athletic needs. As such, we propose that the notions of critical relationships and maltreatment should be extended beyond children and youths to include older athletes.

Nonrelational maltreatment, the second category of maltreatment, also occurs within relationships but in those where a critical relationship does not exist, as may be the case between an athlete and an official, or a coach and an administrator. Bullying and hazing or initiation practices, which occur between peers and teammates, and harassment, which occurs between an authority figure and a subordinate, are also examples of nonrelational maltreatment.

The following section addresses the existing research on maltreatment in sport, with a specific focus on maltreatment experienced within coach–athlete and athlete–athlete relationships given that these are often referred to as significant relationships within the sport context (Brown & Larson, 2009; Jowett & Wachsmuth, 2020). For the purposes of this review, findings with respect to relational and nonrelational maltreatment will be combined.

Research on Maltreatment in Sport

Although concerns about the treatment of athletes date as far back as organized sport itself, research on athlete maltreatment is still in its infancy. Research on maltreatment in sport emerged in response to several high-profile international cases of athletes' experiences of sexual abuse by their coach (Brackenridge, 1997; Brackenridge & Fasting, 2002). While the primary focus of researchers and the public remains on sexual abuse, our understanding of maltreatment in sport has advanced to include a growing awareness of other commonly experienced forms of maltreatment in the sport setting including psychological and physical abuse and neglect.

Sexual Maltreatment

Sexually related offenses have received the most media and research attention, beginning in the early to mid-1990s with victims' revelations from National Hockey League players in Canada and national-level swimmers in the United Kingdom, among others. Since then, a continuous stream of cases of sexual abuse of athletes have emerged across countries and sports. The Larry Nassar trial in the United States, the Barry Bennell case in the United Kingdom, the Bertrand Charest case in Canada, and the Fernando Lopes case in Brazil, as some of many examples, have drawn significant public scrutiny of sport. The disproportionate attention devoted to sexual maltreatment, compared with other forms of maltreatment, may be because sexual maltreatment is more clearly defined in the legal system, particularly when the sexual maltreatment involves minors.

While the primary focus of researchers and the public remains on sexual abuse, our understanding of maltreatment in sport has advanced to include a growing awareness of other commonly experienced forms of maltreatment in the sport setting including psychological and physical abuse and neglect.

Over the past decade, there have been advances in research on sexual maltreatment, including prevalence studies in countries such as Germany, Canada, the United States, the United Kingdom, the Netherlands, and Belgium (Alexander et al., 2011; Ohlert, 2018; Parent et al., 2016; U.S. Center for SafeSport, 2021; Vertommen et al., 2016; Willson et al., 2021). Alexander and colleagues (2011) found 29% of respondents reported sexual maltreatment, whereas 14% of athletes in a study by Vertommen and colleagues (2016) reported at least one experience of sexual harms, and 19% of current and 23% of retired Canadian athletes reported at least one experience of sexual maltreatment (Willson et al., 2021). In the United States, 9% of athletes reported experiencing inappropriate sexual contact in their sport environment, and 34% of athletes experienced unwanted sexual comments or looks. In Sweden, 5.5% of respondents reported coach-related sexual harassment and abuse (Johansson & Lundqvist, 2017); 13% of female and 6% of male athletes in Australia reported sexual maltreatment in sport (Leahy et al., 2002); and 35% of athletes in a German study (Ohlert, 2021), 45% of athletes in a Norwegian study (Fasting et al., 2003), and 8.8% of adolescent athletes in a Quebec study (Parent et al., 2016) reportedly experienced sexual harms. The large variation in prevalence rates, from 5.5% to 45%, can be attributed to differences in populations studied (e.g., elite versus non-elite athletes, child versus all athletes) and the measures and definitions of sexual harms used. For instance, some surveys focused on contact forms of sexual harms such as unwanted sexual touching, while others included noncontact forms of harms, such as sexist jokes and remarks and intrusive sexual glances, in addition to contact forms. More consistent conceptual frameworks and measurement tools to assess the prevalence of sexual maltreatment in sport will advance research in this area.

There has also been an increased focus on specific populations, including male athletes, adult athletes, racialized athletes, athletes with a disability, and those identifying as LGBTQ2I+. Willson and colleagues (2021) surveyed current and retired athletes over the age of 16, where 19.7% of current and 21% of former athletes reportedly experienced sexual maltreatment, indicating these behaviors are also experienced by athletes in late adolescence and emerging adulthood. Hartill (2014) adopted a narrative approach to explore two male athletes' experiences with sexual abuse from their coach as children. The participants identified the barriers to disclosing and reporting, including the guilt and shame associated with the abuse, fear of disclosure and reporting, and specific fears of homosexual labeling, along with the general stigma experienced by sexual assault victims. In a 2021 study of athletes in the United States, Black athletes and bisexual athletes experienced almost twice as much inappropriate sexual contact, and athletes with a disability experienced significantly more inappropriate contact. Similarly, individuals with those same identity characteristics (racialized, sexual minority, disability) reported more sexual assault (U.S. Center for SafeSport).

In a 2021 study of athletes in the United States, Black athletes and bisexual athletes experienced almost twice as much inappropriate sexual contact, and athletes with a disability experienced significantly more inappropriate contact. Similarly, individuals with those same identity characteristics (racialized, sexual minority, disability) reported more sexual assault (U.S. Center for SafeSport).

There is also growing awareness of the potential use of social media as a vehicle by which to perpetrate sexual maltreatment. Sanderson and Weathers (2020) reviewed 99 published media accounts documenting coaches being arrested for sexual behavior using Snapchat and involving athletes. The coaches were primarily male with a mean age of 30 years; the victims were primarily female with a mean age of 15 years. Coaches used this platform to exploit the relationship of trust and closeness they had with their athletes and engaged in grooming—gradually violating relationship boundaries and external barriers and breaking down resistance. With direct and discreet access to athletes, including sharing of explicit photos, the online interactions often, over time, led to a physical relationship. Litchfield and colleagues (2016), using the term *virtual maltreatment*, reported that three prominent forms occur on social media: (1) the admiration of physical beauty and sexualization, (2) threats of physical or sexual contact, and (3) emotional ridicule, all of which are largely unregulated online. Examples of these forms of violence include expressions of desire for sexual relations, often in explicit terms, or referring to women using derogatory language.

Although coaches have often been the focus of research as perpetrators of sexual maltreatment, we mustn't forget that other stakeholders in sport can also be perpetrators, as illustrated by the Nassar case in USA Gymnastics. As a team physician, Nassar perpetrated sexual harms over decades of treating young athletes, crimes for which he is now imprisoned (Kirby, 2018). Additionally, in a Canadian prevalence study of maltreatment among national team athletes (Willson et al., 2021), peers were most frequently cited as the perpetrators of sexual harms.

Sexual maltreatment between peers in sport often occurs through hazing and initiation practices, which have been well documented in research and in the media. Hazing has been defined as "any activity expected of someone joining a group that humiliates, degrades, abuses or endangers, regardless of the person's willingness to participate" (Hoover, 1999, p. 8). While hazing can occur in many forms, sexual violence is a predominant method to initiate teammates. Athletes have reported disturbing hazing activities of a sexual nature, including forced public nudity (e.g., stealing clothes or towels after a shower and making the athlete walk home naked, being taped to a bench while naked), forced penetration with objects (e.g., broomsticks), and being forced to perform sexual acts (Allan & Madden, 2012; Waldron & Kowalski, 2009).

Psychological Maltreatment

Stirling and Kerr (2008) identified three categories of emotional abuse (often used interchangeably with psychological abuse) within the coach–athlete relationship including

- verbal behaviors (e.g., belittling, name calling, humiliating comments, threats, body shaming),
- physical behaviors (e.g., acts of aggression, throwing objects), and
- denial of attention (e.g., intentionally ignoring athletes for poor performance).

Quantitative reports have confirmed the frequent occurrence of these behaviors in sport (Alexander et al., 2011; Stafford et al., 2015; Vertommen et al., 2016; Willson et al., 2021).

Research on psychological maltreatment in sport has been mounting over the past decade. Psychological maltreatment has been revealed as one of the most prominent forms of maltreatment, with 75% of respondents experiencing at least one form of psychological maltreatment in the United Kingdom (Alexander et al., 2011), 65% in the United States (U.S. Center for SafeSport, 2021), and 38% in Belgium and the Netherlands (Vertommen et al., 2016). It was the most frequently reported form of maltreatment in the study by Willson and colleagues (2021), with 58.6% of current and 61.6% of retired athletes reportedly experiencing behaviors of psychological maltreatment. Examples of frequently experienced behaviors include being criticized about performance (Alexander et al., 2011); repeatedly being shouted at in an angry or critical manner; being put down, embarrassed, or humiliated (Alexander et al., 2011; Willson et al., 2021), and being gossiped about or lied about (Willson et al., 2021). Proposals have been made to include body shaming (Willson et al., 2022) and encouraging self-destructive eating behavior to achieve an ideal weight for the sport (Fortier et al., 2020) as forms of psychological maltreatment.

The study of psychological maltreatment of athletes has focused almost exclusively on coaches' behaviors; however, athletes have reportedly experienced psychological maltreatment from their teammates as well. In fact, among Canadian national team athletes, peers were the second most frequently reported perpetrator of psychological maltreatment (Willson et al., 2021) after coaches. Maltreatment between athletes has typically been explored through bullying and hazing. Among children, Collot D'Escury and Dudink (2010) found that 26% in selected soccer and judo programs self-reported experiences with various forms of bullying. For intercollegiate athletes, Storch and colleagues (2003) reported that relational aggression and peer rejection occurred and was significantly associated with maladjustment. Similarly, Mishna and colleagues (2019) explored the ways interuniversity athletes experienced and perpetrated violence among their teammates, with verbal victimization being the most frequent. In another study of eight team captains of interuniversity teams (Kerr, Jewett, et al., 2016), bullying behaviors were perceived as common occurrences, with relational aggression being the most frequently reported form of bullying. Examples of bullying behaviors included teasing related to athletic performance, demeaning teammates through public embarrassment, gossiping about teammates, and excluding teammates from social events. The team captains believed that athletic ability, seniority on the team, age, personality, commitment, and work ethic influenced vulnerability to being bullied and the nature of the responses to bullying behaviors. Athletes have also experienced teasing and criticisms about their bodies from their peers (Stafford et al., 2015). Adverse effects from bullying, including negative affect (sadness, anger, isolation, fear), low self-esteem, decreased enjoyment, and desire to leave the sport, have been reported by athletes (Jewett et al., 2020).

Finally, a common theme with psychological maltreatment is the normalization that occurs with these behaviors. As one athlete expressed, "[psychological maltreatment] was kind of drilled into you from anywhere and everywhere. . . . if you wanted to keep going, then this is what you have to put up with, and everyone put up with it" (Stafford et al., 2015, p. 134). The interuniversity team captains in the study by Kerr, Jewett, and colleagues (2016) considered most of the reported bullying behaviors to be normal and expected experiences among people who spend a considerable amount of time together; further, they perceived bullying to be normalized within the sport culture more so than in other contexts. Similarly, coaches justified these behaviors because they had experienced psychological maltreatment as former athletes, behaviors of psychological maltreatment were commonplace in their sport, and they perceived athletes as accepting of these behaviors (Stirling & Kerr, 2013). Administrators also claimed that psychological maltreatment was part of elite coaching and had been normalized to the point where it couldn't be recognized as harmful (Jacobs et al., 2017).

Physical Maltreatment

Physical maltreatment has not been studied extensively in sport. Reported prevalence rates vary, with between 3% and 24% of athletes reporting at least one experience of physical harm (Alexander et al., 2011; U.S. Center for SafeSport, 2021; Vertommen et al., 2016; Willson et al., 2021). Examples of commonly experienced behaviors included exercise as punishment in response to not paying attention, being late, poor performance, lack of effort, or making mistakes (Kerr, Stirling, et al., 2016), excessive intense training, training through injury (Alexander et al., 2011), physical aggression (Alexander et al., 2011; Willson et al., 2021), and being threatened with physical harm (U.S. Center for SafeSport, 2021). However, Fortier and colleagues (2020) have proposed that using excessive exercise as punishment and being forced or asked to train through injuries, or to perform movements that exceed the athlete's abilities, should be classified as psychological rather than physical maltreatment.

Physical maltreatment may be a less frequently reported experience because of the objective and visible nature of these actions, and organizations typically have explicit standards for physical abuse. As one sport administrator explained, clear boundaries were identified, such as "we do not tolerate kicking, hitting or humiliating, that sort of thing" (Jacobs et al., 2017, p. 132). Two studies that have focused on physical maltreatment in sport specifically found that the most commonly reported form of physical maltreatment was being made to play when they should have been resting (i.e., when injured or exhausted), followed by being shoved, being thrown or shaken, being knocked down, or having an object thrown at them (McPherson et al., 2017; Stafford et al., 2013) by a coach, trainer, or peers (McPherson et al., 2015). In follow-up interviews, athletes described these experiences as normal and expected, and they felt they had been guilted into continuing to train when injured (McPherson et al., 2015; Stafford et al., 2013). It was also highly normalized, as indicated by one athlete: "You don't really think about it because you don't really know any better" (McPherson et al., 2015, p. 47).

The existing research on physical maltreatment between athletes focuses on bullying or overly physically aggressive acts in the sport context and physically harmful acts during initiation rites. Among Canadian elite athletes, peers were the second most frequently reported perpetrator of physical maltreatment (Willson et al., 2021). When Mishna and colleagues (2019) explored the ways in which interuniversity athletes experienced and perpetrated violence among their teammates, physical forms such as being hit, pushed, slapped, or scratched were ranked second to psychological behaviors. Physical harm is also common in hazing incidents, as experienced through such behaviors as being hit or kicked in the shower, being forced to drink urine, being forced to drink alcohol in excess (to the point of passing out or vomiting), or being pushed into lockers or puddles (Waldron & Kowalski, 2009). Moreover, experiences of physical violence through hazing are often dismissed because of a lack of physical injury. Waldron and Kowalski (2009) found that athletes justified these physical behaviors because "they didn't cross the line by hurting or injuring a teammate" (p. 298). These behaviors are similarly disregarded by the media, with common excuses such as "boys will be boys" and "good kids just having fun" (Mathers & Chavez, 2018).

Neglect

Despite the significant, deleterious effects of neglect documented in the child abuse literature, research on neglect in sport is absent. Some examples of neglectful behaviors in the child abuse literature include failure to provide food or water, failure to provide adequate supervision, and failure to attend to medical needs (Brittain, 2006). To date, only one of the three existing prevalence studies of maltreatment in sport included an independent measure of neglect, finding that 66% of current athletes and 76% of retired athletes reported experiencing at least one neglectful behavior (Willson et al., 2021). When repeated experiences of various forms of maltreatment were assessed in this same study, neglect emerged most frequently after psychological maltreatment. The most frequently reported behaviors of neglect within the coach–athlete relationship included lack of attention to the athlete's health, career, or educational needs and a general feeling of being ignored (Willson et al., 2021). Clearly, experiences and consequences of neglect remain an important area for further research.

Intersectional Nature of Maltreatment

Considerations of maltreatment should also include ways that different forms of maltreatment may occur concurrently as well as ways that experiences may vary according to the level of sport and identity characteristics of the athlete. Evidence exists of the types of maltreatment occurring concurrently. Willson and colleagues (2021) found significant correlations between all types of maltreatment, meaning the likelihood of each type increased when other forms of maltreatment were present. Vertommen and colleagues (2016) found that 4% of athletes experienced all types of maltreatment. Importantly, psychological maltreatment needs to be recognized as a stand-alone form of maltreatment as well as a form of maltreatment that is inherently part of every other type of maltreatment. In fact, 80% of athletes who reportedly experienced physical maltreatment and 67% of athletes who reportedly experienced sexual maltreatment also reported incidents of psychological maltreatment (Vertommen et al., 2016). Only 1.9% of athletes reported physical maltreatment exclusively, and only 4.3% of athletes reported sexual maltreatment exclusively (Vertommen et al., 2016). Additionally, athletes who competed at higher levels of sport competition (e.g., elite or international) reported more experiences compared with athletes in lower levels of sport engagement (Alexander et al., 2011; Vertommen et al., 2016). This has been attributed to an increased emphasis on performance outcomes at this level and a win-at-all-costs mentality (Jacobs et al., 2017).

Existing prevalence studies also indicated that certain populations reported higher incidence of maltreatment in sport, including immigrant groups, athletes with a disability (Vertommen et al., 2016), and individuals identifying as LGBTQ2I+ (Vertommen et al., 2016; Willson et al., 2021). Females reported significantly more experiences of all forms of maltreatment than male athletes (Willson et al., 2021). Literature on gender-based violence, which includes in its definition "violence that is enacted on certain populations disproportionately" (European Commission, 2014, p. 47), suggests that normative role expectations, unequal power relationships, and the cultural context contribute to the occurrence of violence (Bloom, 2008). Future research on athlete maltreatment must adopt an intersectional lens to advance our understanding of the ways systems of privilege and oppression interact to influence experiences, consequences, and prevention of athlete maltreatment.

The existing research on maltreatment in sport clearly challenges commonly held assumptions of sport as a "moral oasis" (Brackenridge, 2001) or "inherently good" (Coakley, 2011). Given that coach–athlete and athlete–athlete relationships can be characterized as either beneficial or harmful, a key question to be addressed is what determines whether the experiences of such relationships will be positive or negative for the athlete? We propose that the ways in which power is used will affect whether the athlete benefits or experiences harm from these relationships.

Power Is Foundational to Maltreatment

At the root of athlete maltreatment experiences is the misuse of power. As such, to understand the occurrence, experiences, and consequences of maltreatment, the power dynamics between the athlete and others in the athlete's life must be considered. Power is generally viewed as the ability to influence others and can be used in both constructive and destructive ways (Lukes, 1993). If one's power is used positively, then it can have many benefits for the recipients (Jowett, 2017; Jowett & Wachsmuth, 2020), as seen when athletes learn life skills through their coach, when athletes gain athletic experience, or when teammates function as a cohesive unit.

Researchers and practitioners have promoted an approach to sport that is characterized by an environment in which power is used positively by those in positions of trust and authority and is shared with athletes in a developmentally appropriate manner. This approach has had several labels, including humanistic coaching (Lombardo, 1987), autonomy-supportive coaching (Mageau & Vallerand, 2003), and athlete-centered coaching (Clarke et al., 1994; Kidman, 2005). Jowett's 3+1Cs model of a quality coach–athlete relationship (chapter 1) has been used to capture positive relationships built on trust, respect, appreciation, commitment, and cooperation. These approaches to coaching are grounded in the philosophy that athlete development should be fostered from a holistic perspective (Kidman, 2005), shifting the priority from winning at all costs to the pursuit of winning outcomes while respecting the needs and rights of athletes (Clarke et al., 1994). A key tenet of such approaches is that power is shared in age- and stage-appropriate ways, and athletes exercise agency and power by contributing to the decisions that affect them. However, when used negatively in coach–athlete or athlete–teammate relationships, power may be used to diminish an athlete's sense of worth, trust of others, health status, and enjoyment of the sport (Battaglia et al., 2017; Kerr et al., 2020; Kuhlin et al., 2020; Stirling & Kerr, 2009). When the power imbalance is used by the coach as a way to coerce, manipulate, diminish, or degrade an athlete, vulnerability of the athlete to maltreatment may increase.

At the root of athlete maltreatment experiences is the misuse of power. As such, to understand the occurrence, experiences, and consequences of maltreatment, the power dynamics between the athlete and others in the athlete's life must be considered.

Power imbalances have also been identified between peers in sport. For example, athletes have discussed the power relations between their teammates, reporting that athletes who demonstrated leadership qualities and who spoke up for the team and had strong relationships with coaches and support staff—typically team captains—held power on their team and were more respected (Tam, 2020). Similarly, Kerr and colleagues (2016) identified several ways in which athletes hold power over teammates, including athletic ability, age, seniority on a team, commitment to the sport or team, and work ethic. Power is a driving force behind hazing practices and has been reportedly used as a rite of passage and a way to ensure new athletes "know their place on the team," so that returning athletes can feel they have power over incoming athletes. In an exploration of athletes who had perpetrated hazing, an athlete described how hazing reinforced team rank: "It was a way of reserving certain privileges for seniors and it made you feel more special 'cause you're a senior. You do it to someone so it brings them down in order to lift yourself up" (Waldron et al., 2011, p. 118). In an exploration of power between peers, Tam (2020) found that athletes used sexual encounters to gain social status; having sex with a successful athlete, for example, was perceived to increase one's social status. Moreover, nonathletes reportedly sought sexual relations with varsity athletes to gain social status and power (Tam, 2020).

French and Raven's work (1959) is informative in identifying sources of power and its use. Table 4.1 identifies types of power and examples of positive and negative power using findings from the extant literature on maltreatment in sport.

Social Relationships Within a Culture of Control

Although the focus of this chapter thus far has been on the interpersonal relationships between athletes and their coaches and teammates, it is critical to acknowledge that interpersonal relationships exist within and are influenced by the broader culture of sport, a culture that has been characterized as controlling. Given the focus on performance outcomes and winning within organized sport, athletes' performances often become the basis for funding and for the employment status of coaches and other sport leaders. In fact, sport sociologists have expressed concerns about athletes being "docile bodies" (Shogan, 1999) controlled for the benefit of others in the sport sector (Cole et al., 2004).

The processes of identifying and developing talent in athletes are typically focused on methods of optimizing performance potential with considerations of early specialization, intense training and competition schedules, a singular focus, and relegation of authority to coaches (Brackenridge, 2001; Côté & Gilbert, 2009; David, 2005). This performance-oriented focus is often at odds with personal development, health, and well-being (Barker-Ruchti & Schubring, 2016; Miller & Kerr, 2002; Preston & Fraser-Thomas, 2018). As an example, coaches reportedly use psychologically abusive behaviors because they believe these behaviors are effective in developing athletic talent (instrumental reasons) (Stirling, 2013), building mental toughness, and contributing to winning (Jacobs et al., 2017). Jacobs and colleagues (2017) reported that coaches in their study admitted they did everything they could to have control, and while they acknowledged the possibility of giving athletes flexibility to contribute to decision making, they also believed it was easier and more expedient to "close the doors, tell them to go to bed at 9 pm, no fries, no ice cream" (p. 135). One coach suggested "a coach has to score and if an athlete has to be sacrificed to accomplish this, then that's how it is" (Jacobs et al., 2017, p. 137).

The culture of control is also illustrated by findings that athletes are reluctant to disclose or report their experiences of maltreatment. In the study of Canadian national team athletes, only 16% of current athletes and 13% of retired athletes reported their experiences of maltreatment; athletes chose not to disclose or report because of fears of negative repercussions, including experiencing cuts to their funding and losing a position on the team (Willson et al., 2021). The control exercised over athletes was highlighted by a Canadian national team athlete who, when explaining why they did not report experiences of maltreatment, said the following:

> Knowing we can be replaced and our careers are on the line, you are regularly forced to ignore issues or maltreatment out of fear. I have witnessed blackmail, intimidation, favouritism, experienced verbal and mental abuse personally. We are silenced or put down if you ask questions. I am fearful that after I speak out, I will be punished. (p.8)

Fear of retaliation was also cited by athletes in the United States as a reason for not submitting a formal report or complaint (U.S. Centre for Safe-

TABLE 4.1 Examples of Positive and Negative Uses of Power

Types of power	Examples of negative use of power	Examples of positive use of power
Legitimate: results from an elected, selected, or appointed position of authority and often underpinned by social norms	"You're somebody if you're coached by him. . . . because he coaches the best people in the country no-one questions him" (Brackenridge, 1997, p. 122)	"Creating an environment where the athletes become experienced in solving problems, making decisions, steering directions"; "gradually giving the reins or the leadership to the athletes by receiving feedback, planning sessions, and developing their own leadership group" (Harvey, 2017, p. 84)
Reward: the ability to offer or deny rewards to others for doing what is wanted or expected of them	"No one could challenge her [coach] because she was being so successful putting athletes on teams and stuff." (Stirling & Kerr, 2009, p. 232)	"Focusing on internal motivation of the individual, he knows he is becoming a better player, improves, they have more input into the game. They get more satisfaction. Individual effort increases and the player is rewarded with more success. Individual development leads to team development and the results come." (Pill, 2017, p. 98)
Expert: what one knows, experience, and special skills or talents	"Whatever the coach said, whatever they told me to do was gold, and I was afraid to not do it." (Stirling & Kerr, 2009, p. 233)	Encouraging athletes to become experts in their sport; "I find the most effective learning comes through questioning the player, 'what did you do there?' 'why did you move there? What were your thought and reasoning?'" (Pill, 2017, p. 96)
Referent: affiliations we make and the groups and organizations we belong to, as well as likeability	"So, the bully sees them as a weaker target. . . . I guess it would be someone who is quiet, shy . . . kind of an outsider on the team. . . . But, it should be said that just because someone doesn't necessarily 'fit in' on a team, they deserve to be bullied." (Kerr, Jewett, et al., 2016, p. 141)	Quality coach–athlete relationships are marked by closeness (mutual respect, trust, appreciation, liking), commitment (close relationship over time), complementary interpersonal behaviors, and co-orientation (i.e., common understanding or expectations of partnership). (Jowett & Shanmugam, 2016)
Coercive: threat of physical, social, emotional, political, or economic means to gain compliance from another	"You're just taught to never question anything they do, or you'll be the one to pay the price for it later." (Clark, 2017)	"As a coach, it's no longer a top-down approach, I guess it's a unified approach. It's not me saying 'we need to do this', [my athletes] have said you wanted to do it, so go ahead and do it." (Alder, 2017, p. 64)
Informational: ability of an agent of influence to bring about change through the resource of information	"He was such a successful coach in tennis and I knew I could get really good if I listened to him. Basically, I just trusted everything he said and I didn't question his coaching." (Stirling & Kerr, 2014, p. 124)	Involving athletes in the information-generating process (e.g., asking athletes "What went well about today's training? What do you wish had been different about today's training? What will you do tomorrow to make a difference?" (Kerr et al., 2017, p. 31)

Sport, 2021), reinforcing the notion that athletes have little control and can feel powerless against sport leaders. Similarly, a review of British Gymnastics revealed numerous forms of maltreatment including belittling, extreme weight management and body shaming, use of excessive physical force, and coercive control. Reportedly, the performance outcome focus of British Gymnastics and emphasis on national and international success was proposed as contributing to experiences of maltreatment (Whyte Review, 2020). The authors of the report also concluded that the environment of control meant that athletes lacked opportunities and safe avenues to raise their concerns and were fearful of negative repercussions if they did raise them (Whyte Review, 2020).

The findings of an independent review into the abuses of gymnasts in New Zealand (Howman et al., 2021, p. 36) also emphasize a culture of control and lack of agency experienced by athletes:

> A consistent theme expressed by gymnasts is they feel disempowered and lack a voice in a sport where adults make decisions about issues that directly impact on and involve them. There is currently no way for them to confidentially have their voices heard in a way that does not carry risk of retribution or isolation.

The authors recommend that athletes be empowered to make choices and decisions in age-appropriate ways.

While a substantial body of research has addressed coaches as perpetrators of maltreatment, it is critical to acknowledge that coaches are part of a broader system and are typically hired and fired based on the performance of their athletes. For example, sport administrators reportedly believed that a coach's priority is to promote athletic success, and therefore, the focus should be on winning rather than positive development (Jacobs et al., 2017). Additionally, when instances of harms have been brought to the sport organizations' attention, the administrators blame the context; for example, one staff member said, "We have to make do with those we have," implying there are no alternative coaches who would be better suited or that other coaches would likely engage in such behaviors as well (Jacobs et al., 2017, p. 134).

While one may wonder what role parents play in protecting their sons and daughters from maltreatment, parents, too, are socialized into accepting harmful but normalized practices. Parents of young athletes reportedly felt anguish seeing what their children are exposed to but felt they were forced into accepting these behaviors as a requirement of being in elite sport (Kerr & Stirling, 2012). Additionally, when parents questioned or complained about the harm their children were experiencing, retribution resulted for the athletes; as a result, the athletes stopped complaining to their parents and parents learned to be compliant, a response they later deeply regretted (Kerr & Stirling, 2012).

Athletes often experience multiple forms of maltreatment in their sport environment simultaneously, indicating this is a systemic issue. For example, in an analysis of maltreatment experiences reported by Canadian national team athletes, all forms of relational maltreatment had significant positive correlations with each other (Willson et al., 2021). Such findings should shift our focus from individual perpetrators of maltreatment or the nature of interpersonal relationships to the characteristics of the environment that account for the acceptance, enabling, or even promoting of relationships characterized by maltreatment.

The culture of control in Canadian sport was challenged through the Dubin Commission, which was established in the wake of the Ben Johnson (100 m sprinter) case. After winning the gold medal in the 100-meter final of the 1988 Summer Olympics, Johnson was disqualified after a positive test for banned substances. The Dubin Commission was initiated to explore the drug scandal, but the focus expanded to an investigation of the culture of Canadian sport. Findings of this commission revealed that a hyperfocused culture of performance and excellence, which had come from the federal government, national sport organizations, sponsoring corporations, and other stakeholders, had created a win-at-all-costs mentality (Dubin, 1990). The Dubin Commission determined that athletes were heavily influenced to make self-sacrificing decisions (in this case, the use of illicit substances) because of the external pressures to win. Dubin encouraged the examination of the definition of excellence, which was almost exclusively measured by medal counts and international success, and commented that "the pursuit of excellence does not mean that we want our athletes to win at any costs" (Dubin, 1990, p. 506).

Despite these advancements, evidence indicates that the focus of sport remains on performance excellence, international rankings, and medal counts. For example, the funding of sports is based primarily on the performance of the athletes (Own the Podium, n.d.), without consideration of the methods used to achieve high performance, thus highlighting the continued prioritization of performance and podium finishes over athlete health and well-being (Kikulis, 2013).

The ongoing revelations of athlete maltreatment, along with subsequent investigations into the handling of maltreatment cases, illustrate that the sport organizations responsible for the oversight of athlete health and well-being have too often failed in fulfilling these responsibilities. These failures have included ignoring athletes' voices and punishing athletes for noncompliance or for speaking up about their concerns. The fact that perpetrators such as Nassar in the United States and Bennell in the United Kingdom continued to commit their crimes over extended periods, leaving so many victims, can only mean that those in positions of authority knew or suspected something and failed to act on their responsibilities (Howley, 2018). As we learned in the Nassar case, both the national sport organization and the university where Nassar was employed had received complaints over the years and had failed to act on these complaints—failures that cost millions of dollars in fines and the firing of those in positions of authority (Associated Press, 2020), in addition to the pain and suffering experienced by the athletes and their families. Notably, athletes who had expressed their discomfort and concerns about receiving treatment from Nassar were dismissed on the basis of the credibility of the physician. The power held by those in positions of authority in sport has not only contributed to cultures of control that diminished athletes' voices but has led to athletes' distrust in those who are responsible for establishing safe environments for athletes.

Athletes Take Back Power

In response to experiences of maltreatment, athletes have found ways to challenge the culture of control and take power back. This section analyzes how athletes have historically used their power to create changes in sport, including how they have used the legal system, athlete representation in organizations, and their voices, both as individuals and collectives.

Use of Law and Arbitration

One of the ways athletes have brought about change is through the use of law and arbitration. In the 1990s, soccer player Jean-Marc Bosman was restricted to staying with his current club because of transfer fees, despite a lack of opportunity and wages (Exner, 2019; Korr, 2002). The courts decided the transfer fee was a breach of the rules of free movement of capital, goods, and labor within the European Union and overruled the organization's decision (Exner, 2019; Korr, 2002). This ruling affected all leagues in the European Union, and organizations had to subsequently change their rules, with many international organizations following suit (Exner, 2019). A more recent case pertaining to maltreatment involved American gymnasts coming forward with their experiences of sexual abuse from their team doctor, Larry Nassar (Hampel, 2019). This case started when a former athlete, Rachael Denhollander, came forward with her experiences of sexual abuse by Nassar, which sparked hundreds of other athletes to join in and share their stories as well. Interestingly, while Denhollander was the first to formally involve the police, there is evidence that other athletes had previously made complaints to their sport organizations. Maggie Nichols reported her experience to her sport organization in 2015, which she believes negatively affected the rest of her elite gymnastics career (Zaccardi, 2018). The 2018 trial against Nassar included testimonies from over 100 athletes and resulted in his receiving a sentence of up to 175 years in prison (Cacciola & Mather, 2018).

Arbitration is often needed when disputes cannot be resolved within an organization. However, traditional courts are not well equipped to handle sport-specific disputes because of the lack of sport-specific knowledge; this has led to the creation of sport-specific arbitration systems (McLaren, 1998). In Canada, the Sport Dispute Resolution Centre of Canada (SDRCC) was established with the goal of providing an independent dispute resolution system for national-level athletes and a formal channel for athletes to voice their concerns around team selection, carding, discipline, contracts, and harassment (Jodouin, 2005; SDRCC, n.d.). Similar arbitration has been established internationally; for instance, the Court of Arbitration for Sport was formed as a division of the International Olympic Committee but has since distanced itself and become more independent (Jodouin, 2005). While these avenues exist, the processes are often financially costly and time consuming, which is problematic given the short length of athletes' careers (Houlihan, 2004; Schwab, 2018).

Given these difficulties, along with well-documented challenges experienced by athletes when seeking redress through their sport organizations (Willson et al., 2022), some countries are establishing frameworks for complaint processes that are independent from the sport organizations. For example, the U.S. Center for SafeSport offers independent investigative and adjudication processes for Olympic and Paralympic athletes. Similarly, in Canada, the newly established Office of the Sport Integrity Commissioner (OSIC, 2022) receives, investigates, and adjudicates certain complaints about maltreatment from those in the Olympic and Paralympic sector. Of significance, both North American organizations leave the vast proportion of sport participants—those below the level of national team athletes—without recourse. Further, evidence suggests that those from equity-denied groups believe they are not well served by these processes (Gurgis et al., 2022).

Formal Athlete Representation

Another avenue athletes have used to exercise their power and enact change is formalized athlete representation in their sport organizations. This provides athletes with a legitimized role to provide feedback to an organization and contribute to decisions being made about athletes. Having athlete representatives on a sport organization's board of directors and committees means athletes can have input into the codes of conduct, team selection criteria, and discipline measures that affect the athletes' sport experience (Clarke et al., 1994). Several countries and organizations have created formal representative bodies, including the International Olympic Committee's Athletes' Commission. In Canada and the United States, rules state that athletes must make up 20% of the votes on the board of directors in sport organizations (Team USA, n.d.; Thibault & Babiak, 2005); however, there are no data to confirm whether this requirement is being upheld.

Feedback from athletes has suggested it is difficult for them to speak out against the prevailing views of the organization, especially when they are now representing the organization's values as part of their duties on the board, and they often get only one vote (Koss, 2011). Houlihan (2004) observed that athlete representatives on boards are "preferred to be seen rather than heard" (p. 422), and too often, the role is tokenistic rather than empowering. Other barriers faced by athlete representatives include time investment, a lack of requisite education to be informed about the important issues, and balancing their engagement in the organization with their athletic careers (Tavares, 2008; Thibault & Harvey, 2013).

Use of Athletes' Voices and Platforms

A third way athletes have demonstrated their power is through the use of their voices and platforms to speak out or protest. Athletes have historically protested for two different reasons: for their rights as athletes and for social justice issues. An example of protesting for athlete rights is Ara Abrahamian, a Swedish wrestler who laid his medal on the podium in protest of the refereeing during the Beijing Olympics in 2008 (Chappelet, 2020). Another example is Beckie Scott, a Canadian cross-country skier who, during the 2002 Olympics, publicly spoke about concerns that her international federation was not doing enough to protect against doping, resulting in extraordinary backlash from her organization (Kihl et al., 2007). In an interesting turn of events, several athletes subsequently tested positive for banned substances, and years after the Games, Scott was awarded the gold medal (Kihl et al., 2007).

Examples of social justice protests include Tommie Smith and John Carlos raising their fists on the podium at the 1968 Summer Olympics to bring recognition to Black rights in the United States (Chappelet, 2020; Kaufman, 2008; Zirin, 2005), Muhammad Ali taking a stand against the Vietnam war (Kaufman, 2008; Rhoden, 2007; Zirin, 2005), and Colin Kaepernick taking a knee to bring attention to police brutality of Black people in the United States (Boykoff & Carrington, 2020; Chappelet, 2020). In all these examples, the result was backlash for the athletes: Smith and Carlos were immediately removed from the Olympic Village and stripped of their medals (Chappelet, 2020; Kaufman, 2008), Ali was banned from his sport for three years (Zirin, 2005), and Kaepernick remained unsigned following his season of protests, effectively ending his career in the NFL (Beaton, 2020). Interestingly, over time, all of these athletes have subsequently been reappraised as heroes for their causes.

For some athletes, using their voices to protest what are perceived to be nonsport issues, such as anti-Black racism, is a way to highlight the holistic nature of their being (Cooper et al., 2019). For example, Ariel Atkins of the Women's National Basketball Association (WNBA) explained that taking a knee to protest anti-Black racism sends the message that "we're not just basketball players, we're so much more than that" (Grablick, 2020). Similarly, the National Hockey League, the National Basketball Association, and Major League Baseball, all very popular and lucrative male professional leagues in North America, demonstrated support for the Black Lives Matter movement by suspending games (Sadler, 2020). Although the attention these athletes drew to this social justice issue was widespread and powerful, the question about whether or not this enhanced attention contributes to lasting change remains.

More recently, athletes have expressed their voices on social media platforms as a vehicle for change making. For example, in the wake of the documentary *Athlete A*, which investigated the culture of abuse in USA Gymnastics, athletes from around the world came forward on their social media channels with their experiences of abuse in sport. The hashtag gymnastalliance has been used for athletes to share horrific practices incurred in their sport (Macur, 2020).

For some athletes, using their voices to protest what are perceived to be nonsport issues, such as anti-Black racism, is a way to highlight the holistic nature of their being.

There are some lessons to be learned from the ways athletes have used their power to enact change and inform efforts to eradicate maltreatment. Using the legal system to fight for justice has led to some positive long-term outcomes, including the prioritization of efforts to prevent maltreatment across sport organizations in the wake of the Larry Nassar trial. However, it can also be a long and financially costly process (Houlihan, 2004). Additionally, this option is primarily used once an injustice has occurred as a way to rectify a situation and is therefore reactive rather than proactive.

Athlete representation is a positive way in which athletes can promote change in their organizations if the organization and athletes are equally committed. Organizations need to ensure there are effective and legitimate ways for athletes to have adequate decision-making power, including equal voting rights on the board and having their perspectives heard and taken into consideration. Additionally, athletes must be educated about the issues, must have the time to invest, and must be empowered to use their voices in this way, so they can be confident when voicing their opinions to the people in positions of power in their organizations.

One way in which athlete representation could be used in practice, for example, is to have athletes evaluate the policies and codes of conduct designed to prevent and address maltreatment. Athletes could provide valuable feedback to organizations about the implementation of and adherence to policies and codes on the ground, as well as provide suggestions for improvements. Athletes are the ones most affected by maltreatment in sport, so involving them in decisions made by the organizations could be an effective means of moving sport toward being a safer environment.

Perhaps the most effective way for athletes to use their power is through their voices and platforms. For example, when 995 national team athletes shared their experiences of maltreatment in Canadian sport (Willson et al., 2021), the data collected guided subsequent conversations on maltreatment across sport organizations and were used to inform safe sport educational modules (Coaching Association of Canada, n.d.) and a Universal Code of Conduct to Prevent and Address Maltreatment (SIRC, 2020). In spite of these advancements, significant work remains, and it is essential that athletes continue to use their voices to dismantle the culture of control and to push for safer sport environments.

Future Research Directions

Within the body of research on maltreatment in sport, unanswered questions exist in regard to effective interventions to prevent maltreatment. Despite the promotion of athlete-centered approaches to sport, these have, for the most part, not gained traction within the sport community, thus leaving open the question of how power may be distributed and shared effectively within interpersonal relationships to prevent harmful experiences. Additionally, with athletes exercising their agency and power via social media channels, it will be important for future research to explore the effectiveness and impact of these efforts on preventing and addressing maltreatment experiences. Do these social media advocacy efforts influence policy and programmatic changes and the shifting of power within interpersonal relationships in sport? Will these social media campaigns contribute to lasting changes in advancing safe sport experiences for athletes?

Practical Implications

For those who are sport practitioners, whether coaches, sport administrators, or policy makers, it's important to recognize and acknowledge that athletes continue to experience various forms of maltreatment in sport and that most of these experiences fail to come to the surface because they are normalized, there are inadequate mechanisms for addressing concerns, and athletes fear negative repercussions for their careers. To advance the promise and potential of sport, it's critical to find ways to invite, hear, and incorporate athletes' voices. Some ways to do this include engaging current or retired athlete representation on all committees of sport organizations and developing safe spaces for current athletes to talk about and evaluate their experiences. Sport organizations should also include athletes on their board of directors as voting members to ensure their opinions are formally acknowledged. In addition, coaches should take a more athlete-centered approach to sport, which can include active listening and engaging athletes in decision making, practice planning, goal setting, problem solving, and evaluating training and competition performances (Jowett, 2007, 2017; Kidman, 2010). With such an approach to coaching, the performance and well-being of both the athlete and coach are likely to be enhanced; after all, when there is high-quality well-being and health, strong performances are likely to follow suit.

Summary

This chapter highlights the forms of maltreatment that occur in sport and the ways in which power and a culture of control underlie occurrences of maltreatment. Although many initiatives have been implemented to prevent maltreatment by attempting to shift power to athletes, these have met with limited success. Given the apparent lack of success in shifting power to athletes, athletes have taken it upon themselves to take back power by engaging in athlete advocacy. Sport has a long history of athletes engaging in advocacy to stimulate changes in sport and in society more broadly; these efforts have included the legal system and arbitration, formal athlete representation, and athletes using their voices and platforms to draw attention to issues. Recently, with the proliferation of social media, athletes have raised their concerns about experiences of maltreatment and existing power structures in sport through social media campaigns. The effectiveness and impact of these campaigns to prevent and address maltreatment in sport will need to await future research.

DISCUSSION QUESTIONS

1. What forms of maltreatment exist in sport, what behaviors characterize each form of maltreatment, and how common is each form?
2. Think about your own experiences in your role(s) in sport (e.g., coach, athlete, parent, sport administrator). What types of power have you experienced in both positions of greater and lesser power?
3. What initiatives have been advanced to promote athlete-centered sport, and what are some plausible explanations for their lack of success?
4. Describe some of the ways in which power and a sense of agency have historically been demonstrated by athletes and how these methods have changed more recently.

5

Parental Involvement in Youth Sport

Camilla J. Knight, PhD; Chris G. Harwood, PhD; Olivier Y. Rouquette, PhD; and Nicholas L. Holt, PhD

LEARNING OBJECTIVES

On completion of this chapter, the reader should have the following:

- Knowledge of how parents are involved in sport
- Understanding of key research and associated theories pertaining to parental involvement in sport
- Appreciation of the influence parents have on children's and adolescents' sporting experiences and psychosocial development
- Knowledge of the impact children, significant others (e.g., coaches), and the youth sport environment have on parental involvement
- Understanding of how research pertaining to parents applies in practice

Parents have the largest and most enduring impact on their children's participation and experiences in sport (Harwood, Thrower, et al., 2019; Holt & Knight, 2014). In turn, children have a reciprocal influence on parents' experiences (Dorsch, Smith, & McDonough, 2015). Parental influence varies depending on their parenting cognitions, practices, and styles, which are in turn dictated by the culture in which parents were raised and are raising their children (Bornstein, 2012). Consequently, the specific ways in which parents are involved in their children's sporting and nonsporting lives vary between individuals and across cultures. Through this chapter, we examine the complexity of parental involvement in youth sport. In particular, we unpack the consequences of parents' involvement on children's experiences and psychosocial outcomes. Further, we explore the factors that affect parents when supporting children in sport, as well as strategies to enhance the ways parents are involved.

Key Theories and Research

Over the last 50 years, but particularly in the last decade, there has been a substantial increase in research examining parental involvement in organized youth sport (Knight, 2019). Within such research, the term *organized youth sport* is usually considered "adult-organized and controlled athletic programs for young people" (Dorsch et al., 2021). In the current chapter, when the term *youth sport* is used, it refers to organized activities aligned with this definition. Further, despite some notable exceptions considering parental involvement in college sports (e.g., Dorsch et al., 2016), the majority of research is focused on young people under the age of 18 years, and thus this age range is the focus of the chapter. The terms *child* and *children* are used throughout because we are discussing parental involvement in relation to parents' own children.

In general, the enduring focus of research examining parental involvement in youth sport has been on *how* parents are involved and the associated consequences (Dorsch et al., 2021). Specifically, guided by theories such as expectancy-value theory (Eccles et al., 1983, 1984), achievement goal theory (AGT; Nicholls, 1984), competence motivation theory (Harter, 1978), and self-determination theory (SDT; Deci & Ryan, 1985) researchers have sought to identify how the comments parents make and the behaviors they display affect outcomes such as children's motivation, enjoyment, anxiety, and perceptions of pressure (see Rouquette et al., 2020, for a review). However, as summarized in figure 5.1, increasing consideration has also been given to the factors that may mediate the relationship between different parental behaviors and child outcomes, as well as the individual, relational, and environmental factors that directly and indirectly influence parental involvement.

Parental Involvement and Influence

Parents fulfill numerous tasks within youth sport, ranging from providing emotional support and feedback to funding participation, transporting children to competitions and training, and identifying opportunities (Côté, 1999; Wolfenden & Holt, 2005). How parents fulfill these tasks (i.e., the specific behaviors they display and the comments they make) affect children's psychosocial development, as well as their ongoing engagement and performance in sport (Sheridan et al., 2014). Specifically, drawing on expectancy value theory (Eccles et al., 1983, 1984), it has been recognized that parents' involvement, and subsequently the ways they can influence children's experiences and development, falls into three categories: *interpreters*, *providers*, and *role models*. As interpreters, providers, and role models, parents directly and indirectly communicate their beliefs about their child's sporting competence—and thus their child's likelihood of achieving success in sport—as well as their attitudes and beliefs about the value or importance of sport. Children's perceptions of these beliefs and attitudes, and subsequently their expectations for success and the value of participating in sport, will influence their sport choices, performance, and persistence (Rouquette et al., 2020).

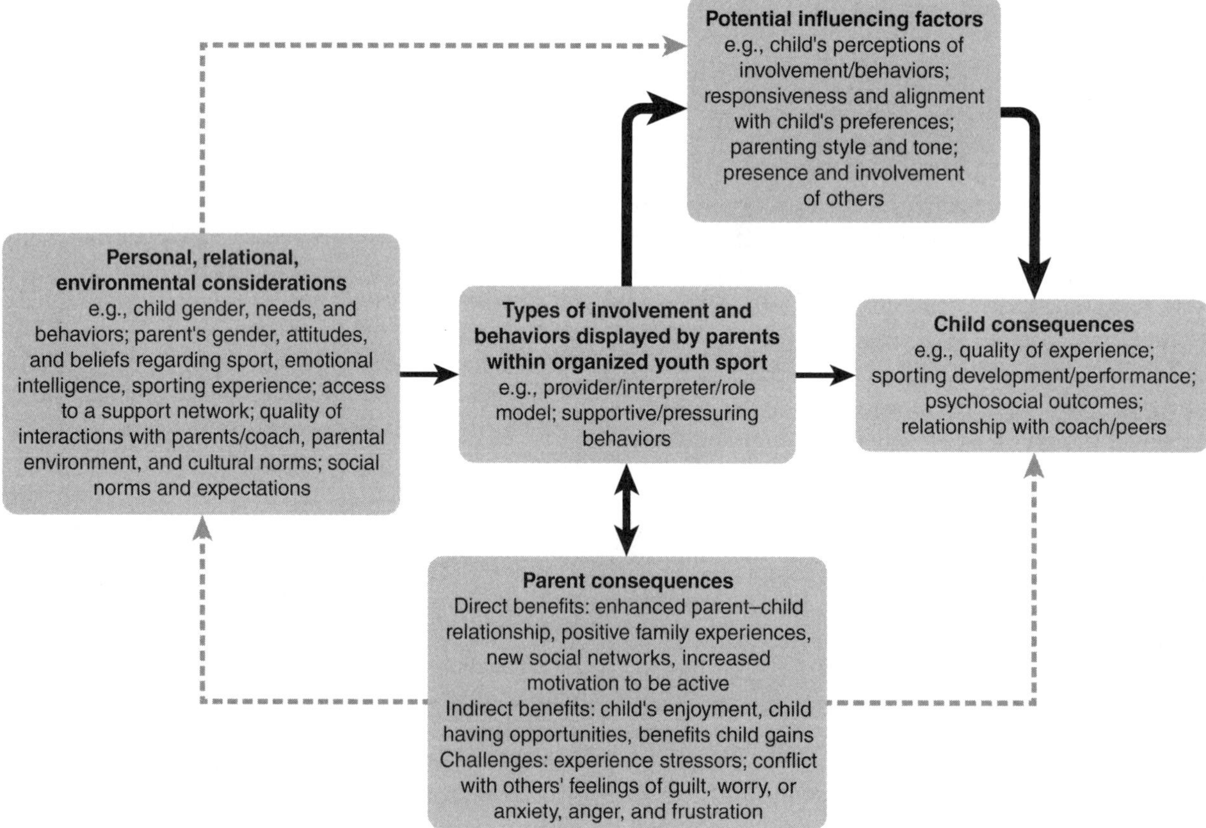

FIGURE 5.1 A proposed model of parental involvement in youth sport.

- *Parents as interpreters.* Parents may help children interpret their sporting experiences through their feedback or discussions before, during, or after training and competitions (e.g., Elliott & Drummond, 2015; Knight, Little, et al., 2016; Tamminen et al., 2017). For instance, whether parents reward children (i.e., provide positive feedback, give treats or gifts) for effort, performance, or winning after a competition will influence how children interpret these behaviors or outcomes and subsequently perceive them as important when they are participating. By influencing children's interpretation of their experiences, parents influence children's expectations of success, their self-perceptions (i.e., perceived competence), and the value and emotions (i.e., enjoyment) they associate with sport participation (Fredricks & Eccles, 2005).
- *Parents as providers.* The provider role incorporates parents' behaviors that enable, support, and encourage children's involvement and participation in sport. Within sport, parents fulfill the provider role in numerous ways—for instance, by encouraging their children to participate in sport (Brustad, 1993), providing transport to training and competitions (Wolfenden & Holt, 2005), and financially supporting their children's sport involvement (Dunn et al., 2016). Parents' provision, and encouragement, of sporting opportunities not only enables children to participate in sport but also indicates that parents value sport participation. Subsequently, parents' provider behaviors effect the likelihood that children will be interested in participating and continue their engagement in sport (Warmenhoven et al., 2020).
- *Parents as role models.* Parents may influence children's experience as role models, particularly by taking part in sport or physical activity themselves (Fredricks & Eccles, 2004). Moreover, it has been suggested that children observe the behaviors parents display at youth sport competitions, such as the comments they make toward the referee, and model their own behaviors in response (Holt & Knight, 2014). It should be noted, however, that limited research has studied this aspect of parents as role models. When parents are active, their children witness these behaviors and may subsequently participate themselves (e.g., Bois et al., 2005; Brustad, 1996). Moreover, if parents display poor sporting behaviors at competitions, it can affect the moral and sporting behaviors children display (e.g., Danioni et al., 2017).

Consequences of Parental Involvement

Given the roles parents play in children's sporting lives and the subsequent influence they can have, considerable attention has been given to identifying the consequences arising from different types of parental involvement or behaviors (Charbonneau & Camiré, 2019; Strandbu et al., 2019; Teques et al., 2018). Much of the early work considering the consequences of parental involvement drew on achievement goal theory (AGT; Nicholls, 1984) to understand the influence of parent-initiated (White, 1996) or parent- and coach-initiated (White et al., 1998) motivational climates on children's goal orientations as well as competitive trait anxiety. Findings indicated that children higher in task orientation and lower in ego orientation had parents who emphasized a motivational climate valuing learning and enjoyment rather than success and minimal necessary effort (White, 1996). Meanwhile, children with high ego orientation and low task orientation reported the highest levels of competitive trait anxiety (White, 1998).

Parents have the largest and most enduring impact on their children's participation and experiences in sport.

AGT has continued to underpin research in this area, helping to explain, for instance, why children adopt achievement goals and belief patterns similar to their parents (see Dorsch et al., 2021, for a summary). However, self-determination theory (SDT; Deci & Ryan, 1985) has increasingly been used. Specifically, drawing on SDT, researchers have sought to develop an understanding of how parents' feedback and encouragement (or lack thereof) may influence children's intrinsic motivation. This research has highlighted the importance of parents' engagement in autonomy-supportive behaviors to enhance self-determined motivation (e.g., Hein & Joesaar, 2015).

Drawing together the extensive body of literature that examines the consequences of parental involvement, it has been suggested that parental support, considered as behaviors that facilitate a child's sport participation (Leff & Hoyle, 1995), might lead to positive outcomes. Support may be conceived as the following, among others:

- Offering sport opportunities (Lauer et al., 2010)
- Providing financial and instrumental support (Dunn et al., 2016; Ross et al., 2015)
- Demonstrating unconditional love and emotional support (Gould et al., 2006; Ross et al., 2015)

Such supportive behaviors have been associated with increasing children's motivation and enjoyment as well as influencing their continuous sport participation (Atkins et al., 2013; O'Rourke et al., 2014).

In contrast, when children perceive pressure from their parents, defined as an unattainable expectation toward a child's sport participation (Leff & Hoyle, 1995), it can negatively influence experiences and development (Lauer et al., 2010). Pressure may arise when

- parents have excessive expectations for their children to play or excel in sport (Fraser-Thomas & Côté, 2009; Fraser-Thomas et al., 2008; Gould et al., 2006),
- sport is valued more than other developmental domains such as school or family life (Fraser-Thomas et al., 2008; Gould et al., 2008),
- support provision is conditional to children's sporting performances or outcomes (Chan et al., 2019; Ross et al., 2015), and
- parents criticize children's performances (Gould et al., 2006).

Such behaviors are associated with children reporting increases in anxiety and stress, displaying poor sporting behavior and reduced motivation, and being at greater risk of burnout or dropout (Fraser-Thomas et al., 2008; Kaye et al., 2015).

However, despite the purported links between certain parental behaviors and child outcomes, the specific relationships between these behaviors and outcomes are not as evident as often suggested (Keegan et al., 2014). That is, although it has been widely accepted that pressuring behaviors lead to negative outcomes and supportive behaviors lead to positive outcomes, the distinction between pressuring and supportive behaviors is not always clear-cut (Dorsch et al., 2016). In fact, there is an ever-growing body of evidence that the same parental behaviors can lead to both positive and detrimental outcomes for young athletes (Dorsch et al., 2016; Fraser-Thomas & Côté, 2009). Consideration of individual, relational, and contextual factors may be required to understand the relationship between parental behaviors and the outcomes experienced by children.

Perceptions of Pressure and Support

Research has shown it is not simply the provision of support or pressure from parents that leads to different psychosocial outcomes; rather, children's *perceptions* of support or pressure are also important (Stein et al., 1999). For instance, Babkes and Weiss (1999) identified that parents' reported attitudes and behaviors were not related to children's psychosocial outcomes. Rather, children who *perceived* their parents had higher beliefs about their competency, provided positive contingent responses to their successes in sport, and served as positive role models had higher perceptions of competence, intrinsic motivation, and sport enjoyment. Such findings align with Harter's (1978, 1981) competence motivation theory, which suggests that parents (or significant others) can directly influence children's perceptions of competence through the feedback they provide. Meanwhile, through feedback accumulated over time in relation to children's effort, attempts, and progress in an achievement domain (such as sport), children gradually develop an internalized self-reward system and develop their perceived competence. When children perceive themselves as in control and competent, either as a result of direct feedback and encouragement or drawing on their internalized self-reward system, they are more likely to be intrinsically motivated to pursue optimal challenges.

Children's Preferences and Parental Responsiveness

Studies of children's preferences for parental involvement, particularly at competitions, provide a clear indication of the types of behaviors they would like to see from parents (Knight et al., 2010, 2011; Knight, Little, et al., 2016; Omli & Wiese-Bjornstal, 2011). For instance, children generally prefer their parents to be supportive during competitions. However, the specific ways in which they want this support to be displayed and what constitutes support may vary depending on the timing and the competition situation (e.g., if the child is winning, losing, playing well) (Knight et al., 2010; Knight & Holt, 2014; Omli & Wiese-Bjornstal, 2011), the perceived importance of the competition, children's perception of their performance (Knight & Holt, 2014), and the relative privacy in which a conversation takes place (Tamminen et al., 2017).

The distinction between pressuring and supportive behaviors is not always clear-cut.

Given such preferences, it is likely that the extent to which parental support is responsive to an individual child influences the outcomes that arise (e.g., Clarke et al., 2016; Knight & Holt, 2014). Responsiveness describes how people in a relationship attend to and support each other's needs and goals (Reis & Gable, 2015). The construct of perceived responsiveness includes three key components:

- Understanding, which accounts for the perception that the partner (e.g., parent) comprehends an individual's core self (e.g., needs, desires)
- Validation, which accounts for the perception that the partner respects or values an individual's view of the self (e.g., expresses liking and encouragements, values abilities and opinions)
- Caring for, which accounts for the perception that the partner expresses warmth, affection, and interest to the individual (Reis et al., 2004; Reis & Gable, 2015)

Research has demonstrated that when athletes perceived higher levels of parental responsiveness while discussing their sport-related goals, they had higher levels of self-efficacy to accomplish their goals, and that self-efficacy and self-esteem mediated the association between perceived parental responsiveness and thriving (Rouquette, Knight, Lovett, & Heuzé, 2021). Subsequently, another study involving young male rugby players showed that players' higher perception of their parents' responsiveness was related to higher levels of thriving and lower worries about sport performance while mediated by their self-esteem (Rouquette, Knight, Lovett, Barrell, et al., 2021).

Emotional Style and Tone

Parenting styles reflect parents' global attitudes and values and create the emotional climate in which specific parenting practices are displayed (Darling & Steinberg, 1993). As such, the parenting style a parent adopts, as well as the emotional tone that exists within family interactions (i.e., presence of warmth or hostility), may alter the impact of specific parenting practices or behaviors on children (Bee & Boyd, 2012; Darling & Steinberg, 1993; Dorsch et al., 2016). The most well-known typology of parenting styles was developed by Baumrind (1971a, 1971b) who differentiated parenting styles based on a parent's degree of control or authority over their child. In this typology, three types of parenting style are specified: authoritarian, permissive, and authoritative. This was subsequently expanded into a bidimensional construct based on demandingness and responsiveness, leading to the identification of four parenting styles: *authoritarian* (i.e., demanding and unresponsive), *authoritative* (i.e., demanding and responsive), *indulgent* (i.e., not demanding and responsive), and *rejecting/neglecting* (i.e., not demanding and not responsive). Grolnick (2003) proposed a three-dimensional construct of parenting styles based on self-determination theory (Ryan & Deci, 2017). The three dimensions of parenting styles proposed by Grolnick (2003) are *autonomy support*, *involvement*, and *structure*.

Evidence suggests that the adoption of an authoritative or autonomy-supportive parenting style is associated with more positive psychosocial outcomes (Harwood & Knight, 2015; Holt et al., 2009; Pynn et al., 2019; Wright et al., 2019). Considering the apparent benefits of adopting an autonomy-supportive parenting style, Holt and colleagues (2021) sought to understand how sport parents executed this approach in their home. They identified that parents engaged in flexible conversations in which children were provided an opportunity to have a voice; supported children's decisions, recognizing that they often make the right choices; set firm boundaries regarding appropriate and inappropriate behaviors and actions; and held their children to certain expectations. With regard to emotional tone, children's reports of warmth (i.e., the tendency to be supportive, affectionate, and sensitive in the relationships) and positive affect from parents are more positively associated with their perception of support. Meanwhile, children's reports of conflict and negative affect from parents are related to their perception of pressure (Dorsch et al., 2016).

Relationship Quality

Research suggests that the quality of the relationship between a parent and a child might also alter the appropriateness of different types of involvement and influence athletes' experiences and psychosocial outcomes in sport (e.g., Carr, 2013; Ullrich-French & Smith, 2006). For instance, drawing on attachment theory (Bowlby, 1973), which proposed that individuals are biologically predisposed to form selective bonds and enter into social interaction with proximal caring figures (i.e., parents), Felton and Jowett (2013, 2015) identified that the quality of attachment security with parents (and coaches), mediated by the fulfillment (or thwarting) of the basic psychological needs within the parental or coaching relational context, influenced children's performance, skill self-concept, and well-being. Subsequently, Felton and Jowett (2017) showed that decreases in children's secure attachment with parents negatively predicted psychological need satisfaction within the parental relational context, as well as vitality and self-esteem, and positively predicted negative affect. (More information about attachment theory can be found in chapter 3.)

Presence and Involvement of Others

Other family members, coaches, and peers can influence children's sporting experiences and psychosocial outcomes (Sheridan et al., 2014), as well as mediate the impact of parental behaviors (e.g., Keegan et al., 2009; Ullrich-French & Smith, 2006). For instance, aligned with a family systems approach, which recognizes the combined influences of all family members on an individual's life (Dorsch, 2017), Clarke and colleagues (2016) identified that different family members shape parent–child interactions and the consequences of parents' behaviors within the context of academy football. Similarly, the behaviors of coaches can interact with parents' behaviors and potentially alter how parents influence children's experiences or outcomes (Assor & Tal, 2012; Felton & Jowett, 2015). For instance, Gaudreau and colleagues (2016) investigated the interaction between autonomy support from parents and coaches on children's sport motivation, need satisfaction, and athletic success. Their results demonstrated a *compensatory-protective effect* with positive outcomes for children who perceived high levels of autonomy support from their parents regardless of the coach's level of autonomy support. Furthermore, children who perceived that their parents provided lower levels of autonomy support still demonstrated positive psychosocial outcomes when they perceived high levels of autonomy support from their coach.

Influences on the Types of Involvement Parents Display

Broadly aligned with ecological systems theory (Bronfenbrenner, 2005), which highlights the importance of considering how increasingly complex and bidirectional interactions between an individual and the people, objects, and symbols in their environment may influence an individual's behaviors and development, there is an increasing recognition that *how* parents are involved in sport is affected by personal, relational, and environmental influences, as well as the interaction between these.

Personal Considerations

At the personal level, research has highlighted the influence parents' attitudes, beliefs, and expectations (Eccles et al., 1983), family structure and circumstances (Fearon & Belsky, 2004), and gender (Bee & Boyd, 2012) can have on parenting practices and behaviors. Such factors similarly influence parents' involvement within organized youth sport (Knight, 2019), including the following:

- *Child's gender* can influence parenting practices and behaviors (e.g., Brown et al., 1989). For instance, parents provide boys with more opportunities to play sport and place a greater emphasis on performance compared with girls (Fredricks & Eccles, 2005), whereas girls may perceive higher support from their parents and less pressure from their fathers than boys (Leff & Hoyle, 1995).
- *Child's needs and behaviors* may also dictate what a parent wants or must do within a youth sport setting (e.g., Holt et al., 2009). As an example, it is apparent that at youth sport competitions, children's performance and behavior often influence the types of comments parents make during and after games (e.g., Elliott & Drummond, 2017; Tamminen et al., 2017). Particularly, when children are visibly upset parents will empathize with their child, which may alter their responses (Holt et al., 2008).
- *Parents' gender* may influence the opportunities parents provide and the actual and

perceived types of involvement they display within sport (e.g., Dorsch et al., 2016; Kay, 2007). For example, mothers appear to make more comments during competitions than fathers, and these may also be more positive (Bowker et al., 2009).

- *Parents' personality* (e.g., Goldstein & Iso-Ahola, 2008) may influence the opportunities and support they provide (e.g., Fredricks & Eccles, 2005; Green & Chalip, 1998). Parents with higher overall levels of perfectionism are more likely to encourage sport specialization than moderate perfectionistic parents (Wright et al., 2019).
- *Parents' attitudes and beliefs regarding sport participation*—that is, the value parents place on sport participation and the benefits they expect children to gain from sport, as well as perceptions of children's sport competence and likelihood of success—may lead to parents' providing different opportunities to their children. They may also lead to parents' altering the amount of tangible and emotional support they offer and the types of feedback they provide (Stefansen et al., 2018; Watchman & Spencer-Cavaliere, 2017).
- *Parents' emotional intelligence and coping effectiveness* can influence their involvement. Youth sport, particularly competitions, can be emotionally demanding and associated with a range of stressors (Harwood, Thrower, et al., 2019; Lienhart et al., 2020). The extent to which parents have effective strategies to cope with the situations they encounter, as well as their levels of emotional intelligence, will likely influence the types of comments they make from the sidelines (Knight & Holt, 2013a; Pynn et al., 2019; Teques et al., 2018).
- *Parents' sporting experiences and knowledge* seem to influence the depth of their involvement (Stefansen et al., 2018), as well as the types of comments parents make at competitions (Elliott & Drummond, 2017; Holt et al., 2008). Moreover, parents who had positive experiences of sport as children are more likely to encourage their own children to participate (e.g., Knight, Dorsch, et al., 2016; Watchman & Spencer-Cavaliere, 2017).

The value parents place on sport participation and the benefits they expect children to gain from sport, as well as perceptions of children's sport competence and likelihood of success, may lead to parents' providing different opportunities to their children.

Relational and Environmental Considerations

Beyond the personal factors just identified, parents are influenced both positively and negatively by others within and beyond the sporting environment, as well as factors related to the youth sport context and broader society (Knight, 2019):

- *Access to a support network*, comprising either other family members or other parents, may be particularly helpful because it enables parents to share specific tasks, such as transporting children to training or competitions (Burgess et al., 2016; Furusa et al., 2020). This reduces parents' requirement to complete these tasks and may also minimize the stressors they encounter (e.g., Newport et al., 2021), which may lead to more positive parent–child interactions.
- *Challenging interactions with other parents* may be a source of stress (e.g., Harwood, Thrower, et al., 2019; Lienhart et al., 2020), increase feelings of frustration or concern among parents (Hayward et al., 2017), and heighten the emotional intensity of a game or event (Holt et al., 2008). Consequently, the presence of other parents may influence the types of comments parents make at competitions (Holt et al., 2008). The comments made by other parents can also either lead to parents increasing their active involvement, so that they can monitor what others are saying, or it can lead to parents reducing their involvement so they can avoid having to interact with other parents (Knight, Dorsch, et al., 2016).
- *Positive parent–coach relationships* can enhance parents' access to information about their child's sport and make them feel more supported in their role (Knight & Holt, 2013b). Consequently, parents may be better able to keep their child's sport in perspective,

provide more appropriate types of support, develop a desirable emotional climate, and facilitate more positive athlete–coach relationships (Jowett & Timson-Katchis, 2005; Knight & Holt, 2014).

- *Lack of interaction between parents and coaches, perceptions of coach favoritism, or concerns regarding coaching practices* may increase parents' feelings of stress and cause conflict in the athletic triangle. It can also result in feelings of frustration, anger, or uncertainty (Clarke & Harwood, 2014; Harwood et al., 2010). Subsequently, parents may feel they need to take on a more active coaching role, provide more technical or tactical feedback, or even remove children from certain programs or sports (Knight, Dorsch, et al., 2016).
- *Game criticality and specific competition situations* can influence involvement during competitions. Games that are perceived to be of more importance or situations in a game that are particularly important can increase the number of comments made and influence the nature of these comments (Holt et al., 2008). Perceptions of injustice regarding refereeing decisions as well as concerns about injuries can also lead to feelings of anger or frustration (Goldstein & Iso-Ahola, 2008; Pynn et al., 2019), which may influence parents' feedback and sideline behavior.
- *Policies pertaining to parental behaviors at competitions,* as well as witnessing actions taken by leagues in response to unacceptable parental behaviors, may restrict or limit the verbal reactions by parents at competitions (Holt et al., 2008). However, a study of the influence of policies on parental involvement within the Australian Football League demonstrated that policies had limited impact on parents' behaviors (Elliott & Drummond, 2015).
- *The sport environment* can, over time, lead to parents' changing their attitudes and beliefs pertaining to their child's sport, which may subsequently lead to changes in parents' behaviors or involvement (Clarke & Harwood, 2014; Dorsch et al., 2009). A study of parental involvement over the first 15 months of their child's participation in sport showed that parents experience changes in their thoughts, feelings, and behaviors, including how they interacted with their child, their emotional investment in their child's sport, and the behaviors they displayed at competitions (Dorsch, Smith, Wilson, et al., 2015).
- *The cultural norms* regarding but not limited to parents' involvement within particular sports can also dictate how parents are involved (cf. Misener, 2020). As an example, when comparing the sideline behaviors of a parent whose children participated in different sports (e.g., indoor vs. outdoor and individual vs. team sports), it was apparent that the particular sport context influenced the number of comments parents made (Dorsch, Smith, Wilson, et al., 2015). Moreover, parents may find themselves "living the part of the athlete parent" (McMahon & Penney, 2015, p. 8), whereby they adopt behaviors that align with the cultural practices inherent within their child's sport.
- *Social norms and expectations regarding what makes a good parent* may influence the sporting activities parents encourage their children to participate in, as well as their subsequent level of involvement in these sports (Pynn et al., 2019; Watchman & Spencer-Cavaliere, 2017). For instance, in Norway, parents indicated that they initiated children's sport involvement, purchased equipment, and took active roles in their participation by attending events and discussing performances because this was "a natural part of being a responsible parent" (Stefansen et al., 2018, p. 166).

Consequences of Children's Participation on Parents

Just as parents' involvement in their children's sport can have positive and negative consequences for children, children's participation in sport can result in positive and negative consequences for their parents (Sutcliffe et al., 2021). These may differ depending on a child's age and the stage of their sporting participation, as well as the level at which a child is competing (e.g., Dorsch, Smith, Wilson, et al., 2015; Harwood & Knight, 2009a; Sutcliffe et al., 2021). Moreover, it is likely that parents may simultaneously encounter both benefits and challenges associated with their child's sport participation (e.g., Wiersma & Fifer, 2008).

Benefits and Opportunities

When encouraging and supporting their child's sporting involvement, parents can experience both direct and indirect benefits. Direct benefits include the following:

- The development and maintenance of quality relationships with their child as a result of taking an active role in their child's interests for an extended period (Stefansen et al., 2018; Tamminen et al., 2017; Wiersma & Fifer, 2008)
- An opportunity to develop their social network, spending time with like-minded people (Bean et al., 2019) and sharing positive experiences within their family network (Clarke et al., 2016; Dorsch, Smith, & McDonough, 2015)
- Increased motivation to engage in sport and physical activity themselves (Eriksson et al., 2008) as well as positive mental health benefits (Sutcliffe et al., 2021)
- A perception that they are positively fulfilling the "good parenting ideal" by providing their child with opportunities to participate in structured, safe, adult-regulated activities (Pynn et al., 2019; Watchman & Spencer-Cavaliere, 2017)

In contrast to the direct benefits for parents, indirect benefits are often related to their child's development and experience, such as seeing their child enjoy participating (Misener, 2020; Newport et al., 2021) and enabling their child to access opportunities that are not available to others through their sport participation, which can have positive consequences for their future (Newport et al., 2021). Additionally, knowing their child is gaining social, psychological, and physical benefits (Wiersma & Fifer, 2008) and witnessing their child develop life skills (Neely et al., 2017) are viewed particularly positively.

Challenges and Demands

Nevertheless, supporting children's involvement in sport can also present challenges for parents. For instance, parents can encounter a range of competitive, organizational, developmental, and parent-personal stressors (Harwood et al., 2010; Harwood & Knight, 2009a, 2009b; Harwood, Thrower, et al., 2019; Lienhart et al., 2020). These stressors can have undesirable consequences, including psychological ill-being (Bean et al., 2019). Parents may also find themselves in conflict with other parents, coaches, and their child because of their behaviors or involvement (Jowett & Timson-Katchis, 2005; Lauer et al., 2010). Such conflict may have short-term consequences on, for instance, children's relationship with their coach, as well as long-term negative implications for parent–child relationships (Lauer et al., 2010). Finally, parents' socialization into the performance sport culture may lead to their accepting questionable or unsafe coaching practices or engaging in behaviors they subsequently regret (Lally & Kerr, 2008).

Parents' socialization into the performance sport culture may lead to their accepting questionable or unsafe coaching practices or engaging in behaviors they subsequently regret.

Further, involvement in youth sport can lead to parents' experiencing negative emotions (Bean et al., 2019). For instance, the time commitment required of parents can limit time spent with their other children, resulting in feelings of guilt (Harwood & Knight, 2009a). The amount of money committed to their child's sport participation may become a source of worry and anxiety (Harwood & Knight, 2009b). Attendance at competitions, particularly witnessing perceived injustice, injury, disappointment, or poor behavior from their child, can lead to negative emotions, such as anger, frustration, or embarrassment (Dorsch et al., 2009; Goldstein & Iso-Ahola, 2008; Omli & Wiese-Bjornstal, 2011).

Enhancing Parental Involvement in Youth Sport

It has been suggested that parents should be seeking involvement that "increases the chances for children to achieve their sporting potential, have a positive psychosocial experience, and develop a range of positive developmental outcomes" (Harwood & Knight, 2015, p. 25). What constitutes such involvement will change over time, as children and parents develop, needs change, and different experiences and challenges arise (Harwood & Knight, 2015; Knight & Holt, 2016; Newport et al., 2021). Displaying desirable types of involvement is not easy because, as already detailed, how parents are involved and the impact of their involvement are influenced by a range of personal, relational, and contextual factors, and the requirement for involvement changes over time. Moreover, supporting children's involvement, while associated with benefits, can also result in parents' encountering several challenges. As such, to be involved in the most optimal manner, parents must develop and demonstrate specific intrapersonal skills (e.g., coping skills, emotional intelligence), interpersonal skills (e.g., maintaining quality relationships with other parents and coaches), and organizational skills (e.g., strategies to cope with time and financial demands) (Harwood & Knight, 2015; Knight & Holt, 2014; Pynn et al., 2019).

Although many parents have some of these skills and are involved in their children's sporting lives in a positive manner (Côté, 1999; Holt et al., 2008), some parents are involved in less-than-optimal ways (e.g., Ross et al., 2015). Consequently, the development and evaluation of parent education and support have been deemed important, particularly in performance settings and programs, and a variety of initiatives are emerging within the published literature. An early example involved a Mastery Approach to Parenting (MAP) workshop focused around creating a task-involving motivational climate through appropriate parental behavior and communication strategies in youth basketball (Smoll et al., 2007). After their parents' attendance, children reported lower levels of pre-competition anxiety.

Some years later, a cluster of authors took a reflective practitioner approach by offering accounts of working with sport parents and delivering parent education programs in gymnastics and soccer (Lafferty & Triggs, 2014; Richards & Winter, 2013; Vincent & Christensen, 2015). As a collective, these articles championed the need to provide parents with detailed information about the sport, make parents aware of their roles and responsibilities, and improve parents' knowledge and awareness of verbal and nonverbal communication. Understanding achievement goals and identifying coping strategies to manage the demands and emotions they experienced reflected core content within these accounts.

In addition, these authors offered some important tips for researchers and practitioners working with parents, including the following (Richards & Winter, 2013; Vincent & Christensen, 2015):

- Keep sessions short to maintain concentration.
- Use coaches and management to drive participation and gain buy-in.
- Include week-long breaks to allow for reflection and implementation.
- Utilize session facilitators possessing knowledge, familiarity, and expertise in the sport.
- Design sessions with specific parents in mind.
- Conduct sessions while children are training to reduce logistical barriers to participation.

Adding to this body of suggestions is a community case study by Dorsch, King, and colleagues (2019) offering qualitative insights from coaches, parents, and administrators around the barriers, facilitators, and desired content of sport parent education in a local community setting. Of particular importance is the need to tailor content and support based on the type of program their child is participating in (i.e., recreational vs. performance), their child's stage of development and experience in the sport, and the specific needs of parents (Newport et al., 2021; Thrower et al., 2016).

It is worth noting that only recently have more rigorous empirical interventions surfaced that have investigated whether specific educational programs with parents can enhance both their own experience of sport and that of their children. A summary of these is provided in table 5.1. As indicated in the results summary, the evaluated parent-education programs have all demonstrated some benefit for parents or children or both. However, it should be noted that, in general, participant numbers have been small. In some studies, this was a methodological decision (i.e., using a qualitative approach to gain an in-depth insight into the experiences of few parents), while in others it occurred because of the challenges of recruiting parents to either take part in the programs or to complete pre- and poststudy evaluations.

Interestingly, although there has been a growing focus on research evaluations of parent-targeted interventions, evaluations of interventions targeting individuals who work with parents (i.e., coaches, club officials, members of sport organizations) are noticeably lacking. Given that effective parent–coach relationships are consistently highlighted as an important component of optimal parental involvement (e.g., Harwood & Knight, 2015; Harwood, Knight et al., 2019; Knight & Holt, 2014) and that many suggestions have been made regarding how coaches could better engage with parents (see *International Journal of Sport Science and Coaching*, Volume 6, Issue 1, for a special issue focused on this), the lack of evidence-based and evaluated interventions, particularly targeted at coaches, is particularly surprising. Similarly, barring notable exceptions (e.g., Elliott & Drummond, 2015) critical

TABLE 5.1 A Summary of Recent Parent Education Interventions

Authors	Study design and aim	Intervention summary	Broad overview of findings
Dorsch et al. (2017)	A quasi-experimental study evaluating the impact of an evidence-based education program for parents within youth soccer	81 parents participated across three groups: a full program (18 parents), partial program (36 parents), and non-implementation (27 parents). Parents in the full program received a 33-page sport parent guide and a 45-minute sport parent seminar. Parents in the partial intervention received only the booklet. Topics covered included youth sport participation, developmental processes, communication, working with coaches, and sport parent behavior.	The children of those parents in the full implementation condition reported more support and warmth and less pressure and conflict after the intervention than those children of parents in the partial or non-implementation groups.
Thrower et al. (2017)	An organizational action research study comprising the development, implementation, and evaluation of a face-to-face parent education program for parents of junior tennis players; six 1-hour workshops for youth parents over a 12-week period	The intervention comprised six 1-hour workshops, delivered over a 12-week period. The topics included in the intervention were the importance of parents supporting their child, organizational information, child development, talent development, competition rules, and ongoing learning.	Parents reported improved knowledge and confidence in their ability to support their child and make developmental decisions. This appeared to serve as a buffer against stress and enhanced their overall experiences and enjoyment of the sport. Parents also perceived themselves to engage in more task-oriented behavior and communication with their child in competitive situations.
Thrower et al. (2019)	A convergent parallel mixed-methods design to evaluate a series of web-based educational workshops that could be digitally accessed at a parent's convenience	Similar to their face-to-face education program, the topics covered supporting their child, organizational information, child and talent development, competition roles, and continued learning and support.	Aligned with the face-to-face program findings, parents reported improved emotional experiences of competitions as well as enhanced confidence not only in their tennis-specific roles but also in their perceptions of general parenting efficacy.
Lisinskiene and Lochbaum (2019)	A 12-month intervention with 10 families (parent and child of 5-6 years old) enrolled together in a bespoke martial arts program	Parents and their children received one sport training session per week in conjunction with one sport parent educational session per month, as well as a psychological support session for parents that focused on video recorded observations of their interactions with their child in the class.	Within- and postintervention interviews with parents revealed how supporting the quality of their ongoing involvement with their child was perceived to augment parent–child attachment, the quality of the parent–child relationship, and associated improvements in social and family life.

(continued)

Table 5.1 *(continued)*

Authors	Study design and aim	Intervention summary	Broad overview of findings
Azimi and Tamminen (2020)	A qualitative study evaluating an intervention aiming to enhance parent–child communication and parental involvement	The intervention comprised one 45-minute parent education session, scaffolded by a follow-up parent guidebook that led to 6 weeks of parental reflective practice on parent–child communications in sport. The workshop included discussion about parents' roles in sport, parent–athlete interactions, parents' behavior in sport, developmental changes in parent–child communication, and preferred parental behavior.	Qualitative findings from 10 parent and child interviews underscored greater parental awareness of their communication styles and positive behavioral trends. However, quantitative data from selective inventories showed no significant pre- to postintervention changes in perceptions of parent support and pressure, parenting style, or quality of parent–child communication from either child or parent viewpoints.
Tamminen et al. (2020)	An evaluation of the Respect in Sport Parent Program (RiSPP) within the Ontario Minor Hockey Association over three seasons	The RiSPP comprises a series of educational videos (an hour in total) and supplemental material focused on a broad range of youth sport topics including setting realistic expectations, handling winning and losing, maintaining balance, injury management, managing emotions, establishing positive relationships, and creating a safe environment. This program was mandatory for parents to take as part of league participation.	Data were obtained from children whose parents had either been involved or not involved in the program. Although modest in magnitude, the authors found evidence for improved prosocial behaviors toward teammates, less antisocial behaviors toward opponents, and a trend toward positive improvements in initiative, goal setting, and cognitive skills.

evaluations of policies or practices implemented to regulate or change parents' behaviors (e.g., silent Sundays, red-carding parents, barriers around pitches and fields, parent codes of conducts), as well as activities targeting changes in the youth sport culture and perceptions of sport parents (e.g., NSPCC Parents in Sport Week), are absent from the literature. This absence is notable given that enhancing parental involvement is a priority for many sport organizations (e.g., Holt et al., 2018), and many are implementing activities and policies with parents, despite a lack of evaluation and limited underpinning evidence of their effectiveness.

Future Research Directions

Despite the sustained and substantial growth in youth sport parenting research, there remain numerous avenues for further study.

- The sport psychology literature does not adequately explain how parents can proactively contribute to their children's psychosocial development (Harwood, Knight, et al., 2019). Such research would need to account for the characteristics of parents and children and also the sport context (e.g., competitive level, coach influence).
- Lack of population diversity is a problem in sport parenting research (Knight, 2019), and it is particularly necessary to pay more attention to the culture–parenting nexus. Although there may be some universal elements of parenting cognitions and practices across cultures (Bornstein, 2012), they may be shaped by varying cultural values (see, e.g., Kagitcibasi's [2013] autonomy-relatedness framework).
- Research examining parental experiences in sport has predominantly used qualitative methods. Quantitative research can be useful for examining correlates, predictors, and outcomes of various aspects of parent-

ing. For instance, based on data from 9,367 parents, Sutcliffe and colleagues (2021) identified that parents with adolescents in youth sport reported more life stress and time pressure than parents of nonathletes. Other variables, such as socioeconomic status (SES), race or ethnicity, and access to facilities may moderate the relationship between parental mental health and child sport participation (Vella et al., 2014) and would benefit from examination.

- Another issue that requires further attention is the stability of parenting. Most sport psychology studies offer only a snapshot of parenting at a given time. There may be both stable and habitual *and* mutable (changing) patterns of parenting, influenced by parental traits and the changing needs of the child over time (Bornstein et al., 2008). Children's behaviors may reciprocally influence their parents' approach to parenting (Holt et al., 2009). Indeed, parental control tends to decrease during later adolescence (Levy-Warren, 1999). There may also be day-to-day fluctuations in parenting in sport, varying based on parents' own experiences or mood.
- There remains a need for research evaluating the effects of interventions. Some researchers have developed and evaluated sport parent education programs (e.g., Thrower et al., 2017, 2019). Others have evaluated existing community-based parent education programs (e.g., Elliott & Drummond, 2015; Tamminen et al., 2020). However, programs that go beyond efforts to inform parents about the appropriateness of particular behaviors and, instead, focus on equipping parents with knowledge and skills that can be beneficial in sport and in family life (e.g., emotional intelligence abilities; Pynn et al., 2019) are limited.

Taking a humanistic perspective of parents as valued support resources, who are well intentioned and highly capable, creates opportunities for coach–parent collaboration and effective coach–parent relationships.

- Finally, developing and evaluating interventions that target a broader range of stakeholders, rather than just parents, may be valuable. For instance, interventions focused on improving how coaches, clubs, and sport organizations support and work with parents are needed. Further, evaluating the impact cultural or environmental changes have on parents' involvement may provide valuable insights that move beyond the current focus on educating parents to improve their behaviors.

Practical Implications

As long as there are young people engaging in sport, there will be parents exerting an influence on processes and outcomes. Yet despite their pivotal roles, research in sport psychology is characterized more by studies *of* parents than *with* parents. Such an approach likely exists because researchers often have child outcomes as their focus and thus draw on theories (e.g., SDT, AGT) that position parents simply as influences in children's lives, with limited consideration of the parents themselves. Lamentably, this mirrors a societal discourse of keeping parents at arm's length by coaches and national governing bodies, of dealing with as opposed to working with parents (Harwood, Knight, et al., 2019). The applied implications from this chapter for coaches, practitioners, and organizations suggest a time for change.

All individuals who engage with parents within youth sport settings (i.e., coaches, practitioners, club officials) need information and guidance regarding the importance of integrating parents within youth sport and the complexity of parental involvement. With an enhanced appreciation of parents, practitioners and coaches should directly engage with parents to understand their background and empathize with any specific circumstances that may influence the quality of support to the child. Taking a humanistic perspective of parents as valued support resources, who are well intentioned and highly capable, creates opportunities for coach–parent collaboration and effective coach–parent relationships.

Moreover, given the complexity of sport parenting, it may be beneficial for practitioners to work with parents on developing the dimensions of sport parenting expertise proposed by Harwood and Knight (2015). Starting from an early stage of involvement in sport, practitioners (internal and external to organizations) can raise parents' awareness of the intrapersonal, interpersonal, emotional, and organizational qualities that will promulgate effective support to their child [and others] across stages of athletic development. It is clear parents experience different stressors at different stages, and their support needs change as they transition, maneuver, and pivot through the social and organizational intricacies of youth sport (Newport et al., 2021). For practitioners, this highlights the value of individualized, ongoing work with parents, distinct from or in tandem with any support that may be provided to children or coaches.

Such implications will occur only where the policies and practices of youth sport federations or governing bodies reflect the value of holistic and integrated child athlete development and duty of care. Achieving such an objective means taking a positive approach to parents and skillfully empowering them by applying the findings from academic scholarship. Such progress would bridge any research-to-practice gaps and ensure that any knowledge translation is actually used by practitioners and coaches.

Summary

Parents have a substantial, enduring impact on children's participation in organized youth sport. Moreover, through their involvement, parents can increase the likelihood that their children will experience positive or negative psychosocial and performance outcomes. However, despite attempts to create clear distinctions between good or appropriate and bad or inappropriate parental behaviors, research shows that parental involvement is far more complicated than this. How parents are involved within organized youth sport, as well as the outcomes that arise because of parents' involvement, is influenced by personal, relational, and contextual factors. Moreover, children's involvement in sport can lead to parents' experiencing changes in their thoughts, feelings, and behaviors, and parents may require support or guidance to optimize their involvement in their child's sporting lives.

DISCUSSION QUESTIONS

1. Why are researchers and practitioners concerned with parental involvement in sport?
2. Thinking about your own involvement in sport as a young athlete, how did your parents influence your experience? What could they have done to further support your development?
3. Consider your parents' experience of supporting you in sport. What situational or contextual factors do you think influenced their involvement and the support they provided to you?
4. Drawing on the research and theories that have been used to help understand parental involvement in sport, what considerations are needed to optimize parental involvement?
5. You are consulting with a sport organization regarding parental involvement. What key pieces of advice would you offer to help it maximize positive parental involvement within their sport?

PART II

Leadership in Sport

Social psychology research in sport identifies effective leadership as a central factor in athlete development and performance success. Several decades of study have provided the foundation for understanding the key components of effective leadership, and research continues to advance both theory and practice. Since the first edition of this book (published in 2007), there have been numerous advancements in sport leadership research relating to coaches as well as alternative leaders (e.g., captains). Initially, social cognitive perspectives of leadership (e.g., multidimensional model of leadership, mediational model of leadership) dominated research and practice within the sport context; more recently, transformational leadership theory and social identity approaches adapted from other fields (e.g., business, military) have been applied to sport research. Further, earlier research focused predominantly on the coach or team manager as a source of leadership, whereas more recent studies have explored diverse leadership roles embedded within sport settings (e.g., parents, peers, mentors, officials). In team settings there are several individuals who may serve in a leadership position; in particular, the influence of athlete leadership has gained wider recognition. Part II of this volume comprises four independent yet related chapters that collectively highlight the development of leadership theory, research, and practice in sport.

In chapter 6, Foundations of Sport Leadership, Sebastian Harenberg and Harold Riemer present an overview of the history and concept of sport leadership that have provided the basis for two foundational and fundamental models for the study of leadership in sport—namely, the multidimensional model of coach leadership and the mediational model of leadership. The main components and propositions of these models are presented, with a comprehensive overview of the measurement tools used in the associated research. The multidimensional and mediational models are noted as important milestones in developing understanding of sport leadership; they have served as a foundation for theory building and facilitated advances in research. Although the models presented in this chapter are well established and extensively tested, the authors conclude that further study using these models still offers promising lines of research. Suggestions for future research are put forward, and practical implications of the current research findings are discussed.

In chapter 7, Transformational Leadership in Sport, Jennifer Turnnidge and Adam Kelly present transformational leadership theory as a framework to study leadership in sport. The main dimensions of transformational leadership are highlighted, with a comprehensive overview of the current research landscape as it pertains to the role of transformational leadership for athlete development and across various social agents (e.g., coaches, parents, peers, and officials). Turnnidge and Kelly provide a detailed discussion of the diverse methodologies that feature in current research and outline potential tools for use in future studies extending across a range of research directions. The chapter identifies practical implications of the research and highlights the need for researchers and practitioners to work together to advance understanding of transformational leadership among a diverse range of sport leaders.

In chapter 8, The Social Identity Approach to Leadership, Matthew Slater and Anthony Miller contend that sport leadership can be well served by considering a group dynamic perspective that appreciates togetherness. This chapter presents a concise overview of the principles of the social identity approach to leadership; it compares and contrasts aspects of social identity with other approaches to the study of sport leadership and critically discusses issues surrounding measurement. Slater and Miller discuss the growing interest of empirical studies investigating the social identity approach to leadership in sport; they put forward proposed avenues for future research endeavors as well as practical recommendations for those who wish to develop their leadership skills.

In chapter 9, Athlete Leadership in Sport, Todd Loughead, Krista Munroe-Chandler, Katherine Hirsch, and Matthieu Boisvert highlight the role and importance of athlete leadership. Previous chapters in this volume identify coaches as the central source of leadership within their teams; however, they are not athletes' sole source of leadership. Athletes also seek assistance from their teammates; therefore, athletic peers are an important source of leadership within team settings. This chapter offers a clear definition of athlete leadership as well as a precise overview of the conceptual frameworks and models used to guide research. In particular, the working ecological model for the study of athlete leadership is presented. Methods used to assess athlete leadership are outlined together with a detailed discussion of existing research endeavors. The chapter concludes with suggested directions for future research and proposed recommendations for fostering athlete leadership; this includes recommendations for the implementation of athlete leadership development programs and peer mentoring.

6

Foundations of Sport Leadership

Sebastian Harenberg, PhD, and Harold Riemer, PhD

LEARNING OBJECTIVES

On completion of this chapter, the reader should have the following:

- Understanding of the definitions and history of the study of leadership in sport
- Knowledge of the tenets of two foundational models of leadership in sport
- A comprehensive overview of the research associated with each model
- Understanding of the limitations and future research directions associated with these models

Regardless of culture or context, a coach's leadership is often seen as a critical component in determining an athlete's or team's success. In fact, in most organizational environments, leadership is considered a major factor in effectiveness and performance (Bormann et al., 2016; Fransen et al., 2020). While sport participants and fans see a direct connection between leadership and performance, many would be unable to articulate what it takes to be an effective leader (other than the fact that they win). This chapter examines some of the theory and research associated with sport-related leadership.

As a preface to a sport-specific discussion about leadership, a brief overview of the concept is worthwhile. We begin with a look at the common elements of almost every formal definition of leadership.

First, leadership generally takes place in organizations (e.g., a team, a club), and leaders must therefore deal with *individuals* as well as *groups of individuals*. Both individual and group dynamics are in play. Second, leadership involves *behaviors*; leaders mold, change, or direct individuals, and as such, leadership is always about what a leader actually does. Third, leadership requires *human interaction*, which, in turn, is predicated upon *effective communication*. Finally, leadership is always focused on moving an individual or group in a *particular direction*; the leader seeks to influence and motivate others toward goal achievement.

Taken together, leaders do a great deal. They ensure the team meets the expectations of the organization they are a part of (e.g., the franchise, the athletic department, the sport federation). Leaders increase each individual's, and the group's, productivity or performance. Leaders focus on individual and group satisfaction, help shape individual and team objectives and goals, and work to build or maintain group or organizational culture. Most of these aspects are captured in the plethora of definitions of leadership. For example, Barrow (1977) views leadership as "a behavioral process of influencing individuals or groups towards set goals" (p. 232). Similarly, Northouse (2007) defined leadership as "a process whereby an individual influences a group of individuals to achieve common goals" (p. 3).

Historical Perspectives

The scholarly disciplines of management and organizational psychology have a rich tradition of leadership research. Theory and research in sport have built on this knowledge. Early work in the area focused on leadership styles and specific behaviors that result in effective leadership (e.g., Kurt Lewin's work: Lewin et al., 1939; work in the 1950s and '60s at Ohio State University: Hemphill, 1950; Halpin & Winer, 1957; at the University of Michigan: Katz & Kahn, 1951; and at Harvard University: Bales & Slater, 1955). Out of this body of work, we came to understand (1) that how a leader makes decisions is important and (2) that ensuring the task is completed while taking the needs of individual team members into account is critical to leadership success.

Building on this early research, four theoretical frameworks formed the foundation for much of our current understanding and research on leadership:

- Fiedler's (1967) model of leadership effectiveness suggested that any leadership style or behavior could be effective as long as it matched the situation, and that it was often easier to adapt the situation to fit the leader rather than try to make the leader adapt to the situation.
- Evan's (1970) and House's (1971; House & Dressler, 1974) *path-goal theory of leadership* was built on Vroom's (1964) *expectancy theory* (i.e., individuals are motivated to pursue a particular behavior because they expect it will lead to a valued outcome). House argued that a leader's role was to motivate team members to pursue organizational goals by clarifying team goal accomplishments to result in outcomes valued by the individual team members. House's major contribution was to show that different team members required different approaches to leadership.
- Osborn and Hunt's (1975) *adaptive-reactive theory of leadership* focuses on how the organization in which the team or group functions affects both the leader and the individual team members. Fundamentally, leaders have to balance organizational demands (i.e., adapt) with those of the individual or group (i.e., react).
- Yukl's (1971) *discrepancy model of leadership* contributed some important understandings. He conceptualized key concepts (i.e., decision making, task-focused leadership, and person-focused leadership) as independent of each other. In other words, Yukl argued it was possible to have "benevolent autocrats" and "malevolent democrats" (p. 419). In addition, Yukl suggested satisfaction with leadership was governed by the difference between a team member's preference for a particular leadership approach and the individual's actual experience with the leader. A person's preferences were determined by their personality and various situational variables (i.e., importance of a decision to a member, level of commitment to group goals). Finally, Yukl argued that leaders affect group performance levels by influencing a team member's motivation, their skill development and acquisition, and the quality of the decisions made by the leader.

Other contributions to our understanding of leadership include *transactional or exchange leadership* (e.g., Burns, 1978; Bass, 1985) and *transformational leadership* (Bass, 1985). Transactional leadership focuses on exchange relationships between the leader and the team member, or the team as a whole: "transactional leaders give followers something they want in exchange for something the leaders want" (e.g., athletic scholarship, a supportive environment, respect for the athlete's abilities) (Kuhnert & Lewis, 1987, p. 649). The major contribution of transactional approaches to leadership is that mutual need dependence is necessary for success (Kellerman, 1984).

Transformational leadership (Bass, 1985) suggests that effective leaders connect with their individuals and teams as a whole in a unique way that results in extraordinary individual and group performance (Yammarino et al., 1997). Note that transformational leadership is similar to *new leadership* (Bryman, 1992), *visionary leadership* (Sashkin, 1988), and *charismatic leadership* (Conger, 1989). Such leadership sees individuals adopt the goals or vision of the team, organization, or leader as their own; team members tend to be motivated by higher-order needs (as outlined by Maslow, 1943, and others), and they perform well above what is expected. Highly successful coaches have often been described in terms suggesting they may be transformational (e.g., convincing athletes to adopt a particular vision, goal, strategy, or tactic as their own, or to buy into the system). Consequently, transformational leadership has been a central construct of sport leadership research for decades (see chapter 7 in this book).

To some extent, all of the foundational ideas about leadership have found their way into the more sport-specific models of leadership. We would even suggest most of those ideas are consistent with the average sport psychology student's view of important ideas when it comes to explaining effective leadership. In the following pages, we explore two of the most popular theoretical approaches to sport leadership: Chelladurai's (1980) *multidimensional model of leadership (MML)* and Smoll and Smith's (1989) *mediational model of leadership (MEDM)*. For detailed exploration of other sport-related approaches to leadership, please see chapters 7, 8, and 9.

The Multidimensional Model of Leadership (MML)

The multidimensional model of leadership (MML) has three basic elements:

- Antecedents of leader behaviors
- Leader behaviors
- Outcomes of leader behaviors

Before examining each of these elements in more detail, a short overview of the central proposition of the model would be useful; an illustration is shown in figure 6.1. The model's central hypothesis (often referred to as the *congruence/discrepancy hypothesis*) suggests that a team's performance and the individual athlete's level of satisfaction are a function of the extent to which a leader's actual leadership behavior is *congruent* with (i.e., consistent with, not discrepant with, or not different from) the preferred leadership behavior of the athlete and the requirements and constraints placed on leader behavior (arrows 1, 2, and 3). This relationship is generally thought to be positive. That is, the more a leader's actual behavior matches both the athlete's preferred types of behaviors and the behaviors required of the leader given the particular situation, the greater the levels of performance and satisfaction are expected to be. Other model propositions are detailed later in the chapter.

Let's continue our look at the model by providing more detail about the three key elements. We begin with the antecedents of leader behaviors: *situational* and *personal characteristics* of the athletes and coach. Situational characteristics refer to the *contextual* and *environmental* influences on a leader or team member in any given context. For example, a struggling team will require different leadership than a successful one, and the environmental demands or constraints of a professional franchise would be very different from those of a local sport club

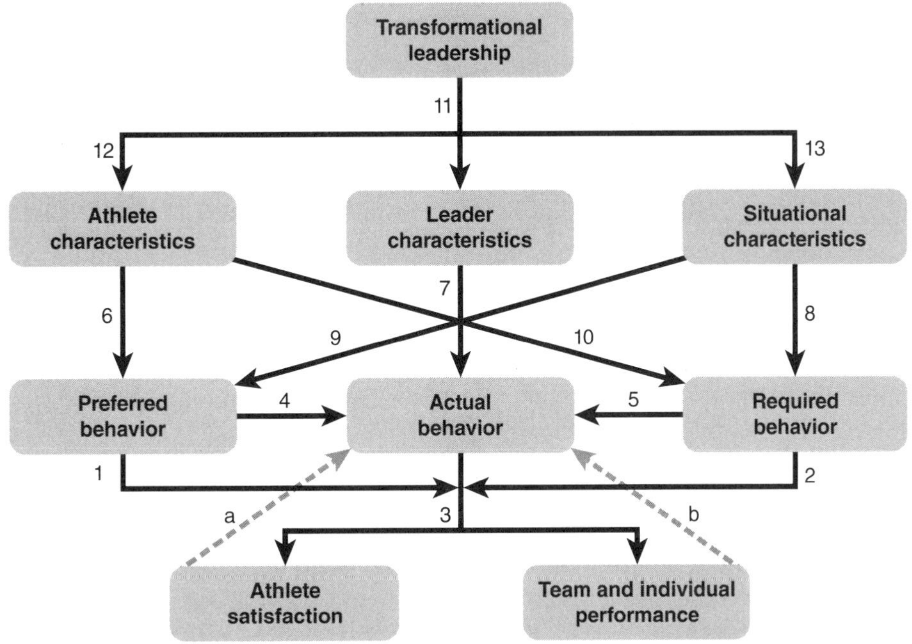

FIGURE 6.1 The multidimensional model of leadership by Chelladurai (1980).

Adapted by permission from P. Chelladurai, *Managing Organization for Sport and Physical Activity: A Systems Perspective* (Scottsdale, AZ: Holcomb-Hathaway, 2001). © P. Chelladurai.

made up of U15 athletes. The *athletes' characteristics* would include their individual personalities, their task-related resources (e.g., ability, skill), and the expectations individual members have of the team and the coach. It's reasonable to expect that differential levels in any of the noted characteristics would want or need a different type of leadership (e.g., male teams often have differing expectations of their coach than do teams of females). Finally, *leader characteristics* (e.g., personality, abilities, experience, expectations) are also important. For example, we would expect that new leaders would bring very different expectations and skills to the group than a seasoned and veteran leader would. To some extent, all of these characteristics (i.e., situational, the athlete's, and the coach's) may be influenced by certain leadership behaviors, in particular, transformational leadership (and arguably servant leadership as well) (arrows 11, 12, and 13). Recall that transformational leadership is thought to cause transformative change at the individual, group, and even organizational levels.

The second element of the model concerns *leader behaviors*. Preferred behavior refers to the type of leadership desired by the individual members of the team or group. Note that athlete characteristics and situational requirements (arrows 6 and 9) influence these preferences. For example, more experienced athletes may prefer to be treated differently from those who are new to the sport or group (Chelladurai & Carron, 1983). Required behaviors represent expected behaviors determined largely by situational factors and are influenced by characteristics of the situation and of the athletes or team (arrows 8 and 10). For example, what a leader does just before a final playoff game for the league championship will likely be different from their behaviors prior to the very first exhibition game of the season. Actual behavior is effectively how a coach or leader leads through actions, behaviors, and style. That bundle of behaviors is influenced primarily by the characteristics (including experiences) of the leader (arrow 7).

The final element of the model is the *outcomes*. The model proposes two primary outcomes (i.e., athlete satisfaction, performance); however, other important outcomes (e.g., coach–athlete relationship, team culture, climate) may be included. The model proposes that the outcomes are a function of the interaction between preferred, actual, and required behaviors (arrows 1, 2, and 3) (i.e., the extent to which they are congruent or aligned; refer to the central hypothesis).

In addition to the central hypothesis noted previously, the MML makes several other propositions about how the various behaviors interact:

- First, how a leader leads (or a coach coaches) depends on their understanding of the preferences (expectations) of the individual team members (and the collective), as well as the leader's perceptions of the constraints imposed by the situation in which the group is operating (arrows 4 and 5). If the situation allows, knowledge about the athletes' preferred leadership approach may help the coach adjust their actual behaviors to align more closely with those expectations.
- The MML anticipates an interaction between the characteristics of the coach, the team members, and the situation as influencing (i.e., predicting) what the preferred, actual, and required leadership behaviors might be. At its core, the model views expectations, requirements, and displayed leadership behavior as dynamic and dependent on the interplay of various antecedents.
- The leader will receive feedback from the outcomes (e.g., athlete satisfaction, performance, climate) that may be used to adjust actual leadership behavior as required (arrows a and b).
- The model also proposes that a transformational leader (and the behaviors that accompany that sort of leadership) changes athletes, the coaching staff, and even the situation (arrows 11, 12, and 13). Coaches may adopt transformational leadership qualities, which may significantly influence the leader's own values and purpose in coaching. Through transformational leadership, a coach may change the vision of a team or organization and also influence values, traditions, and culture. As such, transformational leadership may influence a variety of the situational characteristics. Transformational coaches are thought to instill trust in their athletes and are likely to influence the characteristics of athletes as well. We would argue that servant leadership has the ability to influence the model in a similar manner. Those interested in a greater understanding of the role of transformational leadership can look to chapter 7 of this textbook. Those interested in more information about servant leadership might begin by reading

an essay by Robert Greenleaf (1970), "The Servant as Leader."

Measurement

Research tied to the MML often makes use of the Leadership Scale for Sports (LSS; Chelladuari & Saleh, 1980), a self-reported Likert-type instrument that measures the perceptions of and preferences for five leadership behaviors on 40 items:

1. *Training and instruction* describes behaviors intended to improve performance by developing athletes' physical and mental skills.
2. *Democratic behavior* measures the extent to which a coach lets athletes participate in decision making.
3. *Autocratic behavior* can be viewed as the polar opposite of democratic behavior (i.e., the coach's exclusion of athletes from decision making and emphasis on authority).
4. *Social support* describes the behavior focusing on athletes' interpersonal needs.
5. *Positive feedback* is the extent to which a coach acknowledges and compliments a player's performance.

Response options are as follows: never, seldom (25% of the time), occasionally (50% of the time), often (75% of the time), and always. Research has demonstrated the validity and reliability of the LSS (for an overview, see Chelladurai & Riemer, 1998). The scale has been translated into various languages. Although the 40-item scale is widely used, shorter versions have recently been published (Teques et al., 2020). The reliability and validity of the abbreviated versions have yet to be demonstrated.

Research Associated With the MML

The MML has been the theoretical foundation for hundreds of studies. Most of this research has evaluated (1) the relationship between the antecedents (i.e., characteristics of the athlete, situation, and leader) and perceptions of leader behavior or (2) the impact of leader behavior on outcomes. In the following sections, we look at the impact of specific antecedents on leaders' perceptions as well as the impact of leadership on a variety of outcomes.

Athlete Characteristics

Investigations into the link between athlete characteristics and leader behaviors have tended to focus on several factors. Historically, the most commonly researched characteristic is biological sex (i.e., male vs. female), with mixed results. Several studies have reported that male athletes preferred autocratic behavior compared with female athletes (e.g., Chelladurai & Saleh, 1978; Pitts et al., 2018; Riemer & Toon, 2001; Wang, 1997). Pitts and colleagues (2018) also reported that females tended to prefer positive feedback, although the actual differences were relatively small. Riemer and Toon (2001) reported that female athletes preferred more social support compared with male athletes. Other studies have reported no differences based on sex (e.g., Terry & Howe, 1984).

Several explanations for the mixed findings are possible. First, the differences were based on biological sex rather than gender; using a gender continuum may add a different perspective since preferences may be more tied to masculine or feminine traits—these traits are not restricted or tied to a person's biology. Riemer and Toon (2001) also argued that very few studies have considered the gender (sex) of the coach in this context as well. Accordingly, Pfeffer and Gallitschke (2008) showed that female soccer athletes who were coached by a male coach perceived more democratic behavior, social support, and positive feedback compared with female athletes who were coached by a female coach. The authors suspected that the differences may be explained by perceived role expectations and norms. In particular, female coaches may gravitate toward the gender-typical culture within a sport, which is often more masculine.

Another important characteristic is the maturity or age of an athlete. Hersey and Blanchard (1969) argued that leaders need to adapt their leadership behaviors to the maturity level of those on their team or in their work group. Maturity was defined as "the capacity to set high but attainable goals, willingness and ability to take responsibility, and education and/or experience of an individual or group" (p. 161). Chelladurai and Carron (1983) applied this perspective to sport by hypothesizing that younger and less athletically mature athletes would prefer high levels of relationship-oriented behaviors while older and more mature athletes would prefer low levels of such behaviors. They also suggested that task-oriented leadership behaviors (e.g., training and instruction; positive feedback) would become more important (i.e., preferred) as one moved from athletic immaturity through midlevel maturity and then decrease in importance again for those who were very mature (i.e., a curvilinear relationship, or inverted U). Maturity has been operationalized by researchers in a variety of ways: age, experience, and level of competition.

- *Age.* Terry and Howe (1984) reported no significant relationship between age and leadership preferences in their sample of intercollegiate and sport-club athletes. However, Serpa (1990) reported that younger female Portuguese basketball players (aged 12-15) preferred less autocratic behavior and more social support and democratic behavior than did their older counterparts (aged 17-29). No significant differences between the age groups were found for training and instruction and positive-feedback behaviors.
- *Experience.* Erle (1981) found that athletes with more experience in their sport indicated a greater preference for positive feedback, while Chelladurai and Carron (1983) observed a greater preference for autocratic behavior and social support among those with more experience.
- *Competitive level.* Terry and Howe (1984) reported that elite athletes preferred more democratic behavior and social support and less positive feedback than did sport-club athletes. Riemer and Toon (2001) also reported that athletes with more ability (playing at a higher competitive level, such as National Collegiate Athletic Association [NCAA] Division I vs. Division III) preferred less positive feedback than those with less ability. It is worth noting that in their 1983 study, Chelladurai and Carron operationalized athletic maturity using (1) competitive level (i.e., high school midget, high school junior, high school senior, and university intercollegiate basketball players), (2) years of experience playing basketball, and (3) age. In all three instances the results were essentially the same. First, a statistically significant linear trend for social-support (relationship-oriented) behavior was found. That is, preferences increased for this behavior as maturity level, experience, and age increased. Second, in the case of training and instruction (i.e., task-oriented leadership), preferences decreased from the high school midget group (i.e., 14-15 years of age) through the high school senior group (i.e., 18-19 years of age), and then increased again among university athletes (i.e., 18-24 years of age). A similar trend was seen when age and experience were the independent variables. These findings were inconsistent with the hypotheses proposed by Chelladurai and Carron (1978) and Hersey and Blanchard (1969).

However, from a big picture perspective, all the results suggest that preferences an athlete has for a particular leadership behavior do change as an athlete matures (regardless of how you define maturity). The preference for positive feedback (i.e., the focus on task-related behaviors) seems to decrease and the preference for social support (i.e., a focus on relationship behaviors) increases with maturity. While the results associated with training and instruction were mixed, this type of behavior was generally one of the most preferred across groups.

Preferences an athlete has for a particular leadership behavior do change as an athlete matures (regardless of how you define maturity).

Another individual characteristic that has been examined is motivation orientation. Erle (1981) reported that task-motivated individuals (i.e., those focused on improvement relative to previous performances) preferred more training and instruction behavior, while affiliation-motivated athletes (i.e., concerned with the maintenance of happy relationships within the group; Ball & Carron, 1976) and extrinsically motivated athletes (i.e., undertaking behaviors to attain an end state separate from the actual behavior; Vallerand & Ratelle, 2002) preferred more social-support behavior. Similarly, Chelladurai and Carron's (1981) research suggested that athletes exhibiting a high need for information and structure in the environment (i.e., cognitive structure) prefer more training and instruction behavior and less autocratic behavior than those who are low on this particular need. They also reported that athletes high on the trait of impulsivity (tendency to be impulsive) preferred more social support than those low on this trait.

Situational Characteristics

The most commonly examined situational characteristic is task type. In particular, authors have looked at leadership perceptions in interdependent (e.g., football, hockey) versus independent (e.g., track, tennis) sports or activities. Building on House's (1971) work, Chelladurai and Saleh (1978) suggested task dependency (i.e., does success depend on working with others) and task variability (i.e., the variability of the external environment during a game or performance) would influence leadership preferences. Specifically, interdependent- and open-sport athletes (e.g., soccer) would prefer more training and instruction and positive feedback than those involved in independent and closed sports (e.g., 100 m sprint), and independent-sport athletes would prefer more democratic and social-support behavior and less autocratic behavior.

The research examining this proposed connection between the nature of the task and leadership has produced interesting results:

- Chelladurai and Saleh (1978) reported that interdependent- and closed-sport athletes (e.g., rowing, synchronized swimming) preferred the greatest levels of training and instruction (inconsistent with the theory).
- Terry and Howe (1984) reported that independent-sport athletes preferred more democratic and less autocratic behavior than interdependent-sport athletes (consistent with the theory).
- Terry and Howe (1984) and Kang (2003) also found that athletes in team sports (i.e., greater task dependence) preferred more training and instruction and positive feedback than individual-sport athletes (consistent with the theory).
- Kang (2003) reported individual-sport athletes (i.e., less task dependence) preferred more democratic behavior than did team-sport athletes (consistent with the theory).
- Pyun and colleagues (2010) reported no differences between interdependent and independent sports (inconsistent with the theory), but when biological sex was considered as a mediator, the nature of the task influenced leadership preferences.

Taken together, the research has generally shown that the nature of the task does affect preferences for leadership. The more recent work suggests that the impact of the task on preferences may be more complicated than previously thought; other individual or group characteristics may interact with (i.e., moderate or mediate) the nature of the task to influence preferences for leadership behavior.

A second situational characteristic of interest has been the role culture may play on leadership preferences. Terry and Howe (1984) investigated the preferences of elite athletes and found no differences based on country of origin. However, the authors noted that the majority of athletes participating in the research were from countries that shared similar cultural backgrounds and philosophies of sport (e.g., Canada, Great Britain, and the United States).

Chelladurai and colleagues (1988) argued that two different perspectives might explain Terry and Howe's results:

- First, that culture (defined as "attitudes, beliefs, and values of a society"; see Fayerweather, 1959, p. 7) influences a coach's leadership behaviors. If cultures differ significantly, one would also anticipate leadership behaviors to differ.
- The concept of (industrial) *convergence* describes when the process of industrialization forces organizations, regardless of the type of cultural, political, or economic system they operate in, to perform and compete (e.g., make a profit, outperform competitors). The organizations have a tendency to adopt similar designs and management structures (e.g., Child & Tayeb, 1983; Pascale, 1978). Chelladurai and colleagues (1988) argued that this perspective would suggest that "coaches and athletes from different cultures would have similar behavioral dispositions since they are involved in athletics, which are also governed by performance requirements" (p. 376). To test the explanations would necessitate the comparison of two cultures that are sufficiently different from each other.

Chelladurai and colleagues (1988) did this when they compared the leadership preferences of Japanese and Canadian university physical education students. Overall, Japanese students preferred more supportive leadership. Interestingly, Japanese students who participated in Western sports (i.e., volleyball, basketball) preferred more democratic behavior than Canadians, while those Japanese students who participated in Eastern sports (i.e., judo, kendo) preferred a more aloof and authoritarian leadership style than both Canadians and Japanese students of Western sport. The results indicate that culture and sport type affect leadership preferences and that sport type moderates cultural influences (Chelladurai, 1993). However, we would suggest that sport type may be influenced by its culture of origin.

In summary, all the studies indicate that culture does influence leadership preferences. More importantly, sport type (i.e., where sport originates, task variability, task dependence) and competitive orientation of the participants interact with culture to influence leadership preferences. This is certainly consistent with the information in the previous section about athlete characteristics.

Leader Characteristics

While much of the MML-related research has focused on athlete or sport-setting characteristics, and their impact on reported preferences for leadership behavior, less research has looked at the connection between certain coaching or leadership characteristics and how that might influence an athlete's perceptions of the leader's coaching-related behaviors. This may be a function of the more recent development of measurement tools to assess specific leader characteristics thought to influence perceptions and leadership behaviors.

Anderson (2018) explored whether a coach's *passion* was related to perceptions of leadership. In particular, she found that harmonious passion (e.g., autonomous engagement in an activity) was a significant predictor of leadership behaviors, while obsessive passion (e.g., the feeling of being compelled to do an activity) was not. Anderson's work indicates that adaptive rather than maladaptive personality traits may facilitate positive coaching behavior. The influence of the coach's personality is captured in a quote from former NHL hockey player Mark Messier: "The team often will take the personality of the coach." In other words, players may identify with certain personality characteristics in the coach's leadership behavior and potentially adopt those traits. However, more research in this area is clearly warranted to confirm these suggestions.

Cruz and Kim (2017) examined the influence of the coach's biological sex on the leadership preferences in elementary and high school badminton players. The authors found that male athletes with female coaches preferred more democratic behavior, autocratic behavior, and social support than male players with male coaches. Female players with male coaches preferred more democratic behavior, autocratic behavior, and social support than female players with female coaches. While the findings of the study were significant, most differences were rather small. Nonetheless, the findings may indicate that a coach's sex is an important factor, particularly when coaching athletes of the opposite sex. These results were consistent with the findings of Riemer and Toon (2001), who found an interaction effect (between the sex of the coach and the sex of the athlete) that influences preferences.

In summary, the characteristics of the coach may influence leader behaviors. To date, only a few studies have explored this topic, leaving the potential for more investigation. For example, countries differ in coaching philosophies. Consequently, coaches from different ethnic and national backgrounds may show different leader behaviors. Other psychological characteristics may also be worth exploring (e.g., different levels of competitiveness of coaches). Clearly more research in this area is warranted.

Outcomes

The central proposition of the MML is that if an athlete's preferences for leadership behavior(s), the behaviors required of the coach by the organization, and the actual behavior demonstrated by the leader all align (i.e., are congruent), greater levels of athlete satisfaction and performance will result. This is also called the congruence hypothesis. To date, no research has evaluated this complex premise in its entirety. Rather, most researchers have focused on certain elements of the hypothesis by examining, primarily, the effect of the interaction between preferences for leadership behaviors with actual leadership behavior (the latter measured through athlete perceptions of a coach's leadership) on satisfaction.

Older studies (Chelladurai, 1984; Horne & Carron, 1985; Schliesman, 1987) evaluated the impact of the interaction (i.e., the congruence) by measuring the difference between preference for, and perceptions of, leadership behavior (referred to as discrepancy scores). The results were very inconsistent and failed to provide clear evidence whether this part of the congruence hypothesis should be confirmed or rejected.

There are several possible explanations for the inconsistencies. Riemer and Chelladurai (1995) argued that the calculation of difference or discrepancy scores is problematic for the statistical evaluation of the congruence hypothesis and proposed that interaction values between perceived and preferred scores (i.e., a person's perception score multiplied by the preference score) would be a better approach. Moreover, Riemer and Toon (2001) added that most studies examining the congruence hypothesis have employed single-item measures of the outcome variable (i.e., satisfaction or performance), which makes it difficult to tease out specific relationships. For example, alignment of a coach's behavior with an athlete's preferences, say, for training and instruction behavior may not result in greater satisfaction when only overall satisfaction is measured. Riemer and Toon (2001) go on to note the following:

> The lack of evidence for the congruence hypothesis does not negate it. Its validity might be a function of situational conditions (e.g., task variability, task dependency, team size etc.) or how actual behaviour is operationalized. The absence of a congruence effect might also have resulted from the combination of a relatively small sample size and conservative treatment of the data—an effect was present but not detected. (p. 252)

Since the MML suggests there are a variety of antecedents for athlete preferences, coach behavior, and required behavior, it is not inconsistent that congruence would be affected in some way by the situational conditions or individual characteristics. Moreover, as noted previously, no one has attempted to evaluate the entirety of the congruence hypothesis in a single study. This is likely for at least two reasons. First, it is difficult to operationalize (and adequately measure) all of the elements (preferences, actual behavior, organization or situational requirements). Second, given the complexity, the sample size would need to be substantial, particularly since some of the outcome measures (in the case of performance in particular) would require group-level analysis.

Association of Leader Behaviors With Outcomes

A large body of literature has connected leadership with various adaptive group outcomes. The central outcomes listed in Chelladurai's MML are athlete satisfaction and performance, which we review now.

Satisfaction

Generally, all dimensions of leadership, except autocratic behavior, have been associated with athlete satisfaction in several studies (Chelladurai et al., 1988; McMillin, 1990). Other studies showed individual dimensions of leadership (e.g., positive feedback, social support; Dwyer & Fischer, 1990; Weiss & Friedrichs, 1986) to be associated with athlete satisfaction. In addition, Dwyer and Fischer (1990) showed that autocratic behavior was a negative predictor of athlete satisfaction.

To summarize the findings, Kim and Cruz (2016) conducted a meta-analysis on the relationship between leadership and satisfaction. The authors combined the evidence from 11 studies with a total sample size of 2,492 athletes. Most of the studies were conducted in a collegiate setting. The meta-analysis confirmed that all dimensions of leadership, with the exception of autocratic behavior, were positively associated with satisfaction. The authors followed up their analysis by examining biological sex as a moderator. Interestingly, the association between leader behaviors and satisfaction was substantially larger in female athletes than in male athletes. The authors attributed the difference in effect to female athletes' preference for leader behaviors (e.g., positive feedback, social support) that are typically associated with higher athlete satisfaction. This was the first study to examine biological sex as a moderator in the leadership–satisfaction relationship, so more research is needed to confirm the findings.

Performance

Compared with satisfaction, far less research has examined the link between leadership and performance. To a certain extent this is ironic because athletic performance, particularly in competitive sport, is considered a key responsibility of coaches. Evidence for the leadership–performance link is mixed. Weiss and Friedrichs (1986) found that perceived social support was the strongest negative predictor of a team's win–loss record. The greater the perception of social support, the lower the record of performance. Horne and Carron (1985) reported that as perceptions of positive feedback increased, so did athletes' perceptions of their own level of subjective performance.

Moen and colleagues (2014) demonstrated that athletes who were more satisfied with their performance progress (note: we could argue that this is really satisfaction rather than performance) rated their coaches higher in all leadership dimensions. The only exception was autocratic behavior, which might be because of the directive nature of this behavior. Garland and Barry (1988) defined performance based on playing time (i.e., regulars, substitutes, survivors). While all five dimensions of leadership behavior were found to be significant predictors of performance, lower levels of performance were associated with higher perceptions of autocratic behavior. This finding was consistent with Robinson and Carron's (1982) work, which reported that less successful players perceived their coaches as being more autocratic.

Several researchers have compared members of winning and losing teams in an effort to operationalize performance. Gordon (1988) compared players' perceptions of leadership behavior from successful and unsuccessful university soccer teams. Members of the successful teams perceived greater levels of training and instruction, autocratic behavior, social support, and positive feedback. However, Serpa and colleagues (1991) reported that members of the first-place team at the 1988 world championships perceived greater levels of autocratic behavior and less positive feedback, social support, and democratic behavior than did players from the last-place team.

Taken together, there are some indications that leader behaviors may be associated with performance. Yet the findings should be interpreted with caution because performance is difficult to conceptualize and quantify. As we noted, most research has focused on playing time, win-loss records, and perceptions of performance progress as an indicator. However, those approaches provide, at best, a limited picture of what performance is. This is particularly true in a team-sport context, where both individual and group-level performance are present (i.e., an individual can have a great performance but the team still loses).

There are some indications that leader behaviors may be associated with performance. Yet the findings should be interpreted with caution because performance is difficult to conceptualize and quantify.

A more comprehensive theoretical approach, paired with one or more validated measurement tools, would bring more clarity with regard to this outcome. Karreman and colleagues (2015) initiated some work to conceptualize performance as a theoretical construct. Yet a validated and reliable tool to measure a theoretical model of athletic performance remains absent from the literature. Another challenge related to the use of performance as an outcome is the complexity of analysis involved; it generally would require both individual and group-level analysis (and by extension, a very large sample). Continued work in this area will enhance our abilities to better understand the true impact of leadership on performance.

Mediational Model of Leadership (MEDM)

At the heart of the mediational model of leadership (MEDM, see figure 6.2) (Smoll & Smith, 1989; Smoll et al., 1977) are three simple elements: coaching behaviors (i.e., what the coach actually does), athletes' perception and recall (i.e., how coaching behaviors are perceived and recalled), and athletes' evaluative reactions (e.g., attitudes toward the coach and the sport). The model suggests that the relationship between coaching behaviors and athletes' evaluative reactions is mediated by athletes' perceptions and recall, which are made up of affective-cognitive processes (e.g., motivation for participation). Smith and Smoll (1984) expanded the model to include more complex antecedents of basic building blocks. Among those are the characteristics of the coach (e.g., goals, experience, gender) and the athlete (e.g., age, gender) as well as situational factors (e.g., practice vs. game, playoffs vs. regular season). Finally, the coach's perception of the athletes' attitudes also mediates the coach's behavior(s), as well as the athlete's reactions to those behaviors. The model notes how the primary variables are influenced by various antecedents; reciprocal relationships between variables are also a feature of the model (see figure 6.2).

Coach's Individual Difference Variables

Smoll and Smith (1989) argued that a coach's goals and behavioral intentions (i.e., cognitive decisions preceding actual behavior) account for the differences in coaching behavior. Examined in the work of Vroom (1964) and others, goals and intentions are believed to flow from instrumentalities. Instrumentalities in this context refer to the product of (1) an individual's perceptions of the probability of a particular behavior's leading to a particular outcome or future state and (2) the value (i.e., valence) a person assigns to that particular outcome or future state. They are thought to be most predictive of how a coach intends to coach. That is, if a particular historical behavior has consistently resulted in a particular outcome the coach values (or does not value at all), the historical behavior is likely to occur again (or not occur). For example, a coach may follow a specific sequence of instruction to teach specific tactical behavior (e.g., zone defense in basketball). If the coach deems that this sequence was instructed well and fulfilled its purpose, the coach is likely to reuse the sequence. Smith and colleagues (1977) reported a moderate correlation between instrumentalities and coaching behavior. Interestingly, an association with observed

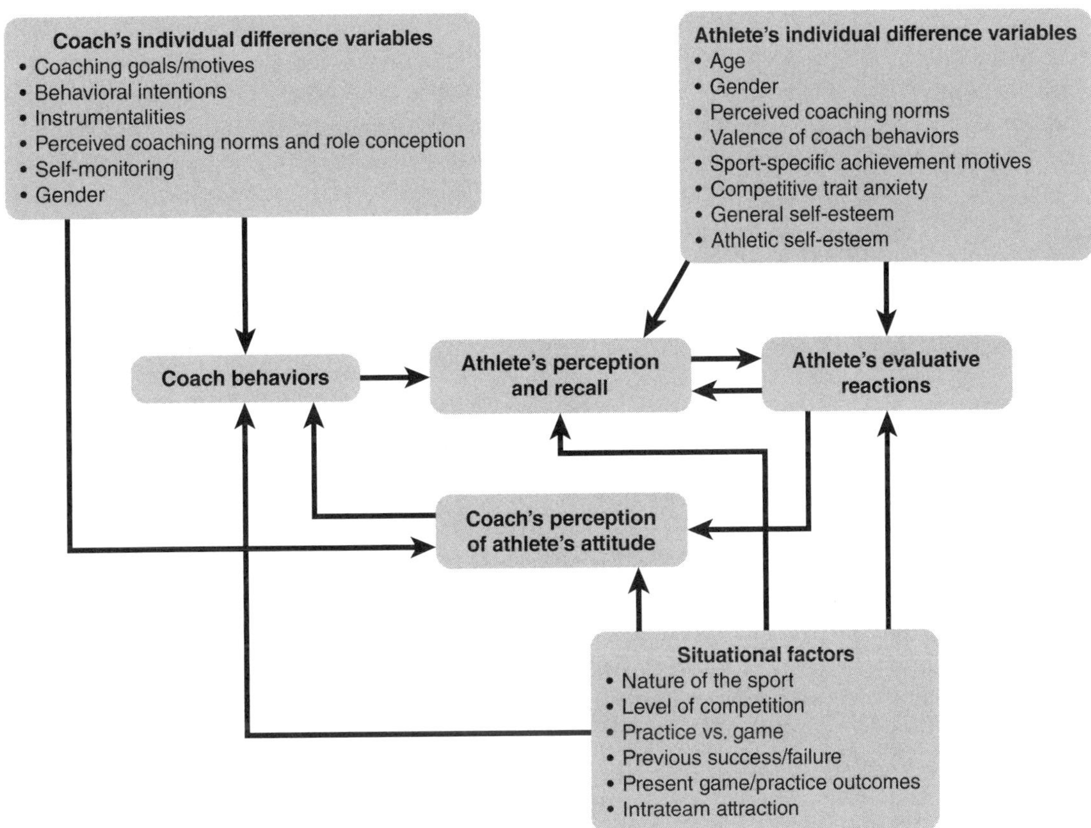

FIGURE 6.2 Mediational model of leadership (Smoll & Smith, 1989).

Adapted by permission from F.L. Smoll and R.E. Smith, "Leadership Research in Youth Sports," in *Psychological Foundations of Sport*, edited by J.M. Silva and R.S. Weinberg (Champaign, IL: Human Kinetics, 1984), 383.

or athlete-perceived leader behavior was not found, which warrants future investigation.

Smoll and colleagues (1977) also believe that social factors play a role in determining these behavioral intentions—in particular, the conceptions a leader has of the coaching role and the leader's perceptions of the norms associated with their coaching role. For example, not every coach sees their responsibilities the same. Gould and Martens (1979) examined the diversity of amateur coaches' perceptions of their roles. It became evident that some coaches defined their role as outcome based (i.e., winning games) and applied an autocratic leadership approach. Others viewed their role as a promoter of fun and development. Such coaches may apply a more supportive, positive, and democratic approach to coaching athletes. These stark differences in the perception of the role of the coach will directly influence behavioral intentions. A coach with an autocratic, punitive style may punish athletes for losing a game, while a more positive coach may find more educational solutions to a loss (e.g., viewing video footage, talking about mistakes).

What a coach believes about how athletes in general, and their own athletes in particular, are motivated is also critical. Smith and colleagues (1977) assessed the beliefs of coaches about achievement goals in their athletes. Through cluster analysis, two main groups emerged. One group of coaches saw the most value in intrinsic athletic motives. These included the joy of playing the game or sport and perfecting necessary skills. Another group valued extrinsic motives more, which included impressing peers or parents. It is very likely that the perception of the importance of athlete motives will subsequently influence how the coach leads. More research examining the coach's perceptions of the importance of athletes' motives is clearly needed to better understand the complexity of the relationship.

The previous examples are a selection of a long list of possible individual characteristics of the coach that may influence leader behaviors. Other factors may include the coach's emotional regulation and ability to self-monitor, which may clearly influence the structure of practice situations and response to athletes' needs. Much like the research on the MML, the influence of individual characteristics of coaches on leader behavior and athlete perceptions of such behavior in the MEDM has been underexamined and deserves more research attention.

Athlete's Individual Difference Variables

A variety of constructs are thought to influence an athlete's perceptions of, and responses to, a coach's actions, including age, gender, and normative beliefs about coaching behaviors. The valence (or the value) an athlete attaches to particular behaviors is considered to be a function of these antecedents. Valence is also thought to be influenced by situational factors (e.g., team size, type of sport) as well as experiential factors (e.g., maturity of athlete, level of competition) (Smith et al., 1977). Finally, achievement-related motivations for performing well, including the desire to succeed and the fear of failure, are also said to influence athlete perceptions and recall. Smoll and Smith (1989) argued that some personality variables operated as moderators of athlete perceptions and reactions. Some of those may include competitive trait anxiety; more anxious athletes would tend to perceive the coach as more punitive and less encouraging. Second, general self-worth and athletic self-esteem are considered moderators of athletic perceptions and reactions to leader behaviors. Smith and colleagues (1977) had reported differences in athlete behavior as a function of these constructs.

Situational Factors

Situational factors influence all primary variables in the model. There was early evidence that the nature of a particular sport (e.g., basketball vs. baseball; Smith et al., 1983) might influence these variables differently. There is additional evidence, from studies grounded in other leadership theories, that task variability and task dependency (which vary by sport, and even within sports because of the nature of the position) support this proposition (e.g., Chelladurai & Saleh, 1978; Riemer & Chelladurai, 1995). Other viable situational factors include practice versus games, historical team success and failure, current game and practice developments (e.g., is the team behind, has it lost its lead), the level of competition (i.e., U18 AAA vs. U18C), and the extent to which members of the group get along (socially and competitively).

Measurement

While the mediational model and its propositions make sense conceptually, and one can even point to anecdotal evidence supporting many of the proposed relationships, it has not been adequately tested to establish its validity; many of the complex relationships suggested by the model have yet to be verified. Techniques such as structural equation modeling are available to empirically verify some or all of the hypotheses advanced by the model (Smoll & Smith, 1989).

Most research focused on evaluating the MEDM has used the Coaching Behavior Assessment System (CBAS; Smith et al., 1977). The scale assesses the frequency of 12 different types of coaching behaviors (B1-B12). Smith and Smoll (2006) argue that the main advantage of the scale is the ranking of the frequency of displayed behaviors rather than the perception of such behaviors. Most of the alternative scales in the literature rely on athletes' perceptions of leadership.

The 12 CBAS categories are either reactive behaviors (reactions to an athlete's actions; e.g., good or bad aspects of performance) or spontaneous behaviors (behaviors initiated entirely by the coach; i.e., not in response to an athlete's action) (Carron & Eys, 2012). All behaviors are displayed in table 6.1.

A coach's reactive behaviors are classified further into three subcategories: reaction to an athlete's (1) desirable performance, (2) mistakes or errors, and (3) misbehaviors. When an athlete performs well, coaches usually praise or use other positive reinforcements (B1) or ignore through nonreinforcement (B2). Mistakes and errors may result in encouragement (B3), correction of the technique (B4), or punishment (B5). Sometimes coaches punish and then correct the mistake or error (B6) or ignore the mistake altogether (B7). An athlete's misbehaviors are addressed through the maintenance of control (e.g., highlighting the negative consequences for misbehaviors; B8).

Spontaneous behaviors can be classified as (1) game-related behaviors or (2) game-unrelated behaviors. During a game, coaches usually instruct athletes on technical aspects (B9), provide encouragement (B10), and organize and coordinate the

TABLE 6.1 Response Categories of the Coaching Behavior Assessment System

Response category	Behavioral description
CLASS I: REACTIVE BEHAVIORS	
RESPONSES TO DESIRABLE PERFORMANCE	
B1: Reinforcement (R)	A positive, rewarding reaction (verbal or nonverbal) to a good play or good effort
B2: Nonreinforcement (NR)	Failure to respond to a good performance
RESPONSES TO MISTAKES	
B3: Mistake-contingent encouragement (EM)	Encouragement given to a player following a mistake
B4: Mistake-contingent technical instruction (TIM)	Instruction on how a player should correct a mistake
B5: Punishment (P)	Negative reaction, verbal or nonverbal, following a mistake
B6: Punitive technical instruction (TIM+P)	Technical instruction following a mistake given in a punitive or hostile manner
B7: Ignoring mistakes (IM)	Failure to respond to a player mistake
RESPONSE TO MISBEHAVIOR	
B8: Keeping control (KC)	Reactions intended to restore or maintain order among team members
CLASS II: SPONTANEOUS BEHAVIORS	
GAME-RELATED BEHAVIORS	
B9: General technical instruction (TIG)	Spontaneous instruction in the techniques and strategies of the sport (not following a mistake)
B10: General encouragement (EG)	Spontaneous encouragement (not following a mistake)
B11: Organization (O)	Administrative behavior that sets the stage for play by assigning duties, responsibilities, positions, and so on
GAME-UNRELATED BEHAVIORS	
B12: General communication (GC)	Interactions with players unrelated to the game

Adapted by permission from F.L. Smoll and R.E. Smith, "Leadership Research in Youth Sports," in *Psychological Foundations of Sport*, edited by J.M. Silva and R.S. Weinberg (Champaign, IL: Human Kinetics, 1984), 375.

team's efforts (B11). Lastly, coaching behaviors that are game unrelated include any communication that does not revolve around the sport or game (B12) (Carron & Eys, 2012).

Because of the generality of coaching behaviors captured in the scale, the CBAS is usable across sports and contexts. For example, the scale can be used for comparison of leader behaviors in practice and game situations as well as for comparison across different sports. It should be noted that although the CBAS is over 40 years old, there is little evidence supporting its reliability or validity (Conroy & Coatsworth, 2007).

Interestingly, the CBAS has not been used as a measurement for coaching behaviors by others, or even a great deal. One reason is likely tied to the logistics involved in collecting observational data in a reliable and valid fashion (e.g., establishing inter- and intrarater reliability). Another reason may be that the scale measures observations of coaching behaviors by those outside of the coach–athlete system rather than an athlete's perceptions of the coach's behavior (e.g., Leadership Scale for Sports; Williams et al., 2003).

Smith and colleagues (1979) developed two additional versions of the CBAS. The first measure, the CBAS Perceived Behavior Scale (CBAS-PBS), assesses athletes' perceptions of leader behaviors that are captured in the CBAS. Interestingly, the CBAS-PBS has been used much more frequently than the original version of the scale. The second scale is the CBAS Coach-Perceived Behavior Scale (CBAS-CPBS), which examines coaches' perspectives of their own behavior. Taken together, the three scales (CBAS, CBAS-PBS, CBAS-CPBS) capture leader behaviors from the perspectives of an observer, athlete, or self-evaluative view of the coach.

Research Associated With the Mediational Model of Leadership

The research group led by Ron Smith and Frank Smoll examined the relationship between coaching behaviors and athletes' reactions in a series of studies (Curtis et al., 1979; Smith & Smoll, 1990; Smith et al., 1978, 1983). The group coded the behaviors (85,000+) of 80 youth sport coaches. Interview data from over 1,000 children were also collected to capture the athletes' perspectives of coaching behaviors and their sport experiences. Generally, the data indicated that encouragement, technical instruction, and organization of the team were associated with positive athlete outcomes. Coaching behaviors that were seen as controlling were generally related to negative athlete experiences.

Using these field studies, Smith and colleagues (1979) developed coaching protocols for evidence-based coaching behaviors (i.e., Coach Effectiveness Training; CET) and conducted an intervention study with 34 Little League coaches. Eighteen coaches were assigned to the intervention group and 16 to the control group. The coaches in the intervention group received structured material and feedback to educate them about beneficial coaching behaviors. The control group did not receive this material. The coaching behaviors of all coaches were assessed, along with athletes' perceptions of the coaching behaviors. The results clearly indicated that the intervention was effective; coaches in the intervention group demonstrated more positive behaviors (i.e., reinforcements), and athletes in the intervention group perceived higher reinforcements and encouragement and less punishment and nonreinforcement compared with those in the control groups.

In 1993, Smith and colleagues conducted a second study using the CET in eight youth baseball coaches. The participants received a preseason workshop on supportive coaching behavior. This group was compared against 10 coaches who had not received the workshop. The outcomes of athletes' enjoyment and self-esteem were measured. Athletes from the intervention group enjoyed their sport experience more and had higher self-esteem compared with athletes from the control condition. The findings highlighted the importance of supportive coaching behaviors for positive motivational and emotional development in youth athletes.

Based on their initial findings, Smith and Smoll (2006) developed the Mastery Approach to Coaching, an interventional workshop for coaches to foster motivation and skill building while reducing anxiety. The approach has been tested for its effectiveness using experimental and quasi-experimental designs, showing important positive outcomes for athletes and coaches. Those include better relationships with coaches and teammates, reductions in competitive anxiety, and greater tendencies toward mastery achievement orientation (Conroy & Coatsworth, 2007).

In general, research on the MEDM highlights how important it is for coaches (particularly in a youth context) to engage in positive behaviors (e.g., using supportive behavior and reinforcements). Studies have linked supportive coaching to various positive athlete outcomes. For example, providing important technical instructions may contribute to effective athlete development and, as a result, may also lead to the development of positive self-concept and confidence (Smith & Smoll, 1991; Smoll & Smith, 1989). From this perspective, the mediational model can be seen as a foundation for supportive coaching theories and measures that have come along more recently (e.g., Autonomy-Supportive Coaching Questionnaire; Conroy & Coatsworth, 2007).

Summary of the Models

The multidimensional model and the mediational model are important milestones in our understanding of sport leadership. While there are similarities between the models (e.g., both focus on coaching behaviors) there are some notable differences. For example, Eys and Carron (2012) argue that Chelladurai's multidimensional model focuses on behaviors that will vary depending on the situation (which necessarily changes based on a variety of team and environmental factors, such as preference of followers, win–loss record). The interaction between the needs of the organization, the coach, and the athlete is central to the understanding of the situational complexity and an important proposition (and, we would argue, contribution) of the multidimensional model. On the other hand, the mediational model is a general framework for more universal behaviors. That is, a limited number of coaching behaviors tend to be displayed in a particular situation; the important contribution of the mediational model is that these behaviors are actually observable and do not need to be assessed via athletes' perceptions.

The differences between the models are most visible in the primary measurement tools that first accompanied the models. The CBAS measures how often 12 different behaviors are observed. The LSS assesses the perceptions and preferences of certain leadership behavior qualities by athletes. The LSS can also evaluate expectations regarding those qualities from an organizational perspective and also a coach's self-perceptions of their own behaviors (although these latter perspectives have rarely been included in research). In addition, as Chelladurai (2007) correctly noted, the multidimensional model has traditionally been perceived as the framework of choice when examining adult athletes (primarily college aged or elite), while the mediational model has been associated with youth sport and has been built from a youth sport perspective. Nonetheless, there is no theoretical rationale to suggest that these models are not applicable in contexts other than those in which they have historically been applied (Chelladurai, 2007).

We would suggest that the models do not compete with each other. Rather, they view coaching leadership from slightly different, but certainly not inconsistent, perspectives. The mediational model is built largely on the foundational work of Vroom to better explain and understand individual human motivations and subsequent behaviors (see Vroom, 1964). In short, the MEDM begins with its focus on the athlete. The MML, on the other hand, is based largely on work that focuses primarily on the role of the leader or coach and the role they play in guiding the team and facilitating the achievement of group-level goals. It is also worth noting there are many conceptual similarities, such as the role individual differences, task characteristics, and other elements of the situation play in influencing athlete and coach behaviors (or preferences, etc.).

Regardless of the notable differences, both models are important milestones in sport leadership research. Since their initial publication decades ago, both models have served as a fundamental basis for theory building and research endeavors in sport leadership. As research in this area advances, it is important to rely on the contributions of established theories and models while exploring new ideas and perspectives in sport leadership. In the next section we look at some of the future directions.

Future Research Directions

The MML and MEDM made important propositions and advanced our understanding of leadership in sport. While there is a plethora of research using the models as a theoretical basis, some elements of the models deserve more research attention. For example, the congruence between desired, required, and actual leader behavior is an important consideration for the assessment of leadership for the future. Although this congruence may be debated, we need to advance our knowledge of how the requirements of a situation and preferences of athletes may be related to leader behaviors. This will help us better understand the complexities of the interaction and collaboration between athletes and coaches to move a team forward.

When reviewing the literature, we noticed an absence of research attention toward testing other key propositions of the models. Scientifically, the merit of theories can be appraised only if their propositions or hypotheses are tested repeatedly. Only then can we determine whether the propositions on which we build our current understanding of leadership are accurate. Moreover, more recent leadership approaches (e.g., identity leadership) found their way from other fields (e.g., organizational psychology) into the sport realm. While the theoretical diversification of leadership approaches in sport should be welcomed, the tenets of such theories stem from research conducted in different leadership contexts. This presents a serious limitation to the historical and current development of leadership theories in sport. As Rainer Martens (1979) noted: "Sport psychology will surely be a healthier field when we recognize that the internal psychological processes that occur when people engage in sport must be understood within the social context of sport" (p. 96). The challenge made by Martens over 40 years ago is still applicable. Accordingly, we encourage future leadership research to build on the MML, MEDM, and other theoretical propositions, but with a focus on original theory building within the context of sport. Next, we outline some of the areas where we see future research gaps in the realm of sport.

Organizational Context

Most sport leadership research has focused exclusively on the interactions between coaches and athletes as well as behaviors that occur in a team context. While these topics cover important aspects of sport leadership, as Chelladurai's MML noted (but has largely been ignored), leadership occurs in a broader context beyond the immediate team (e.g., club, organization, association) (Arthur et al., 2018). Sport organizations (e.g., youth sport clubs) often encompass more than one team and present a larger, and more complex, context in which sport leadership functions. For example, organizations may provide concrete and specific guidelines of desired coaching behavior norms and provide direction through organizational vision, mission, and culture. Certainly both of the models we have examined suggest that multiple constituencies determine or influence how a coach will coach. Other scholars have also noted the important role organizational culture plays in mediating leadership in a sport context (or other contexts, for that matter; see Wagstaff & Burton-Wylie, 2018). We encourage scholars and practitioners to further consider the importance of the organizational context when examining leadership in sport, particularly in the context of the MML and MEDM.

Social Identity

Sport leadership effectiveness is closely connected with the creation, management, and advancement of a shared social identity (Haslam et al., 2020). Recent research in sport has adopted "identity leadership" as a core construct in the social psychology of sport teams (Evans et al., 2021). For a larger overview, please see chapter 8 of this book. The identity approach sees leadership playing an important role in enhancing the extent to which athletes socially identify with the team. This can be done in several ways. First, leaders should be an exemplary (or prototypical) representative of the group (i.e., a good example to the group of desirable behavior). Second, leaders need to think and behave in ways that reflect the group's values. Third, leaders increase social identity by developing group values that encourage the group to common action (e.g., team first, teammates before self). Finally, leaders can embed the social identity into the reality of the group (e.g., using language that reflects the group's values) (Stevens et al., 2021). The social identity approach suggests certain group processes (e.g., identity, cohesion, conflict) need to be seen as emergent states that continuously mediate leadership efforts and effectiveness within sport teams.

We view the social identity approach, similar to Chelladurai's (1993) proposition, to include transformational leadership as an antecedent to leadership behaviors. If leaders can facilitate a social identity, this will influence the situational requirements, displayed behaviors, and preferences of athletes. For example, a team with a strong social bond may be able to navigate through challenging moments (e.g., a loss in a final) more constructively. Conflicts and other adverse consequences may be preventable or lessened in severity. To test these propositions, future research is clearly needed in this area.

Team Formation and Management

As noted in the MML, the role of a coach in a sport team context includes at least two critical functions: (1) satisfying the demands of the organization and (2) fulfilling the needs and aspirations of team members (Eys & Carron, 2012). For organizations that focus on competitive success (i.e., the pursuit of excellence; Chelladurai, 2012), the coach is often tasked with important managerial tasks, one of which concerns the formation and management of the team composition. Essentially, coaches are the gatekeepers as to which athletes will join and remain on the team. Coaches also determine who will be rewarded with playing time—a powerful tool (Turman, 2006). Managerial tasks, particularly selection, have been explored in a youth sport context (e.g., Capstick & Trudel, 2010; Harenberg et al., 2020; Neeley et al., 2016, 2017, 2018). However, these important tasks and associated behaviors (e.g., communication of selection) are not directly reflected in any leadership theories, including the MML and MEDM, or measures to date. The power of a coach over an athlete is a substantial consideration in their relationship. For example, if the coach benches a regular starting athlete without any justification, the athlete may react negatively to the decision and may even question the ability of the coach. In essence, the fit between the coaching decision, communication, and athlete's preference of communication is incongruent. Accordingly, Fiedler (1967) has suggested that constructive selection should be determined to ensure a good fit between the player and coach. These are important managerial responsibilities of a coach and warrant more investigation and integration in future theoretical leadership models of sport.

Practical Implications

As we have noted throughout the chapter, leadership remains a widely discussed and ever-evolving field of study. How then can those in the real world apply the theoretical knowledge and information presented in this chapter? Although we could make many recommendations, we focus on three.

First, coaches should consider the merits of engaging in a more democratic approach to leadership, particularly with those athletes who are capable of taking on the responsibility that comes with shared involvement in the leadership process. Such an approach may include greater involvement in setting the group's direction and increasing the areas in which athletes can make more autonomous decisions. One of the positive outcomes of such an approach is that it encourages greater autonomy on the part of the individual, as well as personal accountability to the group. It will also increase their buy-in to the team or collective direction (something we know is critical from the research related to goal setting). However, to do this effectively, coaches will need to provide information about the constraints and expectations placed on leaders by the organization and other important considerations in the environment. That will mean increasing lines of communication between coaches and players (i.e., creating an increasingly transparent environment) so that all those in the group can effectively participate in the leadership process. For example, communicating more openly about situational requirements being imposed on the coach or even explaining certain behaviors to athletes by communicating situational needs and their corresponding coaching style should result in a better collective understanding of what is necessary or important, as well as in higher athlete engagement overall. We are not suggesting that accountability disappear. Rather, athletes should be allowed to share in the leadership and hold themselves, as well as the group, accountable—a shift away from the micromanaging of an athlete's or team's life on the part of the coach (i.e., authoritarian or autocratic) to a macromanagement of the group, by the group. While such an approach will necessarily take more time, and some decisions may be delegated to the coach by the collective, the goal of building a strong group, aligned in purpose, is well worth the costs.

Coaches should consider the merits of engaging in a more democratic approach to leadership, particularly with those athletes who are capable of taking on the responsibility that comes with shared involvement in the leadership process.

Second, it is important that coaches not underestimate the importance of the more managerial tasks of coaching and the role they play in leadership success (e.g., scheduling the practices, communicating who has made the team, coordinating the work of the support team). Most of these tasks are not typically assessed in our formal evaluation of leaders, but when students are asked to identify characteristics of effective leaders, being organized is almost always mentioned. In fact, leadership is determined by the many behaviors a coach displays, regardless of whether those are on the field or in the office. Everything coaches do, even the mundane, should be seen as leadership and may influence other important processes for the team (e.g., social identity, cohesion).

Finally, the MEDM and MML, along with other leadership theories covered in other chapters of this book, provide an important theoretical foundation for understanding leadership from different perspectives. While it is critical for researchers to look for evidence in support of the theoretical tenets, it is equally important for practitioners not to dismiss theories out of hand. Theories are, after all, someone using evidence collected to date in an attempt to explain a set of phenomena. In our context, they are attempts to explain what key factors determine whether a coach (and their team) will be effective or not. Leadership is hard; it is also complex. Practitioners should certainly rely on their own experiences, but they must also pay attention to the framework in which their experiences reside—that is where theory is so very helpful. Theories offer insight, make very real recommendations for applied leadership behavior, and also point to areas leaders need to consider (which they may not identify organically if they are focused only on their own experiences). Using an evidence-based approach in your own personal approach to leading is enhanced by a foundational understanding of theories in the area. It also requires knowledge of how human beings think and act as individuals and in groups. Good leaders must never stop learning and growing in their understanding of current theoretical thought and evidence in the field.

Summary

In this chapter, we have introduced two important theoretical models of sport leadership: the multidimensional model and the mediational model of leadership. We have outlined where the models overlap and where they diverge. One important perspective of these, as well as other (if not most) theoretical perspectives of leadership, is that leadership is a social construct that involves a complex interaction between the leader, those being led, and the context in which the leading occurs (e.g., the situation, the context, the organization). Moreover, all three of these components influence, and are simultaneously influenced by, each other. Both the multidimensional model and the mediational model represent an attempt to highlight some of the key ways in which the components interact with each other to influence important individual and group-level outcomes. Remember, leadership is always about accomplishing some kind of goal, and generally more than one outcome simultaneously.

We see encouraging trends for future research in sport leadership, including working toward a deeper understanding of organizational influences, an expanded understanding of leader behaviors to include managerial duties, and exploration of important new leader behaviors (e.g., social identity approach). These directions will certainly lead to a deeper understanding of the complexity of leadership within sport teams. At the same time, there are many new learnings in the business or managerial literature that need to be considered and ultimately integrated into our understanding of sport-related leadership. We have highlighted some ideas throughout the chapter.

Finally, while advancements in the field are promising, there is still much work to be done. Although the two models we have focused on are more than 40 years old, some critical propositions of both models have yet to be tested (e.g., congruence hypothesis). Additionally, research on some key hypotheses of the models have resulted in inconsistent results. To advance research on leadership in sport, we must dedicate time and effort toward more fully evaluating the theoretical connections proposed by the models. This may warrant the development of new measures, which is time consuming and difficult. Only then will we be able to critically evaluate the contribution of each model to our understanding of leadership and how each model may provide a framework for future novel and innovative theories in the field of sport-related leadership.

DISCUSSION QUESTIONS

1. Discuss which elements are integral when defining leadership.
2. Discuss the central propositions of the multidimensional model of leadership in sport.
3. Think about your own experiences as a coach or an athlete. What situational and personal factors might determine the types of leadership behaviors a coach prefers to engage in?
4. Discuss the central propositions of the mediational model in sport.
5. Describe the measures that were developed within the MML and the MEDM. How do these measures differ?
6. What are the differences between the models, and how do they complement each other?
7. Think about your experiences as a player or coach. Which model fits better to your leadership style? Why?

7

Transformational Leadership in Sport

Jennifer Turnnidge, PhD, and Adam L. Kelly, PhD, CSci

LEARNING OBJECTIVES

On completion of this chapter, the reader should have the following:

- Knowledge of the four dimensions of transformational leadership
- Understanding of the critical link between transformational leadership and athlete development
- Appreciation of the role of transformational leadership within the context of social groups in sport
- Awareness of current methodologies used to study transformational leadership in sport and directions for future research
- Understanding of practical applications of transformational leadership in sport

Across various disciplines, leadership has long been a topic of interest for researchers and practitioners. Indeed, issues related to leadership have received significant attention from philosophers, historians, sociologists, educators, psychologists, health care practitioners, and organizational partners. Leadership is also prominently featured in popular culture, such as film and television, blogs and websites, and social media. Given the ubiquitous nature of leadership, it is worthwhile to examine leadership within the sport context. This may be particularly relevant given the myriad of leadership roles embedded within sport settings, including coaches, parents, peer leaders (e.g., captains), officials, and organizational leaders.

Broadly, researchers have explored how leaders shape the sport environment and the ways leaders can influence the outcomes derived from sport participation, such as performance, participation, and personal development. A growing body of literature consistently highlights the important role leadership plays in creating positive experiences in sport. To this end, it is important for researchers and practitioners to gain a deeper understanding of how to enact effective leadership in practice.

The aim of this chapter is to explore the potential contribution of transformational leadership (TFL; Avolio, 1999; Bass, 1985) to the study of leadership in sport. Specifically, this chapter will (1) provide a brief overview of the theoretical conceptualization of TFL, as situated within the broader full-range leadership model (Bass & Riggio, 2006), (2) discuss the methodological approaches for studying TFL in sport, (3) elaborate on how TFL may be a viable framework for understanding the leadership behaviors of key invested partners in sport, including coaches, parents, peers, officials, and organizations, (4) highlight directions for future research, and (5) outline practical implications for leadership in sport.

Leadership Frameworks in Sport

Numerous conceptual frameworks have explored leadership within the sport environment, including the multidimensional model of leadership (MML; Chelladurai, 1993, 2007; see chapter 6), the mediational model of leadership (Smith & Smoll, 2007; Smoll et al., 1978; see chapter 6), and the social identity approach to leadership (Hogg, 2001). The MML focuses on coach leadership and characterizes leadership according to a coach's decision-making style (democratic or autocratic), motivational tendencies (social support and positive feedback), and instructional behaviors (training and instruction). Research employing this model has typically used questionnaires to assess how three interacting states of coaches' leadership behaviors—the required coach behavior, the athlete's preferred coach behavior, and the actual coach behavior—can influence athletes' sport experiences, such as cohesion and aggression (e.g., Murray, 2006; Shields et al., 1995). Collectively, studies using the MML highlight the important influence that coaches' leadership behaviors can have on athlete development.

A growing body of literature consistently highlights the important role leadership plays in creating positive experiences in sport.

Another prominent leadership model in sport is the mediational model (Smith & Smoll, 2007), which explores how the associations between coaches' leadership behaviors and athlete outcomes are mediated by situational factors (e.g., practices vs. games, level of competition), cognitive processes, and individual athlete differences. Using observational methods, Smith, Smoll, and colleagues (e.g., Smith & Smoll, 1990; Smith et al., 1983) explored how coaches' reactive behaviors (e.g., responding to mistakes) and spontaneous behaviors (e.g., general encouragement) can influence athlete outcomes, such as perceptions of the coach and peer relationships. This line of research also informed the development of a coach education program that focuses on the behavioral strategies (e.g., providing encouragement and instruction and minimizing the use of punishment) that leaders can use to create quality sport experiences. Findings indicated that this program can effectively change coaches' leadership behaviors and that these changes were associated with positive athlete outcomes, such as higher levels of fun and lower levels of attrition (e.g., Smoll et al., 1993). Overall, studies employing the mediational model lend insight into the potential influence of coaches' leadership behaviors on developmental outcomes and provide practical interventions to enhance the quality of coaches' leadership behaviors.

Haslam and colleagues (2010) advocated that coaches' leadership resides in leaders' ability to influence the process of social identity. Specifically, the social identity approach to leadership focuses on how leaders can help athletes find meaning in their team membership. Researchers have employed novel methods, such as media analysis and experimental designs, to investigate how coach and athlete leaders can facilitate athlete outcomes, including identity and confidence (e.g., Fransen et al., 2015; Slater et al., 2015). In doing so, studies using this model illustrate how broader psychological theories can inform our understanding of leadership in sport. Moreover, these studies highlight the potential benefits of a diverse range of methodologies for studying leadership.

Each of these models has greatly contributed to our understanding of leadership in sport. Nonetheless, concerns have been raised regarding the comprehensiveness of the behaviors captured within these models (e.g., Chelladurai, 2007). As such, researchers have advocated exploring alternative approaches to the study of leadership in sport (Rowold, 2006; Turnnidge & Côté, 2018).

Transformational Leadership

One approach that may be useful for examining leadership in sport is the full-range leadership model (Avolio, 1999; Bass, 1985). Informed by Burns' (1978) pivotal work on political leadership, this model suggests that leadership behaviors can be understood along two axes: one axis ranging from passive to active, and the other axis ranging from least effective to most effective. This model is made up of three distinct forms of leadership: laissez-faire, transactional, and TFL behaviors (see figure 7.1).

Laissez-faire refers to a passive and ineffective form of leadership in which leaders are unresponsive to followers' needs (e.g., avoiding one's responsibilities, withholding feedback). This form of leadership has been associated with negative outcomes, such as role stress, psychological fatigue, and reduced well-being (Barling & Frone, 2017; Kelloway et al., 2005). Moving along the axes, transactional leadership encompasses assigning consequences for certain types of behaviors (i.e., contingent reward) or moni-

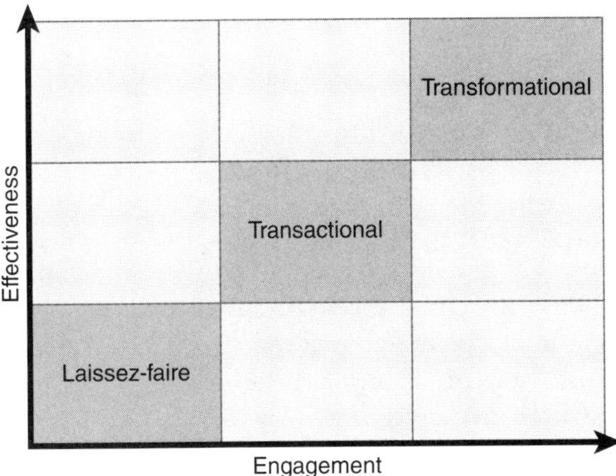

FIGURE 7.1 Full-range leadership model.

Adapted from B.M. Bass and R.E. Riggio, *Transformational Leadership*, 2nd ed. (New York: Psychology Press, 2006), 10.

toring followers to detect deviations from specific standards (i.e., management by exception). Transactional leadership focuses on providing rewards and punishments in relation to followers' abilities to meet leaders' expectations or standards. Although previous studies suggest that these behaviors can be an important component of leadership, they may be insufficient for optimal follower development (Judge & Piccolo, 2004). This relates to the *augmentation hypothesis*, which suggests that TFL can build upon the foundation of transactional leadership to enhance development (Bass, 1998).

At the end of the two axes is transformational leadership, which represents an approach to leadership designed to empower, challenge, and inspire followers (Bass & Riggio, 2006). Although there are various interpretations of TFL (Bass, 1985; Callow et al., 2009; Podsakoff et al., 1990), this chapter focuses on the conceptualization of TFL put forward by Bass (1985; Bass & Riggio, 2006). Very broadly, this model suggests that TFL comprises four dimensions (collectively known as the four Is):

- Idealized influence (leaders foster respectful and trusting relationships by acting as a role model and by demonstrating personally held beliefs)
- Inspirational motivation (leaders inspire and motivate followers by holding high expectations and communicating a compelling vision of the future)
- Intellectual stimulation (leaders encourage followers to approach problems from different perspectives and empower followers to contribute novel ideas)
- Individualized consideration (leaders show genuine care and concern for each individual's unique needs, abilities, and contributions)

Transformational leadership may be well suited to sport because of the *cascade effect* (Bass, 1985), which suggests that transformational leaders serve as role models who can encourage their followers to use TFL behaviors themselves.

Overall, these behavioral dimensions are intended to facilitate positive developmental experiences among one's followers. For instance, by enhancing followers' understanding of their collective vision and expressing belief in followers' capabilities to achieve their goals, it is posited that leaders can improve followers' motivation. Charbonneau and colleagues (2001) explored this possibility in their investigation of coaches' use of transformational leadership behaviors within the university sport context. Results indicated that intrinsic motivation mediated the relationship between coaches' TFL and sport performance, thus suggesting that coaches who use TFL behaviors may positively influence athletes' motivation. Given the potential for TFL behaviors to shape developmental experiences, it is worthwhile to further explore the applicability of TFL within the sport context.

TFL offers an appealing lens for examining leadership in sport since it has been associated with a myriad of positive developmental outcomes across several disciplines, including organizational, educational, health care, military, and sport settings (Turnnidge & Côté, 2018). For example, previous studies reveal positive association between TFL and followers' outcomes, such as well-being (e.g., Arnold et al., 2007), motivation (e.g., Piccolo & Colquitt, 2006), and helping behaviors (e.g., Tsai et al., 2009).

TFL may also be well suited to sport because of the *cascade effect* (Bass, 1985), which suggests that transformational leaders serve as role models who can encourage their followers to use TFL behaviors themselves. Given that sport is often advocated as a fertile context for developing leadership skills (Gould et al., 2013), it would be beneficial to provide athletes with opportunities to learn about leadership experientially and vicariously through their interactions with sport leaders (e.g., coaches, parents, peers, officials, and organizational administrators).

Methodological Considerations for TFL in Sport

The purpose of this section is to explore the methodologies that have been used to study TFL in sport. Understanding how this research is conducted is critical to ensure the findings from TFL research can be relevant and applicable in real-world sport settings. This section discusses the strengths and limitations of current methodological approaches and offers considerations for future research.

Questionnaire-Based Approaches

Across various disciplines, the research on TFL has been largely dominated by the use of questionnaires to provide a quantitative examination of perceptions of TFL. Commonly used questionnaires include the following:

- Multifactor Leadership Questionnaire (MLQ-5X; Bass & Avolio, 1990)
- Global Transformational Leadership Scale (Carless et al., 2000)
- Transformational Teaching Questionnaire (Beauchamp et al., 2010)
- Transformational Leadership Behavior Inventory (Podsakoff et al., 1990)
- Differentiated Transformational Leadership Inventory (DTLI; Callow et al., 2009)
- Differentiated Transformational Leadership Inventory for Youth Sport (DTLIYS; Vella et al., 2012)

Although several of these scales are informed by the conceptualization of TFL described previously by Bass and colleagues (Bass, 1985; Bass & Riggio, 2006), it is important to note that others are informed by a differentiated approach to TFL (e.g., Callow et al., 2009; Podsakoff et al., 1990; Vella et al., 2012). Using this approach, leadership is assessed across six behavioral dimensions (Callow et al., 2009):

- Individual consideration
- Inspirational motivation
- Intellectual stimulation
- Fostering acceptance of group goals
- High-performance expectations
- Contingent reward

Within the leadership literature, there is some debate as to whether TFL should be viewed as a global or a differentiated construct (for more details, see Antonakis et al., 2003; Arthur & Tomsett, 2015; Arthur et al., 2017). Using a global approach, researchers collapse the subscales of the lower-order dimensions (i.e., the four Is) to create one higher-order scale that represents TFL overall. Conversely, the differentiated approach emphasizes the analysis of the lower-order dimensions of TFL. Previous research suggests a potential benefit of the differentiated approach is that it enables examination of the specific mechanisms by which the dimensions of TFL may influence follower outcomes (Jowett & Arthur, 2019). The issues surrounding these two approaches to TFL may be exacerbated by common-method biases due to the overreliance on questionnaires, as well as the multicollinearity (i.e., high correlations) between the subscales of existing questionnaires (Arthur et al., 2017). As such, it may be worthwhile for future research to refine sport-specific measures for TFL and to explore alternative methodologies for studying leadership in sport to help address this debate. Moreover, researchers who wish to employ TFL should consider how these different approaches align with their intended research aims, conceptualization of TFL, and preferred measurement tools.

The majority of studies have used self-report questionnaires to assess leadership (e.g., Charbonneau et al., 2001; Vella et al., 2013a). Although this approach has yielded important insight, there are some limitations to consider (Arthur et al., 2017). For instance, issues have been raised regarding questionnaires, including multicollinearity between subscales, inconclusive findings regarding the factor structure, and access to questionnaire-based tools. Another issue relating to current measurement tools is that several questionnaires (e.g., MLQ-5X) include items in which followers are asked to attribute positive outcomes to certain leadership behaviors. For example, items often ask participants to reflect on whether leaders use behaviors that facilitate developmental outcomes such as trust, respect, or team perceptions (Arthur et al., 2017; Meyer et al., 2016). It is thus recommended that tools be refined to separate the outcomes of leadership from the behaviors that contribute to these outcomes.

Questionnaire-based studies may also be limited by using only one type of data source. For instance, it is common for studies to have followers complete questionnaires assessing both the independent variables (i.e., leaders' TFL behaviors) and dependent variables (i.e., followers' outcomes). To strengthen the methodological quality of leadership studies, researchers (e.g., Arthur et al., 2017; Barling, 2014). have advocated for the use of different data sources (e.g., leader, follower, and observer reports) or tools (e.g., questionnaires, interviews, observations).

Qualitative Approaches

In an effort to address these concerns, sport researchers have attempted to diversify the methodological tools to assess leadership. Qualitative approaches have also been used to inform the sport leadership literature (Hodge et al., 2014; Mills & Boardley, 2016; Newland et al., 2015; Smith et al., 2017). For example, Smith and colleagues (2017) employed semi-structured interviews to explore professional cricket players' perceptions of TFL behaviors among their captains and head coaches. Results shed light on the complex nature of TFL among different invested partners in the sport environment. Specifically, findings highlighted that coaches and captains used TFL behaviors in different but complementary ways. Indeed, coaches were perceived to be responsible for setting high expectations, whereas captains reinforced these expectations through their role modeling behaviors. Coaches' and captains' TFL behaviors were also influenced by the setting in which leadership-based interactions occur. Consistent with this contention, results suggested that coaches used individual consideration in training, whereas captains displayed individual consideration during competition. These findings highlight how qualitative approaches can provide in-depth information concerning the processes that shape sport leadership. Moreover, qualitative approaches can offer insight into how leadership is exhibited and experienced by different invested partners in sport (e.g., parents, coaches, athletes, organizational administrators). Given the relatively small body of qualitative research in this area, there is ample opportunity to use a broader range of qualitative methods (e.g., focus groups, diary studies, artifact analysis) and analytical approaches (e.g., thematic, discourse, narrative) to enhance our understanding of leadership in sport.

Observational Approaches

Another methodological approach that has been used to study leadership in sport is behavioral observation. One of the challenges for sport leaders is to translate the theory of TFL into everyday practice. To help leaders understand how TFL can be manifested in daily interactions, Turnnidge and Côté (2019) developed a microanalytic observational coding system to capture coaches' leadership behaviors in youth sport settings: the Coach Leadership Assessment System (CLAS). Informed by literature reviews, qualitative interviews, and observations, the 17 behavioral categories of the CLAS were developed to assess coaches' leadership behaviors across five higher-order leadership dimensions:

- TFL (11 codes)
- Transactional (2 codes)
- Neutral (1 code)
- Laissez-faire (1 code)
- Toxic (2 codes)

The TFL dimension consists of 11 distinct transformational coaching behaviors mapped to the four Is of idealized influence, inspirational motivation, intellectual stimulation, and individualized consideration. Figure 7.2 shows an overview of the codes of the CLAS). The coding system CLAS also analyzes coaches' leadership behaviors in relation to their content (e.g., instruction and feedback, organization, and general communication), recipient (e.g., team, small group, individual), and context (e.g., warm-up, scrimmage, and cool-down).

The CLAS helped operationalize the theoretical constructs of the full-range leadership model, with an emphasis on TFL, within the context of coach–athlete interactions in sport. In doing so, this instrument provides a unique behavioral account of coaches' leadership behaviors and offers an alternative to assessing participants' subjective experiences of leadership. Further, by capturing transactional, laissez-faire, and toxic coaching behaviors in addition to TFL behaviors, the CLAS provides a unique opportunity to assess the full range of coaches' leadership behaviors. This is important and may provide a more complete picture of the behaviors leaders employ when they are not being transformational.

In line with this assertion, Lefebvre and colleagues (2019) employed the CLAS to examine how coaches use leadership behaviors in youth sport settings. The behaviors of seven male head coaches of soccer teams were systematically observed and coded over two training sessions and one competition. Findings suggested that approximately 75% of the coaches' coded behaviors were neutral in nature, whereby coaches were either engaged in silent observation or interacting with their athletes with no discernible leadership tone. Results also

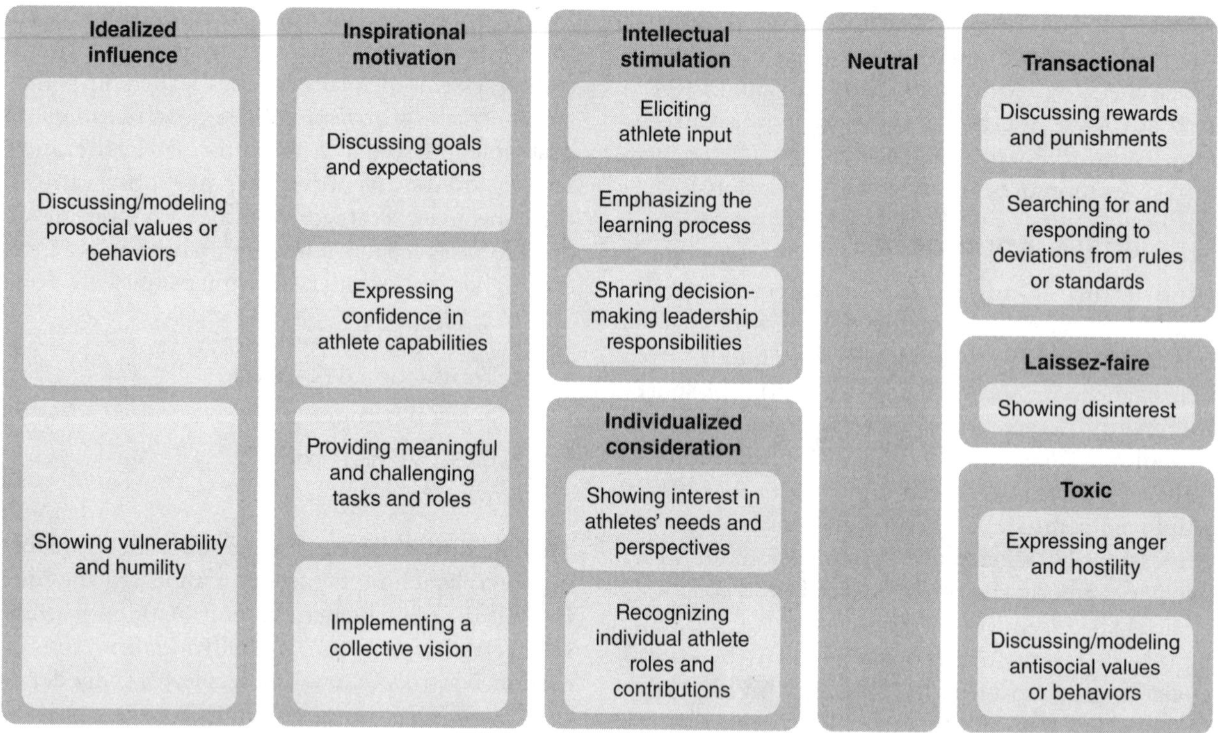

FIGURE 7.2 Behavioral dimensions of the Coach Leadership Assessment System (Turnnidge & Côté, 2019).

indicated that coaches engaged in a broad range of leadership behaviors, with higher levels of TFL and transactional behaviors and lower levels of laissez-faire and toxic behaviors. When engaging in TFL, findings suggested that coaches most frequently displayed individualized consideration and inspirational motivation behaviors and less frequently displayed idealized influence and intellectual stimulation. These results shed new light on how TFL can be manifested in real-time interactions and illustrated the potential for coaches to improve both the quantity and quality of their leadership-based interactions with young athletes. However, it is important to acknowledge the descriptive nature of these findings. Since no outcomes were assessed, questions remain regarding how these behavioral patterns may influence athletes' developmental outcomes.

Intervention-Based Approaches

Despite an overreliance on descriptive studies, it is worth noting that exciting advances are occurring. Notably, researchers have employed interventions to enhance leadership in sport settings. For instance, researchers have adapted coaching and leadership interventions to target coaches' TFL behaviors (Lawrason et al., 2019; Vella et al., 2013b). Lawrason and colleagues (2019) found preliminary support for a coach development program focused on these behaviors. This program involves a combination of lectures, videos, group discussions, and action planning activities. In their pilot evaluation of the program, Lawrason and colleagues observed and coded the leadership behaviors of eight soccer coaches pre- and postintervention using the CLAS. Results found that coaches spent more time using idealized influence, inspirational motivation, and intellectual stimulation postintervention. Although these improvements were not statistically significant, analyses indicated medium to large effect sizes, suggesting there may be a meaningful, practical improvement in TFL behaviors. Nonetheless, it is important to recognize the preliminary nature of these findings and the small sample size of the pilot study. As such, these results should be interpreted with caution, and continued investigations are required to further this line of research.

Populations and Contexts Under Study

In addition to examining the methods used to study TFL, it is important to critically reflect on the populations and contexts in which it has been investigated. In their review of the TFL literature in sport, Arthur and colleagues (2017) suggest that samples in TFL research have been relatively heterogeneous in relation to location (e.g., North America, Asia, Australia, and Europe) and sport context (e.g., martial arts, ice hockey, soccer, Ultimate, and multisport samples). Nonetheless, there is a need to ensure the populations and contexts under study represent the diverse spectrum of invested partners in sport in relation to age, socioeconomic status, competitive level, gender, race, and ability status. The perspectives of diverse partners should be explored in relation to both their own leadership behaviors and their experiences of others' leadership behaviors. This is particularly important since experiences in sport settings are shaped by the contextual needs (e.g., developmental level) of both the participants and the program (e.g., Côté & Gilbert, 2009).

Studies interested in TFL have predominantly focused on coach leadership (Arthur et al., 2017). Although coaches represent a crucial and highly visible leader in sport environments, it is important to recognize the diverse spectrum of invested partners who occupy leadership roles in sport. This includes parents, athletes, officials, and organizational administrators. By expanding our focus to a broader range of leaders, researchers and practitioners can develop a more complete and nuanced understanding of leadership in sport. In addition to examining the leadership behaviors of each of these partner groups, it is also integral to investigate their experiences of leadership.

TFL and Sport Leaders

This section delves deeper into the existing empirical research on the leadership behaviors of different invested partners in sport, as well as discusses potential future directions and practical applications for TFL.

Coach TFL

Coaches represent the most studied leaders in the sport environment. Previous studies suggest that coaches' TFL is positively linked with several individual- and group-level outcomes, including coach effectiveness (Rowold, 2006), psychological well-being (Stenling & Tafvelin, 2014), effort (Callow et al., 2009), aggression (Tucker et al., 2010), cohesion (Callow et al., 2009; Cronin et al., 2015; Smith et al., 2013), and performance (Bormann & Rowold, 2016; Charbonneau et al., 2001). Within the youth sport context, Vella and colleagues (2013a) suggested that TFL may foster personal development in youths because higher ratings of coach TFL behaviors using the DTLI-YS (Vella et al., 2012) were associated with the development of personal and social skills, cognitive skills, goal-setting skills, and initiative. Further, Vella and colleagues (2013b) found that educational workshops can enhance coaches' use of TFL behaviors, namely intellectual stimulation and appropriate role modeling. Moreover, findings indicated that changes in coaches' TFL behaviors were associated with higher reported levels of goal setting and cognitive skills. Collectively, these studies lend support to the notion that TFL may be a salient avenue for promoting positive athlete outcomes. Moreover, these findings suggest that the full-range leadership model (Bass & Riggio, 2006) may provide a useful foundation for evidence-informed coach education.

Researchers have also examined the potential mechanisms underpinning the relations between coaches' TFL behaviors and athletes' developmental outcomes, including motivation (Charbonneau et al., 2001), coach competency (Kao & Tsai, 2016), need satisfaction (Stenling & Tafvelin, 2014), sacrifice (Cronin et al., 2015), and team aggression (Tucker et al., 2010). For example, Tucker and colleagues (2010) used the Global Transformational Leadership Scale to examine the influence of coaches' use of TFL behaviors on aggression among adolescent ice hockey players. Results demonstrated that the team's aggression mediated the association between the coach's TFL behaviors and athlete aggression, thereby suggesting that coaches may indirectly influence athlete aggression by discouraging aggressive team norms.

Research has also examined how TFL may indirectly influence group outcomes through mediating mechanisms. Cronin and colleagues (2015) used the DTLI (Callow et al., 2009) to investigate the potential mechanisms underpinning the association between TFL and cohesion. Findings suggested that intrateam communication and inside sacrifices (i.e., transcending self-interest for the good of the group) mediated the association between TFL and cohesion. Baird and colleagues (2020) extended our understanding of TFL at the group level by examining athletes' perceptions of coaches' TFL across multiple time points in relation to task cohesion and team potency beliefs. Using a novel mobile application to assess team dynamics among competitive youth athletes, the authors found a positive relation between overall TFL and task cohesion at both the within- and between-person levels. Conversely, coach TFL was significantly linked with team potency at the between-person level, but not at the within-person level. These findings highlight both the utility of innovative methodological approaches and the need to continue exploring the dynamic nature of TFL using longitudinal designs.

Researchers have also explored potential moderators of these associations, including athlete characteristics (e.g., athlete narcissism: Arthur et al., 2011; Callow et al., 2009) and contextual variables (e.g., experience: Beauchamp et al., 2010; and team performance: Callow et al., 2009). Although the examination of potential moderators and mediators provides insight into the black box of leadership, researchers have advocated the need to test these factors competitively to assess which factors are most salient for facilitating positive developmental outcomes. Moreover, while the studies discussed in this section focus primarily on the role of TFL in coaches' relationships with their athletes, it is also possible that coaches may employ TFL behaviors with different partners (e.g., athletes, parents, officials, and organizational administrators). Consequently, researchers and practitioners are encouraged to explore coaches' use of TFL beyond the coach–athlete relationship. Such studies would help capture the complex and dynamic nature of sport leadership. Finally, questions remain regarding the relations between specific TFL behaviors and athlete outcomes. As such, it would be beneficial for researchers to investigate the potentially unique relations between each of the TFL dimensions and athlete outcomes.

Parent TFL

Previous research consistently highlights that parents or other primary caregivers are crucial in influencing the ways athletes experience sport activities (see chapter 5 on parental involvement in sport for more detail). Parents facilitate critical components of youth sport participation, such as providing tangible support (e.g., registration and travel fees, equipment purchases, volunteerism) and emotional support (e.g., encouragement, feedback; Ryan Dunn et al., 2016). Parents' social interactions within the sport environment have also been shown to influence the quality of youth sport experiences and the developmental outcomes derived from sport participation (e.g., Cumming & Ewing, 2002). Given the integral role parents play in sport, it may be valuable to examine parents' behaviors through a leadership lens.

Previous research consistently highlights that parents or other primary caregivers are crucial in influencing the ways athletes experience sport activities.

Evidence suggests that young athletes can be influenced by adults' use of TFL behaviors. Using the MLQ-5X (Bass & Avolio, 1990), Zacharatos and colleagues (2000) employed a global perspective to examine TFL behaviors in sport. Results indicated that adolescents who observed their parents exhibiting TFL behaviors in turn manifested TFL behaviors themselves when interacting with their teammates in sport. Furthermore, adolescents who employed these behaviors in their interactions were rated as more effective, satisfying, and effort-evoking leaders by their coaches and peers. This study highlights (1) that parents can employ TFL behaviors and (2) the potential benefits of using these behaviors to develop leadership in youths. Further, these findings lend support to the cascade effect (Bass, 1985) and the notion that followers can learn to use TFL behaviors through imitating important role models (Barling, 2014; Lehmann-Willenbrock et al., 2015).

Parents' use of TFL behaviors has also been examined in relation to adolescents' health behaviors. For example, Morton and colleagues (2011) adopted a global approach to develop the Transformational Parenting Questionnaire. Using this tool, 857 adolescents rated the leadership behaviors of their mothers and fathers. Results found positive relations between mothers' and fathers' transformational parenting behaviors, adolescents' self-regulatory efficacy for physical activity and healthy eating, and life satisfaction. These findings indicate there may be value in a similar exploration of parents' TFL behaviors in sport settings.

Given the limited research to date on parents' TFL behaviors in sport, it may be useful to reflect on how parents' leadership behaviors may influence athletes' developmental outcomes. During the early stages of athletes' sport participation, athletes rely heavily on parents as a source of information and feedback (Horn & Weiss, 1991). With this in mind, parents' use of inspirational motivation behaviors, such as expressing confidence in athletes' capabilities or discussing goals and expectations, may shape athletes' perceptions of their own competence. Moreover, by using intellectual stimulation behaviors, such as emphasizing the learning process, parents may positively contribute to athletes' adoption of a mastery-oriented approach to achievement.

Another way parents may serve as leaders for athletes is by setting standards or role modeling (Vealey & Chase, 2016). Parental modeling of physical activity and sport participation (e.g., Brustad, 1993; Sebire et al., 2016), moral behavior and life skills (e.g., self-regulation of emotions, using respectful behaviors; Arthur-Banning et al., 2009), and work ethic (Eccles & Harold, 1991) can serve as important behavioral cues for athletes. For example, in their examination of motivational outcomes in youth soccer players, Babkes and Weiss (1999) found that athletes who perceived their parents to be positive role models reported higher levels of perceived competence, enjoyment, and intrinsic motivation in soccer. It may thus be particularly useful to examine the influence of parents' use of idealized influence behaviors in their interactions with their athletes.

Parents can also play a pivotal role in the sport environment through their involvement in the administration or coaching of sport programs (Barber et al., 1999). Given that parents are often asked to engage in a variety of leadership roles within sport organizations, it is crucial for researchers and practitioners to explore ways of optimizing the quality of their leadership-based interactions with a range of invested partners. For instance, it may be interesting to explore how parents employ TFL behaviors when leading volunteer initiatives or organizing team events. Overall, parents' leadership behaviors represent a fruitful avenue for future research and practical interventions.

Peer TFL

Given that peer leaders have been identified as a critical element of the sport environment (Fransen et al., 2014; Hoffman & Loughead, 2016), it is important to explore how peer leaders employ TFL behaviors. To this end, Price and Weiss (2011) used the MLQ-5X (Bass & Avolio, 1990) to explore the characteristics of peer leaders among 191 adolescent female soccer players and the influence of peer leaders' TFL on athlete outcomes. Results found that peer leaders were characterized by higher levels of soccer competence, peer acceptance, behavioral conduct, and intrinsic motivation. Moreover, effective peer TFL was linked with higher perceptions of task and social cohesion and collective efficacy. These results lend valuable insight into the characteristics of peer leaders as well as their potential influence on athlete development. In doing so, they may help inform selection processes of peer leaders in sport. These finding also underscore the importance of providing leadership opportunities for athletes.

Price and Weiss (2013) further investigated the influence of coach and peer TFL on adolescent soccer players' individual and team outcomes. Findings demonstrated that while both coach and peer TFL were linked with athletes' perceptions of task cohesion, peer TFL was more influential for athletes' perceptions of social cohesion. This finding illustrates how the use of TFL by social agents may hold important implications for athlete development in sport. This also relates to the findings of Smith and colleagues (2017) described previously, which found that peer leaders can use TFL in different yet complementary ways. Collectively, these studies highlight the value of examining the intersections between different leaders' (e.g., coaches and peers) behaviors within the sport environment.

One potential avenue for future research on peer leaders is to examine how TFL may be used by different types of athlete leaders. Fransen and colleagues (2014) categorized athlete leadership into

- task leaders (responsible for aiding in goal attainment, making tactical decisions),
- motivational leaders (responsible for emotional regulation on the field, encouraging teammates to reach team objectives),
- social leaders (responsible for promoting the development of high-quality, interpersonal relationships between teammates), and
- external leaders (responsible for acting as a liaison between teammates and external organizations, such as the team's sport club).

Evidence suggests that all four types of leaders can shape team processes, such as conflict (Dupuis et al., 2006), resilience (Morgan et al., 2015), and performance (Fletcher & Arnold, 2011). Given the diverse nature of these leadership types, it may be worthwhile to explore how TFL may be manifested in each of these roles. For example, do motivational leaders use more inspirational motivation-related behaviors, or do social leaders use more individualized consideration behaviors?

It may also be beneficial to explore how peers' TFL behaviors are enacted in everyday sport settings. For instance, researchers could build on the observational work with coaches to develop instruments to assess athletes' real-time leadership behaviors. For example, an athlete leader may use more intellectual stimulation behaviors while discussing team strategies during a practice, and display more individualized consideration behaviors while discussing their favorite movies in the dressing room. By examining peer leadership in different settings (e.g., participating in practice or competition, resting on the bench, talking with teammates during social events), researchers may gain a deeper understanding of the situational influences on leadership behaviors.

Official TFL

Although often overlooked in sport research, officials represent another important leader in sport (Tucker et al., 2006). Tasked with applying the rules and procedures to create fair and equitable sport environments, officials can act as leaders by encouraging coaches and players to engage in prosocial behaviors and by imposing consequences when transgressions occur (Tucker et al., 2006). For example, previous studies suggest that officials can influence coaches' communication behaviors (Cunningham et al., 2014; Mellick et al., 2005) and athletes' positive sporting behaviors (Arthur-Banning et al., 2007). As such, it may be worthwhile to explore how officials' use of TFL may influence developmental outcomes in sport.

By examining peer leadership in different settings (e.g., participating in practice or competition, resting on the bench, talking with teammates during social events), researchers may gain a deeper understanding of the situational influences on leadership behaviors.

To explore this possibility, Tucker and colleagues (2006) randomly assigned head coaches of competitive hockey teams to receive one of two questionnaires that asked them to recall (1) a situation in which a referee with whom they were familiar apologized for making a mistake during a game or (2) a situation in which a referee with whom they were familiar did not apologize for making a mistake during a game. Coaches were also asked to reflect on the leadership qualities of that referee. Ninety-four coaches responded to the survey (43 for the apology condition and 51 for the no apology condition). Results indicated that referees who were perceived as having apologized for mistakes were rated as more transformational than when no apology was made. These findings illustrate that officials can be viewed as transformational within the sport environment and that apologies may be one avenue through which leaders can foster perceptions of TFL among sport partners. Although these findings provide preliminary insight into how TFL may be relevant for sport officials, much more research is needed in this area.

Organizational TFL

Although TFL has often been examined at the micro level (i.e., coach–athlete, parent–child relationships), it is important to recognize that these relationships are nested within broader societal contexts (e.g., within sport clubs, associations, countries). As such, it is important to examine how TFL may be manifested by the leaders of sport organizations. One such study explored the use of TFL among sport organizations' athletic directors. Lee and colleagues (2018) used questionnaires to assess 244 intercollegiate head coaches' perceptions of athletic directors' TFL, affective commitment, and organizational citizenship behaviors. Results demonstrated that TFL was positively linked with affective commitment, which in turn was positively linked with organizational citizenship behaviors. These findings shed light on a mechanism by which organizational leaders can influence partner outcomes. The research parallels the work of Thoonen and colleagues (2001) in educational contexts, which found that principals' use of inspirational motivation was associated with teachers' outcome interdependence, whereas their use of individualized consideration and intellectual stimulation was linked with task interdependence. Overall, these studies indicate that the use of TFL by organizational leaders can shape partner relationships. Nonetheless, since there is a paucity of research in this area, there is a need for researchers and practitioners to further investigate TFL at the organizational level.

To better understand the role of TFL in sport organizations, it may be useful to investigate the culture of sport organizations, including their artifacts, their values, and the behaviors of partners within the organization (e.g., Schein, 2004). Researchers are also encouraged to explore organizational leadership across a wide variety of sport contexts, including community-based, volunteer driven organizations and professional sport organizations. Such studies may yield valuable insight into how TFL may be influenced by contextual constraints and may help uncover the dynamic relations that exist between organizational leadership and partner outcomes.

Future Research Directions

Based on the research reviewed throughout this chapter, a growing body of literature supports the notion that TFL is a salient lens for understanding leadership in sport and its potential influence on athlete development. Although the theoretical and conceptual frameworks described in this chapter provide insight into the role of TFL in sport, further development of TFL research in sport is vital. First, future research needs to consider the unique micro- and macroenvironments of sport and the way in which these environments evolve over athletes' developmental trajectories. Given the dominance of cross-sectional study designs, questions remain regarding the long-term effects of TFL. It would thus be beneficial for future research to adopt longitudinal approaches to the study of leadership in sport. Moreover, it is unclear how the influence of different partners' TFL behaviors may change over the course of athletes' developmental trajectories. For example, it may be interesting to examine potential differences in the influence of parental and peer leadership behaviors on athlete development in the early years of sport participation compared with adolescence. The adoption of longitudinal approaches may lend valuable insight into the dynamic nature of leadership and its influence on athlete development.

The application of diverse methodologies represents another important avenue for future TFL research to redefine how leadership is studied. With regard to quantitative approaches, social network analysis (e.g., Freeman, 2004) may provide novel theories, methods, and analyses that could enhance our understanding of leadership in sport. For example, researchers could construct social networks of athletes at different points along athletes' developmental trajectories and explore how these social networks are associated with leadership roles and developmental outcomes. On the other hand, social network analysis could be used within sport organizations to examine how the leadership behaviors of sport administrators may influence organizational processes (e.g., knowledge sharing) and organizational culture.

Another quantitative tool that may be useful for future TFL research is the state space grid (SSG; Lewis et al., 1999) method, which allows for in-depth analysis of real-time interpersonal interactions (Erickson et al., 2011). The SSG method provides researchers with an opportunity to investigate the dynamic and reciprocal nature of TFL-based interactions because it focuses on the temporal course of interactions while accounting for the behaviors of multiple actors (e.g., the coach and athlete, the parent and child, peers, the coach and official). As such, this technique may provide insight into how different invested partners (e.g., athletes, coaches, parents) (1) use TFL behaviors, (2) respond to TFL behaviors, and (3) elicit TFL behaviors from others. By exploring the content and structure of TFL-based interactions, future research may contribute to a more in-depth understanding of the leadership process.

The use of such innovative methodological tools may be particularly important because the majority of previous studies were conducted with a unidirectional flow of influence (Avolio, 2007). Using this approach, followers are often positioned as passive recipients of leadership behaviors. However, followers play an active role in shaping leadership behaviors and can have a significant influence on the construction of leadership relationships and the outcomes derived from these relationships. Thus, methodological approaches should aim to capture the dynamic nature of leadership.

The field may also benefit from the use of more qualitative approaches. Indeed, qualitative techniques such as interviews, focus groups, observations, and document analysis may lend new insight into invested partners' TFL behaviors. For example, case studies may offer an avenue for exploring the intersection of different TFL-based interactions within specific settings (e.g., in a specific team, club, or organization). Another worthwhile direction could involve the adoption of narrative approaches, which may shed light on (1) the stories invested partners use to understand, make meaning of, and relate to their leadership experiences and (2) how these stories can be situated and understood in relation to familial, institutional, and cultural narratives (Caine et al., 2013). The growing body of knowledge emanating from qualitative research may capture a more nuanced picture of the leadership processes in sport.

As illustrated throughout this chapter, TFL can be measured through a variety of tools (e.g., questionnaires, systematic observation coding systems, interviews). Although the dominant approach is self-report questionnaires, a diverse range of methodologies would more accurately capture the nuances of TFL in sport. As such, self-report measures may be most valuable in combination with methods such as observations (qualitative or quantitative measures of behaviors), diary methods, artifact analysis, qualitative interviews or focus groups, or descriptive information about how TFL is used in a variety of sport contexts.

Finally, it would be beneficial for future research to engage in knowledge mobilization to examine how evidence-informed products and tools can be applied in real-world sport programs. One example of TFL-based knowledge mobilization research is the development, implementation, and evaluation of educational programs intended to develop TFL behaviors in leaders (e.g., Barling et al., 1996; Beauchamp et al., 2011; Lawrason et al., 2019; Vella et al., 2013b). These studies suggest that educational programs may be a promising avenue for disseminating TFL-informed research. Nonetheless, further research is needed to continue exploring the effectiveness of these interventions in changing TFL behaviors and influencing developmental outcomes in larger samples and in a wider variety of sport contexts. It would also be worthwhile to explore how a broader assortment of TFL-informed knowledge products and tools (e.g., marketing, guidelines, policies, and legislation) can be implemented and adapted by sport organizations over time.

Practical Implications

Drawing on the research discussed in this chapter, it is evident that TFL may be a valuable lens for understanding leadership in sport. Accordingly, it is important to explore how TFL can be applied in real-world sport settings. To this end, this section explores ways partners could apply the four dimensions of TFL. First, idealized influence involves behaviors such as modeling personal values and beliefs. This dimension may be particularly important for partners to apply in practice since studies illustrate the importance of role modeling for developing leadership. Parents, coaches, officials, peers, and organizational administrators can apply this principle by making an active effort to demonstrate their personal values in their everyday settings. For instance, a captain who values teamwork could translate this value into action by modeling appropriate behaviors (e.g., helping others, giving feedback, organizing team events) or discussing the importance of such behaviors (e.g., having conversations with their peers about working together). Adult leaders (e.g., coaches, parents, officials) may also consider how they model their values in different contexts. For example, a coach who values respect should model respectful behaviors in their interactions with athletes, parents, officials, and community members.

Second, inspirational motivation includes behaviors such as having discussions about what others would like to achieve, how they will achieve it, and why these achievements are important. For example, organizational leaders may have meetings with parents to discuss expectations for parental behaviors. Officials can also discuss their expectations and standards for the competition with coaches and captains. It should be noted that inspirational motivation can be tailored to the context. To do so, leaders can consider who leads the interaction (e.g., adult vs. athlete), who is involved (e.g., officials, coaches, parents), and the content (e.g., are the expectations or achievements being discussed related to technique, teamwork, or balancing sport with hobbies, school or work, and family). Leaders can also enhance the quality of inspirational motivation-based interactions by ensuring that the expectations and desired achievements are meaningful to all partners.

Third, intellectual stimulation may be a particularly important dimension for leaders to consider since it can help shift sport from leader- to follower-centered approaches. For instance, parents can use intellectual stimulation to empower youths to make decisions to engage in sport activities that are relevant and meaningful for them. Coaches can also engage in intellectual stimulation by providing athletes with opportunities to make choices and decisions during practices and competitions and to take on a variety of leadership roles (e.g., formal roles such as captains, or informal roles such as peer mentorship or leading the design of practice activities). There are also numerous ways that organizational partners can adopt intellectual stimulation, such as by offering opportunities for athletes, parents, and coaches to provide input on organizational decision making. Organizational partners can also provide athletes and parents with opportunities to engage in leadership roles within sport organizations.

Lastly, individualized consideration may be enacted in practice by leaders who show others they genuinely care about who they are and what they do. For example, organizational partners may adapt practice schedules to accommodate a coach's family or work commitments. Coaches, parents, officials, and peer leaders can enact individualized consideration by listening to each other's concerns and discussing each other's interests. By gaining a deeper understanding of others' needs, leaders can more effectively create positive developmental experiences in sport.

Summary

Overall, this chapter has sought to highlight the importance of TFL for sport research, review the methodologies and empirical research that shape our current understanding of TFL in sport, and highlight exciting avenues for future research. Researchers and practitioners are challenged to work together to deepen our understanding of TFL among a diverse range of sport leaders. Advances in the methodological approaches to the study of TFL are needed to better understand the contribution of TFL in sport. It is our hope that this chapter will spark increased interest in this important topic.

DISCUSSION QUESTIONS

1. Think of your best leader in sport. What behaviors did they use that align with the four dimensions of TFL? How did they make you feel?
2. What are the 11 transformational coaching behaviors of the CLAS, and how do they fit within the four Is?
3. What criteria should we use to select and evaluate leaders in sport?
4. How could you develop an intervention that aims to create a transformational coaching environment?
5. Design a study to assess the development of TFL over time. What methods would you use?

8

The Social Identity Approach to Leadership

Matthew J. Slater, PhD, and Anthony Miller, PhD

LEARNING OBJECTIVES

On completion of this chapter, the reader should have the following:

- Understanding of the principles of the social identity approach to leadership
- Knowledge of current research on the social identity approach to leadership
- Capacity to identify gaps in literature that has examined the social identity approach to leadership
- Knowledge of current interventions based on the social identity approach to leadership

> A sense of followership is the glue for any group of people who want to outperform competitors.
>
> —Sir Alex Ferguson
> (previous manager of
> Manchester United Football Club)

Winning 38 domestic and international trophies across an uninterrupted 26-year spell as manager of Manchester United Football Club, Sir Alex Ferguson is often regarded as the most successful football manager ever. The opening quote speaks to how his leadership enabled Manchester United to outperform other teams through a "sense of followership." It was, perhaps, this sense of followership, or "glue," that psychologically bound the team together, including athletes, assistant coaches, and science and medicine staff. Followership—or a shared social identity, to put it more formally as it is theoretically operationalized—is what scholars researching the social identity approach to leadership place at the core of successful leadership. Put another way, successful leadership guides athletes' thoughts, decisions, and actions to be not only for themselves but to contribute to something bigger—a higher purpose (e.g., a sport team, a historic club or organization, a culture, a nation, or the legacy of sport in general, such as inspiring others at the Olympic Games). Such leadership leans into the complexity of group dynamics and the context, resulting in athletes' seeing their sport team's interests as their own because the team becomes an integral part of their sense of self (e.g., as "we" Patriots or "we" Lionesses). In sum, from a social identity perspective, leadership success hinges on a leader's ability to create, embody, advance, and embed a shared sense of social identity.

It is this focus on group dynamics and context, and in particular a shared *social identity*, that sets identity leadership apart from other approaches to leadership (such as those outlined in chapters 6 and 7). In this chapter, we set out how individuals in sport teams go about "leading for togetherness" by examining the contemporary empirical evidence and theoretical developments in the social identity approach. To achieve this vision, we first introduce the social identity approach more broadly, then outline four principles of the approach. Here too we compare and contrast the social identity approach with other leadership approaches and critically discuss issues surrounding the measurement. Next, we examine the growing empirical evidence supporting the social identity approach to leadership in sport, which sets the scene for proposed avenues for future research endeavors in this literature. Finally, we outline the practical applications of the social identity approach with the view that these ideas can be tried and tested by coaches, sport psychology consultants, performance directors, and others to develop leadership excellence.

Understanding the Social Identity Approach

The social identity approach encompasses social identity theory (Tajfel & Turner, 1979) and self-categorization theory (Turner et al., 1987), emphasizing the importance of group processes in understanding individual and group cognition and behavior. First, we begin with social identity theory. Addressing Mayo's (1949) proposal that the psychology of an individual is a product of their personal and social identities, the social identity approach contends that in social contexts people can define themselves as individuals (i.e., personal identity; "I" and "me") *and* as group members (i.e., a shared social identity; "we" and "us"). Personal identity explains an individual's perception of themselves as unique and different from other people. Alternatively, social identity refers to an "individual's knowledge that he [or she] belongs to certain social groups together with some emotional value and significance to him [or her] of this group membership" (Tajfel, 1972, p. 292). In other words, the self is personal in the sense that all individuals have their own unique personality, but more than this, people can (and do) define themselves based on the attributes they share with others—known as their social identities. Crucially, it is both an individual's personal identity and their range of social identities (i.e., group memberships) that make up a significant part of their self-concept (Haslam, 2004). Not all groups are perceived as important and meaningful, but all groups have the capacity to be internalized into the self. Developing this some more, taking Tajfel's (1972) point and applying it to a sporting context, when an athlete defines themselves in terms of their sport team (which is an example of a specific social identity—the in-group), they will be motivated to do all they can to ensure their team is distinct from, and better than, other sport teams (known as out-groups).

Successful leadership guides athletes' thoughts, decisions, and actions to be not only for themselves but to contribute to something bigger—a higher purpose.

Following early conceptualizations of social identity theory, self-categorization theory soon followed to expand on two areas in particular: (1) when individuals would define themselves within one of their social identities and (2) the consequences of defining the self in this collective way (Turner et al., 1987). As Haslam, Fransen, and Boen (2020) outlined, the proposals within self-categorization theory do this in at least three important ways:

- First, depersonalization is added. Depersonalization is what makes group behavior possible in that individuals categorize themselves as part of the group they share with others (they think "we" and "us" rather than "I" and "me"). Accordingly, this is the basis of working together as a team—there is potential that athletes can act for each other, themselves, and the group all at the same time.
- Second, given that individuals have a unique, individual personality but multiple social identities, self-categorization theory embellishes how particular social identities become salient. In other words, individuals can step into certain social identities in particular contexts, and in sport, this is understood to be a result of an interaction between an athlete's internal readiness to use a particular social identity and its external fit with the context.
- Third, the ramifications of social identity salience are made clear. When an athlete is operating within their sport team identity, there is perceived interchangeability with other members of that group (i.e., other athletes, coaches, science and medicine staff that are part of "us"—our sport team). This sense of connection and that "we are bound together" promotes many positive individual- and group-level outcomes, including influence, communication, and coordination of efforts.

Despite its promise, the social identity approach had, until recently, been comparatively overlooked in the context of sport. It is only since 2014 that this research field has begun to thrive, stimulated by a number of sport scholars' placing the social context at the forefront of their empirical investigations (see, for reviews, Haslam, Fransen, & Boen, 2020; Rees et al., 2015; Slater et al., 2014). To further understand this application to sport, we can turn to the empirical evidence. Researchers have found that athletes who perceive high levels of social identity with their sport team (i.e., high levels of psychological connection) are more likely to report greater self-worth, commitment, and effort (Martin et al., 2017), are more likely to be more task and socially cohesive (Fransen et al., 2016), and ultimately may perform better (Slater, Haslam, & Steffens, 2018). The focus by researchers on the social identity approach in sport is growing. Up until 2014, 271 articles had been published examining social identity in sport (Haslam, Fransen, & Boen, 2020). By the end of 2018, this total had grown to 483 publications, and by 2022, researchers' energies had culminated in an edited book (Haslam, Fransen, & Boen, 2020) and three international congresses attended by over 200 people across the globe.

In sum, the key contribution of the social identity approach reflects the notion that sport is very much a "we thing"—that is, derived from being a member of a group. The social identity approach to leadership takes these ideas forward and applies them to better understand successful leadership. Researchers have proposed and demonstrated that leaders' capacity to motivate others to progress toward a collective vision rests on their capacity to create, embody, advance, and embed a shared sense of "us" (Haslam, Reicher, & Platow, 2020; Steffens et al., 2014). Typically, in sport, *leaders* refers to formal roles including the coach and captain, but researchers have also highlighted the important role of informal leaders. Loughead, Hardy, and Eys (2006) defined athlete leadership as "an athlete occupying a formal or informal role within a team who influences a group of team members (i.e., a minimum of two team members) to achieve a common goal" (p. 144). Accordingly, athlete leaders may be a formal leader (e.g., a team captain), or an informal leader (e.g., a player who influences their teammates despite not having a formal leadership role; see chapter 9). Irrespective of whether an individual is a formal or informal leader, based on the social identity approach, there are four principles of effective leadership (figure 8.1): (1) leaders as identity *prototypes*, (2) leaders as identity *advancers*, (3) leaders as identity *entrepreneurs*, and (4) leaders as identity *impresarios* (Haslam, Reicher, & Platow, 2020; Slater et al., 2014; Steffens et al., 2014). The four principles are defined by Steffens and colleagues as follows:

1. Identity *prototypes*: "Being one of us." Representing the unique qualities that define the group and what it means to be a member of this group. Embodying those core attributes of the group that make this group special as well as distinct from other groups. Being an exemplary and model member of the group (p. 1003).
2. Identity *advancers*: "Doing it for us." Advancing and promoting core interests of the group. Standing up for and, if threatened, defending group interests (and not personal interests or those of other groups). Championing concerns and ambitions that are key to the group as a whole. Contributing to the realization of group goals. Acting to prevent group failures and to overcome obstacles to the achievement of group objectives (p. 1004).
3. Identity *entrepreneurs*: "Crafting a sense of us." Bringing people together by creating a shared sense of "we" and "us" within the group. Making people feel they are part of the same group and increasing cohesion and inclusiveness within the group. Clarifying people's understanding of what the group stands for (and what it does not stand for) by defining core values, norms, and ideals (p. 1004).
4. Identity *impresarios*: "Making us matter." Developing structures, events, and activities that give weight to the group's existence and allow group members to live out their membership. Promoting structures that facilitate and embed shared understanding,

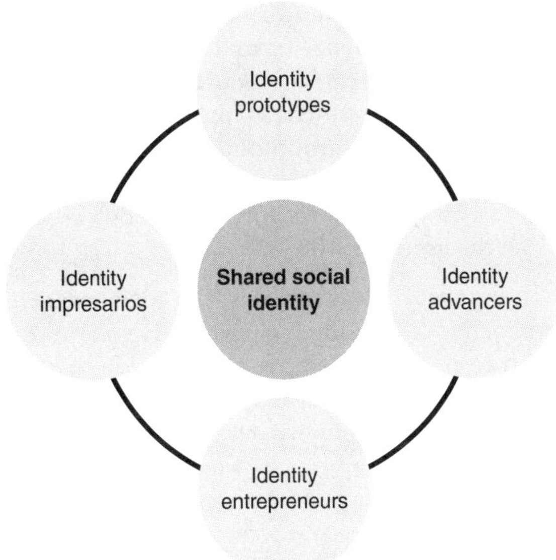

FIGURE 8.1 The four principles of the social identity approach to leadership.

> coordination, and success (and not structures that divide or undermine the group). Providing a physical reality for the group by creating group-related material and delivering tangible group outcomes. Making the group matter by making it visible not only to group members but also to people outside the group (p. 1005).

In organizational settings, the social identity approach to leadership is considered in its infancy (Dinh et al., 2014). Before its application to sport and exercise, for instance, 31 research articles on the social identity approach to leadership were published in 10 top-tier organizational journals between the years of 2000 and 2012 (Dinh et al., 2014). Bringing these research endeavors and those preceding 2000 together, Haslam and colleagues (2011) were the first to synthesize the four interrelated principles of the social identity approach to leadership. These four principles describe behaviors that individuals in sport teams can demonstrate. The principles are linked and can be enacted to develop a shared social identity, yet they are distinct in terms of how they are defined and measured, as well as how they contribute to team effectiveness. At that point (2011), there was no formal validation of these proposals because there was no measure associated with the social identity approach to leadership. On the heels of Haslam and colleagues' 2011 textbook, a validated measurement instrument capturing the four principles of the social identity approach to leadership was developed: the Identity Leadership Inventory.

Measurement of the Four Principles of the Social Identity Approach

The Identity Leadership Inventory (ILI; Steffens et al., 2014) has provided a validated instrument to capture the extent to which followers believe their leader is engaging in the four principles of the social identity approach to leadership. In other words, in a sporting context, athletes may complete the measure by rating their head coach, for example (although leadership is not reserved only for formal leaders in the social identity approach; Fransen et al., 2014), on the extent to which they create, advance, represent, and embed a shared social identity in their sport team. In the initial development and validation manuscript, Steffens and colleagues (2014) documented content, construct, discriminant, and criterion validity across three cultures of the United States, China, and Belgium, including one study in sport. The full version of the ILI includes 15 items and asks followers to rate questions that point to each of the four principles. There is a short form, too, that comprises four items, with *Group X* replaced with the name of the sport team:

1. This leader is a model member of [Group X] = identity prototype ("Being one of us").
2. This leader acts as a champion for [Group X] = identity advancer ("Doing it for us").
3. This leader creates a sense of cohesion within [Group X] = identity entrepreneur ("Crafting a sense of us").
4. This leader creates structures that are useful for [Group X] members = identity impresario ("Making us matter").

The publication of the ILI has led to a growth in research on the social identity approach to leadership across a range of domains. For example, in a global study in 20 countries (representing all six inhabited continents), van Dick and colleagues (2018) translated the ILI into 13 different languages and investigated the psychometric properties of the instrument. The results indicated that the measure was valid across cultures, further supporting its use, and all translated versions are freely available online. It's clear that one of the emerging strengths within the social identity approach to leadership literature is the consistent adoption of the ILI, a goal that has been facilitated through transparency, openness, and access to the measure for all scholars.

Comparing the Social Identity Approach With Other Approaches

At this juncture, we can begin distinguishing the social identity approach to leadership from other leadership approaches in sport. In terms of similarities, the social identity approach, in a similar vein to transformational approaches (i.e., individualized consideration as one of the four Is; Bass & Riggio, 2006) and the coach–athlete relationship model (chapter 1), does account for relational elements within the leadership process. One point of differentiation reflects the theoretical focus within the social identity approach to the social self (i.e., individuals have both personal and social identities, as explained earlier). The individualized consideration element of transformational leadership provides a useful comparison because it primarily reflects the individual needs of the athletes, which is an important part of successful leadership. In contrast, the social identity approach centers on collective (encompassing the sport team as a whole) *and* personal consideration, reflecting that the group can be internalized as part of the self.

In addition, empirical investigations provide evidence that leadership as outlined by the social identity approach is distinct from other popular approaches. Van Dick and colleagues' (2018) global project demonstrated that the extent to which followers perceived leaders to engage in the four principles was uniquely associated with pertinent group outcomes, such as social identification, trust, and job satisfaction, beyond transformational leadership, authentic leadership, and leader–member exchange. This study was not in sport, and thus future researchers could examine whether these relationships apply with coaches and athletes. Yet the data imply that the social identity approach is distinct from other approaches to leadership, and engagement in the four principles is associated with unique benefits.

Third, it remains the case that approaches to leadership in sport typically shine an individualistic lens on the individual leader or a dyadic lens between a coach and an athlete. For example, the coach–athlete relationship model (chapter 1) focuses on the dyadic relationship between coach and athlete. In contrast, researchers within the social identity approach examine leadership more broadly by, for example, focusing on other team members who can show successful leadership, notwithstanding whether they have a formal leadership role or not. Thus, the lens is wider and captures the broader view that leadership success hinges upon the group processes at play—in particular, the social identity dynamics—within a social group (Haslam, 2004).

Leadership success hinges upon the group processes at play—in particular, the social identity dynamics—within a social group.

Developing this point some more, often within sport, leadership approaches focus on the formal leader, usually the coach. Beyond this, the social identity approach to leadership has similarities to shared leadership (see Fransen, Barker, & Slater, 2020) and outlines how any group member can have an influence and therefore show leadership, whether formally in a leadership role or not. This approach, which is democratically leaning, links the social identity approach and shared leadership at least in part, but theoretical differences remain. Shared leadership does not account for the social identities of coaches or athletes, while the social identity approach places these group dynamics at the theoretical core. Further, shared leadership asserts that having multiple athlete leaders can be helpful for team functioning and performance (see chapter 9), while the social identity approach would indicate that success remains bound up within the social identity dynamics at play and the leadership of the coach. While evidence has shown that informal athlete leaders may be more effective leaders than formal athlete leaders on sport teams (e.g., captains; Fransen et al., 2014), and that coaches who display identity leadership bring about positive outcomes (e.g., Miller et al., 2020), some evidence (Fransen, McEwan, & Sarkar, 2020) indicates that coaches, formal athlete leaders (e.g., captains), and informal athlete leaders all uniquely positively influence players' social identification.

Finally, within the identity leadership approach there is a strong emphasis on theory *and* practice. In particular, taking theory to practice, identity leadership includes an evidence-based leadership development program that coaches and athletes alike can engage with to enhance their identity leadership (e.g., the three Rs: reflect, represent, realize [Haslam, Reicher, & Platow, 2020; Slater & Barker, 2019]; the five Rs [Mertens et al., 2020]). The focus on both theory and practice is similar to other approaches to leadership in sport such as the mediational model, which provides intervention for coaches to engage with (see chapter 6). Other leadership approaches have focused less on practice, such as transformational leadership (chapter 7), which does not clearly outline a theoretically based intervention program, and the corresponding empirical evidence to develop leadership success in sport.

Now that we have highlighted some of the theoretical similarities and points of contrast between the social identity approach and other leadership models in sport, we move to analyzing the research undertaken in this field. In the following section, we examine the growing body of research that has investigated the influence of the social identity approach to leadership across a range of key variables in sport (e.g., motivation, attendance, burnout).

Research on the Social Identity Approach to Leadership in Sport

Away from sport, a large body of research literature has indicated that individuals who are perceived to lead in a way that creates a shared social identity are more trusted (Geissner & van Knippenberg, 2008), influential (Subašic et al., 2011), and effective overall (van Knippenberg & van Knippenberg, 2005). Since 2014, leadership researchers have both confirmed and expanded these insights in the sport domain. In other words, growing evidence in sport settings has supported the assertion that leaders who create, embody, advance, and embed a collective sense of "us" are more effective. In what follows, we discuss this expanding research literature on the social identity approach to leadership in sport.

Performance Director and Coach Leadership

In an early examination of the applicability of the social identity approach to leadership in sport, research by Slater and colleagues (2015) examined Olympic leaders' media communication surrounding the London 2012 Olympic Games. Six prominent leaders were analyzed using inductive and deductive thematic analysis from 100 days prior to, during, and for 30 days following the Olympic Games:

- Lord Seb Coe (chairperson of the 2012 Olympic and Paralympic Games)
- Andy Hunt (Team GB chef de mission)
- Charles van Commenee (performance director of British athletics)
- Sir David Brailsford (performance director of British cycling)
- David Tanner (performance director of British rowing)
- Michael Scott (performance director of British swimming)

The analysis created five higher-order themes that displayed a range of social identity processes: creation of team identities, team values, team vision, performance consequences, and "we" achieved. In other words, leaders at the London 2012 Olympic Games and performance directors consistently communicated a positive, distinctive, and enduring sense of social identity in their language. Following this initial work examining Olympic leaders' media communication, researchers have adopted a systematic strategy for examining the social identity approach to leadership with coaches and athletes.

From an attendance and motivation perspective, researchers have found identity leadership to be influential in developing sport and exercise attendance (Stevens et al., 2018), mobilization of effort (Slater et al., 2019; Slater, Turner, et al., 2018), and athletic performance (i.e., power output; Stevens et al., 2019). In laboratory settings, Stevens and colleagues (2019) demonstrated that compared with low-identity entrepreneurship, recreational athletes led by a leader displaying high-identity entrepreneurship improved their power output on a 3.1-mile (5 km) cycling time trial. Further, the development of high (vs. low) relational identification between coaches and athletes has been associated with greater intentional mobilization of effort (Slater, Turner, et al., 2018). Developing shared identity content (i.e., the meaning and values members associated with their group; Turner, 1991) has also been found to be pertinent for followers' behavioral mobilization of effort (i.e., the number of minutes dedicated to a task requested by the leader; Slater et al., 2019). Often in laboratory leadership research, an individual external to the research team acts as the leader, while the performance tasks may lack realism. Thus, while a laboratory provides a controlled environment, what may be less clear is how these findings may play out with coaches and athlete leaders of competing sport teams.

Miller and colleagues (2020) investigated the social identity approach to leadership with coaches and their athletes both cross-sectionally and longitudinally. In particular, the researchers were interested in the influence of coach social identity leadership on athletes' resource appraisals (e.g., athletes' confidence) ahead of competition and on their performance, as well as examining the key aspects that may explain any relationships found. Analysis indicated that adult athletes across a range of sports reported positive associations between perceived social identity approach to leadership and resource appraisals (e.g., self-efficacy, perceived control, social support). In other words, the more their coach demonstrated the four principles of the social identity approach to leadership, the greater the athletes' psychological resources to deal with the demands of competition. Cross-sectionally, these relationships were underpinned by social and relational identification. Over the course of a competitive season, perceptions of the social identity approach to leadership in netball, soccer, and rugby athletes were not associated with resource appraisals other than self-efficacy, and this was mediated by relational (but not social) identification. Accordingly, there appear to be benefits of coaches' engaging in the social identity approach to leadership for athletes' psychological resources (e.g., self-efficacy) as they approach competition, and this is explained by social and relational identification. But the picture is more mixed temporally. Across a competitive season, there may be benefits on athletes' self-efficacy through relational identification but not on other resource appraisals. Thus, this area is still ripe for future research endeavors. Particularly, a focus on youth athletes is warranted, while researchers may wish to also stratify their sample to ensure suitable numbers of males and females, amateurs and professionals, and athletes from different types of sport (e.g., coactive vs. interactive) are represented.

The more their coach demonstrated the four principles of the social identity approach to leadership, the greater the athletes' psychological resources to deal with the demands of competition.

Athlete Leadership

Building on the predominance of leadership research in sport targeting the coach, there is a body of literature examining athlete leadership roles and outcomes (see chapter 9). As Loughead and colleagues (2006) noted in their definition of athlete leadership, players on sport teams have a formal role (e.g., captain) or informal role on the team and can be influential on teammates.

As part of the development and validation paper of the ILI, Steffens and colleagues (2014) conducted a study in sport focused on athlete leadership. The authors recruited 421 adult athletes in Belgium who competed in four team sports: basketball, soccer, volleyball, or handball. Rather than focusing on the coach as the formal leader, athletes were asked to consider their team captain. The results indicated that the captain's identity prototypicality, advancement, entrepreneurship, and impresarioship (i.e., the four dimensions of the social identity approach to leadership) played a unique role across a range of group dynamic and leadership outcomes. More specifically, identity prototypicality was associated with their influence within the sport team, identity advancement was associated with team members' confidence, identity entrepreneurship was associated with social identification on the team, and identity impresarioship was associated with the team's task cohesion.

More broadly, too, research evidence on athlete leadership corroborates the notion that athlete leaders' capacity to develop a shared sense of "we" and "us" within sport teams provides a foundation for team effectiveness (e.g., Fransen et al., 2014, 2016). Fransen, McEwan, and Sarkar (2020) conducted a cross-sectional study of handball players by asking them to rate the identity leadership of their coach, captain, and informal athlete leaders. They found that perceptions of how much coaches, captains, and informal athlete leaders engaged in identity leadership were associated with greater psychological safety, which in turn provided the foundation for high levels of team functioning and athlete health. The short form of the ILI was completed by athletes, and therefore we are unable to discern the relative influence of each of the four principles of the social identity approach to leadership. Yet different relationships were found across the three leaders. For example, informal leaders were more influential in the performance pathway, while coaches were more so in the health pathway. Thus, a more nuanced picture emerges beyond the notion that everyone engaging in the social identity approach to leadership will bring about the same individual- and group-level positive ramifications for all. This is a point for future researchers to explore.

One of the collective strengths of the early and developing body of literature on the social identity approach to leadership in sport reflects researchers' attention to the underlying mechanisms (i.e., mediators) that may go some way toward explaining the evidenced associations (e.g., Fransen, McEwan, & Sarkar, 2020; Miller et al., 2020; Stevens et al., 2019). The mechanisms through which the enactment of the four principles influences variables such as performance, effort, and attendance may include both relational (i.e., with the leader) and social identification. For example, Stevens and colleagues (2019) found that the enactment of identity leadership has a positive effect on sport and exercise attendance through social identification. Zhu and colleagues (2015) identified that leaders who strengthen followers' social identification are likely to improve followers' performance too. Specifically, because leaders can influence followers to internalize a group as part of their self-concept, this becomes the basis for follower attitude, behavior, and mobilization to engage with the group they identify with and, in turn, perform better. As an antecedent to group-level identification, and as an influence on variables such as attendance and performance, relational identification with a leader has also been found to play a role.

Relational Identification

Sluss and Ashforth (2007, p. 15) defined relational identification as "a (partial) definition of oneself in terms of a given role-relationship—what the relationship means to the individual." They posited that to identify with a collective (i.e., group identification), an individual must identify with the individuals that embody and sustain the role-relationship. Simply, an individual is likely to see the collective (i.e., group identification) as an extension of the dyadic role-relationship (Sluss & Ashforth, 2007). To illustrate, an athlete may need to first perceive a strong psychological connection with their coach, which then gives rise, at least in part, to the athlete's identification with the broader sport team. In other words, under the leadership of Jurgen Klopp, perhaps the Liverpool players need to identify strongly with Jurgen Klopp, which is then the platform for identification with the Liverpool football team.

Echoing this argument, outside of sport, Sluss and colleagues (2012) demonstrated that strong relational identification with a leader can, in turn, positively influence group identification. A heightened level of relational identification has been shown to influence follower creativity (Gu et al., 2015), perceptions of social support (White et al., 2020), and positive appraisals of motivated performance situations (i.e., important stress-inducing events such as a competitive sport match; Slater, Turner, et al., 2018). Yet only the study by Slater, Turner, and colleagues (2018) was conducted in sport. Indeed, relational identification has been largely overlooked in sport leadership research examining the social identity approach. Perhaps this is because relational identification is not as clearly theoretically integrated within the social identity approach to leadership compared with the four principles that are conceptualized to lead to a shared social identity. Figure 8.2 reflects a proposed model of how relational identification may integrate within the social identity approach to leadership as a separate construct to social identification, but this requires empirical testing.

Indeed, relational identification could be an important aspect to examine. Two studies that have investigated relational identification are Slater, Turner, and colleagues (2018) and Miller and colleagues (2020). According to Slater, Turner, and colleagues (2018), low levels of relational identification with a leader led to threat (i.e., maladaptive) physiological stress reactivity when an athlete was approaching a competitive scenario, holding negative health implications too. However, despite a controlled experimental program of research, the researchers concluded that competing athletes need to be examined in an ecologically valid setting.

Further demonstrating how both relational and social identification can influence appraisals of motivated performance situations temporally and with competing athletes, Miller and colleagues (2020) showed that perceptions of coach identity leadership positively influenced dyadic relationships between coach and athlete. As a result, athletes were then likely to see the group as an extension of the dyadic relationship, leading to greater group identification. It's plausible that the relationship with the coach may have been integrated into the athletes' sense of self. In other words, dyadic relationships become meaningful and significant for athletes and a part of their self-concept. This is likely to generate social identification because both the coach and athlete share the group membership (of the sport team), the coach is a key part and influence within that sport team, and it is in both of their interests that the team does well.

From this identification (relational and group), athlete efficacy, perceived control, and approach goals were bolstered on approach to a competitive sport match. In addition, compared with poor relational identification, perceiving a strong relational identification with a coach positively influenced

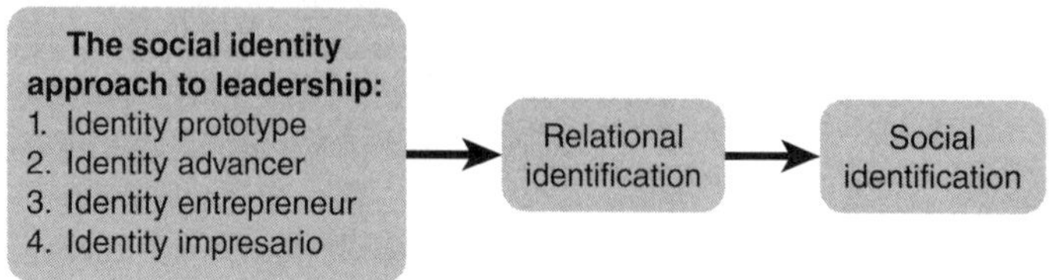

FIGURE 8.2 The four principles of the social identity approach to leadership may give rise to relational identification and then social identification.

athletes' efficacy, perceived control, approach goals, and cognitive performance within competitive situations (Slater, Turner, et al., 2018). The social identity approach to leadership positively influences not only appraisals of events but also athletes' psychological safety to speak up, freedom to take risks, team-level resilience, satisfaction with performance, and perceptions of burnout (Fransen, McEwan, & Sarkar, 2020). Evidently, coaches, captains, and athletes engaging in the social identity approach to leadership are likely to see multiple positive outcomes, and researchers in sport have only just begun to scratch the surface of this exciting field.

In reviewing the contemporary and growing literature on the social identity approach to leadership in sport, a number of shortcomings pave the way for future research endeavors. First, literature has tended to focus on adult sport teams (and not youth). Second, there has been a focus on motivation- and performance-related outcomes rather than health (but this is emerging). Third, researchers have conducted experimental work and cross-sectional studies but few longitudinal designs. Fourth, in designing studies, researchers have focused on psychological outcomes and could consider objective measures of effort, performance, and health. Finally, less attention has been given to the practical applications of leadership development programs. With these limitations in mind, in the subsequent section we outline a number of fruitful avenues for future research endeavors to expand our knowledge of the social identity approach to leadership in sport.

Future Research Directions

Although researchers examining the social identity approach have increased our understanding of effective leadership, there are many sport populations (e.g., youth athletes), topics of interest (e.g., general health and stress reactivity), study designs (e.g., objective outcome measures and longitudinal designs), and practical applications (e.g., identity leadership development programs) that remain understudied. First, research is necessary to understand whether identity leadership constructs are applicable in youth sport settings. The ILI (Steffens et al., 2014; van Dick et al., 2018) has been used and validated globally within an adult population, but the lack of instrument development for youth populations has inhibited our understanding of this population. In other words, a revised youth version of the ILI would be valuable to open research avenues within youth sport contexts. The focus of positive youth development is a key strand of sport psychology and one that, to date, identity leadership researchers have overlooked.

Most recently, researchers have found evidence that in addition to the influence of the social identity approach to leadership on motivational-related outcomes (e.g., Stevens et al., 2019), health-related outcomes such as stress reactivity (Miller et al., 2020; Slater, Turner, et al., 2018), burnout, and well-being (Fransen, McEwan, & Sarkar, 2020) are affected by athletes' perceptions of the extent to which their leader engages in identity leadership. For example, there is scope to understand how the four principles, relational identification, and social identification influence physiological reactivity to stressful situations. Slater, Turner, and colleagues (2018) demonstrated that poor relational identification led to maladaptive physiological responses to competitive scenarios, and as such, there is scope to understand whether the four identity leadership dimensions as outlined in the model (Haslam, Reicher, & Platow, 2020; Steffens et al., 2014) influence psychophysiological stress reactivity in response to an imminent competitive situation. Drawing from the social cure literature (Haslam et al., 2018), there is certainly research attention to be directed even more so to the role of social factors such as the social identity approach to leadership and on athletes' more general health and well-being. Indeed, this potential avenue for future research focuses on both subjective and objective markers of, for example, stress reactivity, and a focus on objective outcomes of identity leadership more generally could be of interest.

Future researchers may wish to examine the distinction and theoretical integration between the four principles of the social identity approach to leadership, social identification, and relational identification. Figure 8.2 outlines one hypothesized process that is supported by initial evidence in sport (Miller et al., 2020) and outside of sport (Zhu et al., 2015), but more empirical evidence is needed. It is also plausible that athletes' perceiving their coach to be leading in line with the four principles stimulates both social and relational identification simultaneously (rather than relational leading to social identification).

Following Slater and colleagues' (2019) assessment of behavioral mobilization and Stevens and colleagues' (2019) use of a cycling time trial performance as key dependent variables, future identity leadership studies would do well to continue in this vein and assess objective outcomes.

This way, a more comprehensive account of the effects of the social identity approach to leadership could be ascertained. Along with considering outcome measures, researchers may consider improving other methodological elements, such as the design. For instance, there are growing studies in the laboratory that take the first step toward causation (e.g., Slater et al., 2019; Slater, Turner, et al., 2018; Stevens et al., 2019), and these inform both theory and practice. Yet field studies tend to rely on cross-sectional designs. Thus, continuing experimental work in the laboratory and encouraging field experiments, together with a focus on longitudinal designs, would certainly be a step toward increasing our knowledge of the influence of the social identity approach to leadership on pertinent outcomes temporally (e.g., over an entire season, or throughout the duration of a competition). Along similar lines, the field research, although mainly cross-sectional (e.g., Fransen, McEwan, & Sarkar, 2020; Miller et al., 2020, study 1), has for the most part sought to analyze underpinning mechanisms (i.e., social and relational identification) with the view of going beyond the description of associations. This focus on path models and mediation analyses should be continued and, where possible, should involve temporal assessment of variables.

In the next section we focus on the practical applications of identity leadership. Indeed, a clear evidence-based framework to take theory to practice is a key strength of the social identity approach to leadership (Haslam, Reicher, & Platow, 2020). That said, compared with experimental (e.g., Stevens et al., 2019) and field studies of associations between concepts (e.g., Fransen, McEwan, & Sarkar, 2020), few examples of applied intervention studies aim to develop leadership skills (for exceptions, see Fransen, Haslam, et al., 2020; Mertens et al., 2020; Slater & Barker, 2019). Accordingly, future applied researchers may wish to implement identity leadership-based interventions using randomized controlled trials to better assess the effectiveness of such leadership development programs. It would be further valuable to increase the diversity of the populations involved in such work. As with many areas of sport psychology literature, there is a predominant focus on Western cultures within the identity leadership literature, and a more holistic approach would be welcomed.

A clear evidence-based framework to take theory to practice is a key strength of the social identity approach to leadership.

Practical Implications

This chapter has outlined the thriving and robust evidence pointing to the positive influence of leaders' engaging in the social identity approach to leadership for both individual outcomes (e.g., mobilization of effort; Slater et al., 2019) and group-level outcomes (e.g., team functioning; Fransen et al., 2014). Despite this valuable starting point, there are clearly many nuances to the associations and, as outlined in the section on future research, a significant amount of empirical work to be done going forward. Collectively, it can be advocated that coaches, performance directors, science and medicine staff, and athletes who wish to develop their leadership skills, as well as sport psychology consultants who can facilitate this development, should take a careful look at the social identity approach. In particular, the practical application of the social identity approach to leadership has centered on the 3R model (Haslam et al., 2011).

Haslam and colleagues initially proposed the 3R model (reflecting, representing, realizing) to develop the social identity approach to leadership. The 3R model comprises three stages:

- *Reflecting* involves listening and observing to understand the identities that matter to group members and what it means to individuals to be part of the group.
- *Representing* involves ensuring that leadership decisions and actions champion the collective identity and the leader acts as a role model for the group.
- *Realizing* involves embedding in reality the collective identity and achieving or making progress toward the collective vision.

According to Slater (2019), there are multiple objectives within each phase (see figure 8.3), and in practice, the 3R model can be delivered in a number of ways. On the one side, sport psychology consultants could work one-on-one with the coach. This approach has yet to receive empirical examination but would involve the coach then completing tasks with their team in between sessions with the sport psychology consultant. On the other side, sport psychology consultants can facilitate interactive workshops with coaches, support staff, and athletes

Reflecting

- Understand the group memberships that athletes and staff have
- Understand the values athletes and staff associate with the team and their vision for the team
- Understand the unique characteristics of the team
- Understand the team's history, including successes and failures

Representing

- Develop and agree on a set of shared values and a collective vision
- Develop and agree on behaviors aligned with common values
- Put the team's interests first (e.g., in decision making)

Realizing

- Live out the team's shared values
- Live up to behaviors and evaluate these in an ongoing manner
- Achieve a collective vision
- Achieve togetherness (i.e., a shared social identity)

FIGURE 8.3 Objectives of the 3R phases of reflecting, representing, and realizing.
Based on Slater (2019).

on sport teams for each of these phases (Slater & Barker, 2019). Session content may include the following (Slater, 2019):

- The reflecting workshop might cover social identity mapping (Cruwys et al., 2016), emphasizing the importance of reflecting on and discussing the team's core values and interests, as well as beginning to gather ideas for the collective vision.
- In the representing workshop, the team agrees on shared values and identifies behaviors that align with them.
- The realizing session may highlight the importance of goal setting for success, creating an action plan to achieve the team's vision through identifying any barriers that may need to be overcome.

At the time of writing, only one study published in sport adopted the 3R model in practice. Slater and Barker (2019) provide promising initial evidence of the usefulness and effect of the 3R model, but at present there is insufficient testing of the three Rs in sport to be conclusive. Over two years in an international disability football context, Slater and Barker created a senior leadership team (SLT) of three staff members and four athletes to facilitate the 3R program. The athletes invited to be part of the SLT were empowered to complete the same activities (e.g., social identity mapping) with their teammates who are not directly involved in the SLT, in a train-the-trainer approach. These athletes would then feed in the information from the wider athlete team in the following SLT session, to ensure the involvement of everyone.

Slater and Barker delivered the 3R program twice, first to a national team and then to a Paralympic team in the second year. In the first year, results indicated that compared with baseline data, athletes reported medium effect size increases in social identification, engagement in the social identity approach to leadership of staff, and mobilization of effort; there were large effect size increases in the hours of practice away from formal training. Statistically these effects were not significant at the $p < .05$ level because of the small sample size. In the second year, compared with baseline data, athletes reported large effect size increases in social identification and engagement in the social identity approach to leadership of staff, along with medium increases in mobilization of effort and the hours of practice away from formal training.

In sum, there was promising support for the efficacy of the 3R model to develop perceived leadership, social identification, and mobilization of effort. As such, if a coaching staff in disability sport would like to bring their team together, they may aim to create, embody, advance, and embed a shared social identity, and the 3R model provides promise in doing so. Despite the model's being repeated with a largely new team in the second year to aid confidence in replication, there is clearly a need to apply the 3R model across all standards of sport, encompassing diverse cultures and types of sport to further examine the effectiveness.

Developing the 3R model further, Haslam and colleagues (2017) conducted a preliminary application of a 5R model with Allied Health team managers in Australia. Although this study is outside of sport, it includes two new phases in addition to the three core workshops on reflecting, representing, and realizing. The two new phases are as follows:

- In a first workshop, those involved were educated on the importance of social identity processes (i.e., *readying*).
- In a final workshop, progress toward the vision and goals was assessed and monitored (i.e., *reporting*).

These two new phases ensured that, at the outset, participants were educated sufficiently on the approach they would be engaging with, while at its conclusion they were able to review and monitor progress (or otherwise). The study's pre- and post-measures indicated that managers felt an improvement in their ability to engage in the social identity approach to leadership, along with a marginal increase in their social identification (Haslam et al., 2017). Despite this promising initial evidence, there were no data from the managers and followers on their perceptions of engagement in better or worse leadership. There are opportunities for future researchers to develop these ideas further in sport.

Summary

Our vision for this chapter was to set out how individuals on sport teams go about "leading for togetherness" by examining the contemporary empirical evidence and theoretical developments in the topic area of the social identity approach to leadership. The social identity approach to leadership centers on four principles (Haslam, Reicher, & Platow, 2020), whereby leaders

1. endorse the unique qualities that define a group they lead (i.e., identity prototypical),
2. advance and promote the core interests of the group (i.e., identity advancement),
3. bring people together by creating a shared sense of "we" and "us" (i.e., entrepreneur of identity), and
4. organize events and activities that give weight to the group's existence (i.e., impresario of identity).

Research on the social identity approach to leadership in sport is beginning to thrive. What already exists in the literature indicates that engaging in the principles of the social identity approach to leadership has positive implications for identification (relational and group), which in turn influences a multitude of variables such as self-efficacy, control, approach focus (Miller et al., 2020), physiological stress (Slater, Turner, et al., 2018), psychological safety, and burnout (Fransen, McEwan, & Sarkar, 2020). In this chapter, we hope we have paved the way with a road map for future research on the social identity approach to leadership in sport. There is certainly a range of exciting initial findings to further unpack, along with exciting opportunities for future researchers to latch onto. We believe such opportunities should, where possible, capture objective markers, adopt longitudinal designs, and focus on mechanisms to explain temporal relationships as well as new contexts, including youth sport and greater cultural diversity. As outlined in the quote by Sir Alex Ferguson at the start of this chapter, perhaps the social identity approach to leadership demonstrates how "a sense of followership is the glue for any group of people who want to outperform competitors."

DISCUSSION QUESTIONS

1. Describe the two theories that the social identity approach to leadership is based on.
2. Explain the four principles of the social identity approach to leadership.
3. Reflecting on your own experiences in sport, discuss whether you have had leaders who displayed the social identity approach to leadership or not (and the influence this had on you and your team). If you are a coach or captain, you could discuss how you have displayed the social identity approach to leadership.
4. Develop a study to take the identity leadership in sport literature forward. What would be your research question(s) and methodology?
5. Outline what interventions can be employed to develop identity leadership and how they bring about enhanced perceptions of leadership.
6. Develop a range of activities that could be used within the 3R model.

9

Athlete Leadership in Sport

Todd M. Loughead, PhD; Krista J. Munroe-Chandler, PhD;
Katherine E. Hirsch, MHK; and Matthieu M. Boisvert, MHK

LEARNING OBJECTIVES

On completion of this chapter, the reader should have the following:

- Knowledge of the conceptual models used to study athlete leadership
- Understanding of the methods used to assess athlete leadership
- Appreciation of the existing research literature on athlete leadership
- Understanding of the various approaches to developing athlete leadership

Leadership is regarded as important for achieving effective team functioning, and coaches are important sources of leadership within their teams. Coaches provide leadership in developing their athletes (e.g., personal growth, discipline), creating a positive team environment, and emphasizing the team as a collective. Further, coaches are largely responsible for constructing their own approach for leading their teams. For example, some coaches may value technical skill development, while others are more concerned with the social development of their athletes. Despite their role as a team leader, it is unreasonable to expect coaches to be able to fulfill each of their athletes' needs. As a result, athletes seek assistance from their teammates (Duguay et al., 2019). This is referred to as *athlete leadership*, which is a form of peer leadership characterized by interaction with other individuals. Loughead and colleagues (2006) noted that peer leaders are critical for enhancing team dynamics. Peer leadership is useful within sport teams because it is a form of social support that athletes are likely to perceive as beneficial and less threatening than that provided by an authority figure such as a coach (Gross & McMullen, 1983). Typically, athletes who provide peer leadership are at a slightly more advanced stage of tenure than those they are leading (Loughead et al., 2006). As such, teammates can easily identify with and relate to them (Duguay et al., 2018; Ender & Newton, 2000). Consequently, athlete leaders are sources of positive social influence by serving as teammates and role models.

This chapter is divided into six sections. The first section provides a definition of athlete leadership by conceptualizing the construct as being shared among many athletes. The second section begins by summarizing current theories and models used to study athlete leadership and concludes with the advancement of two recent conceptualizations of athlete leadership as a shared phenomenon. The third section highlights the approaches used to measure and assess athlete leadership along with considerations for designing an athlete-focused leadership inventory. The fourth section synthesizes the research conducted within athlete leadership by summarizing the characteristics of athlete leaders, the outcomes associated with having effective athlete leadership, and the sharedness of athlete leadership. Next, we highlight some potential areas for future research to help advance this emerging construct. Lastly, we conclude this chapter by presenting research that has examined the development of athlete leadership at the intercollegiate and youth levels, along with peer mentoring.

Athlete Leadership Defined

Historically, leadership theory and research in sport have been dominated by a leader-centered perspective reflecting an individualistic approach to understanding leadership. However, this perspective fails to capture a central aspect of leadership: It is a dynamic process carried out in a group or team context that is shaped by the interactions between multiple interdependent individuals (DeRue & Ashford, 2010). Athlete leadership aligns with this perspective and is defined as the process of athletes' fulfilling formal or informal leadership roles within a team and influencing team members to achieve a common goal (Loughead et al., 2006). Therefore, athlete leadership is a fluid, inclusive, and interactive form of leadership (Loughead et al., 2021). For instance, athletes can occupy a formal leadership role (i.e., assigned to a leadership position by the team) or an informal leadership role (i.e., assume a leadership role based on interactions with team members). In theory, the definition of athlete leadership implies that multiple athletes can provide leadership to their team. As a result, athlete leadership is shared among team members.

Gibb (1954) was one of the early scholars to note the importance of leadership's being shared among team members when he stated, "Leadership is probably best conceived as a group quality, as a set of functions which must be carried out by the group" (p. 884). As such, DeRue (2011) noted that shared leadership is a complex, adaptive process that involves a series of leading and following interactions. For example, within the context of a sport team, teammates will fulfill a leadership role when it is appropriate (i.e., leading) and will step back in other situations to allow other teammates to lead (i.e., following). With this approach to shared athlete leadership, teammates can exert leadership influence and provide guidance to one another as needed. Therefore, shared athlete leadership can be defined as an emergent and dynamic team process comprising mutual influence and shared responsibility dispersed among team members, who lead each other toward the achievement of team goals.

Athlete leadership is a fluid, inclusive, and interactive form of leadership.

According to the aforementioned definition, shared athlete leadership highlights four key characteristics:

- *Lateral influence among teammates.* There are two sources of athlete leadership—formal and informal (Loughead et al., 2006).
- *Emergent property of a team.* The leadership influence is pooled from team members (Duguay et al., 2019); it does not emanate from either the formal or informal athlete leader but is shared collectively among teammates.
- *Distribution of influence.* Athlete leadership is distributed among multiple athletes rather than being concentrated on one single leader (Duguay et al., 2019). The first two characteristics indicate that shared athlete leadership focuses on leadership influence from potentially all team members, whereas this third characteristic highlights how leadership is dispersed among teammates.
- *Dynamic nature of shared leadership.* Athlete leadership can be assumed by different athletes either at the same time or at varying points in the team's season (Duguay et al., 2020).
- Although the definitions of athlete leadership and shared athlete leadership are similar, shared athlete leadership is the process of two or more athletes providing athlete leadership. Contrastingly, athlete leadership does not always present itself in a shared way, despite there being opportunities for multiple leaders to exhibit leadership (i.e., shared leadership). That is, when multiple athletes fulfill a leadership role, this is considered shared athlete leadership. In many ways, the definition of shared athlete leadership helps clarify the original definition of athlete leadership.

Theoretical Models and Conceptual Frameworks

Within the field of athlete leadership, two of the most used models for examining leadership behaviors are Chelladurai's (1978, 2007) multidimensional model of leadership (MML) and Avolio's (1999) full range of leadership model (FRLM). As for the MML, it is a linear model composed of antecedents, throughputs, and outcomes. The antecedents directly influence the throughputs (operationalized as leader behaviors). The three categories of antecedents include leader, member, and situational characteristics:

- *Leader characteristics:* trait and personality characteristics of the leader such as age, expertise, gender, and experience

- *Member characteristics:* attributes such as gender, age, personality, and ability
- *Situational characteristics:* environmental factors such as norms, group goals, task type, and group composition

The throughputs are operationalized as the required, preferred, and perceived leader behaviors:

- *Required leader behaviors:* needed in certain situations and directly influenced by the antecedents of situational and member characteristics
- *Preferred leader behaviors:* actions individuals wish to see from their leaders
- *Perceived leader behaviors:* actual behavior (influenced by the antecedents as well as required and preferred behaviors); it is hypothesized that the leader behavior displayed will influence outcomes such as performance and athlete satisfaction

Refer to chapter 6 for more detailed discussion of the MML.

The second common model for studying athlete leadership behaviors is the FRLM (Avolio, 1999). This model encompasses three broad categories of leadership behaviors that range from ineffective to effective. First, the most ineffective and passive form of leadership is *laissez-faire*, described as the absence of leadership, whereby leaders avoid taking any action. A second more active and effective form of leadership behaviors are displayed in *transactional leadership*. This type of leadership focuses on the exchanges that occur between leaders and followers in order to meet their own self-interests. From a behavioral standpoint, it can take the form of contingent reward in which the leader clarifies to the follower what the follower needs to do in order to be rewarded for their effort. In addition, transactional leadership can also take the form of active management by exception, where the leader monitors the performance of followers and takes corrective action if the follower fails to meet the necessary standards. Or it can take the form of passive leadership where the leader adopts passive management by exception by waiting for problems to arise before taking any corrective action. Third, *transformational leadership* (chapter 7) is an expansion of transactional leadership and is characterized by the leader's moving the follower beyond self-interest using four leadership behaviors: *idealized influence*, *individual consideration*, *inspirational motivation*, and *intellectual stimulation*.

Avolio (1999) argued that effective leaders will use both transactional and transformational leadership behaviors with their followers. For instance, early in the leader–follower relationship, transactional leadership can be effective for establishing trust. This is accomplished by both parties holding up their end of the exchange (i.e., task completion by the follower and reward by the leader). Consequently, trust is built, and the leader can continue to influence the follower and eventually use transformational leadership behaviors where they help transform the follower into an eventual leader (Avolio, 1999).

While the MML and FRLM have been vital in advancing athlete leadership research, these two conceptual frameworks are primarily theorized at the dyadic level, used to explain an athlete leader's influence over teammates but not necessarily the influence on team-level processes. However, two new conceptual models for studying athlete leadership may be used to better understand these group processes.

The first is derived from work by Yukl (2012), who synthesized over 50 years of research examining effective leadership behaviors. Yukl notes that his hierarchical taxonomy contains leadership behaviors used to influence the performance of groups. He advanced a hierarchical taxonomy that contains four metacategories labeled as task-oriented, relations-oriented, change-oriented, and external leadership, and within those four categories are 15 leadership behaviors. Maechel and colleagues (2020) tested Yukl's four metacategories within the context of athlete leadership and found good model fit. The testing of this four-dimensional model for athlete leadership included defining the 15 leadership behaviors proposed by Yukl to make them appropriate to athlete leadership plus an additional 5 leadership behaviors based on the existent athlete leadership literature for a total of 20 leadership behaviors.

- *Task-oriented leadership* behaviors are those in which the objective is to accomplish the job in an efficient manner. There are five athlete leadership behaviors associated with task-oriented leadership: clarifying goals, establishing team structure, decision making, maintaining standards of performance, and training.
- *Relations-oriented leadership* refers to increasing human and social capital where the emphasis is on increasing intrapersonal resources and developing interpersonal relationships. There are seven athlete leadership behaviors: personal development, managing

conflict, promoting teamwork, recognizing good performance, providing individual support, role modeling, and empowering.

- As for *change-oriented leadership*, this meta-category refers to activities that advocate for change, such as articulating an inspiring vision, encouraging innovation, and inspiring collective learning. There are four athlete leadership behaviors: inspirational motivation, intellectual stimulation, advocating change, and fostering collective learning.
- Lastly, *external leadership* refers to acquiring the necessary information and resources, along with promoting and defending the interests of the team. There are four athlete leadership behaviors: networking, representing the team, external monitoring, and information gathering.

Taken together, the elements of this four-dimensional model provide conceptual clarity with regard to the relevance and structure of where these 20 leadership behaviors fit within this model (see table 9.1).

TABLE 9.1 Four-Dimensional Model of Athlete Leadership

Dimension	Athlete leadership behavior	Description
Task-oriented functions	Clarifying goals	Helps the team focus on its goals
	Establishing team structure	Clarifies and coordinates team activities; determines the steps and resources necessary to accomplish these activities
	Decision making	Identifies team-related problems and facilitates decisions to resolve them
	Maintaining standards of performance	Makes sure the team's and team members' performances are meeting or exceeding expectations
	Training	Helps team members develop their skills and tactics
Relations-oriented functions	Personal development	Provides feedback, advice, and mentoring in order to help individual team members develop
	Managing conflict	Fosters a constructive way of dealing with conflicts that may arise to maximize the team's effectiveness
	Promoting teamwork	Promotes teamwork and engagement among team members
	Recognizing good performance	Recognizes and praises team members for good performance
	Providing individual support	Shows concern for individual members, provides support, and gains trust from team members
	Role modeling	Sets an example that is consistent with the values of the team for teammates to follow
	Empowering	Considers the suggestions of teammates and involves them in important decisions
Change-oriented functions	Inspirational motivation	Promotes a positive vision concerning the future of the team
	Intellectual stimulation	Challenges team members to think about problems in new ways
	Advocating change	Explains why change is desirable for the team
	Fostering collective learning	Encourages learning between team members to help the team develop
External-oriented functions	Networking	Develops or maintains favorable relationships with others outside the team who can provide useful information or assistance
	Representing the team	Represents the team's interests in meetings with coaching staff, administrators, or key stakeholders
	External monitoring	Observes the environment to identify opportunities for the team or to protect it from distractions and unnecessary demands
	Information gathering	Assesses information about the team's performance and shares relevant information with the team

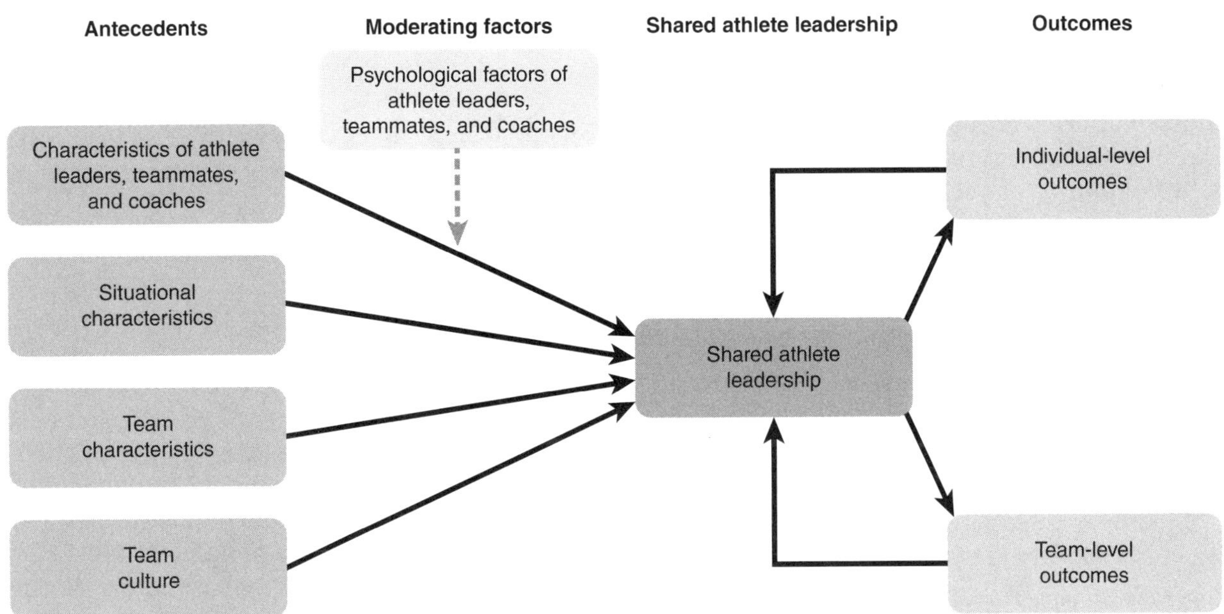

FIGURE 9.1 A working model for the study of athlete leadership.

Adapted by permission from T.M. Loughead, K.J. Munroe-Chandler, M.M. Boisvert, and K.E. Hirsch, "Athlete Leadership," in *Sport, Exercise and Performance Psychology: Research Directions to Advance the Field*, edited by E. Filho and I. Basevitch (New York: Oxford University Press, 2021). Reproduced with permission of the Licensor through PLSclear.

The second more recent model, advanced by Loughead and colleagues (2021), is a working model of athlete leadership based on the extant literature (see figure 9.1). It is not meant as a definitive model of athlete leadership but one that provides an initial framework for organizing and integrating information concerning this construct. As social psychology researchers, we believe an ecological perspective is needed for understanding and explaining athlete leadership. This perspective implies that athlete leadership behaviors result from the interaction of both the individual and situational determinants. Consequently, in planning research and intervention efforts, researchers need to consider not only the individual athletes but also important situational and social forces that act on the athletes who are members of sport teams. As such, a central component of this working ecological model is the notion that athlete leadership is a shared phenomenon.

The definition of athlete leadership from Loughead and colleagues (2006) along with several studies (e.g., Duguay et al., 2016, 2018) indicate that numerous athletes display leadership and do so using a broad spectrum of behaviors. In addition to the athletes' sharing leadership behaviors, our ecological model incorporates factors that focus on *psychological* (i.e., characteristics and psychological factors of athlete leaders, teammates, and coaches; individual-level outcomes), *social* (i.e., situational characteristics; team-level outcomes), and *organizational* (i.e., team characteristics, team culture) levels of influence to provide a comprehensive framework for integrating multiple theoretical perspectives, such as Avolio's (1999) FRLM, Chelladurai's (1978, 2007) MML, and Yukl's (2012) model. We believe shared athlete leadership is optimized when athletes understand that effective team functioning is a product of understanding the team environment and, consequently, exhibiting the necessary leadership behaviors. That is, effective leadership is produced by educating athletes on leadership behaviors while also considering a team's dynamics. Therefore, we believe our ecological model—which combines both individual- and team-level factors—will be useful for achieving effective leadership. This working model holds promise for guiding future research, and we look forward to its continued development as researchers use it as a theoretical framework.

Measurement of Athlete Leadership

Researchers have used two general quantitative approaches when examining athlete leadership: questionnaires and social network analysis (SNA). The first approach has resulted in the use of traditional self-report questionnaires to measure the frequency of athlete leadership behaviors. The development of the MML (Chelladurai, 1978, 2007) corresponded with the advancement of the Leadership

Scale for Sports (LSS; Chelladurai & Saleh, 1980; see chapter 6). While the LSS was originally developed to measure coaching behaviors, it has been adapted to assess athlete leadership behaviors (Loughead & Hardy, 2005). Specifically, the 40 items assess five different dimensions of leader behaviors:

- *Training and instruction* reflects the behaviors of an athlete leader targeted at improving the performance of teammates and instructing them in the skills and tactics of the sport.
- *Democratic behavior* assesses the degree to which an athlete leader includes team members in the decision-making process.
- *Autocratic behavior* reflects the degree to which an athlete leader is independent in decision making.
- *Social support* measures the degree to which an athlete leader is engaged in satisfying the interpersonal needs of others.
- *Positive feedback* assesses the degree to which an athlete leader praises and encourages teammates for good performance.

Originally developed for use in a military setting, the Differentiated Transformational Leadership Inventory (DTLI; Callow et al., 2009; see chapter 7) has been used to assess athlete leadership behaviors. The DTLI's 27 items measure one transactional and six transformational athlete leadership behaviors. When assessing athlete leadership, here are the seven leadership behaviors:

- *Contingent reward*, the only transactional leadership behavior, reflects the athlete leader's tendency to provide positive reinforcement when teammates perform as expected.
- *Individual consideration* reflects the degree to which an athlete leader pays individual attention to teammates' feelings and needs.
- *Inspirational motivation* is the extent to which athlete leaders energize teammates and view the future with optimism about achieving team objectives.
- *Intellectual stimulation* measures an athlete leader's ability to challenge teammates' assumptions and promote creativity.
- *Fostering acceptance of group goals and promoting teamwork* assesses the degree to which an athlete leader promotes cooperation and goal setting among teammates.
- *High-performance expectations* assesses the expectation for excellence and high performance on the part of team members.
- *Appropriate role modeling* evaluates the extent to which athlete leaders set good examples for teammates.

While the LSS and the DTLI have been primarily used to measure athlete leadership behaviors, both inventories were originally developed to assess sport coaching and military contexts, respectively. Confirmatory factor analysis of the LSS and DTLI have shown both inventories to be valid and reliable for measuring athlete leadership (see Callow et al., 2009; Vincer & Loughead, 2010). Further evidence supports the usefulness of measuring the athlete leadership behaviors contained in these two inventories. Specifically, Duguay and colleagues (2018) asked athletes to rate on a 5-point scale how important it was for their athlete leaders to exhibit these leadership behaviors (higher scores reflected greater importance). For eight of the leadership behaviors, the scores were above 4, and the other three behaviors scored higher than 3 on the 5-point scale. Taken together, the results show that the leadership behaviors contained within the LSS and DTLI are important for athlete leaders to exhibit. Despite their validity and reliability, it is unknown whether these two inventories capture all the leadership behaviors exhibited by athletes.

In addition to examining the leadership behaviors of athletes, researchers have studied the characteristics of athlete leaders using the Sport Leadership Behavior Inventory (SLBI; Glenn & Horn, 1993). The characteristics identified were deemed desirable for athlete leaders to possess and were developed based on an interactional approach to leadership effectiveness. Interactional theories suggest the examination of athlete leaders' characteristics should be specific to this population. Thus, the SLBI taps into 19 personal characteristics by asking participants to rate each of their teammates on a 7-point Likert scale ranging from 1 (*never*) to 7 (*always*). Examples of the descriptions used to characterize these leadership attributes include athlete leaders being determined, positive, motivated, consistent, organized, responsible, skilled, confident, honest, and respected.

In a review of transformational leadership in sport (including both coach and athlete leader studies), Arthur and colleagues (2017) noted several measurement issues related to the use of questionnaires. First, relying on single-source questionnaire measures as independent variables can lead to omitted variable bias, simultaneous bias, and common-source common-method bias. They further argued that measuring leadership with a global single-score index is problematic given the multidimensionality of leadership. The use of objective measures of coaches' (or in this case athlete leaders') behaviors that would not be affected by raters' perception has been suggested as an alternative to questionnaires (Arthur et al., 2017). What is said in speeches, pep talks, and press conferences (at elite levels) could be coded for charismatic tactics.

Further, if the LSS and DTLI are to be used as measures of athlete leadership, item analysis should be conducted to determine their appropriateness for measuring this characteristic. For instance, the LSS item "Encourages team members to make suggestions for ways of conducting practices" may be attributed more to coaches than athlete leaders since the latter may not have the ability or authority to dictate practices or training sessions. Moreover, it is possible other aspects of leadership have yet been discovered (Avolio, 1999). In our in-depth interviews with athletes about behaviors they believe constitute effective athlete leadership, leadership behaviors from both the LSS and DTLI were present. However, other leadership behaviors unique to athlete leadership also emerged. Therefore, one promising avenue for the inclusion of additional leadership behaviors is Yukl's (2012) four-dimensional model of leadership. Maechel and colleagues (2020) tested Yukl's four-dimensional model within the context of athlete leadership and found that all four dimensions significantly predicted perceived athlete leadership effectiveness. Thus, to capture the full extent of athlete leadership behaviors, a specific questionnaire targeting all four functions is imperative.

Social network analysis (SNA) is the second quantitative approach for measuring athlete leadership. SNA is a research method that examines the relationships individuals and teams form with each other (Borgatti et al., 2018). For instance, to assess athlete leadership, SNA uses a roster method approach whereby teammates are listed and athletes are asked to rate the frequency with which each teammate provides leadership. Consequently, SNA assesses athlete leadership between members, thereby providing a different perspective in relation to other athlete leadership measures already noted. Social networks are defined as a set of network members (nodes) that are connected by one or more types of relations (ties) (Wasserman & Faust, 1994).

In the context of team sports, SNA methods allow for the simultaneous examination of relations between team members (e.g., cohesion, friendship, leadership) and individual-level attributes (e.g., age, playing position, leadership status) (Lusher et al., 2010). It has been suggested that *degree centrality* (individual level), *degree centralization* (network level), and *density* (network level) are the most relevant measures of the sharedness of leadership in social network research (Gockel & Werth, 2010). As such, a node with a high *in-degree centrality* is indicative of a player who is looked to often by teammates for leadership. With respect to *network centralization*, a low degree of shared leadership is observed when influence stems from one player (high network centralization), whereas a high degree of shared leadership is observed when influence is distributed more equally (low network centralization). Finally, *density* indicates the average leadership influence within the teams (Gockel & Werth, 2010).

Despite the scant research using this type of quantitative approach to athlete leadership, researchers have found that (1) over the course of a season there were increases in the overall amount of task and social leadership (Duguay, Hoffmann, et al., 2020), (2) the leadership responsibilities on a team were shared by numerous athletes (Duguay et al., 2019; Fransen et al., 2015b), (3) teammates felt more socially connected to their team when high-quality leadership is available (Fransen et al., 2015a), and (4) having high-quality athlete leadership was positively associated with stronger feelings of team cohesion (Loughead et al., 2016).

While these SNA studies advanced our understanding of athlete leadership, most of them used aggregated data from sport teams. Consequently, only one study included the specific sociograms (a graphic representation of the social network) associated with each of the teams (Duguay et al., 2019). Researchers must continue to analyze the athlete leadership networks of individual teams in order to gain a better understanding of team functioning. Moreover, given that leadership takes time to develop, longitudinal designs (rather than the typical cross-sectional design) would allow for the exploration of the temporal nature of leadership.

Athlete Leadership Research

Athlete leadership research over the last two decades has broadened our understanding of athlete leaders and leadership behaviors they exhibit. We begin with a review highlighting the characteristics of athlete leaders. We then examine the athlete leadership behaviors associated with athlete- and team-level outcomes. Finally, we review the research examining the sharedness of athlete leadership.

Characteristics of Athlete Leaders

As noted in the MML (Chelladurai, 1978, 2007) and the working model of athlete leadership (Loughead et al., 2021), the antecedent of athlete characteristics is important for understanding the leadership behaviors exhibited by athletes. As such, researchers investigating the characteristics of athlete leaders have focused on the perspectives of coaches, athletes, and athlete leaders. Coaches identify athlete leaders as team members who are older (Bucci et al., 2012), more tenured, and starters (Loughead et al., 2006). Coaches also value a number of traits in their athlete leaders, including being highly skilled (Moran & Weiss, 2006), having a strong work ethic, and working well with the coaching staff (Bucci et al., 2012). Further, athletes who are ambitious, honest, generous, and competitive are perceived more favorably as leaders by their coaches (Bucci et al., 2012). Similarly, coaches also report athlete leaders are those who display the characteristics of being independent, confident in their abilities, and understanding toward their teammates (Moran & Weiss, 2006), yet who are humble, mature, optimistic, and approachable (Imholte et al., 2019).

Athlete leadership research over the last two decades has broadened our understanding of athlete leaders and leadership behaviors they exhibit.

In regard to research asking athlete leaders themselves, these individuals indicated that strong interpersonal communication and task-related skills are of great importance for effective leadership (Dupuis et al., 2006; Wright & Côté, 2003). These characteristics have been echoed by their teammates. Specifically, teammates noted that athletes who are viewed as great leaders were conscientious, extraverted, articulate, and trustworthy (Fransen, Haslam, et al., 2020). Further these characteristics were moderated by leadership function (task, social, external, and motivational). For instance, high-quality task leaders were perceived to be self-confident, self-assured, perceptive, dominant, and diligent and exhibited less neuroticism than their teammates. High-quality external leaders were more sensitive, outgoing, dominant, perceptive, self-confident, and self-assured than their teammates. High-quality motivational leaders were more outgoing, diligent, self-confident, self-assured, and determined than their teammates (Fransen, Haslam, et al., 2020). Preferences for certain leader characteristics also differed by gender, with male athletes valuing task experience and athlete leaders who are trustworthy, whereas female athletes preferred strong interpersonal and communication skills from their athlete leaders (Holmes et al., 2010).

Although researchers have identified numerous characteristics of athlete leaders, very little research has examined whether these characteristics influence the choice of displaying specific leadership behaviors as hypothesized in the MML (Chelladurai, 1978, 2007) and the working model of athlete leadership (Loughead et al., 2021). Therefore, a possibility for future research is the examination of these characteristics in relation to leadership behaviors as measured by a traditional leadership inventory (e.g., LSS or DTLI) or using SNA asking athletes to identify leader characteristics displayed by themselves and their teammates.

Outcomes of Effective Athlete Leadership

Researchers have reported positive associations between athlete leadership behaviors and individual- and team-level outcomes. In terms of individual-level outcomes, researchers examining the youth sport context noted that the frequency of athlete leadership characteristics, as measured by the SLBI (Glenn & Horn, 1993), was positively associated with stronger friendships among teammates (Moran & Weiss, 2006), feeling competent about their skills, and being more intrinsically motivated (Price & Weiss, 2013). When assessing athlete leadership behaviors in youth sport, researchers who used the LSS (Chelladurai & Saleh, 1980) identified that training and instruction, social support, positive feedback, and democratic behavior were positively related to athlete satisfaction (Paradis & Loughead, 2012). In a qualitative investigation of informal athlete leadership in professional sport, Imholte and colleagues (2019) found that informal athlete leaders who exhibited the leadership behavior of social support were helpful to their teammates in managing negative emotions. Moreover, formal athlete leaders reported using leadership behaviors to help their teammates develop positive life skills (e.g., social skills; Santos et al., 2019).

As for team-level outcomes, athlete leadership behaviors have been shown to be positively related to collective efficacy (e.g., Price & Weiss, 2013) and cohesion (e.g., Vincer & Loughead, 2010). For instance, athletes from intercollegiate- and club-level teams reported feeling more task and socially cohesive with their team when receiving social support and positive feedback from their athlete leaders (Vincer & Loughead, 2010). Furthermore, democratic behavior was positively associated with task cohesion, while autocratic behavior was negatively associated with both task and social cohesion. Similarly, Callow and colleagues (2009) investigated how the transformational leadership behaviors of team captains, as measured by the DTLI, influenced the perceptions of cohesion. The authors found that the transformational leadership behaviors of fostering acceptance of group goals and promoting teamwork, individual consideration, and high-performance expectations were positively associated with task cohesion. The leadership behaviors of fostering acceptance of group goals and promoting teamwork were positively associated with social cohesion. Further research on transformational leadership was conducted on competitive female youth soccer players (Price & Weiss, 2013), wherein athletes completed a transformational leadership inventory, the Multifactor Leadership Questionnaire-5X (Bass & Avolio, 1997)—an inventory similar to the DTLI (Callow et al., 2009)—along with measures of cohesion and collective efficacy. Transformational leadership was positively associated with task cohesion, social cohesion, and collective efficacy. This indicates leaders who exhibited behaviors that provided social support, inspired their teammates, and helped them problem-solve had teammates who reported higher levels of group cooperation, group support, and group harmony.

In general, the study of athlete leadership has shown that the behavior of athletes can have positive effects on both individual teammates and the group as a whole. These positive effects are not generated by one athlete on a team but by numerous athletes. As noted at the beginning of this chapter, we view athlete leadership as being best conceived as a shared phenomenon. This paradigm reflects a shift in the focus of leadership research—from understanding it as a leader-centered construct to understanding it as the collective (i.e., team) leading itself, dubbed *shared leadership*.

Shared Athlete Leadership

Given that numerous athletes on teams occupy and share various leadership roles, researchers have examined how coaches can promote and foster the dynamic nature of shared athlete leadership and the benefits of having this form of leadership. To our knowledge, Duguay, Loughead, and colleagues (2020) were among the first to explicitly examine how shared athlete leadership is nurtured and developed within sport teams. To accomplish their purpose, the authors interviewed 15 intercollegiate coaches as to how they facilitated the development of shared athlete leadership. Four themes were identified (see table 9.2). The first theme related to the importance coaches played in facilitating the development of shared athlete leadership, such that coaches viewed *empowering their athletes* as key in fostering shared leadership. De Cruz (2019) noted that empowerment is key in developing shared leadership since it supports athletes' sense of competence and facilitates motivation. The second theme consisted of coaches using leadership groups and alternative leadership structures. Coaches believed that being a leader on a sport team is too big a role for one athlete to occupy and as such felt leadership groups and structures were valuable. Coaches promoted the use of shared athlete leadership using various leadership structures. The size of these leadership groups varied from maintaining a typical structure of one team captain but having each player serve as a captain throughout the season (e.g., captain rotations) to having larger athlete leadership groups such as leadership teams, leadership councils, and athlete leaders for different roles (e.g., academic captains, weight room captains). The leadership structure adopted by the coaches was dependent on factors such as the maturity of the athletes and the number of veteran players on the team.

The third theme related to how coaches created a positive team environment for shared athlete leadership to flourish. One approach noted by the coaches was to eliminate the status differences between athletes (e.g., newer vs. more established players) by making sure athletes felt they had a voice within the team by having open lines of communication, developing trust, and engaging in team-building activities. The fourth theme consisted of a positive team environment allowing for leadership to flourish. In order to accomplish this, coaches needed to intentionally develop athlete leadership within their teams. The coaches used multiple methods

TABLE 9.2 Four Approaches for Coaches to Develop Shared Athlete Leadership

Theme	Description	Example
Empower athletes.	This precursor to shared athlete leadership has coaches encourage athletes to feel confident and competent when taking on leadership opportunities.	A coach emphasizes the importance of athletes' contributing to decision-making processes and using their voice.
Use leadership groups and alternative leadership structures.	Coaches establish athlete leadership structures in which athlete leadership responsibilities are distributed among multiple athletes.	A coach initiates a process wherein all team members elect members from various roles or tenure to serve on leadership council.
Create a positive team environment.	Coaches create or facilitate a team-oriented, inclusive environment in which all athletes feel valued.	A coach instills a process of more senior athletes' serving the team (e.g., setting up equipment) rather than rookie team members.
Deliberately develop athlete leadership.	Coaches make efforts throughout the season to foster the leadership behaviors of athletes on their team.	Regular meetings are held with the coach and athlete leader(s) to discuss ways to improve athlete leadership behaviors. These meetings may also be held with a mental performance consultant.

to develop shared athlete leadership, including offering shared experiential learning opportunities such as small and large team discussions, providing books and articles on leadership to their athletes, delivering leadership development workshops, and modeling shared leadership among the coaching staff.

Aside from the fact that most coaches used some form of shared athlete leadership groups, there was little consensus on their implementation. These variations in athlete leadership structures align with current input-throughput-outcome sport leadership models. For instance, in Chelladurai's (1978, 2007) MML, which has been used to examine the leadership of both coaches and athletes, leadership is influenced by various antecedents including situational (e.g., type of sport, level of competition, team goals), leader (e.g., age, gender, leadership philosophy), and member (e.g., maturity level, experience, ability) characteristics (see chapter 6). In considering such sport leadership models alongside the findings of Duguay, Loughead, and colleagues (2020), there is no one-size-fits-all strategy when it comes to developing a structure of shared athlete leadership. What appears to be critical is that coaches adopt shared athlete leadership group structures that meet the needs, values, and culture of their teams. Promoting shared athlete leadership structures affects perceptions of coaching, as shown by Fransen, Mertens, and colleagues (2020), who demonstrated a positive relationship between shared athlete leadership and perceptions of coach leadership quality. More specifically, athletes on teams with high density and moderate centralization (i.e., several athlete leaders share leadership responsibilities) have more favorable perceptions of their coaches' task, social, and motivational leadership. Taken together, teams reap many benefits from having athlete leaders who share the leadership responsibilities.

Another important aspect to consider in better understanding shared leadership is *time*. The component of time highlights that shared leadership is a dynamic construct allowing different team members to participate in the team's leadership. Using an SNA approach, Duguay, Hoffmann, and colleagues (2020) examined an elite adolescent ice hockey team to assess for changes in task and social leadership over the course of a season. The results demonstrated that as the season progressed task leadership changed (i.e., who was doing this type of leadership), but the degree of centralization did not increase (i.e., the number of players doing this type of leadership did not increase). In contrast, the team's social leadership structure became significantly more shared over time as the season proceeded, with more players exhibiting this type of leadership. Similarly, using an SNA approach, Duguay and colleagues (2019) examined the degree of athlete leadership sharedness in four female soccer teams. In each of these four soccer teams, athlete leadership was shared among team members. However, the degree of sharedness varied for each team, meaning some teams had more athletes participate in the leadership of their team, while other teams had fewer athletes. These results may be related back to Chelladurai's (1978, 2007) MML in that leadership is influenced by various antecedents including situational, leader, and member characteristics that support the notion of a no one-size-fits-all approach to the structure of shared athlete leadership. Despite the difference in the amount of sharedness, one finding was consistent in all four teams. Every athlete was viewed by at least one other teammate as providing leadership to them. This finding highlights the importance of developing the leadership potential in all athletes.

Shared athlete leadership within leadership types (e.g., multiple social leaders) and between leadership types (e.g., different leaders for social and task functions) is associated with several benefits. In a qualitative investigation of university athletes, participants expressed that having a high degree of shared leadership (i.e., athlete leaders encompass 85% of the team) leads to more available leadership (e.g., athletes can pick which leader to approach in specific situations), individual-level outcomes (e.g., satisfaction, confidence), team-level outcomes (e.g., communication, cohesion, effort), and greater frequencies of favorable leadership behaviors (e.g., idealized influence, social support) (Crozier et al., 2013). Further, Morgan and colleagues (2013, 2015) have shown that shared leadership facilitates team resilience. Coaches also report that having shared leadership groups can enhance support for coaches and athletes, decision making, team culture, and leadership succession and, ultimately, improve team performance (Haddad et al., 2021). In particular, Haddad and colleagues (2021) interviewed 16 coaches from the four professional domestic sport leagues in Australia: National Rugby League, Australian Rules, Super Rugby, and A League. Coaches believed there were numerous benefits of having shared athlete leadership groups, including managing the team more effectively by distributing the leadership workload to the players. The coaches also noted that team functioning was enhanced through the reinforcing of the team's culture by the leadership group and better decision making as a collective. These all contributed to the coaches' belief that the team's performance was better as a result of having a strong leadership group.

The perceived benefits noted from these qualitative studies have also been supported by quantitative studies. In relation to team-level outcomes, athlete leadership operationalized as task, social, external, and motivational leadership functions have been positively associated with team identification and collective efficacy (Fransen et al., 2014). Leo and colleagues (2019) expanded on these findings by investigating relationships between the sharedness of task, social, and motivational leadership functions and their ties to several team-level outcomes. Their findings indicated positive associations among shared task athlete leadership and collective efficacy, task cohesion, and performance and negative associations with role, task, and relationship conflict. Shared social athlete leadership was positively associated with social cohesion and perceived performance and negatively associated with role and task conflict. Lastly, shared external athlete leadership was positively associated with social cohesion and a desire to continue playing sport. While these quantitative findings are encouraging, researchers are urged to examine the four metacategories and 20 leadership behaviors proposed by Maechel and colleagues (2020) in order to expand the functions performed by athlete leaders.

Future Research Directions

To continue advancing the field of athlete leadership, it is critical to use a variety of theoretical frameworks. To date, the majority of research examining leadership behaviors has used components of Chelladurai's (1978, 2007) MML and Avolio's (1999) FRLM. While these frameworks have been and will continue to be useful, researchers are encouraged to adopt other theories and frameworks to fully understand the construct of athlete leadership. For instance, Yukl's (2012) four metacategories appear to be relevant, so developing the 20 athlete leadership behaviors associated with those four metacategories seems like a fruitful endeavor (Maechel et al., 2020). To date, researchers have examined athlete leadership behaviors and their relationship to individual- and team-level outcomes. However, athlete leadership is more complex than this relationship to individual and outcomes. We have advanced a working ecological framework (see figure 9.1) to encourage researchers to examine the components of the model but more importantly to stimulate ideas for conceptualizing a framework that is unique to athlete leadership. To assist in the examination of the relationships contained within our working framework, an athlete leadership-specific inventory is required. On this front, the majority of current athlete leadership inventories (e.g., LSS and DTLI) measure the frequency of the leadership behavior being displayed. Another alternative to consider is the effectiveness or quality of the leadership behavior being exhibited by the athletes.

Practical Implications

Research examining athlete leadership development is currently limited. To our knowledge, there are only nine published articles dedicated to the development of athlete leadership. This lack of research attention is surprising given the proliferation of empirical evidence (e.g., meta-analyses) on the effectiveness of leadership development in nonsport leadership studies (e.g., Avolio et al., 2009; Collins & Holton, 2004). In fact, leadership is considered one of the most important life skills that athletes should acquire and develop to help them achieve success in sport and life (Gould et al., 2006).

The existing athlete leadership development literature has drawn inspiration from a variety of sources. Certain leadership development programs are theoretically grounded, while others rely on the personal experiences of the professionals (i.e., researcher, consultant) implementing the program. The current athlete leadership development literature can be divided into two main categories based on the type of participants targeted: intercollegiate and youth athletes.

Intercollegiate Athletes

Voight (2012) conducted a season-long athlete leadership development program with two NCAA Division I volleyball teams, targeting the leadership development of team captains and assistant captains. The goals of this program were to

- improve team performance through better leadership,
- improve team communication and functioning,
- teach the captains and assistants about leading the team on a daily basis including practices and games, and
- foster the personal leadership development of captains and assistants.

In order to fulfill the goals of this program, a 15-stage approach to leadership development was created and implemented by the author. These stages included discussing the positives and negatives of being a leader, the responsibilities of being a leader, how to make effective decisions as a leader, how to self-reflect, and assessment of leadership and team needs. The program was implemented by a leadership consultant via email, videoconferencing, and in-person communication with the team captains, team, and coaching staff. The 15 stages also included debriefing questions on opportunities and challenges as a leader, team progress reports, development of a vision statement, and reflections by the captains over the season. At the end of the season, the author interviewed two captains and two assistants, asking them to describe their perceptions of having gone through this leadership development program. In terms of the benefits of the program, the leaders believed it helped empower them, increased the team and individual performances, and enhanced the team's cohesion.

While the Voight (2012) approach focused on formal leaders, Duguay and colleagues (2016) used a shared athlete leadership approach. Their program, grounded in the MML (Chelladurai, 1978, 2007) and the FRLM (Avolio, 1999), developed all athletes of two volleyball and basketball teams regardless of their leadership status. In four workshops presented over the course of the season, participants learned how they could exhibit the leadership behaviors assessed by the LSS (Chelladurai & Saleh, 1980) and DTLI (Callow et al., 2009), and how these leadership behaviors affected a team's dynamics. In each workshop the participants received (1) a presentation of the leadership behaviors to be learned, (2) a demonstration of these leadership behaviors in action, and (3) the opportunity to practice these leadership behaviors. Throughout the workshops, activities (e.g., role playing, case studies) highlighted how the leadership behaviors benefited the participant personally but also how they benefited the team's dynamics (cohesion, communication, motivation, and satisfaction). Additionally, each participant was given an athlete leadership handbook to support the material covered in the workshops.

The results showed that the leadership program positively affected most of the athlete leadership behaviors targeted. More precisely, participants reported using 8 of the 10 leadership behaviors (i.e., training and instruction, democratic behavior, social support, positive feedback, appropriate role model, inspirational motivation, high-performance expectations, and fostering acceptance of group goals and promoting teamwork) significantly more often after completing the leadership development program. The results also demonstrated increases in athlete satisfaction concerning team integration and team performance along with increases in task-involving peer motivational climate from pre- to postintervention. Lastly, although cohesion and communication showed increasing trends from pre- to postintervention, the increase was not statistically significant, likely because of a ceiling effect. Therefore, the athlete leadership development program was able to maintain levels of cohesion and communication over the course of the season (Duguay et al., 2016).

Youth Athletes

Using the same program developed by Duguay and colleagues (2016), Boisvert and colleagues (2022) studied a male youth ice hockey team over the course of a season. The results from pre- and postintervention measures showed that the leadership program helped maintain levels of athlete leadership, cohesion, and collective efficacy throughout the year. In addition, a focus group interview at the end of the season revealed that the leadership program was beneficial in helping players improve their leadership behaviors, along with maintaining perceptions of cohesion and collective efficacy. Additionally, players mentioned the program improved communication among team members and helped them deal with conflict more effectively. The results of this study are encouraging since the participating team had a difficult season, with a winning percentage of 16%. Thus, it appears the leadership development program was able to buffer some of the effects of losing by preserving leadership and some of the team's dynamics.

Gould and Voelker (2010) developed the Captain's Leadership Training Program (CLTP), which has been used in various athlete leadership development studies (e.g., Blanton et al., 2014; Pierce et al., 2018). The CLTP teaches high school athletes how to be effective team captains. The program is delivered as a one-day workshop separated into three breakout sessions over the course of the day. Additionally, each participant is given a leadership guidebook (*Becoming an Effective Team Captain: Student-Athlete Guide*) to reinforce the learning that occurred in this one-day workshop. The six-chapter guidebook contains information about the leadership skills covered throughout the program, including role modeling, effective communication, motivation, team building and cohesion, and handling tough situations. At the end of the workshop, participants are asked to evaluate the content of the breakout sessions including the effectiveness of the instructors. The feedback from these evaluations indicate that the CLTP is helpful in developing leadership and that the workshops are an enjoyable experience facilitated by instructors who are knowledgeable about the topics. The authors also discussed potential future directions including the importance of developing a concurrent program for coaches who can monitor the progress of the participants once they complete the leadership development program. Furthermore, the authors also indicate that future research should include a follow-up component to reinforce the leadership skills learned in the program.

Nearly every athlete leadership development program has been conducted face-to-face (i.e., researcher or practitioner physically present to deliver the program). While this method of delivery is beneficial, it is limited in the number of athletes it can reach. An avenue for future research is the use of web-based technologies to increase the reach of athlete leadership development programs. The process of creating online leadership development platforms can vary depending on both the type of learning (e.g., synchronous or asynchronous) and the goals of the program (Mishra & Koehler, 2006). *Asynchronous learning* refers to instances where participants are not connected online at the same time; it can be facilitated through various formats, such as modules. Asynchronous learning provides flexibility and convenience to the participant but lacks the interpersonal nature provided through interactions with the instructor and other participants (Vonderwell, 2003).

An avenue for future research is the use of web-based technologies to increase the reach of athlete leadership development programs.

In contrast, *synchronous learning* provides the opportunity for real-time online communication, through technologies such as videoconferencing on platforms such as Zoom (Finkelstein, 2006). Synchronous communication can enhance people's sense of social presence so that communication feels real, even though mediated by technology (McInnerney & Roberts, 2004). Synchronous conferencing technologies can simulate the sense of community and social interactions experienced in face-to-face instruction (Kear et al., 2012). Regardless of the type of learning, the use of technology offers significant advantages, such as reach, convenience, low cost, and eco-friendliness. Once online athlete leadership development programs have been established and tested, the next logical step from a research perspective is to conduct a comparative analysis of learner satisfaction and learning outcomes in online and face-to-face leadership learning environments.

Peer Mentoring

Another method for fostering leadership is peer athlete mentoring. *Peer athlete mentoring* is defined as a dynamic process in which a more experienced and knowledgeable athlete, known as the mentor, serves as a trusted role model to another athlete, referred to as the mentee, helping the mentee achieve their goals along with supporting their personal growth and development (Hoffmann et al., 2017). While many athletes benefit from being in a mentoring relationship, it is important to note that not every athlete experiences these benefits. In fact, nearly 40% of Canadian intercollegiate athletes never considered another athlete as a peer mentor (Hoffmann & Loughead, 2016), and one in five of a sample of Canadian national team and intercollegiate athletes have never been peer mentored (Hoffmann & Loughead, 2019).

Hoffmann (2019) proposed strategies for practitioners (i.e., coaches, mental performance consultants) interested in facilitating the development of peer athlete mentoring relationships. In particular, Hoffmann suggested two broad approaches. The first approach allows mentoring relationships to develop informally. Informal mentoring relationships are preferable because of their natural occurrence between mentor and mentee (Hoffmann, 2019). Informal mentoring stems from a process of mutual discovery where mentors and mentees identify with one another. From a practical standpoint, practitioners can hold meetings at the beginning of the season to discuss how peer mentorship can be beneficial to the team's vision and goals. These types of meetings help lay the groundwork for informal peer mentoring relationships to occur naturally between athletes (Hoffmann, 2019).

The second approach is to formalize peer mentoring relationships among the athletes (Hoffmann, 2019). Blake-Beard and colleagues (2007) outlined three approaches to fostering formal mentoring relationships: (1) practitioner-assigned matching, (2) choice-based matching, and (3) assessment-based matching. First, coaches and practitioners can pair mentors and mentees based on their own subjective evaluations of which athletes represent a suitable pairing. This approach can be effective but comes with the risk of athletes feeling left out of the matching process (Hoffmann, 2019). In that case, practitioners can elect to formalize peer mentoring relationships through choice-based matching. This approach enables mentors and mentees to mutually agree to undertake a mentoring relationship. However, a pitfall of this method is the potential of only a few mentoring relationships emerging, leaving others without a mentor or mentee (Blake-Beard et al., 2007). Lastly, practitioners can pair athletes through assessment-based matching. Compatibility can be determined using data derived from assessment tools such as personality or emotional intelligence instruments (e.g., NEO Five-Factor Inventory; Costa & McCrae, 1992). For this approach to be successful, compatibility between mentor and mentee is crucial.

Regardless of the approach used to foster mentoring relationships between athletes, practitioners can also make use of technology. Consequently, electronic mentoring, or e-mentoring, can be a means of communication between athletes (Hoffmann, 2019). Evidence suggests that e-mentoring produces many similar benefits to traditional mentoring relationships (Hoffmann, 2019). Video communication technology (e.g., Zoom, Microsoft Teams) is a potential avenue through which to develop and maintain peer athlete mentoring relationships, particularly when meeting face-to-face is unfeasible. While the viability of e-mentoring has not been studied between athletes, a sport coaches e-mentoring program has highlighted some of the benefits and barriers of this form of mentoring. Specifically, Grant and colleagues (2020) found that coaches derived three advantages of e-mentoring: open communication, acquiring sport-specific knowledge, and a sense of professional fulfillment on the part of the coach mentor. In terms of barriers, this type of mentoring resulted in technological difficulties with using the online platform, distance in geographical proximity that did not permit face-to-face meetings, and difficulties in scheduling regular weekly or monthly meetings.

Summary

In comparison with other topics in the field of social psychology in sport, athlete leadership has a relatively short history. Nonetheless, researchers have highlighted the importance of this construct to the sporting environment, mainly through the effect of athlete leadership on team dynamics. The goals of the chapter were to provide a definition of athlete leadership, stressing the importance of the shared nature of this construct, along with theoretical frameworks that have guided previous research and models that could be used in future research. Further, we provided a succinct overview of the inventories and methods used to test the relationships from these frameworks. We also underlined some of the research examining athlete leadership and drew attention to development programs and peer athlete mentoring opportunities for those interested in enhancing the leadership within their teams. Finally, we suggested some possibilities for future research, with the goal of the continued development of this construct.

DISCUSSION QUESTIONS

1. Research suggests that athlete leadership is shared among numerous athletes on a team. How can coaches and teammates ensure that athletes have the opportunity to serve in a leadership role?
2. What are some of the methods used to measure athlete leadership? What are some of the benefits and drawbacks of these methods?
3. Synthesize the research to date regarding athlete leadership. Based on that synthesis, identify areas of future research and justify its importance in order to move the field of athlete leadership forward.
4. Why is it important for teams to have leadership emanating from the athletes? What are the advantages and disadvantages of having too many or too few leaders?

PART III

Motivational Considerations in Sport

Within the field of social psychology in sport, motivation is a crucial contributor to athletic performance, leading researchers from around the world to examine how motivation can be influenced by the dynamic interplay between athletes, coaches, and the team environment. In this part, chapters delve into approaches to studying the social influences on motivation, through extensions of traditional motivational climate research, through the consideration of how researchers and practitioners meet athletes' core psychological needs, and by introducing more recent concepts—to sport psychology, at least—such as a caring climate. The contributions also explore the possibilities, offered by novel perspectives and methods, for generating new insights and possibilities in the study of how the people surrounding athletes might influence their motivation. Understanding the key components of a motivational climate in sport, and how one can create empowering environments that foster growth, learning, and success, is essential for both coaches and athletes alike.

In chapter 10, Empowering and Disempowering Coach-Created Motivational Climates, Joan Duda, Isabel Balaguer, and Paul Appleton explore how athlete perceptions of feeling empowered or disempowered can be associated with a range of important outcomes spanning emotion, motivation, and sustained engagement versus dropout. Beginning with a review of the foundational literature in achievement goal theory, and its findings pertaining to task climates and ego climates, the text progresses to review recent developments achieved when integrating achievement goals with self-determination theory. In recent years, the literature has seen an increase in applied interventions that have supported coaches in modifying their coaching styles, and this body of research is reported, reviewing coaches' impacts on athletes' perceptions and behaviors. Overall, this chapter reflects the extension of almost 40 years of motivational climate research grounded in the task–ego distinction from achievement goal theory, in new and exciting directions.

In chapter 11, Caring Climate, Lori Gano-Overway and Mary Fry consider the importance of athletes' feeling cared for and valued during their sporting endeavors, and the ways that coaches and teams can promote this experience. *Trust, connection, belonging,* and *support* are terms commonly used in modern sport, yet understanding how to foster these attributes, and the benefits of doing so, continue to be detailed in research. The authors also examine the effects of coaches who prioritize their athletes' well-being and holistic development, and how this type of environment can enhance motivation and performance. A brief history of the concept of caring climate leads to an overview of qualitative and psychometric studies that have contextualized and refined the concept for application in sport. Because it is a more recent research topic in sport, the authors suggest how coaches may adjust their practices in light of this new knowledge, and also signpost the requirements for future research to continue developing our understanding.

In chapter 12, Need-Supportive, Thwarting, and Indifferent Coach Interpersonal Styles, Nikos Ntoumanis, Eleanor Quested, and Hamsini Sivaramakrishnan examine the impact of different coaching practices on athlete motivation, through the lens of recent developments in self-determination theory, and explore how coaches can support athletes' core psychological needs for competence, autonomy, and relatedness. Similarly, researchers have studied how athletes may feel these needs are being thwarted or overlooked, and how this experience affects athlete motivation, confidence, and performance. As a relatively new extension to a popular theory, this chapter also details new measurement instruments that enable the study of coaches who are perceived to support, ignore, or thwart athletes' psychological needs. This chapter reflects recent developments, extending a highly established and popular theory of motivation, and so offers exciting opportunities and insights as to how even well-known theories are still able to be extended and refined.

Finally, in chapter 13, The Climate as a Collective Adaptive System, Richard Keegan and David Smith use the lens of complex systems science—an approach that is already firmly established in other fields of science, such as meteorology and advanced computer modeling—to offer up new avenues for researching motivational climates in sport. Each of the preceding chapters has considered the social influences of athlete motivation in sport, using different theoretical lenses to examine the same subject. As well as considering methodological opportunities for reconciling these competing theories and concepts, the authors discuss the applied recommendations that result from considering social interactions as a less predictable complex system, as opposed to more stable "if, then" formulas for controlling motivation.

10

Empowering and Disempowering Coach-Created Motivational Climates

Joan L. Duda, PhD; Isabel Balaguer, PhD; and Paul R. Appleton, PhD

LEARNING OBJECTIVES

On completion of this chapter, the reader should have the following:

- Awareness of what is a motivational climate within sport
- Understanding of the concepts of task-involving and ego-involving motivational climates (as described in achievement goal frameworks) in sport and their associated processes and outcomes
- Familiarity with the characteristics of the motivational climate from a self-determination theory perspective and research findings regarding their correlates
- Understanding of the rationales for a more theoretically integrated approach to the motivational climate and the definitions of what constitute overarching empowering and disempowering features of the social environment
- Appreciation of how variability in the empowering and disempowering features of the empowering motivational climate has been measured and what these two dimensions predict
- Awareness of the *Empowering Coaching*™ training program (content, approach), which is grounded in the integrated conceptualization of the motivational climate and its impacts

From the grassroots to the elite level of sport competition, the significance of the behaviors and attitudes of the coach to the cognitive, emotional, and behavioral responses of athletes is readily apparent. From studies in sport psychology as well as anecdotal accounts, we understand that coaches have an impact on how athletes feel about their sport, including their confidence, motivation, experienced anxiety, enjoyment of the sport, desire to continue or drop out, moral functioning, and overall well-being.

We can learn much about what coaches do by reading autobiographies, biographies, and interviews of successful coaches as well as qualitative research studies of elite coaches' behaviors, knowledge, training approaches, and strategies (e.g., Burns et al., 2019). In their interviews of professional and Olympic "serial winning" coaches, Lara-Bercial and Mallett (2016) reflected that the practices of such coaches are marked by "driven benevolence" and encompass "the creation of an optimal environment where [their athletes] can thrive" (p. 236).

Unfortunately, from research including stories conveyed by current or past sport competitors, we also see a troubling picture indicating coaches can have a negative impact on those they coach (e.g., Kavanagh et al., 2017; Kerr et al., 2019).

To help us make sense of it all, researchers have worked to develop definitions, theories, and data to characterize the antecedents, mechanisms, and impacts of coaching practices. How can we best capture and describe the variability in the actions and expressed attitudes of coaches? Based on research, what are the outcomes associated with different coach behaviors? And *why* do such differences in ways of coaching lead to variability in athletes' responses?

In addressing the features and potential effects of positive and negative coach behaviors, this chapter focuses on the differential psychological environments, or motivational climates (Ames, 1992), that coaches create. We characterize these psychological environments in regard to their motivation-relevant attributes and describe an extended conceptualization of the motivational climate.

We first tie our examination of the motivational climate to two popular theoretical frameworks: achievement goal theory (AGT; Duda & Balaguer, 2007) and self-determination theory (SDT; Mageau & Vallerand, 2003). We define the relevant features of the motivational climate according to AGT and then SDT, in regard to predicting motivational processes and ensuing outcomes. In the case of each theoretical framework, we highlight research findings about the characteristics of the motivational climates associated with athletes' reporting positive and adaptive outcomes (e.g., enjoyment, feelings of vitality, engagement) versus more negative and maladaptive outcomes (e.g., burnout, dropout).

Subsequently, we introduce a more integrated framework that pulls together subdimensions of the motivational climate emphasized by both AGT and SDT (Duda, 2013; Duda & Appleton, 2016). We provide empirical, conceptual, and practical rationales for the amalgamation of these subdimensions into what are termed overarching empowering and disempowering facets of the motivational climate. The chapter then summarizes recently developed measurement tools (questionnaire, observational system) that assess the empowering and disempowering features of the motivational climate. We then review major findings regarding the correlates of empowering and disempowering coach behaviors.

Our attention next turns to the content and features of a training program that has been delivered to coaches (i.e., *Empowering Coaching*™), which is grounded in the integrated model and aims to promote more motivationally adaptive motivational climates in sport (and reduce disempowering coach behaviors). We describe the key content and approach embedded in the *Empowering Coaching*™ training and reflect on some projects entailing the delivery and evaluation of the training.

We conclude the chapter by providing some directions for future research based on the theoretically integrated model of the (empowering and disempowering) motivational climate (Duda, 2013; Duda & Appleton, 2016). Further avenues for applied work grounded in this model are also provided.

Motivational Climate in Achievement Goal Theory

As applied to sport, achievement goal frameworks hold that differences in the achievement goals emphasized influence the motivational patterns exhibited by sport participants (Ames, 1992; Dweck, 1999; Nicholls, 1989). According to achievement goal theory (AGT), to appreciate which achievement goals are given importance, we need to ask questions. What are athletes concerned about when they participate in sport? What do the athletes want to achieve? On what bases do they feel competent and successful?

According to Nicholls (1989) and others (e.g., Roberts, 2012), a hallmark of achievement activities (such as sport) is a focus on demonstrating skill or competence. When athletes feel they have exhibited high competence in their sport, they are then more likely to feel personally successful at the activity. Different achievement goals are assumed to reflect differences in how such demonstrated competence is conceived or understood. That is, what are the criteria underlying an athlete's judgments of whether or not they have shown a high (or low) level of sport ability?

In the original achievement goal frameworks (Ames, 1992; Dweck, 1999; Nicholls, 1989), two major goal perspectives were proposed that reflect two different ways of judging one's level of competence: a task goal perspective and an ego goal perspective. When an athlete is primarily centered on a task goal, perceptions of competence are primarily self-referenced (e.g., a basketball player working to improve their positioning around the boards and increase their rebounds per game). Meeting the demands of the task, exerting effort, and improving one's strategic approach or skill level bring about a sense of success in this case. When primarily focused on an ego goal, athletes are concerned with demonstrating superior competence (e.g., attempting to outscore their teammates). That is, they feel highly competent and successful when they show they are better than others (opponents, teammates) or do well in regard to normative standards in the sport (e.g., break someone else's record, or realize a good ranking). The experience of personal improvement and the exertion of high effort will not automatically translate into perceptions of high competence if an ego goal predominates. Indeed, an athlete with a pronounced focus on ego goals might feel even more capable and successful if they could exhibit outstanding performance without having to give their best effort.

AGT (Ames, 1992; Nicholls, 1989) holds that there are individual differences in the tendency to focus on task and ego goals (i.e., task and ego goal orientations, respectively), and social situational factors also come into play. In regard to the former and as found to be the case in educational settings (Nicholls, 1989), task and ego orientations tend to be orthogonal, or independent (Duda & Whitehead, 1998). This means there are athletes who are oriented toward both task and ego goals, athletes who have one prevailing goal orientation, and athletes who place neither goal in prominence.

With respect to the latter factor assumed to influence task and ego goal emphasis, the social psychological environments created by the behaviors and views of significant others (such as the coach) can be differentiated in regard to the achievement goals promoted (Ames, 1992). Ames (1992) introduced the term *motivational climate* to capture the achievement goals accentuated in the social psychological environment and suggested that this environment can be more or less *task involving* and *ego involving*. In Ames' view, the motivational climate is multidimensional and comprises different structures and leader behaviors. How is success defined by those creating the climate? What aspects of performance are reinforced? How are individuals evaluated and recognized? What are the bases of recognition?

Numerous AGT-based studies in sport have focused on the processes and outcomes predicted by participants' perceptions of the motivational climate. AGT-grounded research has recognized that parents (White et al., 1992), peers (Vazou et al., 2005), and other significant figures (such as teachers) also create motivational climates. Sport studies, however, have tended to focus on the perceived motivational climate as created by the coach and its correlates. In most of these studies, the degree to which athletes feel the coach-created motivational climate is more or less task and ego involving has been captured via the Perceived Motivational Climate in Sport Questionnaire (PMCSQ-2; Newton et al., 2000). Assessing perceptions of a task-involving motivational climate overall, PMCSQ-2 items capture more specific and underlying features of a perceived task-involving motivational climate: (1) the coach emphasizes effort and athletes' personal improvement; (2) the coach contributes to all players' feeling they have an important role on the team; and (3) the coach fosters cooperation among team members. The questionnaire also assesses perceptions of how ego involving the motivational climate is deemed to be. This overarching perspective stems from specific characteristics of such a climate: (1) the coach is punitive in response to mistakes; (2) the coach favors the most skilled players (thus emphasizing differences in ability), and (3) the coach cultivates rivalry among team members (important to be better than others).

In general, the results of studies examining variables associated with perceptions of the motivational climate have been broadly consistent with the predictions of AGT (Ames, 1992). As summarized in a systematic review of this literature (which included numerous studies centered on the climate as created by the coach) by Harwood and colleagues (2015), perceptions of a task-involving motivational climate were linked to numerous outcomes reflecting an adaptive achievement pattern and more positive cognitive and emotional responses in athletes. Perceiving a task-involving, coach-created climate has been found to positively predict sport participants' task orientation (Fabra et al., 2021) and their autonomous reasons for engaging in sport (e.g., Ruiz et al., 2017). Past work has found a perceived ego-involving motivational climate (again with a plethora of studies focused on the coach-created motivational climate) to correspond to a more maladaptive achievement pattern, more negative cognitive and emotional responses, and greater ego orientation (Harwood et al., 2015).

Most of the research examining the correlates of task-involving and ego-involving motivational climates in sport has been cross-sectional—that is, all the variables of interest are assessed at one moment in time (Duda & Balaguer, 2007; Harwood et al., 2015). However, longitudinal designs are being more regularly adopted to address key research questions about the perceived motivational climate from an AGT lens. As such, it is possible to test how changes in perceptions of the motivational climate predict changes in the targeted motivational processes and outcomes. For example, Ruiz and colleagues (2019) examined the temporal interplay between perceptions of the motivational climate created by the coach, athletes' motivation for participating in sport, and emotional states (pleasant states, anger, and anxiety) as experienced before practice. Changes in task-involving climate scores positively predicted changes in autonomous motivation and negatively predicted changes in the intensity of dysfunctional anxiety and anger. Changes in perceptions of an ego-involving motivational climate positively related to changes in controlled motivation and experienced anger deemed to be dysfunctional (i.e., having a negative impact on performance).

Over the course of a season, Fabra and colleagues (2021) examined the relationship of perceptions of the task- and ego-involving aspects of the perceived motivational climate to young football players' goal orientations, self-esteem, and degree of contingent self-esteem (i.e., the degree to which athletes' perceptions of self-worth are tied to their athletic performance). They were also interested in whether changes in the latter psychological outcomes predicted intentions to drop out. Changes in the task-involving features of the motivational climate, from the beginning to the end of the season, positively predicted changes in reported task orientation. That is, the more task involving players felt the climate was, the more players reported a higher task orientation. Parallel findings held for changes in perceptions of ego-involving climate and players' ego orientation. As the young athletes' degree of task orientation increased during the season, their self-esteem was higher, and their level of contingent self-esteem reduced. Increases (from the start to the finish of the season) in ego orientation positively predicted changes in contingent self-esteem. The players who were more likely to report greater intentions to drop out, over time, were those whose self-esteem decreased and contingent self-esteem increased as the season progressed.

Taken in their totality, the research on perceived task-involving and ego-involving motivational climates suggests clear benefits of trying to promote the former and reduce the latter. Such evidence provides a sound justification to design and test interventions aimed at promoting more task-involving and less ego-involving motivational climates (e.g., Cecchini et al., 2014; McLaren et al., 2015; Smith et al., 2007).

Motivational Climate in Self-Determination Theory

Self-determination theory (SDT; Ryan & Deci, 2002, 2017) primarily focuses on people's reasons for engagement, which vary in their degree of self-determination. SDT places emphasis on what are considered core psychological needs, the factors that support versus thwart them, and the impacts of doing so (including implications for motivation quality). The theory makes an important distinction between *autonomous motivation* (individuals participate because they enjoy and want to, for the activity's inherent value or worth, or because the activity can bring personally valued meanings or benefits) versus *controlled motivation* (individuals participate because they feel obliged, someone is telling them to, or for the extrinsic rewards). According to SDT, individuals can also be *amotivated*. In this case, they are participating in an activity but feel there is no viable autonomous or controlled reason for being involved.

Taken in their totality, the research on perceived task-involving and ego-involving motivational climates suggests clear benefits of trying to promote the former and reduce the latter.

Whether an athlete manifests more or less of each form of motivational regulation is assumed to be determined by the degree to which their basic psychological needs are satisfied or frustrated in any given situation or context. The three psychological needs emphasized in SDT are as follows: (1) the need to feel competent (i.e., can meet or handle the demands placed on us), (2) the need to have a sense of autonomy (e.g., that one has input, volition, choice), and (3) the need to feel related to others in a safe, trusting, and respectful way (Ryan & Deci, 2002, 2020).

As conceptualized within SDT (Ryan & Deci, 2002, 2017, 2020), the prediction of motivation (how self-determined) and associated outcomes is dependent on the degree to which the social psychological environment contributes to satisfaction and/or frustration of the three basic psychological needs. Thus, although the concept of motivational climate is not formally used in SDT, the theory can be used to further differentiate motivational climates in regard to whether participants' perceptions of competence, autonomy, and relatedness are promoted or undermined.

As was the case for AGT research, work grounded in SDT has examined the social psychological environment as shaped by various significant others (e.g., teachers, parents, exercise instructors, health care providers; Ryan & Deci, 2020). Relevant to the focus of this chapter, however, considerable SDT-based research has been done on the implications of the environment created by the coach. When a coach acts in a way that supports athletes' feelings of competence, autonomy, and relatedness, athletes are more likely to report greater autonomous motivation and well-being and to exhibit optimal engagement (Adie et al., 2008, 2012; Alvarez et al., 2009; Brown et al., 2021).

An *autonomy-supportive* coach tends to provide meaningful choices to their athletes and solicits their input, acknowledges their perspectives, and provides a rationale when making a request (Mageau & Vallerand, 2003). *Socially supportive* coaches promote athletes' *feelings of relatedness* by being there to help, showing they respect them and care for them (regardless of the performance of the athlete), and being genuinely interested in the athlete. SDT also considers the degree to which an activity leader provides structure. Structure, which can promote feelings of competence and autonomous motivation, is evident when the coach makes expectations clear and gives informative feedback in an autonomy-supportive manner (Reeve et al., 2004).

Recent work in sport grounded in SDT has investigated the implications of athlete perceptions of both autonomy-supportive and controlling coach behaviors on athletes' reported satisfaction or frustration regarding the basic need for competence, autonomy, and relatedness. A coach who is seen as controlling tends to intimidate athletes, is autocratic in exchanges with athletes (i.e., tells them what to do), and uses extrinsic (including social) rewards to make the athletes do what the coach wants (Bartholomew et al., 2011). When athletes' psychological needs are frustrated by a coach, they perceive the coaches' behaviors as efforts to make them feel incompetent, with little or no sense of autonomy ("like a pawn on a chessboard") and feel disconnected and disregarded in regard to the coach (and perhaps teammates as well). It is important to note that athletes can view their coaches to be actively frustrating their psychological needs, even if the coaches' behaviors are unintentional.

Consistent with the tenets of SDT (Ryan & Deci, 2017), past research has found perceptions of controlling instructor behaviors, and need frustration, to correspond to less self-determined motivational processes and negative outcomes (Bartholomew et al., 2011). In their longitudinal research on young male soccer players across a competitive season, for example, Balaguer and colleagues (2012) found that perceived increases in coaches' autonomy-supportive behaviors corresponded to the athletes' reporting greater need satisfaction and less need frustration over this time period. When the players reported higher need satisfaction, they also experienced greater vitality (i.e., feelings of psychological energy) and fewer burnout symptoms. On the other hand, increases in the players' perceptions of a controlling motivational climate corresponded to players' reporting greater need frustration across the season. Greater need frustration was associated with increases in player burnout. Parallel findings were reported in a longitudinal study by Gonzalez and colleagues (2017), which also considered potential team effects on the relationships examined (via multilevel modeling). Curran and colleagues (2016) found basic psychological need satisfaction and frustration to mediate the relationships between autonomy-supportive and controlling coaching behaviors to athletes' reported engagement over three time points during a competitive youth soccer season.

SDT-based interventions in sport have primarily centered on the promotion of coach autonomy support (Raabe et al., 2019). For example, Cheon and colleagues (2015) trained coaches in autonomy-supportive principles and strategies and examined the effects on the coaches as well as their athletes during the 2012 Paralympic Games. According to objective ratings and athletes' perceptions, intervention coaches were more autonomy supportive as a result of the training. When contrasted with control group athletes, motivation quality and indicators of engagement and functioning were maintained over time in the athletes whose coaches had undergone the training program. The intervention athletes were also reported to have won more medals. Langan and colleagues (2015) delivered an SDT-based intervention to Gaelic football coaches, again primarily focused on the promotion of autonomy support. No significant effects on players' motivation or reported burnout were observed, but the authors did find that their training program was feasible and delivered with fidelity.

The Integrated Empowering and Disempowering Model

Both AGT and SDT have developed over the last several decades and provided the conceptual foundation for extensive bodies of research in sport. This literature has offered insight into what coaches (and influential others) do to influence athletes' degree of self-determined motivation and related outcomes. No question, AGT and SDT have furthered researchers' and practitioners' understanding of different features of the motivational climate relevant to athletes' views of and responses to their sport experience.

With an appreciation and awareness of this work, Duda and colleagues have proposed a conceptualization of the motivational climate that aims to include and integrate concepts and predictions from both AGT and SDT (Duda, 2013; Duda & Appleton, 2016; Duda et al., 2018; see figure 10.1). In this integrated conceptualization, the motivational climate is assumed to be multidimensional, hierarchically structured, and characterized overall as being more or less empowering versus disempowering. An *empowering* motivational climate is task involving, autonomy supportive, and socially supportive. Motivational climates that are highly ego involving and controlling are considered to be *disempowering*. Structure is not ignored in the evolution of this approach (e.g., it is a subdimension of the MMCOS observational system, which is grounded

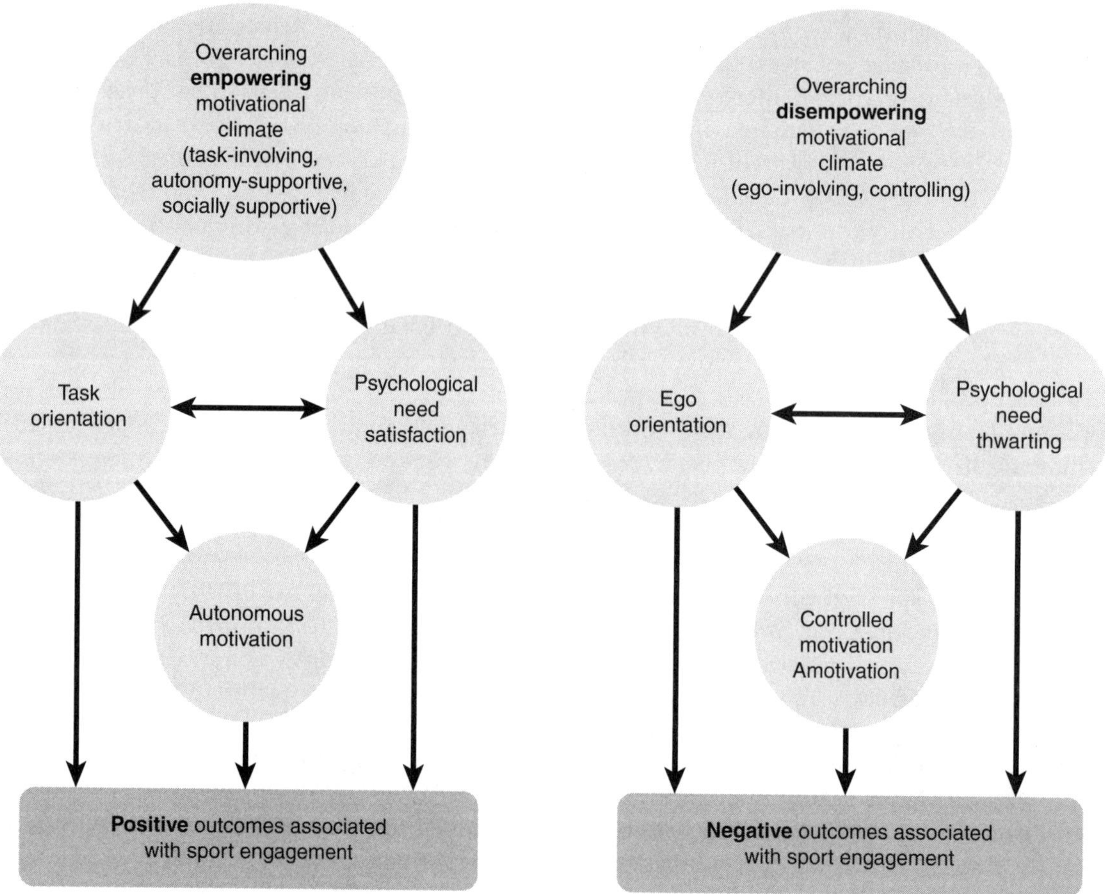

FIGURE 10.1 Integrated conceptualization of the differential features, processes, and outcomes associated with overarching empowering and disempowering motivational climates.

in the integrated model; Smith et al., 2015), but the other AGT and SDT climate subdimensions have been given more prominence to date.

The integrated model incorporates motivation-related processes (e.g., goal orientations, need satisfaction, need frustration, autonomous or controlled motivation, and amotivation from SDT) that are expected to be promoted by more or less empowering and disempowering motivational climates (Duda, 2013; Duda & Appleton, 2016). Pulling from AGT, the integrated approach assumes that coaches' behaviors, which fuel athletes' emphasis on task criteria for judging whether they have been competent, are an important ingredient of an empowering motivational climate. It is also held that athletes' task orientation would be promoted when they train and compete in a strongly empowering environment. Converse but conceptually parallel predictions are made for the impact of a pronounced disempowering motivational climate. That is, coach behaviors that are likely to attenuate a focus on task-involved goal criteria and/or accentuate ego-involved goal emphasis contribute to a disempowering environment. Perceptions of a disempowering motivational climate are expected to maintain or even foster athletes' ego orientation.

When athletes are strongly task oriented and their feelings of autonomy, relatedness, and task-involved competence are satisfied, it is predicted that autonomous motivation is also encouraged. When sport participants experience high need satisfaction and have greater autonomous motivation (aligned with what is suggested by SDT), positive outcomes are expected.

In contrast, when the needs for autonomy, relatedness, and a task-involved sense of competence are not satisfied (or are frustrated) and athletes' ego goals are emphasized, controlled motivation (and even amotivation) are likely to be fostered. In such cases, we would predict that athletes are more likely to experience ill-being and report indicators of compromised functioning.

Rationale for Integrated Model

The impetus to develop and embrace a more theoretically integrated model of the motivational climate stemmed from a variety of considerations (Duda, 2013; Duda & Appleton, 2016; Duda et al., 2018). The earlier work of the first author (see Duda, 2013, for a summary) was grounded in AGT, particularly the contributions of Nicholls (1989). Over time she and her students and colleagues began to incorporate constructs from SDT (Deci & Ryan, 2000; Ryan & Deci, 2002) along with the constructs embedded in AGT. Early empirical studies supported the notion that basic psychological needs represented one mechanism by which task- and ego-involving motivational climates predict differential outcomes. Past research also supported the initiative to include SDT-based dimensions of the social environment (such as autonomy support) when determining the processes and outcomes predicted by task- and ego-involving motivational climates.

As highlighted earlier, previous AGT- and SDT-based research on the concomitants of the dimensions of the motivational climate provided another justification for pulling together these related but still different features of the social environment. Considerable literatures (in sport and other domains) indicate positive processes and outcomes to be associated with perceptions of environments that are task involving, autonomy supportive, and social supportive (marked by involvement or caring) (Fry et al., 2019). Moreover, AGT- as well as SDT-grounded studies have pointed to the (same or similar) negative, maladaptive processes and outcomes linked to perceptions of highly ego-involving and controlling motivational climates, respectively.

Studies grounded in SDT often describe positive associations between autonomy support and social support or involvement (e.g., Hornstra et al., 2021). Research considering these two SDT-emphasized features of the social environment, and also assessing how task involving the motivational climate in question is, have identified positive intercorrelations between the three dimensions, which suggests they share considerable variance (e.g., r = .68-.79) (Appleton et al., 2016). The controlling and ego-involving aspects of coach behaviors are also conceptually as well as empirically linked (r = .60) (Appleton et al., 2016) albeit not redundant.

A final reason for proposing a more theoretically integrated model of the motivational climate is primarily practical (Keegan et al., 2017). When you speak to coaches about specific behaviors that are autonomy supportive (e.g., providing meaningful choices to the athletes, providing rationales for requested or recommended actions) and task involving (e.g., pointing out when the athlete is trying or is improving), these dimensions can be readily grasped as different although all-empowering strategies. The same goes when referring to disempowering behaviors. That is, the coach might want to be more aware of when they are comparing athletes to each other (ego-involving behavior), which is outwardly different from a coach's using intimidation to get what they want or using rewards in a controlling fashion (controlling behaviors).

This point regarding the practical distinctions in coaching behaviors (reflecting different subdimensions emphasized by AGT or SDT but falling under an overarching conceptualization of empowering and disempowering climates) is also supported in an observational study of coaches in training and competition (Smith et al., 2016). Overall findings indicated that grassroots football coaches were more empowering and less disempowering in training than was the case in matches. To better appreciate the differences in what the coaches were doing, however, it was informative to capture the particular behaviors that significantly varied across competitive and practice settings in accordance with an AGT as well as an SDT lens. For example, coaches were significantly more likely to provide a rationale and opportunity for player input (two autonomy-supportive strategies based on SDT) and emphasize task-focused competence feedback (a task-involving promotion strategy, according to AGT) in training when contrasted with a competitive situation. In competition (vs. a practice setting), coaches were significantly more likely to employ overt personal or physical control and devalue their athletes' perspective (two controlling strategies, based on SDT) but did not exhibit more ego-involving behaviors (from an AGT perspective).

Assessment of the Empowering and Disempowering Features of the Motivational Climate

Central to research testing Duda's (2013) integrated model has been the development and validation of measures capturing empowering and disempowering motivational climates (and underlying subdimensions) in sport (see table 10.1 for a summary). Initial efforts focused on the Empowering and Disempowering Motivational Climate Questionnaire (EDMCQ; Appleton et al., 2016), which was developed to measure athletes' perceptions of coaches' empowering and disempowering behaviors and communication strategies as demarcated by AGT and SDT.

Measures to capture the various assumed aspects or components of an empowering and disempowering climate exist in the literature (e.g., the Perceived Motivational Climate in Sport Questionnaire-2 to assess perceptions of task- and ego-involving climates; Newton et al., 2003). But to capture the full range of empowering and disempowering features of the climate that are central to Duda's model with established AGT- or SDT-based scales would prove lengthy and thus time consuming for athletes to complete. The development of the EDMCQ addresses this limitation by identifying (via statistical analyses, and based on the responses of a sample of young British sport participants) a reduced number of items that most closely represent the assumed dimensions of the empowering and disempowering climate model. Appleton and colleagues' (2016) findings suggest that in its current format, the EDMCQ may be best represented by two composite factors, whereby task-involving, autonomy-supportive, and socially supportive items load onto an empowering factor, and ego-involving and controlling items load onto a disempowering factor.

More recently, this two-factor structure has been supported using data from adolescent athletes in Lithuania (Sukys, 2020) and secondary school physical education students in Wales (Milton et al., 2018). Researchers have also provided support for the scale's invariance across five languages, two time points, experimental groups (Appleton et al., 2023), and gender (Milton et al., 2018). The EDMCQ's predictive validity and internal reliability have also been supported. Overall, evidence suggests that the EDMCQ-C is a promising psychometric questionnaire for assessing athletes' perceptions of empowering and disempowering motivational climates. More work is needed to adequately capture the assumed underlying subdimensions, however, and support the presumed hierarchical structure of the measure.

Although originally developed to capture athletes' perceptions of the motivational climate, the EDMCQ has been adapted (via changing the reference of the items) to capture coaches' self-reported adoption of empowering and disempowering strategies. In a study with coaches from five European countries, Solstad and colleagues (2020) examined the psychometric properties (i.e., factor structure and cross-cultural equivalence) of the coach-adapted version of the EDMCQ. Supporting previous findings relating to the original version of the EDMCQ, Solstad and colleagues' analyses did not support the multidimensional, hierarchical factor structure of the EDMCQ. Instead, they

TABLE 10.1 Tools for Assessing Empowering and Disempowering Motivational Climates

Measure	Source	Climate dimensions measured	Items and rating scale	Summary of psychometric evidence
EDMCQ (athletes' perceptions)	Appleton et al. (2016)	*Empowering* Task involving Autonomy supportive Social supportive *Disempowering* Ego involving Controlling	34 items Responses measured on a 5-point Likert scale (1 = strongly disagree, 5 = strongly agree)	Support for two-factor model (empowering and disempowering), with model holding across groups. Scales have internal reliability and predictive validity, and demonstrate invariance.
EDMCQ-Coach (coaches' self-report)	Solstad et al. (2020)	*Empowering* Task involving Autonomy supportive Social supportive *Disempowering* Ego involving Controlling	19 items Responses measured on a 5-point Likert scale (1 = strongly disagree, 5 = strongly agree)	Support for two-factor model (empowering and disempowering) and internal reliability of the scales across five countries.
MMCOS (observers' ratings)	Smith et al. (2015)	*Empowering* Task involving Autonomy supportive Relatedness supportive *Disempowering* Ego involving Controlling Relatedness thwarting *Other* Structure	34 coaching strategies reflecting 7 dimensions of empowering and disempowering climates Potency rating given on 4-point scale (0 = not at all, 3 = strong potency) for strategies, 7 dimensions, and in terms of the overall empowering and disempowering climate	Reliability and indicators of validity supported across multiple countries.

found support for a reduced 19-item measurement model, with each item contributing to its higher-order factor (empowering or disempowering) to a similar degree across the five countries.

Alongside the EDMCQ, the Multidimensional Motivational Climate Observation System (MMCOS) was developed to more objectively assess empowering and disempowering features of the motivational climate (Smith et al., 2015). Valid and reliable objective rating systems that assess characteristics of the motivational climate are important because the resulting data can be used to overcome common method variance (De Meyer et al., 2013) (e.g., when we observe inflated associations between variables because they are all assessed via the same method, such as questionnaires). Other benefits include providing a comparison to self-reported data regarding the features of the motivational climate obtained from questionnaires (such as the EDMCQ), and informing the evaluation of interventions aimed at modifying coach behavior and communication strategies (Smith et al., 2015). Within the sport science literature, observational systems do exist to capture features of the motivational climate from an AGT perspective (e.g., Boyce et al., 2009) and according to SDT (e.g., Webster et al., 2013).

The tendency in the literature has been for such observational systems to assess the frequency of different coaching behaviors emphasized by AGT,

SDT, or the climate dimensions proposed by either theory in isolation from one another. In contrast, the MMCOS captures the quality or psychological potency of empowering and disempowering behaviors displayed by the coach that reflect the broad array of AGT- and SDT-emphasized climate subdimensions. Specifically, the motivational climate is coded in the MMCOS according to the higher-order empowering and disempowering factors, seven lower-order dimensions (autonomy support, controlling, task involving, ego involving, relatedness support, relatedness thwarting, and structure), and 32 coach strategies identified within previous AGT- and SDT-based sport research (Smith et al., 2015) (see figure 10.2). Because the emphasis is on obtaining potency ratings—on a scale from 0 (not at all), 1 (weak potency), 2 (moderate potency), to 3 (strong potency)—the MMCOS allows researchers to capture the intensity or quality of the coach's delivery and how pervasive the coach-created environment is deemed to be in terms of its motivational meaning rather than simply counting the number of times any of the empowering and disempowering coaching behaviors were observed.

Smith and colleagues (2015) reported on the initial development of the MMCOS assessment of empowering and disempowering motivational climates (and underlying AGT and SDT subdimensions) using data from coaches in England, Greece, and France. Coders' ratings, following their review of video recordings of coaches engaging with their grassroots soccer players in training, were highly correlated and nonsignificantly different. They also reflected an adequate degree of reliability (i.e., different coders were more or less seeing and hearing the same things). The data also suggested that, overall, the MMCOS was marked by factorial validity, and predictive validity was established for a number of the lower-order environmental dimensions. Fabra and colleagues (2018) provided further support for the MMCOS's reliability and evidence of factorial and predictive validity in a sample of Spanish grassroots coaches. Evidence regarding the concurrent validity of the MMCOS stemmed from a study by Smith and colleagues (2016); significant differences emerged in the empowering and disempowering characteristics of the motivational climate manifested in training and matches.

Finally, in an attempt to triangulate assessments of the motivational climate grounded in Duda's (2013) model, Smith and colleagues (2016) tested the interrelationships between athletes' and coaches' perceptions (as assessed with the EDMCQ) and observers' ratings (as assessed via the MMCOS) of the empowering and disempowering motivational climate operating on one's team. Analyses of data from grassroots football coaches and their young players from England, France, Greece, and Spain suggested some consistency in perceptions of empowering and disempowering features of the climate when measured from multiple sources. Smith and colleagues (2016) also compared the fit of two competing models that predicted athletes' scores on autonomous motivation: One model

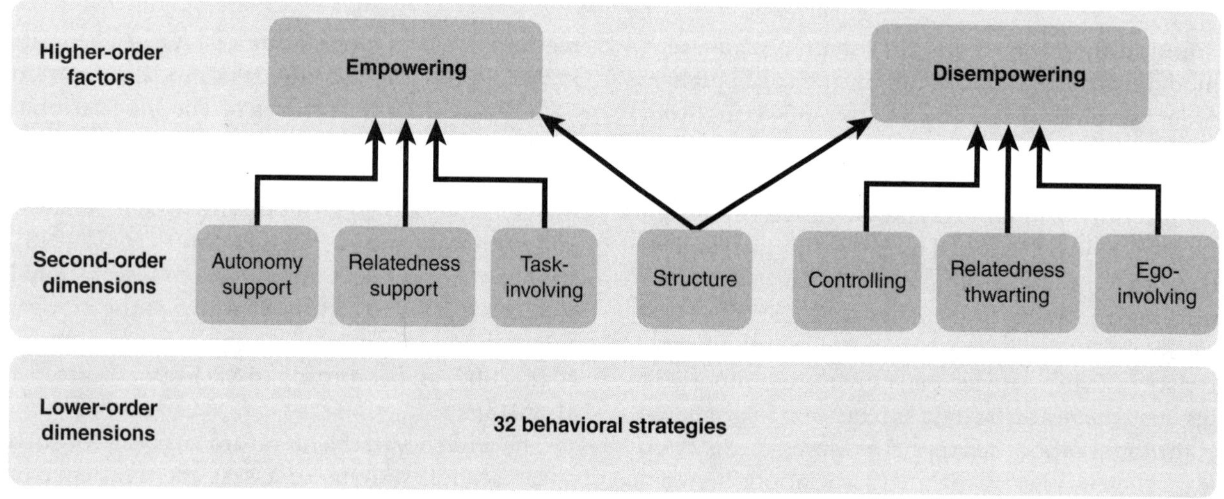

FIGURE 10.2 Hierarchical structure of the Multidimensional Motivational Climate Observation System (MMCOS).
Adapted from N. Smith, D. Tessier, Y. Tzioumakis, et al., "Development and Validation of the Multidimensional Motivational Climate Observation System," *Journal of Sport & Exercise Psychology* 37, no. 1 (2015): 4-22.

included just athletes' perceptions of empowering and disempowering motivational climates as predictor variables, and a second model included all three measurements of the climate (i.e., athlete, coach, observational ratings). Analyses suggested the second model was a better fit, providing evidence that researchers may benefit from assessing empowering and disempowering motivational climates using athletes', coaches', and observers' perceptions. Although there is some overlap between what is gleaned from these assessment tools, taking into account the two perspectives (athlete and coach) and the two methods (questionnaire and observation system) seems to provide a more insightful picture regarding the coach-created motivational climate and its potential impact on youth sport participants.

The results of Smith and colleagues (2016) are consonant with Cooper and Allen (2020), who employed a multiple methods approach to examine the motivational climate manifested in adventure sports in the views of adult participants, their coaches, and observers. The overall picture was relatively consistent in indicating the sport sessions were typically delivered in a strongly empowering—and weakly disempowering—manner.

Outcomes of Empowering and Disempowering Motivational Climates in Sport

The findings to date in studies specifically grounded in Duda's empowering climate approach (Duda, 2013; Duda & Appleton, 2016; Duda et al., 2018) have been consonant with theoretical predictions (see Birr, Hernandez-Mendo, Monteiro, & Rosado, 2023, for a recent scoping review). Perceptions of an empowering motivational climate have been found to positively predict enjoyment (Krommidas et al., 2016), with autonomous motivation mediating that relationship (Mosqueda et al., 2019), and players' self-efficacy, with positive self-talk supported as a mediator (Zourbanos et al., 2016). In a study of youth sport participants, Fenton and colleagues (2017) reported a perceived empowering motivational climate to positively relate to autonomous motivation, which corresponded to greater enjoyment of the sport. Greater enjoyment of football positively predicted objectively assessed moderate to vigorous physical activity. Legg and colleagues (2018) found features of an empowering motivational climate to predict positive youth development outcomes within and outside of sport.

Providing support for the differential pathways (empowering or disempowering climate, need satisfaction or frustration, motivation, goal orientations, and outcomes) assumed in Duda's (2013) model, Ruiz and associates (2021) reported autonomous motivation and task orientation mediation the positive association between empowering climate and desirable emotions. Perceptions of a disempowering motivational climate corresponded to greater ego orientation and controlled motivation, which was associated with more unpleasant emotions (such as anxiety, dejection). Castillo-Jimenez and colleagues (2022) found need satisfaction and self-determined motivation to partially explain the observed positive relationship between perceptions of an empowering climate and intentions to continue. Perceptions of a disempowering motivational climate significantly predicted athletes' intentions to drop out of their sport via heightened need frustration and lower levels of self-determined motivation. Taking a novel approach by focusing on eSports, Lopes Angelo and associates (2022) found professional players' perceptions of an empowering motivational climate to link positively to need satisfaction and indirectly relate to autonomous motivation. Need satisfaction and autonomous motivation (along with amotivation) significantly predicted intentions to continue in eSports and reported well-being. A perceived disempowering motivational climate corresponded to greater need frustration. More recently, Moulds and colleagues (2023) reported that empowering climates were associated with actual continuation, and disempowering climates associated with actual drop-out in young Australian swimmers.

Martinez-Gonzalez and associates (2021) examined the relevance of the empowering and disempowering features of the motivational climate to how athletes respond when faced with unattainable personal sport goals. Results revealed an empowering motivational climate to positively predict more autonomous goal motives, which partially explained the positive relationship between empowering climates and goal reengagement when one's goals became impossible to realize. When athletes perceived the motivational climate to be more disempowering, they were more likely to report controlled motives for their personal goal pursuit. The emphasis placed on controlled goal motives was not associated with goal reengagement. In a recent study with German athletes, Ohlert, Schimitz,

Schäfer-Pels, and Allroggen (2022) examined the relationship between athletes' perceptions of the coach-created empowering and disempowering climates and their experiences of sexual violence. Results from a MANOVA revealed that athletes who had experienced or observed sexual violence within their sport rated the coach-created empowering climate subfactors within their training group as lower and the disempowering climate subfactors as higher. Ohlert and colleagues concluded that a climate high in empowering features and low in disempowering features might be a protective factor against sexual violence in sport groups.

Employing a longitudinal design, Solstad and associates (2018) were interested in the relationships between coaches' perceptions of the degree to which the motivational climate they created was more or less empowering or disempowering, need satisfaction, and their reported well-being. A person-centered approach was adopted (using latent profile analysis), and three distinct motivational climate profiles (most empowering, less empowering, and least empowering) were revealed, based on the coaches' scores on the empowering and disempowering subscales of the EDMCQ (Appleton et al., 2016). Coaches who felt the motivational climate they fostered at the beginning of the season was marked by more empowering and less disempowering features (i.e., the most empowering profile) reported greater need satisfaction and positive affect and lower negative affect at the season's end.

Promoting More Adaptive Motivational Climates

It is advocated that interventions have a theoretical underpinning so we can better ascertain the what and why of the intervention content (embedded strategies and approach) being adopted. In their systematic review of the impact of interpersonal coach education interventions, Langan and colleagues (2013) called for further implementation and testing of such intervention efforts. They also argued for the importance of such interventions being theory based rather than theory inspired.

Aligned with Duda's theoretically integrated model of the motivational climate (Duda, 2013; Duda & Appleton, 2016; Duda et al., 2018), a training program (*Empowering Coaching*™; www.empoweringcoaching.co.uk) for coaches from grassroots through elite has been developed. Not surprisingly, key content within the training program is directed toward facilitating coaches' understanding and awareness of differences between autonomous and controlled motivation and the importance of athletes' feeling competent (as primarily defined via task-involving criteria), feeling a sense of autonomy, and feeling like they belong, are cared for, and respected to the quality of their motivation. The training also aims to make coaches more aware of the reasons why such motivational processes (autonomous motivation) and perceptions (need satisfaction) are important to optimize if we want to promote sustained, optimal, health-conducive sport participation. Within *Empowering Coaching*™, coaches are encouraged to think through and reflect on what constitutes their own and others' positive and questionable coaching strategies and the implications of such for sport participants and the coaches themselves.

Another key aspect of the training is that the coaches have an opportunity to consider and plan *how* they can be more empowering in training and competition and address likely barriers to their creating a more adaptive motivational climate in training and competitions in the future. Within *Empowering Coaching*™ training, classroom-based learning materials and activities designed to promote coaches' confidence and increase their likelihood of becoming more empowering and less disempowering include interactive games for understanding, a supplemental workbook, video clips, and guided small-group discussions. When and where feasible, follow-up opportunities (from the classroom-based workshop) to put more empowering strategies in practice take place.

Implementation and Impact of *Empowering Coaching*™ Training

The first major project that implemented the *Empowering Coaching*™ training program in youth sport was the Promoting Adolescent Physical Activity (PAPA) project. It could be argued that, to date, the PAPA project is the largest and most ambitious coach education study implemented in youth sport. This project involved delivering *Empowering Coaching*™ and conducting an associated research project across five countries (England, France, Greece, Norway, and Spain). The project also included the formation of a consortium involving researchers from eight European universities.

At its heart, the PAPA project (www.projectpapa.org) entailed the following:

- Translating the approximately six-hour classroom-based version of the *Empowering Coaching*™ training program from English into French, Greek, Norwegian, and Spanish and tailoring it for coaches of grassroots football players (ages 10-14 years)
- Translating and delivering a training program so that (football) tutors in the respective countries could be trained to deliver the targeted *Empowering Coaching*™ workshop to grassroots coaches with acceptable levels of fidelity
- Evaluating the fidelity and impact of *Empowering Coaching*™ over time on players and their coaches (in contrast to coaches who did not receive the training and their players) via both quantitative and qualitative methods

Duda and colleagues (2013) and Van Hoye and colleagues (2013) provide more information regarding particulars of the protocols adopted in the PAPA project. Viladrich and associates (2013) and Papaioannou and colleagues (2013) provide examples of research conducted within PAPA to examine the suitability of the questionnaires used to assess key outcomes *across* the five countries (i.e., measurement invariance). Earlier in this chapter, we summarize similar efforts in regard to measures of the perceived motivational climate (Appleton et al., 2016) and the observational assessment of the motivational climate (Smith et al., 2015) developed in PAPA.

Within *Empowering Coaching*™, coaches are encouraged to think through and reflect on what constitutes their own and others' positive and questionable coaching strategies and the implications of such for sport participants and the coaches themselves.

Findings emanating from the PAPA project are summarized elsewhere (e.g., Duda & Appleton, 2016). Overall, in regard to perceptions of the motivational climate in the view of the players and coaches and as objectively assessed across four of the countries (England, France, Greece, and Spain), the intervention reduced the perceived disempowering features of the motivational climate, increased the objectively assessed empowering aspects pre- to postworkshop, and decreased the disempowering characteristics over the course of the season.

Following the delivery of the *Empowering Coaching*™ training in the PAPA project, Castillo and colleagues (2015) examined Spanish coaches' perceptions of the impact and implementation of the training. The coaches reported that the content of the workshop was innovative and promoted rethinking their approaches to training. They also felt they understood and were able to integrate empowering principles and strategies in both training and competition.

Larsen and colleagues (2014) interviewed a subsample of coaches from Norway and France who had participated in the *Empowering Coaching*™ workshop within the PAPA project. Questions asked tapped into their views about the program and its implications for their coaching practice. Overall, coaches from both countries embraced the philosophical bases of *Empowering Coaching*™. They felt that training promoted strategies to enhance players' intrinsic motivation, enjoyment when playing, and likely long-term participation.

Sovik and colleagues (2016) evaluated the implementation of the *Empowering Coaching*™ program within the PAPA project specifically in Norway. This study shed light on the fidelity of program implementation when *Empowering Coaching*™ was delivered by coach tutors (members of regional or national football federations) who were trained by the respective research teams. This is an important feature of the PAPA project, because so often in the literature, it is the researchers themselves who deliver the AGT- or SDT-based training to coaches (e.g., Cheon et al., 2015). Sovik and associates concluded that overall (and especially in the case of experienced tutors), the program was delivered with moderate to high fidelity (and overall high quality). Some of the tutors made some adaptations when delivering the workshop, but these were still aligned with *Empowering Coaching*'s goals and underlying theoretical model.

In collaboration with the charity StreetGames in the United Kingdom, a tailored version of the *Empowering Coaching*™ training (i.e., Empowering Coaching for Doorstep Sport) was given to coaches and volunteers who were delivering sport sessions to young people from economically disadvantaged communities in various regions in England and Wales. Changes in the perceived motivational climate before and after the training—as well as on the young people's motivation, engagement, and well-being—were assessed. The bespoke *Empowering Coaching™* training was deemed to increase coaches' use of empowering strategies and decrease disempowering strategies in the views of the young people and the coaches and volunteers. The coaches reported that such changes in motivational strategies resulted in greater retainment and more quality engagement in the children.

In a study conducted in international schools in Mexico, Mosqueda and colleagues (under review) examined the effects of an extended delivery of *Empowering Coaching™* training on team cohesion (task and social). The intervention led to increases in the student-athletes' perceptions that the coach-created climate became more empowering over time. Such changes in the motivational climate held positive implications for the level of cohesion experienced.

Future Research Directions

The research and applied work based on Duda's (2013) integrated model is growing, and certainly further work is needed to build on this platform and extend knowledge of how to create more empowering and less disempowering motivational climates and the implications of doing so.

In their systematic review of research on the intrapersonal correlates of perceptions of the task- and ego-involving features of the motivational climate in sport, Harwood and colleagues (2015) indicated that further investigation is warranted on the motivational climates created by significant other influences besides the coach, such as parents and peers. We would make the same recommendation in regard to advocating more work on the correlates of empowering and disempowering motivational climates. Aligned with the suggestions of McCann and colleagues (2021), subsequent research should consider the range of motivational influences that coaches, parents, and peers may have and take into account the particular sport culture and development stage of the sport participant. We also would add to the list of relevant social agents who may create or contribute to more or less empowering and disempowering motivational climates such as club managers, sport governing bodies, partners (in the case of older athletes), and health care staff.

Subsequent research should consider the range of motivational influences that coaches, parents, and peers may have and take into account the particular sport culture and development stage of the sport participant.

It is difficult to imagine a coach working with athletes who is not affiliated with a community league, sport club, school or university, or perhaps a regional or national governing body or sport association. As such, coaches are influenced by motivational climates in which they themselves do their coaching, and these climates would be expected to influence how they perceive their job or role and how they behave (and which motivational climate they create) for their athletes. In the work setting, Gillet and colleagues (2012) found perceptions of support provided by the organization itself, as well as the autonomy support provided by one's supervisor, to be predictive of workers' need satisfaction and thwarting, satisfaction with their job, and personal well-being. In future research, it would be interesting to examine the relationship of empowering and disempowering motivational climates (manifested in the club, the sport organization, and perhaps the sport community) on coaches. Drawing from Gillet and colleagues (2012), Bartholomew and colleagues (2017), and also the work of Stebbings and colleagues (2015), we would expect empowering and disempowering climates to have differential effects on coaches' need satisfaction or frustration, motivation to coach, well-being, desire to continue in their role, and the climate they are creating for the athletes with whom they work.

Practical Implications

The lines of work summarized in this chapter reflect how theoretical frameworks can lay the bases for intervention in sport. Drawing from AGT, SDT, and Duda's (2013) integrated conceptualization, one way to promote more positive sporting experiences (for the sport participants and the coaches) is to work with coaches to help them better understand the motivational impact of their behaviors. Their regular patterns of interaction with athletes form a motivational climate. Existing theories and related research provide information about the features that make such motivational climates more positive and what characteristics are likely to result in motivational climates being more detrimental. Pulling from theoretical knowledge and evidence, we also know quite a lot about *why* we see such differential outcomes, and it is helpful if we share this insight with coaches.

All in all, the work summarized in this chapter indicates it is best when coaches create an environment in which athletes can motivate themselves (i.e., be autonomously motivated to train and compete) rather than coaches' needing to motivate their athletes. We want to work with coaches and help them build a motivational climate geared toward having athletes feel capable and focused on working hard and improving (the climate is task involving), view themselves as cared for and respected (it is socially supportive), and believe they have a voice and options (it is autonomy supportive) when it comes to their sport engagement. It is also beneficial to empower coaches to self-reflect on their behaviors and be aware of and understand the consequences of disempowering practices—even if well intended.

Summary

Drawing from personal accounts conveyed in the media by athletes, from personal reflections on our own sport experiences, and from what is gleaned when sport psychology consultants work with athletes, it is clear that coaches matter. Coaches have an impact on how athletes think, how they feel, and how they behave . . . within and even outside of sport. But how can we describe what coaches do in a meaningful way, and how do different coach behaviors lead to more positive—or more negative—sport experiences? Theories such as AGT and SDT facilitate capturing key features of the motivational climate coaches create in their day-to-day interactions with their athletes. These theories enhance understanding of the processes by which different coaching behaviors are likely to lead to positive and sustained sport engagement or compromised participation.

This chapter described and made the case for an integrated model of the motivational climate that pulls together constructs and predictions from AGT *and* SDT. This integrated model has set the stage for the development of comprehensive assessments of the perceived and observed empowering and disempowering features of the coach-created motivational climate. The model provides a conceptual backdrop for a systematic and targeted training program for coaches; the research to date on *Empowering Coaching*™ is hopeful and enlightening. The evidence shows it is possible to make a difference and have sporting environments be better places. Future work should consider how we can also work with and offer bespoke training on empowering principles to other significant individuals who contribute to the broader motivational landscape affecting sport participants.

DISCUSSION QUESTIONS

1. What do you think would be arguments for examining variability in the behaviors of coaches?
2. Considering the AGT and SDT subdimensions or characteristics of both environments, provide specific illustrations of how an empowering coach would typically coach. Contrast this with the usual coaching practices of a primarily disempowering coach.
3. How would you suggest we assess the empowering and disempowering coach-created motivational climate in your favorite sport?
4. Drawing from the literature, what are some of the consequences of exhibiting empowering coaching behaviors in sport? What are likely to be the implications of a highly disempowering ego-involving climate on athletes' cognitive, affective, and behavioral responses?
5. What are some directions for future research on the empowering and disempowering coach-created motivational climate in sport settings?

11

Caring Climate

Lori Gano-Overway, PhD, and Mary Fry, PhD

LEARNING OBJECTIVES

On completion of this chapter, the reader should have the following:

- Knowledge of how *caring* and the *caring climate* are defined in the field
- Comprehension of the theoretical and conceptual underpinnings of the caring climate
- Understanding of personal and situational factors that could influence engagement in caring practices and one's perceptions of the caring climate
- Ability to describe the major findings outlining outcomes in contemporary caring climate research
- Knowledge of the most promising avenues for future research related to the caring climate
- Understanding of ways to be more intentional in implementing a caring climate in their own practice

"I have found that once a student-athlete trusts that I really care for them primarily as a human, then as an athlete, that's when the magic happens" (Maine, 2019). This quote from recently retired UCLA gymnastics coach Valorie Kondos Field—known as Miss Val—illustrates the importance some coaches place on caring. Gordon and colleagues (1996) defined *caring* as "a set of relational practices that foster mutual recognition and realization, growth, development, protection, empowerment, and human community, culture, and possibility" (p. xiii). Miss Val exhibited caring, as her athletes highlighted in the following quotes (Maine, 2019):

> She asked me right away what I wanted to do after gymnastics. . . . No one had ever asked me that before. . . . I realized Miss Val, and the entire coaching staff, didn't just want me to win in gymnastics, but in life too. . . . They have my best interests at heart. They want me to be not an excellent gymnast, but an excellent person.
>
> —Margzetta Frazier

> Because of her, I've learned to enjoy every single day that I have, because tomorrow's not guaranteed, and I think Miss Val embodies that. . . . People ask about her legacy, but I think she's already left it with the close bond she has with everyone she touches in her life.
>
> —Katelyn Ohashi

Miss Val has developed a personal relationship with each athlete that steps outside of her own frame of reference—that is, she cares. However, this caring extends beyond them as individuals; in other words, the athletes perceive a broader caring climate.

According to Newton and colleagues (2007), a *caring climate* is "the extent to which individuals perceive a particular setting to be interpersonally inviting, safe, supportive, and able to provide the experience of being valued and respected" (p. 70). At its core, a caring climate is about being relational and being in community with others. There are glimpses of this in the athletes' quotes and in the description of Miss Val's coaching practices. Specifically, Maine (2019) describes her greeting players as they enter the gym, checking in on how life is going, giving high fives to the gymnastics team's support squad, asking gymnasts' opinions on their training, and encouraging them to find joy. Miss Val is attending to others, helping them feel a part of the team, and recognizing who they are as people. In doing so, athletes described how she had ignited or reignited their joy and passion for gymnastics. Miss Val demonstrates a practical example of the caring climate in the sport setting. In this chapter, we elaborate on why the caring climate, as illustrated in Miss Val's approach, is important in developing athletes as moral, healthy, and competent individuals and in creating a positive sport experience.

Over the last 15 years, researchers have explored caring in sport coaching, athletes' perceptions of the caring climate, and the influence it has on athletes. The purpose of this chapter is to describe the contemporary research regarding caring climate within the sport context. The chapter begins by discussing the conceptual frameworks that have informed the defining elements of the caring climate and helps the reader distinguish it from the coach–athlete relationship and other social psychological climates. Using the current research findings, the next section of the chapter introduces a caring climate model, identifying caring practices that can lead to perceptions of the caring climate, as well as explores antecedents to and outcomes associated with the caring climate. The final sections of the chapter outline areas of future research and considerations for how coaches might use this information to more intentionally develop a caring climate.

At its core, a caring climate is about being relational and being in community with others.

Conceptual Frameworks Associated With the Caring Climate

In conceptualizing the caring climate within physical activity contexts, Newton and colleagues (2007) turned to research and philosophical writings within the educational setting—more specifically, the philosophical work of Noddings (1992, 2003a) and intervention research conducted by Battistich and colleagues (e.g., Battistich & Solomon, 1997) in the Child Development Program. In this section, we review each of these frameworks, how they are incorporated into the caring climate, and what makes the caring climate a unique construct compared with other relational interactions and social psychological climates.

The Caring Relation

Noddings' (2003a) *caring relation* is a way of being in relation with another person, which is sustained over time and has implications for sense of belonging, caring behaviors, affective responses, ethical actions, and motivation. The caring relation involves both the one-caring (e.g., the coach) engaging in *engrossment* and *motivational displacement* toward the cared-for (e.g., the athlete), and the cared-for engaging in *recognition* of the caring actions of the one-caring. According to Noddings, the caring relation begins with engrossment, which involves attentiveness and receptivity. An illustrative example of Noddings' description of engrossment is when a coach observes, converses with, and listens to the athlete through an empathetic lens—that is, the coach seeks to understand the athlete's perspective, recognizes the athlete's emotions, and connects with those emotions to feel what the athlete is experiencing. In doing so, the coach comes to understand the other person's needs, wants, and goals. According to Noddings, this new understanding and emotional connection (i.e., engrossment) often results in motivational displacement, or feeling compelled to respond to the other. For instance, a coach notices an athlete rarely interacts with other members of the team and is often seen alone and appears unhappy before or after practice. In casual conversation, the coach learns the athlete does not know many of teammates. The actions of engrossment result in the coach connecting with similar feelings of sadness the athlete may be feeling and lead the coach to express concern and consider actions to help the athlete feel a part of the team. In this instance, the coach turns motivational energy (thoughts, feelings, and behaviors) toward helping the athlete by organizing activities for the athletes to get to know one another better. In doing so, the coach provides an example to the team of how to care and creates a sense of belongingness for the athlete and others on the team. For the caring relation to continue to exist, however, Noddings notes the need for the cared-for (e.g., athlete) to recognize the actions or responses of the one-caring. This recognition occurs when the cared-for acknowledges, responds, self-discloses, or reciprocates in response to the one caring (Noddings, 2003a). In the example described, it may be a change in demeanor, greater interaction, or a smile exhibited by the athlete. The coach's action also provides an example of how to engage with others that the coach may see replicated by the athlete or other members of the team. In the end, the caring action helps another person learn to care (Noddings, 2003a) as well as grow and become self-actualized (Mayeroff, 1971).

Noddings (2003a) noted that embedded in the caring relation is ethical caring (e.g., obligation to care) informed by natural caring (e.g., experiences with naturally caring moments, such as when someone is hurting). In this way, Noddings (2003a) argued that the one-caring feels obliged to act and does not ignore or reject the call to move toward ethical caring. Applying this to the previous example, the coach experiences a sense of obligation to care for the athlete who feels isolated because it is the right thing to do informed by an empathic response as well as a memory of what it felt like to be part of a team based on previous natural caring experiences. Noddings (1992, 2003a) also contended that the one-caring can further develop ethical caring in others by modeling caring, engaging in dialogue to develop mutual understanding and care, providing opportunities to practice care, and confirming an individual action may have a better motive, thus seeing the best in another. Therefore, while the caring relation is a didactic relationship, she acknowledged that the modeling, dialogue, and practice of care may extend beyond the caring relation to create a moral caring climate, or rather the establishment of "a climate in which caring relation can flourish" (Noddings, 2008, p. 166) and we teach each other to care.

The Caring Community

Similar to Noddings, Battistich and colleagues (1997) had a goal of developing caring individuals within the school environment. Specifically, they stated, "we want the outcomes of participating in the school community to be students who care about others, are socially responsible, and value justice and integrity as much as academic achievement" (p. 148). In creating caring communities of learners within classrooms and schools, the Child Development Program focused on five components (Battistich, 2008b):

- Collaborative learning
- Embedding helping activities
- Developing empathy
- Fostering social competencies for living in community
- Deploying developmental discipline

While implementing this program depended on the development of teacher–child relationships, the program planners were clear that the goals of the program would be more likely to occur when students "are able to participate actively in a cohesive, caring group with a shared purpose; that is, a community" (Battistich et al., 1997, p. 138). Battistich (2008a) further argued, "While a positive teacher-student relationship is necessary, it is not sufficient. The teacher also must create an environment where relationships among students are caring and supportive" (p. 85).

The Caring Climate

The caring climate within the sport realm integrates the work of Noddings (1992, 2003a) and Battistich (2008a, 2008b). It is a climate where the coach is "in relation" with each athlete and engages in actions unique to each athlete supporting their growth as a moral, competent, and healthy person. The climate is also based on a collaborative effort with the intention to teach care (i.e., care for and care about), encourage self-development, and create a sense of community. The coach works with athletes to nurture a welcoming and accepting environment where all members of the team feel valued, while also encouraging athletes to support one another in achieving their potential in and out of sport. How the caring climate is implemented is likely to be unique to each coach, and based on the individual and collective relationships with athletes on the team. As Noddings (1992) stated, "Caring is a way of being in relation, not a set of specific behaviors" (p. 17). While there are principles that guide caring practices, it is not possible to assess specific strategies that work for all individuals in all situations. The likely complexity of trying to assess whether and how specific caring behaviors may influence outcomes has made it more difficult to design and test interventions in this area. Therefore, the caring climate has instead been assessed based on athletes' perceptions of *general caring*.

Differentiating the Caring Climate From Other Social Psychological Climates

Aspects of caring can be seen in other work examining social psychological climates. One social psychological climate that has received much attention is the task-involving climate (see chapter 10). Achievement goal theorists acknowledge that the task-involving climate is primarily *competence-based* recognizing, reinforcing, and evaluating success based on effort, improvement, and skill mastery (Duda & Balaguer, 2007). However, some elements of caring have been incorporated. For example, Newton and colleagues' (2000) perceived task-involving motivational climate measure included subscales associated with fostering cooperation among teammates and valuing the important role of each team member, each of which has some connection to the caring climate. We would argue that coaches who emphasize these features with their athletes are engaging in caring behaviors because they are encouraging athletes to focus on working together and supporting one another to reach their potential and recognize each other's contribution to the team. Further, coaches who strive to help athletes develop their capacities as athletes, a characteristic of task-involving climates, can be engaging in motivational displacement as when caring coaches turn their energies toward helping athletes reach their potential. Therefore, there are elements of caring behavior, but it does not fully encompass the caring climate.

How the caring climate is implemented is likely to be unique to each coach, and based on the individual and collective relationships with athletes on the team.

While we endorse the creation of both a caring and task-involving climate within sport settings (Fry et al., 2020)—as we believe the combined features of both climates together contribute to an optimal climate—for the purposes of this chapter we are focusing primarily on the literature central to the caring climate. However, in a few studies the research methodology combines the caring and task-involving features of the climate (i.e., coaches are trained to create a caring and task-involving climate); we believe this research is important to note and will distinguish it throughout the chapter.

In addition to the research centered on achievement goal perspective theory, self-determination theory is a popular framework that has elements of caring. Specifically, theorists Ryan and Deci (2017) point to a relatedness-supportive climate as part of the social factors that can influence basic psychological needs. Relatedness-supportive climates are based on a secure attachment and support from another who is in a leadership position. The empowering motivational climate (chapter 10), which combines elements of self-determination theory and achievement goal theory, integrates the task-involving with an autonomy-supportive and a socially-supportive climate (Duda & Appleton, 2016). The socially-supportive climate is purported to occur when the coach "cares and values each" member of the team as a person (Duda & Appleton, 2016, p. 375). While the caring climate may conceptually, and sometimes empirically, overlap with these climates, a caring climate represents a qualitatively different endeavor on the part of the coach to develop a community of care, informed by relational and communal elements, that is then expressed and experienced by all members of the group.

Model of the Caring Climate

To further describe the caring climate and associated outcomes, we introduce a model based on our conceptualization of the climate, the philosophical and conceptual underpinnings of the caring climate noted previously, and research conducted in caring and caring climate in sport (see figure 11.1). While the caring climate is assessed based on

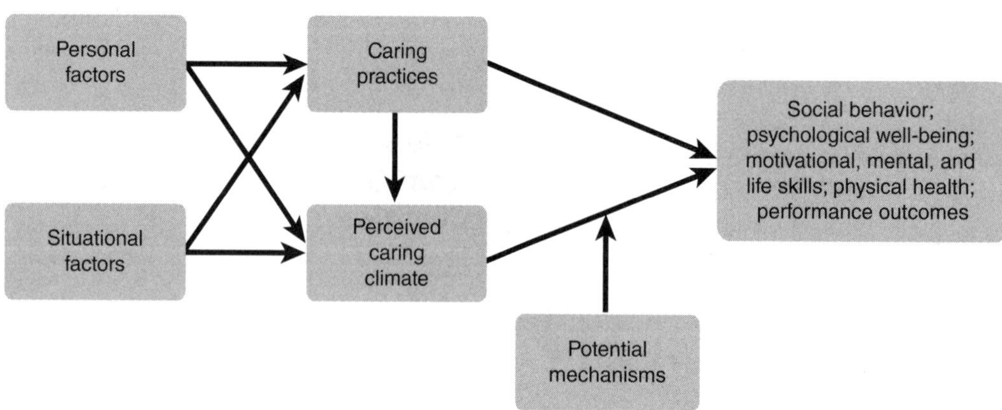

FIGURE 11.1 Caring climate model.

the athletes' perception of the climate, theory and research in this topic are grounded in the assumption that this perception is based on the athletes' recognition of caring practices implemented by the coach. We contend that *both* coaches' caring practices *and* athletes' perceptions of the climate can be influenced by personal and situational factors. Further, the coaches' caring practices and perceived caring climate are purported to influence a variety of athlete outcomes. In the following paragraphs, we elaborate on the components of the model and review supporting research.

Antecedents to Caring

We begin our discussion of the model by considering antecedents (i.e., factors that may influence coaches' engagement in the caring climate or athletes' perceptions of caring). These antecedents are divided into two types: personal factors and situational factors.

Personal Factors

Personal factors play a role in determining engagement in or perceptions of caring. While many personal factors could be postulated, we will describe the current conceptual and empirical work that points to *previous experiences*, *emotional intelligence*, and *self-reflection* as potential personal factors. As noted earlier, Noddings (2003a) proposed that ethical caring within the caring relation emerges from one's previous experiences with natural caring. Therefore, previous experiences of being cared for, seeing others model care, or practicing care can influence a person's ability to engage in the caring relation, whether it be practicing care or recognizing care.

Another personal factor that may influence an individual's ability to employ caring practices is emotional intelligence. Emotional intelligence entails identifying and expressing emotions, understanding emotions, and regulating emotions (Mayer & Salovey, 1997). Individuals who possess emotional intelligence may be more attuned to the emotional needs of others, take their perspective, and be empathic, all of which could influence caring actions. Magyar and colleagues (2007) found partial support for this as youth sport leaders' ability to regulate their own emotions predicted caring, which the authors postulated could positively influence leaders' ability to be present for youth and be more likely to recognize their emotional needs.

Aspects of personal experience, emotional intelligence, and self-reflection, the third potential personal factor, are apparent in Jones' (2009) autoethnographic story of his interaction with a young footballer. In his recollection, he notices the emotional reaction of the athlete as they pass in the hall, reflects upon this emotion and moment, and based on his understanding and his own emotional response from previous experiences takes the initiative to engage in a caring action. Therefore, the ability to reflect in the moment may be necessary to capture the need for care. These preliminary conceptual remarks and research findings provide some evidence that personal factors can foster or impede caring practices. However, additional research is needed to further characterize the role of personal experience, emotional intelligence, and self-reflection and explore the role of other personal factors (e.g., leadership style). Further, the current research has explored only personal factors associated with coaches' caring practices, meaning work investigating what personal factors may influence athletes' perceptions of caring is warranted.

Situational Factors

When examining caring practices exhibited by coaches, research points to the role situational factors may have in fostering or impeding care. These factors may be associated with the cultural context, the structural and contextual power within sport, the sport culture, a program's emphasis on effort or winning, program resources, and demands of coaching. While scholarly work is limited, researchers have found that some of these factors play a role. Cronin and colleagues (2019) found the highly competitive and micropolitical environment within an elite football program made caring more difficult. The strength and conditioning coach, highlighted in their narrative, struggled to care as the focus turned toward winning and protecting one's job. These factors did not prevent caring, but they constrained his ability to do so. The situational factors also extended to the athlete highlighted in the research study; as he focused on getting back to competition, undermining care for his own well-being, and limited his capacity to reciprocate care. Claunch and Fry (2016) described the initial resistance of three college football coaches in adopting a caring and task-involving climate as the coaches did not see how the approach was aligned with a highly competitive sport context. A large driving force that led these coaches to experiment with this approach was the low retention rate in the program (i.e., 20% over several years). In participating in the intervention, the coaches acknowledged their approach undermined their ability to establish strong relationships with the athletes and dehumanized players. In the end, they discovered that caring supported their goals within the competitive context. In fact, the retention rate rose to 94% following the season-long intervention. Another difficulty in caring related to the high-performance context was raised by Dohsten and colleagues (2020) in their interviews with coaches. Some coaches recognized they cared more about high-performance athletes than other athletes. The coaches also found it difficult to balance caring for athlete well-being and health with performance concerns.

These initial findings highlight the importance of investigating how situational factors encourage or hamper caring practices among coaches and athletes. The findings also point to the need for further work in this area to reinforce these outcomes and determine how caring practices interact with the situational factors. Finally, while we contend the features of the caring and task-involving climate are complementary, combining them does create difficulty for researchers and theorists in untangling which situational factors may influence caring versus task-involving practice and how; but in the end, it may provide better insight for practitioners developing a complex climate.

Caring Practices

As noted earlier, a core tenet of the conceptual model is that athletes' perceptions of the caring climate are based on the caring actions and behaviors of coaches and teammates. As such, the next part of the caring climate model relates to the caring practices enacted. Drawing on the conceptual underpinnings of the caring climate, we contend these caring practices are associated with the caring relation, and developing a caring community emanating first from the sport coach but then extending to other members of the team.

Elements of the caring relation and caring community have been incorporated into physical activity practice for quite some time. In particular, Hellison (1978) argued for a humanistic approach to physical activity instruction that emphasized the needs of the participants. Over time, this humanistic philosophy evolved into an approach for teaching personal and social responsibility (TPSR), emphasizing development of values and life skills through experiential learning, opportunities for dialogue and reflection, empowerment, and relationship building (Richard & Shiver, 2020). In describing the core values of the TPSR approach, Hellison (2011) noted the importance of holistic development within a child-centered context that promotes "human decency and positive relationships with others" (p. 18). Therefore, his daily program format included relational time where program leaders, like coaches, focused on getting to know their athletes, recognizing their strengths, asking for their input, honoring their decisions, and possibly encouraging them to reflect on better ways of being (i.e., improving their level of responsibility). In reviewing this approach, we acknowledge there are connections to the caring relation (e.g., engrossment), teaching care (i.e., modeling, dialogue, practice, confirmation), and developing a caring community (e.g., embedding helping activities, developing social competencies, exhibiting norms associated with caring). Therefore, caring practices are not new to the physical activity environment. However, further conceptual and theoretical frameworks and research were needed to support this approach and the underpinnings of the caring climate.

More recently, researchers have specifically explored caring practices identified by coaches and their athletes associated with the caring relation. At the youth level, youth performance coaches discussed recognizing and responding to the needs of their athletes (Cronin & Armour, 2017), and a youth football coach described his attentiveness to the needs of a player (Jones, 2009). Researchers (Annerstedt & Lindgren, 2014; Fisher et al., 2017; Knust & Fisher, 2015; Lindgren & Barker-Ruchti, 2017) shared how high-performance coaches engaged in the caring relation by

- getting to know athletes through listening, checking in, and remaining available;
- engaging in positive interactions with athletes;
- negotiating expressed needs with a focus on accountability;
- helping athletes develop skills to be their own coach;
- supporting holistic development with an emphasis on ethical care; and
- noting a willingness to learn from athletes.

Qualitative researchers have also interviewed both coaches and their athletes, reinforcing the previously listed caring behaviors and further establishing that athletes recognized and reciprocated the caring actions of their coaches (Cronin et al., 2019; Gano-Overway, 2023; Gano-Overway & Carson Sackett, 2021). These collective findings demonstrate how coaches engage in engrossment and motivational displacement as well as how athletes recognize this care, supporting the tenets of the caring relation.

Researchers have also characterized caring practices that align more closely with aspects of developing a caring community. Annerstedt and Lindgren (2014), using a case study approach, examined the strategies used by Swedish national handball coach Bengt Johansson. They highlighted his desire to get to know his players deeply, care for their well-being, and develop a safe and secure team built on sharing and reinforcing values of respect, trust, and common courtesy. Annerstedt and Lindgren clarified that these values were not rules but rather agreed upon norms that guided all team members. Other researchers described how high-performance coaches referred to their teams as families, where the circle of care extended to support staff along with athletes; noted the importance of creating a positive community based on the norms of trust and respect; encouraged athletes to help one another achieve excellence; and modeled the respect and ethical behavior they hoped to see in their athletes (Gano-Overway & Carson Sackett, 2021; Knust & Fisher, 2015; Lindgren & Barker-Ruchti, 2017).

A core tenet of the conceptual model is that athletes' perceptions of the caring climate are based on the caring actions and behaviors of coaches and teammates.

While most studies have focused on high-performance coaches, research by Gano-Overway (2023) provided insight into how former athletes recognized a community of care created by their high school coaches. In the narrative of one athlete's experiences with her swim coach, Gano-Overway describes how the swim coach helped the swimmer feel part of the team and recognize her value to the team as well as helped all the athletes learn how to support one another. Overall, research findings suggest that coaches develop a caring community by

- fostering community values (e.g., respect, care, trust, empathy, and kindness);
- modeling, communicating, and confirming these values;
- providing opportunities to practice care;
- developing a welcoming, accepting, and inviting environment;
- valuing every team member's contribution to the team; and
- collaborating with and learning from one another.

In considering the caring practices, Noddings (2010) emphasized the importance of what motivates the caring act. While some coaches may be compelled to care because it serves their own interests (e.g., helps facilitate athletic performance and builds team cohesion) or strictly out of duty (e.g., a coach is supposed to care), we contend that individuals exhibit caring when they are motivated to care because of the relational and communal aspects associated with the caring climate. In providing an overview of philosophical elements that can inform developing a caring climate in the youth sport setting, Gano-Overway (2013) discussed how the African ethic *ubuntu* may mirror aspects of a caring community. At its core *ubuntu* is developing humanness in ourselves and others through relation and community (Metz & Gaie, 2010). From this perspective, what motivates coaches to care may be their desire to help others and themselves be better people and create a strong community.

With regard to ethical caring, Noddings (2010) contended empathy played a role. For example, when a coach listens to and observes an athlete, the coach not only comes to understand the athlete and their needs but also connects to the emotions the athlete is feeling. Feshbach (1997) described empathy as "an emotional response that emanates from the emotional state of another individual, and although empathy is defined as a shared emotional response, it is contingent on cognitive as well as emotional factors" (p. 35). This shared emotional response is the driving force for the coach to engage in motivational displacement (Noddings, 2010). Therefore, empathy is a motivator for one to engage in caring and is one part of caring. Research in sport is limited but provides some initial insights. For example, Annerstedt and Lindgren (2014) described the importance the Swedish national coach placed on viewing "the world from the perspective of his players" (p. 35). Coach Johansson specifically stated, "A coach must be able to feel empathy and understanding and be able to treat every human being with respect in any situation he or she experiences" (p. 35).

While current findings provide direction on what caring practices coaches are engaged in and athletes perceive, it is still not clear that all these practices are actually caring or promote adaptive outcomes. Consider the following questions related to some of the caring practices previously noted.

- When a coach listens to and supports athlete development, will this always be a caring practice? What information does the coach attend to? Are coaches really attending to the expressed needs of the athletes, or does the coach make a value judgment on what they need to attend to?
- Does the coach empathize and support all expressed needs, or is the coach's motivational displacement based on their own cultural values? That is, do coaches express empathy only toward those needs they can resonate with, which may be based on their own personal experience and cultural values?
- How much of the athlete's own culture is embraced in the climate, leading them to feel welcomed and accepted, particularly if the coach is not knowledgeable about the culture?

These and other questions note the complexity of studying caring practices and the need to link the caring practices indicated by coaches with athletes' perceptions of the caring climate, independent observations of the climate, and adaptive outcomes as well as a critical analysis of the influence of personal and situational factors.

Perceptions of the Caring Climate

While we acknowledge caring practices influence athletes' affect, behavior, and cognition, we also propose that perceptions of the caring climate are more closely linked to athlete outcomes. Hence, what is enacted and valued by coaches is several steps along the causal chain, whereas athletes' perceptions are much more closely associated with their experiences. As Noddings (1992, 2003a, 2010) asserted, the caring relation is only complete when the cared-for recognizes caring. This approach is mirrored in various social psychological research traditions, emphasizing the importance of the individual's *perception* that the environment has an influence on emotions, thoughts, and actions (e.g., Duda & Appleton, 2016; Newton et al., 2000; Nicholls, 1989; Ryan & Deci, 2017). Perceptions of caring in sport have been assessed by the Caring Climate Scale (CCS; Newton et al., 2007). Within the CCS, athletes self-report what their coaches and team are typically like. Items include athletes' perception of the coach (i.e., coaches get to know, listen, help, welcome, accept, and respect athletes) and general perceptions associated with being part of the team (i.e., athletes feel welcomed, accepted, and safe). The CCS has demonstrated good validity, measuring general caring as it purports to measure (Cetinkaya & Mutluer, 2019; Iwasaki & Fry, 2016; Newton et al., 2007), and internal consistency, having survey items that correlate with one another, suggesting they are measuring the same construct (Fry & Gano-Overway, 2010; Gould et al., 2012; Hall et al., 2017).

Athlete Outcomes Experienced in Caring Sport Climates

A primary focus of research on caring in sport over the last decade has been on the outcomes athletes experience when they perceive a caring climate, often assessed using the CCS. As noted in the caring climate model (table 11.1), these outcomes relate to social behavior, psychological well-being, motivation, mental skills and life skills, physical health, and performance. In this section, we highlight the research addressing each of these outcomes.

Social Behavior Outcomes

Athletes who perceive a caring climate report having better relationships with their peers in the program. Specifically, when they perceived a caring climate, athletes were more likely to report

- liking their teammates (Fry & Gano-Overway, 2010),
- having more friends on the team (Stark & Newton, 2014),
- experiencing a greater sense of belonging (Byrd & Martin, 2016; Gerabinis et al., 2018),
- having greater attachment to and compassion for their peers (Fontana et al., 2017; Stark & Newton, 2014),
- feeling like their teammates care about their well-being (Brown et al., 2019), and
- experiencing greater social self-esteem (Hogue et al., 2021).

In addition to more positive interactions with peers, when perceiving a caring environment, athletes reported fewer negative peer influences and experienced less social exclusion (Gould et al., 2012).

The positive relationships that typically occur in a perceived caring climate extend beyond the athletes' relationships with one another. Athletes have reported (1) experiencing closer relationships with their coaches (Fry & Gano-Overway, 2010), (2) feeling greater attachment to their dance instructors (Stark & Newton, 2014), and (3) feeling that their coaches care about their well-being (i.e., as

TABLE 11.1 Athlete Outcomes Experienced in Caring Sport Climates

Social behavior	Psychological well-being	Motivational outcomes	Mental and life skills	Physical health	Performance
OUTCOMES POSITIVELY ASSOCIATED WITH A CARING CLIMATE					
• Like teammates • Teammates as friends • Feel sense of belonging • Attached to and compassion for peers • Social self-esteem • Closer relationship or attachment with coaches • Prosocial and caring behaviors	• Positive affect • Feel a sense of hope and happiness • Ability to regulate positive and negative emotional responses	• Enjoyment • Commitment to continue playing • Continuing participation in the future • Effort	• Coping skills • Initiative • Teamwork and social skills • Mindfulness • Confidence in ability to explore future careers after sport • Proactive learning about future career options	• Share concussion symptoms with coaches • Care about their physical health • Play only when fully healed from concussion • Perceived teammates and coaches cared about personal health	• More assists and fewer turnovers • Belief that they reached their potential during the season
OUTCOMES NEGATIVELY ASSOCIATED WITH A CARING CLIMATE					
• Negative peer influences • Social exclusion • Antisocial behaviors • Bullying	• Negative affect • Sadness • Depressive symptoms • General life stress • Shame • Cognitive and somatic anxiety • Feel judged, humiliated, or self-conscious				

human beings) beyond their role as athletes (Brown et al., 2019).

Athletes who perceive more caring on their teams also report engaging in caring behaviors toward one another. In cross-sectional research, perceptions of a caring climate have been associated with young athletes indicating they engage in prosocial (Gano-Overway et al., 2009) and caring behaviors with their peers and coaches (Fry & Gano-Overway, 2010; Iwasaki & Fry, 2013). Researchers have also reported a negative association between youngsters' perceptions of a caring climate in sport and physical education with antisocial and bullying behaviors (Gano-Overway, 2014; Gano-Overway et al., 2009).

Overall, small to moderate positive correlations have been reported, suggesting that when athletes perceive a caring climate, those athletes, in turn, are more likely to report engaging in positive relationships with members of the team and engaging in prosocial and general caring behaviors. Based on research in this area, we propose that when coaches engage in caring practices, and athletes perceive these practices, the athletes may be likely to internalize the behaviors observed and experienced (i.e., use their personal experiences with natural caring) to respond and/or reciprocate. We acknowledge that continued research is needed to further test these conceptual tenets that extend beyond cross-sectional research. To date, no findings have indicated the emergence of negative associations between athletes' perceptions of the caring team climate and variables related to athletes' relationships with coaches and teammates, and/or their engagement in prosocial and compassionate behaviors.

Psychological Well-Being Outcomes

Perceptions of a caring climate have also been associated with healthy psychological functioning, represented by the experience of greater positive parameters of well-being and fewer negative parameters. Stark and Newton (2014), for example, found adolescent dancers' perceptions of a caring climate in their studios were positively associated with their positive affect and negatively related with negative affect. In an experimental study, Hogue and colleagues (2017) reported middle school students, who were introduced to a novel physical task, expressed greater positive affect and less negative affect in a caring and task-involving climate condition than in an ego-involving condition. Additional parameters of psychological well-being (i.e., hope and life happiness) have also been linked to a perceived caring climate for both youth sport campers (Fry et al., 2012) and college athletes (Scott et al., 2021).

Various negative parameters seem to be buffered when athletes experience a caring climate. For example, perceptions of a caring climate in physical education classes and youth sport have been negatively associated with sadness, depressive symptoms, and general life stress (Fry et al., 2012; Gould et al., 2012; Hogue et al., 2019). Further, when participants in a lab-based study and physical education environment perceive a caring climate, they were less likely to experience shame or cognitive and somatic anxiety or to feel judged, humiliated, or self-conscious (Hogue et al., 2013, 2019). Collegiate baseball players' perceptions of a caring climate accounted for 25% of their mental health scores (Erdesz et al., 2023). There is also a developing pattern of findings linking athletes' perceptions of a caring team climate to their ability to regulate their positive and negative emotional responses (Fry et al., 2012; Gano-Overway et al., 2009). It appears that when athletes perceive a caring climate, they are more likely to report an ability to express joy and happiness when good things happen and an ability to better manage negative emotions.

The evidence is consistent that a caring climate is associated with positive indicators of an athlete's psychological well-being.

When considered together, the evidence is consistent that a caring climate is associated with positive indicators of an athlete's psychological well-being. Because one in five individuals experiences a mental illness each year (National Institute of Mental Health, 2019), the well-being of young people should be of foremost concern. Therefore, continuing to examine how sport environments can be structured to help athletes feel cared for and learn to care for others in ways that will support their mental health is warranted. Doing so would augment the value of sport as a venue to help athletes experience a strong and consistent state of psychological well-being.

With regard to psychological well-being and future research directions, there is much to consider. Cross-sectional research demonstrates that perceptions of a caring climate are consistently related to positive parameters of well-being, yet longitudinal research that examines questions such as the following will be valuable avenues for future inquiry:

- Do athletes who start a season with mental health issues show improvement after being in a caring sport team climate?
- Does being in a caring climate promote psychological well-being that extends beyond the sport season?
- How could qualitative research with parents examine the impact of their child's sport participation (i.e., in a caring climate) and their perceptions of their child's mental health?
- From athletes' perspectives, how does the caring climate on their teams affect their psychological well-being?

Current research has laid a tiny foundation for the work to come.

Motivational Outcomes

When athletes perceive a caring climate, they consistently report greater enjoyment. This relationship has been reported among adolescent volleyball, basketball, and soccer players and in high school athletes in off-season training programs (Chamberlin et al., 2016; Fry & Gano-Overway, 2010; Gerabinis et al., 2018; Iwasaki & Fry, 2013) as well as individuals participating in laboratory physical activity experiments where the caring and task-involving climates are combined (Hogue et al., 2013, 2017). Being in an environment where athletes perceive a caring connection to the coach and team heightens the likelihood they will perceive the experience to be more enjoyable.

Athletes' perceptions of a caring climate have been positively associated with their commitment to continue playing on their respective sport teams

(Fry & Gano-Overway, 2010) and to continue their sport and physical activity participation in the future (Gerabinis et al., 2018; Hall et al., 2017; Iwasaki & Fry, 2013; Newton et al., 2007). For example, Chamberlin and colleagues (2016) found that high school athletes' perceptions of a caring climate in their voluntary summer conditioning programs were positively associated with their belief that both they and their teammates were highly committed to off-season training, took the program seriously, and valued the benefits their commitment produces. Being on a team where athletes perceived a strong caring climate appeared to promote positive thoughts of wanting to continue to be part of their respective groups and a desire to maximize their sport experiences.

Athletes' perceptions of a caring climate have been positively associated with effort. For example, participants consistently indicate they try harder when they perceive a caring climate (Chamberlin et al., 2016; Hogue et al., 2013; Iwasaki & Fry, 2013). In our view, this is an important finding since effort is a quality that coaches highly value and athletes can control. Nevertheless, research is needed to investigate whether coaches who are intentional about building a caring community within their team are in turn helping to enhance this important marker of sport participation for athletes. If continued research demonstrates a strong link from the caring climate to athletes' levels of effort, this becomes a key factor in understanding how to help athletes reap the physical benefits of sport, experience challenge over time, and remain committed to their sport endeavors, because effort is required to augment these outcomes.

Mental and Life Skills Outcomes

Some evidence exists to link the perceived caring climate to athletes' adoption of and use of mental and life skills. Fry and colleagues (2021), in a study with over 500 Division I athletes at universities in the United States, found athletes' perceptions of a caring climate were positively associated with their coping skills (e.g., coping with adversity, attaining peak performance under pressure, using goal setting, being free from worry, optimizing mental preparation and concentration, being highly motivated, reflecting confidence, and being coachable). Researchers also reported a significant link between adolescent athletes' perceptions of their team climate to their tendency to take greater initiative, display stronger teamwork and social skills, and be mindfully engaged within their sport (Gerabinis et al., 2018; Gould et al., 2012; Iwasaki & Fry, 2016). Hogue and colleagues (2019, 2021) demonstrated a positive relationship between participants' perceptions of a caring climate and their ability to cope with stress. Athletes' ability to plan for their future once they have completed their sport careers has also been investigated. Poux and Fry (2015) reported Division I collegiate athletes who perceived a caring climate were more likely to indicate confidence in their ability to explore future careers after sport and be proactive in learning more about potential future career options. Overall, the perceived caring climate is associated with a variety of mental and life skills that may equip athletes for both their sport and life participation. However, it is still necessary to unravel why the caring climate may support athletes' use of mental and life skills. Research using intervention and longitudinal research designs will be key for continuing to explore these relationships.

Physical Health Outcomes

Hogue and colleagues (2013, 2017, 2019) have established a line of experimental research examining individuals' physiological stress responses in two distinct climates, a caring and task-involving climate versus an ego-involving climate. A proxy for assessing this physiological stress response was to measure cortisol, a naturally occurring hormone that is part of the stress response and has many important functions including anti-inflammatory properties (Newell-Price & Auchus, 2020). Across these experimental studies, adolescents and college students were introduced to a novel physical task in a 30-minute session where cortisol was measured every 15 minutes for approximately 90 minutes, to capture the hormonal response over time. The researchers found the caring and task-involving climate condition prompted significantly reduced cortisol levels (as assessed by repeated measures analyses), and the ego-involving climate condition elicited a heightened cortisol response. Hogue and colleagues (2019) also examined another marker of anti-inflammatory activity, salivary tumor necrosis factor alpha receptor II (sTNFARII). When individuals were assigned to the caring and task-involving climate condition, sTNFARII increased, and this, together with the reduced cortisol levels, suggests a decreased physiological stress response occurs when individuals experience a caring and task-involving climate. Thus, when faced with a challenging stressor, a caring and task-involving climate can positively affect both the psychology and physiology of an individual. However, future research will need to explore what aspect of the climate resulted in these changes and whether it is possible to tease them apart.

In addition to direct measures of physiological responses, researchers have linked a caring climate to athletes' valuing their own health. Brown and colleagues (2019) reported that when athletes perceived a caring climate, they were more likely to indicate they would be forthcoming in sharing their concussion symptoms with coaches. They also found the high school soccer players who perceived a caring climate were more likely to indicate they cared about their health, would not want to play until they had fully healed from a concussion, and cared more about their health than winning a soccer game. They were also more likely to report that both their teammates and coaches cared about their personal health. These findings suggest that perceptions of a caring climate correspond with an environment where health is prioritized.

Performance Outcomes

Noddings (1992) was clear that individuals should not engage in caring behaviors toward others to induce particular favorable outcomes, because caring is, first and foremost, a relational act, meant to focus on developing ethical caring in oneself and others. While it is clear from this chapter that we agree with Noddings, we have also experienced some pushback from coaches who have concerns that enhancing a caring climate may actually impair teams' performance because of misperceptions that caring is equivalent to being soft, being nonchalant, or having an "anything goes" approach. Therefore, there is a need to examine the connection between the caring climate and performance. We would argue, as has Fisher and colleagues (2019), that performance may be inherently optimized in a caring climate because athletes are receiving genuine support from their coaches and teammates to strive to be their best. As has been previously highlighted, when athletes perceive a caring climate, they reflect adaptive motivational responses, experience more rewarding relationships with all involved, report greater psychological well-being, and report more use of coping strategies and mental skills. These positive outcomes may set athletes up to consistently perform their best.

Research examining the association between a caring climate and performance is limited but not completely absent from the literature. Frederick (2017) found collegiate basketball players' perceptions of a caring climate had teams with more assists and fewer turnovers. Further, Reid-Pinson (2018) reported college recreational athletes' perceptions of a caring climate were positively associated with their belief that, both as individual athletes and as a team, they reached their potential across the sport season. While further research on the link between a caring climate and objective performance is needed, evidence suggests there may be a connection.

Mechanisms Explaining the Connection Between a Perceived Caring Climate and Athlete Outcomes

The literature on athlete outcomes indicates that perceptions of a caring climate are linked to physical and mental health, personal and athletic development, moral behaviors associated with ethical caring (e.g., social behaviors and empathy), and indicators of motivation. However, what explains the relationship between the climate and outcomes? The final element of the caring climate model includes possible mechanisms that may explain the relationship between the perceived caring climate and athlete outcomes. Initial research has pointed to the role of empathy, affective self-regulatory efficacy, and reciprocity.

Empathy

Earlier in this chapter, the role of empathy as a potential mechanism of caring was briefly reviewed when considering why coaches may care. The rationale and logic can be applied to why athletes may engage in caring for others and in prosocial behaviors. Further, Eisenberg and colleagues (e.g., Eisenberg et al., 2015) have contended that empathy *can* be a motivator for prosocial behavior. Gano-Overway and colleagues (2009) found perceptions of a caring climate among campers attending a summer sport camp were positively associated with empathic self-efficacy (i.e., their belief in their ability to be empathic toward others). In turn, empathic self-efficacy was positively associated with prosocial behaviors, such as helping another camper, and negatively related to antisocial behaviors like calling someone names or threatening to hurt someone. These findings provide preliminary evidence of the motivating effect of empathy. However, the results do not demonstrate cause and effect and do not clarify whether the cognitive and/or affective components of empathy play a role. While Gano-Overway (2014) found cognitive empathy, or understanding another person's emotions, mediated the relationship between perceived caring and prosocial behavior in middle school physical education classes, Feshbach (1997) has indicated an intertwining of cognitive and affective responses is needed for empathy to influence prosocial or antisocial behaviors. Future research should explore how the caring climate contributes to indicators of empathy and how empathy influences social behaviors.

Affective Self-Regulatory Efficacy

Another potential mechanism is affective self-regulatory efficacy, or an individual's belief they can manage their positive and negative emotions (Bandura, 2006). In a youth sport context, researchers (Fry et al., 2012; Gano-Overway et al., 2009) have found positive and negative self-regulatory efficacy mediated the relationship between perceived caring and outcomes. Specifically, Gano-Overway and colleagues (2009) found the ability to regulate and express positive emotions was more likely to be associated with youth sport campers' ability to empathize with others. Fry and colleagues (2012) showed how affective self-regulatory efficacy mediated the relationship between the perceived caring climate and the emotions of hope, happiness, sadness, and depression. While this work is informative, additional research will need to further substantiate the link to empathy and mental health issues as well as investigate whether affective self-regulatory efficacy influences the relationship between perceptions of the caring climate and other athlete outcomes.

Future research should explore how the caring climate contributes to indicators of empathy and how empathy influences social behaviors.

Reciprocity

In describing the caring relation, Noddings (2003a) pointed to the cared-for receiving and responding to the caring actions observed. The cared-for is not obligated to respond in a particular way nor demanded to respond by the one caring. Rather, the response indicates the caring relation exists and is being nurtured by those in the relationship. However, the desire to reciprocate may contribute to motivation, social behaviors, and psychological well-being. Reciprocity has been demonstrated in collegiate and high school sport settings. For example, Gano-Overway and Carson Sackett (2021) interviewed a highly successful collegiate coach and her former athletes about the type of climate she created and how athletes experienced it. One of the findings noted was a sense of gratitude experienced based on the interactions with and actions of the coach. Athletes described how this sense of gratitude motivated them to meet her expectations and emulate her model of hard work as well as support the connectedness she created within the team—that is, it encouraged them to reciprocate. However, other forms of reciprocation also exist. Gano-Overway (2023) described how one high school athlete expressed how her coach's caring built her confidence, which motivated her to stay on the team and work hard in practice and improved her emotional response. While these findings point to gratitude and confidence as ways athletes demonstrated reciprocity that could lead to outcomes like motivation and emotional well-being, these are tentative assertions needing further testing.

We have presented evidence that empathy, affective self-regulatory efficacy, and reciprocity may explain the link between the perceived caring climate and athlete outcomes, but additional research is needed to explore these mechanisms to determine their veracity as well as determine which mechanisms connect with which outcomes. Further research is needed to explore other possible mechanisms (e.g., norms, learning through observation).

Future Research Directions

Considerable progress has been made in exploring the nature of caring in sport over the last 15 years. A valuable mix of both quantitative and qualitative approaches has been employed, resulting in the following:

- The development of a psychometrically strong measure to assess athletes' perceptions of the climate
- Identification of important motivational, social, psychological, and physiological athlete outcomes
- In-depth coach interviews at a variety of sport levels to better understand how coaches conceive of and enact caring and why they embrace caring
- Laboratory-controlled studies where trained leaders effectively created caring and task-involving climates

Still, there are numerous limitations of the current research, some of which have been identified earlier, and many directions for future inquiry.

To begin, research has emphasized developing a valid and reliable measure of the perceived sport caring climate and considering the host of positive outcomes athletes experience in a strong caring climate. While the CCS has shown to be a valid and reliable instrument, continued exploration is warranted. For example, research has examined only individual perceptions of the caring climate. Is there a team-level perception of the climate? Exploring both individual and team-level effects of the perceived caring climate on athlete outcomes using multilevel modeling is warranted. Additionally, there is a need to better understand how athletes construe caring within their teams over time and what personal and situational factors may influence athletes' perceptions.

Clearly, another major limitation of the caring climate research stems from the use of the CCS to examine athlete outcomes using primarily a cross-sectional design that lacks a perspective to provide a deeper understanding of how caring takes shape and is manifested over time. Future mixed-methods intervention research is needed to examine the process that occurs for teams across a season. For instance, coaches trained in developing a caring climate can be observed and interviewed regarding their implementation of a caring climate while also examining how athletes recognize care (e.g., by gathering athletes' perceptions of the climate at different time points across the sport seasons) and documenting the dynamic processes associated with the athletic season (e.g., win–loss record, distribution of playing time, amount of time athletes interact with coaches on a personal level). Equally critical is considering how athletes begin to see themselves as significant participants in fostering a caring community as well as assessing athlete outcomes.

An additional avenue for future research is developing a better understanding of how coaches can receive training to further expand the caring climate. Hogue and colleagues have successfully created highly caring and task-involving climates in laboratory studies, but more ecologically valid studies, like the season-long intervention to assist coaches in adopting a caring and task-involving climate conducted by Claunch (2016) and Claunch and Fry (2016), are needed. This is particularly important because there is a need to help coaches develop a caring climate that works within their context and with their athletes. In addition, as Noddings (2003b) has noted, caring involves developing relationships that extend over time. While some research has begun to explore this impact in sport (Gano-Overway, 2023; Gano-Overway & Carson Sackett, 2021), further work is needed to identify coaches' desire and ability to engage in caring practices with their athletes over time and the personal and situational factors that may play a role.

Another area for continued research is examining the caring climate across age groups and sport contexts. Fisher and colleagues' research on collegiate sport expands the research often conducted in youth sport or experimental settings (Fisher et al., 2017; Knust et al., 2015). However, Fontana and colleagues' (2017) study with adult recreational athletes is one of the few to explore a caring climate in adults who continue to participate in sport. Similar work with coaches at all levels, athletes, and parents will be critical moving forward.

Athletes' perceptions are valuable, but equally important are observational studies that note observed behaviors of coaches and athletes (i.e., that reflect strong caring practices), as well as the behaviors that support a caring community. These observations could be compared with athletes' perceptions of their team climate. It is also important to understand how caring is construed by individuals from various sports, cultures, race and ethnic groups, socioeconomic statuses, genders, and so on. Thus, caring research could be strengthened and extended in multiple ways. For instance, the role of culture may influence coaching practices or perceptions of caring. Would coaches and athletes from more collectivistic cultures place an emphasis on developing harmony and unity within a caring community, while individualistic cultures place an emphasis on developing personal relationships with athletes where collaboration and questioning the coach to understand training is the norm? Another example would be including a wide range of sports (e.g., rugby) because each can reflect its own unique characteristics and culture, which may have implications for how caring is manifested and recognized.

A final consideration for future study is to expand the caring climate research by incorporating a social justice lens (Kochanek & Erickson, 2020). An underlying premise of the caring climate is that all athletes are made to feel welcome, valued, and respected. However, how coaches create this type of climate while considering their own cultural competence and social justice perspective has not been examined. Further, it may be that athletes on highly caring teams develop a greater commitment to actively work toward creating a more just and accepting playing field both within sport and in society. Yet personal and situational factors may create limits on whether this occurs. Finally, Kochanek and Erickson (2020) noted the importance of taking a critical look at positive youth development outcomes from a social justice perspective. In the case of the caring climate, this would involve how social behaviors and developmental outcomes can be extended to consider critical contribution, where athletes are encouraged to challenge systems of oppression to benefit all individuals.

In summary, we agree with Nichol and colleagues (2019), who suggested that "It is essential that future research aims to further coach knowledge and stimulate reflection in relation to how, when, why, and under which circumstances [coaching] practice influences athlete outcomes" (p. 24). Therefore, future research efforts should consider how the caring climate is implemented and perceived, including the impact of personal and situational factors, why caring practices and perceptions of the caring climate influence particular athlete outcomes, and under what circumstances caring practices will lead to adaptive versus maladaptive outcomes. Addressing these issues with a variety of research designs and methodologies that triangulate data among the many stakeholders within the sport setting will further our understanding of the components of the caring climate model.

Practical Implications

While there is still much to learn about how to create and sustain a caring climate within sport, the research reviewed in this chapter does provide insight into how coaches and administrators can get started creating a caring climate. However, we are very cognizant that caring is a way of being in relation with others rather than specific strategies (Noddings, 1992). Therefore, we encourage coaches to reflect on the following questions based on caring practices outlined in the research:

- How tuned in are you to the needs, motives, interests, and goals of your athletes? How tuned in are the athletes to each other's needs? (engrossment)
- How often do you feel compelled (give your time, energy, and resources) to support or help an athlete? How often do you observe this among other members of the team? (motivational displacement)
- Would the team describe the climate as caring? Do you feel cared for on your team? (recognition)
- How do you practice care with your athletes and help them do so with one another? (modeling, dialogue, and reinforcement)
- What norms, core values, and expectations focus on caring? How do you discuss and reinforce these? (caring norms and expectations)
- How do athletes know they are welcomed and accepted members of the team? (welcoming and accepting)
- How do you let athletes know they are valued and their contribution to the team is important? (valued contribution)
- What situational factors in your sport environment might limit or assist your ability to care?
- What personal attributes may you need to strengthen to further assist in your ability to care?
- What are your motives for creating a caring climate?

Coaches' responses to these questions can help them reflect on how caring is currently enacted and the caring climate outlined in this chapter can provide ideas for action.

Here is an example of this reflection. A softball coach may respond that she gets to know her athletes and does a lot of team-building activities to help players get to know one another. She also expresses that she understands her players well because she spends time listening to their needs and motives, and she works to support their development. While she does note that the team is like a family and the players seem to enjoy one another's company, she is not convinced they all feel welcome, accepted, and valued. She would like to see the players support one another more and she has realized she does not have core values or expectations around caring, and they are not really discussed or reinforced. Using the knowledge of the caring climate model and associated research outlined in this chapter, this softball coach may consider the following actions:

- Aligned with the caring relation, she could spend more time talking about caring and have the athletes engage in caring behaviors toward others (e.g., community service activities or creating a mentor–mentee program on the team so older athletes can mentor and support younger athletes).

- Using her observational skills, she could get a sense of whether all athletes are welcomed and accepted on the team and engage in conversations with team leaders to learn more. If all do not feel welcome and accepted, she could consider ways to make everyone feel welcome, consider ways to remove barriers for why some people may not feel accepted, remind all athletes of their role on the team, and find public ways to communicate the important and valuable contribution each athlete makes on a regular basis.
- To further develop a welcoming and accepting environment where all feel valued, she may want to consider how often she interacts with each player on the team and how supportive she is of all members (e.g., how often does she engage in engrossment and motivational displacement with all players?).
- She could also continue developing a caring community by adding caring concepts into her core values and expectations and identifying ways to communicate and reinforce these on a regular basis.

If the coach has difficulty identifying actions associated with a caring climate, she could review resources that offer strategies for consideration (see Fry, 2010; Gano-Overway & Guivernau, 2018). However, in applying any of these actions, the coach will need to consider her own personal and situational factors along with the athletes she coaches. Finally, how she implements the ideas will be unique to her situation.

While the reflective activity can provide a starting point for ways to implement caring practices, we encourage coaches to not change everything at once. It would be better to take action on one or two ideas and implement them in coaching practice. After trying out actions to foster community or be in relation with others, coaches can check in, either via a self-reflection or through conversations with other coaches, administrators, and athletes. As part of this check-in process, coaches are able to identify which actions are working and why. They can then make appropriate changes or consider further action. The key is for coaches to gauge where they are in developing relationships with each athlete on their team and how they are augmenting their caring community over time. This cyclical process is similar to the general process for improving coaching practice outlined by the International Sport Coaching Framework (International Council for Coaching Excellence et al., 2013) and is further discussed by Fry and colleagues (2020) specific to creating a caring and task-involving climate.

Summary

When coaches have success with fostering a caring climate (i.e., athletes perceive a caring climate), athletes are more likely to have positive sport experiences and opportunities for holistic development. Scholars have provided insight into the ways coaches exhibit caring practices, which include the caring relation and caring community conceptual frameworks. Researchers are also starting to provide a glimpse into how personal and situational factors foster or impede caring practices. Further, researchers have begun to identify potential motives for caring and mechanisms that connect recognition of care to a variety of athlete outcomes. As this research continues to unfold, researchers and practitioners are gaining a better understanding of the role of the caring climate in the sport domain and its influence on the health, development, and well-being of athletes.

DISCUSSION QUESTIONS

1. How is the caring climate defined, and what role does the caring relation and caring community play in framing caring practices in sport?
2. What are some of the personal characteristics of coaches and the situational factors of the context that influence coaches' ability to care?
3. Describe a caring climate you have experienced. What benefits did you as a coach or athlete reap from being in this caring community? How does your experience align with the research presented in the chapter?
4. What are some directions for future research related to the caring climate?

12

Need-Supportive, Thwarting, and Indifferent Coach Interpersonal Styles

Nikos Ntoumanis, PhD; Eleanor Quested, PhD;
and Hamsini Sivaramakrishnan, MSc

LEARNING OBJECTIVES

On completion of this chapter, the reader should have the following:

- Understanding of the historical developments in the conceptualization of coach interpersonal styles, based on self-determination theory
- Knowledge of the antecedents and consequences of coach interpersonal styles
- Appreciation of the different instruments for assessing coach interpersonal styles
- Understanding of practical ways to create more need-supportive and fewer need-thwarting and indifferent coaching environments in sport

Gareth Southgate, a former English professional soccer player, became the manager for the struggling English national soccer team soon after they finished at the bottom of their group in the first stage of the 2014 World Cup. Southgate was described in the media as someone who was bringing a new "culture" to the team (Wallace, 2017). Examples of this new culture included allowing players to make decisions on the field, asking them questions, challenging them in different ways, and asking them to address him by his first name as opposed to "the boss." Two years later, the English soccer team reached the semifinal of the 2018 World Cup, losing to Croatia in extra time. Although many factors contribute to sporting success, the coach's influence is indisputably an important element. How do coaches influence their athletes' motivation and achievement? Coaches can support or undermine the motivation of their athletes and hence affect the quality of athletes' emotional experiences, their decision to persist or drop out, and other important consequences (e.g., use of performance-enhancing substances, moral behavior) by engaging in qualitatively different types of behaviors and communications with the athletes. In the self-determination theory literature (SDT; Ryan & Deci, 2017) terms such as *interpersonal style*, *communication style*, and *behaviors* have been used more or less interchangeably to describe how individuals in position of authority or expertise (e.g., sport coaches) influence the motivation of the people they interact with via certain actions, decisions, or vocalizations (Ntoumanis et al., 2018).

In this chapter, we first present a historical overview of how coaches' interpersonal styles have been conceptualized and measured in the SDT literature. We also make a case for a three-by-three conceptual framework in which interpersonal styles are described by their function (supporting, indifferent, and thwarting) and the psychological needs they target (autonomy, competence, and relatedness). We also summarize diverse evidence regarding the variety of motivation-related outcomes predicted by different interpersonal styles. Furthermore, we present research on the contextual and personal antecedents of such styles. Lastly, we offer suggestions for future research and outline practical implications from research conducted on coach interpersonal styles.

Theory and Research

Self-determination theory (SDT; Ryan & Deci, 2017) is a theory of human motivation that has been extensively applied in the sport domain. According to Ryan and Deci (2017), all individuals have three basic psychological needs. These needs are *autonomy* (feeling willingness and self-endorsement), *competence* (experience of mastery and accomplishment of desired outcomes), and *relatedness* (feelings of meaningful connection to others). SDT-based research has explored factors in the social environment (including interpersonal styles) that may nurture or undermine these needs, leading to different types of motivation and well-being. Originally, SDT researchers conceptualized and measured two interpersonal styles: *autonomy support*, which is an adaptive interpersonal style, and *control*, which is a maladaptive style (Deci & Ryan, 1987). As will be explained in this chapter, the terminology used to describe interpersonal styles (as well as the number and dimensions of those styles) has evolved over the years. Interpersonal styles are posited to predict the satisfaction or frustration of the three basic psychological needs, in conjunction with the content of the goals individuals pursue (e.g., intrinsic goals such as personal development, or extrinsic goals such as fame and wealth).

SDT proposes a variety of types of motivation that regulate behavior, which reflect different degrees of self-determination (autonomous and controlled). These behavioral regulations are determined by psychological need satisfaction and frustration, as well as by motivational predispositions toward autonomy or control. Lastly, different psychological and behavioral outcomes have been measured in the SDT literature, some adaptive (e.g., engagement, high self-esteem) and others maladaptive (e.g., dropout, exhaustion). These outcomes are predicted by behavioral regulations, goal content, and psychological needs. The interrelations between interpersonal styles, psychological needs, goal content, motivation, and outcomes are illustrated in figure 12.1 (see also Bhavsar et al., 2020, for more details on the components of SDT).

Interpersonal Styles in Sport: Autonomy Support and Control

Cognitive evaluation theory (CET; Ryan & Deci, 2017), the first mini-theory of SDT, focuses on the role of autonomy support and control in supporting

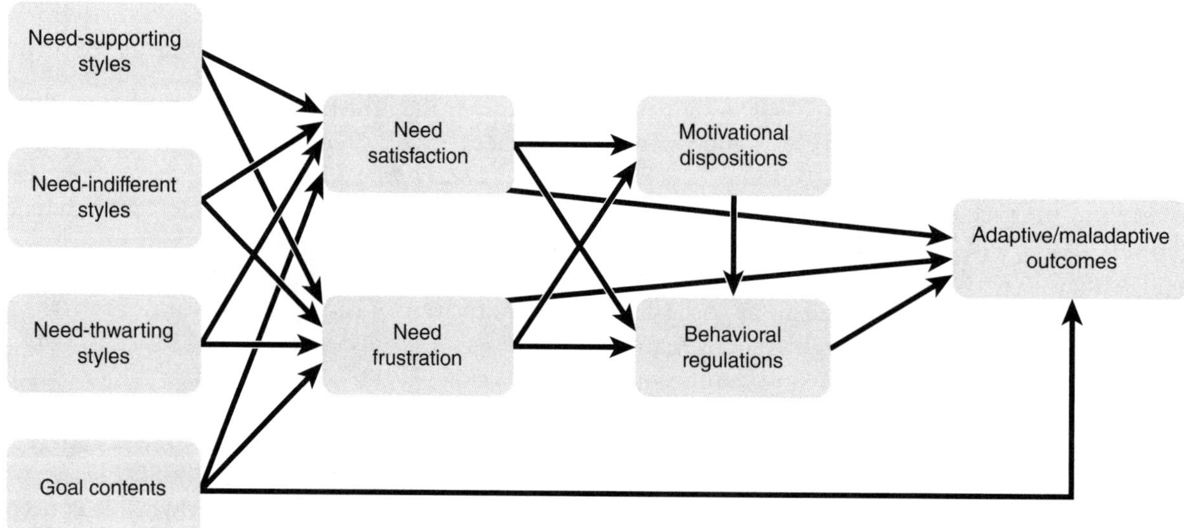

FIGURE 12.1 Interrelations between various SDT variables.

or thwarting the needs for competence and autonomy, and hence promoting or undermining intrinsic motivation, respectively. CET-based research has explored the role of autonomy support and control in a variety of contexts, including education, parenting, and sport (e.g., Deci et al., 1981; Grolnick et al., 1997). Individuals in position of authority or expertise, such as coaches, may support others' (e.g., athletes') autonomy by providing them with choice, offering rationales for task engagement, acknowledging their feelings, providing them with opportunities to demonstrate initiative, allowing them opportunities in decision making, and trying to understand their perspective (Mageau & Vallerand, 2003; Ntoumanis & Mallet, 2014). In contrast to autonomy support, a controlling interpersonal style thwarts the need for autonomy. Controlling coaches tend to pressure their athletes to think, feel, or behave in specific ways. Bartholomew and colleagues (2009) reviewed the extant literature and identified several dimensions of coaches' controlling strategies. Broadly, these controlling behaviors were classified as

- tangible rewards to manipulate athletes' behaviors,
- controlling feedback to convey expectations,
- excessive personal control to impose coaches' opinions,
- intimidation behaviors to ensure athlete compliance,
- promoting athletes' ego involvement (e.g., with normative comparisons), and
- conditional regard, such as affection, only when athletes behave according to the coaches' expectations.

Some of the work in sport using CET has focused on the role of sport scholarships. For instance, collegiate athletes who receive scholarships perceive these scholarships as reducing their autonomy, and hence they are less intrinsically motivated (Medic et al., 2007). More recently, it was found that athletic scholarships are negatively associated with intrinsic motivation for sport and enjoyment later on in adulthood, even several decades later, highlighting the enduring impact and long-term consequences of interpersonal control on intrinsic motivation (Moller & Sheldon, 2020). An autonomy-supportive style enhances the internalization of a behavioral regulation and promotes more self-determined forms of motivation and better outcomes in athletes. For example, Almagro and colleagues (2010) showed that coach autonomy support can predict athletes' autonomy need satisfaction, which in turn predicts intrinsic motivation and sport adherence. Autonomy support has also been linked with greater athlete engagement, lower levels of depression, and increased psychological well-being (Sol Alvarez et al., 2009). In contrast, intrusive and pressurizing forms of control have been found to relate to negative outcomes such as controlled motivation, decreased engagement and well-being, and even burnout (Bartholomew et al., 2011; Ryan & Deci, 2000; Vansteenkiste & Ryan, 2013).

Early theorizing and research suggested that autonomy-supportive and controlling styles are bipolar; for instance, a coach can be either autonomy supportive or controlling (Soenens & Vansteenkiste, 2010). Subsequently, empirical evidence challenged this assumption and showed that autonomy support and control are correlated but independent constructs; over time coaches can be both autonomy supportive and controlling to different degrees (e.g., Balaguer et al., 2012; Bartholomew et al., 2010). For instance, a coach may involve athletes in the goal-setting process and provide a rationale for tasks but simultaneously also use controlling feedback and conditional regard.

Cultivating Autonomy-Supportive Interpersonal Style

Given the adaptive outcomes associated with an autonomy-supportive interpersonal style, interventions have been designed to help promote coaches' autonomy-supportive behaviors. For instance, Cheon and colleagues (2015) conducted a coach-focused field-based experiment during the 2012 London Paralympic Games, evaluating the impact of a three-part autonomy-supportive intervention program, consisting of a combination of presentations, a group discussion, and a one-to-one meeting with each coach. Their findings suggested that athletes in the control group perceived their coaches as being less autonomy supportive and more controlling, and they reported a significant increase in need frustration. In contrast, athletes in the experimental group reported perceiving their coaches as more autonomy supportive and less controlling (there were no changes in need satisfaction and need frustration). It was also reported that athletes of coaches in the experimental group won significantly more medals when compared with those in the control group.

Mahoney and colleagues (2016) evaluated the potential of implementing an autonomy-supportive intervention for coaches in order to foster mental toughness in adolescent rowers. They found that an eight-week intervention (comprising a two-hour coach workshop on using autonomy-supportive behaviors delivered in each of the first two weeks, followed by six weeks of providing relevant supplementary materials) did not significantly influence athletes' perception of their coaches' using more autonomy-supportive and less controlling behaviors. The intervention also did not appear to increase athletes' perceived psychological need satisfaction and mental toughness. The authors suggested, based on the athletes' perception of their coaches and independently observed coach behaviors, that coaches might have already been engaging in autonomy-supportive behaviors prior to the intervention. Therefore, it may be important for future interventions to consider selecting coaches who would most benefit from such interventions. The authors also highlighted the need to tailor theory-based instructional material to suit the needs of specific sports, in order to make them more engaging and increase their potential efficacy.

Given the adaptive outcomes associated with an autonomy-supportive interpersonal style, interventions have been designed to help promote coaches' autonomy-supportive behaviors.

Beyond Autonomy Support and Control: Need-Supportive and Need-Thwarting Styles

The majority of SDT sport-based research concerned with the motivation-related impact of the social context has focused on perceived autonomy-supportive and controlling styles. However, several studies have shown that autonomy-supportive behaviors can also support the needs for competence and relatedness (e.g., Ntoumanis, 2012; Quested et al., 2013; Ryan & Deci, 2000). This is possibly because many features of autonomy support have relevance for competence and relatedness need satisfaction. For example, *acknowledging an athlete's perspective* may fulfill athletes' basic need for relatedness as well as autonomy, because the athlete may feel more respected and cared for, if their coach is trying to see situations from the athlete's point of view. *Involvement in decision making* could be expected to increase athletes' feelings of competence, because this involvement suggests the coach considers the athlete to have the necessary knowledge and capabilities in their sport. However, there are other motivationally relevant coach behaviors not captured by the dimensions of autonomy support or control that may support or thwart competence and relatedness. For that reason, sport researchers (e.g., Bhavsar et al., 2019; Rocchi & Pelletier, 2017) extended beyond the focus on autonomy support and control and began examining other facets of the social environment that might predict athletes' competence (e.g., structure and chaos) and relatedness (e.g., social support and hostility).

In recent years, behaviors likely to support competence, such as structure, have received research attention (Curran et al., 2013). The term *structure* originated in the parenting literature (e.g., Grolnick & Ryan, 1989) and has also been extensively examined in educational settings (e.g., Jang et al., 2010). Structure is present when information is provided clearly and consistently, with the aim of supporting attainment of the individual's goals. In a structured environment, coaches can support competence by helping athletes set challenging but achievable goals; providing thorough, positive, and constructive feedback; helping athletes recognize their progress; and showing belief that the athlete can achieve their goals (e.g., Matosic et al., 2016; Pulido et al., 2018). In terms of competence thwarting, SDT research has focused on the construct of chaos. Skinner and colleagues (2005) regarded a chaotic social environment as being disorganized, confusing, and inconsistent. In the sport literature, competence thwarting is considered to include coach interactions that emphasize athletes' incompetence and likelihood of failure or mistakes, or belittle what the athlete has or could achieve (Pulido et al., 2018; Rocchi et al., 2017).

With regard to relatedness support, the terms *interpersonal involvement*, *social support*, and *warmth* have been used in the parenting and education literatures (Grolnick & Ryan, 1989; Sarason et al., 1987; Skinner et al., 2005). In the sport literature, coaches are regarded to be supportive of athletes' relatedness when they show care, respect, and empathy; are available when needed; and foster connections among athletes (e.g., Appleton et al., 2016; Bhavsar et al., 2019). In contrast, when coaches are cold, unfriendly, hostile, belittling, and unavailable in times of need, and show active dislike for an athlete, their interpersonal style is described as relatedness thwarting (e.g., Pulido et al., 2018; Smith et al., 2015).

Correlates of Need-Supportive and Need-Thwarting Styles

There is a burgeoning evidence base supporting the benefits of a need-supportive coaching style and demonstrating the drawbacks of a need-thwarting style. In early work in the sport context, the dimensions of coach behavior have been typically examined independently of each other. For example, outcomes such as athlete need satisfaction, autonomous motivation, dropout, and engagement, as well as indicators of physical and psychological welfare, have been predicted independently by autonomy-supportive, socially supportive, and structured coaching environments (e.g., Felton & Jowett, 2013; Quested et al., 2013; Smith et al., 2015). Other research has examined interactions between different need-supportive dimensions. For instance, how structure is enacted can determine the degree to which it contributes to or detracts from autonomy need support, because structure can be provided in such a way as to emphasize autonomy or to emphasize control (Ntoumanis, 2012). Curran and colleagues (2013) explored this interaction hypothesis in a study of 245 youth soccer players. Their findings showed that perceived autonomy support affected the strength of association (i.e., was a statistical moderator) between structure and athlete outcomes; structure was most adaptive for athletes when coach autonomy support was high.

Delrue and colleagues (2019) proposed a circumplex model to provide an alternative viewpoint of how autonomy support, control, structure, and chaos interrelate. This approach presents these constructs within a circumplex structure (termed a *helicopter view*). The model operates on two dimensions, one representing need support to thwarting, and the other representing directedness, ranging from the coach to the athlete taking more of the lead. The model structure includes eight approaches to coaching (clarifying, guiding, attuning, participating, awaiting, abandoning, domineering, and demanding). This approach provides a less abrupt and more gradual representation of coach behaviors, indicating that autonomy support, control, structure, and chaos are less distinct, theoretically and operationally, than has been historically inferred in the SDT literature.

There is a burgeoning evidence base supporting the benefits of a need-supportive coaching style and demonstrating the drawbacks of a need-thwarting style.

Interventions to Promote Need-Supportive Styles

Building on the evidence base supporting the potential to train coaches to be autonomy supportive, SDT researchers have begun examining whether it is possible to train coaches to adopt more relatedness and competence-supportive behaviors. For instance, Reynders and colleagues (2019) examined whether an intervention consisting of four need-supportive coach workshops could upskill coaches in how to be autonomy supportive and to provide structure. Following baseline measures of coach (n = 43) and athlete (n = 346) perceptions of coach behaviors, as well as athlete motivation and engagement, the intervention group received a workshop every 3 weeks over a 9-week period, whereas the control group received no intervention. Intervention workshops addressed three topics: how to be need supportive in training, how to be need supportive in competition, and how to introduce and monitor rules. The intervention used best practice examples, illustrated via videos and through discussion, to convey ways to be autonomy and competence supportive. Postintervention follow-up measures were held at 3 and 12 weeks. Both coaches and athletes in the intervention arm reported increases in perceived coach autonomy support but no change in controlling coach behaviors. Athletes also perceived increases in the coaches' use of structure. Intervention arm athletes reported an increase in autonomous motivation but no changes in controlled motivation. These findings indicate that promoting need support does not necessarily counter coaches' use of need-thwarting behaviors. We speculate that interventions may be most effective if coaches are upskilled in how to increase need-supportive behaviors and how to reduce need-thwarting ones.

This approach was trialed by Ntoumanis and colleagues (2021) in an intervention study that focused on reducing athletes' doping willingness. The intervention, delivered in three countries to 130 coaches (of 919 athletes), covered not only how and why to be more need supportive but also how to recognize and reduce need-thwarting coaching behaviors when communicating with athletes about doping. Findings showed that athletes whose coaches were in the intervention arm reported reduced willingness to take prohibited substances, reduced need frustration, and anti-doping knowledge. Coaches in the intervention arm reported greater efficacy in creating an anti-doping culture and dealing with doping-relevant situations, increases in perceived effectiveness of need-supportive behaviors, and decreased perceptions of effectiveness of need-thwarting behaviors.

Antecedents of Need-Supportive and Need-Thwarting Styles

Most of the SDT research on interpersonal styles has focused on how those styles influence psychological needs, forms of motivation, and diverse cognitive, affective, and behavioral outcomes. Nevertheless, there is some evidence, albeit scarce in sport, on the perceived antecedents of those styles. Research on this topic is important; need-supportive training programs should take into consideration some of these antecedents (e.g., personal beliefs about autonomy), which can potentially limit the effectiveness of such programs.

In 2016 Matosic and colleagues presented the first review of antecedents of need-supportive and need-thwarting styles. They identified only five studies from the sport context (published up to 2015), a rather low number; those studies focused on autonomy support and control (i.e., autonomy thwarting). For instance, Stebbings and colleagues (2012) surveyed coaches in the United Kingdom and showed, via structural equation modeling, that the contextual factors of perceived job security and opportunities for professional development predicted greater coach psychological need satisfaction, well-being, and (self-reported) autonomy-supportive coaching style. In contrast, work–life conflict was a predictor of need frustration and psychological ill-being, as well as of (self-reported) controlling style.

Given the small number of eligible studies in the sport domain, Matosic and colleagues expanded their review to include relevant studies from the parental and educational domain, and they explained how findings from these domains could be relevant to understanding antecedents of coach interpersonal styles. They included 35 published sources in their review and identified three broad categories of antecedents: *contextual factors*, *perceptions of others' behaviors and motivation*, and *personal factors*. Sociocontextual factors were split into socioenvironmental (e.g., cultural norms, job security) and external pressures (e.g., administrative pressures, performance evaluations). Examples of the second category included perceptions of whether others (e.g., athletes) are self-determined or controlled in their motivation, and the extent of their emotional and behavioral engagement. In terms of the third category of antecedents—personal factors—examples were one's own autonomous or controlled motivation (e.g., to coach), well-being or ill-being, and beliefs about the efficacy or the widespread adoption of a particular style.

Empirical studies have examined antecedents of additional styles proposed by SDT or expanded the list of antecedents identified in the Matosic and colleagues' (2016) review. For instance, Rocchi and Pelletier (2017), using data from two samples of Canadian coaches, found that reports of support and thwarting of each of the three needs were predicted by the coaches' autonomous and controlled motivation to coach, respectively. These motivations were in turn predicted by the coaches' job-related need satisfaction and frustration and, indirectly, by perceived administrative support, athlete motivation, colleague support, and time constraints. Kim and colleagues (2019) surveyed a sample of Korean coaches and found that self-reported controlling coaching was predicted by low-quality coach–athlete relationships and by obsessive passion for coaching. In contrast, harmonious passion for coaching predicted high-quality coach–athlete relationships, which in turn were associated with perceived autonomy-supportive style. Lastly, Matosic and colleagues (2017) found that perceived controlling coaching, as reported by a sample of coaches in the United Kingdom, was predicted by high levels of narcissism and low empathetic concern about athletes.

In summary, there is growing evidence in the sport literature of diverse personal and contextual antecedents of coach interpersonal styles. However, this evidence is limited (1) compared with what is known in other life domains about the antecedents of such styles and (2) to autonomy support and thwarting; very little is known about the antecedents of support and thwarting of competence and relatedness.

Making the Case for a Need-Indifferent Style

As described earlier in the chapter, the distinction between need-supportive and need-thwarting styles has received a substantial amount of empirical support in the SDT literature, including in sport settings. Nevertheless, it is possible that this distinction ignores a third style, which neither supports nor thwarts the athletes' psychological needs. Bhavsar and colleagues (2019) first advocated for, and provided empirical evidence for, an interpersonal style that is *need indifferent*.

Bhavsar and colleagues (2019) explained that previous conceptualizations and measurements of interpersonal style did not differentiate between leaders' behaviors and vocalizations that actively suppress others' psychological needs (e.g., coaches intimidating athletes) and those that are passive or indifferent to those needs (e.g., being unresponsive to athletes' preferences). They exemplified this distinction by referring to the construct of chaos, which has been traditionally considered in the wider SDT literature as a facet of need thwarting (Skinner et al., 2005). A chaotic coaching style is unstructured and inconsistent; although it might slow down athletes' skill development, it is not a style that *actively blocks* athletes' psychological needs (Vansteenkiste & Ryan, 2013). Hence, a chaotic environment is more representative of a need-*indifferent* than a need-*thwarting* environment. Similarly, a distinction can be made between a coach who is rejecting and dismissive of their athletes (i.e., need thwarting) and a coach who is emotionally unavailable (i.e., need indifferent).

Alongside need support and need thwarting, a need-indifferent style provides a more comprehensive framework of how significant social agents (e.g., coaches) influence others' (e.g., athletes') needs for autonomy, competence, and relatedness. This conceptualization of interpersonal styles is illustrated in table 12.1 via the three-by-three model of coach interpersonal behaviors. In this SDT-informed model, interpersonal styles are distinguished in terms of their function (support, thwart, indifferent) and the psychological needs they target (autonomy, competence, and relatedness), resulting in nine potential interpersonal styles adopted by significant others.

The supporting and thwarting styles have been described earlier in this chapter. To illustrate need indifference, coaches can be autonomy indifferent by not showing interest in athletes' opinions and thoughts. Coaches can be competence indifferent by being chaotic or by neglecting to create conditions that will optimally challenge each of their athletes. Lastly, relatedness-indifferent coaches are inattentive to the quality of the coach–athlete relationship, and neglectful of providing emotional or other types of support to their athletes when such support is needed. Bhavsar and colleagues (2019) argued that a need-indifferent style is likely to be less motivationally damaging than a thwarting style but more detrimental than a need-supportive style. This is because a need-indifferent style would not be expected to actively undermine athletes' psychological needs as a thwarting style does; nevertheless, an indifferent style does not foster such needs as a need-supportive style does.

TABLE 12.1 Three-by-Three Model of Interpersonal Styles

PSYCHOLOGICAL NEED	FUNCTION: Supporting	FUNCTION: Indifferent	FUNCTION: Thwarting
AUTONOMY	Autonomy support	Autonomy indifferent	Autonomy thwarting
COMPETENCE	Competence support	Competence indifferent	Competence thwarting
RELATEDNESS	Relatedness support	Relatedness indifferent	Relatedness thwarting

Note: This table is available at https://osf.io/fzxwj/ under a CC-BY4.0 license and can be freely reproduced.

Although these conceptual arguments were not specific to any particular life domain, the evidence they provided was limited to sport only. Via a series of three studies, Bhavsar and colleagues developed and provided initial validity evidence for a scale that assesses athletes' perceptions of supporting, indifferent, and thwarting coach styles, using the 22-item Tripartite Measure of Interpersonal Behaviors-Coach (TMIB-C). The scale development process included a review of available instruments, input from experts in SDT, and interviews with athletes. The quantitative data obtained by the authors from different samples of young adult Australian athletes did not support a nine-factor structure. Although the three need functions were not clearly differentiated, the three functions were; hence the authors advocated a three-factor structure for the

TMIB-C (overall need support, need indifference, and need thwarting). The scores from this scale demonstrated, across two independent samples, good model fit, factor loadings, modest factor correlations, and adequate internal reliability.

In terms of evidence of nomological networks, Bhavsar and colleagues (2019) found that, as expected, athletes' dedication to sport and their irrelevant thought processing were best predicted by perceptions of coach need support and need indifference, respectively. Feelings of exhaustion were predicted to the same degree by both need thwarting and (unexpectedly) need indifference. Further, as expected, (1) satisfaction of each of the three needs was best predicted by perceptions of need-supportive coaching, and (2) frustration of the needs for autonomy and competence were best predicted by perceptions of need-thwarting coaching. Frustration of the need for relatedness was predicted by both thwarting and indifferent coaching.

Preliminary evidence for the role of a need-indifferent style is also emerging in other life domains. For instance, similar to the Bhavsar study, a three-factor model structure (need support, need thwarting, and need indifferent) was the best fit to the data provided by several samples of English- and French-speaking employees (Huyghebaert-Zouaghi et al., 2020). Model fit was tested with structural equation modeling fit indices that compared the three-factor model to alternative factor model structures. Quested and colleagues (2018) used an observational tool to code the behaviors of exercise instructors, before and after an SDT-informed intervention, and reported large effect sizes in the change scores for all three styles.

In conclusion, there is increasing evidence (in sport and other life domains) that a need-indifferent style can be measured alongside need-supportive and need-thwarting styles, and that such a style can predict important outcomes, independent of the other two styles. However, the evidence suggests that although such styles can be distinguished in terms of their function (support, thwart, indifferent), they cannot be easily differentiated in terms of the needs they target (autonomy, competence, and relatedness). As such, we suggest that different analytical approaches are needed to capture the three-by-three model, an issue we discuss later in this chapter.

There is increasing evidence (in sport and other life domains) that a need-indifferent style can be measured alongside need-supportive and need-thwarting styles, and that such a style can predict important outcomes, independent of the other two styles.

Measurement and Statistical Approaches

In this section we briefly review some of the instruments that have been used in the literature to measure and analyze quantitative data on coach interpersonal styles from a SDT perspective.

The majority of tools used to assess coach interpersonal styles have focused on athlete perceptions of the prominent behaviors of their coach. In early SDT-based research in sport, measures were borrowed from other contexts and adapted for use with athletes. The autonomy-supportive features of the environment were most assessed, and the most popular way to do so was by using items from the Health Care Climate Questionnaire (HCCQ; Williams et al., 1996). The full version of this scale captures not only perceptions of autonomy-supportive behaviors but also things medical practitioners may say or do that support competence or relatedness. A shorter seven-item version of the HCCQ has often been used, isolating only those items tapping support for autonomy (e.g., Adie et al., 2008; Fenton et al., 2014).

Assessment of how athletes perceive competence- and relatedness-supportive coaching behaviors received scant attention in the early days of the sport-based SDT literature. This was partly attributed to a lack of sport-specific or easily adaptable measures for the sport context (Curran et al., 2013). Until recently, the few studies assessing these constructs relied on adaptations of scales developed in other settings. For example, in their assessment of motivation-related predictors of young athletes' welfare, Reinboth and colleagues (2004) measured perceptions of relatedness support using the Social Support Questionnaire (Sarason et al., 1987). In the same study, coach-provided support for competence was assessed by using the coach involvement items from the Perceived Motivational Climate in Sport Questionnaire-2 (Newton et al., 2000), an achievement goal theory–based measure. Curran and colleagues (2013) assessed how athletes perceived coaches' provision of structure using an adaptation of the Teacher as a Social Context Questionnaire (Belmont et al., 1988). However, the authors highlighted the potential limitations of using an assessment tool not developed for the sport context and called for a validated and sport-specific assessment tool for structure.

Wilson and colleagues (2009) developed the first sport-specific multidimensional measurement tool to assess the perceived need-supportive features of the sporting environment, the Interpersonal Supportiveness Scale-Coach (ISS-C). The scale includes 18 items assessing perceptions of autonomy support, involvement, and structure, using a 7-point scale to respond to items such as "my coach clarifies training expectations." During the validation work, there was reasonable support for the psychometric properties of the ISS-C; however, the need-support subscales were highly correlated (e.g., involvement and autonomy support; $r = 0.94$), raising the question of whether a multidimensional approach to represent the three facets of need support is most appropriate.

There have since been a few other efforts to assess perceptions of need-supportive and need-thwarting dimensions of the coaching interpersonal style. The 24-item Interpersonal Behaviours Questionnaire (IBQ) was adapted for sport by Rocchi and colleagues (2017). Athlete data supported the six-factor internal structure; however, the scale has been criticized for using items to tap need thwarting, which, conceptually, would be more likely to be classified as indifferent (Bhavsar et al., 2019). The Coaches' Interpersonal Style Questionnaire (CIS-Q; Pulido et al., 2018) assesses 22 items, including the six need-supportive and -thwarting dimensions of coaching behavior. The validity of the need-thwarting items has been called into question because they are worded more to assess athlete experiences of need frustration rather than social environmental features that are likely to cause it (Bhavsar et al., 2019). A further limitation pertaining to the IBQ Sport and CIS-Q is the moderately high correlations between the interpersonal styles. Noting the limitations of the existing scales, Bhavsar and colleagues (2019) set out to develop a tripartite scale to assess how athletes perceive the need-supportive, need-thwarting, and need-indifferent behaviors of coaches. See page 179 for a description of the 22-item Tripartite Measure of Interpersonal Behaviors-Coach (TMIB-C).

All self-report instruments are prone to social desirability and other types of bias (e.g., response, recall) (DeVellis, 2017). Further, athlete reports of coach behaviors often conflict for the same coach or do not correlate meaningfully with observed coach behaviors (Rocchi & Pelletier, 2018). Hence, researchers have used observational methodologies to create observation tools for assessing the motivational features of the coaching environment. The most recent instruments have been multidimensional and have coded both the adaptive (i.e., need supportive) and maladaptive (i.e., need thwarting) features of coach interpersonal styles. Observational scales enable researchers to dissect what it was about a particular behavior that contributed toward its being need supportive or thwarting. Because the social-cognitive perspective underpins motivational theories such as SDT, observational scales enable the comparison of what actually happens versus what is perceived or experienced. For example, Smith and colleagues' Multidimensional Motivational Climate Observation System (MMCOS; 2015) included assessment of potency (i.e., psychological meaning of an observed behavior with motivational significance). In the Coach Interpersonal Style Observational System (CISOS), Pulido and colleagues (2019) assessed both verbal and structural behaviors as well as types of tone (controlling, neutral, supportive).

Observation scales have long been considered highly important tools for helping researchers understand what coaches do and how athletes are affected (Roberts & Treasure, 2012). For example, such tools can be useful for assessing change in observable behaviors over time (e.g., before or after a need-supportive intervention). However, there are also limitations to such instruments; for instance, accurate coding is dependent on the researchers' thorough understanding of the tool itself and the underpinning theoretical principles. In particular, coding of relatedness-supportive behaviors is challenging and may be at risk of subjectivity from coders (Smith et al., 2015).

Future Research Directions

In this section we propose some other avenues for future research on interpersonal styles. One obvious direction is to examine the construct overlap (conceptual and measurement) of SDT-proposed styles with other constructs that tap coach influence on athletes' motivation. Such constructs include variants of motivational environments such as empowering, caring, and motivational climates based on achievement goal theory (e.g., see other chapters in this book; Jaakola et al., 2016). They also include constructs from the leadership literature such as transformational leadership (chapter 7), leadership based on social identity theory (chapter 8), and other leadership theories less researched in sport (e.g., charismatic: Banks et al., 2017; transactional: Antonakis et al., 2003). All these constructs make different assumptions about how significant others' (e.g., coaches) influence operates, yet there is overlap among many of them in terms of item content. Shaffer and colleagues (2016) have provided a useful guide to tackle what they called "construct proliferation," focusing on assessing discriminant validity of constructs that are ostensibly different but potentially very similar. In addition to discriminant validity, establishing criterion validity would be a very important step in this process (e.g., identifying how much unique variance of important athlete- and coach-related outcomes overlapping constructs predict).

Another avenue for future research is to examine how interpersonal styles relate to team processes and outcomes. The vast majority of SDT work on interpersonal styles has focused on individual outcomes; however, team dynamics are very important in sport. For instance, examining the relations between coach interpersonal styles and team-level outcomes such as resilience (Gucciardi et al., 2018), cognition (Grand et al., 2016), and adaptation (Maynard et al., 2015) would be an original avenue for future research. In addition, most of the SDT work on interpersonal styles has focused on the effects of these styles on athlete outcomes; yet evidence in other contexts suggests that being autonomy supportive can benefit not only those who receive such support but also those who provide it (Deci et al., 2006). An examination of how being need supportive can benefit a coach (e.g., in terms of their own well-being, work-related outcomes, psychological need satisfaction, and autonomous motivation to coach), and how being need indifferent and thwarting to athletes can eventually backfire, is a very much needed longitudinal research project. The interface between personality and interpersonal styles also deserves greater research attention. For instance, narcissism has been examined in relation to being an antecedent of coach interpersonal styles (Matosic et al., 2017), but it can also be examined at the athlete level. Sedikides and colleagues (2019) suggested that narcissists who are in a subordinate (rather than an authority) position may fluctuate highly from seeking control to seeking autonomy support, particularly those with vulnerable narcissism. Other personality antecedents of coach interpersonal style can also be explored (e.g., the big five; see the work of Reeve et al., 2018, with teachers).

Practical Implications

The intervention studies conducted in sport and other life settings (e.g., Ntoumanis et al., in press; Su & Reeve, 2011; Vasconcellos et al., 2020) have shown it is possible to train individuals in position of authority or expertise to become more autonomy supportive and need supportive. However, in many of these studies it is unclear how key components of the intervention were delivered. To address this and other concerns, Teixeira and colleagues (2020) developed a taxonomy of 21 motivation and behavior-change techniques used in SDT-informed interventions in the health domain. Seven techniques from this taxonomy capture each of the three needs. Examples include providing a meaningful rationale and choice (autonomy support), acknowledging perspectives and showing unconditional regard (relatedness support), and clarifying expectations and offering constructive, clear, and relevant feedback (competence support). Most of these techniques have been reported in past interventions in sport, exercise, and physical education settings. Applied researchers and sport practitioners can consult this taxonomy to identify specific techniques that significant others in sport (e.g., coaches, parents) can adopt to be need supportive.

A limitation of the Teixeira and colleagues (2020) classification system is that need-thwarting techniques were not identified. Given that need-thwarting (and potentially need indifferent) styles can be motivationally detrimental, the addition of such techniques in future revisions of this classification system is essential. Nevertheless, applied researchers and practitioners can consult existing sources to identify specific ways significant others in sport can be less thwarting or indifferent. For instance, Hancox and colleagues (2015) identified motivationally adaptive strategies (LARS; Listening, Advising, Relating to participants, Structuring a class in ways that support participants' psychological needs) and motivationally maladaptive strategies (PEAS; Pressuring language, Empty communication, Appearing cold, Structuring a class in ways that undermine participants' psychological needs) that fitness instructors should aim to use more and less, respectively. The LARS strategies are captured in the taxonomy by Teixeira and colleagues. The PEAS strategies include specific behaviors such as criticizing and belittling others, appearing cold and indifferent, using "no pain, no gain" language, and imposing goals and rules. All

LARS and PEAS techniques should be relevant to the sport context.

The implementation of need-supportive training can be augmented by the use of behavior-change techniques, such as planning, goal setting, and barrier identification (Michie et al., 2013), to identify opportunities of when, where, or how often specific techniques should be delivered (e.g., how often and when to provide choice to athletes). For an example of combining SDT training with behavior-change techniques in training exercise instructors, see Hancox and colleagues (2018). A further consideration is that changing interpersonal styles can be a time-consuming process, even for those who are willing to change. The literature on the antecedents of such styles (reviewed earlier in this chapter) has identified a number of barriers, including beliefs, cultural norms, and personal dispositions toward autonomy. Ntoumanis and colleagues (2018) discussed a number of solutions for overcoming such barriers. Given that pressures from work colleagues and sport administrators have been identified as predictors of need-thwarting style (Matosic et al., 2016), intervention work to promote more need-supporting and fewer thwarting and indifferent styles in sport should also consider targeting, where feasible, the broader social environment surrounding sport coaches. Parents are, indisputably, part of that social environment, particularly in youth sport, and can influence children's motivation (e.g., Lienhart et al., 2020). Applied research and practice informed by SDT should also attempt to include parents in future intervention studies on interpersonal styles. Examining the generalizability of need-supportive training, which has to date been focused on coaches, to other significant social agents in sport is a question of significant applied importance.

Summary

There is strong evidence in the SDT literature that coaches can adopt styles that support or thwart athletes' basic psychological needs, to differing degrees. We reviewed empirical evidence, both correlational and experimental, showing that this influence on psychological needs can result in bright motivational pathways (satisfied needs result in autonomous motivation and positive outcomes) and dark motivational pathways (frustrated needs result in controlled motivation or amotivation and negative outcomes). Such a pattern of findings seems to hold up irrespective of whether coach interpersonal styles are measured by athletes' perceptions, coaches' self-reports, or third-party observations of coaching practices. We also discussed how more recent evidence suggests the existence of a third style, need indifferent, and why this additional style might matter. To this end, we presented a three-by-three model of interpersonal styles describing their functions (supportive, indifferent, and thwarting) and the psychological needs they target (autonomy, competence, and relatedness). We lastly discussed the antecedents of such styles and how to develop intervention programs that target some of these antecedents, or directly target coaches' behaviors and vocalizations, to foster a more need-supportive style.

DISCUSSION QUESTIONS

1. Discuss how conceptual and measurement advances in the self-determination theory literature have helped researchers to better understand the complexities associated with the representation of coach interpersonal styles.
2. What are the main antecedents of coach interpersonal styles? Explain how and why they predict the likelihood of coaches' adopting different styles.
3. What are some of the well-studied consequences of different interpersonal styles? Explain how and why such styles result in different affective, cognitive, and behavioral outcomes.
4. Discuss some practical ways of helping coaches adopt a more need-supportive style and reduce need-thwarting and need-indifferent styles.

13

The Climate as a Collective Adaptive System

Richard J. Keegan, PhD, and David J.C. Smith, MSc

LEARNING OBJECTIVES

On completion of this chapter, the reader should have the following:

- Clear understanding of trends in motivational climate research and an awareness of opportunities to advance understanding in this area
- Insights into where current methods for studying the social determination of motivation in athletes are reaching the limits of possibilities for advancing understanding regarding motivational climates
- Understanding of the possibilities for drawing from research methods from the science of complex adaptive systems
- Awareness of the implications of the complex systems framework for future research and applied practice

Carly is a youth basketball coach. She has coached the same group of players through four consecutive age groups and built up a team that consistently performs well and who also like each other. They had jelled. The team focused on improving every game, helping each other on this journey, and valuing effort and commitment above all else. As a result, of course, they won a lot of games.

As the team transitioned into high school, even though the same players stayed, everything seemed to change. All the work Carly and her assistant coaches had done to set expectations and norms seemed to have been forgotten, or even rejected; players criticized each other and resorted to bullying and cheating to compete for game time. The parents seemed to reinforce this competitive ethos, and the atmosphere soured. A relatively simple, and quite predictable, transition had changed her team and knocked them out of their groove.

Is this story plausible? Can a social group reach a consistent steady state but then suddenly fall out of it? Can a social group flip states, seemingly inexplicably and quite suddenly? Can new unwritten rules and expectations emerge without being introduced by the leader or coach? If so, then we have identified that *attractor states*, *instability*, *phase transitions*, and *emergence* are all typical aspects of social life. These terms are central to the idea of complex systems and are discussed later in the chapter. First, however, we consider how such attributes of social groups can make researching them so challenging.

This chapter takes a different approach to many others in this book, whose job has been to offer a clear summary of research in their specific topic area. In contrast, motivational climate research appears to have reached something of a steady state, or plateau, in recent years as already detailed in similar textbooks (Harwood et al., 2015; Keegan, 2019). These texts have detailed how—using broadly consistent theories, measures, and analysis techniques—we may have reached the limit of what can be understood without diversifying in some way. Conceptually, several chapters in this book offer complementary models of how the social climate around sport can promote motivation, better experiences, and more optimal outcomes (chapters 10, 11, and 12), and this is important and valuable understanding. For the main part, however, these different research fields within the social psychology of sport tend to favor similar methods—particularly psychometrics surveys—and those previous chapters were not necessarily intended to critically reflect on measures, methods, and analytic approaches on offer. The current chapter, however, is.

Given that we are largely taught similar content in our degrees—regarding psychometric measures, common statistical models, and the like—merely identifying the problem of depending on these (as Harwood et al. [2015] and Keegan [2019] have done) does not necessarily progress us toward a solution. So this chapter connects the current research themes on motivational climate to a different approach: that of *complex systems science* (Eagle & Pentland, 2005; Holland, 2006). Here we map how the social influences on athlete motivation may be better viewed as a complex, dynamic process—playing out over time, rather than a parsimonious, dichotomous model. This chapter adopts a broader interpretation of motivational climates, spanning several approaches already detailed in the preceding chapters. The assumptions and methods discussed herein could also be applied to many other concepts throughout this book.

Challenges in Theory and Research

The preceding chapters have provided authoritative summaries of key conceptual and theoretical advancements, regarding how social interactions influence athlete motivation. Chapter 10 overviewed the progression from achievement goal theory into more recent empowering versus disempowering climates, incorporating a range of concepts from self-determination theory in their updating of conceptual models. Chapter 11 detailed a sustained program of work that has characterized the concept of caring climates and, similarly, linked this construct to important outcomes, including athletes' motivation. Chapter 12 described the rich history of research in self-determination theory, as well as recent developments in the way social environments can support, thwart, or neglect athletes' psychological needs. Without doubt, these theories, models, and concepts are meaningful and important, having benefited from empirical attempts to characterize and refine them, and they show strong promise for improving the experience of athletes of all ages and levels. These approaches help us understand how we can frame, monitor, and adjust the social milieu around sport to optimize athlete motivation. Similarly, however, there remain inherent limitations on the meaningfulness and usefulness of research in these topics—science is always progressing. What follows, therefore, is a rapid, almost unreasonably superficial, summary of criticisms that have been developed within this literature (e.g., Elliot, 1999; Hassmén et al., 2016; Keegan et al., 2014a, 2014b). The subsequent sections seek to offer solutions to these concerns.

A systematic review conducted by Lacerda and colleagues (2021) found that although studies in motivational climate adopted different measurement tools and theoretical approaches, they primarily focused on variations of self-determination theory (Ryan & Deci, 2002) and achievement goal theory (Nicholls, 1989). Studies typically used questionnaires such as the Perceived Motivational Climate in Sport Questionnaire (PMCSQ, Walling et al., 1993; PMCSQ-2, Newton et al., 2000) or the Parent-Initiated Motivational Climate Questionnaire (PIMCQ-2, White, 1996). These measures sometimes—*but not always*—refer to the perceived motivational influences created by specific social agents such as coaches, parents, and peers. Nevertheless, some scales are interpreted as assessing the coach-created climate when questions make little or no reference to the coach (cf. Harwood et al., 2015). The full array of motivational influences in a social context is very unlikely to be determined by only one person, such as a coach.

Similarly, such measures, by the very nature of the statistics involved in creating them, simplify the social context into a small number of categories (i.e., factors—usually two to six) and assume that all people will perceive and report these experiences in very similar ways (otherwise it would not work as a measure). In reality, the social milieu that determines athletes' motivation is not simple (i.e., only a few categories): it is not parsimonious. This book has already reviewed multiple theories of the same phenomenon: how social interactions influence motivation. While there may be some convergence in concepts (e.g., Duda's integrative model, see chapter 10), we must consider that many related, competing concepts are in play when groups of people interact to influence each other's motivation. Further, motivational climate is unlikely to be dependably experienced in the same way across cultures and contexts. Most of our research takes place in so-called WEIRD settings: Western, Educated, Industrialized, Rich, and Democratic; these are not representative of the full diversity of settings where sport takes place.

In addition to these issues, such questionnaires (generated at huge effort and using sophisticated methods) tend to ask the same group of 20 to 40 questions, plus many more to assess whatever else is being measured. Consequently, athletes usually complete them only once—which is quite reasonable, of course—but it means we could miss seeing changes over time, as well as how they might link to other important outcomes. As summarized by Harwood and colleagues (2015), when we conduct research using a battery of questionnaires *completed on one occasion* by athletes, we do tend to generate consistent findings. We may even be at a point where there is little benefit in doing similar cross-sectional studies, unless we greatly vary the types of participants and populations.

In reality, the social milieu that determines athletes' motivation is not simple (i.e., only a few categories): it is not parsimonious.

Nonetheless, even these relatively consistent findings have a concerning limitation. Participants on the same team, or in the same setting, perceive it very differently (Cumming et al., 2008; Sproule et al., 2007). Athletes with the same coach give very different responses. Further, when Smith and colleagues (2015) developed an observational tool for examining motivational climate, the resulting instrument—which showed good reliability and validity—demonstrated either no relationship or negligible correlations with what was perceived subjectively (e.g., $r = 0.07, 0.12$ etc.). So there remains a gap between objective and observable attributes of the motivational climate versus what is perceived. By consequence, we are somewhat limited to concluding that *when* an athlete perceives a particular configuration of climate (e.g., mastery, empowering, need supportive), *then* they experience good things. Whereas if they perceive other combinations (performance or ego, disempowering, need thwarting), they experience bad things. As to how those perceptions are generated, we continue to struggle. As such, Smith and colleagues (2007) commented on the need to "clarify relations between particular intervention elements and various outcome measures" (p. 54). Elliot (1999) also speculated that "it is also possible that some of the antecedent variables *combine* together to jointly and *interactively* predict achievement goal adoption" (p. 176). That sounds much more difficult to study scientifically. It sounds *complex*.

There have, however, been some experimental interventions of motivational climate, or variations of it (e.g., Smith et al., 2007). The main drawback is that they recommend sweeping changes to athlete or team practices, losing the ability to detect fine-grained associations of what change caused which impacts. So, if it is not the case that simply implementing a few precisely defined techniques derived from a tightly specified theory is what worked—but rather a broader approach, dependent on coaches using their discretion in navigating moment to moment—is that support for the particular underlying theory over another (e.g., achievement goals, self-determination)? Coaches and practitioners may also ask researchers, "In the absence of clear, dependable, consistent techniques, how can this process be steered, maintained, and navigated?"

The papers of Keegan and colleagues (see next section) simultaneously called for such an unpacking of the motivational climate (or atmosphere) as well as enabling it—by extensively detailing the raw ingredients that athletes reported as influencing their motivation. Before these papers and findings, the best return on investment was to use cross-sectional questionnaire and correlation methods. After these papers, it is now possible to examine the situational influences and interactions of specific social interactions in determining motivation (i.e., momentary utterances, emotional reactions, paying attention to certain players over others). Further, it may become possible to explore how these exchanges accrue over time and to finally gain traction on the issue of socialization of achievement goals, identified by Duda (2001). Drawing an analogy to food and cooking, we are at a juncture where we depend only on the postmeal perceptions of diners to understand what "good food" is. But we are arriving at the opportunity to engage with the producers—the farmers, chefs, and the like—to understand what the raw ingredients are, and how they are combined and presented to achieve those experiences.

In a similar vein, we examine the motivation of an athlete based on one moment at a time, say, after a particularly exhaustive training session. This is a snapshot afforded to us of how the athlete feels within that moment, yet without engaging with the coaches, teammates, or parents, as well as the athlete's personal life and environmental context leading up to that moment; all of which may have an influence on the athlete's motivation. As Keegan and colleagues (2014b, p. 561) concluded: "Any developments in our ability to capture the complexity in the social determination of athlete motivation would, arguably, represent a much more significant advancement for the field than any further studies suggesting that one concept (or collection of concepts) correlates with another concept."

Make no mistake, however, that researchers working in motivational climate and related topics are already taking steps to address many of these limitations. They likely would have done so anyway, without prompting by the critiques listed. Further, it is important to recognize that the way research is funded, administered, assessed, and legislated also heavily constrains the speed at which researchers can progress from the descriptive work (developing, measuring, associating) into the more sophisticated work of testing, predicting (over time), and offering refined, specific guidance.

Developments to Enable Progress

Between 2009 and 2015, Keegan and colleagues (2009, 2010, 2014a) generated a series of studies attempting to answer the question of what exactly coaches, parents, and peers do to influence athletes' motivation. Three studies detailed these behaviors, as experienced by the athletes, at three career stages. A fourth study synthesized and compared all these findings with the rest of the relevant literature and considered the implications for theory development, research approaches, and applied practice (Keegan et al., 2014b). The approach has also been replicated in adult physical activity participation (Keegan et al., 2016) and in the specific context of football (soccer) academies (McCann et al., 2021). The findings of these papers detailed specific observable behaviors and attitudes or trends that athletes picked up on from each social agent (in this case, coaches, parents, and peers). Table 13.1 summarizes the motivationally relevant influences described, which were diverse and expanded consideration beyond parsimonious models and into seven broad areas: competition climate, training climate, evaluation climate, emotional climate, authority climate, social support climate, and relatedness climate. When combined, these climates were conceptualized using a meteorological metaphor (figure 13.1).

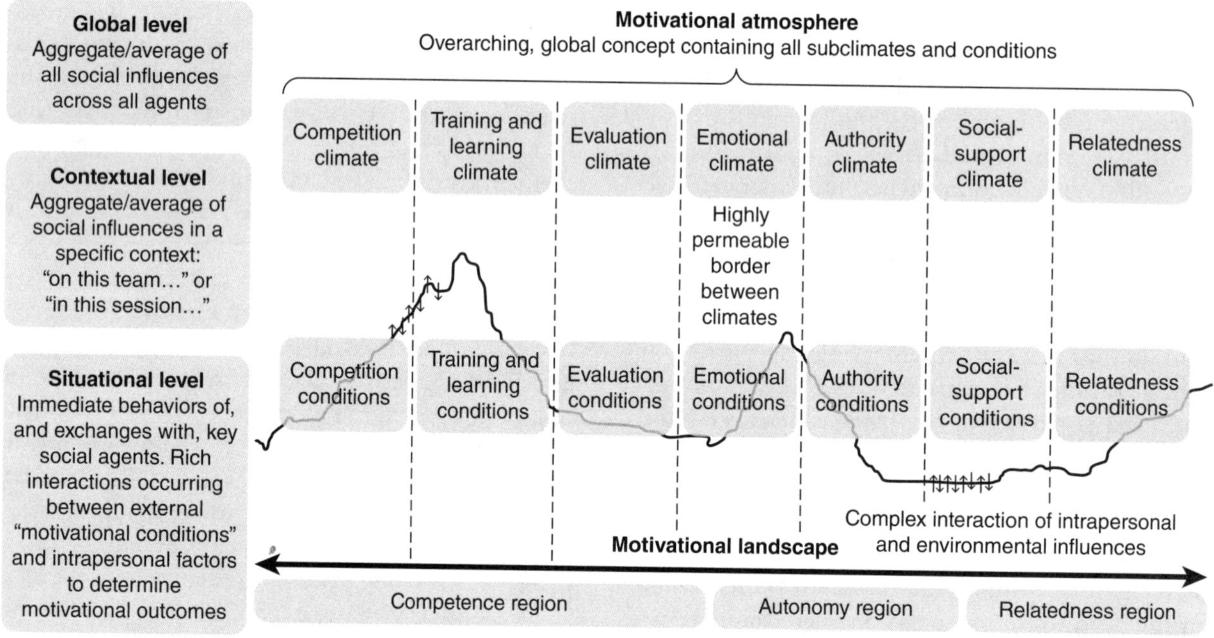

FIGURE 13.1 A heuristic model suggesting potential processes, relationships, and terminology for the study of social and environmental influences on motivation. Momentary motivation ("the landscape") is proposed to be shaped by a complex interaction of the social motivational processes identified in this study ("the atmosphere") and the intrapersonal motivational variables identified elsewhere (the motivational "geology"). NB: The atmosphere contains several smaller climates.

TABLE 13.1 Main Sources of Motivationally Relevant Influences

	Explanation	Coaches	Parents	Peers
Competition climate	Social interactions immediately before, during, and immediately after athletes' engagement in competitive performances	• Emphasizing mastery and improvement • Emphasizing effort • Focusing on competitive success • Pressurizing behaviors • Energizing behaviors (e.g., passionate speeches)	• Emphasizing mastery and improvement • Emphasizing effort • Focusing on competitive success • Pressurizing behaviors	• Emphasizing mastery and improvement • Emphasizing effort • Focusing on competitive success • Pressurizing behaviors • In-competition decisions (e.g., who to pass to)
Training climate	The situations in which training and learning occurred, as separated from competition (in preparation for competition)	• Equal treatment • Pedagogical (teaching) style - Groupings - Task design - One-to-one coaching - Modeling, demonstrating - Informational support • Selections for competition	• Equal treatment • Pedagogical (teaching) style	• Emphasizing effort in training • Emphasizing competitive success in training • Team promoting improvement • Engaging in positive rivalries to push each other • Collaborative learning
Evaluation climate	The ways in which athletes' performance is assessed and feedback is provided	• Evaluation criteria - Personal mastery - Normative comparison - Fault finding • Verbal feedback - Positive - Negative - Balanced - Honesty - Summative vs. formative - Public vs. private - Timing: immediate vs. delayed - Personally relevant • Behavioral reinforcement - Reinforcing effort - Reinforcing outcomes - Punishing mistakes	• Evaluation criteria - Personal mastery - Normative comparison - Fault finding • Verbal feedback - Positive - Negative - Balanced - Honesty - Summative vs. formative - Public vs. private - Timing: immediate vs. delayed • Behavioral reinforcement - Reinforcing effort - Reinforcing outcomes - Punishing mistakes	• Evaluation criteria - Personal mastery - Normative comparison - Fault finding • Verbal feedback - Positive - Negative - Balanced - Honesty - Summative vs. formative - Public vs. private - Timing: immediate vs. delayed
Emotional climate	The emotional and affective displays of key social agents—not only about athletic performance	• Negative emotional responses - Negative responses to mistakes - Negative responses to defeats - Competitive body language • Tolerance - Mistakes tolerated - Defeats tolerated - Joke about or de-emphasize mistakes • Positive, supportive climate - Encouragement following mistakes - Happiness following success - Warm, friendly style • Emotional intensity • Emotional range • Sincerity of emotions	• Negative emotional responses - Negative responses to mistakes - Negative responses to defeats - Competitive body language • Tolerance - Mistakes tolerated - Defeats tolerated • Positive, supportive climate - Happiness following success	• Negative emotional responses - Negative responses to mistakes - Negative responses to defeats • Tolerance - Joke about or de-emphasize mistakes • Positive, supportive climate - Happiness following success - Calming influence

(continued)

Table 13.1 *(continued)*

	Explanation	Coaches	Parents	Peers
Authority climate	The manner in which those in positions of authority or responsibility (mainly coaches and parents) fulfill this role	• Facilitating autonomy • Controlling style • Maintaining discipline • Importance of previous experience or success • Responses to competition pressures (e.g., more controlling) • Forming good relationships • Reflexive, adaptive style • Conflicting, inconsistent coaching	• Facilitating autonomy • Controlling style • Maintaining discipline • Previous experience of the sport • Importance of previous experience or success • Differences between parents • Giving a sense of perspective	• Facilitating autonomy
Social support climate	Behaviors that contribute directly and indirectly to the athlete's participating in and benefitting from sport	–	• Emotional support • Material support (e.g., equipment) • Conditional vs. unconditional support • Unconditional support • Investing in the athlete • Managing athlete's career • Spectating support	• Emotional support • Conflict (presence, severity, and resolution) • Adapting own behavior to accommodate colleagues • Spectating support
Relatedness climate	All the elements of sport participation associated with seeking both friendship or affiliation and belonging or group membership	• Coach affiliation: feels like a friend or ally • Coach dedication and commitment • Coach complementarity: their behaviors and style complement the athletes'	–	• Associating competence with friendship: "we all want to be friends with the good players" • Friendship and affiliation • Group identity and sense of belonging • Group culture: history

Adapted from R.J. Keegan, C.M. Spray, C.G. Harwood, and D.E. Lavallee, "A Qualitative Synthesis of Research Into Social Motivational Influences Across the Athletic Career Span," *Qualitative Research in Sport, Exercise and Health* 6, no. 4 (2014): 537-567. Distributed under the terms of the Creative Commons Attribution 4.0 International License (http://creativecommons.org/licenses/by/4.0/).

Motivational Atmosphere and the Meteorology Metaphor

The meteorological model was developed to more adequately represent the rich complexity of social and interpersonal influences on athlete motivation. In attempting to capture the full range of behaviors and attitudes that may influence motivation, the model offers both a horizontal range and vertical height. The horizontal element ranged from competition and training climates at one end to social support and relatedness climates at the other. The vertical height reflected Vallerand's (1997) distinction between global, contextual, and situational influences. As such, the model delineates levels of abstraction: a broad, global *motivational atmosphere* contains a series of *contextual climates* (competition, training, evaluation, emotion, authority, social support, and relatedness). These contextual climates are effectively the aggregate of many instances of momentary or situational *motivational conditions.* Local conditions include the immediate influences that interact with the athlete's traits and dispositions, which are cast as the landscape in this model. From such a viewpoint, specific local motivational conditions may be objectively observed and would make sense in attempting to study and model how social factors influence athlete motivation—as opposed to broad, subjective perceptions gathered at single points in time. This shift in assumptions, perspectives, and mental models points us toward complexity—we can quickly see how studying such a system in the form of isolated momentary snapshots may be missing important details and insights (Abraham, 1995; Guastello & Liebovitch, 2009).

The meteorological analogy that emerged from this analysis might seem cumbersome and complicated, but it is worth noting that meteorologists are frequently able to predict the weather with surprising accuracy (Holland, 2006; Miller & Page, 2009). To achieve this success, however, meteorologists require a detailed understanding of the atmosphere, climates, and conditions, along with their nuances, interactions, and interdependence. A simple dichotomy (e.g., hot vs. cold, wet vs. dry) can be a useful heuristic, but it does not adequately differentiate between atmosphere, climate, and conditions. Neither does it afford the scientist a full and functional understanding of the phenomenon under study. As such, research in this topic—motivational climate—is at something of a crossroads: facing a choice between the parsimony offered by simple models and subjective rating scales versus embracing the complexity of social interactions in shaping motivation (Abraham, 1995; Guastello & Liebovitch, 2009). The remainder of this chapter considers the burgeoning body of research regarding complex adaptive systems, to demonstrate that measurement, analysis, and scientific progress are indeed possible without needing to impose simplicity. We seek to offer an alternative approach.

Applying Methods From Complex Adaptive Systems to Motivational Climate Research

The developments just described are entirely understandable when we consider the nature of how research is organized and analyzed. We must operationalize concepts into measures that we can then realistically use and understand, and we historically use statistical assumptions that rely on linear statistics and linear models: depicting change as a straightforward concept (cf. Hassmén et al., 2016). That is, the output of a system is directly proportional to the input. So, for example, more force propels a ball proportionately farther, but does more coach passion always lead to proportionately better athlete motivation? Rather than accepting the necessary simplification (termed *reductionism*) of these complex phenomena using simple linear models, one might alternatively argue that those approaches have served their purpose: they have taken us to where we are now and generated sufficient knowledge to help numerous coaches and athletes in sport. To truly legitimize a reductionist approach would require the assumption that any system of individual parts working together is inherently mechanical, meaning we can understand how the system works by examining the individual parts (Abraham, 1995; Guastello & Liebovitch, 2009). So to what extent do we accept that this is the true nature of a motivational climate? If we think it may well be complex, then it is time to adopt new methods—especially because developments in science and technology now enable new forms of research and analysis, such as more frequent monitoring of subjective and objective measures (e.g., Chevance et al., 2020; Saw et al., 2016).

The Nature of Complex Adaptive Systems

In the last few decades, coinciding with the rise of advancing computing technologies, research in complex adaptive systems has gathered pace. These developments allow us to better conceptualize and describe behaviors that are inherently either themselves complex or occurring within a complex environment. In complex systems, the system is defined as the makeup of individual elements and the interactions of those elements with each other and the environment. Because these parts can interact, as well as learn and adapt, the output of the system is greater than (or at least very different from) the simple sum of the inputs. The most obvious example in sport is when a team of superstar athletes is beaten by a well-organized team of lesser-known players. Behaviors and patterns emerge within a system that would simply not exist from the individual elements themselves. Examples include team cohesion, social norms, shared language, slang, and of course, motivational climates. The elements of such a system interact with each other, share information, change each other, and cannot be removed without fundamentally altering the dynamics of the system itself. Defenders talk to midfielders about where gaps are appearing, and midfielders talk to attackers about new ideas to score a point—and the information being shared is constantly changing in response to events that have just happened. (Did the last attack work? Are we winning or losing? How long is left to play?) The resiliency of a system is how well it can adapt to any kind of change, flaw, or external intrusion without collapsing upon itself (Abraham, 1995; Guastello & Liebovitch, 2009).

In order to map complex systems onto motivational climate research, we may ask several key questions. How is an individual's perceived motivational climate generated? And how is a group's shared perception of climate generated? Are there multiple elements interacting, such as people (in multiple roles), behaviors, rules, backgrounds, and contexts? Do these things (e.g., people, rules, processes) learn, remember, and adapt according to what has happened before? Is it difficult to predict how these interactions will lead to a motivational climate until after it's happened, with the same behavior sometimes leading to wildly different experiences? As an example, coach criticism of skill execution was reported by one participant as fear inducing and harmful to motivation, whereas another participant in the same focus group reported the same behavior as showing the coach really cared and was thus a boost to motivation (as described by participants in Keegan et al., 2010). We may need to consider that recommending specific actions or behaviors regardless of context may not generate the desired results—an issue that is not well accommodated when seeking simple cause and effect but that is explicitly acknowledged within the complex systems approach.

A complex adaptive systems approach embraces outliers and changes within a system by acknowledging that systems are not solely deterministic, nor completely random.

Research using complex adaptive systems has been applied to explain scientific concepts in diverse disciplines, including evolutionary biology, physics, geology, sociology, and meteorology (Guastello & Liebovitch, 2009). A complex adaptive systems approach embraces outliers and changes within a system by acknowledging that systems are not solely deterministic, nor completely random. As such, even if short-term outcomes are predictable, over the long term they are inherently unpredictable; but patterns that might not be easily observed do emerge in what first appears to be noise or randomness (Abraham, 1995; Guastello & Liebovitch, 2009). Within complex adaptive systems, the constructs used to observe, understand, and describe change within a system include

- attractors,
- phase transitions,
- chaos, or instability,
- emergence, and
- self-similarity, or fractals.

Each of these is explained a little more in the following paragraphs.

Ways We Understand Complex Adaptive Systems

The term *attractors* describes configurations of a system that appear to hold steady, almost as if the system gravitates back to that configuration. Such an attractor can be fixed (i.e., focused on a single point), such as training to win or learning a specific task. It can also be a stable cycle that repeats (e.g., the weekly transitions from focusing on learning during training to winning during competition). Thus, even within a fluid, evolving social system, there can be periods of stability and predictability, and this is a recognized phenomenon in complex systems research. Nevertheless, the situation may also change, perhaps unexpectedly. For example, a team that lacks focus on learning and development may do an about-face after they tire of losing frequently. Such a quick change would be consistent with the notion of *phase transitions*—when a system rapidly changes how it behaves and appears very different. A classic example of this characteristic is the way pure water can be observed as solid ice, liquid water, or gaseous steam—yet it is the same thing, fundamentally. This framing can help us understand (and even expect) that the same team of players and coaches may enact very different motivational climate behaviors and perceptions if conditions around them change.

Just before and during a phase transition, the equations and expectations describing how a system or group behaves are no longer accurate and what worked before may no longer apply. Around such phase transitions we might expect to see some instability; the phase transition between a fixed and cyclical attractor will typically return to a stable state, but if the system becomes increasingly unstable, another attractor may be present, which is captured by the notion of chaos. If the system undergoes a phase transition to a chaotic state, then the system itself becomes disorganized and unstable to the point that its behavior is inherently unpredictable, and it will remain so as long as the volatility continues. For example, violent disturbances in air and water cause turbulent air flows, and the system remains in a chaotic attractor state until the flow of fluid slows down (cf. Guastello & Liebovitch, 2009). Imagine, for a moment, what kind of overstimulating or overstressful conditions might put a team's motivational climate into such a chaotic attractor state. Could such a thing happen? How could we detect and measure it?

As the conditions upholding an attractor state change, sometimes it becomes possible to recognize that a system is becoming unstable, or disrupted. If a team has found a good configuration, such a situation can be undesirable (e.g., a player leaves or is injured). But likewise, sometimes coaches may choose to deliberately introduce instability (e.g., by changing the focus of training, or what is recognized and rewarded). A dominant player might be benched to encourage other players to grow as leaders, or practice games might introduce challenging worst-case scenarios to teach a team how to adapt, as well as how to enact their normal or preferred tactics. Such changes would alter the goal structures of the motivational climate, and while the system may fall back to the most favored attractor state, seeking out such disruptions describes how a social system might be destabilized and moved into a new configuration (Guastello & Liebovitch, 2009).

In expressing how these characteristics come about—and recognizing that it is difficult if not impossible to dependably introduce intervention X to achieve outcome Y—the term *emergence* is used to describe how patterns and configurations of a system take shape. Sometimes a substantial effort to generate change can achieve very little, and other times a seemingly small change can see a whole system or team change behavior. If the patterns are not easily controlled or even predictable, then they might be said to emerge. This term also reflects the observation that even very simple interacting agents, such as the birds in a starling murmuration—following very simple rules such as "minimize the distance to the nearest other bird"—can still generate higher properties, such as the fluid shapeshifting seen in such murmurations. Many parents will have seen similar behavior in young soccer players, amassing around the ball and not spreading out to exploit the space. Emergence arises when a system exhibits behaviors or patterns from the interaction between elements that otherwise do not exist among the elements themselves. As such, emergence is a fundamental component of complex systems and is dependent on the interactivity and synergy of the elements within the system as well as with the environment. Emergence is the result of

- the actions of many individuals, interacting with each other;
- the history of individuals and their interactions;
- the complexity of said interactions (do they exchange a lot of information or a little, and in what ways?);
- any higher-level structures such as a team existing within a club, within a league, within a governing body; and
- the extent to which those higher structures influence the athletes and coaches as they interact (Guastello & Liebovitch, 2009).

Returning to metaphors we have used within this chapter, emergence helps us frame the ways that water vapor might combine with other elements within the environment to form a thunderstorm, or the way food ingredients combine to build flavors that cannot be experienced solely within the raw ingredients—including flavors that reflect different cooking processes. Asking athletes to classify their experiences into either performance or mastery climates precludes us from pursuing a deeper understanding of how those perceptions—and their likely consequences—can be generated. When we combine the notions of attractors with emergence, an additional property can be described denoting self-organization—which is to say that without necessarily having any structure enforced, a complex system (e.g., a group of children playing an informal game without adults or official equipment) will likely still self-organize—to define some aims, criteria for success, and recognition and reward structures (e.g., how points are scored). Indeed, this behavior can often be observed in school playgrounds around the world and in other systems focusing on unstructured play; it is even recognized as a pedagogical approach to physical education (Kinder et al., 2020). Notably, in such approaches, it is not the sporting or motor skills that are prioritized so much as the ability of learners to collaborate in negotiating rules, aims, and enforcement systems.

The final key term we consider here in mapping motivational climates onto a complex systems approach is *fractals*. Where a system, such as the social structures surrounding a sport team, can be understood at different levels of scale, the notion of fractals denotes that familiar patterns appear to repeat across those levels. Examples of fractal structures are found in many complex systems, such as the branches of a tree (from the tree trunk down to the support fibers on the leaves) or even within the cardiovascular system (i.e., the branching pattern of blood vessels from the aorta down to the capillaries) (Guastello & Liebovitch, 2009). One might argue, for example, that key concepts from our theories of motivation and motivational climate—concepts such as mastery, performance, empowerment, caring, and psychological need support—can be detected within momentary behaviors, situational conditions, and general perceptions of the climate, and indeed as global attributes of a sport, or all sport. In this way, we might assert that these constructs capture fractal patterns. For example, in the meteorological model (figure13.1), these levels are adopted to offer an understanding of how momentary interactions combine to build a climate, a wider atmosphere. Repeated momentary behaviors accumulate to influence an individual athlete's perception, and they may also combine to set a group's collective memory of "how things are done on this team," or role modeling behavior for other coaches to follow. Similarly, achievement goal theory offers the same dichotomous conceptualization of achievement goals at all three levels: situational goal adoption, personal or trait goal orientation, and motivational climate: task or mastery versus ego or performance.

Where a system, such as the social structures surrounding a sport team, can be understood at different levels of scale, the notion of fractals denotes that familiar patterns appear to repeat across those levels.

Almost 30 years ago, and in a widely accepted framework, Vallerand (1997) specified that the same motivational construct exists at three levels: global (e.g., ever-present from the viewpoint of the actor, and usually taken to mean personality or traits), context (distinct spheres of activity, such as school, sport, relationships), and situational (the motivation experienced while engaged in an activity). In principle, global and contextual measures should be expected to exhibit temporal stability (potentially displaying test-retest reliability, for example), whereas situational measures should arguably not. One challenging aspect for us, as theorists and researchers, is that multiple repeating patterns or attributes can be observed across these varying levels (Guastello & Liebovitch, 2009): the mastery-performance distinction, the approach-avoidance distinction (Gómez-López et al., 2020; Morris & Kavussanu, 2008), the caring climate concept, the supporting versus thwarting of psychological needs, and the empowering nature of the climate—and undoubtedly more. Each property could be observed or involved in specific instances, in characterizing a team's broader climate or in considering the global motivationally relevant attributes of a sport, club, or organization. The nature of fractals is their self-similarity across these different scales (Guastello & Liebovitch, 2009). A key insight at this juncture is that fractals are another property of complex adaptive systems that are easily compatible with what we know about the social influences on athlete motivation, both resolving some tensions and also offering us opportunities and ideas for how to extend research in this topic area.

In the previous text, we considered motivational climate theory and research—and critiques of those—against the framework of complex systems. If the reader is convinced that a real motivational climate represents more than just a simplified perspective of the athlete's subjective perceptions, then an alternative approach is needed. So far, we have argued that a complex systems approach can accommodate the conceptual and ontological demands of this shift in thinking—by mapping what we know about motivational climate research against commonly recognized attributes of complex systems. But in order to benefit from this analysis and catalyze future research efforts, we need to offer solutions too: We can adapt research methods and analysis techniques from complex adaptive systems research to study the social processes determining an athlete's motivation.

Future Research Directions

Complexity is a well-recognized topic within science, and there is a range of methods and approaches to support its meaningful scientific study. Entire textbooks have been generated to help students and researchers understand how best to study complex systems (e.g., Fuchs, 2013; Miller & Page, 2009; Mitleton-Kelly et al., 2018). As Keegan (2019) and Hassmén and colleagues (2016) have argued, ignoring these developments and persisting with linear models—based around parsimonious concepts, normally distributed data, and the expectation of highly generalizable findings—is likely to involve more complex mental gymnastics than simply acknowledging that social interactions affecting motivation are complex. Even within the assumptions of general linear models, however, other methods such as objective measurement (not only subjective perceptions), longitudinal designs, pre- to post-test designs, and randomized controlled trials are all possible and may extend understanding of motivational climate (Harwood et al., 2015). But these have tended to be the source of challenging or inconsistent findings in motivational climate research (e.g., Keegan et al., 2009; Smith et al., 2015; Smith et al., 2007). We assert that these issues may reflect underlying complexity, and therefore methods that recognize the implications of complexity are needed.

Four Proposed Methods for Observing and Changing Complex Adaptive Systems

Chevance and colleagues (2020) articulated core considerations for making the transition to studying behavior change in a complex system. First, they prompted us to shift our thinking from low- to high-resolution behavioral assessments—such as from assessing generalized perceptions of momentary interactions (and yes, momentary perceptions). This shift enables the capturing of the potential dynamic nature of behaviors and their determinants, including their relative variability or stability over time, as well as the exploration of questions relating to spatial and temporal patterning. Frequent high-resolution sampling (i.e., taking small amounts of data from people but very often, over time) would permit greater insights as well as reduce the likelihood of erroneous conclusions due to the use of an inappropriate sampling frequency.

Second, they recommended a shift from group-only to group- and individual-level statistical inference: from seeking group-level analyses to considering patterns and trends for the individual, within the group. They argued that such a shift can facilitate fast, efficient, and cost-effective learning and also provide direct benefits to the person who provided the data (e.g., personal insights into how they are reacting; what works vs. what does not, for them personally)—remembering that research ethics often require us to articulate the clear benefit for the participants. Studying individual-level patterns also facilitates a deeper exploration of individual differences, beyond—for example—treating personality traits as covariates in a model or offering a regression coefficient for the particular moment the data were sampled. This shift also discourages us from assuming that a pattern observed at the group or average level applies to all individuals within it (see also Fisher et al., 2018; Hekler et al., 2019).

Third, Chevance and colleagues recommended a shift from narrative models (i.e., away from observing what we are able to detect about real people using available methods) to dynamic computational models (i.e., toward building synthetic models of the groups or people we seek to study, to see if we can first replicate observed patterns, and then eventually steer and control them—in the simulation, at least!). As well as reducing the burden placed on research participants, this shift would enable the development of formalized and more precise behavioral hypotheses, taking temporal, contextual, and individual aspects into account. Likewise, it would produce transparent theories that can be refuted, revised, or extended—not least because the models, code, and data could be shared, explored, and tested among research teams. Using computer models—or agent-based modeling—would also facilitate the testing of hypotheses that would otherwise be difficult to explore because of practical limitations (e.g., phenomena that unfold across the life span).

Finally, the team recommended a shift from static set-and-forget approaches to adaptive approaches continuously tuning interventions. Such a change would allow provision of the right type and intensity of support to individuals at the right time (ethically good), and the answering of complex questions such as what type of support works, in what circumstances, and for whom (see also Keegan et al., 2014b). Highly tailored support via digital tools (or a combination of computer and human support) is currently offered only through intensive involvement of practitioners and experts who may be able to offer immediate in situ feedback. However, shifting to the use of research methods that both assess and also feed back to the user would enable the development of innovative technologies to—over time—more consistently and efficiently deliver improved outcomes for the athletes.

Qualitative and Mixed Methods

We can start by considering options that are already familiar to sport and exercise psychology research. Qualitative research is now relatively commonplace in sport and exercise psychology (Poucher et al., 2020). While many quantitative studies necessitate simple or parsimonious assumptions in order to use typical measures and analysis techniques, many forms of qualitative research effectively reject that such assumptions can be justified for their particular research question. Sample research topics include understanding the experiences of unique individuals, diverse groups, and cultures (that could not be compared against norms developed using American and European samples) and—of course—questions pertaining to the construction, experience, and consequences of meaning in social groups. Qualitative data might include reflective interviews looking back at prior events, more immediate reflections after or even within sporting participation, observer ratings of events, and media and video files of competition and training. Qualitative researchers gather rich, in-depth data and apply various forms of bespoke—usually inductive—analysis to focus on the research question in hand. On occasion, qualitative data can be supplemented with quantitative metrics and analysis, and in reality, a large volume of unstructured quantitative data might still be approached using qualitative analysis—to characterize and explore rather than to accurately measure and compare (Anguera et al., 2017).

The unstructured and dense nature of qualitative data can be quite challenging to analyze, but understanding that one may be dealing with complexity may be illuminating.

The unstructured and dense nature of qualitative data can be quite challenging to analyze, but understanding that one may be dealing with complexity may be illuminating. Looking for recurrent patterns (fractals), stable states and processes (attractors), apparently causeless events and processes (emergence), and sudden shifts in the story (phase changes) can transform how one views and analyzes qualitative data. In a similar shift to what is recommended for quantitative studies, qualitative research can also adopt a longitudinal approach and follow participants through key developments and journeys such as persisting with a team for a long time, with different coaches or staff and the turnover of players coming and going (e.g., Cresswell & Eklund, 2007; Ryba et al., 2020). Indeed, following people through their journeys—using both qualitative and quantitative data—is strongly aligned with the next two recommendations: experience sampling methods and time series analysis.

Experience Sampling Methods

The experience sampling method (Larson & Csikszentmihalyi, 1983; Sather, 2014) is a relatively intensive longitudinal research method that involves asking participants to report on their thoughts, feelings, behaviors, and environment on multiple occasions over time (Bolger & Laurenceau, 2013). It can also go under other names, such as the daily diary method or ecological momentary assessment. Participants record information in the moment, in response to a prompt or cue such as an alarm, phone alert, or pager alert (Csikszentmihalyi & Larson, 2014). Responses can be logged in a paper diary or journal, in an app, or on a web page. The response format could take the form of validated psychometric scales, open-ended questions, voice and video notes, or anything else used to assess their condition in that place and time. Experience sampling studies can also be automated and refined using app-based technology (van der Krieke et al., 2016).

It is worth contrasting this approach against using similar measures to assess someone's experience, thoughts, attitudes, and so on *only once*, as is common in motivational climate research. A second notable point is that experience sampling is relatively widely used in clinical practice, offering the ability to assess exactly what each client needs to have monitored, at a time more relevant and proximal to key events and real-life experiences, and even able to feed directly into treatment outcomes (e.g., increasing self-awareness and personal insight—cf. Maher et al., 2018). As with qualitative data, there is no set widely approved method of analyzing this type of data, but instead the researcher is required to consider what question is being asked and what type of approach might provide a meaningful answer to that question.

Time Series Analysis

Once quantitative data have been collected over a sustained period of time, we can consider time series analysis to extract meaningful statistics and other characteristics of the data. Many of the methods used in time series analysis are based on, or at least comparable with, the more popular methods taught in psychology undergraduate classes. *Autocorrelation* examines the extent to which a measure correlates with itself over time and can reveal repeating patterns or the frequency of rhythms. *Cross-correlation* examines the associations between variables over time, searching for repeating patterns between two signals. Data can be compared before and after some important event or intervention, described as an *interrupted time series*. *Spectral analysis* searches across a spectrum or entire range—of time points, performance levels, or similar—to look for peaks and troughs in some other variable such as fatigue or motivation. And *wavelet analysis* searches the time series data for particular shapes of waves, by seeing where the mathematical function describing those waves becomes a good fit to the data (or not, of course!).

As a simple example, perhaps an athlete's motivation wanes through the course of a week and then increases as competition approaches. Over time that signal could be detected. Or perhaps it dips significantly after their session with one particular coach—again, that would be a shape of wave that could be defined and then searched for in the data. All of these, and more, are accessible analysis techniques, within striking distance of what we are taught in most psychology courses, but not currently applied to motivational climate research.

Idiographic Versus Nomothetic Approaches

Most research in sport and exercise psychology assumes a *nomothetic* approach: seeking to produce general statements and laws that generalize across contexts, to account for observed patterns. With a nomothetic approach, one conducts careful and systematic observation and experimentation to derive results that can be applied more broadly outside the realm of study. Researchers pursuing nomothetic research are likely to work with large survey data sets or other forms of statistical data and to conduct quantitative statistical analysis as their method of study: What works at time point A and with group X should generalize to also apply to time point B and group Y. While this may be applicable to many physical laws, social psychology is different. Motivational climate is different.

An *idiographic* method focuses on individual cases or events. A case here might refer to a person, a team, or an organization. When performing qualitative research, ethnographic researchers observe the minute details of their participants' everyday lives to develop a big picture of a specific group of people or community. Similar research methods can be used employing both nomothetic and idiographic assumptions. As an example, principal component analysis (also known as exploratory factor analysis) is commonly used to look for generalized patterns, capturing underlying latent variables and patterns that characterize the responses of an entire large group. The resulting model is an average of all involved; it does not accommodate outliers and exceptions very well (termed *R-technique*; Cattell, 1952). The same basic mathematics can be applied to time series data from a single individual to build a model of the factors this one person experiences over time, rather than an average model for all respondents at one specific time point (termed *P-technique*; Cattell, 1963). A study by Strohacker and colleagues (2021) suggested that P-technique may be more informative than R-technique when it comes to informing and refining training goals for individual exercisers.

Researchers applying P-technique factor analyses to psychometric personality data have also demonstrated that individual factor structures can be relatively diverse compared with generalized results uncovered using R-technique (Fournier et al., 2008, 2009; Wright et al., 2016), resulting in unique structural features termed *interpersonal signatures* (Fournier et al., 2009). Could there be any benefit to seeking out such intrapersonal signatures in motivational climate research? For example, could this approach help us understand why very similar coach behaviors affect athletes differently, or why the perceived motivational climate reported by athletes on the same team is so often fundamentally different (even more so than for athletes on different teams)?

Mathematical Modeling

Mathematical techniques exist to seek out and identify the attractor states discussed earlier. For example, Lichtenstein (2018) reviewed studies using *deterministic chaos theory* to identify attractors in time series analysis data. Such investigations have already been applied in psychology, particularly the organizational psychology of characterizing a group's structure (Meyer et al., 1993), dynamic states (Levie & Lichtenstein, 2010), or an optimal business model (Osterwalder & Pigeneur, 2010). Similarly, Cheng and Van de Ven (1996) and Van de Ven and colleagues (1999) identified phase transitions in an organization and developed an explanation for how these changes were caused. In sport this might look like the changes we observe as teams form, negotiate norms, and transition into coherent, smoothly functioning units—often appearing unrecognizable in the way they interact and anticipate each other during this time. The main change needed to enact such studies in motivational climate research is a shift from single time point cross-sectional data to a data sample covering at least 50 time points: frequent monitoring as detained in the experience sampling method (ESM). Similarly, mathematical models exist to help detect and describe fractals within a complex system (i.e., to detect self-similarity between levels of a system; cf. Abraham, 1995). Using this approach, Thomas and colleagues (2012) were able to detect similarities in the way urban areas develop in different regions of Europe. The algorithm for seeking fractals can also be approached qualitatively (e.g., by explicitly seeking similarities, metaphors, and resonances in how seemingly different system elements behave). This quickly connects to how the models of Vallerand (1997) and Keegan and colleagues (2014) for understanding motivation both describe resonances and consistencies across situational, contextual, and global levels. Seeking fractals can help us theorize about and build better models, once we know we are dealing with a complex system.

In a similar movement away from cross-sectional snapshots, we might consider the way optimal motivation and adaptive behaviors can spread through a sporting team. If, for example, members of a clique within the team are simultaneously experiencing introjected motivation (avoiding external disapproval, seeking external approval), they might also be more likely to act out: discouraging each other from exerting maximal effort, or self-handicapping (withholding effort to avoid looking bad if one fails). But what if one of this small group begins to experience more *identified* motivation (relating to internally held but learned values or contingencies), or even *integrated* regulation (relating to behaviors that have become so internalized they can be deemed to satisfy psychological needs)? Could their behavior be perceived by their peers as sufficient to alter their own perceptions of motivational climate, and thus (potentially) their own affect, goal adoptions, and values? Would this perhaps feed back toward the first player who changed and reinforce their own development? At what point would the whole clique tip over into being a positive influence on the whole team?

With different methods, assumptions, and statistics, we can study motivational climate much more effectively, in ways that may actually allow us to guide coaches on what behaviors would work best, with which athletes, in what circumstances.

As before, there are methods for detecting this positive feedback effect, which is another component of complex adaptive systems, better known as *feedback loops*. In an open feedback loop, in its simplest form, if one athlete "infects"—on average—more than one other athlete with their positive (or negative) motivational regulation, we would observe *exponential growth*. Exponentials—either skyrocketing growth or its opposite, diminishing returns—are common in the study of complex systems; they are easily detected, of course, and are the reason logarithms are useful in mathematics. Exponentials—*power laws*—also give rise to common heuristic laws and rules such as the famous 80:20 rule—that 80% of benefit comes from 20% of the effort. Over time, researchers in complex systems have compared the benefit of using Gaussian distributions (normal bell curves) with Paretian distributions (exponential curves), finding that exponential patterns are a better fit for many social systems (which a motivational climate arguably is—e.g., Andriani & McKelvrey, 2009; Crawford et al., 2015). With different methods, assumptions, and statistics, we can study motivational climate much more effectively, in ways that may actually allow us to guide coaches on what behaviors would work best, with which athletes, in what circumstances.

There is another perhaps even more left-field option, however: In some cases we may not even need to take up the time and effort of kind participants volunteering their time in order to learn something about their motivation. Researchers in adjacent fields of research have become adept at building computer models that can predict how a system of things might behave: in this case a team, sport, game, or season. *Agent-based modeling* involves attempting to synthetically replicate aspects of how a group or system acts by encoding rules into agents—sometimes different rules, such as coach rules versus player rules, or workers versus bosses—and then allowing a computer to play out how these agents interact. For example, simulated starling murmurations—which famously achieve elegant, seemingly coordinated patterns—have been shown to work by programming each agent with only three rules: (1) Nearby birds would move farther apart, (2) birds would align their direction and speed, and (3) more distant birds would move closer (Reynolds, 1987). Several such models using agents to generate a simulation of a bigger system have been created and refined, enabling important insights into how human systems not only behave but also shift between patterns of behavior (Carley, 1999; Carley and Hill, 2001; Davis et al., 2007).

Lichtenstein (2018) noted that because they are easier to implement (no need for human ethics, no recruitment, no dropout), easier to report transparently (open data, open models, easily inspected by reviewers), and easier to replicate, agent-based models may also be easier to publish than longitudinal studies of real people. Such an approach may allow researchers to investigate motivationally harmful behaviors—such as stern criticism, aggression, or abuse—without breaching ethical imperatives to not harm people (because there are no people affected—it's a computer model). The beauty of agent-based modeling is that it uses emergence, which is the basis of complexity in that simple individual behavior can lead to complex group behavior. Emergence is difficult to observe in real time in many circumstances because of the sheer scale of time and complexity. Through agent-based modeling, we can observe how an agent (e.g., an athlete) might behave in response to different types of motivation based on the amount of influence a coach, a parent, or a random spectator has on that agent's own motivation. From a simple rule-governing interaction of this agent among others, such as teammates or opponents, we can then observe how motivational climate is influenced through the evolution of a sports game as it plays out.

Practical Implications

The section Four Proposed Methods for Observing and Changing Complex Adaptive Systems offers advice on how to steer change in light of recognizing that social interactions are complex. The central practical implication of acknowledging complexity in motivational climates is that coaches and practitioners must move away from expecting clear golden rules. Almost every strategy or behavior we might recommend could be nullified by a change in circumstances, or reframed by shifts in the accompanying, preceding, or following events. That sounds pessimistic perhaps, but humans already navigate this uncertainty every day in normal social interactions. Instead, there are guiding principles that steer our attempts to motivate athletes, and there are clear dashboard indicators of motivation such as attention, energy, effort, and enjoyment. Armed with that knowledge and awareness, combined with a change in expectation that we are only influencing and not definitively determining motivation, coaches and practitioners may be better able to navigate the complexity that is inherent in social interactions—including motivational climates.

Summary

Motivational climate research has been characterized on several occasions since approximately 2008 (at least) as having reached a plateau. The pattern of findings reported in the systematic review of Harwood and colleagues (2015) persists and indeed changes very little with the addition of new studies. With some exceptions, the measurement tools used to assess motivational climate are both small in number and also have not evolved over time (Lacerda et al., 2021). The tendency to use these psychometric measures to measure one-off cross-sectional perceptions and correlate them has also changed little; but they also present limitations on how much we can learn about motivational climate—and how useful it is (Hassmén et al., 2015). This chapter briefly reviewed those findings but has not labored that point because they are already well described in other chapters and reviews.

The main argument against diversifying the concepts, methods, and analysis techniques we deploy to study motivational climate is that the concept refers only to the subjective perceptions of the athletes, not the objective reality, and then these perceptions are to be understood only in terms of parsimonious models. Effectively, under that viewpoint, if we want to study these phenomena another way, we must call it something else—and to this end the terms *motivational atmosphere* (global system) and *motivational conditions* (immediate situations) have also been offered (cf. Keegan et al., 2014b). Where researchers have used other methods, such as systematic observation systems, randomized controlled trials, or qualitative methods, the findings regarding motivational climate have failed to consistently align with the parsimonious frameworks and underlying assumptions. Athletes of the same coach perceive a different climate, and perceptions of athletes do not associate to the observers' independent reports.

To resolve these difficulties, researchers have started unpacking the way motivational climate is generated, perceived, and managed—especially using qualitative methods. Those studies suggest that the social systems and interactions that affect athlete motivation are complex: Specifically, they are complex adaptive systems. Fortunately, complexity is a rapidly evolving field of science, with appropriate and developing methods for studying complex phenomena. If the reader is convinced that perhaps the motivational climate is, indeed, a complex adaptive system, then the methods introduced herein may offer a more fruitful and enriching way forward for both researching and also simply understanding motivational climate.

DISCUSSION QUESTIONS

1. Describe what comprises a motivational climate.
2. Reflecting on your own experiences in sport, describe a time when a team or group you worked with generated the best motivational climate you've experienced. What about the worst? Can you tease out some key differences between them?
3. Compare two leading models or theories of motivational climate, and establish their respective pros and cons.
4. What are the strengths and weaknesses of research on motivational climate? Do the studies exhibit certain trends or tendencies in their methods, and what might be the risks of these?
5. Develop a study to take the motivational climate in sport literature forward—what would be your research question(s) and methodology?
6. Outline what interventions can be employed to develop an optimal motivational climate and how they bring about enhanced experiences for the athletes within them.

PART
IV

Key Social and Cognitive Processes in Sport

Following from the previous part exploring the social influences on motivation, this part extends similar consideration to the social determination of other experiences and perceptions central to sport psychology. The social psychology of sport encompasses a wide range of topics, including social support, efficacy beliefs, stress, emotion regulation, mental health, team cohesion, and the question of what represents effective coaching. In this part, our expert contributors examine these important topics; their close dependence on, and emergence within, social interactions and phenomena; and their impact on athletes and performance.

In chapter 14, Influence of Social Support on Athletes, Chris Hartley and Pete Coffee explore the crucial role that social support plays in enhancing athlete well-being and performance. They discuss the main theoretical approaches to studying social support as well as recent trends in this research topic within sport, giving consideration to the impact of experiencing social support on athlete performance, motivation, confidence, and behavior. An important distinction is explored between receiving social support versus what is perceived by the recipient, and the different findings these two forms of support generate. The ways social support can be enacted and then experienced, and the subsequent consequences of perceiving social support, are unpacked, with the inclusion of a model for helping to plan and monitor or review social support within a team. The model is designed to inform future applied work and research that evaluates applied interventions.

In chapter 15, Efficacy Beliefs Within Relational and Group Contexts in Sport, Mark Beauchamp, Colin Wierts, and Ben Jackson provide readers with a contemporary update on research regarding how the social environment can influence athletes' efficacy beliefs. While *self-efficacy* is a term often used synonymously with *confidence*—an attribute highly prized in sport and many other achievement settings—the chapter considers multiple forms of efficacy: regarding one's role, one's team, the quality of coaching, and more. The authors explore how beliefs about one's ability to perform within the context of the team and with others can both be influenced through social interaction, and also the flow-on, effects on athletes' experience, cognitions, and behavior—including performance. From there, readers are provided with the authors' expert summaries of the current best applied recommendations for supporting athletes' efficacy beliefs in sport.

In chapter 16, Stress, Coping, Emotion, and Emotion Regulation in Sport, Katherine Tamminen and Faye Didymus examine the links between social influences—such as relationship, feedback, and authority structures—and athletes' experiences of stress and coping during athletic performance. Reflecting centuries of claims that sport develops character, the authors explore the potential for the social context in sport to teach and reinforce strategies athletes may use to cope and to regulate their emotions. After reviewing contemporary theory and research in stress and coping, the authors provide insights into how researchers study the social influences on stress and coping in sport, and offer the latest advice for how coaches, managers, and parents may support better coping, less stress, and better experiences through sport.

In chapter 17, Psychosocial Aspects of Mental Health in Sport, Paul Gorczynski, Cindy Miller Aron, and Claudia Reardon explore the risks, protective factors, and contemporary approaches for supporting mental health in sport. The authors examine the importance of promoting mental health in athletes and the psychosocial factors that contribute to mental health in sport. The strategy of promoting mental health literacy across entire teams and organizations is a particular focus, and ways of achieving this by working together with diverse coaches and support staff feature in the applied recommendations contained within this chapter.

In chapter 18, Team Cohesion, Mark Eys, Shauna Burke, and Mark Beauchamp delve into the ways that research conceptualizes, studies, and attempts to steer team cohesion and its impact on athletic performance. The chapter explores the factors that contribute to team cohesion and how cohesion can be fostered and developed within teams. As well as pausing to consider some potential pitfalls of focusing too much, or inappropriately, on cohesion, the authors use their extensive expertise to synthesize the literature in this topic, offering future research directions and up-to-date best evidence recommendations for applied practice in sport settings.

Finally in chapter 19, Coaching Effectiveness in Youth Sport, Jean Côté, Caroline Hummell, Leisha Strachan, and Jessica Fraser-Thomas explore the important role that coaches play in enhancing athlete development and performance. Using a system approach to capture the concepts and determinants of effective coaching research, they examine the various coaching styles, strategies, and practices that have been shown to be effective in youth sport and provide insights into how coaches can enhance their effectiveness. After reviewing and synthesizing this body of literature, the authors offer guidance for how future research can meaningfully extend this literature and reflect on the current best practice recommendations for optimizing coaching effectiveness in youth sport settings.

14

Influence of Social Support on Athletes

Chris Hartley, PhD, and Pete Coffee, PhD

LEARNING OBJECTIVES

On completion of this chapter, the reader should have the following:

- Critical understanding of social support and its role in the sport environment
- Understanding and synthesis of contemporary findings about the influence of social support on athletes
- Understanding of the main theoretical perspectives and models that explain how social support operates
- Understanding of the issues and opportunities related to the investigation and measurement of social support
- Awareness of avenues for future research directions and implications for applied practice

Elsewhere in this book, readers will have learned extensively about the vital roles of relationships in sport (see part I), leadership behaviors (see part II), and the considerable impact that an empowering, caring, and holistic sport climate and environment can have on athletes (see part III). In this chapter, we explore how these important topics reflect the art of supporting people—the socially supportive relationships, actions, and resources that are exchanged and available from others within the sport environment.

Social support is essential to the fabric of sport. Indeed, in recent years the sporting world has increasingly asked whether the support provided for the health, well-being, and performance of athletes is appropriate or optimal. An increasing number of news stories and empirical research studies are reporting that athletes who fail to develop interests and careers outside of sport are struggling with mental health concerns, cultures of abuse, and the social stigma associated with speaking up and asking for help when they most need it. Occasionally, the presence of harmful support may not only lead to poor performance among athletes but may even *increase* levels of stress, burnout, or even dropout from sport altogether. As such, a lack of social support—or even the presence of ineffective support—may contribute to a range of undesirable physical and psychological outcomes in sport.

Consequently, researchers, practitioners, and sport organizations have been working to better understand how they can adequately and effectively safeguard and support the mental health (e.g., Henriksen et al., 2020; Moesch et al., 2018; Reardon et al., 2019; Schinke et al., 2017), dual career progression (e.g., Hong & Coffee, 2018; Knight et al., 2018), and holistic welfare of their athletes more generally (e.g., Sly et al., 2020). As we will see, this burgeoning and important area—the socially supportive relationships, actions, and resources from others—underpins all the preceding concerns. We argue that a better understanding of how we can help and support others in sport is pivotal to the roles of coaches, teammates, parents, sport science practitioners, sport organizations, and more generally anyone involved in sport.

The purpose of this chapter is to introduce readers to the influence of social support on athletes. The chapter starts with an introduction to the concept of social support, its constituent components, and its underpinning dimensions, along with a synthesis of available empirical evidence of its observed effects in sport. We then provide an overview of the main theoretical approaches to explain how social support operates and examine the mixed evidence for and against these theoretical perspectives. The chapter then moves on to a discussion of ways to investigate and measure social support, followed by an overview of future directions for research. Based on the preceding content, the chapter finishes with a discussion of implications for applied practice.

Theory and Research

Over the past 50 years of research across psychology (e.g., Burleson & MacGeorge, 2002; Cohen & Wills, 1985; Lane & Fink, 2015; Moss, 1973; Thoits, 1995), social support has come to be regarded as a core component of interpersonal relationships and can even be considered a key resource for health and well-being (Cohen, 2004; Cohen et al., 2000; Liu et al., 2016; Uchino, 2004, 2009). In sport, social support is a principal variable related to performance and well-being in athletes (Aitchison et al., 2021; Bianco & Eklund, 2001; Chen, 2013; Connaughton et al., 2008; Kristiansen & Roberts, 2010; Rees, 2016; Rees & Hardy, 2000). For instance, perceptions of social support have been associated with the following:

- Superior performance (Freeman & Rees, 2008, 2009; Gillet et al., 2009; Rees & Freeman, 2010; Rees et al., 2007)
- Self- and collective efficacy (Coffee et al., 2017; Rees & Freeman, 2009)
- Self-confidence (Freeman et al., 2011; Freeman & Rees, 2010; Holt & Hoar, 2006; Rees & Freeman, 2007)
- Flow (Bakker et al., 2011; Rees & Hardy, 2004; Rees et al., 1999)
- More effective self-talk behaviors (Zourbanos et al., 2011)
- Improved training adherence (Way et al., 2012)
- Self-determined motivation and behaviors (Alvarez et al., 2009)

Researchers also consider social support to play a preventative or protective role in sport, because it is associated with a reduced risk for injury (Bianco, 2001; Carson & Polman, 2012), cognitive interference (Hatzigeorgiadis & Biddle, 2000; Sarason et al., 1983; Sarason & Sarason, 1986), burnout (Defreese & Smith, 2013, 2014; Hartley & Coffee, 2019; Lu et al., 2016; Shang & Yang, 2021), and poor career transitions (Park et al., 2013; Willard & Lavallee, 2016).

Despite the accumulation of survey-based evidence for the beneficial effects of social support in sport, readers may also identify with potential detrimental effects (e.g., from support that is unsolicited, poorly timed, or inappropriate). Indeed, the methods typically used in this type of research tend to average out peoples' experiences and can overlook unique moments and events (cf. Hassmén et al., 2016). Consider a basketball player who is practicing her jump shot—which she finds challenging—only to have her coach or fellow teammate, with good intentions, stop play and draw the whole team's attention to what she is "doing wrong." Ineffective social support has, as such, been shown by researchers to undermine goal pursuit, draw attention to one's incompetence, and damage self-esteem (e.g., Bolger & Amarel, 2007; Fitzsimons & Finkel, 2011; Gleason et al., 2008; Rafaeli & Gleason, 2009).

Qualitative researchers have also indicated it is possible to receive too much support in sport (Knight & Holt, 2014). Consider a lacrosse player who sustained a season-ending shoulder injury during a match. His parents and coaches might—understandably—try to console him by saying the injury looked really painful, telling him it was a shame his hard work during the off-season would not pay off because of the injury, and suggesting elaborate plans for his return to training to get "stronger and better than before." Is all this "support" welcomed?

Accordingly, in some situations, the experience of social support has been shown to worsen one's responses to injury, facilitate feelings of burnout, and increase the risk for dropout from sport (Gould et al., 1996; Sheridan et al., 2014; Udry et al., 1997). Findings like this highlight a paradox where social support can be both a facilitator and a barrier to managing challenges posed by the sport environment (Brock & Lawrence, 2009; Haslam et al., 2012; Kellezi & Reicher, 2012). To understand why these effects may occur and what constitutes effective social support, the following sections introduce ways in which we can define and understand social support as a construct.

Defining the Construct

Within the general and sport psychology literature, many theories acknowledge that social support is a complex construct—there are multiple ways to construe and define it (Veiel & Baumann, 1992). For the purposes of this text, however, social support is defined as the existence of socially supportive *relationships*, the supportive and helping *actions* associated with those relationships, and/or the exchange of physical and/or psychological *resources* intended to benefit the individual (Lakey, 2010; Rees, 2016). We can see how this definition relates to the structural quantity and quality of relationships within one's network and how extensively integrated one is within them. We can also see how the supportive actions and resources provided and perceived to be available from these networks serve particular functions. For example, support recipients may experience different degrees of satisfaction and/or stress reduction with different types of socially supportive behaviors or providers (e.g., emotional support from a parent, such as hugs and reminders of being cared for, and tangible forms of support from a national governing body, such as transportation or financial remuneration) (Cohen, 1988; Cohen et al., 2000). We now break down and conceptualize these components of social support—namely, the structural component of social integration and the functional components of perceived and received support.

Social Integration

The structural component of social support can be thought of as the framework of social relationships that athletes are connected to—the mere existence and number of social interconnections in their social support network (Cohen, 1988; Holt & Hoar, 2006). For example, this network may refer to the multiple teams an athlete is a member of (e.g., both regional and national squads), their personal relationships, and the multidisciplinary support team they are embedded within. To date, *social integration* has been assessed in terms of the number of relationships and groups an athlete belongs to, the degree to which they engage with those relationships, and their perceived integration within those relationships (e.g., how embedded they *feel* within their groups; Brisette et al., 2000; Stroebe & Stroebe, 1996).

Social support is defined as the existence of socially supportive relationships, the supportive and helping actions associated with those relationships, and/or the exchange of physical and/or psychological resources intended to benefit the individual.

Evidence suggests that being highly socially integrated has many health and well-being benefits (Haslam et al., 2016), including enhanced resistance to disease and lower levels of anxiety and depression (Cohen et al., 1997; Cohen & Wills, 1985; Cruwys et al., 2014). Having a higher number of support providers in sport has also been associated with having fewer injuries (Anderson & Williams, 1999; Covassin et al., 2014). Indeed, the number of groups we are a part of *and* the degree to which we are socially integrated within them have both been associated with longer living and protective benefits against risk factors such as smoking and obesity (Berkman & Syme, 1979; Holt-Lunstad et al., 2010)—yet many individuals tend to underestimate the importance of social integration (Haslam et al., 2018).

As might be becoming clear from this text, however, the *mere existence* of socially supportive relationships does not necessarily equate to receiving any supportive or helping actions nor, indeed, the physical and psychological resources associated with them (Burleson & MacGeorge, 2002). Consider how, for example, teammates or family members offer different support (both in quantity and quality) to athletes when they need it. Indeed, qualitative researchers have reported that the presence of certain coaches may impair, rather than benefit, an athlete's performance (Kristiansen & Roberts, 2010). As such, there is clearly a distinction between the mere *existence* of social ties versus the particular *functions* served by those social ties (Burleson & MacGeorge, 2002), which is explored next.

Received Support

In contrast to social integration, we can imagine that many athletes—despite having a large selection of supportive others available—will likely engage with a select few of those supportive relationships that attend to their needs. *Received support* refers to the *experience* of receiving help and support from one's friends, family, teammates, and coaches (to name a few) (Rees & Freeman, 2010). For example, an injured athlete may require help and support from several sources including their medic, physiotherapist, family, and friends, as well as their sport's national governing body (Bianco & Eklund, 2001). However, athletes may differ in their perception of how helpful the supportive actions from a support provider are (e.g., because of their perceived competence) (Coussens et al., 2015). In this regard, received support more specifically refers to a recipient's unique *perception* of a supportive act (e.g., "I think he helped me") (Sarason et al., 1990; Uchino, 2009), whereas—technically—*enacted* support refers to *manifest* supportive actions (i.e., a verifiable act of support; e.g., "He transported me to training") (Goldsmith, 2004). Similarly, athletes might receive *invisible support*—that which occurs in the background of which they are unaware (e.g., a travel coordinator booking flights and hotel rooms for away games) (Girme et al., 2013; Moll et al., 2017).

Within the literature, received support has come to be regarded as a mixed blessing. On the one hand, higher levels of received support have been associated with better golf performance (Rees & Freeman, 2009; Rees et al., 2007), self-confidence (Freeman et al., 2014; Rees & Freeman, 2007), use of self-talk (Zourbanos et al., 2011), enhanced recovery from hardship and injury (Mitchell et al., 2014; Wadey et al., 2012), and positive beliefs about adolescent sport (Lubans et al., 2011). On the other hand, received support has also been associated with exacerbating burnout in sport (Hartley & Coffee, 2019) and increasing risk of dropout in youth sport (Sheridan et al., 2014). The contrasting effects of received support on outcomes in sport may be due to receivers' interpretations of acts of support or their relationships with providers of support. For example, some athletes may interpret support received from coaches, parents, and peers as pressure to perform. Others may experience a reduced sense of accomplishment or exhaustion if support is provided by someone they dislike, if it is unsolicited, or if it simply fails to address the needs of the situation. In sum, in both the general (Gleason et al., 2008; Rafaeli & Gleason, 2009) and sport psychology literatures, received support has shown both positive and negative associations with outcome variables (Boat & Taylor, 2015; Freeman & Rees, 2008, 2009; Lakey & Orehek, 2011; Rees & Freeman, 2007; Rees & Hardy, 2004).

Evidence suggests that, compared with received support, higher levels of perceived support are more consistently associated with beneficial effects on outcomes in sport.

Perceived Support

Finally, *perceived support* refers to the perception that support is available *if and when needed*. For example, simply knowing a coach *could* help if an athlete needed technical guidance on their golf swing might be enough to prevent the athlete from experiencing stress when out on the course—without the athlete's actually receiving any support (Madden et al., 1989; Sarason et al., 1990). Evidence suggests that, compared with received support, higher levels of perceived support are more consistently associated with beneficial effects on outcomes in sport (Rees, 2016; Rees & Hardy, 2004). For instance, higher levels of perceived support are consistently associated with improved performance (Boat & Taylor, 2015; Freeman & Rees, 2008, 2009), higher flow states (Bakker et al., 2011), challenge appraisals (Freeman & Rees, 2009), higher resilience scores (Sarkar & Fletcher, 2014), higher levels of self-confidence (Freeman et al., 2011; Freeman & Rees, 2010; Rees & Freeman, 2007), and lower levels of burnout (Defreese & Smith, 2014; Hartley & Coffee, 2019; Lu et al., 2016; Shang & Yang, 2021).

Critical Synthesis of Received and Perceived Support

The empirical evidence in both sport and general psychology suggests that perceived support is more consistently associated with beneficial outcome variables (Freeman & Rees, 2008, 2009), whereas the effects of received support can be more mixed (or even unhelpful; Abgarov et al., 2012; Defreese & Smith, 2013; Hartley & Coffee, 2019; Haslam et al., 2017; Knight & Holt, 2014). It is inconclusive as to why these different effects have been observed in the literature to date. Tentative explanations for these equivocal findings might be that one's *perceptions* of social support availability are based on cognitive abstractions (i.e., a perception that may or may not align directly with manifest and enacted support provision). These perceptions of support may also be influenced by other factors—lower levels of distress or self-esteem might negatively influence the beneficial impact of perceived support, for example (Girme et al., 2013; Marigold et al., 2014). In contrast, judgments about received support may be made more instantaneously in context (Sarason et al., 1990), meaning received support may therefore fail to meet the demands of the situation by not living up to one's expectations and perceptions of support (Haslam et al., 2017; Rees & Freeman, 2010; Sarason & Sarason, 1986). It may also exceed them.

The existence of reciprocal effects between perceived and received support (Uchino, 2009) may also contribute to their observed differences, yet this has not been consistently examined in the literature. Specifically, our baseline perceptions of support may depend on our historic and ongoing experiences of receiving support. An athlete who is experiencing a persistent lack of support (low received support) against abuse in their sport may, over time, develop perceptions of low support availability; however, this same athlete could gain a lot from receiving appropriate support to decrease such abuse.

Another point to consider is that while perceived and received support are considered distinct constructs and show unique effects on a range of outcomes in both health and sport domains (e.g., Freeman & Rees, 2008; Lakey & Cohen, 2000; Rees & Freeman, 2007; Uchino, 2009), the degree of common variance observed between both can vary depending on the measures used (e.g., from 12% to 41% in some studies; Freeman & Rees, 2008; Haber et al., 2007; Hartley & Coffee, 2019). This suggests that, depending on the measure, there might be some overlap between the measurement of perceived and received support, making it hard to ascertain the extent of their uniqueness. As such, researchers need to be clear in how they conceptualize and measure social support to ensure distinct constructs (received vs. perceived) are being investigated: otherwise, such inconsistencies can occur and be difficult to explain or understand (Bianco & Eklund, 2001; Holt & Hoar, 2006).

Dimensions of Social Support

Looking back at our initial definition of social support (i.e., consisting of relationships, actions, and resources), we can see that social integration captures the more structural elements of social support relationships, while perceived and received support capture the more functional elements served by those relationships (i.e., the actions and resources; Cohen, 1988; Rees, 2016). In other words, rather than having a redundant number of structural social ties and relationships (which may or may not offer any beneficial actions and resources), it may be sufficient for an athlete to be integrated with a selection of *functional* relationships that provide for all their needed supportive actions and resources (Abgarov et al., 2012; Sanders & Winter, 2016). However, an additional angle from which we can examine social support is with regard to its specificity.

First, we can consider social support at broader, more general levels—for example, by investigating an athlete's *general* sense of being supported (e.g., overall, how much support is perceived to be available or how one would rate the overall satisfaction with, or quality of, support received). Indeed, several studies have reported high correlations among different types of supportive behaviors, and higher-order (more general) support factors are able to account for such correlations (Freeman et al., 2011, 2014; Sarason et al., 1990). Second, we can also consider social support at narrower, more specific levels—for example, by investigating *specific* helping behaviors by asking, "How often did someone make you feel loved and cared for?" (emotional support). In this regard, social support can be grouped under four distinct categories of supportive behaviors (also called dimensions) (Cutrona & Russell, 1990; Rees & Hardy, 2000).

Because of the unique demands and resources posed by different environments, the precise wording of social support dimensions is noted to differ between domains of psychology. Within sport, Rees and Hardy (2000) interviewed elite-level athletes and identified the following support dimensions as being relevant to the sport environment: emotional, esteem, informational, and tangible. While these dimensions have been increasingly adopted in the sport literature (e.g., Coffee et al., 2017; Freeman et al., 2011, 2014), the relevance of dimensions might vary across subgroupings (e.g., across sports, cultures, or competitive levels; Aitchison et al., 2021) or simply be labeled differently. *Emotional support* refers to the provision of comfort and security (e.g., causing an athlete to know they are loved and cared for). *Esteem support* refers to attempts made at bolstering and reassuring a sense of competence. *Informational support* refers to guidance and instruction (e.g., regarding failures and performance slumps, as well as technical issues with training and competition). Finally, *tangible support* refers to concrete instrumental assistance, where resources and conditions necessary for athletic functioning are facilitated (e.g., financial support, transportation to and from training venues; Cutrona & Russell, 1990; Rees & Hardy, 2000; Rees et al., 2007).

While some unique associations have been found between individual dimensions of support and outcome variables such as self-confidence, performance, and dimensions of burnout (Freeman et al., 2011, 2014; Freeman & Rees, 2009; Lu et al., 2016; Rees & Freeman, 2007; Rees & Hardy, 2004), these dimensional effects are somewhat inconsistent and contradictory (Hartley & Coffee, 2019)—some dimensions have been found to have both effective *and* ineffective influences on the same outcome across independent samples. Theoretical explanations for why these dimensional effects may occur are offered through considering optimal matching and provider–recipient factors (explained in the next section). Simply, for support to be effective, it may need to be matched to the demands and stressors of a situation and be provided by an appropriate individual.

Principal Theoretical Frameworks for How Social Support Operates

While there is no single established theory of how social support operates, many theoretical approaches have been derived from social, motivational, developmental, and cognitive frameworks (summarized in Lakey & Cohen, 2000; Sheridan et al., 2014). In sport, three of the most prominent theoretical models for how social support operates are grounded in theories of stress and coping (e.g., Lazarus, 1999; Lazarus & Folkman, 1984; Meijen et al., 2020)—largely because stress plays an inherent role in the sport environment, and social support has the potential to lessen the negative effects of stress (e.g., Gallagher et al., 2021). In this regard, social support may help athletes thrive in the presence of stress, yet it may also be ineffective or even be the source of stress (e.g., when it is poorly matched to the demands posed by environmental stressors) (Cutrona & Russell, 1990; Gustafsson et al., 2017; Sarkar & Fletcher, 2014). We therefore start this section with an overview of stress and coping perspectives (further elaborations on stress and coping in social settings can be found in chapter 16).

The transactional model of stress (Cohen & Wills, 1985; Lazarus & Folkman, 1984) suggests that the presence of perceived support intervenes directly during the primary appraisal of stressors (i.e., to help decide "Is this a *threat* or a *challenge* for me?") (Cohen et al., 2000; Lazarus, 1999). It is therefore posited that perceived support is of primary relevance to the main effects model (explained shortly). Building on this, the transactional stress and coping perspective suggests the intervention of *both* perceived and received support may be needed to buffer the effects of stress actually experienced. This may be achieved by, for example, bolstering one's perceived capabilities and resources to cope with potential threats during secondary stress appraisal (i.e., to help decide "Can I cope with this stress?") (Bianco & Eklund, 2001; Lazarus & Folkman, 1984). More recently, stress and coping perspectives of social support have been informed by the revised theory of challenge and threat states in athletes (Meijen et al., 2020), which places emphasis on the degree to which challenge and threat states are facilitated by psychosocial coping resources (such as perceived support) during stress reappraisal. For example, an athlete might rightly perceive a stressor—such as being deselected—to be threatening; but knowing their coach and teammates will keep them included in team training and activities might lead to better situational congruence with their desired goal states, thereby helping the athlete see the threat as being surmountable and thus facilitating a challenge state.

Main Effects Model

The effects of social support in sport may typically be demonstrated through a statistical main effect of social support on outcomes—thereby also being referred to as direct effects (Cohen et al., 2000; Cohen & Wills, 1985). In other words, the main effects model proposes social support to have a direct effect on outcomes, irrespective of whether an individual is under high or low levels of stress (see figure 14.1) (Bianco & Eklund, 2001; Cohen & Wills, 1985; Freeman & Rees, 2010). For example, the mere belief that an athlete's teammates are on hand to provide support if needed may be enough to decrease feelings of burnout in sport (Hartley & Coffee, 2019; Shang & Yang, 2021). Perceived support is more consistently associated with main effects compared with received support in this regard (Cohen et al., 2000; Freeman et al., 2011; Freeman & Rees, 2008, 2009, 2010; Rees & Hardy, 2004).

FIGURE 14.1 In the main effects model, social support has a direct effect on outcomes.

The dominant method of statistical analysis used for identifying and explaining main effects may have led to the adoption of main effects as a named model of social support. As such, while the model may offer practical insights into the direct benefits of social support, its explanatory utility may be somewhat lacking since it does not elaborate on the mechanisms responsible for those direct effects. Although the mechanisms underpinning social support's effects are somewhat inconclusive, researchers assert that social support exerts its beneficial main effects through a range of cognitive, emotional, behavioral, and physiological mechanisms (Cohen et al., 2000; Lakey & Cohen, 2000; Lane & Fink, 2015). This is somewhat captured by the stress prevention model (a similar pathway that is not mutually exclusive from the main effects model) (Barrera, 1986), where the main effects of social support may be exerted through a range of mediating variables—for example, an enhanced sense of situational control, self-esteem, self-efficacy, or mental toughness, or by facilitating flow states and motivation (Bakker et al., 2011; Cohen et al., 2000; Freeman & Rees, 2009; Rees & Freeman, 2009; Shang & Yang, 2021; Thoits, 2011). Coping styles have also been shown to partially mediate the effects of social support on well-being indicators (Liu et al., 2016). Importantly, however, the main effects model fails to account for the influence that high or low levels of stress may have on the effects of social support, for which we now turn to a discussion of the stress-buffering model.

Stress-Buffering Model

Further drawing on the stress and coping perspective, Bianco and Eklund (2001) argued that when a stressor is deemed to be stressful (i.e., when the environmental demands outweigh available coping resources), both perceived support and received support are likely needed to intervene and assist with successful coping. As such, the stress-buffering model suggests that the effects of social support on outcomes are related to the levels of stress being experienced (see figure 14.2). In other words, researchers have suggested that higher levels of social support might be more beneficial for individuals under higher levels of stress (the support therefore buffers the stress), whereas it may be less beneficial for those not experiencing stress (Cohen et al., 2000; Cohen & Wills, 1985).

Although both perceived and received support are theorized to act through the stress-buffering model (Bianco & Eklund, 2001), the empirical support for this model is mixed. Perceived support is more consistently associated with stress-buffering effects as well as main effects (Cohen et al., 2000; Freeman et al., 2011; Freeman & Rees, 2008, 2009, 2010; Rees & Hardy, 2004), while there is only limited evidence for received support to act as a stress buffer in sport (Hartley & Coffee, 2019; Mitchell et al., 2014; Rees & Freeman, 2007; Rees et al., 2007). A further limitation of the main and stress-buffering models is their failure to explain why social support may have neutral or even harmful effects (e.g., when it is poorly matched to the demands posed by environmental stressors) (Cutrona & Russell, 1990).

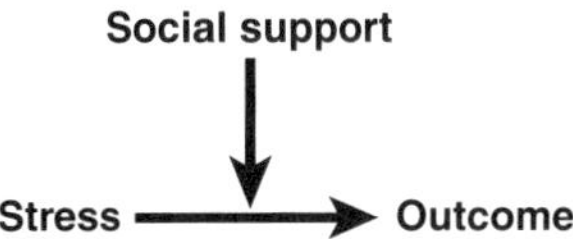

FIGURE 14.2 In the stress-buffering model, effects of social support on outcomes are related to the levels of stress being experienced.

Optimal Matching Model

Tied more specifically to the stress-buffering model, the optimal matching model (also referred to as a hypothesis) provides a theoretical means to explain when certain dimensional effects are observed and to specify the conditions needed for effective social support (Cutrona & Russell, 1990). Specifically, it is theorized that in order for social support to be effective and to achieve effective coping, specific dimensions of support need to be optimally matched to the demands posed by specific stressors (Cohen & McKay, 1984; Cohen & Wills, 1985; Cutrona & Russell, 1990). An optimal match may assist an athlete in successfully reducing their levels of stress and experiencing other support-related benefits (Berg & Upchurch, 2007; Holt & Hoar, 2006). Perceived controllability of the stressor plays an important role in this regard. Cutrona and Russell (1990) suggested that problem-focused coping (e.g., achieved through informational and tangible forms of support) may be best suited to controllable stressors because it may enhance one's ability to address the root cause of the problem. In contrast, emotion-focused coping (e.g., achieved through emotional and esteem forms of support) may be best suited to uncontrollable stressors because it may assist with emotional coping and recovery from the problem's consequences (Mitchell et al., 2014; Uchino, 2004). See figure 14.3 for a summary of the optimal matching model.

While the optimal matching hypothesis offers an appealing explanation for when stress buffering is likely to occur, it has also received mixed empirical support (Mitchell et al., 2014; Rees et al., 2007, 2010), possibly because the same dimensions of support can serve both divergent and convergent functions depending on the context (Burleson & MacGeorge, 2002). For example, most social support exchanges are likely to convey a combination of several dimensions of support rather than a singular dimension (e.g., carrying an athlete's kit bag while discussing tactics about the impending game might simultaneously provide esteem, informational, and tangible forms of support). Furthermore, while one dimension of support may be optimally matched to the demands of a stressor in one context, it may prove useless or even stressful in another. Nonetheless, the sentiment that support should be well matched to the demands of the situation is—in our appraisal—arguably valid and important (Burleson, 2003; Burleson & MacGeorge, 2002). In this regard, readers might be advised to sensitively tailor social support to the person in context as opposed to providing blanket social support irrespective of an athlete's particular needs and the salient context. Doing so may allow for a more optimal choice (e.g., over type of supportive behavior) and manner of support delivery by the provider, and thereby pave the way for more favorable interpretation of that support by the recipient.

As a final point, while the optimal matching hypothesis may explain when social support has neutral effects, it fails to explain how and why social support may have *harmful* effects (e.g., by being the source of stress) (Hartley et al., 2020; Kristiansen & Roberts, 2010), for which we turn our attention to provider–recipient factors.

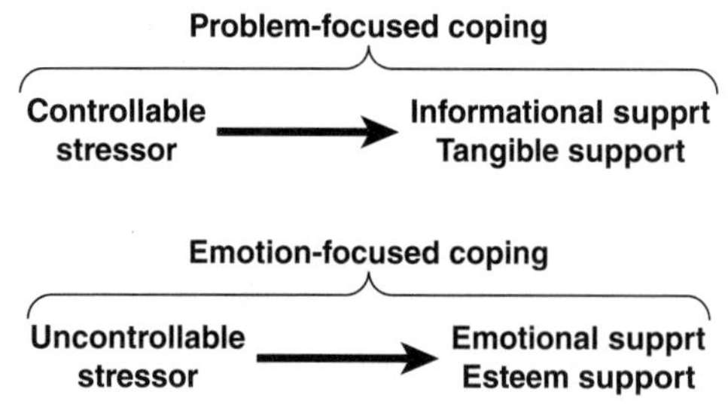

FIGURE 14.3 An example of an optimal match between stressor and social support dimensions, as based on Cutrona and Russell's optimal matching hypothesis (1990).

Provider–Recipient Factors

Several important provider–recipient factors influence the effectiveness of social support and may go some way toward explaining why empirical observations may (or may not) align with the aforementioned theoretical perspectives. First, the alignment or misalignment of provider and recipient *characteristics*—such as age, gender, rapport, mood, and perceived expertise—may influence the effectiveness of support (Bianco, 2001; Hassell, et al., 2010; Hayward et al., 2017; Judge et al., 2012; Kristiansen & Roberts, 2010). Although this is yet to be explicitly investigated and synthesized in the sport literature, it could be that perceived or actual provider–recipient characteristics influence the adequacy of support and satisfaction with it (e.g., Dehle et al., 2001). Compared with a coach, for example, a parent's lack of sport-specific expertise might mean they underprovide credible informational support while overproviding emotional forms of support to their child athlete. Consequently, this may mean the child athlete's sport-related needs are not met and they experience lower levels of satisfaction with support. These provider–recipient factors may also change over time (e.g., the support-related needs of younger athletes and their dependency on parental support may change as they get older) (Harwood & Knight, 2015; Hayward et al., 2017).

Second, the *manner* in which support is provided may have a potent influence on its effects, yet this is not captured by extant theoretical frameworks. For example, esteem support can be provided in verbal forms (e.g., saying, "Well done") and physical forms (e.g., a pat on the back)—and it is likely that one form may have a more beneficial impact than the other depending on context. Relatedly, the timing of when support is provided may have considerable impact. For instance, receiving unsolicited or prematurely timed support may undermine autonomy, be experienced as controlling, and contribute to feelings of incompetence (Bolger & Amarel, 2007). Conversely, receiving support after the need for it has passed may contribute to feelings of resentment, damage the degree of trust between provider and recipient, and contribute to perceptions of lower support availability in future (Uchino, 2009). As alluded to earlier, tactful support provision may also occasionally involve invisible social support, where something helpful is done without the athlete's awareness of it (Girme et al., 2013). For instance, Moll and colleagues (2017) demonstrated how esteem support was more effective when communicated visibly, whereas informational support was more effective when communicated invisibly.

Third, *group dynamics* and *shared social identities* have also been demonstrated to influence the observed effects of social support in sport (e.g., Levine et al., 2005; Nicholson et al., 2011; Slater et al., 2013). In this regard, the social identity approach—as specified by both social identity and self-categorization theories (Tajfel & Turner, 1979; Turner et al., 1987)—offers a theoretical perspective through which to conceptualize the influence of provider–recipient factors on social support. This approach posits that the groups we belong to—and the social identities that accompany membership of those groups—structure our experiences of social support in sport (e.g., "Do *we* have the support needed?" as opposed to "Do *I* have the support needed?") (Rees et al., 2015). Relatedly, social identities specify how group norms and cultures within the sport environment can shape social support and the way it is provided toward in-group members (favorably) versus out-group members (unfavorably) (Levine et al., 2005; Slater et al., 2013). Likewise, social identities may shape the types of support perceived to be desirable and effective for in-group members (e.g., Hartley et al., 2022; Nicholson et al., 2011), and this may differ between groups (e.g., emotional support may be deemed more acceptable and important for some sports, whereas other sports may value informational support more highly) (Haslam, 2004; Haslam et al., 1998). As such, the social identity approach offers a theoretical perspective to explain when, how, and why social support may be ineffective and even be the *source* of stress (e.g., partly due to the identity-based implications behind the provision and receipt of social support) (Hartley et al., 2020). Future investigation into the role of social identities in sport may help explain why—despite the existence of athlete mental health and dual career support programs—athletes still experience stress and stigma when accessing support (and relatedly why some avoid support services) (Brown et al., 2018; Butler et al., 2018).

Investigating Social Support

Studies across the general and sport psychology literature have adopted varied approaches to investigating and measuring social support. From a quantitative perspective, early research in sport adopted several social support questionnaires originally developed in social and health psychology (Freeman, 2020): the Inventory of Socially Supportive Behaviors (ISSB; Barrera et al., 1981), the Social Support Questionnaire (SSQ; Sarason et al., 1983), the Interpersonal Support Evaluation List (Cohen et al., 1985), the Social Provisions Scale (Cutrona & Russell, 1987), and the Social Support Survey (SSS; Richman et al., 1993). Of most frequent use has been the SSQ and the SSS.

The SSQ provides measures of network (structural and social integration) support (SSQ-N) and satisfaction with support (SSQ-S). Across 27 items (different situations), respondents list the initials of people they would turn to for support and their relationship with them. SSQ-N is calculated by the mean number of people listed across the 27 items. Further, for each item, respondents are asked to rate how satisfied they are with the support, from 1 (very dissatisfied) to 6 (very satisfied). SSQ-S is calculated as the mean of the satisfaction scores across the 27 items. In the development of the SSQ, Sarason and colleagues (1983) reported a strong factor structure, low correlations with social desirability, and good test–retest correlations. A six-item version of the SSQ was subsequently developed (Sarason et al., 1987).

The SSS assesses eight dimensions of social support (task appreciation, task challenge, listening support, emotional challenge, emotional support, tangible assistance, reality confirmation, and personal assistance), and respondents are asked to complete four items in reference to each dimension. These four items measure the following:

- The number of providers of that support
- Satisfaction with that support (1 = very dissatisfied to 5 = very satisfied)
- Difficulty in obtaining more of that support (1 = very difficult to 5 = very easy)
- The importance of that support to one's overall well-being (1 = very unimportant to 5 = very important)

In the development of the SSS, Richman and colleagues (1993) reported good construct validity (including content validity and concurrent validity) and good test–retest reliability.

Within the sport literature, several idiosyncratic psychometric measurements have also been created to examine social support in sport contexts (e.g., Freeman & Rees, 2008; Lubans et al., 2011;

Zourbanos et al., 2011). While this allowed for domain-specific measurement of social support (Rees et al., 1999; Holt & Hoar, 2006), the development of such measures may have contributed toward disparate findings in the sport literature (Holt & Hoar, 2006; Vangelisti, 2009). That is, it is unclear whether findings are due to the relationship of interest or due to the unique properties of each measure. To enhance our understanding of social support and aid literature synthesis, Freeman and colleagues (2011, 2014) argued for the importance of using theory-based sport-specific measures. As such, several sport-specific measures of social support have been developed for assessing perceived support (the 16-item Perceived Available Support in Sport Questionnaire [PASS-Q]; Freeman et al., 2011), received support (the 22-item Athletes' Received Support Questionnaire [ARSQ]; Freeman et al., 2014), and team members' individual perceptions of support available to their team (the 16-item Team-referent Availability of Social Support Questionnaire [TASS-Q]; Coffee et al., 2017). These sport-specific measures are also dimensional (i.e., they assess emotional, esteem, information, and tangible support) (Rees & Hardy, 2000) and have demonstrated good validity and reliability indices across independent samples (e.g., Freeman et al., 2014; Hartley & Coffee, 2019; Lu et al., 2016).

Quantitative approaches to the study of social support arguably offer an incomplete understanding of the construct and its effects in sport, and the investigation of social support can also be approached from a qualitative perspective. For example, interviews may help researchers to better understand the types of supportive behaviors that are important in the sport environment (e.g., Rees & Hardy, 2000) and to develop a more athlete-centered understanding of their social support experiences (e.g., Alvarez et al., 2009; Greenleaf et al., 2001; Kristiansen & Roberts, 2010). For instance, Aitchison and colleagues (2021) conducted interviews to explore the social support experiences of elite para-athletes and the influence thereof on their well-being and performance. Qualitative approaches may also provide researchers with a more nuanced and contextualized insight into when, how, and why particular social support effects and outcomes exist (e.g., Hartley et al., 2022). For instance, qualitative approaches can explore why being primed to think about supportive acts in more or less abstract ways (e.g., "Why did he help you?" vs. "What did he do to help you?") can have different effects on task outcomes (e.g., more vs. less beneficial, respectively) (Lee & Ybarra, 2017). Qualitative approaches may also provide richer insights into the aforementioned shortcomings of extant theoretical perspectives (e.g., understanding why social support may be the source of stress as well as the key to reducing it)—for example, by examining how social norms may contribute to stress and how this causes social support to backfire when it is seen to conflict with those norms (e.g., by instigating identity-based threat) (Hartley et al., 2022; Wainwright et al., 2017).

Quantitative approaches to the study of social support arguably offer an incomplete understanding of the construct and its effects in sport, and the investigation of social support can also be approached from a qualitative perspective.

Researchers may also consider adopting more diverse investigative methods to examine the social integration of athletes, the nature of those social relationships, and the implications this may have for access to socially supportive actions and resources. These topics are yet to be thoroughly investigated in sport, and such methods may generate unique insights (cf. Hassmén et al., 2016). For instance, social identity mapping (Cruwys et al., 2016) invites individuals to identify and portray a subjective representation of the key physical or psychological groups they consider themselves to be a member of (e.g., their family, church, sport club) and to indicate the nature of the relations between those groups (whether they are complementary or antagonistic). These groups are, in turn, likely to be the basis for individuals' social support networks and will likely structure individuals' experiences of providing, perceiving, and receiving social support (Steffens et al., 2016). Similarly, social network analysis represents a set of tools for understanding and visualizing the structural social ties and relationships between a network of individuals (Wasserman & Faust, 1994). Social network analysis has been used in sport psychology research (e.g., Fransen et al., 2015; Lusher et al., 2010) and may likewise provide valuable insights into social support structures within sport environments and their influence on a range of outcomes (Nixon, 1993).

Future Research Directions

This section provides suggestions for how to advance our theoretical and empirical understandings of social support in sport. Of relevance to the preceding discussions, we argue that gaining a better understanding of social support's mechanisms (i.e., when, how, and why social support may result in both effective and ineffective outcomes) may advance our theoretical understanding and models of social support and help explain the inconsistencies observed in the literature.

Conducting research into social support mechanisms within specific environments of interest—within particular sport teams, organizations, or cultures—may reveal how to best safeguard and support those groups. Such concurrent investigations in the study of social support mechanisms requires researchers to develop, implement, and evaluate theory-driven social support interventions in sport. While there has been some progress in studying the beneficial effects of individual-level social support interventions (e.g., for enhancing golf performance) (Freeman et al., 2009; Rees & Freeman, 2010), we encourage researchers to look beyond athlete-centered support transactions and to instead consider support resources, systems, and procedures holistically within sport—for instance, evaluating the provision and receipt of social support within athlete welfare, dual career, and mental health support programs; implementing social support–related changes that would improve the perceived and observed effects of such programs; and evaluating the impact of such changes at recipient, provider, and organizational levels. Relatedly, researching ways to support the efficacy of such interventions through better understanding the facilitating or constraining influence of systemic factors and the prevailing social environment would have practical implications (e.g., social norms might influence engagement with certain types of support behaviors) (Butler et al., 2018; Hartley et al., 2020, 2022).

Building on these ideas, we provide several methodological considerations for future social support research. First, much of the extant social support literature in sport has been cross-sectional. Moving beyond this to adopting longitudinal designs (e.g., collecting data at multiple time points, or collecting phenomenological life span data) may help researchers better establish the immediate and ongoing effects of social support.

Second, much extant research in sport has relied on correlation-based approaches to determine social support's main and stress-buffering effects (e.g., DeFreese & Smith, 2013, 2014; Hartley & Coffee, 2019; Lu et al., 2016), and research that can more firmly replicate and validate these effects (notably experimental methods) is lacking. For example, researchers may choose to adopt controlled lab methods that examine the neurophysiological effects of social support on stress appraisal and coping (e.g., by monitoring the levels of stress biomarkers) (Frisch et al., 2014; Gallagher et al., 2021; Meijen et al., 2020; see chapter 16), or to innovatively adopt social network analysis to investigate the factors needed for optimal social integration.

Finally, there has been a narrow approach to much social support research, with a focus primarily on recipients' experiences of social support. In reality—and as implied in the name of the construct—social support is a *social* phenomenon that is ultimately structured and influenced by a range of providers *and* recipients (similar to motivational climate; see chapter 10) (Hayward et al., 2017). It is therefore important that researchers capture both perspectives—of those involved in the provision *and* the receipt of social support—because this might reveal more about the optimal provision of support and how such resources are understood, engaged with, and experienced from the recipient's perspective (e.g., Hartley et al., 2022).

Practical Implications

There are tangible implications for applied practice arising from this chapter. Indeed, we argue that several principles of social support practice may help athletes, coaches, practitioners, and sport organizations to better understand the art of supporting people. Embedding these principles into the sport environment may, in turn, better promote performance, well-being, and duty of care.

First, perceptions of support being available *if needed* seems, in most cases, to be more beneficial than actually receiving support. That is not to say that practitioners should avoid providing support for fear of "getting it wrong." It does, however, emphasize the importance of cultivating healthy perceptions of support availability. As such, we suggest practitioners educate and inform their target audience about *what* support is available if needed (e.g., listing the available forms of emotional, esteem, informational, and tangible support), *how* they should engage with it (e.g., which support providers to speak to and how they can request such support), and clearly explain *why* it is available and beneficial (e.g., that it may benefit their health, well-being, and performance). As a practical example from the first author's applied experiences, there is value in encouraging athletes, coaches, and parents to explicitly discuss this topic. It may, for example, lead to the writing and signing of support agreements to facilitate shared understandings and accountability between providers and recipients for the dos and don'ts of social support practice within their environments.

Second, the effects of social support may vary greatly because of the prevailing context and provider–recipient factors, in both more and less adaptive ways. As such, it may be helpful for practitioners to consider (1) how the support provided fits the needs of the prevailing context and (2) the most appropriate way of delivering support. With regard to the former point, we recommend that practitioners consider logistics (e.g., location, visibility, timing of supportive interactions), athlete needs (e.g., the type of support behavior—perceived, received, or dimensions of support), and the support-related outcomes of interest (i.e., whether addressing the outcome will be considered helpful and meaningful or undermining and stressful). Such considerations may ensure that the implications behind social support do not undermine its effects (e.g., ensuring that technical instruction in front of an athlete's teammates is not misconstrued as a sign of criticism or an attempt to assert dominance).

Regarding the most appropriate way to provide support, we argue that this can be more easily achieved through the medium of well-developed interpersonal and reflective skills. At an anecdotal level, we have both personally encountered incidents where well-designed and well-intentioned acts of support failed to have their intended effects because of a lack of social tact and oratory skill. Furthermore, considering the influence of provider–recipient factors (as discussed earlier—characteristics, shared group memberships, and social identities) might also inform practitioners about appropriate and potentially more effective ways of offering social support—for example, by providing invisible social support, or support that aligns with the cultural and group norms of the target audience (Butler et al., 2018), or even realizing that, occasionally, the most appropriate form of support is to do nothing.

Finally, we have already mentioned how one's historic and ongoing experiences of receiving support are likely to influence one's perceptions of support availability (Uchino, 2009). These ongoing experiences may also, in some instances, create barriers to accessing future support (e.g., being teased or being forensically questioned when asking for help may create a barrier to asking for help in the future) and thus negatively affect the welfare of athletes. This effect of personal history speaks to the importance of building safe, trusting, and reliable working relationships and environments—because these ultimately shape and influence the effectiveness of the support practitioners offer (e.g., Sharp et al., 2015). As such, we would invite whole teams (e.g., of athletes, parents, coaches, multidisciplinary support staff), organizational groups, and collectives (e.g., human resources departments, managers, directors, national governing bodies, and organizations) to consider how the structures, procedures, and cultures of their sport environments may both facilitate and constrain the effectiveness of social support (Hartley et al., 2020; Haslam, 2004). For example, the cultural values espoused by one famous sport organization—the All Blacks, New Zealand's national men's rugby team—have emphasized how "better people make better All Blacks" and how this shapes their day-to-day functioning. It would be worthwhile for individuals to reflect on how such norms and values may influence the social support practices observed within their own environments. Indeed, we argue that reflecting on these social nuances (e.g., individual perceptions, interpersonal provider–recipient dynamics, organizational support norms, and cultures) will enable the provision of effective social support that safeguards and facilitates the health, well-being, and performance of people in sport.

Summary

This chapter has provided insight into the influence of social support on athletes. We've sought to facilitate a critical understanding of social support and its role in the sport environment through an introduction to the concept and its influence on a range of outcomes related to performance and well-being in sport. We offered a critical synthesis of contemporary findings about the influence of social support in sport, followed by an overview of the main theoretical perspectives (i.e., main effects, stress-buffering, and optimal matching models and provider–recipient factors) that explain how social support operates. This was followed by a discussion of the issues and opportunities related to the investigation and measurement of social support. We have closed by considering avenues for future research directions, important methodological considerations for future work in this area, and implications for applied practice arising from this chapter.

DISCUSSION QUESTIONS

1. What are some of the ways we can define social support in sport, and what are the main constituent components and dimensions of social support?
2. Based on available empirical evidence, which of the following is more consistently associated with beneficial sport-related outcomes—perceived or received support? Discuss why this might be the case.
3. What theories and models have researchers used to explain how social support operates in sport? Discuss whether you feel current models and theoretical approaches are adequate.
4. What are the ways we can investigate and measure social support in sport, and what are some of the associated advantages and disadvantages of these methods?
5. How might the implications for applied practice from this chapter be implemented into a sport environment of your choosing? Describe what this would look like in practice.

15

Efficacy Beliefs Within Relational and Group Contexts in Sport

Mark R. Beauchamp, PhD; Colin M. Wierts, PhD; and Ben Jackson, PhD

LEARNING OBJECTIVES

On completion of this chapter, the reader should have the following:

- Understanding of the conceptual bases for different efficacy constructs that exist within close relationships and groups in sport
- Ability to identify the sources of efficacy cognitions as well as the consequences for individuals (athlete, coach), dyads (athlete–athlete, coach–athlete), and groups (teams) in sport
- Awareness of contemporary efficacy studies focused on relationships and group settings and potential directions for future research
- Understanding of the associated practical implications for athlete, team, and coach functioning

Self-efficacy refers to an individual's "belief in one's capabilities to organize and execute the courses of action required to produce given attainments" (Bandura, 1997, p. 3); in sport, it is an important predictor of positive cognitions, affective responses, and behaviors. Self-efficacy relates to a person's perceived abilities to perform tasks independently of others. Within most sport contexts, however, athletes spend a great deal of time training, performing, and working with others (e.g., teammates, coaches), and in such environments, efficacy beliefs should also be considered in relation to the interactive and interdependent tasks that athletes perform.

The purpose of this chapter is to review the efficacy literature as it corresponds to behavioral enactment within close relationships (e.g., coach–athlete, athlete–athlete) and group settings in sport. Although self-efficacy theory (Bandura, 1977, 1997) provides the theoretical underpinning for the study of efficacy beliefs within relational and group settings, this chapter is not a review of self-efficacy research per se. Reviews of the self-efficacy construct are provided elsewhere (see Jackson et al., 2020). This chapter centers on efficacy beliefs that manifest within close relationships and group contexts in sport and physical activity settings.

Self-efficacy theory exists within the broader theoretical framework provided by social cognitive theory (Bandura, 1986), in which individuals are considered to be both products and producers of their environment, personality, and actions. Specifically, Bandura (1997) used the term *triadic reciprocal causation* to describe the functional dependence that occurs among these three factors and reiterated the underlying theme that permeates this book—that athletes, coaches, and teammates influence and are influenced by others within their social environment. Within Bandura's (1986) social cognitive framework, self-efficacy theory is concerned with how people develop judgments and expectations about their own capabilities to meet various demands and challenges. When one also considers sports that require interaction between athletes (i.e., competing dyads such as doubles tennis partnerships, most sport teams), efficacy beliefs can additionally be observed in relation to the role responsibilities athletes undertake while interacting with other team members (Bandura, 1999), the capabilities of one's partner to perform specific tasks (Lent & Lopez, 2002), or even the capabilities of a group or team as a whole (Bandura, 2000). In addition, while each of these efficacy appraisals describes cognitions held by athletes, an established body of research points to the fact that coaches' efficacy beliefs may have important implications for the learning and performance of their athletes (Feltz et al., 1999). Within the organizational psychology literature, researchers have used the term *leadership efficacy*, which is analogous to the way in which coaching efficacy has been operationalized in sport (e.g., Hoyt et al. 2003). However, in sport, leaders also include those other than the coach, namely on-field or on-court leaders, and their efficacy beliefs have the potential to shape the actions and behaviors of the holder of those beliefs as well as their teammates (e.g., Fransen, Vanbeselaere, et al., 2014; Watson et al., 2001). In this chapter, we explore how these disparate forms (see table 15.1) of coach and athlete efficacy beliefs manifest themselves within close relational and group contexts in sport, consider how they arise, and examine to what extent they affect both individual and collective functioning.

Role Efficacy Within Sport Teams

Roles refer to sets of expectations about behaviors for a position in a social structure (Biddle & Thomas, 1966; Shaw & Costanzo, 1982; Sherif & Sherif, 1953). For sport teams to succeed, members need to successfully perform their task-related formal role responsibilities. As Bandura (1999) remarked, "If people are to work together successfully, the members of a group have to perform their roles with a high degree of efficacy" (p. 227). Most of the research in this area relates to formal or positional roles. Bray and colleagues (Beauchamp & Bray, 2001; Bray, Balaguer, & Duda, 2004; Bray & Brawley, 2002; Bray et al., 2002) embraced the basic tenets of self-efficacy theory (Bandura, 1997) and were the first to substantively examine the construct of role efficacy in sport. Bray and colleagues (2002) considered role efficacy to represent athletes' confidence in their capabilities to successfully carry out formal interdependent role responsibilities within a group. One of the purposes of their study was to investigate the conceptual uniqueness of role efficacy, by examining role efficacy in relation to both self-efficacy and collective efficacy (a construct we return to later in the chapter). As hypothesized, athletes' efficacy beliefs about performing their interdependent role responsibilities were found to be related to, but also distinct from, their confidence to perform independent tasks (i.e., self-efficacy) such as shooting and dribbling. In addition, role efficacy was found to be empirically distinct from collective efficacy.

In light of evidence that self-efficacy beliefs consistently relate to achievement outcomes, it is perhaps not surprising that researchers have examined the relations between role efficacy and role performance effectiveness (Beauchamp et al. 2002; Bray, Balaguer, & Duda, 2004; Bray & Brawley, 2002). As one example, Beauchamp and colleagues (2002) investigated adolescent rugby players' role efficacy beliefs in relation to their performance of offensive and defensive role responsibilities. In line with self-efficacy theory (Bandura, 1997), the results revealed that players' efficacy expectations for performing their offensive and defensive responsibilities explained significant variation in coach ratings of role performance effectiveness.

After generating a handful of studies on role efficacy in the early 2000s, research on the role efficacy construct has been relatively sparse over the past decade within sport settings. Most of the research on role efficacy has been correlational in nature, which precludes inferences of causality. Given the experimental evidence linking self-efficacy beliefs to achievement behaviors in sport (Wright et al., 2016), we propose that those concerned with supporting athlete development and achievement (e.g., coaches, sport psychology practitioners) consider targeting role efficacy beliefs as a means of enhancing athletic performance on interdependent (i.e., interactive) sport teams. To fully ascertain the utility of this approach, however, high-quality experimental research is clearly needed.

Collective Efficacy Within Sport Teams

While role efficacy beliefs describe the confidence of a team member that they can perform specific role responsibilities, collective efficacy relates to team members' perceptions about the team's *collective* abilities. Specifically, Bandura (1997) defined collective efficacy as the "group's shared belief in their conjoint capabilities to organize and execute the courses of action required to produce given attainments" (p. 476). Within this definition, three

TABLE 15.1 Efficacy Beliefs Within Relational and Group Contexts in Sport

Construct	Definition	Example
Self-efficacy	A person's confidence in their own capabilities to perform independent tasks (Bandura, 1997)	"I just remember the race going out super quick, and I'm saying, 'You are in the best shape of your life.'" (Canadian distance runner Mohammed Ahmed, describing his third-place finish in the men's 5,000 m track and field event, 2019 World Athletics Championships; quoted on CBC Sports, 2020)
Role efficacy	A person's confidence in their own capabilities to carry out formal interdependent role responsibilities within a group (Bray et al., 2002)	"The fit is just really good in Winnipeg. I felt really confident in my role there and with the group of guys, it's a good team and we're going to be a good team for a long time." (Dylan DeMelo, describing his role after moving to the Winnipeg Jets in the National Hockey League; quoted in Brooks, 2020)
Collective efficacy	A group's confidence in their collective capabilities to perform collective tasks (Bandura, 1997)	"We knew we were up against very strong opponents. But we went out on the golf course and believed in ourselves and what we stand for as a team." (Thomas Bjorn, captain of the European golf team, on their Ryder Cup victory over the United States; quoted in Clarey, 2018)
Coaching efficacy (type 1)	A coach's confidence in their own capabilities to facilitate the learning and development of athletes (Feltz et al., 1999)	"I feel young, but I'm not overly conscious of my age and the role that I'm in. It's like a player going into the Olympics: If you know you've put the work in, then you feel ready and confident. I feel the most calm and composed in this role. Had I done it three years ago, maybe I wouldn't feel the same way." (Bev Priestman, describing the confidence she has gained from past experiences to be the head coach for the Canadian women's national soccer team, before the 2020 Olympic Games; quoted in Molinaro, 2021)
Coaching efficacy (type 2)	A coach's confidence in their players' abilities to perform given tasks (Chase et al., 1997)	"I feel really good about this group of players. These players all have something very special to bring." (U.S. women's soccer coach Jill Ellis, commenting on her players' capabilities at the start of the 2018 season; quoted in U.S. Soccer, 2018)
Proxy efficacy	A person's confidence in an intermediary's capabilities, such as a coach or doctor, to function on their behalf (Bray et al., 2001)	"Every program he gives to a client is designed for them and their specific body needs. He knows me very well at this point." (Professional ice hockey player Nathan MacKinnon, describing the ability of his trainer, Andy O'Brien, to provide him with a personalized training program to help him be physically ready for each season; quoted in Shultz, 2020)
Other-efficacy	A person's belief in their partner's capabilities to perform given behaviors (Lent & Lopez, 2002)	"Sam is an experienced All Black with eight years in the team now and is a 'follow me' type of leader and a very good thinker in the game." (New Zealand All Blacks rugby coach Ian Foster, describing player Sam Cane after revealing him as his new team captain; quoted on RugbyPass, 2020)
Relation-inferred self-efficacy (RISE)	An athlete's appraisal of how their capabilities are viewed by another person such as a playing partner or coach (Lent & Lopez, 2002)	"It's the first time that I've had a coach believe in me through the offseason like this." (Case Keenum of the NFL's Los Angeles Rams, describing his coach's belief in him; quoted in Alarcon, 2016)

concepts are worth emphasizing. First, collective efficacy is a *shared perception* that involves a certain degree of consensus and represents individual members' beliefs about the group. Second, collective efficacy involves beliefs about the group's *conjoint capabilities*, which refers to the enactment of highly integrative tasks that involve the team as a whole (e.g., a set-piece play in rugby). Third, Bandura's (1997) definition is concerned with the *organization and execution* of courses of action. Zaccaro and colleagues (1995) elaborated on this aspect of Bandura's definition by suggesting that collective efficacy involves the "allocation, coordination, and integration" (p. 309) of a group's resources. Implicit within both Bandura's definition and Zaccaro and colleagues' suggestion is the notion that collective efficacy involves beliefs about tasks requiring high levels of interdependence that combine to result in group execution. Given that collective efficacy is grounded within the broader framework provided by self-efficacy theory, Bandura (1997) suggested that the sources of collective efficacy are likely to be similar to other forms of efficacy beliefs. This means that although the antecedents of collective efficacy may operate at the group level (cf. Chan, 1998), the underlying mechanisms will likely be similar to those that influence both self-efficacy and role efficacy expectations.

Collective Efficacy: Measurement Considerations

As noted by Myers and Feltz (2007), the slightly different definitions of collective efficacy forwarded by Bandura (1997) and Zaccaro and colleagues (1995) have produced competing views surrounding the measurement of collective efficacy in sport, resulting in four common methods of assessment (see Myers & Feltz, 2007):

1. Each individual's self-efficacy beliefs are aggregated, at the group level, to form a collective efficacy score.
2. Participants respond to collective efficacy items preceded by a stem that asks the individual about their confidence in the group's or team's ability; scores are either aggregated at the group level or analyzed at the individual level.
3. Participants respond to collective efficacy items preceded by a stem that asks the individual how confident their team or group is in their ability; scores are either aggregated at the group level or analyzed at the individual level.
4. An interview is conducted with team members to determine one score of collective efficacy.

Approaches 2 and 3 are, by far, the most common for assessing collective efficacy in sport teams. The main difference between these approaches is the entity the individual is rating. Using approach 2, the individual rates their *own* confidence in the group or team to carry out specific behavior, whereas when using approach 3, the individual is asked to be an informant of their *team's* confidence to carry out specific behaviors. Although collective efficacy research in sport sees regular use of both approaches, there are subtle but important differences that can have potential consequences for understanding the meaning of scores derived from collective efficacy measures (Messick, 1995). Consider the following thought experiment. An athlete can have low confidence in their group to carry out a specific behavior and simultaneously believe their team, as a whole and in general, is confident in its ability to carry out those same behaviors. By considering the two previous assessment protocols, in the context of this thought experiment, it is evident that they essentially measure two related (Myers & Feltz, 2007) but notably distinct constructs. The implications are that the *meanings* derived from each method are not entirely comparable and should not be interpreted as such.

Researchers have presented varying suggestions regarding the use of approaches 2 and 3. Short and colleagues (2005) made the argument for using approach 3 because it represents the emergent collective belief of a team. However, in a review of methodology surrounding collective efficacy assessment, Myers and Feltz (2007) contended that although there may not be substantive differences between these approaches in terms of their predictive utility of team performance, they recommended approach 2 because rating one's confidence in a team is a more *directly accessible* appraisal—to the rater—than making *inferences* about the beliefs of others within a team. Myers and Feltz (2007) noted that the methods in approaches 2 and 3 are comparable in their predictive utility. Although predictive utility represents one important facet of measurement validity, from the perspective of validity theory (see Messick, 1995; Zumbo, 2009) researchers need to be attentive to three things—(1) the *meaning* of scores derived from a given instrument, (2) the specific study's research question, and (3) the context in which they are asking their research question—before deciding to use a particular form of assessment. This need for careful consideration is particularly pertinent when studying collective efficacy.

For example, when assessing many individual athletes, and outcomes related to personal performance, motivation, and well-being variables, it may be more appropriate to use approach 2 given individual confidence in a team might be more relevant for individual-level outcomes. In contrast, when assessing all members of a team who have been competing together for a long time (e.g., national teams) and team-level outcomes such as win percentage, it may be more fitting to use approach 3 because athletes will likely have a relatively more sophisticated understanding of their team as a collective entity. Nevertheless, what is particularly pertinent is that researchers ensure direct alignment between the research questions being studied and the selected method of collective efficacy assessment, and not assume that all measures will tap into the same underlying construct.

A second assessment issue corresponds to the dimensionality of collective efficacy. Arguably, the most frequently used collective efficacy questionnaire in sport psychology is the Collective Efficacy Questionnaire for Sports (CEQS; Short et al., 2005), which assesses the degree to which an athlete perceives their team is confident in five aspects—team ability, effort, persistence, preparation, and unity. Although the CEQS was initially developed to assess five factors, more recently Fransen, Kleinert, and colleagues (2014) presented factor analytic evidence that a two-factor solution is more appropriate with Flemish athletes and coaches. Items used to assess effort, persistence, preparation, and unity contributed to one factor, which they termed *process-oriented collective efficacy*, and items used to assess ability represented the second factor, which they termed *team outcome confidence*. In future research, investigators should provide evidence via factor analysis supporting their chosen dimensionality of collective efficacy assessment (Zumbo, 2007).

What is particularly pertinent is that researchers ensure direct alignment between the research questions being studied and the selected method of collective efficacy assessment, and not assume that all measures will tap into the same underlying construct.

Sources of Collective Efficacy

Previous experiences of success were theorized by Bandura (1997) to be the most powerful source of collective efficacy beliefs. A number of studies provide evidence for this relationship (Feltz & Lirgg, 1998; Myers, Payment, & Feltz, 2004). In a study with women's ice hockey teams, for example, Myers, Payment, and Feltz (2004) found that previous performance positively predicted collective efficacy, even after accounting for the effects of previous levels of collective efficacy. In a two-part study of male soccer players (Fransen, Decroos, et al., 2015), subjective team performance during the first half of the game was significantly related to collective efficacy and team outcome confidence at the beginning of the halftime break (study 1). These findings were replicated in study 2, and moreover, subjective team performance during the second half of the game was significantly related to both collective efficacy and team outcome confidence after the game had finished. More recently, Habeeb and colleagues (2019) examined the reciprocal relationships between efficacy beliefs (collective, other-, and self-) and performance within 73 cheerleading dyads (male base and female flyer) performing five successive stunt tasks. Objectively rated performance was consistently related to prospective collective, self-, and other-efficacy beliefs for both bases and flyers. The findings of Fransen, Decroos, and colleagues (2015) and Habeeb and colleagues (2019) demonstrate that task performance during competition has a substantive effect on subsequent collective efficacy beliefs.

A growing body of literature points to the fact that leadership behaviors are also important determinants of collective efficacy beliefs. Watson and colleagues (2001) found that teams with more confident leadership, in the form of both appointed and emergent leaders, had greater levels of collective efficacy. Transformational leadership (cf. Bass & Avolio, 1994), which involves behaviors that exert influence by elevating followers' goals and provides members with the confidence to go beyond minimally acceptable expectations, also significantly and positively relates to collective efficacy perceptions in athletes (Price & Weiss, 2013).

Another way in which leaders can foster group members' beliefs in their team is by establishing group distinctiveness, through a sense of "us" (Haslam et al., 2011). Fransen and colleagues (Fransen, Haslam, et al., 2015; Fransen et al., 2016) conducted a series of experimental studies to examine how leaders influence athletes' collective efficacy beliefs by enhancing athletes' social identification (i.e., positively appraising their membership with the group). Specifically, when leaders expressed high confidence in their group, it had a contagion effect on athletes' collective efficacy beliefs (process and outcome confidence). Moreover, these effects were mediated by the degree to which group members positively identified with their team (Fransen, Haslam, et al., 2015; Fransen et al., 2016).

Bandura (1997) and Lindsley and colleagues (1995) contended that vicarious experiences may also be an important source of efficacy beliefs at the group level. A program of research presented by Bruton and colleagues (Bruton et al., 2014, 2019) provided evidence to support the use of observational learning (Bruton et al., 2016) as a means to improve collective efficacy beliefs, as well as the delivery methods that maximize intervention effectiveness. In a two-part intervention study (Bruton et al., 2014), individuals exposed to positive video footage (of themselves performing) and neutral video footage (not of themselves performing) reported greater collective efficacy than those receiving video footage of themselves performing negatively (study 1). In study 2, individuals exposed to video footage of themselves performing well reported greater increases in collective efficacy than individuals exposed to video footage of teams from a different sport (who were also playing well). In a more recent study, Bruton and colleagues (2019) reported that using individual- and team-level observational learning content can have positive effects on collective efficacy. At the individual level, each individual athlete watched successful in-game action of themselves only, whereas in the team condition athletes watched their team perform successfully, without themselves personally included in the footage. When taken together, these findings point to the practical value of having athletes watch film footage of successful collective *and* personal task execution as a means of bolstering collective efficacy.

Another team-level source of collective efficacy corresponds to *teamwork*. In their theoretical and integrative review of team effectiveness and teamwork, McEwan and Beauchamp (2014) defined teamwork in sport as "a dynamic process involving a collaborative effort by team members to effectively carry out the independent and interdependent behaviors that are required to maximize a team's likelihood of achieving its purposes" (p. 233). McEwan and Beauchamp (2014) outlined two broad components of teamwork: *management of team maintenance* (behaviors aimed at ensuring the group stays intact) and *regulation of team performance* (behaviors aimed at ensuring team goals are realized). Management of team maintenance comprises behaviors designed to (1) provide *psychological support* and (2) support *integrative conflict management*. Regulation of team performance comprises behaviors that involve (1) *preparation*, (2) *execution*, (3) *evaluation*, and (4) *adjustment*. Consistent with work in organizational settings that suggests collective efficacy is an emergent state stemming from teamwork (Tasa et al., 2007), McEwan (2020) found that all five of the dimensions of teamwork described above were positively related to athletes' collective efficacy beliefs in their team's capabilities.

Outcomes of Collective Efficacy

In addition to examining previous success as a source of collective efficacy, researchers have also investigated team performance as a behavioral outcome. In sport settings, collective efficacy has been found to positively predict team performance (Myers, Feltz, & Short, 2004), even after controlling for the effects of prior performance (Myers, Payment, & Feltz, 2004). Support for this prospective collective efficacy–team performance relationship has also been found with professional basketball teams (Heuzé et al., 2006). In female collegiate ice hockey teams, Myers and colleagues (2007) demonstrated that the relationship between collective efficacy (measured before each game) and cumulative performance (period 1; period 1 and 2; period 1, 2, and 3) was positive and invariant across each time period. These findings suggest that collective efficacy beliefs contribute to total game performance as well as performances throughout a game. In related experimental research, Bray, Gyurcsik, and colleagues (2004) pointed to an explanatory pathway through which collective efficacy beliefs might influence team performance. Specifically, Bray's study involved having participants perform a group strength task (i.e., holding a medicine ball aloft), and found that collective efficacy predicted group performance and that group goals mediated this relationship. This means that collective efficacy beliefs enhance team performance outcomes by virtue of more efficacious teams setting more challenging group goals.

Several researchers have also sought to examine the potential relations between collective efficacy beliefs and team members' affective states. For example, Greenlees and colleagues (1999) examined the relationships between collective efficacy, precompetition anxiety, and positive affect within six rugby union teams. Results revealed that collective efficacy was negatively related to members' levels of cognitive state anxiety and positively related to positive affect. Outside sport, findings from other domains of psychology suggest that collective efficacy may also act as a buffer of stressor–strain relationships (Jex & Bliese, 1999) and may be related to other salient outcomes, including member satisfaction (Caprara, Barbaranelli, Borgogni, Steca, et al., 2003) and commitment (Caprara, Barbaranelli, Borgogni, Petitta, et al., 2003).

Coaching Efficacy in Sport

An underlying theme of this book is that coaches play a prominent role in facilitating the development and behaviors of athletes and teams. Further—similar to athletes—coaches also hold efficacy beliefs that influence the learning, development, and performance of their athletes. Some of the extant coaching efficacy research has focused on coaches' confidence in their own abilities to facilitate the learning and development of their athletes (Feltz et al., 1999), whereas other research has been directed toward coaches' confidence in their players' abilities to perform given tasks (Chase et al., 1997). Most research has focused on the former, whereas the latter might be more accurately considered a form of proxy agency (see table 15.1—a coach's confidence in *other people's* capabilities).

Theory and Measurement of Coaching Efficacy

Feltz and colleagues (1999) developed a conceptual model for a coach's confidence in their own capabilities to affect the learning and development of their players. This conceptual model was based on Bandura's (1977) theorizing, as well as Denham and Michael's (1981) model of teacher efficacy, and it was subsequently operationalized in the form of the Coaching Efficacy Scale (Feltz et al., 1999). Feltz and colleagues identified four dimensions of coaching efficacy, which included coaches' confidence in their

- ability to coach during competition and lead their team to successful performance (game-strategy efficacy),
- ability to affect the psychological skills and states of their athletes (motivation efficacy),
- instructional and diagnostic skills (technique efficacy), and
- ability to influence the personal development of their athletes (character-building efficacy).

Feltz and colleagues (1999) provided partial support for the factor structure of measures derived from the Coaching Efficacy Scale and their multidimensional conceptualization of coaching efficacy. More recently though, Myers, Wolfe, and Feltz (2005) suggested that the original factor structure (e.g., Feltz et al., 1999) of measures derived from the Coaching Efficacy Scale did not fully support the four-factor model, and there was a lack of discriminant validity between the technique efficacy and game-strategy efficacy factors. By analyzing data collected from previous studies, Myers and colleagues determined the four-factor model was superior to a three-factor (specifying technique efficacy and game-strategy efficacy items on one factor) and one-factor model, but they recommended altering the definition of technique efficacy to "instruction and diagnosing issues within practice" (as opposed to competition) in order to decrease its conceptual overlap with game-strategy efficacy and improve model fit.

Following these recommendations, Myers and colleagues (2008) produced a revised version of the original Coaching Efficacy Scale, which altered the operational definition of technique efficacy to include instructional and diagnostic skills during practice, and included an additional physical conditioning efficacy factor—a coach's belief in their ability to physically prepare their athletes appropriately for sport participation—resulting in the Coaching Efficacy Scale II—High School Teams. The five-factor structure of scores derived from this instrument was supported by Myers and colleagues (2008, 2011), who concluded that it represents a viable replacement of the Coaching Efficacy Scale, especially for use with high school coaches. When taken together, this body of work points to the fact that dimensions of coaching efficacy exist that are distinct from one another. From a practical perspective, those concerned with coach education and training might consider developing competencies in each of these five areas, which might translate into coaches' becoming more confident and self-assured in their overall coaching capabilities.

Sources of Coaching Efficacy

Feltz and colleagues (1999) suggested that in accordance with theory (see Bandura, 1997), coaches' efficacy expectations would likely be influenced by specific antecedents. Feltz and colleagues found that coaching efficacy was predicted by coaches' past experiences of mastery and success, coaching experience, athletes' skill levels, and social support from the school and community (see also Myers, Vargas-Tonsing, & Feltz, 2005). Myers and colleagues (2011) examined 13 correlates of coaching efficacy, including coach education, variants of coach and athletic experience, a variety of performance outcomes, and six sources of social support from significant others. All 13 potential correlates were significantly related to at least one of the coaching efficacy factors. The only two proposed sources that were positively related to all five factors of coaching efficacy were coaching education and improvement of athletes. Boardley (2018) also concluded that coach education is a consistent correlate of coaching efficacy. Building on this correlational research base, some experimental evidence lends support for the potential of coaching education programs to enable coaches to feel efficacious in influencing their athletes. For example, Malete and Feltz (2000) provided a sample of high school coaches with an education program titled Program for Athletic Coaches' Education (Seefeldt & Brown, 1990), and coaching efficacy significantly improved within the experimental group when compared with a control group.

In a meta-analysis of the sources of coaching efficacy, Myers and colleagues (2017) reported small to moderate relationships between four sources of coaching efficacy (i.e., coaching experience and preparation, prior success, perceived skill of athletes, and social support) and technique efficacy, game-strategy efficacy, character-building efficacy, and motivation efficacy. Effect sizes were stronger when studies had a higher percentage of females than males and when studies included collegiate coaches compared with high school and youth coaches. It is unclear why those sources were stronger predictors in studies that had more women coaches (than men), or why those effects were more pronounced for collegiate-level coaches than youth coaches. The authors speculated that a potential reason for the finding related to gender as a moderator could be that female coaches are more accurate in their efficacy appraisals, resulting in stronger correlations. Regarding coaching level as a moderator, Myers and colleagues (2017) suggested that some types of coaching information not modeled in their meta-analysis may be more pertinent for youth coaches (e.g., player improvement) with regard to bolstering their coach efficacy beliefs. As such, they suggested that future research examine additional sources of coaching efficacy that might have greater relevance at different levels (e.g., youth versus collegiate).

Outcomes of Coaching Efficacy

In terms of outcomes related to coaching efficacy, Feltz and colleagues (1999) found that coaches with higher levels of coaching efficacy provided more praise and encouragement behaviors and fewer instruction and organization behaviors than coaches with low coaching efficacy. Players also reported greater satisfaction with coaches with higher coaching efficacy and had better winning percentages than players performing under coaches with low coaching efficacy. Hwang and colleagues (2013) and Sullivan and colleagues (2012) demonstrated that coaching efficacy was significantly related to adaptive leadership behaviors. Researchers have also found that coaching efficacy is positively related to university coaches' commitment to coaching (Kent & Sullivan, 2003) and is positively related to the frequency with which coaches employ various behaviors designed to enhance the efficacy of their players (Myers, Vargas-Tonsing, & Feltz, 2005).

Coaching efficacy may also influence athletes' collective efficacy beliefs. In a laboratory study, Hoyt and colleagues (2003) found that leaders' confidence to lead (i.e., leader efficacy) was significantly related to their confidence in their team's abilities, which in turn was positively associated with followers' perceptions of collective efficacy. Although that study involved a nonsport task, research in sport by Chase and colleagues (1997) provided additional evidence for the potential *transference* effects of coaches' efficacy (in their players' capabilities) on subsequent player behavior. They found that coaches' confidence in their team's capabilities was related to two indicators of team performance in basketball—free throws and turnover performance. Although Chase and colleagues did not test collective efficacy as a mediator of the coach efficacy–team performance relationship as Hoyt and colleagues did, we contend that when coaches communicate their efficacious expectations to a team, the team will likely in turn become more efficacious, resulting in more accomplished performances. Future research could test this proposal.

Additional Forms of Relational Efficacy in Sport

Individuals form efficacy beliefs not only about the groups of which they are members but also in relation to specific individuals, or significant others, and make inferences about how others view their abilities. Lent and Lopez (2002) presented a conceptual model for the study of efficacy beliefs within relational contexts. They suggested that when people perform within close relationships (e.g., performance dyads), self-efficacy beliefs interact with the beliefs people hold about the capabilities of their relationship partners. They referred to this latter form of efficacy as *other-efficacy* and defined this as "an individual's beliefs about his or her significant other's ability to perform particular behaviors" (p. 264). Lent and Lopez (2002) also suggested that one should consider peoples' reflections on how they are viewed by their partners. Specifically, they described the beliefs a person has about how their capabilities are viewed by a significant other as a form of *relation-inferred self-efficacy* (RISE). In doubles tennis for example, an athlete might believe their partner is very confident in their capabilities to play doubles (i.e., high RISE), or conversely they may believe their partner lacks confidence in their capabilities. Lent and Lopez theorized that these relational efficacy beliefs contribute to relationship satisfaction, commitment, effort, and performance-directed behaviors, and they referred to the potential interaction of self-efficacy, other-efficacy, and RISE as a *tripartite* view of efficacy beliefs within relational contexts.

We contend that when coaches communicate their efficacious expectations to a team, the team will likely in turn become more efficacious, resulting in more accomplished performances.

Jackson and colleagues (Jackson & Beauchamp, 2010; Jackson et al., 2007, 2010) provided support for Lent and Lopez's (2002) contentions regarding the importance of other-efficacy and RISE beliefs in relation to perceptions of relationship quality through use of actor–partner interdependence modeling (Kenny et al., 2006). With such models, individuals' scores on a dependent variable are a function not only of their own scores (actor effect) on select independent variables but of their partner's scores (partner effect) as well. Within youth tennis partner dyads, other-efficacy (actor effects) was significantly related to relationship satisfaction (Jackson et al., 2007). Jackson and colleagues (Jackson & Beauchamp, 2010; Jackson et al., 2010) also examined tripartite efficacy beliefs in coach–athlete dyads. Coach and athlete other-efficacy was a robust correlate (actor and partner effects) of various interpersonal outcomes such as commitment, effort, and perceived relationship quality. These effects also tended to be stronger for athletes than coaches. Moreover, coaches' RISE perceptions predicted their own (actor effects) and athletes' (partner effects) perceptions of positive relationship outcomes such as commitment and relationship quality (Jackson & Beauchamp, 2010; Jackson et al., 2010). This means that when coaches think athletes are confident in their coaching capabilities, it can shape how satisfied coaches are with their relationship and can also transfer to their athletes' level of satisfaction with the relationship.

Several researchers have provided evidence that when athletes believe significant others have high confidence in their abilities (i.e., RISE perceptions), they report higher self-efficacy in relation to their own abilities. In junior tennis partner dyads, higher perceptions of RISE, as well as other-efficacy, were significantly related to self-efficacy (Jackson et al., 2007). In another study, athletes' RISE beliefs in relation to both their coach and teammates were significantly related to self-efficacy and indirectly related to their intentions to continue playing their sport and stay on their team via their self-efficacy beliefs (Jackson et al., 2014). In a study with youth athletes, perceptions of coaches' verbal and nonverbal RISE-relevant behaviors were indirectly related to self-efficacy via their own RISE perceptions (Saville & Bray, 2016). Moreover, Saville and Bray (2018) developed a communication workshop for alpine ski coaches with the intent of developing RISE-relevant behaviors. There was a significant increase in coaches' self-efficacy, outcome expectations, and perceived knowledge regarding RISE behaviors. From a practical perspective, this means coach education programs should include instruction on how to improve RISE-relevant behaviors (e.g., having coaches set high expectations and goals for the athlete and overtly acknowledge their athlete's strengths to the athlete).

Habeeb and colleagues (2017) examined how efficacy beliefs (self-, other-, and collective) within cheerleading dyads (male base and female flyer) are affected by the partner, and how these effects interact with role dependency (high dependence on a partner vs. low dependence on a partner) and task difficulty. Male bases (low dependency role) are more self-focused because they provide support for the flyer, and flyers (high dependency role) are more other-focused because they rely on the base to provide a proper toss so they can execute their stunt. Habeeb and colleagues found that flyers' ratings of other-efficacy and collective efficacy were more strongly affected by their partner during difficult tasks, whereas this was not the case for bases. In considering these findings, we suggest that when athletes particularly depend on their partners to perform a difficult task, they are more likely to pay attention to their partners' abilities, which consequently influences the perception of their partners' and the collective group's abilities.

When athletes particularly depend on their partners to perform a difficult task, they are more likely to pay attention to their partners' abilities, which consequently influences the perception of their partners' and the collective group's abilities.

Researchers have also examined the relationship between other-efficacy and performance. Within the sport of equestrian eventing, Beauchamp and Whinton (2005) found that riders' confidence in their own capabilities (i.e., self-efficacy) and their confidence in their horses' capabilities (i.e., other-efficacy) were each able to explain unique variance in riding performance. Building on this initial (observational) work, Dunlop and colleagues (2011) conducted a randomized experiment that manipulated other-efficacy beliefs of women students at a Canadian university performing a dyadic dance-based video game. Individuals who received positive feedback about their partners (enhanced other-efficacy condition) reported higher other-efficacy than those who received negative feedback about their partners (inhibited other-efficacy condition). Individuals in the enhanced other-efficacy condition also outperformed those in the inhibited other-efficacy condition. Accordingly, when individuals perform with a teammate or partner, it is important (for their own personal performance) that they have confidence in their own abilities *as well as* their partner's abilities.

Just as athletes can have confidence in a teammate or coach to carry out their responsibilities, they may also at times rely on the guidance of (or divest responsibility to) another individual. For example, a golfer's caddy will walk the entire course prior to a tournament to map out course measurements (e.g., how far a bunker is from a tee shot) and examine course conditions. Although the golfer will do some of these tasks (e.g., examine putting greens) during practice rounds, they rely heavily on their caddy to know the dimensions of the course. In describing his notion of *proxy efficacy*, Bandura (1997) contended that individuals develop and hold confidence beliefs regarding the capacity of an intermediary to function on their behalf. Bray and colleagues (Bray et al., 2001; Bray, Gyurcsik, et al., 2004) operationalized Bandura's construct of proxy efficacy and examined exercise participants' confidence in their class leader to help them achieve their goals. In one study, Bray and colleagues (2001) found that exercisers' confidence in their exercise leader (i.e., proxy efficacy) was related to their self-efficacy expectations and that proxy efficacy was able to explain significant variance in future exercise adherence above and beyond self-efficacy beliefs. The authors concluded that "proxy efficacy beliefs may play an important role in bolstering exercisers' beliefs about their own abilities to successfully perform the necessary elements of a strenuous aerobic workout within structured group classes" (p. 432). Although this study was conducted in an exercise context, the findings point to how having confidence in a coach or personal trainer may rub off on an athlete by shaping their confidence in their own capabilities.

Future Research Directions

The study of efficacy beliefs within relationship and group contexts represents an area of inquiry that is ripe for in-depth exploration. Much behavior in sport exists within social contexts that involve numerous influential agents (e.g., coaches, teammates, family, friends). Our review of the current literature illustrates that people hold a range of efficacy beliefs corresponding to the diverse tasks that involve those agents. Although researchers have articulated, defined, and investigated these distinct forms of efficacy to some extent, more research is required to understand how each of these forms of efficacy belief interrelate, how they develop, and what implications they hold for individual and collective functioning (vis-à-vis cognition, affect, and behavior).

With regard to interrelations among efficacy constructs, several lines of inquiry are encouraged. First, researchers have shown that leadership behaviors are influential in raising followers' collective efficacy beliefs (Fransen, Decroos, et al., 2015; Fransen et al., 2016; Hoyt et al., 2003). However, researchers have yet to ascertain how leadership behaviors affect members' perceptions about their role-related capabilities. Formal roles are typically assigned by the coach to meet the task-specific demands of the group (Mabry & Barnes, 1980). As such, and in line with the transference effects found by Hoyt and colleagues (leaders' efficacy beliefs shape subsequent confidence among team members in their own collective capabilities), it seems likely that if coaches and on-field leaders are confident in team members' capabilities, those athletes may in turn feel confident in their abilities to perform their various formal *role responsibilities*. At this time, we are unaware of any experimental research in sport that has tested the effect of an intervention to bolster athletes' role efficacy beliefs or role performance effectiveness. Given the effectiveness of interventions that target self-efficacy (Collins et al., 2019; Higgins et al., 2014; Williams & French, 2011), work that develops and evaluates role efficacy interventions in sport would be particularly worthwhile.

Another potential area of interest relates to extending the experimental work of Fransen and colleagues (Fransen, Haslam, et al., 2015; Fransen et al., 2016), described earlier in the chapter, which found that leaders' confidence in their team members can have a contagion effect on collective efficacy via team identification. Fransen and colleagues examined social identification through short-term experimental designs. However, athletes' social identification with their teams or groups likely changes over the course of their tenure with a particular team. A worthwhile future line of inquiry is to examine the longer-term impact of social identity leadership interventions delivered to coaches and athlete leaders that develop their skills in creating a shared group identity and sense of "us" (see Haslam et al., 2011, for a review). For example, researchers could examine the dynamic relationship between social identity leadership interventions and athletes' social identities, collective efficacy, and performance using longitudinal designs and multilevel growth modeling (Gaudreau et al., 2020).

Finally, our review of the literature on this topic leads us to conclude that researchers should examine the effects of teamwork interventions on different forms of efficacy beliefs. A pilot study demonstrated that teamwork training can have positive effects on athletes' perceptions of the multiple dimensions of teamwork (McEwan & Beauchamp, 2020). Going forward, it would be valuable to study the utility of teamwork interventions to bring about other emergent efficacy beliefs such as role efficacy, intrateam relational efficacy (other-efficacy and RISE), and resultant performance outcomes.

Practical Implications

From an applied perspective, the results of the research covered within this chapter suggest a number of considerations for those interested in facilitating behavioral enactment within relational and group settings in sport. One need only examine the various sources that researchers have ascribed to each type of efficacy to identify practical strategies for how that form of efficacy can be enhanced. For example, if a coach is particularly interested in raising the team's collective efficacy, they could do the following:

- Structure practices so that team members draw from successful experiences of performing specific maneuvers
- Exude confidence in the team's capabilities when communicating with them
- Foster a team's social identity that "we're in this together"
- Compile video footage (i.e., a series of highlights) so the team can see themselves performing specific collective systems or maneuvers effectively (i.e., collective self-modeling)
- Employ interventions designed to enhance teamwork (e.g., role-clarity strategies)

The same principles also apply to facilitating the other forms of efficacy covered in this chapter. For example, if a coach is interested in raising a player's role efficacy, they could devise strategies such as ensuring the player is (1) given sufficient experience to practice their role responsibilities away from the pressure of competition, (2) clear about their role responsibilities, and (3) provided with appropriate role models for the successful execution of specific role responsibilities. Alternatively, if a sport psychology practitioner is concerned with enhancing a team captain's leadership efficacy, the practitioner could encourage the captain to model leadership behaviors on those of an efficacious leader or encourage the coach to exude confidence in the captain's leadership capabilities.

The research findings highlighted in this chapter point to the viability of directing efficacy-enhancement interventions at the coach, the athlete, or the team as a whole. Regardless, when developing such interventions, one should be acutely aware of the temporal nature of the efficacy cognition being targeted (Bandura, 1997). Efficacy beliefs are likely to change with time, especially as the target (i.e., athlete, coach, team) begins to access different sources of efficacy information and develops different levels of success and failure across a range of performance contexts. As Lindsley and colleagues (1995) demonstrated, the efficacy–performance relationship is cyclic in nature and can spiral upward or downward. In sport settings, this can work in favor of athletes (if the spiral is upward) or against athletes (if the spiral is downward). Practitioners (e.g., coaches, sport psychology practitioners) are encouraged to be aware of any efficacy–performance spiral and intervene if necessary, especially if the spiral is downward.

Summary

The overall purpose of this chapter was to provide a comprehensive review of the extant efficacy literature related to behavioral enactment within relational (e.g., coach–athlete, athlete–athlete) and group settings. Each of the efficacy constructs covered in this chapter is grounded within the broader theoretical framework provided by self-efficacy theory (Bandura, 1977, 1997) and as such is likely to be determined by multiple sources of information. In general, relational and group conceptions of efficacy have been found to be positively related to improved athlete, team, and coach functioning. Although some of the efficacy constructs covered in this chapter have been the focus of much research attention (e.g., collective efficacy), other forms have received relatively less attention (e.g., other-efficacy, RISE). Given that efficacy beliefs are potent social cognitions that are also amenable to change (cf. Bandura, 1997), future research is needed to understand how best to develop these perceptions and harness desirable individual and collective outcomes in sport.

DISCUSSION QUESTIONS

1. Research conducted on coaching efficacy, proxy efficacy, and other-efficacy suggests that confidence in a significant other may affect an athlete's personal sense of efficacy. To what extent might a parent's confidence in a child's capabilities affect the confidence of that child?
2. What are some of the key sources of collective efficacy beliefs in sport teams? If a coach or sport psychology consultant is interested in developing a team-building intervention to raise the team's collective efficacy, what sort of strategies might they use? Who should facilitate the intervention (coach or sport psychology practitioner) and why?
3. What are some of the key sources of coaching efficacy? Given the importance of retaining the involvement of coaches in youth sport in particular, how might national sport federations, governing bodies, and coach development programs go about supporting (and, where appropriate, bolstering) the efficacy beliefs of such coaches?
4. In light of the potential for efficacy–performance relationships to spiral (upward as well as downward), what strategies might a sport psychology practitioner or coach implement when members of a sport dyad (such as a coxless pair in rowing) begin to display a lack of confidence in each other's capabilities? Similarly, if an upward efficacy spiral develops, what might a coach or sport psychology practitioner do to guard against complacency?

16

Stress, Coping, Emotion, and Emotion Regulation in Sport

Katherine A. Tamminen, PhD, and Faye F. Didymus, PhD

LEARNING OBJECTIVES

On completion of this chapter, the reader should have the following:

- Knowledge of both foundational and contemporary approaches to understanding stress, emotions, coping, and emotion regulation
- Appreciation of individual and interpersonal approaches to understanding stress in sport
- Understanding of the impact that emotions have between individuals in dyadic and group settings such as team sport
- Understanding of the ways individuals may influence the stressor appraisals, emotions, coping, and emotion regulation of others

Consider an athlete who is performing poorly in competition: No matter what they do, they keep getting more angry and more upset with themselves and their performance, and they cannot seem to do anything right. To deal with their performance problems and anger, the athlete may try to regulate their emotions in a number of ways. They might use self-talk to refocus their attention on technique, or they might try to breathe deeply and relax between moments of competition. However, the athlete's experience in competition does not occur in a vacuum, insulated from the people around them: Sport is a social setting where other people can and do influence the athlete's emotions and experiences. The athlete's experience of stress, coping, and emotion regulation is occurring within the social context of sport. Perhaps a teammate approaches them during a time-out to check in and see how they're feeling. The teammate might point out that the athlete has been working really hard, or mention things the athlete has been doing well during the game, despite their poor performance. How might this teammate's actions influence the upset athlete's emotions? The athlete may feel relieved and reassured that they can still do some things well, even if other aspects of their performance are suffering. Alternatively, in a different scenario, a teammate might approach the athlete who is performing poorly and shout at them in a frustrated, angry manner, pointing out the errors the athlete has been making. In this scenario, the athlete may feel even more angry at themselves, as well as experiencing shame or guilt for feeling they are letting teammates down.

The study of stress, coping, emotions, and emotion regulation has typically been approached from an individualistic perspective in sport, wherein researchers have sought to examine how athletes experience, express, and manage their own emotions and cope with stressors on their own (e.g., Gaudreau et al., 2010; Nicholls et al., 2006). However, sport is inherently a social setting where coaches, teammates, and opponents, for example, can influence athletes' stressors, emotions, coping, and emotion regulation. In recent years, there has been an expansion of research that approaches these topics from an interpersonal perspective, which is informed by social psychology and provides a nuanced and complex picture of the interpersonal processes that affect an athlete's performance in sport. In this chapter, we consider the following questions: How do social influences affect appraisals of stressors? How are emotions experienced and expressed in social contexts in sport? How do emotion regulation and coping occur between individuals in the context of sport?

The athlete's experience in competition does not occur in a vacuum, insulated from the people around them: Sport is a social setting where other people can and do influence the athlete's emotions and experiences.

Defining Key Terms

To begin, it is important to provide some definitions of key terms that serve as a starting point for the study of stressors, coping, emotions, and emotion regulation. *Stress* is a broad term that refers to a variety of processes and variables; it reflects the relationship between the person and their environment as they continually adapt to changing conditions in their lives (Lazarus, 1999). According to this conceptualization, *stressors* are defined as internal or external events, situations, or environmental demands that are appraised as taxing or exceeding the person's resources or endangering their well-being (Lazarus & Folkman, 1984). Importantly, stressors are appraised according to their personal relevance or meaningfulness for the individual or the group(s) they belong to (primary appraising), as well as in relation to the individual's resources for dealing with the situation or event (secondary appraising). Appraising an upcoming competition as a threat, for example, may result in disruptions to the athlete's attentional focus, an increased heart rate, physiological changes throughout the body, and emotions such as anxiety or fear.

Emotions are discrete and episodic experiences, typically short in duration (compared with moods, for example, which last longer than emotions), that produce noticeable changes in behaviors, thoughts, sensations, and physiological arousal (e.g., Ekman, 1992; Frijda & Mesquita, 1994; Lazarus, 1999). *Coping* refers to "constantly changing cognitive and behavioural efforts to manage specific external and/or internal demands that are appraised as taxing or exceeding the resources of the person" (Lazarus & Folkman, 1984, p. 141), while *emotion regulation* is defined as "the processes by which individuals influence which emotions they have, when they have them, and how they experience and express these emotions" (Gross, 1998, p. 275). Therefore, emotion regulation is concerned with *what* emotions people are experiencing and *how* they are experiencing, expressing, and regulating them. Conversely, the focus of coping is primarily on the conscious efforts (thoughts and behaviors) that people make to try to manage or regulate the stressors or emotions they are experiencing.

These definitions are grounded in transactional theories of stress such as Lazarus' (1999) cognitive–motivational–relational theory (CMRT) of stress and emotion and the revised theory of challenge and threat states in athletes (TCTSA; Jones et al., 2009; Meijen et al., 2020). Theories such as these have been used extensively in sport psychology research and practice to understand how athletes appraise stressors, the responses associated with different appraisals, the emotions athletes experience, and the strategies athletes use to cope with stressors or regulate their emotions. Research on psychological stress in sport has typically been informed by transactional perspectives that view "the person and the environment in a dynamic, mutually reciprocal, bidirectional relationship" (Lazarus & Folkman, 1984, p. 293). Researchers who have examined appraising most often apply these theories at the intraindividual level with athletes (e.g., Didymus & Fletcher, 2012, 2014; Doron & Martinent, 2017), coaches (e.g., Didymus, 2017; Dixon et al., 2017), or parents (Harwood et al., 2019).

While such research has made helpful advances in understanding appraising among individuals, it has overlooked the often inherently social nature of stress. The focus on individual athletes' appraisals, emotions, and coping in previous research could be because sport psychology as an applied field has emphasized the understanding of processes and principles that can be targeted for intervention to improve performance. For example, understanding how an athlete copes effectively with performance-related stressors is important to determine ways of helping the athlete cope more effectively and perform consistently well in competitions. However, this focus on the individual's appraisal and coping processes and outcomes has tended to neglect the social context in which appraisals, emotions, and coping take place. Figure 16.1 visualizes the relationships in an athlete's life that form the athlete's social context.

This shortcoming of the extant evidence base exists despite long-standing knowledge that social roles and relationships are developed, altered, and maintained via encounters of daily stressors; that social functioning is in part determined by the effectiveness with which daily encounters are appraised and managed (Lazarus & Folkman, 1984); and that stressors often have social beginnings (e.g., Hoar et al., 2010). Take the example of an athlete who consistently appraises their coach's well-intended feedback as a threat. Such appraisals over a prolonged period of time could lead to misunderstanding, hurt feelings, and relationship dissatisfaction. This example highlights the importance of considering the interpersonal nature and consequences of appraising and coping with stressors in sport. Although many theorists acknowledge that appraisals, emotions, and coping take place in social contexts and have interpersonal consequences (Lazarus, 1999; Vallerand & Blanchard, 2000), only recently has there been sustained research attention on these topics as social processes.

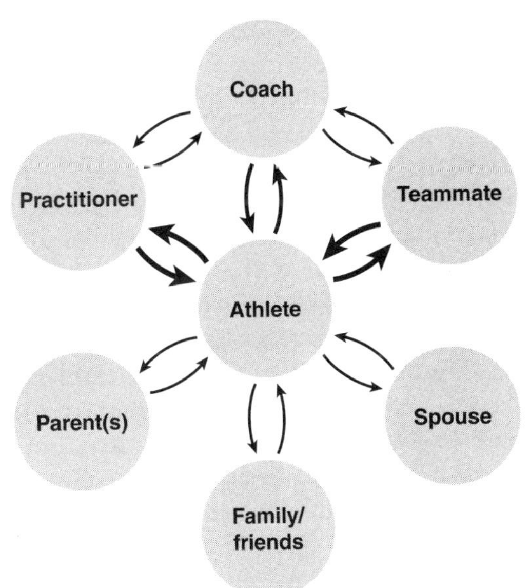

FIGURE 16.1 Stress, coping, emotions, and emotion regulation exist within social networks. Athletes' emotional expressions and their efforts to manage their emotions and cope with stressors are influenced by people around them, including coaches, sport practitioners, teammates, spouses, parents, and family and friends.

Appraising Stressors in Group Settings

Stressors can be appraised in different ways by individuals who are in motivated performance situations (e.g., a sport competition) (Jones et al., 2009; Meijen et al., 2020). Within most research on this topic, there are two independent but related processes that individuals engage with when evaluating stressors: primary and secondary appraising (Lazarus, 1999). During *primary appraising*, the individual decides whether or not the situation is stressful (i.e., personally relevant and meaningful). When the stressor is evaluated as stressful, there are four possible outcomes: threat, challenge, harm or loss, and benefit (see Lazarus, 1999). Threat and harm or loss appraisals typically have negative implications, because they assess actual or potential harm that may occur, while challenge and benefit appraisals are likely to have more beneficial implications for the individual and their performance, because they have the potential for gain or growth in an encounter (Lazarus & Folkman, 1984). During *secondary appraising*, athletes consider the degree of control they have over the stressor, what coping resources they have available, and the likelihood of a coping strategy's managing the stressor effectively (Lazarus & Folkman, 1984). As such, appraising is a highly complex phenomenon that incorporates many evaluative processes that can occur simultaneously, both consciously or subconsciously, and that change over time; this complexity makes the study and measurement of appraising difficult.

Literature on appraising in the context of two or more people is limited in sport. There is, however, more literature in general and relationship psychology that explores the interpersonal nature of appraising. For example, the presence of a supportive partner has been shown to shape appraisals and augment available coping resources among heterosexual couples (Meuwly et al., 2012). Indeed, stressors can be perceived as less threatening when appraised in the presence of a helpful other. Comparable findings have been reported in literature on social support in sport, whereby esteem support (i.e., facilitating an individual's sense of competence) can reduce threat appraisals (Freeman & Rees, 2009) and perceived support can augment positive appraisals of stressors (DeFreese & Smith, 2013).

While it is clear from general psychology research that the notion of interpersonal cognition is not new (Lazarus & Folkman, 1984), it is only recently that sport, performance, and exercise psychology researchers have begun to forge understanding in this area. This is in part due to methodological and measurement constraints that have inhibited the address of more complex research questions relating to the social and interpersonal aspects of stress-related cognition. Some researchers (Wolf et al., 2015) have, however, made progress toward the consideration of appraising as a socially tied construct by examining appraisals in the context of team sport. The results of this research suggest that those who perceive their team as more cohesive may be more likely to appraise stressors as a challenge, which has beneficial effects on emotions and performance. In other research, Doron and Bourbousson (2017) used audiovisual recordings alongside verbalizations during postmatch interviews with male basketball players; the athletes reviewed the recordings of their performance to explore stressors and appraisals among their teammates. The findings highlighted that stressors can be appraised by individual players and, at the same time during a game, by other team members, and that stressors can be perceived to influence both team and individual functioning. These insights lend support to the notion of moment-to-moment *emotional contagion* (i.e., the spread or transfer of emotions between people) in team sports (Barsade, 2000) and highlight the need for further research on the interpersonal manifestation of appraising.

While it is clear from general psychology research that the notion of interpersonal cognition is not new (Lazarus & Folkman, 1984), it is only recently that sport, performance, and exercise psychology researchers have begun to forge understanding in this area.

Emotions as Social Phenomena

Just as appraisals of stressors are influenced by social contexts (Wolf et al., 2015), the experience and expression of emotions can also be influenced by the presence of others (Tamminen, Palmateer et al., 2016), as well as by the affiliations athletes feel with members of their group or team (Campo, Mackie, et al., 2019). There are several ways to consider emotions as social phenomena and to examine how emotions are experienced within groups and teams. *Group-based emotions* are experienced as a function of an individual's social identity as an athlete or team member; these emotions are typically reported in response to events or stressors that are appraised as affecting the athlete's team or group (Goldenberg et al., 2014). Initial qualitative research with Canadian varsity athletes documented their experiences of group-based emotions such as pride associated with being a member of a team or a representative of their country, or happiness when seeing a teammate perform well (Tamminen, Palmateer, et al., 2016). Subsequent research has also demonstrated that athletes' social identities as both athletes and team members are associated with their emotions as experienced in sport settings (Campo, Mackie, et al., 2019). However, the link between group-based emotions and athletes' individual performances remains unclear (Campo, Champely, et al., 2019; Campo et al., 2018), and further research is needed to determine whether group-based emotions have substantive impacts on athletes' performances.

A second way emotions may be considered as social phenomena is by examining them collectively. *Collective emotions* are also considered a type of group-based emotions; however, they are experienced with others at the same time (Goldenberg et al., 2014; Tamminen, Palmateer, et al., 2016). Within sport, athletes have described the atmosphere in the team dressing room after a competition as an example of collective emotions: "After any win that emotion is pretty uniform throughout the room. Guys are all happy, dancing around, celebrating and stuff" (Tamminen, Palmateer, et al., 2016, p. 32). Similarly, the emotions experienced as a group after losing a competition provide an example of collective emotions: "At the end of the game we literally all just went to the bench and just sat and cried and our coach just talked to us then he started crying" (Tamminen, Palmateer, et al., 2016, p. 32). The key difference between collective emotions and group-based emotions is that collective emotions occur when people are physically in the same space together, whereas individuals do not necessarily need to be physically present in the same place to experience group-based emotions connected to one's team (von Scheve & Ismer, 2013). For example, sport fans watching an athlete representing their country at the Olympics may feel a swell of pride or joy when the athlete wins in competition, despite not being physically present at the event.

A third way emotions can be viewed as social phenomena is by considering how athletes within teams or groups might experience the spread of emotions throughout the team; this phenomenon is referred to as *emotional contagion* (Barsade, 2000). The implications of emotions spreading throughout teams has been highlighted in teams' performance outcomes. For example, in a study of team collapse in sport competition (i.e., where multiple players within a team exhibit sudden and extreme underperformance), Wergin and colleagues (2018) found that athletes described negative emotional contagion among athletes during their team's collapse. Linkages between the positive moods of cricket players during competition have been associated with improved performance (Totterdell, 2000), and soccer players' celebrations of successful goals have been associated with their team's eventual success in competitions (Moll et al., 2010). Researchers have offered evidence for gender differences in emotional contagion susceptibility, suggesting that women athletes report they are more likely than men to be susceptible to the emotions displayed by leaders within their team (Cotterill et al., 2020). It is unknown whether these differences could be attributed to women athletes being more aware of others' emotions compared with men, or whether leaders on women's teams are more emotionally expressive than leaders on men's teams. Further research is needed to examine the mechanisms for these effects. These findings do, however, support the idea of emotional contagion within teams and suggest that some athletes may be more likely to be influenced by the emotions of others. Collectively, these three examples—group-based emotions, collective emotions, and emotional contagion—reflect ways that athletes may experience and be influenced by emotions in social settings in sport.

Extending beyond explorations of how emotions are experienced in group settings, researchers have begun to investigate the extent to which emotional experiences in groups or teams may be shaped or influenced by individual members, such as coaches or team leaders (e.g., van Kleef et al., 2019). This line of inquiry has direct relevance to sport and performance settings because it would be useful to understand how team leaders or coaches might change the emotional experience of the members of the team (Kim et al., 2021; van Kleef et al. 2019). If a team of athletes is experiencing a collapse in their collective performance within a competition, the negative emotions experienced by the athletes may exacerbate the team's poor performance (Wergin et al., 2018). Therefore, understanding how athletes or coaches can change the direction of the emotional climate within the team could prove valuable in preventing further performance decrements. There has been limited research on the intentional strategies that coaches and leaders can use to change the emotional climate within teams. However, coaches' pregame speeches (Vargas & Short, 2011) and coaches' and leaders' emotional expressions (Staw et al., 2019; van Kleef et al., 2019) have been associated with athletes' effort and subsequent performance in competition. Future research can extend this work by testing different types of speeches and emotional expressions that vary in tone and intensity to determine the most effective means of influencing the emotional climate within a team and promoting positive performance outcomes.

Coping as a Social Process

Our discussions of appraising and emotions as social phenomena, and the possibility of athletes or coaches being able to influence the emotions of a group, lead us to consideration of coping as a social process. As is the case with most stress-related phenomena, coping has typically been investigated from an individual perspective in sport, despite acknowledgment for many years that stress has close social ties and is entwined with human relationships, networks, and support systems (Hanin, 2007; Vallerand, 1983; Vallerand & Blanchard, 2000). Research examining the interpersonal nature of coping has typically been with general population samples, including marital relationships (e.g., Bodenmann et al., 2006), couples coping with significant life events (e.g., cancer) (Kayser et al., 2007), and parent–child relationships (e.g., Körner et al., 2013). Researchers who work in these contexts use various terms to refer to interpersonal coping, including dyadic, communal, and relational coping. *Dyadic coping* is "a process in which the stress signals of one partner and the coping reactions of the other partner to these signals (both verbal and nonverbal) are taken into consideration" (Bodenmann, 1997, p. 138). From this perspective, communication of the stressor from one person to another is essential, and one partner's well-being is dependent on that of the other partner as well as on their social environment. *Communal coping*, on the other hand, is defined as the "pooling of resources and efforts of several individuals (e.g., couples, families, or communities) to confront adversity" (Lyons et al., 1998, p. 580), while *relational coping* includes the participation of two partners together in the coping process (Kayser et al., 2007). Although several definitions are used across this body of research, many of the terms for describing interpersonal coping mean similar things and have in common the involvement of more than one person in efforts to manage stressors.

Research on interpersonal coping has often focused on making theoretical advancements that help to frame understanding and guide the development of research questions. For example, theories relating to

- relationship-focused coping (Coyne & Fiske, 1992),
- interpersonal regulatory processes (DeLongis & O'Brien, 1990; O'Brien & DeLongis, 1997),
- coping congruence (Revenson, 1994, 2003),
- communal coping (Lyons et al., 1998), and
- systemic-transactional coping (Bodenmann, 1995, 1997, 2005)

have each been offered as advancements to the original—and often intrapersonally focused—theories of psychological stress (e.g., Lazarus & Folkman, 1984; Pearlin & Schooler, 1978).

In the first qualitative study to focus explicitly on dyadic coping in sport, Staff and colleagues (2017) explored how coaches and athletes work together to cope with stressors; they identified factors that led to (i.e., antecedents) and occurred as a result of (i.e., outcomes) dyadic coping. The findings indicated that, for the coaches, athletes, and researchers involved with the study, the essence of dyadic coping was "the sharing of demands experienced by an individual as a means to supplement and develop coping strategies for both members of the dyad" (Staff et al., 2017, p. 95). A lock-and-key fit between the coach and the athlete, friendship and trust, and communication of a stressor were antecedents necessary for dyadic coping to occur. Poczwardowski and colleagues (2020) also found that, among a sample of elite beach volleyball players, dyadic coping was an important component of relationship complementarity (i.e., the mutual distribution of power and control between partners, and the degrees of collaborative efforts, cooperation, and responsiveness to achieve successful performance). The volleyball players in this study emphasized the importance of balancing each other's strengths and compensating for each other's weaknesses as part of a single mechanism of dyadic coping that involved both members of the partnership.

Promoting dyadic coping may contribute to the development of positive, nurturing environments that facilitate protection and support for both athletes and coaches.

Other research demonstrates associations between athletes' and coaches' dyadic coping, relationship quality, and appraisals of stressors. For example, among a sample of 158 coach–athlete dyads, relationship quality mediated the relationship between dyadic coping and appraisals of stressors, and this effect was greater for coaches than it was for athletes (Nicholls & Perry, 2016). In addition, when coach–athlete dyads reported more positive dyadic coping (i.e., supportive, delegated, or common forms of dyadic coping), they also experienced greater relationship satisfaction and often viewed stressful events as a challenge as opposed to a threat. These findings are noteworthy because challenge appraisals are thought to be associated with superior performance, as well as less anxiety and conscious processing, than threat appraisals (Moore et al., 2013; Turner et al., 2013).

Most recently, Staff and colleagues (2020) developed a substantive grounded theory to capture the development and manifestation of dyadic coping among coaches and athletes. This theory proposes that coaches and athletes must communicate (either verbally or nonverbally) with the other person about a stressor to initiate dyadic coping. Once this communication has occurred, coaches and athletes will appraise the stressor, and if this appraisal suggests the stressor is significant and meaningful, they will initiate dyadic coping to protect themselves and their relationship. The theory also highlights that dyadic coping can be moderated by personal characteristics (e.g., personality), relationship characteristics (e.g., length of time working together), and organizational characteristics (e.g., leadership behaviors). Outcomes of dyadic coping are thought to be related to performance, personal development, psychological well-being, and relationship satisfaction (Staff et al., 2020). Thus, dyadic coping is one mechanism by which these factors could be enhanced. Promoting dyadic coping may contribute to the development of positive, nurturing environments that facilitate protection and support for both athletes and coaches (Staff et al., 2017).

Complementing this work studying dyadic coping in sport, some researchers have taken a communal perspective to examine coping from a conceptually different but similarly interpersonal viewpoint. In one such study, Neely and colleagues (2017) focused on female youth athletes and their parents as they coped with deselection from competitive sport (soccer, basketball, volleyball, and ice hockey). They used a descriptive phenomenological approach that was guided by a framework of communal coping (Lyons et al., 1998) to analyze semi-structured interviews. The findings highlighted that deselection was a shared stressor and, interestingly, that parents' and youth athletes' responsibilities for coping changed over time. Initially, parents assumed responsibility for protecting their child from the potentially negative emotional ramifications of deselection, and then athletes and their parents worked together to cooperatively manage each other's reactions. These findings suggest there is value in communal coping during deselection from sport and raise interesting questions about the similarities and differences between what is termed communal coping in this study versus dyadic coping in others.

In another qualitative study of communal coping, Leprince and colleagues (2018) explored shared stressors and communal coping strategies among 10 athletes who competed in either football, rugby, volleyball, ice hockey, or basketball. The findings of this work highlighted four themes of communal coping:

- Problem-focused communal efforts (e.g., information sharing)
- Relationship-focused coping (e.g., motivational support)
- Communal management of emotions (e.g., interpersonal emotion regulation)
- Communal goal withdrawal (e.g., task disengagement)

These findings are consistent with other research in this area, in that the athletes used a range of strategies to cope with stressors (c.f. Nicholls & Polman, 2007). However, the insight offered by this study also highlights the potential for team athletes to engage with collaborative coping efforts when encountering shared stressors. We note, however, that this research gathered insights from only one member of each team, rather than exploring more deeply the communal coping efforts of numerous members of the same team. In doing so, the way the data were gathered was somewhat incongruent with the concepts the study was trying to explore. Future research should address this and other methodological constraints by, for example, conducting in-depth examinations of communal coping among multiple members of the same team.

Emotion Regulation as a Social Process

Researchers examining interpersonal emotion regulation in sport seek to understand how individuals may try to influence one another's emotions and the impacts of these actions on athletes' performance. An intrapersonal (or individualistic) perspective of emotion regulation focuses on the strategies athletes use to regulate their own emotions, whereas an interpersonal perspective broadens the focus beyond the athlete's own actions to consider how interactions with other people may influence emotions and performance outcomes. Key questions to consider in understanding emotion regulation within social settings are as follows:

- How does emotion regulation occur between people in sport?
- Why do people try to influence the emotions of one another in sport?
- What is the impact of interpersonal emotion regulation for athletes?

Interpersonal emotion regulation refers to efforts to deliberately try to influence the emotions of another person (Dixon-Gordon et al., 2015; Niven, 2017; Tamminen & Neely, 2020). Strategies that may be considered interpersonal emotion regulation efforts include actions attempting to improve or worsen the emotions or mood of another person. For example, a teammate may point out the things an athlete is doing well in an effort to improve the athlete's emotions, while another teammate may criticize or yell at the athlete in an attempt to make them feel bad about their performance. The definition also suggests that interpersonal emotion regulation consists of actions and interactions that are motivated by the goal of regulating another person's emotional expressions or experiences, regardless of the actual impact on the recipient's emotions (Dixon-Gordon et al., 2015).

Within sport settings, athletes have reported a number of ways they try to positively influence the emotions of their teammates, including providing positive or technical feedback to teammates, using humor, cueing teammates about their emotions, engaging in prosocial actions with teammates, and undertaking indirect or unseen actions to decrease negative emotions of other athletes (Tamminen & Crocker, 2013). In a study of ice hockey players, Friesen and colleagues (2015) described several verbal and behavioral strategies that coaches and athletes used to attempt to influence the emotions of teammates. These included providing positive appraisals of teammates' performances, distracting teammates, using humor, engaging in deception (e.g., misleading teammates about the importance of the game), calling out teammates on their poor performance, and threatening athletes with punishments for poor performance. A case study of university volleyball athletes provided further information about strategies athletes used to try to worsen the emotions of teammates, such as calling out teammates in practice if they are not working hard enough, and physically or tactically picking on teammates to force them to make further mistakes (Palmateer & Tamminen, 2018). Considering these findings in relation to stressors, emotions, coping, and emotion regulation, these strategies athletes report using may be directed at changing their teammates' appraisals of the situation (Lazarus & Folkman, 1984), or they may be characterized as efforts to increase or decrease their teammates' positive and negative emotions (e.g., emotion regulation) (Gross, 1998).

On the surface it may appear mean-spirited to try to cause a teammate to feel worse about themselves if they are not performing well, yet athletes may engage in these emotion-worsening strategies for instrumental reasons (Campo et al., 2017). That is, athletes may hold beliefs that worsening the emotions of teammates or inducing guilt could cause them to try harder and ultimately contribute to a better performance within the team. Indeed, research by Campo and colleagues (2017) documented that rugby players engaged in interpersonal emotion regulation to try to improve the emotions of teammates and to improve their own emotions (for discussions of the purposes for emotion regulation, see Netzer et al., 2015; Tamir, 2016). There is also evidence that coaches engage in emotion management with their athletes for performance-related purposes (Braun & Tamminen, 2019; Donoso-Morales et al., 2017). Although limited research has investigated the instrumental (e.g., performance related) versus hedonic (e.g., to make athletes feel better) reasons for engaging in interpersonal emotion regulation, sport provides a unique social context for future research investigating the motives people have when trying to influence others' emotions.

Sport provides a unique social context for future research investigating the motives people have when trying to influence others' emotions.

Interpersonal emotion regulation is interconnected with athletes' own self-regulation of their emotions (Tamminen, Gaudreau, et al., 2016), and this may be particularly important among team leaders. For example, athletes have reported that they control their own emotions "for the sake of the team" (Tamminen & Crocker, 2013, p. 741) by monitoring their own body language and censoring their own emotional and verbal expressions, as well as by isolating themselves from teammates, reappraising the situation, and holding in their own emotions (Campo et al., 2017; Palmateer & Tamminen, 2018). These findings indicate that athletes are often keenly aware of the potential for emotional contagion that could spread within a team and influence the team's performance. Furthermore, this research illustrates how athletes' emotional self-regulation and coping efforts to deal with their own stressors and emotions (Lazarus, 1999) are often intertwined with their sense of the team environment and their efforts to regulate their teammates' emotions.

Athletes' interpersonal emotion regulation efforts have been linked to sport enjoyment and commitment among adolescent athletes (Tamminen, Gaudreau, et al., 2016), such that athletes' engaging in more actions to try to improve the emotions of their teammates was associated with their own higher enjoyment and commitment in sport. Research among university athletes indicates that patterns of interpersonal emotion regulation to improve or worsen teammates' emotions fluctuate over time before and after a competition, and that patterns of interpersonal emotion regulation among teammates are associated with the team's likelihood of winning in competition (Tamminen et al., 2019). Specifically, the team's success was predicted by decreases in affect-worsening interpersonal emotion regulation actions among teammates in the days leading up to the competition. Thus, success in competition may be dependent on maintaining a positive atmosphere within the team. This could be achieved by, for example, teammates' avoiding actions that worsen one another's emotions in the lead-up to competition. These findings provide initial evidence that athletes' actions to improve or worsen the emotions of their teammates are associated with individual and team outcomes in sport.

The research on interpersonal emotion regulation in sport has thus far documented the strategies individuals may use to try to improve or worsen the emotions of others, as well as the motives for engaging in these actions, and the psychological and performance outcomes associated with these processes. Additionally, researchers have begun to identify some of the factors influencing processes of interpersonal emotion regulation in sport. For example, qualitative interviews with high-performance volleyball players revealed that athletes' relationships with teammates and the personalities of different teammates played a role in determining whether they attempted to regulate the emotions of another player on the team (Palmateer & Tamminen, 2018). Similarly, athletes' preferences for regulating their own emotions, their role on the team, and social norms within the sport environment have been proposed as factors that could influence athletes' interpersonal emotion regulation with teammates (Palmateer & Tamminen, 2018; Tamminen & Crocker, 2013; Tamminen, Palmateer, et al., 2016).

Some quantitative research has provided evidence of additional factors associated with athletes' use of interpersonal emotion regulation, including gender, starting status, competitive experience (Palmateer et al., 2017; Tamminen et al., 2015), and perceptions of esteem support available from teammates (Tamminen et al., 2019). However, further research is needed to understand the factors that influence interpersonal emotion regulation between teammates. Interpersonal emotion regulation is likely to differ depending on the sport being played. For example, a sport such as baseball may have ample opportunities for players to try to regulate one another's emotions while players are sitting on the bench, but when the team is spread out on the field these opportunities would be less frequent. Conversely, volleyball players are more closely positioned to one another during the entire game, and teams often come together after each point, providing more opportunities for interpersonal emotion regulation between teammates.

Overview and Synthesis of Current Literature

The study of appraising, coping, emotions, and emotion regulation in sport is rapidly evolving to incorporate social perspectives and concepts. This development is important in reflecting the social environment of sport and understanding how the appraisal, experience, and regulation of stressors and emotions are influenced by social factors. Overall, researchers have investigated social and interpersonal influences in relation to multiple aspects of athletes' appraisals of stressors, emotional experiences, coping, and emotion regulation, and in relation to various outcomes including sport performance, commitment, motivation, enjoyment, social identity, and relationship satisfaction.

Figure 16.2 provides an overview of key concepts from research conducted in sport settings, and we have mapped these onto the concepts of appraising, emotions, coping, emotion regulation, and associated outcomes. First, this model summarizes findings indicating that athletes' appraisals of stressors may be influenced by their goals, values, and needs that arise as a function of their social relationships and social identity, as well as the ways athletes' appraisals may be influenced by their sense of social support and relationships with others. Second, this model depicts the ways athletes' emotional experiences are influenced by others: Individual experiences of emotions may be influenced by others' actions, athletes may experience group-based or collective emotions, and athletes may experience emotional contagion because emotions can spread throughout a team or group of people. Third, this model indicates interpersonal influences on athletes' coping and emotion regulation: Athletes' coping and self-regulation may be influenced by social norms, athletes may engage in interpersonal emotion regulation actions, and athletes may engage in dyadic or communal coping to deal with stressors. Finally, this model summarizes outcomes that are influenced by interpersonal and social processes: Sport performance, commitment, motivation, social identity, and relationship satisfaction have all been found to be related to interpersonal and social aspects of appraising, coping, emotions, and emotion regulation.

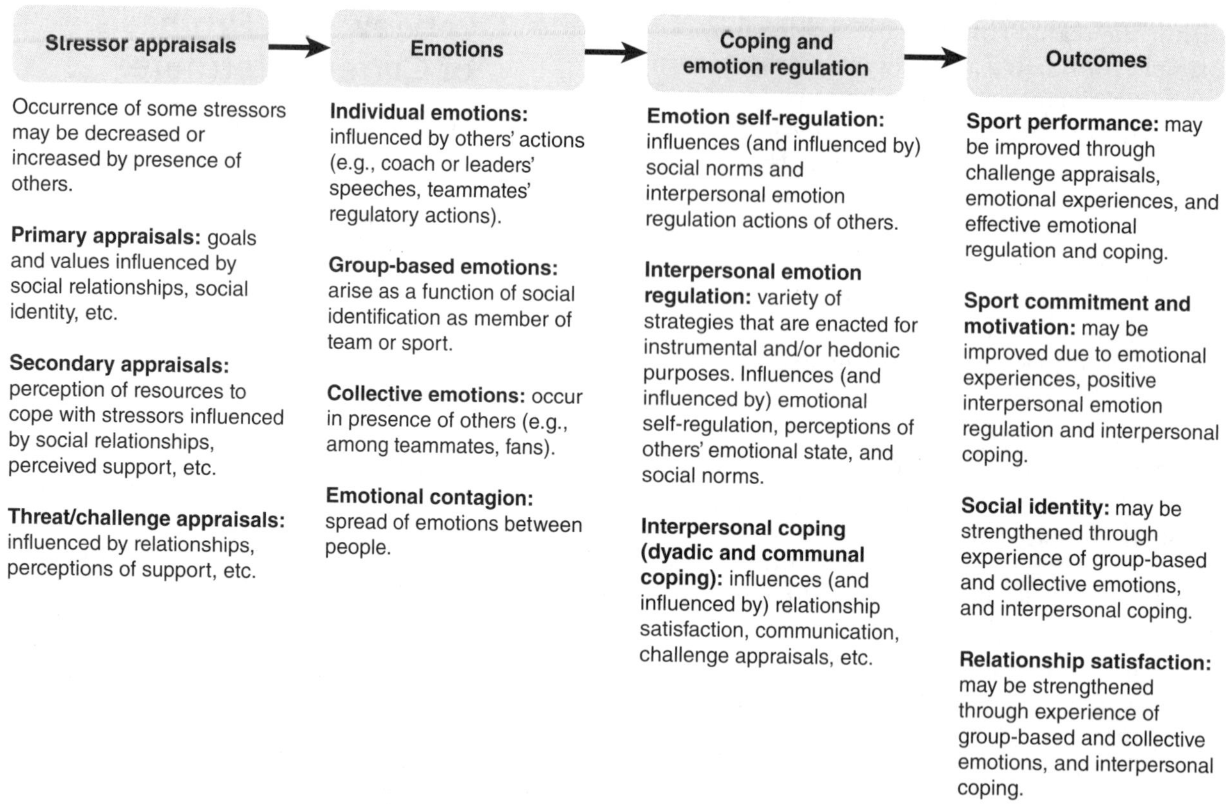

Stressor appraisals → **Emotions** → **Coping and emotion regulation** → **Outcomes**

Stressor appraisals	Emotions	Coping and emotion regulation	Outcomes
Occurrence of some stressors may be decreased or increased by presence of others.	**Individual emotions:** influenced by others' actions (e.g., coach or leaders' speeches, teammates' regulatory actions).	**Emotion self-regulation:** influences (and influenced by) social norms and interpersonal emotion regulation actions of others.	**Sport performance:** may be improved through challenge appraisals, emotional experiences, and effective emotional regulation and coping.
Primary appraisals: goals and values influenced by social relationships, social identity, etc.	**Group-based emotions:** arise as a function of social identification as member of team or sport.	**Interpersonal emotion regulation:** variety of strategies that are enacted for instrumental and/or hedonic purposes. Influences (and influenced by) emotional self-regulation, perceptions of others' emotional state, and social norms.	**Sport commitment and motivation:** may be improved due to emotional experiences, positive interpersonal emotion regulation and interpersonal coping.
Secondary appraisals: perception of resources to cope with stressors influenced by social relationships, perceived support, etc.	**Collective emotions:** occur in presence of others (e.g., among teammates, fans).	**Interpersonal coping (dyadic and communal coping):** influences (and influenced by) relationship satisfaction, communication, challenge appraisals, etc.	**Social identity:** may be strengthened through experience of group-based and collective emotions, and interpersonal coping.
Threat/challenge appraisals: influenced by relationships, perceptions of support, etc.	**Emotional contagion:** spread of emotions between people.		**Relationship satisfaction:** may be strengthened through experience of group-based and collective emotions, and interpersonal coping.

FIGURE 16.2 Overview of interpersonal influences on appraisals, emotions, coping, and emotion regulation. Note: This process is recursive and dynamic, changing over time and across situations and contexts. This diagram presents a simplified overview to depict some of the main concepts that have been investigated in sport.

Future Research Directions

Moving forward in this area, there are several important avenues for research. First, research is required to examine the uses and purposes of interpersonal emotion regulation strategies among athletes and among other members of athletes' social contexts, such as coaches, physiotherapists, and parents. It is possible that athletes may prefer or benefit from particular types of interpersonal emotion regulation strategies employed by coaches versus teammates (Palmateer & Tamminen, 2018), and it would be useful to understand how members of an athlete's social environment may influence their appraisals and overall emotional experiences in sport (Wolf et al., 2015). For example, if athletes are consistently feeling that teammates, coaches, and parents are worsening their emotions or contributing to feelings of guilt over poor performance, what impacts do these interactions have on the athlete's mental health, well-being, and performance? It would also be valuable to examine whether the emotion-improving actions of just one other person such as a parent, coach, teammate, or physiotherapist could buffer potentially detrimental effects (cf. Gaudreau et al., 2016). Furthermore, research on athletes' motives for engaging in interpersonal emotion regulation with teammates could provide valuable information about people's use of affect-improving or affect-worsening behaviors in other cooperative or competitive contexts. For example, this information could be applied in academic or workplace settings to promote more effective interpersonal functioning as well as individual and team performance outcomes.

A second important area of future research involves exploring the socialization of emotion regulation to understand how social norms for the expression and regulation of emotions develop within sport, and how these processes occur at a microlevel within teams and specific sport cultures. Much of the research examining coping and emotion regulation as social processes in sport has been largely descriptive to explore how these processes operate. Indeed, limited research has investigated associations between communal coping, dyadic coping, or interpersonal emotion regulation and psychological, social, and performance outcomes in sport. Further research is required to understand the impact of these processes on athletes' individual well-being and performance, and on interpersonal outcomes such as the quality of relationships with teammates or coaches and group functioning and performance.

Relatively little research has explored the moderators and mediators of these processes, so advancing hypotheses about the conditions under which interpersonal coping and/or interpersonal emotion regulation would be associated with better or worse outcomes, or conditions under which these factors have no effect on important outcomes, is warranted. For example, longitudinal studies with teams over one or more competitive seasons may identify periods when interpersonal coping and interpersonal emotion regulation are most needed to protect against declining performance (e.g., during slumps in team performance; after major losses). Such research could support the development of targeted, theoretically informed interventions to promote more effective interpersonal coping for better performance outcomes. Researchers seeking to examine the development of social norms surrounding emotional expression could embrace ethnographic and case study approaches to examine these processes over time and within specific sport contexts. For example, research is needed to examine how emotional expressions are influenced by social norms in sports that endorse hypermasculinity and aggression (e.g., rugby, Giazitzoglu, 2020; football, Steinfeldt et al., 2011), and their resultant impacts on athletes' mental health and well-being.

There is a paucity of applied research evaluating the outcomes of interventions related to the interpersonal influences on appraisals of stressors, emotions, coping, and emotion regulation in sport. Researchers working with sport teams could develop and test interventions to modify athletes' appraisals (e.g., shared stressors vs. individual stressors), emotions (e.g., group-based emotions), coping strategies (e.g., promoting engagement in interpersonal coping), and emotion regulation (e.g., promoting different types of interpersonal emotion regulation) to determine how these may be improved to promote better performance and psychosocial outcomes in sport. These interventions will help characterize the extent to which team and individual performance can be improved, as well as developing understanding about the athletes and teams that may benefit from intervention. Teams with athletes who demonstrate poor interpersonal coping or ineffective interpersonal emotion regulation may benefit the most from such interventions.

There is also scope for advancing the measurement of appraising, communal coping, dyadic coping, emotions, and interpersonal emotion regulation in sport settings. With few exceptions (e.g., the Communal Coping Strategies Inventory for Competitive Team Sports; Leprince et al., 2019), most measures used in sport have been adapted from nonsport settings, and there may be important information missing from these assessments that is relevant to athletes' interpersonal interactions. Thus, the development of contextually relevant measures would be useful for researchers in this field. Much of the qualitative research on the topics explained in this chapter has used interview methods and cross-sectional research designs. Broadening the scope of methods used to examine stress-related phenomena from interpersonal perspectives is warranted.

In addition to advocating for further research examining the interpersonal and social influences on athletes' appraisals, emotions, coping, and emotion regulation and their associated outcomes in an isolated manner, there is also a need for examining these processes in interconnected, holistic ways. For example, researchers could examine how athletes' appraisals of stressors are influenced by their social identities or as a result of inferences about teammates' stressor appraisals. Appraisals could be linked to individual and group-based emotional experiences and also to athletes' individual and interpersonal coping and emotion regulation actions, as well as with performance and psychosocial outcomes. By understanding the social influences on the separate components of athletes' appraisals, emotions, coping, and emotion regulation, as well as by understanding how these parts work together and are interconnected, we may gain a better understanding of the complexity of these processes as they occur in the real world to influence important outcomes in sport and performance settings.

Practical Implications

Recent research on appraisals of stressors, coping, emotions, and emotion regulation that emphasize social and interpersonal perspectives provides valuable information to improve applied practice in sport. In general, these perspectives broaden our consideration of how stressors are appraised in dyads and in groups, how emotions may influence (and are influenced by) other people within teams, and how people cope with stressors or manage emotions in group contexts. Coaches and sport psychology practitioners should be aware that athletes' appraisals of stressors may influence others' appraisals of stressors in group settings (Wolf et al., 2015) and that stress and emotions can spread throughout a team and affect athletes' confidence and performance in competition (Moll et al., 2010; Totterdell, 2000). Given the findings from research on interpersonal emotion regulation and communal coping, coaches and athletes should be educated about the impact of their actions on others' emotions (Braun & Tamminen, 2019; Friesen et al., 2015; Kim et al., 2021) and should learn strategies for supporting communal coping with shared stressors (Leprince et al., 2019; Staff et al., 2020). Providing coaches and athletes (particularly leaders on the team) with information about these processes could improve the emotional climate of the team, improve performance outcomes, and enhance athletes' collective efficacy and confidence in training and competition.

Viewing appraisals of stressors, emotions, coping, and emotion regulation as social and interpersonal processes also provides direction for sport psychology practitioners working with coach–athlete dyads and coach–parent–athlete triads. Rather than focusing solely on helping individuals improve their appraisals, coping, or emotion regulation, practitioners working with dyads or triads should be mindful of the interpersonal dynamics influencing these processes. Thus, practitioner approaches underpinned by family systems theories (Winek, 2010) or models of couples counseling (Gurman, 2011) could be fruitful for working within the context of relationships between coaches, parents, and athletes or between dyads of athletes (e.g., rowers, figure skaters, tennis players). Strategies for working with athletes and coaches could, for example, include examination of the interpersonal impacts of each person's actions and the patterns of interaction within the dyad that contribute to exacerbating or improving appraisals of stressors.

Summary

This chapter brings to the fore the importance of studying stress-related concepts as interpersonal phenomena. It is clear from decades of research in general, social, and relationship psychology that individuals' experiences of stress have close social ties and are entwined with human relationships, networks, and support systems. To fully embrace and explore the highly social nature of sport, researchers and practitioners must move beyond the examination of stress-related phenomena as intrapersonal concepts and toward more complex, interpersonal explorations. To facilitate such developments, measurement and methodological advancements will be required.

DISCUSSION QUESTIONS

1. Think back to an experience in sport that you found stressful. Can you recall how you evaluated the situation in terms of its significance for your well-being and performance? You may, for example, have seen the situation as a threat, challenge, harm or loss, or benefit.
2. Thinking about the stressful situation you reflected on in the previous question, how did you cope with it? Did anyone else help or hinder your coping efforts?
3. Reflecting on your own experiences in sport, have you ever felt happy about your own performance when the rest of the team was upset about a loss? Did you have to conceal or change your own emotional expressions to conform to the emotions that were expected of you?
4. How do you think the quality of the relationship between teammates or between coaches and athletes could influence their coping?
5. How would athletes' preferences for regulating their own emotions influence the way they may try to influence others' emotions? How would athletes' preferences for emotion regulation influence the receipt of emotion regulation efforts from teammates or coaches?

17

Psychosocial Aspects of Mental Health in Sport

Paul Gorczynski, PhD; Cindy Miller Aron, LCSW; and Claudia L. Reardon, MD

LEARNING OBJECTIVES

On completion of this chapter, the reader should have the following:

- Ability to describe mental health, well-being, and common mental health symptoms and disorders in sport
- Familiarity with the epidemiology of mental health symptoms and disorders in sport
- Understanding of socioecological factors that contribute to mental health symptoms and disorders in sport
- Ability to define mental health literacy
- Appreciation of interdisciplinary perspectives toward enhancing mental health literacy in sport

Mental health symptoms and disorders have an impact on athletes, coaches, and referees (Reardon et al., 2019). They are associated with increased risk of and recovery from physical injuries and diminished performance in sport. Mental health symptoms and disorders affect both current and retired individuals in sport. The consequences of mental health symptoms and disorders also affect an individual's social health, potentially resulting in strained or fractured relationships with teammates, coaches, and staff, as well as family and friends (Reardon et al., 2019). Such consequences are not limited just to performance in sport but have an impact on the individual's whole life. Overall, the costs associated with not understanding and addressing mental health symptoms and disorders in sport are tremendous, and there is a need for closer alignments between what research evidence and many aspects of applied practice show us.

This chapter provides a definition of mental health and how it plays an important role in the overall well-being of athletes, coaches, and referees. Primarily, the mental health symptoms and disorders common among athletes, coaches, and referees are defined and discussed with respect to prevalence and treatment. Socioecological models are discussed in relation to better understanding individual and social factors responsible for poor mental health in sport. Multidisciplinary socioecological strategies aimed at enhancing the mental health literacy of athletes, coaches, and referees are presented. Although research in mental health in sport continues to evolve and progress, areas of mental health literacy in sport are still in their infancy. The chapter concludes with suggestions for future research and implications for future practice.

Mental Health, Well-Being, and Mental Health Symptoms and Disorders

Mental health in sport has received considerable attention from athletes, coaches, referees, fans, journalists, researchers, and mental health practitioners from around the world. Left unaddressed, mental health symptoms and disorders can have a tremendous impact on individuals, with consequences for physical, psychological, and social health—both within and outside of sport (Hainline & Reardon, 2019). Most notably, the International Olympic Committee convened a group of mental health experts, including researchers, practitioners, and Olympians, to provide a comprehensive understanding of mental health symptoms and disorders in elite athletes, including their prevalence, underlying causes, and treatments (Hainline & Reardon, 2019; Reardon et al., 2019). The consensus statement was grounded in a psychosocial perspective, acknowledging both the individual and the environment in contributing to mental health symptoms and disorders and as a theoretical framework from which to work toward the promotion of mental health. Such a perspective provided an opportunity for the holistic examination of biological, psychological, interpersonal, and environmental factors in different contexts and at different times that may have an effect on mental health (Henriksen et al., 2010; Lehman et al., 2017).

Taking this approach demonstrated that such factors are dynamic and fluctuate as individuals grow and develop, both within and outside of sport (Lehman et al., 2017). It also allowed for the examination of mental health from a life span perspective, where talent development in elite sport was recognized as multidimensional and occurring in athletic and nonathletic pursuits (Wylleman et al., 2013). The statement was designed to spur on essential research in multiple areas of mental health and sport and provide practical guidance to mental health practitioners. To date, there have been many consensus, position, and expert statements regarding the mental health of athletes, coaches, and referees (see Breslin et al., 2019; Chang et al., 2020; Gorczynski et al., 2019; Gorczynski & Webb, 2022; Henriksen et al., 2019, 2020; Moesch et al., 2018; Schinke et al., 2018; Van Slingerland et al., 2019). Given the consequences of mental health symptoms and disorders, all statements have generally spoken to the need to better understand mental health, as well as the various factors associated with mental health symptoms and disorders so as to improve diagnosis, prevention, and treatment. So, what is mental health and well-being? How do they differ from mental health symptoms and disorders?

Mental health allows individuals to identify a purpose in life, set key goals, establish pathways to success, and work in a productive manner where challenges in life are acknowledged and processed.

The World Health Organization (WHO, 2001, p. 1) defined mental health as "a state of well-being in which every individual realizes his or her own potential, can cope with the normal stresses of life, can work productively and fruitfully, and is able to make a contribution to her or his community." Like other aspects of health, mental health is viewed as a resource, something that allows individuals to flourish. From this perspective, overall, mental health allows individuals to identify a purpose in life, set key goals, establish pathways to success, and work in a productive manner where challenges in life are acknowledged and processed.

Mental health is a component of overall health and is not merely the absence of mental health symptoms and disorders. As noted by the WHO (2018a), "Mental health is an integral part of health; indeed, there is no health without mental health." The WHO (2001) definition of mental health has recognized and advocated continuous positive and productive functioning in life, rooted in Western values and beliefs of labor (Galderisi et al., 2015). Of course, it should be acknowledged that perspectives toward mental health, and its definition, are shaped by culture and vary around the world (Galderisi et al., 2015). Galderisi and colleagues (2015) have proposed a new global definition of mental health, one that encourages individuals to use their abilities that are harmonious with the values of their society and culture. This new definition recognizes the dynamic nature of emotional states in response to adverse life events as well as the ability to empathize with others. Some individuals may also view mental health through spiritual or religious perspectives (Gureje et al., 2015). For athletes, being mentally healthy is often viewed through the lens of productivity and hard work, which are integral to skill mastery as well as their overall perspectives of success. The same, of course, can be said for coaches, referees, and everyone else in the arena.

The state of well-being, referred to in the WHO (2001) definition of mental health, can be described in many different ways (Dodge et al., 2012). Well-being is a multifaceted construct, one that has evolved over the years and that continues to evolve. It was first labeled by Bradburn (1969) as a state where an individual experienced a greater degree of positive affect over negative affect. Here, affect was understood along its positive and negative valences where emotions and moods were either pleasant or unpleasant—happy or sad, so to speak. Conversely, a state of low well-being was one where an individual would feel a greater degree of negative affect over positive affect. Over time, the affective components of well-being remained a part of the definition, which came to include other elements such as life satisfaction and quality of life (Diener & Suh, 1997; Shin & Johnson, 1978). Other researchers have added even more aspects to the definition, including autonomy, mastery, positive relationships, life purpose, one's potential, and the acceptance of self (Dodge et al., 2012; Ryff, 1989).

Today, a new definition of well-being encompasses and extends these considerations so as to acknowledge their new dynamic nature: moving from functional impairment to thriving and resilience. Dodge and colleagues (2012) proposed a view of well-being as a balance point between one's physical, psychological, and social resources and physical, psychological, and social challenges. This definition acknowledges the fulcrum that is key to well-being, where well-being is in a constant state of flux and where resources and challenges are always being carefully weighed and balanced against each other. Here, considering the athlete, this translates into the need to recognize and understand one's physical, psychological, and social talents, and then to weigh them carefully against the challenges of competition. To progress and to win, the athlete must continually adapt, learn, and then relearn various skills. In essence, the athlete must make use of combined physical, psychological, and social resources to constantly acknowledge and address diverse and complex challenges. This perpetual disequilibrium of well-being, teetering carefully between success and the need to learn, can help athletes improve and push themselves to greatness. Such a push may be what's necessary to find, sustain, or restore flow, or a psychological state of optimal experience (Csikszentmihalyi, 1990). Simply being an athlete presents a constant challenge to one's well-being. One may even argue that this constant state of disequilibrium is what is at the heart of the Olympic motto "Citius, Altius, Fortius," or put more plainly in English, "faster, higher, stronger" (Olympic.org, n.d.).

But what happens when the dynamic balancing act of well-being becomes stuck in a state of excess resource usage or depletion (e.g., self-esteem, self-efficacy, agency)? This leads to boredom, or perhaps reckless behavior that may result in the athlete taking unnecessary risks, which may lead to injury. Or what if the dynamic balance of well-being becomes stuck in a position where the athlete faces an excess of challenges? Here, the athlete would be unable to cope, no longer resilient, unable to progress, and unable to win. Such challenges would negatively affect their cognitions, emotions, and behaviors and would result in strained relationships and occupational functioning and dysfunction in daily life. The athlete would be said to be experiencing mental health symptoms, and if delineated over established periods of time, with specific criteria met for frequency and severity, those symptoms could potentially qualify as disorders (American Psychiatric Association, 2013; WHO, 2018b).

Prevalence of Mental Health Symptoms and Disorders

Mental health symptoms and disorders are a concern for elite athletes. Systematic reviews and meta-analyses that have investigated mental health symptoms and disorders of current and retired elite athletes have shown a high prevalence of symptoms of distress, anxiety, depression, alcohol misuse, and sleep disturbance (Gouttebarge et al., 2019; Reardon et al., 2019; see figure 17.1). For current elite athletes, prevalence has ranged from 19% (alcohol misuse) to 34% (anxiety and depression), while for retired elite athletes, prevalence ranged from 16% (distress) to 26% (anxiety and depression) (Gouttebarge et al., 2019). Other recent systematic reviews and meta-analyses of elite athletes have shown similar findings (Gorczynski et al., 2017; Rice et al., 2019).

Despite providing epidemiological evidence as to the prevalence of mental health symptoms and disorders, current systematic reviews and meta-analyses offer little information about the key individual and environmental correlates associated with, and that are determinants of, such mental health symptoms and disorders. For instance, demographic information extracted from the studies in such reviews has shown little evidence associated with mental health and specific population characteristics. Specifically, mental health information pertaining to female sex, nonbinary gender identity, sexuality, ethnicity, race, indigeneity, (dis)ability, class, and geography (e.g., low- and middle-income countries) is underrepresented in the literature (Henriksen et al., 2020; Reardon et al., 2019; Swartz et al., 2019). Calls have been made for a more inclusive, transcultural model of understanding and treating mental health symptoms

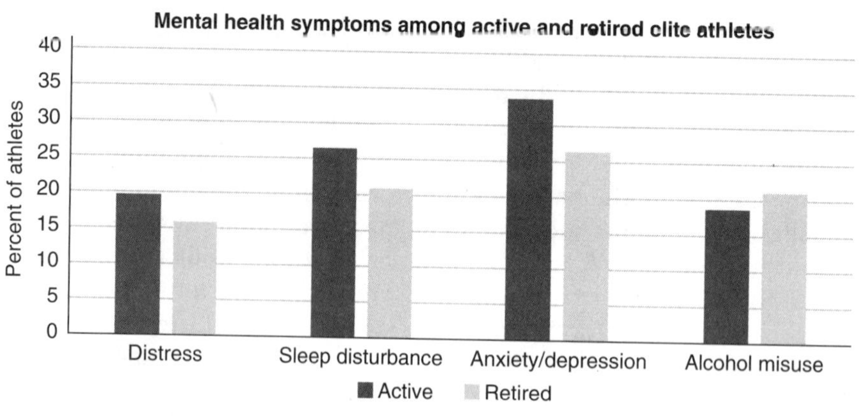

FIGURE 17.1 Mental health symptoms among active and retired elite athletes.

Data from V. Gouttebarge, J.M. Castaldelli-Maia, P. Gorczynski, et al., "Occurrence of Mental Health Symptoms and Disorders in Current and Former Elite Athletes: A Systematic Review and Meta-Analysis," *British Journal of Sports Medicine* 53, no. 11 (2019): 700-707. Distributed under the terms of the Creative Commons Attribution 4.0 International License (http://creativecommons.org/licenses/by/4.0/).

and disorders in professional sport (Bennett, 2021; Wilkerson et al., 2020). Additionally, mental health symptoms and disorders are reported for different sports using different assessment instruments, without standardization of whether assessments were done by the individual or through a clinical diagnosis (Reardon et al., 2019). These relative shortfalls in the current evidence are a problem, once we recognize that such information is essential to better understanding, preventing, and treating mental health symptoms and disorders (Castaldelli-Maia et al., 2019; Reardon et al., 2019). Such a deficit of knowledge has led to a poor understanding of the multiple socioecological factors associated with mental health symptoms and disorders and how best to address them.

Research that has investigated mental health symptoms and disorders in sport has done so from the perspective of elite athletes, with little work exploring the mental health symptoms and disorders of other key individuals in the arena, such as coaches and referees (Bissett et al., 2020; Webb & Gorczynski, 2020). Additionally, the mental health of individuals in sport at community and recreational levels, as opposed to elite and other higher levels, has not been addressed (Vella & Swann, 2021). Although careful attention has been paid to understanding the performance and organizational stressors coaches encounter, no evidence exists on the prevalence of mental health symptoms and disorders in this population (Bissett et al., 2020). This is particularly problematic because the stress coaches feel can have a profoundly negative impact on the performance of their athletes (Thelwell et al., 2016, 2017). Further research to help understand the mental health of coaches is essential given coaches play an important role in the overall development of their athletes, and in their organizations, and can help with the promotion of mental health and help seeking (Kroshus et al., 2018; Mazzer & Rickwood, 2015).

From the perspective of referees, Gorczynski and Webb (2022) have identified only a limited number of epidemiological studies that have explored the mental health symptoms and disorders of referees in any sport, at any level, anywhere in the world. Despite overwhelming evidence that referees experience considerable stress stemming from abuse and harassment before, during, and after their games, their mental health has been mostly ignored. Unfortunately, such a deficit of knowledge in this target population has already had severe consequences; a lack of support for mental health symptoms and disorders has become the most common reason referees quit their jobs (Webb, 2020).

Socioecological Perspectives Toward Mental Health Symptoms and Disorders in Sport

Socioecological models (e.g., McLaren & Hawe, 2005; McLeroy et al., 1988; Sallis et al., 2006) help individuals better understand the multiple factors that influence their health. Born out of ecological systems theory (Bronfenbrenner, 1979), such models recognize the importance of broader social factors (e.g., ethnicity, class, environment) that have an influence on the individual with respect to their health (Bronfenbrenner, 1979; Golden & Earp,

2012). In a sense, the individual exists within, and is inextricable from, a wider social system—able to access numerous behavioral settings and interact with other individuals, organizations, and communities, all the while influenced by political forces, attitudes, and cultural practices that change with time (Bronfenbrenner, 1979). For instance, professional athletes need to traverse between their homes, hotels, and training and competitive facilities, while interacting with friends, partners, families, coaches, support staff, trainers, and other health professionals. Some professional athletes also need to consider other environments, such as school or other occupational settings, and additional individuals such as teachers or professors and employers. These professional athletes will be guided by local, regional, national, and international organizations and bodies that oversee their respective sports, bound by various geographic districts and countries, each with their own unique laws.

The nature of sport changes constantly, requiring individuals to be mindful of how attitudes, values, beliefs, and formal and informal rules shift with time. Here, think of how perspectives have shifted and changed in sport with respect to gender identity, race, ethnicity, and (dis)ability. Although there has been progress with greater inclusivity and diversity in sport, other cultural practices of exclusion still persist (e.g., disclosure of sexuality of athletes). Such socioecological models force us to explore a variety of factors with respect to the etiology of mental health symptoms and disorders (Dick, 2011; Uher & Zwicker, 2017). Such models also recognize the diverse and multiple roles individuals have in life. As Schinke and Stambulova (2017, p. 73) note, it is important to consider the context when examining individuals in sport, "given that people are influential and influenced products in their environments." For athletes, coaches, and referees, the holistic life span perspective acknowledges the whole person, not just the individual role one occupies in a particular sport setting (Stambulova & Wylleman, 2014; Wylleman et al., 2013).

The nature of sport changes constantly, requiring individuals to be mindful of how attitudes, values, beliefs, and formal and informal rules shift with time. Here, think of how perspectives have shifted and changed in sport with respect to gender identity, race, ethnicity, and (dis)ability.

Research has shown that the following individual-level factors have an influence on mental health symptoms and disorders in elite athletes (for a review, see Castaldelli-Maia et al., 2019; Küttel & Larsen, 2019; Reardon et al., 2019):

- Family history
- Female sex
- Personality
- Competitive anxiety
- Health status
- Severity of injury
- Surgery
- Adverse life events
- Career satisfaction

From an environmental perspective, the following factors have an impact on an athlete's mental health (Castaldelli-Maia et al., 2019; Küttel & Larsen, 2019; Reardon et al., 2019):

- Sporting pressure
- Sporting type (i.e., individual, aesthetic)
- Poor team dynamics
- Player status and deselection
- Retirement uncertainty
- Nonaccidental violence (i.e., harm arising from harassment and abuse)

Regarding the latter, Mountjoy and colleagues (2016) illustrated the effects of nonaccidental violence, be it psychological, physical, sexual, or through neglect. Specifically, situated in a competitive sporting culture, nonaccidental violence exploits power differentials between individuals based on sex, gender identity, race, ethnicity, sexuality, indigeneity, (dis)ability, age, athletic ability, athletic longevity, organizational status, faith, and class. Nonaccidental violence delivered through contact, noncontact, social media, negligence, bullying, or hazing has consequences on the athlete and the organization. For the athlete, this may result in physical, cognitive, behavioral, emotional, relational, and economic consequences. For instance, an exploration of the USA Gymnastics program described the consequences associated with years of systemic sexual exploitation on the lives of thousands of girls and women and their families (Fasting et al., 2002; Fisher & Anders, 2020; Freeman, 2018).

As noted by Mountjoy and colleagues (2016), none of these factors—be they individual or environmental—

occurs in isolation, and sometimes the cumulative and compounded effect of multiple factors acting on the individual can result in mental health symptoms and disorders.

Of course, individual and environmental factors not only influence mental health symptoms and disorders but also have an impact on how individuals understand and perceive their mental health, as well as how they seek support (Castaldelli-Maia et al., 2019). Coyle and colleagues (2017) found that elite athletes have a poor understanding of mental health symptoms and disorders, have negative attitudes toward mental health symptoms and disorders, and are generally not able to articulate how to seek support. Furthermore, their research has illustrated that elite athletes have a sense of hesitancy with respect to disclosing mental health symptoms and disorders and a lack of trust in their coaches and sport psychology consultants for fear that any admission of mental health symptoms and disorders would result in deselection from their team. Such perspectives are not unique to athletes; they have recently been captured for football referees in the United Kingdom (Webb et al., 2021). Other factors associated with poor help-seeking behaviors include public and self-stigma, low mental health literacy, negative past experiences with respect to pharmacological and psychological interventions, busy schedules, and hypermasculinity (Castaldelli-Maia et al., 2019).

One mental health promotion strategy aimed at addressing both the causes of mental health symptoms and disorders and helping individuals in sport seek support is mental health literacy (Gorczynski et al., 2021). As noted by Castaldelli-Maia and colleagues (2019) and Küttel and Larsen (2019), strategies rooted in mental health literacy help address low knowledge of mental health symptoms and disorders, public and self-stigma, and access to mental health support. Mental health literacy strategies can help identify positive, supportive, and trusting relationships, within teams and organizations. They can identify where individuals can go for support. They can also be used to clarify individual, team, and organizational needs, values, beliefs, and goals, and how mental health should be taken into account. Such strategies also acknowledge the important roles of coaches in supporting athletes with mental health support. Mental health literacy strategies can also benefit other individuals involved in sport, such as support staff and referees. Overall, mental health literacy can help establish a framework for early intervention that is responsive to the needs of not only athletes but also other individuals in sport (Purcell et al., 2019; Sebbens et al., 2016). As noted by Kutcher and colleagues (2016), mental health literacy represents the foundation of mental health promotion, the prevention of mental health symptoms and disorders, treatment, and support through recovery (Kutcher & Wei, 2020). It should also be noted that such programs are in their infancy and are undergoing development to address the diverse needs of individuals involved in sport.

Mental Health Literacy

Mental health literacy is defined as the "knowledge and beliefs about mental disorders [that] aid their recognition, management or prevention" (Jorm et al., 1997, p. 182). Overall, mental health literacy is concerned with how individuals understand mental health symptoms and disorders and how they seek support. It takes into consideration knowledge of mental health symptoms and disorders, knowledge of management strategies for mental health symptoms and disorders, how to address mental health stigma, how to help others seek mental health support, and how to follow through with one's own intentions to seek mental health support (Jorm, 2000). As a construct, mental health literacy has evolved from health literacy. Initially, health literacy was concerned with basic literacy skills and ensuring that individuals were able to read, understand, and act on printed information to improve their own health (American Medical Association, 1992; Dewalt et al., 2004; Nutbeam et al., 1993). The focus of these early health literacy strategies was around addressing elements of physical health, such as improving diet, preventing skin cancer, performing self-examinations, and finding information from available sources (Nutbeam et al., 1993; Jorm, 2000). Soon, health literacy evolved to encompass both cognitive and social skills, ensuring that individuals could not only enhance their own lives but also work collectively with others to improve the health of their communities (Kutcher et al., 2016; WHO, 1998).

Health literacy has become both proactive and reactive, acknowledging sociological models of health with a full understanding of the various determinants of health. Like health literacy, mental health literacy has moved from simply educating individuals about mental health symptoms and disorders and ways to set appointments with mental health practitioners, to encompass key cognitive and social skills necessary to help prevent as well as address mental health symptoms and disorders (Gorczynski et al., 2021; Kutcher et al., 2016). This evolution has provided individuals the key skills necessary to advocate for their own mental health and the mental health of others. In essence, research examining mental health literacy has embraced a full understanding of the determinants of *mental* health.

In sport, research has shown that mental health promotion strategies rooted in mental health literacy are associated with positive effects (Breslin et al., 2017; Bu et al., 2020). The work has mostly focused on the mental health symptoms and disorders of athletes, with very little attention paid to coaches and referees (Breslin et al., 2017; Gorczynski et al., 2021). Through their systematic review of mental health literacy interventions, Breslin and colleagues (2017) demonstrated that such interventions have been associated with improved knowledge of mental health symptoms and disorders, improved knowledge of mental health professionals, reductions in public stigma, greater confidence to follow through with referrals, and increased intentions to seek mental health support. A study conducted with university student athletes showed that mental health literacy programs based on mental health knowledge, empathy, stigma counterstereotyping, and help-seeking contact resulted in increased mental health knowledge, decreased self-stigma, and improved attitudes to seek help and intentions to seek counseling (Chow et al., 2020).

Research with coaches has shown the importance of general help-seeking behaviors to overall well-being, suggesting that coach education programs could benefit from giving coaches a better sense of available mental health services and how such services may be accessed (Gorczynski et al., 2020). Such benefits would not only apply to coaches but potentially extend to athletes and staff members who work with those coaches. With respect to UK soccer referees, greater mental health literacy has been associated with a greater likelihood to seek help for mental health symptoms and disorders and a greater sense of well-being (Gorczynski & Thelwell, 2022). Results have also shown that mental health literacy was inversely associated with depressive symptoms.

Despite the benefits associated with mental health literacy in sport settings, caution must be taken when interpreting the results (Breslin et al., 2017; Bu et al., 2020; Gorczynski et al., 2021). Overall, research results are based on only a handful of studies that have mostly used small sample sizes. Changes in knowledge, attitudes, and help seeking have been shown to have small and medium effect sizes. Additionally, all mental health literacy interventions were delivered differently, often with no control groups, with no follow-up, and evaluated through nonrigorous methods without the use of valid or reliable psychometric scales (Breslin et al., 2017). Furthermore, mental health literacy interventions have not been mindful of cultural competencies, in a sense not taking into consideration "the importance of social and cultural influences on patients' health beliefs and behaviors" (Betancourt et al., 2003, p. 297). Recognizing and understanding the diverse mental health needs of athletes, coaches, referees, and other individuals in sport is essential for creating mental health strategies that are inclusive, supportive, and welcoming (Gorczynski et al., 2021). Sport organizations have a responsibility to address individual and environmental factors that may contribute to mental health symptoms and disorders as well as to provide access to mental health information and services. Maintaining cultural competence with respect to mental health literacy in sport is a practice that needs constant review given that cultural beliefs and behaviors change with time (Crabtree, 2019; Kirmayer, 2013).

Recognizing and understanding the diverse mental health needs of athletes, coaches, referees, and other individuals in sport is essential for creating mental health strategies that are inclusive, supportive, and welcoming.

Future Research Directions

Epidemiology is the cornerstone of good public health practice (Porta, 2014; Ries et al., 2009). Having a clear understanding of a disease condition for a particular population requires a clear understanding of its distribution, patterns, and determinants in order to create effective interventions against it. The goal of epidemiology is to understand the etiology of a disease condition so that strategies may be designed to enable prevention and treatment and ultimately help protect people (Bahr et al., 2020). Data on the distribution, patterns, and determinants of a disease condition can provide key information that can be used to help design, evaluate, and disseminate evidence-based interventions. Epidemiology can drive policy and enhance practice (Choi et al., 2005). To do so, studies must progress from *descriptive* epidemiology, where an understanding of the distribution and patterns of a disease condition is gained, to *analytic* epidemiology, where an understanding of the determinants of a disease condition is gained (Eaton & Merikangas, 2000; Ries et al., 2009).

From a mental health perspective within sport, be it the mental health symptoms and disorders of athletes, coaches, or referees, this evidence is slowly being compiled, as made clear through the published consensus, position, and expert statements noted earlier. With the support of the International Olympic Committee, the work of Reardon and colleagues (2019) has helped bring together key studies related to the distribution, patterns, and determinants of mental health symptoms and disorders in elite athletes. The consensus statement has also brought together evidence as to the best strategies known to prevent and treat mental health symptoms and disorders in this target population. Similar strategies are now necessary for coaches and referees. The key question is how best to ensure the creation and evolution of evidence-based interventions, such as mental health literacy, within sport. This is discussed in the sections that follow.

The behavioral epidemiological framework (Sallis et al., 2000) provides a series of steps for creating and delivering evidence-based interventions for public health. The framework moves carefully from basic research to program and policy development and later dissemination. Overall, the framework provides information about particular behaviors and health-related outcomes, and then leverages that information to further influence future behaviors and health-related outcomes. The framework relies on descriptive and analytic epidemiological studies, in addition to the evaluation of interventions, to put forward effective programs and policies for improving public health. The behavioral epidemiology framework has five phases (Sallis et al., 2000). Gorczynski and colleagues (2019) have proposed the following five phases specific to mental health literacy intervention development in sport, with examples provided.

Phase 1: Link Mental Health Literacy and Mental Health Outcomes in Elite Sport

In the first phase, both descriptive and analytic epidemiological studies are necessary to assess the strength of associations between mental health literacy and mental health outcomes. Here, mental health literacy scores must be shown to be significantly and positively associated with well-being and significantly and negatively associated with mental health symptoms and disorders. For instance, this may mean that greater mental health literacy scores are associated with higher levels of well-being and lower levels of distress or other mental health symptoms and disorders. Furthermore, different components of mental health literacy, be it knowledge, attitudes, or intentions to seek support, must be shown to be associated with mental health outcomes. Here, a careful examination of which aspects of mental health literacy have significant relationships with mental health outcomes is needed. Such studies have been conducted for athletes, coaches, and referees (Breslin et al., 2017; Bu et al., 2020; Chow et al., 2020; Sullivan et al., 2019); however, studies need to be replicated to confirm captured evidence.

Phase 2: Develop and Use Valid and Reliable Measures

A major recommendation from the IOC consensus statement on mental health in elite athletes was to establish valid and reliable tools to screen athletes for mental health symptoms and disorders in order to help them receive the care they need (Reardon et al., 2019). It was recommended that such screening be done not only during the active careers of athletes but during retirement as well (Reardon et al., 2019). Such tools would provide opportunities for further learning of mental health symptoms and disorders and help establish preventative mental health literacy strategies to enhance mental health. The authors noted in their consensus statement that careful attention must be given to measuring mental health outcomes that are specific to a sport context. Psychometric scales need to be both valid and reliable measures of mental health (Gouttebarge et al., 2021). With regard to validity, scales need to demonstrate both content (face and construct) and criterion (concurrent and predictive) validity. With reliability, scales must show they are consistent over time (test–retest), across questions (internal consistency), and administrators (interrater). With respect to mental health literacy, the Mental Health Literacy Scale has shown both validity and reliability (O'Connor & Casey, 2015). Unfortunately, not all measures of mental health literacy used within sport-related studies have been demonstrated to be valid and reliable, let alone to capture the main elements of mental health literacy (Breslin et al., 2017; Bu et al., 2020). Given this bias, the results of such studies must be viewed with caution.

With respect to the measurement of mental health symptoms and disorders, several valid and reliable psychometric scales have been used with athletes but not coaches or referees. As noted by Reardon and colleagues (2019), researchers should be mindful to minimize response bias and use a variety of diagnostic evaluation methods such as chart reviews and clinical interviews with qualified mental health professionals. To further assist clinicians and others in sport in the detection and management of mental health symptoms and disorders, the Mental Health Working Group of the IOC created two tools: (1) the Sport Mental Health Assessment Tool-1 (SMHAT-1) and (2) the Sport Mental Health Recognition Tool-1 (SMHRT-1) (Gouttebarge et al., 2021). The SMHAT-1 is used by trained mental health professionals to identify elite athletes who may be at risk of or already experiencing mental health symptoms and disorders. The SMHAT-1 helps ensure referral of athletes to needed mental health support provided by trained mental health professionals. The SMHRT-1 is used by friends, family, and other members of the athlete's entourage to better understand and spot early warning signs of potential mental health symptoms and disorders, as well as promote dialogue and help seeking. The SMHRT-1 may be helpful in improving intentions among athletes to speak to mental health professionals.

Phase 3: Identify Determinants

Collecting key demographic and environmental information helps in the creation of effective interventions, by enabling the comparison of patterns and the tailoring of intervention strategies. Analytic epidemiological evidence is needed to better understand risk factors and determinants of mental health symptoms and disorders in sport, and specifically how mental health literacy interventions can be designed to target such factors. Here, detailed information collected on individual and environmental factors is required, including age, sex, gender, gender identity, sexuality, class, race, ethnicity, (dis)ability, geography, training level, league, league level, time of season, off-season, time in relation to the competition (i.e., before, during, after), and retirement (Gorczynski & Webb, 2022). With such information, it is possible to design mental health literacy interventions while taking into account modifiable factors (e.g., training level) and nonmodifiable factors (e.g., age).

Research by Küttel and Larsen (2019) has demonstrated numerous individual and environmental factors related to the mental health of athletes. The results of their scoping review, with respect to their quantitative and qualitative mapping, illustrated limited data collected about demographic information, however. For instance, most research on protective and risk factors associated with mental health has been conducted on men between the ages of 16 and 26 who play team sports and are active (as opposed to retired) in their careers. Additionally, most research has been conducted in Europe, North America, and Australia. As demonstrated by Küttel and Larsen (2019), there is a need for more detailed demographic information about the diversity of athletes. Although there are efforts to improve data collection in athletes, again as noted previously, limited data exist for coaches and referees. Unfortunately, such limited pools of data will not help create effective mental health literacy interventions.

Phase 4: Evaluate Mental Health Literacy Interventions to Improve Mental Health Outcomes

Mental health literacy interventions should be constructed after detailed data have been collected through descriptive and analytic epidemiological studies. Interventions should address specific individual and environmental factors in an evidence-based manner. The current state of evidence concerning mental health literacy interventions clearly demonstrates a nonsystematic epidemiological approach to intervention design and a nonrigorous set of methods of intervention evaluation (Breslin et al., 2017; Bu et al., 2020).

Phase 5: Translate and Distribute Mental Health Literacy Interventions

The results of descriptive and analytic epidemiological studies along with studies of mental health literacy interventions need to be made publicly available, with data sharing among researchers made possible to allow study replication and the aggregation of data for systematic reviews and meta-analyses. Following the Medical Research Council's framework for complex intervention design (Craig et al., 2008; O'Cathain et al., 2019), for instance, researchers can enact an active process for the implementation of research findings in practice. The framework guides researchers to systematically develop health interventions, test them for their efficacy and effectiveness, and help disseminate them to the general public. Within this framework, as part of the dissemination phase, research findings are made easy to understand, are accessible and specific, and are underpinned by evidence. The framework is housed in a circular structure that requires continual updating. The active involvement of researchers and key stakeholders ensures that interventions are updated regularly and kept culturally relevant.

Practical Implications

As mental health literacy strategies are developed to address various individual and environmental factors associated with mental health symptoms and disorders, a collaborative and multidisciplinary approach is needed to move the field forward (Reardon et al., 2019). This requires the combined efforts of not only mental health professionals, including psychiatrists, clinical psychologists, sport psychology consultants, educational psychologists, social workers, general physicians, sports medicine physicians, and neurologists, but also researchers with diverse skill sets, including those with expertise in both qualitative and quantitative methods. As noted by Gorczynski and colleagues (2021), athletes, coaches, referees, and others who operate in professional sport need to be at the center of the process of developing key mental health literacy interventions. Their expert knowledge will ensure that interventions are not only feasible but also worthwhile, because buy-in from these specific target groups is key to ensuring effective interventions. Furthermore, their input will result in interventions that are culturally competent. Moving forward together will ensure that a systematic and evidence-based approach is used to understand, prevent, and treat mental health symptoms and disorders.

Gorczynski and colleagues (2021) have proposed multiple strategies for collaborative and multidisciplinary research and practice to help address mental health symptoms and disorders through socioecological strategies rooted within mental health literacy. These strategies advocate for mental health literacy interventions that are developmentally appropriate, pedagogically sound, aware of everyone's mental health, and culturally competent.

Summary

Overall, the study of mental health, well-being, and mental health symptoms and disorders in elite sport is in its infancy. Although considerable attention is being devoted to elite athletes, research with coaches and referees is surely lagging. Efforts must be made to better understand the prevalence of mental health symptoms and disorders in all sport populations, with careful attention paid to ensure studies are done in a manner that minimizes biases and uses a rigorous process. Researchers need to embrace a socioecological approach, one that acknowledges the complexity of individual and environmental factors that influence mental health symptoms and disorders in all those who find themselves in the arena. Strategies such as mental health literacy show much promise in allowing individuals to better understand mental health and to create pathways to prevent and treat mental health symptoms and disorders. Rooting future research and practice in a collaborative and multidisciplinary approach and relying on rigorous frameworks of intervention design are keys to the development of such strategies and the overall improvement of mental health in sport.

DISCUSSION QUESTIONS

1. Define mental health, well-being, and mental health symptoms and disorders.
2. What is mental health literacy?
3. Describe the main features of socioecological models.
4. What is the holistic life perspective, and why is it important within the study of mental health and sport?
5. How can multiple mental health professions operate together within the study and practice of mental health and sport?

18

Team Cohesion

Mark Eys, PhD; Shauna M. Burke, PhD; and Mark R. Beauchamp, PhD

LEARNING OBJECTIVES

On completion of this chapter, the reader should have the following:

- Introductory understanding of the theoretical and conceptual bases of cohesion for sport teams
- Ability to describe how cohesion relates to key antecedents and outcomes in sport
- Comprehension of potentially negative aspects of task and social cohesion
- Understanding of future research directions in the study of cohesion in sport
- Knowledge of strategies for developing greater cohesion in sport teams

> Former Bulls Coach Phil Jackson said he had to ask Jordan to tone it down during practice if he was too hard on his teammates. "He'd get feisty in a practice and maybe go up against people," Jackson said. "I'd have to talk a little bit about toning it down and make amends and keep that level of team camaraderie. That's your role, too, as part of this, in being a captain." (Butler, 2020, paras. 8-9)

At the height of the first wave of the global COVID-19 pandemic, one of the most popular sport documentaries was released, providing an in-depth look at the final season in the dynasty of the National Basketball Association's Chicago Bulls. *The Last Dance* focused predominantly on the influence of Michael Jordan as the team's and league's star player during the 1990s. It also provided the narratives of the coach (Phil Jackson), organizational leaders (e.g., general manager Jerry Krause), and other players (e.g., Scottie Pippen) occupying a variety of roles within the team. As the opening quote exemplifies, a running theme throughout the documentary was the relationships Jordan fostered with his teammates as they pursued league championships. The expectations he held for himself, other group members, and the organization, as well as the manner in which he communicated these expectations, challenged the unity of the group and created tension across all levels (i.e., players, coaches, and administration). In short, viewers of *The Last Dance* were exposed to vivid examples of the dynamics of group cohesion at work.

Cohesion, which is used synonymously in the media with terms such as *team unity*, *closeness*, and *camaraderie*, is defined as an emergent state that "is reflected in the tendency for a group to stick together and remain united in the pursuit of its instrumental objectives and/or for the satisfaction of member affective needs" (Carron et al., 1998, p. 213). Research efforts have located this emergent state within broader frameworks of group dynamics with equally important components that create structure (e.g., roles) and facilitate group processes (e.g., teamwork) (Eys, Evans, & Benson, 2020; McEwan & Beauchamp, 2014).

Ultimately, the examples provided in *The Last Dance* give rise to several questions about group cohesion, which are addressed in this chapter. How important is group cohesion toward individual and group outcomes? And if it is important, how do teams develop a sense of unity and togetherness? As Swoboda (2020) observed: "Inarguably, Jordan was the Bulls' most valuable player during those championship years. But he couldn't do it alone. Basketball, like business, requires teams to make critical decisions in real time, constantly reacting to new, often momentary challenges and opportunities" (para. 6).

Theory and Research

We all belong to a number of groups throughout our lives. For example, we are born into a family unit, and as we grow, the number and types of groups to which we belong also tend to grow and change. But what constitutes a group? In other words, what differentiates a collection of individuals, such as those waiting together at a bus stop, from a group to which we belong and experience a meaningful sense of "groupness" such as a family unit or sport team? To answer these important questions, we can turn to the influential work of Tajfel and Turner and colleagues, who conceived the *social identity approach*, which encompasses social identity theory and self-categorization theory (e.g., Tajfel, 1974; Tajfel & Turner, 1979; Turner, 1982, 1985; Turner & Oakes, 1989).

Precursors to Group Cohesion: Entitativity and Social Identification

Within the social identity approach, the first theoretical construct to consider as a potential underpinning of group cohesion is *entitativity*. In a 1958 paper about the characteristics of groups as social entities, Campbell defined entitativity as "the degree of having the nature of an entity, of having real existence" (p. 17). So, whereas it would be unlikely that those waiting together at a bus stop would feel part of a real group, athletes on a sport team would be much more likely to experience a sense of meaningful groupness with others on the team. Research in exercise psychology provided support for this conclusion, showing that exercisers who feel they are part of a real group (i.e., they socially identify as a group member and experience a strong sense of the group's entitativity) display greater enjoyment and exert more effort during exercise tasks (e.g., Beauchamp & O'Rourke, 2020; Evans et al., 2019).

As it pertains to the second theoretical construct, *social identification*, individuals begin to feel more a part of a real group when they identify psychologically as a group member. Throughout the years, sport and exercise psychology researchers have acknowledged that social identity principles provide an important foundation upon which we might understand group cohesion and sport-related behavior (e.g., Beauchamp, 2019; Beauchamp & O'Rourke, 2020; Carron & Spink, 1993; Rees et al., 2015). For example, when people categorize themselves as a group member and begin to develop a sense of shared identity with others in the group—based on certain characteristics or perceived similarities—they quite readily distinguish between "us" (the in-group) versus "them" (the out-group) (Turner, 1982). In turn, this sense of unity (i.e., us versus them) and self-identity as a group member can lead to greater collective actions and stronger psychological bonds (cohesion) among team members (Hogg, 1993; Rees et al., 2015).

Overall, when people both consider themselves to be members of a group and socially identify with other group members (and experience a sense of belonging), they are more likely to feel attracted to the group and perceive the group to be united. That is, both entitativity and social identification represent salient antecedents of group cohesion in sport. This is supported by experimental research (Van Vugt & Hart, 2004) as well as recent observational research in sport (Worley et al., 2020). Despite these examples, additional research is needed to further examine the possible interrelationships of social identity principles and group cohesion in sport settings (a point reiterated in the section on future research directions). Sport research has been conducted from a strong and well-established framework of group cohesion, which has provided important insights regarding numerous correlates of team cohesion. This conceptual model is discussed next.

Conceptual Model and Assessment of Team Cohesion

Figure 18.1 provides a schematic representation of the conceptual model Carron and colleagues (1985) developed to represent cohesion in sport teams. They proposed that each team member develops and holds perceptions about their team that are related to (1) the group as a totality and (2) the manner in which the group satisfies personal needs and objectives. These perceptions are labeled as follows:

- Group integration: the closeness and bonding within the group as a whole, as well as the degree of unification of the group

- Individual attractions to the group: personal motivations acting to attract and retain the individual in the group, as well as their personal feelings about the group
- As figure 18.1 also illustrates, Carron and colleagues suggested there are two fundamental focuses of a group member's perceptions:
  - A task orientation: general orientation or motivation toward achieving the group's objectives
  - A social orientation: general orientation or motivation toward developing and maintaining social relationships and activities within the group

The result of conceptualizing cohesion this way is four manifestations of cohesiveness:

- Group integration-task (GI-T)
- Group integration-social (GI-S)
- Individual attractions to the group-task (ATG-T)
- Individual attractions to the group-social (ATG-S)

When this conceptual model was proposed, the primary target was adult sport participants (>18 years old). More recent explorations (Eys et al., 2009; Martin et al., 2012) found that younger athletes (10-17 years old) viewed cohesion in broader terms (i.e., task and social cohesion), and their perceptions related to personal (i.e., attractions to the group) and group foci (i.e., group integration) were indistinguishable.

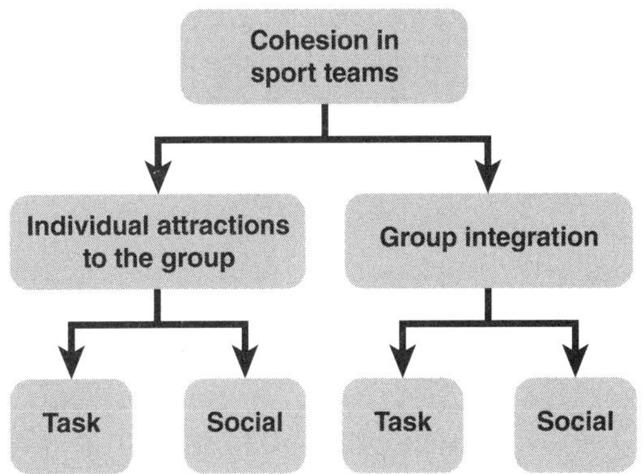

FIGURE 18.1 Conceptual model of cohesion for sport teams.

Adapted by permission from A.V. Carron, W.N. Widmeyer, and L.R. Brawley, "The Development of an Instrument to Assess Cohesion in Sport Teams: The Group Environment Questionnaire," *Journal of Sport Psychology* 7, no. 3 (1985): 244-266.

In elaborating on their conceptual model, Carron and colleagues (1998) suggested that a fundamental characteristic of cohesion is its *multidimensionality*. That is, cohesion in sport teams is not a unitary construct; it has a number of dimensions. Figure 18.1, of course, reflects this characteristic. A second fundamental characteristic of cohesion is that it is *dynamic*, meaning it is not a stable, relatively permanent property. Cohesion in a group changes in both its extent and its various forms (e.g., task cohesiveness, social cohesiveness) throughout the life span of the group (the need for longitudinal study designs to examine these changes over time is discussed in the section on future research directions). A third fundamental characteristic is that cohesion is *instrumental*. Groups do not stick together solely to stick together; they have a raison d'être. All groups (e.g., musical groups, work groups, families, and sport teams) form and intend to stay together for a purpose. Even groups that may be considered purely social in nature have an instrumental basis for their formation. Finally, cohesion has an *affective* dimension. The social bonding or task unity that develops in groups is pleasing to individual group members. Groups that are devoid of the affective dimension are characterized by conflict, lack of harmony, and even breakups (e.g., divorce).

The four-dimension conceptual model of cohesion was used as the foundation for the Group Environment Questionnaire (GEQ; Carron et al., 1985). The GEQ is an 18-item self-report survey that has been the primary tool for estimating athletes' perceptions of cohesion in sport, particularly for young adult English-speaking populations. However, alternative questionnaires have been developed for younger athletes (i.e., Youth Sport Environment Questionnaire [Eys et al., 2009]; Child Sport Cohesion Questionnaire [Martin et al., 2012]) in addition to the creation of several translated versions of the GEQ (e.g., French; Questionnaire sur l'Ambiance du Groupe [Heuzé & Fontayne, 2002]).

Self-report surveys such as these have several advantages (e.g., ease of collection, quantifying of subjective experiences) and disadvantages (e.g., social desirability, tendency toward cross-sectional usage), and this methodological approach has been heavily relied on to investigate cohesion in sport. Researchers in other fields (e.g., organizational psychology) have suggested that recording more objective indicators may provide useful estimations of cohesion (Grossman et al., 2015; Salas et al., 2015). These include, for example, collecting information on interaction duration and frequency among group members (via sociometric electronic tags) or other targeted observations of the team. However, Eys and Brawley (2018) cautioned that "the measures taken to complement or converge with validated self-report should be appropriate to answer a specific cohesion research question versus arbitrarily being added to current measurement approaches" (p. 11). Regardless of approach, it remains a challenging task to capture an intangible emergent group property like cohesion with a reasonable degree of accuracy and reliability.

Correlates of Cohesion in Sport

Research over the past 35 years has identified a number of important group and individual variables associated with task and social cohesion. In the present chapter, performance, situational, individual, leadership, and team correlates of cohesion are discussed.

Team Performance

A large quantity of research on the team cohesion–team success relationship has been conducted in sport psychology. Carron and colleagues (2002) undertook a meta-analysis of 46 studies that examined the association between team cohesiveness and team success through the years 1975 to 2000. Subsequently, Filho and colleagues (2014) conducted a follow-up meta-analysis to examine results emanating from 16 studies conducted from 2000 to 2010. Overall, cohesion and performance are positively related. Carron and colleagues found an overall moderate to large effect size (*ES* = .645) while Filho and colleagues found a moderate relationship (*ES* = .340). Furthermore, this association was found for both task and social cohesion in both studies. One might expect that task cohesion would be a more important correlate of overall task effectiveness (i.e., performance) of a team; however, these findings suggest that coaches and athletes should not underestimate the potential benefits of setting up a positive social atmosphere for the group to enhance team success.

Both sets of researchers also undertook an examination of potential moderators of the cohesion–performance relationship. As the term suggests, a moderator is a factor that modifies (changes) the relationship between an independent variable (e.g., cohesion) and a dependent variable (e.g., team success). Once a general relationship is established, researchers are often interested in determining whether that relationship holds under all circumstances. As one example, type of sport may play a role in terms of the strength of the relationship between cohesion and performance. It is reasonable to assume that cohesion may be important for team success in interactive sports (e.g., basketball) but less so in independent (e.g., track and field) and coacting sports (e.g., tennis) (Carron & Chelladurai, 1981). Carron and his colleagues actually found that cohesion is equally important for independent/coactive (*ES* = .766) and interactive (*ES* = .657) teams.

In a series of studies, Evans and colleagues (2012, 2013; Evans & Eys, 2015) further examined how different interdependencies exist and influence the group environment within traditional independent sports (e.g., cross-country skiing, wrestling), providing several possible reasons for the positive link between cohesion and performance. For example, independent sport athletes often share coaches, training facilities, and, in many cases, collective goals (e.g., an overall team points competition in golf) that require cooperation and good relations to perform to the best of one's ability (Evans et al., 2012).

As a second example, the group dynamics literature is replete with instances where gender has been found to be a moderator of fundamental relationships. The Carron and colleagues (2002) and Filho and colleagues (2014) meta-analyses found that the cohesion–performance relationship is no exception. For example, in the earlier meta-analysis, the association between cohesion and performance was significantly greater for female teams (*ES* = .949) than it was for male teams (*ES* = .556). The accumulated results led Filho and colleagues to suggest that future research may "focus on asking 'why' (e.g., Why do women and men differ in cohesion dynamics?) to provide an explanation of the mediating mechanisms underlying gender idiosyncrasies" (p. 174). A qualitative study subsequently explored these potential differences through the perspectives of German and Canadian coaches who had experience leading both male and female sport teams over the course of their careers (Eys et al., 2015). All coaches indicated that cohesion is very important for both male and female sport teams. However, there were notable perceived differences in terms of the particulars of the sport environment for male and female sport teams, including how role differentiation and status are experienced and influential toward developing cohesion; approaches to conflict and adversity; and the direction of the cohesion–performance relationship.

The latter finding is concerned with the question "Does cohesion lead to performance, or does performance lead to cohesion?" The likely answer is "both." Evidence from the two meta-analyses points to the likelihood that the relationship is circular. Eys and colleagues (2015) suggested, based on their qualitative findings, that a testable proposition is whether the cohesion–performance direction is a stronger pathway for female sport teams, whereas the performance–cohesion direction is the driver for male sport teams. Preliminary evidence for elite male youth soccer teams lends some support for the latter proposition. In a study examining the experiences of 352 Czech and Slovak youth soccer players (22 teams), midseason performance predicted late-season perceptions of both task and social cohesion (but not the other way around) (Benson et al., 2016). In essence, winning promoted positive group perceptions. Overall, many questions remain regarding the link between cohesion and performance, and the future research directions section of this chapter highlights specifically the need to understand the potential mechanisms underlying this relationship.

"Does cohesion lead to performance, or does performance lead to cohesion?" The likely answer is "both."

Situational Correlates of Cohesion

Both theory and research provide some indication and evidence, respectively, that cohesion contributes to team functioning (Carron et al., 2002; Filho et al., 2014). As such, it is logical to explore the situational precursors that could promote or detract from positive evaluations of one's group. As an example, early research efforts in sport took a quasi-experimental approach to examine the effect of team size on cohesion. Widmeyer and colleagues (1990) created a three-on-three recreational basketball league with teams consisting of three, six, or nine members. The results showed that task cohesion decreased as roster size increased, and the researchers speculated this may have been due to increased needs for coordination with larger groups or decreased opportunities for participation on an individual basis. In contrast to this finding, however, social cohesion was highest in the six-person groups. Widmeyer and colleagues suggested that in the three-person teams, the lack of substitutes might not have left sufficient time and opportunities to develop social relationships.

Another contextual variable that contributes to perceptions of cohesion is motivational climate (see chapter 10), which refers to the "social situation created by significant others [that] varies in terms of the achievement goals emphasized" (Duda & Balaguer, 2007, p. 120). These important others can be coaches, peers, and parents. The motivational climate can be task oriented such that there is a focus on effort, improvement, and fostering cooperation within the group. In contrast, an ego-oriented environment stresses social comparison, rivalry, and outperforming others (Duda, 2001; Harwood et al., 2014). As it pertains to cohesion, two cross-sectional studies were consistent in demonstrating that when coaches created a more task-oriented motivational climate, athletes' perceptions of task and social cohesion were stronger (Eys et al., 2013; Horn et al., 2012). Furthermore, McLaren and colleagues (2015) devised a quasi-experimental study in which soccer coaches took part in a motivational climate workshop to develop behaviors more in line with creating a task-oriented climate. They found that the athletes whose coaches participated in these workshops (vs. athletes whose coaches were placed in control groups) perceived not only a stronger task climate across the season but also greater task and social cohesion.

Individual Correlates of Cohesion

The general experience of being a member of a group has numerous effects on individual cognitions, emotions, and behaviors (Baumeister & Leary, 1995). From a *cognition* perspective, in task-cohesive teams, members are more egalitarian in accepting responsibility for unfavorable results. For example, Brawley and colleagues (1987) had athletes use their teammates as a benchmark to estimate the degree of personal responsibility for the team's win or loss. The athletes who rated their team high in task cohesiveness assumed a level of personal responsibility that was equal to that of the average team member regardless of outcome (i.e., winning or losing). However, those athletes who rated their team low in task cohesion showed a self-protective pattern of attribution by accepting less responsibility for the loss than the average team member.

Individual role perceptions are another cognitive factor shown to be related to cohesion. One cognition is role ambiguity, which refers to the lack of clear, consistent information regarding one's role (Kahn et al., 1964). Intercollegiate basketball players who believed their team was more task cohesive were likely to perceive less role ambiguity regarding the scope of their responsibilities (Eys & Carron, 2001). Furthermore, athletes commit more strongly to their role responsibilities when they are part of more cohesive teams. Across two studies, Coleman and colleagues (2021) demonstrated that cohesion perceptions predicted the degree to which athletes wanted to, and thought they ought to, commit to their roles (i.e., affective and normative bases for role commitment; see Eys, Beauchamp, et al., 2020, for a framework of role commitment).

Terry and colleagues (2000) provided an example of a positive *affective* relationship with cohesion. These researchers examined cohesion in relation to mood among rugby players, rowers, and netball players. Consistently across the samples, higher levels of cohesion were related to lower levels of depression, anger, and tension as well as higher perceptions of vigor.

Finally, cohesion has positive individual *behavioral* outcomes. For example, social loafing refers to a reduction in effort by an individual when working in a group versus working alone (Latané et al., 1979). When Høigaard and colleagues (2006) examined perceptions of youth competitive soccer players, they determined that social loafing was less likely among individuals experiencing greater attractions to task aspects of the group (ATG-T). Also, cohesion ultimately represents sticking together and thus is related to a variety of adherence indicators, including reduced absenteeism and lateness (Carron et al., 1988) and a greater likelihood of athletes returning to their teams the following season (Spink et al., 2010).

Leadership Correlates of Cohesion

In theory and as evidenced in research, coaches' behaviors are associated with team cohesion. Specific behaviors have varied across studies, but generally, higher levels of training and instruction behavior, social support behavior, and positive feedback from coaches are associated with higher levels of cohesion (e.g., Juntumaa et al., 2007).

Furthermore, several researchers (e.g., Callow et al., 2009; Smith et al., 2013) have stressed the importance of considering transformational leadership behaviors (see chapter 7) in relation to group perceptions. Transformational leaders build relationships with members of the team via "personal, emotional, and inspirational exchanges, with the goal of developing followers to their fullest potential" (Callow et al., 2009, p. 396); specific behaviors include those that promote individualized consideration, inspirational motivation, intellectual stimulation, acceptance of group goals, high performance expectations, and appropriate role modeling (Hardy et al., 2010). These transformational behaviors are related to both task and social cohesion (Callow et al., 2009), and the relationship can be explained in part by a greater frequency of positive communication practices (Smith et al., 2013).

There are further extensions and connections to consider regarding the leadership–cohesion research. First, Jowett and Chaundy (2004) demonstrated that team cohesion is not influenced by leader behaviors alone; athletes' perceptions of the coach–athlete relationship (commitment, closeness, complementarity; see chapters 1 and 2) contribute to task and social cohesion as well. Furthermore, coaches are not the only leaders in the group to have an effect on group cohesion. Positive perceptions of peer leaders (i.e., athlete leaders) are also associated with stronger task and social cohesion within sport teams (Price & Weiss, 2013; see chapter 9).

Team Correlates of Cohesion

The previous sections identified important connections between cohesion and team performance, situational factors athletes experience in their environment, intraindividual variables, and leadership. Cohesion is also linked with other group-level perceptions held by athletes. Two team-related correlates of cohesion that have received research attention are collective efficacy and team norms. According to Zaccaro and colleagues (1995), collective efficacy represents "a sense of collective competence shared among individuals when allocating, coordinating, and integrating their resources in a successful concerted response to specific situational demands" (p. 309). Zaccaro and colleagues suggested that characteristics of the group itself, such as group cohesion, influence its sense of collective efficacy. Subsequent studies supported this contention. For example, after their investigation with French professional basketball teams, Heuzé and colleagues (2006) suggested that integration (i.e., cohesion), both on and off the playing surface, is important in developing a sense of collective competence.

Group norms are standards for behavior expected of group members; they are influential because they (1) inform members about the expectations of the group and (2) integrate those members more closely within the group's structure (Eys, Evans, & Benson, 2020). If members view their team as united concerning task and social aspects (i.e., high cohesion), it is reasonable to expect they would agree with and conform to standards of behavior that are deemed acceptable for that group. In a lab-based study (Gammage et al., 2001), participants read scenarios depicting combinations of cohesion and norm levels in team sports. Participants indicated how much effort the actor in the scenario would likely expend. The situation found to contribute to the best effort was characterized by high cohesion and a high norm for productivity.

Coaches are not the only leaders in the group to have an effect on group cohesion. Positive perceptions of peer leaders (i.e., athlete leaders) are also associated with stronger task and social cohesion within sport teams.

Potential Downsides of Cohesion

Although cohesion generally is a positive group property, it does have the potential to be negative under some circumstances. Hardy and colleagues (2005) asked athletes to indicate whether they felt there were disadvantages to high social or task cohesion on a team and, if so, to identify those disadvantages. Over half of athletes reported potential disadvantages to high social cohesion, while approximately one-third of the sample reported disadvantages to high task cohesion. Some of the disadvantages to high social cohesion included wasting task-related time, difficulties focusing and committing to task-related goals, problematic communication between friends, and the potential for social isolation of those outside the main group. Potential drawbacks of social cohesion were further highlighted in a case study with a junior-level ice hockey team, in which the researchers concluded that group polarization, groupthink, and pressures to conform were possible negative by-products (Rovio et al., 2009).

Disadvantages associated with high task cohesion in sport teams include strained social relations, communication problems, reduced personal enjoyment, and increased perceived pressures (Hardy et al., 2005). This latter notion that high cohesion can lead to increased pressure, stress, or anxiety for athletes has interested several groups of researchers, who derived opposing hypotheses regarding this link. Prapavessis and Carron (1996) were the first to consider the relationship between cohesion and competitive state anxiety (precompetitive cognitive and somatic anxiety). They hypothesized that there could be both psychological costs and benefits to being a member of a cohesive team. Being a member of a cohesive group might (1) reduce competitive state anxiety because there would be less threat of evaluation because of a higher diffusion of responsibility or (2) increase competitive state anxiety because "the pressure to carry out responsibilities and satisfy the expectations of highly valued teammates is maximized" (p. 66). The results showed that athletes who perceived their teams as more cohesive experienced less intense competitive state anxiety symptoms, a decidedly positive result relative to the possible disadvantage suggested by participants in the Hardy and colleagues (2005) study.

However, it is not only the intensity of the typical cognitive (e.g., concern) and somatic (e.g., heart racing) symptoms of anxiety that are important to consider, but also how individuals interpret these occurrences (Fletcher & Fletcher, 2005). For example, one individual may interpret an elevated heart rate as particularly threatening and negative (promoting anxiety), whereas someone else may view it as an indicator of readiness and excitement. Studies following from the Prapavessis and Carron (1996) study demonstrated that athletes holding stronger perceptions of cohesion were more likely to view cognitive and somatic symptoms as facilitative to performance (Eys et al., 2003; Wolf et al., 2015a).

Overall, the relationship between cohesion and stress or anxiety is complicated. Revisiting Prapavessis and Carron's (1996) propositions that cohesion could have psychological costs or benefits when encountering stressful situations, the evidence suggests it has both. Wolf and colleagues (2015b) found that stronger perceptions of cohesion were related to heightened primary appraisals of stressors (i.e., what is at stake) such that the importance of the competition was viewed as greater, while at the same time secondary appraisals (i.e., what can be done) were facilitated, indicating greater coping resources to deal with the stressful situation. In this way, higher levels of cohesion may produce a greater chance that demanding situations are viewed as a challenge (vs. a threat).

Future Research Directions

A robust body of literature in sport is devoted to understanding the role of the emergent state of cohesion. However, given its importance in relation to individual and team variables (e.g., adherence and performance), continued calls for research highlight several potential future directions. For example, research findings from the Carron and colleagues (2002) and Filho and colleagues (2014) meta-analyses permit us to reliably conclude that task and social cohesion are related to team success. Although as Carron and colleagues pointed out:

> One unfortunate byproduct of any meta-analysis . . . is that the results may be assumed to provide the final answer on any issue. . . . Science proceeds in stages from description to explanation to prediction to control. Meta-analyses provide a summary at the descriptive stage. They do not offer insights into questions associated with the "why" or "when" of a relationship. (pp. 183-184)

For example, is higher cohesion associated with better performance because it contributes to improved role commitment or better adherence to team norms for productivity? Are there conditions in which one direction of the relationship is stronger (i.e., performance leads to cohesion or vice versa)? Gathering evidence in response to questions like this would provide a better mechanistic understanding of group processes as well as generate broader theoretical consequences.

Relatedly, it would be useful to revisit the theoretical roots of the conceptual model of cohesion to better understand how self-categorization processes and social identity contribute to athletes' perceptions of unity within their team. Previous work in sport has provided preliminary support for these connections. For example, Spink and colleagues (2015) disentangled athletes' perceptions of groupness (in other words, entitativity) from cohesion to determine that these two perceptions interact to influence intentions to return. Further, stronger team identification is associated with higher task and social cohesion (De Backer et al., 2011). There is an opportunity to consider these concepts collectively in future work that tests propositions by Beauchamp and O'Rourke (2020) that greater perceptions of entitativity, or groupness, provide the basis for stronger team identification, which subsequently contributes to greater task and social cohesion. Furthermore, there is a need to examine whether interventions that explicitly strive to develop a sense of identification with the group, and are supported and assessed through experimentation, subsequently improve cohesion. As discussed in the subsequent applied section, developing shared leadership might be a viable theory-driven, evidence-informed approach to intervention. It would be useful to see if shared leadership interventions develop social identification, and thereafter influence cohesion and performance in a positive manner. In short, a social identity approach to understanding group processes is gaining traction within sport psychology.

One suggestion for research that has persisted for some time is the need to consider cohesion perceptions across the life span of the group (Eys & Brawley, 2018). One prominent characteristic of cohesion is that it is dynamic, though the majority of research in sport has approached its examination via cross-sectional or limited time point designs. Examples of longitudinal investigations are emerging. In a physical activity context, Dunlop and colleagues (2013) demonstrated unique patterning for task and social cohesion perceptions of participants in exercise classes. Furthermore, Baird and colleagues (2020) asked athletes to complete weekly assessments of task cohesion, transformational leadership, and group potency during a sport season. Across 11 weeks, their results demonstrated a lack of stability in these perceptions, and that increasing perceptions of transformational leadership were associated with greater perceptions of task cohesion. However, studies employing these longitudinal approaches, currently few and far between, are needed to understand the dynamism of cohesion.

Finally, although we discuss practical approaches to developing cohesion in the following section, very little attention has been paid to the development of evidence-based intervention programs to enhance the dynamics of sport teams. The research focus in group dynamics in sport has primarily been descriptive and correlational in nature. Coaches and sport psychology researchers must develop intervention protocols collaboratively to enhance team cohesion and other group processes, and then evaluate the efficacy and effectiveness of those protocols to better understand what works and why.

Practical Implications

The studies on the potential liabilities of cohesion offer an interesting perspective, and future research should continue to pursue this question. However, as the majority of researchers, sport psychology practitioners, coaches, and athletes would attest, the benefits of a cohesive team far outweigh any disadvantages that might be present. Hence, the current section details evidence-based and theoretically sound interventions that may help promote cohesion in sport teams.

Team Building

The primary approach to target the development of task and social cohesion is *team building*. Brawley and Paskevich (1997) defined team building as "a method of helping the group to: (a) increase effectiveness; (b) satisfy the needs of members; or (c) improve work conditions" (pp. 13-14). In sport settings, team-building approaches often seek to foster a sense of unity around the team's task and social activities, on the basis that such cohesion is expected to promote extra effort, coordination, and indeed subsequent team functioning outcomes.

To guide team-building efforts, Carron and Spink (1993) presented an implementation model (see figure 18.2) that included a number of group environment, group structure, and group process variables, which they theorized would, if optimized, lead to higher levels of cohesion. Originally targeting exercise groups, this model was subsequently employed within several team-building studies in sport (e.g., Newin et al., 2008; Prapavessis et al., 1996; Stevens & Bloom, 2003). The group environment constitutes the psychological climate that pervades the team, and in particular reflects conceptions of how members perceive themselves to be similar to one another and distinct from other groups. Group distinctiveness can be developed organically, but it can also be targeted through intervention by promoting a sense of "us" or "we." An example is the use of clothing or team attire to emphasize connection to one's own team as well as distinction from other teams.

Group structure was conceptualized in Carron and Spink's (1993) model as involving members' respective playing positions, status, norms, and roles, along with specific perceptions related to those concepts (e.g., role clarity, role commitment). Finally, group processes were conceptualized by Carron and Spink as throughput variables that mediate the effects of the group environment and group structure in relation to cohesion. Those throughput variables constitute intrateam interactions (e.g., cooperation), communication, and personal member sacrifice. Before discussing the extant research that has evaluated team-building interventions seeking to build group cohesion, it is worth critically reflecting on the utility, but also the limitations, of this implementation model. Specifically, although some of the group-based constructs embedded within the model (e.g., role clarity, communication) have been identified as correlates of group cohesion (e.g., Prapavessis & Carron, 1997), there is a paucity of experimental evidence supporting the purported claims within this model that the putative input variables causally influence the throughput variables, which in turn causally influence cohesion. Instead, while we recognize the

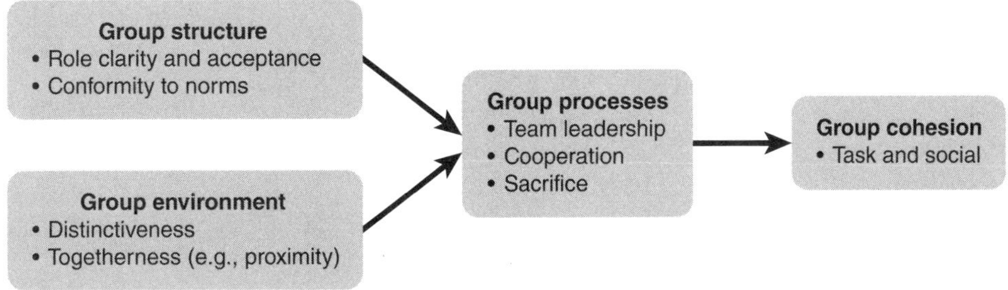

FIGURE 18.2 Implementation model for team building in sport groups.

Reprinted from M.A. Eys, M.B. Evans, and A. Benson, *Group Dynamics in Sport*, 5th ed. (Morgantown, WV: Fitness Information Technology, 2020), 265. Used with permission from FiT Publishing/West Virginia University. Based on A.V. Carron and K.S. Spink, "Team Building in an Exercise Setting," *The Sport Psychologist* 7 (1993): 8-18.; H. Prapavessis, A.V. Carron, and K.S. Spink, "Team Building in Sport," *International Journal of Sport Psychology* 27 (1996): 269-285.

importance of demonstrating positive results for participants and researchers alike, we argue that insights into the purported sequential chain that underpins this model are limited by the tendency of most team-building interventions in sport to simply target as many of the group environment, structure, and process variables as possible.

So how effective have those team-building interventions been at enhancing both group cohesion and team performance? To address this question, Martin and colleagues (2009) conducted a meta-analysis of the literature containing team-building interventions in sport settings. Although the team-building interventions covered by that review (e.g., team goal setting, adventure education) were found to generally result in substantive improvements (g = .71) in team performance, the effects on group cohesion were nonsignificant for task cohesion and small for social cohesion (g = .21). As such, it is conceivable that those interventions were relatively ineffectual at developing cohesion (especially task cohesion). That said, those null or weak effects in relation to cohesion were also juxtaposed against significant (and meaningful) effects on measures of team performance, which suggests that team performance might well improve via mechanisms other than cohesion. Indeed, as a second noteworthy point, it is conceivable that other explanatory processes might be responsible for teams performing well (i.e., operating as distinct mediators). For instance, examples abound of sport teams excelling despite their constituent members not being highly cohesive.

Teamwork

One approach to team development that may hold promise in promoting both cohesion *and* team performance effectiveness corresponds to efforts designed to promote better *teamwork*. Teamwork represents the behaviors among members that are enacted to achieve the team's goals; it has been defined as "a dynamic process involving a collaborative effort by team members to effectively carry out the independent and interdependent behaviors that are required to maximize a team's likelihood of achieving its purposes" (McEwan & Beauchamp, 2014, p. 233). Within both the organizational psychology literature (Mathieu et al., 2008) and more recently within sport (McEwan & Beauchamp, 2014), cohesion is considered to represent an emergent state that derives from, and contributes to, teamwork. Within occupational settings, when group-based interventions have sought to optimize teamwork behaviors, those initiatives tend to improve both cohesion and team performance (LePine et al., 2008). From a practical perspective, a robust way of nurturing cohesion and achievement outcomes is to focus on those core behaviors required of team members to collectively perform effectively.

Within sport settings, McEwan and Beauchamp (2014) presented a conceptual model of teamwork that differentiated between the behaviors required to manage team maintenance and those required to regulate team performance. This framework drew from work in organizational psychology (Mathieu et al., 2008; Rousseau et al., 2006) in which (1) management of team maintenance is composed of strategies for *psychological support* (e.g., providing emotional support) and *conflict management* (e.g., developing codes of conduct), and (2) regulation of team performance includes *preparation* (e.g., specifying goals), *execution* (e.g., coordinating actions), *evaluation* (e.g., performance monitoring), and *adjustment* (e.g., brainstorming solutions to team challenges) behaviors. McEwan and colleagues (2018) also developed a measure of teamwork based on this conceptual model and, of direct relevance to this chapter, subsequently found that athletes' teamwork behaviors were related to higher levels of both task and social cohesion (McEwan, 2020).

Identity Leadership

Informed by the tenets of the social identity approach described earlier in this chapter, when coaches and athlete leaders are able to foster a shared sense of belonging, team identification is fostered that subsequently elevates levels of group cohesion (Fransen et al., 2016). Fostering group member identification involves more than just promoting a sense of unity (i.e., cohesion); group identification also involves members' sense of self becoming intertwined with the social groups to which they belong. This approach would be termed *identity leadership*.

Recently, Fransen and colleagues (2020) presented the $5R^S$ Shared Leadership Program, which targets the development of shared leadership within sport teams and also seeks to optimize shared leadership processes through

- readying (awareness raising related to team identity),
- reflecting (reflecting on a team's core values),
- representing (identifying team aspirations),
- realizing (implementing strategies), and
- reporting (monitoring goal progress).

Initial qualitative work in sport points to the feasibility and acceptability of this program (Fransen et al., 2020), with experimental evidence also pointing to its efficacy with basketball teams (Mertens et al., 2020). Specifically, Mertens and colleagues conducted an experimental study that involved having teams in the intervention condition identify the intrateam leadership structure (through a mapping exercise), appoint the best leaders in their leadership role, and then promote their identity leadership skills. Athlete leaders' identity leadership skills were found to improve along with team members' identification with their team. Athletes in the intervention condition also displayed more self-determined motivation and commitment than those in the comparison condition. Although the authors did not assess cohesion as an explanatory variable, these results (vis-à-vis enhanced intrateam commitment) suggest that interventions that look to promote shared identity leadership (and exhorting a sense of "us" and togetherness) have considerable potential to foster group cohesion, member motivation, and effort, and consequently team performance.

Summary

In this chapter, we pointed out that cohesion in sport teams is a multidimensional construct composed of individual attractions to the group (task and social) and group integration (task and social). Individual and team correlates were introduced and potential negative consequences of high cohesion were presented. Although the mere existence of a group or team implies a degree of cohesion, its level may not be optimal. As such, multiple approaches to building and working as a team were discussed, with an eye toward maximizing team cohesiveness and effectiveness. Future research may take several directions. For example, providing greater insight into the dynamic nature of task and social cohesion, reconnecting cohesion with its social identity roots, and developing and evaluating sound intervention protocols are necessary steps in continuing a strong tradition of group cohesion research in sport.

DISCUSSION QUESTIONS

1. Considering the discussion related to entitativity and social identity, what factors differentiate a collection of individuals from a real group?
2. According to the conceptual model of cohesion outlined by Carron and colleagues (1985), what are the four manifestations of cohesiveness, and how do they differ?
3. What are some potential moderators of the cohesion–performance relationship, and how have they been shown to affect this relationship?
4. Potential liabilities are associated with high task and social cohesion. Identify some of these liabilities from your experiences as an athlete. What signs should coaches, sport psychology consultants, and athletes look for in order to avoid the potential disadvantages of high cohesion?
5. Team building is one approach to enhancing team cohesion. Identify and describe another team development approach that was presented in the chapter.

19

Coaching Effectiveness in Youth Sport

Jean Côté, PhD; Caroline Hummell, MSc; Leisha Strachan, PhD; and Jessica Fraser-Thomas, PhD

LEARNING OBJECTIVES

On completion of this chapter, the reader should have the following:

- Appreciation of the use of a system perspective to integrate the determinants and outcomes of effective coaching
- Understanding of three types of coaching approaches: outcome centered, athlete centered, and person centered
- Knowledge of conceptual models that focus on coaches' interpersonal knowledge and behaviors to enhance positive youth development (PYD) through sport
- Understanding of potential best practices of the person-centered approach that may foster long-term outcomes

Activities that provide enjoyment and sustained concentration, such as organized sports, contribute to the development of personal assets and initiative (Larson, 2000). Coaches and coach-athlete relationships, in particular, provide an environment that is not only rife with opportunity for quality developmental experiences but also engages a large proportion of youth in sport. A growing body of literature supports the role of coaches as agents of change for youths' physical and psychosocial development through sport (Fraser-Thomas et al., 2005). Therefore, to realize the benefits associated with sport involvement, researchers have focused their attention on the influence that coaches bring to the planning and implementation of positive sport initiatives for youth. As such, this chapter examines coaching effectiveness through the lens of positive youth development (PYD).

We begin by providing a brief overview of the PYD literature and describing a structure that integrates the determinants and outcomes of effective coaching. Second, we describe three types of coaching approaches—outcome centered, athlete centered, and person centered—that favor various types of coaches' knowledge and privilege different elements for the development of athletes in sport. Third, we review conceptual models that focus on coaches' interpersonal knowledge and behaviors that have been shown to provide an additive effect to coaches' professional knowledge behaviors for enhancing PYD through sport. Finally, we suggest the person-centered approach as a coaching style that encourages young athletes to grow as individuals while sustaining their participation in sport and enhancing their performance. This last section of the chapter provides some guidelines for coaches at the levels of the physical environment, activities, and social dynamics to help young athletes achieve success while nurturing high-quality relationships based on trust and respect.

Theory and Research

Previous research in the field of human development has produced a rich literature describing the dynamic and synergistic relationships that exist between an individual and their context (e.g., Bronfenbrenner, 1999; Ford & Lerner, 1992; Smith & Thelen, 2003). These system frameworks have been successfully adopted within sport research to describe development as a result of athletes' interactions with elements of their social and physical environments (e.g., Côté et al., 2014, 2020; Dorsch et al., 2020; Henriksen et al., 2010; Holt et al., 2017). Indeed, these conceptual frameworks highlight the complexity of athlete development by suggesting that athletes' physical environments, their relationships with important social agents, and the unique context surrounding athletic activities will inevitably mediate experiences and outcomes over different timelines. We describe a system approach next, and we use this viewpoint in the remainder of this chapter, to better situate the role of coaches in the overall development of athletes.

Activities that provide enjoyment and sustained concentration, such as organized sports, contribute to the development of personal assets and initiative.

A System Perspective of Athlete Development

The field of positive youth development (PYD) through sport has focused on the growth of positive skills that can facilitate young people's development inside and outside of the sport context (Gould & Carson, 2008). Fraser-Thomas and colleagues (2005) and Petitpas and colleagues (2005) were among the first to apply PYD frameworks in sport by highlighting individual and contextual factors that are present or may be developed through sport. Recently, the Personal Assets Framework (PAF; Côté et al., 2016, 2020; Vierimaa et al., 2017) has been proposed and used as a standard framework for positive youth sport program delivery. The PAF is rooted in a developmental system approach (e.g., Bronfenbrenner, 1999; Dorsch et al., 2020; Lerner et al., 2000) and explicitly emphasizes interactions between personal, relational, and organizational factors as necessary for understanding development through sport. A unique feature of the PAF, when compared with other conceptual frameworks, is how it delineates the determinants and the outcomes of athletes' development over different timelines. More specifically, the dynamic elements situated within the PAF (i.e., determinants), which have been recently revised, are (1) appropriate settings, (2) quality social dynamics, and (3) personal engagement in activities (Côté et al., 2020). When these dynamic elements—represented as gears—are optimally arranged, they can work in concert to foster positive assets in developing athletes. Importantly, each proposed subdimension extends proximally to distally, with those positioned closest to an athlete having the most immediate impact. All three dynamic elements need to work in unison to influence the cultivation of a sport context that fosters optimal growth and development in young athletes.

While the PAF offers a set of determinants (i.e., gears) that influence engagement in sport, it also suggests specific outcomes that sequentially result from developmentally appropriate settings, activities, and relationships (e.g., Côté et al., 2019; Vierimaa et al., 2017). More precisely, the concept of interest (Hidi & Renninger, 2006) shapes the immediate experience of athletes after a specific activity, such as playing a game or being involved in a practice. If interest is sustained over a longer period of time, then repeated positive experiences translate over a season (e.g., three to nine months) into the development of personal assets such as confidence, competence, connection, and character (i.e., the 4Cs). Subsequently, the long-term outcomes of engagement in sport can be achieved through continued participation, personal development, and performance (i.e., the 3Ps). One of the most important features of the PAF is that long-term athlete development (i.e., the 3Ps) cannot occur without sport programs that sustain athletes' interest and focus on the development of personal assets (i.e., the 4Cs) as short-term goals. Coaches are key social agents who exist within sport programs; therefore, their behaviors play a critical role in the facilitation of athletes' immediate personal assets.

Conceptualizing coaching roles in the overall development of young people becomes complex when trying to determine what constitutes an effective (or ineffective) coach. In the past, researchers examined coaching effectiveness through the lens of the pedagogical and teaching behaviors of coaches (Cushion et al., 2010). However, a coach's ability to establish and sustain interpersonal relationships with their athletes is a key component of effective coaching and has not always been salient in the coaching research (Erickson & Côté, 2016; Lefebvre et al., 2016). For instance, Horn (2008) asserted that an effective coach should be able to foster positive psychosocial outcomes in their athletes in addition to standard performance outcomes and suggests how this could be improved through more focused research that examines coaches' behaviors.

As such, Côté and Gilbert (2009) developed a comprehensive definition of coaching effectiveness that addresses some of the concerns related to the narrow scope of the existing coaching research. They defined coaching effectiveness as "the consistent and integrated application of professional, interpersonal, and intrapersonal knowledge and behaviours to facilitate athlete outcomes pertaining to competence, confidence, connection, and character in specific sport contexts" (Côté & Gilbert, 2009, p. 316; figure 19.1).

Gilbert and Côté (2013) further defined coaches' knowledge by suggesting that *professional knowledge* is the technical and tactical sport-specific knowledge—and behaviors—that a coach possesses. *Interpersonal knowledge* relates to a coach's ability to form quality relationships with those they interact with, whereas *intrapersonal knowledge* is more self-reflective in nature and refers to a coach's awareness of themselves in the sport environment. Together, these three types of knowledge and corresponding behaviors were found to affect the immediate and personal assets highlighted in the PAF—the maintenance of interest and the development of personal assets such as competence (e.g., skill development),

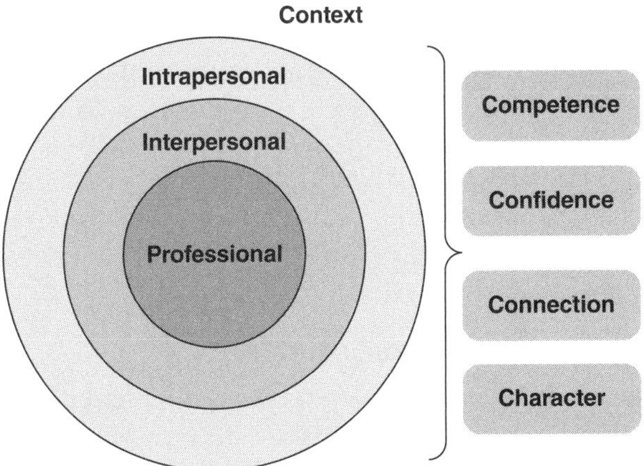

FIGURE 19.1 Visual representation of coaching effectiveness definition.

Adapted from J. Côté and W. Gilbert, "An Integrative Definition of Coaching Effectiveness and Expertise," *International Journal of Sports Science & Coaching* 4, no. 3 (2009): 307-323.

confidence (e.g., increased levels of self-esteem), connection (e.g., relating to others), and character (e.g., moral development) (Vierimaa et al., 2017).

When combined, Côté and colleagues' (2020) PAF and Côté and Gilbert's (2009) coaching definition suggest that coaches' focus on interpersonal assets—in conjunction with the development of sport-specific skills—will eventually lead to the long-term outcomes that are used in many sport programs as the ultimate indicators of success (i.e., the achievement of athletes' performance, continued participation, and personal development through sport). Coaches who focus collectively on these short-term assets instead of focusing exclusively on one long-term outcome (most often performance), suggest a coaching style that values process over results. In the next section, we review three styles of coaching that emphasize process and outcomes differently.

Outcome-Centered, Athlete-Centered, and Person-Centered Coaching

When viewed holistically, a substantial body of research on coaching encapsulates the inconsistency of terms used to define coaching approaches that, typically, are either task oriented or people oriented (e.g., Cassidy, 2010; Falcão et al., 2020). Although research does not support a sole task-oriented or outcome-centered approach to coaching, Avner and colleagues (2017) suggested that people-oriented approaches often represent rhetoric as opposed to practical reality. This section of the chapter describes three different approaches to coaching that vary in terms of the emphasis placed on outcomes or people.

Outcome-Centered Coaching

Outcome-centered coaching represents a task-oriented approach to leadership that has long been a predominant method of measuring coaching success or effectiveness and by extension has guided many coaches' philosophies and approaches (Denison, 2010). Outcome-centered coaches are mainly concerned with the ultimate results that athletes achieve under their supervision. The effectiveness of an outcome-centered approach is most often evaluated by athletes' level of achievement (e.g., win–loss percentage) but could also be evaluated through other outcomes such as frequency of participation or athletes' personal attributes (e.g., leadership). While these consequences could be attributed to the coaching process, an outcome-centered approach will use only outcomes as a measure of success while ignoring the coaching knowledge and behaviors that led to these outcomes. Horn (2008) reviewed studies on effective coaching and proposed a definition of coaching effectiveness solely based on athletes' outcomes:

> Effective coaching . . . results in either successful performance outcomes (measured either in terms of win–loss percentages, individual player development, or success at the national or international level) or positive psychological responses on the part of the athletes (e.g., high perceived ability, high self-esteem, intrinsic motivational orientation, or high level of sport enjoyment and satisfaction). (p. 240)

Although this definition summarizes what is expected to result from effective coaching (i.e., performance results or positive psychological responses), there is no reference to what coaches should do to achieve these outcomes. Further, Horn's (2008) definition proposed two mutually exclusive outcomes (note the *or*), indirectly suggesting little connection between factors (i.e., processes) that may lead to various outcomes. In one sense, Horn's (2008) definition provided us with a macro-level view of effective coaching outcomes; since then, coaching approaches have been examined at a more micro level.

Coaching effectiveness can be achieved through interpersonal interactions that emphasize athletes' development of the 4Cs: competence, confidence, connection, and character.

Athlete-Centered Coaching

Athlete-centered coaching was first proposed in the early 2000s, emerging as an alternative to the outcome-centered approach that had increasingly been criticized for its win-at-all-costs mentality and adoption of professional sport models at a youth sport level (Kidman, 2005). Drawing on the philosophical underpinnings of humanism (Rogers, 1969), athlete-centered coaching has a focus on humanizing athletes in a holistic manner—fostering athletes' physical, cognitive (e.g., critical thinking), psychological (e.g., self-esteem), social (e.g., communication), and affective or spiritual development (Kidman, 2010). Further, athlete-centered coaching places the athlete as an active participant in the learning process, with the coach empowering the athlete to take a more central position in their sport experiences. Athlete-centered coaching has been described as the process by which athletes "gain and take ownership of knowledge, development, and decision making that will help them to maximize their performance and their enjoyment" (Kidman & Lombardo, 2010, p. 13). Accordingly, specific strategies that inform an athlete-centered coaching approach have been suggested in the literature. These strategies include methods that engage athletes in learning and decision making through questions, facilitate an appropriate team culture, use different forms of play (e.g., teaching games for understanding), and work in small groups (e.g., shared leadership) with rotating team roles (Kidman & Lombardo, 2010).

Despite a common use of the term *athlete-centered coaching* by practitioners, researchers have expressed concerns about the potentially atheoretical nature of this approach—lacking a firm connection to specific underlying theory or empirical evidence—leading to challenges in implementing athlete-centered coaching. For example, Bowles and O'Dwyer (2020) engaged in a collaborative self-study, finding that past experience influenced both coaches' and athletes' abilities to deliver and engage with the athlete-centered approach—particularly in a competitive team environment. These findings were in line with Zehntner and McMahon's (2014) work identifying issues around coaches' and athletes' personally infused cultural ideologies, their questions around performance successes associated with the approach, and disciplinary power issues within sport organizations. While the above work indicates some resistance to move away from outcome-centered coaching approaches focused primarily on performance, there is evidence of growing receptiveness to new coaching approaches that incorporate elements of the athlete-centered approach and theoretical frameworks that focus on youth development through sport.

Person-Centered Coaching

A *person-centered* approach to coaching acknowledges the importance of the interpersonal element situated within the Côté and Gilbert (2009) coaching effectiveness definition. While the importance of coaches' professional knowledge is emphasized throughout the coaching literature (Cushion et al., 2010) and indirectly linked with the outcome-centered and athlete-centered approaches, Abraham and colleagues (2006) suggested that research consider other elements of effective coaching rather than focusing solely on technical and tactical sport-specific knowledge.

As a result, research over the past decade has begun to look beyond coaches' professional knowledge and behaviors, showing that the integration and application of interpersonal knowledge and behaviors are imperative for enhancing coaching effectiveness (Allan & Côté, 2016; Erickson et al., 2011). More specifically, coaching effectiveness can be achieved through interpersonal interactions that emphasize athletes' development of the 4Cs: competence, confidence, connection, and character (Côté et al., 2020; Vierimaa et al., 2012). The original model put forward by Little (1993) included the 4Cs; this model was later expanded to include a fifth C—*caring* (Lerner et al., 2005) or *compassion* (Jelicic et al., 2007). Nonetheless, for research in youth sport, Côté and colleagues (2010) have recommended a return to the original 4Cs model. This recommendation stemmed from a review of the sport literature in which the authors concluded that caring, compassion, and character were not well differentiated in the sport domain and could be easily collapsed into an encompassing single C (Côté et al., 2010). As indicators of PYD in the youth sport context, the 4Cs are defined as follows: *competence*—an athlete's technical, tactical, and physical ability in sport; *confidence*—an athlete's belief in their ability to be successful in sport; *connection*—the quality of relationships and degree of interaction with others in sport (e.g., coaches, peers); and *character* (encompassing caring and compassion)—engagement in prosocial behaviors and avoidance of antisocial behaviors (see Vierimaa and colleagues 2012 for a review). Given that, in the broader context of youth development, the Cs are intended to represent the personal assets of optimally developing youth, policies and programs must correspondingly be in place to assist families, communities, and schools in working toward these ideal outcomes.

Following the integration of the 4Cs into Côté and Gilbert's (2009) definition of coaching effectiveness and the Personal Assets Framework (PAF; Côté et al., 2016, 2020; Vierimaa et al., 2017), these assets are also at the heart of a person-centered approach to coaching. If the development of personal assets such as confidence, competence, connection, and character (i.e., the 4Cs) are developed through regular coach–athlete interactions, then the long-term outcomes of engagement in sport will be achieved in the form of continued participation, personal development, and performance (i.e., the 3Ps). One of the most important postulates of the coaching effectiveness definition and the PAF model is that long-term athlete development (i.e., the 3Ps) requires coaches who prioritize the development of the person over outcomes such as winning and performance.

Contrasting Coaching Styles

In brief, outcome-centered, athlete-centered, and person-centered coaching exemplify different coaching styles that translate into different markers of coaching effectiveness. Outcome-centered coaching uses the long-term results of athletes in terms of performance, participation, and personal development as the main indicator of coaching effectiveness. Athlete-centered coaching focuses on pedagogical principles that help coaches design sport systems in which athlete learning is central to coaching effectiveness. As an extension of athlete-centered coaching, a person-centered approach uses developmental frameworks to refocus coaching and sport as a relational activity in which the development of the person is the primary aim of sport. Person-centered coaches will see their relationships with athletes as the driver of athletes' success and the achievement of long-term outcomes (i.e., performance, participation, and personal development) as a by-product of athletes' development. To achieve this goal, we need to take a closer look at the characteristics of interpersonal coaching behaviors, guided by current practical and applied frameworks that outline specific actions for coaches.

Additive Effect of Interpersonal Coaching Knowledge and Behaviors

A person-centered coach seeks to facilitate athletes' acquisition of immediate personal assets (i.e., the 4Cs) through the application of their interpersonal knowledge and behaviors (i.e., developing and maintaining quality relationships with athletes) (Côté & Gilbert, 2009). As an ongoing stream of research from Jowett and colleagues continues to demonstrate (e.g., Jowett, 2007; Jowett & Meek, 2000; Jowett & Ntoumanis, 2004), quality coach–athlete relationships are critical because they have been linked to various athlete outcomes including intrinsic motivation (Adie & Jowett, 2010), passion for sport (Lafrenière et al., 2008), and satisfaction with training and performance (Jowett & Nezlek,

2012). Furthermore, studies have shown that coach–athlete relationships are multidirectional in nature (referred to as coach–athlete dyads) and that even specific aspects concerning the interpersonal nature of emotional processes (e.g., being consistent, tone of voice used with athletes) can influence athletes' psychosocial development (Allan & Côté, 2016; Erickson et al., 2011). Consistent with these findings, Becker (2012) proposed that coaching behaviors are more likely to be effective when they involve characteristics that are supportive, appropriate, individualistic, clear, and consistent. Similarly, aligning with interpersonal knowledge (described earlier), the behaviors proposed by Becker (2012) suggest that coaches' use of personalized and caring behaviors may be most effective at developing positive outcomes in athletes.

Coaches' interpersonal behaviors can be conceptualized through varying existing models and frameworks. Three coaching models that provide a comprehensive lens for understanding coaches' interpersonal behaviors through a person-centered approach to coaching are (1) mastery-oriented coaching (Smoll & Smith, 1989; Smoll et al., 1978), (2) autonomy-supportive and empowering coaching (Duda, 2013; Mageau & Vallerand, 2003), and (3) transformational leadership (Turnnidge & Côté, 2018; Vella et al., 2013). Each of these three coaching models is reviewed in the following sections and discussed more in depth in chapter 7 of this book.

Mastery-Oriented Coaching

Mastery-oriented coaching (Smith et al., 2007) acknowledges how cognitive processes, differences between individuals (e.g., age), and situational factors (e.g., competition level) mediate the relationships between coach behaviors and athlete outcomes (Smoll & Smith, 1989; Smoll et al., 1978). In line with achievement goal theory (AGT; Nicholls, 1989), this framework posits that coaches can contribute to perceptions of two types of motivational climates: a mastery-oriented climate or an ego-oriented climate (Smith et al., 2007). *Mastery-oriented climates* are described as environments whereby success is defined through an individual's level of self-improvement, maximum effort, and task mastery (Ames, 1992). Mastery climates can be beneficial for athletes because they focus on effort and view mistakes as a source of valuable feedback; they are associated with lower anxiety and increased intrinsic motivation (Dweck & Leggett, 1988). In comparison, *ego-oriented climates* focus primarily on winning and elicit toxic and punitive behaviors from coaches when athletes make mistakes (Duda & Ntoumanis, 2005). An ego-oriented motivational climate is also characterized by the perception that teachers or coaches vary their treatment of players based on ability differences, rivalry, and a focus on outperforming one's competitors (Newton et al., 2000). Overall, coaching research points to the benefits of promoting mastery-oriented climates, particularly when we look at what athletes and participants perceive the climate to be (e.g., Harwood et al., 2015), but also with some promising findings in interventions such as the Mastery Approach to Coaching (MAC; Smith et al., 2007).

One shortcoming of this research and associated interventions (i.e., Coach Effectiveness Training [CET], Smith et al., 1979; MAC, Smith et al., 2007) is that it is focused mainly on the facilitation of motivational sport climates through the assessment of professional behaviors such as instruction, feedback, and organization. It appears that a more intricate understanding of how coaches specifically interact with their athletes while using professional behaviors, such as instruction or feedback, is necessary. To that end, the next section provides a review of coaching models (i.e., autonomy-supportive coaching, Mageau & Vallerand, 2003; empowering coaching, Duda, 2013) and discusses how specific types of interpersonal coaching behaviors promote the emergence of a positive motivational climate.

Autonomy-Supportive and Empowering Coaching

Self-determination theory (SDT; Deci & Ryan, 2013) suggests that coaches' behaviors can be viewed in terms of two interpersonal styles: autonomy supportive or controlling. Theoretically, a coach who is *autonomy supportive* would consider—and be responsive to—athletes' perspectives and preferences, provide choice in practices and games, and be receptive and welcoming to input from athletes regarding the decision-making process (Mageau & Vallerand, 2003; Mageau et al., 2009). On the other hand, a coach who is *controlling* pressures athletes, exhibits coerciveness, and uses intimidation tactics with athletes (Bartholomew et al., 2010). Researchers in this area have focused on examining autonomy-supportive coaching behaviors specifically; findings consistently associate these behaviors with athletes reporting positive experiences and outcomes, as well as more optimal or adaptive motivational climates (e.g., Coatsworth & Conroy, 2009; Mageau & Vallerand, 2003).

For instance, coaching behaviors that support athletes' sense of autonomy have been shown to be associated with athletes' intrinsic and autonomous extrinsic motivation; increases in these types of motivation have been correlated with increases in athlete psychological needs satisfaction and player well-being and performance, as well as decreases in athlete burnout (Mageau & Vallerand, 2003). Coaches who were perceived as showing more autonomy-supportive behaviors have also tended to have athletes with higher levels of self-esteem, positive identity, and prosocial behaviors (Coatsworth & Conroy, 2009; Hodge & Lonsdale, 2011). In light of this pattern of findings, Occhino and colleagues (2014) suggested that three factors—a coach's personal orientation, coaching context, and perceptions of athletes' behaviors and motivation—directly influence coaches' use of autonomy-supportive coaching behaviors.

Coaches can contribute to perceptions of two types of motivational climates: a mastery-oriented climate or an ego-oriented climate.

In an effort to further advance this line of research, Duda (2013) introduced the concept of *empowering coaching*. While heavily influenced by SDT in regard to the effects of coaching on athlete autonomy, competence, and relatedness, empowering coaching also uses AGT and additional empirical research to consolidate the importance of coaches' interpersonal behaviors for the total development of athletes. An empowering coaching environment is one that is task oriented, autonomy supportive, and socially supportive in order to enhance the psychological needs satisfaction of athletes and increase their overall well-being (Duda, 2013). The conceptual model described to be underlying empowering coaching considers "what" coaches can emphasize (i.e., the goal content in terms of players' participation); the "why," or reasons for athletes' engagement (i.e., goal motives); and the "how" regarding coaches' influence on their athletes (i.e., via their facilitation or compromising of players' sense of autonomy) (Sheldon et al., 2004; Vansteenkiste et al., 2004).

Similar to autonomy-supportive coaching, empowering coaching environments also hold potential for influencing athlete development. Reinboth and colleagues (2004) found that autonomy-supportive, task-involving, and socially supportive features of the coaching environment predict autonomy, competence, and relatedness needs satisfaction in athletes. For instance, Quested and Duda (2010) examined antecedents of burnout among 219 elite dancers enrolled in vocational training and found that when athletes perceived task-involving environments, it positively predicted psychological needs satisfaction in dancers, whereas perceived ego-involving environments were negatively correlated with competence and relatedness. Other studies have found that task-involving climates, where empowering coaching behaviors are used, can elicit increased task cohesion among athletes (Heuzé et al., 2006).

While the findings from studies examining autonomy-supportive coaching and empowering coaching point to the importance of coaches' interpersonal behaviors, it appears there is a lack of a clear taxonomy of autonomy-supportive or empowering coaching behaviors that can be used to inform the development and implementation of coaching resources and interventions. A perspective that does provide classification of coaches' interpersonal behaviors is transformational leadership (e.g., Bass & Riggio, 2006); this concept has been well researched in sport and is suggested as a useful avenue for examining coach–athlete interactions (Chelladurai, 2007).

Full-Range Leadership Model and Transformational Leadership

Theoretical coaching models have expanded beyond autonomy-supportive, mastery-oriented, and empowering coaching and have also considered the application of a leadership approach to coaching. One comprehensive leadership model that has been applied in different contexts and is now being adapted to sport coaching is transformational leadership (Bass & Riggio, 2006; Turnnidge & Côté, 2018). Transformational leadership is derived from a broader leadership framework known as the full-range leadership model (Bass & Riggio, 2006); it examines leadership by taking into consideration two axes: active to passive and effective to ineffective. As discussed in chapter 7, along these axes fall three distinct leadership behaviors: laissez-faire, transactional, and transformational.

Transformational leadership is considered the most active and effective style. More specifically, transformational leadership adopts a follower-centered approach that enables the growth and development of followers into leaders by attending to their individual needs (Bass & Riggio, 2006). This is accomplished by empowering them and by aligning the goals of the individual followers, the leader, and the group. The original full-range leadership model has since been adapted to the coaching context by incorporating two additional distinct leadership behaviors—toxic leadership and neutral leadership (Turnnidge & Côté, 2019).

In an effort to provide a more comprehensive framework for examining the nature of coach leadership, Turnnidge and Côté (2019) used qualitative interviews, video observation, and expert review to suggest 11 transformational leadership behaviors that are specific to a person-centered approach to coaching (e.g., transformational coaching). The line of research on transformational coaching (e.g., Lawrason et al., 2019; Lefebvre et al., 2021; Turnnidge & Côté, 2017, 2018, 2019) showcases 11 transformational behaviors specific to coaching that align closely with coaching styles such as mastery, autonomy-supportive, and empowering coaching. The 11 transformational coaching behaviors are categorized by one of the four dimensions of transformational leadership (referred to as the 4Is): (1) idealized influence, (2) inspirational motivation, (3) intellectual stimulation, and (4) individualized consideration (Turnnidge & Côté, 2019). *Idealized influence* occurs when coaches discuss and model prosocial values and show vulnerability and humility. *Inspirational motivation* is displayed when coaches discuss goals and expectations, express confidence in athletes' potential, promote team concept, and enhance the meaning of activities by connecting them to a bigger picture. *Intellectual stimulation* involves eliciting athlete input, sharing decision-making and leadership responsibilities, and emphasizing the learning process. Finally, *individualized consideration* refers to behaviors that show interest in athletes and recognize roles and accomplishments. For more details about measurement and research related to these behaviors, please refer to chapter 7 of this book.

Overall, the 11 behaviors of transformational coaching provide a comprehensive framework that is unique to the sport environment and includes elements that are not explicitly addressed by other conceptualizations of coaches' interpersonal behaviors (e.g., showing vulnerability and humility; discussing and modeling prosocial values and behaviors).

Indeed, transformational coaching is a valuable concept for discussing the determinants of effective interpersonal interactions between coaches and athletes. Furthermore, transformational coaching concretely personalizes a person-centered approach to coaching, for which a practical intervention, the Transformational Coaching Workshop, has been developed and tested for effectiveness (Lawrason et al., 2019; Turnnidge & Côté, 2017).

Future Research Directions

The literature on athlete development and coaching effectiveness reviewed and integrated in this chapter raised some research questions that need further investigation. For example, researchers interested in understanding and optimizing how coaches influence overall athlete development may ask questions such as the following: What knowledge and behaviors best describe and differentiate outcome-centered, athlete-centered, and person-centered coaching? Can we develop specific measurement tools and methods that examine how coaches affect a diversity of athletes' assets and outcomes over short and long periods of time? What mobilization initiatives are best suited to make changes to coaching education and programs?

First, the integration of coaching research and working toward the overall acceptance of constructs among researchers that represent coaching effectiveness is an important area for future research. A growing body of knowledge emanating from various disciplines such as sport psychology, sociocultural studies, sport pedagogy, and sport management has influenced the direction of coaching research in the last several years. It appears that, independent of disciplines, researchers interested in coaching should consider broad conceptual approaches such as outcome-centered, athlete-centered, and person-centered coaching and build upon recent methodological innovation to advance the field, instead of maintaining research silos. For example, the state space grid method (Erickson & Côté, 2013), recently applied in coaching research (e.g., Erickson & Côté, 2016), represents a shift in thinking about social processes. Briefly, state space grids allow researchers to present a visual aid that depicts the relationships between two variables synchronized in time. This innovative method of studying coach–athlete interactions has the potential to shed light on different types of coaching behaviors and allow for a more distinctive taxonomy of effective and less effective coaching practices and behaviors.

Second, when considering athlete development through the PAF lens, it is vital to consider the unique micro and macro environment of determinants that youth sport coaches can or cannot change. In other words, coaches can change athletes' interests, personal assets, and long-term engagement by modifying certain elements of the physical environment, nurturing some aspects of the social dynamics, and structuring activities that foster enjoyment and skill development. However, some features of the environment, social dynamics, and activities (e.g., the city in which one coach lives, the family of a given athlete) are more constant, and coaches need to adopt to these stable factors. The PAF provides a practical blueprint for coaches and sport organizations to make decisions about areas of intervention and a conceptual framework for researchers to design impactful studies (e.g., Erikstad et al., 2021).

With this in mind, coaches should focus on the changeable determinants of the PAF, and researchers should develop specific measurement tools and innovative research approaches to examine how coaches effectively promote changes in athletes over different periods. This temporality functions on many time scales—from the course of a single practice to more developmental spans such as the course of a season or the additive effects of several seasons—and requires coaches to adapt and engineer the training and competition environment to produce consistent performance and developmental outcomes. Therefore, the integration and validation of tools that assess coaches' impact on athletes' development in sport on different time scales and outcomes is an important next step.

Finally, a vital future direction involves ensuring that contemporary coaching research can have a direct positive influence on the development of young athletes. When considering the numerous domains of applied research, there are indeed established strategies for designing research and implementing interventions in ways that facilitate optimal uptake. As one example, translation research may help identify a broader scope of realms through which coaches could be effectively trained. Notably, whereas approaches to translate sport findings often include interventions with coaches (e.g., Smith et al., 2007; Turnnidge & Côté, 2017) that are effective in small-scale studies, more attention should be given to the external validity of these interventions. In other words, coaching interventions should be designed to ensure they not only are effective but also reach important populations and can be implemented and adopted over time by targeted sport organizations (Evans et al., 2015).

Practical Implications: Person-Centered Coaching Within the PAF

While a person-centered approach to coaching has support for its ability to establish quality relationships and aid in the emergence of positive athlete outcomes, we have not yet, in the chapter, explained how this coaching approach can be situated within the PAF, and so in this section we detail and justify this synergy. The three gears of the PAF (i.e., appropriate settings, quality social dynamics, personal engagement in activities) provide a framework to (1) outline the key challenges for youth sport coaches to adopt a person-centered approach and (2) propose potential means of approaching these challenges, based on research in the field. It is important to recognize the diversity of contexts in which youth sport coaches operate (e.g., recreational, competitive, high performance; seasonal, year-round; community based, nonprofit, private; volunteer, paid), in addition to the challenges athletes, coaches, programmers, and administrators often encounter. The intent of the following guidelines is not to prescribe specific one-size-fits-all roles for coaches but rather to offer insights for consideration in the implementation of a person-centered approach to coaching using evidence from established coaching models. The essential elements that contribute to interest, motivation, and positive assets among developing athletes at each organizational level of the PAF are presented here.

Appropriate Settings

Appropriate settings refer to the physical contexts that athletes occupy while participating in sport. To achieve optimal development, it has been suggested that the physical place should be structured to promote clear and consistent boundaries and expectations, while providing age-appropriate monitoring and supervision (Lerner et al., 2000). Although many sport programs are competitively engineered to enhance both the performance and the development of young athletes (i.e., rules, facilities, and equipment are modified) (Burton et al., 2011; McCalpin et al., 2017), person-centered coaches can still modify the practice environment to promote competence, confidence, and connections between athletes. Principles of nonlinear pedagogy (Machado et al., 2019) would suggest, for example, that a youth basketball coach could alter the size of the court during a practice or the number of players involved in a drill. These imposed constraints in the learning environment would provide athletes with greater opportunities to interact with the ball, and with each other, and potentially offer a more positive experience.

A physical setting that fosters holistic development, positive relationships, and learning empowers youth with the tools to pursue a wide array of physical pursuits with confidence and competence. Coaches' careful considerations of the physical setting can stimulate athletes' interest and encourage personal relevance by offering opportunities to engage in diverse activities, interactions, and roles, all while maintaining a sense of autonomy and freedom to safely explore the sport setting.

Social Dynamics

Research in education and youth sport consistently points to the importance of a mastery motivational climate (e.g., Smith et al., 2007; Smoll et al., 2007) and a multiple goals approach (e.g., Harackiewicz et al., 2008; Harwood et al., 2015; Hulleman et al., 2008) as an optimal social environment for success. Another feature, autonomy-supportive relationships, also contributes to self-determined motivation and enhanced well-being in sport (e.g., Adie et al., 2008; Smith et al., 2007).

As detailed earlier in this chapter, the behaviors of transformational coaching may also be an appropriate lens for understanding coaching behaviors of youth sport coaches because researchers have investigated the relationships between transformational leadership behaviors and athletes' performance, participation, and personal development at both an individual and team level. Youth sport coaches who use transformational leadership behaviors improve sport performance via the mediating effects of intrinsic motivation (Charbonneau et al., 2001). Coaches' use of transformational leadership has recently been linked with developmental outcomes in youth athletes such as the growth of personal, social, and cognitive skills; goal setting abilities; and initiative (Vella et al., 2013). Furthermore, transformational leadership can be linked with team outcomes, because coaches' transformational leadership behaviors positively influence task and social cohesion in team sports (Callow et al., 2009). A recent intervention study with youth soccer coaches provided some preliminary support for the effectiveness of a transformational coaching workshop (Lawrason et al., 2019) that can help coaches include more effective interpersonal behaviors in their coaching. Indeed, coaches spent more time displaying idealized influence, inspirational motivation, intellectual stimulation, and instruction or feedback behaviors following the workshop. Coaches also spent less time displaying neutral and organizational or management behaviors after the workshop.

Another resource that helps coaches learn about the 4Cs and how to develop quality relationships in sport programs is Project SCORE (Sport Connect and Respect). Coaches who have used this resource have reported an increased awareness of their coaching behaviors and opportunities for development for their athletes and themselves (Strachan et al., 2016). The development of Project SCORE also highlights the importance of accessibility for sport leaders and coaches to learn about PYD through sport (Strachan et al., 2020).

There is mounting evidence that interpersonal interventions with coaches can improve coach–athlete relationships and the quality of social dynamics within the broader sport system. In conflict with this pattern, however, a systematic review classifying 285 coaching interventions into higher-order and lower-order domains indicated that most education programs for coaches focused on professional knowledge and behaviors (i.e., skill and performance, health and well-being; $n = 261$), with minimal consideration to developing coaches' interpersonal knowledge and behaviors ($n = 18$) (Lefebvre et al., 2016). Consequently, studies like this help us identify a need to be more deliberate about designing, implementing, and evaluating coaching interventions that will help coaches improve their interpersonal behaviors to increase the likelihood of developing athletes' personal assets such as the 4Cs.

Personal Engagement in Activities

To achieve long-term positive outcomes in sport, the developmental model of sport participation suggests that (1) diversity should precede specialization in sport, (2) play and practice activities should be balanced, and (3) a mixture of adult-led and youth-led activities should be included (Côté et al., 2014). Through each of these processes, youth are afforded opportunities to explore their options, discover what they like and what they are good at, and develop a range of competencies that enable engagement in a variety of physical pursuits, ultimately contributing to talent development. Furthermore, coaches who deliver activities that focus on the personal assets of the athletes are more likely to promote interest, motivation, and continued engagement in physical activity and sport. When designing activities, person-centered coaches need to make sure that youths feel (1) they are capable and effective (e.g., competence and confidence), (2) they are working toward a collective cause or are connected with others (e.g., connection), and (3) their sport participation is governed by moral behaviors that include courage, honesty, and empathy (e.g., character). Altogether, personal engagement in activities that reflect these essential elements will promote a person-centered approach to coaching.

Summary

Those most proximally involved with young athletes, namely coaches, have the greatest potential to influence their personal development and, subsequently, their long-term engagement in sport (i.e., the 3Ps). Because athlete development involves distinct stages and learning contexts, coaches must be aware of the overriding sport context and the variables that affect their work. The different determinants and outcomes of the PAF (Côté et al., 2016, 2020) allow coaches to assess specific coaching situations and ultimately use a person-centered approach to contribute to their athletes' overall development.

While coaching effectiveness is conceptualized as the integrated application of a coach's professional, interpersonal, and intrapersonal knowledge and behaviors (Côté & Gilbert, 2009), the coaching research points to the benefits of coaches' abilities to develop and sustain interpersonal relationships with their athletes for facilitating positive sport experiences (Erickson & Côté, 2016; Lefebvre et al., 2016). The 4Cs provide a concise yet comprehensive framework with which to measure performance (competence) and psychosocial outcomes (confidence, connection, and character) in coaching. Together, these four constructs represent a person-centered approach to coaching that incorporates the traditional goals of youth sport programs (e.g., skill development and performance), with an added emphasis on positive psychosocial development.

DISCUSSION QUESTIONS

1. Outline and discuss the key features of the Personal Assets Framework (PAF).
2. In your own words, what is the definition of coaching effectiveness? Provide a unique example of each component of the definition.
3. Describe coaching behaviors that could be associated with the development of the 4Cs.
4. What is meant by a person-centered approach to coaching? What are the main differences between person-centered, outcome-centered and athlete-centered coaching?

PART V

The Athlete in the Wider Sport Environment

This part contains an eclectic mix of chapters to capture the breadth and depth of social psychology in sport. Numerous psychosocial factors shape the quality of experiences, developmental processes, and performance outcomes of those involved in sport. Some of these factors have become more prominent within the sport psychology literature in recent years and have been the focus of considerable research attention since the first edition of this book (e.g., the influence of environmental and sociocultural factors on resilience in competitive sport; the importance of critical perspectives related to gender and gender differences; the barriers and challenges experienced by both girls and boys and women and men in sport). The creation of safe sport cultures has also been a burgeoning topic in an attempt to prevent misconduct and abusive behavior within and across the sport ecosystems. The final part of this volume includes seven chapters featuring, alongside the topics just mentioned, career transitions of elite athletes, moral behavior, resilience, thriving, and talent development.

In chapter 20, Career Transitions of Elite Athletes, Paul Wylleman, Simon Defruyt, Jolan Kegelaers, Koen De Brandt, Sofie Smismans, and Suzan Blijlevens consider the career transitions of elite athletes by presenting a holistic and life span perspective on athletes' dual and postathletic careers. The authors present the holistic athletic career (HAC) model, describing the normative developmental stages and transitions of athletes at the athletic, psychological, psychosocial, academic and vocational, financial, and legal levels. Through the description of related research, readers can gain an understanding of the major challenges of transition periods and the associated barriers athletes encounter during crucial stages of their athletic careers. The chapter concludes with suggestions for advancing research within dual career environments as well as suggestions and strategies for supporting athletes during potentially challenging transition periods.

In chapter 21, Creating Safe Cultures in Sport, Daniel Rhind and Frank Owusu-Sekyere outline the nature, scope, and importance of safe sport for all, then explore key models and frameworks that guide and facilitate safe sport, including the International Safeguards for Children in Sport and the safeguarding culture model. Additionally, the conceptualization and measurement of safeguarding culture is addressed, whereby the importance of internal and external contextual factors are highlighted; the chapter concludes with suggestions for future research and practice. Moving the field forward, Rhind and Owusu-Sekyere outline the value of integrating research, theory, and practice to ensure that education, policies, and practice underpin safe cultures in sport.

In chapter 22, Antecedents and Consequences of Moral Behavior in Sport, Maria Kavussanu, Ian Boardley, and Nicholas Stanger begin with key definitions of prosocial and antisocial behaviors in sport followed by a review of literature that has examined antecedents and predictors of prosocial and antisocial behavior. The authors then review work on the outcomes and consequences of these behaviors for both individual and team functioning, including the consequences of teammate and opponent antisocial behavior. There is more research to be carried out around the effects of antisocial teammate behavior on athletes' objective performance. Employing experimental and longitudinal designs to examine such effects would be advantageous. To close this chapter, a range of practical considerations for coaches, physical education teachers, parents, and other key stakeholders are offered for promoting prosocial, and deterring antisocial, behavior in athletes.

In chapter 23, Environmental and Sociocultural Influences on Resilience in Competitive Sport, Mustafa Sarkar and Sally Hilton consider definitions, concepts, and theories of individual and team resilience and offer a comprehensive overview of research in this field. The discussion of research is focused on individual resilience and sociocultural factors, team resilience, and relational influences, as well as the consideration of coach resilience in terms of coaches' personal resilience and their influence on the resilience of their athletes. Furthermore, five main future research areas to advance knowledge in the context of environmental and sociocultural influences related to resilience in competitive sport are proposed. This chapter concludes with some insight into the practical ways coaches can help develop resilience and shape the sport environment.

In chapter 24, Systems That Promote Thriving in Sport, Daniel Brown, Michael Passaportis, Christopher Wagstaff, and Rachel Arnold provide an overview of the emerging body of thriving research in sport. As such, they offer a detailed explanation of the term *thriving* along with its theoretical mechanisms, an insight into the psychosocial enablers of thriving in athletes, and a contemporary overview of research in the area. Given that the concept of thriving in the context of sport is relatively new, there remains many interesting questions to explore. Specifically, while the importance of promoting thriving in athletes has been recognized, it is also pertinent that future research consider other stakeholders such as coaches. The chapter concludes with suggestions for promoting thriving in athletes and coaches, as well as more widely in sport organizations.

In chapter 25, Gender Perspectives, Nicole LaVoi and Courtney Boucher define key terms related to gender and gender-related research, offer a concise overview of theory including the ecological model, and provide a detailed review of current research, as well as potential caveats to be addressed. Specifically, the chapter focuses on three key areas, including girls' and women's participation in sport and barriers faced, challenges experienced by women coaches, and purported gender differences between coaching females and males. The chapter concludes with suggestions for future research and practical applications that may support and advance the field of sport psychology in meaningful ways. For example, LaVoi and Boucher highlight the necessity for education to consider sociocultural competency training, to ensure that gender and racial stereotypes are not reproduced.

In chapter 26, Talent Development and Performance, Dave Collins and Jamie Taylor discuss conceptual considerations and approaches to talent development and review emerging research into effective talent development, with a focus on exploring the development of an athlete's skill set, the role of feedback, and the optimizing of challenge. An in-depth overview of suggestions for future research within the area of talent development is presented, and applied implications are highlighted. Specifically, several considerations for applied practice are discussed, with consideration of the stakeholders engaged in talent development (e.g., coaches, sport psychology consultants, parents) and those supporting the development of practitioners.

20

Career Transitions of Elite Athletes

Paul Wylleman, PhD; Simon Defruyt, PhD; Jolan Kegelaers, PhD; Koen De Brandt, PhD; Sofie Smismans, PhD; and Suzan Blijlevens, PhD

LEARNING OBJECTIVES

On completion of this chapter, the reader should have the following:

- Understanding of the life-span and holistic perspective on athletes' development
- Understanding of the main multilevel transitions and associated barriers athletes are confronted with in crucial periods of the athletic career
- Knowledge of the competency-enhancing empowerment approach in career support
- Insight into the ecological perspective on athletes' environments
- Knowledge of the working models, taxonomies, and instruments that can be used on a micro (competency enhancement) level and meso (environmental) level in career support services

Research on athletes' career development has reached a state of maturity in looking at the elite athlete as a whole person developing over the entire life span. This has led to a shift from a singular focus on the athletic domain to a more multidomain perspective, taking into account athletes' psychological, psychosocial, academic and vocational, financial, and legal development (Wylleman, 2019; Wylleman & Rosier, 2016). Athletic development and success are thus no longer seen as the single end goal but rather as one among a number of developmental goals that constitute the whole life career of athletes, during competition as well as after athletic retirement (Wylleman et al., 2020).

Taking into account the importance of education and employment in an individual's development, it should not be surprising that researchers have also focused on the significance of the dual elite sport and education career as well as of the postathletic career as part of this holistic perspective on elite athletes' development (e.g., Guidotti et al., 2015; Park et al., 2013; Stambulova & Wylleman, 2019). This research not only detailed the multilevel challenges and barriers athletes encounter during these phases in their development but also shed light on the role of support provision and of the environmental context in facilitating these career pathways. In view of its impact on athletes' development, this chapter presents a holistic perspective on athletes' dual and postathletic careers, taking both a microlevel approach, related to competency development, and a meso-level approach focusing on how the environment (e.g., sport organizations, schools, family members) can facilitate athletes' development. In conclusion, evidence-based instruments and future research directions emerging from these approaches are presented.

Athletes' Holistic Development: Challenges and Required Support

In this section, a key model in describing athletes' holistic and life-span development is introduced. Then research findings about two important periods in athletes' lives are discussed, taking into account the challenges and barriers of multiple life domains. Finally, research findings and suggestions for practice are discussed on dual career support initiatives toward elite athletes.

Life-Span Perspective on the Athletic and Postathletic Career

Based on research data on the career development of active as well as former talented, professional, and elite athletes, and originally presented as the developmental model on transitions faced by athletes (Wylleman & Lavallee, 2004), the holistic athletic career model (HAC; Wylleman, 2019) was developed. This life-span model describes the normative developmental stages and transitions of athletes at the athletic, psychological, psychosocial, academic and vocational, financial, and legal levels (figure 20.1).

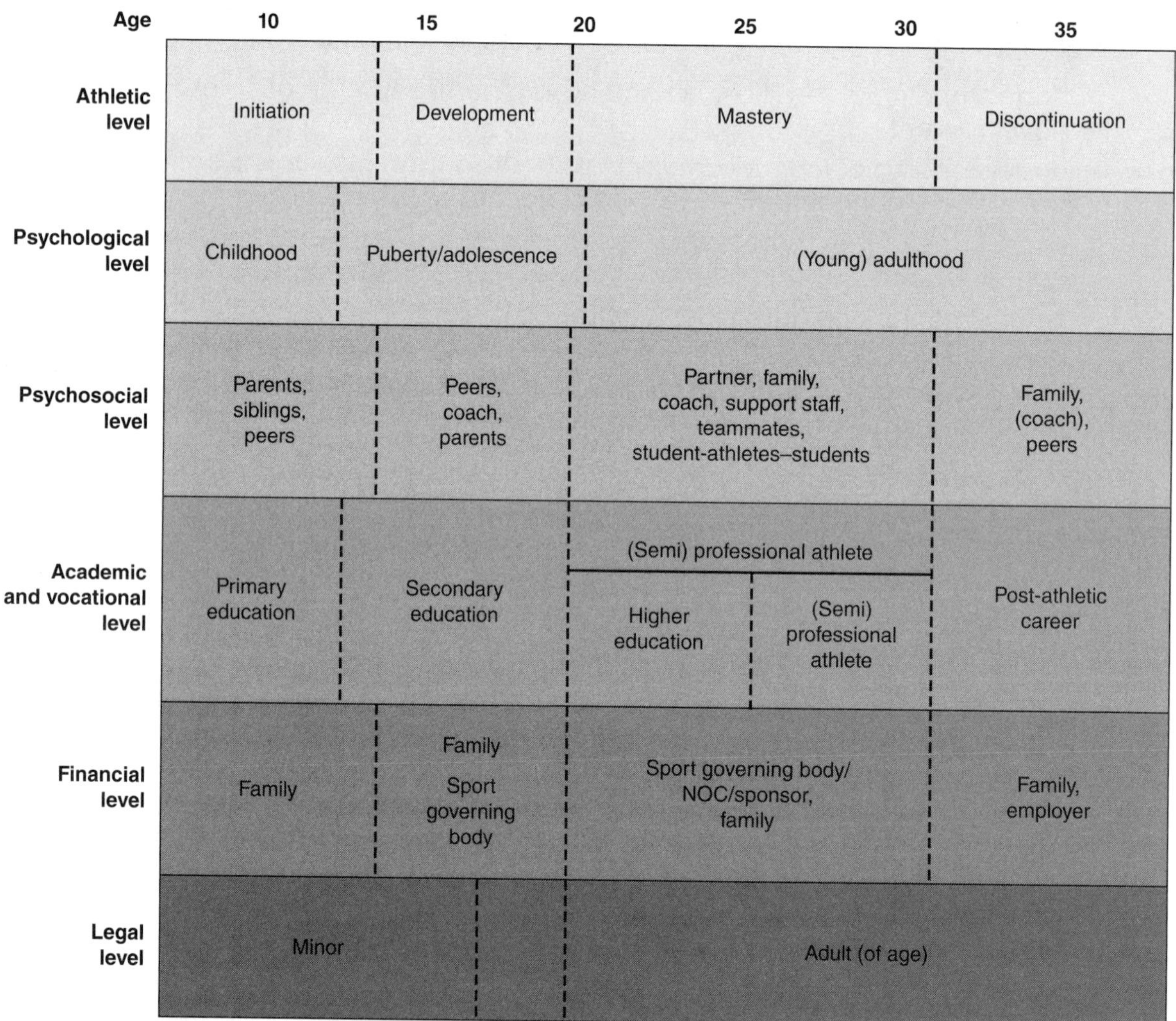

FIGURE 20.1 Holistic Athletic Career model.

The top layer represents the stages and transitions athletes face in their athletic development and includes four stages that are tentatively linked to approximated ages:

- Initiation stage, during which the young athlete is introduced to organized competitive sport (6-7 years of age)
- Development stage, during which the athlete is recognized as talented; entails an intensification of training and participation in competitions (12-13 years of age)
- Mastery stage, which reflects the athlete's participation at the highest competitive level (18-19 years of age)
- Discontinuation stage, which describes the elite athlete's transition out of competitive sport (28-30 years of age)

Although these stages are normative in nature, major differences may occur between sports; for example, from age 18 to 19, the mastery stage among female gymnasts may be coming to an end (Kerr & Dacyshyn, 2000), while for male rowers the mastery stage may just be starting (Wylleman et al., 1993).

The second layer represents the developmental stages and transitions occurring at the psychological level and is based on conceptual frameworks for psychological development, such as Erikson's (1963) developmental stages, Piaget's (1971) stages of cognitive development, and Havighurst's (1973) developmental tasks over the life span. The stages of psychological development include childhood, adolescence, and adulthood.

The third layer represents the stages and changes identified in earlier research (e.g., Rees & Hardy, 2000; Rice, 1998) that can occur in athletes' psychosocial context relative to their athletic involvement. It situates those people whom athletes perceive as being the most significant during the particular stages. These changing contexts include the athletic triangle (athlete–parents, athlete–coach, and coach–parents relationships) (e.g., Wylleman, 2000; Wylleman et al., 2003), the athlete's relationships within the athletic family (e.g., Hellstedt, 1995), peer relationships (e.g., Smith, 2003; Weiss & Stuntz, 2004), marital or lifetime partner relationships (e.g., Jowett & Meek, 2000), and other interpersonal relationships significant to athletes.

Transitions and associated challenges in one domain can have a concurrent, interactive, and reciprocal effect on other levels of development.

The fourth layer reflects academic and vocational stages and transitions, including the transitions into primary education, secondary education, higher education, vocational training, and a post-athletic career (Bussmann & Alfermann, 1994; Petitpas et al., 1996; Wylleman et al., 1993). Especially in the past decade, the importance of educational and vocational development of athletes has gained attention, because many athletes are combining elite sport with higher education or other employment (e.g., Wylleman & Rosier, 2016; Smismans et al., 2020).

The fifth layer reflects the financial development of athletes. Athletes (like all humans) start with a financial dependence on their parents, (often) move to a paid income through their sport once they move to senior level, and then at the end of their careers, find themselves in need of earning a (new) income source. While this layer is more practical in nature, it is important to take into account, because it can have an impact on athletes' career decisions (Tekavc et al., 2015; Wylleman, 2019).

Finally, the sixth layer, which was added to the model recently, describes athletes' legal development. Especially when athletes move into adulthood, legislation has an impact on their development and responsibilities (Wylleman, 2019).

The model underscores that transitions and associated challenges in one domain can have a concurrent, interactive, and reciprocal effect on other levels of development (Wylleman & Rosier, 2016). A transition is hereby defined as "an event or a non-event which results in a change in assumptions about oneself and the world and, thus, requires a corresponding change in one's behaviour and relationships" (Schlossberg, 1981, p. 5). The transitions depicted in the model are normative in nature (i.e., expected and predictable). Examples of such normative transitions include the junior–senior transition at the athletic level, the transition into adolescence at the psychological level, and the transition from secondary to higher education at the academic level. However, the HAC model equally acknowledges that nonnormative transitions (i.e., unexpected or unpredictable) can occur at the levels of development as well (e.g., injury at athletic level, death of a family member at psychosocial level) (Wylleman, 2019).

In order to maintain a healthy, balanced, and successful development, athletes need to cope with multilevel transitions. The effectiveness with which athletes are able to cope with these normative and nonnormative transitions depends on how internal resources (e.g., motivation or competencies) and external resources (e.g., social support) are available and used in relation to these transitional demands (Stambulova, 2003). A lack of resources or failure to cope with one or more transitions may in fact lead to crises and long-term negative consequences, such as dropout from elite sport, depression, or substance abuse (Stambulova et al., 2009).

Major Challenging Transition Periods and Associated Barriers

As reflected in the HAC model, two major transition periods can be expected to be strongly challenging, because normative transitions occur concurrently at different levels of development. The main demands and barriers associated with these transition periods are discussed in this section, further illustrating the importance of a holistic life-span perspective.

Transition Period One (TP1): Stepping Up to the Next Level

Often within a narrow time frame, athletes move from developmental to master athletic level, move from adolescence to adulthood, move from secondary to higher education, and move into the adult legal level. These developments, in turn, cause the psychosocial environment to change drastically (e.g., new friends in university, new teammates at senior level) and can involve associated financial challenges as well. Not only the sum of the previously mentioned transitions but especially the interaction of the demands and barriers on the developmental levels can make transition periods extremely challenging (e.g., Gledhill & Harwood, 2015; Pummell et al., 2008; Ryba et al., 2016). The demands and barriers of these transition periods are discussed next per level of development, bearing in mind that these level-specific demands and barriers have a concurrent and reciprocal impact on each other as well (Wylleman & Rosier, 2016).

Athletic Moving to the mastery level, often referred to as the junior-to-senior transition (Wylleman et al., 2016), brings forth a significant increase in training load and additional competitive standards and expectations (MacNamara & Collins, 2010; Pummell et al., 2008; Ryba et al., 2015; Stambulova et al., 2009, 2012). Associated with the additional pressure, overtraining (Gomez et al., 2018) and injuries are increasingly prevalent within this phase (Brown et al., 2015; MacNamara & Collins, 2010; Tekavc et al., 2015). Only one out of three elite athletes makes a successful transition to the senior level, making it a crucial transition in the athletic life span (Gulbin et al., 2010; Wylleman & Rosier, 2016).

Psychological In this transition period, athletes move from adolescence to early adulthood, a period in which their identity further develops and many common mental disorders (e.g., anxiety, depression) can arise (De Girolamo et al., 2012; Kessler et al., 2007). Research in the sport domain has shown that the highest onset of mental health disorders in elite athletes typically occurs during this specific transition period, more specifically between the ages of 17 and 21 years (Åkesdotter et al., 2020). During this phase, athletes' identity development can be strongly influenced by the developments in their athletic pathway. Athletes who tend to put everything into their sports, without any other distractions (e.g., hobbies, social contact, education), might be at higher risk of identity foreclosure. Because of this lack of exploring other interests or life domains, those athletes might have more difficulties coping with stress during (e.g., putting things in perspective when they fail at an important tournament) or at the end of their careers (e.g., coping with a career-ending injury) (Cartigny et al., 2021; Van Rens et al., 2019).

Psychosocial Elite athletes move into completely new social contexts (both in the athletic field and academic domain) and thus have to get acquainted with many people at once (e.g., Brown et al., 2015; Wylleman & Rosier, 2016). Furthermore, the additional time required to maintain social connections with friends and family in a qualitative way may become stressful because of the increased time pressure in their dual careers (Debois et al., 2015; MacNamara & Collins, 2010), potentially causing conflict situations or feelings of severe loneliness when relationship issues are avoided (Geraniosova & Ronkainen, 2015; Miller & Kerr, 2002). Finally, in this phase, athletes often experience difficulties due to their social comparisons with peers who are not involved in sports. For example, as they see how many of these peers engage in more outgoing activities (e.g., music festivals, parties), they might feel they are missing out on regular life activities (Defruyt et al., 2020).

Academic and Vocational The transition from secondary to higher education is challenging because student-athletes are confronted with a less structured environment that requires them to be more self-regulatory than in secondary education. The volume of the educational material grows substantially, while the structure provided by the system is less strict, especially in comparison with the well-structured systems of elite sport schools in secondary education (MacNamara & Collins, 2010; Tekavc et al., 2015). Because of the additional athletic and academic requirements, time pressure is extremely relevant for many dual career (DC) athletes going into higher education (Cosh & Tully, 2014, 2015). This time pressure is visible not only in the daily training load, making it difficult to attend all courses, but also in games and tournaments, which can interfere with exam periods or internships (Brown et al., 2015; Kıvanç, 2018).

Although the reasons to engage in higher education can be diverse for elite athletes (Defruyt et al., 2020), research shows that in many cases, elite athletes start the combination with controlled motives (e.g., pressured by parents, feelings of guilt). Many athletes perceive the educational pathway as externally regulated (e.g., pushed by the environment) or as an introjected engagement (e.g., would feel guilty not to pursue a diploma) rather than being intrinsically motivated to pursue education or seeing the potential added value of it (e.g., competency development or the value of a diploma) (Christensen & Sørensen, 2009; Defruyt et al., 2020; McGillivray & McIntosh, 2006). Not only the decision to study but often also the specific study domain chosen can be based on extrinsic reasons. For example, athletes often choose a study subject for practical reasons (e.g., travel time to training field) and the feasibility of the study program (e.g., a subject of study with many obligatory courses are often impossible for them to follow) (Debois et al., 2015; Tekavc et al., 2015). As such, many athletes fully prioritize the more intrinsically valued athletic pathway (Cosh & Tully, 2014; Romar, 2012; Tekavc et al., 2015), potentially leading to bad results and academic dropout from the athletes' perspectives, or even prejudice toward elite athletes in general from higher education stakeholders' perspectives (Christensen & Sørensen, 2009; Geraniosova & Ronkainen, 2015; Oros & Hanţiu, 2016).

The lack of support from the coach can lead athletes to not begin or even drop out of higher education.

Financial In this period, athletes move to adulthood and thus often to financial independence, requiring a stable income. Although some athletes make enough money through their sport, many elite athletes remain partly financially dependent on their parents (Geraniosova & Ronkainen, 2015). However, for those who do not earn enough through their sport and cannot rely on their parents, it can become extremely challenging because they must engage in additional employment, sometimes even in combination with an academic career in higher education (i.e., the triple sport–education–vocation career) (Ryba et al., 2015; Tekavc et al., 2015).

Legal Athletes' legal rights and duties change slightly as they reach the age of 16, and again and more fundamentally on their 18th birthday. These legal changes can be related to national legislation (e.g., legal age for drinking alcohol in Europe vs. the United States) and may have an impact on athletes' lives (e.g., financial independence), on their sporting lives (e.g., impact of financial independence on their sport contracts), or on their sport involvement (e.g., legislation around doping). While legal changes can provide additional autonomy (e.g., possibility of attaining driver's license, gaining autonomous decision making, having a vote in elections), it also involves additional accountability (in cases of crime, doping whereabouts, additional doping controls) and administrative changes (social security, tax requirements, insurances) (Wylleman, 2019).

Interaction of the Domains To illustrate the interactive and reciprocal nature of all the challenges and potential barriers, a typical example is discussed here. In many contexts, some coaches may have an unsupportive attitude toward athletes' dual careers combining elite sport and higher education (Cosh & Tully, 2015; Ryan, 2015). Such unsupportive attitudes occurring in the athletic context can lead to tensions at the psychosocial level (i.e., conflict with the coach or with parents, who often defend the more long-term value of education) (Debois et al., 2015) as well as feelings of role strain and associated stress at the psychological level related to their roles in sport and higher education (Gledhill & Harwood, 2015; Skrubbeltrang et al., 2016). In turn, the lack of support from the coach can lead athletes to not begin or even drop out of higher education (Defruyt et al., 2020), compromising vocational opportunities in the long term as well (Torregrossa et al., 2015).

Transition Period Two (TP2): Heading Toward the New Career

Eventually, elite athletes come to a point where they leave competitive sport (i.e., athletic retirement) and make their transition to a new postathletic career. In this phase, again, transitions and related potential barriers co-occur and interact at the levels of development.

Athletic At the athletic level, athletes retire from elite sport, leading to a strongly reduced training load and the absence of competition schedules (Wylleman, 2019). This not only drastically changes their daily routines but can also influence their physical condition if they do not detrain properly, potentially leading to health issues (e.g., injuries, weight gain) and difficulties with changing body images (Kuettel et al., 2017; Stambulova et al., 2009).

Psychological At the psychological level, elite athletes are confronted with a changing identity and self-image (e.g., from describing oneself as an athlete to describing oneself as a former athlete and in search of a job). Those athletes who, while being active, focused purely on their athletic careers (i.e., identity foreclosure) might be more likely to experience difficulties adapting to a "new life" and "new identity" (Park et al., 2013). Furthermore, if athletes start a job that is completely unrelated to the sport domain (e.g., in retail, science, engineering), athletes can think they need to start from scratch (e.g., having never experienced a specific organizational culture) and thus possibly experience feelings of uselessness or incompetence, in some instances even leading to a fundamental identity crisis (Reints, 2011; Wylleman et al., 2020). Unfortunately, in line with these multilevel difficulties and associated psychological stress and identity issues, a high number of retired elite athletes report mental health disorders (e.g., depression, anxiety, sleeping disturbance, adverse alcohol use) (Gouttebarge et al., 2016, 2017; Van Ramele et al., 2017).

Psychosocial At the psychosocial level, elite athletes might experience a drastic change in their social environment as they move away from their sport-related environment. Especially if athletes relied solely on their sport-related support network during the athletic career while neglecting their psychosocial environment in other domains (e.g., lifetime partner, friends outside of sport), they might experience difficulties coping with this change (Demulier et al., 2013; Kuettel et al., 2017). On the other hand, after retirement athletes might have more time to spend with their closest family. At the same time, the lifetime partner or the family members themselves may find it difficult to adapt to having the athlete back in their lives on a full-time basis, requiring them to change their daily routines (Wylleman, 2019).

Vocational Transitioning to the postathletic career at the vocational level may be quite challenging. In looking for a new job, athletes often hold unrealistic expectations of job opportunities, expecting that employers are keen on hiring them despite their lack of specific job experience (B-WISER, 2018). Furthermore, at the age of athletic retirement, while most of their contemporaries have gone through a job search several times before, many elite athletes have no experience at all in developing a CV, cover letter, and so on (Wylleman et al., 2020). Moving into a new job and its requirements also pushes athletes into increased responsibilities, changing wage conditions, and changing daily work–life rhythm (e.g., fixed hours). Moreover, former athletes might perceive the lack of specific and challenging goals within a new job troubling (e.g., Wylleman et al., 2020). For most athletes with a higher-education diploma, a significant time gap may exist between finalizing their academic study and actually choosing to engage in their first employment after retirement. Considering this occupational delay, these athletes can have difficulties catching up with the most recent developments in the field (Wylleman & Rosier, 2016).

Financial After a long period of gaining income directly or indirectly related to their athletic pathway, most athletes move to a different income structure, possibly falling back on their savings or family first, then moving to a new employer in a later phase (Wylleman, 2019). The often well-established financial support in elite sport presents itself as a double-edged sword in this transition, because many elite athletes may have developed a supported lifestyle, which might come under pressure once the professional contract and associated sponsorship deals disappear (Kuettel et al., 2017). The potential financial problems put additional pressure on the search for a new job and can additionally complicate the transition to a new career (Reints, 2011; Wylleman, 2019).

Interaction of the Domains As stated earlier, it is important to consider the interaction of challenges and barriers at the different levels of development. For example, an athlete who failed to prepare for the end-of-career transition and who did not engage in education might take longer to find a new job, be faced with financial setbacks, and experience increased levels of stress and other psychosocial difficulties (B-WISER, 2018; Torregrossa et al., 2015).

Helping Athletes Cope With Major Transitions and Associated Barriers

Notwithstanding the many interacting challenges and potential barriers co-occurring at the levels of development in these transition periods, applying an integrative approach (e.g., developing a broader identity, using proactive career planning, providing quality dual career support) to these challenges in the different life domains will be beneficial to athletes' holistic development, before as well as after retirement. Among other things, it can lead to healthy psychosocial development, qualitative career planning trajectories, enhanced employability, the development of multiple valuable identities, healthy athletic careers, and financial security (e.g., Aquilina, 2013; Price et al., 2010; Torregrossa et al., 2015). Consequently, the objective is not to avoid or take away all challenges and barriers, but rather to (1) facilitate an autonomy-supportive, empowering approach to supporting athletes, enabling them to develop the competencies necessary to prepare for and cope with these transitional challenges, and to (2) optimize the structure of the context and the resources available to elite athletes with regard to these challenges (De Brandt, 2017; Defruyt, 2019).

Preparing Athletes Through Empowerment and Competency Development

The discourse on how to support athletes coping with transitions has shifted during the past years from a focus on ad hoc support (e.g., providing academic flexibilities, reducing training load) to a more proactive approach focusing on preparation and competency enhancement (e.g., Stambulova et al., 2015; Wylleman et al., 2017). This more elaborate, proactive approach in supporting athletes throughout their careers is illustrated by zooming in on the evolutions in dual career support approaches and on support approaches with regard to the postathletic career.

Empowerment in Dual Career Support Initial research on DCs focused on the requirements and structures enabling elite athletes to combine elite sport with education. While crossnational cooperation in establishing such quality support structures for DC athletes is key, research has shown that the contexts can vary heavily between countries, making it necessary to gain insight into nation-specific support structures as well (De Knop et al., 1999). For example, Henry (2013) described the national differences with regard to the role of the government in creating the required support structures for elite athletes to engage in a DC in higher education:

- A state-central system with defined legal obligations for the DC stakeholders, meaning DC arrangements for sport clubs, educational institutions, and governing bodies are formulated within prescriptive legislation (e.g., Spain)
- State-sponsored formal systems established on permissive legislation, meaning there is financial support from the state to facilitate DC support structures, without formal legal obligations for the stakeholders (e.g., Belgium)
- A representation of athletes' educational interests by sporting bodies, meaning athletes depend on the sport clubs to negotiate facilitative measures from schools and universities (e.g., Greece)
- No formal structures, meaning athletes need to negotiate themselves with their sport organizations and educational institutions to acquire facilitative measures to combine education with elite sport (e.g., Italy)

Although research on crossnational (e.g., De Knop et al., 1999) and national (e.g., Aquilina & Henry, 2010; Henry, 2013) structural support and facilitation of dual career possibilities is important, it is not sufficient, because it does not focus on describing the processes and resources necessary to develop DC supportive environments. As such, with the publication of the EU guidelines on the dual careers of athletes (European Commission, 2012), a more elaborate and proactive approach, focusing on high-quality, competency-enhancing dual career support, was further advised. In line with these guidelines, DC research projects (e.g., funded by the Erasmus+ Sport program of the European Union) and the implementation of additional guidelines (European Commission, 2015; Kornbeck, 2017) enhanced the resources and interest in proactive DC research and practices.

The generally accepted philosophy is based on putting athletes at the steering wheel of their own DC pathway (Samuel & Tenenbaum, 2013). Within the established structural support systems, athletes should thus be allowed to learn from experiences (positive and negative) in order to develop crucial dual career competencies (Brown et al., 2015; Stambulova et al., 2015). The removal of all potential barriers to support athletes in their DCs might impede the development of these competencies (e.g., due to lack of challenges, becoming used to being served), whereas coping with multilevel challenges and getting out of the comfort zone (e.g., making an integrated plan, doing their own cooking) helps athletes become more proactive and develop a wide range of competencies (De Brandt et al., 2018; MacNamara & Collins, 2010). Consequently, DC support shifts its focus to enhancing athletes' competencies, while at the same time providing experiential learning in coping with the multilevel transitions (De Brandt, 2017; De Brandt et al., 2018; Defruyt, 2019). Competency-enhancing interventions range from optimizing attributional styles (Parker et al., 2016), planning, time management, and goal-setting attitudes (Hardcastle et al., 2015) to cooking skills (Ellis et al., 2017).

Other interventions focused on preparing athletes for stressful life events by implementing stress-management interventions (Harris et al., 2003; Sallen et al., 2018) or by providing psychological skills training programs focused on growth mindset principles (Golby & Wood, 2009). For example, in this last study, 16 DC rowers received three interactive sessions to develop mental skills and mental techniques (e.g., self-talk, thought control, concentration). Over the course of these interventions, mental toughness, perceived self-efficacy, self-esteem, and positive affect were positively influenced. Although all these interventions showed some degree of effectivity, none of the studies measured the impact on the longer term. Future researchers are encouraged to take into account more encompassing competency-enhancement programs (e.g., evaluating a structural support program with multiple interventions instead of just a specific intervention), using more elaborate designs (e.g., prospective longitudinal design), and assessing long-term outcomes as well (e.g., performance in sport and studies).

Furthermore, none of the previously mentioned studies built their interventions around DC-specific competencies or used DC-specific instruments to measure the impact of the intervention. The development of the Dual Career Competency Questionnaire for Athletes could be very useful in this regard (DCCQ-A) (De Brandt et al., 2018). Based on research with more than 3,350 European student-athletes and 45 DC experts, the DCCQ-A identifies student-athletes' perceived importance and possession of four DC competencies: DC management (e.g., planning and time management), career planning (e.g., long-term vision), emotional awareness (e.g., stress management), and social intelligence and adaptability (e.g., social skills and networking). The four competencies of the DCCQ-A were identified using ESEM (De Brandt et al., 2018) and were validated in relation to challenging DC situations (e.g., De Brandt, 2017; Linnér et al., 2019; Perez-Rivases et al., 2020). Furthermore, the DCCQ-A holds considerable promise as a monitoring tool to measure and discuss athletes' DC competencies (e.g., Alcaraz et al., 2020). The theoretical underpinnings and practical value of the DCCQ-A are being further tested in other countries (e.g., Brazil, Turkey) and within the online application DualCareerTools.

Preparation for the Next Career Empowering athletes is key, not only in a DC but also in preparation for and during the transition to the next career (Reints, 2011; Wylleman, 2019). There is need for a nuanced perspective, with a view on the next career as a process requiring planning and empowerment in preparation for, during, and in follow-up to the transition (Wylleman et al., 2020). More specifically, in this process approach, there is a differentiation between three consecutive end-of-career phases (B-WISER, 2018; Smismans et al., 2020; Wylleman et al., 2020):

- *Still active in elite sport (i.e., active phase).* Research has shown that the quality of the transition to the postathletic career depends heavily on how well athletes are already prepared. Among others, career planning, engaging in a dual career, developing multiple interests, taking into account a sound focus on other aspects of life while competing, and enjoying a good professional relationship with the coach have all shown a positive impact on the adaptation to retirement from elite sport (B-WISER, 2018; Park et al., 2013; Torregrossa et al., 2015).

- *Retired from sport and not yet in a new postathletic career (i.e., retirement phase).* Athletes face many challenges at different levels of development in this phase. Among others, psychosocial support, professional support programs, and financial stability are key in this phase (B-WISER, 2018; Park et al., 2013).
- *In a new postathletic career (i.e., new career phase).* Engaging in a new profession after the athletic career is seen as a separate phase because it is a fundamental transition that often requires a set of completely new insights and routines. Among others, the support of the new employer and role models can help former athletes with this transition (B-WISER, 2018; Wylleman et al., 2020).

Those three consecutive phases are approached as positive phases with specific challenges that can help the athlete's broader development, rather than viewing the transition as a single negative life event (Wylleman et al., 2020). Without ignoring that athletes face demands at different levels of development in these career phases (e.g., Wylleman, 2019), this approach focuses on the necessary competencies and the social and structural support needed to overcome those multilevel demands from a proactive perspective (Stambulova, Ryba, & Henriksen, 2020).

In line with this, action research approaches have led to guidelines to proactively support elite athletes in those consecutive phases of the transition to a next career (Wylleman et al., 2020). For example, the Athlete Competency Questionnaire for Employability (ACQE; Smismans et al., 2020) was developed to measure athletes' competencies required to optimize their employability across the three phases. This instrument consists of 28 items that measure four competencies: career and lifestyle management, career communication, career resilience, and career engagement and flexibility (Smismans et al., 2020). The instrument can help athletes and their support providers evaluate, monitor, and optimize the competencies of importance in the general labor market. Initial statistical validation of this instrument has proven to be satisfactory, and the application of the instrument (in different countries and contexts) in both workshops and individual counseling has been of assistance to athletes preparing for or coping with the transition to a new career. The ACQE can help athletes think about what competencies they have developed during their athletic careers and how they can transfer these to the labor market (B-WISER, 2018; Smismans et al., 2020).

Empowering athletes is key, not only in a DC but also in preparation for and during the transition to the next career.

Ecological Approach to Career Support

Notwithstanding that a competency-enhancing approach is key in supporting athletes throughout their career, a broader perspective is necessary to capture environmental and societal factors as well. The holistic ecological perspective captures a broader view on athletes' development by bringing together micro (e.g., athletes' choices, competencies, motivations), meso (e.g., interpersonal relationships, interactions with support staff), and macro (e.g., the culture of a country, policy factors) levels of athletes' lives (Henriksen & Stambulova, 2017). This environmental approach has recently gained considerable attention in the context of dual career research and practice. During the Erasmus+ Sport project Ecology of Dual Careers (ECO-DC, 2020), two empirical models (i.e., the dual career development environment model [DCDE] and the dual career environment success factors model [DC-ESF]) were developed and applied to better understand dual career environments in six European countries (ECO-DC, 2020; Henriksen et al., 2020). In addition, the ECO-DC project identified two other research-based outcomes that can aid practitioners in understanding and optimizing their environments: (1) a taxonomy of dual career environments and (2) a tool to assess 10 essential features of successful dual career environments.

Taxonomy of Dual Career Environments Dual career environments can be very different, especially within the complex context of Europe. While the typology described by Henry (2013) provides a first insight into how DC policies can vary among countries, it does not consider the more specific differences between dual career contexts. The need for more information on the specificities of these DC environments urged researchers to develop a taxonomy of dual career development environments (Morris et al., 2020). The taxonomy takes into account features of and questions related to the environment:

- The career stage or transition supported (e.g., development or mastery phase): What phase or age does the context provide support for?
- The nature and scope of the environment (e.g., sport-led, education- or vocation-led, or combined dual career system): What is the main scope of the environment, and does it focus mainly on sport, mainly on education, or on both?
- The type of support provided (e.g., fixed or flexible): Is the DC support integrated within the environment, or is it provided ad hoc?
- A centralized or decentralized DC system: Are education and elite sport provided within one context (centralized) or provided in different contexts and facilitated by different stakeholders (decentralized)?
- The type of state involvement (see Aquilina & Henry, 2010): What role does the state play in facilitating dual careers?

Based on a study of 57 environments from seven European countries and using a procedure with documentary analysis, interviews with experts in the DC field, cross-case analysis, and research discussions, eight types of European dual career development environments were identified:

- In combined dual career support systems, both sport and education are fully integrated. In these contexts, organizations are purposefully established to provide integrated support for sport and education. Examples include the Talented Athlete Scholarship Scheme (TASS) in the United Kingdom and Team Denmark Universities.
- Three types of dual career systems are mainly led by sport:
    - *Professional and private club programs.* The clubs provide support and flexibilities for educational purposes. Examples include the educational support programs provided by FC Barcelona and Everton (football).
    - *Player union programs.* Player unions defend athletes' rights within the sport environment, and some of these unions have integrated educational and vocational support or even vocational courses for athletes in their support practices. Examples of player unions with well-established dual career support programs are Rugby Players Ireland, 4player (Denmark), and Study4Player (Finland).
    - *National sport programs.* In this federation-based support system, educational and vocational support is provided on a national level within a specific sport environment. A good example is the Sport Scotland Institute of Sport.
- Finally, in four specific systems, the main support system is built around education:
    - *Sport-friendly schools.* Some regional educational institutions allow athletes to engage in elite sport in their own clubs by providing flexibilities and ad hoc support. Examples include Sandagymnasiet in Sweden and TASS-accredited schools and colleges in the United Kingdom.
    - *Elite sport schools and colleges.* These schools are developed specifically for elite athletes and provide elite sport coaching and education (with adapted schedules) within one context. Examples include the elite sport schools in Belgium (e.g., Stedelijk Lyceum Topsport, Koninklijk Atheneum Voskenslaan) and Marselisborg Gymnasium in Denmark.
    - *Sport-friendly universities.* Sport-friendly higher-education institutions provide flexibilities and ad hoc support to let athletes engage in elite sport (in their own club or federation). Examples include Vrije Universiteit Brussel and Autonomous University of Barcelona (UAB).
    - *Defense force programs.* In these work-based programs established by the defense forces, athletes are granted vocational flexibilities to be able to engage in elite sport activities. Such support programs are available in the military of, among others, Belgium, the United Kingdom, Finland, and the Netherlands.

The taxonomy in figure 20.2 is a helpful resource for researchers and practitioners to get a better view of the European dual career landscape and to position and compare environments (ECO-DC, n.d.).

Essential Features of Successful Dual Career Environments Based on a cross-case analysis of European DC development environments, involving a series of focus groups discussing the similarities between a range of cases on DC environments from seven different countries, the ECO-DC consortium identified 10 essential features of successful DC development environments (Storm et al., 2021): dedicated DC support team, integration of effort across the whole environment, clear understanding of DC issues and support from across the environment, role models and mentorship, access to expert support, a whole person approach, an empowerment approach, flexible DC solutions, care of DC athletes' mental health and well-being, and an open and proactive approach to the development of the environment. As a follow-up, a monitoring tool was developed for stakeholders within DC environments to assess these 10 essential features and identify areas for improvement (ECO-DC, 2020). The initial validation of the Dual Career Development Environment Monitoring Tool (DCDEM) shows satisfactory psychometric properties and highlights the potential value of the instrument to evaluate, monitor, and optimize DC environments (De Brandt et al., in preparation). Ideally, the DCDEM will allow different stakeholders (e.g., athletes, support staff, parents) to provide and compare their perspectives about their DC environments.

Future Research Directions

Summarizing the previous sections, research and practices on career transitions and athletes' development reached a mature level with regard to the following:

- The life-span and holistic perspective on athletes' development
- Knowledge of the main multilevel transitions and associated barriers athletes are confronted with during and beyond their athletic careers
- The development and application of the competency-enhancing empowerment approaches in career support (micro level)
- Working models, taxonomies, and instruments that can be used on an environmental level in career support services (meso and macro levels)

Nevertheless, several topics require additional research attention to further advance the field of career research (Stambulova & Wylleman, 2019).

While the EU guidelines on dual careers of elite athletes have emphasized that researchers and practitioners should focus on the mental health of dual career athletes (European Commission, 2012), research on the bidirectional relationship between

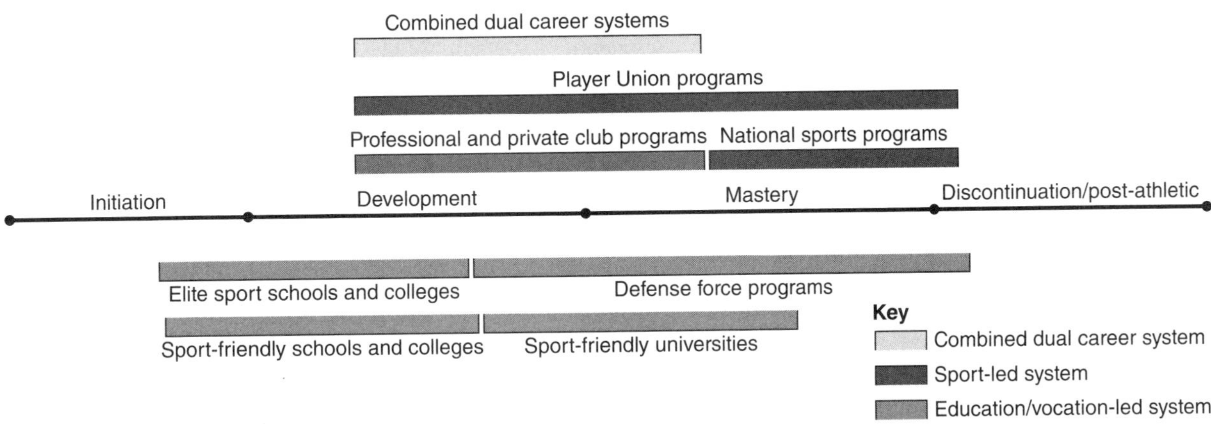

FIGURE 20.2 Dual career development environments across Europe, primarily targeting the athletic stage of Wylleman and colleagues' (2004) model of career development.

Reprinted by permission from Ecology of Dual Careers, "Ecology of Dual Careers Work Package 1 Report, 20," Liverpool John Moores University, March 2023, accessed April 3, 2023, https://www.ljmu.ac.uk/-/media/ljmu/projects/dualcareers/files/wp1-report.pdf.

dual careers and mental health has remained sparse (Kuettel & Larsen, 2019; Stambulova & Wylleman, 2019). In fact, both DC athletes and support providers have expressed the need for more knowledge on and evidence-based support practices regarding mental health (ECO-DC, 2020; Wylleman et al., 2017, 2018). Moreover, attention for DC athletes' mental health might be as relevant as ever given the recent COVID-19 pandemic. Scholars have highlighted that the pandemic could form a crisis transition for many athletes, including increased stress and anxiety, social isolation, loneliness, loss of goals, and even forced retirement out of sport (Gorczynski & Aron, 2020; Schinke et al., 2020; Stambulova, Schinke, et al., 2020). In line with this urge for more research on mental health within DC contexts, the project Dual Careers for Mental Health (DC4MH) has recently been launched. DC4MH aims to optimize mental health within European dual careers by developing, implementing, and evaluating evidence-based mental health promotion recommendations and tools. The project will focus on the following:

- Mental health structures: How can organizations integrate mental health support within their structure?
- Mental health monitoring: How can mental health be monitored in an evidence-based manner?
- Mental health literacy: How can athletes and stakeholders be better educated around the topic of mental health?
- Resilience building: How can athletes be proactively trained to foster resilience?

Several studies have already focused on athletes' mental health during the transition out of sport (e.g., Reints, 2011; Gouttebarge et al., 2017; Van Ramele et al., 2017). However, these studies have predominantly adopted a deficit perspective (i.e., measuring common mental disorders and associated risk factors). In line with suggestions of Wylleman and colleagues (2020), future research should focus on the facilitators in this process (e.g., the role of physical exercise, positive psychology interventions) and on the positive mental health outcomes (e.g., emotional and psychosocial well-being) of the transition process. Especially more prospective longitudinal research might provide more insights into the processes and resources that can help athletes positively adapt to the postathletic career. Such an approach might not only pave the way for a more positive approach to the transition out of sport (Wylleman et al., 2020) but also assist practitioners in helping athletes achieve and sustain a successful postathletic life and career (Knights et al., 2016).

Future studies should also focus on gaining more insight into the DC elite sport and employment pathway (Stambulova & Wylleman, 2019). Practitioners, such as career support providers and employers, play a central role in making such combinations possible (B-WISER, 2018). While B-WISER (2018) results indicated the existence of a number of good practices (e.g., cooperation networks, quality coaching, development services, employment flexibilities), research on athletes engaging in a DC of elite sport and employment remains scarce. Specific future research avenues could include the following:

- The specific challenges and barriers athletes in a dual career of sport and work encounter and the resources needed to cope with those challenges
- Athletes' motives to pursue a DC of sport and work
- Employers' perspectives on employing athletes who are still active in their elite sporting careers
- Sustainable support initiatives to provide athletes the necessary facilities needed to combine the demands of an elite sporting career with those of another professional career
- Case studies targeting athletes in a dual career of sport and work to provide an in-depth exploration of the complexity and uniqueness of such a DC in its real-life context

Finally, at an environmental level, researchers are encouraged to link the DC models (DC-ESF, taxonomy of DC environments, essential features of DC environments) to other approaches that are not necessarily linked to the DC context. For example, it might be interesting to look at the influence of type of sport (early specialization vs. late specialization) on how DC environments should optimally be organized (Morris et al., 2020). It seems reasonable to expect that DC support in gymnastics (early specialization) requires a more centralized approach (cf. taxonomy of DC environments) and more explicit attention on mental health (cf. essential features of DC environments) from secondary or even primary education onward. Whereas in rowing, for example, it might be more crucial to have support structures in place at higher education levels (e.g., sport-friendly universities), with additional attention on role models showing it is possible to combine rowing with higher education (cf. essential features of DC environments).

Linking or integrating these environment models to the broader context of elite sport policy might also be worth considering. For example, the Sport Policy factors Leading to International Sport Success (SPLISS) clusters elite sport national policies into nine areas, with postathletic career support being one of the pillars (De Bosscher et al., 2006). By integrating the instrument on essential features of DC environments in the pillar of career support, future studies could evaluate the link of these features with the other pillars (e.g., with financial resources, general elite sport structures, talent identification and development) and investigate the impact of these DC features on broader policy outcomes (e.g., sport performances, educational outcomes).

Practical Implications

For practitioners, it is crucial to look at athletes from a holistic and developmental perspective (Wylleman, 2019). Additional attention might be required in preparation of and during periods where athletes' transitions occur concurrently at different levels of development. For most athletes, the junior to senior transition and the transition to the next career can be seen as such challenging transition periods (e.g., Rosier, 2020; Torregrossa et al., 2015; Wylleman & Rosier, 2016).

While the multilevel transitions and associated barriers are challenging, this does not imply that career support stakeholders should try to take away all of these potential barriers (e.g., advise athletes not to engage in a dual career). A proactive empowerment approach, taking into account the specific context or environment, means athletes are supported (e.g., through individual counseling or workshops integrating the holistic perspective on athletes) to develop the competencies necessary to cope with their multilevel transitions themselves, while respecting their own autonomous choices (Defruyt, 2019; Wylleman et al., 2017). Encouraging athletes to explore and get involved in different domains (e.g., other hobbies, education, internships, work) and preparing them to cope with the multilevel transitions (e.g., by providing workshops on resilience) will help athletes grow as athletes and as whole persons. On the other hand, forcing them to focus only on sport, and taking away all other barriers, might put them at risk of identity foreclosure, narrow worldviews, trouble putting things in perspective, or trouble adapting to athletic retirement (Aquilina, 2013; Lavallee, 2019; McQuown Linnemeyer & Brown, 2010).

As illustrated throughout this chapter, research on DC support has brought forward many crucial findings with regard to required competencies, good practices, and broader perspectives on support environments (e.g., Defruyt et al., 2019; Stambulova & Wylleman, 2019). This has led to working models, taxonomies, and assessment instruments for environments (ECO-DC, 2020); development of handbooks and toolboxes (B-WISER, 2018; Wylleman et al., 2017), and development of educational curricula (Defruyt, 2019; Hong & Coffee, 2018). At this moment, however, much of the evidence-based information remains underused, lacking a structural and high-quality implementation within an applied context (Wylleman et al., 2020). A crucial step is the development and institutionalization of evidence-based educational programs, as well as the certification of the DC support profession (Defruyt, 2019).

This development can be supported using the increasing number of online tools related to career transition support. In light of the flexibility required to reach athletes with their busy schedules, and in light of the recent coronavirus developments, these approaches will only grow in importance in the coming years (Wylleman et al., 2020). Interesting examples of evidence-based online tools that support athletes' careers include online educational video games (e.g., play2PREVENT developed a doping prevention video game); European career toolkits to help DC organizations manage, train, and counsel DC stakeholders (e.g., Starting 11 and B-WISER are two projects that provide many interesting tools and reports); and online instruments with direct visual feedback (e.g., DualCareerTools brings together instruments aimed at evaluating and developing the competencies important for athletes' career development and their support providers). These and other online tools are crucial for supporting athletes' career development in the context of busy schedules, the coronavirus pandemic, and the associated need for more digitalization.

Summary

Research on career transitions requires a holistic and life-span perspective, looking at athletes' development from a multilevel and whole-life perspective. Two crucial transition periods are anticipated to be extra challenging, because transitions at the different levels of development coincide: (1) the transition period that requires moving to the next athletic level (the junior–senior transition), psychological level (adolescence to adulthood), educational level (secondary education to higher education), and legal level (moving to adult regulations) and (2) the transition period that requires athletes to retire from sport (athletic retirement), change the psychosocial environment (leave elite sport environment), move into a new vocation, and change the financial income structure.

To support athletes with these and other transitions, career support research has increasingly focused on empowerment approaches. Furthermore, environmental perspectives are gaining in importance, taking into account the complex contexts surrounding elite athletes. Future studies should focus on mental health within DC environments and how this relates to athletes' DC barriers, athletes' DC competencies, and the broader environment.

From a practical perspective, while many evidence-based taxonomies and instruments are available in the domain of athlete career support, these remain underused because of the lack of structural education and certification for DC support practitioners. In further professionalizing this DC support practice, the application of online tools will become increasingly crucial.

DISCUSSION QUESTIONS

1. What are the main transitions and associated barriers that athletes are confronted with?
2. How can the holistic athletic career model help athletes (and support providers) cope with the multilevel challenges throughout their careers?
3. How could you integrate a more proactive competency-enhancing empowerment approach in your career or practice?
4. What type of dual career environment are you in? (See figure 20.2.)
5. How do you evaluate your environment on the essential features of career support environments? What are the main strengths of your environment? What could be better?

21

Creating Safe Cultures in Sport

Daniel J.A. Rhind, PhD, and Frank Owusu-Sekyere, PhD

LEARNING OBJECTIVES

On completion of this chapter, the reader should have the following:

- Knowledge of the nature, scope, and importance of safe sport
- Understanding of key models and frameworks concerning the development and maintenance of safe sport
- Understanding of the factors that may facilitate or jeopardize safe sport
- Understanding of how research can contribute to safe sport through informing policies, education, and practice

Safe sport is characterized by "an athletic environment that is respectful, equitable and free from all forms of non-accidental violence to athletes" (Mountjoy et al., 2016, p. 1119). This includes respecting children's rights to protection, participation, and provision. It also ensures that the best interests of children in sport are paramount, there is no discrimination, all children can enjoy holistic development, and children's voices are heard.

The importance of creating safe sport has been powerfully illustrated by a series of high-profile cases of abuse. Some examples follow:

- Allegations centered around British Gymnastics have described a toxic culture characterized by fear. One gymnast described her experiences of being an elite child athlete in the sport as follows (Sky Sports News, 2020): "Mental and physical abuse was entirely the norm. Our coach mimicked the most extreme abuse as if it were a training method. We were taught to be more scared of our coach than of the skill we were attempting and that that was the only way to achieve it."
- The report by Human Rights Watch in partnership with the World Players Association (Human Rights Watch, 2020), focused on sport in Japan, highlighted a series of examples of physical abuse. One athlete explained: "I was hit so many times, I can't count. . . . we were all called to the coach and I was hit in the face in front of everyone. I was bleeding, but he did not stop hitting me. I did say that my nose was bleeding, but he did not stop."
- Larry Nassar, the USA Gymnastics team doctor, was found guilty of sexually abusing hundreds of gymnasts since the early 1990s (Fisher & Anders, 2020).
- Gigi Alford (2019), sport and human rights director at World Players Association explained:

> As the USA Gymnastics tragedy shows, the institutional culture of placing profits and medals above people is what enables sexual predators to thrive in the silence and shadows of sport's resistance to institutional accountability. This is not solely a problem in the United States, but a global one that has rocked the world of sport most recently in South Korea, as well as the United Kingdom, the Netherlands, Canada and more—and these are just the ones we know about. What is clear everywhere, from the grassroots to the very top, is that the power imbalance in sport—immense for all athletes and compounded for those who are children—creates prime conditions for child sexual abuse, exploitation and harassment.

This chapter outlines the importance of having athletic environments that are respectful, equitable, and free from nonaccidental violence, defined as safe sport (Mountjoy et al., 2016), at the individual, interpersonal, and organizational levels. Factors that can facilitate or jeopardize safe sport are discussed, and strategies for developing and maintaining safe sport are outlined. The conceptualization and measurement of safeguarding culture is discussed along with the implications for research and practice.

Rights in Sport

Fundamental to safe sport is ensuring that the rights of young athletes are respected. The United Nations Convention on the Rights of the Child (United Nations, 1989) outlines the wide range of rights that should be respected and promoted for all children. These rights fall into three broad categories. First, children have rights related to protection (e.g., from violence, harassment, and abuse). Second, they have rights to participation (e.g., in relation to leisure and play). Finally, children have rights to provision (e.g., access to appropriate education and health care). The convention is built on four fundamental principles:

- All decisions should be made with the best interests of the child as a priority.
- No child should experience discrimination.
- All children have the right to life, survival, and development.
- All children's voices should be heard.

These rights should be respected in all contexts, including sport. However, the ways these internationally recognized rights and conventions are applied to sport had not traditionally been clearly explained, understood, or acted upon. To address this gap, the World Players Association (2017) developed and launched the Universal Declaration of Player Rights (UDPR). This identifies 17 key rights, all sourced under international human rights standards, that should be respected for all athletes. In order to drive a global movement toward protecting and promoting athletes' rights, including child athletes, it was critical that the specific rights that should be respected be clearly identified. The rights of particular relevance to the focus of this chapter state that every athlete

Fundamental to safe sport is ensuring that the rights of young athletes are respected.

- has the right to a sporting environment that is well governed, free of corruption, manipulation, and cheating, and that protects, respects, and guarantees the fundamental human rights of everyone involved in or affected by sport, including the player (right 1);
- is entitled to equality of opportunity in the pursuit of sport without distinction of any kind and free of discrimination, harassment, and violence (right 3);
- who is a minor is entitled to the opportunity to freely pursue sport in an inclusive, adapted, and safe manner, and to have their rights as a child protected, respected, and guaranteed (right 4);
- is entitled to a safe and secure workplace and sporting environment that promotes the player's safety, physical and mental health, and social well-being. They must be treated and supported with utmost integrity by health care professionals when injured or ill, and have direction and control over that treatment and support (right 9).

By realizing these rights for all young athletes, we can ensure that athletic environments are respectful, equitable, and free from nonaccidental violence, and hence are offering safe sport (Mountjoy et al., 2015). Note that safe sport has clear synergies with a range of other social psychological concepts that help develop healthy individuals, healthy relationships, and healthy environments. Related topics include the satisfaction of basic needs, the quality and maintenance of effective coach–athlete relationships, social support, and motivational climate. There are significant bodies of literature on each of these topics, and you can read about each of them in more depth within other chapters of this book.

The Importance of Safe Sport

Safe sport is important for all stakeholders at every level. At the individual level, safe sport should reduce the prevalence of a range of potential negative outcomes of an environment that is not respectful, equitable, or free from nonaccidental violence. Examples include injury, depression, anxiety, addictive behaviors, substance misuse, and disordered eating (Mountjoy et al., 2015; Roberts et al., 2016). Safe sport can also facilitate the psychosocial development of children (Allen et al., 2015). At the interpersonal level, safe sport should help prevent the development of relationships characterized by abuse (Alexander et al., 2011; Kavanagh et al., 2020; Rhind et al., 2015). This includes mitigating the risk of sexual abuse (Brackenridge et al., 2008), emotional abuse (Stirling & Kerr, 2008), and physical abuse (Brackenridge & Rhind, 2010). It should also facilitate environments that promote the development and maintenance of effective relationships (Rhind & Jowett, 2010; see also chapter 4). At the contextual level, a focus on safe sport can help prevent the development of structures or procedures that could be harmful for athletes. Examples include the promotion of overtraining of athletes, systematic doping, or passively encouraging hazing and initiation practices through not taking appropriate action. There is also the risk of medical mismanagement if appropriate support, guidance, and treatment are not in place (Mountjoy et al., 2015).

For the organization, the absence of safe sport can have significant reputational risks when cases of concern are disclosed and publicized. On the contrary, an organization that promotes safe sport can benefit in each of these areas through creating structures and procedures that facilitate healthy relationships that should, in turn, enhance participation and performance. There are also significant reputational benefits through emphasizing the strategic importance of safe sport for the organization.

It is important to emphasize that safe sport is not just about preventing negative experiences and outcomes. It extends to the promotion of positive experiences and outcomes for everyone involved. This holistic approach is particularly important because everyone is responsible and has an influence on the creation and maintenance of safe sport. This can be done directly through acting in ways that facilitate or jeopardize safe sport. However, it can also be done indirectly in terms of how bystanders respond to the actions of other people in the context (Raakman et al., 2010). Bystanders can help achieve safe sport through recognizing and rewarding practices that promote it. Likewise, when safe sport is being threatened, bystanders can play a critical role by recognizing and reporting their experiences. Safe sport should therefore be of primary interest to all stakeholders.

Influencing Factors: The Seesaw Model of Safeguarding

A range of factors may combine to put a young athlete at greater risk. Rhind and Owusu-Sekyere (2018) have conceptualized this with the analogy of a seesaw (see figure 21.1), the kind typically found in a children's playground. A seesaw works most effectively when the users on either end are approximately equal in size. This balancing act is an analogy for the existence and management of risks to safe sport. At one end are the risk factors, and at the other end are the strategies used by all stakeholders to mitigate these risks and create a safe environment. There is a range of stakeholders including the athlete, coach, family members, teammates, other bystanders, safeguarding officers, and those in leadership roles within the organization. The safe sport strategies need to be effectively implemented and supported by all stakeholders such that all risks are mitigated. The risks are conceptualized at the individual, interpersonal, and contextual levels.

At the *individual level*, research suggests that a range of personal characteristics are associated with increased risks in sport. These include having a disability, being from an ethnic minority, or being lesbian, gay, or bisexual (Vertommen et al., 2016).

At the heart of the *interpersonal* risk factor is the concept of power. A person in a position of trust (e.g., a coach) over another (e.g., an athlete) can acquire power from six key bases (Raven, 1992):

- Coercive (e.g., through applying physical, social, or economic force)
- Reward (e.g., providing benefits such as funding or team selection)

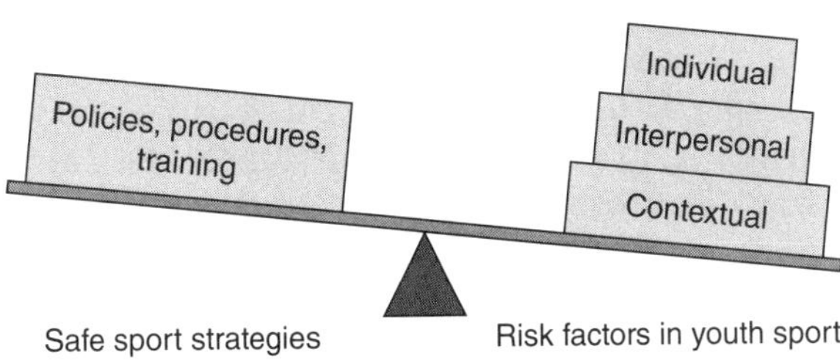

FIGURE 21.1 The seesaw model of safeguarding.

Adapted from D.J.A. Rhind and F. Owusu-Sekyere, "Evaluating the Impacts of Working Towards the International Safeguards for Children in Sport," *Sport Management Review* 23, no. 1 (2020): 104-116.

- Legitimate (e.g., the power associated with the role of the coach within the organization)
- Referent (e.g., through the relationships, groups, or networks to which an individual belongs)
- Expert (e.g., associated with an individual's skills and experience)
- Information (e.g., through having knowledge that another person needs)

This interpersonal power can be used by the coach to influence the feelings, thoughts, behaviors, and general lifestyle of an athlete (Brackenridge et al., 2008). This can lead to positive outcomes (e.g., appropriate training programs) as well as negative outcomes (e.g., an abusive relationship). It is important to emphasize that this is a dyadic relationship within which both the coach and the athlete can access, or be given access to, these bases of power. Young athletes do have agency within this relationship, and they need to be supported to access and use their power within this relationship and the broader context.

Factors related to the context can also increase people's vulnerabilities. These include structures, procedures, and cultures that either facilitate or threaten safe sport. In terms of structures, an organization needs to have effective governance with clear lines of responsibility and oversight. Procedures relate to how safeguarding concerns are reported and managed. If people are not able to voice concerns, and if concerns are not effectively managed, then such procedures can render individuals at risk. Cultures can also develop within organizations that are characterized, for example, by emotionally abusive practices that can be viewed as normal and acceptable. Such cultures can encourage participants to internalize, accept, or even justify threats to their welfare (Papaefstathiou et al., 2012). For example, an investigation into the sexual abuse carried out by Larry Nassar by Ropes and Grey (2018) concluded that the United States Olympic Committee (USOC) and United States of America Gymnastics (USAG) permeated a "self-limiting" and "loose governance model" in which Nasser "thrived." There was a "marked disconnect at both institutions between adopted policies and effective action" that "permitted the unchecked growth of policies, practices and cultural norms that were not reflective of a child-first approach and led to the absence of effective, on-the-ground protective measures."

Another important contextual factor is the level at which the child is competing (Brackenridge & Rhind, 2010). Research suggests that risks can increase as one progresses through the competitive levels (Alexander et al., 2011; Vertommen et al., 2016). Indeed, this may have previously been a blind spot because of a tendency to idealize elite young athletes and therefore assume they are not at risk (Coyle et al., 2017).

In line with Rhind and Owusu-Sekyere's (2018) seesaw analogy, these individual, relational, and contextual risk factors can combine to tip the balance of probability toward safe sport being jeopardized. This analogy emphasizes the interplay between factors that safeguard children and those that increase risk. Therefore, safeguarding is tasked with tipping the balance of probability in favor of the protection of children, in order to minimize the probability that these risk factors will result in actual harm to participants in sport. The next section considers how safe sport can be achieved and how young athletes can be safeguarded from potential risks.

Promoting Safe Sport

There is a growing consensus of the need for safe sport. For example, Baroness Tanni Grey-Thompson led the Duty of Care in Sport Review (2017) and stated the following:

> Recent media reports and anecdotal evidence from across a range of sports has led to questions about whether welfare and safety really are being given the priority they deserve in elite sport. At a time of success for British sport in terms of medals, championships, and profile, this raises challenging questions about whether the current balance between welfare and winning is right and what we are prepared to accept as a nation. (p. 4)

This report raised significant questions and has contributed to ongoing debates around the meaning of safe sport and how it can best be promoted. The importance of this topic has also been recognized by the leaders of key organizations, such as FIFA president Gianni Infantino.

> FIFA has established guiding principles and minimum requirements that will help leaders and organizers in our sport to ensure a safe and nurturing environment for the youngest members of the football family. Such an environment, far from a privilege, is every child's right. (FIFA, 2019)

It has also been recognized that everyone has a role to play in ensuring that athletes are safe and can enjoy healthy relationships and environments where their rights are protected. Thomas Bach, president of the International Olympic Committee, stated that "the safety and wellbeing of athletes are paramount to the IOC and the Olympic Movement. It is the responsibility of all of us to keep athletes safe and to guard their rights" (IOC, 2017).

A global review of violence prevention programs in sport commissioned by UNICEF (Brackenridge et al., 2012) highlighted how the vast majority of work related to what we now call safe sport had been conducted in single countries, typically in Europe or North America (e.g., Chroni et al., 2012). There had traditionally been a problem-oriented approach through a focus on understanding the nature and scope of abuse in sport. A series of projects led by Professor Celia Brackenridge and Dr. Daniel Rhind (Brackenridge & Rhind, 2014; Rhind & Owusu-Sekyere, 2018) has resulted in a paradigm shift in the field. This paradigm shift was stimulated by a new solutions-oriented approach; its global perspective builds on the insights gained through the traditional problem-focused approach to help create safe sport for all. This work has resulted in a set of guidelines known as the International Safeguards for Children in Sport.

International Safeguards for Children in Sport

The International Safeguards for Children in Sport outline the strategies that all organizations should have in place to ensure that the rights of all young athletes are respected (Rhind & Owusu-Sekyere, 2018). They reflect international declarations, the United Nations Convention on the Rights of the Child, relevant legislation, government guidance, good practice, and existing child protection and safeguarding standards. The international safeguards are summarized in table 21.1.

TABLE 21.1 International Safeguards for Children in Sport

Safeguard	Description	Rationale
1. Developing your policy	Any organization providing or with responsibility for sport activities for children and young people under the age of 18 should have a safeguarding policy. This statement of intent demonstrates a commitment to safeguard children involved in sport from harm, and it provides the framework within which procedures are developed.	A safeguarding policy makes clear to all what is required in relation to the protection of children and young people. It helps create a safe and positive environment for children and shows that the organization is taking its duty of care seriously. It also takes into account factors that may leave some children more vulnerable.
2. Procedures for responding to safeguarding concerns	Procedures describe the operational processes required to implement organizational policy and provide clear step-by-step guidance on what to do in different circumstances. They clarify roles and responsibilities as well as lines of communication. Effective systems are required that help process any complaints or concerns and support any victims of violence. You should build on existing systems and understand your role with regard to relevant national systems and legislation.	For safeguarding to be effective, procedures need to be credible for children. Procedures help ensure a prompt response to concerns about a child's safety or well-being. They also help you comply with and implement legislation and guidance. Violence against children is distressing and can be difficult to deal with. Organizations have a duty to ensure that advice and support are in place to help people play their part in safeguarding children.
3. Advice and support	Essential information and support must be provided to those responsible for safeguarding children. Children and young people are advised on where to access help and support.	You have a duty to ensure advice and support are in place so that children know who they can turn to for help.

(continued)

Table 21.1 *(continued)*

Safeguard	Description	Rationale
4. Minimizing risks to children	Measures to assess and minimize the risks to children must be in place.	Some people who work or seek to work in sport in a paid or voluntary capacity pose a risk to children. Children are also at risk when unrealistic expectations are placed on them and when they are placed in unsuitable situations or asked to participate in unsuitable activities, including age-inappropriate activities and overtraining. It is possible to minimize these risks by putting safeguards in place.
5. Guidelines for behavior	These codes of conduct describe what an acceptable standard of behavior is and promote current best practice.	Children's sport should be carried out in a safe, positive, and encouraging atmosphere. Standards of behaviour set a benchmark of what is acceptable for all.
6. Recruiting, training, and communicating	It is necessary to recruit appropriate members of staff, create opportunities to develop and maintain the necessary skills, and communicate about safeguarding.	Everyone in contact with children has a role to play in their protection. They can only do so confidently and effectively if they are aware of and understand key skills and have the opportunity to develop, practice, and implement them. Organizations providing sporting activities for children have a responsibility to provide training and development opportunities for staff and volunteers.
7. Working with partners	Organizations should promote their measures to safeguard children and influence partner organizations to adopt and implement them.	A number of sport organizations have both a strategic and a delivery role in relation to children and young people. Where organizational partnership, membership, funding, or commissioning relationships exist or develop with other groups, the organization should use its influence to promote the implementation of safeguarding measures. The organization should provide or signpost support and resources in relation to implementing adequate safeguarding measures. The organization should actively promote the adoption of the International Safeguards for Children in Sport.
8. Monitoring and evaluating	All relevant groups must monitor compliance and effectiveness on an ongoing basis.	Organizations need to recognize patterns of risk and must know whether safeguarding is effective and where improvements and adaptations are needed.

There has been global uptake of the international safeguards. They have been endorsed by over 400 organizations who work with more than 50 million children in sport worldwide. This includes leading sport organizations (e.g., Manchester City and Manchester United), sport for development organizations (e.g., Moving the Goalposts and Right to Play), coaching organizations (e.g., Coaches Across Continents), and governing organizations (e.g., International Netball Federation). Interest regarding the international safeguards has been fueled by the Safe Sport Day that was launched on August 8, 2020. This date was selected because there are eight safeguards, and hence the eighth day of the eighth month seemed fitting. There are now calls to have this event recognized as United Nations International Day for Safe Sport, which would facilitate further change through raising global awareness.

Measuring the Adoption of the International Safeguards

It is a well-known adage that what gets measured gets managed. It is therefore important to identify the indicators of safe sport. Rhind and Owusu-Sekyere (2020) used the concept of activation states, a heuristic device that lets researchers plot the level of activation with respect to safeguarding across four key dimensions:

- Voices (what people say about safeguarding)
- Knowledge (what people know about safeguarding)
- Feelings (what people feel about safeguarding)
- Action (what people do or have done in relation to safeguarding)

The inclusion of these dimensions affords an examination of both psychological and social processes. The level of activation for each dimension is identified as opposed, inactive, active, reactive, active, or proactive. Examples of each level across the four dimensions are provided in table 21.2.

Activation states were used in a two-year project to evaluate the impact of working toward the International Safeguards for Children in Sport (Rhind & Owusu-Sekyere, 2020). Thirty-two organizations were recruited to trial the implementation of these strategies. These organizations worked in a diverse range of geographical settings in Africa, Asia, Europe, Oceania, and North and South America. They were also diverse in terms of size (e.g., local, national, or international) and purpose (e.g., elite performance, participation, sport for development, and governance). The activation states proved particularly helpful in terms of tracking changes within these organizations.

The following pairs of quotes each come from the same individual at the start and end of the implementation phase (Rhind & Owusu-Sekyere, 2020).

- Voices (start: opposed): "People are against this kind of work when it is talked about as coming from the attitude of 'we come from the empire and we know what is best for you.'"
- Voices (end: active): "We get much less resistance. When we get new people there may be some questions as they have just not come across safeguarding before. Everyone else is much more invested and they see how important it is."
- Knowledge (start: inactive): "The children are not made aware of various rights they are entitled to. Generating awareness is a tough challenge that we face on a regular basis."
- Knowledge (end: active): "Everyone knows that they need to adhere to the safeguards that are in place and sign the code of conducts for safeguarding children. People now know that there are procedures to be followed regarding safeguarding concerns. Parents understand that participants engaged in our programs need consents signed for them to take part in our activities."
- Feelings (start: opposed): "Scolding children is not seen as abuse. Having a child run around a field 5 times is not a problem. We are coming from a culture in which these are seen as ok. These are the feelings that we have to engage with."
- Feelings (end: active): "Since starting the Safeguards project, we have gone from a position of people saying that they cannot

TABLE 21.2 Activation States

Dimension	Opposed	Inactive	Reactive	Active	Proactive
Voices	Talks negatively	Does not discuss	Reluctantly discusses	Talks positively	Talks enthusiastically
Knowledge	Actively avoids learning	Has no knowledge	Reluctant to learn	Knows requirements of their role	Engages with learning beyond their role
Feelings	Has negative feelings	Has no strong feelings	Lacks confidence	Feels positive	Feels enthusiastic
Action	Actively avoids safeguarding	Takes no action	Reluctantly acts	Acts in line with their role	Goes beyond their role

believe you are making me do this to one where they say I would not put my child in a club that did not do this."

- Actions (start: inactive): "Within our organisation, in terms of formal protocols there are very few."
- Actions (end: active): "Before the policy we would finish meetings and girls would be going home, some of them late in the dark. Now we know that at 3pm we have to finish so everyone has enough time to get home before it's dark."

These activation states offer an insight into the extent to which safeguarding measures have been adopted. It is through effective adoption of the International Safeguards that organizations can work to respect the rights for all young athletes. In contrast, the absence of any effective safeguarding measures within an organization can result in the violation of rights.

A key element of any organization working with young athletes is the culture. Organizational culture is often cited as playing a key role in facilitating safe sport, and it has been highlighted as a critical contributing factor during investigations of rights violations in sport (Grey-Thompson, 2017; Phelps et al., 2017). It was therefore important that a theoretically grounded conceptualization of culture be developed to guide research and practice.

Conceptualizing Safeguarding Culture

Safety culture has been defined as "the assembly of underlying assumptions, beliefs, values and attitudes shared by members of an organisation, which interact with an organization's structures and systems and the broader contextual setting to result in those external, readily visible, practices that influence safety" (Edwards et al., 2013, p. 77).

This concept has been applied in a wide variety of industries such as construction, aviation, health care, and energy production (Filho & Waterson, 2018; Cull et al., 2013). Rhind and Owusu-Sekyere (2021) built on this definition of safety culture, with a specific focus on rights and using the term *safeguarding culture*. Qualitative research was conducted with 77 participants working in diverse sport organizations around the world. One participant encapsulated the meaning of safeguarding culture in explaining the following: "It's much more engrained you know. Safeguarding becomes like a habit almost, you don't think about it, and it's just a matter of course that you do it. So, for that to happen it's got to go beyond policies" (Owusu-Sekyere et al., 2021). Through this research, the safeguarding culture in sport model has been proposed.

Owusu-Sekyere and colleagues (2021) proposed a model to conceptualize safeguarding culture in sport. This conceptualization is grounded in Bandura's social cognitive theory and the concept of reciprocal determinism (Bandura, 1986), where the emphasis is placed on the constant interplay between human behavior, the environment, and personal factors (e.g., feelings and thoughts). Subsequently, at the center of Owusu-Sekyere and colleagues' (2021) model are three key influencing factors: the safety management system, stakeholder engagement, and leadership commitment. These factors are theorized to interact to shape the prevalent safeguarding culture. These interactions are theorized to be shaped by internal and external contextual factors. The next section briefly describes the factors within the model.

Safety Management Systems

This relates to the structural elements of safeguarding being in place within an organization. It includes having effective policies, incentives to promote safe behaviors, safeguarding training, effective communication channels regarding safeguarding, proactive approaches to prevent and mitigate risks, and an effective system to monitor and evaluate safeguarding within the organization.

Stakeholder Engagement

This aspect emphasizes the importance of engaging with everyone who affects the safeguarding culture of the organization, including people who work or volunteer for the organization, children, and parents. These are referred to as internal stakeholders. It also refers to the wide variety of external stakeholders, which may include people from funding bodies, governing organizations, sponsors, or event organizers. All of these stakeholders can influence the safeguarding culture, and it is important that they go beyond concepts such as minimum standards and compliance. Engagement should occur across knowledge and awareness; attitudes, values, and beliefs; and motivation.

Leadership Commitment

Safeguarding culture can be facilitated through the commitment of leaders throughout the organization. This relates to leadership of stakeholders as well as of the safety management system (SMS). Stakeholder leadership describes how leaders empower, mentor, and support people to engage with safe sport. Leadership of the SMS describes the actions taken by leaders to develop, implement, and oversee the strategies to keep people safe. This includes encouraging safe practices as well as taking appropriate measures when people are not acting in line with safe sport.

Contextual Factors

The interactions between the stakeholders, leadership, and SMS are fundamentally shaped by a host of contextual factors. These can relate to factors internal to the organization as well as broader external factors. Internal factors can be related to the available resources, the mission, and the values of the organization as well as the physical environments in which people interact. External factors concern norms regarding how children are treated, the existence and enforcement of legislation, the effectiveness of social services, and the media.

Future Research Directions

Despite the progress that has been made, there remains considerable scope for further research related to creating safe sport for everyone involved, irrespective of their age or role. Future directions can be identified regarding the antecedents, applications, and outcomes of safeguarding. In terms of antecedents, research is required to understand the factors that create risks to safe sport. This work, which could be guided by the seesaw model outlined in figure 21.1, could consider the characteristics of individuals associated with increased risk, such as those with a disability or of a certain age (Vertommen et al., 2016). Strategies for creating safe sport also merit further research. Studies can explore the applicability of the safeguarding culture model previously discussed. The nature and scope of the interactions between each factor within the model can be investigated—in particular, how the interplay between the safety management system, the engagement of stakeholders, leadership commitment, and contextual factors influences the activation states of particular groups. For example, how can the implementation of safeguarding measures influence the feelings, knowledge, and behaviors of all key stakeholders (e.g., coaches, athletes, and parents)?

Research is also required on how the effective application of safe sport is shaped by the given context. This could include the geographical location, the size and purpose of the organization, and the type and level of sport. The experiences of all stakeholders (e.g., athletes, coaches, parents, managers, and all other support staff) need to be captured and analyzed regarding how effective safeguarding is developed, implemented, and maintained. This would help elucidate the outcomes of safe sport for individuals (e.g., well-being and performance), relationships (e.g., quality and communication), and organizations (e.g., reputation and achieving strategic goals).

There is also a strong rationale to go beyond the focus on safe sport for young athletes to create inclusive safe sport that safeguards everyone involved. This can extend to all athletes in sport of all ages. Traditionally, research and practice in this field have focused on children; the initial work concentrated on child protection and drew on associated concepts from other sectors such as social work. Significant progress in this field is primarily due to the leadership of key organizations such as UNICEF UK and the National Society for the Prevention of Cruelty to Children, which understandably have a focus on children. However, an individual does not automatically become safe on their 18th birthday. As a result, work is required to understand the transition to adulthood and how participants can be safeguarded during this period and throughout their lives. The fundamental principles of safe sport should be relevant to everyone. However, there is a range of reasons as to why adult-specific research and policies are required.

First, adults may face a different set of issues in sport than do children. For example, adults may be more likely to be subject to professional contracts and to extra attention, both in the training and competition context and online. There may be a greater range of stakeholders who have vested interests in an adult athlete such as an agent, club managers, the national governing body, sponsors, or fans. This may give rise to different safeguarding concerns. Second, there are typically legislative changes. For example, there will be an age of maturity at which people can legally engage in sexual activity (e.g., 16 years old). Beyond this age, people are viewed as being able to consent to sexual activity. However, given the power dynamics at play (see chapter 4), the extent to which adult athletes can actually consent within critical relationships can be questioned. Finally, another critical difference between safeguarding adults and safeguarding children is an adult's right to self-determination. In a safeguarding context, self-determination means an adult may choose not to act at all to protect themselves when they are subject to harm. It is only in extreme circumstances that the police or social services may intervene. This typically happens only when an adult is assessed to lack capacity, or when children may be indirectly affected. This conceptualization of consent and capacity is a critical issue, particularly in relation to the salient safeguarding culture and the power dynamics of any interpersonal relationships (see chapter 4). Research is thus merited into how safeguarding adults differs from safeguarding children and how safe sport can be developed for all.

There is also a need for a multidisciplinary and interdisciplinary approach to the creation of safe sport. Traditionally, research, theory, and practice regarding safeguarding in sport have developed in silos. As a result, there is clear potential to explore the links within the range of other key topics covered in this book, such as coach–athlete relationships, motivational climate, and facilitating performance.

Practical Implications

The international safeguards help organizations respect the rights of all young athletes through creating a safeguarding culture. The international safeguards and the safeguarding culture model thus work in tandem. This can be illustrated through considering how this applies to the safeguarding policy of an organization (safeguard 1; see table 21.1). Based on the model, this is more likely to be effective if the following are in place:

- *Safety management system.* The policy needs to be readily available and embedded within key structures (e.g., clearly linked to the values and mission of the organization).
- *Stakeholder engagement.* People should be consulted during the development and ongoing review of the policy.
- *Leadership commitment.* Those in leadership roles should publicly endorse the policy and ensure there is clear oversight regarding people's adherence to the policy.
- *Context.* The policy should be tailored to both the internal context of the organization (e.g., the type of sport) and the external context (e.g., the legislative, political, and social influences).

An audit can also be conducted against the International Safeguards for Children in Sport. For example, thinking about your role in sport as an athlete, coach, parent, or other role, you can reflect on the following questions:

- Do you know the organization's policy on safeguarding?
- Do you know the procedures for reporting any safeguarding concerns?
- Do you know who to turn to for advice and support related to safeguarding?
- Do you think about the risks that may be associated with your role in sport and take steps to mitigate these proactively?
- Are you aware of, and do you follow, any codes of conduct related to safeguarding?
- Do you engage with the safeguarding aspects of any recruitment processes or ongoing training?
- Do you have relationships with other people who can support your safeguarding role both internally (e.g., other athletes, coaches, safeguarding managers) and externally (e.g., social services, charities)?
- Do you reflect on how effective you have been in relation to your safeguarding role?

Answers (or lack of?) to such questions can help identify areas in which progress can be made. As a result, you can set short- and longer-term goals to maintain or improve your safeguarding knowledge and practices. Along with at the individual level, this auditing process can be conducted for groups (e.g., coaches) or an organization as a whole.

There have already been important implications of the international safeguards and the safeguarding culture model. Drawing on this work, FIFA launched its Guardians toolkit to support its 211 national football associations on their safeguarding journey toward safe sport. The IOC has developed a designated safeguarding officer certificate. This is a nine-month program that develops the knowledge, confidence, and skills of people who will perform this key coordinating role within national and international federations.

Summary

Safe sport is characterized by "an athletic environment that is respectful, equitable and free from all forms of non-accidental violence to athletes" (Mountjoy et al., 2016, p. 1119). This approach should help respect the fundamental rights of all children. A range of factors at the individual, interpersonal, and contextual levels can result in a young athlete's being at risk. There is a growing consensus across key organizations of the importance of creating and maintaining safe sport for all. This chapter has outlined how key developments, such as the International Safeguards for Children in Sport and the safeguarding culture model, can help deliver these aspirations. This multifaceted issue requires a similarly multifaceted approach through all stakeholders working together. Researchers will play a key role in proposing theories, creating an evidence base, and evaluating safeguarding strategies to inform the drive toward creating safe cultures in sport.

DISCUSSION QUESTIONS

1. What do you think are the key risk factors that could jeopardize safe sport at the individual, interpersonal, and contextual levels?
2. How would you develop effective procedures for managing safeguarding concerns (safeguard 2) based on the safeguarding culture model?
3. Imagine you have taken on the role of safeguarding officer at your local sport club. What three things could you do to help create safe sport within the club?
4. What do you think is the most important research question related to creating safe sport for young athletes?

22

Antecedents and Consequences of Moral Behavior in Sport

Maria Kavussanu, PhD; Ian D. Boardley, PhD; and Nicholas Stanger, PhD

LEARNING OBJECTIVES

On completion of this chapter, the reader should have the following:

- Understanding about the key definitions of prosocial and antisocial behavior in sport
- Knowledge and understanding about potential predictors of prosocial and antisocial behavior in sport
- Appreciation of the various outcomes for the recipients of prosocial and antisocial behavior in sport
- Familiarity with avenues for further research on morality in sport
- Awareness of the main implications for sport practitioners (e.g., coaches) for promoting prosocial—and deterring antisocial—behavior in athletes

As a context where social interaction is inevitable, sport provides participants with many opportunities to engage in behaviors that could have positive or negative consequences for others' welfare (Kavussanu, 2012). Many readers will recall seeing double Olympic triathlon gold medalist Alistair Brownlee stopping in the 2016 World Triathlon Series finals to assist his brother Jonny, who had collapsed, almost carrying him to the finish line. Similarly, violent incidents such as the bench-clearing brawl that broke out between the Australia and Philippines men's national basketball teams in 2018 live long in the memory of those who see them. We refer to these types of acts as *prosocial* and *antisocial* behaviors, respectively. Specifically, prosocial behavior has been defined as voluntary behavior intended to help or benefit another individual or group of individuals (Eisenberg & Fabes, 1998); examples in sport include helping a player off the floor and congratulating a teammate. Antisocial behavior has been defined as behavior intended to harm or disadvantage another individual or group of individuals (Kavussanu et al., 2006; Sage et al., 2006); examples in sport include trying to injure an opponent and verbally abusing a teammate.

Prosocial and antisocial sport behaviors have been defined in terms of their potential consequences for the recipient (see Kavussanu, 2012) and correspond to the two dimensions of morality described by Bandura (1999): proactive and inhibitive. *Proactive morality* is the power to behave humanely (i.e., do good things), whereas *inhibitive morality* is the power to refrain from behaving inhumanely (i.e., refrain from doing bad things). Our perspective is grounded in Bandura's (1991) social cognitive theory of moral thought and action, which views behavior as the cornerstone of morality. In addition, Bandura (1991) explained that individuals develop moral standards through socialization via interactions with, and observations of, significant others. Moral standards regulate behavior through anticipated self-evaluative reactions. People tend to behave in ways that align with their moral standards, and experience self-satisfaction when they do so, and refrain from engaging in behaviors that contravene their moral standards, because this would bring self-disapproval (e.g., feelings of guilt or shame).

Empirical research has shown that prosocial and antisocial behaviors in sport can be directed toward both opponents and teammates and vary as a function of the recipient (Kavussanu & Boardley, 2009). In a large-scale study of 110 sport teams, Kavussanu and Boardley (2009) found that most of the prosocial behaviors that take place toward opponents are helping behaviors (e.g., helping an opponent off the floor or helping an injured opponent). This finding makes sense if we consider that in team sport, athletes come in close contact with their opponents, and when injurious acts take place, it is often one's opponent who is closer to the victim and in a position to help. In contrast, the prosocial behaviors most frequently identified as taking place toward teammates were congratulating and encouraging a teammate, a finding that has been confirmed in observational research (e.g., Kavussanu et al., 2009). Prosocial behaviors toward teammates could have achievement-related consequences for the recipient. For example, encouraging a teammate after a mistake could help the teammate perform better, with subsequent benefits for the team. Thus, the prosocial behaviors that most commonly take place toward teammates and opponents in team sport are qualitatively different from each other.

People tend to behave in ways that align with their moral standards, and experience self-satisfaction when they do so, and refrain from engaging in behaviors that contravene their moral standards, because this would bring self-disapproval (e.g., feelings of guilt or shame).

Antisocial behaviors toward teammates and opponents are also distinct (Kavussanu & Boardley, 2009; Kavussanu et al., 2009). Antisocial behaviors toward teammates tend to be verbal behaviors (e.g., arguing with, or swearing at, a teammate), reflecting the nature of team sport, whereby in the pursuit of team goals, frustration is commonly expressed and disagreements between teammates take place. In contrast, antisocial behaviors toward opponents are verbal *and* physical. Some of these behaviors (e.g., verbally abusing an opponent) could also constitute *sledging*, a term that originated in cricket and has been defined as "the practice whereby players seek to gain an advantage by insulting or verbally intimidating the batter" (Joseph & Cramer, 2011, p. 237). A similar term is *trash talking*, which refers to verbal barbs that are directed at the opponent with the aim to gain a competitive advantage (Dixon, 2007). Acts such as trying to injure an opponent constitute physical aggression, whereas intentionally breaking the rules of sport can be viewed as cheating. Thus, antisocial behaviors that are directed at one's opponents are quite diverse. In this chapter, we review studies that have examined these types of behaviors, as well as physical aggression, because they fall under the broader umbrella term of *antisocial conduct*.

Much of the research presented in this chapter has used the Prosocial and Antisocial Behavior in Sport Scale (PABSS; Kavussanu & Boardley, 2009), which measures prosocial and antisocial behaviors toward teammates and opponents. First, we discuss studies that have examined antecedents of prosocial behavior, followed by research investigating antecedents or predictors of antisocial behavior. Next, we review work on the outcomes or consequences of these behaviors for the recipient. We continue with research investigating the concept of bracketed morality and conclude with a section on future research directions and implications for practice.

At the outset, we should note that our review is not exhaustive. It is meant to give a flavor of the progress that has been made in this area of research rather than provide a complete review of all relevant research on moral behavior in sport. The latter would have been an impossible task, in light of the space limitations of this chapter.

Understanding Prosocial Behavior

Researchers have investigated a range of variables as predictors of prosocial behavior in sport. Most studies have examined how constructs derived from achievement goal theory (Ames, 1992; Nicholls, 1989) or self-determination theory (Deci & Ryan, 2000) are related to prosocial behavior, guided by these two major theories of motivation. Others have been guided by social identity theory (Tajfel, 1981) and sport-specific models of coaching behavior

(Bolter & Weiss, 2012, 2013). These studies have revealed some interesting findings, which we discuss in this section.

Two of the most reliable predictors of prosocial behavior in sport are task orientation and mastery climate, two constructs of achievement goal theory (Ames, 1992; Nicholls, 1989). This theory posits that two major achievement goals operate in achievement contexts such as sport—namely, *task* and *ego* orientation (Nicholls, 1989)—and these goals reflect the criteria one tends to use to define success and evaluate competence. Individuals high in task orientation tend to use self-referenced criteria to evaluate competence and feel successful when they try hard, improve, and master a new skill, whereas those high in ego orientation tend to feel competent when they show superiority over others (Nicholls, 1989). Task orientation has been positively related to prosocial behavior toward teammates and opponents, whereas ego orientation tends to be unrelated or weakly and inversely associated with this behavior (e.g., Kavussanu & Boardley, 2009; Sage & Kavussanu, 2008).

Similar links have been revealed for motivational climate, which involves the criteria used to evaluate success in achievement contexts; these criteria are communicated to athletes by significant others, such as coaches, via their behavior (Ames, 1992). Coaches create a *mastery* motivational climate when they communicate to athletes that they value personal progress by rewarding effort, recognizing individual progress, and creating equal opportunities for success. In contrast, a *performance* climate is created when coaches place value on normative success and communicate this with a variety of practices such as rewarding athletes who outperform, or show superior ability, over others. Mastery motivational climate has been positively associated with prosocial behavior in sport, whereas performance climate tends to be unrelated or weakly and inversely related to this behavior (e.g., Boardley & Kavussanu, 2009; Stanger et al., 2018). A meta-analysis examining intrapersonal correlates of motivational climate revealed a significant positive relationship between perceived mastery motivational climate and prosocial functioning (i.e., prosocial attitudes, intentions, and behavior) across 15 studies (Harwood et al., 2015). In contrast, the relationship between perceived performance climate and prosocial functioning across 11 studies was weak and not significant. This suggests that coaches who wish to promote prosocial behavior within the context of sport should focus their efforts on creating a mastery motivational climate.

Several studies have shown that the positive relationship between mastery climate and prosocial behavior tends to be stronger toward teammates than opponents in both adolescent and adult team-sport athletes (e.g., Boardley & Kavussanu, 2009; Stanger et al., 2018). Moreover, in adolescent athletes, perceived mastery climate has been linked to prosocial behavior toward opponents via affective social support (i.e., emotional and esteem support) and perspective taking, and with prosocial behavior toward teammates only via affective social support (Stanger et al., 2018). These findings provide initial evidence that the link between mastery climate and prosocial behavior may be partly explained by athletes' perceiving the environment to be more caring and more encouraging; the link of mastery climate with prosocial behavior toward opponents may be due to this goal structure's facilitating athletes' tendency to adopt the perspective of others. However, because of the cross-sectional nature of this study, more research using longitudinal designs is needed before firm conclusions can be drawn regarding the processes through which mastery climate may influence prosocial behavior in sport.

Autonomous motivation and autonomy support, two constructs derived from self-determination theory (Deci & Ryan, 2000), are also relevant to, and have been investigated as, predictors of prosocial behavior in sport (Hodge & Gucciardi, 2015; Hodge & Lonsdale, 2011). Autonomous motivation exists when involvement in the activity emanates from one's sense of self (e.g., choosing to take part in sport because one enjoys or values the activity and its benefits). In an autonomy-supportive climate, coaches support autonomy in athletes (e.g., by providing athletes with choices) (Deci & Ryan, 1985). In line with the tenets of self-determination theory, an autonomy-supportive coaching climate has been positively linked to prosocial behavior toward teammates indirectly via autonomous motivation (Hodge & Lonsdale, 2011) and via satisfaction of the needs for competence and relatedness (Hodge & Gucciardi, 2015). In addition, autonomous motivation has been positively associated with prosocial behavior toward both teammates and opponents in masters athletes (Sheehy & Hodge, 2015), but only toward teammates in university athletes (Hodge & Lonsdale, 2011). In general, an autonomy-supportive climate tends to evidence stronger links with prosocial behavior toward teammates than toward opponents (Hodge & Gucciardi, 2015; Hodge & Lonsdale, 2011). This may be due to the different types of prosocial behaviors directed toward teammates and opponents, which are helping behaviors for opponents but can also be achievement-conducive behaviors for teammates.

A limitation of these studies is that they are cross-sectional. This was addressed in a recent study (Cheon et al., 2018) that implemented an autonomy-supportive intervention program with physical education teachers and examined whether this program influenced students' behaviors during class. Teachers who took part in the program increased their autonomy-supportive behaviors and decreased their controlling behaviors, and their students experienced greater need satisfaction and engaged in more prosocial behaviors than the control group, which consisted of a group of teachers who did not receive the intervention. These findings suggest that an autonomy-supportive climate created by physical education teachers may increase students' prosocial behavior by satisfying students' needs for autonomy, relatedness, and competence, the three central needs posited in self-determination theory. This study provided good evidence for a causal relationship between autonomy support and prosocial behavior in a physical activity context.

Coaches who wish to promote prosocial behavior within the context of sport should focus their efforts on creating a mastery motivational climate.

In addition to studies guided by achievement goal theory (Ames, 1992; Nicholls, 1989) and self-determination theory (Deci & Ryan, 2000), researchers have examined prosocial behavior from the perspective of social identity theory (Bruner et al., 2014, 2018). Social identity has been described as "that part of an individual's self-concept [that] derives from his/her knowledge of his/her membership of a social group (or groups), together with the value and emotional significance attached to that membership" (Tajfel, 1981, p. 255). Three dimensions of social identity have been examined in sport research: cognitive centrality (i.e., the importance of being a group member), in-group affect (i.e., positive feelings about group membership), and in-group ties (i.e., perceived sense of belonging, bonding, and similarity with team members). In-group ties and in-group affect were positively associated with prosocial behavior toward teammates in high school team sports (Bruner et al., 2014), while in youth ice hockey players, all three dimensions of social identity were positively linked to prosocial behavior toward teammates (Bruner et al., 2018); no such relationships were identified with prosocial behavior toward opponents. Thus, young athletes are more likely to act prosocially toward their teammates when they feel that being part of the team is important to their self-concept, feel strong ties with their team, and are happy to be a member of the team.

Researchers have also examined coach behaviors that can influence fair play and sporting behavior, proposing the construct of good and poor sportspersonship (Bolter & Weiss, 2012). Bolter and Weiss (2012, 2013) identified six coach behaviors that could influence sportspersonship: setting expectations; reinforcing good sportspersonship; teaching good sportspersonship; modeling good sportspersonship; punishing poor sportspersonship; and prioritizing winning over good sportspersonship. Across two studies of youth team-sport athletes (Bolter & Kipp, 2018; Bolter & Weiss, 2013), players who perceived that their coach set expectations and reinforced, taught, and modeled good sportspersonship reported more frequent prosocial behavior toward their teammates and their opponents. The coach behavior of modeling good sportspersonship was also positively linked with prosocial behavior toward teammates indirectly via relatedness. Thus, coaches can facilitate prosocial behavior in young athletes, and modeling good sportspersonship may also promote a stronger connection between players, which may explain this relationship.

In summary, several studies have shown that mastery climate, autonomous motivation, autonomy-supportive coaching style, and social identity are positively associated with prosocial behavior toward teammates, with most of these constructs positively—albeit weakly—linked with prosocial behavior toward opponents. Task orientation and sportspersonship coaching behaviors tend to be similarly linked with prosocial behaviors toward both teammates and opponents. Strategies targeted at promoting a mastery and autonomy-supportive climate, and coaches' sportspersonship behaviors, as well as strengthening team members' social identity, should facilitate prosocial behavior toward teammates in sport, with some potentially positive effects on prosocial behavior toward opponents.

However, it is important to note that most of this research is cross-sectional, limiting the conclusions we can draw about causality.

Understanding Antisocial Behavior

Much recent research has focused on understanding the factors that facilitate or inhibit antisocial behavior in sport (see Kavussanu & Al-Yaaribi, 2021; Kavussanu & Stanger, 2017). Common theories underpinning such research are Bandura's (1991) social cognitive theory of moral thought and action, achievement goal theory (Ames, 1992; Nicholls, 1989), and self-determination theory (Deci & Ryan, 2000). In this section, we discuss predictors of antisocial behavior in sport. Psychological or social-environmental factors that are likely to facilitate antisocial behavior are discussed first, followed by factors that are likely to inhibit such behavior. We use the terms *positive predictors* and *negative predictors*, respectively, to refer to these two sets of factors.

Positive Predictors

One of the most consistent and widely researched predictors of antisocial behavior in sport is moral disengagement, a construct described by Bandura (1991) in his social cognitive theory of moral thought and action. Moral disengagement refers to eight cognitive mechanisms that allow us to circumvent our internalized moral standards, thereby facilitating unethical behavior without experiencing the unpleasant self-sanctions (e.g., guilt, shame) that typically arise from such behavior. The eight mechanisms are

- moral justification,
- euphemistic labeling,
- advantageous comparison,
- diffusion of responsibility,
- displacement of responsibility,
- distortion of consequences,
- attribution of blame, and
- dehumanization.

These mechanisms operate by cognitively restructuring the behavior, reducing one's responsibility for the act, ignoring or distorting the detrimental consequences of the conduct, and dehumanizing or blaming one's victim (Bandura, 1991). Moral disengagement has shown strong positive relationships with antisocial behavior, particularly toward opponents, in numerous studies (for reviews see Kavussanu & Al-Yaaribi, 2021; Kavussanu & Stanger, 2017).

In one experiment, Stanger and colleagues (2013) randomly assigned student-athletes to either an experimental or a control group; they used a scenario to induce attribution of blame, one of the moral disengagement mechanisms (i.e., the scenario provided the conditions for this mechanism to operate) in the experimental group. Compared with the control group, participants in the experimental group reported greater likelihood to behave antisocially, and this effect was partially explained by reduced anticipated guilt (Stanger et al., 2013). This provides support for Bandura's (1991) contention that moral disengagement increases the likelihood of antisocial behavior by reducing anticipated guilt when engaging in such action.

One study examined the temporal sequencing of the relationships between moral disengagement and antisocial behavior (Boardley et al., 2020). Specifically, competitive adolescent team-sport players completed measures of moral disengagement and antisocial behavior at the start (2 weeks), middle (6-8 weeks), and end (12-16 weeks) of the season. Reciprocal relationships between moral disengagement and antisocial behavior toward opponents were identified: Moral disengagement positively predicted longitudinal changes in antisocial behavior toward opponents from the start to the middle and from the middle to the end of the season. These findings support Bandura's (1991) proposition that moral disengagement enables individuals to act transgressively. Null findings for antisocial behavior directed at teammates suggest these behaviors may be more legitimized in team sport compared with antisocial acts directed at opponents, thereby reducing the need to rationalize these behaviors. It may also be that moral disengagement is more relevant to antisocial behavior toward opponents.

Moral disengagement has been investigated as a potential mediator of the effects of motivational factors on antisocial behavior, namely ego orientation and performance motivational climate, two constructs of achievement goal theory (Ames, 1992; Nicholls, 1989). Ego orientation involves the tendency to evaluate competence using normative criteria, while performance climate is its situational counterpart. Both variables have been consistently and positively associated with antisocial behavior toward teammates and opponents in numerous studies, with stronger links typically shown for antisocial behavior toward opponents than teammates (see Kavussanu & Al-Yaaribi, 2021). In one study of male soccer players, ego orientation was also indirectly linked to antisocial behavior via moral disengagement, and the link was stronger for behavior directed toward opponents than teammates (Boardley & Kavussanu, 2010). Similarly, performance climate has been linked with antisocial behavior toward teammates and opponents indirectly via moral disengagement in youth team-sport athletes (Stanger et al., 2018).

Controlled motivation and climate, two constructs of self-determination theory, have also been examined in relation to antisocial behavior. Controlled motivation exists when athletes take part in sport for extrinsic reasons, such as to obtain rewards and prizes or to avoid feelings of guilt and shame (Deci & Ryan, 1985). In a controlling climate, coaches implement coercive and pressuring practices such as using controlling language, manipulation, and guilt induction, and they rely on obedience to impose a specific and preconceived way of thinking and behaving on their athletes (e.g., Bartholomew et al., 2009). Controlled motivation has been positively associated with antisocial behavior toward teammates and opponents in masters athletes (Sheehy & Hodge, 2015) and university student-athletes (Hodge & Lonsdale, 2011), both directly and indirectly via moral disengagement (Hodge & Lonsdale, 2011). Similarly, perceived controlling coach and teammate climates have been positively and indirectly linked to antisocial behavior toward teammates and opponents, via moral disengagement (Hodge & Gucciardi, 2015). Thus, athletes may engage in more frequent antisocial behavior in response to pressure created by controlling climates, and they may rationalize this through moral disengagement.

One of the most consistent and widely researched predictors of antisocial behavior in sport is moral disengagement, a construct described by Bandura (1991) in his social cognitive theory of moral thought and action.

In sum, moral disengagement has been a popular explanatory variable in researchers' efforts to understand the effects of motivational factors on antisocial behavior toward teammates and opponents in sport. However, most studies investigating moral disengagement as an explanatory variable between motivational constructs and antisocial behavior have been cross-sectional, limiting the conclusions we can draw regarding causality. Longitudinal and experimental evidence is gradually emerging and suggests that moral disengagement plays an important role in facilitating antisocial behavior toward opponents (e.g., Boardley et al., 2020; Stanger et al., 2013).

Negative Predictors

Researchers have also examined variables that can potentially reduce or inhibit antisocial behavior in sport. Moral identity and empathy are two of these variables. Aquino and Reed (2002) defined moral identity as "a self-conception organized around a set of moral traits" (p. 1424) and identified nine traits as essential characteristics of a moral person (i.e., caring, compassionate, fair, friendly, generous, helpful, hardworking, honest, and kind). They also distinguished between the internalization and symbolization dimensions of moral identity. Researchers in sport have primarily examined the internalization dimension of moral identity, which reflects the extent to which the moral self-schema is perceived as central to one's identity (e.g., Aquino & Reed, 2002), and have found it to be inversely associated with antisocial behavior toward teammates and opponents (see Kavussanu, 2019). Some evidence also suggests this relationship may be due to increased anticipated guilt. Kavussanu and colleagues (2015) used an experimental design to investigate whether the relationship between moral identity and antisocial behavior is mediated by anticipated guilt. They allocated 86 undergraduate sport and exercise science students to either a moral identity group (i.e., a group where participants' moral identity was primed) or a control group. Participants in the moral identity group reported higher anticipated guilt if they were to engage in an antisocial behavior toward an opponent and lower likelihood to behave antisocially. Anticipated guilt was a partial mediator of the effects of moral identity on antisocial behavior. These findings highlight the important role of anticipated guilt in reducing antisocial behavior and the role that moral identity could play in activating this emotion.

Empathy is an other-oriented response, which is congruent with another person's situation or perceived welfare (Batson et al., 1997). People who are high in empathy can take another person's perspective and tend to experience concern for unfortunate others (Davis, 1983). Empathy has been negatively linked to antisocial behavior in several cross-sectional studies (see Kavussanu, 2019; Kavussanu & Stanger, 2017). In a recent study, perspective taking (i.e., the cognitive component of empathy) was inversely and indirectly associated with antisocial behavior toward opponents and teammates via moral disengagement (Stanger et al., 2018). This suggests that the ability to take someone else's perspective may reduce the propensity to morally disengage, with a subsequent reduction in antisocial behavior. However, the mediating role of moral disengagement between empathy and antisocial behavior needs to be confirmed in longitudinal or experimental studies.

Experimental evidence points to the causal role of empathy in reducing aggression. In one experiment, Stanger and colleagues (2012) allocated 71 undergraduate sport and exercise students to a high-empathy group (instructed to adopt their opponent's perspective and consider how they would feel if they had the opportunity to intentionally hurt an opponent) or a low-empathy group (asked to adopt an objective perspective and remain emotionally detached from the hypothetical opponent). Compared with the low-empathy group, the high-empathy group reported higher anticipated guilt if they were to harm their opponent and lower likelihood to commit the aggressive act.

Research has also revealed interesting interaction effects between empathy, sex, and provocation. Using the same empathy manipulation as the aforementioned experimental study (Stanger et al., 2012), Stanger and colleagues (2016) investigated the effects of empathy on student-athletes' aggressive behavior (i.e., giving an electric shock up to their pain threshold) in a competitive reaction time task against a (fictitious) opponent during conditions of low and high provocation. Empathy reduced aggression in both men and women at low provocation, but when athletes were highly provoked (i.e., they received higher electric shock) during the task, empathy reduced aggression only in women. Thus, provocation overrode the suppressing effect of empathy on aggression in men. In addition, guilt mediated the suppressing effect of empathy on aggression only in men at low provocation. Thus, empathy may activate the regulatory moral emotion of anticipated guilt, which in turn should decrease the tendency to engage in antisocial behavior under certain conditions.

In sum, athletes who have high empathy and a strong moral identity are less likely to engage in antisocial behaviors toward both teammates and opponents. These findings have important practical implications and point to the importance of strengthening moral identity and empathy in sport to reduce antisocial behavior in sport.

Consequences of Prosocial and Antisocial Behaviors

Prosocial and antisocial behaviors can have consequences for the psychological and physical well-being of the recipient (Kavussanu & Boardley, 2009). However, it is possible that these behaviors also have consequences that go beyond one's psychological and physical welfare—for example, they could influence performance, commitment to sport participation, and team functioning. Most researchers have examined outcomes or potential consequences of teammate behavior for one's teammates (e.g., Al-Yaaribi & Kavussanu, 2017, 2018). Researchers have also examined effects of some antisocial behaviors (e.g., sledging) on one's opponents (e.g., Joseph & Cramer, 2011; Ring et al., 2019). In addition, some studies have measured teammate behaviors personally experienced by individual teammates (e.g., Al-Yaaribi et al., 2016), whereas others have investigated the prevalence of these behaviors within the team, thereby referring to them as in-group antisocial behaviors or practice norms (e.g., Benson et al., 2017). It is to this research we now turn, discussing work on prosocial behavior first, followed by research on antisocial behavior.

Prosocial Behavior

Encouraging and supporting one's teammates, giving them positive and constructive feedback, and congratulating them for good play are the prosocial behaviors that tend to occur most frequently in team sport (Kavussanu, 2012; Kavussanu & Boardley, 2009; Kavussanu et al., 2009). These behaviors could have a positive impact not only on the individual athlete but also on the whole team. A range of cognitive, affective, and behavioral consequences of prosocial behavior toward teammates have been examined and are discussed in this section.

Al-Yaaribi and colleagues (2016) were the first to investigate consequences of teammate behavior for the recipient. They asked male and female adult soccer and basketball players how often they perceived their teammates engaged in prosocial behavior toward them during the match they had just played and to indicate their experiences during the match. In both samples, athletes who perceived their teammates acting prosocially toward them during the match reported more enjoyment and effort and perceived they had better performance. In addition, in the basketball players, prosocial teammate behavior was positively related to commitment both directly and indirectly via enjoyment, effort, and perceived performance. These findings were corroborated in a second study of adolescent male soccer players, with participants asked about their experiences during training and competition across the course of a season (Al-Yaaribi & Kavussanu, 2018). In addition, when these soccer players perceived that their coaches created a mastery motivational climate, the positive links between prosocial teammate behavior and both enjoyment and perceived performance were stronger. Thus, a mastery motivational climate accentuated the positive effects of prosocial teammate behavior on the recipient's enjoyment and perceived performance.

A limitation of these studies is their cross-sectional design. This limitation was addressed in an experiment that used simulated team competition in a basketball free throw shooting task (Al-Yaaribi et al., 2018). Participants were partnered with a person pretending to be the participant's teammate who enacted verbal behaviors, creating a prosocial (e.g., "you can do it"), antisocial (e.g., "you are letting me down"), or neutral (e.g., "the floor is hard") condition. The goal assigned to the two-member team was to score as many baskets as possible in two minutes, with the participant as shooter and the "teammate" collecting rebounds and returning the ball to the participant. The prosocial behavior group reported more happiness and had better basketball free throw shooting performance compared with the control group. These findings provided the first experimental evidence for the beneficial influence of prosocial behavior for one's teammates.

Other important consequences for individual and team functioning in sport are group cohesion, which consists of task and social cohesion, and collective efficacy. *Task cohesion* refers to the degree to which team members are united in working together toward achieving team goals, while *social cohesion* refers to perceptions regarding social relationships with those on the team (e.g., being friends with those on the team) (e.g., Carron et al., 1985; Eys et al., 2009). *Collective efficacy* is the shared belief among a group in its aggregate capability to organize and execute the required actions to generate given levels of achievement (Bandura, 1997). Prosocial teammate behavior positively predicted task cohesion in male and female team-sport players (Al-Yaaribi & Kavussanu, 2017), and this relationship was partly explained by positive affect, which refers to the degree to which someone feels enthusiastic, active, and alert and has high energy, full concentration, and pleasurable engagement (Watson et al., 1988). In another study, prosocial teammate behavior was positively related to both task and social cohesion, while task cohesion mediated the relationship between prosocial teammate behavior and collective efficacy (Pizzi & Stanger, 2020).

Finally, prosocial teammate behavior has implications for social identity, a concept discussed in a previous section as a predictor of prosocial behavior (Bruner et al., 2014, 2018). In a qualitative study of male and female youth ice hockey players, Bruner and colleagues (2017) found that participants believed social identity was strengthened when their teammates engaged in prosocial behaviors (e.g., helping an injured teammate off the ice, sharing a water bottle during a break) toward them. In a second study of male and female youth ice hockey players, Benson and Bruner (2018) found that experiencing more prosocial teammate behaviors on a given day was associated with stronger social identity. Taken together, these studies suggest that increasing intrateam prosocial behavior has the potential to enhance social identity.

In sum, experiencing prosocial behavior from one's teammates has been linked with desirable affective (i.e., enjoyment, positive affect, happiness), behavioral (i.e., effort, performance), and group-related (i.e., social identity, cohesion) outcomes. Thus, evidence indicating that prosocial teammate behavior can have beneficial effects on both individual and group functioning is gradually being accumulated.

Antisocial Behavior

Antisocial behavior toward one's teammates also occurs in sport (Kavussanu & Boardley, 2009), and behaviors such as arguing, swearing, verbally abusing, and showing frustration at teammate performance are included in this class of behaviors. In this section, we review research examining consequences of antisocial behavior for the recipient, starting with consequences of teammate antisocial behavior, and continuing with consequences of opponent antisocial behavior.

Consequences for Teammates

Antisocial behavior is likely to have a negative impact on both individual and team functioning. In their study of adult soccer and basketball players (discussed in the previous section), Al-Yaaribi and colleagues (2016) found a positive relationship with anger, a negative relationship with effort and perceived performance, and a negative indirect relationship between antisocial teammate behavior and performance via lower effort. In addition, lower effort and perceived performance explained a negative relationship between antisocial teammate behavior and commitment to continue playing for the team. These findings were replicated in a second study of adolescent male soccer players, who were asked about their experiences with their team across a season (Al-Yaaribi & Kavussanu, 2018). Importantly, when participants perceived a stronger performance motivational climate created by the coach, antisocial teammate behavior was a stronger negative predictor of perceived performance. In other words, performance climate accentuated the negative effect of antisocial teammate behavior on perceived performance.

Another consequence that may result from experiencing antisocial behavior from one's teammates is burnout, which pertains to the psychological, emotional, and physical withdrawal from a previously enjoyable activity in response to chronic stress (Smith, 1986). Burnout in sport has been operationalized as a higher-order construct underpinned by three subdimensions: perceived emotional and physical exhaustion, reduced sense of accomplishment, and sport devaluation (Raedeke & Smith, 2001). Al-Yaaribi and Kavussanu (2017) found that when adolescent male soccer players perceived their teammates as acting antisocially toward them, they were more likely to report burnout; the positive link between antisocial teammate behavior and burnout was partially mediated by negative affect ("a general dimension of subjective distress and unpleasurable engagement that subsumes a variety of aversive mood states, including anger, contempt, disgust, guilt, fear, and nervousness"; Watson et al., 1988, p. 1063). This study also revealed a negative association between antisocial teammate behavior and task cohesion, a finding replicated by Pizzi and Stanger (2019), who also showed negative links between antisocial teammate behavior and both social cohesion and collective efficacy in team-sport athletes. Taken together, these findings suggest that experiencing antisocial behavior from one's teammates could have adverse implications for team functioning. However, it was not possible to establish the direction of causality in these studies because of their cross-sectional nature.

In the experiment conducted with adult basketball players discussed in the previous section, Al-Yaaribi and colleagues (2018) showed that experiencing antisocial behavior from one's "teammate" increased anger and lowered happiness and attention compared with the control group during a two-minute basketball free throw shooting competition. Interestingly, performance was also better in the antisocial behavior group, a finding that contrasts with the negative relationships between antisocial teammate behavior and perceived performance reported in field studies (e.g., Al-Yaaribi & Kavussanu, 2017; Al-Yaaribi et al., 2016). One difference between this experiment and the field studies is that performance was assessed over a much shorter period. It may be that antisocial teammate behavior confers benefits for short- but not long-term performance. It is also possible that the limited existing affiliation with the (confederate) teammate in this experiment influenced performance in a positive way, whereas antisocial teammate behavior from an established teammate may result in less positive outcomes for one's performance.

The recipient's own antisocial behavior and their social identity could also be influenced by the antisocial behavior of one's teammates. In daily diary research with youth ice hockey players, increased daily frequency of experienced antisocial teammate behavior was positively associated with increases in participants' self-reported antisocial behavior toward teammates (Benson & Bruner, 2018). Further, there seemed to be a protective effect from prosocial teammate behavior. That is, the relationship between experienced and self-reported antisocial behavior toward teammates was weaker when participants reported experiencing more frequent prosocial behavior from their teammates. In addition, social identity was weaker on days participants experienced more frequent antisocial behavior from their teammates. In another study, ice hockey players who reported low or moderate frequency of antisocial behavior toward their teammates described how they felt this behavior undermined their social identity (Bruner et al., 2017). In contrast, players reporting more frequent intrateam antisocial behavior dismissed any damaging effects, possibly because they have learned to rationalize and downplay possible negative effects owing to the frequency with which they experienced this behavior. Finally, Benson and colleagues (2017) found a positive association between in-group antisocial norms and personal engagement in antisocial teammate behavior with female team-sport athletes; this effect was stronger with increased social identity.

Consequences for Opponents

Very few studies have investigated the effects of antisocial behavior on opponents. These studies have focused on a specific antisocial behavior, namely sledging, which is behavior aimed to insult or verbally intimidate the opponent in order to gain a competitive advantage (Joseph & Cramer, 2011). Sledging has been investigated in both qualitative and experimental studies, and it is this research that we review here.

Joseph and Cramer (2011) conducted semi-structured interviews with 10 elite cricket batsmen, exploring the effects and coping strategies they used. The cricketers described several negative effects of sledging, namely that it led to them being distracted, anxious, overaroused, and insulted, and that it altered their state of mind and reduced their batting ability. However, some players were able to respond positively to sledging and used coping strategies such as self-talk, routines, and expressing frustration. Interestingly, some participants felt that sledging could have a positive effect on batsmen (e.g., by increasing motivation and determination during performance). Thus, although it seems overall that sledging results in negative outcomes for recipients, some players do appear able to respond positively to it. It would be interesting in future research to examine the athlete characteristics (e.g., mental toughness) that moderate the effects of sledging on one's emotions and behavior, as well as the potential positive consequences of sledging on opponents.

Experiencing antisocial behavior from one's teammates has been positively linked with anger, negative affect, and burnout and negatively associated with effort, social identity, and cohesion. More frequent experiences of antisocial teammate behavior may also cause players to engage in more frequent antisocial acts toward teammates.

In another qualitative study, Davis and colleagues (2018) conducted semi-structured interviews with 12 professional male cricketers. Participants were asked to recall an instance where their opponent became physically or verbally aggressive toward them when they were batting, and to report the emotions they experienced in response to this behavior. They all experienced interactions during competitive matches that were aimed to disrupt their performance and felt both anger and anxiety as a result of these interactions. In addition, participants indicated they used sledging in order to disrupt concentration and induce anxiety by intimidating the batsman, and they viewed sledging as an inherent part of elite-level cricket. Similar to the findings of Joseph and Cramer (2011), some participants reported positive effects of sledging, such as increased sense of awareness and attentional focus, which resulted from the emotions experienced as a consequence of sledging. Thus, qualitative research suggests that sledging could lead to negative emotions and affect attention but also have unintentional positive consequences for the recipient.

Ring and colleagues (2019) experimentally investigated the effects of sledging on opponents' anger, attention, and basketball free throw performance. Participants were randomly assigned to either an insult (i.e., behavior designed to affront or upset the performer), a distraction (i.e., behavior aimed at drawing attention away from the task), or a control (i.e., neutral comments) condition. In each condition, a confederate acted as an opponent, enacting verbal behaviors reflecting the assigned condition. The goal was to score as many baskets as possible in 10 attempts. As anticipated, the insult condition induced more anger than the distraction and control conditions, and both the distraction and insult conditions increased distraction in comparison to the control condition. However, there were no effects on performance, a finding that does not support qualitative evidence that sledging affects one's performance (e.g., Joseph & Cramer, 2011). It is possible that sledging was perceived as not sufficiently severe to affect performance directly during this task, or participants may have employed coping strategies to deal with the sledging (e.g., Davis et al., 2018). Thus, the negative effects of sledging on performance remain to be confirmed in experimental research.

In sum, experiencing antisocial behavior from one's teammates has been positively linked with anger, negative affect, and burnout and negatively associated with effort, social identity, and cohesion. More frequent experiences of antisocial teammate behavior may also cause players to engage in more frequent antisocial acts toward teammates. Findings regarding performance vary, with cross-sectional evidence showing a negative effect on perceived performance and experimental evidence showing a positive effect on actual performance. Finally, sledging can lead opponents to be angry and distracted, or to potentially become more motivated and determined, and its effects on performance remain unclear.

Bracketed Morality

A relatively unexplored area of research in relation to prosocial and antisocial behavior in sport is *bracketed morality*, which refers to the adoption of less mature patterns of moral exchange in sport compared with daily life (Bredemeier & Shields, 1986). Drawing on their seminal work with basketball players, Bredemeier and Shields (1986) proposed that when one enters the realm of sport, the responsibility to act in a moral manner is suspended, and egocentrism becomes a valued principle. One way bracketed morality has been examined in recent studies is by investigating the degree to which prosocial and antisocial behavior in sport differs from behavior in other contexts. In these studies, the comparative context was education (i.e., university or school), and moral behavior was examined using either an adapted version of the PABSS, which measures behaviors toward teammates and opponents in sport (e.g., Kavussanu et al., 2013; Kavussanu & Ring, 2021), or hypothetical scenarios depicting situations likely to occur in sport and university contexts (Kavussanu & Ring, 2016). In this section, we discuss this research as it pertains to prosocial and antisocial behavior.

In the studies using the PABSS (Kavussanu & Boardley, 2009), it is important to reiterate that the four subscales measuring prosocial and antisocial behavior toward teammates and opponents tapped into different types of behavior, reflecting the distinct acts that are typically observed in team sport. Specifically, the prosocial teammate behaviors (e.g., congratulating a teammate) are supportive acts that are conducive to team achievement, whereas the prosocial opponent behaviors (e.g., helping an opponent off the ground) are helping acts that do not have clear achievement-related consequences for the recipient. Similarly, the antisocial teammate behaviors are verbally aggressive acts (e.g., verbally abusing a teammate), whereas the antisocial opponent behaviors are a combination of aggression (e.g., trying to injure an opponent), gamesmanship (e.g., intentionally distracting an opponent), and cheating (e.g., intentionally breaking the rules). In addition, there has been variation in the recipient of moral behavior between the two contexts. In sport, the recipient was either a teammate or an opponent; whereas in school or university, the recipient was always a classmate, because the teammate versus opponent distinction was relevant in sport but not in school or university. These differences are important to consider when interpreting the findings of this line of research. Next we discuss the findings as they pertain to prosocial behavior, followed by the findings regarding antisocial behavior.

Prosocial Behavior

In the first study to investigate the concept of bracketed morality in relation to moral behavior in sport, Kavussanu and colleagues (2013) asked university student-athletes to indicate how often they engaged in prosocial behaviors toward their teammates (e.g., encouraging, congratulating, giving positive and constructive feedback to a teammate) and opponents (e.g., helping a player off the floor, helping an injured player) in sport. Participants also indicated the frequency of engaging in these same behaviors toward their fellow students at university. In two independent samples of male and female athletes, recruited from a variety of team sports, prosocial behavior was more frequent toward teammates in sport than it was toward other students at university (e.g., more often encouraging a teammate than a student). The opposite pattern was observed for prosocial behavior toward opponents (e.g., less often helping an opponent off the floor than helping a student in need) in one of the two samples. These results were replicated in two independent samples of adolescent soccer players ranging in age from 13 to 17 years old, who reported frequency of moral behavior in sport and school throughout the soccer season and school year, respectively (Kavussanu & Ring, 2021). Importantly, context differences in prosocial behavior were consistent across all age groups as well as across males and females.

These findings point to the unifying role team sport can have on athletes. The higher prosocial behavior toward one's teammates compared with the same behavior toward other students suggests that team sport can have a positive influence on prosocial behavior. Athletes who are part of a sport team strive for the same goal, and this common purpose might lead them to act prosocially toward each other by encouraging and supporting one another. These team dynamics are not present among students at university, where there are typically no goals for which students in the same class collectively strive. It would be interesting for future research to examine common goal striving as a potential mechanism underlying the patterns of prosocial behavior revealed in athletic and academic contexts.

The findings also highlight the important role of groups in regulating moral behavior. A large body of literature indicates that the in-group versus out-group classification influences individuals' behavior (e.g., Hewstone et al., 2002). People tend to act more favorably toward members of the in-group and less favorably toward members of the out-group. According to social identity theory (Tajfel et al., 1981), being a member of a group leads one to develop a positive social identity through comparing and distinguishing the self along dimensions of value. Research suggests that relative to school or university, the competitive context of sport is likely to suppress prosocial behavior toward one's opponents, who belong to the out-group, but promote prosocial behavior toward one's teammates, who represent the in-group. Sport is a unique context, where one is typically part of a team competing against other teams. The differential findings for teammates and opponents underline the importance of this distinction when examining bracketed morality in sport.

Antisocial Behavior

The findings for antisocial behavior toward *teammates* in sport and fellow students or classmates at university or school have been less consistent in the studies discussed in the previous section. This behavior did not differ between contexts in university student-athletes competing in a variety of team sports (Kavussanu et al., 2013) or in older adolescent male soccer players (Kavussanu & Ring, 2021). However, it was less frequent in sport than school in younger male and female adolescent soccer players (Kavussanu & Ring, 2021), a finding which is in line with the in-group and out-group explanation discussed in the previous section. A limitation of this research (Kavussanu & Ring, 2021) is that participants were drawn from different age groups, rather than the same athletes being followed over time to examine changes in antisocial behavior across adolescence in the two contexts. Thus, variables specific to each age cohort may have been responsible for the different results in the two samples. Future research should attempt to replicate the present findings using a longitudinal design.

It is also possible that specific features of the context influence behavior toward teammates in sport and students in school, and differences exist in specific behaviors. This hypothesis could be investigated by presenting athletes with hypothetical situations in the two contexts and asking them to indicate the likelihood they would engage in the behavior in these situations. This methodology was used by Kavussanu and Ring (2016), who presented male and female university student-athletes with two hypothetical scenarios indicating how likely they were to criticize "a teammate who made a mistake during a regular game, which cost the team the game" and "a fellow student who made a mistake during a class presentation which cost the group a high mark" (p. 270). Participants indicated they would be less likely to criticize the teammate than the student in these hypothetical situations. It may be that achieving high marks in a class group presentation at university is more important than losing a regular game, where the stakes are not that high. Thus, circumstances surrounding the behavior are important to consider when comparing the two contexts. Further research is needed to understand antisocial behavior toward teammates and how it varies between contexts.

Antisocial behavior was more frequent toward *opponents* in sport than toward other students or classmates in male and female university athletes from a variety of team sports (Kavussanu & Ring, 2016; Kavussanu et al., 2013), in adolescent female soccer players (regardless of age), and in older adolescent male soccer players (Kavussanu & Ring, 2021). However, this behavior was less frequent in sport than school in early adolescent males.

Overall, the largest and most consistent context difference identified across samples was in antisocial behavior toward opponents compared with the same behavior toward students or classmates. The reasons for this discrepancy were further explored by considering factors that varied between contexts. Moral disengagement was higher in sport compared to university and school, and this difference partially explained the context difference in athletes' antisocial behavior (Kavussanu & Ring, 2021; Kavussanu et al., 2013). Thus, participants may have acted more antisocially toward their opponents in sport than toward their classmates at school or fellow students at university *because of* their higher moral disengagement in sport relative to school or university (cf. Kavussanu et al., 2013). Perhaps certain features of sport (e.g., the presence of officials) facilitate certain mechanisms of moral disengagement (e.g., displacement of responsibility) in this context. These findings suggest that by intervening on moral disengagement we may be able to reduce the gap in antisocial behavior between the two contexts. However, it is important to remember that these findings are from cross-sectional studies.

In sum, bracketed morality exists in the context of team sport. Perhaps unsurprisingly, team-sport athletes tend to act more prosocially toward their teammates and more antisocially toward their opponents in sport than they do toward their fellow students or classmates at school or university; they also tend to behave more prosocially toward their fellow students at school or university than they do toward their opponents in sport.

Future Research Directions

In the past 10 years, much progress has been made in our understanding of factors that could facilitate prosocial and inhibit antisocial behavior in sport. In addition, recent findings of studies investigating the potential consequences of these behaviors underline the importance of this area of research for both individual and team functioning. Despite the progress made, there is much that remains to be done in future research.

One limitation of the evidence base is that most of the research has been cross-sectional. This limits our understanding of the causal direction of relationships, as well as the time course required for effects to be manifested. More studies employing experimental and longitudinal designs are needed. Such designs would allow us to answer more advanced research questions, thus enhancing our understanding of the processes governing moral behavior in sport. For example, although variables such as moral disengagement have been examined as an explanatory (or mediating) factor in many studies, the cross-sectional design of these studies can only provide evidence that the tested models are consistent with the data supporting indirect relationships. Longitudinal studies with three data collection time points and rigorously designed experimental studies that manipulate both the predictor and the mediator would provide stronger evidence for causality. In addition, more research is needed to design field-based interventions to increase prosocial behavior and decrease antisocial behavior in sport (see Cheon et al., 2018). These studies will help determine whether the variables measured in cross-sectional and longitudinal studies, or manipulated in laboratory experiments, can be manipulated in real-world settings and influence moral behavior.

Studies are needed to enhance our understanding of the effects of antisocial teammate behavior on athletes' performance, in light of some findings showing negative effects of this behavior on perceived performance in cross-sectional research (Al-Yaaribi et al., 2016) but positive effects in experimental research (Al-Yaaribi et al., 2018). Longitudinal and experimental studies using objective measures of performance could help elucidate the inconsistency in these findings. This should also address common method bias (Podsakoff et al., 2003), another limitation evident in cross-sectional studies, where the same participants complete measures of both the predictor and the outcome variables. The shared method used to measure predictors and outcomes could result in an inflated correlation between the variables. It would also be interesting to investigate whether the task duration and the frequency and intensity of teammate behaviors moderate the effects of antisocial teammate behavior on performance. For example, long-term frequency of antisocial teammate behavior could lead to extreme anger responses, which in turn may impair performance. Such effects may not result from isolated incidents of antisocial behavior toward one's teammates.

Researchers could also investigate moderators of previously identified relationships. It would be interesting to examine whether the relationships between prosocial and antisocial behaviors, and their predictors and outcomes, are influenced by other variables such as gender, sport type, and features of the social environment, such as coach behavior. For example, in young athletes who may be more sensitive to peer criticism, antisocial teammate behavior may have more profound effects on enjoyment and sport commitment than it would have on older players. Prosocial teammate behavior may also have stronger effects on enjoyment, effort, and performance in team sports than individual sports, where interactions are more frequent among players and a part of both competition and training. Researchers could also examine the role of the big five personality factors (i.e., agreeableness, conscientiousness, extraversion, openness, and neuroticism) on moral behavior in sport and whether certain features of the social environment moderate any relationships between certain dispositional variables and moral behavior. For instance, in environments where antisocial behavior is prevalent, the suppressing effect of empathy on antisocial behavior could be attenuated, similar to the findings for aggression in males under conditions of high provocation (e.g., Stanger et al., 2016).

Although some studies have investigated coach behavior in relation to moral behavior (e.g., Bolter & Weiss, 2012), other aspects of coaching behavior could also be examined, such as ethical leadership, manifested in the degree to which coaches act in an ethical manner and treat players with respect. This style of leadership refers to normatively appropriate conduct that is shown through interpersonal relationships and actions, and the promotion of this type of conduct to followers (Brown et al., 2005). To be perceived as an ethical leader, one must be seen as both a moral person (i.e., principled, respectful of others, honest, caring, trustworthy, and open to input) and a moral manager, by setting and communicating ethical standards, and holding others accountable when those standards are violated (Trevino et al., 2003). It would be interesting to investigate the relationship between ethical leadership and moral behavior in sport.

Finally, more research is needed to understand the effects of sledging, a form of antisocial behavior, on athletes' performance. Although sledging is meant to have a negative effect on performance, the research evidence so far has not provided firm support for this hypothesis, and it is not clear whether the null findings are due to methodological limitations (i.e., the intensity of sledges) or because sledging simply does not influence performance. More research is needed to further understand the effects of sledging on performance and whether the emotions (e.g., anger) it elicits have a negative or even a positive effect on performance (e.g., Davis et al., 2018; Ring et al., 2019).

Practical Implications

A range of practical implications for coaches, physical education teachers, parents, and other key stakeholders involved in sport can be offered based on the research reviewed in this chapter. Coaches and physical education teachers who wish to promote prosocial behavior and deter antisocial behavior in athletes could create a motivational climate that is mastery oriented and autonomy supportive. They could reward effort, recognize self-improvement, offer private rather than public feedback, and provide athletes with choices and opportunities to take initiative and be involved in decision making. At the same time, coaches should avoid behaviors that could promote peer or intrateam rivalry or behaviors that overtly pressure and manipulate athletes to think and behave in preconceived ways, such as intimidation (e.g., reliance on punishments) and guilt induction.

Coaches could also try to strengthen empathy and moral identity in their athletes. Empathy could be facilitated by tasks that assist in understanding the perspective of others, how others may feel, and how our actions may influence the psychological and physical well-being of others. Coaches and other stakeholders could create a caring environment where athletes feel supported and psychologically safe to share their thoughts and feelings (e.g., Gano-Overway et al., 2009). To strengthen moral identity, coaches could emphasize the importance of being a moral sportsperson, such as involving athletes in the development of appropriate codes of conduct about how people should behave and support one another. By clearly defining what are desirable and inappropriate behaviors, coaches can encourage athletes to engage in, or avoid, certain behaviors.

Coaches, athletes, and parents should model prosocial behaviors frequently, helping others to vicariously experience the behaviors and the positive consequences that stem from them. They should also model reacting calmly when they are the recipients of antisocial behavior, thus refraining from antisocial behavior even in pressing circumstances. Failing to do so may suggest that antisocial behavior is acceptable in certain situations. Sport governing bodies could also consider including modules on promoting intrateam moral behavior within coach education programs, potentially promoting coaching behaviors such as those described within this section of the chapter.

Summary

Prosocial and antisocial behaviors are behaviors that can have positive or negative consequences for the recipient's psychological and physical welfare. These acts are common in sport and can be directed toward teammates and opponents. Task orientation, mastery climate, autonomous motivation, and autonomy-supportive climate are some of the factors that have been most consistently and positively associated with prosocial behavior in sport, with stronger relationships evidenced with behavior toward teammates. Ego orientation, performance climate, controlled motivation, and controlling climate are some of the factors most consistently linked with antisocial behavior in sport. Moral disengagement has been identified as a potential mediator of the effects of these variables on antisocial behavior, with stronger effects for behavior toward opponents. Prosocial and antisocial behaviors also have important consequences for the recipient. Prosocial behavior experienced from one's teammates can lead to positive affective behavioral and cognitive consequences, whereas the opposite pattern is true for antisocial teammate behavior. Therefore, aiming to promote prosocial and deter antisocial behaviors could facilitate intrateam functioning, well-being, and performance.

DISCUSSION QUESTIONS

1. Define prosocial behavior and antisocial behavior in sport, and identify some examples of each type of behavior toward teammates and opponents.
2. Which factors could promote prosocial behavior in sport?
3. Which factors could promote antisocial behavior in sport? Which factors could inhibit or reduce such behavior?
4. What are some of the main outcomes associated with prosocial and antisocial teammate behavior for the recipient in sport?
5. What are some possible explanations for the inconsistent findings of research examining performance as an outcome for the recipient of antisocial teammate behavior?
6. What are some ways in which coaches could promote prosocial and reduce antisocial behavior in their athletes?

23

Environmental and Sociocultural Influences on Resilience in Competitive Sport

Mustafa Sarkar, PhD, and Sally J. Hilton, DCPsych

LEARNING OBJECTIVES

On completion of this chapter, the reader should have the following:

- Understanding of how resilience has been defined and conceptualized and ability to critically reflect on its associated drawbacks and advantages
- Ability to discuss theoretical models of individual and team resilience, specifically focusing on environmental and sociocultural influences
- Ability to describe and evaluate research regarding resilience in competitive sport
- Ability to identify evidence-based avenues for future research in the context of environmental and sociocultural influences
- Ability to discuss evidence-based implications for applied practice in terms of helping coaches develop resilience

Why is it that some athletes and teams are able to withstand the pressures of competitive sport and attain peak performances, whereas others succumb to the demands and underperform? The study of resilience aims to address this question. Resilience and its development have arguably become one of the most talked about topics in competitive sport in recent years. Often after major sporting events, athletes offer examples of the significant role of resilience in performing under pressure. In support of this statement, the importance of resilience was emphasized in the Duty of Care in Sport UK government review published by Baroness Grey-Thompson in 2017. Specifically, in the section on mental welfare, the report stated that "the routine element of elite sport, where the regimen is one of continuous training, performance, and selection, brings significant mental resilience challenges for both participants and coaches" (p. 22), and for those on a high-performance pathway, "mental resilience is not something that all participants and coaches automatically have and this should be developed with the same consideration that physical resilience is built" (p. 23). An interesting observation within this latter statement is the implied assumption of locating responsibility of resilience development within the individual (i.e., resilience is something participants should "have"), with limited consideration given to the environmental and sociocultural conditions surrounding the individual (see Ungar, 2008, 2011, 2012).

Despite the straw man's argument that resilience relates only to cognitive-affective processes manifested in an individual's behaviors, scholars have repeatedly emphasized the importance and impact of environmental and sociocultural factors (see, e.g., Fletcher & Sarkar, 2013; Morgan et al., 2015; Sarkar, 2018; Sarkar & Hilton, 2020). Drawing on the burgeoning body of research in this area, in this chapter we review the research on resilience in competitive sport, focusing on environmental and sociocultural influences. Specifically, we first outline definitional, conceptual, and theoretical issues in relation to both individual and team resilience, before providing an overview of resilience research in relation to athletes, teams, and coaches. We go on to identify areas for future research before concluding with implications for applied practice.

Individual Resilience: Definitions, Concepts, and Theories

At the individual level, numerous definitions of resilience have been proposed in the psychology research literature based on alternative conceptualizations of resilience as a trait or as a process (Fletcher & Sarkar, 2013). When resilience is conceived as a trait, it has been suggested that it represents a constellation of characteristics that enable individuals to adapt to the circumstances they encounter (Connor & Davidson, 2003). To illustrate, psychological resilience has been defined as "the positive role of individual differences in people's response to stress and adversity" (Rutter, 1987, p. 316). Such individual differences were found to include personal qualities such as optimism, self-esteem, and problem solving (Rutter, 1985). In relation to this trait conceptualization, these individual differences, which are more commonly referred to as *protective factors* in the resilience literature, have been examined extensively by scholars seeking to identify the qualities of resilient individuals (see Luthar, 2006; Masten & Reed, 2002). However, the danger of this trait notion is that resilience becomes a "dirty word." To illustrate, in the context of the United Kingdom's National Health Service (NHS), Oliver (2017) argued the following:

> There's nothing wrong with helping doctors build "resilience" . . . but absorbing any unacceptably and avoidably negative conditions makes resilience a dirty word. It shifts the blame and responsibility for doctors' struggles away from what are often over-politicised, understaffed, underfunded, badly organised systems and onto individuals. (p. 358)

Indeed, the emphasis on individual resilience has been argued to support a neoliberal agenda (Joseph, 2013) in which individuals are made responsible for their personal well-being while structural inequalities (such as poverty, racism, and lack of access to resources) are disregarded, rendering individuals "responsible for dealing with collective challenges that should be dealt with by collective structures, such as the state" (van Breda, 2018, p. 7). Friedman and Robbins (2012) cite the influence of positive psychology (e.g., Peterson & Seligman, 2004) in presenting resilience as a value-free virtue, noting the unintended negative consequences of resilience when it is assumed to be an individual character strength, decontextualized from the circumstances in which it is demonstrated. They draw attention to the program teaching resilience in the U.S. Army, which according to the authors, risks creating "desensitized warfighters who are immune to appropriately catastrophizing the horrors of war, which are truly catastrophic, and trained instead to compartmentalize their emotions to obediently perform the bidding of extant power structures" (p. 98). Such a critique highlights ways that resilience can be misused to perpetuate existing power structures and put the onus on individuals to adapt to, rather than resist, intolerable circumstances.

Mahdiani and Ungar (2021) develop this line of argument and question if resilience is always adaptive and functional or whether it has the potential to be maladaptive, concluding that "in particular contexts, resilience can be wrongly deployed as an inducement to tolerate disparity and inequality, accepting the deferral of demands for change, or as an excuse to assign individuals who lack power the responsibility to change their lives" (p. 151).

In contrast to the trait perspective—which locates the responsibility of resilience within the individual—resilience has also been defined as a "dynamic process encompassing positive adaptation within the context of significant adversity" (Luthar et al., 2000, p. 543). This *process conceptualization of resilience* recognizes it as a capacity that develops over time in the context of person–environment interactions (Egeland et al., 1993). Specifically, the process conceptualization of resilience recognizes that the effects of protective factors will vary contextually (from situation to situation) and temporally (throughout a situation and across an individual's life span). Thus, although an individual may react positively to adversity at one point in their life, it does not mean the person will react in the same way to stressors at other points in their life (cf. Davydov et al., 2010; Rutter, 2006). As Rutter (1981) observed, "If circumstances change, resilience alters" (p. 317).

As previously mentioned, an important issue when examining resilience is the environmental and sociocultural context in which an individual operates. Some researchers have critiqued the construct of resilience on the basis of its failure to adequately acknowledge contextual and cultural factors in terms of both understanding what represents a positive outcome as well as the contribution of contextual conditions to such outcomes. To illustrate, it has been suggested that understandings of positive adaptation reflect culturally valued and normative understandings of what represents a good outcome (e.g., Kaplan, 2013) while overlooking outcomes that may not conform to societal norms of healthy functioning but may nonetheless represent resilience in the absence of conventionally prosocial options. For example, Ungar (2004a) notes the potential for "hidden resilience" among troubled youth, whereby attempts at adaptation may be culturally nonnormative but nonetheless represent attempts at overcoming adversity. Ungar (2004b) argues for a socially constructed understanding of resilience, which challenges dominant discourses on what constitutes an acceptable expression of health and involves "less focus on predetermined outcomes to judge the success of growth trajectories and more emphasis on understanding the functionality of behaviour when alternative pathways to development are blocked" (Ungar, 2011, p. 8).

Resilience can be misused to perpetuate existing power structures and put the onus on individuals to adapt to, rather than resist, intolerable circumstances.

Adopting a socially constructed view of resilience recognizes, therefore, that there is no universal or objective determination around what represents positive adaptation and that such determinations are dependent upon what is contextually desirable. In sport, for example, the desired (and therefore resilient) outcome typically relates to performance indicators, such as maintaining performance under pressure or after a setback (Fletcher & Sarkar, 2012). However, where the desired outcome is mental well-being, other indicators will be used to demonstrate resilience. For example, leaving a toxic sport environment may be regarded as resilient when participation is detrimental to mental health, whereas staying in spite of such conditions may be regarded as resilient if the desired outcome is understood solely in terms of performance. As such, what is understood as resilience in a particular context reflects what is valued in that context.

In line with the process conceptualization of resilience, a body of work produced by Ungar and colleagues at Dalhousie University has explored a social ecological perspective. This view targets the social and physical environment as the locus of resources for growth and regards resilience as dependent on the capacity of the individual's physical and social ecology to potentiate positive development under stress (Ungar, 2012). Ungar argues that social ecological factors such as family, school, neighborhood, community services, and cultural practices are equally as influential as individual psychological factors when people face adversity. Such a perspective supports a shift in focus from the individual toward the environment. Within the sport context, this challenges organizations to examine their own practices and the availability of resources within the environment to support resilient outcomes. This perspective also invites organizations to recognize the ways sport cultures can influence how resilience is understood and operationalized locally. Research has highlighted sporting subcultures that promote hypermasculine ideals and denial of vulnerability among athletes (e.g., Brownrigg et al., 2018; Coulter et al., 2016) and coaches (e.g., Olusoga & Kenttä, 2017). It is therefore important that the imperative to demonstrate resilience does not exclude the expression of vulnerability or compel individuals to adapt to toxic environments. To sum, from a definitional and conceptual perspective, as Sarkar and Page (2022) argued, before developing resilience in competitive sport, it is important for athletes, coaches, and practitioners to ensure clarity of what resilience is and is not, and

> it is especially worth noting that rather than being a fixed trait that individuals either have or don't have (which puts the individual at the heart of resilience development), resilience is a context-specific capacity that can be developed and trained over time (which recognizes the role of the environment in developing resilience). (p. 41)

From a theoretical perspective, two models of individual resilience in athletes have been developed, namely the conceptual model of sport resilience (Galli & Vealey, 2008) and the grounded theory of psychological resilience and optimal sport performance (Fletcher & Sarkar, 2012). Galli and Vealey (2008) interviewed college and professional athletes about their perceptions and experiences of resilience using Richardson (2002) and Richardson and colleagues' (1990) resiliency model as a guiding theoretical framework. According to the model, the resilience process begins with a state of biopsychospiritual homeostasis, or a comfort zone, where a person is in balance physically, mentally, and spiritually. Disruption from this homeostatic state occurs if an individual has insufficient resources (i.e., protective factors) to buffer them against stressors, adversities, or life events. In time, an individual who has experienced disruption will adjust and begin the reintegration process. Within Galli and Vealey's study, five general dimensions emerged that described the resilience experience of athletes:

- Breadth and duration of the resilience process
- Agitation (i.e., the use of a variety of coping strategies to deal with a wide range of unpleasant emotions and mental struggles)
- Personal resources (e.g., positivity, determination, competitiveness, commitment, maturity, persistence, and passion for the sport)
- Sociocultural influences (e.g., social support and cultural factors)
- Positive outcomes (e.g., learning, perspective, realization of support, and motivation to help others)

Based on these dimensions, a conceptual model of sport resilience was created. In the context of the present chapter, interestingly, Galli and Vealey (2008) noted that athletes' perceptions of their experiences support the notion of resilience as an ever-evolving process of interactions between the person and their environment (Egeland et al., 1993; Luthar & Zelazo, 2003). The model generated from this study refutes the popular notion of resilience as a trait (i.e., athletes who "have" resilience) and expands the concept to include environmental influences as well as internal processes. However, in terms of a critical evaluation of the study, Richardson's model is not without its limitations, including the linear stage framework evident within its structure, the absence of meta-cognitive processes (i.e., one's ability to evaluate their own thoughts) and meta-emotive processes (i.e., one's ability to evaluate their own feelings), and its bias toward coping-oriented processes (cf. Fletcher & Sarkar, 2013).

To address the limitations of Galli and Vealey's (2008) work, several groups of researchers (e.g., Fletcher & Sarkar, 2012; White & Bennie, 2015) have employed inductive qualitative designs to explore resilience free from the constraints of a preconceived model. To illustrate, Fletcher and Sarkar (2012) developed a grounded theory of psychological resilience and optimal sport performance. They interviewed 12 Olympic gold medalists to explore and explain the relationship between psychological resilience and optimal sport performance. Stressors identified ranged from ongoing daily demands (e.g., balancing work and training) to significant life events (e.g., bereavement) and were classified under three main categories: *competitive* (e.g., loss of form), *organizational* (e.g., sport politics), and *personal* (e.g., family). The findings revealed that numerous psychological factors (relating to a positive personality, motivation, confidence, focus, and perceived social support) protected the world's best athletes from the potential negative effect of stressors by influencing the processes of challenge appraisal and meta-cognitions. These constructive cognitive reactions promoted facilitative responses that led to the realization of optimal sport performance. In the context of the present chapter, it is worth noting that all the participants described prolonged periods in their sporting careers during which they were required to withstand the pressures they encountered. This supports the conception of resilience as a "dynamic process encompassing positive adaptation within the context of significant adversity" (Luthar et al., 2000, p. 543).

Overall, the grounded theory supports elements of both process and trait conceptualizations of resilience. Furthermore, in contrast to the majority of existing theories, including the conceptual model of sport resilience (Galli & Vealey, 2008), Fletcher and Sarkar's (2012) findings emphasize that the influence of psychological factors should be conceived in relation to the specific stressors encountered and the context in which they arise. Since high achievers actively seek to engage with challenging situations that present opportunities for them to raise their performance level, the authors proposed that research and practice in this area should pay careful attention to the matching of psychological factors with the environmental demands.

Team Resilience: Definitions, Concepts, and Theories

Resilience researchers in various domains of psychology have shifted their attention from individuals toward the study of groups and teams (see, e.g., Alliger et al., 2015; Bennett et al., 2010; Morgan et al., 2013, 2015). Reinforcing the need to consider group-level resilience, Bennett and colleagues (2010) remarked that "resilience may be viewed as much a social factor (existing in teams and groups) as an individual trait" (p. 225). In a similar fashion to the construct of individual resilience, a variety of definitions of team resilience have been proposed in the psychology research literature. West and colleagues (2009) defined team resilience as "the capacity to bounce back from failure, setbacks, conflicts, or any other threat to well-being that a team may experience" (p. 253). Elsewhere, in a review of team resilience exploring how teams flourish under pressure, Alliger and colleagues (2015) defined team resilience as "the capacity of a team to withstand and overcome stressors in a manner that enables sustained performance; it helps teams handle and bounce back from challenges that can endanger their cohesiveness and performance" (p. 177). More recently, Gucciardi and colleagues (2018) defined team resilience "as an emergent outcome characterised by the trajectory of a team's functioning, following adversity exposure, as one that is largely unaffected or returns to normal levels after some degree of deterioration in functioning" (p. 729).

Although there is variability in how team resilience is defined and conceptualized, a recent scoping review by Chapman and colleagues (2020) noted broad agreement among scholars in the features of team resilience as encompassing the presence of some form of disturbance in the form of stressors, setbacks, pressure, challenge, or adversity, and that definitions also addressed team functioning in the face of such demands. Team functioning was largely operationalized through references to the maintenance of team performance, although in some cases a more holistic understanding was offered to include well-being or thriving.

In the specific context of elite sport, based on focus group discussions with elite team members from a range of sports, Morgan and colleagues (2013) defined team resilience as "a dynamic, psychosocial process which protects a group of individuals from the potential negative effect of stressors they collectively encounter. It comprises of processes whereby team members use their individual and collective resources to positively adapt when experiencing adversity" (p. 552). In line with the process conceptualization of individual resilience, it is important to highlight that team resilience was described as a dynamic phenomenon since it was regarded as, for example, being "dependent upon what time of season it is" or whether there was "an injury in the team." The majority of participants in this study also described how team resilience arose from a variety of social interactions. To illustrate, during challenging times, the "support" or "friendship" aspect was influenced by "everybody along the chain" and dependent on "what kind of leadership there is." Most participants also emphasized how resilience was typically a changing process because of the "ups and downs" of "riding the roller coaster of sport." All of these elements were captured within the definition as "a dynamic, psychosocial process" supporting the process conceptualization, and capturing the relational aspects, of team resilience.

In terms of team resilience theory, a number of researchers have noted the emergent nature of team resilience. Emergent team states are described by Ilgen and colleagues (2005) as "constructs that develop over the life of the team and impact team outcomes" (p. 520). Emergent states differ from team processes since they do not describe the nature of team member interactions. Rather, they are defined as "constructs that characterize properties of the team that are typically dynamic in nature and vary as a function of team context, inputs, processes, and outcomes" (Marks et al., 2001, p. 357). As such, rather than representing team interaction or actions that lead toward outcomes, emergent states are understood as products of team experiences (including team processes) describing cognitive, motivational, and affective states of teams.

Although not sport specific, numerous theoretical models of team resilience offering an emergent state perspective have been proposed. Such models attempt to integrate divergent conceptualizations of team resilience and offer multilevel perspectives that consider the relationship between individual-level and team-level resilience. For example, Bowers and colleagues (2017) draw upon the input-mediator-output-input (IMOI) model (Ilgen et al., 2005) to organize findings from the research literature into inputs, mediators (i.e., team processes and emergent states), and outputs associated with resilience. The authors propose inputs from the individual, team, and organizational levels (e.g., optimism, norms, diffused power) that drive team processes (e.g., planning, leadership, adaptability, monitoring, and shared decision making). Team processes are argued to lead to first-order emergent states including team cohesion, collective efficacy, and shared mental models. These emergent states combine to enable team resilience, which allows the team to achieve positive outcomes (e.g., psychological health, error avoidance, goal attainment) and buffer negative outcomes. As such, the authors argue for a conceptualization of team resilience as a second-order emergent state (see figure 23.1), suggesting it arises as a result of other emergent states and team processes rather than being a process in itself.

Gucciardi and colleagues (2018) extend Bowers and colleagues' (2017) work by considering the interrelationships of key factors (e.g., inputs, processes, emergent states, and outcomes) in terms of *how* and *why* they interact to foster the emergence of team resilience. In other words, the authors seek to go beyond identification of the "ingredients" of resilience to consider the "recipe." They propose a multilevel model of team resilience, suggesting it originates in the resources of individual team members and emerges as a team-level construct through dynamic person–situation interactions that are triggered by adverse events. While the authors view team resilience as an emergent outcome, they note that such an outcome is shaped by traits, capacities (e.g., human capital resources), and processes and attempt to explain how these components contribute to the emergence of team resilience in one unifying framework. Within this model, adversity is the catalyst for the emergence process, with individual inputs (human capital resources) and team-level inputs (such as leadership, norms, and shared mental models) transformed into outcomes via team processes such as planning, reflection, and coordination. The nature of the relevant human capital resources (knowledge, skills, abilities, other characteristics) depends on the objective of the team, and therefore the salient inputs for team resilience emergence will be context specific. The authors noted they would expect some human capital resources to generalize across contexts, but not all, given differences in the nature of team objectives and adversities faced.

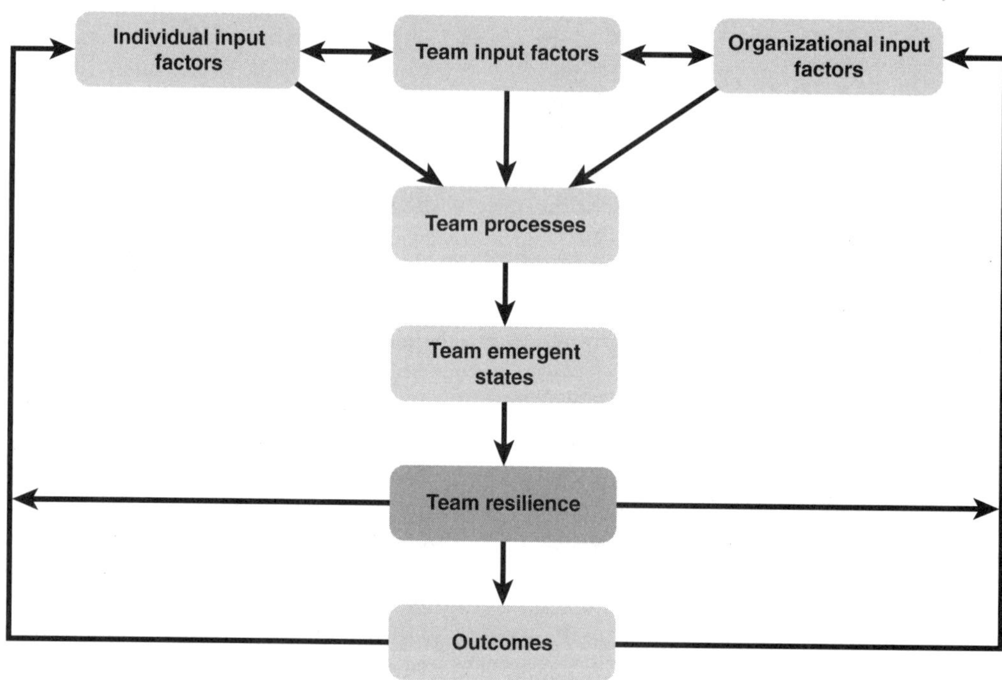

FIGURE 23.1 Team resilience as a second-order emergent state: a theoretical model.

Reprinted from C. Bowers, C. Kreutzer, J. Cannon-Bowers, and J. Lamb, "Team Resilience as a Second-Order Emergent State: A Theoretical Model and Research Directions," *Frontiers in Psychology* 8, (2017): 1360. Distributed under the terms of the Creative Commons Attribution 4.0 International License (http://creativecommons.org/licenses/by/4.0/).

A subsequent model proposed by Hartwig and colleagues (2020) aligns with and builds upon Gucciardi and colleagues' (2018) conceptual work, which also explains team resilience as an emergent team state arising from dynamic team interactions in response to adversity. Drawing upon multilevel theory (Kozlowski & Klein, 2000) and the IMOI framework (Ilgen et al., 2005), Hartwig and colleagues offer an integrative multilevel model of team resilience. In terms of input factors, the authors include enablers at the *individual* level (e.g., communication skills, expertise, resilience) and *team* level (e.g., team adaptability, team member relationship, group structure), as well as *contextual factors* (e.g., leadership, organizational culture). Resilient team processes are understood to emerge from these input factors. These include communication, cooperation, and coordination as well as minimizing, managing, and mending behaviors (categories drawn from Alliger et al., 2015), showing that different kinds of adversity management behaviors are required at different times. The authors highlight a number of mediating team states (including psychological safety and collective efficacy) that sit between inputs and resilient outcomes, with desirable outcomes including health, performance, and team functioning. The authors suggest a number of mechanisms for cross-level effects between individual and team resilience, suggesting team members' individual resilience may function as an antecedent of team resilience and that, conversely, team resilience may operate as a resource for team members' individual resilience. They suggest individual resilience supports team resilience through contributing to team member resources, as well as strengthening each other's resilience through social learning, with a shared perception of team resilience enhancing individual self-efficacy. They also argue that the group may serve as a social resource and provide social identity.

An emergent conceptualization of team resilience puts the focus on identifying the salient context-specific inputs and processes from which resilience emerges as a by-product.

In sum, an emergent conceptualization of team resilience puts the focus on identifying the salient context-specific inputs and processes from which resilience emerges as a by-product. As such, although not sport specific, such models have the potential to be applied to competitive sport contexts. However, while these models highlight the interactional processes that are essential in transforming individual resources into team resources, they offer limited consideration of the features of the environment that contribute to team resilience emergence.

Research in Competitive Sport: Individual Resilience and Sociocultural Influences

In terms of individual resilience research in sport, there has been varied empirical evidence regarding the impact of sociocultural influences. Mummery and colleagues (2004) explored the impact of three protective factors (self-concept, social support, coping style) against three performance-related outcomes (i.e., initially successful performance; resilient performance involving an initial failure followed by subsequent success; nonresilient performance involving an initial failure followed by subsequent failure) in a national swimming championship. In terms of social support, interestingly, findings revealed that resilient performers had lower perceptions of social support than the other two groups. This finding is contrary to predictions that would arise from existing resilience research in the domains of general and sport psychology. The authors noted that the resilient performers were not lacking in perceived social support, recording a mean score of 4.5 out of a possible 6 on the MSPSS significant others scale (Zimet et al., 1988). Rather, the score by the resilient performers group was simply lower than that of the other two groups. Thus, a conclusion that a lack of social support leads to resilient performance would be incorrect.

Instead, the authors noted we should look for reasons why the nonresilient group reported unexpectedly high levels of social support. It may be that the measure of social support revealed a certain level of dependence in the participant. Specifically, since the competition in question occurred at a site geographically removed from the majority of participants' homes, it is possible that the nonresilient participants did not have immediate access to the social support they reported. It may be that the competitors reporting less perceived social support were able to act more independently at a competition where family, friends, and significant others may not have been in attendance. Although this study provided an initial insight into resilience in sport performers, it is worth noting that the research focused on a limited number of psychosocial characteristics (self-concept, social support, coping style) that precluded participants from providing a broader insight into the trait and process elements of resilience.

Taking a more holistic approach to resilience inquiry, Galli and Vealey (2008) explored athletes' perceptions and experiences of resilience. From the five general dimensions that described the resilience experience of the athletes (described earlier), sociocultural influences (including social support and cultural factors) were an important underlying factor that seemed to influence the athletes' resilience process. Supportive others facilitated (and in some cases hindered) the resilience process. The presence of support (or the lack thereof) appeared to strongly influence athletes' ability to successfully cope with their unpleasant feelings. In addition, cultural factors were also evident for the two African American athletes in the study. Specifically, these athletes cited race as being a significant obstacle for them at various points in their lives, and subsequently bolstering the personal resources they used to deal with adversity.

Building on Galli and Vealey's (2008) study, Fletcher and Sarkar (2012) sought to explore and explain the relationship between psychological resilience and optimal sport performance. Results indicated that numerous psychological factors (including perceived social support) protected the world's best athletes from the potential negative effect of stressors by influencing their challenge appraisal and meta-cognitions (described earlier). Olympic champions perceived that high-quality social support was available to them, including support from family, coaches, teammates, and support staff. This finding, taken together with those of previous investigations (e.g., Freeman & Rees, 2009, 2010), demonstrates the stress-buffering effects of perceived social support and suggests it is an important aspect of resilience in elite sport. The study indicated that trust and respect formed the basis of perceived social support for the various social agents, particularly during the latter stages of athletes' careers when such relationships had been established.

Using quantitative methods, Lu and colleagues (2016) examined the conjunctive effects of athletes' resilience and coaches' social support on the relationship between life stress and burnout in 218 student-athletes participating in team and individual sports. Findings revealed that resilience and coaches' social support conjunctively moderated the stress–burnout relationship. Specifically, the interaction of athletes' resilience with coaches' informational and tangible social support moderated athletes' stress–burnout relationship in high and low life stress conditions. Under low life stress, athletes with high resilience but low informational support, or low resilience but high informational support, were less prone to burnout than those who are both low in resilience and informational social support. As to coaches' tangible social support, there were two conjunctive moderations. In the high life stress condition, athletes who were both high in resilience and tangible support were less susceptible to burnout than those with high resilience but low tangible support. However, in the low life stress condition, findings revealed that athletes with high resilience but low tangible support were less prone to burnout than those low in both resilience and tangible support. To apply their research and specifically to facilitate social support, the authors noted that sport professionals should incorporate different sources of social support, such as coaches, parents, teachers, and peers, as well as different types of social support, such as informational, emotional, tangible, and esteem social support, into their system. They also suggested that sport professionals should help athletes by matching specific types of social support with specific stressors (cf. Rees & Hardy, 2004).

To advance our understanding of individual resilience in competitive sport, there exists an urgent need to develop a sport-specific measure of resilience (Sarkar, 2014; Sarkar & Fletcher, 2013). From a research perspective, one of the most common scales used to measure resilience in athletes is the Connor-Davidson Resilience Scale (CD-RISC; Connor & Davidson, 2003). Although the CD-RISC has sound psychometric properties in terms of reliability and validity (Gonzalez et al., 2016; Gucciardi et al., 2011) and has been used in the competitive sport context (see, e.g., Lu et al., 2016), it considers only generic resilient qualities and not how these attributes come to the fore in specific contexts (Gonzalez et al., 2016; Gucciardi et al., 2011; Sarkar & Fletcher, 2013).

Research in Competitive Sport: Team Resilience and Relational Influences

In terms of team resilience research in sport, there is a growing body of empirical evidence highlighting the impact and importance of relational influences. As noted, Morgan and colleagues (2013) conducted the first study of team resilience in sport. In addition to developing a definition of team resilience, the study also identified the resilient characteristics of elite sport teams: group structure (i.e., conventions that shape group norms and values), mastery approaches (i.e., shared attitudes and behaviors that promote an emphasis on team improvement), social capital (i.e., the existence of high-quality interactions and caring relationships within the team), and collective efficacy (i.e., the team's shared beliefs in its ability to perform a task). Emphasizing the importance of relational influences on team resilience, the authors concluded that these characteristics are a distinct set of resources peculiar to groups, suggesting individual resilience does not necessarily guarantee resilience at the group level. Indeed, the results support Luthar's (2006) claim that "resilience rests, fundamentally, on relationships" (p. 780) and show that this is particularly pertinent for teams seeking to excel at the highest levels of sport. Morgan and colleagues went on to argue that because of "the contextual and temporal nature of team resilience, future studies should aim to identify the processes that underpin the resilience characteristics" (p. 558). To address this gap in our understanding of team resilience, Morgan and colleagues (2015) subsequently explored the psychosocial processes underpinning team resilience in elite sport. Using narrative inquiry, they analyzed the autobiographies of eight members of the 2003 England rugby union World Cup–winning team. Findings revealed five main psychosocial processes underpinning team resilience: transformational leadership, shared team leadership, team learning, social identity, and positive emotions. The results indicate that these processes enabled the England rugby team to effectively use their cognitive, affective, and relational resources to act as leverage points for team resilience when facing stressors.

Findings revealed five main psychosocial processes underpinning team resilience: transformational leadership, shared team leadership, team learning, social identity, and positive emotions.

As such, research investigating team resilience in elite sport has begun to describe what resilient teams look like (i.e., their characteristics) and how they function (i.e., their processes). However, less is known about the psychosocial enablers and cues that stimulate such mechanisms and the associated pathways to team resilience (Morgan et al., 2017; Wagstaff et al., 2016). In their discussion of future research directions, Morgan and colleagues (2015) proposed that "creative qualitative approaches such as ethnography offer intriguing possibilities to study 'first-hand' the underlying team resilience mechanisms . . . and how they are developed" (p. 99). Thus, through prolonged fieldwork, Morgan and colleagues (2019) conducted a season-long (11 months) ethnography to explore the psychosocial enablers and strategies that promote the development of team resilience within a high-level sport team. The sample consisted of a leading English national league–winning semiprofessional rugby union team. Multiple data collection methods were employed (i.e., observation, interviewing, field notes, reflexive diary) as part of a holistic ethnographic approach. An iterative process of content data analysis was employed to identify key themes. Findings revealed five categories comprising multiple practical strategies, actions, and enablers for team resilience development:

- Inspiring, motivating, and challenging team members to achieve performance excellence
- Developing a team regulatory system based on ownership and responsibility
- Cultivating a team identity and togetherness based on a selfless culture
- Exposing the team to challenging training and unexpected or difficult situations
- Promoting enjoyment and keeping a positive outlook during stressors

The findings of this study provide sport psychology consultants, coaches, and those working in teams with multiple psychosocial enablers and strategies for developing team resilience.

To advance our understanding of team resilience in competitive sport from a research perspective, there is a need for large-scale quantitative studies to better understand the relationships between team resilience and contextually relevant positive outcomes (e.g., performance and well-being). In terms of conducting and implementing this research, there is a need to measure team resilience in competitive sport. A sport-specific measure was developed by Decroos and colleagues (2017). Specifically, the Characteristics of Resilience in Sports Teams Inventory (CREST) offers a state-like measure of team-level resilient characteristics and vulnerabilities. Research has demonstrated evidence for the reliability and validity of the measure across various nations and cultures (see, e.g., Decroos et al., 2017; Fransen et al., 2020; Gorgulu et al., 2018; Yang et al., 2020). To gain further understanding of team resilience as a process, the CREST measure could be used to examine adverse events and a sport team's pre- and postadversity functioning over time.

Research in Competitive Sport: Coach Resilience

In recent years, resilience researchers in sport have shifted their attention from athletes and teams toward the study of coaches, in terms of both coaches' personal resilience and their influence on the resilience of athletes (see, e.g., Kegelaers & Wylleman, 2019; Kegelaers, Wylleman, Blijlevens et al., 2020; Sarkar & Hilton, 2020; White & Bennie, 2015). In one of the first resilience studies to examine coaches, White and Bennie (2015) investigated gymnast and coach perceptions about the development of resilience through gymnastics participation. Underpinned by a qualitative design, 22 female gymnasts and seven gymnastics coaches participated in semi-structured interviews. Data analysis revealed that aspects of the gymnastics environment created stress and exposed gymnasts to many challenges in training and competition. Features of the sport environment, such as interpersonal relationships and positive coach behaviors, supported gymnasts through these challenges and encouraged them to overcome failure.

Building on White and Bennie's (2015) study, Kegelaers and Wylleman (2019) explored how coaches can foster resilience in elite athletes. Semi-structured interviews were conducted with four elite athletes, four elite-level coaches, and two sport psychology consultants from a diverse range of sports including tennis, judo, gymnastics, swimming, cycling, athletics, fencing, and triathlon. Thematic analysis revealed six major themes reflecting resilience training strategies. Three themes reflected proactive (i.e., before the occurrence of a stressor) strategies (i.e., fostering motivation, mental preparation, and promoting life balance) and three themes reflected reactive (i.e., after the occurrence of a stressor) strategies (i.e., evaluating setbacks, promoting a positive mindset, and implementing lessons). Furthermore, the use and effectiveness of these strategies were believed to be influenced by coaches' interpersonal skills (i.e., quality of coach–athlete relationship and an individualized approach). The study was limited to a cross-sectional design (i.e., at one point in time), and the authors suggested that future research might adopt a longitudinal design by organizing multiple interviews over the course of a season. Furthermore, although the study focused on the role of the coach in the development of resilience in athletes, coaches themselves are not exempt from the need to display resilience in the face of adversity (Young, 2014). Indeed, coaches experience a wide range of stressors during their daily work and should be considered performers in their own right (Olusoga et al., 2012; Thelwell et al., 2008). As such, the authors proposed that future research might investigate the resilient qualities that allow coaches to positively adapt to the stressors they experience.

Taking these suggestions on board, Sarkar and Hilton (2020) explored psychological resilience in world-class coaches and how they develop resilience in athletes. A longitudinal qualitative design was adopted because of the dynamic and temporal nature of resilience. Five Olympic medal-winning coaches (four males and one female) were interviewed twice over a 12-month swimming season. Reflexive thematic analysis was employed to analyze the data. Findings revealed 14 higher-order themes, which were categorized into the following three general dimensions:

- Coach stressors (managing the Olympic environment, preparing for major events, coach personal well-being, directing an organization)
- Coach protective factors (progressive coaching, coaching support network, maintaining work–life balance, secure working environment, durable motivation, effective decision making)

- Enhancing resilience in athletes (developing a strong coach–athlete relationship, creating a facilitative environment, developing a resilience process, athlete individual factors)

The results demonstrate the interplay between coach stressors and protective factors over time, which offers an original and significant contribution to the resilience literature by providing a unique insight into the dynamic and temporal nature of resilience in Olympic medal-winning coaches. While this study focused on psychological resilience in world-class coaches and how they develop resilience in athletes, the authors noted there is a need to investigate coaches' impact on resilience in teams. Indeed, coaches play a pivotal role in influencing team resilience, particularly in relation to transformational and shared leadership, devising team learning strategies, and cultivating a distinctive social identity (Morgan et al., 2015, 2017, 2019).

Building on this recommendation, Kegelaers Wylleman, Blijlevens and colleagues (2020) explored national team head coaches' experiences of team resilience. More specifically, the study was aimed at (1) identifying team-level resilient qualities and vulnerabilities and (2) exploring how coaches might develop team resilience in preparation for international competition. Semi-structured interviews with three national team head coaches were analyzed using interpretative phenomenological analysis (IPA). Results indicated that team resilience during competition can be characterized by a collective resilient attitude and strong and shared leadership, while avoiding breakdowns in communication, failing leadership, and the inability to adapt flexibly. Furthermore, coaches should strategically develop resilience by focusing on learning from experiences, anticipating setbacks, and using planned disruptions. This latter suggestion for developing resilience is discussed later in the section Practical Implications.

Coaches play a pivotal role in influencing team resilience, particularly in relation to transformational and shared leadership, devising team learning strategies, and cultivating a distinctive social identity.

Future Research Directions

The literature reviewed in this chapter suggests that resilience is likely to be a fruitful avenue for sport researchers to explore. Here, we discuss five main areas we believe will advance knowledge in the context of environmental and sociocultural influences on resilience.

First, in terms of participants, there is need to understand the perceptions and experiences of resilience for the "team behind the team" in competitive sport. As previously mentioned, resilience researchers in sport have shifted their attention from athletes and teams toward the study of coaches (see, e.g., Kegelaers & Wylleman, 2019; Kegelaers, Wylleman, Blijlevens et al., 2020; Sarkar & Hilton, 2020; White & Bennie, 2015), but there is a need to extend this line of inquiry to those operating in sport science and management roles, including senior management, heads of performance, strength and conditioning coaches, sport scientists (e.g., performance analysts, sport psychology consultants), and physiotherapists. Indeed, a study by Arnold and colleagues (2019) found the team behind the team to experience a wide range of stressors relating to features of working life (e.g., relationships, contractual, performance development, and logistical issues) during their daily work and argued they should be considered performers in their own right (see also Olusoga et al., 2012; Thelwell et al., 2008). As noted by Arnold and colleagues (2019), understanding more about resilience as it relates to support staff is particularly important given the part they play in facilitating athletic success as well as in ensuring support staff are optimally supported.

Second, in terms of the scope of discussion, there is a need to explore resilience at the organizational level (Wagstaff et al., 2016). Although there has been a burgeoning body of research investigating individual (Bryan et al., 2019) and team resilience (Morgan et al., 2017) in competitive sport, there has been very limited research examining organizational resilience. In the only study to date in the competitive sport context, Fasey and colleagues (2021) constructed a definition of organizational resilience and identified resilient characteristics of elite sport organizations using the Delphi method with 62 expert panelists working in or with elite sport organizations or having academic experience of resilience in various contexts. By proposing a definition of organizational resilience that is appropriate for and endorsed by those in elite sport organizations, and identifying resilient characteristics of elite sport organizations, this study provides an important foundation for future research and practice endeavors in this area. The body of knowledge remains at a nascent stage, and empirical examination of organizational resilience is rather scant in the sport psychology context. In particular, more research is needed to understand the complex relationships between individual, team, and organizational resilience. This is particularly important given the impact of the organizational and cultural environment on those within it, and the availability of resources within the organizational context that contribute to the resilience of athletes and teams (Wagstaff et al., 2020).

Third, in line with the process conceptualization of resilience, when investigating resilience in competitive sport, there is a need for more longitudinal research designs that temporally represent dynamic fluctuations within both an individual's psyche and the sociocultural environment. From a quantitative perspective, identifying such patterns will require relatively sophisticated data analytic approaches, such as latent growth mixture modeling, to examine resilience pathways and trajectories and to provide assessments of resilience over time (Galatzer-Levy & Bonnano, 2016). From a qualitative perspective, the extant sport resilience literature has typically employed single interviews or focus groups to explore individual, team, and coach resilience (see, e.g., Fletcher & Sarkar, 2012; Galli & Vealey, 2008; Kegelaers & Wylleman, 2019; Kegelaers, Wylleman, Blijlevens et al., 2020; Morgan et al., 2013; White & Bennie, 2015). One of the few resilience studies to have employed a longitudinal qualitative design is Sarkar and Hilton (2020), who explored coaches' resilience via interviews at two specific time points (September and April) over a 12-month swimming season to illustrate the interplay between coach stressors and protective factors over time. However, the authors noted that although the longitudinal qualitative design was considered a strength of the study, a potential limitation could be the limited period of investigation (i.e., two interviews over a 12-month season) and that future researchers should explore resilience in Olympic coaches with multiple (i.e., three or four) interviews over a longer time period (e.g., a four-year Olympic cycle) to better understand the dynamic and temporal nature of resilience.

Fourth, in terms of methodological perspectives, ethnography could be a particularly valuable approach in understanding environmental and sociocultural influences of resilience over time. Indeed, it has already been demonstrated to be a useful methodology for understanding resilience in competitive sport (e.g., Morgan and colleagues 2019), particularly in terms of capturing the contextual and dynamic nature of team resilience. By being embedded in the context, the researcher is provided with the opportunity for in situ observation and interaction, leading to an "inductive, detailed, in-depth description of cultural practices" (Atkinson, 2016, p. 49) grounded in the experiences of group members, and therefore enhancing the likelihood of generating successful interventions (Krane & Baird, 2005). Going forward, ethnography offers intriguing possibilities to study firsthand the underlying resilience mechanisms, at the individual, team, and organizational levels, and how they are developed over time.

Fifth, from a methodological perspective, narrative methods can be drawn upon to capture the contribution of contextual factors and to attend to the temporal features of resilience (Morgan et al., 2015). Narrative approaches involve collecting and analyzing stories (Etherington, 2004), and they provide a particularly good fit for researchers adopting a social constructionist or social ecological perspective of resilience. Narrative analysis studies both the individual and the culturally available meta-narratives against which personal narratives are framed (Spector-Mersel & Knaifel, 2018) and is thereby revealing of how psychological processes are influenced by the surrounding sociocultural structures (Carless & Douglas, 2017). As such, narrative analysis pays attention to both the individual and the cultural, to both agency and structure (Carless & Douglas, 2017). This is particularly relevant within resilience research that explores the power individuals exercise over their lives as well as the impact of systems that can constrain and limit the availability of resources and opportunity (van Breda, 2018).

Narrative methods can also be of use in capturing temporal dimensions of experience. For example, Douglas and Carless (2009) explored two women golfers' stories of participation and withdrawing from professional golf through life history interviews conducted over six years. The work captured the ways elite sport culture shaped the participants' identities around a single-minded dedication to sporting success, and their subsequent efforts to reinstate a coherent identity following the conclusion of their professional careers when such a performance narrative was no longer viable.

This work demonstrates how people reconstruct their stories and generate new understandings over time, with the availability of new experiences and narrative resources. This approach may be particularly pertinent in capturing the storied elements of resilience in terms of the culturally available narratives people draw on when making sense of adversities and their consequences and how this is reconstructed over time.

Practical Implications

In this final section, we conclude with some implications for applied practice. Although practitioners may find it tempting to focus on individuals' ability to withstand pressure, in line with the notion that resilience is a capacity that can be developed (over time) in the context of person–environment interactions, more attention needs to be paid to creating environments that athletes can thrive in as both a person and a performer (Fletcher & Sarkar, 2016; Sarkar, 2018). Of fundamental importance to developing high-performance environments are the notions of challenge and support. Challenge involves everyone (leaders, coaches, support staff, and athletes) having high expectations of one another, and it helps instill accountability and responsibility. Support refers to enabling people to develop their personal qualities, and it helps promote learning and build trust. In the context of resilience development, Fletcher and Sarkar (2016) differentiated between four types of environment: stagnant environment, unrelenting environment, comfortable environment, and facilitative environment (see figure 23.2). In an unrelenting environment, too much challenge and not enough support will compromise well-being; conversely, in a comfortable environment, too much support and not enough challenge will inhibit performance. In a facilitative environment, however, high challenge and high support are balanced, resulting in resilience being optimally developed. Importantly, individuals and organizations should take *shared* responsibility for developing resilience for performance *and* well-being (Sarkar, 2018; Sarkar & Page, 2022).

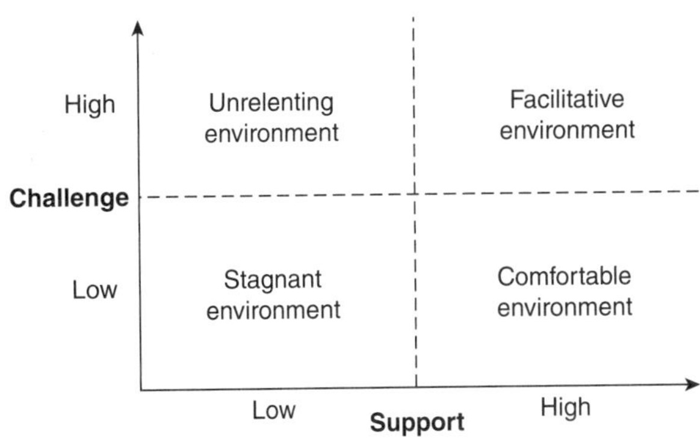

FIGURE 23.2 A challenge–support matrix for developing resilience.

Reprinted by permission of Taylor & Francis Ltd, http://www.tandfonline.com, from D. Fletcher and M. Sarkar, "Mental Fortitude Training: An Evidence-Based Approach to Developing Psychological Resilience for Sustained Success," *Journal of Sport Psychology in Action 7*, no. 3 (2016): 142.

Sport psychology practitioners can help leaders, coaches, and support staff provide an appropriate balance between challenge and support by engaging in pressure inurement training (Fletcher & Sarkar, 2016; see also Kegelaers et al., 2021; Kent et al., 2022; van Rens et al., 2021). Pressure inurement training involves gradually increasing the pressure on individuals via challenge and manipulation of the environment. Practitioners will need to carefully monitor how individuals react to these manipulations, both in terms of their psychological responses and other outcomes (i.e., well-being and performance). When the pressure exceeds the available resources, individuals are likely to react with more debilitative responses and negative outcomes, in which case increased motivational feedback and support should be provided, together with possibly temporarily decreasing the challenge. Conversely, when individuals react with more facilitative responses and positive outcomes, indicating they have adapted to the pressure, then increased developmental feedback and challenge should be imposed.

One approach to imposing challenge is to use planned disruptions (i.e., structured and deliberate activities whereby athletes are exposed to increased or changing demands under controlled conditions; Kegelaers, Wylleman, & Oudejans et al., 2020). Kegelaers, Wylleman, Oudejans and colleagues (2020) found that high-performance coaches use a combination of nine types of planned disruptions (i.e., location, competition simulation, punishments and rewards, physical strain, stronger competition, distractions, unfairness, restrictions, and outside the box). These strategies familiarize athletes with pressure, create awareness, develop or refine personal resources, and promote team processes. Three additional considerations emerged relating to *how* these planned disruptions were used in practice—namely, the surprise use of planned disruptions, periodization, and the impact on personal relationships. Importantly, from a support point of view, planned disruptions should be progressively adaptable and developmentally appropriate, with athlete, staff, and organization buy-in and rationale (before) and debrief (after), and provided in a psychologically safe environment.

To support resilience from a social ecological perspective, Ungar (2018) has provided a manual for designing programs that build resilience. Although primarily targeting those working with disadvantaged youth, the principles of program design may have wider applicability, especially in terms of directing attention toward systemic issues and the availability of resources within the social and physical environment. The manual proposes seven ingredients for successful program design (building relationships, encouraging powerful identities, providing participants with opportunities for power and control, promoting social justice, improving access to basic material needs, developing a sense of belonging, and encouraging a sense of culture and historical roots) to ensure that programs nurture and sustain resilience, as well as step-by-step instructions for effective program creation. While not written with competitive sport in mind, such a manual can nonetheless provide a useful starting point for thinking about resilience intervention from a systems perspective. Specifically, Ungar (2018) noted that all resilience-promoting programs should pay attention to (1) risk exposure, (2) desired outcomes, and (3) protective processes and that when designing a program to build resilience, it is important to be clear which risk factors a program addresses, which protective processes are likely to contribute to change, and which desirable outcomes are most important (in this case) to athletes, coaches, support staff, and the team or organization (figure 23.3 is an adapted exercise from the manual to help identify stressors, protective resources, and desirable outcomes for resilience program design, with a sport-specific example provided).

Summary

Despite the straw man's argument that resilience relates only to cognitive-affective processes manifested in individuals' behaviors, scholars have repeatedly emphasized the importance and impact of environmental and sociocultural factors (see, e.g., Fletcher & Sarkar, 2013; Morgan et al., 2015; Sarkar, 2018; Sarkar & Hilton, 2020). Drawing on the burgeoning body of research in this area, in this chapter we reviewed the research on resilience in competitive sport focusing on environmental and sociocultural influences. To this end, the narrative was divided into four main sections. The first considered how both individual and team resilience has been defined, conceptualized, and theorized. Specifically, we discussed the drawbacks and dangers of defining and conceptualizing resilience as a trait and the advantages and opportunities of defining and conceptualizing resilience as a process from a social ecological perspective. The second section provided an overview of resilience research at the individual and team level, focusing on environmental and sociocultural influences regarding resilience in athletes, teams, and coaches. The third section highlighted five main avenues for future research in the context of environmental and sociocultural influences we believe will advance knowledge in this area. In the fourth section, we concluded with some implications for applied practice. Specifically, we discussed some practical ways of helping coaches shape the environment (in terms of providing an appropriate balance of challenge and support) to develop resilience, and we discussed how coaches can devise a program to support resilience from a social ecological perspective.

Identifying Stressors (Risk Factors), Protective Resources (Processes), and Desirable Outcomes

Think about a program you'd like to design or have already designed or participated in. Complete the table below, carefully considering how the design of the program can improve people's capacity to deal with pressure in the future. Pay particular attention to the context (i.e., what is the issue we want to solve within this particular context, at this time, for this group of participants).

- Brief program description: decompression following major tournament
- Who are the participants: athletes

What stressors or adversities are participants exposed to?	What protective resources (processes) can the program promote to help participants deal with pressure better?	What are the program's desired outcomes?
Dealing with disappointment	Drawing on previous experiences of coping Space and opportunity for debrief, individual and team reflection, and feedback Analysis of performance and learning for the future Identifying future goals and reevaluation Referral for further support (e.g., counseling) if required	Positively processing emotions Learning from experiences
Adapting to home environment or normal life	Reconnecting with family- or home-based support network Connecting with mentors or senior team members for advice Regular check-ins from support staff Focusing on physical and mental rest and recovery Identifying areas of meaning and value in life away from sport	Positive adjustment

PROGRAM CONSIDERATIONS

How can the proposed program build resources and strengths across multiple levels (e.g., individual, team, organization)?

Could it be adapted to work with coaches and support staff?

How can the program be broken down into phases or stages and consider appropriate timing?

- Debrief dealing with immediate issues and feelings
- Focusing on rest and recovery
- Processing emotion and reflecting
- Looking forward

FIGURE 23.3 An adapted exercise to identify stressors, protective resources, and desirable outcomes for resilience program design.

This example (i.e., the program description and the identification of stressors, protective resources, and desirable outcomes) was in part drawn from the following articles:

English Institute of Sport (EIS, August 2021). *Performance Decompression: Post-Games Celebration and Support.* https://www.eis2win.co.uk/article/performance-decompression-post-games-celebration-and-support

Howells, K., & Lucassen, M. (2018). 'Post-Olympic blues'–The diminution of celebrity in Olympic athletes. *Psychology of Sport and Exercise, 37,* 67-78.

Adapted by permission from M. Ungar, *What Works: A Manual for Designing Programs That Build Resilience* (Resilience Research Centre, 2018), 27, https://resilienceresearch.org/files/WhatWorks-Ungar-WebVersion.pdf.

DISCUSSION QUESTIONS

1. What are some of the drawbacks and dangers of defining and conceptualizing resilience as a trait, and what are some of the advantages and opportunities of defining and conceptualizing resilience as a process from a social ecological perspective?
2. Discuss the theoretical models of individual and team resilience, specifically focusing on environmental and sociocultural influences.
3. Synthesize the research regarding resilience in competitive sport (individual resilience, team resilience, and coach resilience).
4. Based on this synthesis, identify avenues of future research in the context of environmental and sociocultural influences in order to advance knowledge in this area.
5. Discuss some practical ways of helping coaches shape the environment (in terms of providing an appropriate balance of challenge and support) to develop resilience.
6. Discuss how coaches can devise a program to support resilience from a social ecological perspective.

24

Systems That Promote Thriving in Sport

Daniel J. Brown, PhD; Michael J.R. Passaportis, PhD; Christopher R.D. Wagstaff, PhD; and Rachel Arnold, PhD

LEARNING OBJECTIVES

On completion of this chapter, the reader should have the following:

- Understanding of the approaches to conceptualizing thriving in sport
- Knowledge of the theoretical mechanisms that are thought to underpin thriving in sport
- Awareness of contemporary research on the intrapersonal, interpersonal, and organizational variables associated with thriving in sport performers
- Appreciation of the strategies used to promote thriving in sport performers

Elite sport environments are characterized by complexity, turbulence, and volatility (Wagstaff, 2017) and have the potential to significantly influence individuals' well-being and performance (Fletcher & Wagstaff, 2009). As such, the climatic and cultural aspects of sport require careful monitoring and influencing to optimize human experiences and promote individual, team, and organizational thriving. Understanding the interplay between individual and environmental thriving factors has intuitive value for a range of stakeholders in sport, and yet the examination of psychosocial constructs such as thriving have, until recently, been elided within sport psychology. Within this chapter, we aim to give the reader an overview of this emerging body of thriving research by providing (1) an explanation of what is meant by the term *thriving*, (2) a critical review of the theoretical mechanisms and promoting factors underpinning the occurrence of thriving in sport, and (3) a selection of recommendations for future research and applied practice.

What Is Thriving?

The topic of thriving has received much attention from researchers studying across the human life span (e.g., infants, older adults) and within various contexts (e.g., sport, work) (Brown, Arnold, Fletcher, & Standage, 2017). Cumulatively, this work has provided a significant advancement toward Seligman and Csikszentmihalyi's (2000) aspiration of "a psychology of positive human functioning . . . that achieves a scientific understanding and effective interventions to build thriving in individuals, families, and communities" (p. 13). But what does it mean to thrive, and what does it look like within these diverse groups?

Human Thriving

Some of the earliest usages of the terms *thriving* and *thrive* appear in the medical literature, where *failure to thrive* initially described a pediatric syndrome characterized by growth failure, signs of severe malnutrition, and developmental delay in infants (Bullard et al., 1967; Haynes et al., 1984), and more recently a geriatric condition evidenced by consistent weight loss and a decline in cognitive and physical function (Braun et al., 1988). In line with this use of the term *failure to thrive* as a negative or suboptimal state, thriving was, in turn, positioned as a positive or desired state characterized by growth, development, and optimal functioning (Tremethick, 1997; Walker & Grobe, 1999). This general description of thriving has subsequently been reflected in research when used in the context of youth development, where thriving has been described as a developmental concept denoting healthy and purposeful change (Bundick et al., 2010; Lerner et al., 2003), and in the thriving at work literature, where thriving is characterized by learning and vitality (Porath et al., 2012; Spreitzer et al., 2005).

Elite sport environments are characterized by complexity, turbulence, and volatility (Wagstaff, 2017) and have the potential to significantly influence individuals' well-being and performance (Fletcher & Wagstaff, 2009).

In addition to the developmental interpretations of thriving, the term has also been used to reflect being successful, often in the context of difficulty (see, e.g., Jackson et al., 2011; Narel et al., 2019). For example, when a person was faced with adversity, thriving was thought to represent successfully overcoming the adverse event and achieving a level of psychological or physical functioning beyond previous levels (e.g., enhanced knowledge or a sense of security in personal relationships) (Carver, 1998; O'Leary & Ickovics, 1995). Moreover, Bakker and colleagues (2010) depicted thriving as the experience of task enjoyment and commitment to an organization despite the occurrence of high job demands, and Sarkar and Fletcher (2014) explored how high achievers thrive and perform at extraordinary levels when actively seeking challenging situations to engage with.

Taking this wider literature into consideration, Brown, Arnold, Fletcher, and Standage (2017) argued that human thriving should be broadly defined as "the joint experience of development and success" (p. 168). They describe the developmental component of thriving as relating to progressive enhancements across physical, psychological, or social dimensions (e.g., learning adaptive coping strategies), and the success component as being evidenced through a variety of contextually and temporally relevant outcomes (e.g., attainment scores for school-aged children).

To experience both development and success and to thrive, an individual needs to be functioning optimally. Within the literature, this optimal functioning has been variously described as "effective holistic functioning" (Brown, Arnold, Fletcher, & Standage, 2017, p. 169), "being fully functioning" (Ryan & Deci, 2017, p. 241), and "positive functioning at its fullest range—mentally, physically, and socially" (Su et al., 2014, p. 256). Collectively, these characterizations reflect two key attributes of thriving-related functioning—namely, that functioning will be (1) at the highest possible level (i.e., effective, fullest range) and (2) across multiple dimensions (i.e., holistically, fully). These features are displayed in figure 24.1, where data are provided for five participants on three possible functioning indicators: subjective performance, social connection, and psychological well-being. Participant 1 would be considered thriving because they have recorded consistently high levels across all functioning indicators (i.e., close to or reporting 10/10 for subjective performance, social connection, and psychological well-being). In contrast, participants 2 and 4 would not be considered thriving, as they have recorded high levels on only some of the indicators. Participants 3 and 5 would also not be considered thriving; although their levels are consistent across multiple dimensions, these levels have not reached a sufficiently high mark.

The dimensions of functioning used to determine thriving are contingent on the context (e.g., education, sport, work) and lens (e.g., context specific vs. life in general) being studied (Brown et al., 2020). For example, within a performance domain such as sport, the performing arts, or the military, functioning dimensions are likely to include measures of performance (i.e., task-specific functioning; Brown, Arnold, Fletcher, & Standage, 2017) and well-being (i.e., optimal psychological functioning and experience; Ryan & Deci, 2001), with performers experiencing high levels across all dimensions to thrive.

With the movement toward understanding thriving as an experience, as opposed to a medical diagnosis, the occurrence of thriving becomes subjec-

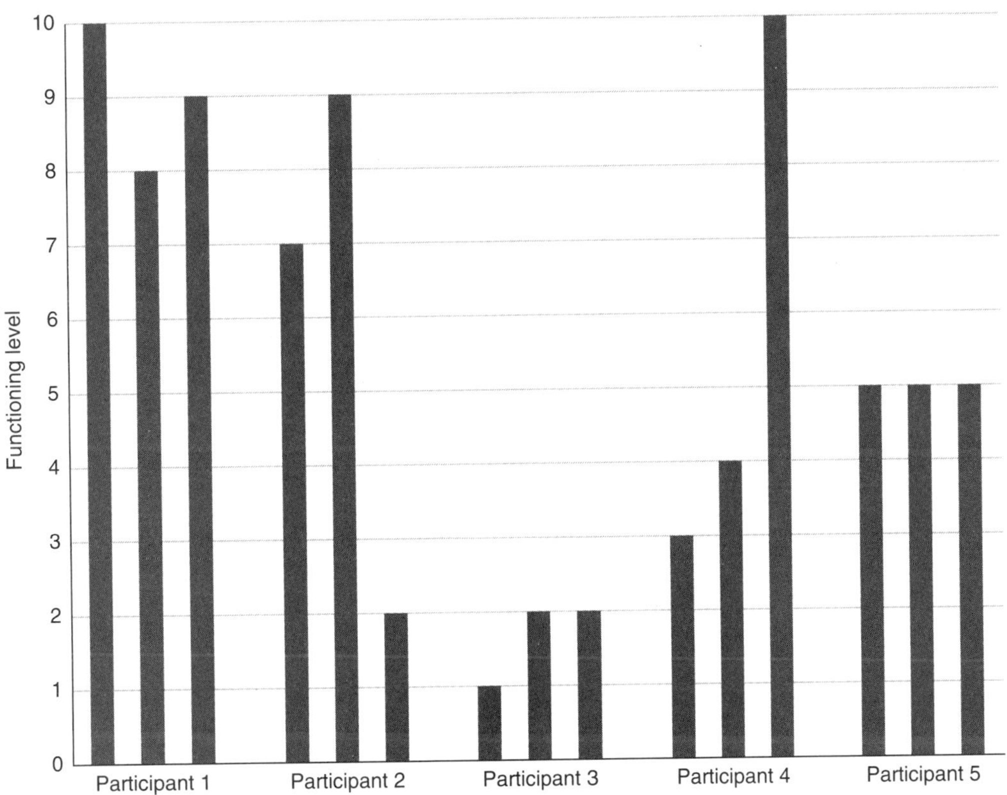

FIGURE 24.1 Functioning levels for five participants.

tively determined. In the case of the five participants from figure 24.1, participant 1 was determined as thriving based on their personal (i.e., subjective) responses to three functioning indicators. However, individuals can also subjectively determine and describe their own experiences of thriving. This was the case in Brown and colleagues (2018), where elite sport performers, along with coaches and sport psychology practitioners, described what it was like to thrive in elite sport; in this instance, thriving was perceived to comprise a sustained high level of performance and dimensions of well-being.

Thriving in Sport

Although some scholars have adopted a functioning-based approach to understanding thriving in sport (see, e.g., Brown, Arnold, Standage, & Fletcher, 2017; McNeill et al., 2018), several alternative interpretations have also been offered (see figure 24.2). The earliest direct use of the terms *thriving* and *thrive* in sport research can be found in the work on mental toughness. Within this work, Jones and colleagues (2002) identified *thriving on the pressure of competition* as an attribute of mental toughness in international adult performers, and Bull and colleagues (2005) similarly described how mentally tough cricketers were those individuals who could *thrive on competition*. Since this work emerged, thriving has been more readily perceived as an independent outcome, with its occurrence examined in relation to parenting (Rouquette, Knight, Lovett, & Heuzé, 2021a) and coaching (Gucciardi et al., 2017) behaviors, as well as competitive sporting encounters (Brown, Arnold, Standage, Turner, & Fletcher, 2021), and following a geographic relocation (Harris et al., 2012b) or retirement from sport (van Rens & Filho, 2020). Adopting this outcome-focused position has meant that researchers could quantitatively examine and qualitatively explore the predictors for thriving. Moreover, this work has shed light on potential strategies and techniques that might promote thriving in a variety of sporting contexts.

ASSOCIATIONS WITH MENTAL TOUGHNESS

- Thriving on challenge or pressure is believed to represent a dimension of mental toughness (Bull et al., 2005; Gucciardi et al., 2009; Jones et al., 2002; Mahoney et al., 2014).
- Mental toughness is considered to be an indicator of thriving in youth sport (Gucciardi & Jones, 2012).

THRIVING AS A RESPONSE TO ADVERSITY AND CHALLENGE

- Thriving represents an elevation in functioning resulting from an adverse event such as injury (Wadey & Hanton, 2014).
- Thriving represents the final phase of a successful transition or a positive outcome following a transition (Diehl et al., 2020; Harris et al., 2012a, 2012b; van Rens & Filho, 2020).

APPLICATIONS OF A POSITIVE YOUTH DEVELOPMENT LENS

- Thriving in adulthood represents an end state derived from the development of interpersonal and personal life skills in adolescent athletes (Jones & Lavellee, 2009).
- Thriving involves the mutual enhancement of an individual and their environment, as well as a developmental construct along an upward trajectory whereby individuals pursue optimal development across all life domains (Kerr et al., 2017).

THRIVING AS FULL AND HOLISTIC FUNCTIONING

- Thriving represents a sustained high level of functioning and performance (Sarkar & Fletcher, 2014).
- Thriving is characterized by both high-level performance or personal accomplishment and dimensions of well-being (Brown et al., 2018; Brown, Arnold, Standage, & Fletcher, 2017, 2021; Brown, Arnold, Standage, Turner, & Fletcher, 2021; Davis et al., 2022; McHenry et al., 2022; McNeill et al., 2018; Passaportis et al., 2022).

APPLICATIONS OF A THRIVING AT WORK PERSPECTIVE

- Thriving is characterized by the experience of vitality and learning (Gucciardi et al., 2015, 2017; Kinoshita et al., 2021, 2022).

THRIVING AS FLOURISHING PERSONALLY AND RELATIONALLY

- Thriving is characterized as positive affect, vitality, life satisfaction, and health quality (Rouquette, Knight, Lovett, Barrell, & Heuzé, 2021; Rouquette, Knight, Lovett, & Heuzé, 2021a, 2021b).

FIGURE 24.2 Interpretations of thriving in sport.

How Do We Promote Thriving in Sport?

Within their review of the human thriving literature, Brown, Arnold, Fletcher, and Standage (2017) categorized three types of psychosocial variables considered to influence thriving: personal enablers, contextual enablers, and process variables. *Personal enablers* include the attitudes, cognitions, and behaviors of an individual that help them thrive (e.g., optimism; Carver, 1998). *Contextual enablers* describe the social agents within, and characteristics of, an environment that can foster continued task engagement and subsequent thriving (e.g., trusting relationships; Carmeli & Spreitzer, 2009). Lastly, *process variables* were the theoretical mechanisms through which enablers may facilitate thriving (Brown, Arnold, Fletcher, & Standage, 2017); these theoretical mechanisms will be the focus of the next section.

Theoretical Mechanisms

To understand how thriving occurs in sport, it is important to identify the factors that precede it because these will likely represent the mechanisms through which more distal factors (e.g., enablers) act. Two variables that have been proposed as the theoretical mechanisms of thriving are basic psychological needs and stress appraisals.

Basic Psychological Needs

Humans possess a small number of universal needs that, if satisfied, can result in optimal functioning and thriving regardless of cultural setting or moment in time (Ryan & Deci, 2017; Sheldon, 2009). These *needs* can be considered the essential nutrients for growth, integrity, and well-being, with basic physiological needs integral for bodily health and safety and basic psychological needs vital for psychological interest, development, and wellness (Ryan & Deci, 2017). While various candidate psychological needs have been proposed (e.g., security; self-actualization, or meaning; Sheldon et al., 2001), the greatest empirical support has been found for the need for autonomy, competence, and relatedness, as outlined in self-determination theory (Ryan & Deci, 2017; see also chapter 12). Autonomy describes the human need to "self-regulate one's experiences and actions" (Ryan & Deci, 2017, p. 10) (i.e., for one's behaviors to be volitional and congruent with one's interests and values). Competence describes one's need to feel mastery and the ability to operate effectively within important life contexts, and relatedness captures one's need to feel a sense of belonging, significant, and socially connected to others (Ryan & Deci, 2017). Further, Ryan and Deci (2017) argued that the collective satisfaction of these three needs is "a *necessary condition* for human thriving" (p. 242).

Four studies have examined the suggested role of basic psychological needs on the occurrence of thriving in sport. In the first of these studies, Brown, Arnold, Standage, and Fletcher (2017) aimed to identify sport performers who thrived in demanding competitive encounters and to test whether thriving could be predicted from a variety of personal enablers (e.g., resilient qualities), contextual enablers (e.g., social support), and process variables (e.g., basic psychological need satisfaction). A sample of 535 sport performers completed measures of functioning via scales for subjective performance, hedonic well-being, and eudaimonic well-being. Factor mixture analysis was then used to identify groups of individuals who had scored similarly. One of the groups scored highly across all three scales and was labeled as thriving. When examining the role of possible predictor variables, basic psychological need satisfaction was found to be a significant, positive predictor of performers' membership in the thriving group when compared with the above-average group (who had scores marginally above the sample mean), the below-average group (who had scores marginally below the sample mean), and the low-functioning group (who had scores well below the sample mean).

Further support for the predictive relationship between basic psychological needs and thriving has been found in more recent studies conducted by Brown, Arnold, Standage, Turner, and Fletcher (2021); Brown, Arnold, Standage, and Fletcher (2021); and Kinoshita and colleagues (2022). Within their study in youth sport, Kinoshita and colleagues (2022) found that basic psychological need satisfaction positively predicted thriving when measured using indices of vitality and learning; however, this study was limited by its cross-sectional design, which precluded the robust assessment of causality. This limitation was overcome in the prospective study conducted by Brown, Arnold, Standage, Turner, and Fletcher (2021), who collected daily diary entries on players' perceptions of basic psychological need satisfaction in advance of an important field hockey match, thereby separating the collection of predictor data from in-match thriving data. The results showed that prematch levels of need satisfaction significantly predicted in-match thriving, with those players reporting the highest levels of need satisfaction also reporting the highest levels of functioning. The strongest support for the predictive relationship between need satisfaction and thriving, however, is from the longitudinal study by Brown, Arnold, Standage, and Fletcher (2021). Within this latter study, athletes completed questionnaires on levels of need satisfaction and thriving on three occasions, and the results from longitudinal structural equation modeling showed that satisfaction of the basic psychological needs had a consistent, facilitative effect on thriving when measured on the repeated occasions, as well as significant indirect effects on future thriving up to 28 days later. Taken together, the results from these studies support the arguments of self-determination theory and position basic psychological need satisfaction as an important factor in the occurrence of thriving in sport.

Stress Appraisal

An additional process variable via which personal and contextual enablers may influence thriving is a challenge appraisal. According to the widely used transactional model of stress (Lazarus & Folkman, 1984), there are three different types of primary appraisal that individuals may make when encountering a stressor. These are *irrelevant* (i.e., the situation has no implication for well-being and no potential for loss or gain), *benign-positive* (i.e., the situation has the potential to enhance well-being), and *stressful* (i.e., the situation is significant to well-being). If the encounter is appraised as stressful, then theory posits that four transactional alternatives can be experienced: *challenge, benefit, harm or loss*, and *threat* (Lazarus, 1999; Lazarus & Folkman, 1984). To explain these, Didymus and Jones (2021, p. 65) stated the following:

> Challenge appraisals arise when personal significance of the stressor is in proportion to the available coping resources and, thus, gain may result from the situation. Benefit and harm/loss appraisals occur when an individual perceives that enhancement of, or damage to, well-being has already occurred. Threat appraisals arise when personal significance outweighs coping resources and, thus, damage to the individual's well-being is anticipated.

Taken together, the results from these studies support the arguments of self-determination theory and position basic psychological need satisfaction as an important factor in the occurrence of thriving in sport.

Challenge appraisals have been associated with thriving given that they create opportunities for positive change and encourage engagement with tasks to experience potential growth, development, and mastery (see Bakker et al., 2010; Carver, 1998; O'Leary & Ickovics, 1995). In relation to thriving, these tasks may come in the form of life adversities or life opportunities (Feeney & Collins, 2015).

In the sport context, Brown, Arnold, Standage, and Fletcher (2017) provided support for the theoretical relationship between challenge appraisal and thriving when they found that performers who were more likely to thrive perceived their competitive sporting encounters as a challenge, compared with those who experienced low functioning. Specifically, perceiving sporting encounters as a challenge was found to significantly decrease the likelihood that performers would be members of a low-functioning profile compared with a thriving profile. These findings have subsequently been reinforced by Brown, Arnold, Standage, Turner, and Fletcher (2021), who found that levels of challenge appraisal increased in the week preceding an important match, with prematch levels shown to positively predict in-match thriving. These initial findings on thriving in sport advance extant work in sport psychology that has found direct links between challenge appraisal and components of thriving, such as performance or well-being (see, e.g., Didymus & Fletcher, 2017a, 2017b; Turner et al., 2013), and examined the mediating role of appraisal in explaining the relationship between various personal and contextual enablers and individual thriving indicators (see, e.g., Edwards & Edwards, 2012; Freeman & Rees, 2009; Rees et al., 2016).

Enablers of Thriving in Athletes

Within the emerging thriving literature, researchers identified a variety of intrapersonal, interpersonal, and organizational factors that appear important for enabling thriving in sport performers. Given the primary focus of this text is the *social psychology* of sport and the associated interpersonal relationships and contextual systems that exist to influence the experiences of sport performers, this section focuses predominantly on the social agents and organizational influences on thriving in sport (i.e., contextual enablers). Yet it would be remiss to not also briefly mention the intrapersonal variables that are likely to influence how these social factors are received or interpreted by an individual.

Intrapersonal Variables

Typically labeled as *personal enablers* within the thriving literature (e.g., Brown, Arnold, Fletcher, & Standage, 2017), intrapersonal variables describe the attitudes, behaviors, and thoughts of an individual that may, in this case, help them thrive. With regard to attitudes, thriving can be driven by possessing personal desire and motivation to succeed (e.g., Brown et al., 2018) and wanting to learn from new environments (e.g., Harris et al., 2012b). Examples of behaviors include using self-regulatory processes (e.g., goal setting; McNeill et al., 2018) and being socially competent (e.g., empathizing skills; Jones & Lavellee, 2009); examples of thoughts or cognitions include maintaining balance and perspective (e.g., Sarkar & Fletcher, 2014). Within their study of high achievers, Sarkar and Fletcher (2014) identified five intrapersonal factors associated with thriving in challenging situations, with the additional characteristics to balance and perspective being positive and proactive personality, experience and learning, sense of control, flexibility, and adaptability. Supplementing these intrapersonal factors was one interpersonal factor, which was the perception and receipt of social support.

Interpersonal Variables

In addition to the intrapersonal factors just discussed, there are several *contextual enablers* believed to facilitate thriving in sport performers. For purposes of communication, the discussion that follows will distinguish contextual enablers into influential social agents within sport performers' environments and physical features of the environment (e.g., facilities). More specifically, we explore how interpersonal relationships formed with coaches, teammates and peers, and parents may support mechanisms for promoting thriving with sport performers.

Coaches The coach–athlete relationship is a pivotal part of sport performers' social environments and can have significant and lasting effects on both athletes' sporting development and performance success (Jowett & Shanmugam, 2016; see also chapter 1). For example, through their relationships with sport performers, coaches have the potential to satisfy or frustrate the athletes' basic psychological needs through their use of need-supportive (e.g., responsive to the perspectives of the individuals they coach) or need-thwarting behaviors (e.g., high levels of control) (Ryan & Deci, 2017; see also chapter 12). Despite a perception that coaches who display need-supportive behaviors may facilitate thriving in their athletes, only two studies have explicitly examined how coach behaviors influence thriving outcomes. Gucciardi and colleagues (2017) used a conceptualization of thriving adapted from the thriving at work literature, where thriving is characterized by vitality and learning (see Spreitzer et al., 2005), and found that controlling coach behaviors (e.g., controlled use of rewards, negative conditional regard) were inversely related to experiences of thriving in adolescent netballers. Alternatively, Brown, Arnold, Standage, and Fletcher (2017) used a sport-specific conceptualization of thriving, indexed by levels of subjective performance and well-being, and showed no significant predictive effects between perceived coach need support or thwart variables and athletes' membership to a thriving profile in their varied sample of sport performers.

Coaches can also influence basic psychological need satisfaction (and subsequent thriving) through their position as key attachment figures for athletes (see Davis & Jowett, 2010; Felton & Jowett, 2013). For example, Felton and Jowett (2013) found that need satisfaction from the coach partially mediated the negative relationships between avoidant attachment style and vitality and positive affect—that is, high avoidant attachment led to lower basic psychological need satisfaction, which partially led to lower vitality and positive affect. This relationship was further examined by Davis and colleagues (2021), where basic psychological need satisfaction was found to fully mediate the positive effect of secure attachment to the coach on thriving in athletes, and to fully mediate the negative effects of avoidant and anxious attachment styles.

Further to the quantitative research outlined earlier, sport performers' qualitative accounts emphasize the significance of supportive relationships with coaches in their experience of thriving (Brown et al., 2018), with the depth and sincerity of these connections proving to be important. To elaborate on the importance of the depth of these connections, Harris and colleagues (2012b) reported that professional footballers who demonstrated genuine warmth toward others forged relationships with coaches, thereby increasing their propensity to thrive (i.e., have a positive experience of transition) following disruptive geographical dislocations. McHenry and colleagues (2022) found elite figure skaters credited honest and open relationships with coaches as significantly influencing their sporting performance and well-being, while Brown and Arnold (2019) found that professional rugby players were more likely to thrive when they were able to foster meaningful connections with coaching staff, characterized by honesty, sincerity, care, and a coach's personal understanding of the player. In their exploration of Olympic and Paralympic sport organizations, Passaportis and colleagues (2022) noted that a coach–athlete-centered approach (cf. Jowett et al., 2017) facilitated meaningful, inclusive, and empowering relationships between athlete and coach. The formation of such relationships enhanced the sport experience, performance, and well-being of the athletes.

The apparent importance of creating meaningful connections for thriving in sport is not surprising given coaches and athletes often form strong dyadic relationships that influence both members' individual and collective goals (Jowett, 2017). Indeed, as Kerr and colleagues (2017) noted, the bidirectionality of these relationships indicates that both athletes and coaches can influence each other's experiences of thriving. With regard to promoting coach thriving, the central tenets of this approach include the enhancement of holistic health and well-being, individual agency, extended responsibility, partnership relationships, and teaching by guiding. Further, the authors suggest facilitators of coach thriving can be conceptualized at three levels: personal (coaches' or athletes' behaviors or qualities), interpersonal (nature and quality of the coach–athlete relationship), and contextual (the sport organization or actual sport environment). In terms of what characterizes thriving in coaches, McNeill and colleagues (2018) described a profile of thriving coaches as those who scored highest across functioning indicators for personal accomplishment, psychological well-being, emotional well-being, and social well-being, and scored lowest on emotional exhaustion and depersonalization dimensions. While the aforementioned work on coach thriving in sport has been insightful, it will be important for scholarly advances on this topic moving forward to ensure that thriving is consistently conceptualized and that the similarities and differences between athletic and coach thriving are further examined and disentangled.

Teammates and Peers Forming interpersonal relationships with teammates and peers reflects a salient part of an athlete's social environment (cf. Martin et al., 2016). Belonging to a group and working among colleagues provides an individual with a potential source of support and guidance, and it equips them with the resources to face challenges and complete daily tasks (Brown, Arnold, Fletcher, & Standage, 2017). Within the sporting context, interpersonal connections with coparticipants are important to the psychosocial experiences of athletes (Donohue et al., 2007), and social support from teammates has been found to be central to the promotion of thriving in elite sport (Brown et al., 2018). In an exploration of thriving in professional sporting environments, Brown and Arnold (2019) described how rugby union players spoke to the effect of promoting equality within their training and playing squads, which allowed new and younger members to fully integrate into the squad and encouraged mentorship and guidance from senior players, all of which would be considered to increase both individual and team performance. Additionally, fostering collective goals and establishing strong bonds between teammates brought about enjoyment, a sense of belonging, and a sense of feeling valued, and it enabled thriving among the players (Brown & Arnold, 2019). Further, Passaportis and colleagues (2022) found that teammates who perceived high levels of understanding, openness, and trust within their training and competition environments felt a greater sense of cohesion among their teammates. This in turn facilitated greater collective action (e.g., information sharing, collaborative problem solving), which has been associated with high levels of performance and well-being in elite sport (see, e.g., Henriksen et al., 2010). These accounts appear to reflect the mechanisms of thriving proposed within self-determination theory, whereby social agents (i.e., the teammates) provide relatedness support and, in so doing, increase the perceptions of relatedness satisfaction within the athletes (Ryan & Deci, 2017).

A critical consideration for researchers and practitioners working in team-sport environments is understanding the dynamic and interconnected experiences of those operating within it. For example, implementing a technique to increase mentoring between senior and younger players may foster thriving in the latter individuals; however, it may also increase selection competition for the senior player and undermine their subsequent experience of thriving. Moreover, several of the findings from Brown and Arnold's (2019) study allude to the interdependency of thriving within team-sport settings, yet little is known about whether or how an individual who is thriving within a team can influence the thriving of a teammate (for a discussion see McGuire et al., 2023). Better understanding of the interplay between individual, dyadic, and collective thriving seems to be an important area for researchers to reflect on and investigate in the future.

Parents Parents tend to retain a high level of input in their children's sporting lives up to and including the adolescent years, but as they get older, children typically wish to acquire greater autonomy over decision making (Holt & Knight, 2014; Knight & Holt, 2013; see also chapter 3). By drawing from the large body of research in this area, one can speculate as to potential mechanisms through which parents may influence thriving. For instance, parents may attempt to be need supportive once their children start to push for autonomy, because allowing children a sense of agency may facilitate thriving. In earlier years, parents can promote athletes' need for autonomy by selecting sport activities *with* their children rather than for them, ensuring they are age and stage appropriate and fun focused (Harwood & Knight, 2015). Parents also need to be flexible and adaptable to their children's needs, because athletes' preferences for different parental behaviors change depending on the stage or moment in competition (Knight et al., 2011). By appropriately adapting their behavior, including nonverbal gestures, to the children's needs, parents can foster a sense of competence and support (Felber Charbonneau & Camiré, 2020).

In a study examining parents' observed and perceived responsive support and thriving outcomes (i.e., positive affect, vitality, life satisfaction, and health quality), parental support was shown to be associated with positive self-perceptions and optimal well-being in young athletes (Rouquette, Knight, Lovett, & Heuzé, 2021a). The athletes' need for relatedness is perceived through the manner of support shown from parents, most frequently via participating in and attending events (Dorsch et al., 2009). Parents can foster feelings of relatedness and provide emotional support through consistently being present at their children's sporting events; yet Felber Charbonneau and Camiré (2020) warned against enacting need-thwarting behaviors in these situations if the child perceives this as controlling. Therefore, parents and children should be encouraged to articulate their expectations and desires to ensure that needs are met and that thriving can occur.

With the limited work that has explicitly examined the influence of parents on athletes' thriving, it is clear that further research is needed to substantiate the hypothesized associations between parent behaviors, athlete basic psychological need satisfaction, and athlete thriving. Moreover, while parents may represent key family members for facilitating thriving in youth athletes, the parent–athlete relationship evolves as the athlete matures, with other familial and personal relationships (e.g., romantic relationships with partners, parenting relationships with children) taking precedence for thriving in adulthood (Brown, Arnold, Fletcher, & Standage, 2017). It would therefore be important to gain a better understanding of the changing influence of these relationships on athlete thriving as the sport performer becomes older and, perhaps, as they progress through higher competitive standards.

Organizational Variables

Thus far in this chapter, we have drawn on literature relevant to the intrapersonal and interpersonal enablers of thriving in the sport context. While these factors are undoubtedly important, it is also important to examine the multilevel, dynamic, and systemic processes that influence thriving in sport. That is, it is essential to acknowledge the *interconnectedness* of these factors across time and a range of individuals, teams, organizations, and societal and cultural contexts.

It is essential to acknowledge the *interconnectedness* of these factors across time and a range of individuals, teams, organizations, and societal and cultural contexts.

Sport Systems In 2009, Fletcher and Wagstaff reviewed six lines of inquiry pointing to the salience of organizational issues, many of which are pertinent for thriving: factors affecting Olympic success; organizational stress; perceptions of roles; organizational success factors; performance environments in elite sport; and organizational citizenship behavior. Later, Wagstaff and colleagues (Wagstaff et al., 2012a, 2012b, 2012c) reviewed the literature relating to positive organizational psychology in sport (POPS) and conducted a program of research examining factors relating to flourishing in sport organizations. For example, Wagstaff and colleagues' (2012c) nine-month ethnography on an Olympic national sport organization highlighted the development and maintenance of interpersonal relationships as being the critical building blocks for optimal organizational functioning. Moreover, individuals better able to monitor and manage their emotions were more likely to forge and maintain successful relationships. The use of these emotion abilities and regulation strategies enabled what Wagstaff and colleagues (2012c) termed *psychosocial capital* (i.e., enhanced levels of engagement and social relationships) and displays of prosocial behavior within the organization. While not explicitly focused on thriving, the seminal program of research on POPS has helped create a shared agenda on positive psychological experiences and optimal functioning. Indeed, this shared agenda provided the foundations for Passaportis and colleagues' (2022) exploration of the environmental factors that influence thriving within an Olympic and Paralympic sport organization. Like Wagstaff and colleagues (2012c), this study highlighted how interpersonal relationships founded on understanding, openness, and trust can enable organizations to create psychosocial environments that facilitate thriving.

In addition to the influence of formal sport organizations on thriving, sport communities establish and maintain norms while providing support at the team and organizational level that fosters a sense of belongingness among individuals (see Dorsch et al., 2022). This is often referred to as *sense of community*, which is salient for thriving given this may support the need for relatedness (McMillan & Chavis, 1986; Sarason, 1974). Indeed, a sense of community through sport has been linked to thriving-related outcomes such as better health (e.g., Warner et al., 2017). As noted by Dorsch and colleagues, given the potential range of characteristics (e.g., size, initiatives, access, infrastructure) that can affect how communities support sport, as well as community factors that shape how sport is designed and delivered, it is critical to understand how communities fit within sport systems.

Another mechanism by which systems influence thriving in sport is through the societal-level factors that shape the meanings individuals and groups give to behaviors, attitudes, experiences, and outcomes in sport, and how they integrate those meanings into norms and ultimately the design and delivery of sport (Bowers & Green, 2013). For example, researchers such as Coakley (2002) and Whitley and colleagues (2019) have noted that in societies characterized by socioeconomic inequality, sports for youths from wealthier families tend to focus on skills and future opportunities (e.g., college or professional participation), whereas sport programs for youths from lower income families tend to focus on social control and personal deficit reduction. Hence, in the pursuit of thriving sport systems it is important to recognize that the perceived significance of sport in societies depends on popular beliefs about the connection between sport and an individual's psychosocial development, social acceptance, and the achievement of educational and occupational success (see Dorsch et al., 2022).

While the value of systemic approaches for understanding thriving in sport has been acknowledged by many scholars (see Wagstaff, 2017, 2019), scholars have yet to explicitly examine the construct of thriving from this perspective. Nevertheless, Dorsch and colleagues (2022) outlined an integrated heuristic model of the youth support system that may provide thriving researchers with valuable insights. To elaborate, they outlined how the *family subsystem* (comprised of an athlete, parents, and siblings), the *team subsystem* (comprised of an athlete, peers, and coaches), and the *environmental subsystem* (comprised of organizations, communities, and societies) have the potential to influence athletes' behaviors, attitudes, experiences, and outcomes in youth sport. Dorsch and colleagues' model builds directly from a systems perspective and its tenets of holism, feedback loops, and roles. Specifically, they argue that the people and contexts that surround an athlete in youth sport should be considered collectively, and that these have important functional roles for individual outcomes (e.g., thriving) that are negotiated over time. The model offers a socially integrated perspective that might also be a useful template for thriving work given its incorporation of proximal and distal processes within youth sport.

Cultures Another organizational and systemic factor that might influence thriving relates to the cultural environment in sport. While sport psychology consultants have called for the study of organizational culture within sport psychology for some time (e.g., Fletcher & Wagstaff, 2009), it has been the field of sport management that had, until recently, led the way (see Girginov, 2006; Kaiser et al., 2009; Maitland et al., 2015). Nevertheless, regarding the early research examining organizational culture in the field of sport psychology, the typical approach adopted has been to conceptualize it through a performance enhancement lens (cf. Cruickshank et al., 2014; Maitland et al., 2015). Indeed, researchers have considered organizational culture as a source of strain for athletes (Arnold et al., 2013); as a factor influencing the denial, ignorance, and acceptance of abuse (Mountjoy, 2019); and as a significant influence on talent development (for a review, see Henriksen & Stambulova, 2017), the development of a high-performance culture (see Henriksen, 2015), performance outcomes at the Olympic Games (see Gould et al., 2002), organizational functioning (e.g., Fletcher & Wagstaff, 2009), and performance leadership (see Fletcher & Arnold, 2011). For instance, adopting a holistic ecological approach in several independent studies, Henriksen and Stambulova (2017) investigated successful athletic talent development environments and paid considerable attention to the organizational context of the environment. Collectively, this program of work showed that a hierarchal system that values open communication, promotes athlete autonomy, and supports athletes in their education and continuous development is more likely to experience sporting success.

A new wave of work on organizational culture is characterized by a more inclusive and balanced approach to studying this concept, beginning with Wagstaff and Burton-Wylie's (2018) review of conceptual, definitional, and methodological considerations for organizational culture, which illuminated some of the debates and challenges within the field of organizational culture. Feddersen and colleagues (2020) used a combined action research and grounded theory design over a 16-month longitudinal study to outline the process of how a destructive organizational culture emerged and was perpetuated in an Olympic sport. The authors reported that radical changes and antagonism in the power relations between the governing body and stakeholders characterized this process. Moreover, denial of responsibility and social weighting neutralized the stigma of perpetuating antagonism.

Champ and colleagues (2020) reported the findings of a three-year ethnography within a football academy and used creative nonfiction vignettes to reveal that youth players were encouraged to develop their self-stories focused on a single-minded dedication to professional football. The limited identity-related resources offered at both the club and cultural level were detrimental for players in terms of their well-being and long-term psychological development. Hence, the influence of the organizational culture in this study represented an obstacle to healthy identity development and arguably, although not noted by the authors, thriving. Further, McDougall and colleagues' (2020a) findings emphasize different patterns of meaning in sport stakeholders' narratives of organizational culture, suggesting a need to develop a broader, more inclusive concept of culture, so as not to minimize, dismiss, or misunderstand other types and sources of sport culture content that are not shared, clear, homogenized, coherent, or leader led (McDougall et al., 2020a, 2020b; Wagstaff & Burton-Wylie, 2018). Clearly, while these rich and insightful accounts do not explicitly focus on thriving per se, they offer salient opportunities to better understand how valuable a cultural lens within sport organizations might benefit those attempting to understand and influence thriving at the individual and collective levels.

In sum, using an organizational or systems lens affords scholars the opportunity to identify feedback loops, as well as the narratives and metaphors people use to describe their organizations and develop a shared language of thriving. This work can offer explorations of human and system thriving with consideration of structure, boundaries, power, hierarchy, function, resource and information sharing, and subgrouping within organizations that might provide valuable insights into social environments in sport and their interconnected, complex, and dynamic nature.

Future Research Directions

With research on thriving in sport still in its relative infancy, many necessary and interesting avenues exist for future research. In this section, we discuss three broad areas that warrant consideration: the assessment of thriving, thriving beyond the individual athlete performer, and the development of evidence-based interventions to promote thriving.

Assessment of Thriving

The alternative interpretations adopted to study thriving in sport pose several challenging issues for researchers and practitioners. First, by adopting differing interpretations and definitions, we are unsure as to whether researchers are studying the same psychological construct. For example, while some researchers identify and advocate performance as being a central indicator of thriving in sport (e.g., Brown, Arnold, Standage, & Fletcher, 2017; McNeill et al., 2018), others do not include performance in their measurement (e.g., Rouquette, Knight, Lovett, & Heuzé, 2021a) or argue that performance should be considered an outcome of thriving (e.g., Kinoshita et al., 2022). This, in turn, prevents reliable and valid measurement. Second, the absence of a consistent measurement approach precludes reliable testing of the variables associated with thriving, including predictors and outcomes. Third, without being able to identify robust predictors of thriving, researchers are unable to design and test interventions to bring about its occurrence. Moving forward, it is recommended that scholars adopt a functioning-based interpretation of thriving and that researchers select indices of functioning most relevant to their context of investigation (see Brown, Arnold, Fletcher, & Standage, 2017; Brown et al., 2020; McNeill et al., 2018; Ryan & Deci, 2017). Within sport, this should include task-specific functioning (i.e., performance) as well as optimal psychological functioning and experience (i.e., well-being).

The inclusion of performance in the assessment of thriving evokes further questions about how best to measure one's execution of a particular action or skill (e.g., subjectively vs. objectively; global performance vs. skill specific). As aforementioned, thriving should be considered a subjective experience and is thus personally determined and labeled. As such, it is important that any measurement of thriving be collected from a subjective perspective, including the measurement of performance (e.g., How would you rate your performance in today's match?) and well-being. In so doing, this may result in a scenario where the athlete's personal evaluation of thriving differs from that of observers (e.g., coaches, practitioners), which may on the one hand create a negative questioning narrative and undermine the lived experiences of the performer, yet on the other hand positively highlight a potential misalignment in the performance expectations of the athlete and coach.

An additional challenge is the expected association between objective performance (e.g., match outcome or ranking) and thriving. For example, if a player's team won, would they not have to have thrived? Similarly, would it not be expected that a player whose team lost a match failed to thrive? In making these assertions, we neglect the personal and subjective experience of the player, whose perceptions of their own performance may differ from the overall outcome of the team. To date, only one exploratory study has examined the relationship between objective competition performance and thriving, finding a trivial, nonsignificant correlation between the two variables (see Davis et al., 2021). Further examining this relationship will no doubt represent an interesting area for future research.

Thriving Beyond the Individual Athlete Performer

While recognizing the importance of promoting thriving in athletes, it is also pertinent to consider other stakeholders operating within sport. Indeed, coaches and sport science and medicine staff can have a substantial influence on athletes' experiences and play a significant role in both athletic and organizational success (Wagstaff et al., 2016). The literature on these populations' psychological functioning in sport, however, has tended to focus on indicators of ill-being (e.g., burnout, strain), particularly given the numerous demands they face in their roles (cf. Arnold et al., 2019; Fletcher & Scott, 2010; Olusoga et al., 2009), or to a more limited extent, on the embedded structures and practices that might make it difficult for women to thrive in sport (see, e.g., Cui, 2007; Norman & Rankin-Wright, 2018). Thus, future research should consider more positive elements of coaches' and support staffs' functioning in elite sport as well as additional enablers and barriers of thriving in such populations.

Furthermore, there remains an opportunity to advance the extant thriving literature relating to environmental and contextual enablers, by looking beyond the unidirectional examination of environment to personal factors regarding thriving. To elaborate, researchers have used self-determination theory to examine environmental factors in terms of the extent to which they support or thwart *individual* needs and success (see Ryan & Deci, 2017). Yet it is important to note that individual thriving is rarely the exclusive or collectively agreed outcome pursued in sport. Instead, team, organizational, community, societal, and cultural thriving are viable and meaningful pursuits in and via sport and should be explored as outcomes if not prioritized over individual or relational thriving given their greater potential societal benefit (e.g., social justice). To achieve this, researchers should consider examining multilevel structures within their data sets as well as the influence of predictors that operate and explain variance in thriving at each level (e.g., individual, team, organization; see McGuire et al., 2023).

Development of Evidence-Based Interventions to Promote Thriving

This third area for future research draws on both the robust conceptualization and measurement of thriving and the acquisition of thriving knowledge across individual, group, and organizational levels to develop multilevel interventions for the promotion of thriving. These interventions may target personal enablers of thriving (e.g., personal resilient qualities) to promote individual performance and well-being, or contextual enablers (e.g., interpersonal relationships, organizational factors) to promote thriving across individuals, groups, or the organization as a whole. When designing these interventions, practitioners should also consider the theoretical mechanisms that have been shown to predict thriving (i.e., basic psychological need satisfaction, challenge appraisal). Moreover, any interventions should be tested longitudinally in conditions that maximize both internal validity (i.e., to ensure that the intervention was responsible for changes in the outcome) and external validity (i.e., to ensure that the effects are representative of those in the population and set in the real world) (see Brown & Fletcher, 2017).

Athletes' experiences of thriving can be fostered through their own journey of personal development and growth via the creation of attitudes, behaviors, and thoughts supportive of performance and well-being, but this developmental voyage can also be facilitated by the actions of key social agents (e.g., coaches) and the organizations within which the athletes participate and compete.

Practical Implications

Although interventions for thriving are yet to be empirically tested, a variety of techniques and strategies have been identified within the sport literature as supporting the joint experience of high-level performance and well-being. These approaches concern both thriving in athletes and in others operating in sport organizations, and they typically target the personal enablers (i.e., intrapersonal variables), contextual enablers (i.e., interpersonal relationships, organizational factors), and process variables (i.e., theoretical mechanisms) associated with thriving.

Promoting Thriving in Athletes

To facilitate thriving in sport performers, Brown and Arnold (2019) suggested it is important that sport organizations establish a collective culture, underpinned by an integrated, inclusive, and trusting training environment that provides opportunities for interaction between groups. A number of potential methods to facilitate these interactions were posited, including organizing opportunities for teammates to socialize away from training, encouraging informal touchpoints such as regular coffee meetups after training, and asking players to alternate who they sit with during team meetings (Brown & Arnold, 2019). Yet it is important not to attempt to exercise excessive control over the social environment in search of creating a collective culture; Wagstaff and colleagues (2017) stress the need to allow individuality within sport organizations and advise caution in discouraging subgroups or cultures. Moreover, from a coaching perspective, Brown and Arnold (2019) suggest that coaches should endeavor to make themselves accessible to players so as to form effective relationships with all sport performers under their care, facilitate enjoyment, and provide players with agency to enable thriving.

With regard to promoting thriving in athletes via the enhancement of personal enablers, Sarkar and Fletcher (2014) describe how practitioners should help individuals cultivate a commitment to personal development and mastery, and to seek out appropriately challenging situations to prepare individuals to thrive in future demanding situations. In youth sport contexts, it may prove important for coaches and parents to support young athletes in fostering both hedonic motives (i.e., seeking pleasure, fun, and comfort) and eudaimonic motives (i.e., seeking excellence and to achieve one's best) to allow them to achieve both positive psychological experiences (i.e., well-being) and performance outcomes (cf. Kinoshita et al., 2022). Moreover, Jones and Lavellee (2009) highlight the importance of reflection in the development of life skills through the enhancement of personal awareness and self-understanding. It is clear, therefore, that athletes' experiences of thriving can be fostered through their own journey of personal development and growth via the creation of attitudes, behaviors, and thoughts supportive of performance and well-being, but this developmental voyage can also be facilitated by the actions of key social agents (e.g., coaches) and the organizations within which the athletes participate and compete.

Promoting Thriving in Coaches and Others Within Sport Organizations

Sport organizations can play a significant role in enabling thriving for key stakeholders (e.g., athletes, coaches, support staff, fans). Indeed, in their special issue, Green and Ghaye (2018) provide numerous examples of how football businesses are increasingly searching for innovative ways to meet organizational needs and maximize stakeholder thriving. These examples include coordinating development initiatives (Solntsev & Osokin, 2018), having a cohesive and strategic vision (Kitchin & Crossin, 2018), optimally managing relationships (Finnegan et al., 2018), monitoring rule and format adaptations (Bullough, 2018), and ensuring a holistic and segment-specific marketing strategy (Huiszoon et al., 2018).

With specific reference to coaches, it would be worthwhile focusing on strengthening their capacity to self-regulate and manage their perceptions of stress to allow them to overcome and thrive on the demands they experience. Indeed, McNeill and colleagues (2018) profiled Canadian developmental and high-performance sport coaches and found that coaches within a thriving profile reported significantly higher self-regulation capacities and lower perceived stress than those categorized as at risk or within depleted profiles. Thus, to improve self-regulation, coaches are encouraged to adopt high but realistic well-being standards for themselves, identify barriers that might make prioritizing their psychological health difficult, and continually monitor their own emotional states (McNeill et al., 2018). To better manage their perceptions of stress, McNeill and colleagues (2018) suggest that coaches modify their cognitive appraisals, develop effective coping strategies, and build in sufficient recovery periods. As well as placing the responsibility for improved functioning on the coaches themselves, the sport organization can also play a role in coaches' thriving. Specifically, those operating at the organizational level can look to monitor expectations placed on remunerated coaches, guard coaches' working hours, and ensure they have sufficient resources and training opportunities to meet demands encountered (McNeill et al., 2018).

Summary

This chapter has sought to introduce readers to the topic of thriving and to provide an overview of theory and research within the area. Thriving can be broadly defined as the joint experience of development and success, which can be best understood by the exhibition of full and holistic functioning across context-relevant indicators (e.g., performance and well-being in sport). Within a sporting context, basic psychological need satisfaction and challenge appraisal have been shown to predict thriving and thus represent potential pathways through which coaches and practitioners can promote thriving in their athletes. As research continues to progress in the area of thriving, it will be important for researchers to offer a clear conceptualization of what they interpret thriving to mean and to use measurement tools that reliably evaluate the effectiveness of interventions delivered across individual, group, or organizational levels.

DISCUSSION QUESTIONS

1. Think about a team sport of your choice and two playing positions within that team. What skill or performance indicators would best illustrate task-specific functioning for those two positions? Which indicators would be relevant for both, and which would be position specific?
2. Based on the arguments presented in this chapter and from the articles referenced, provide an argument for and against including performance in the assessment of thriving.
3. Why is it that a challenge appraisal may predict thriving in sport performers?
4. In what ways can peers, coaches, and parents support an athlete's basic psychological need for relatedness?
5. How might an organizational-level intervention simultaneously promote thriving in players and coaches?

25

Gender Perspectives

Nicole M. LaVoi, PhD, and Courtney Boucher, PhD

LEARNING OBJECTIVES

On completion of this chapter, the reader should have the following:

- Knowledge of major constructs related to gender scholarship in sport psychology
- Understanding of the critical link between theory and research
- Comprehension of review and caveats to be addressed in gender research and praxis in sport and exercise psychology
- Knowledge of the ecological model of barriers for girls and women in sport
- Understanding of how gender affects girls' and women's participation in and through sport
- Critical perspectives of gender difference and similarity

In this chapter, gender within social psychology in sport is outlined in three areas of research: girls' and women's participation in sport; barriers faced and challenges experienced by women coaches in the occupational landscape of sport; and purported gender differences between coaching females and males. Many more intersections could be addressed, but for the sake of space and scope for this chapter, these three areas were chosen based on our expertise, the fact girls and women face more barriers in sport than boys and men, and the fact we are often asked about these topics. Of note, any chapter on gender in sport psychology should give proper recognition and attribution to seminal colleagues who have shaped the discipline. Two feminist sport psychology gender scholars who stand out and deserve special recognition for their contributions to the literature are Dr. Diane Gill (see Gill, 2001, 2020), who laid the foundation of gender-related research on sport psychology for decades, and Dr. Vikki Krane, who studies the intersections of sex, gender, sexual orientations, sexual identities, and sexual prejudice in sport (see Krane, 2018). Their work provides a deeper and more comprehensive dive into all the areas of gender and sport psychology, which are beyond the scope of this chapter.

Key Concepts

To begin, it is important to define key terms in gender-related research, including *gender, stereotypes, bias, stereotype threat, homophobia, homonegativism, heterosexism*, and *heteronormativity*. This section also outlines what gender-related research comprises, and what it does not include.

Gender

Biological sex, gender, gender identity, and *sexual identity* (or *orientation*) are terms that are commonly conflated and used interchangeably. According to the American Psychological Association (2011), *sex* refers to the physical and biological aspects that distinguish being male or female (i.e., sex chromosomes, internal reproductive organs, external genitalia), while *gender* refers to the sociocultural attitudes, behaviors, feelings, experiences, and characteristics associated with being male and female. Examining gender pertains to how socially constructed and arbitrary conceptions of masculinity and femininity influence the sport experiences of all stakeholders—athletes, coaches, leaders, and parents. *Gender identity* is an individual's inner concept of self as male, female, a blend of both, or neither. One's gender identity can be the same (cisgender) or different (transgender) from the cultural expectations of the sex assigned at birth. *Gender expression* encompasses the way in which an individual expresses their gender identity, typically through mannerisms, appearance, dress, and behavior. *Sexual identity* is an individual's emotional, romantic, or sexual attraction to others. Gender and sexual identities and expressions are numerous but not necessarily linked, and a dynamic set of gender-related terminology exists that reflects the entire gender spectrum, rather than a traditional gender binary of male or female, which helps individuals accurately express identities. Gender-related research, although not typically in mainstream sport psychology, also pertains to how the structure of sport has traditionally privileged men and masculinity and problematized or marginalized females in sport contexts.

Psychologists often think about gender at the individual level, primarily as an identity, expression, or role learned in childhood through families, schools, and peers. Sociologists view gender as a social system, not just something that is inherent, natural, and individual. From a sociological perspective, gender is a system of social practices that categorize people along a gender binary and then arrange social life along that difference (Rauscher & Cooky, 2018). This social system is the primary way people are categorized (into groups of boys, men, girls, or women), most commonly into a binary rather than a continuum; it shapes opportunities, access to resources, and life experiences, both directly and indirectly (Rauscher & Cooky, 2018). Importantly, a binary classification system maintains gender-based inequality by ranking males and masculinity above females and femininity (Lorber, 1994).

Examining gender pertains to how socially constructed and arbitrary conceptions of masculinity and femininity influence the sport experiences of all stakeholders—athletes, coaches, leaders, and parents.

Sport is a socially constructed, gendered activity that is traditionally considered within a structured gender binary. While Kane (1995) and other scholars have contested the idea of a gender binary—arguing a continuum—sport is rarely presented or constructed in this way. For example, there are girls' or women's teams and there are boys' or men's teams. Some sports are seen as masculine, feminine, or neutral activities (Hardin & Greer, 2009; Klomsten et al., 2005). Female athletes may be more likely to follow ideals, conform, and participate in sports deemed "appropriate" based on dominant feminine norms, such as gymnastics or dance, as opposed to traditionally masculine sports such as American football or ice hockey (Hardin & Greer, 2009; Messner, 2002). Scholars argue that sociocultural norms and stereotypes for sporting females are shifting (Cooky & LaVoi, 2012), and perhaps this has been accelerated because of COVID-19 changes in the sport industry that have given women athletes unprecedented visibility (Lebel et al., 2020), but sustainable systems change is contested and slow.

Since sport is dominated and controlled by men and intertwined with traditional notions of masculinity, for decades women in sport have had to challenge traditional gender norms—but they are stigmatized, harassed, discriminated against, and labeled "deviant" for doing so (Blinde & Taub, 1992). Because not every sportswoman (or sportsman) engages in behaviors and roles consistent with gender norms, mechanisms exist to ensure that masculinity is seen as both different from, and superior to, femininity (Anderson, 2005; Ross & Shinew, 2008). Traditionally defined masculine traits include leadership, independence, confidence, and aggression while feminine traits are constructed as gentle, nurturing, relational, sensitive, and caring (Bem, 1974; Donnelly & Twenge, 2017). Traits associated with femininity and perceived as feminine position women as the weaker and inferior sex, making sport a space for men but not for gentle women, and while gender scholars argue stereotypes are dated, data indicate gender stereotypes and power hierarchies in sport are alive and well (Chalabaev & Sarrazin, 2020). Gender scholars typically embrace a critical feminist perspective that places gender inequality; the roles, rights, opportunities, interests, and conditions of girls and women; and the origins and consequences of gender relations and hierarchies that privilege men and boys at the center of inquiry. Gender scholars also advocate for ideological, structural, and organizational changes that move toward gender equality, in sport specifically as per this chapter, but also in society in general.

Stereotypes and Gender Bias

Stereotypes are mistaken fixed generalizations and beliefs about an individual or class of people based on how they look on the outside, which can lead to prejudice and bias. *Gender bias* is defined by the idea that one gender (most typically male) is preferred over another. Gender bias affects how women are perceived, evaluated, and treated differently than men. Because of traditional gender norms and the presence of male dominance in sport, gender biases and stereotypes are also widely prevalent. Chalabaev and colleagues (2013) make an important distinction between gender roles and stereotypes—*gender roles* are "prescriptions" (e.g., men are supposed to run faster than women) and *stereotypes* are "descriptions" (e.g., men run faster than women). Gender stereotypes surrounding traditional masculinity and femininity and athleticism can affect girls and women in sport many different ways. Metheny's (1965) groundbreaking work on sport typing inspired scholars (e.g., Kane & Snyder, 1989; Klomsten et al., 2005; Matteo, 1986, 1988) to better understand how gender stereotypes influence sport participation and the sports that girls and women and boys and men choose to play. Numerous stereotypes, often called false narratives, exist about girls and women in sport including that girls and women don't like sport as much as boys and men do, girls and women are less competitive than boys and men, girls and women who play masculine-typed sports are lesbians, women don't want to coach as much as men, and women can't coach and have a family. Based on the data in physical activity contexts, stereotypes manifest into discrimination, internalization of stereotypes, and identity threat for marginalized individuals (Chalabaev & Sarrazin, 2020). The production and reproduction of gender stereotypes and biases are problematic in a variety of ways that will be highlighted in subsequent sections.

Despite changing sociocultural norms, outdated gender stereotypes and beliefs and attitudes about gender that make sport an unwelcoming and unsafe place for those in gender or sexual orientation minorities are persistent.

Stereotype Threat

Stereotype threat is defined as a socially premised psychological threat that arises when one is in a situation or doing something for which a negative stereotype about one's group applies (Steele & Aronson, 1995). According to stereotype threat, members of a marginalized group acknowledge that a negative stereotype exists in reference to their group, and they demonstrate apprehension about confirming the negative stereotype by engaging in particular activities. In short, it is the fear of stigmatized individuals to be judged or treated stereotypically. It is also situation specific—people experience it only when they are in a setting where a negative stereotype about their group is salient to them. In the context of sport, activation of a negative stereotype is harmful to learning a new sport skill for girls (Heidrich & Chiviacowsky, 2015) and to performance in cognitive and motor domains (Smith & Martiny, 2018). A meta-analysis illuminated that gender stereotypes affect the choice of sport activities of women, and this was stronger for sports typed and considered masculine (Gentile et al., 2018). Research in sport and exercise psychology and stereotype threat is nascent, but existing data consistently point to the fact that stereotypes in situations where one's competence is evaluated may be "sufficient to detract females' sport and motor performance" (Chalabaev & Sarrazin, 2020, p. 30). Despite changing sociocultural norms, outdated gender stereotypes and beliefs and attitudes about gender that make sport an unwelcoming and unsafe place for those in gender or sexual orientation minorities are persistent (LaVoi & Glassford, 2021).

Homophobia, Homonegativism, Heterosexism, and Heteronormativity

Homophobia is a culturally constructed irrational fear or prejudice against individuals who identify as homosexuals, while *homonegativism* is negative treatment of individuals who are nonheterosexual. *Heterosexism* is defined as the discrimination or prejudice against gay people on the assumption that heterosexuality is the normal sexual orientation. *Heteronormativity* is the belief that heterosexuality is the default, preferred, or only normal mode of sexual orientation expression. While sport privileges men first and foremost, it also privileges individuals who identify as heterosexual (Krane & Barber, 2005). Because of the aforementioned male power and hegemonic masculinity that permeate sporting spaces, sport has always been a homophobic space (Calhoun et al., 2011). The stereotype of a lesbian presence in sport perpetuates and evokes a stereotype threat that affects all girls and women and denies them respect, decency, and power (Iannotta & Kane, 2002; Norman, 2012).

Theory and Research

Gender-related aspects of sport and exercise psychology (SEP) research have predominantly focused on girls and women in sport (Gill, 2020; LaVoi, 2012) and far less on boys and men. Three lines of research pertaining to girls and women are summarized later in the chapter. In 1988, sport sociologist Ann Hall argued that in North America the tendency is to think *gender* means *woman*, and this remains mostly true in SEP over 30 years later. The experiences, correlates, and outcomes for females in sport are worthy topics of inquiry and may, but should not be assumed to, differ from the experiences of males because of social and cultural contexts of participation, historic influences, and gender socialization. Sport researchers and practitioners are advised to consider and apply the information in this chapter in culturally competent ways, resist generalizations, and ask research questions that do not reify damaging and outdated gender stereotypes. For example, instead of asking why girls and women lack confidence (arguably this is a "blame the women" narrative) or have a negative body image—unarguably predictors of sport participation—instead examine what interpersonal, organizational, and sociocultural variables influence the development of self-confidence and body image for females, and how those systems can be changed.

Ecological Systems Theory

The ecological systems theory (Bronfenbrenner, 1977, 1979, 1993) posits that human development reflects the influence of several environmental systems including individual, social, environmental, societal, and cultural. This seminal theory has influenced how researchers approach the study of human beings and their environments. A commonly used framework to understand the facilitators and barriers girls and women face in sport is derived from the ecological systems theory (Bronfenbrenner, 1979). The ecological systems theory incorporates a multilevel model that focuses on four distinct yet interwoven levels. These levels include individual, interpersonal, organizational and environmental, and societal (Bronfenbrenner, 1979). The ecological systems theory has been applied to sport for specific groups, such as underserved girls (LaVoi, 2018a; Thul & LaVoi, 2011), including immigrant girls (Thul et al., 2018), and women sport coaches (Burton & LaVoi, 2016; Cunningham et al., 2019; LaVoi, 2016; LaVoi & Dutove, 2012), as well as mentoring of women in sport coaching (Banwell et al., 2020). Using the ecological framework in this context allows for the examination of both supports and barriers that girls and women face and aid in the understanding of their experiences, because according to the data, the barriers that girls and women face in sport far outweigh the supports (LaVoi, 2016; LaVoi, 2018a; LaVoi & Dutove, 2012).

Employing an ecological framework allows examination and understanding of barriers and supports for females from multiple and interwoven levels of influence, from the most proximal (i.e., closest to the individual) to the most distal (i.e., societal), and how those factors influence the developmental trajectory of sport participation or one's coaching profession. The societal level of the ecological model includes dominant ideologies, stereotypes, bias, homophobia relating to issues of discrimination, and prejudice. The organizational and environmental level includes structures of power, culture, norms, policies, programs, and opportunities that help or hinder girls' participation in sport or women's career trajectory. The interpersonal level includes relationships and social influences of people such as coaches, parents, peers, siblings, colleagues, teammates, staff, and family. The most proximal, the individual level, includes how self-perceptions, personality, agency, and personal intersectional identity variables influence and interact with the other levels. All girls and women are not a monolith, and depending on intersectional identities, they will experience the system very differently, including sport participation.

Gender and Sport Participation

The gendered participation data are clear on two fronts. First, girls are provided less opportunity to be physically active and participate in sport than are boys, and they also face more barriers to participation, which can lead to disparate health and developmental outcomes (LaVoi, 2018a). Underserved girls (i.e., lesbian, queer, trans, immigrant, nonwhite, lower social class, physically impaired) face more barriers and are the least physically active groups, which exacerbates health and development asset accrual. The multilevel and numerous ecological barriers girls face are outlined in detail within the Tucker Center research report *Developing Physically Active Girls: A Multidisciplinary Approach* (LaVoi et al., 2018) and will be summarized here. At the societal level, girls face enduring gender stereotypes, gender bias, and homophobia, and for nonwhite girls, these gender-related biases intersect with racism. At the organizational level, fewer and lesser-quality programs are offered for girls, spaces are less safe for girls, and boys dominate the public and sporting spaces that do exist. At the interpersonal level, physical activity and sport participation are often less valued by parents for girls than for boys, girls are expected to conduct more domestic labor than is expected of their brothers and to care for younger siblings, and families may lack resources to support girls' participation. Given that a majority of youth, club, and high school coaches are men (LaVoi, 2009), girls often experience coaches who lack education, blatantly or inadvertently demean girls, monitor their bodies, sexually harass or sexually abuse them, criticize rather than provide constructive feedback, and let their own gender bias affect how they coach girls (Fisher & Anders, 2019; Slater & Tiggerman, 2011).

Some physical education teachers also transmit damaging stereotypes that limit the behaviors of boys and girls, but particularly girls, in what has been called the hidden curriculum (Duncan, 2007). Similarly, some parents and coaches champion that sport is a natural, predestined extension for boys to release their energy, aggression, and competitiveness, and in contrast, girls are perceived as naturally more sensitive, vulnerable, and group oriented (Messner, 2011), which likely affects the opportunities afforded girls and how girls are treated and coached. Adolescent immigrant Muslim girls report coaches lack cultural competence and fail to understand religious beliefs and modesty practices (Thul et al., 2018). At the individual level, the values, beliefs, and attitudes of girls are influenced by the system around them. Some girls internalize gender stereotypes, which impedes or influences their choices and unfortunately perpetuates the status quo. Girls should not be blamed for choosing not to participate. The data show that girls love sport just as much as boys, but because of the barriers inherent in their experiences, it is not surprising that girls enter into sport later and then drop out of sport earlier than boys.

Girls should not be blamed for choosing not to participate. The data show that girls love sport just as much as boys, but because of the barriers inherent in their experiences, it is not surprising that girls enter into sport later and then drop out of sport earlier than boys.

Second, adults are central in providing opportunities, structuring sport, and coaching girls, in addition to providing optimal experiences by creating the right motivational climate where health, developmental, and positive psychosocial assets can accrue. These evidence-based practices are covered in depth in other chapters. However, the power of same-gender, same-identity role models is a salient factor in girls' aspiration and motivation to play sport (Midgley et al., 2021), not to mention that males and male sport would benefit greatly from the presence of women coaches as role models. Yet because of the dearth of women coaching role models and the scarce media coverage of women's sport, girls and boys often do not have exposure to active, athletic, confident female role models. Similar to girls' participation, women who coach face numerous barriers in the ecological system that impede and influence their career trajectory.

Gender and Sport Coaching

Decades of research indicates that the majority of coaching positions are held by men at every level, in nearly every sport around the globe (Robertson, 2016). Given the importance of same-gender, same-identity role models in sport contexts (Midgley et al., 2021)—something afforded to nearly all boys and men in sport—it is imperative that girls and women have the opportunity to be coached by women at some point in their active lives. Decades of research and the multitude of barriers women sport coaches face are well documented and summarized by the ecological model of barriers and supports for women coaches (LaVoi & Dutove, 2012) and more recently in the seminal book *Women in Sports Coaching* (Burton & LaVoi, 2016; LaVoi, 2016).

At the societal level, women sport coaches face stereotypes, gender bias, homophobia, ageism, ableism, and the mommy penalty (career problems women face after having a child due to gender bias). Dr. Leanne Norman and colleagues have documented how sport, primarily in the United Kingdom and Europe, promotes and maintains a gender order unfavorable to women, who often feel powerless; how women must continually prove themselves; and how often women sport coaches experienced a hostile and intimidating culture (Norman, 2010; Norman & Rankin-Wright, 2018; Norman et al., 2018). Particularly, women who identify as lesbian often experienced oppressive heterosexist and homophobic sport cultures that were gender and sexuality blind (Norman, 2013, 2014, 2016), which downplays or disregards gender differences and reinforces existing gender inequalities. Norman's findings are reflective of the gendered nature of sport around the world. Much work remains to ensure all sport cultures are gender responsive and strive to create a safe, respectful, equitable environment that accounts for the fact girls and women experience the world differently than do boys and men.

One tangible way heteronormativity and homophobia are manifested in sport occupational spaces and affect women is through family narratives within coaching biographies. Nontraditional, diverse sexual orientation narratives (i.e., same-sex couples) within online college coaching biographies are rare and have not become more common despite changing sociocultural norms and laws pertaining to gay rights in the last decade (Calhoun et al., 2011; LaVoi & Glassford, 2021; LaVoi, Boucher, & Silbert, 2019). Precisely because heterosexism permeates sport, women (and men) do not feel comfortable or safe including a same-sex relationship in their biography, which erases the visibility of lesbian coaches (Calhoun et al., 2011). Similarly, perceptions of characteristics associated with an ideal head coach are more closely aligned with stereotypical masculine characteristics (e.g., confident, forceful, assertive), and data indicate the head coach position is more closely aligned with the masculine gender role, which Madsen and colleagues (2017) argued might influence women to pursue assistant coach positions and "could prevent women from pursuing such opportunities, lead athletes to prefer male head coaches, and prevent athletic directors from hiring women as head coaches" (p. 135).

At the organizational level, barriers for women sport coaches include wage gap inequality, deeply embedded organizational norms that privilege men, homologous reproduction from those in power who recruit and hire, limited opportunity for upward career progression, policies that do not support coaches who are mothers, coach education that is unwelcoming to women, tokenism, and marginalization (Kane & LaVoi, 2018). At the interpersonal level, barriers include the old boys' club, in some cases an unsupportive life partner, athlete gender bias against women that privileges men, and weak mentorship, sponsorship, and gender allyship. For example, researchers found the pressure to conform to traditional gender roles influenced female collegiate athletes to view sport and sport careers as masculine and therefore perceive their female coaches negatively (Madsen, 2016).

At the individual level are the competencies, values, beliefs, and choices of women, shaped by the ecological system in which they exist and work. For example, the gendered culture of sport where women are marginalized and perceived as secondary, organizational policies that do not support women, a weak support network for women coaches, and very few visible female coaching role models affect women coaches' sense of self and confidence (Norman, 2014). In sum, the system of sport does not, and is not set up to, value and support women coaches across the career trajectory (LaVoi & Boucher, 2021), including coach education and development that scarcely challenges and often reproduces gender stereotypes, gender hierarchies, and unfavorable sporting and occupational cultures (de Haan & Norman, 2020; Norman & Rankin-Wright, 2018).

Sport Coaching: Challenging Versus Reproducing Gender Stereotypes

Coaching is a social-relational process in which athletes can be empowered or experience bias and stereotypes, or both. As stated earlier, coaches and sport instructors including physical education teachers can purposefully or inadvertently reproduce gender stereotypes. For example, when coaches hold stereotypical beliefs, such as girls are less competitive, less skilled, and less physically able than boys, coaches may alter their behaviors by giving misguided feedback or reinforcement because of their lowered expectations (LaVoi, 2018a). Conversely, if coaches believe sport makes boys into men by teaching them to compete, be tough, suppress emotion, act aggressively, and dominate others (e.g., characteristics aligned with masculinity), these gendered beliefs will influence how male athletes are taught, socialized, and coached compared with females. Evoking negative gender stereotypes about female athletes with males improves the males' sport performance (Chalabaev & Sarrazin, 2020), but this practice simultaneously reinforces misogyny and sexist, homophobic stereotypes that have no place in sport. Research indicates that psychologically males and females are more similar than different (Hyde,

2005; Hyde et al., 2019), but an essentializing sex difference paradigm in sport (Gill, 2020), in sport coaching (LaVoi et al., 2007; Messner, 2011), and about women sport coaches (LaVoi & Goorevich, in press) persists. While psychology scholars have moved away from sex differences research, sport psychology has been slower to move away from the focus on sex differences (Gill, 2020).

Lumping all males or all females into stereotypical behavioral categories, such as "females are more relational and emotional than males," erases the fact that human behavior regardless of sex or gender or sexual or gender identity, is not fixed and runs along a continuum. Some males are more emotional than some females, but that is rarely discussed and even rarer is it taught in coaching education. A plethora of books on coaching girls were developed to help coaches be more effective, but in reality they reproduce damaging gender stereotypes and undermine the empowerment possibilities sport can provide (LaVoi et al., 2007). A reminder that gender is an arbitrary construct of what it means to be masculine and feminine in a particular historical time and space and is part of a negotiated and subjective identity that influences optimal performance, experience, and development of an individual. It is but one variable that affects how individuals interact with each other, but it is an important one. For practitioners, a more effective way to teach, coach, or consult is to focus on the individual, regardless of gender. Unfortunately, stereotypes begin when girls first enter sport and follow them throughout their sporting careers, which limits the ability and capacity of women to hold leadership positions within the sporting context (Sartore & Cunningham, 2007). The cycle and effect of gender stereotypes are insidious, and only through awareness and education, including coach development, will this begin to change.

As outlined in the previous section, engagement in gender research is necessary and important work. However, some caveats for conducting gender research in sport psychology (Carter, 2020; Fisher & Anders, 2019; Gill, 2020; LaVoi, 2012) will help guide future research and are outlined in the next section.

Caveats for Gender-Related Sport and Exercise Psychology Research

First, doing gender research does not simply mean "add females and stir"; inclusion of females in the sample criteria is not sufficient to qualify research as gender related. Stated simply, including girls and women does not automatically qualify as gender scholarship. Second, gender-related research in most major sport and exercise psychology (SEP) textbooks is mentioned in passing; presented as a marginal, add-on, or special issue topic, typically placed at the end of the publication; or not covered at all (Gill, 2020; Gill & Kamphoff, 2010). Gender, like other social constructions such as culture, class, race, able bodies, and sexual orientation, is not privileged within SEP knowledge as is motivation, self-regulation skills, self-perceptions, and group dynamics (Fisher et al., 2009a), and the work of sport psychology scholars who walk interdisciplinary lines and focus inquiry on social justice, identities, power, and structural influences is often marginalized (Butryn et al., 2014; Gill, 2020). In response to continued marginalization, some sport psychology scholars created safe and inclusive intellectual spaces for this work, including a group in the United States who in 2016 formed and now annually host the Social Justice Through Sport and Exercise Psychology Symposium (see www.socialjusticesep.com).

Third, frequently within gender-related SEP research, girls and women are framed as problematic. For example, fear of success, attributional patterns, eating disorders, and lack of confidence or self-efficacy are often framed as problems pertaining primarily to females. Duncan (2007) summarized a multitude of research that indicated girls' lack of interest, motivation, or effort in sport is often explained by coaches and physical educators as the "problem with girls." The same is true in popular sport coaching books, in that coaching females is problematized and framed as an issue that needs to be fixed, dealt with, or overcome, and coaching females is different from coaching males, while similarities are rarely highlighted (LaVoi et al., 2007). Similarly, the underrepresentation of women in positions of power in sport is often blamed on women by oft-repeated false narratives including women don't apply, there aren't enough qualified women, and women won't move for a job (LaVoi, 2016). When girls and women are blamed and problematized, the system and cultures of sport and the people in power in the system who marginalize females do not need to be interrogated, fixed, or changed. Additionally, the gendered essentialist framing erases and marginalizes the experiences of boys and men, who experience detriments in psychosocial outcomes. For example, if one believes the common narrative that sport makes boys into men, a practitioner might reproduce and teach (explicitly or inadvertently) toxic masculinity that limits boys' emotional, social, and relational behaviors to fit the dominant gender norms.

Fourth, female athletes are commonly and constantly compared against boys and men and the male norm (i.e., females are less competitive than males, females are more social, females lack the "killer instinct," females are more emotional). Beliefs of inherent social-psychological gender differences often originate from personal beliefs or experiential knowledge rather than evidence. Hall (2002) points out that researchers often seek to delineate how females are different from males, but the reverse question is rarely posed. Gill (2020) writes, "Gender scholarship in psychology has shifted from early research on sex differences and gender roles to more current approaches in line with our framework, emphasizing intersecting identities and cultural relations" (p. 1135); however, an essentialistic gender difference perspective persists among many practitioners in sport contexts. And as Gill (2001) noted, "Sport psychology does not have well-developed feminist theories or models" (p. 364), and Carter (2020) more recently acknowledged and reinforced the existence of the sparse literature and minimal acceptance of feminist sport psychology. Feminist sport psychology is defined by a primary focus on systems, organizational structures, and an emphasis on multiple and intersecting cultural identities, power relations, and advocacy for social justice in order to dismantle the systems of privilege that enable and (re)produce sexist discrimination (Carter, 2020). In addition, feminist sport psychology consultants shift "attention away from a narrow focus on elite sport to a wider range of women and to marginalized groups" (Carter, 2020, p. 29).

Meta-analysis of gender difference across numerous psychological qualities supports a gender similarity hypothesis, and any gender differences that do exist are small or very small (Hyde, 2016; Hyde et al., 2019). Difference hypotheses are typically tested with quantitative statistics, and results provide irrefutable evidence that males and females are different—while similarities are often ignored, erased, or not discussed. Examining gender using quantitative, reductionist, positivistic methods is predicated on the assumptions of cause-and-effect relationships and objective scientific processes. In reality, many other factors besides the sex or gender of the athlete influence sport confidence levels, and the affect, cognition, behavior, and experience of any individual in sport contexts. This is not to say psychosocial differences between male and female athletes do not exist, but researchers should use caution and not inadvertently reproduce gender stereotypes or marginalize female athletes through the types of research questions and methods employed. Relatedly, researchers should not assume all females (or males) are identical and make blanket generalizations that reinforce stereotypes (Peters & Williams, 2009).

When girls and women are blamed and problematized, the system and cultures of sport and the people in power in the system who marginalize females do not need to be interrogated, fixed, or changed. Additionally, the gendered essentialist framing erases and marginalizes the experiences of boys and men, who experience detriments in psychosocial outcomes.

Gender-related research fits most effectively with qualitative methodologies (i.e., interviews, case studies, focus groups) where complex gendered interactions, identities, experiences, and life histories of female (and male) athletes can be illuminated. Researchers interested in gender-related questions should examine the individual *within* the social, political, cultural, and historical context that influences the sport and physical activity experiences of both males and females, using the systems approach outlined previously. Methods and theoretical frameworks that help researchers place the individual within complex ecological or what some call multisystem layers of social influence will help forward and deepen gender-related SEP research.

Fifth, gender stereotypes about what is appropriate and inappropriate behavior based on dominant gender norms (i.e., being aggressive and competitive is not ladylike or feminine, playing certain contact sports like rugby or football is inappropriate for females) limit and restrict the full potential and development of all athletes. Often in gender-related SEP research, the focal point is on female athlete conformity or deviation from femininity, while the masculinity of male athletes is rarely questioned or examined. Given that historically SEP researchers have embraced a limited approach to examining gender, a blurring of disciplinary boundaries is necessary if this area of inquiry is to progress. Reconstructing SEP by infusing physical cultural studies or sociology has not been widely used or accepted in sport psychology (Butryn et al., 2014; Fisher et al., 2009a; Gill, 2020) nor gone uncontested. Other social scientific approaches offer a way for SEP researchers to study and integrate gender within their work, because gender is located on and performed by the physical body. Conducting gender-related research in the ways just described does little to advance the field of SEP. Gill (2020) calls for both researchers and practitioners to become "culturally competent professionals [who] recognize multiple, intersecting identities and power relations, and apply those understandings to develop programs that are inclusive and empowering" (p. 1144). Despite multiple calls to action to use cultural studies and feminist perspectives (Carter, 2020; Fisher et al., 2003, 2009b, 2019; Gill, 2020; LaVoi, 2012), progress toward systemic inclusion of gender in sport and exercise psychology is limited. The exception includes a small but committed group of scholars and practitioners.

Two decades ago, cultural sport psychology (CSP) grew out of sport psychology, and CSP scholars encouraged those in the discipline to include and think about how "cultural factors such as power, social structure, identity, gender, and religion . . . impact individual sport experiences" and how to work toward justice and combat oppression, exploitation, inequities, violence, and abuse (Fisher & Anders, 2019, p. 129). The book *Feminist Applied Sport Psychology: From Theory to Practice* is a groundbreaking and salient contribution to feminist and womanist approaches in sport psychology that incorporates gender scholarship as well as multicultural, critical race, and social justice perspectives, theories, and methodologies for sport psychology researchers and practitioners seeking deeper understanding (Carter, 2020).

Future Research Directions

Many questions remain at the intersection of SEP and gender-related research. Situating the individual within the familial, interpersonal, organizational, environmental, and sociocultural context in which they work, play, and live will further understanding about the individual's emotions, thoughts, values, beliefs, behavior, and yes, also sport performance. Recognition of similarities between individuals within any group—racial, gender, religion, or any other intersectional identity—does not mean everyone in that group is a monolith. For example, not all girls are the same; neither are all Black individuals, or all individuals who identify as heterosexual or trans. Consideration of multiple and intersectional identities within the ecological system is imperative for moving SEP knowledge forward. Gender research in SEP needs to include boys and men and deepen understanding of how traditional notions of masculinity can lead to detrimental psychosocial outcomes in sport contexts. Given that girls and women in sport face numerous and a greater number of barriers to sport participation and career entry and advancement and not much is known in this domain, additional research is needed about supports at every level of the ecological model. As other scholars have indicated, additional research on psychosocial, health, and performance outcomes of stereotype threat is warranted (Chalabaev & Sarrazin, 2020), especially in marginalized populations who experience intersecting oppressions (e.g., Black and Indigenous women). More knowledge is needed about what, who, and how the system can support and value women and girls of *all* identities.

Cultural sport psychology scholars implore and challenge researchers and practitioners to first engage in serious reflexivity and self-reflection of their own biases, power, and privilege (Carter, 2020; Fisher & Anders, 2019). LaVoi, McGarry, and Fisher (2019) outlined areas of inquiry that researchers can undertake to activate a change agenda for women sport coaches in particular. The following are some examples:

- Include experiences of women coaches with intersecting, multiple, or marginalized social identities, and reflect on how dominant theories and methods incorporate or exclude them.
- Focus explicit attention on gender, intersectional identities, and power at the organizational and sociocultural levels.
- Shed light on and investigate successful educational programming, as well as decision makers and individuals in power who are doing it right, and create cultures that value and support women.
- Incorporate cultural diversity and relational analyses to move toward feminist practice.

Similarly, LaVoi (2018a) noted future research directions for girls and women in sport and physical activity (for a comprehensive list, see the full report):

- Forward understanding of the multitude of barriers, the cultural context, the lived experiences of girls with various intersectional identities, and the outcomes of participation for underserved girls.
- Evaluate sport-based youth development programs for girls that are proliferative.
- Illuminate how girls and women experience body confidence in movement cultures, and how those cultures are created by coaches.

Practical Implications

One practical application of the knowledge in this chapter is to develop cultural competencies in coach education and strengthen that knowledge in applied sport psychology, specifically drawing on the subdisciplines of cultural sport psychology, physical cultural studies, sociology, feminist scholarship, and other related domains. For example, Norman (2016) argued that coach education and sport organizations must include all sociocultural aspects (e.g., gender, gender identity, race, ableism) of programming and be precise in how concepts on equality, equity, inclusion, and diversity are taught. Diversity and inclusion training is trending in corporate environments, and sport and exercise psychology professionals who work with athletes, coaches, and sport administrators, and who also teach in university settings, would do well to seek similar sociocultural competency training so as not to inadvertently reproduce damaging gender (and racial) stereotypes. For example, in the United States, organizations such as Athlete Ally and Return On Inclusion have developed diversity, equity, and inclusion (DEI) training for sport stakeholders and organizations. Sport and exercise psychology practitioners and researchers should also undergo professional development to learn about, assess, and reflect on their own biases and privilege to more effectively serve the athletes, coaches, and sport stakeholders they work with (Carson et al., 2020; Carter, 2020; Fisher & Anders, 2019).

A move beyond the female deficit model that blames girls and women for inherent biases in the system that impede their full participation in sport contexts, whether it be participatory or occupational, must be forwarded. Systems change is needed based on evidence-based best practices, and this must involve interrogation of power and privilege based on positional and social capital and intersectional identities. To that end, diversification of occupational positions of power in sport is needed at every level and at every position to better serve and represent diverse athlete-participant populations. Individual-level asset-building interventions, leadership skills, and programming are needed—for example, to improve the body positivity, self-regulation (controlling anxiety, arousal, stress), or self-perceptions (self-esteem, body image, confidence) of girls and women in sport. However, interventions should simultaneously address the system that created the context where girls and women are in need of asset-building programming.

Summary

In this chapter major constructs related to gender scholarship and caveats for conducting gender-related research in sport psychology were summarized. Understanding of the critical link between theory and research is vital, particularly the usage of the ecological model to deepen research pertaining to how an individual's lived experiences are influenced by the multiple levels of the system and their intersectional identities. Research was summarized as to how gender affects girls' sport participation and women sport leaders, and how gender essentialist beliefs can reproduce damaging gender stereotypes that influence human interactions. Future research ideas and practical applications were advanced that will help move the field of sport psychology forward in meaningful ways, including toward social justice.

DISCUSSION QUESTIONS

1. With the understanding of gender stereotypes and stereotype threat, what are actionable ways to better recognize and counter harmful stereotypes?
2. Girls and women in gender-related sport and exercise psychology research, consulting, and coaching education are often framed as problematic. How can girls and women in sport be *reframed* in research and in common narratives to avoid reinforcing gender essentialist beliefs and putting blame on girls and women?
3. Gender-related research and discussion of gender by practitioners often focuses on gender differences between girls and women and boys and men that often lead to the reproduction of harmful gender stereotypes. In what ways can we focus on the similarities between girls and women and boys and men?
4. As discussed, the ecological systems model has been applied to sport for underserved girls and for women coaches. How might the ecological systems model be used to understand the barriers to accessing and participating in physical activity faced by girls? Disabled girls? Coaches who are mothers? Queer athletes? Women of color?
5. To better serve girls and women through sport and physical activity, what are some accountability measures that could be implemented in your community to encourage systems change?
6. Can you think of any additional future research questions or actions?

26

Talent Development and Performance

Dave Collins, PhD, and Jamie Taylor, PhD

LEARNING OUTCOMES

On completion of this chapter, the reader should have the following:

- Awareness of the performance now versus development conundrum, which is a common feature of talent development (TD) environments
- Awareness of and ability to critically examine the consequent tensions in practice, including the developmental use of challenge, the necessity for skills development, and the optimal use of feedback
- Ability to apply the principles of effective nested planning and TD environments to the design and conduct of TD practice
- Awareness of the TD milieu and the consequent implications for talent pathway practitioners
- Knowledge of the contexts of TD and how they affect decision making for the athlete, coach, practitioner, and parent
- Ability to consider how the shaping of shared mental models can optimize TD in pathways
- Awareness of the important considerations in giving feedback, including timing, nature, and emotional state of the recipient

For many sports, growing your own performer, as opposed to the rather more expensive tactic of buying in from other sources, has become an essential component of the business. Even in soccer, where budgets are often astronomical, the reputational and income capital that can be accrued from effective talent development (TD) academies means most of the largest clubs around the world indulge themselves with an academy. Indeed, it becomes world news when a club decides to limit such activity. For example, the famous German club Bayern Munich announced a cut to their program (Austin, 2020) only three years after opening a new state-of-the-art facility to much fanfare.

Such decisions are perhaps unsurprising, especially because numerous studies have attested to the challenges of early identification and its conversion to senior talent (Güllich, 2014). The problem is identified clearly by Güllich and Cobley (2017); procedures that generate performance at a junior level often seem to associate with failure to achieve as a senior. In contrast, a change of emphasis at the developmental stage seems to be much more effective in generating high performance as a senior, which is after all what the process is really about (Barth & Güllich, 2020). Of course, even when the primary focus is the future realization of potential, there are still concerns that must be addressed, brought into sharper focus by the growing number of cases citing abusive behaviors by coaches and support staff (Feddersen et al., 2020). Interestingly, while often portrayed as due to overemphasis on success (e.g., medals), we see this as a rare phenomenon *but also* one that has always been in existence. In short, there have always been coaches who see the TD process as "all about them and their ego" and engage in excessive behaviors as a result.

In our experiences of academy settings, most coaches and systems are focused on the broader development of the youngster—indeed, all those not seduced by the ego trip of youth performance! As this chapter will show, this is advantageous for both the general development of the individual and their eventual levels of achievement. In short, much like effective physical education, focusing on developing as athlete *and* person offers a truly developmental and adaptive performance experience.

This positive and desirable focus carries several implications, many of which are critically considered in this chapter. For example, we present the concept of nested planning (cf. Abraham & Collins, 2011; Martindale & Collins, 2012), a tool that encourages the coach or manager to consider and address the needs of today embedded within a structure that looks to the medium- (meso) and longer-term needs of the athlete. This encourages the coach to make decisions about practices and methods with an eye on the three nested agendas, all of which must be satisfied if the performer is to progress effectively.

As a result, this chapter presents a number of issues around TD. First, we discuss the conceptual considerations necessary in the domain before exploring approaches in the literature for developing talent. We offer emerging areas of research, including development of an athlete's skill set, the role of feedback, and the optimizing of challenge. We then consider the role of athlete experience, calling for a broader and more nuanced perspective on the factors that influence development. Finally, as coach-practitioners, we offer considerations for real-world practice.

Much like effective physical education, focusing on developing as athlete *and* person offers a truly developmental and adaptive performance experience.

Effective Talent Development

Talent development focuses on the realization of potential through longer-term performance; it is the process of building for the future, as opposed to achieving good performances today (cf. Collins & MacNamara, 2017). Given the importance of this topic, there is clearly plenty of research and quite a bit of theory available. Rather than fill the entire book with a long list of these perspectives, however, we have limited ourselves to five as follows:

- The essential underpinning role of individual skills
- How these skills are best developed
- How feedback can be timed and presented for best effect
- The essential role of challenge and optimizing its impact
- Fitting all these into an effective TD environment, or TDE

All these interacting factors offer underpinnings to the applications and implications discussed later in the chapter.

Essential Underpinning Role of Individual Skills

Researchers and practitioners acknowledge the consequences of aiming for performance today as opposed to the future. Many offer ideas on how these goals can be accomplished, offering specific methods such as growth mindset (Dweck, 2006), grit (Duckworth, 2007), and resilience (Fletcher & Sarkar, 2012). Whichever type of *performance* (*P*) desired or method needed (*O* for *outcome*), all permutations can be achieved through a mixture of *processes* (*P*) based on individual skills. Described in a review of the state of play, the performance-outcome-process, or POP, model (Collins et al., 2019) suggests that developing a set of skills—a hand of cards—enables athletes to select and apply different combinations to address each challenge. One such set of skills are the psychological characteristics of developing excellence, or PCDEs (MacNamara et al., 2010a, 2010b).

Pertinent for the purpose of this chapter, the benefits of a skill set approach such as the PCDEs are receiving increasing support (e.g., Hill et al., 2018; Saward et al., 2020). As such, our standpoint is that skill development, deployment, practice, and refinement should be an essential feature of the athlete development diet.

The PCDE model has been refined over the years but currently stands at the following 10 skills:

- Commitment
- Focus and distraction control
- Realistic performance evaluation
- Role clarity
- Self-regulation
- Planning and self-organization
- Goal setting and self-reward
- Quality practice
- Effective and controllable imagery
- Seeking and using social support

These 10 skills (cf. MacNamara et al., 2010a, 2010b) are evaluated in athletes, and recently in younger children, by a purpose-built questionnaire: the Psychological Characteristics of Developing Excellence Questionnaire (Hill et al., 2018; Laureys et al., 2021), which offers a profile built around seven factors:

- Adverse response to failure
- Imagery and action preparation
- Self-directed control and management
- Perfectionistic tendencies
- Seeking and using social support
- Active coping
- Clinical indicators

The idea is that any of the outcomes needed in young athletes to realize their potential, such as mental toughness or resilience, can be achieved through different combinations of PCDEs, applied in a bespoke and personalized fashion to meet the challenge. Collins and colleagues (2019) explain the advantages of this approach in their POP model. For the present, however, we stress that the skill set approach fits with the other approaches but also enables a flexible and adaptable approach to challenges.

Teaching and Developing an Appropriate Skill Set

The advantages of developing a flexible skill set rather than just one or two more focused, almost monochrome approaches are hopefully clear. The model suggests that a set of skills, such as but not limited to the PCDEs (other lists could be developed), should be used to achieve the outcomes that enable the desired performance. Change any of the contexts and the optimal blend will change. Importantly, this means the same athlete can use different skill combinations as their needs change. For example, the typical challenges faced by athletes in the TD context are often very different if they reach the senior level of performance (e.g., increased media exposure, performance pressure) (Taylor & Collins, 2021a). Since such changes are almost inevitable, this psychological flexibility is very important.

If this approach is to work, we need to decide on an appropriate set of skills (ideally grounded in evidence), teach and develop those skills (Collins et al., 2016a), and provide plenty of opportunities for the developing athlete to test their skills against a variety of challenges. Once again, the literature offers a range of possibilities. In simple terms, these fall into three broad categories. First is *the importance of challenging experiences*. The Great British Medallists study (Rees et al., 2016) suggests that top performers (i.e., winners of multiple medals) have all experienced significant life challenges in association with sporting success (e.g., the death of a parent or being bullied at school). The second broadly relates to *attitudes youngsters bring to the situation* (cf. growth mindset; Dweck, 2006). In contrast, the third is *the skill set idea already introduced*. In fact, Collins and MacNamara (2017) suggest that all three can be seen as skill related, with diversity only on how and when the skills are developed. The main consideration is when, relative to challenge, the skills evolve. In this case, a growing literature sees the importance of teaching skills ahead of sporting challenges rather than life challenges, then reviewing and refining as a result of how well the challenge was addressed (cf. Savage et al., 2021).

Optimizing Feedback: Timing, Nature, and Emotional Concomitants

Crucial for directing effort and for developing skill sets such as the PCDEs is the coach's use of feedback (cf. Taylor & Collins, 2021b). Fortunately, recent work shows a returning focus to this well-established technique. One issue is the exact role of the different types of feedback and when they are administered. A key determining factor in the overall impact is the recipient's emotional state, both before and after feedback (Molloy et al., 2019). Notably, both positive and negative feedback have an important part to play; indeed, perhaps the latter is even more critical!

Our work makes this clear, drawing on a wide range of literature from both performance and education (Taylor & Collins, 2020). In simple terms, the emotional impact of feedback depends on the recipient's sensemaking of the subject. As a result, it is difficult to clearly distinguish between the impact of feedback (positive or negative) through observation alone, especially for the aspirational elite (Taylor & Collins, 2021b). In the broadest terms, a positive response to feedback is genuinely reinforcing for the athlete (as long as it is appropriate and not overdone) but doesn't seem to change the performer's behavior, except in that they might try to do the same thing again.

The coach, parent, or support staff member will carefully consider both the short- and long-term goals of the process (as with the nested planning process), consider the different blends of tools that might be used, then select and apply them.

In marked contrast, as long as it is not overdone, a negative affective response to feedback is likely to motivate the recipient to search for solutions—in simple terms, ways to avoid the often traumatic emotions of being criticized (Taylor & Collins, 2021b). Notably, this idea underpins elements of the suggested adage that "talent needs trauma" (Collins & MacNamara, 2012). Indeed, we suggest that without some upset along the pathway, the developing athlete will emerge with stunted growth. In fact, there are clear cases of those who do not feel challenged until it is too late on the pathway (Collins et al., 2016b). Please note, we are talking about feedback impacts in the longer term. This stands in contrast to research that has shown associations between positive emotions (resulting from praise) and proximate performance (e.g., Moen et al., 2018). Unfortunately, these obvious relationships, together with a general (and building?) disposition to be positive and supportive with athletes, may have inhibited a more considered approach to the optimal impacts of feedback. In summary, negative feedback (as long as it is proportionate) is an effective *and essential* component in athlete development. Of course, the key question is what is proportionate, and how can the right level be determined for any individual?

Optimizing Challenge: Balancing the Highs and Lows

Moving on from emotion, we must stress how important it is to consider (and where possible orchestrate) the emotional state in which each individual receives their feedback. Expanding the need for appropriateness in negative feedback, it is worth considering how negative the experience or challenge should be, in what aspects of the athlete's experience it should occur, and how the balance of challenge and success is best achieved.

The first element to consider is the degree of optimal negativity. This, we suggest, is highly individualistic and relates to how prepared the athlete is—in short, their level of self-efficacy. For this reason, and reflecting earlier comments, our work has highlighted the importance of teaching and testing skills in advance of challenge wherever possible (cf. Collins et al., 2016a). Indeed, elite athletes will rarely, if ever, see corrective feedback as negative—the acid test being they are aware of what is needed to improve and reasonably confident they can accomplish it. Even in development, these comments suggest that the feedback sandwich (surrounding critical comments with positives) is not a good idea. Notably, this method has been challenged for quite a while (Schwartz, 2013) even though partial support still pops up (Prochazka et al., 2020). Be that as it may, we suggest that the case for teaching skills to developing athletes from an early stage is well supported (Taylor & Collins, 2019).

The second is where challenge or negative feedback can best occur; as suggested earlier, this is best focused on the performance domain. Interestingly, a meta-analysis also found that traumatic challenges were most effective in influencing performance when they occurred in the specific domain (John et al., 2019; Savage et al., 2021). So evidence seems to be in favor of setting and making good use of challenge in the performance domain.

The final element comes down to the balance of challenge and success (negativity and positivity) and optimizing this for each athlete. Recent work shows that this relies on a considered combination of monitoring athlete perceptions and coach decision making (Taylor & Collins, 2021a). As with so much in coaching and interpersonal interactions, making the best decisions as coach, leader, or parent is essential.

Drawing on work in applied sport psychology and case conceptualization, we have used the term *professional judgment and decision making*, or PJDM (cf. Collins & Collins, 2015) to label and describe this process. When done correctly, the coach, parent, or support staff member will carefully consider both the short- and long-term goals of the process (as with the nested planning process shown in figure 26.1), consider the different blends of tools that might be used, then select and apply them. Importantly, the PJDM process also includes a follow-up at a predetermined time and against expected outcomes (Collins & Collins, 2020).

Of course, it is important to acknowledge that the use of sport to teach life skills is not without question. For example, Ronkainen and colleagues (2020) stress the additional benefits of adopting an existential approach to learning in youth sport. Once again, however, we suggest that readers consider the weight of evidence in making conclusions.

Optimizing the TDE

When optimizing the TDE, the factors presented previously need to be effectively integrated. Previous authors have provided excellent checklists for TDE design (e.g., Henriksen et al., 2010; Martindale et al., 2005). Accordingly, in this section we focus on the effective integration of ideas, using the structural model proposed by Webb and colleagues (2016). This, known colloquially as the ping-pong model, is shown in figure 26.1.

In the version on the left (the direct route), athletes are kept to a straight and narrow pathway, with sometimes authoritarian and directive coaching pushing them toward a clearly stated ideal for senior performance. As shown, progress is usually quick and targets very clear. The athlete may lack the capacity for adaptability, however, which many suggest is an important characteristic. In the middle option (the meandering route) changes of coach from stage to stage means the athlete is taken on a journey. A wide variety of inputs are made, often from somewhat different epistemological stances. As a result, those athletes who make it through such a pathway are very adaptable. Unfortunately, however, the high variation in challenge can derail many. The third option, presented on the right, offers a Goldilocks route, the idea being that the level of variation is "just right."

Of course, the Goldilocks content, and the degree of variation, can be very different, both across athletes and contexts or even with different levels of variation at different ages. In our experience, a set of core content with some degree of variation is usually most effective, offering the coach some guidelines but also allowing for some personal input and creativity.

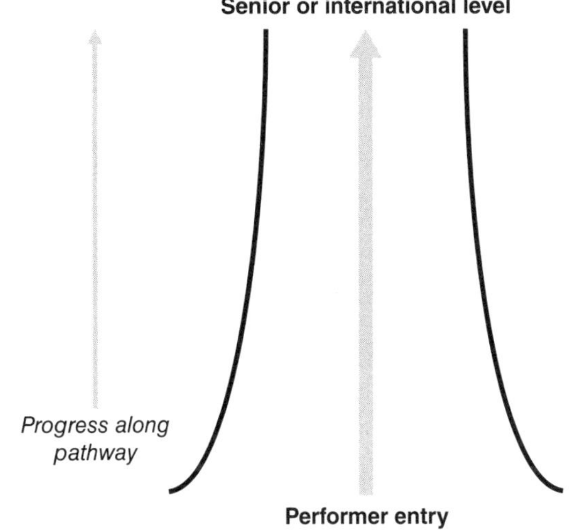

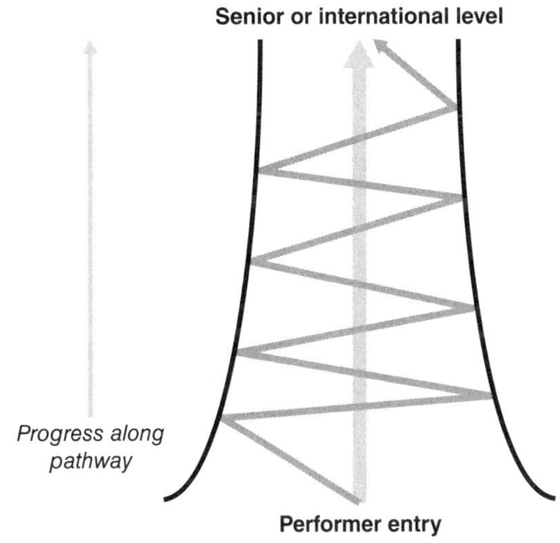

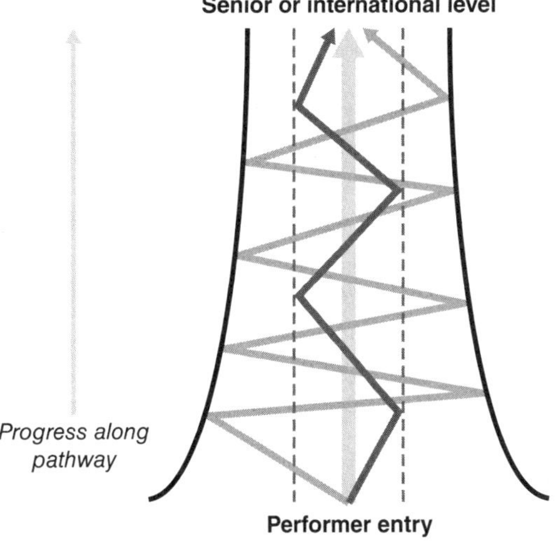

FIGURE 26.1 Conceptual models of different TD pathways.

Reprinted by permission from D. Collins and A. Cruickshank, *Sport Psychology Essentials* (Champaign, IL: Human Kinetics, 2023), 218.

Future Research Directions

Readers should take several messages from the previous section. Most particularly, many methods are available to the practitioner, and as with ideas of wider coaching in general, choosing between them to decide on the optimal blend for the context is a key requirement (cf. PJDM; Collins & Collins, 2015). There is a clear need for the TD practitioner and pathway to consider ways in which the optimal balance and dose of these tools (e.g., use of challenge and feedback) can be deployed to optimize athlete development, well-being, and ultimately performance over the long term. For example, challenging feedback offered to a young athlete may motivate a focus on technique change, leading to a short-term decline in performance but essential for long-term progress.

To facilitate this shift in practice, and reflecting the underlying principles of PJDM, we suggest a long overdue need for TD research to move beyond the descriptive and consider the mechanisms that underpin development and associated phenomena (Baker et al., 2020). For example, research into relative age effect (RAE) shows a higher proportion of earlier born athletes are selected into talent pathways, but it also shows, at the population level, a relative lower likelihood of reaching elite status when compared with their later born peers (Kelly et al., 2021; McCarthy et al., 2016). Although working with these dynamics is an essential part of TD practice, few have considered the underlying mechanisms of RAE, or *why* this occurs (e.g., McCarthy et al., 2022). There are several methodological approaches to understanding RAE and other phenomena in TD; for example, longitudinal research is important to avoid issues like survivorship bias. Yet there are the obvious challenges of finding the right people and tracking them over time. Ultimately, perhaps the real shift is more a matter of epistemology (how we arrive at a justified belief). For research to make a genuine difference to practice, we need greater focus on a more mechanistic and nuanced approach—in essence, *why* is something happening? (Collins et al., 2019). For example, if we really want to understand the experience of athletes over the long term, through the highs and lows, qualitative methods (such as in-depth, longitudinal interview-based approaches) are important to deepen understanding, especially in relation to the athlete's experience of TD (e.g., Taylor et al., 2021).

As noted earlier, an area that merits further research is the role that challenge plays in the process of TD, especially given evidence from a number of competing views that it appears pivotal in the developmental process (Collins et al., 2016b; Rees et al., 2016; Sarkar & Fletcher, 2017). Heeding calls for a focus on mechanisms, and a more granular approach to TD research, recent work has sought to understand how challenge influences the individual experience of the athlete. Pursuit of high performance will lead to significant emotional disruption for the individual performer (Taylor & Collins, 2020). Of course, the role of challenge (and specifically the use of the word *trauma* (cf. Collins & MacNamara, 2012) has attracted questioning and criticism, although it appears as an increasingly common thread in the outputs of numerous researchers and authors (Wadey & Howells, 2020).

This raises another important direction for future research: the need for conceptual clarity across the domain, especially as the impact of coaching on athlete welfare rightly becomes an increased focus for research (see chapter 21) (Kerr & Stirling, 2017). This conceptual clarity and focus on the mechanisms appear critical given the need for athletes to have a bumpy journey (Collins et al., 2016a), where developmental challenges such as nonselection may be a critical proving experience supportive of long-term development (Savage et al., 2017). In contrast, however, other research suggests that the benching of athletes can be considered punitive and hinder their developmental needs (Battaglia et al., 2017). In short, at least on superficial inspection, there appears to be a wide gulf between ideas (or perhaps even ideals) in this field. On the face of it, we might consider these findings contradictory; but we would suggest this as an example of the importance of context. It highlights the need for a mechanistic focus for research and practice on the perceptions of the athlete and their interpretation. In other words, what is the impact of these sorts of practices, and if they seem to work positively, how may this best be optimized?

In the research sense, we would do well to consider how an individual perceives an event, rather than classifying coach or support staff behavior and attempting to identify a uniform response, subsequently offering generalized advice (e.g., Carpentier & Mageau, 2013). In the practical sense, the coach or practitioner needs to be keenly aware of the individual athlete experience and shape it accordingly for optimal development. It seems obvious that the balance between challenge and collapse can often be a subtle one (Taylor & Collins, 2019). Of course, the context of a recreational athlete will be very different from that of a highly committed academy footballer, focused on reaching the highest levels of international performance. However, we need to be careful with this apparently straightforward distinction, because recreational athletes may be pursuing excellence in other areas of their lives (e.g., education), perhaps generically benefiting in the long run from challenging or even traumatic experiences (e.g., Williams & MacNamara, 2020). This is implicit in the often repeated notion that sport builds character. Despite some level of face validity, this lacks empirical support, with challenging experience appearing to test previously developed skill rather than directly provoking development (Savage et al., 2017). There is, therefore, an ethical and performance imperative for sport at all levels to pay attention to the broader psychological development of the athlete. As stated earlier, we suggest that PCDEs offer an empirically supported and practical way of doing this (Collins & MacNamara, 2017). Ultimately, however, given the complexities, there is a need to carefully delineate the *purpose* of an athlete's participation as a key variable in both research and practice and not generalize research findings across every sporting domain, or every individual in a particular classification.

The Talent Development Context

A challenge of actively shaping the experience of the individual performer within a TD milieu is typically characterized by a wide variety of stakeholders and often competing agendas (Bjørndal & Ronglan, 2018). This means the broader experience of the athlete is influenced by a variety of interpersonal and systemic interactions. These include the support they receive from coaches, parents, and support staff as well as the systemic features of the talent pathway, such as selection criteria and competition schedules. Consequently, for optimal impact, there is a need for systemic and organizational principles that influence multiple levels of stakeholders to optimally support their progress (Pankhurst et al., 2013).

By developing these shared principles and shaping shared mental models (SMMs) throughout a talent system, it is possible to curate an appropriate and coherent experience for an athlete. This curation has been proposed as ideally characterized by levels of difference, but not too much difference, as athletes move through a pathway (Taylor & Collins, 2020; Webb et al., 2016). In contrast, the lack of a systemic and principled approach may lead to a pathway that supports only the progress of athletes with high levels of motivation, because they need to navigate a long and winding road to elite status. When they arrive, however, they are likely to have high levels of adaptability and independence as an outcome of the pathway experience.

As shown earlier in figure 26.1, the ideal pathway has been characterized as offering a Goldilocks approach, offering appropriate levels where the athlete experience at various stages and times is different, but not *too* different. Critically, what is deemed appropriately different is highly context dependent, and what might be appropriate for a 14-year-old engaged in multiple sports and talent pathways is contextually different from what is right for an 18-year-old academy pole-vaulter committed solely to long-term development as an athlete. If research is to make a difference in real-world TD, there is a need to further consider the impact of the systemic features of TD pathways and their impact on athlete experience. Context needs and differences should be framed against long-term needs and the demands of the milieu, rather than a set of implicit or universal criteria held by the researcher.

This is particularly important because the present context has set multiple challenges for coaches and administrators in high-level sport. Of course, much of this is welcome and well overdue. There is little doubt that some behavior has been at best questionable and at worst illegal and abusive. We would suggest, however, that each case must be carefully considered. High-performance environments are essentially challenging, while even normal child-rearing practice must include some element of discombobulation (Taylor et al., 2022b). For this and several other reasons, we have proposed the RIB model as the basic structure for considering coaching behavior. In keeping with ideas established quite a while ago in coaching (e.g., Abraham & Collins, 1998), basing evaluations solely on observed behavior is likely to generate spurious data in either direction. Hence the need to consider the *rationale*, *intent*, and *behavior* in tandem. We suggest this as an addition to the principles that underpin effective management in TDEs.

Of course, to operationalize these systemic and organizational principles across a talent pathway, it appears clear that the different levels of an organization are both horizontally and vertically integrated. *Integration* refers to the extent to which processes and inputs are systematically combined to create a whole. Horizontally, this would be characterized by the mutually supportive practice of multiple stakeholders across time for an athlete. To exemplify, a number of stakeholders might work together to optimize the development experience of a 16-year-old swimmer. This working practice would necessarily engage those within the TDE, but necessarily and importantly, it will go beyond the TD organizational chart to encompass teachers, parents, and other influential figures. A distinct but clearly related concept, vertical integration refers to the ways a talent pathway can systemically and coherently offer developmental experiences to athletes that build from previous involvement toward long-term needs (Abraham & Collins, 2011; Taylor & Collins, 2020, 2022).

Our use of the term *coherence* is also deserving of explicit consideration. *Coherence* refers to the extent to which the interpersonal communication around an athlete holds logical connection and is mutually reinforcing. It has been identified in multiple models as a critical feature of effective TDEs (Henriksen & Stambulova, 2017; Martindale et al., 2005). This can be seen vertically, throughout a talent system, for example, with senior coaches engaging in regular effective communication with age-group coaches. It can also be seen horizontally, across a level of performance and multiple environments, which offers an appropriate and mutually reinforcing message to the athlete (Webb et al., 2016). Importantly, when these concepts are appropriately operationalized, they are likely to promote an optimal balance of support for the athlete. Taking this into account, a wide body of research has considered TD practice in a single environment (e.g., Henriksen, 2010; Larsen et al., 2020). There is now a need, however, to go beyond the walls of individual TDEs (Taylor et al., 2022) and investigate the breadth of "all aspects of the coaching situation" (Martindale et al., 2005, p. 354). Given the context of TD and concern for the dynamic balance between performance now and performance later, a breakdown in coherence around an athlete is likely to lead to stakeholders' holding different expectations and offering confusing support to the athlete.

We hope the elements within this section make the need clear for SMMs at all levels and across all stakeholders. Our point is that SMMs are essential for the smooth and coherent conduct of TDEs: without this, even the most motivated and considered of providers will inevitably end up pulling the athlete in different directions.

Given that optimal athlete experience is facilitated by a relatively large number of stakeholders, athlete needs are best met by developing SMMs within and across pathways (Taylor & Collins, 2020). SMMs are the "overlapping mental representations of knowledge by members of a team" that support the working practice of groups (Van den Bossche et al., 2011, p. 285). They are ideally developed at a number of levels, including top-down (from sport or organization leaders) and bottom-up processes (input from a range of stakeholders). The ideal outcome is coherence of experience for the athlete (Henriksen & Stambulova, 2017; Martindale et al., 2005). SMMs should be shaped around the needs of the individual athlete, their stage of performance, the pathway, the organization, and the wider sport. The process of doing so will build individual knowledge structures that help groups of people work together (McComb & Simpson, 2014). In the TD context, it would be typical to see athlete reviews and action planning involving interdisciplinary teams being used to build SMMs at the individual level (cf. Collins et al., 2016a). It is less common to see this type of approach being used across and between levels of performance or organizations, taking account of the totality of the athlete's experience, as might be done in the education setting (e.g., Wiliam, 2013). As a result, breakdowns in coherence can be frequent, given differences between levels of performance and the variety of stakeholders involved (Taylor et al., 2021).

Practical Implications

Although identifying ourselves as pracademics not wanting to promote a further divide between research and practice, we recognize the widespread perception of such. We therefore suggest a number of considerations for practice and those who support the development of practitioners.

Over the last 20 years, prescriptive models of TD, along with a host of other dubious ideas, have influenced the development of practitioners (e.g., long-term athlete development; Balyi & Hamilton, 2004). Along with other dubious practices, approaches that are linear and rigid in nature are recognized as suboptimal at best (Bailey & Collins, 2013; Bailey et al., 2018). Unfortunately, the desire for the simple solution remains and is exacerbated by research that is either descriptive or esoteric in nature (Collins et al., 2019). Drawing on the concept of PJDM, we suggest that the multiple stakeholders engaged in TD need to be engaged and supported to develop their decision making if performers are to have an optimal experience through the talent pathway.

Although the phrase *athlete centered* (Kidman, 2010) is common, it is often used to prescribe a range of coaching behaviors that are seen as *the* right way. This is perhaps a consequence of athlete empowerment's rarely receiving the critical attention it deserves (Alder, 2018). If TD pathways are to truly enable an athlete to "own the direction, [be] accountable for that direction and [take] responsibility for their actions and performance" (Penney & Kidman, 2014, pp. 2-3), this should surely be woven into a long-term developmental journey. True independence, we argue, should be seen as more than a social phenomenon in latter stages. Applied work and empirical research would suggest that an athlete's independence appears to be a critical factor in their later performance (Collins et al., 2016b). This may be an even more critical feature of athlete development given the complexity of the TD milieu and the demand it places on the athlete's psychosocial skill set (Bjørndal & Ronglan, 2018; Taylor & Collins, 2021a).

The complex demands of coaching in the TD milieu and its requisite knowledge bases and skill set have routinely been ignored in coach development, where "knowledge light" and competency-based approaches have dominated.

This complexity has historically been recognized in the coaching domain, often characterized as being multifaceted, presenting the coach with a variety of complex demands and decisions (Jones & Standage, 2006). Emerging evidence suggests that the context of the athlete offers an analogous level of complexity, necessitating a variety of complex decisions as they move through a pathway (Taylor et al., 2021). For example, as athletes navigate an often complex milieu, they may need to make decisions about the type of coach to work with, what advice to listen to, and from whom. These decisions have potential to profoundly influence their ultimate performance trajectory and well-being. Therefore, in addition to the previously identified need for a focus on the development of PCDEs (Larsen et al., 2014; MacNamara et al., 2010a, 2010b), athletes also need skills to make decisions about their own development. Evidence in the rugby league context would suggest that developmental athletes have a relatively limited skill set to navigate the knowledge sources they experience. Sensemaking of feedback tended to focus on the power of the provider, their relationship, or their playing background, notably omitting the validity of what was said (Taylor et al., 2021). Practically, we recommend that coaches and support staff support the development of an athlete's epistemological chain. The epistemological chain is the link between beliefs about knowledge and learning and one's actions (Grecic & Collins, 2013). In addition, this forms a critical element of a truly athlete-centered experience, enabling the performer to make independent decisions based on various knowledge sources.

In considering how this approach to athlete development might be pursued, we now consider the role of support figures around the TD athlete, a factor that is clearly critical, especially given the range and breadth of support required as an athlete moves through a pathway (Taylor et al., 2021). The implications for these support figures will now be considered, beginning with the coach.

Coaches

While it is clear that the athlete needs to make a variety of complex decisions based on the *social* milieu of TD, the coach has to contend with the additional complexity of *biopsycho* processes that influence athlete development (Bailey et al., 2010). The result of these developmental processes is that determinants of performance are hyperdynamic, in most cases varying significantly over time (van der Sluis et al., 2019). These layers of complexity place a substantial decision-making load on the individual coach, balancing the needs of performing now and later. Consequently, optimal support for the athlete requires a level of PJDM and the adaptive expertise to navigate complexity (Bohle Carbonell et al., 2014).

Adaptive expertise can be contrasted with routine expertise that demands the ability to perform routine tasks without error. It therefore requires the flexible, creative, and innovative use of domain-specific, metacognitive, and innovative skills, drawing on a significant declarative knowledge base (Mees et al., 2020). A typical problem for the TD coach is the management of a training group at various stages of maturation. On the face of it, encouraging a later physically developing athlete to train down in a lower age group might appear to be an obvious thing to do. Yet using simple rules of thumb like this ignores the need for adaptive expertise and does not take account of the potentially negative psychosocial consequences of doing so.

The complex demands of coaching in the TD milieu and its requisite knowledge bases and skill set have routinely been ignored in coach development, where "knowledge light" and competency-based approaches have dominated (Collins et al., 2015; Cushion & Nelson, 2013). Similarly, it appears that coaches have a preference for engagement with peers as a means of developing their practice (Stoszkowski & Collins, 2016). This has led to a self-reinforcing cycle where suboptimal simple approaches are initially offered and then reinforced by the preferences of the coach. An example is the predominance of theoretical positions in the field of skill acquisition (e.g., Davids et al., 2013), dominating both coach development and social media. Positions such as this are often represented as the *totality* of coaching practice, neglecting other critical developmental necessities, with many presented as the only way to operate. Given the significant challenge posed by the nature of TD, it would seem inappropriate to represent one way of working or to suggest a range of simplistic solutions as best practice to coaches.

To support this, a position paper has pointed to the need for coaches to develop a level of criticality to support their ongoing development (Stoszkowski et al., 2020). Thus, if coaches are to help athletes develop psychobehavioral skills and optimize feedback and use of challenge, they will need to draw on a variety of sources to develop their knowledge base and use it effectively. Thus, a developmental diet that fosters a level of critical interaction with knowledge sources should be a pressing concern for those who develop coaches.

Sport Psychology Consultants

Stressing the critical role of above-the-neck skills, many of the previous recommendations for coaches are just as applicable for support staff. For the sport psychology consultant working in TD, however, there are further implications beyond the development of the psychobehavioral skill set emphasized throughout this chapter. Additionally, given what we know about the potential benefits of a range of emotional states for the performer (Taylor & Collins, 2020), the psychology consultant has a balance to strike as an emotional expert. Thus, rather than always comforting during periods of negative emotion, in times of potentially adaptive negative emotion the psychology consultant offers support in the form of "good company" to effect an adaptive response (Berger, 2004). During a period of negative affect, this would see a psychology consultant, as part of an interdisciplinary group, helping the performer make sense of their experience and reflect in depth for the purpose of learning and development. Ultimately, the intention is the harnessing of affective states for optimal development (Gasper & Clore, 2002).

This is not to suggest that the sport psychology consultant ignore the welfare of the individual. It is simply to highlight the dual focus of performance and well-being, requiring monitoring the psychoemotional state of the performer during challenging periods for signs their emotional experience has become more chronic than acute (McEwen, 1998). Consequently, if an athlete experiences negative affect for an extended period, or is subject to prolonged or uncontrollable stressors, there is a need for a different approach (Parihar et al., 2011). This would suggest the need for the consultant to develop their own empathic accuracy (cf. Lorimer & Jowett, 2010). The consequent recognition of affective states should support a consultant's PJDM and ability to make effective practice decisions, based on the needs of the individual.

An additional concern for the consultant is the multiple stakeholders that characterize the TD milieu. To reach the ideal of a coherent experience for the athlete, integrated working practice between members of the athlete's support team (e.g., parents, coaches, sport science staff, peers) is a necessity (Taylor et al., 2022a). The often used maxim of "working with and through the coach" is an appropriate reference point to ensure the athlete experience is appropriately curated by all support figures. Relatedly, the sport consultant also helps the athlete independently navigate the complexity of the milieu. This support should come in two forms: (1) by offering insight and advice on interpersonal conduct to enable appropriate use of a range of support figures and (2) by developing an effective sensemaking process, ideally helping the performer to independently make sense of and make decisions based on the advice they receive (Taylor et al., 2021).

Throughout the chapter, we have highlighted the significant biopsychosocial complexities of the TD process. To optimally support the groups of practitioners working with TD athletes, researchers have a critical role to play in countering the overly simplistic narrative being offered. Accordingly, we suggest a double-ended approach. First is to perform research focused on the real-world problems of practice, thus offering insight to the practitioner (Cruickshank & Collins, 2017). This means being ambitious, asking practically valuable questions, and reporting findings in as simplistic a manner as possible—but clearly no simpler. The second approach is for academia to model the same level of criticality we expect from practitioners, helping them see the strengths *and* weaknesses of ideas. There is a clear practical and ethical imperative for journals to encourage the writing and publication of response papers. We should not be afraid of the necessary discourse and robust competition of ideas to help deepen our understanding of TD and encourage the broader development of the domain.

Parents

Although parents have been recognized in the literature for many years (e.g., Bloom, 1985; Harwood & Knight, 2015), it is only recently that sport has begun paying specific attention to their role in the process of TD. This has led to the emergence of the specialist parental adviser and generalized TD parent guidance in sport. Catchall advice, however well intentioned, has the potential to generate incoherence for the athlete if disconnected from the aims and objectives of the TD organization, especially if the advice is from the parent (Pankhurst et al., 2013). For this reason, we suggest caution, with a blanket approach offered for all parents regardless of domain. As stated earlier, the support needs of all young people are different. Indeed, the parenting of a truly ambitious young performer will be very different from that of an engaged young person with no ambitions of further development beyond participation. It also appears that the parenting challenge changes over the course of time and in line with the experience of the athlete (Newport et al., 2020). Thus, generalized advice offered to all parents is both inappropriate and unadvised, ultimately incongruent with the need for a focus on expertise in sport parenting (Harwood & Knight, 2015).

A critical role of the TD organization or coach is to offer specialized support to parents, helping them understand the differential needs of young people aiming for high performance. Support should help parents take into account the motivations of highly driven and ambitious children, while at the same time balancing dual career objectives and preventing identity foreclosure (Kuttel, 2022). We further suggest that parents should ideally influence their child's long-term performance aims by offering appropriate encouragement, without contradicting the messaging of practitioners (Taylor et al., 2021). For example, a coach may choose to approach a competition with a view of offering minimal support and guidance to athletes as a test of previously developed psychobehavioral skills. Parents might mitigate this developmental test by offering instruction or advice to their children (Omli & Wiese-Bjornstal, 2011) or even by undermining the coach's approach if they believe winning to be most important for their child's progress.

Summary

The talent development process is complex, with lots of moving parts. Ideally, these are integrated and working in the same direction. The key take-home messages for scientists and practitioners include the following:

- All involved need to be clear about the outcome deliverables. Are we working for success now, developing for the future, or looking for a weighted combination of both?
- Despite some apparent contradictions, most scholars are agreed on the need for developing and deploying a set of skills. Make sure all involved know what the skills are and are aware of how to facilitate the young player in self-regulation.
- There are no magic formulas or quick fixes. Deciding between options to optimize the pathway for individuals is the key skill of the TD coach.
- Young developing athletes will feel under pressure. Indeed, this is an essential feature of the effective pathway *but not all the time*. Once again, decision making and timing are crucial considerations.

DISCUSSION QUESTIONS

1. What are the key features to be considered when planning and providing feedback to a developing athlete?
2. How might the structure of pathway provision (content and method) vary as athletes progress? If there is more than one option, what factors should influence this variation?
3. How does a parent's role need to change through the pathway? How might an organization, team, or coach support this?
4. What are some key considerations in deciding on the level, timing, and monitoring of challenge?

Afterword

Anne-Marie Elbe, PhD

This second edition of *Social Psychology in Sport* showcases once again the fascinating and ever-evolving study of psychosocial factors influencing athletic performance and behavior. The book thoughtfully acknowledges the complexity of the social world of sport and outlines the conditions under which social behavior and emotions in sport occur. What a task it surely has been for Louise Davis, Richard Keegan, and Sophia Jowett to put together the recent developments in this area of research in one book—and in such depth and breadth. It is a true accomplishment to successfully combine theoretical and applied perspectives, to include such a variety of both qualitative and quantitative research, and at the same time to create a book that is so readable and understandable for its audience. This book includes clear descriptions and definitions of the topics, concise theoretical overviews, new research ideas, and discussions of practical applications of the research. In addition, readers will strongly appreciate the learning objectives at the beginning of each chapter as well as the discussion questions at the end.

When reading the chapters in the second edition of *Social Psychology in Sport*, what stands out most is how much the field has developed in the past years. The book now contains 26 chapters, which are a wonderful mix of updated "old" topics (such as the coach–athlete relationship, interpersonal communication and conflict, leadership, team cohesion, and motivational climate) and entirely new topics. One aspect these new topics focus on are the challenges that athletes and their coaches, peers, and parents face. Examples of these challenges are the psychosocial aspects of mental health issues and how the use of power in sport-related relationships can lead to athlete maltreatment. At the same time, positive approaches to conquer these challenging sides of sport are portrayed in detail. These include topics such as systems that promote thriving, environmental and sociocultural influences of resilience, and how to create safe cultures in sport. The contributors and editors have successfully woven together theoretical frameworks, the most current empirical research, and their implications for applied practice, which is something few books in our field accomplish.

This book clearly demonstrates what an established field the social psychology of sport has become and, at the same time, draws attention to future avenues of research. The chapters highlight the multitude of reliable and valid sport-specific instruments that are available to measure social psychological constructs. Furthermore, the chapters illustrate how the development of these instruments has led to a rich body of knowledge. This knowledge, however, has often been generated from cross-sectional studies predominantly conducted with athletes and coaches (i.e., the micro level). In the future, I would expect an even stronger focus on the macro level (e.g., how do sport organizations, sport governing bodies, and other social agents have an impact on the social climate, communication, or leadership?). At the same time, investigations of the macro level's influence on social phenomena calls for a more holistic research approach that would also entail utilization of diverse research methods. By employing qualitative research methods (e.g., observations, interviews), the underlying mechanisms for the existing correlational results could be further explored. Including additional quantitative methods such as psychophysiological measurements could further explore the emotional effects of stress, conflicts, and coping, for example. Also, the use of more complex analytical methods (e.g., social network analysis) could deepen the understanding of macro-level influences of various social phenomena. Additionally, more evidence-based studies with a longitudinal or experimental design can be expected in the future. The need for these studies is outlined in a number of the chapters and would further advance and solidify our knowledge base as well as the derived practical implications.

In addition to advancements on a methodological level, I would also expect deeper exploration of specific topics. First, I anticipate that upcoming studies will place a stronger focus on cultural issues, a void several of the authors pointed out with regard to the role of parents, social and motivational climate, and leadership. It can be assumed that the relevance of investigating cultural aspects and topics such as identity and acculturation will be further sparked by the ever-growing waves of migration due to war and climate change. Second, the world has recently lived through a pandemic that may have sustainably affected human interactions in sport, which warrants investigation. I hypothesize that the lives of athletes, coaches, and other social agents have already been affected by increased digitalization and the more frequent use of modern communication technology and platforms. If this in turn will affect social relationships, how and why this potentially will occur, and which role sport psychology could play in ensuring that digitalization and technology have a positive impact on interactions in sport, could be another future avenue of interest.

In conclusion, social psychology in sport is a complex and multifaceted field that continues to evolve and expand as new research is conducted. I am sure this handbook will once again become a strong resource for students, researchers, and practitioners in the field and will contribute to theory-driven applied practice as well as inspire future research. The volume provides readers a rich source of inspiration for upcoming studies by portraying how the field has advanced in the past 15 years. The second edition of *Social Psychology in Sport* provides a valuable overview to the topic and will most certainly spark interest in further learning.

References

Chapter 1

Aggarwal, U., & Bhargava, S. (2010). The effects of equity sensitivity, job stressors and perceived organizational support on psychological contract breach. *Journal of Business Perspective, 14*(1/2), 45-55.

Allen, M.S., Greenlees, I., & Jones, M.V. (2013). Personality in sport: A comprehensive review. *International Review of Sport and Exercise Psychology, 6*, 184-208. https://doi.org/10.1080/1750984X.2013.769614

Antonini Philippe, R., Sagar, S.S., Huguet, S., Paquet, Y., & Jowett, S. (2011). From teacher to friend: The evolving nature of the coach-athlete relationship. *International Journal of Sport Psychology, 42*(1), 1-23.

Aşçi, F.H., Kelecek, S., & Altintaş, A. (2015). The role of personality characteristics of athletes in coach-athlete relationships. *Perceptual and Motor Skills, 121*(2), 399-411. https://doi.org/10.2466/30.PMS.121c17x9

Bartholomew, K.J., Ntoumanis, N., & Thøgersen-Ntoumani, C. (2010). The controlling interpersonal style in a coaching context: Development and initial validation of a psychometric scale. *Journal of Sport and Exercise Psychology, 32*(2), 193-216. https://doi.org/10.1123/jsep.32.2.193

Baudin, N., Aluja, A., Rolland, J.P., & Blanch, A. (2011). The role of personality in satisfaction with life and sport. *Psicologia Conductual, 19*(2), 333.

Baxter, L.A., & Montgomery, B.M. (1998). A guide to dialectical approaches to studying personal relationships. In B.M. Montgomery & L.A. Baxter (Eds), *Dialectical approaches to studying personal relationships* (pp. 1-15). Erlbaum.

Bishop, C. (2020). *The long win: The search for a better way to succeed.* Practical Inspiration Publishing.

Brummelman, E., Nelemans, S.A., Thomaes, S., & Orobio de Castro, B. (2017). When parents' praise inflates, children's self-esteem deflates. *Child Development, 88*, 1799-1809. https://doi.org/10.1111/cdev.12936

Caspi, A., Roberts, R.W., & Shiner, R.L. (2005). Personality development: Stability and change. *Annual Reviews of Psychology, 56*, 453-484. https://doi.org/10.1146/annurev.psych.55.090902.141913

Claxton, A., O'Rourke, N., Smith, J.Z., & DeLongis, A. (2012). Personality traits and marital satisfaction within enduring relationships: An intra-couple discrepancy approach. *Journal of Social and Personal Relationships, 29*(3), 375-396. https://doi.org/10.1177/0265407511431183

Côté, J., Yardley, J., Hay, J., Sedgwick, W., & Baker, J. (1999). An exploratory examination of the Coaching Behaviour Scale for Sport. *Avante, 5*(3), 82-92.

Davis, L., Jowett, S., Sormen, D., & Ekelund, R. (2022). The role of quality relationships and communication strategies for the fulfilment of secure and insecure athletes' basic psychological needs [Manuscript under review].

Davis, L., Jowett, S., & Tafvelin, S. (2019). Communication strategies: The fuel for quality coach-athlete relationships and athlete satisfaction. *Frontiers in Psychology, 10*, 2156. https://doi.org/10.3389/fpsyg.2019.02156

de Haan, D., & Norman, L. (2020). Mind the gap: The presence of capital and power in the female athlete-male-coach relationship within elite rowing. *Sports Coaching Review, 9*(1), 95-118. https://doi.org/10.1080/21640629.2019.1567160

Dryer, D.C., & Horowitz, L.M. (1997). When do opposites attract? Interpersonal complementarity versus similarity. *Journal of Personality and Social Psychology, 72*(3), 592. https://doi.org/10.1037/0022-3514.72.3.592

Edmondson, A.C., & Harvey, J.F. (2017). *Extreme teaming: Lessons in complex, cross-sector leadership.* Emerald Group Publishing.

Felton, L., & Jowett, S. (2013). "What do coaches do" and "how do they relate": Their effects on athletes' psychological needs and functioning. *Scandinavian Journal of Medicine and Science in Sports, 23*(2), 130-139. https://doi.org/10.1111/sms.12029

Felton, L., Jowett, S., Begg, C., & Zhong, X. (2021). A multistudy examination of the complementarity dimension of the coach-athlete relationship. *Sport, Exercise, and Performance Psychology, 10*(1), 27. https://doi.org/10.1037/spy0000209

Gosai, J., Jowett, S., & do Nascimento-Júnior, J.R.A. (2023). When leadership, relationships and psychological safety promote flourishing in sport and life. *Sports Coaching Review*, 1-21. https://doi.org/10.1080/21640629.2021.1936960

Gosai, J., Jowett, S., & Rhind, D.J. (2021). Coaching through a "gender lens" may reveal myths that hinder female athletes: A multistudy investigation. *International Sport Coaching Journal, 1*(AoP), 1-12. https://doi.org/10.1123/iscj.2021-0046

Gosselin, D. (2002). Gender issues related to males coaching female athletes. http://assets.teamusa.org/assets/documents/attached_file/filename/15749/gender_issues_in_coaching.pdf

Hampson, R., & Jowett, S. (2012). Effects of coach leadership and coach-athlete relationship on collective efficacy. *Scandinavian Journal of Medicine and Sport Sciences, 24*(2), 454-460. https://doi.org/10.1111/j.1600-0838.2012.01527.x

Heller, D., Watson, D., & Ilies, R. (2004). The role of person versus situation in life satisfaction: A critical examination. *Psychological Bulletin, 130*, 574-600. https://doi.org/10.1037/0033-2909.130.4.574

Hinde, R.A., Tamplin, A., & Barrett, J. (1993). A comparative study of relationship structure. *British Journal of Social Psychology, 32*(3), 191-207. https://doi.org/10.1111/j.2044-8309.1993.tb00995.x

Jackson, B., Dimmock, J.A., Gucciardi, D.F., & Grove, J.R. (2011). Personality traits and relationship perceptions in coach-athlete dyads: Do opposites really attract? *Psychology of Sport and Exercise,* 12, 222-230. https://doi.org/10.1016/j.psychsport.2010.11.005

Jones, R.L., Edwards, C., & Viotto Filho, I.T. (2016). Activity theory, complexity and sports coaching: An epistemology for a discipline. *Sport, Education and Society, 21*(2), 200-216. https://doi.org/10.1080/13573322.2014.895713

Jones, R.L., & Wallace, M. (2006). The coach as 'orchestrator': More realistically managing the complex coaching context. In R.L. Jones (Ed), *The sports coach as educator: Re-conceptualising sports coaching* (pp. 69-82). Routledge.

Jowett, S. (2007). Interdependence analysis and the 3 + 1Cs in the coach–athlete relationship. In S. Jowett & D. Lavallee (Eds.), *Social psychology in sport* (pp. 63-77). Human Kinetics.

Jowett, S. (2008). Outgrowing the familial coach - athlete relationship. *International Journal of Sport Psychology, 39,* 20-40.

Jowett, S. (2009). Validating coach-athlete relationship measures with the nomological network. *Measurement in Physical Education and Exercise Science, 13,* 1-18.

Jowett, S. (2017). Coaching Effectiveness: The Coach-Athlete Relationship at its Heart. *Current Opinion in Psychology, 16,* 154-158.

Jowett, S., & Arthur, C. (2019). Effective coaching: The links between coach leadership and coach–athlete relationship. From theory to research to practice. In M.H. Anshel, T.A. Petrie, & J.A. Steinfeldt (Eds.), *APA handbook of sport and exercise psychology. Vol. 1: Sport psychology* (pp. 419-449). American Psychological Association. https://doi.org/10.1037/0000123-022

Jowett, S., & Carpenter, P. (2015). The concept of rules in the coach–athlete relationship. *Sports Coaching Review, 4,* 1-23. https://doi.org/10.1080/21640629.2015.1106145

Jowett, S., & Clark-Carter, D. (2006). Perceptions of empathic accuracy and assumed similarity in the coach–athlete relationship. *British Journal of Social Psychology, 45*(3), 617-637. https://doi.org/10.1348/014466605X58609

Jowett, S., & Cockerill, I.M. (2003). Olympic medallists' perspective of the athlete–coach relationship. *Psychology of Sport and Exercise, 4*(4), 313-331. https://doi.org/10.1016/S1469-0292(02)00011-0

Jowett, S., & Felton, L. (2014). Coach–athlete relationships and attachment styles within sport teams. In M.R. Beauchamp, B. Jackson, & D. Lavallee (Eds.), *Group dynamics in exercise and sport psychology* (pp. 73-90). Routledge.

Jowett, S., Lafrenière, M.A.K., & Vallerand, R.J. (2013). Passion for activities and relationship quality: A dyadic approach. *Journal of Social and Personal Relationships, 30*(6), 734-749. https://doi.org/10.1177/0265407512467748

Jowett, S., & Meek, G.A. (2000). The coach–athlete relationship in married couples: An exploratory content analysis. *The Sport Psychologist, 14*(2), 157-175. https://doi.org/10.1123/tsp.14.2.157

Jowett, S., do Nascimento-Júnior, J.R.A., Zhao, C., & Gosai, J. (2022). Creating the conditions for psychological safety and its impact on quality coach–athlete relationships [Manuscript under review].

Jowett, S., & Nezlek, J. (2012). Relationship interdependence and satisfaction with important outcomes in coach–athlete dyads. *Journal of Social and Personal Relationships, 29*(3), 287-301. https://doi.org/10.1177/0265407511420980

Jowett, S., Nicolas, M., & Yang, S. (2017). Unravelling the links between coach behaviours and coach–athlete relationships. *European Journal of Sports and Exercise Science, 5*(3), 10-19.

Jowett, S., & Ntoumanis, N. (2004). The Coach - Athlete Relationship Questionnaire (CART - Q): Development and initial validation. *Scandinavian Journal of Medicine and Science in Sports, 14,* 245-257.

Jowett, S., & Poczwardowski, A. (2007). Understanding the coach–athlete relationship. In S. Jowett & D. Lavallee (Eds.), *Social psychology in sport* (pp. 3-14). Human Kinetics.

Jowett, S., & Shanmugam, V. (2016). Relational coaching in sport: Its psychological underpinnings and practical effectiveness. In R. Schinke, K.R. McGannon, & B. Smith (Eds), *Routledge international handbook of sport psychology* (pp. 471-484). Routledge.

Jowett, S., & Slade, K. (2021). Understanding the coach–athlete relationship and the role of ability, intentions and integrity. In C. Heaney, N. Kentzer, & B. Oakley (Eds.), *Athletic development: A psychological perspective.* Open University.

Jowett, S., & Wachsmuth, S. (2020). Power in coach–athlete relationships: The case of the women's artistic gymnastics. In G. Kerr (Ed), *Women's artistic gymnastics: Socio-cultural perspectives.* Routledge.

Jowett, S., & Wylleman, P. (2006). Interpersonal relationships in sport and exercise settings: Crossing the chasm. *Psychology of Sport and Exercise, 7*(2), 119-123. https://doi.org/10.1016/j.psychsport.2005.08.001

Jowett, S., Yang, X., & Lorimer, R. (2012). The role of personality, empathy, and satisfaction with instruction within the context of the coach–athlete relationship. *International Journal of Coaching Science, 6*(2), 3-20.

Karney, B.R., & Bradbury, T.N. (1997). Neuroticism, marital interaction, and the trajectory of marital satisfaction. *Journal of Personality and Social Psychology, 72,* 1075-1092. https://doi.org/10.1037/0022-3514.72.5.1075

Kiesler, D.J. (1996). *Contemporary interpersonal theory and research: Personality, psychopathology, and psychotherapy.* Wiley.

Kim, I., Lee, K., & Kang, S. (2019). The relationship between passion for coaching and the coaches' interpersonal behaviors: The mediating role of coaches' perception of the relationship quality with athletes. *International Journal of Sports Science and Coaching, 14*(4), 463-470. https://doi.org/10.1177/1747954119853104

Koestner, R., & Losier, G.F. (2002). Distinguishing three ways of being internally motivated: A closer look at introjection, identification, and intrinsic motivation, In E.L. Deci & R.M. Ryan (Eds.), *Handbook of self-determination research.* University of Rochester Press.

Kozlowski, S.W. (2018). Enhancing the effectiveness of work groups and teams: A reflection. *Perspectives on Psychological Science, 13*(2), 205-212. https://doi.org/10.1177/1745691617697078

Kozlowski, S.W., & Ilgen, D.R. (2006). Enhancing the effectiveness of work groups and teams. *Psychological Science in the Public Interest, 7*(3), 77-124. https://doi.org/10.1111/j.1529-1006.2006.00030.x

Lafrenière, M.A.K., Jowett, S., Vallerand, R.J., & Carbonneau, N. (2011). Passion for coaching and the quality of the coach–athlete relationship: The mediating role of coaching behaviors. *Psychology of Sport and Exercise, 12*(2), 144-152. https://doi.org/10.1016/j.psychsport.2010.08.002

Lafrenière, M.A.K., Jowett, S., Vallerand, R.J., Donahue, E.G., & Lorimer, R. (2008). Passion in sport: On the quality of the coach–athlete relationship. *Journal of Sport and Exercise Psychology, 30*(5), 541-560. https://doi.org/10.1123/jsep.30.5.541

Lehmann, C.M. (2009). Early Greek athletic trainers. *Journal of Sport History, 36*(2), 187-204. www.jstor.org/stable/26405186

Longshore, K., & Sachs, M. (2015). Mindfulness training for coaches: A mixed-method exploratory study. *Journal of Clinical Sport Psychology, 9*(2), 116-137. https://doi.org/10.1123/jcsp.2014-0038

Lorimer, R., & Jowett, S. (2011). Empathic accuracy, shared cognitive focus, and the assumptions of similarity made by coaches and athletes. *International Journal of Sport Psychology,* 42(1), 40-54.

Lorimer, R., & Jowett, S. (2013). Empathic understanding and empathic accuracy in the coach-athlete relationship. In P. Potrac, W. Gilbert, & J. Denison (Eds.), *Routledge handbook of sports coaching.* Routledge.

MacKinnon, V. (2011). Techniques for instructing female athletes in traditionally male sports: A case study of LPGA teaching professionals. *International Journal of Sport and Society, 2*(1), 75-87. https://doi.org/10.18848/2152-7857/CGP/v02i01/54060

Mageau, G.A., & Vallerand, R.J. (2003). The coach-athlete relationship: A motivational model. *Journal of Sports Science, 21*(11), 883-904. https://doi.org/10.1080/0264041031000140374

McCrae, R.R., & Costa, P.T., Jr. (2008). The five-factor theory of personality. In O.P. John, R.W. Robins, & L.A. Pervin (Eds.), *Handbook of personality: Theory and research* (3rd ed., pp. 159-181). Guilford Press.

Metcalfe, J., & Mischel, W. (1999). A hot/cool-system analysis of delay of gratification: dynamics of willpower. *Psychological Review, 106*(1), 3-19.

Navarre, M.J. (2011). *Male college soccer coaches perceptions of gender similarities and differences in coach-athlete and teammate relationships: Introducing the construct of relationship-performance orientation* [Unpublished doctoral dissertation]. University of Minnesota.

Norman, L. (2015). The coaching needs of high performance female athletes within the coach-athlete dyad. *International Sport Coaching Journal, 2*(1), 15-28. https://doi.org/10.1123/iscj.2013-0037

Norman, L., & French, J. (2013). Understanding how high performance women athletes experience the coach-athlete relationship. *International Journal of Coaching Science, 7*(1), 3-24.

O'Connor, J., & Lages, A. (2009). How coaching works: The essential guide to the history and practice of effective coaching. London.

Olympiou, A., Jowett, S., & Duda, J.L. (2008). The psychological interface between the coach-created motivational climate and the coach-athlete relationship in team sports. *The Sport Psychologist, 22*(4), 423-438. https://doi.org/10.1123/tsp.22.4.423

Reis, H.T. (2001). Relationship experiences and emotional well-being. In C.D. Ryff & B.H. Singer (Eds.), *Emotion, social relationships and health* (pp. 57-95). Oxford University Press.

Rhind, D.J.A., & Jowett, S. (2010). Relationship maintenance strategies in the coach-athlete relationship: The COMPASS model. *Journal of Applied Sport Psychology, 22*, 106-121. https://doi.org/10.1080/10413200903474472

Rhind, D.J.A., & Jowett, S. (2011). Linking maintenance strategies to the quality of coach-athlete relationships. *International Journal of Sport Psychology, 41*(1), 55-68.

Rhind, D.J.A., & Jowett, S. (2012). Development of the Coach-Athlete Relationship Maintenance Questionnaire (CARM-Q). *International Journal of Sports Science and Coaching, 7*(1), 121-137. https://doi.org/10.1260%2F1747-9541.7.1.121

Singh, P., Nadim, A., & Ezzedeen, S.R. (2012). Leadership styles and gender: An extension. *Journal of Leadership Studies, 5*(4), 6-19. https://doi.org/10.1002/jls.20239

Solomon, B.C., & Jackson, J.J. (2014). Why do personality traits predict divorce? Multiple pathways through satisfaction. *Journal of Personality and Social Psychology, 106*(6), 978. https://doi.org/10.1037/a0036190

Stafford, L., & Canary, D. J. (1991). Maintenance strategies and romantic relationship type, gender and relational characteristics. *Journal of Social and Personal Relationships, 8*(2), 217-242. https://doi.org/10.1177/0265407591082004

Vallerand, R.J., Blanchard, C., Mageau, G.A., Koestner, R., Ratelle, C., Léonard, M., Gagné, M., & Marsolais, J. (2003). Les passions de l'âme: On obsessive and harmonious passion. *Journal of Personality and Social Psychology, 85*(4), 756-767. https://doi.org/10.1037/0022-3514.85.4.756

Van den Bossche, P., Gijselaers, W., Segers, M., Woltjer, G., & Kirschner, P. (2011). Team learning: Building shared mental models. *Instructional Science, 39*(3), 283-301. https://doi.org/10.1007/s11251-010-9128-3

Vella, S.A., Oades, L.G., & Crowe, T.P. (2013). The relationship between coach leadership, the coach-athlete relationship, team success, and the positive developmental experiences of adolescent soccer players. *Physical Education and Sport Pedagogy, 18*(5), 549-561. https://doi.org/10.1080/17408989.2012.726976

Wachsmuth, S., Jowett, S., & Harwood, C.G. (2018). Managing conflict in coach-athlete relationships. *Sport, Exercise, and Performance Psychology, 7*(4), 371. https://doi.org/10.1037/spy0000129

White, J.S., Schempp, P.G., McCullick, B.A., Berger, B.S., & Elliott, J.M. (2017). Mentoring relationships in sport from the protégé's perspective. *International Journal of Evidence Based Coaching and Mentoring, 15*(1), 152-168.

Woodrow, C., & Guest, D.E. (2017). Leadership and approaches to the management of workplace bullying, *European Journal of Work and Organizational Psychology, 26* (2), 221-233. DOI: 10.1080/1359432X.2016.1243529

Wylleman, P. (2000). Interpersonal relationships in sport: Uncharted territory in sport psychology research. *International Journal of Sport Psychology, 31*(4), 555-572.

Yang, X.S., & Jowett, S. (2013). Conceptual and measurement issues of the complementarity dimension of the coach-athlete relationship across cultures. *Psychology of Sport and Exercise, 14*(6), 830-841. https://doi.org/10.1016/j.psychsport.2013.06.003

Yang, S.X., Jowett, S., & Chan, D.K.C. (2015). Effects of big-five personality traits on the quality of relationship and satisfaction in Chinese coach-athlete dyads. *Scandinavian Journal of Medicine and Science in Sports,* 25(4), 568-580. https://doi.org/10.1111/sms.12329

Zhao, C., & Jowett, S. (2022). Coach transformational leadership and coach-athlete relationship: What is the link? [Manuscript under review].

Chapter 2

Barki, H., & Hartwick, J. (2004). Conceptualizing the construct of interpersonal conflict. *International Journal of Conflict Management, 15*(3), 216-244. https://doi.org/10.1108/eb022913

Becker, A.J. (2009). It's not what they do, it's how they do it: Athlete experiences of great coaching. *International Journal of Sports Science and Coaching, 4*(1), 93-119. https://doi.org/1747-9541.4.1.93

Becker, A.J. (2013). Quality coaching behaviors. In P. Potrac, W. Gilbert, & J. Denison (Eds.), *Routledge handbook of sports coaching* (pp. 184-195). Routledge.

Benson, A., Eys, M., Surya, M., Dawson, K., & Schneider, M. (2013). Athletes' perceptions of role acceptance in interdependent sport teams. *The Sport Psychologist, 27*(3), 269-280.

Canary, D.J., Cupach, W.R., & Serpe, R.T. (2001). A competence-based approach to examining interpersonal conflict: Test of a longitudinal model. *Communication Research, 28*(1), 79-104. https://doi.org/10.1177/009365001028001003

Canary, D.J., & Lakey, S.G. (2006). Managing conflict in a competent manner. In J.G. Oetzel & S. Ting-Toomey (Eds.), *The Sage handbook of conflict communication: Integrating theory, research, and practice* (pp. 185-210). Sage.

Côté, J., & Gilbert, W. (2009). An integrative definition of coaching effectiveness and expertise. *International Journal of Sports Science and Coaching, 4*(3), 307-323. https://doi.org/10.1260%2F174795409789623892

d'Arripe-Longueville, F., Fournier, J.F., & Dubois, A. (1998). The perceived effectiveness of interactions between expert French judo coaches and elite female athletes. *The Sport Psychologist, 12*(3), 317-332. https://doi.org/10.1123/tsp.12.3.317

Davis, L., & Jowett, S. (2014). Coach-athlete attachment and the quality of the coach-athlete relationship: Implications for athlete's well-being. *Journal of Sports Sciences, 32*(15), 1454-1464. https://doi.org/10.1080/02640414.2014.898183

Dieffenbach, K. (2019). Framework for coach education and development. In K. Dieffenbach & M. Thompson (Eds.), *Coach education essentials* (pp. 3-16). Human Kinetics.

Dupuis, M., Bloom, G., & Loughead, T. (2006). Team captains' perceptions of athlete leadership. *Journal of Sport Behavior, 29*(1), 60-78.

Eaves, M., & Leathers, D.G. (2018). *Successful nonverbal communication: Principles and applications* (5th ed.) Routledge.

Evans, A.L., Slater, M.J., Turner, M.J., & Barker, J.B. (2013). Using personal-disclosure mutual-sharing to enhance group functioning in a professional soccer academy. *The Sport Psychologist, 27*(3), 233-243. https://doi.org/10.1123/tsp.27.3.233

Feddersen, N.B., Morris, R., Littlewood, M.A., & Richardson, D.J. (2020). The emergence and perpetuation of a destructive culture in an elite sport in the United Kingdom. *Sport in Society, 23*(6), 1004-1022. https://doi.org/10.1080/17430437.2019.1680639

Gearity, B.T., & Metzger, L.H. (2017). Intersectionality, microagressions and microaffirmations: Toward a cultural praxis of sport coaching. *Sociology of Sport Journal, 34*(2), 160-175. https://doi.org/10.1123/ssj.2016-0113

Gearity, B.T., & Murray, M.A. (2011). Athletes' experiences of the psychological effects of poor coaching. *Psychology of Sport and Exercise, 12*(3), 213-221. https://doi.org/10.1016/j.psychsport.2010.11.004

Gosai, J., Jowett, S., & do Nascimento-Júnior, J.R.A. (2021). When leadership, relationships and psychological safety promote flourishing in sport and life. *Sports Coaching Review,* 1-21. https://doi.org/10.1080/21640629.2021.1936960

Gould, D., & Dieffenbach, K. (2021). Key coaching functions. In D. Gould & C. Mallett (Eds). *Sport coaches' handbook* (2nd ed., pp. 51-72). Human Kinetics.

Greenleaf, C., Gould, D., & Dieffenbach, K. (2001). Factors influencing Olympic performance: Interviews with Atlanta and Nagano US Olympians. *Journal of Applied Sport Psychology, 13*(2), 154-184. https://doi.org/10.1080/104132001753149874

Heelis, W.J., Caron, J.G., & Bloom, G.A. (2020). The experiences of high-performance coaches in the management of difficult athletes. *Psychology of Sport and Exercise, 51,* 101751. https://doi.org/10.1016/j.psychsport.2020.101751

Henriksen, K., Larsen, C.H., & Christensen, M.K. (2014). Looking at success from its opposite pole: The case of a talent development golf environment in Denmark. *International Journal of Sport and Exercise Psychology, 12*(2), 134-149. https://doi.org/10.1080/1612197X.2013.853473

Holt, N., Knight, C., & Zukiwski, P. (2012). Female athletes' perceptions of teammate conflict in sport: Implications for sport psychology consultants. *The Sport Psychologist, 26*(1), 135-154. https://doi.org/10.1123/tsp.26.1.135

Jackson, B., Dimmock, J.A., Gucciardi, D.F., & Grove, J.R. (2011). Personality traits and relationship perceptions in coach-athlete dyads: Do opposites really attract? *Psychology of Sport and Exercise, 12*(3), 222-230. https://doi.org/10.1016/j.psychsport.2010.11.005

Jackson, B., Grove, J.R., & Beauchamp, M.R. (2010). Relational efficacy beliefs and relationship quality within coach-athlete dyads. *Journal of Social and Personal Relationships, 27*(8), 1035-1050. https://doi.org/10.1177%2F0265407510378123

Jackson, B., Knapp, P., & Beauchamp, M.R. (2008). Origins and consequences of tripartite efficacy beliefs within elite athlete dyads. *Journal of Sport and Exercise Psychology, 30*(5), 512-540. https://doi.org/10.1123/jsep.30.5.512

Jehn, K.A., Rispens, S., Jonsen, K., & Greer, L. (2013). Conflict contagion: A temporal perspective on the development of conflict within teams. *International Journal of Conflict Management, 24*(4), 352-373.

Jowett, S., & Carpenter, P. (2015). The concept of rules in the coach-athlete relationship. *Sports Coaching Review, 4*(1), 1-23. https://doi.org/10.1080/21640629.2015.1106145

Jowett, S., & Frost, T. (2007). Race/ethnicity in the all-male coach-athlete relationship: Black footballers' narratives. *International Journal of Sport and Exercise Psychology, 5*(3), 255-269. https://doi.org/10.1080/1612197X.2007.9671835

Jowett, S., & Slade, K. (2021). Understanding the coach-athlete relationship and the role of ability, intentions and integrity. In C. Heaney, N. Kentzer, & B. Oakley (Eds.), *Athletic development: A psychological perspective* (pp. 89-106), Routledge/Open University.

Jowett, S., & Wachsmuth, S. (2020). Power in women artistic gymnastics' coach-athlete relationships. In R. Kerr, N. Barker-Ruchti, C. Stewart, & G. Kerr (Eds.) *Women's artistic gymnastics: Socio-cultural perspectives* (pp. 122-142). Routledge.

Khomutova, A. (2015). Basketball coaches' experience in working with multicultural teams: Central and Northern European perspectives. *Sport in Society, 19*(7), 861-876. https://doi.org/10.1080/17430437.2015.1067777

Komaki, J.L., & Tuakli-Wosornu, Y.A. (2021). Using carrots not sticks to cultivate a culture of safeguarding in sport. *Frontiers in Sports and Active Living, 3*(9), 625410. https://doi.org/10.3389/fspor.2021.625410

Korsgaard, M.A., Ployhart, R.E., & Ulrich, M.D. (2014). The emergence of intragroup conflict: Variations in conflict configurations. In O.B. Ayoko, N.M. Ashkanasy, & K.A. Jehn (Eds.), *Handbook of conflict management research* (pp. 51-65). Elgar. https://doi.org/10.4337/9781781006948

Korsgaard, M.A., Soyoung Jeong, S., Mahony, D.M., & Pitariu, A.H. (2008). A multilevel view of intragroup conflict. *Journal of Management, 34*(6), 1222-1252. https://doi.org/10.1177/0149206308325124

Kristiansen, E., Tomten, S.E., Hanstad, D.V, & Roberts, G.C. (2012). Coaching communication issues with elite female athletes: Two Norwegian case studies. *Scandinavian Journal of Medicine and Science in Sports, 22*(6), 156-167. https://doi.org/10.1111/j.1600-0838.2012.01521.x

Leo, F.M., González-Ponce, I., Sánchez-Miguel, P.A., Ivarsson, A., & García-Calvo, T. (2015). Role ambiguity, role conflict, team conflict, cohesion and collective efficacy in sport teams: A multilevel analysis. *Psychology of Sport and Exercise, 20,* 60-66. https://doi.org/10.1016/j.psychsport.2015.04.009

Loughead, T.M. (2017). Athlete leadership: A review of the theoretical, measurement, and empirical literature. *Current Opinion in Psychology, 16,* 58-61. https://doi.org/10.1016/j.copsyc.2017.04.014

Mellalieu, S., Shearer, D.A., & Shearer, C. (2013). A preliminary survey of interpersonal conflict at major games and championships. *The Sport Psychologist, 27*(2), 120-129. https://doi.org/10.1123/tsp.27.2.120

O'Malley, L., Winter, S., & Holder, T. (2018). "Always picking country over club": A creative non fiction story of an international coach-athlete-coach triad. *Qualitative Research in Sport, Exercise and Health, 10*(2), 223-237. https://doi.org/10.1080/2159676X.2017.1367716

Overall, N.C., & McNulty, J.K. (2017). What type of communication during conflict is beneficial for intimate relationships?

Current Opinion in Psychology, 13, 1-5. https://doi.org/10.1016/j.copsyc.2016.03.002

Paradis, K.F., Carron, A.V, & Martin, L.J. (2014a). Athlete perceptions of intra-group conflict in sport teams. *Sport and Exercise Psychology Review, 10*(3), 4-18.

Paradis, K., Carron, A., & Martin, L. (2014b). Development and validation of an inventory to assess conflict in sport teams: The Group Conflict Questionnaire. *Journal of Sports Sciences, 32*(29), 1966-1978. https://doi.org/10.1080/02640414.2014.970220

Partridge, J.A., & Knapp, B.A. (2016). Mean girls: Adolescent female athletes and peer conflict in sport. *Journal of Applied Sport Psychology, 28*(1), 113-127. https://doi.org/10.1080/10413200.2015.1076088

Potrac, P., & Jones, R. (2009). Power, conflict, and cooperation: Toward a micropolitics of coaching. *Quest, 61*(2), 223-236. https://doi.org/10.1080/00336297.2009.10483612

Purdy, L., Potrac, P., & Jones, R. (2008). Power, consent and resistance: An autoethnography of competitive rowing. *Sport, Education and Society, 13*(3), 319-336. https://doi.org/10.1080/13573320802200693

Rahim, M.A. (2002). Toward a theory of managing organizational conflict. *International Journal of Conflict Management, 13*(3), 206-235. https://doi.org/10.1108/eb022874

Rhind, D.J., & Jowett, S. (2010). Relationship maintenance strategies in the coach–athlete relationship: The development of the COMPASS Model. *Journal of Applied Sport Psychology, 22*(1), 106-121. https://doi.org/10.1080/10413200903474472

Roberts, L.J. (2006). From bickering to battering: Destructive conflict processes in intimate relationships. In P. Noller and J.A. Feeney (Eds.), *Close relationships: Functions, forms and processes* (pp. 325-351). Psychology Press.

Roberts, V., Sojo, V., & Grant, F. (2020). Organisational factors and non-accidental violence in sport: A systematic review. *Sport Management Review, 23*(1), 8-27. https://doi.org/10.1016/j.smr.2019.03.001

Stirling, A.E. (2009). Definition and constituents of maltreatment in sport: Establishing a conceptual framework for research practitioners. *British Journal of Sports Medicine, 43*, 1091-1099. https://doi.org/10.1136/bjsm.2008.051433

Stirling, A.E., & Kerr, G.A. (2008). Elite female swimmers' experiences of emotional abuse across time. *Journal of Emotional Abuse, 7*(4), 89-113. https://doi.org/10.1300/J135v07n04_05

Stirling, A.E., & Kerr, G.A. (2009). Abused athletes' perceptions of the coach–athlete relationship. *Sport in Society, 12*(2), 227-239. https://doi.org/10.1080/17430430802591019

Sullivan, P. (2004). Communication differences between male and female team sport athletes. *Communication Reports, 17*(2), 121-128. https://doi.org/10.1080/08934210409389381

Van de Vliert, E., Nauta, A., Giebels, E., & Janssen, O. (1999). Constructive conflict at work. *Journal of Organizational Behavior, 20*(4), 475-491. https://doi.org/10.1002/(SICI)1099-1379(199907)20:4%3C475::AID-JOB897%3E3.0.CO;2-G

Vealey, R.S. (2017). Conflict management and cultural reparation: Consulting "below zero" with a college basketball team. *Case Studies in Sport and Exercise Psychology, 1*(1), 83-93. https://doi.org/10.1123/cssep.2017-0008

Wachsmuth, S., & Jowett, S. (2020). Conflict and communication in coach–athlete relationships. In D. Hackfort & R.J. Schinke (Eds.) *The Routledge international encyclopedia of sport and exercise psychology. Vol. 2: Applied and practical measures* (pp. 192-212). Routledge.

Wachsmuth, S., Jowett, S., & Harwood, C.G. (2017). Conflict among athletes and their coaches: What is the theory and research so far? *International Review of Sport and Exercise Psychology, 10*(1), 84-107. https://doi.org/10.1080/1750984X.2016.1184698

Wachsmuth, S., Jowett, S., & Harwood, C.G. (2018a). On understanding the nature of interpersonal conflict between coaches and athletes. *Journal of Sports Sciences, 36*(17), 1955-1962. https://doi.org/10.1080/02640414.2018.1428882

Wachsmuth, S., Jowett, S., & Harwood, C.G. (2018b). Managing conflict in coach–athlete relationships. *Sport, Exercise, and Performance Psychology, 7*(4), 371. https://doi.org/10.1037/spy0000129

Wachsmuth, S., Jowett, S., & Harwood, C.G. (2022). Third party interventions in coach–athlete conflict: Can sport psychology practitioners offer the necessary support? *Journal of Applied Sport Psychology, 34*(1), 178-203. https://doi.org/10.1080/10413200.2020.1723737

Wachsmuth, S., Weise, M., Jowett, S., & Höner, O. (2021). Die Trainer-Athlet-Beziehung: Grundstein zum Erfolg? [The coach–athlete relationship: A steppingstone to success?]. *Leistungssport, 51*(1), 5-11.

Wylleman, P., De Brandt, K., & de Knop, P. (2020). Career development. In D. Hackfort & R. Schinke (Eds.), *The Routledge international encyclopedia of sport and exercise psychology. Vol. 2: Applied and practical measures* (pp. 89-106). Routledge.

Yang, S.X., Jowett, S., & Chan, D.K. (2015). Effects of the big-five personality traits on the quality of relationship and satisfaction in coach–athlete dyads. *Scandinavian Journal of Medicine and Science in Sports, 25*(4), 568-580. https://doi.org/10.1111/sms.1232

Chapter 3

Ainsworth, M.D.S., Blehar, M.C., Waters, E., & Wall, S. (1978). *Patterns of attachment: A psychological study of the strange situation*. Erlbaum.

Armsden, G.C., & Greenberg, M.T. (1987). The inventory of parent and peer attachment: Individual differences and their relationship to psychological well-being in adolescence. *Journal of Youth and Adolescence, 16*(5), 427-454. http://doi.org/10.1007/BF02202939

Assor, A., Roth, G., & Deci, E. L. (2004). The emotional costs of parents' conditional regard: A Self-Determination Theory analysis. Journal of personality, 72(1), 47-88. https://doi.org/10.1111/j.0022-3506.2004.00256.x

Baldwin, M.W. (1995). Relational schemas and cognition in close relationships. *Journal of Social and Personal Relationships, 12*(4), 547-552. https://doi.org/10.1177/2F0265407595124008

Baldwin, M.W., & Fehr, B. (1995). On the instability of attachment style ratings. *Personal relationships, 2*(3), 247-261. https://doi.org/10.1111/j.1475-6811.1995.tb00090.x

Bartholomew, K., & Shaver, P.R. (1998). Methods of assessing adult attachment: Do they converge? In J.A. Simpson and W.S. Rholes (Eds.), *Attachment theory and close relationships* (pp. 25-45). Guilford Press.

Bergin, C., & Bergin, D. (2009). Attachment in the classroom. Educational psychology review, 21, 141-170. https://doi.org/10.1007/s10648-009-9104-0

Bischof, M. (1975). A systems approach toward the functional connections of attachment and fear. *Child Development, 46*(4), 801-807. https://doi.org/10.2307/1128384

Bowlby, J. (1969/1982). *Attachment and loss. Vol. 1: Attachment*. Basic Books.

Bowlby, J. (1973). *Attachment and loss. Vol. 2: Separation: Anxiety and anger.* Basic Books.

Bowlby, J. (1977). The making and breaking of affectional bonds. *British Journal of Psychiatry, 130,* 201-210. https://doi.org/10.1192/bjp.130.3.201

Bowlby, J. (1979/2005). *The making and breaking of affectional bonds.* Routledge.

Bowlby, J. (1988). A secure base: Parent-child attachment and healthy human development. Basic Books.

Brennan, K.A., Clark, C.L., & Shaver, P.R. (1998). Self-report measurement of adult attachment: An integrative overview. In J.A. Simpson & W.S. Rholes (Eds.), *Attachment theory and close relationships* (pp. 46-76). Guilford Press.

Bretherton, I. (1985). Attachment theory: Retrospect and prospect. In I. Bretherton & F. Waters (Eds.), *Growing points of attachment theory and research: Monographs of the Society for Research in Child Development, 50*(1-2), 3-35. www.jstor.org/stable/3333824?origin=JSTOR-pdf

Bretherton, I., & Munholland, K.A. (2008). Internal working models in attachment relationships: Elaborating a central construct in attachment theory. In J. Cassidy & P.R. Shaver (Eds.), *Handbook of attachment: Theory, research, and clinical applications* (p. 102-127). Guilford Press.

Carr, S. (2009a). Implications of attachment theory for sport and physical activity research: Conceptual links with achievement goal and peer relationship models. *International Review of Sport and Exercise Psychology, 2*(1), 95-115. https://doi.org/10.1080/17509840902759173

Carr, S. (2009b). Adolescent-parent attachment characteristics and quality of youth sport friendship. *Psychology of Sport and Exercise, 10*(6), 653-661. https://doi.org/10.1016/j.psychsport.2009.04.001

Carr, S. (2012). *Attachment in sport, exercise and wellness.* Routledge.

Carr, S., & Batlle, I.C. (2015). Attachment theory, neoliberalism, and social conscience. *Journal of theoretical and philosophical psychology, 35*(3), 160. https://psycnet.apa.org/doi/10.1037/a0038681

Carr, S., & Fitzpatrick, N. (2011). Experiences of dyadic sport friendships as a function of self and partner attachment characteristics. *Psychology of Sport and Exercise, 12*(4), 383-391. https://doi.org/10.1016/j.psychsport.2011.03.003

Cassidy, J. (1999). The nature of a child's ties. In J. Cassidy and P.R. Shaver (Eds.), *Handbook of attachment: Theory, research and clinical applications* (pp. 3-20). Guilford Press.

Collins, N.L. (1996). Working models of attachment: Implications for explanation, emotion, and behavior. *Journal of Personality and Social Psychology, 71*(4), 810-832. https://doi.org/10.1037/0022-3514.71.4.810

Collins, N.L., & Read, S.J. (1990). Adult attachment, working models, and relationship quality in dating couples. *Journal of Personality and Social Psychology, 58*(4), 644-663. https://doi.org/10.1037/0022-3514.58.4.644

Côté, J., & Gilbert, W. (2009). An integrative definition of coaching effectiveness and expertise. *International Journal of Sports Science and Coaching, 4*(3), 307-323. https://doi.org/10.1260%2F174795409789623892

Davila, J., & Sargent, E. (2003). The meaning of life (events) predicts changes in attachment security. *Personality and Social Psychology Bulletin, 29*(11), 1383-1395. https://doi.org/10.1177/0146167203256374

Davis, L., Jowett, S., Sörman, D., & Ekelund, R. (2022). The role of quality relationships and communication strategies for the fulfilment of secure and insecure athletes' basic psychological needs. Journal of Sports Sciences, 40(21), 2424-2436. https://doi.org/10.1080/02640414.2022.2162240

Davis, L., Brown, D., Arnold, R., & Gustafsson, H. (2021). Thriving through relationships in sport: The role of the parent-child and coach-athlete attachment relationship. *Frontiers in Psychology, 12,* 694599. doi: 10.3389/fpsyg.2021.694599.

Davis, L., and Jowett, S. (2010). Investigating the interpersonal dynamics between coaches and athletes based on fundamental principles of attachment theory. *Journal of Clinical Sport Psychology, 4*(2), 112-132. https://doi.org/10.1123/jcsp.4.2.112

Davis, Louise (2012). The application of attachment theory in the examination of the coach-athlete relationship. Loughborough University. Thesis. https://hdl.handle.net/2134/10151

Davis, L., and Jowett, S. (2013). Attachment styles within the coach athlete dyad: Preliminary investigation and assessment development. *Journal of Clinical Sport Psychology, 7,* 120-145. https://doi.org/10.1123/jcsp.7.2.120

Davis, L., and Jowett, S. (2014). Coach-athlete attachment and the quality of the coach-athlete relationship: Implications for athlete's well-being. *Journal of Sports Science, 32,* 1454-1464. https://doi.org/10.1080/02640414.2014.898183

Davis, L., Jowett, S., and Lafrenière, M.-A.K. (2013). An attachment theory perspective in the examination of relational processes associated with coach-athlete dyads. *Journal of Sport and Exercise Psychology, 35,* 156-167. https://doi.org/10.1123/jsep.35.2.156

DeVellis, R.F. (2003). Scale development: Theory and application (2nd ed.). London: Sage.

Diaconu-Gherasim, L. R., & Duca, D. S. (2018). Parent-Adolescent attachment and interpersonal relationships in sports teams: exploring the gender differences. Gender Issues, 35, 21-37. https://doi.org/10.1007/s12147-017-9190-0

Ein-Dor, T., Reizer, A., Shaver, P.R., & Dotan, E. (2012). Standoffish perhaps, but successful as well: Evidence that avoidant attachment can be beneficial in professional tennis and computer science. *Journal of Personality, 80*(3), 749-768. https://doi.org/10.1111/j.1467-6494.2011.00747.x

Feeney, J.A., Noller, P., & Hanrahan, M. (1994). *Assessing adult attachment.* In M.B. Sperling & W.H. Berman (Eds.), *Attachment in adults: Clinical and developmental perspectives* (pp. 128-152). Guilford Press.

Felton, L., and Jowett, S. (2013a). The mediating role of social environmental factors in the associations between attachment styles and basic needs satisfaction. *Journal of Sports Sciences, 31*(6), 618-628. https://doi.org/10.1080/02640414.2012.744078

Felton, L., and Jowett, S. (2013b). Attachment and well-being: The mediating effects of psychological needs satisfaction within the coach-athlete and parent-athlete relational contexts. *Psychology of Sport and Exercise, 14,* 57-65. https://doi.org/10.1016/j.psychsport.2012.07.006

Felton, L., & Jowett, S. (2015). On understanding the role of need thwarting in the association between athlete attachment and well/ill-being. *Scandinavian Journal of Medicine and Science in Sports, 25*(2), 289-298. https://doi.org/10.1111/sms.12196

Fraley, R.C., Hudson, N.W., Heffernan, M.E., & Segal, N. (2015). Are adult attachment styles categorical or dimensional? A taxometric analysis of general and relationship-specific attachment orientations. *Journal of Personality and Social Psychology, 109*(2), 354-368. http://dx.doi.org/10.1037/pspp0000027

Fraley, R.C., Waller, N.G., & Brennan, K.A. (2000). An item response theory analysis of self-report measures of adult attachment. *Journal of Personality and Social Psychology, 78*(2), 350-365. https://doi.org/10.1037/0022-3514.78.2.350

Güllich, A., Hardy, L., Kuncheva, L., Laing, S., Barlow, M., Evans, L., Rees, T., Abernethy, B., Côté, J., Warr, C., and Wraith, L. (2019). Developmental biographies of Olympic super-elite and elite athletes: A multidisciplinary pattern recognition analysis. *Journal of Expertise, 2*(1), 23-46. www.journalofexpertise.org/articles/volume2_issue1

Hazan, C., & Shaver, P.R. (1987). Romantic love conceptualized as an attachment process. *Journal of Personality and Social Psychology, 52*(3), 511-524. https://doi.org/10.1037//0022-3514.52.3.511

Hazan, C., & Shaver, P.R. (1994). Attachment as an organizational framework for research on close relationships. *Psychological Inquiry, 5*(1), 1-22. https://psycnet.apa.org/doi/10.1207/s15327965pli0501_1

Hazan, C., & Zeifman, D. (1994). Sex and the psychological tether. In K. Bartholomew & D. Perlman (Eds.), *Advances in personal relationships* (Vol. 5, pp. 151-178). Kingsley.

Lai, Y.H., & Carr, S. (2018). A critical exploration of child–parent attachment as a contextual construct. *Behavioral Sciences, 8*(12), 112. https://doi.org/10.3390/bs8120112

Lai, Y.H., & Carr, S. (2020). Is parental attachment security contextual? Exploring context-specific child–parent attachment patterns and psychological well-being in Taiwanese youths. *Journal of Research on Adolescence, 30*(2), 389-405. https://doi.org/10.1111/jora.12531

Li, R., Bunke, S., & Psouni, E. (2016). Attachment relationships and physical activity in adolescents: The mediation role of physical self-concept. *Psychology of Sport and Exercise, 22*, 160-169. https://doi.org/10.1016/j.psychsport.2015.07.003

Lopez, F.G., Mauricio, A.M., Gormley, B., Simko, T., & Berger, E. (2001). Adult attachment orientations and college student distress: The mediating role of problem coping styles. *Journal of Counseling and Development, 79*(4), 459-464. https://doi.org/10.1002/j.1556-6676.2001.tb01993.x

Lopez, F.G., Mitchell, P., & Gormley, B. (2002). Adult attachment orientations and college student distress: Test of a mediational model. *Journal of Counseling Psychology, 49*(4), 460-467. https://doi.org/10.1037/0022-0167.49.4.460

Main, M., & Solomon, J. (1986). Discovery of an insecure-disorganized/disoriented attachment pattern. In T.B. Brazelton and M.W. Yogman (Eds.), *Affective development in infancy* (pp. 95-124). Ablex.

Main, M., & Solomon, J. (1990). Procedures for identifying infants as disorganized/disoriented during the Ainsworth strange situation. In M.T. Greenberg, D. Cicchetti, & E.M. Cummings (Eds.), *Attachment in the preschool years: Theory, research, and intervention* (pp. 121-60). University of Chicago Press.

Mayseless, O. (2010). Attachment and the leader–follower relationship. *Journal of Social and Personal Relationships, 27*(2), 271-280. https://doi.org/10.1177/0265407509360904

Mikulincer, M., Gillath, O., & Shaver, P.R. (2002). Activation of the attachment system in adulthood: Threat-related primes increase the accessibility of mental representations of attachment figures. *Journal of Personality and Social Psychology, 83*(4), 881-895. https://doi.org/10.1037/0022-3514.83.4.881

Mikulincer, M., & Shaver, P.R. (2016). *Attachment in adulthood: Structure, dynamics, and change* (2nd ed.). Guilford Press.

Mikulincer, M., Shaver, P.R., & Pereg, D. (2003). Attachment theory and affect regulation: The dynamics, development, and cognitive consequences of attachment-related strategies. *Motivation and Emotion, 27*(2),77-102. https://doi.org/10.1023/A:1024515519160

Milroy, J.J., Hebard, S., Kroshus, E., & Wyrick, D.L. (2018). Sport-related concussion reporting and coach–athlete attachment among collegiate student-athletes. *Journal of Clinical Sport Psychology, 12*(2), 268-281. https://doi.org/10.1123/jcsp.2017-0029

Parish, M. (2000). *The nature of the patient's tie to the therapist* [Doctoral dissertation]. Adelphi

University. Dissertation Abstracts International, 60, 6378.

Parish, M., & Eagle, M.N. (2003). Attachment to the therapist. *Psychoanalytic Psychology, 20*(2), 271-286. https://doi.org/10.1037/0736-9735.20.2.271

Pincus, D., Freeman, W., & Modell, A. (2007). A neurobiological model of perception: Considerations for transference. *Psychoanalytic Psychology, 24*(4), 623-640 https://do.org:10.1037/0736-9735.24.4.623

Riley, A., & Anderson-Butcher, D. (2012). Participation in a summer sport-based youth development program for disadvantaged youth: Getting the parent perspective. *Children and Youth Services Review, 34*(7), 1367-1377. https://psycnet.apa.org/doi/10.1016/j.childyouth.2012.03.008

Roisman, G.I. (2009). Adult attachment: Toward a rapprochement of methodological cultures. *Current Directions in Psychological Science, 18*(2), 122-126. https://psycnet.apa.org/doi/10.1111/j.1467-8721.2009.01621.x

Shanmugam, V., Jowett, S., & Meyer, C. (2012). Eating psychopathology amongst athletes: Links to current attachment styles. *Eating Behaviours, 13*(1), 5-12. https://doi.org/10.1016/j.eatbeh.2011.09.004

Shaver, P.R., & Hazan, C. (1988). A biased overview of the study of love. *Journal of Social and Personal Relationships, 5*(4), 473-501. https://doi.org/10.1177/0265407588054005

Shaver, P.R., Hazan, C., & Bradshaw, D. (1988). Love as attachment: The integration of three behavioral systems. In R.J. Sternberg and M.L. Bames (Eds.), *The psychology of love* (pp. 68-99). Yale University Press.

Simpson, J.A. (1990). Influence of attachment styles on romantic relationships. *Journal of Personality and Social Psychology, 59*(5), 971-980. https://psycnet.apa.org/doi/10.1037/0022-3514.59.5.971

Simpson, J.A., Rholes, W.S., Campbell, L., & Wilson, C.L. (2003). Changes in attachment orientations across the transition to parenthood. *Journal of Experimental Social Psychology, 39*(4), 317-331. https://psycnet.apa.org/doi/10.1016/S0022-1031(03)00030-1

Simpson, J.A., Rholes, W.S., & Phillips, D. (1996). Conflict in close relationships: An attachment perspective. *Journal of Personality and Social Psychology, 71*(5), 899-914. https://psycnet.apa.org/doi/10.1037/0022-3514.71.5.899

Ullrich-French, S.C., Smith, A.L., & Cox, A.E. (2011). Attachment relationships and physical activity motivation of college students. *Psychology and Health, 26*(8), 1063-1080. https://doi.org/10.1080/08870446.2010.530123

Van der Horst, F.C.P. (2009). John Bowlby and ethology: A study of cross-fertilization. Doctoral thesis, Centre for Child and Family Studies, Leiden University.

Van Ijzendoorn, M., Schuengel, C., & Bakermans-Kranenburg, M. (1999). Disorganized attachment in early childhood: Meta-analysis of precursors, concomitants, and sequelae. *Development and Psychopathology, 11*(2), 225-249. https://doi.org/10.1017/s0954579499002035

Waters, E. (2000). Notes on attachment as grand theory [Unpublished manuscript].

Wei, M., Russell, D.W., Mallinckrodt, B., & Vogel, D.L. (2007). The Experiences in Close Relationship Scale (ECR)-short form: Reliability, validity, and factor structure. *Jour-*

nal of Personality Assessment, 88(2), 187-204. https://doi.org/10.1080/00223890701268041

West, W., Rose, S.M., Spreng, S., Sheldon-Keller, A., & Adam, K. (1998). Adolescent Attachment Questionnaire: A brief assessment of attachment in adolescence. *Journal of Youth and Adolescence, 27*(5), 661-673. https://doi.org/10.1023/A:1022891225542

Chapter 4

Alder, J.P. (2017). Team culture and athlete-centred coaching. In S. Pill (Ed.), *Perspectives on athlete-centred coaching* (pp. 57-69). Routledge.

Alexander, K., Stafford, A., & Lewis, R. (2011). *The experiences of children participating in organized sport in the UK.* Child Protection Research Centre.

Allan, E., & Madden, M. (2012). The nature and extent of college student hazing. *International Journal of Adolescent Medicine and Health, 24*(1), 83-90.

Associated Press. (2020, August 4). How the Larry Nassar trial has affected others. www.washingtonpost.com/health/how-the-larry-nassar-scandal-has-affected-others/2020/08/04/15917e9c-d676-11ea-a788-2ce86ce81129_story.html

AthletesCAN. (n.d.). Retrieved October 25, 2020, from https://athletescan.com/en

Battaglia, A., Kerr, G., & Stirling, A. (2017). Youth athletes' interpretations of punitive coaching practices. *Journal of Applied Sport Psychology, 29*(3), 337-352. https://doi.org/10.1080/10413200.2016.1271370

Barker-Ruchti, N., & Schubring, A. (2016). Moving into and out of high-performance sport: The cultural learning of an artistic gymnast. *Physical Education and Sport Pedagogy, 21*(1), 69-80.

Beaton, A. (2020, September 11). The NFL protests with Colin Kaepernick, who's still unsigned. *Wall Street Journal.* www.wsj.com/articles/the-nfl-protests-with-colin-kaepernick-whos-still-unsigned-11599827958

Bloom, S. (2008). Violence against women and girls: A compendium of monitoring and evaluation indicators. *MEASURE Evaluation. https://www.measureevaluation.org/resources/publications/ms-08-30/at_download/document*

Boykoff, J., & Carrington, B. (2020). Sporting dissent: Colin Kaepernick, NFL activism, and media framing contests. *International Review for the Sociology of Sport, 55*(7), 829-849. https://doi-org.myaccess.library.utoronto.ca/10.1177/1012690219861594

Brackenridge, C. (1997). "He owned me basically. . ." Women's experience of sexual abuse in sport. *International Review for the Sociology of Sport, 32*(2), 115-130. https://doi-org.myaccess.library.utoronto.ca/10.1177/101269097032002001

Brackenridge, C. (2001). *Spoilsports: Understanding and preventing sexual exploitation in sport.* Routledge.

Brackenridge, C., & Fasting, K. (2002). Sexual harassment and abuse in sport: The research context. *Journal of Sexual Aggression, 8*(2), 3-15. https://doi-org.myaccess.library.utoronto.ca/10.1080/13552600208413336

Brittain, C.R. (2006). Defining child abuse and neglect. *Understanding the Medical Diagnosis of Child Maltreatment: A Guide for Nonmedical Professionals,* 149-189.

Brown, B.B., & Larson, J. (2009). Peer relationships in adolescents. In R.M. Lerner & L. Steinberg (Eds.), *Handbook of adolescent psychology. Vol. 2: Contextual influences on adolescent development* (3rd ed., pp. 74-103). Wiley.

Bruner, M.W., Balish, S.M., Forrest, C., Brown, S., Webber, K., Gray, E., McGuckin, M., Keats, M.R., Rehman, L., & Shields, C.A. (2017). Ties that bond: Youth sport as a vehicle for social identity and positive youth development. *Research Quarterly for Exercise and Sport, 88*(2), 209-214. https://doi.org/10.1080/02701367.2017.1296100

Cacciola, S., & Mather, V. (2018, January, 24). Larry Nassar sentencing: "I just signed your death warrant." *New York Times.* www.nytimes.com/2018/01/24/sports/larry-nassar-sentencing.html

Chappelet, J.L. (2020). The unstoppable rise of athlete power in the Olympic system. *Sport in Society, 23*(5), 795-809. https://doi.org/10.1080/17430437.2020.1748817

Clark, A. (2017). *Coaching abuse experiences in young elite female artistic gymnasts: An ethical appraisal* [Master's thesis]. Brock University.

Clarke, H., Smith, D., & Thibault, G. (1994). Athlete-centred sport: A discussion paper. www.athletescan.com/Images/Publications/AthleteCentredDiscussion.doc

Coaching Association of Canada (n.d.). Retrieved October 21, 2020, from https://coach.ca

Coakley, J. (2011). Youth sports: What counts as "positive development?" *Journal of Sport and Social Issues, 35*(3), 306-324.

Cole, C.L., Giardina, M.D., & Andrews, D.L. (2004). Michel Foucault: Studies of power and sport. In R. Giulianotti (Ed.), *Sport and modern social theorists* (pp. 207-223). Palgrave Macmillan.

Collot D'Escury, A.L., & Dudink, A.C. (2010). Bullying beyond school: Examining the role of sports. In S.R. Jimerson, S.M. Swearer, & D.L. Espelage (Eds.), *Handbook of bullying in schools: An international perspective* (pp. 235-248). Routledge/Taylor Francis Group.

Cooper, J.N., Macaulay, C., & Rodriguez, S.H. (2019). Race and resistance: A typology of African American sport activism. *International Review for the Sociology of Sport, 54*(2), 151-181. https://doi.org/10.1177/1012690217718170

Côté, J., & Gilbert, W. (2009). An integrative definition of coaching effectiveness and expertise. *International Journal of Sports Science and Coaching, 4*(3), 307-323. https://doi.org/10.1260/174795409789623892

Crooks, C.V., & Wolfe, D.A. (2007). Child abuse and neglect. In E.J. Mash & R.A. Barkley (Eds.), *Assessment of childhood disorders* (4th ed., pp. 1-17). Guilford Press.

David, P. (2005). *Human rights in youth sport: A critical review of children's rights in competitive sport.* Routledge.

Dubin, C.L. (1990). *Commission of inquiry into the use of drugs and banned practices intended to increased athletic performance.* Canadian Government Publishing Centre.

European Commission. (2014). What is gender-based violence: Gender-based violence can take different forms and mostly affects women and girls. https://ec.europa.eu/info/policies/justice-and-fundamental-rights/gender-equality/gender-based-violence/what-gender-based-violence_en

Evans, B., Adler, A., MacDonald, D., & Côté, J. (2016). Bullying victimization and perpetration among adolescent sport teammates. *Pediatric Exercise Science, 28*(2), 296-303. https://doi.org/10.1123/pes.2015-0088

Exner, J. (2019). *Sporting nationality in the context of European Union law: Seeking a balance between sporting bodies' interests and athletes' rights.* Springer International Publishing. https://doi.org/10.1007/978-3-030-10807-6

Fasting, K., Brackenridge, C., & Sundgot-Borgen, J. (2003). Experiences of sexual harassment and abuse among Norwegian elite female athletes and nonathletes. *Research Quarterly for Exercise and Sport, 74*(1), 84-97. https://doi.org/10.1080/02701367.2003.10609067

French, J.R., & Raven, B. (1959). The bases of social power. In D. Cartwright (Ed.), *Studies in social power* (pp. 150-167). Institute for Social Research.

Fortier, K., Parent, S., & Lessard, G. (2020). Child maltreatment in sport: Smashing the wall of silence: A narrative review of physical, sexual, psychological abuses and neglect. *British Journal of Sports Medicine, 54*(1), 4-7. https://doi.org/10.1136/bjsports-2018-100224

Fry, M.D., & Gano-Overway, L.A. (2010). Exploring the contribution of the caring climate to the youth sport experience. *Journal of Applied Sport Psychology, 22*(3), 294-304.

George, Z. (2020, August 1). An insidious culture? New Zealand gymnastics rocked by allegations of psychological and physical abuse. Stuff. www.stuff.co.nz/sport/300071427/an-insidious-culture-new-zealand-gymnastics-rocked-by-allegations-of-psychological-and-physical-abuse

Gould, D., Collins, K., Lauer, L., & Chung, Y. (2007). Coaching life skills through football: A study of award winning high school coaches. *Journal of Applied Sport Psychology, 19*(1), 16-37. https://doi.org/10.1080/10413200601113786

Grablick, C. (2020, August, 28). Mystics player Tianna Hawkins says team is "playing for social justice" tonight. Dcist. https://dcist.com/story/20/08/28/mystics-tianna-hawkins-jacob-blake-social-justice

Gurgis, J.J., Kerr, G., & Darnell, S. (2022). "Safe sport is not for everyone": Equity-deserving athletes' perspectives of, experiences, and recommendations for safe sport. *Frontiers in Psychology,* 13: 832560. *doi: 10.3389/fpsyg.2022.832560*

Hampel, K. (2019). Whose fault is it anyway: How sexual abuse has plagued the United States Olympic movement and its athletes. *Marquette Sports Law Review, 29*, 547.

Hampson, R., & Jowett, S. (2012). Effects of coach leadership and coach–athlete relationship on collective efficacy. *Scandinavian Journal of Medicine and Science in Sports, 24*(2), 454-460. https://doi.org/10.1111/j.1600-0838.2012.01527.x

Hartill, M. (2014). Exploring narratives of boyhood sexual subjection in male-sport. *Sociology of Sport Journal, 31*(1), 23-43. https://doi.org/10.1123/ssj.2012-0216

Harvey, S. (2017). Developing athlete-centred coaching in high performance field hockey. In S. Pill (Ed.), *Perspectives on athlete-centred coaching* (pp. 79-92). Routledge.

Health Canada. (1999).

Holt, N.L., Deal, C.J., & Pankow, K. (2020). Positive youth development through sport. In G. Tenenbaum & R.C. Eklund (Eds.), *Handbook of sport psychology* (pp. 429-446). Wiley.

Hoover, N.C. (1999). National survey: Initiation rites and athletics for NCAA sports teams. www.alfred.edu/news/html/hazingpdf.html

Houlihan, B. (2004). Civil rights, doping control and the world anti-doping code. *Sport in Society, 7*(3), 420-437. https://doi-org.myaccess.library.utoronto.ca/10.1080/1743042000291712

Howley, K. (2018). Everyone believed Larry Nassar: The predatory trainer may have just taken down USA Gymnastics. How did he deceive so many for so long? The Cut. www.thecut.com/2018/11/how-did-larry-nassar-deceive-so-many-for-so-long.html

Howman, D., Nicol, L., & Vickery, R. (2021). Independent review of gymnastics New Zealand. https://www.gymnasticsnz.com/wp-content/uploads/2021/02/Gymnastics-New-Zealand-Independent-Report-10-February-2021.pdf

Jacobs, F., Smits, F., & Knoppers, A. (2017). "You don't realize what you see!": The institutional context of emotional abuse in elite youth sport. *Sport in Society, 20*(1), 126-143. https://doi-org.myaccess.library.utoronto.ca/10.1080/17430437.2015.1124567

Jewett, R., Kerr, G., MacPherson, E., & Stirling, A. (2020). Experiences of bullying victimisation in female interuniversity athletes. *International Journal of Sport and Exercise Psychology, 18*(6), 818-832. https://doi.org/10.1080/1612197X.2019.1611902

Jodouin, A.L. (2005). The Sport Dispute Resolution Centre of Canada: An innovative development in Canadian amateur sport. *Journal of Legal Aspects of Sport, 15*, 295.

Johansson, S., & Lundqvist, C. (2017). Sexual harassment and abuse in coach–athlete relationships in Sweden. *European Journal for Sport and Society, 14*(2), 117-137. https://doi-org.myaccess.library.utoronto.ca/10.1080/16138171.2017.1318106

Jowett, S. (2007). Expanding the interpersonal dimension: Closeness in the coach–athlete relationship. *International Journal of Sports Science and Coaching, 2*(4), 513-517.

Jowett, S. (2017). Coaching effectiveness: The coach–athlete relationship at its heart. *Current Opinion in Psychology, 16*, 154-158. http://dx.doi.org/10.1016/j.copsyc.2017.05.006

Jowett, S., & Cockerill, I.M. (2003). Olympic medallists' perspective of the athlete–coach relationship. *Psychology of Sport and Exercise, 4*(4), 313-331. https://doi.org/10.1016/S1469-0292(02)00011-0

Jowett, S., & Shanmugam, V. (2016). Relational coaching in sport: Its psychological underpinnings and practical effectiveness. In R.J. Schinke, K.R. McGannon, & B. Smith (Eds.), *Routledge international handbook of sport psychology* (pp. 501-514). Routledge.

Jowett, S., & Wachsmuth, S. (2020). Power in coach–athlete relationships. In R. Kerr, N. Barker-Ruchti, C. Stewart, & G. Kerr (Eds.), *Women's artistic gymnastics: Socio-cultural perspectives* (pp. 121-142). Routledge.

Kaufman, P. (2008). Boos, bans, and other backlash: The consequences of being an activist athlete. *Humanity and Society, 32*(3), 215-237. https://doi.org/10.1177/016059760803200302

Kerr, G., Jewett, R., MacPherson, E., & Stirling, A. (2016). Student-athletes' experiences of bullying on intercollegiate teams. *Journal for the Study of Sports and Athletes in Education, 10*(2), 132-149. https://doi.org/10.1080/19357397.2016.1218648

Kerr, G.A., & Stirling, A.E. (2012). Parents' reflections on their child's experiences of emotionally abusive coaching practices. *Journal of Applied Sport Psychology, 24(2)*, 191-206.

Kerr, G., Stirling, A., & Gurgis, J. (2017). An athlete-centred approach to enhance thriving within athletes and coaches. In S. Pill (Ed.), *Perspectives on athlete-centred coaching* (pp. 24-35). Routledge.

Kerr, G., Stirling, A., MacPherson, E., Banwell, J., Bandealy, A., & Preston, C. (2016). Exploring the use of exercise as punishment in sport. *International Journal of Coaching Science, 10*(2), 35-53. https://doi-org.myaccess.library.utoronto.ca/10.1080/21640629.2016.1175149

Kerr, G., Willson, E., & Stirling, A. (2020). "It was the worst time in my life": The effects of emotionally abusive coaching on female Canadian national team athletes. *Women in Sport and Physical Activity Journal, 28*(1), 81-89. https://doi-org.myaccess.library.utoronto.ca/10.1080/21640629.2016.1175149

Kidd, B. (2013). The philosophy of excellence: Olympic performances, class power and the Canadian state. *Sport in Society: Cultures, Commerce, Media, Politics, 16*, 37-41. https://doi.org/10.1080/17430437.2013.785761

Kidman, L. (2005). *Athlete-centred coaching: Developing inspired and inspiring people.* Innovative Print Communications.

Kidman, L. (2010). *Athlete-centred coaching: Developing decision makers.* Innovative Print Communications.

Kihl, L.A., Kikulis, L.M., & Thibault, L. (2007). A deliberative democratic approach to athlete-centred sport: The dynamics of administrative and communicative power. *European Sport Management Quarterly, 7*(1), 1-30.

Kikulis, L.M. (2013). Contemporary policy issues in high performance sport. In L. Thibault & J. Harvey (Eds.), *Sport policy in Canada* (pp. 97-145). University of Ottawa Press. www.jstor.org/stable/j.ctt5hjk9x.6

Kirby, J. (2018, May 16). The sex abuse scandal surrounding USA Gymnastics team doctor Larry Nassar, explained. Vox. www.vox.com/identities/2018/1/19/16897722/sexual-abuse-usa-gymnastics-larry-nassar-explained

Korr, C.P. (2002). Two paths to player power. *The Sports Historian, 22*(1), 60-78. https://doi.org/10.1080/17460260209443681

Koss, J. (2011). Athletes' rights and Olympic reform: A discussion with Johann Koss, Ann Peel and Alexandra Orlando. *Sport in Society, 14*(3), 309-318.

Kuhlin, F., Barker-Ruchti, N., & Stewart, C. (2020). Long-term impact of the coach–athlete relationship on development, health, and wellbeing: Stories from a figure skater. *Sports Coaching Review, 9*(2), 208-230. https://doi.org/10.1080/21640629.2019.1620016

Leahy, T., Pretty, G., & Tenenbaum, G. (2002). Prevalence of sexual abuse in organised competitive sport in Australia. *Journal of Sexual Aggression, 8*(2), 16-36.

Litchfield, C., Kavanagh, E.J., Osborne, J., & Jones, I. (2016). Virtual maltreatment: Sexualisation and social media abuse in sport. *Psychology of Women Section Review, 18*(2).

Lombardo, B.J. (1987). *The humanistic coach: From theory to practice.* Springfield: Charles C Thomas.

Lukes, S. (1993). Three distinctive views of power compared. In M. Hill (Ed.), *The policy process: A reader.* Harvester Wheatsheaf.

Macur, J. (2020, August 3). Gymnasts worldwide push back on their sport's culture of abuse. *New York Times.* www.nytimes.com/2020/08/03/sports/olympics/gymnastics-abuse-athlete-a.html

Mageau, G.A., & Vallerand, R.J. (2003). The coach–athlete relationship: A motivational model. *Journal of Sports Sciences, 21*(11), 883-904. https://doi.org/10.1080/0264041031000140374

Mathers, S.A., & Chavez, J. (2018). When hazing is not hazing: Media portrayal of hazing: Developing a typology. Introducing the TAIR model. *Social Sciences, 7*(9), 158.

McLaren, R. (1998). A new order: Athletes' rights and the Court of Arbitration at the Olympic Games. *Olympika, 7*, 1-24.

McPherson, L., Long, M., Nicholson, M., Cameron, N., Atkins, P., & Morris, M.E. (2017). Secrecy surrounding the physical abuse of child athletes in Australia. *Australian Social Work, 70*(1), 42-53. https://doi-org.myaccess.library.utoronto.ca/10.1080/0312407X.2016.1142589

Miller, P.S., & Kerr, G.A. (2002). Conceptualizing excellence: Past, present, and future. *Journal of Applied Sport Psychology, 14*(3), 140-153.

Mishna, F., Kerr, G., McInroy, L.B., & MacPherson, E. (2019). Student athletes' experiences of bullying in intercollegiate sport. *Journal for the Study of Sports and Athletes in Education, 13*(1), 53-73. https://doi.org/10.1080/19357397.2019.1581512

Office of the Sport Integrity Commissioner (OSIC) (2022). https://sportintegritycommissioner.ca.

Ohlert, J., Seidler, C., Rau, T., Rulofs, B., & Allroggen, M. (2018). Sexual violence in organized sport in Germany. *German Journal of Exercise and Sport Research, 48*(1), 59-68.

Ohlert, J., Vertommen, T., Rulofs, B., Rau, T., & Allroggen, M. (2021). Elite athletes' experiences of interpersonal violence in organized sport in Germany, the Netherlands, and Belgium. *European Journal of Sport Science, 21*(4), 604-613.

Own the Podium (n.d.). Retrieved August 23, 2022, www.ownthepodium.org/en-CA

Parent, S., Lavoie, F., Thibodeau, M.È., Hébert, M., Blais, M., & Team PAJ. (2016). Sexual violence experienced in the sport context by a representative sample of Quebec adolescents. *Journal of Interpersonal Violence, 31*(16), 2666-2686. https://doi-org.myaccess.library.utoronto.ca/10.1177/0886260515580366

Pill, S. (Ed.). (2017). *Perspectives on athlete-centred coaching.* Routledge.

Pill, S. (2017). Developing thinking players: A coach's experience with GameSense coaching. In S. Pill (Ed.), *Perspectives on athlete-centred coaching* (pp. 93-103). Routledge.

Preston, C., & Fraser-Thomas, J. (2018). Problematizing the pursuit of personal development and performance success: An autoethnography of a Canadian elite youth ice hockey coach. *The Sport Psychologist, 32*(2), 102-113.

Rhoden, W.C. (2007). *Forty million dollar slaves: The rise, fall, and redemption of the Black athlete.* Crown.

Sadler, E. (2020, August 27). NHL postpones all games scheduled for Thursday and Friday. Sportsnet. www.sportsnet.ca/nhl/article/nhl-postpones-games-scheduled-thursday-friday

Sanderson, J., & Weathers, M.R. (2020). Snapchat and child sexual abuse in sport: Protecting child athletes in the social media age. *Sport Management Review, 23*(1), 81-94. https://doi-org.myaccess.library.utoronto.ca/10.1016/j.smr.2019.04.006

Schwab, B. (2018). Embedding the human rights of players in world sport. *International Sports Law Journal, 17*(3-4), 214-232.

Sport Dispute Resolution Centre of Canada (SDRCC). (n.d.). Retrieved October 21, 2020, from www.crdsc-sdrcc.ca/eng/home

Shogan, D. (1999). *The making of high-performance athletes: Discipline, diversity and ethics.* University of Toronto Press.

SIRC (Sport Information Resource Centre) (n.d.). Universal code to prevent and address maltreatment in sport. Retrieved July 24, 2022, from https://mcusercontent.com/95de45c23ac490c5d391e924f/files/7cc4ba0b-7565-43bf-aa4c-c5be146e7d97/UCCMS_v5.1_FINAL_Eng.pdf

Stafford, A., Alexander, K., & Fry, D. (2013). Playing through pain: Children and young people's experiences of physical aggression and violence in sport. *Child Abuse Review, 22*(4), 287-299. https://doi.org/10.1002/car.2289

Stafford, A., Alexander, K., & Fry, D. (2015). "There was something that wasn't right because that was the only place I ever got treated like that": Children and young people's experiences of emotional harm in sport. *Childhood, 22*(1), 121-137. https://doi.org/10.1177/0907568213505625

Stirling, A. (2009). Definitions and constituents of maltreatment in sport: Establishing a conceptual framework for research practitioners. *British Journal of Sports Medicine, 43*, 1091-1099. https://doi.org/10.1136/bjsm.2008.051433

Stirling, A.E., & Kerr, G.A. (2008). Defining and categorizing emotional abuse in sport. *European Journal of Sport Science, 8*(4), 173-181. https://doi.org/10.1080/17461390802086281

Stirling, A.E., & Kerr, G.A. (2009). Abused athletes' perceptions of the coach–athlete relationship. *Sport in Society, 12*(2), 227-239.

Stirling, A.E., & Kerr, G.A. (2013). The perceived effects of elite athletes' experiences of emotional abuse in the coach–athlete relationship. *International Journal of Sport and Exercise Psychology, 11*(1), 87-100.

Stirling, A.E., & Kerr, G.A. (2014). Initiating and sustaining emotional abuse in the coach–athlete relationship: An ecological transactional model of vulnerability. *Journal of Aggression, Maltreatment and Trauma, 23*(2), 116-135.

Storch, E., Werner, N., & Storch, J. (2003). Relational aggression and psychosocial adjustment in intercollegiate athletes. *Journal of Sport Behavior, 26*(2), 155-167.

Tam, A.E. (2020). *Exploring athletes' perspectives on power in sexualized experiences between peers in sport* [Master's thesis]. University of Toronto.

Tavares, O. (2008). "Democracy is not the Holy Grail": Concepts and attitudes of Olympic athletes toward the IOC Athletes Commission. In R.K. Barney, M.K. Heine, K.B. Wamsley, & G.H. MacDonald (Eds.), *Pathways: Critiques and discourse in Olympic research* (pp. 448-459). International Centre for Olympic Studies.

Taylor, D. (2018, February 15). Barry Bennell: The predatory Pied Piper who made stars and shattered lives. *The Guardian*. www.theguardian.com/football/2018/feb/15/barry-bennell-abuse-manchester-city-crewe

Team USA (n.d.). Retrieved October 21, 2020, from www.teamusa.org/Footer/Legal/Governance-Documents

Thibault, L., & Babiak, K. (2005). Organizational changes in Canada's sport system: Toward an athlete-centred approach. *European Sport Management Quarterly, 5*(2), 105-132. https://doi.org/10.1080/16184740500188623

Thibault, L., & Harvey, J. (2013). *Sport policy in Canada*. University of Ottawa Press.

U.S. Center for SafeSport. (2021). Athlete culture and climate survey. https://uscenterforsafesport.org/survey-results

Vella, S., Oades, L., & Crowe, T. (2013). The relationship between coach leadership, the coach–athlete relationship, team success, and the positive developmental experiences of adolescent soccer players. *Physical Education and Sport Pedagogy, 18*(5), 549-561. https://doi.org/10.1080/17408989.2012.726976

Vertommen, T., Schipper-van Veldhocken, N., Wouters, K., Kampen, J.K., Brackenridge, C.H., Rhind, D.J.A., Neels, K., & Van Den Eede, F. (2016). Interpersonal violence against children in sport in the Netherlands and Belgium. *Child Abuse and Neglect, 51,* 223-236. https://doi-org.myaccess.library.utoronto.ca/10.1016/j.chiabu.2016.11.029

Waldron, J.J., & Kowalski, C.L. (2009). Crossing the line: Rites of passage, team aspects, and ambiguity of hazing. *Research Quarterly for Exercise and Sport, 80*(2), 291-302.

Waldron, J.J., Lynn, Q., & Krane, V. (2011). Duct tape, icy hot & paddles: Narratives of initiation onto US male sport teams. *Sport, Education and Society, 16*(1), 111-125. https://psycnet.apa.org/doi/10.1111/j.1939-0025.1984.tb01524.x

Whyte Review. (2020). Whytereview.org.

Willson, E., & Kerr, G. (2022). Body shaming as a form of emotional abuse in sport. *International Journal of Sport and Exercise Psychology, 20*(5), 1452-1470.

Willson, E., Kerr, G., Battaglia, A., & Stirling, A. (2022). Listening to athletes' voices: National team athletes' perspectives on advancing safe sport in Canada. *Frontiers in Sports and Active Living* 4:840221. doi: 10.3389/fspor.2022.840221

Willson, E., Kerr, G., Stirling, A., & Buono, S. (2021). Prevalence of maltreatment among Canadian national team athletes. *Journal of Interpersonal Violence,* 1-23. https://doi.org/10.1177/08862605211045096tps

World Health Organization (n.d.). Child maltreatment. Retrieved August 12, 2022, from www.who.int/news-room/fact-sheets/detail/child-maltreatment

Zaccardi, N. (2018, January 9). Maggie Nichols says she is Larry Nassar victim. NBC Sports. https://olympics.nbcsports.com/2018/01/09/maggie-nichols-larry-nassar-victim-gymnastics

Zirin, D. (2005). *What's my name, fool?: Sports and resistance in the United States*. Haymarket Books.

Chapter 5

Assor, A., & Tal, K. (2012). When parents' affection depends on child's achievement: Parental conditional positive regard, self-aggrandizement, shame and coping in adolescents. *Journal of Adolescence, 35*(2), 249-260. https://doi.org/10.1016/j.adolescence.2011.10.004

Atkins, M.R., Johnson, D.M., Force, E.C., & Petrie, T.A. (2013). "Do I still want to play?" Parents' and peers' influences on girls' continuation in sport. *Journal of Sport Behavior, 36*(4), 329-345.

Azimi, S., & Tamminen, K.A. (2020). Parental communication and reflective practice among youth sport parents. *Journal of Applied Sport Psychology, 0*(0), 1-24. https://doi.org/10.1080/10413200.2019.1705433

Babkes, M.L., & Weiss, M.R. (1999). Parental influence on children's cognitive and affective responses to competitive soccer participation. *Pediatric Exercise Science, 11,* 44-62. https://doi.org/10.1123/pes.11.1.44

Baumrind, D. (1971a). Current patterns of parental authority. *Developmental Psychology, 4*(1, pt 2), 1–103. https://doi.org/10.1037/h0030372

Baumrind, D. (1971b). Harmonious parents and their preschool children. *Developmental psychology, 4*(1), 99-102.

Bean, C., McFadden, T., Fortier, M., & Forneris, T. (2019). Understanding the relationships between programme quality, psychological needs satisfaction, and mental well-being in competitive youth sport. *International Journal of Sport and Exercise Psychology, 0*(0), 1-19. https://doi.org/10.1080/1612197X.2019.1655774

Bee, H., & Boyd, D. (2012). *The developing child*. Pearson Education.

Bois, J.E., Sarrazin, P.G., Brustad, R.J., Trouilloud, D.O., & Cury, F. (2005). Elementary schoolchildren's perceived competence and physical activity involvement: The influence of parents' role modelling behaviours and perceptions of their child's competence. *Psychology of Sport and Exercise, 6*(4), 381-397. https://doi.org/10.1016/j.psychsport.2004.03.003

Bornstein, M.H. (2012). Cultural approaches to parenting. *Parenting: Science and Practice, 12*(2-3), 212-221. https://doi.org/10.1080/15295192.2012.683359

Bornstein, M.H., Tamis-LeMonda, C.S., Hahn, C.-S., & Haynes, O.M. (2008). Maternal responsiveness to young children at three ages: Longitudinal analysis of a multidimensional, modular, and specific parenting construct. *Developmental Psychology, 44*(3), 867-874. https://doi.org/10.1037/0012-1649.44.3.867

Bowker, A., Boekhoven, B., Nolan, A., Bauhaus, S., Glover, P., Powell, T., & Taylor, S. (2009). Naturalistic observations of spectator behavior at youth hockey games. *The Sport Psychologist, 23*(3), 301-316. https://doi.org/10.1123/tsp.23.3.301

Bowlby, J. (1973). *Attachment and loss: Separation, anxiety, and anger* (Vol. 2). Basic Books.

Bronfenbrenner, U. (Ed.). (2005). *Making human beings human: Bioecological perspectives on human development.* Sage.

Brown, B.A., Frankel, B.G., & Fennell, M.P. (1989). Hugs or shrugs: Parental and peer influence on continuity of involvement in sport by female adolescents. *Sex Roles, 20*(7-8), 397-412. https://doi.org/10.1007/BF00287999

Brustad, R.J. (1993). Who will go out and play? Parental and psychological influences on children's attraction to physical activity. *Pediatric Exercise Science, 5*, 210-223. https://doi.org/10.1123/pes.5.3.210

Brustad, R.J. (1996). Attraction to physical activity in urban schoolchildren: Parental socialization and gender influences. *Research Quarterly for Exercise and Sport, 67*(3), 316-323. https://doi.org/10.1080/02701367.1996.10607959

Burgess, N.S., Knight, C.J., & Mellalieu, S.D. (2016). Parental stress and coping in elite youth gymnastics: An interpretative phenomenological analysis. *Qualitative Research in Sport, Exercise and Health, 8*(3), 237-256. https://doi.org/10.1080/2159676X.2015.1134633

Carr, S. (2013). *Attachment in sport, exercise and wellness.* Routledge.

Chan, D.K.C., Keegan, R.J., Lee, A.S.Y., Yang, S.X., Zhang, L., Rhodes, R.E., & Lonsdale, C. (2019). Toward a better assessment of perceived social influence: The relative role of significant others on young athletes. *Scandinavian Journal of Medicine and Science in Sports, 29*(2), 286-298. https://doi.org/10.1111/sms.13320

Charbonneau, E.F., & Camiré, M. (2019). Parental involvement in sport and the satisfaction of basic psychological needs: Perspectives from parent-child dyads. *International Journal of Sport and Exercise Psychology,* 1-17. https://doi.org/10.1080/1612197X.2019.1570533

Clarke, N.J., & Harwood, C.G. (2014). Parenting experiences in elite youth football: A phenomenological study. *Psychology of Sport and Exercise, 15*(5), 528-537. https://doi.org/10.1016/j.psychsport.2014.05.004

Clarke, N.J., Harwood, C.G., & Cushion, C.J. (2016). A phenomenological interpretation of the parent-child relationship in elite youth football. *Sport, Exercise, and Performance Psychology, 5*(2), 125-143. https://doi.org/10.1037/spy0000052

Côté, J. (1999). The influence of the family in the development of talent in sport. *The Sport Psychologist, 13*, 395-417. https://doi.org/10.1123/tsp.13.4.395

Danioni, F., Barni, D., & Rosnati, R. (2017). Transmitting sport values: The importance of parental involvement in children's sport activity. *Europe's Journal of Psychology, 13*(1), 75-92. https://doi.org/10.5964/ejop.v13i1.1265

Darling, N., & Steinberg, L. (1993). Parenting style as context: An integrative model. *Psychological Bulletin, 113*(3), 487-496. https://doi.org/10.1037/0033-2909.113.3.487

Deci, E. L., Ryan, R. M., Deci, E. L., & Ryan, R. M. (1985). Conceptualizations of intrinsic motivation and self-determination. *Intrinsic motivation and self-determination in human behavior,* 11-40.

Dorsch, T.E. (2017). Optimising family involvement in youth sport. In C.J. Knight, C.G. Harwood, & D. Gould (Eds.), *Sport psychology for young athletes* (pp. 106-115). Routledge. https://doi.org/10.4324/9781315545202-10

Dorsch, T.E., King, M.Q., Dunn, C.R., Osai, K.V., & Tulane, S. (2017). The impact of evidence-based parent education in organized youth sport: A pilot study. *Journal of Applied Sport Psychology, 29*(2), 199-214. https://doi.org/10.1080/10413200.2016.1194909

Dorsch, T.E., King, M.Q., Tulane, S., Osai, K.V., Dunn, C.R., & Carlsen, C.P. (2019). Parent education in youth sport: A community case study of parents, coaches, and administrators. *Journal of Applied Sport Psychology, 31*(4), 427-450. https://doi.org/10.1080/10413200.2018.1510438

Dorsch, T.E., Smith, A.L., & Dotterer, A.M. (2016). Individual, relationship, and context factors associated with parent support and pressure in organized youth sport. *Psychology of Sport and Exercise, 23*, 132-141. https://doi.org/10.1016/j.psychsport.2015.12.003

Dorsch, T.E., Smith, A.L., & McDonough, M.H. (2009). Parents' perceptions of child-to-parent socialization in organized youth sport. *Journal of Sport and Exercise Psychology, 31*(4), 444-468. https://doi.org/10.1123/jsep.31.4.444

Dorsch, T.E., Smith, A.L., & McDonough, M.H. (2015). Early socialization of parents through organized youth sport. *Sport, Exercise, and Performance Psychology, 4*(1), 3-18. https://doi.org/10.1037/spy0000021

Dorsch, T.E., Smith, A.L., Wilson, S.R., & McDonough, M.H. (2015). Parent goals and verbal sideline behavior in organized youth sport. *Sport, Exercise, and Performance Psychology, 4*(1), 19-35. https://doi.org/10.1037/spy0000025

Dorsch, T.E., Wright, E., Eckardt, V.C., Elliott, S., Thrower, S.N., & Knight, C.J. (2021). A history of parent involvement in organized youth sport: A scoping review. *Sport, Exercise, and Performance Psychology. 10*(4), 536-557. https://doi.org/10.1037/spy0000266

Dunn, C.R., Dorsch, T.E., King, M.Q., & Rothlisberger, K.J. (2016). The impact of family financial investment on perceived parent pressure and child enjoyment and commitment in organized youth sport: Family investment in youth sport. *Family Relations, 65*, 287-299. https://doi.org/10.1111/fare.12193

Eccles, J., Adler, T., Futterman, R., Goff, S., Kaczala, C., Meece, J., & Midgley, C. (1983). Expectancies, values, and academic behaviors. In J.C. Spence (Ed.), *Achievement and achievement motivation* (pp. 75-146). Freeman.

Eccles, J., Adler, T., & Meece, J.L. (1984). Sex differences in achievement: A test of alternate theories. *Journal of Personality and Social Psychology, 45*(1), 26-43.

Elliott, S.K., & Drummond, M.J.N. (2015). Parents in youth sport: What happens after the game? *Sport, Education and Society, 22*(3), 391-406. https://doi.org/10.1080/13573322.2015.1036233

Elliott, S.K., & Drummond, M.J.N. (2017). During play, the break, and the drive home: The meaning of parental verbal behaviour in youth sport. *Leisure Studies, 36*(5), 645-656. https://doi.org/10.1080/02614367.2016.1250804

Eriksson, M., Nordqvist, T., & Rasmussen, F. (2008). Associations between parents' and 12-year-old children's sport and vigorous activity: The role of self-esteem and athletic competence. *Journal of Physical Activity and Health, 5*(3), 359-373. https://doi.org/10.1123/jpah.5.3.359

Fearon, R.M.P., & Belsky, J. (2004). Attachment and attention: Protection in relation to gender and cumulative social-contextual adversity. *Child Development, 75*(6), 1677-1693. https://doi.org/10.1111/j.1467-8624.2004.00809.x

Felton, L., & Jowett, S. (2013). The mediating role of social environmental factors in the associations between attachment styles and basic needs satisfaction. *Journal of Sports Sciences, 31*(6), 618-628. https://doi.org/10.1080/02640414.2012.744078

Felton, L., & Jowett, S. (2015). On understanding the role of need thwarting in the association between athlete attachment and well/ill-being: Attachment, need thwarting, and well-being. *Scandinavian Journal of Medicine and Science in Sports, 25*(2), 289-298. https://doi.org/10.1111/sms.12196

Felton, L., & Jowett, S. (2017). Self-determination theory perspective on attachment, need satisfaction, and well-being in a sample of athletes: A longitudinal study. *Journal of Clinical Sport Psychology, 11*, 304-323. https://doi.org/10.1123/jcsp.2016-0013

Fraser-Thomas, J.L., & Côté, J. (2009). Understanding adolescents' positive and negative developmental experiences in sport. *The Sport Psychologist, 23*, 3-23. https://doi.org/10.1123/tsp.23.1.3

Fraser-Thomas, J.L., Côté, J., & Deakin, J. (2008). Examining adolescent sport dropout and prolonged engagement from a developmental perspective. *Journal of Applied Sport Psychology, 20*(3), 318-333. https://doi.org/10.1080/10413200802163549

Fredricks, J.A., & Eccles, J.S. (2004). Parental influences on youth involvement in sports. In M.R. Weiss (Ed.), *Developmental sport and exercise psychology: A lifespan perspective* (pp. 145-164). Fitness Information Technology.

Fredricks, J.A., & Eccles, J.S. (2005). Family socialization, gender, and sport motivation and involvement. *Journal of Sport and Exercise Psychology, 27*(1), 3-31. https://doi.org/10.1123/jsep.27.1.3

Furusa, M.G., Knight, C.J., & Hill, D.M. (2020). Parental involvement and children's enjoyment in sport. *Qualitative Research in Sport, Exercise and Health, 0*(0), 1-19. https://doi.org/10.1080/2159676X.2020.1803393

Gaudreau, P., Morinville, A., Gareau, A., Verner-Filion, J., Green-Demers, I., & Franche, V. (2016). Autonomy support from parents and coaches: Synergistic or compensatory effects on sport-related outcomes of adolescent-athletes? *Psychology of Sport and Exercise, 25*, 89-99. https://doi.org/10.1016/j.psychsport.2016.04.006

Goldstein, J.D., & Iso-Ahola, S.E. (2008). Determinants of parents' sideline-rage emotions and behaviors at youth soccer games. *Journal of Applied Social Psychology, 38*(6), 1442-1462. https://doi.org/10.1111/j.1559-1816.2008.00355.x

Gould, D., Lauer, L., Rolo, C., Jannes, C., & Pennisi, N. (2006). Understanding the role parents play in tennis success: A national survey of junior tennis coaches. *British Journal of Sports Medicine, 40*(7), 632-636. https://doi.org/10.1136/bjsm.2005.024927

Gould, D., Lauer, L., Rolo, C., Jannes, C., & Pennisi, N. (2008). The role of parents in tennis success: Focus group interviews with junior coaches. *The Sport Psychologist, 22*(1), 18-37. https://doi.org/10.1123/tsp.22.1.18

Green, B.C., & Chalip, L. (1998). Antecedents and consequences of parental purchase decision involvement in youth sport. *Leisure Sciences, 20*(2), 95-109. https://doi.org/10.1080/01490409809512268

Gurland, S. T., & Grolnick, W. S. (2003). Children's expectancies and perceptions of adults: Effects on rapport. *Child development, 74*(4), 1212-1224

Harter, S. (1978). Effectance motivation reconsidered. Toward a developmental model. *Human Development, 21*, 34-64. https://doi.org/10.1159/000271574

Harter, S. (1981). A model of mastery motivation in children: Individual differences and developmental change. In W.A. Collins (Ed.), *Minnesota symposium on child psychology* (pp. 215-255). Erlbaum.

Harwood, C.G., Drew, A., & Knight, C.J. (2010). Parental stressors in professional youth football academies: A qualitative investigation of specialising stage parents. *Qualitative Research in Sport and Exercise, 2*(1), 39-55. https://doi.org/10.1080/19398440903510152

Harwood, C.G., & Knight, C. (2009a). Understanding parental stressors: An investigation of British tennis-parents. *Journal of Sports Sciences, 27*(4), 339-351. https://doi.org/10.1080/02640410802603871

Harwood, C.G., & Knight, C. (2009b). Stress in youth sport: A developmental investigation of tennis parents. *Psychology of Sport and Exercise, 10*(4), 447-456. https://doi.org/10.1016/j.psychsport.2009.01.005

Harwood, C.G., & Knight, C.J. (2015). Parenting in youth sport: A position paper on parenting expertise. *Psychology of Sport and Exercise, 16*(1), 24-35. https://doi.org/10.1016/j.psychsport.2014.03.001

Harwood, C.G., Knight, C.J., Thrower, S.N., & Berrow, S.R. (2019). Advancing the study of parental involvement to optimise the psychosocial development and experiences of young athletes. *Psychology of Sport and Exercise, 42*, 66-73. https://doi.org/10.1016/j.psychsport.2019.01.007

Harwood, C.G., Thrower, S.N., Slater, M.J., Didymus, F.F., & Frearson, L. (2019). Advancing our understanding of psychological stress and coping among parents in organized youth sport. *Frontiers in Psychology, 10*, 1600. https://doi.org/10.3389/fpsyg.2019.01600

Hayward, F.P.I., Knight, C.J., & Mellalieu, S.D. (2017). A longitudinal examination of stressors, appraisals, and coping in youth swimming. *Psychology of Sport and Exercise, 29*, 56-68. https://doi.org/10.1016/j.psychsport.2016.12.002

Hein, V., & Jõesaar, H. (2015). How perceived autonomy support from adults and peer motivational climate are related with self-determined motivation among young athletes. *International Journal of Sport and Exercise Psychology, 13*(3), 193-204. https://doi.org/10.1080/1612197X.2014.947304

Holt, N.L., Camiré, M., Tamminen, K.A., Pankow, K., Pynn, S.R., Strachan, L., MacDonald, D.J., & Fraser-Thomas, J. (2018). PYDSportNET: A knowledge translation project bridging gaps between research and practice in youth sport. *Journal of Sport Psychology in Action, 9*(2), 132-146. https://doi.org/10.1080/21520704.2017.1388893

Holt, N.L., Jørgensen, H., & Deal, C.J. (2021). How do sport parents engage in autonomy-supportive parenting in the family home setting? A theoretically informed qualitative analysis. *Journal of Sport and Exercise Psychology* (AoH). https://doi.org/10.1123/jsep.2020-0210

Holt, N.L., & Knight, C.J. (2014). *Parenting in youth sport: From research to practice.* Routledge.

Holt, N.L., Tamminen, K.A., Black, D.E., Mandigo, J.L., & Fox, K.R. (2009). Youth sport parenting styles and practices. *Journal of Sport and Exercise Psychology, 31*, 37-59. https://doi.org/10.1123/jsep.31.1.37

Holt, N.L., Tamminen, K.A., Black, D.E., Sehn, Z.L., & Wall, M.P. (2008). Parental involvement in competitive youth sport settings. *Psychology of Sport and Exercise, 9*, 663-685. https://doi.org/10.1016/j.psychsport.2007.08.001

Jowett, S., & Timson-Katchis, M. (2005). Social networks in sport: Parental influence on the coach–athlete relationship. *The Sport Psychologist, 19*(3), 267-287. https://doi.org/10.1123/tsp.19.3.267

Kagitcibasi, C. (2013). Adolescent autonomy-relatedness and the family in cultural context: What is optimal? *Journal of Research on Adolescence, 23*(2), 223-235. https://doi.org/10.1111/jora.12041

Kay, T. (2007). Fathering through Sport. *World Leisure Journal, 49*(2), 69-82. https://doi.org/10.1080/04419057.2007.9674487

Kaye, M.P., Frith, A., & Vosloo, J. (2015). Dyadic anxiety in youth sport: The relationship of achievement goals with anxiety in young athletes and their parents. *Journal of Applied Sport Psychology, 27*(2), 171-185. https://doi.org/10.1080/10413200.2014.970717

Keegan, R.J., Harwood, C.G., Spray, C.M., & Lavallee, D.E. (2009). A qualitative investigation exploring the motivational climate in early career sports participants: Coach, parent and peer influences on sport motivation. *Psychology of Sport and Exercise, 10*(3), 361-372. https://doi.org/10.1016/j.psychsport.2008.12.003

Keegan, R.J., Harwood, C.G., Spray, C.M., & Lavallee, D. (2014). A qualitative investigation of the motivational climate in elite sport. *Psychology of Sport and Exercise, 15*(1), 97-107. https://doi.org/10.1016/j.psychsport.2013.10.006

Knight, C.J. (2019). Revealing findings in youth sport parenting research. *Kinesiology Review, 8*(3), 252-259. https://doi.org/10.1123/kr.2019-0023

Knight, C.J., Boden, C.M., & Holt, N.L. (2010). Junior tennis players' preferences for parental behaviors. *Journal of Applied Sport Psychology, 22*(4), 377-391. https://doi.org/10.1080/10413200.2010.495324

Knight, C.J., Dorsch, T.E., Osai, K.V., Haderlie, K.L., & Sellars, P.A. (2016). Influences on parental involvement in youth sport. *Sport, Exercise, and Performance Psychology, 5*(2), 161-178. https://doi.org/10.1037/spy0000053

Knight, C.J., & Holt, N.L. (2013a). Factors that influence parents' experiences at junior tennis tournaments and suggestions for improvement. *Sport, Exercise, and Performance Psychology, 2*(3), 173-189. https://doi.org/10.1037/a0031203

Knight, C.J., & Holt, N.L. (2013b). Strategies used and assistance required to facilitate children's involvement in tennis: Parents' perspectives. *The Sport Psychologist, 27*(3), 281-291. https://doi.org/10.1123/tsp.27.3.281

Knight, C.J., & Holt, N.L. (2014). Parenting in youth tennis: Understanding and enhancing children's experiences. *Psychology of Sport and Exercise, 15*(2), 155-164. https://doi.org/10.1016/j.psychsport.2013.10.010

Knight, C.J., Little, G.C.D., Harwood, C.G., & Goodger, K. (2016). Parental involvement in elite junior slalom canoeing. *Journal of Applied Sport Psychology, 28*(2), 234-256. https://doi.org/10.1080/10413200.2015.1111273

Knight, C.J., Neely, K.C., & Holt, N.L. (2011). Parental behaviors in team sports: How do female athletes want parents to behave? *Journal of Applied Sport Psychology, 23*(1), 76-92. https://doi.org/10.1080/10413200.2010.525589

Lafferty, M.E., & Triggs, C. (2014). The working with parents in sport model (WWPS-model): A practical guide for practitioners working with parents of elite young performers. *Journal of Sport Psychology in Action, 5*(2), 117-128. https://doi.org/10.1080/21520704.2014.914113

Lally, P., & Kerr, G. (2008). The effects of athlete retirement on parents. *Journal of Applied Sport Psychology, 20*(1), 42-56. https://doi.org/10.1080/10413200701788172

Lauer, L., Gould, D., Roman, N., & Pierce, M. (2010). How parents influence junior tennis players' development: Qualitative narratives. *Journal of Clinical Sport Psychology, 4*(1), 69-92. https://doi.org/10.1123/jcsp.4.1.69

Leff, S.S., & Hoyle, R.H. (1995). Young athletes' perceptions of parental support and pressure. *Journal of Youth and Adolescence, 24*(2), 187-203. https://doi.org/10.1007/BF01537149

Levy-Warren, M.H. (1999). I am, you are, and so are we: A current perspective on adolescent separation-individuation theory. In A.H. Esman, L.T. Flaherty, & H.A. Horowitz (Eds.), *Adolescent psychiatry: Development and clinical studies* (Vol. 24, pp. 3-24). Analytic Press.

Lienhart, N., Nicaise, V., Martinent, G., & Guillet-Descas, E. (2020). Perceived parental behaviours and motivational processes among adolescent athletes in intensive training centres: A profile approach. *Psychology of Sport and Exercise, 49*, 101708. https://doi.org/10.1016/j.psychsport.2020.101708

Lisinskiene, A., & Lochbaum, M. (2019). A qualitative study examining parental involvement in youth sports over a one-year intervention program. *International Journal of Environmental Research and Public Health, 16*(19), 3563. https://doi.org/10.3390/ijerph16193563

McMahon, J.A., & Penney, D. (2015). Sporting parents on the pool deck: Living out a sporting culture? *Qualitative Research in Sport, Exercise and Health, 7*(2), 153-169. https://doi.org/10.1080/2159676X.2014.901985

Misener, K.E. (2020). Parent well-being through community youth sport: An autoethnography of "sideline" participation. *Journal of Sport Management, 34*(4), 329-340. https://doi.org/10.1123/jsm.2019-0201

Neely, K.C., McHugh, T.-L.F., Dunn, J.G.H., & Holt, N.L. (2017). Athletes and parents coping with deselection in competitive youth sport: A communal coping perspective. *Psychology of Sport and Exercise, 30*, 1-9. https://doi.org/10.1016/j.psychsport.2017.01.004

Newport, R.A., Knight, C.J., & Love, T.D. (2021). The youth football journey: Parents' experiences and recommendations for support. *Qualitative Research in Sport, Exercise and Health, 13*(6), 1006-1026. https://doi.org/10.1080/2159676X.2020.1833966

Nicholls, J. G. (1984). Achievement motivation: conceptions of ability, subjective experience, task choice, and performance. *Psychological review, 91*(3), 328-346. https://psycnet.apa.org/doi/10.1037/0033-295X.91.3.328

Omli, J., & Wiese-Bjornstal, D.M. (2011). Kids speak: Preferred parental behavior at youth sport events. *Research Quarterly for Exercise and Sport, 84*(4), 701-711.

O'Rourke, D.J., Smith, R.E., Smoll, F.L., & Cumming, S.P. (2014). Relations of parent- and coach-initiated motivational climates to young athletes' self-esteem, performance anxiety, and autonomous motivation: Who is more influential? *Journal of Applied Sport Psychology, 26*(4), 395-408. https://doi.org/10.1080/10413200.2014.907838

Pynn, S.R., Dunn, J.G.H., & Holt, N.L. (2019). A qualitative study of exemplary parenting in competitive female youth team sport. *Sport, Exercise, and Performance Psychology, 8*(2), 163-178. https://doi.org/10.1037/spy0000141

Reis, H. T., Clark, M. S., & Holmes, J. G. (2004). Perceived partner responsiveness as an organizing construct in the study of intimacy and closeness. In *Handbook of closeness and intimacy* (pp. 211-236). Psychology Press

Reis, H.T., & Gable, S.L. (2015). Responsiveness. *Current Opinion in Psychology, 1*, 67-71. https://doi.org/10.1016/j.copsyc.2015.01.001

Richards, K., & Winter, S. (2013). Key reflections from "on the ground": Working with parents to create a task climate. *Journal of Sport Psychology in Action, 4*(1), 34-44. https://doi.org/10.1080/21520704.2012.733909

Ross, A.J., Mallett, C.J., & Parkes, J.F. (2015). The influence of parent sport behaviours on children's development: Youth coach and administrator perspectives. *International Journal of Sports Science and Coaching, 10*(4), 605-621. https://doi.org/10.1260/1747-9541.10.4.605

Rouquette, O. Y., Knight, C. J., Lovett, V. E., Barrell, D., & Heuzé, J. P. (2021). The positive association between perceived parental responsiveness and self-esteem, anxiety, and thriving among youth rugby players: A multigroup analysis. *Journal of Sports Sciences, 39*(13), 1537-1547. https://doi.org/10.1080/02640414.2021.1883311

Rouquette, O.Y., Knight, C.J., Lovett, V.E., & Heuzé, J.-P. (2020). Parent-athlete relationships: A central but underexamined consideration within sport psychology. *Sport and Exercise Psychology Review, 17*, 47.

Rouquette, O.Y., Knight, C.J., Lovett, V.E., & Heuzé, J.-P. (2021). Effect of parent responsiveness on young athletes' self-perceptions and thriving: An exploratory study in a Belgian

French-community. *Psychology of Sport and Exercise, 52*, 101801. https://doi.org/10.1016/j.psychsport.2020.101801

Ryan, R. M. (2017). *Self-Determination Theory: Basic Psychological Needs in Motivation, Development, and Wellness.* The Guilford Press

Sheridan, D., Coffee, P., & Lavallee, D. (2014). A systematic review of social support in youth sport. *International Review of Sport and Exercise Psychology, 7*(1), 198-228. https://doi.org/10.1080/1750984X.2014.931999

Smoll, F.L., Smith, R.E., & Cumming, S.P. (2007). Effects of coach and parent training on performance anxiety in young athletes: A systemic approach. *Journal of Youth Development, 2*(1), 19-36. https://doi.org/10.5195/JYD.2007.358

Stefansen, K., Smette, I., & Strandbu, Å. (2018). Understanding the increase in parents' involvement in organized youth sports. *Sport, Education and Society, 23*(2), 162-172. https://doi.org/10.1080/13573322.2016.1150834

Stein, G.L., Raedeke, T.D., & Glenn, S.D. (1999). Children's perceptions of parent sport involvement: It's not how much, but to what degree that's important. *Journal of Sport Behavior, 22*(4), 591-601.

Strandbu, Å., Stefansen, K., Smette, I., & Sandvik, M.R. (2019). Young people's experiences of parental involvement in youth sport. *Sport, Education and Society, 24*(1), 66-77. https://doi.org/10.1080/13573322.2017.1323200

Sutcliffe, J.T., Kelly, P.J., & Vella, S.A. (2021). Youth sport participation and parental mental health. *Psychology of Sport and Exercise, 52*, 101832. https://doi.org/10.1016/j.psychsport.2020.101832

Tamminen, K.A., McEwen, C.E., Kerr, G., & Donnelly, P. (2020). Examining the impact of the Respect in Sport Parent Program on the psychosocial experiences of minor hockey athletes. *Journal of Sports Sciences, 0*(0), 1-11. https://doi.org/10.1080/02640414.2020.1767839

Tamminen, K.A., Poucher, Z.A., & Povilaitis, V. (2017). The car ride home: An interpretive examination of parent–athlete sport conversations. *Sport, Exercise, and Performance Psychology, 6*(4), 325-339. https://doi.org/10.1037/spy0000093

Teques, P., Serpa, S., Rosado, A., Silva, C., & Calmeiro, L. (2018). Parental involvement in sport: Psychometric development and empirical test of a theoretical model. *Current Psychology, 37*(1), 234-249. https://doi.org/10.1007/s12144-016-9507-2

Thrower, S.N., Harwood, C.G., & Spray, C.M. (2016). Educating and supporting tennis parents: A grounded theory of parents' needs during childhood and early adolescence. *Sport, Exercise, and Performance Psychology, 5*(2), 107-124. https://doi.org/10.1037/spy0000054

Thrower, S.N., Harwood, C.G., & Spray, C.M. (2017). Educating and supporting tennis parents: An action research study. *Qualitative Research in Sport, Exercise and Health, 9*(5), 600-618. https://doi.org/10.1080/2159676X.2017.1341947

Thrower, S.N., Harwood, C.G., & Spray, C.M. (2019). Educating and supporting tennis parents using web-based delivery methods: A novel online education program. *Journal of Applied Sport Psychology, 31*(3), 303-323. https://doi.org/10.1080/10413200.2018.1433250

Ullrich-French, S., & Smith, A.L. (2006). Perceptions of relationships with parents and peers in youth sport: Independent and combined prediction of motivational outcomes. *Psychology of Sport and Exercise, 7*(2), 193-214. https://doi.org/10.1016/j.psychsport.2005.08.006

Vella, S.A., Cliff, D.P., & Okely, A.D. (2014). Socio-ecological predictors of participation and dropout in organised sports during childhood. *International Journal of Behavioral Nutrition and Physical Activity, 11*(1), 62. https://doi.org/10.1186/1479-5868-11-62

Vincent, A.P., & Christensen, D.A. (2015). Conversations with parents: A collaborative sport psychology program for parents in youth sport. *Journal of Sport Psychology in Action, 6*(2), 73-85. https://doi.org/10.1080/21520704.2015.1054535

Warmenhoven, J., Weissensteiner, J.R., & MacMahon, C. (2020). "Dad! Let's go have a hit . . .": Sources and types of support in female cricket players. *Journal of Science and Medicine in Sport, 23*(10), 991-998. https://doi.org/10.1016/j.jsams.2020.03.012

Watchman, T., & Spencer-Cavaliere, N. (2017). Times have changed: Parent perspectives on children's free play and sport. *Psychology of Sport and Exercise, 32*, 102-112. https://doi.org/10.1016/j.psychsport.2017.06.008

Wiersma, L.D., & Fifer, A.M. (2008). "The schedule has been tough but we think it's worth it": The joys, challenges, and recommendations of youth sport parents. *Journal of Leisure Research, 40*(4), 505-530. https://doi.org/10.1080/00222216.2008.11950150

Wolfenden, L.E., & Holt, N.L. (2005). Talent development in elite junior tennis: Perceptions of players, parents, and coaches. *Journal of Applied Sport Psychology, 17*(2), 108-126. https://doi.org/10.1080/10413200590932416

White, S. A. (1996). Goal orientation and perceptions of the motivational climate initiated by parents. *Pediatric Exercise Science, 8*(2), 122-129.

White, S. A., Kavussanu, M., & Guest, S. M. (1998). Goal orientations and perceptions of the motivational climate created by significant others. *European Journal of Physical Education, 3*(2), 212-228.

Wright, E., Chase, M.A., Horn, T.S., & Vealey, R.S. (2019). United States parents' perfectionism, parenting styles and perceptions of specialization in youth sport. *Psychology of Sport and Exercise, 45*, 101571. https://doi.org/10.1016/j.psychsport.2019.101571

Chapter 6

Anderson, S.N. (2018). *Exploring predictors of the coach–athlete relationship: Passion, perfectionism, and leadership behaviors* [Unpublished master's thesis]. Ithaca College.

Arthur, C.A., Wagstaff, C.R.D., & Hardy, L. (2018). Leadership in sport organizations. In C.R.D. Wagstaff (Ed.), *The organizational psychology of sport: Key issues and practical applications* (pp. 153-175). Routledge.

Bales, R.F., & Slater, P.E. (1955). Role differentiation in small decision-making groups. In T. Parsons & R.F. Bales (Eds.), *The family socialization and interaction process* (pp. 259-306). Free Press.

Ball, J.R., & Carron, A.V. (1976). The influence of team cohesion and participation motivation upon performance success in intercollegiate ice hockey. *Canadian Journal of Applied Sport Science, 1*, 271-275.

Barrow, J.C. (1977). The variables of leadership: A review and conceptual framework. *Academy of Management Review, 2*, 231-251. https://doi.org/10.2307/257906

Bass, B.M. (1985). *Leadership and performance beyond expectations.* Free Press.

Bormann, K.C., Schulte-Coerne, P., Diebig, M., & Rowold, J. (2016). Athlete characteristics and team competitive performance as moderators for the relationship between coach transformational leadership and athlete performance. *Journal of Sport and Exercise Psychology, 38*(3), 268-281. https://doi.org/10.1123/jsep.2015-0182

Bryman, A. (1992). *Charisma and leadership in organizations.* Sage.

Burns, J.M. (1978). *Leadership.* Harper & Row.

Capstick, A.L., & Trudel, P. (2010). Coach communication of non-selection in youth competitive sport. *International Journal of Coaching Science, 4*(1), 3-23.

Carron, A.V., & Eys, M.A. (2012). *Group dynamics in sport* (4th ed.). Fitness Information Technology.

Chelladurai, P. (1980). Leadership in sport organizations. *Canadian Journal of Applied Sport Sciences, 5*, 201-215.

Chelladurai, P. (1984). Discrepancy between preferences and perceptions of leadership behavior and satisfaction of athletes in varying sports. *Journal of Sport Psychology, 6*(1), 27-41. https://doi.org/10.1123/jsp.6.1.27

Chelladurai, P. (1993). Leadership. In R.N. Singer, M. Murphy, & L.K. Tennant (Eds.), *Handbook on research in sport psychology* (pp. 647-671). Macmillan.

Chelladurai, P. (2007). Leadership in sports. In G. Tenenbaum & R. Eklund (Eds.), *Handbook of sport psychology* (pp. 113-135). Wiley.

Chelladurai, P. (2012). Leadership and manifestations in sport. In S. Murphy (Ed.), *The Oxford handbook of sport and performance psychology.* Oxford University Press.

Chelladurai, P., & Carron, A.V. (1983). Athletic maturity and preferred leadership. *Journal of Sport and Exercise Psychology, 5*(4), 371-380. https://doi.org/10.1123/jsp.5.4.371

Chelladurai, P., Imamura, H., Yamaguchi, Y., Oinuma, Y., & Miyauchi, T. (1988). Sport leadership in a cross-national setting: The case of Japanese and Canadian university athletes. *Journal of Sport and Exercise Psychology, 10*, 374-389. https://doi.org/10.1123/jsep.10.4.374

Chelladurai, P., & Riemer, H.A. (1998). Measurement of leadership in sport. In J.L. Duda (Ed.), *Advances in sport and exercise psychology measurement* (pp. 227-256). Fitness Information Technology.

Chelladurai, P., & Saleh, S.D. (1978). Preferred leadership in sports. *Canadian Journal of Applied Sport Sciences, 3*, 85-92.

Chelladurai, P., & Saleh, S.D. (1980). Dimensions of leader behaviour in sports: Development of a leadership scale. *Journal of Sport Psychology, 2*, 34-45. https://doi.org/10.1123/jsp.2.1.34

Child, J.D., & Tayeb, M. (1983). Theoretical perspectives in cross-national research. *International Studies of Management and Organization, 23*, 32-70. https://doi.org/10.1080/00208825.1982.11656351

Conger, J.A. (1989). *The charismatic leader: Behind the mystique of exceptional leadership.* Jossey-Bass.

Conroy, D.E., & Coatsworth, J.D. (2007). Assessing autonomy-supportive coaching strategies in youth sport. *Psychology of Sport and Exercise, 8*, 671-684. https://doi.org/10.1016/j.psychsport.2006.12.001

Curtis, B., Smith, R.E., & Smoll, F.L. (1979). Scrutinizing the skipper: A study of leadership behaviors in the dugout. *Journal of Applied Psychology, 64*, 391-400. https://doi.org/10.1037/0021-9010.64.4.391

Cruz, A.B., & Kim, H.D. (2017). Leadership preferences of adolescent players in sport: Influence of coach gender. *Journal of Sports Science and Medicine, 16*, 172-179.

Dwyer, J.M., & Fisher, D.G. (1990). Wrestlers' perceptions of coaches' leadership as predictors of satisfaction with leadership. *Perceptual and Motor Skills,* 71, 511-517. https://doi.org/10.2466/pms.1990.71.2.511

Erle, F.J. (1981). Leadership in competitive and recreational sport [Unpublished master's thesis]. University of Western Ontario.

Evans, A.L., Slater, M.J., & Edwards, M. (2021). The effects of embedding social identities on perceived leadership outcomes and the intentional mobilization of group members. *Psychology of Sport and Exercise, 53*, 101879. https://doi.org/10.1016/j.psychsport.2020.101879

Evans, M.G. (1970). The effects of supervisory behavior on the path-goal relationship. *Organizational Behavior and Human Performance, 5*(3), 277-298. https://doi.org/10.1016/0030-5073(70)90021-8

Eys, M., & Carron, A. (2012). *Group dynamics in sport.* Fit.

Fayerweather, J. (1959). *The executive overseas.* Syracuse University Press.

Fiedler, F.E. (1967). *A theory of leader effectiveness.* McGraw-Hill.

Fransen, K., McEwan, D., & Sakar, M. (2020). The impact of identity leadership on team functioning and well-being in team sport: Is psychological safety the missing link? *Psychology of Sport and Exercise, 51*, 101763. https://doi.org/10.1016/j.psychsport.2020.101763

Garland, D.J., & Barry, J.R. (1988). The effects of personality and perceived leader behaviors on performance in collegiate football. *The Psychological Record, 38*, 237-247. https://doi.org/10.1007/BF03395019

Gordon, S. (1988). Decision styles and coaching effectiveness in university soccer. *Canadian Journal of Sport Sciences, 13*, 56-65.

Gould, D., & Martens, R. (1979). Attitudes of volunteer coaches toward significant youth sport issues. *Research Quarterly, 3*, 369-380. https://doi.org/10.1080/00345377.1979.10615623

Halpin, A.W., & Winer, B.J. (1957). A factorial study of the leader behavior description. In R.M. Stogdill & A.E. Coons (Eds.), *Leader behavior: Its description and measurement* (pp. 39-51). Bureau of Business Research, Ohio State University.

Harenberg, S., Bottino, A., Ford, R., & Vosloo, J. (2020). 'You are in, you are out' – A classification of selection processes in high performance team sport [Poster presentation]. Association of Applied Sport Psychology Conference, online.

Haslam, S.A., Reicher, S.D., & Platow, M.J. (2020). *The new psychology of leadership: Identity, influence, and power.* Routledge.

Hemphill, J.K. (1950). Relations between the size of the group and the behavior of superior leaders. *Journal of Social Psychology, 32*, 11-22. https://doi.org/10.1080/00224545.1950.9919026

Hersey, P., & Blanchard, K.H. (1969). Life cycle theory of leadership. *Training and Development Journal,* 23(5), 26-34.

Horne, T., & Carron, A.V. (1985). Compatibility in coach–athlete relationships. *Journal of Sport Psychology, 7*, 137-149. https://doi.org/10.1123/jsp.7.2.137

House, R.J. (1971). A path goal theory of leader effectiveness. *Administrative Science Quarterly, 16*(3), 321-339. https://doi.org/10.2307/2391905

House, R.J., & Dressler, G. (1974),"Perceived leadership behavior scales," in Beardon,W.O.and Netemeyer,R.G.(Eds), *Handbook of Marketing Scales*, Sage, Newbury Park, CA, (pp. 305-6).

Karreman, E., Riemer, H., & Harenberg, S. (2015). Team athlete performance: A multidimensional approach. *Applied Research in Coaching and Athletics Annual, 2*, 135-165. Kang, B.J. (2003). *A comparison of preferred coaching leadership behaviors in selected sports by United States and Korean collegiate athletes* [Unpublished master's thesis]. Ball State University.

Katz, D., & Kahn, R.L. (1951). *Human organisation and work motivation in industrial production.* Industrial Relations Research Association.

Kellerman, B. (1984). *Leadership: Multidisciplinary perspectives.* Prentice Hall.

Kim, H.D., & Cruz, A.B. (2016). The influence of coaches' leadership styles on athletes' satisfaction and team cohesion: A meta-analytic approach. *International Journal of Sport Science and Coaching, 11,* 900-909. https://doi.org/10.1177/1747954116676117

Kuhnert, K.W., & Lewis, P. (1987). Transactional and transformational leadership: A constructive/developmental analysis. *Academy of Management Review, 12*(4), 648-657. https://doi.org/10.5465/amr.1987.4306717

Lewin, K., Lippitt, R., & White, R.K. (1939). Patterns of aggressive behavior in experimentally created "social climates." *Journal of Social Psychology, 10*(2), 269-299. https://doi.org/10.1080/00224545.1939.9713366

Martens, R. (1979). About smocks and jocks. *Journal of Sport and Exercise Psychology, 1*(2), 94-99. https://doi.org/10.1123/jsp.1.2.94

Maslow, A. (1943). A theory of human motivation. *Psychological Review, 50,* 370-396.

McMillin, C.J. (1990). The relationship of athlete self-perceptions and athlete perceptions of leader behaviors to athlete satisfaction [Unpublished doctoral dissertation]. University of Virginia.

Moen, F., Hoigaard, R., & Peters, D. (2014). Performance progress and leadership behavior. *International Journal of Coaching Science, 8,* 69-81.

Neely, K.C., Dunn, J.G.H., McHugh, T.-L.F., & Holt, N.L. (2016). The deselection process in competitive female youth sport. *The Sport Psychologist, 30*(2), 141-153. https://doi.org/10.1123/tsp.2015-0044

Neely, K.C., Dunn, J.G.H., McHugh, T.L.F., & Holt, N.L. (2018). Female athletes' experiences of positive growth following deselection in sport. *Journal of Sport and Exercise Psychology, 40*(4), 173-185. https://doi.org/10.1123/jsep.2017-0136

Neely, K.C., McHugh, T.L.F., Dunn, J.G.H., & Holt, N.L. (2017). Athletes and parents coping with deselection in competitive youth sport: A communal coping perspective. *Psychology of Sport and Exercise, 30,* 1-9. https://doi.org/10.1016/j.psychsport.2017.01.004

Northouse, P.G. (2007). *Leadership theory and practice.* Sage.

Osborn, R., & Hunt, J. (1975). An adaptive-reactive theory of leadership: The role of macro variables in leadership research. In J. Hunt & L. Larson (Eds.), *Leadership frontiers* (pp. 27-44). Kent State University.

Pascale, R.T. (1978). Communication and decision making across cultures: Japanese and American comparisons. *Administrative Science Quarterly, 23,* 91-110. https://doi.org/10.2307/2392435

Pfeffer, I., & Gallitschke, M. (2008). Trainerinnen und Trainer im Frauenfußball aus Sicht der Athletinnen. *Zeitschrift für Sportpsychologie, 15,* 88-95. https://doi.org/10.1026/1612-5010.15.3.88

Pitts, T.D., Nyambane, E.D., & Butler, S.L. (2018). Preferred leadership styles of student athletes in a midwest NAIA conference. *The Sport Journal, 20,* 1-12.

Pyun, D.Y., Kwon, H.H., Koon, T.K., & Wang, C.K. (2010). Perceived coaching leadership of youth athletes in Singapore. *Journal of Sport Behavior, 33,* 25-41.

Riemer, H.A., & Chelladurai, P. (1995). Leadership and satisfaction in athletics. *Journal of Sport and Exercise Psychology, 17,* 276-293. https://doi.org/10.1123/jsep.17.3.276

Riemer, H.A., & Toon, K. (2001). Leadership and satisfaction in tennis: Examination of congruence, gender, and ability. *Research Quarterly for Exercise and Sport, 72*(3), 243-256. https://doi.org/10.1080/02701367.2001.10608957

Robinson, T.T. & Carron, A.V. (1982). Personal and situational factors associated with dropping out versus maintaining participation in competitive sport. *Journal of Sport and Exercise Psychology, 4,* 364-378. https://doi.org/10.1123/jsp.4.4.364

Sashkin, M. (1988). *The visionary leader.* Jossey-Bass.

Schliesman, E.S. (1987). Relationship between the congruence of preferred and actual leader behavior and subordinate satisfaction with leadership. *Journal of Sport Behavior, 10,* 157-166.

Serpa, S. (1990). Research work on sport leadership in Portugal [Unpublished manuscript]. Lisbon Technical University.

Serpa, S., Pataco, V., & Santos, F. (1991). Leadership patterns in handball international competition. *International Journal of Sport Psychology,* 22(1), 78-89.

Smith, R.E. & Smoll, F.L. (1984). Leadership in youth sport. In J.M. Silva & R.S Weinberg (eds.) *Psychological Foundations of Sport* (pp. 371-386). Human Kinetcs.

Smith, R.E., & Smoll, F.L. (1990). Self-esteem and children's reactions to youth sport coaching behaviors: A field study of self-enhancement processes. *Developmental Psychology, 26*(6), 987-993. https://doi.org/10.1037/0012-1649.26.6.987

Smith, R.E., & Smoll, F.L. (1991). Behavioral research and intervention in youth sports. *Behavior Therapy, 22*(3), 329-344. https://doi.org/10.1016/S0005-7894(05)80370-3

Smith, R.E., & Smoll, F.L. (2006). Social-cognitive approach to coaching behaviors. In S. Jowett & D. Lavallee (Eds.), *Social psychology in sport* (pp. 75-90). Human Kinetics.

Smith, R.E., Smoll, F.L., & Curtis, B. (1979). Coach effectiveness training: A cognitive-behavioral approach to enhancing relationship skills in youth sports. *Journal of Sport Psychology, 1,* 59-75. https://doi.org/10.1123/jsp.1.1.59

Smith, R.E., Smoll, F.L., & Hunt E.B. (1977). A system for the behavioral assessment of athletic coaches. *Research Quarterly, 48,* 208-214. https://doi.org/10.1080/10671315.1977.10615438

Smith, R.E., Zane, N.W., Smoll, F.L., & Coppel, D.B. (1983). Behavioral assessment in youth sports: Coaching behaviors and children's attitudes. *Medicine and Science in Sports and Exercise, 15,* 208-214. https://doi.org/10.1249/00005768-198315030-00005

Smoll, F.L., & Smith, R.E. (1989). Leadership behaviors in sport: A theoretical model and research paradigm. *Journal of Applied Social Psychology, 19,* 1522-1551. https://doi.org/10.1111/j.1559-1816.1989.tb01462.x

Smoll, F.L., Smith, R.E., Barnett, N.P., & Everett, J.J. (1993). Enhancement of children's self-esteem through social support training for youth sport coaches. *Journal of Applied Psychology, 78*(4), 602-610. https://doi.org/10.1037/0021-9010.78.4.602

Smoll, F.L., Smith, R.E., Curtis, B., & Hunt, E. (1978). Toward a mediational model of coach–player relationships. *Research Quarterly, 49*(4), 528-541. https://doi.org/10.1080/10671315.1978.10615567

Stevens, M., Rees, T., & Cruwys, T. (2021). Social identity leadership in sport and exercise: Current status and future directions. *Psychology of Sport and Exercise,* 55, 101931. https://doi.org/10.1016/j.psychsport.2021.101931

Terry P.C., & Howe, B.L. (1984). The coaching preferences of athletes. *Canadian Journal of Applied Sport Sciences, 9,* 188-193.

Teques, P., Silva, C., Rosado, A., & Serpa, L. (2020). Refining the short version of the Leadership Scale for Sports: Factorial validation and measurement invariance. *Psychological Reports, 124,* 0033294120953560. https://doi.org/10.1177/0033294120953560

Turman, P.D. (2006). Athletes' perception of coach power use and the association between playing status and sport satisfaction. *Communication Research Reports, 23*, 273-282. https://doi.org/10.1080/08824090600962540

Vallerand, R.J., & Ratelle, C.F. (2002). Intrinsic and extrinsic motivation: A hierarchical model. In E.L. Deci & R.M. Ryan (Eds.), *Handbook of self-determination research* (pp. 37-63). University of Rochester Press.

Vroom, V.H. (1964). *Work and motivation.* Wiley.

Wagstaff, C., & Burton-Wylie, S. (2018). Organizational culture in sport: A conceptual, definitional, and methodological review. *Sport and Exercise Psychology Review, 14*(2), 32-52.

Wang, Y.T. (1997). *A comparison of the coach leadership behavior preferred by male and female track and field athletes* [Unpublished master's thesis]. Springfield College.

Weiss, M.R., & Friedrichs, W.D. (1986). The influence of leader behaviors, coach attributes, and institutional variables on performance and satisfaction of collegiate basketball teams. *Journal of Sport and Exercise Psychology, 8*, 332-346. https://doi.org/10.1123/jsp.8.4.332

Williams, J.M., Kenow, L.J., Jerome, G.J., Rogers, T., Sartain, T.A., & Darland, G. (2003). Factor structure of the coaching behavior questionnaire and its relationship to athlete variables. *The Sport Psychologist, 17*, 16-34. https://doi.org/ 10.1123/tsp.17.1.16

Yammarino, F.J., Dubinsky, A.J., Comer, L.B., & Jolson, M.A. (1997). Women and transformational and contingent reward leadership: A multiple-levels-of-analysis perspective. *Academy of Management Journal, 40*(1), 205-222. https://doi.org/10.5465/257027

Yukl, G. (1971). Toward a behavioural theory of leadership. *Organizational Behavior and Human Performance, 6*, 414-440. https://doi.org/10.1016/0030-5073(71)90026-2

Chapter 7

Antonakis, J., Avolio, B.J., & Sivasubramaniam, N. (2003). Context and leadership: An examination of the nine-factor full-range leadership theory using the multifactor leadership questionnaire. *The Leadership Quarterly, 14*, 261-295. http://dx.doi.org/10.1016/ S1048-9843(03)00030-4

Arnold, K.A., Turner, N., Barling, J., Kelloway, E.K., & McKee, M.C. (2007). Transformational leadership and psychological well-being: The mediating role of meaningful work. *Journal of Occupational Health Psychology, 12*(3), 193-203. https://doi.org/10.1037/1076-8998.12.3.193

Arthur, C.A., Bastardoz, N., & Eklund, R. (2017). Transformational leadership in sport: Current status and future directions. *Current Opinion in Psychology, 16*, 78-83. https://doi.org/10.1016/j.copsyc.2017.04.001

Arthur, C.A., & Tomsett, P. (2015). Transformational leadership behavior in sport. In S.D. Mellalieu & S. Hanton (Eds.), *Contemporary advances in sport psychology* (pp. 175-201). Routledge.

Arthur, C.A., Woodman, T., Ong, C.W., Hardy, L., & Ntoumanis, N. (2011). The role of athlete narcissism in moderating the relationship between coaches' transformational leader behaviors and athlete motivation. *Journal of Sport and Exercise Psychology, 33*(1), 3-19. https://doi.org/10.1123/jsep.33.1.3

Arthur-Banning, S.G., Paisley, K., & Wells, M.S. (2007). Promoting sportsmanship in youth basketball players: The effect of referees' prosocial behavior techniques. *Journal of Park and Recreation Administration, 25*(1), 96-114.

Arthur-Banning, S., Wells, M.S., Baker, B.L., & Hegreness, R. (2009). Parents behaving badly? The relationship between the sportsmanship behaviors of adults and athletes in youth basketball games. *Journal of Sport Behavior, 32*(1), 3-18.

Avolio, B.J. (1999). *Full leadership development: Building the vital forces in organizations.* Sage.

Avolio, B.J. (2007). Promoting more integrative strategies for leadership theory-building. *American Psychologist, 62*, 25-33. https://doi.org/10.1037/0003-066X.62.1.25

Babkes, M.L., & Weiss, M.R. (1999). Parental influence on children's cognitive and affective responses to competitive soccer participation. *Pediatric Exercise Science, 11*(1), 44-62. http://dx.doi.org/10.1123/pes.11.1.44

Baird, N., Martin, L.J., & Benson, A.J. (2020). A dynamic view of coach transformational leadership: How leadership perceptions relate to task cohesion and team potency. *Psychology of Sport and Exercise, 51*, 101789. http://dx.doi.org/10.1016/j.psychsport.2020.101789

Barber, H., Sukhi, H., & White, S.A. (1999). The influence of parent-coaches on participant motivation and competitive anxiety in youth sport participants. *Journal of Sport Behavior, 22*(2), 162-180.

Barling, J. (2014). *The science of leadership: Lessons from research for organizational leaders.* Oxford University Press. https://doi.org/10.1093/acprof:oso/9780199757015.001.0001

Barling, J., & Frone, M.R. (2017). If only my leader would just do something! Passive leadership undermines employee well-being through role stressors and psychological resource depletion. *Stress and Health, 33*(3), 211-222. https://doi.org/10.1002/smi.2697

Barling, J., Weber, T., & Kelloway, E.K. (1996). Effects of transformational leadership training on attitudinal and financial outcomes: A field experiment. *Journal of Applied Psychology, 81*, 827-832. http://dx.doi.org/10.1037/0021-9010.81.6.827

Bass, B.M. (1985). *Leadership and performance beyond expectations.* Free Press.

Bass, B.M. (1998). *Transformational leadership.* Erlbaum.

Bass, B.M., & Avolio, B.J. (1990). *Transformational leadership development: Manual for the multifactor leadership questionnaire.* Consulting Psychologists Press.

Bass, B.M., & Riggio, R.E. (2006). *Transformational leadership* (2nd ed.). Psychology Press.

Beauchamp, M.R., Barling, J., Li, Z., Morton, K.L., Keith, S.E., & Zumbo, B.D. (2010). Development and psychometric properties of the transformational teaching questionnaire. *Journal of Health Psychology, 15*, 1123-1134. https://doi.org/10.1177/1359105310364175

Beauchamp, M.R., Barling, J., & Morton, K.L. (2011). Transformational teaching and adolescent self-determined motivation, self-efficacy, and intentions to engage in leisure time physical activity: A randomised controlled pilot trial. *Applied Psychology: Health and Well-Being, 3*, 127-150. http://dx.doi.org/10.1111/j.1758-0854.2011.01048.x

Bormann, K.C., & Rowold, J. (2016). Transformational leadership and followers' objective performance over time: Insights from German basketball. *Journal of Applied Sport Psychology, 28*(3), 367-373. https://doi.org/10.1080/10413200.2015.1133725

Brustad, R.J. (1993). Who will go out and play? Parental and psychological influences on children's attraction to physical activity. *Pediatric Exercise Science, 5*(3), 210-223. http://dx.doi.org/10.1123/pes.5.3.210

Burns, J.M. (1978). *Leadership.* Harper & Row.

Caine, V., Estefan, A., & Clandinin, D.J. (2013). A return to methodological commitment: Reflections on narrative inquiry. *Scandinavian Journal of Educational Research, 57*(6), 574-586. http://dx.doi.org/10.1080/00313831.2013.798833

Callow, N., Smith, M.J., Hardy, L., Arthur, C.A., & Hardy, J. (2009). Measurement of transformational leadership and its relationship with team cohesion and performance level. *Journal of Applied Sport Psychology, 21*, 395-412. http://dx.doi.org/10.1080/10413200903204754

Carless, S.A., Wearing, A.J., & Mann, L. (2000). A short measure of transformational leadership. *Journal of Business Psychology, 14*, 89-405.

Charbonneau, D., Barling, J., & Kelloway, E.K. (2001). Transformational leadership and sports performance: The mediating role of intrinsic motivation. *Journal of Applied Social Psychology, 31*, 1521-1534. https://doi.org/10.1111/j.1559-1816.2001.tb02686.x

Chelladurai, P. (1993). Leadership. In R.N. Singer, M. Murphey, & L.K. Tennant (Eds.), *Handbook of research on sport psychology* (pp. 647-671). MacMillan.

Chelladurai, P. (2007). Leadership in sports. In G. Tenenbaum & R.C. Eklund (Eds.). *Handbook of sport psychology* (3rd ed., pp. 113-135). Wiley.

Côté, J., & Gilbert, W. (2009). An integrative definition of coaching effectiveness and expertise. *International Journal of Sports Science and Coaching, 4*(3), 307-323. https://doi.org/10.1260/174795409789623892

Cronin, L.D., Arthur, C.A., Hardy, J., & Callow, N. (2015). Transformational leadership and task cohesion in sport: The mediating role of inside sacrifice. *Journal of Sport and Exercise Psychology, 37*, 23-36. http://dx.doi.org/10.1123/jsep.2014-0116

Cumming, S.P., & Ewing, M.E. (2002). Parental involvement in youth sports: The good, the bad and the ugly. *Spotlight on Youth Sports, 26*(1), 1-5.

Cunningham, I., Simmons, P., Mascarenhas, D., & Redhead, S. (2014). Skilled interaction: concepts of communication and player management in the development of sport officials. *International Journal of Sport Communication, 7*(2), 166-187. http://dx.doi.org/10.1123/IJSC.2013-0098

Dupuis, M., Bloom, G.A., & Loughead, T.M. (2006). Team captains' perceptions of athlete leadership. *Journal of Sport Behavior, 29*(1), 60-78.

Eccles, J.S., & Harold, R.D. (1991). Gender differences in sport involvement: Applying the Eccles' expectancy-value model. *Journal of Applied Sport Psychology, 3*(1), 7-35. http://dx.doi.org/10.1080/10413209108406432

Erickson, K., Côté, J., Hollenstein, T., & Deakin, J. (2011). Examining coach-athlete interactions using state space grids: An observational analysis in competitive youth sport. *Psychology of Sport and Exercise, 12*, 645-654. https://doi.org/10.1016/j.psychsport.2011.06.006

Fletcher, D., & Arnold, R. (2011). A qualitative study of performance leadership and management in elite sport. *Journal of Applied Sport Psychology, 23*(2), 223-242. https://doi.org/10.1080/10413200.2011.559184

Fransen, K., Haslam, S.A., Steffens, N.K., Vanbeselaere, N., De Cuyper, B., & Boen, F. (2015). Believing in "us": Exploring leaders' capacity to enhance team confidence and performance by building a sense of shared social identity. *Journal of Experimental Psychology: Applied, 21*, 89-100.

Fransen, K., Vanbeselaere, N., De Cuyper, B., Vande Broek, G., & Boen, F. (2014). The myth of the team captain as principal leader: Extending the Athlete Leadership Classification within sport teams. *Journal of Sports Sciences, 32*(14), 1389-1397. https://doi.org/10.1080/02640414.2014.891291

Freeman, L. (2004). The development of social network analysis. *A Study in the Sociology of Science, 1*(687), 159-167. https://doi.org/10.4135/9781446294413.n3

Gould, D., Voelker, D.K., & Griffes, K. (2013). Best coaching practices for developing team captains. *The Sport Psychologist, 27*, 13-26. https://doi.org/10.1123/tsp.27.1.13

Haslam, S.A., Reicher, S.D., & Platow, M.J. (2010). *The psychology of leadership: Identity, influence, and power.* Psychology Press.

Hodge, K., Henry, G., & Smith, W. (2014). A case study of excellence in elite sport: Motivational climate in a world champion team. *The Sport Psychologist, 28*, 60-74. http://dx.doi.org/10.1123/tsp.2013-0037

Hoffmann, M.D., & Loughead, T.M. (2016). Investigating athlete mentoring functions and their association with leadership behaviors and protégé satisfaction. *International Journal of Sport and Exercise Psychology, 14*(1), 85-102. https://doi.org/10.1080/1612197x.2014.999348

Hogg, M.A. (2001). A social identity theory of leadership. *Personality and Social Psychology Review, 5*, 184-200.

Horn, T.S., & Weiss, M.R. (1991). A developmental analysis of children's self-ability judgments in the physical domain. *Pediatric Exercise Science, 3*(4), 310-326. http://dx.doi.org/10.1123/pes.3.4.310

Jowett, S., & Arthur, C. (2019). Effective coaching: The links between coach leadership and coach-athlete relationship—From theory to research to practice. In M.H. Anshel, T.A. Petrie, & J.A. Steinfeldt (Eds.), *APA handbook of sport and exercise psychology. Vol. 1: Sport psychology* (p. 419-449). American Psychological Association. https://doi.org/10.1037/0000123-022

Judge, T.A., & Piccolo, R.F. (2004). Transformational and transactional leadership: A meta-analytic test of their relative validity. *Journal of Applied Psychology, 89*, 755-768. https://doi.org/10.1037/0021-9010.89.5.755

Kelloway, E.K., Sivanathan, N., Francis, L., & Barling, J. (2005). Poor leadership. In J. Barling, K. Kelloway, & M.R. Frone (Eds.), *Handbook of work stress* (pp. 89-112). Sage. https://doi.org/10.4135/9781412975995.n5

Lawrason, S., Turnnidge, J., Martin, L.J., & Côté, J. (2019). A transformational coaching workshop for changing youth sport coaches' behaviors: A pilot intervention study. *The Sport Psychologist, 33*(4), 304-312. http://dx.doi.org/10.1123/tsp.2018-0172

Lee, Y.H., Woo, B., & Kim, Y. (2018). Transformational leadership and organizational citizenship behavior: Mediating role of affective commitment. *International Journal of Sports Science and Coaching, 13*(3), 373-382. http://dx.doi.org/10.1177/174795411772528

Lefebvre, J.S., Turnnidge, J., & Côté, J. (2019). A systematic observation of coach leadership behaviors in Youth Sport. *Journal of Applied Sport Psychology, 33*(3), 377-386. https://doi.org/10.1080/10413200.2019.1609620

Lehmann-Willenbrock, N., Meinecke, A.L., Rowold, J., & Kauffeld, S. (2015). How transformational leadership works during team interactions: A behavioral process analysis. *The Leadership Quarterly, 26*(6), 1017-1033. https://doi.org/10.1016/j.leaqua.2015.07.003

Lewis, M.D., Lamey, A.V., & Douglas, L. (1999). A new dynamic systems method for the analysis of early socio-emotional development. *Developmental Science, 2*(4), 458-476. http://dx.doi.org/10. 1111/1467-7687.00090.

Kao, S., & Tsai, C. (2016). Transformational leadership and athlete satisfaction: The mediating role of coaching competency. *Journal of Applied Sport Psychology, 28*(4),469-482. https://doi.org/10.1080/10413200.2016.1187685

Mellick, M.C., Fleming, S., Bull, P., & Laugharne, E.J. (2005). Identifying best practice for referee decision communication in association and rugby union football. *Football Studies, 8*(1), 42-57.

Meyer, B., Burtscher, M.J., Jonas, K., Feese, S., Arnrich, B., Tröster, G., & Schermuly, C.C. (2016). What good leaders actually do: Micro-level leadership behaviour, leader evaluations, and team decision quality. *European Journal of Work and Organizational Psychology, 25*(6), 773-789. https://doi.org/10.1080/1359432x.2016.1189903

Mills, J.P., & Boardley, I.D. (2016). Expert Premier League soccer managers' use of transformational leadership behaviours and attitude towards sport integrity: An intrinsic case study. *International Journal of Sports Science and Coaching, 11*(3), 382-394. https://doi.org/10.1177/1747954116645011

Morgan, P.B.C., Fletcher, D., & Sarkar, M. (2015). Understanding team resilience in the world's best athletes: A case study of a rugby union world cup winning team. *Psychology of Sport and Exercise, 16*, 91-100. https://doi.org/10.1016/j.psychsport.2014.08.007

Morton, K.L., Barling, J., Rhodes, R.E., Mâsse, L.C., Zumbo, B.D., & Beauchamp, M.R. (2011). The application of transformational leadership theory to parenting: Questionnaire development and implications for adolescent self-regulatory efficacy and life satisfaction. *Journal of Sport and Exercise Psychology,* 33(5), 688-709.

Murray, N.P. (2006). The differential effect of team cohesion and leadership behavior in high school sports. *Individual Differences Research, 4*, 216-225.

Newland, A., Newton, M., Podlog, L., Legg, W.E., & Tanner, P. (2015). Exploring the nature of transformational leadership in sports: A phenomenological examination with female athletes. *Qualitative Research in Sport, Exercise and Health, 7*(5), 663-687. https://doi.org/10.1080/2159676X.2015.1007889

Piccolo, R.F., & Colquitt, J.A. (2006). Transformational leadership and job behaviors: The mediating role of core job characteristics. *Academy of Management Journal, 49*, 327-340. https://doi.org/ 10.5465/AMJ.2006.20786079

Podsakoff, P.M., MacKenzie, S.B., Moorman, R.H., & Fetter, R. (1990). Transformational leader behaviors and their effects on followers' trust in leader, satisfaction, and organizational citizenship behaviors. *The Leadership Quarterly, 1*, 107-142. https://doi.org/10.1016/1048-9843(90)90009-7

Price, M.S., & Weiss, M.R. (2011). Peer leadership in sport: Relationships among personal characteristics, leader behaviors, and team outcomes. *Journal of Applied Sport Psychology, 23*(1), 49-64. http://dx.doi.org/10.1080/10413200.2010.520300

Price, M.S., & Weiss, M.R. (2013). Relationships among coach leadership, peer leadership, and adolescent athletes' psychosocial and team outcomes: A test of transformational leadership theory. *Journal of Applied Sport Psychology, 25*, 265-279. http://dx.doi.org/10.1080/10413200.2012.725703

Rowold, J. (2006). Transformational and transactional leadership in martial arts. *Journal of Applied Sport Psychology, 18*, 312-325. https://doi.org/10.1080/10413200600944082

Ryan Dunn, C., Dorsch, T.E., King, M.Q., & Rothlisberger, K.J. (2016). The impact of family financial investment on perceived parent pressure and child enjoyment and commitment in organized youth sport. *Family Relations, 65*(2), 287-299. https://doi.org/10.1111/fare.12193

Schein, E.H. (2004). *Organizational culture and leadership* (3rd ed.) Jossey-Bass.

Sebire, S.J., Jago, R., Wood, L., Thompson, J.L., Zahra, J., & Lawlor, D.A. (2016). Examining a conceptual model of parental nurturance, parenting practices and physical activity among 5-6 year olds. *Social Science and Medicine, 148*, 18-24. http://dx.doi.org/10.1016/j.socscimed.2015.11.022

Shields, D.L., Gardner, D.E., Bredemeier, B.J., & Bostrom, A. (1995). Leadership, cohesion, and team norms regarding cheating and aggression. *Sociology of Sport Journal, 12*(3), 324-336. https://doi.org/10.1123/ssj.12.3.324

Slater, M.J., Barker, J.B., Coffee, P., & Jones, M.V. (2015). Leading for gold: Social identity leadership processes at the London 2012 Olympic Games. *Qualitative Research in Sport, Exercise and Health, 7*(2), 192-209. https://doi.org/10.1080/2159676x.2014.936030

Smith, M.J., Arthur, C.A., Hardy, J., Callow, N., & Williams, D. (2013). Transformational leadership and task cohesion in sport: The mediating role of intrateam communication. *Psychology of Sport and Exercise, 14*(2), 249-257. https://doi.org/10.1016/j.psychsport.2012.10.002

Smith, M.J., Young, D.J., Figgins, S.G., & Arthur, C.A. (2017). Transformational leadership in elite sport: A qualitative analysis of effective leadership behaviors in cricket. *The Sport Psychologist, 31*(1), 1-15. https://doi.org/10.1123/tsp.2015-0077

Smith, R.E., & Smoll, F.L. (1990). Self-esteem and children's reactions to youth sport coaching behaviors: A field study of self-enhancement processes. *Developmental Psychology, 26*, 987-993. https://doi.org/10.1037/0012-1649.26.6.987

Smith, R.E., & Smoll, F.L. (2007). Social-cognitive approach to coaching behaviors. In S. Jowett & D. Lavallee (Eds.). *Social psychology in sport* (pp. 75-90). Human Kinetics.

Smith, R.E., Zane, N.W.S., Smoll, F.L., & Coppel, D.B. (1983). Behavioral assessment in youth sports: Coaching behaviors and children's attitudes. *Medicine and Science in Sports and Exercise, 15*, 208-214. https://doi.org/10.1249/00005768-198315030-00005

Smoll, F.L., Smith, R.E., Barnett, N.P., & Everett, J.J. (1993). Enhancement of children's self-esteem through social support training for youth sport coaches. *Journal of Applied Psychology, 78*, 602-610. https://doi.org/10.1037/0021-9010.78.4.602

Smoll, F.L., Smith, R.E., Curtis, B., & Hunt, E. (1978). Toward a mediational model of coach-player relationships. *Research Quarterly, 49*(4), 528-541. https://doi.org/10.1080/10671315.1978.10615567

Stenling, A., & Tafvelin, S. (2014). Transformational leadership and well-being in sports; The Mediating role of need satisfaction. *Journal of Applied Sport Psychology, 26*, 182-196. https://doi.org/10.1080/10413200.2013.819392

Thoonen, E.E.J., Sleegers, P.J.C., Oort, F.J., Peetsma, T.T.D., & Geijsel, F.P. (2011). How to improve teaching practices: The role of teacher motivation, organizational factors, and leadership practices. *Educational Administration Quarterly, 47*, 496-536. http://dx.doi.org/10.1177/0013161X11400185

Tsai, W.C., Chen, H.W., & Cheng, J.W. (2009). Employee positive moods as a mediator linking transformational leadership and employee work outcomes. *International Journal of Human Resource Management, 20*, 206-219. https://doi.org/10.1080/09585190802528714

Tucker, S., Turner, N., Barling, J., & McEvoy, M. (2010). Transformational leadership and childrens' aggression in team settings: A short-term longitudinal study. *The Leadership Quarterly, 21*, 389-399. http://dx.doi.org/10.1016/j.leaqua.2010.03.004

Tucker, S., Turner, N., Barling, J., Reid, E.M., & Elving, C. (2006). Apologies and transformational leadership. *Journal of Business Ethics, 63*, 195. http://dx.doi.org/10.1007/s10551-005-3571-0

Turnnidge, J., & Côté, J. (2018). Applying transformational leadership theory to coaching research in youth sport: A systematic literature review. *International Journal of Sport and Exercise Psychology, 16*, 327-342. http://dx.doi.org/10.1080/1612197X.2016.1189948

Turnnidge, J., & Côté, J. (2019). Observing coaches' leadership behaviours: The development of the Coach Leadership Assessment System (CLAS). *Measurement in Physical Education and Exercise Science, 23*(3), 214-226. https://doi.org/10.1080/1091367x.2019.1602835

Vealey, R.S., & Chase, M.A. (2016). *Best practice for youth sport.* Human Kinetics. http://dx.doi.org/10.5040/9781492595267

Vella, S.A., Oades, L.G., & Crowe, T.P. (2012). Validation of the differentiated transformational leadership inventory as a measure of coach leadership in youth soccer. *The Sport Psychologist, 26*(2), 207-223. https://doi.org/10.1123/tsp.26.2.207

Vella, S.A., Oades, L.G., & Crowe, T.P. (2013a). The relationship between coach leadership, the coach-athlete relationship, team success, and the positive developmental experiences of adolescent soccer players. *Physical Education and Sport Pedagogy, 18*, 549-561. https://doi.org/10.1080/17408989.2012.726976

Vella, S.A., Oades, L.G., & Crowe, T.P. (2013b). A pilot test of transformational leadership training for sports coaches: Impact on the developmental experiences of adolescent athletes. *International Journal of Sports Science and Coaching, 8*, 513-530. https://doi.org/10.1260/1747-9541.8.3.513

Zacharatos, A., Barling, J., & Kelloway, E.K. (2000). Development and effects of transformational leadership in adolescents. *The Leadership Quarterly, 11*, 211-226. https://doi.org/10.1016/S1048-9843(00)00041-2

Chapter 8

Bass, B.M., & Riggio, R.E. (2006). *Transformational leadership* (2nd ed.). Erlbaum.

Cruwys, T., Steffens, N.K., Haslam, S.A., Haslam, C., Jetten, J., & Dingle, G. (2016). Social identity mapping: A procedure for visual representation and assessment of subjective multiple group memberships. *British Journal of Social Psychology, 55*(4), 613-642. https://doi.org/10.1111/bjso.12155.

Dinh, J.E., Lord, R.G., Gardner, W.L., Meuser, J.D., Liden, R.C., & Hu, J. (2014). Leadership theory and research in the new millennium: Current theoretical trends and changing perspectives. *The Leadership Quarterly, 25*, 36-62. https://doi.org/10.1016/j.leaqua.2013.11.005

Fransen, K., Barker, J.B., & Slater, M.J. (2020). Leadership and social identity. In D. Hackfort and R. Schinke (Eds.), *The Routledge international encyclopaedia of sport and exercise psychology* (pp. 219-231). Routledge.

Fransen, K., Coffee, P., Vanbeselaere, N., Slater, M., De Cuyper, B., & Boen, F. (2014). The impact of athlete leaders on team members' team outcome confidence: A test of mediation by team identification and collective efficacy. *The Sport Psychologist, 28*(4), 347-360. https://doi.org/10.1123/tsp.2013-0141.

Fransen, K., Decroos, S., Vande Broek, G., & Boen, F. (2016). Leading from the top or leading from within? A comparison between coaches' and athletes' leadership as predictors of team identification, team confidence, and team cohesion. *International Journal of Sports Science and Coaching, 11*(6), 757-771. https://doi.org/10.1177/1747954116676102

Fransen, K., Haslam, S. A., Steffens, N. K., Peters, K., Mallett, C., J., Mertens, N., & Boen, F. (2020). All for us and us for all: Introducing the 5R shared leadership program. *Psychology of Sport and Exercise, 51,* 101762. https://doi.org/10.1016/j.psychsport.2020.101762

Fransen, K., McEwan, D., & Sarkar, M. (2020). The impact of identity leadership on team functioning and well-being in team sport: Is psychological safety the missing link? *Psychology of Sport and Exercise, 51*, 101763. https://doi.org/10.1016/j.psychsport.2020.101763

Giessner, S.R., & van Knippenberg, D. (2008). "License to fail": Goal definition, leader group prototypicality, and perceptions of leadership effectiveness after leader failure. *Organizational Behaviour and Human Decision Processes, 105*, 14-35. https://doi.org/10.1016/j.obhdp.2007.04.002

Gu, Q., Tang, T.L.P., & Jiang, W. (2015). Does moral leadership enhance employee creativity? Employee identification with leader and leader-member exchange (LMX) in the Chinese context. *Journal of Business Ethics, 126*, 513-529. https://doi.org/10.1007/s10551-013-1967-9

Haslam, C., Jetten, J., Cruwys, T., Dingle, G., & Haslam, S.A. (2018). *The new psychology of health: Unlocking the social cure.* Routledge.

Haslam, S.A. (2004). *Psychology in organizations: The social identity approach* (2nd ed.). Sage.

Haslam, S.A., Fransen, K., & Boen, F. (Eds.). (2020). *The new psychology of sport and exercise: The social identity approach.* Sage.

Haslam, S.A., Reicher, S.D., & Platow, M.J. (2011). *The new psychology of leadership: Identity, influence and power.* Psychology Press.

Haslam, S.A., Reicher, S.D., & Platow, M.J. (2020). *The new psychology of leadership: Identity, influence and power* (2nd ed.). Routledge.

Haslam, S.A., Steffens N.K., Peters, K., Boyce, R.A., Mallett, C., & Fransen, K. (2017). A social identity approach to leadership development: The 5R program. *Journal of Personnel Psychology, 16*, https://doi.org/10.1027/1866-5888/a000176

Loughead, T.M., Hardy, J., & Eys, M.A. (2006). The nature of athlete leadership. *Journal of Sport Behavior, 29*, 142-158.

Martin, L.J., Balderson, D., Hawkins, M., Wilson, K., & Bruner, M.W. (2017). Groupness and leadership perceptions in relation to social identity in youth sport. *Journal of Applied Sport Psychology, 29*(3), 367-374. https://doi.org/10.1080/10413200.2016.1238414

Mayo, E. (1949). *The social problems of an industrial civilization.* Routledge & Kegan Paul.

Mertens, N., Boen, F., Steffens, N.K., Cotterill, S.T., Haslam, S.A., & Fransen, K. (2020). Leading together towards a stronger "us": An experimental test of the effectiveness of the 5R Shared Leadership Program ($5R^S$) in basketball teams. *Journal of Science and Medicine in Sport, 23*, 770-775. https://doi.org/10.1016/j.jsams.2020.01.010

Miller, A.J., Slater, M.J., & Turner, M.J. (2020). Coach identity leadership behaviours are positively associated with athlete resource appraisals: The mediating roles of relational and group identification. *Psychology of Sport and Exercise, 51*, 101755. https://doi.org/10.1016/j.psychsport.2020.101755

Rees, T., Haslam, S.A., Coffee, P., & Lavallee, D. (2015). A social identity approach to sport psychology: Principles, practice, and prospects. *Sports Medicine, 45*(8), 1083-1096. https://doi:10.1007/s40279-015-0345-4

Slater, M.J. (2019). *Togetherness: How to build a winning team.* Bennion Kearney.

Slater, M.J., & Barker, J.B. (2019). Doing social identity leadership: Exploring the efficacy of an identity leadership intervention on perceived leadership and mobilization in elite disability soccer. *Journal of Applied Sport Psychology, 31*, 65-86. https://doi.org/10.1080/10413200.2017.1410255

Slater, M.J., Barker, J.B., Coffee, P., & Jones, M.V. (2015). Leading for gold: Social identity leadership processes at the London 2012 Olympic Games. *Qualitative Research in Sport, Exercise and Health, 7*, 192-209. https://doi.org/10.1080/2159676X.2014.936030

Slater, M.J., Coffee, P., Barker, J.B., & Evans, A.L. (2014). Promoting shared meanings in group memberships: A social identity approach to leadership in sport. *Reflective Practice: International and Multidisciplinary Perspectives, 15*(5), 672-685. https://doi.org/10.1080/14623943.2014.944126

Slater, M.J., Coffee, P., Barker, J.B., Haslam, S.A., & Steffens, N.K. (2019). Shared social identity content is the basis for leaders' mobilization of followers. *Psychology of Sport and Exercise, 43*, 271-278. https://doi.org/10.1016/j.psychsport.2019.03.012

Slater, M.J., Haslam, S.A., & Steffens, N.K. (2018). Singing it for "us": Team passion displayed during national anthems is associated with subsequent success. *European Journal of Sport Science, 18*(4), 541-549. https://doi.org/10.1080/17461391.2018.1431311

Slater, M.J., Turner, M.J., Evans, A.L., & Jones, M.V. (2018). Capturing hearts and minds: The influence of relational identification with the leader on followers' mobilization and cardiovascular reactivity. *The Leadership Quarterly,* 29, 379-388. https://doi.org/10.1016/j.leaqua.2017.08.003

Sluss, D.M., & Ashforth, B.E. (2007). Relational identity and identification: Defining ourselves through work relationships. *Academy of Management Review, 32*, 9-32. https://doi.org/10.5465/amr.2007.23463672

Sluss, D.M., Ployhart, R.E., Cobb, M.G., & Ashforth, B.E. (2012). Generalizing newcomers' relational and organizational identifications: Processes and prototypicality. *Academy of Management Journal, 55*, 949-975. https://doi.org/10.5465/amj.2010.0420

Steffens, N.K., Haslam, S.A., Reicher, S.D., Platow, M.J., Fransen, K., Yang, J., Ryan, M.K., Jetten, J., Peters, K., & Boen, F. (2014). Leadership as social identity management: Introducing the Identity Leadership Inventory (ILI) to assess and validate a four-dimensional model. *The Leadership Quarterly, 25*, 1001-1024. https://doi.org/10.1016/j.leaqua.2014.05.002

Stevens, M., Rees, T., Coffee, P., Haslam, S.A., Steffens, N.K., & Polman, R. (2018). Leaders promote attendance in sport and exercise sessions by fostering social identity. *Scandinavian Journal of Medicine and Science in Sports, 28*, 2100-2108. https://doi.org/10.1111/sms.13217

Stevens, M., Rees, T., Steffens, N.K., Haslam, S.A., Coffee, P., & Polman, R. (2019). Leaders' creation of shared identity impacts group members' effort and performance: Evidence from an exercise task. *PLOS One, 14*, 0218984. https://doi.org/10.1371/journal.pone.0218984

Subašić, E., Reynolds, K.J., Turner, J.C., Veenstra, K.E., & Haslam, S.A. (2011). Leadership, power and the use of surveillance: Implications of shared social identity for leaders' capacity to influence. *The Leadership Quarterly, 22*, 170-181. https://doi.org/10.1016/j.leaqua.2010.12.014

Tajfel, H. (1972). Social categorisation. English manuscript of "La categorisation sociale." In S. Moscovici (Ed.), *Introduction à la psychologie sociale* (Vol. 1, pp. 272-302). Larosse.

Tajfel, H., & Turner, J.C. (1979). An integrative theory of intergroup conflict. In S. Worchel & W.G. Austin (Eds.), *The psychology of intergroup relations* (pp. 33-47). Brooks-Cole.

Turner, J.C. (1991). *Social influence.* Open University Press.

Turner, J.C., Hogg, M.A., Oakes, P.J., Reicher, S., & Wetherell, M.S. (1987). *Rediscovering the social group: A self-categorisation theory.* Basil Blackwell.

van Dick, R., Lemoine, J.E., Steffens, N.K., Kerschreiter, R., Akfirat, S.A., Avanzi, L., Dumont, K., Epitropaki, O., Fransen, K., Giessner, S., González, R., Kark, R., Lipponen, J., Markovits, Y., Monzani, L., Orosz, G., Pandey, D., Roland-Lévy, C., Schuh, S., . . . & Haslam, S.A. (2018). Identity leadership going global: Validation of the Identity Leadership Inventory across 20 countries. *Journal of Occupational and Organizational Psychology, 91*(4), 697-728. https://doi.org/10.1111/joop.12223

van Knippenberg, B., & van Knippenberg, D. (2005). Leader self-sacrifice and leadership effectiveness: The moderating role of leader prototypicality. *Journal of Applied Psychology, 90*(1), 25-37. doi: 10.1037/0021-9010.90.1.25.

White, C.A., Slater, M.J., Turner, M.J., & Barker, J.B. (2020). More positive group memberships and social identification are associated with greater resilience in Royal Air Force (RAF) personnel. *British Journal of Social Psychology.* https://doi.org/10.1111/bjso.12385

Zhu, W., He, H., Trevino, L.K., Chao, M.M., & Wang, W. (2015). Ethical leadership and follower voice and performance: The role of follower identifications and entity morality beliefs. *The Leadership Quarterly, 22*, 702-718. http://dx.doi.org/10.1016/j.leaqua.2015.01.004

Chapter 9

Arthur, C.A., Bastardoz, N., & Eklund, R. (2017). Transformational leadership in sport: Current status and future directions. *Current Opinion in Psychology, 16*, 78-83. http://dx.doi.org/10.1016/j.copsyc.2017.04.001

Avolio, B.J. (1999). *Full leadership development: Building the vital forces in organizations.* Sage.

Avolio, B.J., Reichard, R.J., Hannah, S.T., Walumbwa, F.O., & Chan, A. (2009). A meta-analytic review of leadership impact research: Experimental and quasi-experimental studies. *The Leadership Quarterly, 20*(5), 764-784. https://doi.org/10.1016/j.leaqua.2009.06.006

Bass, B.M., & Avolio, B.J. (1997). *Full range leadership development: Manual for the Multifactor Leadership Questionnaire.* Mindgarden.

Blake-Beard, S.D., O'Neill, R.M., & McGowan, E.M. (2007). Blind dates? The importance of matching in successful formal mentoring relationships. In B.R. Ragins & K.E. Kram (Eds.), *The handbook of mentoring at work: Theory, research, and practice* (pp. 617-632). Sage.

Blanton, J.E., Sturges, A.J., & Gould, D. (2014). Lessons learned from a leadership development club for high school athletes. *Journal of Sport Psychology in Action, 5*(1), 1-13. https://doi.org/10.1080/21520704.2013.848827

Boisvert, M.M., Loughead, T.M., & Munroe-Chandler, K.J. (2022). The implementation and evaluation of an athlete leadership development program with male youth hockey players. *Frontiers in Psychology-Performance Science, 13, 648039.* https://doi.org/10.3389/fpsyg.2022.648039

Borgatti, S.P., Everett, M.G., & Johnson, J.C. (2018). *Analyzing social networks* (2nd ed.). Sage.

Bucci, J., Bloom, G.A., Loughead, T.M., & Caron, J.G. (2012). Ice hockey coaches' perceptions of athlete leadership. *Journal of Applied Sport Psychology, 24*(3), 243-259. https://doi.org/10.1080/10413200.2011.636416

Callow, N., Smith, M., Hardy, L., Arthur, C., & Hardy, J. (2009). Measurement of transformational leadership and its relationship with team cohesion and performance level. *Journal of Applied Sport Psychology, 21*(4), 395-412. https://doi.org/10.1080/10413200903204754

Chelladurai, P. (1978). *A contingency model of leadership in athletics* [Unpublished doctoral dissertation]. University of Waterloo.

Chelladurai, P. (2007). Leadership in sports. In G. Tenenbaum & R.C. Eklund (Eds.), *Handbook of sport psychology* (pp. 113-135). Wiley.

Chelladurai, P., & Saleh, S.D. (1980). Dimensions of leader behavior in sports: Development of a leadership scale. *Journal of Sport Psychology, 2*(1), 34-45. https://doi.org/10.1123/jsp.2.1.34

Collins, D.B., & Holton, E.F. (2004). The effectiveness of managerial leadership development programs: A meta-analysis of studies from 1982-2001. *Human Resource Development Quarterly, 15*(2), 217-248. https://doi.org/10.1002/hrdq.1099

Costa, P.T., Jr., & McCrae, R.R. (1992). *NEO-PI-R professional manual.* Psychological Assessment Resources.

Crozier, A.J., Loughead, T.M., & Munroe-Chandler, K.J. (2013). Examining the benefits of athlete leadership in sport. *Journal of Sport Behavior, 36*(4), 346-364.

de Cruz, N. (2019). A conceptual overview of attaining, maintaining, and regaining shared leadership in high performing teams. *Journal of Leadership Education, 18*(1), 213-226. https://doi.org/10.12806/V18/I1/T3

DeRue, D.S. (2011). Adaptive leadership theory: Leading and following as a complex adaptive process. *Research in Organizational Behavior,* 31, 125-150. https://doi.org/10.1016/j.riob.2011.09.007

DeRue, D.S., & Ashford, S. (2010). Who will lead and who will follow? A social process of leadership identity construction in organizations. *Academy of Management Review, 35*(4), 627-647. https://doi.org/10.5465/amr.35.4.zok627

Duguay, A.M., Hoffmann, M.D., Guerrero, M.D., & Loughead, T.M. (2020). An examination of the temporal nature of shared athlete leadership: A longitudinal case study of a competitive youth male ice hockey team. *International Journal of Sport and Exercise Psychology, 18*(5), 672-686. https://doi.org/10.1080/1612197X.2019.1570535

Duguay, A.M., Loughead, T.M., & Cook, J.M. (2019). Athlete leadership as a shared process: Using a social network approach to examine athlete leadership in competitive female youth soccer teams. *The Sport Psychologist, 33*(3), 1-43. https://doi.org/10.1123/tsp.2018-0019

Duguay, A.M., Loughead, T.M., Hoffmann, M.D., & Caron, J.G. (2020). Facilitating the development of shared athlete leadership: Insights from intercollegiate coaches. *Journal of Applied Sport Psychology.* Advance online publication. https://doi.org/10.1080/10413200.2020.1773576

Duguay, A.M., Loughead, T.M., & Munroe-Chandler, K.J. (2016). The development, implementation, and evaluation of an athlete leadership development program with female varsity athletes. *The Sport Psychologist, 30*(2), 154-166. https://doi.org/10.1123/tsp.2015-0050

Duguay, A.M., Loughead, T.M., & Munroe-Chandler, K.J. (2018). Investigating the importance of athlete leadership behaviors and the impact of leader tenure. *Journal of Sport Behavior, 41*(2), 129-147.

Dupuis, M., Bloom, G.A., & Loughead, T.M. (2006). Team captains' perceptions of athlete leadership. *Journal of Sport Behavior, 29*(1), 60-78.

Ender, S.C., & Newton, F.B. (2000). *Students helping students: A guide for peer educators on college campuses.* Jossey-Bass.

Finkelstein, J. (2006). *Learning in real time: Synchronous teaching and learning online.* Jossey-Bass.

Fransen, K., Haslam, S.A., Steffens, N.K., Peters, K., Mallett, C.J., Mertens, N., & Boen, F. (2020). All for us and us for all: Introducing the 5R shared leadership program. *Psychology of Sport and Exercise, 51,* 101762. https://doi.org/10.1016/j.psychsport.2020.101762

Fransen, K., Mertens, N., Cotterill, S.T., Vande Broek, G., & Boen, F. (2020). From autocracy to empowerment: Teams with shared leadership perceive their coaches to be better leaders. *Journal of Applied Sport Psychology, 32*(1), 5-27. https://doi.org/10.1080/10413200.2019.1617370

Fransen, K., Van Puyenbroeck, S., Loughead, T.M., Vanbeselaere, N., De Cuyper, B., Broek, G.V., & Boen, F. (2015a). The art of athlete leadership: Identifying high-quality athlete leadership at the individual and team level through social network analysis. *Journal of Sport and Exercise Psychology, 37*(3), 274-290. https://doi.org/10.1123/jsep.2014-0259

Fransen, K., Van Puyenbroeck, S., Loughead, T.M., Vanbeselaere, N., De Cuyper, B., Broek, G.V., & Boen, F. (2015b). Who takes the lead? Social network analysis as a pioneering tool to investigate shared leadership within sports teams. *Social Networks, 43,* 28-38. https://doi.org/10.1016/j.socnet.2015.04.003

Fransen, K., Vanbeselaere, N., De Cuyper, B., Vande Broek, G., & Boen, F. (2014). The myth of the team captain as principal leader: Extending the athlete leadership classification within sport teams. *Journal of Sports Sciences, 32*(14), 1389-1397. https://doi.org/10.1080/02640414.2014.891291

Gibb, C.A. (1954). Leadership. In G. Lindzey (Ed.), *Handbook of social psychology* (Vol. 2, pp. 877-917). Addison-Wesley.

Glenn, S.D., & Horn, T.S. (1993). Psychological and personal predictors of leadership behavior in female soccer athletes. *Journal of Applied Sport Psychology, 5*(1), 17-34. https://doi.org/10.1080/10413209308411302

Gockel, C., & Werth, L. (2010). Measuring and modeling shared leadership: Traditional approaches and new ideas. *Journal of Personnel Psychology, 9*(4), 172-180. https://doi.org/10.1027/1866-5888/a000023

Gould, D., Chung, Y., Smith, P., & White, J. (2006). Future directions in coaching life skills: Understanding high school coaches' views and needs. *Athletic Insight, 8*(3), 28-38.

Gould, D., & Voelker, D.K. (2010). Youth sport leadership development: Leveraging the sports captaincy experience. *Journal of Sport Psychology in Action, 1*(1), 1-14. https://doi.org/10.1080/21520704.2010.497695

Grant, M.A., Bloom, G.A., & Lefebvre, J.S. (2020). Lessons learned: Coaches' perceptions of a pilot e-mentoring programme. *International Sport Coaching Journal, 7*(1), 22-30. https://doi.org/10.1123/iscj.2018-0058

Gross, A.E., & McMullen, P.A. (1983). Models of help-seeking process. In F.D. Fisher, A. Naples, & B.M. DePaul (Eds.), *New directions in helping and help-seeking* (Vol. 2., pp. 24-58). Academic Press.

Haddad, G., O'Connor, D., & Burns, K. (2021). The decision to adopt a formal athlete leadership group: Qualitative insights from professional football coaches. *Psychology of Sport and Exercise, 52,* 101803. https://doi.org/10.1016/j.psychsport.2020.101803

Hoffmann, M.D. (2019). Considerations for facilitating the development of peer mentoring relationships between athletes. *Journal of Sport Psychology in Action, 10*(1), 59-72. https://doi.org/10.1080/21520704.2018.1509164

Hoffmann, M.D., & Loughead, T.M. (2016). Investigating athlete mentoring functions and their association with leadership behaviours and protégé satisfaction. *International Journal of Sport and Exercise Psychology, 14*(1), 85-102. https://doi.org/10.1080/1612197X.2014.999348

Hoffmann, M.D., & Loughead, T.M. (2019). Preliminary development of a questionnaire to assess peer athlete mentoring functions: The Athlete Mentoring Questionnaire (AMQ). *Measurement in Physical Education and Exercise Science, 23*(1), 10-25. https://doi.org/10.1080/1091367X.2018.1479708

Hoffmann, M.D., Loughead, T.M., & Bloom, G.A. (2017). Examining the experiences of peer mentored athletes competing in elite sport. *The Sport Psychologist, 31*(2), 134-146. https://doi.org/10.1123/tsp.2016-0052

Holmes, R.M., McNeil, M., & Adorna, P. (2010). Student athletes' perceptions of formal and informal team leaders. *Journal of Sport Behavior, 33*(4), 442-465.

Imholte, P.D., Blanton, J.E., & McAlarnen, M.M. (2019). Fun, failure, and fulfillment: A case-study approach to informal athlete leadership in minor league baseball. *The Sport Psychologist, 33*(3), 177-188. https://doi.org/10.1123/tsp.2018-0003

Kear, K., Chetwynd, F., Williams, J., & Donelan, H. (2012). Web conferencing for synchronous online tutorials: Perspectives of tutors using a new medium. *Computers & Education, 58*(3), 953-963. https://doi.org/10.1016/j.compedu.2011.10.015

Leo, F.M., García-Calvo, T., González-Ponce, I., Pulido, J.J., & Fransen, K. (2019). How many leaders does it take to lead a sports team? The relationship between the number of leaders and the effectiveness of professional sports teams. *PLOS One, 14*(6), 0218167. https://doi.org/10.1371/journal.pone.0218167

Loughead, T.M., Fransen, K., Van Puyenbroeck, S., Hoffmann, M.D., De Cuyper, B., Vanbeselaere, N., & Boen, F. (2016). An examination of the relationship between athlete leadership and cohesion using social network analysis. *Journal of Sports Sciences, 34*(21), 2063-2073. https://doi.org/10.1080/02640414.2016.1150601

Loughead, T.M., & Hardy, J. (2005). An examination of coach and peer leader behaviors in sport. *Psychology of Sport and Exercise, 6*(3), 303-312. https://doi.org/10.1016/j.psychsport.2004.02.001

Loughead, T.M., Hardy, J., & Eys, M.A. (2006). The nature of athlete leadership. *Journal of Sport Behavior, 29*(2), 142-159.

Loughead, T.M., Munroe-Chandler, K.J., Boisvert, M.M., & Hirsch, K.E. (2021). Athlete leadership. In E. Filho & I. Basevitch (Eds.), *Sport, exercise, and performance psychology: Research directions to advance the field.* Oxford University Press.

Lusher, D., Robins, G., & Kremer, P. (2010). The application of social network analysis to team sports. *Measurement in Physical Education and Exercise Science, 14*(4), 211-224. https://doi.org/10.1080/1091367X.2010.495559

Maechel, C., Loughead, T.M., & Beckmann, J. (2020). The testing of a four-dimensional model of athlete leadership and its relation to leadership effectiveness. *Frontiers in Psychology, 11*, 1361. https://doi.org/10.3389/fpsyg.2020.01361

McInnerney, J.M., & Roberts, T.S. (2004). Online learning: Social interaction and the creation of a sense of community. *Journal of Educational Technology & Society, 7*(3), 73-81.

Mishra, P., & Koehler, M.J. (2006). Technological pedagogical content knowledge: A framework for teacher knowledge. *Teachers College Record, 108*(6), 1017-1054.

Moran, M.M., & Weiss, M.R. (2006). Peer leadership in sport: Links with friendship, peer acceptance, psychological characteristics, and athletic ability. *Journal of Applied Sport Psychology, 18*(2), 97-113. https://doi.org/10.1080/10413200600653501

Morgan, P.B.C., Fletcher, D., & Sarkar, M. (2013). Defining and characterizing team resilience in elite sport. *Psychology of Sport and Exercise, 14*(4), 549-559. https://doi.org/10.1016/j.psychsport.2013.01.004

Morgan, P.B.C., Fletcher, D., & Sarkar, M. (2015). Understanding team resilience in the world's best athletes: A case study of a rugby union World Cup winning team. *Psychology of Sport and Exercise, 16*(1), 91-100. https://doi.org/10.1016/j.psychsport.2014.08.007

Paradis, K.F., & Loughead, T.M. (2012). Examining the mediating role of cohesion between athlete leadership and athlete satisfaction in youth sport. *International Journal of Sport Psychology, 43*(2), 117-136.

Pierce, S., Blanton, J., & Gould, D. (2018). An online program for high school student-athlete leadership development: Community engagement, collaboration, and course creation. *Case Studies in Sport and Exercise Psychology, 2*(1), 23-29. https://doi.org/10.1123/cssep.2017-0014

Price, M.S., & Weiss, M.R. (2013). Relationships among coach leadership, peer leadership, and adolescent athletes' psychosocial and team outcomes: A test of transformational leadership theory. *Journal of Applied Sport Psychology, 25*(2), 265-279. https://doi.org/10.1080/10413200.2012.725703

Santos, F., Strachan, L., Gould, D., Pereira, P., & Machado, C. (2019). The role of team captains in integrating positive teammate psychological development in high-performance sport. *The Sport Psychologist, 33*(1), 1-35. https://doi.org/10.1123/tsp.2017-0135

Vincer, D.J.E., & Loughead, T.M. (2010). The relationship among athlete leadership behaviors and cohesion in team sports. *The Sport Psychologist, 24*(4), 448-467. https://doi.org/10.1123/tsp.24.4.448

Voight, M. (2012). A leadership development intervention program: A case study with two elite teams. *The Sport Psychologist, 26*(4), 604-623. https://doi.org/10.1123/tsp.26.4.604

Vonderwell, S. (2003). An examination of asynchronous communication experiences and perspectives of students in an online course: A case study. *The Internet and Higher Education, 6*(1), 77-90. https://doi.org/10.1016/S1096-7516(02)00164-1

Yukl, G. (2012). Effective leadership behavior: What we know and what questions need more attention. *Academy of Management Perspectives, 26*(4), 66-85. https://doi.org/10.5465/amp.2012.0088

Wasserman, S., & Faust, K. (1994). *Social network analysis: Methods and applications.* Cambridge University Press.

Wright, A., & Côté, J. (2003). A retrospective analysis of leadership development through sport. *The Sport Psychologist, 17*(3), 268-291. https://doi.org/10.1123/tsp.17.3.268

Chapter 10

Adie, J.W., Duda, J.L., & Ntoumanis, N. (2008). Autonomy support basic need satisfaction and the optimal functioning of adult male and female sport participants: A test of basic needs theory. *Motivation and Emotion, 32*, 189-199.

Adie, J.W., Duda, J.L., & Ntoumanis, N. (2012). Perceived coach-autonomy support, basic need satisfaction and the well- and ill-being of elite youth soccer players: A longitudinal investigation. *Psychology of Sport and Exercise, 13*, 51-59.

Álvarez, M.S., Balaguer, I., Castillo, I., & Duda, J.L. (2009). Coach autonomy support and quality of sport engagement in young soccer players. *Spanish Journal of Psychology, 12*, 138-148. http://dx.doi.org/10.1017/S1138741600001554

Ames, C. (1992). Achievement goals, motivational climate, and motivational processes. In G.C. Roberts (Ed.), *Motivation in sport and exercise* (pp. 161-176). Human Kinetics.

Appleton, P.R., Ntoumanis, N., Quested, E., Viladrich, C., & Duda, J.L. (2016). Initial validation of the coach-created Empowering and Disempowering Motivational Climate Questionnaire (EDMCQ-C). *Psychology of Sport and Exercise, 22*, 53-65.

Appleton, P. R., Viladrich, C., Quested, E., González-García, L. Papaioannou, A. Hall. H. K.,... Duda, J. L. (2023). Measurement invariance of the empowering and disempowering motivational climate questionnaire-coach in youth sport. *Frontiers in Psychology, 13.*

Balaguer, I., González, L., Fabra, P., Castillo, I., Mercé, J., & Duda, J.L. (2012). Coaches' interpersonal style, basic psychological needs, and the well- and ill-being of young soccer players: A longitudinal analysis. *Journal of Sports Sciences, 30*(15), 1619-1629.

Bartholomew, K., Ntoumanis, N., & Thøgersen-Ntoumani, C. (2011). Self-determination theory and the darker side of athletic experience: The role of interpersonal control and need thwarting. *Sport and Exercise Psychology Review, 7*(2), 23-27.

Birr, C., Hernandez-Mendo, A., Monteiro, D., & Rosado, A. (2023). Empowering and disempowering motivational coaching climate: A Scoping Review. *Sustainability, 15*(3), 2820.

Boyce, B.A., Gano-Overway, L.A., & Campbell, A.L. (2009). Perceived motivational climate's influence on goal orientations, perceived competence, and practice strategies across the athletic season. *Journal of Applied Sport Psychology, 21,* 381-394.

Brown, D.J., Arnold, R., Standage, M., Turner, J.E., & Fletcher, D. (2021). The prediction of thriving in elite sport: A prospective examination of the role of psychological need satisfaction, challenge appraisal, and salivary biomarkers. *Journal of Science and Medicine in Sport, 24*(4), 373-379.

Burns, L., Weissensteiner, J.R., & Cohen, M. (2019). Lifestyles and mindsets of Olympic, Paralympic and world champions: Is an integrated approach the key to elite performance? *British Journal of Sports Medicine, 53,* 818-824.

Castillo, I., Ramis, Y., Cruz, J., and Balaguer, I. (2015). Formacion de entrenadores de futbol base en al projecto PAPA. *Revista de Psicología del Deporte, 24,* 131-138.

Castillo-Jimenez, N., Lopez-Walle, J.M., Tomas, I., Tristan, J., Duda, J.L., & Balaguer, I. (2022). Empowering and disempowering motivational climates, mediating psychological processes, and future intentions of sport participation. *International Journal of Environmental Research and Public Health, 19,* 896.

Cecchini, J.A., Fernandez-Rio, J., Mendez-Gimenez, A., Cecchini, C., & Martins, L. (2014). Epstein's TARGET framework and motivational climate in sport: Effects of a field-based, long-term intervention program. *International Journal of Sports Science and Coaching, 9*(6), 1325-1340.

Cheon, S.H., Reeves, J., Lee, J., & Lee, Y. (2015). Giving and receiving autonomy support in a high-stakes sport context: A field-based experiment during the 2012 London Paralympic Games. *Psychology of Sport and Exercise, 19,* 59-69.

Cooper, D., & Allen, J. (2020). "I don't want to give them my brain for the day . . . and then take it back": An examination of the coach-created motivational climate in adult adventure sports. *International Sport Coaching Journal, 7*(2), 175-188.

Curran, T., Hill, A.P., Ntoumanis, N., Hall, H.K., & Jowett, G.E. (2016). A three-wave longitudinal test of self-determination theory's mediation model of engagement and disaffection in youth sport. *Journal of Sport and Exercise Psychology, 38*(1), 15-29.

De Meyer, J., Tallir, I.B., Soenens, B., Vansteenkiste, M., Aelterman, N., Van den Berghe, L., & Haerens, L. (2013). Does observed controlling teaching behavior relate to students' motivation in physical education? *Journal of Educational Psychology, 106,* 541-555.

Deci, E.L., & Ryan, R.M. (2000). The "what" and the "why" of goal pursuits: Human needs and the self-determination of behaviour. *Psychological Inquiry, 11,* 227-268.

Duda, J.L. (2013). The conceptual and empirical foundations of Empowering Coaching™: Setting the stage for the PAPA Project. *International Journal of Sport and Exercise Psychology, 11*(4), 311-318.

Duda, J.L., & Appleton, P.R. (2016). Empowering and disempowering coaching behaviour: Conceptualization, measurement considerations, and intervention implications. In M. Raab, P. Wylleman, R. Seiler, A.-M. Elbe, & A. Hatzigeorgiadis (Eds.), *Sport and exercise psychology research: From theory to practice* (pp. 374-390). Elsevier. https://doi.org/10.1016/B978-0-12-803634-1.00017-0

Duda, J.L., Appleton, P.R., Stebbings, J., & Balaguer, I. (2018). Towards more empowering and less disempowering environments in youth sport. In C.J. Knight, C.G. Harwood, & D. Gould (Eds.), *Sport psychology for young athletes* (pp. 81-93). Routledge.

Duda, J.L., & Balaguer, I. (2007). Coach-created motivational climate. In S. Jowett & D. Lavallee (Eds.), *Social psychology in sport* (pp. 117-130). Human Kinetics.

Duda, J.L., & Whitehead, J. (1998). Measurement of goal perspectives in the physical domain. In J.L. Duda (Ed.), *Advances in sport and exercise psychology measurement* (pp. 21-48). Fitness Information Technology.

Dweck, C.S. (1999). *Self-theories: Their role in motivation, personality, and development.* Psychology Press.

Fabra, P., Balaguer, I., Tomás, I., Smith, N., & Duda, J.L. (2018). Spanish version of the multidimensional motivational climate observation system (MMCOS): Reliability and validity evidence. *Revista de Psicologia del Deporte, 27,* 11-22.

Fabra, P., Castillo, I., González-García, L., Duda, J.L., & Balaguer, I. (2021). Changes in drop out intentions: Implications of the motivational climate, goal orientations and aspects of self-worth across a youth sport season. *Sustainability,13,* 13850. https://doi.org/10.3390/su132413850

Fenton, A.M., Duda, J.L., Appleton, P.R., Barrett, T.G. (2017). Empowering youth sport environments: Implications for daily moderate-to-vigorous physical activity and adiposity. *Journal of Sport and Health Science, 6,* 423-433.

Fry, M., Gano-Overway, L., Guivernau, M., Kim, M., & Newton, M. (2019). *A coach's guide to maximizing the youth sport experience: Work hard, be kind.* Routledge.

Gillet, N., Fouquereau, E., Forest, J., Brunault, P., & Colombat, P. (2012). The impact of organizational factors on psychological needs and their relationships with well-being. *Journal of Business Psychology, 27,* 437-450.

Gonzalez, L., Tomas, I., Castillo, I., Duda, J.L., & Balaguer, I. (2017). A test of basic psychological needs theory in young soccer players: Time-lagged design at the individual and team levels. *Scandinavian Journal of Medicine and Science in Sports, 27,* 1511-1522.

Harwood, C., Keegan, R.J., Smith, J.M.J., & Raine, A.S. (2015). A systematic review of the intrapersonal correlates of motivational climate perceptions in sport and physical activity. (2015). *Psychology of Sport and Exercise, 18,* 9-25.

Hornstra, L., Stroet, K., & Weijers, D. (2020). Profiles of teachers' need-support: How do autonomy support, structure, and involvement cohere and predict motivation and learning outcomes? *Teaching and Teacher Education, 99,* 103257.

Kavanah, E., Brown, L., & Jones, I. (2017). Elite athletes' experience of coping with emotional abuse in the coach–athlete relationship. *Journal of Applied Sport Psychology, 29,* 402-417.

Keegan, R.J., Cotteril, S., Woolway, T., Appaneal, R., & Hutter, V.S. (2017). Strategies for bridging the research-practice "gap" in sport and exercise psychology. *Revista de Psicologia del Deporte, 26,* 75-80.

Kerr, G., Battaglia, A., & Stirling, A. (2019). Maltreatment in youth sport: A systemic issue. *Kinesiology Review, 8*(3), 237-243.

Krommidas, C., Galanis, E., Papaioannou, A., Tzioumakis, G., Zourbanos, N., Keramidas, P., & Digelidis, N. (2016). The relationship of empowering and disempowering coaching climate with enjoyment and quality of life variables in Greek youth soccer. *Inquiries in Sport and Physical Education, 14,* 19-35.

Langan, E., Blake, C., & Lonsdale, C. (2013). Systematic review of the effectiveness of interpersonal coach education interventions on athlete outcomes. *Psychology of Sport and Exercise, 14*(1), 37-49.

Langan, E., Toner, J., Blake, C., & Lonsdale, C. (2015). Testing the effects of a self-determination theory-based intervention with youth Gaelic football coaches on athlete motivation and burnout. *The Sport Psychologist, 29*(4), 293-301.

Lara-Bercial, S., & Mallett, C.J. (2016). The practices and developmental pathways of professional and Olympic serial winning coaches. *International Sport Coaching Journal, 3*(3), 221-239.

Larsen, T., Van Hoye, A., Tjomsland, H, Holsen, I., Bente, W., Heuze, J-P., Samdal, O., & Sarrazin, P. (2014). Creating a supportive environment among youth football players: A qualitative study of French and Norwegian youth grassroots football coaches. *Health Education, 115*, 570-586.

Legg, E., Newland, A., & Bigelow, R. (2018). Somebody's eyes are watching: The impact of coaching observations on empowering motivational climates and positive youth development. *Journal of Park and Recreation Administration, 36*(4), 90-106.

Lopes Angelo, D., Villas Boas, M., Jr., Freitas Correa, M.D., Hernandez Souza, V., Moura, P., Oliveira, R., Reyes Bossio, M., & Ferreira Brandao, M.R. (2022). Basic psychological need satisfaction and thwarting: A study with Brazilian professional players of League of Legends. *Sustainability, 14*, 1701.

Mageau, G.A., & Vallerand, R.V. (2003). The coach–athlete relationship: A motivational model. *Journal of Sports Science, 21*(11), 883-904. https://doi.org/10.1080/0264041031000140374

Martínez-González, N., Atienza, F., Tomás, I., & Balaguer, I. (2021). Perceived coach-created motivational climates as predictors of athletes' goal reengagement: The mediational role of goal motives. *Frontiers in Psychology, 12*, 6227.

McCann, B., McCarthy, P., Cooper, J., Forbes-McKay, K., & Keegan, R.J. (2021). A retrospective investigation of the perceived influence of coaches, parents and peers on talented football players' motivation during development. *Journal of Applied Sport Psychology.* https://doi.org/10.1080/10413200.2021.1963013

McLaren, C.D., Eys, M.A., & Murray, R.A. (2015). A coach-initiated motivational climate intervention and athletes' perceptions of group cohesion in youth sport. *Sport, Exercise, and Performance Psychology, 4*, 113-126.

Milton, D., Appleton, P.R., Bryant, A., & Duda, J.L. (2018). Initial validation of the teacher-created Empowering and Disempowering Motivational Climate Questionnaire in PE (EDMCQ-PE). *Journal of Teaching in Physical Education, 37*, 340-351.

Moulds, K., Fraser, K. K., Karp, J., Kapocius, O., Heathcote, M., Appleton, P. R., & Cobley, S. (in press). Coach-created motivational climate ratings differentiate between dropout and continuation in Australian youth swimming. *International Journal of Sports Science & Coaching.*

Mosqueda, S., López-Walle, J.M., Gutiérrez-García, P., García-Verazaluce, J., & Tristán, J. (2019). Autonomous motivation as a mediator between an empowering climate and enjoyment in male volleyball players. *Sports, 7*(6), 153.

Mosqueda, S., López-Walle, J.M., Tomás, I., Tristán, J., Rodenas, L., Balaguer, I., & Duda, J.L. The effects of a motivational climate training program on the perceived coach created motivational climate, need satisfaction and team cohesion. Manuscript under review.

Newton, M.L., Duda, J.L., & Yin, Z. (2000). Examination of the psychometric properties of the Perceived Motivational Climate in Sport Questionnaire-2 in a sample of female athletes. *Journal of Sport Sciences, 18*(4), 275-290.

Nicholls, J.G. (1989). *The competitive ethos and democratic education.* Harvard University Press.

Ohlert, J., Schmitz, H., Schäfer-Pels, A., & Allroggen, M. (2022). An empowering climate as a protective factor against sexual violence in sport? *Social Sciences, 11*(8), 330.

Papaioannou, A.G., Appleton, P.R., Torregrosa, M., Jowett, G.E., Bosselut, G., Gonzalez, L., Haug, E., Ertesvaag, V., & Zourbanos, N. (2013). Moderate-to-vigorous physical activity and personal well-being in European youth soccer players: Invariance of physical activity, global self-esteem and vitality across five countries. *International Journal of Sport and Exercise Psychology, 11*(4), 351-364.

Raabe, J., Schmidt, K., Carl, J., & Honer, O. (2019). The effectiveness of autonomy support interventions with physical education teachers and youth sport coaches: A systematic review. *Journal of Sport and Exercise Psychology, 41*, 345-355.

Reeve, J., Jang, H., Carrell, D., Jeon, S., & Barch, J. (2004). Enhancing students' engagement by increasing teachers' autonomy support. *Motivation and Emotion, 28*(2), 147-169.

Roberts, G.C. (2012). Motivation in sport and exercise from an achievement goal theory perspective: After 30 years, where are we? In G. Roberts & D. Treasure (Eds.), *Advances in motivation in sport and exercise* (3rd ed., pp. 5-58). Human Kinetics.

Ruiz, M.C., Appleton, P.R., Duda, J.L., Bortoli, L., & Robazza, C. (2021). Social environmental antecedents of athletes' emotions. *International Journal of Environmental Research and Public Health, 18*, 4997.

Ruiz, M.C., Haapanen, S., Tolvanen, A., Robazza, C., & Duda, J.L. (2017). Predicting athletes' functional and dysfunctional emotions: The role of the motivational climate and motivation regulations. *Journal of Sports Sciences, 36*(16), 1598-1606.

Ruiz, M.C., Robazza, C., Tolvanen, A., Haapanen, S., & Duda, J.L. (2019). Coach-created motivational climate and athletes' adaptation to psychological stress: Temporal motivation-emotion interplay. *Frontiers in Psychology, 10*, 617.

Ryan, R.M., & Deci, E.L. (2002). Overview of self-determination theory: An organismic dialectical perspective. *Handbook of Self-Determination Research, 2*, 3-33.

Ryan, R.M., & Deci, E.L. (2017). *Self-determination theory: Basic psychological needs in motivation, development and wellness.* Guilford Press.

Ryan, R.M., & Deci, E.L. (2020). Intrinsic and extrinsic motivation from a self-determination theory perspective: Definitions, theory, practices, and future directions. *Contemporary Educational Psychology, 61*, 101860.

Smith, N., Quested, E., Appleton, P., & Duda, J.L. (2016). Differences in the coach-created motivational environment across training and competition in youth sport. *Journal of Sport Sciences, 35*, 149-158.

Smith, N., Tessier, D., Tzoumakis, Y., Quested, E., Appleton, P., Sarrazin, P., Papaioannou, A., & Duda, J.L. (2015). Development and validation of the Multidimensional Motivational Climate Observation System. *Journal of Sport and Exercise Psychology, 37*(1), 4-22.

Smith, R.E., Smoll, F.L., & Cumming, S. (2007). Effects of a motivational climate intervention for coaches on young athletes' sport performance anxiety. *Journal of Sport and Exercise Psychology, 29*(1), 39-59.

Solstad, B.E., Ivarsson, A., Haug, E.M., & Ommundsen, Y. (2018). Youth sport coaches' well-being across the season: The psychological costs and benefits of giving empowering and disempowering sports coaching to athletes. *International Sport Coaching Journal, 5*(2), 124-135.

Solstad, B.E., Stenling, A., Ommundsen, Y., Wold, B., Heuzé, J.-P., Sarrazin, P., Castillo, I., Cruz, J., Hall, H., Papaioannou, P., & Duda, J.L. (2020). Initial psychometric testing of the coach-adapted version of the empowering and disempowering motivational climate questionnaire: A Bayesian approach. *Journal of Sports Sciences, 38*, 626-643.

Sovik, M.L., Larsen, T.B., Samdal, O., & Tjomsland, H. (2016). Evaluating the implementation of the Empowering Coaching™ programme: Balancing fidelity and adaptation. *Health Education, 116*(3).

Stebbings, J., Taylor, I.M., & Spray, C.M. (2015). The relationship between psychological well- and ill-being, and perceived autonomy support and controlling interpersonal styles: A longitudinal study of sport coaches. *Psychology of Sport and Exercise, 19*, 42-49.

Sukys, S., Kromerova-Dubinskiene, E., & Appleton, P.R. (2020). Validation of the Lithuanian version of the coach-created Empowering and Disempowering Motivational Climate Questionnaire (EDMCQ-C). *International Journal of Environmental Research and Public Health, 17*, 3487.

Van Hoye, A., Fenton, S., Krommidas, C., Heuzé, J.P., Quested, E., Papaioannou, A., & Duda, J.L. (2013). Physical activity and sedentary behaviours among grassroots football players: A comparison across three European countries. *International Journal of Sport and Exercise Psychology, 11*(4), 341-350.

Vazou, S., Ntoumanis, N., & Duda, J.L. (2005). Peer motivational climate in youth sport: A qualitative inquiry. *Psychology of Sport and Exercise, 6*, 497-516.

Viladrich, C., Appleton, P.R., Quested, E., Duda, J.L., Alcaraz, S., Heuzé, J.P., Fabra, P., Samdal, O., Ommundsen, Y., Hill, A.P., Zourbanos, N., & Ntoumanis, N. (2013). Measurement invariance of the Behavioural Regulation in Sport Questionnaire when completed by young athletes across five European countries. *International Journal of Sport and Exercise Psychology, 11*(4), 384-394.

Webster, C.A., Wellborn, B., Hunt, K., LaFleche, M., Cribbs, J., & Lineberger, B. (2013). MPOWER: An observation system for assessing coach autonomy support in high school varsity boys' soccer practices. *International Journal of Sports Science and Coaching, 8*, 741-754.

White, S.A., Duda, J.L., & Hart, S. (1992). An exploratory examination of the Parent-Initiated Motivational Climate Questionnaire. *Perceptual and Motor Skills, 75*, 875-880.

Zourbanos, N., Haznadar, A., Papaioannou, A., Tzioumakis, Y., Krommidas, C., & Hatzigeorgiadis, A. (2016). The relationships between athletes' perceptions of coach-created motivational climate, self-talk, and self-efficacy in youth soccer. *Journal of Applied Sport Psychology, 28*, 97-112.

Chapter 11

Annerstedt, C., & Lindgren, E. (2014). Caring as an important foundation in coaching for social sustainability: A case study of a successful Swedish coach in high performance sport. *Reflective Practice, 15*, 27-39. https://doi.org/10.1080/14623943.2013.869204

Bandura, A. (2006). Adolescent development from an agentic perspective. In F. Pajares & T. Urdan (Eds.) *Self-efficacy beliefs of adolescents* (pp. 1-43). Information Age Publishing.

Battistich, V.A. (2008a). Character education, prevention, and positive youth development. *Journal of Research in Character Education, 6*(2), 81-90.

Battistich, V.A. (2008b). The Child Development Project: Creating caring school communities. In L. Nucci & D. Narvaez (Eds.), *Handbook of moral and character education* (pp. 328-351). Routledge.

Battistich, V., & Solomon, D., Watson, M., & Schaps, E. (1997). Caring school communities. *Educational Psychologist, 32*(3), 137-151. https://doi.org/10.1207/s15326985ep3203_1

Brown, T.C., Fry, M.D., Wilkinson, T.J., Breske, M.P., & Iwasaki, S. (2019). Motivational climate and athletes' likelihood of reporting concussions in a youth competitive soccer league. *Journal of Sport Behavior, 42*(1), 29-47.

Byrd, B., & Martin, J.J. (2016). The relationships among youth running programs' multidimensional climates and social responsibility and belonging. *Journal of Clinical Sport Psychology, 10*(1), 19-31. https://doi.org/10.1123/jcsp.2015-0014

Cetinkaya, T., & Mutluer, C. (2019). Turkish adaptation of Caring Climate Scale and reviewing psychometry properties: Validation and reliability Study. *Journal of Education and Learning, 8*(1). https://doi.org/10.553.9/jel.v8n1p206

Chamberlin, J.M., Fry, M.D., & Iwasaki, S. (2016). High school athletes' perceptions of the motivational climate in their off-season training programs. *Journal of Strength and Conditioning Research, 31*(3), 736-742. https://doi.org/10.1519/JSC.0000000000001533

Claunch, J. (2016). *Motivational climate collaboration between a collegiate Native American volleyball program and a sport psychology researcher* (Publication No. 10130136) [Doctoral dissertation]. University of Kansas. Proquest Dissertations and Theses Global.

Claunch, J., & Fry, M.D. (2016). Native American football coaches' experience of a motivational climate collaboration with sport psychology researchers. *International Journal of Sport Science and Coaching, 11*, 482-495.

Cronin, C., & Armour, K. (2017). "Being" in the coaching world: New insights on youth performance coaching from an interpretative phenomenological approach. *Sport, Education and Society, 22*(8), 919-931. https://doi.org/10.1080/13573322.2015.1108912

Cronin, C., Knowles, Z.R., & Enright, K. (2019). The challenge to care in a Premier League football club. *Sports Coaching Review, 9*(2), 123-146. https://doi.org/10.1080/21640629.2019.1578593

Dohsten, J., Barker-Ruchti, N., & Lindgren, E. (2020). Caring as sustainable coaching in elite athletics: Benefits and challenges. *Sports Coaching Review, 9*(1), 48-70. https://doi.org/10.1080/21640629.2018.1558896

Duda, J.L., & Appleton, P.R. (2016). Empowering and disempowering coaching climates: Conceptualization, measurement considerations, and intervention implications. In M. Raab, P. Wylleman, R. Seiler, A. Elbe, & A. Hatzigeorgiadis (Eds.), *Sport and exercise psychology research: From theory to practice* (pp. 373-388). Academic Press.

Duda, J.L., & Balaguer, I. (2007). Coach-created motivational climate. In S. Jowett & D. Lavallee (Eds.), *Social psychology in sport* (pp. 117-130). Human Kinetics.

Eisenberg, N., Eggum-Wilkens, N.D., & Spinrad, T.L. (2015). The development of prosocial behavior. In D.A. Schroeder & W.G. Graziano (Eds.), *The Oxford handbook of prosocial behavior* (pp. 114-136). Oxford University Press. https://doi.org/10.1093/oxfordhb/9780195399813.001.0001

Erdész, A., Fry, M. D., & Fry, A. C. (2023). College baseball players' perception of their team climate and mental health. *Journal of Human Sport and Exercise*, in press. https://doi.org/10.14198/jhse.2023.184.06

Feshbach, N.D. (1997). Empathy: The formative years—implications for clinical practice. In A.C. Bohart & L.S. Greenberg (Eds.), *Empathy reconsidered: New directions in psychotherapy* (pp. 33-59). American Psychological Association.

Fisher, L.A., Behar, M.P., Larsen, L.K., Fynes, J.M., & Gearity, B.T. (2017). Caring in U.S. National Collegiate Athletic Association Division I sport: The perspectives of 18 female and male head coaches. *International Journal of Sports Science and Coaching, 12*(1), 75-91. https://doi.org/10.1177/1747954116684388

Fisher, L.A., Larsen, L.K., Bejar, M.P., & Shigeno, T.C. (2019). A heuristic for the relationship between caring coaching and elite athlete performance. *International Journal of Sports Science and Coaching, 14*(2), 126-137. https://doi.org/10.1177/1747954119827192

Fontana, M.S., Fry, M.D., & Cramer, E. (2017). Exploring the relationship between athletes' perceptions of the motivational climate to their compassion, self-compassion, shame, and pride in adult recreational sport. *Measurement in Physical Education and Exercise Science, 21*, 101-111. https://doi.org/10.1080/1091367X.2017.1278698

Frederick, C. (2017). *Relationship of motivational climate to performance among NCAA Division 1 men's basketball players* (Publication No. 10283072) [Master's thesis]. University of Kansas. Proquest Dissertations and Theses Global.

Fry, M.D. (2010). Creating a positive climate for athletes from day 1. *Journal of Sport Psychology in Action, 1*(1), 33-44. https://doi.org/10.1080/21520704.2010.518224

Fry, M.D., & Gano-Overway, L.A. (2010). Exploring the contribution of the caring climate to the youth sport experience. *Journal of Applied Sport Psychology, 22*(3), 294-304. http://dx.doi.org/10.1080/10413201003776352

Fry, M.D., Gano-Overway, L.A., Guivernau, M., Kim, M., & Newton, M. (2020). *A coaches' guide to maximizing the youth sport experience: Work hard, Be kind*. Routledge.

Fry, M.D., Guivernau, M., Kim, M., Newton, M., Gano-Overway, L., & Magyar, T.M. (2012). Youth perceptions of a caring climate, emotional well regulation, and psychological well-being. *Sport, Exercise, and Performance Psychology, 1*, 44-57. https://doi.org/10.1037/a0025454

Fry, M.D., Hogue, C.M., Iwasaki, S., & Solomon, G.B. (2021). The relationship between the perceived motivational climate in elite collegiate sport and athlete psychological coping skills. *Journal of Clinical Sport Psychology, 15*, 334-350. https://doi.org/10.1123/jcsp.2020-0002

Gano-Overway, L.A. (2013). The caring climate: How sport environments can develop empathy in young people. In K. Pavlovich & K. Krahnke (Eds.), *Organizing through empathy* (pp. 166-183). Routledge.

Gano-Overway, L.A. (2014). Exploring the connections between caring and social behaviors in physical education. *Research Quarterly for Exercise and Sport, 84*(1), 104-114. http://dx.doi.org/10.1080/02701367.2013.762322

Gano-Overway, L.A. (2023). Athletes' narratives of caring coaches who made a difference. *Sport Coaching Review, 12*(1), 47-67. http://dx.doi.org/10.1080/21640629.2021.1896208

Gano-Overway, L.A., & Carson Sackett, S. (2021). The Mapp Way: Success through combining the motivational and caring climates. *Journal of Applied Sport Psychology, 33*(2), 238-258. https://doi.org/10.1080/10413200.2019.1647476

Gano-Overway, L., & Guivernau, M. (2018). Setting the SCENE: Developing a caring youth sport environment. *Journal of Sport Psychology in Action, 9*(2), 83-93. https://doi.org/10.1080/21520704.2017.1343214

Gano-Overway, L.A., Newton, M., Magyar, T.M., Fry, M.D., Kim, M.S., & Guivernau, M.R. (2009). Influence of caring youth sport contexts on efficacy-related beliefs and social behaviors. *Developmental Psychology, 45*(2), 329-340. https://doi.org/10.1037/a0014067

Gerabinis, P., Hatzigeorgiadis, A., Theodorakis, Y., & Goudas, M. (2018). Sport climate, developmental experiences and motivational outcomes in youth sport. *Journal of Education and Human Development, 7*, 58-65. https://doi.org/10.15640/jehd.v7n3a7

Gordon, S., Benner, P., & Noddings, N. (Eds.). (1996). *Caregiving: Readings in knowledge, practice, ethics, and politics*. University of Pennsylvania Press.

Gould, D., Flett, R., & Lauer, L. (2012). The relationship between psychosocial developmental and the sports climate experienced by underserved youth. *Psychology of Sport and Exercise, 13*(1), 80-87. https://doi.org/10.1016/j.psychsport.2011.07.005

Hall, M.S., Newland, A., Newton, M., Podlog, L., & Baucom, B.R. (2017). Perceptions of the social psychological climate and sport commitment in adolescent athletes: A multilevel analysis. *Journal of Applied Sport Psychology, 29*, 75-87. https://doi.org/10.1080/10413200.2016.1174906

Hellison, D.R. (1978). *Beyond balls and bats: Alienated (and other) youth in the gym*. AAPHER.

Hellison, D.R. (2011). *Teaching personal and social responsibility through physical activity* (3rd ed.). Human Kinetics.

Hogue, C.M., Fry, M.D., & Fry, AC. (2017). The differential impact of motivational climate on adolescents' psychological and physiological stress responses. *Psychology of Sport and Exercise, 30*, 118-127. http://dx.doi.org/10.1016/j.psychsport.2017.02.004

Hogue, C.M., Fry, M.D., & Fry, A.C. (2021). The protective impact of learning to juggle in a caring, task-involving climate versus an ego-involving climate on participants' inflammation, cortisol, and psychological responses. *International Journal of Sport and Exercise Psychology, 19*, 650-667. https://doi.org/10.1080/1612197X.2019.1696868

Hogue, C.M., Fry, M.D., Fry, A.C., & Pressman, S. (2013). The influence of a motivational climate intervention on participants' salivary cortisol and psychological responses. *Journal of Sport and Exercise Psychology, 35*, 85-97. https://doi.org/10.1123/jsep.35.1.85

Hogue, C.M., Fry, M.D., & Iwasaki, S. (2019). The impact of the perceived motivational climate in physical education on adolescent greater life stress, coping appraisals, and experience of shame. *Sport, Exercise, and Performance Psychology, 8*, 273-289. https://doi.org/10.1037/spy0000153

International Council for Coaching Excellence, the Association of Summer Olympic Federations, & Leeds Metropolitan University. (2013). *International sport coaching framework*. Human Kinetics.

Iwasaki, S., & Fry, M.D. (2013). The efforts of sport psychology professionals to assist sport administrators in evaluating youth sport programs. *The Sport Psychologist, 27*(4), 360-371. https://doi.org/10.1123/tsp.27.4.360

Iwasaki, S., & Fry, M.D. (2016). Female adolescent soccer players' perceived motivational climate, goal orientations, and mindful engagement. *Psychology of Sport and Exercise, 27*, 222-231. https://doi.org/10.1016/j.psychsport.2016.09.002

Jones, R. (2009). Coaching as caring (the smiling gallery): Accessing hidden knowledge. *Physical Education and Sport Pedagogy, 14*(4), 377-390. https://doi.org/10.1080/17408980801976551

Knust, S.K., & Fisher, L.A. (2015). NCAA Division I female head coaches' experiences of exemplary care within coaching. *International Sport Coaching Journal, 2*(2), 94-107. https://doi.org/10.1123/iscj.2013-0045

Kochanek, J., & Erickson, K. (2020). Interrogating positive youth development through sport using critical race theory. *Quest, 72*(2), 224-240. https://doi.org/10.1080/00336297.2019.1641728

Lindgren, E., & Barker-Ruchti, N. (2017). Balancing performance-based expectations with a holistic perspective on coaching: A qualitative study of Swedish women's national football team coaches' practice experiences. *International Journal of Qualitative Studies on Health and Well-being, 12*, 1-11. https://doi.org/10.1080/17482631.2017.1358580

Magyar, T.M., Guivernau, M.R., Gano-Overway, L.A., Newton, M., Kim, M, Watson, D.L., & Fry, M.D. (2007). The influence of leader efficacy and emotional intelligence on personal caring in physical activity. *Journal of Teaching in Physical Education, 26*, 310-319. https://doi.org/10.1123/jtpe.26.3.310

Maine, D. (2019, April 16). UCLA gymnastics coach Val Kondos Field's storied (and unconventional) career comes to an end. ESPNW Sports. www.espn.com/espnw/sports/story/_/id/26524115/ucla-gymnastics-coach-valorie-kondos-fField-storied-unconventional-career-comes-end

Mayer, J.D., & Salovey, P. (1997). What is emotional intelligence? In P. Salovey & P. Sluyter (Eds.), *Emotional development and emotional intelligence: Implications for educators* (pp. 3-31). Basic Books.

Mayeroff, M. (1971). *On caring.* Harper & Row.

Metz, T., & Gaie, J.B.R. (2010). The African ethic of ubuntu/botho: Implications for research on morality. *Journal of Moral Education, 39*, 273-290. https://doi.org/10.1080/03057240.2010.497609

National Institute of Mental Health. (2019, February). Major depression. www.nimh.nih.gov/health/statistics/major-depression.shtml

Newell-Price, J.D.C., & Auchus, R.J. (2020). The adrenal cortex. In S. Melmed, R.J. Koenig, C.J. Rosen, R.J. Auchus, & A. Goldfine. (Eds.), *Williams textbook of endocrinology* (14th ed., pp. 480-541). Elsevier.

Newton, M., Duda, J.L., & Yin, Z. (2000). Examination of the psychometric properties of the Perceived Motivational Climate in Sport Questionnaire-2 in a sample of female athletes. *Journal of Sport Science, 18*, 275-290. https://doi.org/10.1080/026404100365018

Newton, M., Fry, M., Watson, D., Gano-Overway, L., Kim, M., Magyar, M., & Guivernau, M. (2007). Psychometric properties of the caring climate scale in a physical activity setting. *Revista de Psicología del Deporte, 16*(1), 67-84. https://doaj.org/article/d43b837f870a43d0b241d10ba76801df

Nichol, A.J., Hall, E.T., Vickery, W., & Hayes, P.R. (2019). Examining the relationships between coaching practice and athlete "outcomes": A systematic review and critical realist critique. *International Sport Coaching Journal, 6*, 13-29. https://doi.org/10.1123/iscj.2017-0105

Nicholls, J.G. (1989). *The competitive ethos and democratic education.* Harvard University Press.

Noddings, N. (1992). *The challenge to care in schools: An alternative approach to education.* Teachers College Press.

Noddings, N. (2003a). *Caring: A feminine approach to ethics and moral education* (2nd ed.). University of California Press.

Noddings, N. (2003b). *Happiness and education.* Cambridge University Press.

Noddings, N. (2008). Caring and moral education. In L. Nucci & D. Narvaez (Eds.), *Handbook of moral and character education* (pp. 161-174). Routledge.

Noddings, N. (2010). *The maternal factor: Two paths to morality.* University of California Press.

Poux, K.N., & Fry, M.D. (2015). Athletes' perceptions of their team motivational climate, career exploration and engagement, and athletic identity. *Journal of Clinical Sport Psychology, 9*, 360-372. http://dx.doi.org/10.1123/jcsp.2014-0050

Reid-Pinson, C.A. (2018). A positive coaching alliance intervention on a college campus with club sport athletes (Publication No. 10934105) [Master's thesis]. University of Kansas. ProQuest Dissertations and Theses Global.

Richard, K.A.R., & Shiver, V.N. (2020). "What's worth doing?": A qualitative historical analysis of the TPSR model. *Journal of Teaching in Physical Education, 39*(3), 300-310. https://doi.org/10.1123/jtpe.2019-0215

Ryan, R.M., & Deci, E.L. (2017). *Self-determination theory: Basic psychological needs in motivation, development, and wellness.* Guilford Press.

Scott, C., Fry, M.D., Wiengarter, H., & Wineinger, T. (2021). Collegiate sport club athletes' perceptions of the climate on their teams and indices of their psychological well-being. *Recreational Sports Journal, 45*,17-26. https://doi.org/10.1177/1558866121995169

Stark, A., & Newton, M. (2014). A dancer's well-being: The influence of the social psychological climate during adolescence. *Psychology of Sport and Exercise, 15*(4), 356-363. https://doi.org/10.1016/j.psychsport.2014.03.003

Chapter 12

Adie, J., Duda, J., & Ntoumanis, N. (2008). Autonomy support, basic need satisfaction and the optimal functioning of adult male and female sport participants: A test of basic needs theory. *Motivation and Emotion, 32*(3), 189-199. https://doi.org/10.1007/s11031-008-9095-z

Almagro, B.J., Sáenz-López, P., & Moreno, J.A. (2010). Prediction of sport adherence through the influence of autonomy-supportive coaching among Spanish adolescent athletes. *Journal of Sports Science and Medicine, 9*(1), 8.

Antonakis, J., Avolio, B.J., & Sivasubramaniam, N. (2003). Context and leadership: An examination of the nine-factor full-range leadership theory using the Multifactor Leadership Questionnaire. *Leadership Quarterly, 14*(3), 261-295. https://doi.org/10.1016/S1048-9843(03)00030-4

Appleton, P., Ntoumanis, N., Viladrich, C., Quested, E., & Duda, J.L. (2016). Initial validation of the coach-created Empowering and Disempowering Motivational Climate Questionnaire (EDMCQ-C). *Psychology of Sport and Exercise, 22*, 53-65. https://doi.org/10.1016/j.psychsport.2015.05.008

Balaguer, I., González, L., Fabra, P., Castillo, I., Mercé, J., & Duda, J.L. (2012). Coaches' interpersonal style, basic psychological needs and the well- and ill-being of young soccer players: A longitudinal analysis. *Journal of Sports Science, 30*, 1619-1629. https://doi.org/10.1080/02640414.2012.731517

Banks, G.C., Engemann, K.N., Williams, C.E., Gooty, J., McCauley, K.D., & Medaugh, M.R. (2017). A meta-analytic review and future research agenda of charismatic leadership. *The Leadership Quarterly, 28*(4), 508-529. https://doi.org/10.1016/j.leaqua.2016.12.003

Bartholomew, K.J., Ntoumanis, N., Ryan, R.M., Bosch, J.A., & Thøgersen-Ntoumani, C. (2011). Self-determination theory and diminished functioning: The role of interpersonal control and psychological need thwarting. *Personality and Social Psychology Bulletin, 37*(11), 1459-1473. https://doi.org/10.1177%2F0146167211413125

Bartholomew, K.J., Ntoumanis, N., & Thøgersen-Ntoumani, C. (2009). A review of controlling motivational strategies from a self-determination theory perspective: Implications for sports coaches. *International Review of Sport and Exercise Psychology, 2*(2), 215-233. https://doi.org/10.1080/17509840903235330

Bartholomew, K., Ntoumanis, N., & Thøgersen-Ntoumani, C. (2010). The controlling interpersonal style in a coaching context: Development and initial validation of a psychometric scale. *Journal of Sport and Exercise Psychology, 32*(2), 193-216. https://doi.org/10.1123/jsep.32.2.193.

Belmont, M., Skinner, E., Wellborn, J., & Connell, J. (1988). *Teacher as social context: A measure of student perceptions of teacher provision of involvement, structure, and autonomy support* (Tech. Rep. No. 102). University of Rochester.

Bhavsar, N., Ntoumanis, N., Quested, E., Gucciardi, D., Thøgersen-Ntoumani, C., Ryan, R., Reeve, J., & Bartholomew, K.J. (2019). Conceptualizing and testing a new tripartite measure of coach interpersonal behaviors. *Psychology of Sport and Exercise, 44*, 107-120. https://doi.org/10.1016/j.psychsport.2019.05.006

Bhavsar, N., Ntoumanis, N., Quested, E., Thogersen-Ntoumani, C., & Chatzisarantis, N. (2020). Self-determination theory. In D. Hackfort & R.J. Schinke (Eds), *The Routledge international encyclopedia of sport and exercise psychology* (Vol. 1, pp. 565-583). Routledge.

Cheon, S.H., Reeve, J., Lee, J., & Lee, Y. (2015). Giving and receiving autonomy support in a high-stakes sport context: A field-based experiment during the 2012 London Paralympic Games. *Psychology of Sport and Exercise, 19*, 59-69. https://doi.org/10.1016/j.psychsport.2015.02.007

Curran, T., Hill, A.P., & Niemiec, C.P. (2013). A conditional process model of children's behavioral engagement and behavioral disaffection in sport based on self-determination theory. *Journal of Sport and Exercise Psychology, 35*(1), 30-43. https://doi.org/10.1123/jsep.35.1.30

Deci, E.L., La Guardia, J.G., Moller, A.C., Scheiner, M.J., & Ryan, R.M. (2006). On the benefits of giving as well as receiving autonomy support: Mutuality in close friendships. *Personality and Social Psychology Bulletin, 32*(3), 313-327. https://doi.org/10.1177/0146167205282148

Deci, E.L., & Ryan, R.M. (1987). The support of autonomy and the control of behavior. *Journal of Personality and Social Psychology, 53*(6), 1024-1037. https://doi.org/10.1037/0022-3514.53.6.1024

Deci, E.L., Schwartz, A.J., Sheinman, L., & Ryan, R.M. (1981). An instrument to assess adults' orientations toward control versus autonomy with children: Reflections on intrinsic motivation and perceived competence. *Journal of Educational Psychology, 73*(5), 642-650. https://doi.org/10.1037/0022-0663.73.5.642

Delrue, J., Reynders, B., Vande Broek, G., Aelterman, N., De Backer, M., Decroos, S., De Muynck, G.-J., Fontaine, J., Fransen, K., van Puyenbroeck, S., Haerens, L., & Vansteenkiste, M. (2019). Adopting a helicopter-perspective towards motivating and demotivating coaching: A circumplex approach. *Psychology of Sport and Exercise, 40*, 110-126. https://doi.org/10.1016/j.psychsport.2018.08.008.

DeVellis, R.F. (2017). *Scale development: Theory and applications* (4th ed.). Sage.

Felton, L., & Jowett, S. (2013). The mediating role of social environmental factors in the associations between attachment styles and basic needs satisfaction. *Journal of Sports Sciences, 31*(6), 618-628. https://doi.org/10.1080/02640414.2012.744078

Fenton, S., Duda, J.L., Quested, E., & Barrett, T. (2014). Coach autonomy support predicts autonomous motivation and daily moderate-to-vigorous physical activity and sedentary time in youth sport participants. *Psychology of Sport and Exercise, 15*(5), 453-463. http://doi.org/10.1016/j.psychsport.2014.04.005

Grand, J.A., Braun, M.T., Kuljanin, G., Kozlowski, S.W., & Chao, G.T. (2016). The dynamics of team cognition: A process-oriented theory of knowledge emergence in teams. *Journal of Applied Psychology, 101*(10), 1353-1385. https://doi.org/10.1037/apl0000136

Grolnick, W.S., Deci, E.L., & Ryan, R.M. (1997). *Internalization within the family: The self-determination theory perspective.* In J.E. Grusec & L. Kuczynski (Eds.), *Parenting and children's internalization of values: A handbook of contemporary theory* (pp. 135-161). Wiley.

Grolnick, W.S., & Ryan, R.M. (1989). Parent styles associated with children's self-regulation and competence in school. *Journal of Educational Psychology, 81*(2), 143-154. https://doi.org/10.1037/0022-0663.81.2.143

Gucciardi, D.F., Crane, M., Ntoumanis, N., Parker, S.K., Thøgersen-Ntoumani, C., Ducker, K.J., Peeling, P., Chapman, M.T., Quested, E., & Temby, P. (2018). The emergence of team resilience: A multilevel conceptual model of facilitating factors. *Journal of Occupational and Organisational Psychology, 91*, 729-768. https://doi.org/10.1111/joop.12237

Hancox, J.E., Quested, E., Thøgersen-Ntoumani, C., & Ntoumanis, N. (2015). An intervention to train group exercise class instructors to adopt a motivationally adaptive communication style: A quasi-experimental study protocol. *Health Psychology and Behavioral Medicine, 3*(1), 190-203. https://doi.org/10.1080/21642850.2015.1074075

Hancox, J.E., Quested, E., Thøgersen-Ntoumani, C., Ntoumanis, N. (2018). Putting self-determination theory into practice: Application of adaptive motivational principles in the exercise domain. *Qualitative Research in Sport, Exercise and Health, 10*(1), 75-91. https://doi.org/10.1080/2159676X.2017.1354059

Huyghebaert-Zouaghi, T., Morin, A.J.S., Ntoumanis, N., Berjot S., & Gillet, N. (2020). *Assessing interpersonal styles of communication in the work context.* Manuscript submitted for publication.

Jaakkola, T., Ntoumanis, N, & Liukkonen, J. (2016). Motivational climate, goal orientation, perceived sport ability, and enjoyment within Finnish junior ice-hockey players. *Scandinavian Journal of Medicine and Science in Sports, 26*(1), 109-115. https://doi.org/10.1111/sms.12410

Jang, H., Reeve, J., & Deci, E. (2010). Engaging students in learning activities: It is not autonomy support or structure but autonomy support and structure. *Journal of Educational Psychology,* 102(3), 588-600. https://doi.org/10.1037/a0019682

Kim, I., Lee, K., & Kang, S. (2019). The relationship between passion for coaching and the coaches' interpersonal behaviors: The mediating role of coaches' perception of the relationship quality with athletes. *International Journal of Sports Science and Coaching, 14*(4), 463-470. https://doi.org/10.1177/1747954119853104

Lienhart, N., Nicaise, V., Martinent, G., & Guillet-Descas, E. (2020). Perceived parental behaviours and motivational processes: Among adolescent athletes in intensive training centres: A profile approach. *Psychology of Sport and Exercise, 49*, 101708. https://doi.org/10.1016/j.psychsport.2020.101708

Mageau, G.A., & Vallerand, R.J. (2003). The coach–athlete relationship: A motivational model. *Journal of Sports Sciences, 21*(11), 883-904. https://doi.org/10.1080/0264041031000140374

Mahoney, J.W., Ntoumanis, N., Gucciardi, D.F., Mallett, C.J., & Stebbings, J. (2016). Implementing an autonomy-supportive intervention to develop mental toughness in adolescent rowers. *Journal of Applied Sport Psychology, 28*(2), 199-215. https://doi.org/10.1080/10413200.2015.1101030

Matosic, D., Ntoumanis, N., & Quested, E. (2016). Antecedents of need supportive and controlling interpersonal styles from a self-determination theory perspective: A review and implications for sport psychology research. In Raab, M., Wylleman, P., Seiler, R., Elbe, A.M., and Hatzigeorgiadis, A. (Eds.), *New perspectives on sport and exercise psychology* (pp. 145-180). Elsevier.

Matosic, D., Ntoumanis, N., Boardley, I.D., Sedikides, C., Stewart, B., & Chatzisarantis, N. (2017). Narcissism and coach interpersonal style: A self-determination theory perspective. *Scandinavian Journal of Science and Medicine in Sport, 27*, 254-261. https://doi.org/10.1111/sms.12635

Maynard, M.T., Kennedy, D.M., & Sommer, S.A. (2015). Team adaptation: A fifteen-year synthesis (1998-2013) and framework for how this literature needs to "adapt" going forward. *European Journal of Work and Organizational Psychology, 24*(5), 652-677. https://doi.org/10.1080/1359432X.2014.1001376

Medic, N., Mack, D.E., Wilson, P.M., & Starkes, J.L. (2007). The effects of athletic scholarships on motivation in sport. *Journal of Sport Behavior, 30*(3), 292-306.

Michie, S., Richardson, M., Johnston, M., Abraham, C., Francis, J., Hardeman, W., Eccles, M.P., Cane, J., & Wood, C.E. (2013). The behavior change technique taxonomy (v1) of 93 hierarchically clustered techniques: Building an international consensus for the reporting of behavior change interventions. *Annals of Behavioral Medicine, 46*(1), 81-95. https://doi.org/10.1007/s12160-013-9486-6

Moller, A.C., & Sheldon, K.M. (2020). Athletic scholarships are negatively associated with intrinsic motivation for sports, even decades later: Evidence for long-term undermining. *Motivation Science, 6*(1), 43-48. https://doi.org/10.1037/mot0000133

Newton, M., Duda, J., & Yin, Z. (2000). Examination of the psychometric properties of the Perceived Motivational Climate in Sport Questionnaire-2 in a sample of female athletes. *Journal of Sports Sciences, 18*(4), 275-290. https/doi.org/10.1080/026404100365018

Ntoumanis, N. (2012). A self-determination theory perspective on motivation in sport and physical education: Current trends and possible future research directions. In G.C. Roberts & D.C. Treasure (Eds.), *Advances in motivation in sport and exercise* (Vol. 3, pp. 91-128). Human Kinetics.

Ntoumanis, N., & Mallet, C. (2014). Motivation in sport: A self-determination theory perspective. In A. Papaioannou & D. Hackfort (Eds.), *Routledge companion to sport and exercise psychology: Global perspectives and fundamental concepts* (pp. 67-82). Taylor & Francis.

Ntoumanis, N., Ng, Y.Y., Prestwich, A., Quested, E., Hancox, J.E., Thøgersen-Ntoumani, C., Deci, E.L., Ryan, R.M., Lonsdale, R.M., & Williams G.C. (2021). A meta-analysis of self-determination theory-informed intervention studies in the health domain: Effects on motivation, health behavior, physical, and psychological health. *Health Psychology Review, 15*(2), 214-244. https://doi.org/10.1080/17437199.2020.1718529

Ntoumanis, N., Quested, E., Patterson, L., Kaffe, S., Backhouse, S.H., Pavlidis, G., Whitaker, L., Barkoukis, V., Smith, B.J., Staff, H.R., & Gucciardi, D.F. (2021). An intervention to optimize coach-created motivational climates and reduce athlete willingness to dope (coachMADE): A three-country cluster randomised controlled trial. *British Journal of Sports Medicine, 55*, 213-219. http://dx.doi.org/10.1136/bjsports-2019-101963

Ntoumanis, N., Quested, E., Reeve, J., & Cheon, S.H. (2018). Need supportive communication: Implications for motivation in sport, exercise, and physical activity. In B. Jackson, J.A. Dimmock, & J. Compton (Eds.), *Persuasion and communication in sport, exercise, and physical activity* (pp. 155-169). Routledge.

Pulido, J.J., Sánchez-Oliva, D., Leo, F.M., Sánchez-Cano, J., & García-Calvo, T. (2018). Development and validation of Coaches' Interpersonal Style Questionnaire. *Measurement in Physical Education and Exercise Science, 22*(1), 25-37. https://doi.org/10.1080/1091367X.2017.1369982.

Pulido, J., Sánchez-Oliva, D., Silva, M., Palmeira, A., & García-Calvo, T. (2019). Development and preliminary validation of the Coach Interpersonal Style Observational System. *International Journal of Sports Science and Coaching, 14*(4), 471-479. https://doi.org/10.1177/1747954119858965

Quested, E., Duda, J.L., Ntoumanis, N., & Maxwell, J.P. (2013). Daily fluctuations in the affective states of dancers: A cross-situational test of basic needs theory. *Psychology of Sport and Exercise, 14*(4), 586-595. https://doi.org/10.1016/j.psychsport.2013.02.006

Quested, E., Ntoumanis, N., Stenling, A., Thogersen-Ntoumani, C., & Hancox, J.E. (2018). The Need-Relevant Instructor Behaviours Scale (NIBS): Development and initial validation. *Journal of Sport and Exercise Psychology, 40*(5), 259-268. https://doi.org/10.1123/jsep.2018-0043

Reeve, J., Jang, H.R., & Jang, H. (2018). Personality-based antecedents of teachers' autonomy-supportive and controlling motivating styles. *Learning and Individual Differences, 62*, 12-22. https://doi.org/10.1016/j.lindif.2018.01.001

Reinboth, M., Duda, J.L., & Ntoumanis, N. (2004). Dimensions of coaching behaviour, need satisfaction, and the psychological and physical welfare of young athletes. *Motivation and Emotion, 28*(3), 297-313. https://doi.org/10.1023/B:MOEM.0000040156.81924.b8

Reynders, B., Vansteenkiste, M., Van Puyenbroeck, S., Aelterman, N., De Backer, M., Delrue, J., De Muynck, G.-J., Fransen, K., Haerens, L., & Vande Broek, G. (2019). Coaching the coach: Intervention effects on need-supportive coaching behavior and athlete motivation and engagement. *Psychology of Sport and Exercise, 43*, 288-300. https://doi.org/10.1016/j.psychsport.2019.04.002

Roberts G.C., & Treasure D. (2012). *Advances in motivation in sport and exercise* (3rd ed). Human Kinetics.

Rocchi, M., & Pelletier, L.G. (2017). The antecedents of coaches' interpersonal behaviors: The role of the coaching context, coaches' psychological needs, and coaches' motivation. *Journal of Sport and Exercise Psychology, 39*(5), 366-378. https://doi.org/10.1123/jsep.2016-0267

Rocchi, M., & Pelletier, L. (2018). How does coaches' reported interpersonal behavior align with athletes' perceptions? Consequences for female athletes' psychological needs in sport. *Sport, Exercise, and Performance Psychology, 7*(2), 141-154. https://dx.doi.org/10.1037/spy0000116

Rocchi, M., Pelletier, L., & Desmarais, P. (2017). The validity of the Interpersonal Behaviours Questionnaire (IBQ) in sport. *Measurement in Physical Education and Exercise Science, 21*(1), 15-25. https://doi.org/10.1080/1091367X.2016.1242488.

Ryan, R.M., & Deci, E.L. (2017). *Self-determination theory: Basic psychological needs in motivation, development and wellness.* Guilford Press.

Ryan, R.M., & Deci, E.L. (2000). The darker and brighter sides of human existence: Basic psychological needs as a unifying concept. *Psychological Inquiry, 11*(4), 319-338. https://doi.org/10.1207/S15327965PLI1104_03

Sarason, I., Sarason, B., Shearin, E., & Pierce, G. (1987). A brief measure of social support: Practical and theoretical implications. *Journal of Social and Personal Relationships, 4*(4), 497-510. https://doi.org/10.1177/0265407587044007

Sedikides, C., Ntoumanis, N., & Sheldon, K.M. (2019). I am the chosen one: Narcissism in the backdrop of self-determination theory. *Journal of Personality, 87*(1), 70-81. https://doi.org/10.1111/jopy.12402

Shaffer, J.A., DeGeest, D., & Li, A. (2016). Tackling the problem of construct proliferation: A guide to assessing the discriminant validity of conceptually related constructs.

Organizational Research Methods, 19(1), 80-110. https://doi.org/10.1177/1094428115598239

Skinner, E., Johnson, S., & Snyder, T. (2005). Six dimensions of parenting: A motivational model. *Parenting: Science and Practice, 5*(2), 175-235. https://doi.org/10.1207/s15327922par0502_3.

Smith, N., Tessier, D., Tzioumakis, Y., Quested, E., Appleton, P., Sarrazin, P., Papaioannou, A., & Duda, J.L. (2015). Development and validation of the multidimensional motivational climate observation system. *Journal of Sport and Exercise Psychology, 37*(1), 4-22. https://doi.org/10.1123/jsep.2014-0059

Soenens, B., & Vansteenkiste, M. (2010). A theoretical upgrade of the concept of parental psychological control: Proposing new insights on the basis of self-determination theory. *Developmental Review, 30*(1), 74-99. https://doi.org/10.1016/j.dr.2009.11.001

Sol Alvarez, M., Balaguer, I., Castillo, I., & Duda, J.L. (2009). Coach autonomy support and quality of sport engagement in young soccer players. *Spanish Journal of Psychology, 12*(1), 138-148. https://doi.org/10.1017/s1138741600001554

Stebbings, J., Taylor, I., Spray, C., & Ntoumanis, N. (2012). Antecedents of perceived coach interpersonal behaviors: The coaching environment and coach psychological well- and ill-being. *Journal of Sport and Exercise Psychology, 34*(4), 481-502.

Su, Y.L., & Reeve, J. (2011). A meta-analysis of the effectiveness of intervention programs designed to support autonomy. *Educational Psychology Review, 23*(1), 159-188. https://doi.org/10.1007/s10648-010-9142-7

Teixeira, P.J., Marques, M.M., Silva, M.N., Brunet, J., Duda, J., Haerens, L., La Guardia, J., Lindwall, M., Londsdale, C., Markland, D., Michie, S., Moller, A.C., Ntoumanis, N., Patrick, H., Reeve, J., Ryan, R.M., Sebire, S., Standage, M., Vansteenkinste, M., . . . Hagger, M.S. (2020). Classification of techniques used in self-determination theory-based interventions in health contexts: An expert consensus study. *Motivation Science, 6*(4), 438-455. http://dx.doi.org/10.1037/mot0000172

Vansteenkiste, M., & Ryan, R.M. (2013). On psychological growth and vulnerability: Basic psychological need satisfaction and need frustration as a unifying principle. *Journal of Psychotherapy Integration, 23*(3), 263-280. https://doi.org/10.1037/a0032359

Vasconcellos, D., Parker, P.D., Hilland, T., Cinelli, R., Owen K.B., Kapsal, N., Ntoumanis, N., Ryan, R.M., Lonsdale, C. (2020). Self-determination theory applied to physical education: A systematic review and meta-analysis. *Journal of Educational Psychology, 112*(7), 1444-1469. https://doi.org/10.1037/edu0000420.

Wallace, S. (2017, March 25). England manager Gareth Southgate asks players to call him Gareth in an effort to foster new culture. *Daily Telegraph.* www.telegraph.co.uk/football/2017/03/25/england-manager-gareth-southgate-asks-players-call-gareth-effort

Williams, G.C., Grow, V.M., Freedman, Z.R., Ryan, R.M., & Deci, E.L. (1996). Motivational predictors of weight loss and weight-loss maintenance. *Journal of Personality and Social Psychology, 70*(1), 115-126. https://doi.org/10.1037//0022-3514.70.1.115

Wilson, P.M., Gregson, J.P., & Mack, D.E. (2009). The importance of interpersonal style in competitive sport: A self-determination theory approach. In C.H. Chang (Ed.), *Handbook of sport psychology* (pp. 259-276). Nova Science.

Chapter 13

Abraham, F.A. (1995). Dynamics, bifurcation, self-organization, chaos, mind, conflict, insensitivity to initial conditions, time, unification, diversity, free will and social responsibility. In R. Robertson & A. Combs (Eds.), *Chaos theory in psychology and the life sciences* (pp. 155-173). Psychology Press. https://doi.org/10.4324/9781315806280

Andriani, P., & McKelvrey, B. (2009). From Gaussian to Paretian thinking: Causes and implications of power laws in organizations. *Organization Science, 20,* 1053-1071. https://doi.org/10.1287/orsc.1090.0481

Anguera, M.T., Camerino, O., Castañer, M., Sánchez-Algarra, P., & Onwuegbuzie, A.J. (2017). The specificity of observational studies in physical activity and sports sciences: Moving forward in mixed methods research and proposals for achieving quantitative and qualitative symmetry. *Frontiers in Psychology, 8,* 2196. https://doi.org/10.3389/fpsyg.2017.02196

Bolger, N., & Laurenceau, J.P. (2013). *Intensive longitudinal methods: An introduction to diary and experience sampling research.* Guilford Press.

Carley, K. (1999). On the evolution of social and organizational networks. In S. Andrews and D. Knoke (Eds.), *Research in the sociology of organizations* (pp. 3-30). JAI Press.

Carley, K., & Hill, V. (2001). Structural change and learning within organizations. In A. Lomi & E.R. Larsen (Eds.), *Dynamics of organisations: Computational modelling and organizational theories* (pp. 63-92). AAAI Press.

Cattell, R.B. (1952). The three basic factor-analytic research designs—their interrelations and derivatives. *Psychological Bulletin, 49*(5), 499-520. https://doi.org/10.1037/h0054245

Cattell, R.B. (1963). The structuring of change by P-technique and incremental R-technique. In Harris C. W. (Ed.), Problems in measuring change. Madison: University of Wisconsin Press, 1963. Pp. 167–198.

Cheng, Y., & Van de Ven, A. (1996). The innovation journey: Order out of chaos? *Organizational Science, 6,* 593-614. https://doi.org/10.1287/orsc.7.6.593

Chevance, G., Perski, O., & Hekler, E.B. (2020). Innovative methods for observing and changing complex health behaviors: Four propositions. *Translational Behavioral Medicine, 11,* 676-685. https://doi.org/10.1093/tbm/ibaa026

Crawford, C.G., Aguinis, H., Lichtenstein, B., Davidsson, P., & McKelvey, B. (2015). Power law distribution in entrepreneurship: Implications for theory and practice. *Journal of Business Venturing, 30,* 696-713. https://doi.org/10.1016/j.jbusvent.2015.01.001

Cresswell, S.L., & Eklund, R.C. (2007). Athlete burnout: A longitudinal qualitative study. *Sport Psychologist, 21,* 1-20. https://doi.org/10.1123/tsp.21.1.1

Cumming, S.P., Smith, R.E., Smoll, F.L., Standage, M., & Grossbard, J.R. (2008). Development and validation of the Achievement Goal Scale for Youth Sports. *Psychology of Sport and Exercise, 9*(5), 686-703. https://doi.org/10.1016/j.psychsport.2007.09.003

Csikszentmihalyi, M., & Larson, R. (2014). Validity and reliability of the experience-sampling method. In M. Csikszentmihalyi (Ed.), *Flow and the foundations of positive psychology.* (pp. 35-54) Springer Publishing. ISBN: 9401790876.

Davis, J., Eisenhardt, K., & Bingham, C. (2007). Developing theory through simulation methods. *Academy of Management Review, 32,* 480-499. https://doi.org/10.5465/amr.2007.24351453

Duda, J.L., & Hall, H.K. (2001). Achievement goal theory in sport: Recent extensions and future directions. In Singer R. N., Hausenblas H. A., Janelle C. M. (Eds.), Handbook of sport psychology. (2nd ed.) New York: Wiley. (pp. 417–443)

Eagle, N., & Pentland, A. (2005). Reality mining: Sensing complex social systems. *Personal and Ubiquitous Computing, 10,* 255-268. https://doi.org/10.1007/s00779-005-0046-3

Elliot, A.J. (1999). Approach and avoidance motivation and achievement goals. *Educational Psychologist, 34,* 169-189. https://doi.org/10.1207/s15326985ep3403_3

Fisher, A.J., Medaglia, J.D., & Jeronimus, B.F. (2018). Lack of group-to-individual generalizability is a threat to human subjects research. *Psychological and Cognitive Sciences, 115*(27), 6106-6115. https://doi.org/10.1073/pnas.1711978115

Fournier, M.A., Moskowitz, D.S., & Zuroff, D.C. (2008). Integrating dispositions, signatures, and the interpersonal domain. *Journal of Personality and Social Psychology,* 94, 531-545. https://doi.org/10.1037/0022-3514.94.3.531

Fournier, M.A., Moskowitz, D.S., & Zuroff, D.C. (2009). The interpersonal signature. *Journal of Research in Personality, 43,* 55-162. https://doi.org/10.1016/j.jrp.2009.01.023

Fuchs, A. (2013). *Nonlinear dynamics in complex systems: Theory and applications for the life-, neuro and natural sciences.* Springer: London https://doi.org/10.1007/978-3-642-33552-5

Gómez-López, M., Chicau Borrego, C., Marques da Silva, C., Granero-Gallegos, A., & González-Hernández, J. (2020). Effects of motivational climate on fear of failure and anxiety in teen handball players. *International Journal of Environmental Research and Public Health, 17,* 592. https://doi.org/10.3390/ijerph17020592

Guastello, S. J., & Liebovitch, L. S. (2009). Introduction to nonlinear dynamics and complexity. In S. J. Guastello, M. Koopmans, & D. Pincus (Eds.), Chaos and complexity in psychology: The theory of nonlinear dynamical systems (pp. 1–40). Cambridge University Press. . https://doi.org/10.1017/CBO9781139058544.002

Harwood, C.G., Keegan, R.J., Smith, J.M.J., & Raine, A.S. (2015). A systematic review of the intrapersonal correlates of motivational climate perceptions in sport and physical activity. *Psychology of Sport and Exercise, 18,* 9-25. https://doi.org/10.1016/j.psychsport.2014.11.005

Hassmén, P., Keegan, R., & Piggott, D. (2016). *Rethinking sport and exercise psychology research: Past, present, and future.* Springer: London https://doi.org/10.1057/978-1-137-48338-6

Hekler, E.B., Klasnja, P., Chevance, G., Golaszewski, N.M., Lewis, D., & Sim, I. (2019). Why we need a small data paradigm. *BMC Medicine, 17,* 133. https://doi.org/10.1186/s12916-019-1366-x

Holland, J.H. (2006). Studying complex adaptive systems. *Journal of Systems Science and Complexity, 19,* 1-8. https://doi.org/10.1007/s11424-006-0001-z

Keegan, R.J. (2019). Achievement goals in sport and physical activity. In T. Horn and A. Smith (Eds.), *Advances in sport and exercise psychology* (pp. 265-287). Human Kinetics. ISBN: 9781492528920.

Keegan, R.J., Harwood, C.G., Spray, C.M., & Lavallee, D.E. (2009). A qualitative investigation exploring the motivational climate in early career sports participants: Coach, parent and peer influences on sport motivation. *Psychology of Sport and Exercise, 10*(3), 361-372. https://doi.org/10.1016/j.psychsport.2008.12.003

Keegan, R., Middleton, G., Henderson, H., & Girling, M. (2016). Auditing the socio-environmental determinants of motivation towards physical activity or sedentariness in work-aged adults: A qualitative study. *BMC Public Health, 16,* 438. https://doi.org/10.1186/s12889-016-3098-6

Keegan, R., Spray, C., Harwood, C., & Lavallee, D. (2010). The motivational atmosphere in youth sport: Coach, parent, and peer influences on motivation in specializing sport participants. *Journal of Applied Sport Psychology, 22*(1), 87-105. https://doi.org/10.1080/10413200903421267

Keegan, R.J., Spray, C.M., Harwood, C.G., & Lavallee, D. (2014a). A qualitative investigation of the motivational climate in elite sport. *Psychology of Sport and Exercise, 15*(1), 97-107. https://doi.org/10.1016/j.psychsport.2013.10.006

Keegan, R.J., Spray, C.M., Harwood, C.G., & Lavallee, D.E. (2014b). A qualitative synthesis of research into social motivational influences across the athletic career span. *Qualitative Research in Sport, Exercise and Health, 6*(4), 537-567. https://doi.org/10.1080/2159676X.2013.857710

Kinder, C.J., Gaudreault, K.L., & Simonton, K. (2020). Structured and unstructured contexts in physical education: Promoting activity, learning and motivation. *Journal of Physical Education, Recreation and Dance, 91*(6), 30-35. https://doi.org/10.1080/07303084.2020.1768181

van der Krieke, L., Jeronimus, B.F., Blaauw, F.J., Wanders, R.B., Emerencia, A.C., Schenk, H.M., de Vos, S., Snippe, E., Wichers, M., Wigman, J.T., Bos, E.H., Wardenaar, K.J., & de Jonge, P. (2016). HowNutsAreTheDutch (HoeGekIsNL): A crowdsourcing study of mental symptoms and strengths. *International Journal of Methods in Psychiatric Research, 25*(2), 123-144. https://doi.org/10.1002/mpr.1495

Lacerda, A., Filgueiras, A., Campos, M., Keegan, R., & Landeira-Fernández, J. (2021). Motivational climate measures in sport: A systematic review. *Spanish Journal of Psychology, 24*(27). https://doi.org/10.1017/SJP.2021.13

Larson, R., & Csikszentmihalyi, M. (1983). The experience sampling method. *New Directions for Methodology of Social and Behavioral Science, 15,* 41-56.

Levie, J., & Lichtenstein, B. (2010). A terminal assessment of stages theory: Introducing a dynamic states approach to entrepreneurship. *Entrepreneurship Theory and Practice, 34,* 314-354. https://doi.org/10.1111%2Fj.1540-6520.2010.00377.x

Lichtenstein, B. (2018). Applying the 15 complexity sciences: Methods for studying emergence in organizations. In E. Mitleton-Kelly, A. Paraskevas, & C. Day (Eds.), *Handbook of research methods in complexity science* (pp. 525-544). Elgar.

Maher, J.P., Rebar, A.L., & Dunton, G.F. (2018). Ecological momentary assessment is a feasible and valid methodological tool to measure older adults' physical activity and sedentary behavior. *Frontiers in Psychology, 9.* https://doi.org/10.3389/fpsyg.2018.01485

McCann, B., McCarthy, P.J., Cooper, K., Forbes-McKay, K., & Keegan, R.J. (2021). A retrospective investigation of the perceived influence of coaches, parents, and peers on talented football players' motivation during development. *Journal of Applied Sport Psychology,* 1-24. https://doi.org/10.1080/10413200.2021.1963013

Meyer, A., Tsui, A., & Hinings, C.R. (1993). Configurational approaches to organizational analysis. *Academy of Management Journal,* 36, 1175-1195. https://doi.org/10.2307/256809

Miller, J.H., & Page, S.E. (2009). *Complex adaptive systems: An introduction to computational models of social life* (Vol. 28). Princeton University Press.

Mitleton-Kelly, E., Paraskevas, A., & Day, C. (2018). *Handbook of research methods in complexity science theory and applications.* Elgar.

Morris, R.L., & Kavussanu, M. (2008). Antecedents of approach-avoidance goals in sport. *Journal of Sports Sciences, 26,* 465-476. https://doi.org/10.1080/02640410701579388

Newton, M., Duda, J.L., & Yin, Z. (2000). Examination of the psychometric properties of the perceived motivational climate in sport questionnaire-2 in a sample of female athletes. *Journal of Sports Sciences, 18*, 275-290. https://doi.org/10.1080/026404100365018

Nicholls, J. (1989). *The competitive ethos and democratic education.* Harvard University Press.

Osterwalder, A., & Pigeneur, Y. (2010). *Business model generation: A handbook for visionaries, game changers and challengers.* Wiley.

Poucher, Z.A., Tamminen, K.A., Caron, J.G., & Sweet, S.N. (2020). Thinking through and designing qualitative research studies: A focused mapping review of 30 years of qualitative research in sport psychology. *International Review of Sport and Exercise Psychology, 13*, 163-186. https://doi.org/10.1080/1750984X.2019.1656276

Reynolds, C.W. (1987). Flocks, herds, and schools: A distributed behavioral model. *Computer Graphics, 21*(4), 25-34. https://doi.org/10.1145/37402.37406

Ryan, R.M., & Deci, E.L. (2002). An overview of self-determination theory: An organismic-dialectical perspective. In E.L. Deci & R.M. Ryan (Eds.), *Handbook of self-determination research* (pp. 3-33). University of Rochester Press.

Ryba, T.V., Wiltshire, G., North, J., & Ronkainen, N.J. (2020). Developing mixed methods research in sport and exercise psychology: Potential contributions of a critical realist perspective. *International Journal of Sport and Exercise Psychology*, 1-21. https://doi.org/10.1080/1612197X.2020.1827002

Sather, T. (2014). Experience sampling method. ASHA Journals Academy. https://doi.org/10.1044/CRED-MEAS-R101-003

Saw, A.E., Main, L.C., & Gastin, P.B. (2016). Monitoring the athlete training response: Subjective self-reported measures trump commonly used objective measures: A systematic review. *British Journal of Sports Medicine, 50*, 281-291. https://doi.org/10.1136/bjsports-2015-094758

Smith, N., Tessier, D., Tzioumakis, Y., Quested, E., Appleton, P., Sarrazin, P., Papaioannou, A., & Duda, J.L. (2015). Development and validation of the multidimensional motivational climate observation system. *Journal of Sport and Exercise Psychology, 37*(1), 4-22. https://doi.org/10.1123/jsep.2014-0059

Smith, R.E., Smoll, F.L., & Cumming, S.P. (2007). Effects of a motivational climate intervention for coaches on young athletes' sport performance anxiety. *Journal of Sport and Exercise Psychology, 29*, 39-59. https://doi.org/10.1123/jsep.29.1.39

Sproule, J., Wang, C.K.J., Morgan, K., McNeill, M., & McMorris, T. (2007). Effects of motivational climate in Singaporean physical education lessons on intrinsic motivation and physical activity intention. *Personality and Individual Differences, 43*, 1037-1049. https://doi.org/10.1016/j.paid.2007.02.017

Strohacker, K., Keegan, R., Beaumont, C.T., & Zakrajsek, R.A. (2021). Applying P-technique factor analysis to explore person-specific models of readiness-to-exercise. *Frontiers in Sports and Active Living, 3*, 169. https://doi.org/10.3389/fspor.2021.685813

Thomas, I., Frankhauser, P., & Badariotti, D. (2012). Comparing the fractality of European urban neighbourhoods: Do national contexts matter? *Journal of Geographic Systems, 14*, 189-208. https://doi.org/10.1007/s10109-010-0142-4

Vallerand, R.J. (1997). Toward a hierarchical model of intrinsic and extrinsic motivation. *Advances in Experimental Social Psychology, 29*, 271-360. https://doi.org/10.1016/S0065-2601(08)60019-2

Van de Ven, A., Pooley, D., Garud, R., & Venkataramen, S. (1999). *The innovation journey.* Oxford University Press.

Walling, M.D., Duda, J.L., & Chi, L. (1993). The Perceived Motivational Climate in Sport Questionnaire: Construct and predictive validity. *Journal of Sport and Exercise Psychology, 15*, 172-183. https://doi.org/10.1123/jsep.15.2.172

White, S.A. (1996). Goal orientation and perceptions of the motivational climate initiated by parents. *Pediatric Exercise Science, 8*, 122-129. https://doi.org/10.1123/pes.8.2.122

Wright, A.G., Hallquist, M.N., Stepp, S.D., Scott, L.N., Beeney, J.E., Lazarus, S.A., & Pilkonis, P.A. (2016). Modeling heterogeneity in momentary interpersonal and affective dynamic processes in borderline personality disorder. *Assessment, 23*, 484-495. https://doi.org/10.1177/1073191116653829

Chapter 14

Abgarov, A., Jeffrey-Tosoni, S., Baker, J., & Fraser-Thomas, J. (2012). Understanding social support throughout the injury process among interuniversity swimmers. *Journal of Intercollegiate Sport, 5*, 213-229. https://doi.org/10.1123/jis.5.2.213

Aitchison, B., Rushton, A.B., Martin, P., Soundy, A., & Heneghan, N.R. (2021). The podium illusion: A phenomenological study of the influence of social support on well-being and performance in elite para swimmers. *BMC Sports Science Medicine and Rehabilitation, 13*, 42. https://doi.org/10.1186/s13102-021-00269-1

Alvarez, M.S., Balaguer, I., Castillo, I., & Duda, J.L. (2009). Coach autonomy support and quality of sport engagement in young soccer players. *Spanish Journal of Psychology, 12*, 138-148. https://doi.org/10.1017/s1138741600001554

Anderson, M.B., & Williams, J.M. (1999). Athletic injury, psychosocial factors and perceptual changes during stress. *Journal of Sports Sciences, 17*, 735-741. https://doi.org/10.1080/026404199365597

Bakker, A.B., Oerlemans, W., Demerouti, E., Slot, B.B., & Ali, D.M. (2011). Flow and performance: A study among talented Dutch soccer players. *Psychology of Sport and Exercise, 12*, 442-450. https://doi.org/10.1016/j.psychsport.2011.02.003

Barrera, M., Jr. (1986). Distinctions between social support concepts, measures, and models. *American Journal of Community Psychology, 14*, 413-445. https://doi.org/10.1007/BF00922627

Barrera, M., Jr., Sandler, I.N., & Ramsay, T.B. (1981). Preliminary development of a scale of social support: Studies on college students. *American Journal of Community Psychology, 9*, 435-447. https://doi.org/10.1007/BF00918174

Berg, C.A., & Upchurch, R. (2007). A developmental-contextual model of couples coping with chronic illness across the lifespan. *Psychological Bulletin, 133*, 920-954. https://doi.org/10.1037/0033-2909.133.6.920

Berkman, L.F., & Syme, S.L. (1979). Social networks, host resistance, and mortality: A nine-year follow-up study of Alameda County residents. *American Journal of Epidemiology, 109*, 186-204. https://doi.org/10.1093/oxfordjournals.aje.a112674

Bianco, T. (2001). Social support and recovery from sport injury: Elite skiers share their experiences. *Research Quarterly for Exercise and Sport, 72*, 376-388. https://doi.org/10.1080/02701367.2001.10608974

Bianco, T., & Eklund, R.C. (2001). Conceptual considerations for social support research in sport and exercise settings: The case of sports injury. *Journal of Sport and Exercise Psychology, 23*, 85-107. http://dx.doi.org/10.1123/jsep.23.2.85

Boat, R., & Taylor, I.M. (2015). Patterns of change in psychological variables leading up to competition in superior versus inferior performers. *Journal of Sport and Exercise Psychology, 37*, 244-256. https://doi.org/10.1123/jsep.2014-0216

Bolger, N., & Amarel, D. (2007). Effects of support visibility on adjustment to stress: Experimental evidence. *Journal of Personality and Social Psychology, 92*, 458-475. https://doi.org/10.1037/0022-3514.92.3.458

Brisette, I., Cohen, S., & Seeman, T.E. (2000). Measuring social integration and social networks. In S. Cohen, L.G. Underwood, & B.H. Gottlieb (Eds.), *Social support measurement and interventions: A guide for health and social scientists* (pp. 53-85). University Press. https://doi.org/10.1093/med:psych/9780195126709.003.0003

Brock, R.L., & Lawrence, E. (2009). Too much of a good thing: Underprovision versus overprovision of partner support. *Journal of Family Psychology, 23*, 181-192. https://dx.doi.org/10.1037%2Fa0015402

Brown, C.J., Webb, T.L., Robinson, M.A., & Cotgreave, R. (2018). Athletes' experience of social support during their transition out of elite sport: An interpretative phenomenological analysis. *Psychology of Sport and Exercise, 26*, 71-80. https://doi.org/10.1016/j.psychsport.2018.01.003

Burleson, B.R. (2003). Emotional support skill. In J.O. Greene & B.R. Burleson (Eds.), *Handbook of communication and social interaction skills* (pp. 551-594). Erlbaum.

Burleson, B.R., & MacGeorge, E.L. (2002). Supportive communication. In M.L. Knapp & J.A. Daly (Eds.), *Handbook of interpersonal communication* (pp. 374-424). Sage.

Butler, T.L., McKimmie, B.M., & Haslam, S.A. (2018). The approach-avoidance dilemma at the heart of group-based support: Evidence that group identification increases willingness to seek support at the same time that identity-based support threat reduces it. *European Journal of Social Psychology, 49*, 31-46. https://doi.org/10.1002/ejsp.2384

Carson, F., & Polman, R. (2012). Experiences of professional rugby union players returning to competition following anterior cruciate ligament reconstruction. *Physical Therapy in Sport, 13*, 35-40. https://doi.org/10.1016/j.ptsp.2010.10.007

Chen, L.H. (2013). Gratitude and adolescent athletes' well-being: The multiple mediating roles of perceived social support from coaches and teammates. *Social Indicators Research, 114*(2), 273-285. https://doi.org/10.1007/s11205-012-0145-2

Coffee, P., Freeman, P., & Allen, M.S. (2017). The TASS-Q: The team-referent availability of social support questionnaire. *Psychology of Sport and Exercise, 33*, 55-65. https://doi.org/10.1016/j.psychsport.2017.08.003

Cohen, S. (1988). Psychosocial models of the role of social support in the etiology of physical disease. *Health Psychology, 7*, 269-297. https://doi.org/10.1037/0278-6133.7.3.269

Cohen, S. (2004). Social relationships and health. *American Psychologist, 11*, 76-84. https://doi.org/10.1037/0003-066x.59.8.676

Cohen, S., Doyle, W.J., Skoner, D.P., Rabin, B.S., & Gwaltney, J.M. (1997). Social ties and susceptibility to the common cold. *Journal of the American Medical Association, 277*, 1940- 1944. https://doi.org/10.1001/jama.1997.03540480040036

Cohen, S., & McKay, G. (1984). Social support, stress, and the buffering hypothesis: A theoretical analysis. In A. Baum, S.E. Taylor, & J.E. Singer (Eds.), *Handbook of psychology and health* (pp. 253-267). Erlbaum.

Cohen, S., Mermelstein, R., Kamarck, T., & Hoberman, H. (1985). Measuring the functional components of social support. In I.G. Sarason & B.R. Sarason (Eds.), *Social support: Theory, research, and applications* (pp. 73-94). Martinus Nijhoff. https://doi.org/10.1007/978-94-009-5115-0_5

Cohen, S., Underwood, L.G, & Gottlieb, B.H. (2000). *Social support measurement and intervention: A guide for health and social scientists.* Oxford University Press. https://doi.org/10.1093/med:psych/9780195126709.001.0001

Cohen, S., & Wills, T.A. (1985). Stress, social support, and the buffering hypothesis. *Psychological Bulletin, 98*, 310-357. https://doi.org/10.1037/0033-2909.98.2.310

Connaughton, D., Wadey, R., Hanton, S., & Jones, G. (2008). The development and maintenance of mental toughness: Perceptions of elite performers. *Journal of Sports Sciences, 26*, 83-95. https://doi.org/10.1080/02640410701310958

Coussens, A.H., Rees, T., & Freeman, P. (2015). Applying generalizability theory to examine the antecedents of perceived coach support. *Journal of Sport and Exercise Psychology, 37*(1), 51-62. https://doi.org/10.1123/jsep.2014-0087

Covassin, T., Crutcher, B., Bleecker, A., Heiden, E.O., Dailey, A., & Yang, J. (2014). Postinjury anxiety and social support among collegiate athletes: A comparison between orthopaedic injuries and concussions. *Journal of Athletic Training, 49*, 462-468. https://doi.org/10.4085/1062-6059-49.2.03

Cruwys, T., Haslam, S.A., Dingle, G.A., Haslam, C., & Jetten, J. (2014). Depression and social identity: An integrative review. *Personality and Social Psychology Review, 18*(3), 215-238. https://doi.org/10.1177%2F1088868314523839

Cruwys, T., Steffens, N.K., Haslam, S.A., Haslam, C., Jetten, J., & Dingle, G.A. (2016). Social identity mapping: A procedure for visual representation and assessment of subjective multiple group memberships. *British Journal of Social Psychology, 55*(4), 613-642. https://doi.org/10.1111/bjso.12155

Cutrona, C.E., & Russell, D. (1987). The provisions of social relationships and adaptation to stress. In W.H. Jones & D. Perlman (Eds.), *Advances in personal relationships* (pp. 37-67). JAI Press.

Cutrona, C.E., & Russell, D.W. (1990). Type of social support and specific stress: Toward a theory of optimal matching. In B.R. Sarason, I.G. Sarason, & G.R. Pierce (Eds.), *Social support: An interactional view* (pp. 319-336). Wiley.

DeFreese, J.D., & Smith, A.L. (2013). Teammate social support, burnout, and self-determined motivation in collegiate athletes. *Psychology of Sport and Exercise, 14*, 258-265. https://doi.org/10.1016/j.psychsport.2012.10.009

DeFreese, J.D., & Smith, A.L. (2014). Athlete social support, negative social interactions and psychological health across a competitive sport season. *Journal of Sport and Exercise Psychology, 36*, 619-630. https://doi.org/10.1123/jsep.2014-0040

Dehle, C., Larsen, D., & Landers, J.E. (2001). Social support in marriage. *American Journal of Family Therapy, 29*, 307-324. https://doi.org/10.1080/01926180152588725

Fitzsimons, G.M., & Finkel, E.J. (2011). Outsourcing self-regulation. *Psychological Science, 22*, 369-375. https://doi.org/10.1177%2F0956797610397955

Fransen, K., Van Puyenbroeck, S., Loughead, T.M., Vanbeselaere, N., De Cuyper, B., Vande Broek, G., & Boen, F. (2015). Who takes the lead? Social network analysis as a pioneering tool to investigate shared leadership within sports teams. *Social Networks, 43*, 28-38. http://dx.doi.org/10.1016/j.socnet.2015.04.003

Freeman, P. (2020). Social support in sport. In G. Tenenbaum & R.C. Eklund (Eds), *Handbook of sports psychology* (4th ed., pp. 447–463). Wiley.

Freeman, P., Coffee, P., Moll, T., Rees, T., & Sammy, N. (2014). The ARSQ: The Athletes' Received Support Questionnaire. *Journal of Sport and Exercise Psychology, 36*(2), 189-202. https://doi.org/10.1123/jsep.2013-0080

Freeman, P., Coffee, P., & Rees, T. (2011). The PASS-Q: The Perceived Available Support in Sport Questionnaire. *Journal of Sport and Exercise Psychology, 33*, 54-74. https://doi.org/10.1123/jsep.33.1.54

Freeman, P., & Rees, T. (2008). The effects of perceived and received support on objective performance outcome. *European Journal of Sport Science, 8*, 359-368. https://doi.org/10.1080/17461390802261439

Freeman, P., & Rees, T. (2009). How does perceived support lead to better performance? An examination of potential mechanisms. *Journal of Applied Sport Psychology, 21*, 429-441. https://doi.org/10.1080/10413200903222913

Freeman, P., & Rees, T. (2010). Perceived social support from team-mates: Direct and stress-buffering effects on self-confidence. *European Journal of Sport Science, 10*, 59-67. https://doi.org/10.1080/17461390903049998

Freeman, P., Rees, T., & Hardy, L. (2009). An intervention to increase social support and improve performance. *Journal of Applied Sport Psychology, 21*, 186-200. https://doi.org/10.1080/10413200902785829

Frisch, J.U., Häusser, J.A., van Dick, R., & Mojzisch, A. (2014). Making support work: The interplay between social support and social identity. *Journal of Experimental Social Psychology, 55*, 154-161. https://doi.org/10.1016/j.jesp.2014.06.009

Gallagher, S., Creaven, A.-M., Howard, S., Ginty, A.T., & Whittaker, A.C. (2021). Gratitude, social support and cardiovascular reactivity to acute psychological stress. *Biological Psychology, 162*, 108090. https://doi.org/10.1016/j.biopsycho.2021.108090

Gillet, N., Vallerand, R.J., Amoura, S., & Baldes, B. (2009). Influence of coaches' autonomy support on athletes' motivation and sport performance: A test of the hierarchical model of intrinsic and extrinsic motivation. *Psychology of Sport and Exercise, 11*, 155-161. https://doi.org/10.1016/j.psychsport.2009.10.004

Girme, Y.U., Overall, N.C., & Simpson, J.A. (2013). When visibility matters: Short-term versus long-term costs and benefits of visible and invisible support. *Personality and Social Psychology Bulletin, 39*, 1441-1454. https://doi.org/10.1177/0146167213497802

Gleason, M.E.J., Iida, M., Shrout, P.E., & Bolger, N. (2008). Receiving support as a mixed blessing: Evidence for dual effects of support on psychological outcomes. *Journal of Personality and Social Psychology, 94*, 824-838. https://dx.doi.org/10.1037%2F0022-3514.94.5.824

Goldsmith, D.J. (2004). *Communicating social support*. Cambridge University Press.

Gould, D., Tuffey, S., Udry, E., & Loehr, J. (1996). Burnout in competitive junior tennis players: II. Qualitative analysis. *The Sport Psychologist, 10*, 341-366. https://doi.org/10.1123/tsp.10.4.341

Greenleaf, C., Gould, D., & Dieffenbach, K. (2001). Factors influencing Olympic performance: Interviews with Atlanta and Nagano US Olympians. *Journal of Applied Sport Psychology, 13*, 154-181. https://doi.org/10.1080/104132001753149874

Gustafsson, H., DeFreese, J.D., & Madigan, D.J. (2017). Athlete burnout: Review and recommendations. *Current Opinion in Psychology, 16*, 109-113. https://doi.org/10.1016/j.copsyc.2017.05.002

Haber, M., Cohen, J., Lucas, T., & Baltes, B. (2007). The relationship between self-reported received and perceived social support. *American Journal of Community Psychology, 39*, 133-144. https://doi.org/10.1007/s10464-007-9100-9

Hartley, C., & Coffee, P. (2019). Perceived and received dimensional support: Main and stress-buffering effects on dimensions of burnout. *Frontiers in Psychology, 10*, 1724. https://dx.doi.org/10.3389%2Ffpsyg.2019.01724

Hartley, C., Coffee, P., & Abhyankar, P. (2022). A provider-recipient perspective on how social identity influences the design, provision, and receipt of social support. *Frontiers in Psychology, 13*, 940747. https://doi.org/10.3389/fpsyg.2022.94074

Hartley, C., Haslam, S.A., Coffee, P., & Rees, T. (2020). Social support. In S.A. Haslam, K. Fransen, & F. Boen (Eds.), *The new psychology of sport and exercise: The social identity approach* (pp. 245-264). Sage.

Harwood, C.G., & Knight, C.J. (2015). Parenting in youth sport: A position paper on parenting expertise. *Psychology of Sport and Exercise, 16*, 24-35. https://doi.org/10.1016/j.psychsport.2014.03.001

Haslam, C., Cruwys, T., Milne, M., Kan, C.H., & Haslam, S.A. (2016). Group ties protect cognitive health by promoting social identification and social support. *Journal of Aging and Health, 28*(2), 244-266. https://doi.org/10.1177/0898264315589578

Haslam, S.A. (2004). *Psychology in organizations: The social identity approach*. Sage.

Haslam, S.A., McMahon, C., Cruwys, T., Haslam, C., Greenaway, K., Jetten, J., & Steffens, N.K. (2018). Social cure, what social cure? The propensity to underestimate the importance of social factors for health. *Social Science and Medicine, 198*, 14-21. https://doi.org/10.1016/j.socscimed.2017.12.020

Haslam, S.A., Reicher, S., & Levine, M. (2012). When other people are heaven, when other people are hell: How social identity determines the nature and impact of social support. In J. Jetten, C. Haslam, & S.A. Haslam (Eds.), *The social cure: Identity, health and well-being* (pp. 157-174). Psychology Press.

Haslam, S.A., Steffens, N.K., Peters, K., Boyce, R.A., Mallett, C.J., & Fransen, K. (2017). A social identity approach to leadership development: The 5R program. *Journal of Personnel Psychology, 16*(3), 113-124. https://doi.org/10.1027/1866-5888/a000176

Haslam, S.A., Turner, J.C., Oakes, P.J., McGarty, C., & Reynolds, K.J. (1998). The group as a basis for emergent stereotype consensus. *European Review of Social Psychology, 8*, 203-239.

Hassmén, P., Keegan, R., & Piggott, D. (2016). *Rethinking sport and exercise psychology research*. Palgrave Macmillan.

Hassell, K., Sabiston, C.M., & Bloom, G.A. (2010). Exploring the multiple dimensions of social support among elite female adolescent swimmers. *International Journal of Sport Psychology, 41*, 340-359.

Hatzigeorgiadis, A., & Biddle, S.J.H. (2000). Assessing cognitive interference in sport: Development of the Thought Occurrence Questionnaire for Sport. *Anxiety, Stress, and Coping, 13*, 65-86. https://doi.org/10.1080/10615800008248334

Hayward, F.P.I., Knight, C.J., & Mellalieu, S.D. (2017). A longitudinal examination of stressors, appraisals, and coping in youth swimming. *Psychology of Sport and Exercise, 29*, 56-68. https://doi.org/10.1016/j.psychsport.2016.12.002

Henriksen, K., Schinke, R., Mccann, S., Durand-Bush, N., Moesch, K., Parham, W.D., Larsen, C.H., Cogan, K., Donaldson, A., Poczwardowski, A., Noce, F., & Hunziker, J. (2020). Athlete mental health in the Olympic / Paralympic quadrennium: A multi-societal consensus statement. *International Journal of Sport and Exercise Psychology, 18*, 391-408. https://doi.org/10.1080/1612197X.2020.1746379

Holt-Lunstad, J., Smith, T.B., & Layton, B. (2010). Social relationships and mortality: A meta-analysis. *PLOS Medicine, 7*, 1000316. https://doi.org/10.1371/journal.pmed.1000316

Holt, N.L., & Hoar, S.D. (2006). The multidimensional construct of social support. In S. Hanton & S.D. Mellalieu (Eds.), *Literature reviews in sport psychology* (pp. 1-27). Nova Science.

Hong, H.J., & Coffee, P. (2018). A psycho-educational curriculum for sport career transition practitioners: Development and evaluation. *European Sport Management Quarterly, 18*(3), 287-306. https://doi.org/10.1080/16184742.2017.1387925

Judge, L.W., Bellar, D., Blom, L.C., Lee, D., Harris, B., Turk, M., McAtee, G., & Johnson, J. (2012). Perceived social support from strength and conditioning coaches among injured student athletes. *Journal of Strength and Conditioning Research, 26*, 1154-1161. https://doi.org/10.1519/jsc.0b013e31822e008b

Kellezi, B., & Reicher, S.D. (2011). Social cure or social curse? The psychological impact of extreme events during the Kosovo conflict. In J. Jetten, C. Haslam, & S.A. Haslam (Eds.), *The social cure* (pp. 217-233). Psychology Press.

Knight, C.J., Harwood, C.G., & Sellars, P.A. (2018). Supporting adolescent athletes' dual careers: The role of an athlete's social support network. *Psychology of Sport and Exercise, 38*, 137-147. http://dx.doi.org/10.1016/j.psychsport.2018.06.007

Knight, C.J., & Holt, N.L. (2014). Parenting in youth tennis: Understanding and enhancing children's experiences. *Psychology of Sport and Exercise, 15*, 155-164. https://doi.org/10.1016/j.psychsport.2013.10.010

Kristiansen, E., & Roberts, G.C. (2010). Young elite athletes and social support: Coping with competitive and organizational stress in "Olympic" competition. *Scandinavian Journal of Medicine and Science in Sports, 20*, 686-695. https://doi.org/10.1111/j.1600-0838.2009.00950.x

Lakey, B. (2010). Basic research in social support suggests new strategies for intervention. In J.E. Maddux & P. Tangey (Eds.), *Social psychological foundations of clinical psychology* (pp. 177-194). Guilford Press.

Lakey, B., & Cohen, S. (2000). Social support theory and measurement. In S. Cohen, L.G. Underwood, & B.H. Gottlieb (Eds.), *Social support measurement and intervention: A guide for health and social scientists* (pp. 29-52). Oxford University Press.

Lakey, B., & Orehek, E. (2011). Relational regulation theory: A new approach to explain the link between perceived social support and mental health. *Psychological Review, 118*(3), 482-495. https://doi.org/10.1037/a0023477

Lane J.A., & Fink, R.S. (2015). Attachment, social support satisfaction, and well-being during life transition in emerging adulthood. *The Counseling Psychologist, 43*(7), 1034-1058. https://doi.org/10.1177%2F0011000015592184

Lazarus, R.S. (1999). *Stress and emotion: A new synthesis.* Springer.

Lazarus, R.S., & Folkman, S. (1984). *Stress appraisal and coping.* Springer.

Lee, D.S., & Ybarra, O. (2017). Cultivating effective social support through abstraction: Reframing social support promotes goal-pursuit. *Personality and Social Psychology Bulletin, 43*(3), 453-464. https://doi.org/10.1177/0146167216688205

Levine, R.M., Prosser, A., Evans, D., & Reicher, S.D. (2005). Identity and emergency intervention: How social group membership and inclusiveness of group boundaries shape helping behavior. *Personality and Social Psychology Bulletin, 31*, 443-453. https://doi.org/10.1177%2F0146167204271651

Liu, W., Li, Z., Ling, Y., & Cai, T. (2016). Core self-evaluations and coping styles as mediators between social support and well-being. *Personality and Individual Differences, 88*, 35-39. http://dx.doi.org/10.1016/j.paid.2015.08.044

Lu, F.J.H., Lee, W.P., Chang, Y., Chou, C., Hsu, Y., Lin, J., & Gill, D.L. (2016). Interaction of athletes' resilience and coaches' social support on the stress-burnout relationship: A conjunctive moderation perspective. *Psychology of Sport and Exercise, 22*, 202-209. https://doi.org/10.1016/j.psychsport.2015.08.005

Lubans, D.R., Morgan, P.J., & McCormack, A. (2011). Adolescents and school sport: The relationship between beliefs, social support and physical self-perception. *Physical Education and Sport Pedagogy, 16*, 237-250. https://doi.org/10.1080/17408989.2010.532784

Lusher, D., Robins, G., & Kremer, P. (2010). The application of social network analysis to team sports. *Measurement in Physical Education and Exercise Science, 14*(4), 211-224. https://doi.org/10.1080/1091367X.2010.495559

Madden, C.C., Kirkby, R.J., & McDonald, D. (1989). Coping styles of competitive middle distance runners. *International Journal of Sport Psychology, 20*, 287-296.

Marigold, D.C., Cavallo, J.V., Holmes, J.G., & Wood, J.V. (2014). You can't always give what you want: The challenge of providing social support to low self-esteem individuals. *Journal of Personality and Social Psychology, 107*, 56-80. https://doi.org/10.1037/a0036554

Meijen, C., Turner, M., Jones, M.V., Sheffield, D., & McCarthy, P. (2020). A theory of challenge and threat states in athletes: A revised conceptualization. *Frontiers in Psychology, 11*(126), 1-17. https://doi.org/10.3389/fpsyg.2020.00126

Mitchell, I., Evans, L., Rees, T., & Hardy, L. (2014). Stressors, social support and the buffering hypothesis: Effects on psychological responses of injured athletes. *British Journal of Health Psychology, 19*, 486-508. https://doi.org/10.1111/bjhp.12046

Moesch, K., Kenttä, G., Kleinert, J., Quignon-Fleuret, C., Cecil, S., & Bertollo, M. (2018). FEPSAC position statement: Mental health disorders in elite athletes and models of service provision. *Psychology of Sport and Exercise, 38*, 61-71. https://doi.org/10.1016/j.psychsport.2018.05.013

Moll, T., Rees, T., & Freeman, P. (2017). Enacted support and golf-putting performance: The role of support type and support visibility. *Psychology of Sport and Exercise, 30*, 30-37. https://doi.org/10.1016/j.psychsport.2017.01.007

Moss, G.E. (1973). *Illness, immunity, and social support interaction.* Wiley.

Nicholson, M., Hoye, R., & Gallant, D. (2011). The provision of social support for elite indigenous athletes in Australian football. *Journal of Sport Management, 25*, 131-142. https://doi.org/10.1123/jsm.25.2.131

Nixon, H.L. (1993). Social network analysis of sport: Emphasizing social structure in sport. *Sociology of Sport Journal, 10*(3), 315-321. https://doi.org/10.1123/ssj.10.3.315

Park, S., Lavallee, D., & Tod, D. (2013). Athletes' career transition out of sport: A systematic review. *International Review of Sport and Exercise Psychology, 6*(1), 22-53. https://doi.org/10.1080/1750984X.2012.687053

Rafaeli, E., & Gleason, M.J. (2009). Skilled support within intimate relationships. *Journal of Family Theory and Review, 1*, 20-37. https://doi.org/10.1111/j.1756-2589.2009.00003.x

Reardon, C.L., Hainline, B., Aron, C.M., Baron, D., Baum, A.L., Bindra, A., Budgett, R., Campriani, N., Castaldelli-Maia, J.M., Currie, A., Derevensky, J.L., Glick, I.D., Gorczynski, P., Gouttebarge, V., Grandner, M.A., Han, D.H., McDuff, D., Mountjoy, M., Polat, A., . . . Engebretsen, L. (2019). Mental health in elite athletes: International Olympic Committee consensus statement. *British Journal of Sports Medicine, 53*(11), 667-699. https://doi.org/10.1136/bjsports-2019-100715

Rees, T. (2016). Social support in sport psychology. In R.J. Schinke, K.R. McGannon, & B. Smith (Eds.), *Routledge international handbook of sports psychology* (pp. 505-515). Routledge.

Rees, T., & Freeman, P. (2007). The effects of perceived and received support on self-confidence. *Journal of Sports Sciences, 25*, 1057-1065. https://doi.org/10.1080/02640410600982279

Rees, T., & Freeman, P. (2009). Social support moderates the relationship between stressors and task performance through self-efficacy. *Journal of Social and Clinical Psychology, 28*, 244-263. http://dx.doi.org/10.1521/jscp.2009.28.2.244

Rees, T., & Freeman, P. (2010). Social support and performance in a golf-putting experiment. *The Sport Psychologist, 24*, 333-348. https://doi.org/10.1123/tsp.24.3.333

Rees, T., & Hardy, L. (2000). An investigation of the social support experiences of high-level sports performers. *The Sport Psychologist, 14*, 327-347. http://dx.doi.org/10.1123/tsp.14.4.327

Rees, T., & Hardy, L. (2004). Matching social support with stressors: Effects on factors underlying performance in tennis. *Psychology of Sport and Exercise, 5*, 319-337. http://dx.doi.org/10.1016/S1469-0292(03)00018-9

Rees, T., Hardy, L., & Freeman, P. (2007). Stressors, social support and effects upon performance in golf. *Journal of Sports Sciences, 25*, 33-42. https://doi.org/10.1080/02640410600702974

Rees, T., Haslam, S.A., Coffee, P., & Lavallee, D. (2015). A social identity approach to sport psychology: Principles, practice, and prospects. *Sports Medicine, 45*(8), 1083-1096. https://doi.org/10.1007/s40279-015-0345-4

Rees, T., Ingledew, D.K., & Hardy, L. (1999). Social support dimensions and components of performance in tennis. *Journal of Sports Sciences, 17*, 421-429. https://doi.org/10.1080/026404199365948

Rees, T., Mitchell, I., Evans, L., & Hardy, L. (2010). Stressors, social support and psychological responses to sport injury in high and low-performance standard participants. *Psychology of Sport and Exercise, 11*, 505-512. https://doi.org/10.1016/j.psychsport.2010.07.002

Richman, J.M., Rosenfeld, L.B., & Hardy, C.J. (1993). The Social Support Survey: A validation of a clinical measure of the social support process. *Research on Social Work Practice, 3*, 288-311. https://doi.org/10.1177%2F104973159300300304

Sanders, P., & Winter, S. (2016). Going pro: Exploring adult triathletes' transitions into elite sport. *Sport, Exercise, and Performance Psychology, 5*, 193-205. https://doi.org/10.1037/spy0000058

Sarason, B.R., Pierce, G.R., & Sarason, I.G. (1990). Social support: The sense of acceptance and the role of relationships. In B.R. Sarason, I.G. Sarason, & G.R. Pierce (Eds.), *Social support: An interactional view* (pp. 97-128). Wiley.

Sarason, I.G., Levine, H.M., Basham, R.B., & Sarason, B.R. (1983). Assessing social support: The Social Support Questionnaire. *Journal of Personality and Social Psychology, 44*, 127-139. https://doi.org/10.1037/0022-3514.44.1.127

Sarason, I.G., & Sarason, B.R. (1986). Experimentally provided social support. *Journal of Personality and Social Psychology, 50*, 1222-1225. https://doi.org/10.1037/0022-3514.50.6.1222

Sarason, I.G., Sarason, B.R., & Pierce, G.R. (1990). Social support, personality and performance. *Journal of Applied Sport Psychology, 2*, 117-127. https://doi.org/10.1080/10413209008406425

Sarason, I.G., Sarason, B.R., Shearin, E.N., & Pierce, G.R. (1987). A brief measure of social support: Practical and theoretical implications. *Journal of Social and Personal Relationships, 4*(4), 497-510. https://doi.org/10.1177/0265407587044007

Sarkar, M., & Fletcher, D. (2014). Psychological resilience in sport performers: A review of stressors and protective factors. *Journal of Sports Sciences, 32*, 1419-1434. https://doi.org/10.1080/02640414.2014.901551

Schinke, R.J., Stambulova, N.B., Si, G., & Moore, Z. (2017). International society of sport psychology position stand: Athletes' mental health, performance, and development. *International Journal of Sport and Exercise Psychology*. https://doi.org/10.1080/1612197X.2017.1295557

Shang, Y., & Yang, S.Y. (2021). The effect of social support on athlete burnout in weightlifters: The mediation effect of mental toughness and sports motivation. *Frontiers in Psychology, 12*, 649677. https://doi.org/10.3389/fpsyg.2021.649677

Sharp, L.-A., Hodge, K., & Danish, S. (2015). Ultimately it comes down to the relationship: Experienced consultants' views of effective sport psychology consulting. *The Sport Psychologist, 29*(4), 358-370. https://doi.org/10.1123/tsp.2014-0130

Sheridan, D., Coffee, P., & Lavallee, D. (2014). A systematic review of social support in youth sport. *International Review of Sport and Exercise Psychology, 7*(1), 198-228. https://doi.org/10.1080/1750984X.2014.931999

Slater, M., Rovira, A., Southern, R., Swapp, D., Zhang, J.J., Campbell, C., & Levine M. (2013). Bystander responses to a violent incident in an immersive virtual environment. *PLOS One, 8*(1), 52766. https://doi.org/10.1371/journal.pone.0052766

Sly, D., Wagstaff, C., & Mellalieu, S. (2020). "It's psychology Jim, but not as we know it!": the changing face of applied sport psychology practice. *Sport, Exercise, and Performance Psychology, 9*(1), 87-101. https://doi.org/10.1037/spy0000163

Steffens, N.K., Jetten, J., Haslam, C., Cruwys, T., & Haslam, S.A. (2016). Multiple social identities enhance health post-retirement because they are a basis for giving social support. *Frontiers in Psychology, 7*, 1519. https://dx.doi.org/10.3389%2Ffpsyg.2016.01519

Stroebe, W., & Stroebe, M. (1996). The social psychology of social support. In E.T. Higgins & A.W. Kruglanski (Eds.), *Social psychology: Handbook of basic principles* (pp. 597-621). Guilford Press.

Tajfel, H., & Turner, J.C. (1979). An integrative theory of intergroup conflict. In W.G. Austin & S. Worchel (Eds.), *The social psychology of intergroup relations* (pp. 33-47). Brooks-Cole.

Thoits, P.A. (1995). Stress, coping, and social support processes: Where are we? What next? *Journal of Health and Social Behavior, 35*, 53-79. https://doi.org/10.2307/2626957

Thoits, P.A. (2011). Mechanisms linking social ties and support to physical and mental health. *Journal of Health and Social Behavior, 52*, 145-161. https://doi.org/10.1177%2F0022146510395592

Turner, J.C., Hogg, M.A., Oakes, P.J., Reicher, S.D., & Wetherell, M.S. (1987). *Rediscovering the social group: A self-categorization theory*. Blackwell.

Uchino, B.N. (2004). *Social support and physical health: Understanding the health consequences of relationships*. Yale University Press. https://doi.org/10.12987/yale/9780300102185.001.0001

Uchino, B.N. (2009). Understanding the links between social support and physical health: A lifespan perspective with emphasis on the separability of perceived and received support. *Perspectives in Psychological Science, 4*, 236-255. https://doi.org/10.1111%2Fj.1745-6924.2009.01122.x

Udry, E., Gould, D., Bridges, D., & Tuffey, S. (1997). People helping people? Examining the social ties of athletes coping with burnout and injury stress. *Journal of Sport and Exercise Psychology, 19*, 368-395. https://doi.org/10.1123/jsep.19.4.368

Vangelisti, A.L. (2009). Challenges in conceptualizing social support. *Journal of Social and Personal Relationships, 26*, 39-51. https://doi.org/10.1177/0265407509105520

Veiel, H.O.F., & Baumann, U. (1992). *The meaning and measurement of social support*. Hemisphere.

Wadey, R., Evans, L., Hanton, S., & Neil, R. (2012). An examination of hardiness throughout the sport injury process: A qualitative follow-up study. *British Journal of Health Psychology, 17*, 872-893. https://doi.org/10.1111/j.2044-8287.2012.02084.x

Wainwright, E., Fox, F., Breffni, T., Taylor, G., & O'Connor, M. (2017). Coming back from the edge: A qualitative study of a professional support unit for junior doctors. *BMC Medical Education, 17*(1), 142. https://doi.org/10.1186/s12909-017-0978-0

Wasserman, S., & Faust, K. (1994). *Social network analysis: Methods and applications*. Cambridge University Press. https://doi.org/10.1017/CBO9780511815478

Way, A., Jones, M.V., & Slater, M.J. (2012). Exploring training adherence in elite school-age athletes. *Qualitative Research in Sport, Exercise and Health, 4*, 154-171. https://doi.org/10.1080/2159676X.2011.653496

Willard, V.C., & Lavallee, D. (2016). Retirement experiences of elite ballet dancers: Impact of self-identity and social support. *Sport, Exercise, and Performance Psychology, 5*(3), 266-279. https://doi.org/10.1037/spy0000057

Zourbanos, N., Hatzigeorgiadis, A., Goudas, M., Papaioannou, A., Chroni, S., & Theodorakis, Y. (2011). The social side of self-talk: Relationships between perceptions of support received from the coach and athletes' self-talk. *Psychology of Sport and Exercise, 12*, 407-414. https://doi.org/10.1016/j.psychsport.2011.03.001

Chapter 15

Alarcon, A. (2016, March 3). Los Angeles Rams might be building around QB Case Keenum. Fansided. https://ramblinfan.com/2016/03/20/los-angeles-rams-might-be-building-around-qb-case-keenum

Bandura, A. (1977). Self-efficacy: Toward a unifying theory of behavioral change. *Psychological Review, 84*(2), 191-215. https://doi.org/10.1037/0033-295X.84.2.191

Bandura, A. (1986). *Social foundations of thought and action: A social cognitive theory.* Prentice Hall.

Bandura, A. (1997). *Self-efficacy: The exercise of control.* Freeman.

Bandura, A. (1999). Social cognitive theory of personality. In D. Cervone & Y. Shoda (Eds.), *The coherence of personality: Social-cognitive bases of consistency, variability, and organization* (pp. 105-241). Guilford Press.

Bandura, A. (2000). Exercise of human agency through collective efficacy. *Current Directions in Psychological Science, 9*, 75-78.

Bass, B.M., & Avolio, B.J. (1994). *Improving organizational effectiveness through transformational leadership.* Sage.

Beauchamp, M.R., & Bray, S.R. (2001). Role ambiguity and role conflict within interdependent teams. *Small Group Research, 32*, 133-157.

Beauchamp, M.R., Bray, S.R., Eys, M.A., & Carron, A.V. (2002). Role ambiguity, role efficacy, and role performance: Multidimensional and mediational relationships within interdependent sport teams. *Group Dynamics: Theory, Research, and Practice, 6*, 229-242.

Beauchamp, M.R., & Whinton, L.C. (2005). Self-efficacy and other-efficacy in dyadic performance: Riding as one in equestrian eventing. *Journal of Sport and Exercise Psychology, 27*, 245-252.

Biddle, B.J., & Thomas, E.J. (1966). *Role theory: Concepts and research.* Wiley.

Boardley, I.D. (2018). Coaching efficacy research: Learning from the past and looking to the future. *International Review of Sport and Exercise Psychology, 11*(1), 214-237. https://doi.org/10.1080/1750984X.2017.1290816

Bray, S.R. (2004). Collective efficacy, group goals, and group performance of a muscular endurance task. *Small Group Research, 35*, 230-238.

Bray, S.R., Balaguer, I., & Duda, J.L. (2004). The relationship of task self-efficacy and role efficacy beliefs to role performance in Spanish youth soccer. *Journal of Sports Sciences, 22*, 429-437.

Bray, S.R., & Brawley, L.R. (2002). Role efficacy, role clarity, and role performance effectiveness. *Small Group Research, 33*, 233-253.

Bray, S.R., Brawley, L.R., & Carron, A.V. (2002). Efficacy for interdependent role functions: Evidence from the sport domain. *Small Group Research, 33*, 644-666.

Bray, S.R., Gyurcsik, N.C., Culos-Reed, S.N., Dawson, K.A., & Martin, K.A. (2001). An exploratory investigation of the relationship between proxy efficacy, self-efficacy and exercise attendance. *Journal of Health Psychology, 6*(4), 425-434.

Bray, S.R., Gyurcsik, N.C., Martin-Ginis, K.A., & Culos-Reed, S.N. (2004). The proxy efficacy exercise questionnaire: Development of an instrument to assess female exercisers' proxy efficacy beliefs in structured group exercise classes. *Journal of Sport and Exercise Psychology, 26*, 442-456.

Brooks, C. (2020, October 7). Dylan DeMelo ready to "win cup in Winnipeg." Full Press Coverage. https://fullpresscoverage.com/2020/10/07/dylan-demelo-ready-to-win-a-cup-in-winnipeg

Bruton, A.M., Mellalieu, S.D., & Shearer, D.A. (2014). Observation interventions as a means to manipulate collective efficacy in groups. *Journal of Sport and Exercise Psychology, 36*(1), 27-39. https://doi.org/10.1123/jsep.2013-0058

Bruton, A.M., Mellalieu, S.D., & Shearer, D.A. (2016). Observation as a method to enhance collective efficacy: An integrative review. *Psychology of Sport and Exercise, 24*, 1-8. https://doi.org/10.1016/j.psychsport.2016.01.002

Bruton, A.M., Shearer, D.A., & Mellalieu, S.D. (2019). Who said "there is no 'I' in team"? The effects of observational learning content level on efficacy beliefs in groups. *Psychology of Sport and Exercise, 45*, 1-11. https://doi.org/10.1016/j.psychsport.2019.101563

Caprara, G.V., Barbaranelli, C., Borgogni, L., Petitta, L., & Rubinacci, A. (2003). Teachers', school staff's and parents' efficacy beliefs as determinants of attitudes toward school. *European Journal of Psychology of Education, 18*, 15-31.

Caprara, G.V., Barbaranelli, C., Borgogni, L., & Steca, P. (2003). Efficacy beliefs as determinants of teachers' job satisfaction. *Journal of Educational Psychology, 95*, 821-832.

CBC Sports. (2020). From humble beginnings to Canada's most decorated distance runner, Moh Ahmed is going the distance. YouTube. www.youtube.com/watch?v=_yOUANRAN-I

Chan, D. (1998). Functional relations among constructs in the same content domain at different levels of analysis: A typology of composition models. *Journal of Applied Psychology, 83*(2), 234-246. https://doi.org/10.1037/0021-9010.83.2.234

Chase, M.A., Lirgg, C.D., & Feltz, D.L. (1997). Do coaches' efficacy expectations for their team predict team performance? *The Sport Psychologist, 11*, 8-23.

Clarey, C. (2018, September 30). Ryder cup 2018: Europe again defends its soil against the U.S. *New York Times*, 1. www.nytimes.com/2018/09/30/sports/golf/ryder-cup.html

Collins, H., Booth, J.N., Duncan, A., Fawkner, S., & Niven, A. (2019). The effect of resistance training interventions on fundamental movement skills in youth: A meta-analysis. *Sports Medicine – Open, 5*(29), 1-14. https://doi.org/10.1186/s40798-019-0188-x

Denham, C.H., & Michael, J.J. (1981). Teacher sense of efficacy: A definition of the construct and a model for further research. *Educational Research Quarterly, 5*, 39-63.

Dunlop, W.L., Beatty, D.J., & Beauchamp, M.R. (2011). Examining the influence of other-efficacy and self-efficacy on personal performance. *Journal of Sport and Exercise Psychology, 33*(4), 586-593. https://doi.org/10.1123/jsep.33.4.586

Feltz, D.L., Chase, M.A., Moritz, S.E., & Sullivan, P.J. (1999). A conceptual model of coaching efficacy: Preliminary investigation and instrument development. *Journal of Educational Psychology, 91*(4), 765-776. https://doi.org/10.1037/0022-0663.91.4.765

Feltz, D.L., & Lirgg, C.D. (1998). Perceived team and player efficacy in hockey. *Journal of Applied Psychology, 83*, 557-564.

Fransen, K., Decroos, S., Vanbeselaere, N., Vande Broek, G., De Cuyper, B., Vanroy, J., & Boen, F. (2015). Is team confidence the key to success? The reciprocal relation between collective efficacy, team outcome confidence, and perceptions of team performance during soccer games. *Journal of Sports Sciences, 33*(3), 219-231. https://doi.org/10.1080/02640414.2014.942689

Fransen, K., Haslam, S.A., Steffens, N.K., Vanbeselaere, N., De Cuyper, B., & Boen, F. (2015). Believing in "us": Exploring leaders' capacity to enhance team confidence and performance by building a sense of shared social identity. *Journal of Experimental Psychology: Applied, 21*(1), 89-100. https://doi.org/10.1037/xap0000033

Fransen, K., Kleinert, J., Dithurbide, L., Vanbeselaere, N., & Boen, F. (2014). Collective efficacy or team outcome confidence? Development and validation of the Observational Collective Efficacy Scale for Sports (OCESS). *International Journal of Sport Psychology, 45*(2), 121-137. https://doi.org/10.7352/IJSP

Fransen, K., Steffens, N.K., Haslam, S.A., Vanbeselaere, N., Vande Broek, G., & Boen, F. (2016). We will be champions: Leaders' confidence in 'us' inspires team members' team confidence and performance. *Scandinavian Journal of Medicine and Science in Sports, 26*(12), 1455-1469. https://doi.org/10.1111/sms.12603

Fransen, K., Vanbeselaere, N., De Cuyper, B., Vande Broek, G., & Boen, F. (2014). The myth of the team captain as principal leader: Extending the athlete leadership classification within sport teams. *Journal of Sports Sciences, 32*(14), 1389-1397. https://doi.org/10.1080/02640414.2014.891291

Gaudreau, P., Schellenberg, B., & Gareau, A. (2020). Multilevel designs and modeling in sport and exercise psychology. In G. Tenenbaum & R.C. Eklund (Eds.), *Handbook of sport psychology* (4th ed., pp. 1074-1096). Wiley. https://doi.org/10.1002/9781119568124.ch52

Greenlees, I.A., Nunn, R.L., Graydon, J.K., & Maynard, I.W. (1999). The relationship between collective efficacy and precompetitive affect in rugby players: Testing Bandura's model of collective efficacy. *Perceptual Motor Skills, 89*, 431-440.

Habeeb, C.M., Eklund, R.C., & Coffee, P. (2017). It depends on the partner: Person-related sources of efficacy beliefs and performance for athlete pairs. *Journal of Sport and Exercise Psychology, 39*(3), 172-187. https://doi.org/10.1123/jsep.2016-0348

Habeeb, C.M., Eklund, R.C., & Coffee, P. (2019). Reciprocal relationships between efficacy and performance in athlete dyads: Self-, other-, and collective constructs. *Journal of Sport and Exercise Psychology, 41*(3), 147-158. https://doi.org/10.1123/jsep.2018-0248

Haslam, S.A., Reicher, S.D., & Platow, M.J. (2011). *The new psychology of leadership: Identity, influence and power.* Psychology Press.

Heuzé, J.-P., Raimbault, N., & Fontayne, P. (2006). Relationships between cohesion, collective efficacy and performance in professional basketball teams: An examination of mediating effects. *Journal of Sports Sciences, 24*(1), 59-68. https://doi.org/10.1080/02640410500127736

Higgins, T.J., Middleton, K.R., Winner, L., & Janelle, C.M. (2014). Physical activity interventions differentially affect exercise task and barrier self-efficacy: A meta-analysis. *Health Psychology, 33*(8), 891-903. https://doi.org/10.1037/a0033864

Hoyt, C.L., Murphy, S.E., Halverson, S.K., & Watson, C.B. (2003). Group leadership: Efficacy and effectiveness. *Group Dynamics: Theory, Research, and Practice, 7*(4), 259-274. https://doi.org/10.1037/1089-2699.7.4.259

Hwang, S., Feltz, D.L., & Lee, J.D. (2013). Emotional intelligence in coaching: Mediation effect of coaching efficacy on the relationship between emotional intelligence and leadership style. *International Journal of Sport and Exercise Psychology, 11*(3), 292-306. https://doi.org/10.1080/1612197X.2013.763489

Jackson, B., & Beauchamp, M.R. (2010). Efficacy beliefs in coach–athlete dyads: Prospective relationships using actor–partner interdependence models. *Applied Psychology, 59*(2), 220-242. https://doi.org/10.1111/j.1464-0597.2009.00388.x

Jackson, B., Beauchamp, M.R., & Dimmock, J.A. (2020). Efficacy beliefs in physical activity settings: Contemporary debate and unanswered questions. In G. Tenenbaum & R.C. Eklund (Eds.), *Handbook of sport psychology* (4th ed., pp. 57-80). Wiley.

Jackson, B., Beauchamp, M.R., & Knapp, P. (2007). Relational efficacy beliefs in athlete dyads: An investigation using actor–partner interdependence models. *Journal of Sport and Exercise Psychology, 29*, 170-189.

Jackson, B., Grove, J.R., & Beauchamp, M.R. (2010). Relational efficacy beliefs and relationship quality within coach–athlete dyads. *Journal of Social and Personal Relationships, 27*(8), 1035-1050. https://doi.org/10.1177/0265407510378123

Jackson, B., Gucciardi, D.F., Lonsdale, C., Whipp, P.R., & Dimmock, J.A. (2014). "I think they believe in me": The predictive effects of teammate- and classmate-focused relation-inferred self-efficacy in sport and physical activity settings. *Journal of Sport and Exercise Psychology, 36*(5), 486-505. https://doi.org/10.1123/jsep.2014-0070

Jex, S.M., & Bliese, P.D. (1999). Efficacy beliefs as a moderator of the impact of work-related stressors: A multilevel study. *Journal of Applied Psychology, 84*, 349-361.

Kenny, D.A., Kashy, D.A., & Cook, W.L. (2006). *Dyadic data analysis.* Guilford Press.

Kent, A., & Sullivan, P.J. (2003). Coaching efficacy as a predictor of university coaches' commitment. *International Sports Journal, 7*, 78-88.

Lent, R.W., & Lopez, F.G. (2002). Cognitive ties that bind: A tripartite view of efficacy beliefs in growth-promoting relationships. *Journal of Social and Clinical Psychology, 21*, 256-286.

Lindsley, D.H., Brass, D.J., & Thomas, J.B. (1995). Efficacy-performance spirals: A multi-level perspective. *Academy of Management Review, 20*, 645-678.

Mabry, E.A., & Barnes, R.E. (1980). *The dynamics of small group communication.* Prentice Hall.

Malete, L., & Feltz, D.L. (2000). The effect of a coaching education program on coaching efficacy. *The Sport Psychologist, 14*, 410-417.

McEwan, D. (2020). The effects of perceived teamwork on emergent states and satisfaction with performance among team sport athletes. *Sport, Exercise, and Performance Psychology, 9*(1), 1-15. https://doi.org/10.1037/spy0000166

McEwan, D., & Beauchamp, M.R. (2014). Teamwork in sport: A theoretical and integrative review. *International Review of Sport and Exercise Psychology, 7*(1), 229-250. https://doi.org/10.1080/1750984X.2014.932423

McEwan, D., & Beauchamp, M.R. (2020). Teamwork training in sport: A pilot intervention study. *Journal of Applied Sport Psychology, 32*(2), 220-236. https://doi.org/10.1080/10413200.2018.1518277

Messick, S. (1995). Validity of psychological assessment: Validation of inferences from persons' responses and performances as scientific inquiry into score meaning. *American Psychologist, 50*(9), 741-749. https://doi.org/10.1037//0003-066X.50.9.741

Molinaro, J. (2021, July 19). Bev Priestman relishes her journey from working-class England to the Olympic stage. CBC Sports. www.cbc.ca/sports/olympics/summer/soccer/priestman-canada-women-s-olympic-soccer-1.6107799

Myers, N.D., & Feltz, D.L. (2007). From self-efficacy to collective efficacy in sport: Transitional methodological issues. In G. Tenenbaum & R.C. Eklund (Eds.), *Handbook of sport psychology* (3rd ed., pp. 799-819). Wiley. https://doi.org/10.1002/9781118270011.ch36

Myers, N.D., Feltz, D.L., & Chase, M.A. (2011). Proposed modifications to the conceptual model of coaching efficacy and additional validity evidence for the Coaching Efficacy Scale II-High School Teams. *Research Quarterly for Exercise and Sport, 82*(1), 79-88. https://doi.org/10.1080/02701367.2011.10599724

Myers, N.D., Feltz, D.L., Chase, M.A., Reckase, M.D., & Hancock, G.R. (2008). The Coaching Efficacy Scale II-High School Teams. *Educational and Psychological Measurement, 68*(6), 1059-1076. https://doi.org/10.1177/0013164408318773

Myers, N.D., Feltz, D.L., & Short, S.E. (2004). Collective efficacy and team performance: A longitudinal study of collegiate football teams. *Group Dynamics: Theory, Research, and Practice, 8*(2), 126-138. https://doi.org/10.1037/1089-2699.8.2.126

Myers, N.D., Paiement, C.A., & Feltz, D.L. (2007). Regressing team performance on collective efficacy: Considerations of temporal proximity and concordance. *Measurement in Physical Education and Exercise Science, 11*(1), 1-24. https://doi.org/10.1080/10913670709337009

Myers, N.D., Park, S.E., Ahn, S., Lee, S., Sullivan, P.J., & Feltz, D.L. (2017). Proposed sources of coaching efficacy: A meta-analysis. *Journal of Sport and Exercise Psychology, 39*(4), 261-276. https://doi.org/10.1123/jsep.2017-0155

Myers, N.D., Payment, C.A., & Feltz, D.L. (2004). Reciprocal relationships between collective efficacy and team performance in women's ice hockey. *Group Dynamics: Theory, Research, and Practice, 8*(3), 182-195. https://doi.org/10.1037/1089-2699.8.3.182

Myers, N.D., Vargas-Tonsing, T.M., & Feltz, D.L. (2005). Coaching efficacy in intercollegiate coaches: Sources, coaching behavior, and team variables. *Psychology of Sport and Exercise, 6*(1), 129-143. https://doi.org/10.1016/j.psychsport.2003.10.007

Myers, N.D., Wolfe, E.W., & Feltz, D.L. (2005). An evaluation of the psychometric properties of the coaching efficacy scale for coaches from the United States of America. *Measurement in Physical Education and Exercise Science, 9*(3), 135-160. https://doi.org/10.1207/ s15327841mpee0903_1

Price, M.S., & Weiss, M.R. (2013). Relationships among coach leadership, peer leadership, and adolescent athletes' psychosocial and team outcomes: A test of transformational leadership theory. *Journal of Applied Sport Psychology, 25*(2), 265-279. https://doi.org/10.1080/10413200.2012.725703

RugbyPass. (2020, May 5). Ian Foster announces his new All Blacks captain. www.rugbypass.com/news/ian-foster-announces-his-new-all-blacks-captain

Saville, P.D., & Bray, S.R. (2016). Athletes' perceptions of coaching behavior, Relation-Inferred Self-Efficacy (RISE), and self-efficacy in youth sport. *Journal of Applied Sport Psychology, 28*(1), 1-13. https://doi.org/10.1080/10413200.2015.1052890

Saville, P.D., & Bray, S.R. (2018). Workshop effects on measures of coaches' cognitions towards integrating relation-inferred self-efficacy communication into practice. *Journal of Sport Behavior, 41*(2), 189-208.

Seefeldt, V., & Brown, E.W. (1990). *Program for athletic coaches' education*. Benchmark Press.

Shaw, M.E., & Costanzo, P.R. (1982). *Theories of social psychology* (2nd ed.). McGraw-Hill.

Sherif, M., & Sherif, C.W. (1953). *Groups in harmony and tension*. Harper & Row.

Short, S.E., Sullivan, P., & Feltz, D.L. (2005). Development and preliminary validation of the Collective Efficacy Questionnaire for Sports. *Measurement in Physical Education and Exercise Science, 9*(3), 181-202.

Shultz, A. (2020, April 10). The real-life diet of the NHL's Nathan MacKinnon, who changed his diet and became a star. GQ: Real Life Diet. www.gq.com/story/real-life-diet-nathan-mackinnon

Sullivan, P., Paquette, K.J., Holt, N.L., & Bloom, G.A. (2012). The relation of coaching context and coach education to coaching efficacy and perceived leadership behaviors in youth sport. *Sport Psychologist, 26*(1), 122-134. https://doi.org/10.1123/tsp.26.1.122

Tasa, K., Taggar, S., & Seijts, G.H. (2007). The development of collective efficacy in teams: A multilevel and longitudinal perspective. *Journal of Applied Psychology, 92*(1), 17-27. https://doi.org/10.1037/0021-9010.92.1.17

U.S. Soccer. (2018). Jill Ellis: "I feel really good about this group of players." YouTube. www.youtube.com/watch?v=-MWKF-n0rYP0

Watson, C.B., Chemers, M.M., & Preiser, N. (2001). Collective efficacy: A multilevel analysis. *Personality and Social Psychology Bulletin, 27*, 1057-1068.

Williams, S.L., & French, D.P. (2011). What are the most effective intervention techniques for changing physical activity self-efficacy and physical activity behaviour—and are they the same? *Health Education Research, 26*(2), 308-322. https://doi.org/10.1093/her/cyr005

Wright, B.J., O'Halloran, P.D., & Stukas, A.A. (2016). Enhancing self-efficacy and performance: An experimental comparison of psychological techniques. *Research Quarterly for Exercise and Sport, 87*(1), 36-46. https://doi.org/10.1080/02701367.2015.1093072

Zaccaro, S.J., Blair, V., Peterson, C., & Zazanis, M. (1995). Collective efficacy. In J.E. Maddux (Ed.), *Self-efficacy, adaptation, and adjustment* (pp. 305-330). Plenum Press.

Zumbo, B.D. (2007). Validity: Foundational issues and statistical methodology. In C.R. Rao & S. Sinharay (Eds.), *Handbook of statistics. Vol. 26: Psychometrics* (pp. 45-79). Elsevier Science.

Zumbo, B.D. (2009). Validity as contextualized and pragmatic explanation, and its implications for validation practice. In R.W. Lissitz (Ed.), *The concept of validity: Revisions, new directions, and applications* (pp. 65-82). Information Age Publishing. https://doi.org/10.1111/j.1745-3984.2011.00155.x

Chapter 16

Barsade, S.G. (2002). The ripple effect: Emotional contagion and its influence on group behavior. *Administrative Science Quarterly, 47*(4), 644-675. https://doi.org/10.2307/3094912

Bodenmann, G. (1995). A systemic-transactional conceptualization of stress and coping in couples. *Swiss Journal of Psychology, 54*(1), 34-49.

Bodenmann, G. (1997). Dyadic coping: A systemic-transactional view of stress and coping among couples: Theory and empirical findings. *European Review of Applied Psychology, 47*(2), 137-141.

Bodenmann, G. (2005). Dyadic coping and its significance for marital functioning. In T.A. Revenson, K. Kayser, & G. Bodenmann (Eds.), *Couples coping with stress: Emerging perspectives on dyadic coping* (pp. 33-50). American Psychological Association.

Bodenmann, G., Pihet, S., & Kayser, K. (2006). The relationship between dyadic coping and marital quality: A 2-year longitudinal study. *Journal of Family Psychology, 20*(3), 485-493. https://doi.org/10.1037/0893-3200.20.3.485

Braun, C., & Tamminen, K.A. (2019). Interpersonal emotion regulation among individual varsity sport coaches and their athletes. *Movement and Sport Sciences – Science and Motricité, 105*, 37-51. https://doi.org/10.1051/sm/2019011

Campo, M., Champely, S., Louvet, B., Rosnet, E., Ferrand, C., Pauketat, J.V.T., & Mackie, D.M. (2019). Group-based emotions: Evidence for emotion-performance relationships in team sports. *Research Quarterly for Exercise and Sport, 90*(1), 54-63. https://doi.org/10.1080/02701367.2018.1563274

Campo, M., Mackie, D., Champely, S., Lacassagna, M., Pellet, J., & Louvet, B. (2019). Athletes' social identities: Their influence on precompetitive group-based emotions. *Journal of Sport and Exercise Psychology, 41*(6), 380-385. https://doi.org/10.1123/jsep.2018-0282

Campo, M., Matinent, G., Pellet, J., Boulanger, J., Louvet, B., & Nicolas, M. (2018). Emotion–performance relationships in team sport: The role of personal and social identities. *International Journal of Sports Science and Coaching, 13*(5), 629-635. https://doi.org/10.1177/1747954118785256

Campo, M., Sanchez, X., Ferrand, C., Rosnet, E., Friesen, A., & Lane, A.M. (2017). Interpersonal emotion regulation in team sport: Mechanisms and reasons to regulate teammates' emotions examined. *International Journal of Sport and Exercise Psychology, 15*(4), 379-394. https://doi.org/10.1080/1612197X.2015.1114501

Cotterill, S.T., Clarkson, B.G., & Fransen, K. (2020). Gender differences in the perceived impact that athlete leaders have on team member emotional states. *Journal of Sports Sciences, 38*(10), 1181-1185. https://doi.org/10.1080/02640414.2020.1745460

Coyne, J.C., & Fiske, V. (1992). Couples coping with chronic and catastrophic illness. In M.A.P. Stephens, S.E. Hobfoll, & J. Crowther (Eds.), *Family health psychology* (pp. 129-149). Hemisphere Publication Services.

DeFreese, J.D., & Smith, A.L. (2013). Teammate social support, burnout, and self-determined motivation in collegiate athletes. *Psychology of Sport and Exercise, 14*(2), 258-265. https://doi.org/10.1016/j.psychsport.2012.10.009

DeLongis, A., & O'Brien, T.B. (1990). An interpersonal framework for stress and coping: An application to the families of Alzheimer's patients. In M.A.P. Stephens, J.H. Crowther, S.E. Hobfoll, & D.L. Tennenbaum (Eds.), *Stress and coping in later-life families* (pp. 221-239). Hemisphere Publication Services.

Didymus, F.F. (2017). Olympic and international level sports coaches' experiences of stressors, appraisals, and coping. *Qualitative Research in Sport, Exercise and Health, 9*(2), 214-232. https://doi.org/10.1080/2159676X.2016.1261364

Didymus, F.F., & Fletcher, D. (2012). Getting to the heart of the matter: A diary study of swimmers' appraisals of organizational stressors. *Journal of Sports Sciences, 30*(13), 1375-1385. https://doi.org/10.1080/02640414.2012.709263

Didymus, F.F., & Fletcher, D. (2014). Swimmers' experiences of organizational stress: Exploring the role of cognitive appraisal and coping strategies. *Journal of Clinical Sport Psychology, 8*(2), 159-183. https://doi.org/10.1123/jcsp.2014-0020

Dixon, M., Turner, M.J., & Gillman, J. (2017). Examining the relationships between challenge and threat cognitive appraisals and coaching behaviours in football coaches. *Journal of Sports Sciences, 35*(24), 2446-2452. https://doi.org/10.1080/02640414.2016.1273538

Dixon-Gordon, K. L., Bernecker, S. L., & Christensen, K. (2015). Recent innovations in the field of interpersonal emotion regulation. *Current Opinion in Psychology, 3*, 36-42. https://doi.org/10.1016/j.copsyc.2015.02.001

Donoso-Morales, D., Bloom, G. A., & Caron, J. G. (2017). Creating and sustaining a culture of excellence: Insights from accomplished university team-sport coaches. *Research Quarterly for Exercise and Sport, 88*(4), 503–512. https://doi.org/10.1080/02701367.2017.1370531

Doron, J., & Bourbousson, J. (2017). How stressors are dynamically appraised within a team during a game: An exploratory study in basketball. *Scandinavian Journal of Medicine and Science in Sports, 27*(12), 2080-2090. https://doi.org/10.1111/sms.12796

Doron, J., & Martinent, G. (2017). Appraisal, coping, emotion, and performance during elite fencing matches: A random coefficient regression model approach. *Scandinavian Journal of Medicine and Science in Sports, 27*(9), 1015-1025. https://doi.org/10.1111/sms.12711

Ekman, P. (1992). An argument for basic emotions. *Cognition and Emotion, 6*(3-4), 169-200. https://doi.org/10.1080/02699939208411068

Freeman, P., & Rees, T. (2009). How does perceived support lead to better performance? An examination of potential mechanisms. *Journal of Applied Sport Psychology, 21*(4), 429-441. https://doi.org/10.1080/10413200903222913

Friesen, A.P., Devonport, T.J., Sellars, C.N., & Lane, A.M. (2015). Examining interpersonal emotion regulation strategies and moderating factors in ice hockey. *Athletic Insight, 7*(2), 143-160.

Frijda, N.H., & Mesquita, B. (1994). The social roles and functions of emotions. In S. Kitayama & H.R. Markus (Eds.), *Emotion and culture: Empirical studies of mutual influence* (pp. 51-87). American Psychological Association.

Gaudreau, P., Morinville, A., Gareau, A., Verner-Filion, J., Green-Demers, I., & Franche, V. (2016). Autonomy support from parents and coaches: Synergistic or compensatory effects on sport-related outcomes of adolescent-athletes? *Psychology of Sport and Exercise, 25*, 89-99. https://doi.org/10.1016/j.psychsport.2016.04.006

Gaudreau, P., Nicholls, A., & Levy, A.R. (2010). The ups and downs of coping and sport achievement: An episodic process analysis of within-person associations. *Journal of Sport and Exercise Psychology, 32*(3), 298-311. https://doi.org/10.1123/jsep.32.3.298

Giazitzoglu, A. (2020). This sporting life: The intersection of hegemonic masculinities, space and emotions among rugby players. *Gender, Work and Organization, 27*(1), 67-81. https://doi.org/10.1111/gwao.12367

Goldenberg, A., Saguy, T., & Halperin, E. (2014). How group-based emotions are shaped by collective emotions: Evidence for emotional transfer and emotional burden. *Journal of Personality and Social Psychology, 107*(4), 581-596. https://doi.org/10.1037/a0037462

Gross, J.J. (1998). The emerging field of emotion regulation: An integrative review. *Review of General Psychology, 2*(3), 271-299. https://doi.org/10.1037/1089-2680.2.3.271

Gurman, A.S. (2011). Couple therapies. In S.B. Messer & A.S. Gurman (Eds.), *Essential psychotherapies: Theory and practice* (3rd ed., pp. 345-386). Guilford Press.

Hanin, Y.L. (2007). Emotions in sport: Current issues and perspectives. In G. Tenenbaum & R.C. Eklund (Eds.), *Handbook of sport psychology* (p. 31-58). Wiley.

Harwood, C.G., Thrower, S.N., Slater, M.J., Didymus, F.F., & Frearson, L. (2019). Advancing our understanding of psychological stress and coping among parents in organized youth sport. *Frontiers in Psychology, 10*, 1600. https://doi.org/10.3389/fpsyg.2019.01600

Hoar, S.D., Crocker, P.R.E., Holt, N., & Tamminen, K.A. (2010). Gender differences in adolescent athletes' coping with interpersonal stressors in sport: More similarities than differences? *Journal of Applied Sport Psychology, 22*(2), 134-149. https://doi.org/10.1080/10413201003664640

Jones, M., Meijen, C., McCarthy, P.J., and Sheffield, D. (2009). A theory of challenge and threat states in athletes. *International Review of Sport and Exercise Psychology, 2*(2), 161-180. https://doi.org/10.1080/17509840902829331

Kayser, K., Watson, L.E., & Andrade, J.T. (2007). Cancer as a "we-disease": Examining the process of coping from a relational perspective. *Families, Systems, and Health, 25*(4), 404-418. https://doi.org/10.1037/1091-7527.25.4.404

Kim, J., Tamminen, K.A., Harris, C., & Sutherland, S. (2021). A mixed-method examination of coaches' interpersonal emotion regulation toward athletes. *International Sport Coaching Journal*. Advance online publication. https://doi.org/10.1123/iscj.2021-0006

Körner, A., Würz, J., Brosseau, D.C., Brähler, E., Kapellen, T., & Kiess, W. (2013). Parental dyadic coping in families of children and adolescents with type 1 diabetes. *Journal of Pediatric Endocrinology and Metabolism, 26*(9-10), 867-875. https://doi.org/10.1515/jpem-2012-0410

Lazarus, R. S. (1999). *Stress and emotion: A new synthesis*. Springer.

Lazarus, R.S., & Folkman, S. (1984). *Stress, appraisal, and coping*. Springer.

Leprince, C., d'Arripe-Longueville, F., Chanal, J., & Doron, J. (2019). Development and preliminary validation of the Communal Coping Strategies Inventory for Competitive Team Sports. *Psychology of Sport and Exercise, 45*, 101569. https://doi.org/10.1016/j.psychsport.2019.101569

Leprince, C., d'Arripe-Longueville, F., & Doron, J. (2018). Coping in teams: Exploring athletes' communal coping strategies to deal with shared stressors. *Frontiers in Psychology, 9*, 1908. https://doi.org/10.3389/fpsyg.2018.01908

Lyons, R.F., Mickelson, K.D., Sullivan, M.J., & Coyne, J.C. (1998). Coping as a communal process. *Journal of Social and Personal Relationships, 15*(5), 579-605. https://doi.org/10.1177/0265407598155001

Meijen, C., Turner, M., Jones, M.V., Sheffield, D., & McCarthy, P. (2020). A theory of challenge and threat states in athletes: A revised conceptualization. *Frontiers in Psychology, 11*, 126. https://doi.org/10.3389/fpsyg.2020.00126

Meuwly, N., Bodenmann, G., Germann, J., Bradbury, T.N., Ditzen, B., & Heinrichs, M. (2012). Dyadic coping, insecure attachment, and cortisol stress recovery following experimentally induced stress. *Journal of Family Psychology, 26*(6), 937-947. https://doi.org/10.1037/a0030356

Moll, T., Jordet, G., & Pepping, G. (2010). Emotional contagion in soccer penalty shootouts: Celebration of individual success is associated with ultimate team success. *Journal of Sports Sciences, 28*(9), 983-992. https://doi.org/10.1080/02640414.2010.484068

Moore, L.J., Wilson, M.R., Vine, S.J., Coussens, A.H., & Freeman, P. (2013). Champ or chump?: Challenge and threat states during pressurized competition. *Journal of Sport and Exercise Psychology, 35*(6), 551-562. https://doi.org/10.1123/jsep.35.6.551

Neely, K.C., McHugh, T.-L.F., Dunn, J.G.H., & Holt, N.L. (2017). Athletes and parents coping with deselection in competitive youth sport: A communal coping perspective. *Psychology of Sport and Exercise, 30*, 1-9. https://doi.org/10.1016/j.psychsport.2017.01.004

Netzer, L., Van Kleef, G.A., & Tamir, M. (2015). Interpersonal instrumental emotion regulation. *Journal of Experimental Social Psychology, 58*, 124-135. https://doi.org/10.1016/j.jesp.2015.01.006

Nicholls, A.R., Holt, N.L., Polman, R.C.J., & Bloomfield, J. (2006). Stressors, coping, and coping effectiveness among professional rugby union players. *The Sport Psychologist, 20*(3), 314-329. https://doi.org/10.1123/tsp.20.3.314

Nicholls, A.R., & Perry, J.L. (2016). Perceptions of coach-athlete relationship are more important to coaches than athletes in predicting dyadic coping and stress appraisals: An actor-partner independence mediation model. *Frontiers in Psychology, 7*, 447. https://doi.org/10.3389/fpsyg.2016.00447

Nicholls, A.R., & Polman, R.C.J. (2007). Coping in sport: A systematic review. *Journal of Sports Sciences, 25*(1), 11-31. https://doi.org/10.1080/02640410600630654

Niven, K. (2017). The four key characteristics of interpersonal emotion regulation. *Current Opinion in Psychology, 17*, 89-93. https://doi.org/10.1016/j.copsyc.2017.06.015

O'Brien, T.B., & DeLongis, A. (1997). Coping with chronic stress: An interpersonal perspective. In B. Gottlieb (Ed.), *Coping with chronic stress* (pp. 161-190). Plenum Press.

Palmateer, T., & Tamminen, K.A. (2018). A case study of interpersonal emotion regulation among a varsity volleyball team. *Journal of Applied Sport Psychology, 30*(3), 321-340. https://doi.org/10.1080/10413200.2017.1367335

Palmateer, T., Tamminen, K.A., Schellenberg, B., & Eys, M. (2017, January). Who regulates their teammates' emotions? Associations between athletes' self- and interpersonal emotion regulation with competitive experience, starting status, gender, and teammate ratings of trust, friendship, ability, and team influence [Poster presentation]. Society for Personality and Social Psychology Conference, San Antonio, TX.

Pearlin, L.I., & Schooler, C. (1978). The structure of coping. *Journal of Health and Social Behavior, 19*(1), 2-21. https://doi.org/10.2307/2136319

Poczwardowski, A., Lamphere, B., Allen, K., Marican, R., & Haberl, P. (2020). The 5C's model of successful partnerships in elite beach volleyball dyads. *Journal of Applied Sport Psychology, 32*(5), 476-494. https://doi.org/10.1080/10413200.2019.1573205

Revenson, T.A. (1994). Social support and marital coping with chronic illness. *Annals of Behavioral Medicine, 16*(2), 122-130. https://doi.org/10.1093/abm/16.2.122

Revenson, T.A. (2003). Scenes from a marriage: Examining support, coping, and gender within the context of chronic illness. In J. Suls & K. Wallston (Eds.), *Social psychological foundations of health and illness* (pp. 530-559). Blackwell.

Staff, H.R., Didymus, F.F., & Backhouse, S.H. (2017). Coping rarely takes place in a social vacuum: Exploring dyadic coping in coach-athlete relationships. *Psychology of Sport and Exercise, 30*, 91-100. https://doi.org/10.1016/j.psychsport.2017.02.009

Staff, H., Didymus, F.F., & Backhouse, S.H. (2020). Dyadic coping in coach-athlete relationships: A grounded theory. *Psychology of Sport and Exercise, 50*, 101741. https://doi.org/10.1016/j.psychsport.2020.101741

Staw, B.M., DeCelles, K.A., & de Goey, P. (2019). Leadership in the locker room: How the intensity of leaders' unpleasant affective displays shapes team performance. *Journal of Applied Psychology, 104*(12), 1547-1557. https://doi.org/10.1037/apl0000418

Steinfeldt, J.A., Wong, Y.J., Hagan, A.R., Hoag, J.M., & Steinfeldt, M.C. (2011). A contextual examination of gender role conflict among college football players. *Psychology of Men and Masculinity, 12*(4), 311-323. https://doi.org/10.1037/a0023722

Tamir, M. (2016). Why do people regulate their emotions? A taxonomy of motives in emotion regulation. *Personality and Social Psychology Review, 20*(3), 199-222. https://doi.org/10.1177/1088868315586325

Tamminen, K.A., & Crocker, P.R. (2013). "I control my own emotions for the sake of the team": Emotional self-regulation and interpersonal emotion regulation among female high-performance curlers. *Psychology of Sport and Exercise, 14*(5), 737-747. https://doi.org/10.1016/j.psychsport.2013.05.002

Tamminen, K.A., Gaudreau, P., McEwen, C.E., & Crocker, P.R.E. (2016). Interpersonal emotion regulation among adolescent athletes: A Bayesian multilevel model predicting sport enjoyment and commitment. *Journal of Sport and Exercise Psychology, 38*, 541-555. https://doi.org/10.1123/jsep.2015-0189

Tamminen, K.A., McEwen, C.E., Gaudreau, P., & Crocker, P.R.E. (2015, February). Predicting interpersonal emotion regulation among adolescent athletes: Associations with emotional self-regulation, gender, team status, and peer climate [Poster presentation]. Society for Personality and Social Psychology Conference, Long Beach, CA.

Tamminen, K.A., & Neely, K.C. (2020). We're in this together: Dyadic and interpersonal aspects of emotions, coping, and emotion regulation in sport. In M.C. Ruiz & C. Robazza (Eds.), *Feelings in sport: Theory, research, and practical implications for performance and well-being.* Routledge.

Tamminen, K.A., Page-Gould, E., Palmateer, T., Schellenberg, B., Thai, S., Eys, M., Sabiston, C., & Crocker, P.R.E. (2019). A daily diary study of interpersonal emotion regulation, the social environment, and team performance among varsity athletes. *Psychology of Sport and Exercise, 45*, 101566. https://doi.org/10.1016/j.psychsport.2019.101566

Tamminen, K.A., Palmateer, T.M., Denton, M., Sabiston, C., Crocker, P.R., Eys, M., & Smith, B. (2016). Exploring emotions as social phenomena among Canadian varsity athletes. *Psychology of Sport and Exercise, 27*, 28-38. https://doi.org/10.1016/j.psychsport.2016.07.010

Totterdell, P. (2000). Catching moods and hitting runs: Mood linkage and subjective performance in professional sport teams. *Journal of Applied Psychology, 85*(6), 848-859. https://doi.org/10.1037/0021-9010.85.6.848

Turner, M.J., Jones, M.V., Sheffield, D., Slater, M.J., Barker, J.B., & Bell, J.J. (2013). Who thrives under pressure? Predicting the performance of elite academy cricketers using the cardiovascular indicators of challenge and threat states. *Journal of Sport and Exercise Psychology, 35*(4), 387-397. https://doi.org/10.1123/jsep.35.4.387

Vallerand, R.J. (1983). On emotion in sport: Theoretical and social psychological perspectives. *Journal of Sport Psychology, 5*(2), 197-215. https://doi.org/10.1123/jsp.5.2.197

Vallerand, R.J., & Blanchard, C.M. (2000). The study of emotion in sport and exercise. In Y.L. Hanin (Ed.), *Emotions in sport* (pp. 3-37). Human Kinetics.

van Kleef, G.A., Cheshin, A., Koning, L.F., & Wolf, S.A. (2019). Emotional games: How coaches' emotional expressions shape players' emotions, inferences, and team performance. *Psychology of Sport and Exercise, 41*, 1-11. https://doi.org/10.1016/j.psychsport.2018.11.004

Vargas, T.M., & Short, S.E. (2011). Athletes' perceptions of the psychological, emotional, and performance effects of coaches' pre-game speeches. *International Journal of Coaching Science, 5*(1), 27-43.

von Scheve, C., & Ismer, S. (2013). Towards a theory of collective emotions. *Emotion Review, 5*(4), 406-413. https://doi.org/10.1177/1754073913484170

Wergin, V. V., Zimanyi, Z., Mesagno, C., & Beckmann, J. (2018). When suddenly nothing works anymore within a team–Causes of collective sport team collapse. *Frontiers in Psychology, 9*, 2115. https://doi.org/10.3389/fpsyg.2018.02115

Winek, J.L. (2010). *Systemic family therapy: From theory to practice.* Sage.

Wolf, S.A., Eys, M.A., Sadler, P., & Kleinert, J. (2015). Appraisal in a team context: Perceptions of cohesion predict competition importance and prospects for coping, *Journal of Sport and Exercise Psychology, 37*(5), 489-499. https://doi.org/10.1123/jsep.2014-0276

Chapter 17

American Medical Association Ad Hoc Committee on Health Literacy. (1992). Report of the Scientific Council on Health Literacy. *JAMA, 281*(6), 552-557.

American Psychiatric Association. (2013). *Diagnostic and statistical manual of mental disorders* (5th ed.). American Psychiatric Publishing.

Bahr, R., Clarsen, B., Derman, W., Dvorak, J., Emery, C.A., Finch, C.F., Hägglund, M., Junge, A., Kemp, S., Khan, K.M., Marshall, S.W., Meeuwisse, W., Mountjoy, M., Orchard, J.W., Pluim, B., Quarrie, K.L., Reider, B., Schwellnus, M., Soligard, T., . . . Chamari, K. (2020). International Olympic Committee consensus statement: Methods for recording and reporting of epidemiological data on injury and illness in sport 2020 (including STROBE Extension for Sport Injury and Illness Surveillance (STROBE-SIIS)). *British Journal of Sport Medicine, 54*(7), 372-389. http://dx.doi.org/10.1136/bjsports-2019-101969

Bennett, M. (2021). Behind the mask: Demedicalising race and mental health in professional football. *The Lancet Psychiatry, 8*(4), 264-266. https://doi.org/10.1016/S2215-0366(20)30418-1

Betancourt, J.R., Green, A.R., Carrillo, J.E., & Ananeh-Firempong, O. (2003). Defining cultural competence: A practical framework for addressing racial/ethnic disparities in health and health care. *Public Health Reports, 118*(4), 293-302.

Bissett, J.F., Kroshus, E., & Hebard, S. (2020). Determining the role of sport coaches in promoting athlete mental health: A narrative review and Delphi approach. *BMJ Open Sport and Exercise Medicine, 6*, 000676. http://dx.doi.org/10.1136/bmjsem-2019-000676

Bradburn, N.M. (1969). *The structure of psychological well-being.* Aldine.

Breslin, G., Shannon, S., Haughey, T., Donnelly, P., & Leavey, G. (2017). A systematic review of interventions to increase awareness of mental health and well-being in athletes, coaches and officials. *Systematic Reviews, 6*(1), 177. https://doi.org/10.1186/s13643-017-0568-6

Breslin, G., Smith, A., Donohue, B., Donnelly, P., Shannon, S., Haughey, T.J., Vella, S.A., Swann, C., Cotterill, S., Macintyre, T., Rogers, T., & Leavey, G. (2019). International consensus statement on the psychosocial and policy-related approaches to mental health awareness programmes in sport. *BMJ Open Sport and Exercise Medicine, 5*, 000585. http://dx.doi.org/10.1136/bmjsem-2019-000585

Bronfenbrenner, U. (1979). *The ecology of human development: Experiments by nature and design.* Harvard University Press.

Bu, D., Chung, P.-K., Zhang, C.-Q., Liu, J., & Wang, X. (2020). Mental health literacy intervention on help-seeking in athletes: A systematic review. *International Journal of Environmental Research and Public Health, 17*(19), 7263. https://doi.org/10.3390/ijerph17197263

Castaldelli-Maia, J.M., de Mello e Gallinaro, J.G., Falcao, R.S., Gouttebarge, V., Hitchcock, M.E., Hainline, B., Reardon, C.L., & Stull, T. (2019). Mental health symptoms and disorders in elite athletes: A systematic review on cultural influences and barriers to athletes seeking treatment. *British Journal of Sports Medicine, 53*(11), 707-721. https://dx.doi.org/10.1136/bjsports-2019-100710

Chang, C., Putukian, M., Aerni, G., Diamond, A., Hong, G., Ingram, Y., Reardon, C.L., & Wolanin, A. (2020). Mental health issues and psychological factors in athletes: Detection, management, effect on performance and prevention: American Medical Society for Sports Medicine position statement—executive summary. *British Journal of Sports Medicine, 54*(4), 216-220. https://doi.org/10.1136/bjsports-2019-101583

Choi, B.C., Pang, T., Lin, V., Puska, P., Sherman, G., Goddard, M., Ackland, M.J., Sainsbury, P., Stachenko, S., Morrison, H., & Clottey, C. (2005). Can scientists and policy makers work together? *Journal of Epidemiology and Community Health, 59*(8), 632-637. https://doi.org/10.1136/jech.2004.031765

Chow, G.M., Bird, M., Gabana, N., Cooper, B.T., & Swanbrow Becker, M.A. (2020). A program to reduce stigma toward mental illness and promote mental health literacy and help-seeking in National Collegiate Athletic Association Division I student-athletes. *Journal of Clinical Sport Psychology*. https://doi.org/10.1123/jcsp.2019-0104

Coyle, M., Gorczynski, P., & Gibson, K. (2017). "You have to be mental to jump off a board any way": Elite divers' conceptualizations and perceptions of mental health. *Psychology of Sport and Exercise, 29*, 10-18. https://doi.org/10.1016/j.psychsport.2016.11.005

Crabtree, S.M. (2019). Reflecting on reflexivity in development studies research. *Development in Practice, 29*(7), 927-935. https://doi.org/10.1080/09614524.2019.1593319

Craig, P., Dieppe, P., Macintyre, S., Michie, S., Nazareth, I., Petticrew, M., & Medical Research Council Guidance. (2008). Developing and evaluating complex interventions: The new Medical Research Council guidance. *BMJ, 337*, a1655. https://doi.org/10.1136/bmj.a1655

Csikszentmihalyi, M. (1990). *Flow: The psychology of optimal performance.* Cambridge University Press.

Dewalt, D.A., Berkman, N.D., Sheridan, S., Lohr, K.N., & Pignone, M.P. (2004). Literacy and health outcomes: A systematic review of the literature. *Journal of General Internal Medicine, 19*(12), 1228-1239. https://doi.org/10.1111/j.1525-1497.2004.40153.x

Dick, D.M. (2011). Gene-environment interaction in psychological traits and disorders. *Annual Review of Clinical Psychology, 7*, 383-409. https://doi.org/10.1146/annurev-clinpsy-032210-104518

Diener, E., & Suh, E. (1997). Measuring quality of life: Economic, social, and subjective indicators. *Social Indicators Research, 40*(1-2), 189-216. https://doi.org/10.1023/A:1006859511756

Dodge, R., Daly, A., Huyton, J., & Sanders, L. (2012). The challenge of defining wellbeing. *International Journal of Wellbeing, 2*(3), 222-235. http:/dx.doi.org/10.5502/ijw.v2i3.4

Eaton, W.W., & Merikangas, K.R. (2000). Psychiatric epidemiology: Progress and prospects in the year 2000. *Epidemiologic Reviews, 22*(1), 29-34. https://doi.org/10.1093/oxfordjournals.epirev.a018022

Fasting, K., Brackenridge, C.H., & Walseth, K. (2002). Consequences of sexual harassment in sport for female athletes. *Journal of Sexual Aggression, 8*(2), 37-48. https://doi.org/10.1080/13552600208413338

Fisher, L.A., & Anders, A.D. (2020). Engaging with cultural sport psychology to explore systemic sexual exploitation in USA gymnastics: A call to commitments. *Journal of Applied Sport Psychology, 32*(2), 129-145. https://doi.org/10.1080/10413200.2018.1564944

Freeman, H. (2018, January 26). How was Larry Nassar able to abuse so many gymnasts for so long? *The Guardian.* www.theguardian.com/sport/2018/jan/26/larry-nassar-abuse-gymnasts-scandal-culture

Galderisi, S., Heinz, A., Kastrup, M., Beezhold, J., & Sartorius, N. (2015). Toward a new definition of mental health. *World Psychiatry, 14*(2), 231-233. https://doi.org/10.1002/wps.20231

Golden, S.D., & Earp, J.A.L. (2012). Social ecological approaches to individuals and their contexts: Twenty years of health education & behavior health promotion interventions. *Health Education and Behavior, 39*(3), 364-372. https://doi.org/10.1177/1090198111418634

Gorczynski P.F., Coyle, M., & Gibson, K. (2017). Depressive symptoms in high-performance athletes and non-athletes: A comparative meta-analysis. *British Journal of Sports Medicine, 51*(18), 1349-1354. http://dx.doi.org/10.1136/bjsports-2016-096455

Gorczynski, P., Currie, A., Gibson, K., Gouttebarge, V., Hainline, B., Castaldelli-Maia, J.M., Mountjoy, M., Purcell, R., Reardon, C.L., Rice, S., Swartz, L. (2021). Developing mental health literacy and cultural competence in elite sport. *Journal of Applied Sport Psychology, 33*(4), 387-401. https://doi.org/10.1080/10413200.2020.1720045

Gorczynski, P., Gibson, K., Clarke, N., Mensah, T., & Summers, R. (2020). Examining mental health literacy, help seeking behaviours, distress, and wellbeing in coaches in the UK. *European Physical Education Review, 26*(3), 713-726. https://doi.org/10.1177/1356336X19887772

Gorczynski, P., Gibson, K., Thelwell, R., Papathomas, A., Harwood, C., & Kinnafick, F. (2019). The BASES expert statement on mental health literacy in elite sport. *The Sport and Exercise Scientist, 59*, 6-7.

Gorczynski, P., & Thelwell, R. (2022). Examining mental health literacy, depressive symptoms, help seeking behaviors, and wellbeing in soccer match officials in the UK. *International Journal of Sport Psychology, 53*(1), 25-35. https://doi.org/10.7352/IJSP.2022.53.025

Gorczynski, P., & Webb, T. (2020). Call-to-action: The need for a mental health research agenda for sports match officials. *Managing Sport and Leisure, 27*(4), 416-420. https://doi.org/10.1080/23750472.2020.1792803

Gouttebarge, V., Bindra, A., Blauwet, C., Campriani, N., Currie, A., Engebretsen, L., Hainline, B., Kroshus, E., McDuff, D., Mountjoy, M., Purcell, R., Putukian, M., Reardon, C.L., Rice, S.M., & Budgett, R. (2021). International Olympic Committee (IOC) Sport Mental Health Assessment Tool 1 (SMHAT-1) and Sport Mental Health Recognition Tool 1 (SMHRT-1): Towards better support of athletes' mental health. *British Journal of Sports Medicine, 55*(1), 30-37. http://dx.doi.org/10.1136/bjsports-2020-102411

Gouttebarge, V., Castaldelli-Maia, J.M., Gorczynski, P., Hainline, B., Hitchcock, M.E., Kerkhoffs, G.M., Rice, S.M., & Reardon, C. (2019). Occurrence of mental health symptoms and disorders in current and former elite athletes: A systematic review and meta-analysis. *British Journal of Sports Medicine, 53*, 700-706. http://dx.doi.org/10.1136/bjsports-2019-100671

Gureje, O., Nortje, G., Makanjuola, V., Oladeji, B.D., Seedat, S., & Jenkins, R. (2015). The role of global traditional and complementary systems of medicine in the treatment of mental health disorders. *The Lancet Psychiatry, 2*(2), 168-177. https://doi.org/10.1016/S2215-0366(15)00013-9

Hainline, B., & Reardon, C.L. (2019). Breaking a taboo: Why the International Olympic Committee convened experts to develop a consensus statement on mental health in elite athletes. *British Journal of Sports Medicine.* http://dx.doi.org/10.1136/bjsports-2019-100681

Henriksen, K., Schinke, R., McCann, S., Durand-Bush, N., Moesch, K., Parham, W.D., Larsen, C.H., Cogan, K., Donaldson, A., Poczwardowski, A., Noce, F., & Hunziker, J. (2020). Athlete mental health in the Olympic/Paralympic quadrennium: A multi-societal consensus statement. *International Journal of Sport and Exercise Psychology, 18*(3), 391-408. http://doi.org/10.1080/1612197x.2020.1746379

Henriksen, K., Schinke, R., Moesch, K., McCann, S., Parham, W.D., Larsen, C.H., & Terry, P. (2019). Consensus statement on improving the mental health of high performance athletes. *International Journal of Sport and Exercise Psychology.* https://doi.org/10.1080/1612197X.2019.1570473

Henriksen, K., Stambulova, N., & Roessler, K.K. (2010). Holistic approach to athletic talent development environments: A successful sailing milieu. *Psychology of Sport and Exercise, 11*(3), 212-222. https://doi.org/10.1016/j.psychsport.2009.10.005

Jorm, A.F. (2000). Mental health literacy: Public knowledge and beliefs about mental disorders. *British Journal of Psychiatry, 177*(5), 396-401. https://doi.org/10.1192/bjp.177.5.396

Jorm, A.F., Korten, A.E., Jacomb, P.A., Christensen, H., Rodgers, B., & Pollitt, P. (1997). "Mental health literacy": A survey of the public's ability to recognise mental disorders and their beliefs about the effectiveness of treatment. *Medical Journal of Australia, 166*(4), 182-186.

Kirmayer, L.J. (2013). Embracing uncertainty as a path to competence: Cultural safety, empathy, and alterity in clinical training. *Culture, Medicine, and Psychiatry, 37*(2), 365-372. https://doi.org/10.1007/s11013-013-9314-2

Kroshus, E., Chrisman, S., Coppel, D., & Herring, S. (2018). Coach support of high school student-athletes struggling with anxiety or depression. *Journal of Clinical Sport Psychology, 13*(3), 390-404. https://doi.org/10.1123/jcsp.2018-0004

Kutcher, S., & Wei, Y. (2020). School mental health: A necessary component of youth mental health policy and plans. *World Psychiatry, 19*(2), 174-175. https://doi.org/10.1002/wps.20732

Kutcher, S., Wei, Y., & Coniglio, C. (2016). Mental health literacy: Past, present, and future. *Canadian Journal of Psychiatry, 61*(3), 154-158. https://doi.org/10.1177/0706743715616609

Küttel, A., & Larsen, C.H. (2019). Risk and protective factors for mental health in elite athletes: A scoping review. *International Review of Sport and Exercise Psychology, 13*(1), 231-265. https://doi.org/10.1080/1750984X.2019.1689574

Lehman, B.J., David, D.M., & Gruber, J.A. (2017). Rethinking the biopsychosocial model of health: Understanding health as a dynamic system. *Social and Personality Psychology Compass, 11*(8), 12328. https://doi.org/10.1111/spc3.12328

Mazzer, K.R., & Rickwood, D.J. (2015). Mental health in sport: Coaches' views of their role and efficacy in supporting young people's mental health. *International Journal of Health Promotion and Education, 53*(2), 102-114. https://doi.org/10.1080/14635240.2014.965841

McLaren, L., & Hawe, P. (2005). Ecological perspectives in health research. *Journal of Epidemiology and Community Health, 59*(1), 6-14. http://dx.doi.org/10.1136/jech.2003.018044

McLeroy, K.R., Bibeau, D., Steckler, A., & Glanz, K. (1988). An ecological perspective on health promotion programs. *Health Education Quarterly, 15*, 351-377.

Moesch, K., Kentta, G., Kleinert, J., Quigon-Fleuret, C., Cecil, S., & Bertollo, M. (2018). FEPSAC position statement: Mental health disorders in elite athletes and models of service provision. *Psychology of Sport and Exercise, 38*, 61-71. https://doi.org/10.1016/j.psychsport.2018.05.013

Mountjoy, M., Brackenridge, C., Arrington, M., Blauwet, C., Carska-Sheppard, A., Fasting, K., Kirby, S., Leahy, T., Marks, S., Martin, K., Starr, K., Tiivas, A., & Budgett, R. (2016). International Olympic Committee consensus statement: Harassment and abuse (non-accidental violence) in sport. *British Journal of Sport Medicine, 50*, 1019-1029. http://dx.doi.org/10.1136/bjsports-2016-096121

Nutbeam, D., Wise, M., Bauman, A., Harris, E., & Leeder, S. (1993). *Goals and targets for Australia's health in the year 2000 and beyond.* Australian Government Publishing Service.

O'Cathain, A., Croot, L., Duncan, E., Rousseau, N., Sworn, K., Turner, K. M., Yardley, L., & Hoddinott, P. (2019). Guidance on how to develop complex interventions to improve health and healthcare. *BMJ open, 9*(8), e029954. https://doi.org/10.1136/bmjopen-2019-029954

O'Connor, M., & Casey, L. (2015). The Mental Health Literacy Scale (MHLS): A new scale-based measure of mental health literacy. *Psychiatry Research, 229*(1-2), 511-516. https://doi.org/10.1016/j.psychres.2015.05.064

Olympic.org. (n.d.). *The Olympic motto.* Retrieved May 15, 2023, from www.olympic.org/the-olympic-motto

Porta, M. (2014). *A dictionary of epidemiology* (6th ed.). Oxford University Press.

Purcell, R., Gwyther, K., & Rice, S. (2019). Mental health in elite athletes: Increased awareness requires an early intervention framework to respond to athlete needs. *Sports Medicine Open, 5*, 46. https://doi.org/10.1186/s40798-019-0220-1

Reardon, C.L., Hainline, B., Aron, C.M., Baron, D., Baum, A.L., Bindra, A., Budgett, R., Campriani, N., Castaldelli-Maia, J.M., Currie, A., Derevensky, J.L., Glick, I.D., Gorczynski, P., Gouttebarge, V., Grandner, M.A., Han, D.H., McDuff, D., Mountjoy, M., Polat, A., . . . Engebretsen, L. (2019). Mental health in elite athletes: International Olympic Committee consensus statement (2019). *British Journal of Sports Medicine, 53*(11), 667-699. https://doi.org/10.1136/bjsports-2019-100715

Rice, S.M., Gwyther, K., Santesteban-Echarri, O., Baron, D., Gorczynski, P.G., Gouttebarge, V., Reardon, C.L., Hitchcock, M.E., Hainline, B., & Purcell, R. (2019). Determinants of anxiety in elite athletes: A systematic review and meta-analysis. *British Journal of Sports Medicine, 53*(11), 722-730. http://dx.doi.org/10.1136/bjsports-2019-100620

Ries Merikangas, K., Nakamura, E.F., & Kessler, R.C. (2009). Epidemiology of mental disorders in children and adolescents. *Dialogues in Clinical Neuroscience, 11*(1), 7-20.

Ryff, C.D. (1989). Beyond Ponce de Leon and life satisfaction: New directions in quest of successful ageing. *International Journal of Behavioral Development, 12*(1), 35-55. https://doi.org/10.1177/016502548901200102

Sallis, J.F., Cervero, R.B., Ascher, W., Henderson, K.A., Kraft, M.K., & Kerr, J. (2006). An ecological approach to creating active living communities. *Annual review of public health, 27*, 297-322. https://doi.org/10.1146/annurev.publhealth.27.021405.102100

Sallis, J.F., Owen, N., & Fotheringham, M.J. (2000). Behavioral epidemiology: A systematic framework to classify phases of research on health promotion and disease prevention. *Annals of Behavioral Medicine, 22*(4), 294-298.

Schinke, R.J., & Stambulova, N.B. (2017). Context-driven sport and exercise psychology practice: Widening our lens beyond the athlete. *Journal of Sport Psychology in Action, 8*(2), 71-75. https://doi.org/10.1080/21520704.2017.1299470

Schinke, R.J., Stambulova, N.B., Si, G., & Moore, Z. (2018). International society of sport psychology position stand: Athletes' mental health, performance, and development. *International Journal of Sport and Exercise Psychology, 16*(6), 622-639. https://doi.org/10.1080/1612197X.2017.1295557

Sebbens, J., Hassmen, P., Crisp, D., & Wensley, K. (2016). Mental health in sport (MHS): Improving early intervention knowledge and confidence in elite sport staff. *Frontiers in Psychology, 7*, 911. https://doi.org/10.3389/fpsyg.2016.00911

Shin, D., & Johnson, D. (1978). Avowed happiness as an overall assessment of the quality of life. *Social Indicators Research, 5*(1),475-492. https://doi.org/10.1007/BF00352944

Stambulova, N.B., & Wylleman, P. (2014). Athletes' career development and transitions. In A. Papaioannou & D. Hackfort (Eds.), *Routledge companion to sport and exercise psychology* (pp. 605-621). Routledge.

Sullivan, P., Murphy, J., & Blacker, M. (2019) The level of mental health literacy among athletic staff in intercollegiate sport. *Journal of Clinical Sport Psychology 13*(3), 440-450. https://doi.org/10.1123/jcsp.2018-0052

Swartz, L., Hunt, X., Bantjes, J., Hainline, B., & Reardon, C.L. (2019). Mental health symptoms and disorders in Paralympic athletes: A narrative review. *British Journal of Sports Medicine, 53*(12), 737-740. http://dx.doi.org/10.1136/bjsports-2019-100731

Thelwell, R.C., Wagstaff, C.R., Chapman, M.T., & Kenttä, G. (2016). Examining coaches' perceptions of how their stress influences the coach–athlete relationship. *Journal of Sport Sciences, 35*(19), 1928-1939. https://doi.org/10.1080/02640414.2016.1241422

Thelwell, R.C., Wagstaff, C.R., Rayner, A., Chapman, M., & Barker, J. (2017). Exploring athletes' perceptions of coach stress in elite sport environments. *Journal of Sport Sciences, 35*(1), 44-55. https://doi.org/10.1080/02640414.2016.1154979

Uher, R., & Zwicker, A. (2017). Etiology in psychiatry: Embracing the reality of poly-gene-environmental causation of mental illness. *World Psychiatry, 16*(2), 121-129. https://doi.org/10.1002/wps.20436

Van Slingerland, K.J., Durand-Bush, N., Bradley, L., Goldfield, G., Archambault, R., Smith, D., Edwards, C., Delenardo, S., Taylor, S., Werthner, P., & Kenttä, G. (2019). Canadian Centre for Mental Health and Sport (CCMHS) position statement: Principles of mental health in competitive and high-performance sport. *Clinical Journal of Sport Medicine, 29*(3), 173-180. https://doi.org/10.1097/JSM.0000000000000665

Vella, S.A., & Swann, C. (2021). Time for mental healthcare guidelines for recreational sports: A call to action. *British Journal of Sports Medicine, 55*(4), 184-185. http://dx.doi.org/10.1136/bjsports-2019-101591

Webb, T. (2020). Sports match official research: An evolving narrative, positioning future research. *Managing Sport and Leisure, 27*(3), 199-206. https://doi.org/10.1080/23750472.2020.1762304

Webb, T., & Gorczynski, P. (2020). Factors influencing the mental health of sports match officials: The potential impact of abuse and a destabilised support system from a global context. In M. Lang (Ed.), *Routledge handbook of athlete welfare* (pp. 289-299). Routledge.

Webb, T., Gorczynski, P., Oftadeh Moghadam, S., Grub, L.S. (2022). Experience and construction of mental health among English female football match officials. *The Sport Psychologist.* https://doi.org/10.1123/tsp.2020-0086

Wilkerson, T.A., Stokowski, S., Fridley, A., Dittmore, S.W., & Bell, C.A. (2020). Black football student-athletes' perceived barriers to seeking mental health services. *Journal of Issues in Intercollegiate Athletics, Winter 2020 Special Issue*, 55-81. http://csri-jiia.org/wp-content/uploads/2020/02/SI_2020_01_03.pdf

Wylleman, P., Reints, A., & De Knop, P. (2013). A developmental and holistic perspective on athletic career development. In P. Sotiaradou & V. De Bosscher (Eds.), *Managing high performance sport* (pp. 159- 182). Routledge.

World Health Organization. (1998). Health promotion glossary. www.who.int/healthpromotion/about/HPR%20Glossary%201998.pdf

World Health Organization. (2018b). International Classification of Diseases for mortality and morbidity statistics (ICD-11). http://icd.who.int

World Health Organization. (2018a). Mental health: Strengthening our response. www.who.int/news-room/fact-sheets/detail/mental-health-strengthening-our-response

World Health Organization. (2001). Strengthening mental health promotion. (Fact sheet No. 220).

Chapter 18

Baird, N., Martin, L.J., & Benson, A.J. (2020). A dynamic view of coach transformational leadership: How leadership perceptions relate to task cohesion and team potency. *Psychology of Sport and Exercise, 51*, 101789. https://doi.org/10.1016/j.psychsport.2020.101789

Baumeister, R.F., & Leary, M.R. (1995). The need to belong: Desire for interpersonal attachment as a fundamental human motivation. *Psychological Bulletin, 117*, 497-529. https://doi.org/10.1037/0033-2909.117.3.497

Beauchamp, M.R. (2019). Promoting exercise adherence through groups: A self-categorization theory perspective. *Exercise and Sport Sciences Reviews, 47*, 54–61. https://doi.org/10.1249/JES.0000000000000177

Beauchamp, M.R., & O'Rourke, J.J. (2020). Group-based physical activity participation. In S.A. Halsam, K. Fransen, & F. Boen (Eds.). *The new psychology of sport and exercise: The social identity approach* (pp. 187-205). Sage.

Benson, A., Siska, P., Eys, M., Priklerova, S., & Slepicka, P. (2016). A prospective multilevel examination of the relationship between cohesion and team performance in elite youth sport. *Psychology of Sport and Exercise, 27*, 39-46. https://doi.org/10.1016/j.psychsport.2016.07.009

Brawley, L.R., Carron, A.V., & Widmeyer, W.N. (1987). Assessing the cohesion of teams: Validity of the Group Environment Questionnaire. *Journal of Sport Psychology, 9*, 275-294. https://doi.org/10.1123/jsp.9.3.275

Brawley, L.R., & Paskevich, D.M. (1997). Conducting team building research in the context of sport and exercise. *Journal of Applied Sport Psychology, 9*, 11–40. https://doi.org/10.1080/10413209708415382

Butler, A. (2020, May 11). 'Last Dance': Michael Jordan tears up talking about Bulls teammates. UPI. www.upi.com/Sports_News/NBA/2020/05/11/Last-Dance-Michael-Jordan-tears-up-talking-about-Bulls-teammates/5941589195445

Callow, N., Smith, M.J., Hardy, L., Arthur, C.A., & Hardy, J. (2009). Measurement of transformational leadership and its relationship with team cohesion and performance level. *Journal of Applied Sport Psychology, 21*, 395-412. https://doi.org/10.1080/10413200903204754

Campbell, D.T. (1958). Common fate, similarity, and other indices of the status of aggregates of persons as social entities. *Behavioral Science, 3*, 14-25. https://doi.org/10.1002/bs.3830030103

Carron, A.V., Brawley, L.R., & Widmeyer, W.N. (1998). The measurement of cohesiveness in sport groups. In J.L. Duda (Ed.), *Advances in sport and exercise psychology measurement* (pp. 213-226). Fitness Information Technology.

Carron, A.V., & Chelladurai, P. (1981). The dynamics of group cohesion in sport. *Journal of Sport Psychology, 3*, 123-139. https://doi.org/10.1123/jsp.3.2.123

Carron, A.V., Colman, M.M., Wheeler, J., & Stevens, D. (2002). Cohesion and performance in sport: A meta-analysis. *Journal of Sport and Exercise Psychology, 24*, 168-188. https://doi.org/10.1123/jsep.24.2.168

Carron, A.V., & Spink, K.S. (1993). Team building in an exercise setting. *The Sport Psychologist, 7*, 8-18. https://doi.org/10.1123/tsp.7.1.8

Carron, A.V., Widmeyer, W.N., & Brawley, L.R. (1985). The development of an instrument to assess cohesion in sport teams: The Group Environment Questionnaire. *Journal of Sport Psychology, 7*, 244-266. https://doi.org/10.1123/jsp.7.3.244

Carron, A.V., Widmeyer, W.N., & Brawley, L.R. (1988). Group cohesion and individual adherence to physical activity. *Journal of Sport and Exercise Psychology, 10*, 119-126. https://doi.org/10.1123/jsep.10.2.127

Coleman, T., Godfrey, M., López-Gajardo, M.A., Leo, F.M., & Eys, M. (2021). Do it for the team: Youth perceptions of cohesion and role commitment in interdependent sport. *Sport, Exercise, and Performance Psychology, 10*, 224-239. https://doi.org/10.1037/spy0000253

De Backer, M., Boen, F., Ceux, T., De Cuyper, B., Høigaard, R., Callens, F., Fransen, K., & Vande Broek, G. (2011). Do perceived justice and need support of the coach predict team identification and cohesion? Testing their relative importance among top volleyball and handball players in Belgium and Norway. *Psychology of Sport and Exercise, 12*, 192-201. https://doi.org/10.1016/j.psychsport.2010.09.009

Duda, J.L. (2001). Achievement goal research in sport: Pushing the boundaries and clarifying some misunderstandings. In C.G. Roberts (Ed.), *Advances in motivation in sport and exercise* (pp. 129-182). Human Kinetics.

Duda, J.L., & Balaguer, I. (2007). Coach-created motivational climate. In S. Jowett & D. Lavallee (Eds.), *Social psychology in sport* (pp. 117-130). Human Kinetics.

Dunlop, W.L., Falk, C.F., & Beauchamp, M.R. (2013). How dynamic are exercise group dynamics? Examining changes in cohesion within class-based exercise programs. *Health Psychology, 32*, 1240-1243. https://doi.org/10.1037/a0030412

Evans, M.B., & Eys, M.A. (2015). Collective goals and shared tasks: Interdependence structure and perceptions of individual sport team environments. *Scandinavian Journal of Medicine and Science in Sports, 25*, 139-148. https://doi.org/10.1111/sms.12235

Evans, M.B., Eys, M.A., & Bruner, M.W. (2012). See the 'we' in 'me' sports: The need to consider individual sport team environments. *Canadian Psychology, 53*, 301-308. https://doi.org/10.1037/a0030202

Evans, M.B., Eys, M.A., & Wolf, S.A. (2013). Exploring the nature of interpersonal influence in elite individual sport teams. *Journal of Applied Sport Psychology, 25*, 448-462. https://doi.org/10.1080/10413200.2012.752769

Evans, M.B., Graupensperger, S., Benson, A.J., Eys, M., Hastings, B., & Gottschall, J.S. (2019). Group structure and entitativity in group fitness: Considering groupness at within- and between-group levels. *Psychology and Health, 34*, 715-732. https://doi.org/10.1080/08870446.2019.1566548

Eys, M., Beauchamp, M.R., Godfrey, M., Dawson, K., Loughead, T.M., & Schinke, R.J. (2020). Role commitment and acceptance in a sport context. *Journal of Sport and Exercise Psychology, 42*, 89-101. https://doi.org/10.1123/jsep.2019-0057

Eys, M., & Brawley, L.R. (2018). Reflections on cohesion research with sport and exercise groups. *Social and Personality Psychology Compass, 12*, 12379. https://doi.org/10.1111/spc3.12379

Eys, M.A., & Carron, A.V. (2001). Role ambiguity, task cohesion, and task self-efficacy. *Small Group Research, 32*, 356-373. https://doi.org/10.1177/104649640103200305

Eys, M.A., Evans, M.B., & Benson, A. (2020). *Group dynamics in sport* (5th ed.). Fitness Information Technology.

Eys, M.A., Hardy, J.T., Carron, A.V., & Beauchamp, M.R. (2003). The relationship between task cohesion and competitive state anxiety. *Journal of Sport and Exercise Psychology, 25*, 66-76. https://doi.org/10.1123/jsep.25.1.66

Eys, M.A., Jewitt, E., Evans, M.B., Wolf, S., Bruner, M.W., & Loughead, T.M. (2013). Coach initiated motivational climate and cohesion in youth sport. *Research Quarterly for Exercise and Sport, 84*, 373-383. https://doi.org/10.1080/02701367.2013.814909

Eys, M.A., Loughead, T.M., Bray, S.R., & Carron, A.V. (2009). Development of a cohesion questionnaire for youth: The Youth Sport Environment Questionnaire. *Journal of Sport and Exercise Psychology, 31*, 390-408. https://doi.org/10.1123/jsep.31.3.390

Eys, M.A., Ohlert, J., Evans, B., Wolf, S., Martin, L., VanBussel, M., & Steins, C. (2015). Cohesion and performance for female and male sport teams. *The Sport Psychologist, 29*, 97-109. https://doi.org/10.1123/tsp.2014-0027

Filho, E., Dobersek, U., Gershgoren, L., Becker, B., & Tenenbaum, G. (2014). The cohesion–performance relationship in sport: A 10-year retrospective meta-analysis. *Sport Science for Health, 10*, 165-177. https://doi.org/10.1007/s11332-014-0188-7

Fletcher, D., & Fletcher, J. (2005). A meta-model of stress, emotions and performance: Conceptual foundations, theoretical framework, and research directions. *Journal of Sports Sciences, 23*, 157. https://doi.org/10.1080/02640410512331334413

Fransen, K., Decroos, S., Broek, G.V., & Boen, F. (2016). Leading from the top or leading from within? A comparison between coaches' and athletes' leadership as predictors of team identification, team confidence, and team cohesion. *International Journal of Sports Science and Coaching, 11*, 757-771. https://doi.org/10.1177/1747954116676102

Fransen, K., Haslem, S.A., Steffens, N.K., Peters, K., Mallett, C.J., Mertens, N., & Boen, F. (2020). All for us and us for all: Introducing the 5R Shared Leadership Program. *Psychology of Sport and Exercise, 51*, 101762. https://doi.org/10.1016/j.psychsport.2020.101762

Gammage, K.L., Carron, A.V., & Estabrooks, P.A. (2001). Team cohesion and individual productivity: The influence of the norm for productivity and the identifiability of individual effort. *Small Group Research, 32*, 3-18. https://doi.org/10.1177/104649640103200101

Grossman, R., Rosch, Z., Mazer, D., & Salas, E. (2015). What matters for team cohesion measurement? A synthesis. In E. Salas, W.B. Vessey, & A.X. Estrada (Eds.), *Team cohesion: Advances in psychological theory, methods and practice* (pp. 147-180). Emerald Group.

Hardy, J., Eys, M.A., & Carron, A.V. (2005). Exploring the potential disadvantages of high team cohesion. *Small Group Research, 36*, 166-187. https://doi.org/10.1177/1046496404266715

Hardy, L., Arthur, C.A., Jones, G., Shariff, A., Munnoch, K., Isaacs, I., & Allsopp, A.J. (2010). The relationship between transformational leadership behaviors, psychological, and training outcomes in elite military recruits. *The Leadership Quarterly, 21*, 20-32. https://doi.org/10.1016/j.leaqua.2009.10.002

Harwood, C., Beauchamp, M.R., & Keegan, R.J. (2014). Group functioning through optimal achievement goals. In M. Beauchamp & M. Eys (Eds.), *Group dynamics in exercise and sport psychology* (pp. 279-297). Routledge.

Heuzé, J.P., & Fontayne, P. (2002). Questionnaire sur l'Ambiance du Groupe: A French-language instrument for measuring group cohesion. *Journal of Sport and Exercise Psychology, 24*, 42-67. https://doi.org/10.1123/jsep.24.1.42

Heuzé, J.P., Raimbault, N., & Fontayne, P. (2006). Relationships between cohesion, collective efficacy and performance in professional basketball teams: An examination of mediating effects. *Journal of Sport Sciences, 24*, 59-68. https://doi.org/10.1080/02640410500127736

Hogg, M.A. (1993). Group cohesiveness: A critical review and some new directions. *European Review of Social Psychology, 4*, 85-111. https://doi.org/10.1080/14792779343000031

Høigaard, R., Säfvenbom, R., & Tønnessen, F.E. (2006). The relationship between group cohesion, group norms, and perceived social loafing in soccer teams. *Small Group Research, 37*, 217-232. https://doi.org/10.1177/1046496406287311

Horn, T., Byrd, M., Martin, E., & Young, C. (2012). Perceived motivational climate and team cohesion in adolescent athletes. *Sport Science Review, 21*, 25-48. https://doi.org/10.2478/v10237-012-0009-3

Jowett, S., & Chaundy, V. (2004). An investigation into the impact of coach leadership and coach–athlete relationship on group cohesion. *Group Dynamics: Theory, Research and Practice, 8*, 302-311. https://doi.org/10.1037/1089-2699.8.4.302

Juntumaa, B., Toms, M., Keskivaara, P., & Elovainio, M. (2007). Coaching and cohesion: The perceptions of adolescents, coaches, and team leaders in Finnish junior hockey. In E.M. Vargios (Ed.), *Educational psychology research focus* (pp. 121-132). Nova Science.

Kahn, R.L., Wolfe, D.M., Quinn, R.P., Snoek, J.D., & Rosenthal, R.A. (1964). *Occupational stress: Studies in role conflict and role ambiguity.* Wiley.

Latané, B., Williams, K., & Harkins, S. (1979). Many hands make light the work: The causes and consequences of social loafing. *Journal of Personality and Social Psychology, 37*, 822-832. https://doi.org/10.1037/0022-3514.37.6.822

LePine, J.A., Piccolo, R.F., Jackson, C.L., Mathieu, J.E., & Saul, J.R. (2008). A meta-analysis of teamwork processes: Tests of a multidimensional model and relationships with team effectiveness criteria. *Personnel Psychology, 61*, 273-307. https://doi.org/10.1111/j.1744-6570.2008.00114.x

Martin, L.J., Carron, A.V., & Burke, S.M. (2009). Team building interventions in sport: A meta-analysis. *Sport and Exercise Psychology Review, 5*, 3-18.

Martin, L.J., Carron, A.V., Eys, M.A., & Loughead, T. (2012). Development of a cohesion questionnaire for children's sport teams. *Group Dynamics: Theory, Research, and Practice, 16*, 68-79. https://doi.org/10.1037/a0024691

Mathieu, J., Maynard, T.M., Rapp, T., & Gilson, L. (2008). Team effectiveness 1997-2007: A review of recent advancements and a glimpse into the future. *Journal of Management, 34*, 410-476. https://doi.org/10.1177/0149206308316061

McEwan, D. (2020). The effects of perceived teamwork on emergent states and satisfaction with performance among team sport athletes. *Sport, Exercise, and Performance Psychology, 9*, 1-15. https://doi.org/10.1037/spy0000166

McEwan, D., & Beauchamp, M.R. (2014). Teamwork in sport: A theoretical and integrative review. *International Review of Sport and Exercise Psychology, 7*, 229-250. https://doi.org/10.1080/1750984X.2014.932423

McEwan, D., Zumbo, B.D., Eys, M.A., & Beauchamp, M.R. (2018). The development and psychometric properties of the Multidimensional Assessment of Teamwork in Sport. *Journal of Sport and Exercise Psychology, 40*, 60-72. https://doi.org/10.1123/jsep.2017-0193

McLaren, C.D., Eys, M.A., & Murray, R.A. (2015). A coach-initiated motivational climate intervention and athletes' perceptions of group cohesion in youth sport. *Sport, Exercise, and Performance Psychology, 4*, 113-126. https://doi.org/10.1037/spy0000026

Mertens, N., Boen, F., Steffens, N.K., Cotterill, S.T., Haslam, S.A., & Fransen, K. (2020). Leading together towards a stronger 'us': An experimental test of the effectiveness of the 5R Shared Leadership Program (5R^S) in basketball teams. *Journal of Science and Medicine in Sport, 8*, 770-775. https://doi.org/10.1016/j.jsams.2020.01.010

Newin, J., Bloom, G.A., & Loughead, T.M. (2008). Youth ice hockey coaches' perceptions of a team-building intervention program. *The Sport Psychologist, 22*, 54-72. https://doi.org/10.1123/tsp.22.1.54

Prapavessis, H., & Carron, A.V. (1996). The effect of group cohesion on competitive state anxiety. *Journal of Sport and Exercise Psychology, 18*, 64-74. https://doi.org/10.1123/jsep.18.1.64

Prapavessis, H., & Carron, A.V. (1997). Sacrifice, cohesion, and conformity to norms in sport teams. *Group Dynamics: Theory, Research, and Practice, 1*, 231-240. https://doi.org/10.1037/1089-2699.1.3.231

Prapavessis, H., Carron, A.V., & Spink, K.S. (1996). Team building in sport. *International Journal of Sport Psychology, 27*, 269-285.

Price, M.S., & Weiss, M.R. (2013). Relationships among coach leadership, peer leadership, and adolescent athletes' psychosocial and team outcomes: A test of transformational leadership theory. *Journal of Applied Sport Psychology, 25*, 265-279. https://doi.org/10.1080/10413200.2012.725703

Rees, T., Haslam, S.A., Coffee, P., & Lavallee, D. (2015). A social identity approach to sport psychology: Principles, practice, and prospects. *Sports Medicine, 45*, 1083-1096. https://doi.org/10.1007/s40279-015-0345-4

Rousseau, V., Aube, C., & Savoie, A. (2006). Teamwork behaviors: A review and an integration of frameworks. *Small Group Research, 37*, 540-570. https://doi.org/10.1177/1046496406293125

Rovio, E., Eskola, J., Kozub, S.A., Duda, J.L., & Lintunen, T. (2009). Can high group cohesion be harmful? A case study of a junior ice-hockey team. *Small Group Research, 40*, 421-435. https://doi.org/10.1177/1046496409334359

Salas, E., Grossman, R., Hughes, A.M., & Coultas, C.W. (2015). Measuring team cohesion: Observations from the science. *Human Factors, 57*, 365-374. https://doi.org/10.1177/0018720815578267

Smith, M.J., Arthur, C.A., Hardy, J., Callow, N., & Williams, D. (2013). Transformational leadership and task cohesion in sport: The mediating role of intrateam communication. *Psychology of Sport and Exercise, 14*, 249-257. https://doi.org/10.1016/j.psychsport.2012.10.002

Spink, K.S., Ulvick, J.D., McLaren, C.D., Crozier, A.J., & Fesser, K. (2015). Effects of groupness and cohesion on intention to return in sport. *Sport, Exercise, and Performance Psychology, 4*, 293-302. https://doi.org/10.1037/spy0000043

Spink, K.S., Wilson, K.S., & Odnokon, P. (2010). Examining the relationship between cohesion and return to team in elite athletes. *Psychology of Sport and Exercise, 11*, 6-11. https://doi.org/10.1016/j.psychsport.2009.06.002

Stevens, D.E., & Bloom, G.A. (2003). The effect of team building on cohesion. *Avante, 9*, 43-54.

Swoboda, C. (2020, May 29). *Why 'The Last Dance' is must-see TV for business leaders.* Forbes. www.forbes.com/sites/chuckswoboda/2020/05/29/why-the-last-dance-is-must-see-tv-for-business-leaders/?sh=2403a9775f59

Tajfel, H. (1974). Social identity and intergroup behavior. *Social Science Information, 13*, 65-93.

Tajfel, H., & Turner, J.C. (1979). An integrative theory of intergroup conflict. In W.G. Austin & S. Worchel (Eds.), *The social psychology of intergroup relations* (pp. 33-47). Brooks-Cole.

Terry, P.C., Carron, A.V., Pink, M.J., Lane, A.M., Jones, G.J.W., & Hall, M.P. (2000). Perceptions of group cohesion and mood in sport teams. *Group Dynamics, 4*, 244-253. https://doi.org/10.1037/1089-2699.4.3.244

Turner J.C. (1982). Towards a cognitive redefinition of the social group. In H. Tajfel (Ed.), *Social identity and intergroup relations* (pp. 15-40). Cambridge University Press.

Turner, J.C. (1985). Social categorization and the self-concept: A social cognitive theory of group behaviour. In E.J. Lawler (Ed.), *Advances in group processes* (pp. 77-122). JAI Press.

Turner, J.C., & Oakes, P.J. (1989). Self-categorization theory and social influence. In P.B. Paulus (Ed.), *The psychology of group influence* (pp. 233-275). Erlbaum.

Van Vugt, M., & Hart, C.M. (2004). Social identity as social glue: The origins of group loyalty. *Journal of Personality and Social Psychology, 86*, 585-598. https://doi.org/10.1037/0022-3514.86.4.585

Widmeyer, W.N., Brawley, L.R., & Carron, A.V. (1990). The effects of group size in sport. *Journal of Sport and Exercise Psychology, 12*, 177-190. https://doi.org/10.1123/jsep.12.2.177

Wolf, S.A., Eys, M.A., & Kleinert, J. (2015). Predictors of the precompetitive anxiety response: Relative impact and prospects for anxiety regulation. *International Journal of Sport and Exercise Psychology, 13*, 344-358. https://doi.org/10.1080/1612197X.2014.982676

Wolf, S.A., Eys, M.A., Sadler, P., & Kleinert, J. (2015). Appraisal in a team context: Perceptions of cohesion predict competition importance and prospects for coping. *Journal of Sport and Exercise Psychology, 37*, 489-499. https://doi.org/10.1123/jsep.2014-0276

Worley, J.T., Harenberg, S., & Vosloo, J. (2020). The relationship between peer servant leadership, social identity, and team cohesion in intercollegiate athletics. *Psychology of Sport and Exercise, 49*, 101712. https://doi.org/10.1016/j.psychsport.2020.101712

Zaccaro, S.J., Blair, V., Peterson, C., & Zazanis, M. (1995). Collective efficacy. In J. Maddux (Ed.), *Self-efficacy, adaptation, and adjustment* (pp. 305-328). Plenum.

Chapter 19

Abraham, A., Collins, D., & Martindale, R. (2006). The coaching schematic: Validation through expert coach consensus. *Journal of Sports Sciences, 24*(6), 549-564. https://doi.org/10.1080/02640410500189173

Adie, J.W., Duda, J.L., & Ntoumanis, N. (2008). Autonomy support, basic need satisfaction and the optimal functioning of adult male and female sport participants: A test of basic needs theory. *Motivation and Emotion, 32*(3), 189-199. https://doi.org/10.1007/s11031-008-9095-z

Adie, J.W., & Jowett, S. (2010). Meta-perceptions of the coach-athlete relationship, achievement goals, and intrinsic motivation among sport participants. *Journal of Applied Social Psychology, 40*(11), 2750-2773. https://doi.org/10.1111/j.1559-1816.2010.00679.x

Allan, V., & Côté, J. (2016). A cross-sectional analysis of coaches' observed emotion-behaviour profiles and adolescent athletes' self-reported developmental outcomes. *Journal of Applied Sport Psychology, 28*(3), 321-337. https://doi.org/10.1080/10413200.2016.1162220

Ames, C. (1992). Classrooms: Goals, structures, and student motivation. *Journal of Educational Psychology, 84*(3), 261. https://doi.org/10.1037/0022-0663.84.3.261

Avner, Z., Markula, P., & Denison, J. (2017). Understanding effective coaching: A Foucauldian reading of current coach education frameworks. *International Sport Coaching Journal, 4*(1), 101-109. https://doi.org/10.1123/iscj.2016-0108

Bartholomew, K.J., Ntoumanis, N., & Thøgersen-Ntoumani, C. (2010). The controlling interpersonal style in a coaching context: Development and initial validation of a psychometric scale. *Journal of Sport and Exercise Psychology, 32*(2), 193-216. https://doi.org/10.1123/jsep.32.2.193

Bass, B.M., & Riggio, R.E. (2006). *Transformational leadership* (2nd ed.). Psychology Press.

Becker, A. (2012). Quality coaching behaviours. In P. Potrac, W. Gilbert, & J. Denison (Eds.), *Routledge handbook of sports coaching* (pp. 184-195). Routledge.

Bowles, R., & O'Dwyer, A. (2020). Athlete-centered coaching: Perspectives from the sideline. *Sports Coaching Review, 9*(3), 231-252. https://doi.org/10.1080/21640629.2019.1649901

Bronfenbrenner, U. (1999). Environments in developmental perspective: Theoretical and operational models. In S.L. Friedman & T.D. Wachs (Eds.), *Measuring environment across the life span* (pp. 3-28). American Psychological Association.

Burton, D., Gillham, A.D., & Hammermeister, J. (2011). Competitive engineering: Structural climate modifications to enhance youth athletes' competitive experience. *International Journal of Sports Science and Coaching, 6*, 201-217. https://doi.org/10.1260/1747-9541.6.2.201

Callow, N., Smith, M.J., Hardy, L., Arthur, C.A., & Hardy, J. (2009). Measurement of transformational leadership and its relationship with team cohesion and performance level. *Journal of Applied Sport Psychology, 21*(4), 395-412. https://doi.org/10.1080/10413200903204754

Cassidy, T. (2010). Holism in sports coaching: Beyond humanistic sport psychology. *International Journal of Sports Science and Coaching, 5*(4), 439-443. https://doi.org/10.1260/1747-9541.5.4.439

Charbonneau, D., Barling, J., & Kelloway, E.K. (2001). Transformational leadership and sports performance: The mediating role of intrinsic motivation. *Journal of Applied Social Psychology, 31*(7), 1521-1534. https://doi.org/10.1111/j.1559-1816.2001.tb02686.x

Chelladurai, P. (2007). Leadership in sports. In G. Tenenbaum & R.C. Eklund (Eds.), *Handbook of sport psychology* (3rd edition, pp. 113-135). Wiley.

Coatsworth, J.D., & Conroy, D.E. (2009). The effects of autonomy-supportive coaching, need satisfaction, and self-perceptions on initiative and identity in youth swimmers. *Developmental Psychology, 45*, 320-328. https://doi.org/10.1037/a0014027

Côté, J., Allan, V., Turnnidge, J., Vierimaa, M., & Evans, B. (2019). The environment, relationships, and activities that shape youth development and interest in sport. In T. Horn & A. Smith (Eds.), *Advances in sport and exercise psychology* (4th edition, pp. 467-482). Human Kinetics

Côté, J., Bruner, M., Erickson, K., Strachan, L., & Fraser-Thomas, J. (2010). Athlete development and coaching. In J. Lyle & C. Cushion (Eds.), *Sports coaching: Professionalisation and practice* (pp. 63-84). Elsevier.

Côté, J., & Gilbert, W. (2009). An integrative definition of coaching effectiveness and expertise. *International Journal of Sports Science and Coaching, 4*(3), 307-323. https://doi.org/10.1260/174795409789623892

Côté, J., Turnnidge, J., & Evans, M.B. (2014). The dynamic process of development through sport. *Kinesiologia Slovenica, 20*(3). www.proquest.com/docview/1679123868/abstract/BDD0B41ABE5A4D5CPQ/1?accountid=6180

Côté, J., Turnnidge, J., Murata, A., McGuire, C., & Martin, L. (2020). Youth sport research: Describing the integrated dynamics elements of the Personal Assets Framework. *International Journal of Sport Psychology, 51*, 562-578. https://doi.org/10.7352/IJSP.2020.51.562

Côté, J., Vierimaa, M., & Turnnidge, J. (2016). A personal assets approach to youth sport. In K. Green & A. Smith (Eds.), *Routledge handbook of youth sport* (pp. 243-256). Routledge.

Cushion, C., Nelson, L., Armour, K., Lyle, J., Jones, R., Sandford, R., & O'Callaghan, C. (2010). *Coach learning and development: A review of literature.* Sports Coach UK.

Deci, E.L., & Ryan, R.M. (2013). *Intrinsic motivation and self-determination in human behavior.* Springer Science & Business Media.

Denison, J. (2010). Planning, practice and performance: The discursive formation of coaches' knowledge. *Sport, Education and Society, 15*(4), 461-478. https://doi.org/10.1080/13573322.2010.514740

Dorsch, T.E., Smith, A.L., Blazo, J.A., Coakley, J., Côté, J., Wagstaff, C.R.D., Warner, S., King, M. Q. (2022). Toward an integrated understanding of the youth sport system. *Research Quarterly for Exercise and Sport*, 105-119. https://doi.org/10.1080/02701367.2020.1810847Duda, J.L. (2013). The conceptual and empirical foundations of Empowering Coaching™: Setting the stage for the PAPA project. *International Journal of Sport and Exercise Psychology, 11*(4), 311-318. https://doi.org/10.1080/1612197X.2013.839414

Duda, J.L., & Ntoumanis, N. (2005). After-school sport for children: Implications of a task-involving motivational climate. In J.L. Mahoney, J. Eccles, and R. Larson (Eds.), *Organized activities as contexts of development: Extracurricular activities, after-school and community programs* (pp. 311-330). Erlbaum.

Dweck, C.S., & Leggett, E.L. (1988). A social-cognitive approach to motivation and personality. *Psychological Review, 95*(2), 256. https://doi.org/10.1037/0033-295X.95.2.256

Erickson, K., & Côté, J. (2013). Observing coach-athlete interactions in real time: The state space grid method. In P. Potrac, W. Gilbert, & J. Denison (Eds.), *Routledge handbook of sports coaching* (pp. 108-120). Routledge.

Erickson, K., & Côté, J. (2016). A season-long examination of the intervention tone of coach-athlete interactions and athlete development in youth sport. *Psychology of Sport and Exercise, 22*(1), 264-272. https://doi.org/10.1016/j.psychsport.2015.08.006

Erickson, K., Côté, J., Hollenstein, T., & Deakin, J. (2011). Examining coach-athlete interactions using state space grids: An observational analysis in competitive youth sport. *Psychology of Sport and Exercise, 12*(6), 645-654. https://doi.org/10.1016/j.psychsport.2011.06.006

Erikstad, M.K., Johansen, B.T., Johnsen, M., Haugen, T., & Côté, J. (2021). "As many as possible for as long as possible"—A case study of a soccer team that fosters multiple outcomes. *The Sport Psychologist, 1*(AoP), 1-11. https://doi.org/10.1123/tsp.2020-0107

Evans, M.B., McGuckin, M., Gainforth, H.L., Bruner, M.W., & Côté, J. (2015). Coach development programmes to improve interpersonal coach behaviours: A systematic review using the re-aim framework. *British Journal of Sports Medicine, 49*(13), 871-877. http://dx.doi.org/10.1136/bjsports-2015-094634

Falcão, W.R., Bloom, G.A., & Sabiston, C.M. (2020). The impact of humanistic coach training on youth athletes' development through sport. *International Journal of Sports Science and Coaching, 15*(5-6), 610-620. https://doi.org/10.1177/1747954120933975

Ford, D.H., & Lerner, R.M. (1992). *Developmental systems theory: An integrative approach.* Sage.

Fraser-Thomas, J., Côté, J., & Deakin, J. (2005). Youth sport programs: An avenue to foster positive youth development. *Physical Education and Sport Pedagogy, 10*(1), 19-40. https://doi.org/10.1080/1740898042000334890

Gilbert, W.D., & Côté, J. (2013). Defining coaching effectiveness: A focus on coaches' knowledge. In P. Potrac, W. Gilbert, & J. Denison (Eds.), *Routledge handbook of sports coaching* (pp. 147-159). London: Routledge.

Gould, D., & Carson, S. (2008). Life skills development through sport: Current status and future directions. *International Review of Sport and Exercise Psychology, 1*(1), 58-78. https://doi.org/10.1080/17509840701834573

Harackiewicz, J.M., Durik, A.M., Barron, K.E., Linnenbrink-Garcia, L., & Tauer, J.M. (2008). The role of achievement goals in the development of interest: Reciprocal relations between achievement goals, interest, and performance. *Journal of Educational Psychology, 100*(1), 105. https://doi.org/ 10.1037/0022-0663.100.1.105

Harwood, C.G., Keegan, R.J., Smith, J.M., & Raine, A.S. (2015). A systematic review of the intrapersonal correlates of motivational climate perceptions in sport and physical activity. *Psychology of Sport and Exercise, 18*, 9-25. https://doi.org/10.1016/j.jsams.2014.11.074

Henriksen, K., Stambulova, N., & Roessler, K.K. (2010). Holistic approach to athletic talent development environments: A successful sailing milieu. *Psychology of Sport and Exercise, 11*, 212-222. https://doi.org/10.1016/j.psychsport.2009.10.005

Heuzé, J.P., Sarrazin, P., Masiero, M., Raimbault, N., & Thomas, J.P. (2006). The relationships of perceived motivational climate to cohesion and collective efficacy in elite female teams. *Journal of Applied Sport Psychology, 18*(3), 201-218. https://doi.org/10.1080/10413200600830273

Hidi, S., & Renninger, K.A. (2006). The four-phase model of interest development. *Educational Psychologist, 41*, 111-127. https://doi.org/10.1207/s15326985ep4102_4

Hodge, K., & Lonsdale, C. (2011). Prosocial and antisocial behavior in sport: The role of coaching style, autonomous vs. controlled motivation, and moral disengagement. *Journal of Sport and*

Exercise Psychology, 33(4), 527-547. https://doi.org/10.1123/jsep.33.4.527

Holt, N.L., Neely, K.C., Slater, L.G., Camiré, M., Côté, J., Fraser-Thomas, J., MacDonald, D., Strachan, L., & Tamminen, K.A. (2017). A grounded theory of positive youth development through sport based on results from a qualitative meta-study. *International Review of Sport and Exercise Psychology, 10*(1), 1-49. https://doi.org/10.1080/1750984X.2016.1180704

Horn, T.S. (2008). Coaching effectiveness in the sport domain. In T.S. Horn (Ed.), *Advances in sport psychology* (3rd ed., pp. 239-267). Human Kinetics.

Hulleman, C.S., Durik, A.M., Schweigert, S.B., & Harackiewicz, J.M. (2008). Task values, achievement goals, and interest: An integrative analysis. *Journal of Educational Psychology, 100*(2), 398. http://dx.doi.org/10.1037/0022-0663.100.2.398

Jelicic, H., Bobek, D.L., Phelps, E., Lerner, R.M., & Lerner, J.V. (2007). Using positive youth development to predict contribution and risk behaviors in early adolescence: Findings from the first two waves of the 4-H Study of Positive Youth Development. *International Journal of Behavioral Development, 31*(3), 263-273. https://doi.org/10.1177/0165025407076439

Jowett, S. (2007). Interdependence analysis and the 3+1Cs in the coach–athlete relationship. In S. Jowett & D. Lavallee (Eds.), *Social psychology in sport* (pp. 15-27). Human Kinetics.

Jowett, S., & Meek, G.A. (2000). The coach–athlete relationship in married couples: An exploratory content analysis. *The Sport Psychologist, 14*(2), 157-175. https://doi.org/10.1123/tsp.14.2.157

Jowett, S., & Nezlek, J. (2012). Relationship interdependence and satisfaction with important outcomes in coach–athlete dyads. *Journal of Social and Personal Relationships, 29*(3), 287-301. https://doi.org/10.1177/0265407511420980

Jowett, S., & Ntoumanis, N. (2004). The Coach–Athlete Relationship Questionnaire (CART-Q): Development and initial validation. *Scandinavian Journal of Medicine and Science in Sports, 14*(4), 245-257. https://doi.org/10.1111/j.1600-0838.2003.00338.x

Kidman, L. (2005). *Athlete-centred coaching: Developing inspired and inspiring people.* IPC.

Kidman, L. (2010). *Athlete-centred coaching: Developing decision makers.* IPC.

Lafrenière, M.K., Jowett, S., Vallerand, R.J., Donahue, E.G., & Lorimer, R. (2008). Passion in sport: On the quality of the coach–athlete relationship. *Journal of Sport and Exercise Psychology, 30*(5), 541-560. https://doi.org/10.1123/jsep.30.5.541

Larson, R.W. (2000). Toward a psychology of positive youth development. *The American Psychologist, 55*(1), 170-183. https://doi.org/10.1037//0003-066X.55.1.170

Lawrason, S., Turnnidge, J., Martin, L.J., & Côté, J. (2019). A transformational coaching workshop for changing youth sport coaches' behaviors: A pilot intervention study. *The Sport Psychologist, 1*(AoP), 1-9. https://doi.org/10.1123/tsp.2018-0172

Lefebvre, J.S., Evans, M.B., Turnnidge, J., Gainforth, H.L., & Côté, J. (2016). Describing and classifying coach development programmes: A synthesis of empirical research and applied practice. *International Journal of Sports Science and Coaching, 11*(6), 887-899. https://doi.org/10.1177/1747954116676116

Lefebvre, J.S., Turnnidge, J., & Côté, J. (2021). A systematic observation of coach leadership behaviors in youth sport. *Journal of Applied Sport Psychology,* 33(3), 377-386. https://doi.org/10.1080/10413200.2019.1609620

Lerner, R.M., Fisher, C.B., & Weinberg, R.A. (2000). Toward a science for and of the people: Promoting civil society through the application of developmental science. *Child Development, 71,* 11-20. https://doi.org/10.1111/1467-8624.00113

Lerner, R.M., Lerner, J.V., Almerigi, J.B., Theokas, C., Phelps, E., Gestsdottir, S., Naudeau, S., Jelicic, H., Alberts, A., Ma, L., Smith, L.M., Bobek, D.L., Richman-Raphael, D., Simpson, I., DiDenti Christiansen, E., & von Eye, A. (2005). Positive youth development, participation in community youth development programs, and community contributions of fifth-grade adolescents: Findings from the first wave of the 4-H study of positive youth development. *Journal of Early Adolescence, 25*(1), 17-71. https://doi.org/10.1177/0272431604272461

Little, R.R. (1993). What's working for today's youth: The issues, the programs, and the learnings [Paper presentation]. Institute for Children, Youth, and Families Fellows' Colloquium, Michigan State University.

Machado, J.C., Barreira, D., Galatti, L., Chow, J.Y., Garganta, J., & Scaglia, A.J. (2019). Enhancing learning in the context of street football: A case for nonlinear pedagogy. *Physical Education and Sport Pedagogy, 24*(2), 176-189. https://doi.org/10.1080/17408989.2018.1552674

Mageau, G.A., & Vallerand, R.J. (2003). The coach–athlete relationship: A motivational model. *Journal of Sports Sciences, 21*(11), 883-904. https://doi.org/10.1080/0264041031000140374

Mageau, G.A., Vallerand, R.J., Charest, J., Salvy, S.J., Lacaille, N., Bouffard, T., & Koestner, R. (2009). On the development of harmonious and obsessive passion: The role of autonomy support, activity specialization, and identification with the activity. *Journal of Personality, 77*(3), 601-646. https://doi.org/10.1111/j.1467-6494.2009.00559.x

McCalpin, M., Evans, B., & Côté, J. (2017). Young female soccer players' perceptions of their modified sport environment. *The Sport Psychologist, 31*(1), 65-77. https://doi.org/10.1123/tsp.2015-0073

Newton, M., Duda, J.L., & Yin, Z. (2000). Examination of the psychometric properties of the Perceived Motivational Climate in Sport Questionnaire-2 in a sample of female athletes. *Journal of Sports Sciences, 18*(4), 275-290. https://doi.org/10.1080/026404100365018

Nicholls, J.G. (1989). *The competitive ethos and democratic education.* Harvard University Press.

Occhino, J.L., Mallett, C.J., Rynne, S.B., & Carlisle, K.N. (2014). Autonomy-supportive pedagogical approach to sports coaching: Research, challenges and opportunities. *International Journal of Sports Science and Coaching, 9*(2), 401-415. https://doi.org/10.1260/1747-9541.9.2.401

Petitpas, A.J., Cornelius, A.E., Van Raalte, J.L., & Jones, T. (2005). A framework for planning youth sport programs that foster psychosocial development. *The Sport Psychologist, 19,* 63-80. https://doi.org/10.1123/tsp.19.1.63

Quested, E., & Duda, J.L. (2010). Exploring the social-environmental determinants of well-and ill-being in dancers: A test of basic needs theory. *Journal of Sport and Exercise Psychology, 32*(1), 39-60. https://doi.org/10.1123/jsep.32.1.39

Reinboth, M., Duda, J.L., & Ntoumanis, N. (2004). Dimensions of coaching behavior, need satisfaction, and the psychological and physical welfare of young athletes. *Motivation and Emotion, 28*(3), 297-313. https://doi.org/10.1023/B:MOEM.0000040156.81924.b8

Rogers, C.R. (1969). *Freedom to learn.* Merrill.

Sheldon, K.M., Ryan, R.M., Deci, E.L., & Kasser, T. (2004). The independent effects of goal contents and motives on well-being: It's both what you pursue and why you pursue it. *Personality and Social Psychology Bulletin, 30*(4), 475-486. https://doi.org/10.1177/0146167203261883

Smith, L.B., & Thelen, E. (2003). Development as a dynamic system. *Trends in Cognitive Sciences, 7*(8), 343-348. https://doi.org/10.1016/S1364-6613(03)00156-6

Smith, R.E., Smoll, F.L., & Cumming, S.P. (2007). Effects of a motivational climate intervention for coaches on young athletes' sport performance anxiety. *Journal of Sport and Exercise Psychology, 29*(1), 39-59. https://doi.org/10.1123/jsep.29.1.39

Smith, R.E., Smoll, F.L., & Curtis, B. (1979). Coach effectiveness training: A cognitive-behavioral approach to enhancing relationship skills in youth sport coaches. *Journal of Sport Psychology, 1*(1), 59-75. https://doi.org/10.1123/jsp.1.1.59

Smoll, F.L., & Smith, R.E. (1989). Leadership behaviors in sport: A theoretical model and research paradigm. *Journal of Applied Social Psychology, 19*(18), 1522-1551. https://doi.org/10.1111/j.1559-1816.1989.tb01462.x

Smoll, F.L., Smith, R.E., & Cumming, S.P. (2007). Effects of a motivational climate intervention for coaches on changes in young athletes' achievement goal orientations. *Journal of Clinical Sport Psychology, 1*(1), 23-46. https://doi.org/10.1123/jcsp.1.1.23

Smoll, F.L., Smith, R.E., Curtis, B., & Hunt, E. (1978). Toward a mediational model of coach- player relationships. *Research Quarterly, 49*(4), 528-541. https://doi.org/10.1080/10671315.1978.10615567

Strachan, L., MacDonald, D.J., & Côté, J. (2016). Project SCORE! Coaches' perceptions of an online tool to promote positive youth development in sport. *International Journal of Sports Science and Coaching, 11*(1), 108-115. https://doi.org/10.1177/1747954115624827

Strachan, L., Santos, F., & MacDonald, D.J. (2020). Insights into creating and implementing Project SCORE!: Lessons learned and future pathways. *Journal of Sport Psychology in Action,* 1-13. https://doi.org/10.1080/21520704.2020.1798574

Turnnidge, J., & Côté, J. (2017). Transformational coaching workshop: Applying a person-centered approach to coach development programs. *International Sport Coaching Journal, 4*, 314-325. https://doi.org/10.1123/iscj.2017-0046

Turnnidge, J., & Côté, J. (2018). Applying transformational leadership theory to coaching research in youth sport: A systematic literature review. *International Journal of Sport and Exercise Psychology, 16*(3), 327-342. https://doi.org/10.1080/1612197X.2016.1189948

Turnnidge, J., & Côté, J. (2019). Observing coaches' leadership behaviours: The development of the Coach Leadership Assessment System (CLAS). *Measurement in Physical Education and Exercise Science, 23*(3), 214-226. https://doi.org/10.1080/1091367X.2019.1602835

Vansteenkiste, M., Simons, J., Lens, W., Sheldon, K.M., & Deci, E.L. (2004). Motivating learning, performance, and persistence: The synergistic effects of intrinsic goal contents and autonomy-supportive contexts. *Journal of Personality and Social Psychology, 87(*2), 246-260. https://doi.org/10.1037/0022-3514.87.2.246

Vella, S.A., Oades, L.G., & Crowe, T.P. (2013). A pilot test of transformational leadership training for sports coaches: Impact on the developmental experiences of adolescent athletes. *International Journal of Sports Science and Coaching, 8*(3), 513-530. https://doi.org/10.1260/1747-9541.8.3.513

Vierimaa, M., Erickson, K., Côté, J., & Gilbert, W. (2012). Positive youth development: A measurement framework for sport. *International Journal of Sports Science and Coaching, 7*(3), 601-614. https://doi.org/10.1260/1747-9541.7.3.601

Vierimaa, M., Turnnidge, J., Bruner, M., & Côté, J. (2017). Just for the fun of it: Coaches' perceptions of an exemplary community youth sport program. *Physical Education and Sport Pedagogy, 22*(6), 603-617. https://doi.org/10.1080/17408989.2017.1341473

Zehntner, C., & McMahon, J. (2014). The impact of a coaching/sporting culture on one coach's identity: How narrative became a useful tool in reconstructing coaching ideologies. *Sports Coaching Review, 3*(2), 145-161. https://doi.org/10.1080/21640629.2015.1051883

Chapter 20

Åkesdotter, C., Kenttä, G., Eloranta, S., & Franck, J. (2020). The prevalence of mental health problems in elite athletes. *Journal of Science and Medicine in Sport, 23*(4), 329-335. http://doi.org/10.1016/j.jsams.2019.10.022

Alcaraz, S., Jordana, A., Pons, J., Borrueco, M., Ramis, Y., & Torregrossa, M. (2020). Maximum Information, Minimum Discomfort (MIMO): Shortening questionnaires to take care of participants in sport psychology. *Informacio Psychologica, 119*, 49-64. http://doi.org/10.14635/IPSIC.2020.119.7

Aquilina, D. (2013). A study of the relationship between elite athletes' educational development and sporting performance. *International Journal of the History of Sport, 30*(4), 374-392. http://doi.org/10.1080/09523367.2013.765723

Aquilina, D., & Henry, I. (2010). Elite athletes and university education in Europe: A review of policy and practice in higher education in the European Union member states. *International Journal of Sport Policy and Politics, 2*(1), 25-47. http://doi.org/10.1080/19406941003634024

Brown, D.J., Fletcher, D., Henry, I., Borrie, A., Emmett, J., Buzza, A., & Wombwell, S. (2015). A British university case study of the transitional experiences of student-athletes. *Psychology of Sport and Exercise, 21*, 78-90. http://doi.org/10.1016/j.psychsport.2015.04.002

Bussmann, G., & Alfermann, D. (1994). Drop-out and the female athlete: A study with track-and-field athletes. In D. Hackforth (Ed.), *Psycho-social issues and interventions in elite sport* (pp. 89-128). Lang.

B-WISER. (2018). Main findings of the B-WISER project. www.bwiser.eu/wp-content/uploads/2019/01/B-Wiser_3- luik_A5_2018.pdf

Cartigny, E., Fletcher, D., Coupland, C., & Bandelow, S. (2021). Typologies of dual career in sport: A cluster analysis of identity and self-efficacy. *Journal of Sports Sciences, 39*(5), 583-590. https://doi.org/10.1080/02640414.2020.1835238

Christensen, M.K., & Sørensen, J.K. (2009). Sport or school? Dreams and dilemmas for talented young Danish football players. *European Physical Education Review, 15*(1), 115-133. http://doi.org/10.1177/1356336X09105214

Cosh, S., & Tully, P.J. (2014). "All I have to do is pass": A discursive analysis of student athletes' talk about prioritising sport to the detriment of education to overcome stressors encountered in combining elite sport and tertiary education. *Psychology of Sport and Exercise, 15*(2), 180-189. http://doi.org/10.1016/j.psychsport.2013.10.015

Cosh, S., & Tully, P.J. (2015). Stressors, coping, and support mechanisms for student athletes combining elite sport and tertiary education: Implications for practice. *The Sport Psycholgist, 29*, 120-133. http://doi.org/10.1123/tsp.2014-0102

De Bosscher, V., De Knop, P., Van Bottenburg, M., & Shibli, S. (2006). A conceptual framework for analysing sports policy factors leading to international sporting success. *European Sport Management Quarterly, 6*(2), 185-215. http://doi.org/10.1080/16184740600955087

De Brandt, K. (2017). *A holistic perspective on student-athletes' dual career demands, competencies, and outcomes* [Doctoral dissertation]. Vrije Universiteit Brussel.

De Brandt, K., Kuettel, A., Ramis, Y., Morris, R., Torregrossa, M., Wylleman, P., Stambulova, N., Ryba, T. (in preparation). Development and initial validation of the Dual Career Development Environment Monitoring Tool.

De Brandt, K., Wylleman, P., Torregrossa, M., Schipper-van, N., Minelli, D., Defruyt, S., & De Knop, P. (2018). Exploring the factor structure of the Dual Career Competency Questionnaire for Athletes in European pupil- and student-athletes. *International Journal of Sport and Exercise Psychology.* http://doi.org/10.1080/1612197X.2018.1511619

De Girolamo, G., Dagani, J., Purcell, R., Cocchi, A., & McGorry, P.D. (2012). Age of onset of mental disorders and use of mental health services: Needs, opportunities and obstacles. *Epidemiology and Psychiatric Sciences, 21,* 47-57.

De Knop, P., Wylleman, P., Van Hoecke, J., & Bollaert, L. (1999). Sports management—a European approach to the management of the combination of academics and elite-level sport. In S. Bailey (Ed.), *Perspectives: The interdisciplinary series of physical education and sport science. Vol. 1: School sport and competition* (pp. 49-62). Meyer & Meyer Sport.

Debois, N., Ledon, A., & Wylleman, P. (2015). A lifespan perspective on the dual career of elite male athletes. *Psychology of Sport and Exercise, 21,* 15-26. http://doi.org/10.1016/j.psychsport.2014.07.011

Defruyt, S. (2019). *Dual career support providers: Competencies, support strategies and education* [Doctoral dissertation]. Vrije Universiteit Brussel.

Defruyt, S., Wylleman, P., Kegelaers, J., & De Brandt, K. (2020). Factors influencing Flemish elite athletes' decision to initiate a dual career path at higher education. *Sport in Society, 23*(4), 660-677. http://doi.org/10.1080/17430437.2019.1669324

Defruyt, S., Wylleman, P., Stambulova, N., Cecić Erpič, S., Graczyk, M., & De Brandt, K. (2019). Competencies of dual career support providers (DCSPs): A scenario-specific perspective. *International Journal of Sport and Exercise Psychology.* http://doi.org/10.1080/1612197X.2019.1655773

Demulier, V., Le Scanff, C., & Stephan, Y. (2013). Psychological predictors of career planning among active elite athletes: An application of the social cognitive career theory. *Journal of Applied Sport Psychology, 25,* 341-353. http://dx.doi.org/10.1080/10413200.2012.736444.

ECO-DC. (n.d.). *Ecology of dual careers work package 1 report, 20.* Retrieved May 16, 2023, from www.ljmu.ac.uk/-/media/ljmu/projects/dualcareers/files/wp1-report.pdf

ECO-DC. (2020). *Ecology of dual careers: Final report.*

Ellis, J., Brown, K., Ramsay, S., & Falk, J. (2017). Changes in student-athletes' self-efficacy for making healthful food choices and food preparation following a cooking education intervention. *Journal of Nutrition Education and Behavior.* http://doi.org/10.1016/j.jneb.2017.10.002

Erikson, E.H. (1963). *Childhood and society.* Stonton.

European Commission. (2012). *EU guidelines on dual careers of athletes: Recommended policy actions in support of dual careers in high-performance sport.*

European Commission. (2015). *Study on the minimum requirements for dual career services.*

Geraniosova, K., & Ronkainen, N.J. (2015). The experience of dual career through Slovak athletes' eyes. *Physical Culture and Sport. Studies and Research, 65*(1), 31-40. http://doi.org/10.1515/pcssr

Gledhill, A., & Harwood, C. (2015). A holistic perspective on career development in UK female soccer players: A negative case analysis. *Psychology of Sport and Exercise, 21,* 65-77. http://doi.org/10.1016/j.psychsport.2015.04.003

Golby, J., & Wood, P. (2009). The effects of psychological skills training on mental toughness and psychological well-being of student-athletes. *Psychology, 7*(7), 901-913. http://doi.org/10.4236/psych.2016.76092

Gomez, J., Bradley, J., & Conway, P. (2018). The challenges of a high-performance student athlete. *Irish Educational Studies, 37*(3), 329-349. http://doi.org/10.1080/03323315.2018.1484299

Gorczynski, P., & Aron, C.M. (2020). Social isolation and loneliness in elite athletes during a pandemic. *Revista Argentina de Clinica Psicològia, 3,* 58-61. http://doi.org/10.24205/03276716.2020.909

Gouttebarge, V., Jonkers, R., Moen, M., Verhagen, E., Wylleman, P., & Kerkhoffs, G. (2017). The prevalence and risk indicators of symptoms of common mental disorders among current and former Dutch elite athletes. *Journal of Sports Sciences, 35*(21), 2148-2156. http://doi.org/10.1080/02640414.2016.1258485

Gouttebarge, V., Kerkhoffs, G., & Lambert, M. (2016). Prevalence and determinants of symptoms of common mental disorders in retired professional rugby union players. *European Journal of Sport Science, 16*(5), 595-602. http://doi.org/10.1080/17461391.2015.1086819

Guidotti, F., Cortis, C., & Capranica, L. (2015). Dual career of European student-athletes: A systematic literature review. *Kinesiologia Slovenica, 21*(3), 5-20.

Gulbin, J., Oldenziel, K., Weissensteiner, J., & Gagné, F. (2010). A look through the rear view mirror: Developmental experiences and insights of high performance athletes. *Talent Development and Excellence, 2*(2), 149-164.

Hardcastle, S.J., Tye, M., Glassey, R., & Hagger, M.S. (2015). Exploring the perceived effectiveness of a life skills development program for high-performance athletes. *Psychology of Sport and Exercise, 16,* 139-149. http://doi.org/10.1016/j.psychsport.2014.10.005

Harris, H.L., Altekruse, M.K., & Engels, D.W. (2003). Helping freshman student athletes adjust to college life using psychoeducational groups. *Journal for Specialists in Group Work, 28*(1), 64-81. http://doi.org/10.1177/019339202250079

Havighurst, R.J. (1973). History of developmental psychology: Socialization and personality development through the life span. In P.B. Baltes & K.W. Schaie (Eds.), *Life-span developmental psychology: Personality and socialization* (pp. 3-24). Academic Press.

Hellstedt, J.C. (1995). Invisible players: A family systems model. In S.M. Murphy (Ed.), *Sport psychology interventions* (pp. 117-146). Human Kinetics.

Henriksen, K., & Stambulova, N. (2017). Creating optimal environments for talent development: A holistic ecological approach. In J. Baker, S. Cobley, J. Schorer, & N. Wattie (Eds.), *Routledge handbook of talent identification and development in sport.* Routledge.

Henriksen, K., Storm, L.K., Kuettel, A., Linnér, L., & Stambulova, N. (2020). A holistic ecological approach to sport and study: The case of an athlete friendly university in Denmark. *Psychology of Sport and Exercise, 47,* 101637. http://doi.org/10.1016/j.psychsport.2019.101637

Henry, I. (2013). Athlete development, athlete rights and athlete welfare: A European Union perspective. *International Journal of the History of Sport, 30*(4), 356-373. http://doi.org/10.1080/09523367.2013.765721

Hong, H.J., & Coffee, P. (2018). A psycho-educational curriculum for sport career transition practitioners: Development and evaluation. *European Sport Management Quarterly, 18*(3), 287-306. http://doi.org/10.1080/16184742.2017.1387925

Jowett, S., & Meek, G.A. (2000). The coach athlete relationship in married couples: An exploratory content analysis. *The Sport Psychologist, 14*, 157-175.

Kerr, G., & Dacyshyn, A. (2000). The retirement experiences of elite, female gymnasts. *Journal of Applied Sport Psychology, 12*, 115-133.

Kessler, R.C., Amminger, G.P., Aguilar-Gaxiola, S., Alonso, J., Lee, S., & Üstün, T.B. (2007). Age of onset of mental disorders: A review of recent literature. *Current Opinion in Psychiatry, 20*(4), 359-364. http://doi.org/10.1097/YCO.0b013e32816ebc8c

Kıvanç, S. (2018). Does sports and school run together? A needs analysis of university student-athletes. *Journal of Physical Education and Sports Studies, 10*(2). http://doi.org/10.30655/besad.2018.10

Knights, S., Sherry, E., & Ruddock-Hudson, M. (2016). Investigating elite end-of-athletic-career transition: A systematic review. *Journal of Applied Sport Psychology, 28*(3), 291-308. http://doi.org/10.1080/10413200.2015.1128992

Kornbeck, J. (2017). Bosman and athlete welfare: The sports law approach, the social policy approach, and the EU guidelines on dual careers. *Liverpool Law Review, 38*(3), 307-323. http://doi.org/10.1007/s10991-017-9203-9

Kuettel, A., Boyle, E., & Schmid, J. (2017). Factors contributing to the quality of the transition out of elite sports in Swiss, Danish, and Polish athletes. *Psychology of Sport and Exercise, 29*, 27-39. http://doi.org/10.1016/j.psychsport.2016.11.008

Kuettel, A., & Larsen, C.H. (2019). Risk and protective factors for mental health in elite athletes: A scoping review. *International Review of Sport and Exercise Psychology*, 1-35. http://doi.org/10.1080/1750984X.2019.1689574

Lavallee, D. (2019). Engagement in sport career transition planning enhances performance. *Journal of Loss and Trauma, 24*(1), 1-8. http://doi.org/10.1080/15325024.2018.1516916

Linnér, L., Stambulova, N.B., Lindahl, K., & Wylleman, P. (2019). Swedish university student-athletes' dual career scenarios and competences. *International Journal of Sport and Exercise Psychology*. http://doi.org/10.1080/1612197X.2019.1611898

MacNamara, Á., & Collins, D. (2010). The role of psychological characteristics in managing the transition to university. *Psychology of Sport and Exercise, 11*(5), 353-362. http://doi.org/10.1016/j.psychsport.2010.04.003

McGillivray, D., & McIntosh, A. (2006). 'Football is my life': Theorizing social practice in the Scottish professional football field. *Sport in Society, 9*(3), 371-387. https://doi.org/10.1080/17430430600673381

McQuown Linnemeyer, R., & Brown, C. (2010). Career maturity and foreclosure in student athletes, fine arts students, and general college students. *Journal of Career Development, 37*(3), 616-634. http://doi.org/10.1177/0894845309357049

Miller, P.S., & Kerr, G. (2002). The athletic, academic and social experiences of intercollegiate student-athletes. *Journal of Sport Behavior, 25*(4), 346-367.

Morris, R., Cartigny, E., Ryba, T.V., Wylleman, P., Henriksen, K., Torregrossa, M., Lindahl, K., & Cecić Erpič, S. (2020). A taxonomy of dual career development environments in European countries. *European Sport Management Quarterly*. http://doi.org/10.1080/16184742.2020.1725778

Oros, S., & Hanţiu, I. (2016). Guidelines of the dual career management in sport. *Civilization and Sport, 17*(3), 211-218.

Park, S., Lavallee, D., & Tod, D. (2013). Athletes' career transition out of sport: A systematic review. *International Review of Sport and Exercise Psychology, 6*(1), 22-53. http://doi.org/10.1080/1750984X.2012.687053

Parker, P.C., Perry, R.P., Hamm, J.M., Chipperfield, J.G., & Hladkyj, S. (2016). Enhancing the academic success of competitive student athletes using a motivation treatment intervention (attributional retraining). *Psychology of Sport and Exercise, 26*, 113-122. http://doi.org/10.1016/j.psychsport.2016.06.008

Perez-Rivases, A., Pons, J., Regüela, S., Viladrich, C., Pallarès, S., & Torregrossa, M. (2020). Spanish female student-athletes' perception of key competencies for successful dual career adjustment. *International Journal of Sport and Exercise Psychology*. http://doi.org/10.1080/1612197X.2020.1717575

Petitpas, A., Brewer, B.W., & Van Raalte, J.L. (1996). Transitions of the student-athlete: Theoretical, empirical, and practical perspectives. In E.F. Etzel, A.P. Ferrante, & J.W. Pinkney (Eds.), *Counseling college student-athletes: Issues and interventions* (pp. 137-156). Fitness Information Technology.

Piaget, J. (1971). *Biology and knowledge: An essay on the relations between organic regulations and cognitive processes*. University of Chicago Press.

Price, N., Morrison, N., & Arnold, S. (2010). Life out of the limelight: Understanding the non-sporting pursuits of elite athletes. *International Journal of Sport and Society, 1*(3), 69-79.

Pummell, B., Harwood, C., & Lavallee, D. (2008). Jumping to the next level: A qualitative examination of within-career transition in adolescent event riders. *Psychology of Sport and Exercise, 9*(4), 427-447. http://doi.org/10.1016/j.psychsport.2007.07.004

Rees, T., & Hardy, L. (2000). An investigation of the social support experiences of high-level sports performers. *The Sport Psychologist, 14*, 327-347.

Reints, A. (2011). *Validation of the holistic athletic career model and the identification of variables related to athletic retirement* [Doctoral dissertation]. Vrije Universiteit Brussel.

Rice, P.F. (1998). *Human development: A life-span approach*. Prentice Hall.

Romar, J. (2012). An analysis of Finnish skiing school students' academic education and athletic success. *Acta Universitatis Palackianae Olomucensis Gymnica, 42*(1), 35-41. www.gymnica.upol.cz/index.php/gymnica/article/viewArticle/310

Rosier, N. (2020). *A holistic perspective into the factors contributing to the continued development of junior elite athletes into senior elite level* [Doctoral dissertation]. Vrije Universiteit Brussel.

Ryan, C. (2015). Factors impacting carded athlete's readiness for dual careers. *Psychology of Sport and Exercise, 21*, 1-7. http://doi.org/10.1016/j.psychsport.2015.04.008

Ryba, T.V., Aunola, K., Kalaja, S., Selänne, H., Ronkainen, N.J., Nurmi, J.-E., & Zourbanos, N. (2016). A new perspective on adolescent athletes' transition into upper secondary school: A longitudinal mixed methods study protocol. *Cogent Psychology, 3*. http://doi.org/10.1080/23311908.2016.1142412

Ryba, T.V., Stambulova, N.B., Ronkainen, N.J., Bundgaard, J., & Selänne, H. (2015). Dual career pathways of transnational athletes. *Psychology of Sport and Exercise, 21*, 125-134. http://doi.org/10.1016/j.psychsport.2014.06.002

Sallen, J., Hemming, K., & Richartz, A. (2018). Facilitating dual careers by improving resistance to chronic stress: Effects of an intervention programme for elite student athletes. *European Journal of Sport Science, 18*(1), 112-122. http://doi.org/10.1080/17461391.2017.1407363

Samuel, R.D., & Tenenbaum, G. (2013). Athletes' decision-making in career change-events. *The Sport Psychologist, 27,* 78-82.

Schinke, R., Papaioannou, A., Maher, C., Parham, W.D., Larsen, C.H., Gordin, R., & Cotterill, S. (2020). Sport psychology services to professional athletes: Working through COVID-19. *International Journal of Sport and Exercise Psychology, 18*(4), 409-413. http://doi.org/10.1080/1612197X.2020.1766182

Schlossberg, N.K. (1981). A model for analyzing human adaptation to transition. *The Counseling Psychologist, 9,* 2-18.

Skrubbeltrang, L.S., Olesen, J.S., & Christian, J. (2016). How to stay becoming—living up to the code of conduct in a sports class. *Ethnography and Education, 11*(3), 371-387. http://doi.org/10.1080/17457823.2015.1109467

Smismans, S., Wylleman, P., De Brandt, K., Defruyt, S., Vitali, F., Ramis, Y., Torregrossa, M., Lobinger, B., Stambulova, N.B., & Cecić Erpič, S. (2020). From elite sport to the job market: Development and initial validation of the Athlete Competency Questionnaire for Employability (ACQE). *Cultura, Ciencia y Deporte, 16*(47), 39-48.

Smith, A.L. (2003). Perceptions of peer relationships in physical activity contexts: A road less travelled in youth sport and exercise psychology research. *Psychology of Sport and Exercise, 4,* 25-39.

Stambulova, N.B. (2003). Symptoms of a crisis-transition: A grounded theory study. In N. Hassmen (Ed.), *Svensk Idrottspykologisk Förening* (pp. 97-109). Örebro University Press.

Stambulova, N., Alfermann, D., Statler, T., & Côté, J. (2009). ISSP position stand: Career development and transitions of athletes. *International Journal of Sport and Exercise Psychology, 7*(4), 395-412. http://doi.org/10.1080/1612197X.2009.9671916

Stambulova, N., Franck, A., & Weibull, F. (2012). Assessment of the transition from junior-to-senior sports in Swedish athletes. *International Journal of Sport and Exercise Psychology, 10*(2), 79-95. http://doi.org/10.1080/1612197X.2012.645136

Stambulova, N.B., Ryba, T.V., & Henriksen, K. (2020). Career development and transitions of athletes: The International Society of Sport Psychology position stand revisited. *International Journal of Sport and Exercise Psychology,* 19, 524-550. https://doi.org/10.1080/1612197X.2020.1737836

Stambulova, N.B., Schinke, R.J., Lavallee, D., & Wylleman, P. (2020). The COVID-19 pandemic and Olympic / Paralympic athletes' developmental challenges and possibilities in times of a global crisis-transition. *International Journal of Sport and Exercise Psychology,* 1-10. http://doi.org/10.1080/1612197X.2020.1810865

Stambulova, N.B., & Wylleman, P. (2019). Psychology of athletes' dual careers: A state-of-the-art critical review of the European discourse. *Psychology of Sport and Exercise, 42,* 74-88. http://doi.org/10.1016/j.psychsport.2018.11.013

Storm, L., Henriksen, K., Stambulova N., Cartigny E., Ryba T., De Brandt, K., Ramis, Y., & Cecic Erpic, S. (2021). Ten essential features of European dual career development environments: A multiple case study. *Psychology of Sport and Exercise, 54.* https://doi.org/10.1016/j.psychsport.2021.101918

Tekavc, J., Wylleman, P., & Cecić Erpič, S. (2015). Perceptions of dual career development among elite level swimmers and basketball players. *Psychology of Sport and Exercise, 21,* 27-41. http://doi.org/10.1016/j.psychsport.2015.03.002

Torregrossa, M., Ramis, Y., Pallarés, S., Azócar, F., & Selva, C. (2015). Olympic athletes back to retirement: A qualitative longitudinal study. *Psychology of Sport and Exercise, 21,* 1-7. http://doi.org/10.1016/j.psychsport.2015.03.003

van Ramele, S., Aoki, H., Kerkhoffs, G.M.M.J., & Gouttebarge, V. (2017). Mental health in retired professional football players: 12-month incidence, adverse life events and support. *Psychology of Sport and Exercise, 28,* 85-90. http://doi.org/10.1016/J.PSYCHSPORT.2016.10.009

van Rens, F.E.C.A., Ashley, R.A., & Steele, A.R. (2019). Wellbeing and performance in dual careers: The role of academic and athletic identities. *The Sport Psychologist, 33,* 42-51. https://doi.org/10.1123/tsp.2018-0026

Weiss, M.R., & Stuntz, C.P. (2004). A little friendly competition: Peer relationships and psychosocial development in youth sport and physical activity contexts. In M. Weiss (Ed.), *Developmental sport and exercise psychology: A lifespan perspective* (pp. 165-196). Fitness Information Technology.

Wylleman, P. (2000). Interpersonal relationships in sport: Uncharted territory. *International Journal of Sport Psychology, 31,* 1-18.

Wylleman, P. (2019). A developmental and holistic perspective on transitioning out of elite sport. In M.H. Anshel (Editor-in-Chief), *APA handbook of sport and exercise psychology. Vol. 1: Sport psychology* (pp. 201-216). American Psychological Association.

Wylleman, P., Alfermann, D., & Lavallee, D. (2004). Career transitions in perspective. *Psychology of Sport and Exercise, 5,* 7-20. doi.org/10.1016/S1469-0292(02)00049-3

Wylleman, P., De Brandt, K., & Defruyt, S. (2017). *GEES handbook for dual career support providers.* https://kics.sport.vlaanderen/topsport/Documents/170301_GEES_Handbook_for_dual_career_support_providers.pdf

Wylleman, P., De Knop, P., Menkehorst, H., Theeboom, M., & Annerel, J. (1993). Career termination and social integration among elite athletes. In S. Serpa, J. Alves, V. Ferreira, & A. PaulaBrito (Eds.), *Proceedings of the VIII World Congress of Sport Psychology* (pp. 902906). International Society of Sport Psychology.

Wylleman, P., De Knop, P., Sloore, H., Vanden Auweele, Y., & Ewing, M. (2003). Talented athletes' perceptions of the athlete–coach–parents relationships. *Kinesiologia Slovenica, 2,* 59-69.

Wylleman, P., & Lavallee, D. (2004). A developmental perspective on transitions faced by athletes. In M. Weiss (Ed.), *Developmental sport and exercise psychology: A lifespan perspective* (pp. 507-527). Fitness Information Technology.

Wylleman, P., & Rosier, N. (2016). Holistic perspective on the development of elite athletes. In M. Raab, P. Wylleman, R. Seiler, A.-M. Elbe, & A. Hatzigeorgiadis (Eds.), *Sport and exercise psychology research: From theory to practice* (pp. 269-288). Elsevier. https://doi.org/10.1016/B978-0-12-803634-1.00013-3

Wylleman, P., Rosier, N., De Brandt, K., & De Knop, P. (2016). Coaching athletes through career transitions. In R. Thelwell, C. Harwood, & I. Greenlees (Eds.), *The psychology of sports coaching: Research and practice* (p. 290). Routledge.

Wylleman, P., Smismans, S., Defruyt, S., Kegelaers, J., De Brandt, K., & Blijlevens, S. (2020). *How should athletes be supported before, during and after athletic retirement? Moving from an athletic-centred needs analysis to practical guidelines for career support stakeholders.* https://library.olympic.org/Default/doc/SYRACUSE/470797/how-should-athletes-be-supported-before-during-and-after-athletics-retirement-moving-from-an-athleti

Wylleman, P., Stambulova, N., Torregrossa, M., Schipper-Van Veldhoven, N., & Defruyt, S. (2018). *The development and evaluation of training modules for DC support providers.* https://library.olympic.org/Default/doc/SYRACUSE/177233/the-development-and-evaluation-of-training-modules-for-dual-career-support-providers-a-european-pilo

Chapter 21

Alexander, K., Stafford, A., & Lewis, R. (2011). *The experiences of children participating in organized sport in the UK*. NSPCC.

Alford, G. (2019). Child athletes lose big on lagging rights in sport. www.equaltimes.org/child-athletes-lose-big-on-lagging?lang=en#.YDwVcVX7TbGG

Allen, G., Rhind, D.J.A., & Koshy, V. (2015). Enablers and barriers for male students transferring life skills from the sports hall to the classroom. *Qualitative Research in Sport, Exercise and Health, 7*, 53-67. https://doi.org/10.1080/2159676X.2014.893898

Bandura, A. (1986). *Social foundations of thought and action: A social cognitive theory*. Prentice Hall.

Brackenridge, C.H., Bishopp, D.T., Moussalli, S., & Tapp, J. (2008). The characteristics of sexual abuse in sport: A multidimensional scaling analysis of events described in media reports. *International Journal of Exercise and Sport Psychology, 6*, 385-406. https://doi.org/10.1080/1612197X.2008.9671881

Brackenridge, C.H., Kay, T., & Rhind, D.J.A. (Eds.) (2012). Sport, *children's rights and violence prevention: A source book on global issues and local programmes*. Brunel University Press.

Brackenridge, C.H., & Rhind, D.J.A. (Eds.) (2010). *Elite child athlete welfare: International perspectives*. Brunel University Press.

Brackenridge, C.H., & Rhind, D.J.A. (2014). Institutional responses to child abuse in sport: Reflections on 30 years of science and activism. *Social Sciences, 3*(3), 326-340. https://doi.org/10.3390/socsci3030326

Chroni, S., Fasting, K., Hartill, M., Knorre, N., Martin, M., Papaefstathiou, M., Rhind, D.J.A., Rulofs, B., Toftegaard-Støckel, J., Vertommen, T., & Zurc, J. (2012). *Prevention of sexual and gender harassment and abuse in sport: Initiatives from Europe and beyond*. German Sports Youth.

Coyle, M., Gorczynski, P., & Gibson, K. (2017). "You have to be mental to jump off a board any way": Elite divers' conceptualizations and perceptions of mental health. *Psychology of Sport and Exercise, 29*, 10-18, https://doi.org/10.1016/j.psychsport.2016.11.00556

Cull, M., Rzepnicki, T. L., O'Day, K., & Epstein, R. A. (2013). Applying principles from safety science to improve child protection. Child Welfare, 92(2), 179-195.

Edwards, J.R.D., Davey, J., & Armstrong, K. (2013). Returning to the roots of culture: A review and re-conceptualisation of safety culture. *Safety Science, 55*, 70-88. https://doi.org/10.1016

FIFA. (2019). Football Guardians toolkit. https://resources.fifa.com/image/upload/toolkit-fifa-guardians.pdf?cloudid=nz1lyz3ykaioy7gwfmgssS

Filho, A.P.G., & Waterson, P.E. (2018). Maturity models and safety culture: A critical review. *Safety Science, 105*, 192-211. https://doi.org/10.1016

Fisher, L.A., & Anders, A.D. (2020). Engaging with cultural sport psychology to explore systemic sexual exploitation in USA Gymnastics: A call to commitments. *Journal of Applied Sport Psychology*. https://doi.org/10.1080/10413200.2018.1564944

Grey-Thompson, T. (2017). *Duty of care in sport: Independent report to government*. HMSO.

Human Rights Watch (2020). I was hit so many times I can't count. www.hrw.org/report/2020/07/20/i-was-hit-so-many-times-i-cant-count/abuse-child-athletes-japan#:~:text=(Tokyo%2C%20July%2020%2C%202020,trauma%20resulting%20from%20the%20abusd

IOC. (2017). IOC safeguarding toolkit. www.olympic.org/news/ioc-launches-toolkit-for-olympic-movement-to-safeguard-athletes-from-harassment-and-abuse-in-sport

Kavanagh, E., Rhind, D.J.A., & Gordon-Thomson, G. (2020). Duties of care and welfare practices. In R. Arnold & D. Fletcher (Eds.), *Stress, well-being and performance in sport*. Routledge.

Mountjoy M, Brackenridge C, Arrington M, et al. (2016). International Olympic Committee consensus statement: harassment and abuse (non-accidental violence) in sport. British Journal of Sports Medicine, 50, 1019-1029.

Mountjoy, M., Rhind, D.J.A., Tiivas, A., & Leglise, M. (2015). Safeguarding the child athlete in sport: A review, a framework and recommendations for the IOC youth athlete development model. *British Journal of Sports Medicine, 49*, 883-886. https://doi.org/10.1136/bjsports-2015-094619

Papaefstathiou, M., Rhind, D.J.A., & Brackenridge, C. (2012). Child protection in ballet: Experiences and views of teachers, administrators and ballet students. *Child Abuse Review, 22*, 127-141. https://onlinelibrary.wiley.com/doi/abs/10.1002/car.2228

Owusu-Sekyere, F., Rhind, D. J. A. & Hills, L. (2021). Safeguarding Culture: Towards a new approach to preventing child maltreatment in sport. Sport Management review, 1-23.

Phelps, A., Kelly, J., Lancaster, S., Mehrzad, J., & Panter, A. (2017). *Report of the independent review panel into the climate and culture of the world class programme in British cycling*. UK Sport.

Raakman, E., Dorsch, K., & Rhind, D.J.A. (2010). The development of a typology of abusive coaching behaviours within youth sport. *International Journal of Sports Science and Coaching, 5*, 503-515.

Raven, B.H. (1992). A power interaction model on interpersonal influence: French and Raven thirty years on. *Journal of Social Behavior and Personality, 7*, 217-244.

Rhind, D.J.A., & Jowett, S. (2010). Relationship maintenance strategies in the coach–athlete relationship: The development of the COMPASS model. *Journal of Applied Sport Psychology, 22*, 106-121. https://doi.org/10.1080/10413200903474472

Rhind, D.J.A, McDermott, J., Lambert, E., & Koleva, I. (2015). A review of safeguarding cases in sport. *Child Abuse Review, 24*, 418-426. https://doi.org/10.1008/car-2306

Rhind, D.J.A., & Owusu-Sekyere, F. (2018). *International Safeguards for Children in Sport: Developing and embedding a safeguarding culture*. Routledge.

Rhind, D.J.A., & Owusu-Sekyere, F. (2020). Evaluating the impacts of working towards the International Safeguards for Children in Sport. *Sport Management Review, 23*, 104-116.

Rhind, D.J.A., & Owusu-Sekyere, F. (2021). Safeguarding culture: Towards a new approach to preventing child maltreatment in sport. *Sport Management Review*, 300-322.

Roberts, C., Faull, A.L., & Tod, D. (2016). Blurred lines: Performance enhancement, common mental disorders and referral in the U.K athletic population. *Frontiers in Psychology, 1067*, 61-73. https://doi.org/10.3389

Ropes & Gray. (2018). Independent investigation into Larry Nassar. www.nassarinvestigation.com/ennnn

Sky Sports News. (2020). British Gymnastics. https://news.sky.com/story/british-gymnastics-claims-athletes-beaten-into-submission-amid-culture-of-fear-120225255

Stirling, A.E., & Kerr, G.A. (2008). Elite female swimmers' experiences of emotional abuse across time. *Journal of Emotional Abuse, 7*(4), 89-113. https://doi.org/10.1300

United Nations. (1989). Convention on the Rights of the Child. www.unicef.org.uk/what-we-do/un-convention-child-rights/?sisearchengine=284&siproduct=Campaign_G_02_Our_Work&gclid=EAIaIQobChMI6d-Pl-Du8QIVgtrICh0VIg-TAEAAYAyAAEgJKJvD_BwE

World Players. (2017). World Players Association launches Universal Declaration of Player Rights. www.thefica.com/world-players-association-launches-universal-declaration-of-player-rights

Vertommen, T., Veldhoven, N.S., Wouters, K., Kampen, J.K., Brackenridge, C.H., Rhind, D., & Van Den Eedea, F. (2016). Interpersonal violence against children in sport in the Netherlands and Belgium. *Child Abuse and Neglect, 51*, 223-236. https://doi.org/10.1016/j.chiabu.2015.10.006

Chapter 22

Al-Yaaribi, A., & Kavussanu, M. (2017). Teammate prosocial and antisocial behaviors predict task cohesion and burnout: The mediating role of affect. *Journal of Sport and Exercise Psychology, 39*(3), 199-208. https://doi.org/10.1123/jsep.2016-0336

Al-Yaaribi, A., & Kavussanu, M. (2018). Consequences of prosocial and antisocial behaviors in adolescent male soccer players: The moderating role of motivational climate. *Psychology of Sport and Exercise, 37*, 91-99. https://doi.org/10.1016/j.psychsport.2018.04.005

Al-Yaaribi, A., Kavussanu, M., & Ring, C. (2016). Consequences of perceived prosocial and antisocial behavior for the recipient. *Psychology of Sport and Exercise, 26*, 102-112. https://doi.org/10.1016/j.psychsport.2016.06.012

Al-Yaaribi, A., Kavussanu, M., & Ring, C. (2018). The effects of prosocial and antisocial behaviors on emotion, attention, and performance during a basketball free throw shooting task. *Journal of Sport and Exercise Psychology, 40*(6), 303-311. https://doi.org/10.1123/jsep.2017-0179

Ames, C. (1992). Achievement goals, motivational climate, and motivational processes. In G.C. Roberts (Ed.), *Motivation in sport and exercise* (pp. 161-176). Human Kinetics.

Aquino, K., & Reed, A. (2002). The self-importance of moral identity. *Journal of Personality and Social Psychology, 83*(6), 1423-1440. https://doi.org/10.1037/0022-3514.83.6.1423

Bandura, A. (1991). Social cognitive theory of moral thought and action. In W.M. Kurtines & J.L. Gewirtz (Eds.), *Handbook of moral behavior and development* (pp. 45-103). Erlbaum.

Bandura, A. (1997). *Self-efficacy: The exercise of control.* Freeman.

Bandura, A. (1999). Moral disengagement in the perpetration of inhumanities. *Personality and Social Psychology Review, 3*(3), 193-209. https://doi.org/10.1207/s15327957pspr0303_3

Bartholomew, K., Ntoumanis, N., & Thogersen-Ntoumani, C. (2009). A review of controlling motivational strategies from a self-determination theory perspective: Implications for sports coaches. *International Review of Sport and Exercise Psychology, 2*(2), 215-233. https://doi.org/10.1080/17509840903235330

Batson, C.D., Early, S., & Salvarani, G. (1997). Perspective taking: Imagining how another feels versus imagining how you would feel. *Personality and Social Psychology Bulletin, 23*(7), 751-758. https://doi.org/10.1177/0146167297237008

Benson, A.J., & Bruner, M.W. (2018). How teammate behaviors relate to athlete affect, cognition, and behaviors: A daily diary approach within youth sport. *Psychology of Sport and Exercise, 3*, 119-127. https://doi.org/10.1016/j.psychsport.2017.10.008

Benson, A.J., Bruner, M.W., & Eys, M. (2017). A social identity approach to understanding the conditions associated with antisocial behaviors among teammates in female teams. *Sport, Exercise, and Performance Psychology, 6*(2), 129-142. https://doi.org/10.1037/spy0000090

Boardley, I.D., & Kavussanu, M. (2009). The influence of social variables and moral disengagement on prosocial and antisocial behaviors in field hockey and netball. *Journal of Sports Sciences, 27*(8), 843-854. https://doi.org/10.1080/02640410902887283

Boardley, I.D., & Kavussanu, M. (2010). Effects of goal orientation and perceived value of toughness on antisocial behavior in soccer: The mediating role of moral disengagement. *Journal of Sport and Exercise Psychology, 32*(2), 176-192. https://doi.org/10.1123/jsep.32.2.176

Boardley, I.D., Matosic, D., & Bruner, M.W. (2020). A longitudinal examination of the relations between moral disengagement and antisocial behavior in sport. *Journal of Sport and Exercise Psychology, 42*(2), 123-131. https://doi.org/10.1123/jsep.2019-0127

Bolter, N.D., & Kipp, L.E. (2018). Sportspersonship coaching behaviors, relatedness need satisfaction, and early adolescent athletes' prosocial and antisocial behavior. *International Journal of Sport and Exercise Psychology, 16*(1), 20-35. https://doi.org/10.1080/1612197X.2016.1142461

Bolter, N.D., & Weiss, M.R. (2012). Coaching for character: Development of the Sportsmanship Coaching Behaviors Scale (SCBS). *Sport, Exercise, and Performance Psychology, 1*(2), 32-47. https://doi.org/10.1037/a0026300

Bolter, N.D., & Weiss, M.R. (2013). Coaching behaviors and adolescent athletes' sportspersonship outcomes: Further validation of the Sportsmanship Coaching Behaviors Scale (SCBS). *Sport, Exercise, and Performance Psychology, 2*(1), 32-47. https://doi.org/10.1037/a0029802

Bredemeier, B.J., & Shields, D.L. (1986). Game reasoning and interactional morality. *Journal of Genetic Psychology, 147*(2), 257-275. https://doi.org/10.1080/00221325.1986.9914499

Brown, M.E., Trevino, L.K., & Harrison, D. (2005). Ethical leadership: A social learning perspective for construct development and testing. *Organizational Behavior and Human Decision Processes, 97*(2), 117-134. https://doi.org/10.1016/j.obhdp.2005.03.002

Bruner, M.W., Boardley, I.D., Allan, V., Root, Z., Buckham, S., Forrest, C., & Côté, J. (2017). Examining social identity and intrateam moral behaviors in competitive youth ice hockey using stimulated recall. *Journal of Sports Sciences, 35*(20), 1963-1974. https://doi.org/10.1080/02640414.2016.1243797

Bruner, M.W., Boardley, I.D., Benson, A.J., Wilson, K.S., Root, Z., Turnnidge, J., Sutcliffe, J., & Côté, J. (2018). Disentangling the relations between social identity and prosocial and antisocial behavior in competitive youth sport. *Journal of Youth and Adolescence, 47*, 1113-1127. https://doi.org/10.1007/s10964-017-0769-2

Bruner, M.W., Boardley, I.D., & Côté, J. (2014). Social identity and prosocial and antisocial behavior in youth sport. *Psychology of Sport and Exercise, 15*(1), 56-64. https://doi.org/10.1016/j.psychsport.2013.09.003

Carron, A. V., Widmeyer, W.N., & Brawley, L. R. (1985). The development of an instrument to assess cohesion in sport teams: The Group Environment Questionnaire. *Journal of Sport Psychology, 7*, 244-266. https://doi.org/10.1123/jsp.7.3.244

Cheon, S.H., Reeve, J., & Ntoumanis, N. (2018). A needs-supportive intervention to help PE teachers enhance students' prosocial behavior and diminish antisocial behavior. *Psychology of Sport and Exercise, 35*, 74-88. https://doi.org/10.1016/j.psychsport.2017.11.010

Davis, M.H. (1983). Measuring individual differences in empathy: Evidence for a multidimensional approach. *Journal of Personality and Social Psychology, 44*(1), 113-126. https://doi.org/10.1037/0022-3514.44.1.113

Davis, P.A., Davis, L., Wills, S., Appleby, R., & Nieuwenhuys, A. (2018). Exploring "sledging" and interpersonal emotional-regulation strategies in professional cricket. *The Sport Psychologist, 32*(2), 136-145. https://doi.org/10.1123/tsp.2017-0078

Deci, E.L., & Ryan, R. (1985). *Intrinsic motivation and self-determination in human behavior.* Springer.

Deci, E.L., & Ryan, R.M. (2000). The "what" and "why" of goal pursuits: Human needs and the self-determination of behavior. *Psychological Inquiry, 11*(4), 227-268. https://doi.org/10.1207/S15327965PLI1104_01

Dixon, N. (2007). Trash talking, respect for opponents and good competition. *Sport, Ethics and Philosophy, 1*(1), 96-106. https://doi.org/10.1080/17511320601143025

Eisenberg, N., & Fabes, R.A. (1998). Prosocial development. In N. Eisenberg (Ed.), *Handbook of child psychology. Vol. 3: Social, emotional, and personality development* (pp. 701-778). Wiley.

Eys, M.A., Loughead, T.M., Bray, S.R., & Carron, A.V. (2009). Development of a cohesion questionnaire for youth: The Youth Sport Environment Questionnaire. *Journal of Sport and Exercise Psychology, 31*(3), 390-408. https://doi.org/10.1123/jsep.31.3.390

Gano-Overway, L.A., Newton, M., Magyar, T.M., Fry, M.D., Kim, M.-S., & Guivernau, M.R. (2009). Influence of caring youth sport contexts on efficacy-related beliefs and social behaviors. *Developmental Psychology, 45*(2), 329-340. https://doi.org/10.1037/a0014067

Harwood, C.G., Keegan, R.J., Smith, J.M.J., & Raine, A.S. (2015). A systematic review of the intrapersonal correlates of motivational climate perceptions in sport and physical activity. *Psychology of Sport and Exercise, 18*, 9-25. https://doi.org/10.1016/j.psychsport.2014.11.005

Hewstone, M., Rubin, M., & Willis, H. (2002). Intergroup bias. *Annual Review of Psychology, 53*, 575-604. https://doi.org/10.1146/annurev.psych.53.100901.135109

Hodge, K., & Gucciardi, D.F. (2015). Antisocial and prosocial behavior in sport: The role of motivational climate, basic psychological needs, and moral disengagement. *Journal of Sport and Exercise Psychology, 37*(3), 257-273. https://doi.org/10.1123/jsep.2014-0225

Hodge, K., & Lonsdale, C. (2011). Prosocial and antisocial behavior in sport: The role of coaching style, autonomous vs. controlled motivation, and moral disengagement. *Journal of Sport and Exercise Psychology, 33*(4), 527-547. https://doi.org/10.1123/jsep.33.4.527

Joseph, S., & Cramer, D. (2011). Sledging in cricket: Elite English batsmen's experiences of verbal gamesmanship. *Journal of Clinical Sport Psychology, 5*(3), 237-251. https://doi.org/10.1123/jcsp.5.3.237

Kavussanu, M. (2012). Moral behavior in sport. In S. Murphy (Ed.), *The Oxford handbook of sport and performance psychology* (pp. 364-383). Oxford University Press.

Kavussanu, M. (2019). Toward an understanding of transgressive behavior in sport: Progress and prospects. *Psychology of Sport and Exercise, 42*, 33-39. https://doi.org/10.1016/j.psychsport.2019.01.009

Kavussanu, M., & Al-Yaaribi, A. (2021). Prosocial and antisocial behavior in sport. *International Journal of Sport and Exercise Psychology, 19*(2), 179-202. https://doi.org/10.1080/1612197X.2019.1674681

Kavussanu, M., & Boardley, I.D. (2009). The Prosocial and Antisocial Behavior in Sport Scale. *Journal of Sport and Exercise Psychology, 31*(1), 97-117. https://doi.org/10.1123/jsep.31.1.97

Kavussanu, M., Boardley, I.D., Sagar, S.S., & Ring, C. (2013). Bracketed morality revisited: How do athletes behave in two contexts? *Journal of Sport and Exercise Psychology, 35*(5), 449-463. https://doi.org/10.1123/jsep.35.5.449

Kavussanu, M., & Ring, C. (2016). Moral thought and action in sport and student life: A study of bracketed morality. *Ethics and Behavior, 26*(4), 267-276. https://doi.org/10.1080/10508422.2015.1012764

Kavussanu, M., & Ring, C. (2021). Bracketed morality in adolescent football players: A tale of two contexts. *Psychology of Sport and Exercise, 53*, 101835. https://doi.org/10.1016/j.psychsport.2020.101835

Kavussanu, M., Seal, A.R., & Phillips, D.R. (2006). Observed prosocial and antisocial behaviors in male soccer teams: Age differences across adolescence and the role of motivational variables. *Journal of Applied Sport Psychology, 18*(4), 326-344. https://doi.org/10.1080/10413200600944108

Kavussanu, M., Stamp, R., Slade, G., & Ring, C. (2009). Observed prosocial and antisocial behaviors in male and female soccer players. *Journal of Applied Sport Psychology, 21*(Suppl.), S62-S76. https://doi.org/10.1080/10413200802624292

Kavussanu, M., & Stanger, N. (2017). Moral behavior in sport. *Current Opinion in Psychology, 16*, 185-192. https://doi.org/10.1016/j.copsyc.2017.05.010

Kavussanu, M., Stanger, N., & Ring, C. (2015). The effects of moral identity on moral emotion and antisocial behavior in sport. *Sport, Exercise and Performance Psychology, 4*(4), 268-279. https://doi.org/10.1037/spy0000040

Nicholls, J.G. (1989). *The competitive ethos and democratic education.* Harvard University Press.

Pizzi, G., & Stanger, N. (2020). Consequences of teammate moral behavior: Linking team moral norms with cohesion and collective efficacy. *International Journal of Sport and Exercise Psychology, 18*(4), 437-453. https://doi.org/10.1080/1612197X.2019.1593215

Podsakoff, P.M., MacKenzie, S.B., Lee, J.-Y., & Podsakoff, N.P. (2003). Common method biases in behavioral research: A critical review of the literature and recommended remedies. *Journal of Applied Psychology, 88*(5), 879-903. https://doi.org/10.1037/0021-9010.88.5.879

Raedeke, T.D., & Smith, A.L. (2001). Development and preliminary validation of an athlete burnout measure. *Journal of Sport and Exercise Psychology, 23*(4), 281-306. https://doi.org/10.1123/jsep.23.4.281

Ring, C., Kavussanu, M., Al-Yaaribi, A., Tenenbaum, G., & Stanger, N. (2019). Effects of antisocial behaviour on opponent's anger, attention, and performance. *Journal of Sports Sciences, 37*(8), 871-877. https://doi.org/10.1080/02640414.2018.1532061

Sage, L.D., & Kavussanu, M. (2008). Goal orientations, motivational climate, and prosocial and antisocial behavior in youth football: Exploring their temporal stability and reciprocal relationships. *Journal of Sports Sciences, 26*(7), 717-732. https://doi.org/10.1080/02640410701769716

Sage, L.D., Kavussanu, M., & Duda, J.L. (2006). Goal orientations and moral identity as predictors of prosocial and antisocial functioning in male association football players. *Journal of Sports Sciences, 24*(5), 455-466. https://doi.org/10.1080/02640410500244531

Sheehy, T., & Hodge, K. (2015). Motivation and morality in masters athletes: A self-determination theory perspective. *International Journal of Sport and Exercise Psychology, 13*(3), 273-285. https://doi.org/10.1080/1612197X.2014.956326

Smith, R. (1986). Toward a cognitive-affective model of athletic burnout. *Journal of Sport Psychology, 8*(1), 36-50. https://doi.org/10.1123/jsp.8.1.36

Stanger, N., Backhouse, S.H., Jennings, A., & McKenna, J. (2018). Linking motivational climate with moral behavior in youth sport: The role of social support, perspective taking, and moral disengagement. *Sport, Exercise, and Performance Psychology, 7*(4), 392-407. https://doi.org/10.1037/spy0000122

Stanger, N., Kavussanu, M., Boardley, I.D., & Ring, C. (2013). The influence of moral disengagement and negative emotion in the regulation of antisocial behaviour. *Sport, Exercise and Performance Psychology, 2*(2), 117-129. https://doi.org/10.1037/a0030585

Stanger, N., Kavussanu, M., McIntyre, D., & Ring, C. (2016). Empathy inhibits aggression in competition: The role of provocation, emotion, and gender. *Journal of Sport and Exercise Psychology, 38*(1), 4-14. https://doi.org/10.1123/jsep.2014-0332

Stanger, N., Kavussanu, M., & Ring, C. (2012). Put yourself in their boots: Effects of empathy on emotion and aggression. *Journal of Sport and Exercise Psychology, 34*(2), 208-222. https://doi.org/10.1123/jsep.34.2.208

Tajfel, H. (1981). *Human groups and social and categories: Studies in social psychology.* Cambridge University Press.

Trevino, L.K., Brown, M.E., & Hartman, L.P. (2003). A qualitative investigation of perceived executive ethical leadership: Perceptions from inside and outside the executive suite. *Human Relations, 56*(1), 5-37. https://doi.org/10.1177/0018726703056001448

Watson, D., Clark, L.A., & Tellegen, A. (1988). Development and validation of brief measures of positive and negative affect: The PANAS scales. *Journal of Personality and Social Psychology, 54*(6), 1063-1070. https://doi.org/10.1037/0022-3514.54.6.1063

Chapter 23

Alliger, G.M., Cerasoli, C.P., Tannenbaum, S.I., & Vessey, W.B. (2015). Team resilience: How teams flourish under pressure. *Organizational Dynamics, 44*, 176-184. https://doi.org/10.1016/j.orgdyn.2015.05.003

Arnold, R., Collington, S., Manley, H., Rees, S., Soanes, J., & Williams, M. (2019). "The team behind the team": Exploring the organizational stressor experiences of sport science and management staff in elite sport. *Journal of Applied Sport Psychology, 31*, 7-26. https://doi.org/10.1080/10413200.2017.1407836

Atkinson, M. (2016). Ethnography. In Smith, B. M., & Sparkes, A. C. (Eds.). *Routledge handbook of qualitative research in sport and exercise* (pp. 49-61). Routledge.

Bennett, J.B., Aden, C.A., Broome, K., Mitchell, K., & Rigdon, W.D. (2010). Team resilience for young restaurant workers: Research-to-practice adaptation and assessment. *Journal of Occupational Health Psychology, 15*, 223-236. https://psycnet.apa.org/doi/10.1037/a0019379

Bowers, C., Kreutzer, C., Cannon-Bowers, J., & Lamb, J. (2017). Team resilience as a second-order emergent state: A theoretical model and research directions. *Frontiers in Psychology, 8*, 1360. https://doi.org/10.3389/fpsyg.2017.01360

Brownrigg, A., Burr, V., Bridger, A., & Locke, A. (2018). 'You shut up and go along with it': An interpretative phenomenological study of former professional footballers' experiences of addiction. *Qualitative Research in Sport, Exercise and Health, 10*, 238-255. https://doi.org/10.1080/2159676X.2017.1396557

Bryan, C., O'Shea, D., & MacIntyre, T. (2019). Stressing the relevance of resilience: A systematic review of resilience across the domains of sport and work. *International Review of Sport and Exercise Psychology, 12*, 70-111. https://doi.org/10.1080/1750984X.2017.1381140

Carless, D., & Douglas, K. (2017). Narrative research. *Journal of Positive Psychology, 12*, 307-308. https://doi.org/10.1080/17439760.2016.1262611

Chapman, M.T., Lines, R.L., Crane, M., Ducker, K.J., Ntoumanis, N., Peeling, P., Parker, S.K., Quested, E., Temby, P., Thøgersen-Ntoumani, C., and Gucciardi, D.F., 2020. Team resilience: A scoping review of conceptual and empirical work. *Work and Stress, 34*(1), pp. 57-81. https://doi.org/10.1080/02678373.2018.1529064

Connor, K.M., & Davidson, J.R.T. (2003). Development of a new resilience scale: The Connor-Davidson Resilience Scale (CD-RISC). *Depression and Anxiety, 18*, 76-82. https://doi.org/10.1002/da.10113

Coulter, T.J., Mallett, C.J., & Singer, J.A. (2016). A subculture of mental toughness in an Australian Football League club. *Psychology of Sport and Exercise, 22*, 98-113. https://doi.org/10.1016/j.psychsport.2015.06.007

Davydov, D.M., Stewart, R., Ritchie, K., & Chaudieu, I. (2010). Resilience and mental health. *Clinical Psychology Review, 30*, 479-495. https://doi.org/10.1016/j.cpr.2010.03.003

Decroos, S., Lines, R.L., Morgan, P.B.C., Fletcher, D., Sarkar, M., Fransen, K., Boen, F., & Vande Broek, G. (2017). Development and validation of the Characteristics of Resilience in Sports Teams Inventory. *Sport, Exercise, and Performance Psychology, 6*, 158-178. https://doi.org/10.1037/spy0000089

Douglas, K., & Carless, D. (2009). Abandoning the performance narrative: Two women's stories of transition from professional golf. *Journal of Applied Sport Psychology, 21*, 213-230. https://doi.org/10.1080/10413200902795109

Egeland, B., Carlson, E., & Sroufe, L.A. (1993). Resilience as process. *Development and Psychopathology, 5*, 517-528. https://doi.org/10.1017/S0954579400006131

Etherington, K. (2004). *Becoming a reflexive researcher: Using ourselves in research.* Kingsley.

Fasey, K.J., Sarkar, M., Wagstaff, C.R., & Johnston, J. (2021). Defining and characterizing organizational resilience in elite sport. *Psychology of Sport and Exercise, 52*, 101834. https://doi.org/10.1016/j.psychsport.2020.101834

Fletcher, D., & Sarkar, M. (2012). A grounded theory of psychological resilience in Olympic champions. *Psychology of Sport and Exercise, 13*, 669-678. https://doi.org/10.1016/j.psychsport.2012.04.007

Fletcher, D., & Sarkar, M. (2013). Psychological resilience: A review and critique of definitions, concepts, and theory. *European Psychologist, 18*, 12-23. https://doi.org/10.1027/1016-9040/a000124

Fransen, K., McEwan, D., & Sarkar, M. (2020). The impact of identity leadership on team functioning and well-being in team sport: Is psychological safety the missing link? *Psychology of Sport and Exercise, 51*, 101763. https://doi.org/10.1016/j.psychsport.2020.101763

Freeman, P., & Rees, T. (2009). How does perceived support lead to better performance? An examination of potential mechanisms. *Journal of Applied Sport Psychology, 21*, 429-441. https://doi.org/10.1080/10413200903222913

Freeman, P., & Rees, T. (2010). Perceived social support from team-mates: Direct and stress-buffering effects on self-confidence. *European Journal of Sport Science, 10*, 59-67. https://doi.org/10.1080/17461390903049998

Friedman, H.L., & Robbins, B.D. (2012). The negative shadow cast by positive psychology: Contrasting views and implications of humanistic and positive psychology on resiliency. *The Humanistic Psychologist, 40*, 87-102. https://doi.org/10.1080/08873267.2012.643720

Galatzer-Levy, I.R., & Bonanno, G.A. (2016). It's not so easy to make resilience go away: Commentary on Infurna and Luthar (2016). *Perspectives on Psychological Science, 11*, 195-198. https://doi.org/10.1177%2F1745691615621277

Galli, N., & Vealey, R.S. (2008). "Bouncing back" from adversity: Athletes' experiences of resilience. *Sport Psychologist, 22*, 316-335. https://psycnet.apa.org/doi/10.1123/tsp.22.3.316

Gorgulu, R., Senel, E., Adilogulları, İ., & Yildiz, M. (2018). An adaptation study of measurement properties for the Characteristics of Resilience in Sports Team Inventory. *Education Sciences, 8*, 139. https://doi.org/10.3390/educsci8030139

Grey-Thompson, T. (2017, April). *Duty of care in sport*. British Government Department for Digital, Culture, Media & Sport. https://assets.publishing.service.gov.uk/government/uploads/system/uploads/attachment_data/file/610130/Duty_of_Care_Review_-_April_2017__2.pdf

Gucciardi, D.F., Crane, M., Ntoumanis, N., Parker, S.K., Thøgersen-Ntoumani, C., Ducker, K.J., Peeling, P., Chapman, M.T., Quested, E., & Temby, P. (2018). The emergence of team resilience: A multilevel conceptual model of facilitating factors. *Journal of Occupational and Organizational Psychology, 91*(4), 729-768. https://doi.org/10.1111/joop.12237

Gucciardi, D.F., Jackson, B., Coulter, T.J., & Mallett, C.J. (2011). The Connor-Davidson Resilience Scale (CD-RISC): Dimensionality and age-related measurement invariance with Australian cricketers. *Psychology of Sport and Exercise, 12*, 423-433. https://doi.org/10.1016/j.psychsport.2011.02.005

Gonzalez, S.P., Moore, E.W.G., Newton, M., & Galli, N.A. (2016). Validity and reliability of the Connor-Davidson Resilience Scale (CD-RISC) in competitive sport. *Psychology of Sport and Exercise, 23*, 31-39. https://doi.org/10.1016/j.psychsport.2015.10.005

Hartwig, A., Clarke, S., Johnson, S., & Willis, S. (2020). Workplace team resilience: A systematic review and conceptual development. *Organizational Psychology Review, 10*, 169-200. https://doi.org/10.1177%2F2041386620919476

Ilgen, D.R., Hollenbeck, J.R., Johnson, M., & Jundt, D. (2005). Teams in organizations: From input-process-output models to IMOI models. *Annual Review of Psychology, 56*, 517-543. https://doi.org/10.1146/annurev.psych.56.091103.070250

Joseph, J. (2013). Resilience as embedded neoliberalism: A governmentality approach. *Resilience, 1*, 38-52. https://doi.org/10.1080/21693293.2013.765741

Kaplan, H.B. (2013). Reconceptualizing resilience. In Goldstein, S., Brooks, R. B., (Eds.) *Handbook of resilience in children* (pp. 39-55). Springer.

Kegelaers, J., & Wylleman, P. (2019). Exploring the coach's role in fostering resilience in elite athletes. *Sport, Exercise, and Performance Psychology, 8*, 239-254. https://psycnet.apa.org/doi/10.1037/spy0000151

Kegelaers, J., Wylleman, P., Blijlevens, S., Boonstoppel, A., & Hendriks, M. (2020). Coaches' perspectives on team resilience during major international competition. *International Journal of Sport Psychology, 51*, 221-246. https://doi.org/10.7352/IJSP.2020.51.221

Kegelaers, J., Wylleman, P., Bunigh, A., & Oudejans, R.R. (2021). A mixed methods evaluation of a pressure training intervention to develop resilience in female basketball players. *Journal of Applied Sport Psychology, 33*, 151-172. https://doi.org/10.1080/10413200.2019.1630864

Kegelaers, J., Wylleman, P., & Oudejans, R.R. (2020). A coach perspective on the use of planned disruptions in high-performance sports. *Sport, Exercise, and Performance Psychology, 9*, 29-44. https://doi.org/10.1037/spy0000167

Kent, S., Devonport, T.J., Lane, A.M., & Nicholls, W. (2022). Implementing a pressure training program to improve decision-making and execution of skill among Premier League academy soccer players. *Journal of Applied Sport Psychology, 34*, 691-712. https://doi.org/10.1080/10413200.2020.1868618

Kozlowski, S.W.J., & Klein, K.J. (2000). A multilevel approach to theory and research in organizations: Contextual, temporal, and emergent processes. In K.J. Klein & S.W.J. Kozlowski (Eds.), *Multilevel theory, research, and methods in organizations: Foundations, extensions, and new directions* (pp. 3-90). Jossey-Bass.

Krane, V., & Baird, S.M. (2005). Using ethnography in applied sport psychology. *Journal of Applied Sport Psychology, 17*, 87-107. https://doi.org/10.1080/10413200590932371

Lu, F.J., Lee, W.P., Chang, Y.K., Chou, C.C., Hsu, Y.W., Lin, J.H., & Gill, D.L. (2016). Interaction of athletes' resilience and coaches' social support on the stress-burnout relationship: A conjunctive moderation perspective. *Psychology of Sport and Exercise, 22*, 202-209. https://doi.org/10.1016/j.psychsport.2015.08.005

Luthar, S.S. (2006). Resilience in development: A synthesis of research across five decades. In D. Cicchetti & D.J. Cohen (Eds.). *Developmental psychopathology. Vol. 3: Risk, disorder, and adaptation* (pp. 739-795). Wiley.

Luthar, S.S., Cicchetti, D., & Becker, B. (2000). The construct of resilience: A critical evaluation and guidelines for future work. *Child Development, 71*, 543-562. https://doi.org/10.1111/1467-8624.00164

Luthar, S.S., & Zelazo, L.B. (2003). Research on resilience: An integrative review. In S.S. Luthar (Ed.), *Resilience and vulnerability: Adaptation in the context of childhood adversities* (pp. 510-549). Cambridge University Press.

Mahdiani, H., & Ungar, M. (2021). The dark side of resilience. *Adversity and Resilience Science, 2*, 147-155. https://doi.org/10.1007/s42844-021-00031-z

Marks, M.A., Mathieu, J.E., & Zaccaro, S.J. (2001). A temporally based framework and taxonomy of team processes. *Academy of Management Review, 26*, 356-376. https://doi.org/10.5465/amr.2001.4845785

Masten, A.S., & Reed, M.J. (2002). Resilience in development. In C.R. Snyder & S.J. Lopez (Eds.), *Handbook of positive psychology* (pp. 74-78). Oxford University Press.

Morgan, P.B.C., Fletcher, D., & Sarkar, M. (2013). Defining and characterizing team resilience in elite sport. *Psychology of Sport and Exercise, 14*, 549-559. https://doi.org/10.1016/j.psychsport.2013.01.004

Morgan, P.B.C., Fletcher, D., & Sarkar, M. (2015). Understanding team resilience in the world's best athletes: A case study of a rugby union World Cup winning team. *Psychology of Sport and Exercise, 16*, 91-100. https://doi.org/10.1016/j.psychsport.2014.08.007

Morgan, P.B., Fletcher, D., & Sarkar, M. (2017). Recent developments in team resilience research in elite sport. *Current Opinion in Psychology, 16*, 159-164. https://doi.org/10.1016/j.copsyc.2017.05.013

Morgan, P.B., Fletcher, D., & Sarkar, M. (2019). Developing team resilience: A season-long study of psychosocial enablers and strategies in a high-level sports team. *Psychology of Sport and Exercise, 45*, 101543. https://doi.org/10.1016/j.psychsport.2019.101543

Mummery, W.K., Schofield, G., & Perry, C. (2004). Bouncing back: The role of coping style, social support, and self-concept in resilience of sport performance. *Athletic Insight, 6*, 1-18.

Oliver, D. (2017). David Oliver: When "resilience" becomes a dirty word. *British Medical Journal*, 358. https://doi.org/10.1136/bmj.j3604

Olusoga, P., Maynard, I., Hays, K., & Butt, J. (2012). Coaching under pressure: A study of Olympic coaches. *Journal of Sports Sciences, 30*, 229-239. https://doi.org/10.1080/02640414.2011.639384

Olusoga, P., & Kenttä, G. (2017). Desperate to quit: A narrative analysis of burnout and recovery in high-performance sports coaching. *Sport Psychologist, 31*, 237-248. https://doi.org/10.1123/tsp.2016-0010

Peterson, C., & Seligman, M.E. (2004). *Character strengths and virtues: A handbook and classification* (Vol. 1). Oxford University Press.

Rees, T., & Hardy, L. (2004). Matching social support with stressors: Effects on factors underlying performance in tennis. *Psychology of Sport and Exercise, 5*, 319-337. https://doi.org/10.1016/S1469-0292(03)00018-9

Richardson, G.E. (2002). The metatheory of resilience and resiliency. *Journal of Clinical Psychology, 58*, 307-321. https://doi.org/10.1002/jclp.10020

Richardson, G.E., Neiger, B.L., Jensen, S., & Kumpfer, K.L. (1990). The resiliency model. *Health Education, 21*, 33-39. https://doi.org/10.1080/00970050.1990.10614589

Rutter, M. (1981). Stress, coping and development: Some issues and some questions. *Journal of Child Psychology and Psychiatry and Allied Disciplines, 22*, 323-356. https://doi.org/10.1111/j.1469-7610.1981.tb00560.x

Rutter, M. (1985). Resilience in the face of adversity: Protective factors and resistance to psychiatric disorder. *British Journal of Psychiatry, 147*(6), 598-611. https://doi.org/10.1192/bjp.147.6.598

Rutter, M. (1987). Psychosocial resilience and protective mechanisms. *American Journal of Orthopsychiatry, 57*, 316-331. https://doi.org/10.1111/j.1939-0025.1987.tb03541.x

Rutter, M. (2006). Implications of resilience concepts for scientific understanding. *Annals of the New York Academy of Sciences, 1094*, 1-12.

Sarkar, M. (2014). *The assessment of psychological resilience in sport performers* [Doctoral thesis]. Loughborough University.

Sarkar, M. (2018). Developing resilience in elite sport: The role of the environment. *The Sport and Exercise Scientist, 55*, 20-21.

Sarkar, M., & Fletcher, D. (2013). How should we measure psychological resilience in sport performers? *Measurement in Physical Education and Exercise Science, 17*, 264-280. https://doi.org/10.1080/1091367X.2013.805141

Sarkar, M., & Hilton, N.K. (2020). Psychological resilience in Olympic medal-winning coaches: A longitudinal qualitative study. *International Sport Coaching Journal, 7*, 209-219. https://doi.org/10.1123/iscj.2019-0075

Sarkar, M., & Page, A.E. (2022). Developing individual and team resilience in elite sport: Research to practice. *Journal of Sport Psychology in Action, 13*, 40-53. https://doi.org/10.1080/21520704.2020.1861144

Spector-Mersel, G., & Knaifel, E. (2018). Narrative research on mental health recovery: Two sister paradigms. *Journal of Mental Health, 27*, 298-306. https://doi.org/10.1080/09638237.2017.1340607

Thelwell, R.C., Weston, N.J., Greenlees, I.A., & Hutchings, N.V. (2008). Stressors in elite sport: A coach perspective. *Journal of Sports Sciences, 26*, 905-918. https://doi.org/10.1080/02640410801885933

Ungar, M. (2004a). *Nurturing hidden resilience in troubled youth*. University of Toronto Press.

Ungar, M. (2004b). A constructionist discourse on resilience: Multiple contexts, multiple realities among at-risk children and youth. *Youth and society, 35*, 341-365. https://doi.org/10.1177%2F0044118X03257030

Ungar, M. (2008). Resilience across cultures. *British Journal of Social Work, 38*, 218-235. https://doi.org/10.1093/bjsw/bcl343

Ungar, M. (2011). The social ecology of resilience: Addressing contextual and cultural ambiguity of a nascent construct. *American Journal of Orthopsychiatry, 81*, 1-17. https://doi.org/10.1111/j.1939-0025.2010.01067.x

Ungar, M. (2012). Social ecologies and their contribution to resilience. In Ungar, M. (Ed). *The social ecology of resilience* (pp. 13-31). Springer.

Ungar, M. (2018). What works: A manual for designing programs that build resilience. Resilience Research. https://resilienceresearch.org/files/WhatWorks-Ungar-WebVersion.pdf

van Breda, A.D (2018). A critical review of resilience theory and its relevance for social work. *Social Work, 54*, 1-18. http://dx.doi.org/10.15270/54-1-611

van Rens, F.E., Burgin, M., & Morris-Binelli, K. (2021). Implementing a pressure inurement training program to optimize cognitive appraisal, emotion regulation, and sport self-confidence in a women's state cricket team. *Journal of Applied Sport Psychology, 33*, 402-419. https://doi.org/10.1080/10413200.2019.1706664

Wagstaff, C.R.D., Fasey, K.J., & Sarkar, M. (2020). Resilience in teams and organizations. In D. Hackfort & R.J. Schinke (Eds.), *Routledge international encyclopaedia of sport and exercise psychology. Vol. 1: Theoretical and methodological concepts* (pp. 550-564). Routledge.

Wagstaff, C.R.D., Sarkar, M., Davidson, C.L., & Fletcher, D. (2016). Resilience in sport: A critical review of psychological processes, sociocultural influences, and organizational dynamics. In C.R.D. Wagstaff (Ed.), *The organizational psychology of sport* (pp. 120-149). Routledge.

West, B.J., Patera, J.L., & Carsten, M.K. (2009). Team level positivity: Investigating positive psychological capacities and team level outcomes. *Journal of Organizational Behavior, 30*, 249-267. https://doi.org/10.1002/job.593

White, R.L., & Bennie, A. (2015). Resilience in youth sport: A qualitative investigation of gymnastics coach and athlete perceptions. *International Journal of Sports Science and Coaching, 10*, 379-394. https://doi.org/10.1260/1747-9541.10.2-3.379

Yang, Y., Li, Y., & Sun, Y. (2020). Psychometric evaluation of the Characteristics of Resilience in Sports Team Inventory in China. *PLOS One, 15*, 0234134. https://doi.org/10.1371/journal.pone.0234134

Young, J.A. (2014). Coach resilience: What it means, why it matters, and how to build it. *Coaching and Sport Science Review, 22*, 10-12.

Zimet, G.D., Dahlem, N.W., Zimet, S.G., & Farley, G.K. (1988). The multidimensional scale of perceived social support. *Journal of Personality Assessment, 52*(1), 30-41. https://doi.org/10.1207/s15327752jpa5201_2

Chapter 24

Arnold, R., Collington, S., Manley, H., Rees, S., Soanes, J., & Williams, M. (2019). "The team behind the team": Exploring the organizational stressor experiences of sport science and management staff in elite sport. *Journal of Applied Sport Psychology, 31*(1), 7-26. https://doi.org/10.1080/10413200.2017.1407836

Arnold, R., Fletcher, D., & Daniels, K. (2013). Development and validation of the Organizational Stressor Indicator for Sport Performers (OSI-SP). *Journal of Sport and Exercise Psychology, 35*(2), 180-196. https://doi.org/10.1123/jsep.35.2.180

Bakker, A.B., van Veldhoven, M., & Xanthopoulou, D. (2010). Beyond the demand-control model: Thriving on high job demands and resources. *Journal of Personnel Psychology, 9*(1), 3-16. https://doi.org/10.1027/1866-5888/A000006

Bowers, M.T., & Green, B.C. (2013). Reconstructing the community-based youth sport experience: How children derive meaning from unstructured and organized settings. *Journal of Sport Management, 27*(6), 422-438. https://doi.org/10.1123/jsm.27.6.422

Braun, J.V., Wykle, M.H., & Cowling, W.R. (1988). Failure to thrive in older people. A concept derived. *The Gerontologist, 28*(6), 809-812. https://doi.org/10.1093/geront/28.6.809

Brown, D.J., & Arnold, R. (2019). Sports performers' perspectives on facilitating thriving in professional rugby contexts. *Psychology of Sport and Exercise, 40*, 71-81. https://doi.org/10.1016/j.psychsport.2018.09.008

Brown, D.J., Arnold, R., Fletcher, D., & Standage, M. (2017). Human thriving: A conceptual debate and literature review. *European Psychologist, 22*, 167-179. https://doi.org/10.1027/1016-9040/a000294

Brown, D.J., Arnold, R., Reid, T., & Roberts, G. (2018). A qualitative inquiry of thriving in elite sport. *Journal of Applied Sport Psychology, 30*(2), 129-149. https://doi.org/10.1080/10413200.2017.1354339

Brown, D.J., Arnold, R., Standage, M., & Fletcher, D. (2017). Thriving on pressure: A factor mixture analysis of sport performers' responses to competitive sporting encounters. *Journal of Sport and Exercise Psychology, 39*(6), 423-437. https://doi.org/10.113/jsep.2016-0293

Brown, D.J., Arnold, R., Standage, M., & Fletcher, D. (2021). A longitudinal examination of thriving in sport performers. *Psychology of Sport and Exercise.* Advance online publication. https://doi.org/10.1016/j.psychsport.2021.101934

Brown, D.J., Arnold, R., Standage, M., Turner, J.E., & Fletcher, D. (2021). The prediction of thriving in elite sport: A prospective examination of the role of psychological need satisfaction, challenge appraisal, and salivary biomarkers. *Journal of Science and Medicine in Sport 24*(4), 373-379.. https://doi.org/10.1016/j.jsams.2020.09.019

Brown, D.J., & Fletcher, D. (2017). Effects of psychological and psychosocial interventions on sport performance: A meta-analysis. *Sports Medicine, 41*, 77-99. https://doi.org/10.1007/s40279-016-0552-7

Brown, D.J., Sarkar, M., & Howells, K. (2020). Growth, resilience, and thriving: A jangle fallacy? In R. Wadey, M. Day, & K. Howells (Eds.), *Growth following adversity in sport: A mechanism to positive change in sport* (pp. 59-72). Routledge.

Bull, S.J., Shambrook, C.J., James, W., & Brooks, J.E. (2005). Towards an understanding of mental toughness in elite English cricketers. *Journal of Applied Sport Psychology, 17*(3), 209-227. https://doi.org/10.1080/10413200591010085

Bullard, D.M., Glaser, H.H., Heagarty, M.C., & Pivchik, E. (1967). Failure to thrive in the "neglected" child. *American Journal of Orthopsychiatry, 37*(4), 680-690. https://doi.org/10.1111/j.1939-0025.1967.tb00509.x

Bullough, S. (2018). UEFA champions league revenues, performance and participation 2003-2004 to 2016-2017. *Managing Sport and Leisure, 23*(1-2), 139-156. https://doi.org/10.1080/23750472.2018.1513341

Bundick, M.J., Yeager, D.S., King, P.E., & Damon, W. (2010). Thriving across the life span. In R.M. Lerner, M.E. Lamb, & A.M. Freund (Eds.), *The handbook of life-span development* (pp. 882-923). Wiley.

Carmeli, A., & Spreitzer, G.M. (2009). Trust, connectivity, and thriving: Implications for innovative behaviors at work. *Journal of Creative Behavior, 43*(3), 169-191. https://doi.org/10.1002/j.2162-6057.2009.tb01313.x

Carver, C.S. (1998). Resilience and thriving: Issues, models, and linkages. *Journal of Social Issues, 54*(2), 245-266. https://doi.org/10.1111/0022-4537.641998064

Champ, F.M., Nesti, M.S., Ronkainen, N.J., Tod, D.A., & Littlewood, M.A. (2020). An exploration of the experiences of elite youth footballers: The impact of organizational culture. *Journal of Applied Sport Psychology, 32*(2), 146-167. https://doi.org/10.1080/10413200.2018.1514429

Coakley, J. (2002). Using sports to control deviance and violence among youths: Let's be critical and cautious. In M. Gatz, M.A. Messner, & S.J. Ball-Rokeach (Eds.), *Paradoxes of youth and sport* (pp. 13-30). State University of New York Press.

Cruickshank, A., Collins, D., & Minten, S. (2014). Driving and sustaining culture change in Olympic sport performance teams: A first exploration and grounded theory. *Journal of Sport and Exercise Psychology, 36*(1), 107-120. http://search.ebscohost.com/login.aspx?direct=true&db=s3h&AN=94346682&site=ehost-live

Cui, Y. (2007). Striving and thriving: Women in Chinese national sport organizations. *International Journal of the History of Sport, 24*(3), 392-410. https://doi.org/10.1080/09523360601101378

Davis, L., Brown, D.J., Arnold, R., & Gustafsson, H. (2021). Thriving through relationships in sport: The role of the parent–athlete and coach–athlete attachment relationship. *Frontiers in Psychology.* https://doi.org/10.3389/fpsyg.2021.694599

Davis, L., & Jowett, S. (2010). Investigating the interpersonal dynamics between coaches and athletes based on fundamental principles of attachment. *Journal of Clinical Sport Psychology, 4*, 112-132. https://doi.org/10.1123/jcsp.4.2.112

Didymus, F.F., & Fletcher, D. (2017a). Effects of a cognitive-behavioral intervention on field hockey players' appraisals of organizational stressors. *Psychology of Sport and Exercise, 30*, 173-185. https://doi.org/10.1016/j.psychsport.2017.03.005

Didymus, F.F., & Fletcher, D. (2017b). Organizational stress in high-level field hockey: Examining transactional pathways between stressors, appraisals, coping and performance satisfaction. *International Journal of Sports Science and Coaching, 12*(2), 252-263. https://doi.org/10.1177/1747954117694737

Didymus, F.F., & Jones, M.V. (2021). Cognitive appraisals. In R. Arnold & D. Fletcher (Eds.), *Stress, well-being, and performance in sport* (pp. 63-77). Taylor & Francis.

Diehl, R., Poczwardowski, A., Stambulova, N., O'Neil, A., & Haberl, P. (2020). Transitioning to and thriving at the Olympic Training Center, Colorado Springs: Phases of an adaptive transition. *Sport in Society, 23*(4), 678-696. https://doi.org/10.1080/17430437.2019.1600299

Donohue, B., Miller, A., Crammer, L., Cross, C., & Covassin, T. (2007). A standardized method of assessing sport specific problems in the relationships of athletes with their coaches, teammates, family, and peers. *Journal of Sport Behavior, 30*(4), 375-397.

Dorsch, T.E., Smith, A.L., Blazo, J.A., Coakley, J., Côté, J., Wagstaff, C.R.D., Warner, S., & King, M.Q. (2022). Toward an integrated understanding of the youth sport system. *Research Quarterly for Exercise and Sport, 93*(1), 105-119 https://doi.org/10.1080/02701367.2020.1810847

Dorsch, T.E., Smith, A.L., & McDonough, M.H. (2009). Parents' perceptions of child-to-parent socialization in organized youth sport. *Journal of Sport and Exercise Psychology, 31*(4), 444-468. https://doi.org/10.1123/jsep.31.4.444

Edwards, D.J., & Edwards, S.D. (2012). The evaluation of a psychological skills training programme for rugby players. *African Journal for Physical, Health Education, Recreation and Dance, 18*(3), 525-534. http://search.ebscohost.com/login.aspx?direct=true&db=s3h&AN=80233088&site=ehost-live

Feddersen, N.B., Morris, R., Abrahamsen, F.E., Littlewood, M.A., & Richardson, D.J. (2020). The influence of macrocultural change on national governing bodies in British Olympic sports. *Sport in Society,* 1-17. https://doi.org/10.1080/17430437.2020.1771306

Feeney, B.C., & Collins, N.L. (2015). A new look at social support: A theoretical perspective on thriving through relationships. *Personality and Social Psychology Review, 19*(2), 113-147. https://doi.org/10.1177/1088868314544222

Felber Charbonneau, E., & Camiré, M. (2020). Parental involvement in sport and the satisfaction of basic psychological needs: Perspectives from parent-child dyads. *International Journal of Sport and Exercise Psychology, 18*(5), 655-671. https://doi.org/10.1080/1612197X.2019.1570533

Felton, L., & Jowett, S. (2013). Attachment and well-being: The mediating effects of psychological needs satisfaction within the coach-athlete and parent-athlete relational contexts. *Psychology of Sport and Exercise, 14*(1), 57-65. https://doi.org/10.1016/j.psychsport.2012.07.006

Finnegan, L., McArdle, J., Littlewood, M., & Richardson, D. (2018). Somewhat united: Primary stakeholder perspectives of the governance of schoolboy football in Ireland. *Managing Sport and Leisure, 23*(1-2), 48-69. https://doi.org/10.1080/23750472.2018.1513342

Fletcher, D., & Arnold, R. (2011). A qualitative study of performance leadership and management in elite sport. *Journal of Applied Sport Psychology, 23*(2), 223-242. https://doi.org/10.1080/10413200.2011.559184

Fletcher, D., & Scott, M. (2010). Psychological stress in sports coaches: A review of concepts, research, and practice. *Journal of Sports Sciences, 28*(2), 127-137. https://doi.org/10.1080/02640410903406208

Fletcher, D., & Wagstaff, C.R.D. (2009). Organizational psychology in elite sport: Its emergence, application and future. *Psychology of Sport and Exercise, 10,* 427-434. https://doi.org/10.1016/j.psychsport.2009.03.009

Freeman, P., & Rees, T. (2009). How does perceived support lead to better performance? An examination of potential mechanisms. *Journal of Applied Sport Psychology, 21*(4), 429-441. https://doi.org/10.1080/10413200903222913

Girginov, V. (2006). Creating a corporate anti-doping culture: The role of Bulgarian sports governing bodies. *Sport in Society, 9*(2), 252-268. https://doi.org/10.1080/17430430500491298

Gould, D., Dieffenbach, K., & Moffett, A. (2002). Psychological characteristics and their development in Olympic champions. *Journal of Applied Sport Psychology, 14*(3), 172-204. https://doi.org/10.1080/10413200290103482

Green, M., & Ghaye, T. (2018). "To what extent do football organisations and networks allow individuals to 'thrive'?". *Managing Sport and Leisure, 23*(1-2), 1-6. https://doi.org/10.1080/23750472.2018.1535955

Gucciardi, D.F., Gordon, S., & Dimmock, J.A. (2009). Development and preliminary validation of a mental toughness inventory for Australian football. *Psychology of Sport and Exercise, 10*(1), 201-209. https://doi.org/10.1016/j.psychsport.2008.07.011

Gucciardi, D.F., Jackson, B., Hodge, K., Anthony, D.R., & Brooke, L.E. (2015). Implicit theories of mental toughness: Relations with cognitive, motivational, and behavioral correlates. *Sport, Exercise, and Performance Psychology, 4*(2), 100-112. https://doi.org/10.1037/spy0000024

Gucciardi, D.F., & Jones, M.I. (2012). Beyond optimal performance: Mental toughness profiles and developmental success in adolescent cricketers. *Journal of Sport and Exercise Psychology, 34*(1), 16-36. https://doi.org/10.1123/jsep.34.1.16

Gucciardi, D.F., Stamatis, A., & Ntoumanis, N. (2017). Controlling coaching and athlete thriving in elite adolescent netballers: The buffering effect of athletes' mental toughness. *Journal of Science and Medicine in Sport, 20*(8), 718-722. https://doi.org/10.1016/j.jsams.2017.02.007

Harris, M., Myhill, M., & Walker, J. (2012a). A promising career? The thriving transition cycle. *International Journal of Sports Science, 2*(3), 16-23. https://doi.org/10.5923/j.sports.20120203.01

Harris, M., Myhill, M., & Walker, J. (2012b). Thriving in the challenge of geographical dislocation: A case study of elite Australian footballers. *International Journal of Sports Science, 2*(5), 51-60. https://doi.org/10.5923/j.sports.20120205.02

Harwood, C.G., & Knight, C.J. (2015). Parenting in youth sport: A position paper on parenting expertise. *Psychology of Sport and Exercise, 16,* 24-35. https://doi.org/10.1016/j.psychsport.2014.03.001

Haynes, C.F., Cutler, C., Gray, J., & Kempe, R.S. (1984). Hospitalized cases of nonorganic failure to thrive: The scope of the problem and short-term lay health visitor intervention. *Child Abuse and Neglect, 8*(2), 229-242. https://doi.org/10.1016/0145-2134(84)90012-7

Henriksen, K. (2015). Developing a high-performance culture: A sport psychology intervention from an ecological perspective in elite orienteering. *Journal of Sport Psychology in Action, 6*(3), 141-153. https://doi.org/10.1080/21520704.2015.1084961

Henriksen, K., & Stambulova, N. (2017). Creating optimal environments for talent development: A holistic ecological approach. In J. Baker, S.P. Cobley, J. Schorer, & N. Wattie (Eds.), *Routledge handbook of talent identification and development in sport* (pp. 271-284). Routledge.

Henriksen, K., Stambulova, N., & Roessler, K. (2010). Successful talent development in track and field: Considering the role of environment. *Scandinavian Journal of Medicine and Science in Sports, 20*(2), 122-132. https://doi.org/10.1111/j.1600-0838.2010.01187.x

Holt, N.L., & Knight, C.J. (2014). *Parenting in youth sport: From research to practice.* Routledge.

Huiszoon, P., Martinent, G., & Bodet, G. (2018). Sport governing bodies' influence on non-transactional fan behaviours. *Managing Sport and Leisure, 23*(1-2), 123-138. https://doi.org/10.1080/23750472.2018.1502623

Jackson, D., McDonald, G., & Wilkes, L. (2011). Thriving in the workplace: Learning from innovative practices. In M. McAllister & J.B. Lowe (Eds.), *The resilient nurse: Empowering your practice* (pp. 105-114). Springer.

Jones, G., Hanton, S., & Connaughton, D. (2002). What is this thing called mental toughness? An investigation of elite sport performers. *Journal of Applied Sport Psychology, 14*(3), 205-218. https://doi.org/10.1080/10413200290103509

Jones, M.I., & Lavellee, D. (2009). Exploring the life skills needs of British adolescent athletes. *Psychology of Sport and Exercise, 10*(1), 159-167. https://doi.org/10.1016/j.psychsport.2008.06.005

Jowett, S. (2017). Coaching effectiveness: the coach-athlete relationship at its heart. *Current Opinion in Psychology, 16,* 154-158. https://doi.org/10.1016/j.copsyc.2017.05.006

Jowett, S., & Shanmugam, V. (2016). Relational coaching in sport: Its psychological underpinnings and practical effectiveness. In R.J. Schinke, K.R. McGannon, & B. Smith (Eds.), *Routledge international handbook of sport psychology* (pp. 471-484). Routledge.

Kaiser, S., Engel, F., & Keiner, R. (2009). Structure-dimensional analysis—An experimental approach to culture in sport organisations. *European Sport Management Quarterly, 9*(3), 295-310. https://doi.org/10.1080/16184740903024045

Kerr, G., Stirling, A., & Gurgis, J. (2017). An athlete-centred approach to enhance thriving within athletes and coaches. In S. Pill (Ed.), *Perspectives on athlete-centred coaching* (pp. 24-36). Routledge.

Kinoshita, K., MacIntosh, E., & Sato, S. (2021). A buffering effect of mental toughness on the negative impact of basic psychological need thwarting on positive youth athlete functioning. *The Sport Psychologist, 35*(3), 190-199. https://doi.org/10.1123/tsp.2020-0168

Kinoshita, K., MacIntosh, E., & Sato, S. (2022). Thriving in youth sport: The antecedents and consequences. *International Journal of Sport and Exercise Psychology, 20*(2), 356-376. https://doi.org/10.1080/1612197X.2021.1877327

Kitchin, P.J., & Crossin, A. (2018). Understanding which dimensions of organisational capacity support the vertical integration of disability football clubs. *Managing Sport and Leisure, 23*(1-2), 28-47. https://doi.org/10.1080/23750472.2018.1481764

Knight, C.J., & Holt, N.L. (2013). Strategies used and assistance required to facilitate children's involvement in tennis: Parents' perspectives. *The Sport Psychologist, 27*(3), 281-291. https://doi.org/10.1123/tsp.27.3.281

Knight, C.J., Neely, K.C., & Holt, N.L. (2011). Parental behaviors in team sports: How do female athletes want parents to behave? *Journal of Applied Sport Psychology, 23*(1), 76-92. https://doi.org/10.1080/10413200.2010.525589

Lazarus, R.S. (1999). *Stress and emotion: A new synthesis.* Springer.

Lazarus, R.S., & Folkman, S. (1984). *Stress, appraisal, and coping.* Springer.

Lerner, R.M., Dowling, E.M., & Anderson, P.M. (2003). Positive youth development: Thriving as a basis of personhood and civil society. *Applied Developmental Science, 7*(3), 172-180. https://doi.org/10.1207/S1532480XADS0703_8

Mahoney, J., Ntoumanis, N., Mallett, C., & Gucciardi, D. (2014). The motivational antecedents of the development of mental toughness: A self-determination theory perspective. *International Review of Sport and Exercise Psychology, 7*(1), 184-197. https://doi.org/10.1080/1750984X.2014.925951

Maitland, A., Hills, L.A., & Rhind, D.J. (2015). Organisational culture in sport: A systematic review. *Sport Management Review, 18*(4), 501-516. https://doi.org/https://doi.org/10.1016/j.smr.2014.11.004

Martin, L. J., Evans, M. B., & Spink, K. S. (2016). Coach perspectives of "groups within the group": An analysis of subgroups and cliques in sport. *Sport, Exercise, and Performance Psychology, 5*(1), 52-66. https://doi.org/10.1037/spy0000048

McDougall, M., Ronkainen, N., Richardson, D., Littlewood, M., & Nesti, M. (2020a). Organizational culture beyond consensus and clarity: Narratives from elite sport. *Sport Psychologist, 34*(4), 288-299. http://search.ebscohost.com/login.aspx?direct=true&db=s3h&AN=147461277&site=ehost-live

McDougall, M., Ronkainen, N., Richardson, D., Littlewood, M., & Nesti, M. (2020b). Three team and organisational culture myths and their consequences for sport psychology research and practice. *International Review of Sport and Exercise Psychology, 13*(1), 147-162. https://doi.org/10.1080/1750984X.2019.1638433

McGuire, C. S., Brown, D. J., McEwan, D., Arnold, R., & Martin, L. (2023). Thriving together: Conceptual and methodological considerations for examining thriving in interdependent sport. *International Review of Sport and Exercise Psychology.* Advance online publication. https://doi.org/10.1080/1750984X.2023.2204320

McHenry, L.K., Cochran, J.L., Zakrajsek, R.A., Fisher, L.A., Couch, S.R., & Hill, B.S. (2022). Elite figure skaters' experiences of thriving in the coach–athlete relationship: A person-centered theory perspective. *Journal of Applied Sport Psychology, 34*(2), 436-456. https://doi.org/10.1080/10413200.2020.1800862

McMillan, D.W., & Chavis, D.M. (1986). Sense of community: A definition and theory. *Journal of Community Psychology, 14*(1), 6-23. https://doi.org/10.1002/1520-6629(198601)

McNeill, K., Durand-Bush, N., & Lemyre, P.-N. (2018). Thriving, depleted, and at-risk Canadian coaches: Profiles of psychological functioning linked to self-regulation and stress. *International Sport Coaching Journal, 5*(2), 145-155. https://doi.org/10.1123/iscj.2017-0042

Mountjoy, M. (2019). 'Only by speaking out can we create lasting change': What can we learn from the Dr Larry Nassar tragedy? *British Journal of Sports Medicine, 53*(1), 57. https://doi.org/10.1136/bjsports-2018-099403

Narel, R.L., Yaeger, T., & Soresen, P.F. (2019). Exploring agile thriving teams in continuous change environments. In A.B. Shani & D.A. Noumair (Eds.), *Research in organizational change and development* (Vol. 27, pp. 187-211). Emerald. https://doi.org/10.1108/S0897-301620190000027011

Norman, L., & Rankin-Wright, A. (2018). Surviving rather than thriving: Understanding the experiences of women coaches using a theory of gendered social well-being. *International Review for the Sociology of Sport, 53*(4), 424-450. https://doi.org/10.1177/1012690216660283

O'Leary, V.E., & Ickovics, J.R. (1995). Resilience and thriving in response to challenge: An opportunity for a paradigm shift in women's health. *Womens Health, 1*(2), 121-142.

Olusoga, P., Butt, J., Hays, K., & Maynard, I. (2009). Stress in elite sports coaching: Identifying stressors. *Journal of Applied Sport Psychology, 21*(4), 442-459. https://doi.org/10.1080/10413200903222921

Passaportis, M.J.R., Brown, D.J., Wagstaff, C.R.D., Arnold, R., & Hays, K. (2022). Creating an environment for thriving: An ethnographic exploration of a British decentralised Olympic and Paralympic sport organisation. *Psychology of Sport and Exercise, 62*, 102247. https://doi.org/10.1016/j.psychsport.2022.102247

Porath, C., Spreitzer, G., Gibson, C., & Garnett, F.G. (2012). Thriving at work: Toward its measurement, construct validation, and theoretical refinement. *Journal of Organizational Behavior, 33*(2), 250-275. https://doi.org/10.1002/Job.756

Rees, T., Hardy, L., Güllich, A., Abernethy, B., Côté, J., Woodman, T., Montgomery, H., Laing, S., & Warr, C. (2016). The Great British medalists project: A review of current knowledge on the development of the world's best sporting talent. *Sports Medicine, 46*(8), 1041-1058. https://doi.org/10.1007/s40279-016-0476-2

Rouquette, O.Y., Knight, C.J., Lovett, V.E., Barrell, D., & Heuzé, J.-P. (2021). The positive association between perceived parental responsiveness and self-esteem, anxiety, and thriving among youth rugby players: A multigroup analysis. *Journal of Sports Sciences, 39*(13), 1537-1547. https://doi.org/10.1080/02640414.2021.1883311

Rouquette, O.Y., Knight, C.J., Lovett, V.E., & Heuzé, J.-P. (2021a). Effect of parent responsiveness on young athletes' self-perceptions and thriving: An exploratory study in a Belgian French-community. *Psychology of Sport and Exercise, 52.* Advance online publication. https://doi.org/10.1016/j.psychsport.2020.101801

Roquette, O.Y., Knight, C.J., Lovett, V.E., & Heuzé, J.-P. (2021b). The influence of perceived parental responsiveness on athletes' goal accomplishment, trait cognitive sport anxiety, and thriving: A semi-longitudinal study. *Psychology of Sport and Exercise, 57.* Adance online publication. https://doi.org/10.1016/j.psychsport.2021.102044

Ryan, R.M., & Deci, E.L. (2001). On happiness and human potentials: A review of research on hedonic and eudaimonic well-being. *Annual Review of Psychology, 52*, 141-166. https://doi.org/10.1146/annurev.psych.52.1.141

Ryan, R.M., & Deci, E.L. (2017). *Self-determination theory: Basic psychological needs in motivation, development, and wellness.* Guilford Press.

Sarason, S.B. (1974). *The psychological sense of community: Prospects for a community psychology.* Jossey-Bass.

Sarkar, M., & Fletcher, D. (2014). Ordinary magic, extraordinary performance: Psychological resilience and thriving in high achievers. *Sport, Exercise, and Performance Psychology, 3*, 46-60. https://doi.org/10.1037/spy0000003

Seligman, M.E.P., & Csikszentmihalyi, M. (2000). Positive psychology: An introduction. *American Psychologist, 55*(1), 5-14. https://doi.org/10.1037/0003-066x.56.1.89

Sheldon, K.M. (2009). Providing the scientific backbone for positive psychology: A multi-level conception of human thriving. *Psihologijske Teme, 18*(2), 267-284. https://doi.org/10.31820/pt

Sheldon, K.M., Elliot, A.J., Kim, Y., & Kasser, T. (2001). What is satisfying about satisfying events? Testing 10 candidate psychological needs. *Journal of Personality and Social Psychology, 80*(2), 325-339. https://doi.org/10.1037/0022-3514.80.2.325

Solntsev, I., & Osokin, N. (2018). Designing a performance measurement framework for regional networks of national sports organizations: Evidence from Russian football. *Managing Sport and Leisure, 23*(1-2), 7-27. https://doi.org/10.1080/23750472.2018.1452628

Spreitzer, G., Sutcliffe, K., Dutton, J., Sonenshein, S., & Grant, A.M. (2005). A socially embedded model of thriving at work. *Organization Science, 16*(5), 537-549. https://doi.org/10.1287/orsc.1050.0153

Su, R., Tay, L., & Diener, E. (2014). The development and validation of the Comprehensive Inventory of Thriving (CIT) and the Brief Inventory of Thriving (BIT). *Applied Psychology: Health and Well-Being, 6*(3), 251-279. https://doi.org/10.1111/aphw.12027

Tremethick, M.J. (1997). Thriving, not just surviving: The importance of social support among the elderly. *Journal of Psychosocial Nursing and Mental Health Services, 35*(9), 27-31. https://doi.org/10.3928/0279-3695-19970901-16

Turner, M.J., Jones, M.V., Sheffield, D., Slater, M.J., Barker, J.B., & Bell, J.J. (2013). Who thrives under pressure? Predicting the performance of elite academy cricketers using the cardiovascular indicators of challenge and threat states. *Journal of Sport and Exercise Psychology, 35*(4), 387-397. https://doi.org/10.1123/jsep.35.4.387

van Rens, F.E.C.A., & Filho, E. (2020). Realising, adapting, and thriving in career transitions from gymnastics to contemporary circus arts. *Journal of Clinical Sport Psychology, 14*(2), 127-148. https://doi.org/10.1123/jcsp.2018-0075

Wadey, R., & Hanton, S. (2014). Psychology of sport injury: Resilience and thriving. In F.G. Conner & R. Wilder (Eds.), *Running medicine* (pp. 932-951). Healthy Learning.

Wagstaff, C.R.D. (Ed.). (2017). *The organizational psychology of sport: Key issues and practical applications.* Routledge.

Wagstaff, C.R.D. (2019). Taking stock of organizational psychology in sport. *Journal of Applied Sport Psychology, 31*(1), 1-6. https://doi.org/10.1080/10413200.2018.1539785

Wagstaff, C.R.D., & Burton-Wylie, S. (2018). Organizational culture in sport: A conceptual, definitional, and methodological review. *Sport and Exercise Psychology Review, 14*(2), 32-52.

Wagstaff, C.R.D., Fletcher, D., & Hanton, S. (2012a). Exploring emotion abilities and regulation strategies in sport organizations. *Sport, Exercise, and Performance Psychology, 1*(4), 268-282. https://doi.org/10.1037/a0028814

Wagstaff, C.R.D., Fletcher, D., & Hanton, S. (2012b). Positive organizational psychology in sport. *International Review of Sport and Exercise Psychology, 5*(2), 87-103. https://doi.org/10.1080/1750984x.2011.634920

Wagstaff, C.R.D., Fletcher, D., & Hanton, S. (2012c). Positive organizational psychology in sport: An ethnography of organizational functioning in a national sport organization. *Journal of Applied Sport Psychology, 24*(1), 26-47. https://doi.org/10.1080/10413200.2011.589423

Wagstaff, C.R.D., Gilmore, S., & Thelwell, R.C. (2016). When the show must go on: Investigating repeated organizational change in elite sport. *Journal of Change Management, 16*(1), 38-54. https://doi.org/10.1080/14697017.2015.1062793

Wagstaff, C.R.D., Martin, L.J., & Thelwell, R.C. (2017). Subgroups and cliques in sport: A longitudinal case study of a rugby union team. *Psychology of Sport and Exercise, 30*, 164-172. https://doi.org/10.1016/j.psychsport.2017.03.006

Walker, L.O., & Grobe, S.J. (1999). The construct of thriving in pregnancy and postpartum. *Nursing Science Quarterly, 12*(2), 151-157. https://doi.org/10.1177/08943189922106585

Warner, S., Sparvero, E., Shapiro, S., & Anderson, A. (2017). Yielding healthy community with sport? *Journal of Sport for Development, 5*(8), 41-52.

Whitley, M.A., Massey, W.V., Camiré, M., Blom, L.C., Chawansky, M., Forde, S., Boutet, M., Borbee, A., & Darnell, S.C. (2019). A systematic review of sport for development interventions across six global cities. *Sport Management Review, 22*(2), 181-193. https://doi.org/https://doi.org/10.1016/j.smr.2018.06.013

Chapter 25

American Psychological Association. (2011). Definition of terms: Sex, gender, gender identity, sexual orientation. www.apa.org/pi/lgbt/resources/sexuality-definitions.pdf

Anderson, E. (2005). Orthodox and inclusive masculinity: Competing masculinities among heterosexual men in a feminized terrain. *Sociological Perspectives, 48*(3), 337-355. https://doi.org/10.1525/sop.2005.48.3.337

Banwell, J., Kerr, G., & Stirling, A. (2020). Benefits of a female coach mentorship programme on women coaches' development: An ecological perspective. *Sports Coaching Review, 1(10)* 1-23.

Bem, S.L. (1974). The measurement of psychological androgyny. *Journal of Consulting and Clinical Psychology, 42*(2), 155-162. https://doi.org/10.1037/h0036215

Blinde, E.M., & Taub, D.E. (1992). Women athletes as falsely accused deviants: Managing the lesbian stigma. *Sociological Quarterly, 33*(4), 521-533. https://doi.org/10.1111/j.1533-8525.1992.tb00141.x

Burton, L.J., & LaVoi, N.M. (2016). An ecological/multisystem approach to understanding and examining women coaches. In N.M. LaVoi (Ed.), *Women in sports coaching* (pp. 49-62). Routledge.

Bronfenbrenner, U. (1977). Toward an experimental ecology of human development. *American Psychologist, 32*(7), 513-531. https://doi.org/10.1037/0003-066X.32.7.513

Bronfenbrenner, U. (1979). *The ecology of human development.* Harvard University Press.

Bronfenbrenner, U. (1993). The ecology of cognitive development: Research models and fugitive findings. In R. H. Wozniak & K. W. Fischer (Eds.), *Development in context: Acting and thinking in specific environments* (pp. 3-44). Lawrence Erlbaum Associates, Inc.

Butryn, T., LaVoi, N.M., Kauer, K., Semerjian, T., & Waldron, J. (2014). We walk the line: An analysis of the problems and possibilities of work at the sport psychology-sport sociology nexus. *Sociology of Sport Journal, 31*(2), 162-184. https://doi.org/10.1123/ssj.2012-0169

Calhoun, A.S., LaVoi, N.M., & Johnson, A. (2011). Framing with family: Examining online coaches' biographies for heteronormative and heterosexist narratives. *International Journal of Sport Communication, 4*(3), 300-316. https://doi.org/10.1123/ijsc.4.3.300

Carson, F., McCormack, C., McGovern, P., Ralston, S., & Walsh, J. (2020). Coach like a woman: Learnings from a pilot coach education program. *Women in Sport and Physical Activity Journal, 1*(AoP), 1-6. https://doi.org/10.1123/wspaj.2020-0047

Carter, L. (Ed.). (2020). *Feminist applied sport psychology: From theory to practice.* Routledge.

Chalabaev, A., & Sarrazin, P. (2020). Putting individual motivations into the societal context: The influence of social stereotypes in the physical activity domain. In G. Tenebaum & R.C. Eklund (Eds). *Handbook of sport psychology* (pp. 19-36). https://doi.org/10.1002/9781119568124.ch2

Chalabaev, A., Sarrazin, P., Fontayne, P., Boiché, J., & Clément-Guillotin, C. (2013). The influence of sex stereotypes and gender roles on participation and performance in sport and exercise: Review and future directions. *Psychology of Sport and Exercise, 14*(2), 136-144. https://doi.org/10.1016/j.psychsport.2012.10.005

Cooky, C., & LaVoi, N.M. (2012). Playing but losing: Women's sports after Title IX. *Contexts, 11,* 42-45. https://doi.org/10.1177/1536504212436495

Cunningham, G.B., Ahn, N.Y., Anderson, A.J., & Dixon, M.A. (2019). Gender, coaching, and occupational turnover. *Women in Sport and Physical Activity Journal, 27*(2), 63-72. https://doi.org/10.1123/wspaj.2018-0038

de Haan, D., & Norman, L. (2020). Mind the gap: The presence of capital and power in the female athlete-male-coach relationship within elite rowing. *Sports Coaching Review, 9*(1), 95-118. https://doi.org/10.1080/21640629.2019.1567160

Donnelly, K., & Twenge, J.M. (2017). Masculine and feminine traits on the Bem Sex-Role Inventory, 1993-2012: A cross-temporal meta-analysis. *Sex Roles, 76*(9), 556-565. https://doi.org/10.1007/s11199-016-0625-y

Duncan, M.C. (2007). Sociological dimensions of girls' physical activity participation. In M.J. Kane & N.M. LaVoi (Eds.), *Developing physically active girls: An evidence-based multidisciplinary approach* (pp. 29-50). Tucker Center for Research on Girls & Women in Sport. www.cehd.umn.edu/tuckercenter/library/docs/research/2007-Tucker-Center-Research-Report.pdf

Fisher, L.A., & Anders, A.D. (2019). Engaging with cultural sport psychology to explore systemic sexual exploitation in USA gymnastics: A call to commitments. *Journal of Applied Sport Psychology, 32,* 129-145. https://doi.org/10.1080/10413200.2018.1564944

Fisher, L.A., Butryn, T.M., & Roper, E.A. (2003). Diversifying (and politicizing) sport psychology through cultural studies: A promising perspective. *The Sport Psychologist, 17*(4), 391-405. https://doi.org/10.1123/tsp.17.4.391

Fisher, L.A., Roper, E.A., & Butryn, T.M. (2009a). Engaging cultural studies and "traditional" sport psychology. In R. Schinke & S.J. Hanrahan (Eds.), *Cultural sport psychology* (pp. 23-34). Human Kinetics.

Fisher, L.A., Roper, E.A., & Butryn, T.M. (2009b). Revisiting diversity and politics in sport psychology through cultural studies: Where are we five years later. In R. J. Schinke (Ed.) *Contemporary Sport Psychology,* 105-120. Nova Science.

Gentile, A., Boca, S., & Giammusso, I. (2018). 'You play like a woman!' effects of gender stereotype threat on women's performance in physical and sport activities: A meta-analysis. *Psychology of Sport and Exercise, 39,* 95-103. https://doi.org/10.1016/j.psychsport.2018.07.013

Gill, D.L. (2001). Feminist sport psychology: A guide for our journey. *The Sport Psychologist, 15*(4), 363-372. https://doi.org/10.1123/tsp.15.4.363

Gill, D.L. (2020). Gender and culture. In G. Tenenbaum & R.C. Eckland (Eds.), *Handbook of sport psychology* (4th ed., pp. 1131-1151). Wiley. https://doi.org/10.1002/9781119568124.ch55

Gill, D.L., & Kamphoff, C.S. (2010). Gender in sport and exercise psychology. In J. Chrysler & D. McCreary (Eds.), *Handbook of gender research in psychology* (pp. 563-585). Springer. https://doi.org/10.1007/978-1-4419-1467-5_24

Hall, M.A. (1988). The discourse of gender and sport: From femininity to feminism. *Sociology of Sport Journal, 5*(4), 330-340. https://pdfs.semanticscholar.org/5fdc/22fa1791d18702449119ef6ad775bab63907.pdf

Hall, M.A. (2002). The discourse of gender and sport: From femininity to feminism. In S. Scraton & A. Flintoff (Eds.), *Gender and sport: A reader* (pp. 6-16). Routledge.

Hardin, M., & Greer, J.D. (2009). The influence of gender-role socialization, media use and sports participation on perceptions of gender-appropriate sports. *Journal of Sport Behavior, 32*(2), 207. https://search.proquest.com/openview/5bee287df2238972505b3c32f434e3b1/1?pq-origsite=gscholar&cbl=30153

Heidrich, C., & Chiviacowsky, S. (2015). Stereotype threat affects the learning of sport motor skills. *Psychology of Sport and Exercise, 18,* 42-46. https://doi.org/10.1016/j.psychsport.2014.12.002

Hyde, J.S. (2016). Sex and cognition: Gender and cognitive functions. *Current Opinion in Neurobiology, 38,* 53-56. https://doi.org/10.1016/j.conb.2016.02.007

Hyde, J. S. (2005). The gender similarities hypothesis. *American Psychologist, 60*(6), 581-592. https://doi.org/10.1037/0003-066X.60.6.581

Hyde, J.S., Bigler, R.S., Joel, D., Tate, C.C., & van Anders, S.M. (2019). The future of sex and gender in psychology: Five challenges to the gender binary. *American Psychologist, 74*(2), 171. http://dx.doi.org/10.1037/amp0000307

Iannotta, J.G., & Kane, M.J. (2002). Sexual stories as resistance narratives in women's sports: Reconceptualizing identity performance. *Sociology of Sport Journal, 19*(4), 347-369. https://doi.org/10.1123/ssj.19.4.347

Kane, M.J. (1995). Resistance/transformation of the oppositional binary: Exposing sport as a continuum. *Journal of Sport and Social Issues, 19*(2), 191-218. https://doi.org/10.1177/019372395019002006

Kane, M. J., & LaVoi, N. M. (2018). An examination of athletic administrators' perceptions regarding the absence of female head coaches in women's intercollegiate sports. *Women in Sport and Physical Activity, 1-33*. https://doi.org/10.1123/wspaj.2016-0031

Kane, M.J., & Snyder, E.E. (1989). Sport typing: The social 'containment' of women in sport. *Arena Review, 13*(2), 77-96.

Klomsten, A.T., Marsh, H.W., & Skaalvik, E.M. (2005). Adolescents' perceptions of masculine and feminine values in sport and physical education: A study of gender differences. *Sex Roles, 52*(9-10), 625-636. https://doi.org/10.1007/s11199-005-3730-x

Krane, V. (2018). *Sex, gender, and sexuality in sport: Queer inquiries*. Routledge. https://doi.org/10.4324/9781315114996

Krane, V., & Barber, H. (2005). Identity tensions in lesbian intercollegiate coaches. *Research Quarterly for Exercise and Sport, 76*(1), 67-81. https://shapeamerica.tandfonline.com/doi/pdf/10.1080/02701367.2005.10599263?needAccess=true

LaVoi, N.M. (2009). Occupational sex segregation in a youth soccer organization: Females in positions of power. *Women in Sport and Physical Activity Journal, 18*(2), 25-37. https://doi.org/10.1123/wspaj.18.2.25

LaVoi, N.M. (2012). Trends in gender-related research in sport and exercise psychology. *Revista iberoamericana de psicología del ejercicio y el deporte, 6*(2), 269-281.

LaVoi, N.M. (2016). *Women in sports coaching*. Routledge.

LaVoi, N.M. (2018a). Introduction to the Tucker Center Research Report. In N.M. LaVoi (Ed.), *Developing physically active girls: An evidence-based multidisciplinary approach* (pp. xvii-xxiv). Tucker Center for Research on Girls & Women in Sport. www.cehd.umn.edu/tuckercenter/library/docs/research/2018-Tucker-Center-Research-Report_Developing-Physically-Active-Girls_Full-Report.pdf

LaVoi, N.M. (2018b). Girls' physical activity participation: A best practices model and summary. In N.M. LaVoi (Ed.), *Developing physically active girls: An evidence-based multidisciplinary approach* (pp. 197-213). Tucker Center for Research on Girls & Women in Sport. www.cehd.umn.edu/tuckercenter/library/docs/research/2018-Tucker-Center-Research-Report_Developing-Physically-Active-Girls_Full-Report.pdf

LaVoi, N.M., Becker, E., & Maxwell, H.D. (2007). "Coaching girls": A content analysis of best-selling popular press books. *Women in Sport and Physical Activity Journal, 15*(4), 8-20.

LaVoi, N.M., & Boucher, C. (2021). Supporting and developing women in sport coaching: A career trajectory approach. In L. Norman (Ed.), *Improving gender equity in sport coaching* (pp. 175-197). Routledge.

LaVoi, N.M., Boucher, C., & Silbert, S. (2019). *Head coaches of women's collegiate teams: A comprehensive report on NCAA Division-I institutions, 2018-19*. Tucker Center for Research on Girls & Women in Sport. www.cehd.umn.edu/tuckercenter/library/docs/research/WCCRC-Head-Coaches_All-NCAA-DI-Head-Coaches_2018-19.pdf

LaVoi, N.M., & Dutove, J.K. (2012). Barriers and supports for female coaches: An ecological model. *Sports Coaching Review, 1*(1), 17-37. https://doi.org/10.1080/21640629.2012.695891

LaVoi, N.M., & Glassford, S. (2021). 'This is our family': LGBTQ family narratives in online coaching biographies. *Journal of Homosexuality*. http://dx.doi.org/10.1080/00918369.2021.1921506.

LaVoi N.M., & Goorevich, A. (in press). Refuting gender essentialism in sports coaching. In A. Knoppers & P. Markuula (Eds.), *Handbook on gender and diversity in sport management*. Elgar.

LaVoi, N.M., McGarry, J.E., & Fisher, L.A. (2019). Final thoughts on women in sport coaching: Fighting the war. *Women's Sport and Physical Activity Journal, 27*(2), 136-140. https://doi.org/10.1123/wspaj.2019-0030

LaVoi, N.M., Thul, C.M., & Wasend, M. (2018). Understanding girls in and through physical activity: Assets, identities and disparities. In N.M. LaVoi (Ed.), *Developing physically active girls: An evidence-based multidisciplinary approach* (pp. 1-36). Tucker Center for Research on Girls & Women in Sport. www.cehd.umn.edu/tuckercenter/library/docs/research/2018-Tucker-Center-Research-Report_Developing-Physically-Active-Girls_Full-Report.pdf

Lebel, K., Pegoraro, A., Antunovic, D., Lough, N., LaVoi, N.M. (December 20, 2020). What pro sports should learn from resilient women athlete's post-pandemic. The Conversation. https://theconversation.com/what-pro-sports-should-learn-from-resilient-women-athletes-post-pandemic-151183

Lorber, J. (1994). *Paradoxes of gender*. Yale University Press. https://xyonline.net/sites/xyonline.net/files/2019-08/Lorber%2C%20Paradoxes%20of%20Gender%20%281994%29.pdf

Madsen, R.M. (2016). "Dads play basketball, moms go shopping!" Social role theory and the preference for male coaches. *Journal of Contemporary Athletics, 10*(4), 277.

Madsen, R.M., Burton, L.J., & Clark, B.S. (2017). Gender role expectations and the prevalence of women as assistant coaches. *Journal for the Study of Sports and Athletes in Education, 11*(2), 125-142. https://doi.org/10.1080/19357397.2017.1315994

Matteo, S. (1986). The effect of sex and gender-schematic processing on sport participation. *Sex Roles, 15*(7-8), 417-432. https://doi.org/10.1007/BF00287981

Matteo, S. (1988). The effect of gender-schematic processing on decisions about sex-inappropriate sport behavior. *Sex Roles, 18*(1-2), 41-58.

Messner, M.A. (2002). *Taking the field: Women, men, and sports* (4th ed.). University of Minnesota Press.

Messner, M.A. (2011). Gender ideologies, youth sports, and the production of soft essentialism. *Sociology of Sport Journal, 28*, 151-170. https://doi.org/10.1123/ssj.28.2.151

Metheny, E. (1965). Symbolic forms of movement: The feminine image in sports. *Connotations of Movement in Sport and Dance*, 43-56. W.C. Brown Company.

Midgley, C., DeBues-Stafford, G., Lockwood, P., & Thai, S. (2021). She needs to see it to be it: The importance of same-gender athletic role models. *Sex Roles*, 1-19. https://doi.org/10.1007/s11199-020-01209-y

Norman, L. (2010). Bearing the burden of doubt: Female coaches' experiences of gender relations. *Research Quarterly for Exercise and Sport, 81*(4), 506-517. https://doi.org/10.1080/02701367.2010.10599712

Norman, L. (2012). Gendered homophobia in sport and coaching: Understanding the everyday experiences of lesbian coaches. *International Review for the Sociology of Sport, 47*(6), 705-723. https://doi.org/10.1177/1012690211420487

Norman, L. (2013). The concepts underpinning everyday gendered homophobia based upon the experiences of lesbian coaches. *Sport in Society, 16*(10), 1326-1345. https://doi.org/10.1080/17430437.2013.821255

Norman, L. (2014). A crisis of confidence: Women coaches' responses to their engagement in resistance. *Sport, Education and Society, 19*(5), 532-551. https://doi.org/10.1080/13573322.2012.689975

Norman, L. (2016). The impact of an "equal opportunities" ideological framework on coaches' knowledge and practice. *International Review for the Sociology of Sport, 51*(8), 975-1004. https://doi.org/10.1177/1012690214565377

Norman, L., & Rankin-Wright, A. (2018). Surviving rather than thriving: Understanding the experiences of women coaches using a theory of gendered social well-being. *International Review for the Sociology of Sport, 53*(4), 424-450. https://doi.org/10.1177/1012690216660283

Norman, L., Rankin-Wright, A.J., & Allison, W. (2018). "It's a concrete ceiling; It's not even glass": Understanding tenets of organizational culture that supports the progression of women as coaches and coach developers. *Journal of Sport and Social Issues, 42*(5), 393-414. https://doi.org/10.1177/0193723518790086

Peters, H.J., & Williams, J.M. (2009). Rationale for developing a cultural sport psychology. In R.J. Schinke & S.J. Hanrahan (Eds.), *Cultural sport psychology* (pp. 13-21). Human Kinetics.

Rauscher, L., & Cooky, C. (2018). Sociological dimensions of girls sport and physical activity. In N.M. LaVoi (Ed.), *Developing physically active girls: An evidence-based multidisciplinary approach* (pp. 55-72). Tucker Center for Research on Girls & Women in Sport. www.cehd.umn.edu/tuckercenter/library/docs/research/2018-Tucker-Center-Research-Report_Developing-Physically-Active-Girls_Full-Report.pdf

Robertson, J. (2016). *Coaching leadership: Building educational leadership capacity through partnership* (2nd ed.). New Zealand Council for Educational Research.

Ross, S.R., & Shinew, K.J. (2008). Perspectives of women college athletes on sport and gender. *Sex Roles, 58*(1-2), 40-57. https://doi.org/10.1007/s11199-007-9275-4

Sartore, M.L., & Cunningham, G.B. (2007). Explaining the underrepresentation of women in leadership positions of sport organizations: A symbolic interactionist perspective. *Quest, 59*(2), 244-265. https://doi.org/10.1080/00336297.2007.10483551

Slater, A., & Tiggemann, M. (2011). Gender differences in adolescent sport participation, teasing, self-objectification and body image concerns. *Journal of Adolescence, 34*(3), 455-463. https://doi.org/10.1016/j.adolescence.2010.06.007

Smith, D.M., & Martiny, S.E. (2018). Stereotype threat in sport: Recommendations for applied practice and research. *The Sport Psychologist, 32*(4), 311-320. https://doi.org/10.1123/tsp.2017-0134

Steele, C.M., & Aronson, J. (1995). Stereotype threat and the intellectual test performance of African Americans. *Journal of Personality and Social Psychology, 69*(5), 797. http://mrnas.pbworks.com/f/claude%20steele%20stereotype%20threat%201995.pdf

Thul, C.M., & LaVoi, N.M. (2011). Reducing physical inactivity and promoting active living: From the voices of East African adolescent girls. *Qualitative Journal of Sport and Exercise, 3*(2), 211-237. https://doi.org/10.1080/2159676X.2011.572177

Thul, C.M., LaVoi, N.M., & Wasend, M. (2018). Immigrant girls and physical activity. In N.M. LaVoi (Ed.), *Developing physically active girls: An evidence-based multidisciplinary approach* (pp. 115-134). Tucker Center for Research on Girls & Women in Sport. www.cehd.umn.edu/tuckercenter/library/docs/research/2018-Tucker-Center-Research-Report_Developing-Physically-Active-Girls_Full-Report.pdf

Chapter 26

Abraham, A., & Collins, D. (1998). Examining and extending research in coach development. *Quest, 50*(1), 59-79. https://doi.org/10.1080/00336297.1998.10484264

Abraham, A., & Collins, D. (2011). Taking the next step: Ways forward for coaching science. *Quest, 63*(4), 366-384. https://doi.org/10.1080/00336297.2011.10483687

Alder, J.P. (2018). Team culture and athlete centred coaching. In S. Pill (Ed.), *Perspectives on athlete-centred coaching* (pp. 57-69). Routledge. https://doi.org/https://doi.org/10.4324/9781315102450

Austin, S. (2020). *Bayern Munich to scrap U9 and U10 teams.* https://trainingground.guru/articles/bayern-munich-to-scrap-u9-and-u10-teams

Bailey, R., & Collins, D. (2013). The standard model of talent development and its discontents. *Kinesiology Review, 2*(4), 248-259. https://doi.org/10.1123/krj.2.4.248

Bailey, R.P., Collins, D., Ford, P.A., MacNamara, Á., Pearce, G., & Toms, M. (2010). *Participant development in sport: An academic literature review.* Sports Coach UK.

Bailey, R.P., Madigan, D.J., Cope, E., & Nicholls, A.R. (2018). The prevalence of pseudoscientific ideas and neuromyths among sports coaches. *Frontiers in Psychology, 9*(641). https://doi.org/10.3389/fpsyg.2018.00641

Baker, J., Mosher, A., & Fraser-Thomas, J. (2020). Is it too early to condemn early sport specialisation? *British Journal of Sports Medicine.* https://doi.org/10.1136/bjsports-2020-102053

Balyi, I., & Hamilton, A. (2004). *Long-term athlete development: Trainability in children and adolescents. Windows of opportunity. Optimal trainability.* National Coaching Institute British Columbia & Advanced Training and Performance.

Barth, M., & Güllich, A. (2020). Non-linear association of efficiency of practice of adult elite athletes with their youth multi-sport practice. *Journal of Sports Sciences,* 1-11. https://doi.org/10.1080/02640414.2020.1851900

Battaglia, A.V., Kerr, G., & Stirling, A.E. (2017). Youth athletes' interpretations of punitive coaching practices. *Journal of Applied Sport Psychology, 29*(3), 337-352. https://doi.org/10.1080/10413200.2016.1271370

Berger, J.G. (2004). Dancing on the threshold of meaning: Recognizing and understanding the growing edge. *Journal of Transformative Education, 2*(4), 336-351. https://doi.org/10.1177/1541344604267697

Bjørndal, C.T., & Ronglan, L.T. (2018). Orchestrating talent development: Youth players' developmental experiences in Scandinavian team sports. *Sports Coaching Review, 7*(1), 1-22. https://doi.org/10.1080/21640629.2017.1317172

Bloom, B.S. (1985). *Developing talent in young people.* Ballantine Books.

Bohle Carbonell, K., Stalmeijer, R.E., Könings, K.D., Segers, M., & van Merriënboer, J.J.G. (2014). How experts deal with novel situations: A review of adaptive expertise. *Educational Research Review, 12,* 14-29. https://doi.org/https://doi.org/10.1016/j.edurev.2014.03.001

Carpentier, J., & Mageau, G.A. (2013). When change-oriented feedback enhances motivation, well-being and performance: A look at autonomy-supportive feedback in sport. *Psychology of Sport and Exercise, 14*(3), 423-435. https://doi.org/10.1016/j.psychsport.2013.01.003

Collins, D., Burke, V., Martindale, A., & Cruickshank, A. (2015). The illusion of competency versus the desirability of expertise: Seeking a common standard for support professions in sport. *Sports Medicine, 45*(1), 1-7. https://doi.org/10.1007/s40279-014-0251-1

Collins, D., & Collins, L. (2020). Developing coaches' professional judgement and decision making: Using the 'big 5.' *Journal of Sports Sciences, 39*(1), 115-119. https://doi.org/10.1080/02640414.2020.1809053

Collins, D., & MacNamara, Á. (2012). The rocky road to the top: Why talent needs trauma. *Sports Medicine, 42*(11), 907-914. https://doi.org/10.1007/BF03262302

Collins, D., & MacNamara, Á. (2017). *Talent development: A practitioner guide.* Routledge.

Collins, D., MacNamara, Á., & Cruickshank, A. (2019). Research and practice in talent identification and development—some thoughts on the state of play. *Journal of Applied Sport Psychology, 31*(3), 340-351. https://doi.org/10.1080/10413200.2018.1475430

Collins, D., MacNamara, Á., & McCarthy, N. (2016a). Putting the bumps in the rocky road: Optimizing the pathway to excellence. *Frontiers in Psychology, 7,* 1482. https://doi.org/10.3389/fpsyg.2016.01482

Collins, D., MacNamara, Á., & McCarthy, N. (2016b). Super champions, champions, and almosts: Important differences and commonalities on the rocky road. *Frontiers in Psychology, 6,* 2009. https://doi.org/10.3389/fpsyg.2015.02009

Collins, L., & Collins, D. (2015). Integration of professional judgement and decision-making in high-level adventure sports coaching practice. *Journal of Sports Sciences, 33*(6), 622-633. https://doi.org/10.1080/02640414.2014.953980

Cruickshank, A., & Collins, D. (2017). Beyond 'crude pragmatism' in sports coaching: Insights from C.S. Peirce, William James, and John Dewey: A commentary. *International Journal of Sports Science and Coaching, 12*(1), 70-72. https://doi.org/10.1177/1747954116684226

Cushion, C.J., & Nelson, L. (2013). Coach education and learning: Developing the field. In P. Potrac, W. Gilbert, & J. Denison (Eds.), *Routledge handbook of sports coaching* (pp. 359-374). Routledge.

Davids, K., Araujo, D., Vilar, L., Renshaw, I., & Pinder, R. (2013). An ecological dynamics approach to skill acquisition: Implications for development of talent in sport. *Talent Development and Excellence, 5*(1), 21-34.

Duckworth, A. L., Peterson, C., Matthews, M. D., & Kelly, D. R. (2007). Grit: perseverance and passion for long-term goals. *Journal of Personality and Social Psychology, 92*(6), 1087-1101. https://doi.org/10.1037/0022-3514.92.6.1087

Dweck, C. S. (2006). *Mindset: the new psychology of success.* Random House.

Feddersen, N.B., Morris, R., Littlewood, M.A., & Richardson, D.J. (2020). The emergence and perpetuation of a destructive culture in an elite sport in the United Kingdom. *Sport in Society, 23*(6), 1004-1022. https://doi.org/10.1080/17430437.2019.1680639

Fletcher, D., & Sarkar, M. (2012). A grounded theory of psychological resilience in Olympic champions. *Psychology of Sport and Exercise, 13*(5), 669-678. https://doi.org/10.1016/j.psychsport.2012.04.007

Gasper, K., & Clore, G.L. (2002). Attending to the big picture: Mood and global versus local processing of visual information. *Psychological Science, 13*(1), 34-40. https://doi.org/10.1111/1467-9280.00406

Grecic, D., & Collins, D. (2013). The epistemological chain: Practical applications in sports. *Quest, 65*(2), 151-168. https://doi.org/10.1080/00336297.2013.773525

Güllich, A. (2014). Selection, de-selection and progression in German football talent promotion. *European Journal of Sport Science, 14*(6), 530-537. https://doi.org/10.1080/17461391.2013.858371

Güllich, A., & Cobley, S. (2017). On the efficacy of talent identification and talent development programmes. In J. Baker, S. Cobley, J. Schorer, & N. Wattie (Eds.), *Routledge handbook of talent identification and development in sport.* Routledge. https://doi.org/doi.org/10.4324/9781315668017

Harwood, C.G., & Knight, C.J. (2015). Parenting in youth sport: A position paper on parenting expertise. *Psychology of Sport and Exercise, 16,* 24-35. https://doi.org/10.1016/j.psychsport.2014.03.001

Henriksen, K. (2010). *The ecology of talent development in sport: A multiple case study of successful athletic talent development environments in Scandinavia.* University of Southern Denmark.

Henriksen, K., & Stambulova, N. (2017). Creating optimal environments for talent development: A holistic ecological approach. In J. Baker, S. Cobley, J. Schorer, & N. Wattie (Eds.), *Routledge handbook of talent identification and development in sport.* Routledge. https://doi.org/10.4324/9781315668017

Henriksen, K., Stambulova, N., & Roessler, K.K. (2010). Successful talent development in track and field: Considering the role of environment. *Scandinavian Journal of Medicine and Science in Sports, 20*(2), 122-132. https://doi.org/10.1111/j.1600-0838.2010.01187.x

Hill, A., MacNamara, Á., & Collins, D. (2018). Development and initial validation of the Psychological Characteristics of Developing Excellence Questionnaire version 2 (PCDEQ2). *European Journal of Sport Science, 19*(4), 517-528. https://doi.org/10.1080/17461391.2018.1535627

John, J.M., Gropper, H., & Thiel, A. (2019). The role of critical life events in the talent development pathways of athletes and musicians: A systematic review. *Psychology of Sport and Exercise, 45,* 101565. https://doi.org/10.1016/j.psychsport.2019.101565

Jones, R.L., & Standage, M. (2006). First among equals: Shared leadership in the coaching context. In R.L. Jones (Ed.), *The sports coach as educator: Re-conceptualising sports coaching* (pp. 65-76). Routledge.

Kelly, A.L., Till, K., Jackson, D., Barrell, D., Burke, K., & Turnnidge, J. (2021). Talent identification and relative age effects in English male rugby union pathways: From entry to expertise. *Frontiers in Sports and Active Living, 3*(12). https://doi.org/10.3389/fspor.2021.640607

Kerr, G.A., & Stirling, A.E. (2017). Issues of maltreatment in high performance athlete development. In J. Baker, S. Cobley, J. Schorer, & N. Wattie (Eds.), *Routledge handbook of talent identification and development in sport.* Routledge. https://doi.org/10.4324/9781315668017.ch29

Kidman, L. (2010). *Athlete-centred coaching: Developing decision makers.* IPC.

Kuttel, A. (2022). Integrating athlete and performance-centered approaches. In D. Collins & A. Cruickshank (Eds.), *Sport psychology essentials.* Human Kinetics.

Larsen, C.H., Alfermann, D., Henriksen, K., & Christensen, M.K. (2014). Preparing footballers for the next step: An intervention program from an ecological perspective. *The Sport Psychologist, 28*(1), 91-102. https://doi.org/10.1123/tsp.2013-0015

Larsen, C.H., Storm, L.K., Sæther, S., Pyrdol, N., & Henriksen, K. (2020). A world class academy in professional football. *Scandinavian Journal of Sport and Exercise Psychology, 2*(0). https://doi.org/10.7146/sjsep.v2i0.119746

Laureys, F., Collins, D., Deconinck, F.J.A., & Lenoir, M. (2021). Exploring the use of the psychological characteristics of developing excellence (PCDEs) in younger age groups: First steps in the validation process of the PCDE Questionnaire for Children (PCDEQ-C). *PLOS One, 16*(11), 0259396. https://doi.org/10.1371/journal.pone.0259396

Lorimer, R., & Jowett, S. (2010). Feedback of information in the empathic accuracy of sport coaches. *Psychology of Sport and Exercise, 11*(1), 12-17. https://doi.org/https://doi.org/10.1016/j.psychsport.2009.03.006

MacNamara, Á., Button, A., & Collins, D. (2010a). The role of psychological characteristics in facilitating the pathway to elite performance part 1: Identifying mental skills and behaviors. *The Sport Psychologist, 24*(1), 52-73. https://doi.org/10.1123/tsp.24.1.52

MacNamara, Á., Button, A., & Collins, D. (2010b). The role of psychological characteristics in facilitating the pathway to elite performance part 2: Examining environmental and stage-related differences in skills and behaviors. *The Sport Psychologist, 24*(1), 74-96. https://doi.org/10.1123/tsp.24.1.74

Martindale, A., & Collins, D. (2012). A professional judgment and decision making case study: Reflection-in-action research. *The Sport Psychologist, 26*(4), 500-518. https://doi.org/10.1123/tsp.26.4.500

Martindale, R.J., Collins, D., & Daubney, J. (2005). Talent development: A guide for practice and research within sport. *Quest, 57*(4), 353-375. https://doi.org/10.1080/00336297.2005.1049 1862

McCarthy, N., Collins, D., & Court, D. (2016). Start hard, finish better: Further evidence for the reversal of the RAE advantage. *Journal of Sports Sciences, 34*(15), 1461-1465. https://doi.org/10.1 080/02640414.2015.1119297

McCarthy, N., Taylor, J., Cruickshank, A., & Collins, D. (2022). Happy birthday? Relative age benefits and decrements on the rocky road. *MDPI Sports, 10*(82). https://doi.org/10.3390/sports10060082

McComb, S., & Simpson, V. (2014). The concept of shared mental models in healthcare collaboration. *Journal of Advanced Nursing, 70*(7), 1479-1488. https://doi.org/10.1111/jan.12307

McEwen, B.S. (1998). Stress, adaptation, and disease: Allostasis and allostatic load. *Annals of the New York Academy of Sciences, 840*(1), 33-44. https://doi.org/10.1111/j.1749-6632.1998.tb09546.x

Mees, A., Sinfield, D., Collins, D., & Collins, L. (2020). Adaptive expertise—a characteristic of expertise in outdoor instructors? *Physical Education and Sport Pedagogy, 25*(4), 423-438. https://doi.org/10.1080/17408989.2020.1727870

Moen, F., Myhre, K., Andersen, K.A., & Hrozanova, M. (2018). Emotions and performance in elite women handball. *The Sport Journal, 21*. https://thesportjournal.org/article/emotions-and-performance-in-elite-women-handball

Molloy, E., Noble, C., & Ajjawi, R. (2019). Attending to emotion in feedback. In M. Henderson, R. Ajjawi, D. Boud, & E. Molloy (Eds.), *The impact of feedback in higher education: Improving assessment outcomes for learners* (pp. 83-105). Springer. https://doi.org/10.1007/978-3-030-25112-3_6

Newport, R.A., Knight, C.J., & Love, T.D. (2020). The youth football journey: Parents' experiences and recommendations for support. *Qualitative Research in Sport, Exercise and Health,* 1-21. https://doi.org/10.1080/2159676X.2020.1833966

Omli, J., & Wiese-Bjornstal, D.M. (2011). Kids speak: Preferred parental behavior at youth sport events. *Research Quarterly for Exercise and Sport, 82*(4), 702-711. https://doi.org/10.1080/0270 1367.2011.10599807

Pankhurst, A., Collins, D., & Macnamara, Á. (2013). Talent development: Linking the stakeholders to the process. *Journal of Sports Sciences, 31*(4), 370-380. https://doi.org/10.1080/02640 414.2012.733821

Parihar, V.K., Hattiangady, B., Kuruba, R., Shuai, B., & Shetty, A.K. (2011). Predictable chronic mild stress improves mood, hippocampal neurogenesis and memory. *Molecular Psychiatry, 16*(2), 171-183. https://doi.org/10.1038/mp.2009.130

Penney, D., & Kidman, L. (2014). Opening call for discourse: Athlete centered coaching—a time for reflection on meanings, values and practice. *Journal of Athlete Centered Coaching,* (1), 1-5.

Prochazka, J., Ovcari, M., & Durinik, M. (2020). Sandwich feedback: The empirical evidence of its effectiveness. *Learning and Motivation, 71*, 101649. https://doi.org/https://doi.org/10.1016/j.lmot.2020.101649

Rees, T., Hardy, L., Güllich, A., Abernethy, B., Côté, J., Woodman, T., Montgomery, H., Laing, S., & Warr, C. (2016). The great British medalists project: A review of current knowledge on the development of the world's best sporting talent. *Sports Medicine, 46*(8), 1041-1058. https://doi.org/10.1007/s40279-016-0476-2

Ronkainen, N.J., Aggerholm, K., Ryba, T.V., & Allen-Collinson, J. (2020). Learning in sport: From life skills to existential learning. *Sport, Education and Society,* 1-14. https://doi.org/10.1080/13573322.2020.1712655

Sarkar, M., & Fletcher, D. (2017). Adversity-related experiences are essential for Olympic success: Additional evidence and considerations. In V. Walsh, M. Wilson, & B. Parkin (Eds.), *Progress in brain research* (Vol. 232, pp. 159-165). Elsevier. https://doi.org/https://doi.org/10.1016/bs.pbr.2016.11.009

Savage, J., Collins, D., & Cruickshank, A. (2017). Exploring traumas in the development of talent: What are they, what do they do, and what do they require? *Journal of Applied Sport Psychology, 29*(1), 101-117. https://doi.org/10.1080/10413200.2016.1194910

Savage, J., Cruickshank, A., & Collins, D. (2021). Perspective, control, and confidence: Perceived outcomes of using psychobehavioral skills in the developmental trauma experience. *International Journal of Sport and Exercise Psychology,* 1-20. https://doi.org/10.1080/1612197X.2021.1877323

Saward, C., Morris, J.G., Nevill, M.E., Minniti, A.M., & Sunderland, C. (2020). Psychological characteristics of developing excellence in elite youth football players in English professional academies. *Journal of Sports Sciences, 38*(11-12), 1380-1386. https://doi.org/10.1080/02640414.2019.1676526

Schwartz, R. (2013). The "sandwich approach" undermines your feedback. *Harvard Business Review* (April), 108-110. https://hbr.org/2013/04/the-sandwich-approach-undermin

Stoszkowski, J., & Collins, D. (2016). Sources, topics and use of knowledge by coaches. *Journal of Sports Sciences, 34*(9), 794-802. https://doi.org/10.1080/02640414.2015.1072279

Stoszkowski, J., MacNamara, À., Collins, D., & Hodgkinson, A. (2020). "Opinion and fact, perspective and truth": Seeking truthfulness and integrity in coaching and coach education. *International Sport Coaching Journal,* 1-7. https://doi.org/10.1123/iscj.2020-0023

Taylor, J., Ashford, M., & Collins, D. (2022a). The role of challenge in talent development: Understanding impact in response to emotional disturbance. *MDPI Psychology.* https://doi.org/10.3390/psych4040050

Taylor, J., Ashford, M., & Collins, D. (2022b). Tough love: Impactful, caring coaching in psychologically unsafe environments. *MDPI Sports.* https://doi.org/10.3390/sports10060083

Taylor, J., & Collins, D. (2019). Shoulda, coulda, didnae—why don't high-potential players make it? *The Sport Psychologist, 33*(2), 85-96. https://doi.org/10.1123/tsp.2017-0153

Taylor, J., & Collins, D. (2020). The highs and the lows—exploring the nature of optimally impactful development experiences on the talent pathway. *The Sport Psychologist, 34*(4), 319-328. https://doi.org/10.1123/tsp.2020-0034

Taylor, J., & Collins, D. (2021a). Getting in the way: Investigating barriers to optimising talent development experience. *Journal of Expertise, 4*(3), 315-332.

Taylor, J., & Collins, D. (2021b). Navigating the winds of change on the smooth sea—the interaction of feedback and emotional disruption on the talent pathway. *Journal of Applied Sport Psychology.* https://doi.org/10.1080/10413200.2021.1894505

Taylor, J., & Collins, D. (2022). The talent development curriculum. In C. Nash (Ed.), *Practical sport coaching* (2nd ed., pp. 7791). Routledge. https://doi.org/10.4324/9781003179733-7

Taylor, J., Collins, D., & Cruickshank, A. (2021). Too many cooks, not enough gourmets: examining provision and use of feedback for the developing athlete. *The Sport Psychologist, 36*(2), 89-100. https://doi.org/10.1123/tsp.2021-0037

Taylor, J., MacNamara, À., & Taylor, R.D. (2022). Strategy in talent systems: Top-down and bottom-up approaches. *Frontiers in Sports and Active Living.* https://doi.org/10.3389/fspor.2022.988631

van den Bossche, P., Gijselaers, W., Segers, M., Woltjer, G., & Kirschner, P. (2011). Team learning: Building shared mental models. *Instructional Science, 39*(3), 283-301. https://doi.org/10.1007/s11251-010-9128-3

van der Sluis, J.K., van der Steen, S., Stulp, G., & Den Hartigh, R.J.R. (2019). Visualizing individual dynamics: The case of a talented adolescent. In E. Kunnen, N.D. Ruiter, B. Jeronimus, & M.V. Gaag (Eds.), *Psychosocial development in adolescence.* Routledge.

Wadey, R., Day, M., & Howells, K. (2020). *Growth following adversity in sport: A mechanism to positive change.* Routledge. https://doi.org/https://doi.org/10.4324/9781003058021

Webb, V., Collins, D., & Cruickshank, A. (2016). Aligning the talent pathway: Exploring the role and mechanisms of coherence in development. *Journal of Sports Sciences, 34*(19), 1799-1807. https://doi.org/10.1080/02640414.2016.1139162

Wiliam, D. (2013). Principled curriculum design. In Chambers (Ed.). *Redesigning schooling-3* (pp. 2-46). SSAT.

Williams, G., & MacNamara, Á. (2020). "I didn't make it, but...": Deselected athletes' experiences of the talent development pathway. *Frontiers in Sports and Active Living, 2*, 24. https://doi.org/10.3389/fspor.2020.00024

Index

Note: The italicized *f* and *t* following page numbers refer to figures and tables, respectively.

About the Editors

Louise Davis, PhD, is an associate professor in sport and exercise psychology in the department of psychology at Umeå University in Sweden. Davis gained her PhD in the School of Sport, Exercise, and Health Sciences at Loughborough University and earned her MSc and BSc degrees from Bangor University in the United Kingdom. Her research revolves around psychosocial, developmental, and environmental factors of elite performance and coaching, with a focus on interpersonal relationships in sport. Davis works closely with the Swedish Sport Federation (Riksidrottsförbundet) and has received extensive funding from the Swedish Research Council for Sport Science (Centrum för idrottsforskning). Davis has published in peer-reviewed international journals and authored chapters in edited books. She frequently presents her work at national and international conferences as well as in workshops for coaches, coach educators, and national sport organizations in Sweden. Davis is also an active reviewer for many scientific journals, including *Psychology of Sport and Exercise*, *International Sport Coaching Journal*, *Journal of Sports Science*, and *Sport, Exercise, and Performance Psychology*.

Richard Keegan, PhD, is an associate professor in sport and exercise psychology at the University of Canberra in Australia. He completed MSc and PhD degrees at Loughborough University before beginning his career at the University of Lincoln in the United Kingdom. Keegan's research focuses on motivational processes in sport and exercise, physical literacy, applied sport psychology practice, and readiness monitoring. He is an associate editor for both *Psychology of Sport and Exercise* and *Case Studies in Sport and Exercise Psychology*. Keegan is a psychologist registered in the United Kingdom (HCPC), in Australia (AHPRA), and through the International Society of Sport Psychology (ISSP), where he is a member of the management council. As a practitioner he has worked with athletes across a wide range of levels, from beginners to world champions, and in a range of sports. He has also done officiating as well as supervising and assessing trainee practitioners.

Sophia Jowett, PhD, is a professor of psychology at Loughborough University. Her research interests revolve around interpersonal relationships in sport and sport coaching. Her research—funded by Economic and Social Research Council, British Academy, Nuffield Foundation, and HSBC—has been published in a range of scientific journals, been presented at conferences, and informed coach development across the world. Examples of practical impact include her work with UK Coaching and UK Sport (Coach Development/Women Coaches Leadership Development Project) and national sport organizations.

Jowett is on the editorial board of peer-reviewed scientific journals, including *International Sport Coaching Journal* and *Sports Coaching Review*. She co-edited a special issue of *Psychology of Sport and Exercise* on interpersonal relationships as well as a monograph on the psychology of sports coaching. In 2015, she launched a web-based app known as TANDEM—Working Together for Performance Excellence. In 2019 she launched an online educational program known as CARE (Coach-Athlete Relationship Empowerment). Jowett was a psychologist for the Greek team at the 2004 Olympic Games, and she is an associate fellow and chartered psychologist of the British Psychological Society.

About the Contributors

Paul R. Appleton, PhD, is a senior lecturer in the department of sport and exercise sciences at Manchester Metropolitan University in the United Kingdom. A major focus of Appleton's current work concerns implementing and validating Empowering Coaching and the associated family of education programs in different performance and physical activity settings (e.g., physical education, sport, education, dance). Appleton has published extensively on the assessment of empowering and disempowering motivational climates and their correlates. He also has conducted numerous studies on the antecedents (e.g., parental behaviors) and consequences (e.g., burnout) of perfectionism in sport. Having obtained BSc (1st class) and PhD degrees, Appleton was appointed as a lecturer in the School of Physical Education and Sport Sciences at the University of Bedfordshire (2006-2009), and in 2009, he joined the University of Birmingham as a research and teaching fellow, where he collaborated on and also led a number of research and applied projects centered on the motivational climate, motivational processes, and their implications for differential outcomes in athletes from grassroots through junior elite levels. Appleton is on the editorial board of *Psychology of Sport and Exercise* and the *International Journal of Sport and Exercise Psychology.*

Rachel Arnold, PhD, is a reader in sport and performance psychology in the department for health at the University of Bath in the United Kingdom. She is a chartered psychologist and associate fellow of the British Psychological Society, practitioner psychologist registered with the Health and Care Professions Council, sport and exercise scientist accredited by the British Association of Sport and Exercise Sciences, chartered scientist with the Science Council, and senior fellow of the Higher Education Academy. Alongside her extensive consultancy experience, Arnold has published widely in the area of stress, performance, and well-being, with a focus on examining how and why individuals thrive. Applying her research to sport, organizational, and health settings, her specific research interests include the organizational stress process; performance environments and cultures; leadership and management; and the enhancement of personal, team, and organizational thriving. Arnold has received awards for her research from the Association for Applied Sport Psychology and the British Psychological Society, and she recently coedited the book *Stress, Well-Being, and Performance in Sport.* She has received funding for her research from various bodies including the Medical Research Council, Sport England, the National Institute of Health Research, the Rugby Football Union, and World Rugby.

Isabel Balaguer, PhD, is a professor of social psychology in the faculty of psychology at the University of Valencia in Spain and is director of the Research Group of Sport Psychology at the same university. She is an honorary senior research fellow in the School of Sport, Exercise and Rehabilitation Sciences at the University of Birmingham in the United Kingdom. She teaches graduate and undergraduate courses in social psychology and the social-psychological aspects of sport and exercise. Balaguer's major research interests center on the antecedents and consequences of coach behaviors and the psychosocial predictors of athletes' optimal development. During the last decades she has participated in the design of psychosocial intervention programs in the context of youth sport to promote young people's well-being and the quality of their sport experience. Her high level of research activity is reflected in the publication of several books and more than 150 papers, as well as her participation in numerous national and international conferences. She is actively involved in training leaders (coaches, instructors) in the principles of and strategies embedded in more empowering climates. Isabel is also engaged in applied sport psychology work with athletes, coaches, and parents of athletes in different sports, especially elite-level tennis.

Mark R. Beauchamp, PhD, is a professor of exercise and health psychology in the School of Kinesiology at the University of British Columbia. His research focuses on the psychology of group processes within exercise and sport settings. He is particularly interested in understanding the barriers to, and facilitators of, physical activity behaviour across the age spectrum, and developing effective and scalable physical activity interventions with various populations. His research program has received funding from agencies such as the Canadian Institutes of Health Research, Canadian Foundation for Innovation, and Social Sciences and Humanities Research Council of Canada. He has published over 200 journal articles and book chapters with his work published in outlets such as the *Annals of Behavioral Medicine, Health Psychology,* and the *Annual Review of Psychology.* He is a Chartered Psychologist and Associate Fellow of the British Psychological Society (BPS), and is the editor-in-chief for Sport, Exercise, and Performance Psychology (APA).

Suzan Blijlevens, PhD, has a master's degree in psychology, with a specialization in sport and performance psychology. From 2015 to 2019, she engaged in a collaborative research project between the Vrije Universiteit Brussel, Rijksuniversiteit Groningen, and NOC*NSF, which has led to her dissertation, "Performance Behaviour in Elite Sports." As a postdoctoral researcher, Blijlevens is currently collaborating with the research group Sport Psychology and Mental Support (SPMB). Her main research interest is focused on the psychological development of talented and elite athletes, but she also participates in research on team resilience, collective collapse in teams, and the impact of heat on mental functioning. As part of her PhD, Blijlevens developed a generic learning line on performance behavior, several sport-specific learning lines, and coaching tools (e.g., observation tools, podcasts, handbooks, and an online platform). She is now working with the Dutch Olympic committee (TeamNL), where she is responsible for the further optimalization and implementation of these tools within the elite sport context.

Ian D. Boardley, PhD, is an associate professor of sport and exercise psychology at the University of Birmingham in the United Kingdom. His teaching focuses on moral behavior and doping in sport and exercise, mental health in sport, and interdisciplinary research and research impact. Boardley's research focuses on the psychology of doping in sport and exercise, moral behavior in sport, and coaching efficacy. He has authored more than 60 scientific articles and book chapters, and he regularly presents his research at national and international scientific and professional conferences. Boardley is a member of the UK Anti-Doping Innovation Commission and the steering committee for the British Association of Sport and Exercise Sciences clean sport interest group. He has organized and participated in many sport psychology symposia.

Matthieu M. Boisvert, MHK, is a PhD student at the University of Windsor in Canada. Boisvert's research interests focus on athlete leadership and group dynamics. His master's project involved conducting a leadership development program that targeted the enhancement of athlete leadership behaviors of youth hockey players. Part of Boisvert's doctoral research is the development of an online athlete leadership development platform. He has presented his research at national and international conferences, including the Canadian Society for Psychomotor Learning and Sport Psychology (SCAPPS), the North American Society for the Psychology of Sport and Physical Activity (NASPSPA), the Association for Applied Sport Psychology (AASP), the European Congress of Sport and Exercise Psychology (FEPSAC), the Eastern Canada Sport and Exercise Psychology Symposium (ECSEPS), and the Midwest Sport and Exercise Psychology Symposium (MSEPS).

Courtney Boucher, PhD, earned her master's and is a doctoral candidate, with an emphasis in sport sociology and sociocultural studies in education, in the School of Kinesiology at the University of Minnesota. She is a research assistant in the Tucker Center for Research on Girls and Women in Sport and three-time Pam Borton Fellow for the Promotion of Girls and Women in Sport Leadership. In her research she examines the complex occupational landscape of women sport coaches to develop strategies to reduce and eliminate barriers, as well as the hiring practices of NCAA Division I athletic directors, and she has coauthored the Tucker Center's longitudinal *Women in College Coaching Report Card*. Prior to graduate studies, Boucher was the assistant women's hockey coach at her alma mater, Gustavus Adolphus College, where she earned a BA in chemistry with a minor in political science.

Daniel J. Brown, PhD, is a senior lecturer in sport and exercise psychology at the University of Portsmouth in the United Kingdom and a chartered psychologist of the British Psychological Society (BPS). He is the course leader for the BSc (Hons) sport and exercise psychology program and contributes sport psychology and methodological expertise to taught modules. Brown's research centers on the psychology of human excellence and well-being, with specific focuses on understanding and facilitating thriving in humans, athlete transitions and developmental experiences, and the development and assessment of interventions used in sport and performance psychology. As an early career researcher, he has published regularly in international peer-reviewed journals and authored several book chapters, as well as delivering over 20 scientific and professional presentations at conferences and invited events. Through his research, Brown has achieved various prizes, including the HTA Whiting Undergraduate Dissertation Prize (2011); the 2017 BPS Division of Sport and Exercise Psychology (DSEP) PhD Award; the 2018 Association of Applied Sport Psychology (AASP) Doctoral Dissertation Award; and the 2018 Society for Sport, Exercise and Performance Psychology, APA Division 47 Dissertation Award. He is the current chair of the AASP doctoral dissertation award committee and a member of the BPS DSEP equality, diversity, and inclusion working group.

Shauna M. Burke, PhD, is an associate professor and faculty scholar (2020-2022) in the School of Health Studies at Western University in Canada. Broadly speaking, her research area is child and adolescent health, with a specific focus on childhood obesity, health behaviors (e.g., physical activity, sedentary behavior), and group dynamics and social connectedness. In addition to over 100 presentations, workshops, and invited lectures at national and international scientific conferences, Burke has published several book chapters and close to 70 peer-reviewed articles in reputable journals in the areas of physical activity (e.g., *Psychology of Sport and Exercise, International Journal of Behavioral Nutrition and Physical Activity*), group dynamics (e.g., *BMC Public Health*), health behavior (e.g., *Applied Physiology, Nutrition, and Metabolism*), and public health (e.g., *Public Health Nutrition*). Burke is also coauthor of a widely used Canadian health textbook titled *Core Concepts in Health*, now in its third edition. In the context of the COVID-19 pandemic, Burke is the principal investigator of the iBelong program of research, investigating young people's adherence to public health guidelines, health behaviors, perceptions of social connectedness, and psychological well-being. She has also received numerous prestigious awards in recognition of her excellence in mentorship and teaching.

Sam Carr, PhD, is a senior lecturer in education with the department of education and a research associate with the Centre for Death and Society at the University of Bath in the United Kingdom. Carr was awarded his PhD in educational psychology from Lancaster University in 2005 and is a fellow of the Higher Education Academy. He has a particular interest in human relationships and their role in shaping psychological experiences across the life span and is equally intrigued by (1) the fundamental importance of close attachments and (2) the impacts of broader social and political structures upon attachment development and psychological experiences. Carr has published widely in the area of attachment, connecting and applying the theory to areas such as human–animal relationships, well-being in education, child development, peer relations, foster care, gerontology, and sport, exercise, and health. He has published widely in peer-reviewed international journals and edited books, and he is the author of the monograph *Attachment in Sport, Exercise, and Wellness.*

Pete Coffee, PhD, is a professor of psychology at Heriot-Watt University, researching the social identity approach to sport, exercise, health, and performance settings. His previous and ongoing research in these settings provides insight into several social and physical phenomena including social support, attributions, leadership, and physical activity. Coffee is an HCPC-registered practitioner sport and exercise psychologist, and a chartered psychologist with the British Psychological Society.

Dave Collins, PhD, is a professorial fellow at the University of Edinburgh and director at Grey Matters Performance Ltd. As an academic, Collins has written over 350 peer-reviewed publications and 80 books or chapters. As a practitioner, he has worked with more than 80 world or Olympic medalists plus professional teams and performers. He has also worked as a business and organizational adviser in various fields. Collins has coached to national level in three sports and is a 5th dan karate, director of the Rugby Coaches Association, a fellow of the Society of Martial Arts and BASES, an associate fellow of the BPS, and a former Royal Marine. His research interests extend across the development of performance, coaching, and expertise.

Jean Côté, PhD, is a professor in the School of Kinesiology and Health Studies at Queen's University in Canada, where he served as the director from 2006 to 2019. He is a fellow of the Canadian Society for Psychomotor Learning and Sport Psychology (SCAPPS) and the International Society of Sport Psychology (ISSP). Côté's research interests focus on the interaction between youth, their social dynamics (coaches, parents, peers), and the environment for the development of personal assets and excellence in sport.

Koen De Brandt, PhD, is a postdoctoral researcher and lecturer at the Vrije Universiteit Brussel in Belgium. He is also the coordinator of the university's Topsport en Studie (Top Sport and Study) department, assisting student-athletes in their dual careers. Before De Brandt started working at the VUB, he was active as a professional volleyball player and youth coach. De Brandt has coordinated and assisted in more than 20 international and national projects on athletes' dual careers for, among others, the European Commission, the International Olympic Committee, the Flemish Sport Administration (Sport Vlaanderen), the Brussels-Capital Region, and football club RSC Anderlecht. His current projects focus on athletes' dual careers and mental health (e.g., Erasmus+ Sport project Dual Careers for Mental Health). As a lecturer, De Brandt teaches and assists in courses in the bachelor's and master's program of sport and movement science, including elite sports career planning, high-performance management, mental training and coaching throughout the sports career, specialized sport scientific support, and internships in sport management.

Simon Defruyt, PhD, is a postdoctoral researcher for the research group Sport Psychology and Mental Support (SPMB) of Vrije Universiteit Brussel (VUB) in Belgium. As a postdoctoral researcher, Defruyt focuses on valorizing dual career knowledge, coediting a handbook, and developing instruments and workshops for student-athletes and dual career support providers. From 2015 up to 2019, Defruyt was a doctoral researcher for SPMB. He has a master's degree in organizational psychology and a specialized certificate in sport psychology. In his research, Defruyt focused on the competencies, support strategies, and education of dual career support providers. He coordinated and participated in several European DC projects, including Gold in Education and Elite Sport (GEES), Be a Winner in Elite Sport and Employment Before and After Athletic Retirement (B-WISER), Mind the Gap, and the IOC's "The Development and Evaluation of Training Modules for DC Support Providers." During his PhD, Defruyt coauthored the European handbook for DC support providers, developed education modules for DC support providers, and cocreated an online competence evaluation for DC support providers (www.dualcareertools.com). From an applied perspective, he provides dual career support and workshops for student-athletes in the department Topsport en Studie of the VUB.

Faye F. Didymus, PhD, is a reader in sport and performance psychology within the Institute for Sport, Physical Activity, and Leisure at Leeds Beckett University in the United Kingdom. Her fundamental and applied research focuses on the psychology of performance in sport and related environments. In particular, Didymus is interested in the ways that psychological stress may inhibit or facilitate peak performance among sport coaches and performers. Her most recent research focuses on the cognitive mechanisms underlying stressful transactions; interpersonal stress experiences among athletes, sport parents, and coaches; and the efficacy and effectiveness of stress management interventions in sport.

Kristen Dieffenbach , PhD, CMPC, is the director of the Center for Applied Coaching and Sport Sciences at West Virginia University and an associate professor of athletic coaching education. She is the founding and current president of the United States Center for Coaching Excellence, a fellow in the Association of Applied Sport Psychology, and a graduate of the NSSU Coach Developer Academy. Dieffenbach has been a professional endurance sport coach and a sport psychology and coaching educational consultant for over 20 years, working with developmental through Olympic-level athletes, coaches, and organizations. Her research interests focus on coach developer training, coaching and professionalism, and ethics and moral decision making in coach development.

Joan L. Duda, PhD, is a professor of sport and exercise psychology in the School of Sport, Exercise and Rehabilitation Sciences at the University of Birmingham in the United Kingdom. She is internationally known for her expertise on the motivational climate, motivation, and determinants of optimal functioning and well-being in sport, exercise, and the performing arts. Duda is one of the most cited researchers in her discipline, having published more than 350 papers and book chapters and edited two books. She is also a long-standing sport psychology consultant. Duda has created the evidence-based Empowering Coaching family of training programs, which are being delivered to coaches and parents in the United Kingdom and abroad. She also has extensive applied experience in the development of mental skills and self-regulation in sport, working with athletes and coaches from recreational and junior elite through Olympic and professional levels. Duda is a past president of the European College of Sport Sciences, Association of Applied Sport Psychology and Division 12 (Sport Psychology) of the International Association of Applied Psychology. She is the recipient of the Distinguished Scholar Award from the North American Society for the Psychology of Sport and Physical Activity (2019) and holds an honorary doctoral degree from the Norwegian School of Sport Sciences (2008); the University of Thessaly, Greece (2019); and the University of Malmo, Sweden (2021).

Mark Eys, PhD, is a professor in the department of kinesiology and physical education and the psychology department at Wilfrid Laurier University in Canada. He is a Laurier Research Chair (2019-present) in group dynamics and physical activity and a former Canada Research Chair (2009-2019). His current research interests include role commitment and acceptance in sport, the measurement and correlates of cohesion, and the application of group dynamics across contexts (sport, exercise, organizations). He has published his research in top sport and exercise psychology journals (over 110 peer-reviewed articles), as a coauthor of the book *Group Dynamics in Sport, Fifth Edition* (2020), and as a coeditor of *Group Dynamics in Exercise and Sport Psychology* (2014) and *The Power of Groups in Youth Sport* (2020). Finally, his most recent work focuses on the physical activity and social integration of new Canadians via a partnership development grant (SSHRC 2019-2022) in collaboration with Laurentian University, Focus for Ethnic Women, KW Multicultural Centre, City of Kitchener, Region of Waterloo Public Health, and the Sun Life Financial Centre for Physically Active Communities.

Luke Felton, PhD, is a senior lecturer and the MSc program director at the University of Roehampton in the United Kingdom. His research interests focus around understanding the well-being of athletes, often by exploring the impact of attachment styles and perceptions of basic psychological needs. Felton is particularly interested in studying the role of relationships and the influence they can have on the well-being of an athlete, such as the coach–athlete relationship. Felton has published his research in a range of scientific journals, written and contributed to several book chapters, and has presented at national and international conferences. He is also a chartered psychologist with the British Psychological Society.

Jessica Fraser-Thomas, PhD, is an associate professor in the School of Kinesiology and Health Science at York University in Canada and is a member of the LaMarsh Centre for Child and Youth Research and PYD SportNET. Her research focuses on children's and youths' development through sport, with particular interest in how psychosocial and contextual factors (e.g., coaches, family, culture) influence sport trajectories and outcomes. She is a recipient of the Canadian Society for Psychomotor Learning and Sport Psychology Young Scientist Award, the Province of Ontario Volunteer Service Award, and YMCA Canada's Program Innovation Award.

Mary Fry, PhD, is a professor in sport and exercise psychology at the University of Kansas, as well as the director of the KU Sport and Exercise Psychology Lab. Her research focuses on creating a caring and task-involving climate for individuals (e.g., athletes, coaches, exercisers) in physical activity settings and the social, psychological, and physical benefits of experiencing such a climate. Before pursuing graduate study, Fry taught high school physical education and English and worked as a high school tennis coach for the men's and women's teams in a school district in Texas. She completed her graduate degrees at the University of North Carolina, Greensboro (MS), and Purdue University (PhD). She serves as an associate editor for the *Journal of Sport Psychology in Action*, and she is on the editorial board for the *Journal of Sport, Exercise, and Performance Psychology* and the *Journal of Applied Sport Psychology*. She serves on the national advisory board for the Positive Coaching Alliance and has served on the executive board for the Association for Applied Sport Psychology. Fry and her colleagues authored *A Coach's Guide to Maximizing the Youth Sport Experience: Work Hard, Be Kind.*

Lori Gano-Overway, PhD, is an assistant professor and coaching education minor program director at James Madison University in Virginia. She completed her graduate degrees at Purdue University (MS) and Michigan State University (PhD). Gano-Overway has been involved in coaching education for over 20 years and conducts research on how the social psychological climate can be structured to provide positive experiences for young people and foster positive youth development. As an AASP-certified mental performance consultant, she works with athletes on performance-enhancement issues and collaborates with coaches on creating environments that foster positive experiences and performance-enhancement outcomes for athletes. Gano-Overway serves on the editorial board of the *Journal of Sport Psychology in Action* and the *International Sport Coaching Journal* and is the editor for the *Women in Sport and Physical Activity Journal*. She is also a member of the Virginia High School League coaching education committee, serves on the national advisory board for the Positive Coaching Alliance, and has served as a board member for the United States Center for Coaching Excellence.

Paul Gorczynski, PhD, is a chartered psychologist and associate fellow of the British Psychological Society and a sport and exercise psychologist registered with the Health and Care Professions Council. He works as a senior lecturer of sport and exercise psychology at the University of Greenwich. Gorczynski obtained his doctorate at the University of Toronto. He completed his postdoctoral training at the Centre for Addiction and Mental Health in Toronto, where he was a NARSAD Young Investigator with the Brain and Behavior Research Foundation. His research expertise lies within the promotion of mental health in clinical, education, and elite sport settings. Gorczynski has led several expert statements on mental health literacy and cultural competence in elite sport. He coleads on the Mental Health in Sport training program as well as the Equity, Diversity, and Inclusivity training program as part of the Sport and Exercise Psychology Accreditation Route organized by the British Association of Sport and Exercise Sciences. Gorczynski also consults on research design and ethics within the National Health Service, Health Research Authority, where he is chair for the London-Bloomsbury research ethics committee. In 2018, he was an expert panel member for the International Olympic Committee consensus statement on mental health in elite athletes. From 2021 to 2022, Gorczynski consulted as a Parliamentary Office of Science and Technology fellow for the women and equalities committee in UK Parliament on LGBTQI+ mental health service use.

Sebastian Harenberg, PhD, is an associate professor in the department of human kinetics at St. Francis Xavier University in Canada. His research focuses on sport leadership and group dynamics in sport. In particular, he is interested in team structure, selection process, and competition within interdependent sport teams.

Chris Hartley, PhD, is a lecturer at the University of Stirling in the United Kingdom and is cochair of the Scottish Sport and Exercise Psychology Network. His main areas of interest center on applied sport and performance psychology, social support, and the social identity approach to sport and performance settings. Hartley is an HCPC-registered practitioner sport and exercise psychologist, and a chartered psychologist with the British Psychological Society. He has extensive experience as an applied practitioner working from grassroots to elite professional sport.

Chris G. Harwood, PhD, is a professor of sport psychology at Nottingham Trent University in the United Kingdom. His research interests lie in the psychosocial aspects of athlete development and performance including the roles of the coach, the parents, and the wider social and performance environment. He has published over 150 journal articles, book chapters, and books on these topics as a scientist-practitioner, and he serves on several journal editorial boards, including the *Journal of Applied Sport Psychology*, *International Journal of Sport and Exercise Psychology*, *The Sport Psychologist*, *Psychology of Sport and Exercise*, *Journal of Sport Psychology in Action*, and *Qualitative Research in Sport, Exercise and Health*. A fellow of AASP and BASES, he is a past vice president of the European Federation of Sport Psychology (FEPSAC) from 2007 to 2011 and served as chair of the Psychology Division for BASES from 2014 to 2018. He is currently vice-president and accreditation chair on the managing council of the International Society of Sport Psychology (ISSP). Beyond his academic work, Harwood is an HCPC-registered practitioner psychologist and has held the position of lead psychologist within professional football clubs and for the Lawn Tennis Association. He continues to advise and consult on youth psychological support programs in sport, working with organizations, coaches, athletes, and parents. He still enjoys competing as a national-level veteran player for Leicestershire men's tennis team.

Sally J. Hilton, DCPsych, is a chartered counseling psychologist and integrative psychotherapist specializing in providing psychotherapy to sports people. Hilton works in private practice and supports clients around issues that affect both performance and well-being, working across a broad range of sports, ages, and levels of ability. She completed her doctorate in counseling psychology and psychotherapy by professional studies at Metanoia Institute/Middlesex University, conducting research exploring identity, elite sport, and mental health. Hilton is currently a PhD doctoral candidate at Nottingham Trent University (UK), undertaking a program of research exploring resilience, psychological safety, and fear of failure in international football. She has both a research and practice interest in supporting well-being and high performance within sport contexts, with a particular focus on the impact of sport culture on mental health and resilience.

Katherine E. Hirsch, MHK, is a PhD student studying sport, exercise, and performance psychology in the department of kinesiology at the University of Windsor in Windsor, Ontario, Canada. She is a member of the Sport Psychology and Physical Activity Research Collaborative (SPPARC). Her research is largely focused on creating healthy and positive sport experiences for team-sport athletes. She conducts research that examines the role of athlete leaders in promoting positive group dynamics. This research explores leader fairness constructs and outcomes of fair treatment and unfair treatment, including team cohesion and athlete satisfaction. She also investigates body image and disordered eating in female athletes. In this research, she examines methods that athletes and coaches can use to promote positive body image. Collectively, her research strives to foster safe sport environments so that athletes can focus on the benefits that sport participation has to offer. Hirsch is a member of the Association of Applied Sport Psychology (AASP), Canadian Society for Psychomotor Learning and Sport Psychology (SCAPPS), and North American Society for the Psychology of Sport and Physical Activity (NASPSPA).

Nicholas L. Holt, PhD, is a professor and dean in the faculty of kinesiology at the University of Calgary in Canada. His research focuses on psychosocial aspects of sport participation among children, adolescents, and their families. He has published over 150 journal articles, 38 chapters, and four books. He has received $3.2 million in funding as a principal investigator and another $2.9 million as a coinvestigator to support his work. Holt is a member of the Royal Society of Canada College of New Scholars, Artists, and Scientists. In his spare time, he is a soccer coach and enjoys participating in endurance events.

Caroline Hummell , MSc, is a PhD candidate in the faculty of applied health sciences at Brock University in Canada. Her research examines factors that promote quality relationships in sport, with a specialized focus on mentorship and its influence on positive youth developmental outcomes for athletes.

Ben Jackson, PhD, is a professor in the School of Human Sciences at The University of Western Australia and holds a shared appointment with Telethon Kids Institute (as Research Theme Lead, Brain and Behaviour). Alongside Professor James Dimmock (James Cook University), he also leads the cross-institutional Psychology of Active, Healthy Living (PAHL) Group. The PAHL group develops, delivers, and evaluates community health promotion programs and interventions with an emphasis on knowledge translation and real-world impact. Ben's research output includes more than 150 journal articles and book chapters, and his work is supported by funding from agencies including the Australian Research Council, National Health and Medical Research Council, and Western Australian Department of Health. Ben is a Deputy Editor for *Stress & Health,* an Associate Editor for the *Journal of Sport & Exercise Psychology,* and also serves as an editorial board member for several other journals.

Maria Kavussanu, PhD, is professor of sport and exercise psychology at the University of Birmingham in the United Kingdom. Her research focuses on moral behavior in sport, the psychology of doping, authentic leadership in coaches, and mental health in athletes. Kavussanu has published over 140 journal articles and book chapters. She has received funding for her research from the Economic and Social Research Council, the Nuffield Foundation, the World Anti-Doping Agency, and the International Olympic Committee, as well as research awards from the North American Society for the Psychology of Sport and Physical Activity and the European College of Sport Science. Kavussanu is editor in chief of *Sport, Exercise and Performance Psychology* and has been involved with most sport psychology journals as editorial board member or associate editor. She has delivered keynote addresses at several international conferences including the International Society of Sport Psychology, Spain; the Italian Association of Sport Psychology, Italy; and the 3rd International Congress of Sport and Exercise Psychology, Turkey. In her spare time, she plays tennis and swims.

Jolan Kegelaers, PhD, is a postdoctoral researcher within the research group Sport Psychology and Mental Support of the Vrije Universiteit Brussel in Belgium. He completed his PhD on the development of psychological resilience in talented and elite athletes. His current research interests focus on the promotion of mental well-being in athletes and other performers, as well as the implementation and evaluation of performance psychology within different performance domains. Since September 2018, he has also been active as a postdoc researcher at the Amsterdam University of Applied Sciences, conducting research on the implementation of innovative training methods within sport, music, and dance.

Adam L. Kelly, PhD, CSci, is a senior lecturer and course leader for sport coaching and physical education at Birmingham City University in the United Kingdom. In addition to attaining his PhD from the University of Exeter, Kelly holds the BASES Sport and Exercise Scientist credential and is licensed as a UEFA A Licence coach. Broadly, his research interests examine organizational structures in youth sport to better understand the athlete development process and create more appropriate settings. He is collaborating with a number of regional, national, and international organizations across a range of sports including cricket, football, rugby union, squash, and swimming.

Gretchen Kerr, PhD, is a professor and the dean of the faculty of kinesiology and physical education at the University of Toronto and a codirector of the Canadian Gender Equity in Sport Research Hub. She has devoted her career to researching maltreatment, gender-based violence, and promoting safe, equitable sport opportunities for all. Kerr's recent work includes a prevalence study of maltreatment among national team members, as well as contributions to safe sport training modules for coaches and to the *Universal Code of Conduct to Prevent and Address Maltreatment,* a policy mandated by Sport Canada for all national sport organizations.

Camilla J. Knight, PhD, is a professor of sport psychology and youth sport at Swansea University and an adjunct professor at the University of Agder. She is also the youth sport lead for the Welsh Institute of Performance Science. Knight's research interests are concerned with understanding and enhancing the psychosocial experiences of children in sport, with a particular focus on the influence of parents. She is coauthor of *Parenting in Youth Sport: From Research to Practice* (Routledge, 2014) and coeditor of *Sport Psychology for Young Athletes* (Routledge, 2017). She has published over 25 book chapters on topics related to parental involvement in sport and youth sport, as well as 65 peer-reviewed journal articles. Her work has been presented at over 100 national and international conferences. Knight also consults widely with a range of national and international sport organizations on parental involvement and youth sport participation more broadly. She is a BASES-accredited sport and exercise scientist (psychology support and research).

Nicole M. LaVoi, PhD, is a senior lecturer in social and behavioral sciences in the School of Kinesiology and the director of the Tucker Center for Research on Girls and Women in Sport at the University of Minnesota. Through her multidisciplinary research, she helps solve problems to make a difference in the lives of sport stakeholders—particularly girls and women. As a leading scholar on gender, leadership, coaching education, and women sport coaches, LaVoi has published over 100 book chapters, research reports, and peer-reviewed articles across multiple disciplines. Her seminal work includes the annual *Women in College Coaching Report Card*, *Developing Physically Active Girls: An Evidence-Based Multidisciplinary Approach* (2007, 2018), the Routledge Outstanding Award-winning book *Women in Sports Coaching* (2016), and three Emmy-nominated documentaries on women and girls in sport including *Media Coverage & Female Athletes: Women Play Sports, Just Not in the Media* (2013), which won a regional Emmy for best sport documentary. LaVoi is a cofounder of the Social Justice Through Sport and Exercise Psychology Symposia and annually hosts the Women Coaches Symposium, the largest in the world, and serves on numerous mission-driven boards.

Todd M. Loughead, PhD, is a full professor of sport, exercise, and performance psychology in the faculty of human kinetics and codirector of the Sport Psychology and Physical Activity Research Collaborative (SPPARC) at the University of Windsor in Canada. Loughead's research uses a group dynamics perspective to examine human behavior. Specifically, his interests are investigating athlete leadership and coaching, and how these two sources of leadership influence team functioning. He is also interested in athletes mentoring their peers and its associated benefits, as well as in team cohesion and how this contributes to an enhanced team environment. His research interests have been federally supported by numerous grants, and his current project examines the development of athlete leadership. Loughead consults with coaches, sport teams, and individual athletes at the local, provincial, Olympic, and professional levels. He also assists in the delivery of the UWorkItOut UWin program, an exercise program for university students with mental health concerns. Loughead is a member of the Canadian Sport Psychology Association (CSPA), Association of Applied Sport Psychology (AASP), Canadian Society for Psychomotor Learning and Sport Psychology (SCAPPS), and North American Society for the Psychology of Sport and Physical Activity (NASPSPA).

Anthony Miller, PhD, is a lecturer in sport and exercise psychology in the School of Life Sciences at Staffordshire University in the United Kingdom. Miller's research focuses on the psychophysiological and performance consequences of the social identity approach to leadership in high-performing team sports. He also has a keen interest in the psychology of leadership in high-performing youth sport settings. Miller has published multiple peer-reviewed papers and has published on The Conversation UK. He has spoken at both national and international conferences and is also a consultant within high-performance team sports.

Cindy Miller Aron, LCSW, is senior director of clinical services at Ascend Consultation in Healthcare/Illinois Sport and Performance Institute in Chicago, and an adjunct professor of psychiatry at the University of Wisconsin School of Medicine and Public Health in Madison. She is a content and interventional expert on trauma in sport, particularly focusing on the neurobiological unpinning of somatic and performance complaints. Miller Aron is a national and international advocate for the provision of mental health services in sport. She is a licensed provider for the United States Olympic and Paralympic Committee mental health registry and the NBPA and NFLPA mental health registries. She is a cofounder of the Alliance for Social Workers in Sport, a fellow in the American Group Psychotherapy Association, and current cochair of the annual meeting. She is a co-coordinator of the Association for Applied Sport Psychology eating disorders special interest group and outreach cochair for the International Society for Sports Psychiatry. She is a strong proponent of multidisciplinary care in sport. In 2013, Miller Aron was appointed to the NCAA Inaugural Mental Health Task Force, in 2016 to the NCAA Sexual Violence and Prevention Summit and the NCAA Governors' Commission to Combat Sexual Violence, and in 2018 to the NCAA Sexual Violence Prevention Think Tank. In 2019 she was appointed to the American Medical Society for Sports Medicine Task Force on Sexual Violence in Sport and has been a consultant to the U.S. Center for SafeSport. In 2018 Cindy was appointed to the International Olympic Committee Consensus Group on Mental Health in Elite Athletes as a content expert and as faculty for the International Olympic Committee diploma program. She publishes numerous articles and chapters on the interface of mental health and athletics.

Krista J. Munroe-Chandler, PhD, is recognized for her work in the psychology of sport, exercise, and performance. She is a full professor in the faculty of human kinetics and codirector of the Sport Psychology and Physical Activity Research Collaborative (SPPARC) at the University of Windsor in Canada. Her research interests include imagery use in sport and exercise as well as the application of sport psychology interventions along with her involvement in research of athlete leadership. She runs the UWorkItOut UWin program—an exercise program for university students with mental health concerns—and is the principal investigator on a federally funded research project aimed at developing and implementing an online psychological skills training (PST) program for athletes with a disability. She works with athletes (both able bodied and athletes with a disability) and performers of all ages and levels, helping them achieve their personal performance goals.

Nikos Ntoumanis, PhD, is a professor of motivation science at the University of Southern Denmark. Ntoumanis received his PhD in medical sciences from the University of Exeter in the United Kingdom in 1999. His longest period of employment (2001-2014) has been at the University of Birmingham in the United Kingdom. From 2014 to 2021, he worked at Curtin University in Australia, where he established the Physical Activity and Well-Being Research Group. Ntoumanis' research interests center on personal and contextual factors that optimize motivation and promote performance, morality, psychological well-being, and health-conducive behaviors. Areas of particular interest are physical activity promotion in different community settings, self-regulation of life goals, and psychology of sport, with emphasis on applications of contemporary theories of motivation. His research has been published in various fields of psychology (health, sport, social, developmental, educational) and behavioral and sport medicine, and it has been supported by funding from research councils in the United Kingdom, Australia, and the European Union; the International Olympic Committee; and charities, health departments, and the industry. Nikos is a fellow of the British Psychological Society and the Academy of Social Sciences. In 2019, he was awarded the Distinguished Scholar Award from the Association of Applied Sport Psychology.

Frank Owusu-Sekyere, PhD, is a lecturer in sport and exercise psychology at Kingston University, United Kingdom. He completed his BSc in sport and exercise sciences, MSc in sport and exercise psychology, and PhD in safeguarding in sport at Brunel University in London.

Michael J.R. Passaportis, PhD, is a final-year doctoral student in the School of Sport, Health and Exercise Science at the University of Portsmouth in the United Kingdom. Passaportis' research is centered on exploring the interconnectivity of performance and well-being within multidimensional organizational systems, with a specific focus on the psychosocial factors that influence thriving within elite sport organizations. By incorporating participant expertise to collaboratively create knowledge, his research looks to understand more about the challenges faced by sport science practitioners who are attempting to promote thriving at the complex organizational and systems level. He has been a coauthor on book chapters and delivered presentations at conferences and invited events.

Eleanor Quested, PhD, joined Curtin University in Australia as a senior research fellow in October 2014. Quested received her PhD from the University of Birmingham in the United Kingdom in 2010, where she subsequently spent four years as research fellow and project manager on the European Commission–funded PAPA (Promoting Adolescent Physical Activity) project. Quested's research interests center on applying theories of motivation to foster and sustain health behaviors, health, well-being, personal development, and performance in the contexts of physical activity, sport, dance, and physical education. More specifically, she is interested in the design of interventions that apply theories of motivation and behavior change to engage inactive adults and clinical populations in health behavior change. For example, since arriving in Australia, Quested has established the Aussie Fans in Training intervention for middle-aged men with overweight and obesity, which is delivered in professional Australian football settings. Quested and her team are now adapting that program for men with cardiovascular disease. Her research has been funded by a range of government, industry, and charity funders.

Claudia L. Reardon, MD, holds an MD degree from the University of Wisconsin School of Medicine and Public Health, where she also completed psychiatry residency training. She is a professor at the University of Wisconsin and serves as consulting sport psychiatrist for University of Wisconsin collegiate athletes. Reardon has served as cochair of the International Olympic Committee's work group on mental health in elite athletes, and she codirects the IOC's diploma and certificate programs on mental health in elite sport. She serves on the IOC's Olympic Refuge Foundation think tank. Reardon has also served on the International Society for Sports Psychiatry (ISSP) board of directors since 2010, currently as its education committee chair, and on the National Football League's comprehensive mental health and wellness committee. She has published and presented widely on a number of sport psychiatry–related topics and is coeditor of the book *Clinical Sports Psychiatry: An International Perspective* and editor of the book *Mental Health Care for Elite Athletes.*

Daniel J.A. Rhind, PhD, is a chartered psychologist and a professor in psychology at Loughborough University, United Kingdom. Rhind's research focuses on the realization of human rights in, around, and through sport.

Harold Riemer, PhD, is professor and dean in the faculty of kinesiology and health studies at the University of Regina in Canada. His research and teaching interests lie in the area of leadership generally, in a sport context more specifically, and particularly the impact leadership can have on individuals, teams, and organizations.

Olivier Y. Rouquette, PhD, is a data scientist at Swansea University. He holds a PhD degree in sport science from Swansea University in Wales and in psychology from Université Grenoble Alpes in France. Rouquette's research seeks to develop a better understanding of the influence of significant others (e.g., parents, coaches, peers) on athletes' self-perceptions, performance, and well-being. He is a chartered clinical psychologist (Belgium) and works as a sport psychology consultant for the Sport Performance Assistance Centre (SPAC) and as an expert for the Belgian French-speaking sport administration (ADEPS) with elite athletes, coaches, and federations. Rouquette has also been involved in several sport organizations participating in the development of sport climbing in Belgium.

Mustafa Sarkar, PhD, is an associate professor of sport and performance psychology at Nottingham Trent University in the United Kingdom. His teaching, research, and consultancy focus on the psychology of sporting excellence and its application to other high-performance domains (e.g., business). His work addresses how high achievers thrive on pressure and deliver sustained success, with a particular focus on individual, team, and organizational resilience. In addition to presenting his research at over 30 conferences worldwide (including numerous invited talks), he has published extensively in these areas, including 34 peer-reviewed journal articles and six book chapters. Sarkar sits on the editorial board of six international peer-reviewed journals, and he has won multiple awards for his research and professional practice from organizations such as the British Association of Sport and Exercise Sciences (BASES), the British Psychological Society (BPS), and the Association for Applied Sport Psychology (AASP). As well as presenting and publishing research, as a chartered psychologist (CPsychol), Sarkar works closely with teams and organizations on creating environments and cultures to develop resilience and ultimately enable sustained success and well-being.

Hamsini Sivaramakrishnan, MSc, is a PhD candidate within the Physical Activity and Well-Being Research Group based at the School of Psychology at Curtin University in Australia, and she is a recipient of the Curtin International Postgraduate Research Scholarship. Sivaramakrishnan's research focuses on physical activity promotion for adults through participation in recreational sport programs. Her research explores the importance of cultivating need-supportive coaching environments within sport programs to increase motivation for physical activity and improve the associated mental health outcomes. Sivaramakrishnan completed her MSc in sport and exercise psychology with distinction in 2019 at Loughborough University in the United Kingdom, where she received the Prize for Academic Excellence and Project Prize for Sport and Exercise Psychology. Sivaramakrishnan is also a graduate member of the British Psychological Society.

Matthew J. Slater, PhD, is an associate professor of sport and exercise psychology in the School of Life Sciences at Staffordshire University in the United Kingdom. His research focuses primarily on the psychology of leadership and high-performing teams from a social identity perspective. Slater combines theoretical research with the development and application of psychological interventions to enhance leadership and team functioning. He has published over 40 peer-reviewed papers, including various book chapters, and a book titled *Togetherness: How to Build a Winning Team* (2019). Slater has been invited to speak at national and international conferences. He is a chartered psychologist with the British Psychological Society and is a consultant on leadership and high-performing teams in sport, the military, and business.

Sofie Smismans, PhD, is working as a doctoral researcher and assistant lecturer in the department of movement and sport sciences at Vrije Universiteit Brussel. Smismans graduated from the Vrije Universiteit Brussel in Belgium in 2016 with a master of science degree in physical education and movement sciences and obtained an additional master of science degree in management in 2017. In her doctoral dissertation, Smismans investigates the challenges, barriers, and resources influencing elite athletes' dual career pathway and their transition to a postathletic career. In parallel, Smismans was involved in international projects on athletes' career development and transitions for the European Commission (Be a Winner in Elite Sport and Employment Before and After Athletic Retirement (B-WISER; 2017-2018), Mind the Gap (2018-2020), and the International Olympic Committee ("How Should Athletes Be Supported Before, During, and After Athletics Retirement? Moving From an Athletic-Centred Needs Analysis to Practical Guidelines for Career Support Stakeholders"). As an assistant lecturer, Smismans assists on high-performance management in the master's program of sport and movement science. In addition, she provides support and guidance to students in their sport management internships during both their bachelor's and master's years.

David J.C. Smith, MSc, is a PhD student at the German Sports University of Cologne, following an MSc in sport and exercise psychology from the German Sports University of Cologne and a BSc in sport and exercise science at Metropolitan State University of Denver. He also holds the NSCA Certified Strength and Conditioning Specialist credential and the CSDC Sports Diversity Leader qualification. Over the last 12 years he has worked in the field as a swim coach, strength and conditioning coach, personal trainer, teacher, journalist, and managing editor and has led workshops, lectures, seminars, and webinars in sport psychology, sport science, and sport diversity. His research expertise includes coordinative dynamics, perception and action, dynamical systems, motor skills and control, motivation, diversity, equality, and inclusion, with his first research papers currently under peer review for publication.

Nicholas Stanger, PhD, is a reader in sport and exercise psychology at Leeds Beckett University in the United Kingdom. He has a range of administrative duties and has contributed widely to teaching on the undergraduate and postgraduate provision pertaining to sport and exercise psychology and research methods. He is an expert on morality in sport, has published widely in the area, has presented his work at a range of national and international conferences, and has received external funding for his research (e.g., from the World Anti-Doping Agency). His research interests also include the role that sport plays in the sociomoral development of young people, the psychology of doping, and how emotions can influence cognitive functioning and performance in sport. Stanger is a regular peer reviewer of scientific articles for a range of leading journals in the field and in 2018 was named Outstanding Reviewer of the Year for *Sport, Exercise & Performance Psychology*. He has acted as reviewer for external funding bodies (e.g., the World Anti-Doping Agency Social Science Research Grant Program) and serves on the editorial board for *Sport, Exercise & Performance Psychology* and *Frontiers in Sports & Active Living* (anti-doping sciences section).

Leisha Strachan, PhD, is a professor in the faculty of kinesiology and recreation management at the University of Manitoba in Canada. She is one of the cocreators of Project SCORE (www.projectscore.ca) and also a member of PYDSportNet. Her research is focused on positive youth development through sport and how the 4Cs (competence, confidence, connection, character) could be incorporated to promote positive youth sport spaces through coaching delivery and parent behaviors. Further, Strachan was part of a research team exploring antiracism policies and practices in Winnipeg and the sport experiences of newcomers in the community.

Katherine A. Tamminen, PhD, is an associate professor in sport psychology in the faculty of kinesiology and physical education at the University of Toronto in Canada. Her research in sport psychology focuses on two main areas: (1) stress, coping, and emotion in sport and (2) young athletes' experiences in sport. Her most recent research focuses on interpersonal and social aspects of stress, emotions, and coping in sport, and she also conducts research examining communication and relationships between parents and youth athletes.

Jamie Taylor, PhD, is a senior coach developer at Grey Matters, an assistant professor at Dublin City University, and the performance rugby union coach at Loughborough University in the United Kingdom. His background is as an experienced coach and teacher. Previous roles include coaching the Leicester Tigers, pathway coaching lead at the English Institute of Sport, and teaching. Taylor has consulted across a wide variety of organizations and has worked with over 100 coaches in a developmental capacity. His work includes support for coaches and organizations across football (soccer), rugby, tennis, athletics, and a variety of Olympic sports. He holds a PhD in coaching science and had professional qualifications in teaching, coaching, and mentoring. His research interests are coaching, talent development, and coach development.

Jennifer Turnnidge, PhD, is a health education research associate with the Office of Professional Development and Educational Scholarship at Queen's University in Canada. Turnnidge completed her doctorate degree in the School of Kinesiology and Health Studies at Queen's University. Her research explores how coach–athlete and peer relationships can promote positive development in sport. Specifically, she examines how coaches' leadership behaviors can influence the quality of youths' sport experiences.

Svenja Wachsmuth, PhD, is a junior research group leader in sport psychology and sport coaching at the Institute of Sports Science of the University of Tuebingen in Germany. She previously graduated from the European master's program in sport and exercise psychology and subsequently completed her PhD at Loughborough University in the United Kingdom, investigating experiences of interpersonal conflict within sport relationships. Wachsmuth developed a particular interest in potentially destructive interpersonal interactions that may contribute to the manifestation of dysfunctional sport performance environments. Besides her academic work, she has gained a range of experience working with coaches, athletes, and support staff. Currently, Wachsmuth works as a sport psychology consultant for a national Paralympic team and is regularly involved in coach education and development programs.

Christopher R.D. Wagstaff, PhD, is a professor of applied psychology. He divides his time between research, teaching, and practice. Wagstaff has authored over 100 publications, predominantly on organizational sport psychology. He acts as the editor for *Sport and Exercise Psychology Review* and associate editor for the *Journal of Applied Sport Psychology*, and he sits on the editorial board of *Case Studies in Sport and Exercise Psychology*. He is a past associate editor of the *International Journal of Sport and Exercise Psychology*, *Journal of Sport Psychology*, and *Journal of Applied Case Studies in Sport and Exercise Sciences*. In his teaching role, Wagstaff is the course leader for the masters and professional doctorate courses in sport and exercise psychology at University of Portsmouth in the United Kingdom. From a practice perspective, he is an experienced practitioner psychologist within the United Kingdom's high-performance sport system and acted as head of performance psychology at the English Institute of Sport in the lead-up to the postponed Tokyo 2020 Olympics and is now with Changing Minds UK. Wagstaff is passionate about the development and supervision of trainees and serves on the BPS Division of Sport and Exercise Psychology's executive and training committees.

Colin M. Wierts, PhD, is a post-doctoral fellow in the Behavioural Medicine Laboratory at the University of Victoria (Canada). He previously completed his PhD at the University of British Columbia (UBC). His research interests revolve around issues of motivation, identity, well-being, and measurement in physical activity contexts such as exercise and sport participation. Colin has published his research in a variety of outlets including *Psychology of Sport and Exercise, Psychology and Health,* and the *Journal of Sport and Exercise Psychology,* and has presented his research at a number of national and international meetings.

Erin Willson, MSc, is a PhD student in the faculty of kinesiology and physical education at the University of Toronto in Canada. Her areas of research interest include maltreatment in sport, athlete empowerment, and advocacy. As a former Olympian, she brings a unique perspective to her research endeavors.

Paul Wylleman, PhD, is a clinical psychologist and full professor at the Vrije Universiteit Brussel in Belgium, teaching sport psychology, high-performance management, and mental support for athletes. His research and publications focus on a holistic perspective on the career development and psychological competences of talented and elite athletes, and on mental health and psychology support provision in elite, Olympic, and Paralympic sport. Wylleman heads the university department Topsport and Study, supporting elite student-athletes, as well as the research group Sport Psychology and Mental Support. Wylleman is past president of the European Federation of Sport Psychology (FEPSAC) and was the 2017 Distinguished International Scholar of the Applied Association of Sport Psychology (AASP). Since 2013 he has been the manager of Performance Behaviour at TeamNL (Netherlands' Olympic committee; NOC*NSF), where he heads a team of elite-sport lifestyle coaches, psychologists, and psychiatrists. He was TeamNL's psychologist at the 2016 Rio Olympics, the 2020 Tokyo Olympics, and he is now Expert Psychology with Team Belgium *en route* to the 2024 Paris Olympics.